NCLC Cumulative Title Index, Vols. 1-139

"A Alfred de M." (Sainte-Beuve) **5**:346
"A celle qui est trop gaie" (Baudelaire) **6**:109; **29**:73; **55**:60, 76
A. D. Baratynskoy (Pavlova) **138**:4, 33
"A Félix Guiliemardet" (Lamartine) **11**:272
"A Fontenay" (Sainte-Beuve) **5**:348
"A la manière de Paul Verlaine" (Verlaine) **51**:361
A la manière de plusieurs (Verlaine) **2**:623
"A la musique" (Rimbaud) **4**:485; **35**:289-90
"A la promenade" (Verlaine) **2**:628; **51**:378, 380
"A la très-chère" (Baudelaire) **55**:29
"A l'éternelle madame" (Corbière) **43**:9
"À l'Etna" (Corbière) **43**:27
"A Lord Byron" (Lamartine) **11**:254, 268-69
"A Luigia Pallavicini caduto da cavello" (Foscolo) **8**:268, 270, 277
"A M. Auguste le Prévost" (Sainte-Beuve) **5**:348
"A M. Victor Hugo" (Bertrand) **31**:48
"A M. Victor Hugo" (Musset) **7**:275
"A M. Viguier" (Sainte-Beuve) **5**:348
"A Mademoiselle" (Sainte-Beuve) **5**:348
"A mon ami Leroux" (Sainte-Beuve) **5**:348
"A mon ami Ulric Guttinguer" (Sainte-Beuve) **5**:348
"À mon cotre Le Négrier" (Corbière) **43**:28
"A némésis" (Lamartine) **11**:271, 289
An a priori Autobiography (Brownson) **50**:27
"A quoi rêvent les jeunés filles" (Musset) **7**:260, 264, 268
"A Rescusant" (Thomson) **18**:414
"A. S. Pushkin" (Dobrolyubov) **5**:142
"A Sainte-Beuve" (Musset) **7**:275, 279
"A un dîner d' athées" (Barbey d'Aurevilly) **1**:70, 75, 77-78
"A un poète mort" (Leconte de Lisle) **29**:222, 235
"A une demoiselle" (Corbière) **43**:13
"A une jeune Arabe" (Lamartine) **11**:279
"A une madone" (Baudelaire) **55**:9, 43-4, 67
"A une mendiante Rousse" (Baudelaire) **6**:80; **55**:16, 35, 40
"A une passante" (Baudelaire) **6**:79; **29**:101; **55**:35, 40, 42
"A une raison" (Rimbaud) **35**:295-96, 322-23; **82**:232-33
A. W. Schlegels Vorlesungen über schöne Litteratur und Kunst (Schlegel) **15**:230
"A Zacinto" (Foscolo) **8**:279-80; **97**:57, 68
"Aaron Trow" (Trollope) **101**:233, 235
Abaellino, the Great Bandit (Dunlap) **2**:215
"L'Abbandonata" (Symonds) **34**:355
L'abbaye de Typhaines (Gobineau) **17**:79
"L'abbaye de Vallombreuse" (Lamartine) **11**:255
"The Abbé Aubain" (Mérimée) **6**:354, 364-5, 368-9, 371; **65**:47, 49, 54, 59, 63, 85, 101, 113
"The Abbé Delille and Walter Landor" (Landor) **14**:166, 195
The Abbess: A Romance (Trollope) **30**:319
L'abbesse de Castro (Stendhal) **23**:349, 408-09, 413
L'Abbesse de Jouarre (Renan) **26**:387-89, 415
"Abbey Asaroe" (Allingham) **25**:20
The Abbot (Scott) **15**:300, 312; **69**:303-04, 306, 313; **110**:233
"Abbot of Inisfalen" (Allingham) **25**:13
"The Abbot's Ghost; or, Maurice Treherne's Temptation" (Alcott) **58**:46; **83**:6
Abbotsford (Irving) **2**:373
"Abdala" (Martí) **63**:85, 102
Abdallah (Tieck) **5**:515, 517-18, 523, 527-28
Abdias (Stifter) **41**:335, 366, 367, 391
"The Abdication of Fergus" (Ferguson) **33**:279-80, 293
The Abduction (Becque)
See *L'Enlèvement*
"Abecedarju" (Preseren) **127**:315
Abednego the Money-Leader (Gore) **65**:21
"La abeja y el zángano" (Lizardi) **30**:67
Abel (Alfieri) **101**:18-19
"Abel and Cain" (Baudelaire)
See "Abel et Caïn"
"Abel et Caïn" (Baudelaire) **6**:94
"Abel Jansen Tasman" (Clarke) **19**:231, 236
Aben Humeya (Martínez de la Rosa) **102**:230, 241-46
"The Abencerrage" (Hemans) **71**:276
"Abencerrage" (Hemans) **29**:192
"Der Abend" (Grillparzer) **102**:174
"Der Abend" (Schiller) **39**:338-39, 355
"Abend auf Golgatha" (Keller) **2**:421
"Abendlied an die Natur" (Keller) **2**:421
"Abendlied-augen, meine Lieben Fensterlein" (Keller) **2**:421
"Abendphantasie" (Hölderlin) **16**:184
"Abendrot im Walde" (Meyer) **81**:205
"Abendständchen" (Brentano) **1**:102, 105
"Abendwolke" (Meyer) **81**:146
Aben-Hamet, the Last of the Abencerages (Chateaubriand) **3**:110, 117, 126
"Abenlied" (Claudius) **75**:190
Die Abenteuer in der Sylvesternacht (Hoffmann) **2**:348
"The Abjuration of St. Peter" (Baudelaire)
See "Le reniement de Saint-Pierre"
The Abolitionists (Channing) **17**:24, 32, 35
"L'aboma" (Leconte de Lisle) **29**:225
"Aboriginal Death Song" (Kendall) **12**:192, 201
"Abou Ben Adhem" (Hunt) **1**:414-15, 423; **70**:264
"About Dolly" (Cooke) **110**:33
"About How Ivan Ivanovič Quarreled with Ivan Nikiforovič" (Gogol)
See "The Tale of How Ivan Ivanovich Quarrelled with Ivan Nikiforovich"
About Money (Craik) **38**:127
About the Book—Restricted Action (Mallarmé)
See *L'Action restreinte*
"Abraham Davenport" (Whittier) **8**:509, 523; **59**:360-1
"Abram Morrison" (Whittier) **8**:517
An Abridgment of Universal Geography (Rowson) **69**:114-16
Abroad (Saltykov) **16**:369
"Der Abschied" (Klopstock) **11**:237
"Abschied" (Lenau) **16**:269-70
"Abschied" (Mörike) **10**:453
"Abschied von der Utopie" (Heine) **54**:331
"Abschied von Gastein" (Grillparzer) **102**:174
Abseits (Storm) **1**:540
"Absence" (Bowles) **103**:55
"Absence" (Kemble) **18**:181
"The Absent" (Very) **9**:383-85
The Absentee (Edgeworth) **1**:257, 262-68, 270-72; **51**:77, 79, 88, 90-1, 93, 100, 102, 104-05, 117, 119
Les absents (Daudet) **1**:249
"Abt Vogler" (Browning) **19**:132, 153; **79**:106, 110-11
"Abu Midjan" (Lampman) **25**:188, 199
"La abulea y la nieta" (Silva) **114**:311
"Abundance" (Meyer)
See "Fülle"
"Abuse of the gospel" (Cowper) **94**:72-3
The Abyss (Goncharov)
See *Obryv*
"The Academy of Death. A Fragement" (Freneau) **111**:134
"Acadia" (Longfellow) **103**:296
Accepted Addresses (Sala) **46**:237
"Account of Lord Byron's Residence" (Polidori) **51**:218
Account of New South Wales and the State of the Convicts (Dyer) **129**:115
"An Account of Some Strange Disturbances in an Old House on Aungier Street" (Le Fanu)
See "Some Strange Disturbances in an Old House on Augier Street"
An Account of the Christian Faith on the Principles of the Evangelical Church (Schleiermacher) **107**:268
"Account of the Rural Sentiment Which is Cultivated at the Country Seat of a Man of Fashion" (Mackenzie) **41**:191
"Les accroupissements" (Rimbaud) **35**:271, 282
"An Accursed Race" (Gaskell) **70**:189
"The Accuser Who Is the God of This World" (Blake) **13**:213
"Achan" (Kendall) **12**:192
"Achievements of the Genius of Scott" (Martineau) **26**:350; **137**:309
Achilleis (Goethe) **4**:207, 216
Acia (Turgenev)
See *Asya*
"Acknowledgment" (Lanier) **6**:246; **118**:202, 215
"Acme" (Rossetti) **50**:293
"Acontius and Cydippe" (Morris) **4**:442, 447
Acrobate (Feuillet) **45**:79
"Across the Pea-Fields" (Lampman) **25**:183-84, 209

Across the Plains, with Other Memories and Essays (Stevenson) **5**:410, 414, 419; **14**:331
An Act for Establishing Religious Freedom, Passed in the Assembly of Virginia in the Beginning of the Year 1786 (Jefferson) **11**:170-71, 189, 198, 209; **103**:263
Acté (Dumas) **71**:204
Actes et paroles (Hugo) **3**:262
"Action at Stoney Creek" (Richardson) **55**:342
L'Action restreinte (Mallarmé) **41**:233, 271, 282, 287
Les actionnaires (Scribe) **16**:394
Actions Speaks Louder (Tamayo y Baus)
See *Del dicho al hecho*
Actors and Acting (Lewes)
See *On Actors and the Art of Acting*
Les actrices (Goncourt and Goncourt) **7**:153, 174
"Acts and Scenes" (Landor) **14**:177
"The Acts of the Polish Nation since the Beginning of the World to Its Crucifixion" (Mickiewicz) **3**:390
"Ad Amicos" (Taylor) **89**:317
"Ad Angelo Mai quand'ebbe trovato i libri di Cicerone della Repubblica" (Leopardi) **129**:219, 266, 312, 314-15, 328-29, 346
"Ad Arimane" (Leopardi) **129**:252, 356
"Ad Criticum" (Boker) **125**:77
"Ad leones" (Norwid) **17**:379, 383
Ada Reis (Lamb) **38**:237, 251
Adam and Eve (Clough) **27**:56, 67, 91, 100
Adam Bede (Eliot) **118**:40, 43, 58-62, 103-4, 127, 147
"Adam Buff, the Man without a Shirt" (Jerrold) **2**:395
Adam Greene of Mossgray (Oliphant) **11**:429, 432, 445
"Adam Smith as a Person" (Bagehot) **10**:58
"Adam, the Carrion Crow" (Beddoes) **3**:34
The Adams Papers (Adams) **106**:4
Adams-Jefferson (Jefferson) **103**:192
Addison (Macaulay) **42**:87
"Address" (Barnes) **75**:43
"Address" (Brown) **74**:170-73, 175
"Address" (Emerson)
See "The Divinity School Address"
"An Address Delivered at Lenox on the First of August, 1842, Being the Anniversary of Emancipation in the British West Indies" (Channing) **17**:25
"Address Delivered at the Opening of the New Theatre in Richmond, Va." (Timrod) **25**:363
"An Address Delivered Before the Senior Class in Divinity College, Cambridge" (Emerson)
See "The Divinity School Address"
"An Address Delivered in the Court-house in Concord" (Emerson) **38**:155-56
"Address of a Water Nymph" (Darwin) **106**:182
Address of the Central Council of the Communist League (Marx) **114**:39
Address on the Present Condition, Resources, and Prospects of British North America (Haliburton) **15**:128
Address on the Question of Free Trade (Marx) **17**:333
"Address to a Child" (Wordsworth) **138**:229
"Address to a Lark" (Clare) **86**:155
"An Address to a Wild Deer" (Wilson) **5**:550
"Address to Certain Gold Fishes" (Coleridge) **90**:28
"Address to his auld dog Hector" (Hogg) **109**:202
"An Address to Lord Howe" (Paine) **62**:322
An Address to Miss Phillis Wheatly (Hammon) **5**:261-62, 264-65
"Address to Plenty" (Clare) **9**:72
"An Address to the Fremment of Canada" (Moodie) **113**:308
"An Address to the Friends of Liberty" (Dyer) **129**:103, 129
An Address to the Government of the United States on the Cession of Louisiana (Brown) **74**:88; **122**:116, 119
An Address to the Irish People (Shelley) **18**:341; **93**:373
Address to the Muses (Baillie) **71**:54-5
An Address to the Negroes in the State of New York (Hammon) **5**:262
Address to the Night (Baillie) **71**:51
An Address to the People of Great Britain on the Doctrine of Libels and the Office of Juror (Dyer) **129**:105-6, 113, 137
"Address to the People of South Carolina" (Calhoun) **15**:27
Address to the People on the Death of the Princess Charlotte (Shelley) **93**:272-73
"Address to the Rural Muse" (Clare) **9**:79-80; **86**:160
"Address to the Senators and Representatives of the Free States" (Child) **73**:105
"Address to the Swilcar Oak" (Darwin) **106**:183
"Address to Working Men, by Felix Holt" (Eliot) **118**:37-38, 55-57, 64, 92, 130, 156-57, 160, 176, 180-81, 190
"Addressed to Messrs. Dwight and Barlow, On the Projected Publication of Their Poems in London" (Trumbull) **30**:350
Addresses (Schleiermacher) **107**:303-10, 313-14, 316
"Addresses on the Fundamental Features of the Present Age" (Fichte) **62**:19
Addresses to the German Nation (Fichte)
See *Reden an die deutsche Nation*
"Adélaïde" (Gobineau) **17**:92-3, 103
Adelaide and Theodore (Staël-Holstein)
See *Adélaïde et Théodore*
Adélaïde de Brunswick (Sade) **47**:326
Adélaïde et Théodore (Staël-Holstein) **91**:322, 339
Adelchi (Manzoni) **29**:250-51, 261, 275, 278, 299, 302, 304; **98**:204, 209, 213, 215, 217, 219-20,224-25, 228, 230, 245, 244, 276
Adelgitha; or, The Fruits of a Single Error (Lewis) **11**:305-06
Adelheid von Wulfingen (Kotzebue) **25**:141
Adeline Mowbray; or, The Mother and Daughter (Opie) **65**:157, 168, 171-74, 179, 193-5, 201-2, 206-10, 212, 215, 217
Adelmorn, the Outlaw (Lewis) **11**:296, 302, 304-05
Adelphi (Cowper) **94**:14, 94, 121, 125, 128
"El aderezo de esmeraldas" (Bécquer) **106**:98
"L'adieu" (Lamartine) **11**:282
"Adieu" (Rimbaud) **4**:466, 485; **35**:289-90, 293-94, 303-04, 306-07, 313-14, 320, 324; **82**:223, 229, 236-37, 241, 251-52, 254-55, 262
"Adieu d'une fille è l<'acutecole" (Desbordes-Valmore) **97**:29
"Adieu mystères" (Maupassant) **83**:184
"Adieu to Belashanny" (Allingham) **25**:18
"Adieu!—Adieu!" (Moodie) **113**:348
Les adieux au comptoir (Scribe) **16**:393
Adini (Brown) **74**:7
"Adiós" (Castro) **3**:101; **78**:37, 40-41
"The Adirondacs" (Emerson) **1**:279; **38**:193; **98**:182-83
"Adivinase el dulce y perfumado" (Castro) **78**:41
"Adlercreutz" (Runeberg) **41**:312, 314
"Adlerskaya pesnya" (Bestuzhev) **131**:152
"Admetus" (Lazarus) **8**:411-14, 417-18, 420, 425; **109**:289-90, 294, 319
Admetus, and Other Poems (Lazarus) **8**:412-13, 417-18, 422, 425; **109**:289, 294, 319, 321
"Administrative Nihilism" (Huxley) **67**:64, 66, 97, 105
Admiral Guinea (Stevenson) **5**:411, 421
Adolescent (Dostoevsky)
See *Podrostok*
"Adolf and Annette" (Coleridge) **90**:31, 33, 35-6
Adolphe: An Anecdote Found among Papers of an Unknown Person and Published by M. Benjamin de Constant (Constant) **6**:211, 213-22, 224-25, 228-29
Adonais: An Elegy on the Death of John Keats (Shelley) **18**:320, 329, 344, 349-51, 353-54, 361, 363-64, 373; **93**:322-29, 344
"The Adopted Child" (Hemans) **71**:264
"Adormeciendo a David" (Isaacs) **70**:311
Adrastea (Herder) **8**:307, 313
Adrienne Lecouvreur (Scribe) **16**:389, 412-14
Adrift in New York; or, Tom and Florence Braving the World (Alger) **8**:43; **83**:114
The Adulateur (Warren) **13**:413-16, 419, 425-26, 428
L'adultera (Fontane) **26**:235-37, 241, 243-44, 259, 270-71, 275-76
Adultera (Martí) **63**:84
Advance Notice (Gogol) **5**:233
"Advent" (Rossetti) **2**:559, 562-3; **50**:272; **66**:330
"An Adventure in the East Indies" (Bryant) **6**:181
"The Adventure of Lieutenant Jergounoff" (Turgenev)
See "Istoriya leytenanta Ergunova"
"The Adventure of My Aunt" (Irving) **19**:341
An Adventure of Richelieu (Tamayo y Baus)
See *Una aventura de Richelieu*
"Adventure of the Hansom Cabs" (Stevenson) **5**:394
"The Adventure of the Mysterious Stranger" (Irving) **2**:370; **19**:341
Adventures (Trelawny)
See *Adventures of a Younger Son*
The Adventures of a Brownie (Craik) **38**:122
The Adventures of a Naval Officer; or, Scenes and Adventures in the Life of Frank Mildmay (Marryat) **3**:318-19, 321-22
The Adventures of a Puppet (Collodi)
See *Le Avventure di Pinocchio*
Adventures of a Telegraph Boy (Alger) **8**:43
Adventures of a Younger Son (Trelawny) **85**:314-16, 318-20, 324-25, 327, 330-37, 339, 342-44, 346-48
The Adventures of Arthur O'Leary (Lever)
See *Arthur O'Leary: His Wanderings and Ponderings in Many Lands*
The Adventures of Caleb Williams (Godwin)
See *Things As They Are; or, The Adventures of Caleb Williams*
The Adventures of Captain Bonneville (Irving) **2**:376-77; **95**:258-59
"The Adventures of Frederick Pickering" (Trollope) **101**:235
The Adventures of Hugh Trevor (Holcroft) **85**:192-93, 206-07, 228-31, 236-38, 242-46
Adventures of Nicholas Doświadczynski (Krasicki) **8**:399-401, 404-05
The Adventures of Philip on His Way through the World (Thackeray) **5**:466, 470, 472, 482, 484-85, 488
The Adventures of Pinocchio (Collodi)
See *Le Avventure di Pinocchio*
The Adventures of Robin Day (Bird) **1**:91
The Adventures of the Last Abencérages (Chateaubriand)
See *Aben-Hamet, the Last of the Abencerages*
Adventures of Ulysses (Lamb) **10**:417
"Adventures on Salisbury Plain" (Wordsworth) **111**:267, 346-47
"Advertisement" (Keble) **87**:156, 199
"Advertisement to the First Edition" (Browning) **66**:90
"Advertisement to the Lyrical Ballads" (Wordsworth) **111**:202, 213, 239, 244, 276, 293-94, 306, 314-15, 317, 337, 339, 354-57, 360, 363, 366, 368
"Advice of an Old Woman" (Mörike) **10**:446

"Advice; or, The Squire and the Priest" (Crabbe) **26**:93, 130, 134; **121**:65-6, 71, 73, 76
"Advice to a Raven in Russia" (Barlow) **23**:29-31
"Advice to Authors: By the late Mr. Robert Slender" (Freneau) **111**:81, 132, 156
"Advice to Ladies of a Certain Age" (Trumbull) **30**:349
Advice to the Privileged Orders (Barlow) **23**:17-18, 21-2, 27, 29, 41, 43
Advice to Young Men and (Incidentally) to Young Women (Cobbett) **49**:110, 114, 116, 119, 123, 140, 147-48, 150, 152-53, 159
"Aél" (Gómez de Avellaneda) **111**:4, 27
"Aeneid" (Morris) **4**:420, 441
"Aeolian Harp" (Allingham) **25**:18, 20
"The Aeolian Harp" (Coleridge) **99**:5, 38, 40-1, 59, 92, 101, 105
"The Aeolian Harp" (Zhukovsky) **35**:393
"Aerial Omens" (Whittier) **8**:485
"Aes triplex" (Stevenson) **5**:425
"Aesthetic Poetry" (Pater) **7**:305, 327, 333; **90**:241, 305-06, 326, 346
"The Aesthetic Validity of Marriage" (Kierkegaard) **125**:282
"Aesthetic Value of Greek Comedy" (Schlegel) See "Vom ästhetischen Werte der griechischen Komödie"
The Aesthetics of Ugliness (Sacher-Masoch) **31**:302
Aëthra (Hayne) **94**:136
Af en endnu Levendes Papirer (Kierkegaard) **34**:218, 222, 267-69; **125**:203, 231
Afar in the Forest (Traill) See *Lady Mary and Her Nurse; or, A Peep into the Canadian Forest*
"L'affaire Champonathieu" (Hugo) **10**:378
L'affaire Clémenceau: Mémoire de l'accusé (Dumas) **9**:224, 228-29, 234
L'affaire Lerouge (Gaboriau) **14**:14, 16-17, 19-21, 23-4, 26-33
Affectation (Sheridan) **91**:243
"L'affichage céleste" (Villiers de l'Isle Adam) **3**:581, 590
"The Affliction of Margaret—of—" (Wordsworth) **12**:393, 430-31, 444
Afloat (Maupassant) See *Sur l'eau*
Afloat and Ashore; or, The Adventures of Miles Wallingford (Cooper) **1**:221; **54**:258, 276
L'Africaine (Scribe) **16**:390, 401
The African (Murray) **63**:214
The African Woman (Scribe) See *L'Africaine*
The Africans (Dunlap) **2**:211
Afsluttende uvidenskabelig Efterskrift (Kierkegaard) **34**:199-200, 203-05, 224, 238; **78**:123-25, 148, 154-55, 159-60, 162, 166, 189-90, 195, 197-98, 201, 215, 217, 228, 238, 240, 249-51; **125**:218, 250, 261-63, 265
"After" (Browning) **79**:153
"After a Tempest" (Bryant) **6**:159, 176
After Breakfast (Sala) **46**:237
After Dark (Collins) **1**:173, 180, 186; **93**:46
After Dark—A Tale of London Life (Boucicault) **41**:49
"After Death" (Rossetti) **2**:557, 561; **50**:269, 289, 295-96
"After Great Pain, a Formal Feeling Comes" (Dickinson) **21**:43
After London; or, Wild England (Jefferies) **47**:92-93, 95, 102, 104, 109, 112, 113, 124, 130-33, 142
"After Many Years" (Kendall) **12**:183, 187, 189, 198-99
"After Mist" (Lampman) **25**:210
"After Rain" (Lampman) **25**:169
"After the Burial" (Lowell) **2**:511; **90**:193
"After the Camanches" (Cooke) **110**:9
"After the Death of John Brown" (Thoreau) **7**:406
"After the Deluge" (Rimbaud) See "Après le déluge"
After the Dinner Comes the Reckoning (Ostrovsky) See *Ne vse kotu maslenitsa*
"After the French Liberation of Italy" (Rossetti) **77**:297
"After the German Subjugation of France, 1871" (Rossetti) **77**:297
"After the Hunt" (Kendall) **12**:181, 191
"After the Play" (Gogol) **5**:254; **31**:103
"After the Pleasure Party" (Melville) **3**:363; **91**:184
"After the Shower" (Lampman) **25**:210
"After the Storm" (Herzen) **10**:337
"After the Supper and Talk" (Whitman) **31**:434
"After the Theater" (Gogol) **31**:98
"After the Tornado" (Hayne) **94**:138
"After the Victory" (Isaacs) See "Después da la victoria"
After-Dinner Chat (Silva) See *De sobremesa*
"Aftermath" (Longfellow) **2**:492; **45**:161, 187
"Afternoon at a Parsonage" (Ingelow) **39**:263-65
"Afternoon in February" (Longfellow) **45**:152; **103**:293
Afternoon of a Faun (Mallarmé) See *L'après-midi d'un faune*
"Again a Springtime" (Bertrand) **31**:55
"Again His Voice Is at the Door" (Dickinson) **21**:58
Against Heavy Odds: A Tale of Norse Heroism (Boyesen) **135**:8, 15
"Against Inconsistency in our Expectations" (Barbauld) **50**:3
Against the Dualism of Soul and Body, Flesh and Spirit (Feuerbach) **139**:290
"Against widows" (Lonnrot) **53**:339
"Agamemnon" (Galt) **1**:327
Agamemnon and Orestes (Alfieri) **101**:32
Agamemnone (Alfieri) See *Agamennone*
Agamemnon's Grave (Slowacki) See *Grób Agamemnona*
Agamemnon's Tomb (Lazarus) **109**:294
Agamennone (Alfieri) **101**:4, 8, 32, 42, 73
Agar (Staël-Holstein) **91**:359
"Agassiz" (Lowell) **90**:190, 193, 220
"Agatha" (Eliot) **13**:334
Agatha's Husband (Craik) **38**:110, 120, 128
Agay-Han (Krasiński) **4**:305-06, 309
"Age d'or" (Rimbaud) **4**:484; **35**:269
The Age of Constantine the Great (Burckhardt) See *Die Zeit Constantins des Grossen*
The Age of Reason (Paine) **62**:259, 262, 264, 268-9, 271, 275, 278, 280, 285, 297-8, 309, 311-2, 314, 39, 345-6, 349, 368, 370, 373, 375-6, 379-80, 385-6, 389-93
"The Age of Steam" (Horne) **127**:253
The Age of the Despots (Symonds) **34**:318-19, 346-47, 349, 357, 360-63, 368, 370
Agemennone (Alfieri) See *Agamennone*
"The Agency of Heaven in the Cause of Liberty" (Brackenridge) **7**:44
"The Ages" (Bryant) **6**:158, 161-62, 164, 171, 181, 189, 191; **46**:4, 15
The Ages of the World (Schelling) See *Die Weltalter*
Agezylausz (Slowacki) **15**:371, 378
Agide (Alfieri) **101**:13, 7, 39, 42
Agis (Alfieri) See *Agide*
"The Agitation of the Socialist-Democratic Party in Austria" (Bakunin) **58**:133
"Aglauron and Laurie" (Fuller) **50**:258
Agnes (Oliphant) **61**:173, 188, 209
"Agnes asszony" (Arany) **34**:15, 20
Agnes Bernauer: Ein deutsches Trauerspiel in fünf Aufzügen (Hebbel) **43**:230, 234, 238-40, 244-45, 249, 251, 249, 261-62, 264, 269, 284, 287, 291, 297, 300, 301
Agnes Bernauerin (Ludwig) **4**:350
Agnes Grey: An Autobiography (Brontë) **4**:38-40, 42-43, 48-50, 52-55; **71**:73, 75, 78-82, 84-86, 88-91, 93, 98, 104-09, 111-13, 120, 122-28, 131-39, 144-46, 148, 150, 153-57, 159, 162-63, 165-66, 169, 171-79; **102**:3, 27
Agnes of Sorrento (Stowe) **3**:557, 559, 562, 568
Agnete and the Merman (Andersen) **79**:13, 78, 82
"Agnosticism" (Huxley) **67**:96
"Agnosticism and Christianity" (Huxley) **67**:41
"La agonía del héroe" (Isaacs) **70**:311
L'agonie de la Semillante (Daudet) **1**:247
Agonies (Flaubert) **19**:288
"The Agony of the Hero" (Isaacs) See "La agonía del héroe"
Agrarian Justice (Paine) **62**:262, 271, 296, 301, 373
Agreement of Religion with Reason (Kant) See *Religion within the Limits of Reason Alone*
"Agricultura de la zona tórrida" (Bello) **131**:103-4, 109-13, 119
"Agricultural Address" (Madison) **126**:329
"El agua y el fuego" (Rizal) **27**:425
Ah! (Wergeland) **5**:535
"Ah, I feel wretched . . ." (Bestuzhev) See "Akh, toshno mnye . . ."
"Ah! May the Red Rose Live Alway" (Foster) **26**:298
"Ah, Peggie, since th'art gane away" (Hogg) **109**:200
"Ah Poverties, Wincings, and Sulky Retreats" (Whitman) **81**:315
"Ah! Sun-Flower" (Blake) **13**:181, 221; **37**:15, 26-7, 29, 43, 49, 51, 62, 92
"Ah What Is Love, Our Love, She Said" (Clough) **27**:106
Ahalya Baee (Baillie) **71**:3
"Ahasver, der ewige Jude" (Lenau) **16**:279, 284
Ahavat Zion (Mapu) **18**:286-93, 295, 298-301, 303
Die Ahnen (Freytag) **109**:165, 170-73
Die Ahnfrau (Grillparzer) **1**:382-85, 387, 389, 397; **102**:81, 85, 100, 120-26, 146, 148, 176, 186
Ahnung und Gegenwart (Eichendorff) **8**:214-19, 222, 226-29
"Aho, Aho, Love's Horn Doth Blow" (Beddoes) **3**:34
Aiace (Foscolo) **8**:270
"Aideen's Grave" (Ferguson) **33**:278, 293, 305
"Aids to Reflection" (Coleridge) **9**:147, 155, 205; **54**:79, 107; **99**:112-16
"L'aigle du casque" (Hugo) **3**:276
"Aileen" (Kendall) **12**:193
"Aileen Astore" (Darley) **2**:130
"The Ailing Muse" (Baudelaire) See "La Muse malade"
"Ailleen" (Banim and Banim) **13**:129
"Aimer Paris" (Banville) **9**:30
"The Aims of Education" (Bello) **131**:121
"Ain't I A Woman" (Truth) See "Ar'n't I a woman?"
"Air" (Boyesen) **135**:47
"Air:—spirituosi" (Darwin) **106**:182
"Airiños, airiños, aires" (Castro) **3**:100
"Äiti ja lapsi" (Kivi) **30**:51
"La ajorca de oro" (Bécquer) **106**:97, 108, 120-21, 130-31, 161
"Ajudah" (Mickiewicz) **3**:404
"Akatsuki Zukuyo" (Ichiyō) **49**:353
"Akbar's Dream" (Tennyson) **30**:283
Akëdysséril (Villiers de l'Isle Adam) **3**:583
"Akerman Steppes" (Mickiewicz) See "Stepy Akermańskie"

"Akh, toshno mnye . . ." (Bestuzhev) **131**:149, 180-81
"Akhill" (Zhukovsky) **35**:398
Akinari ibun (Ueda Akinari) **131**:21
"The Akond of Swat" (Lear) **3**:296
"Akrivie Phrangopoulo" (Gobineau) **17**:80, 92-3, 103
"Al Aaraaf" (Poe) **1**:492, 514, 527; **16**:304; **55**:156; **94**:240; **117**:195-96, 216, 221, 225, 227-31, 233, 237, 239, 244, 260, 262, 264-70, 273, 275-78, 281, 301
Al Aaraaf, Tamarlane, and Minor Poems (Poe) **1**:492, 514; **117**:226, 305
"Al escudo de armas de Nueva Granada" (Isaacs) **70**:313
"Al mar" (Gómez de Avellaneda) **111**:30, 33, 56-7, 64-7
"Al mar!" (Isaacs) **70**:303, 313
"Al pie de la estatua" (Silva) **114**:301-3
Al pie de la estatua (Silva) **114**:261
Al! prav se piše kau a ali kaſha (Preseren)
See "Črkarska pravda"
"Al sol" (Espronceda)
See "Himno al sol"
Al través de los libros amó siempre (Silva) **114**:263
Alarcos (Disraeli)
See *The Tragedy of Count Alarcos*
Alarcos (Schlegel) **45**:287, 327
"Alastor" (Browning) **79**:113
"Alastor; or, The Spirit of Solitude" (Shelley) **18**:326-27, 331, 334, 344, 358, 361, 363, 365, 369, 380, 383
Alastor; or, The Spirit of Solitude, and Other Poems (Shelley) **18**:313; **93**:275, 283, 287-88, 290-91, 356, 369-77
"Albanos Traum" (Jean Paul) **7**:234
"L'albatros" (Baudelaire) **55**:18, 48-51, 53, 55-6, 64
Albert and Emily (Beddoes) **3**:33
"Albertine's Wooers" (Hoffmann) **2**:342
Albertus, ou l'âme et le péché: légende théologique (Gautier) **1**:339, 342-43, 347, 350; **59**:17-19, 39, 70
Die Albigenser (Lenau) **16**:263, 266, 268-70, 272, 274-75, 277, 280-81
The Albigenses (Maturin) **6**:325-28, 332-34, 341
"Albion and Marina" (Brontë) **105**:54
"Albor" (Isaacs) **70**:311
"El album" (Larra) **17**:282
Album cubano de lo bueno y lo bello (Gómez de Avellaneda) **111**:7, 30, 33, 57, 64-6
"Album de la ciudad. El Fénix" (Casal) **131**:263
Album de vers et de prose (Mallarmé) **4**:376
Album Verses, with a Few Others (Lamb) **10**:405; **113**:166, 283-84
"Alcaics" (Clough) **27**:104
"Alcedama Sparks; Or, Old and New" (Cooke) **110**:37, 43
"Alceo" (Foscolo) **8**:266, 268
Alceo (Foscolo)
See *Alceus*
Alceus (Foscolo) **97**:51-2
"Alchemy of the Word" (Rimbaud)
See "Alchimie du verbe"
"Alchimie de la douleur" (Baudelaire) **55**:65
"Alchimie du verbe" (Rimbaud) **35**:268, 317-20; **82**:222-23, 227, 231, 237, 240-41, 245, 247
"L'alchimiste" (Bertrand) **31**:48-9
L'Alchimiste (Dumas)
See *The Alchymist*
The Alchymist (Dumas) **11**:47; **71**:192-93
"Alciphron" (Moore) **6**:386
Alcuin: A Dialogue on the Rights of Women (Brown) **22**:23, 45; **74**:7, 9, 14-15, 19, 28-30, 32, 47, 50, 54, 134, 151-57, 182
"Alcyone" (Lampman) **25**:186, 189, 193-94, 216-17, 219
Alcyone and Other Poems (Lampman) **25**:169, 183-84, 199
"La aldeana infiel" (Isaacs) **70**:306
Aldomen (Senancour) **16**:438, 445, 447-48
"Alexander and Zenobia" (Brontë) **4**:44
Alexander the Kind (Eminescu) **33**:265; **131**:292
"Alexander von Humboldt" (Taylor) **89**:308
Alexandru Lăpuşneanu (Eminescu) **33**:265, 267; **131**:292
"Alexis und Dora" (Goethe) **90**:109
"Alfarabi" (Beddoes) **3**:33
"Alfieri and Italian Drama" (Lewes) **25**:285
"Az alföld" (Petofi) **21**:262, 285
"Alföldi utazás" (Madach) **19**:369
Alfonso, King of Castile (Lewis) **11**:302, 305
Alfonso Munio (Gómez de Avellaneda) **111**:4, 12, 24, 28
Alfoxden-Grasmere Journals (Wordsworth)
See *Journals of Dorothy Wordsworth: The Alfoxden Journal, 1798; The Grasmere Journals, 1800-1803*
Alfoxden Journal (Wordsworth) **25**:396, 400, 404-06, 408-09, 411, 412, 416-17, 419
Alfoxden Journal (Wordsworth)
See *Journals of Dorothy Wordsworth: The Alfoxden Journal, 1798; The Grasmere Journals, 1800-1803*
Alfred Hagart's Household (Smith) **59**:295, 299, 314, 319, 332
The Algerine Captive; or, The Life and Adventures of Doctor Updike Underhill: Six Years Prisoner among the Algerines (Tyler) **3**:572-75, 577-78
Älgskyttarne (Runeberg)
See *Elgskyttarne*
The Alhambra (Irving) **2**:371, 377-80, 383-84, 387-88; **19**:332; **95**:239, 280
"Al-Hassan" (Mangan) **27**:284
"Alice Doane's Appeal" (Hawthorne) **17**:137; **39**:180-81; **95**:128, 132, 137, 139
"Alice Fell" (Wordsworth) **12**:430; **111**:213
Alice in Wonderland (Carroll)
See *Alice's Adventures in Wonderland*
Alice; or, the Mysteries (Bulwer-Lytton) **1**:140; **45**:21, 23, 28-9, 68
Alice Through the Looking Glass (Carroll)
See *Through the Looking-Glass and What Alice Found There*
Alice's Adventures in Wonderland (Carroll) **2**:106-15, 118-20; **53**:37-155; **139**:4, 7, 15, 22-26, 32-33, 35, 40, 43-45, 48, 50, 52, 57, 59, 64, 67-68, 72, 76, 80, 83-86, 88-90, 92-94, 96, 98-99, 101, 107-12, 114-21, 124, 126, 131-58
Alice's Adventures Under Ground (Carroll) **139**:35, 44, 86, 108, 112, 138, 140-41, 147
Alide: An Episode of Goethe's Life (Lazarus) **8**:414, 425; **109**:289, 292, 297, 301, 323
Alien Bread (Turgenev)
See *Nakhlebnik*
The Alienated Manor (Baillie) **71**:64
Aline et Valcour (Sade) **3**:468, 478, 481, 491, 495-96; **47**:305, 309, 311, 314-16, 328, 335
Alix (Feuillet) **45**:75, 79
"All About Lovers" (Parton) **86**:367
"All Alone Along the Road I Am Walking" (Lermontov)
See "Alone I Go along the Road"
"All Along the Village Street" (Petofi)
See "A faluban utcahosszat"
"All' amica risanata" (Foscolo) **8**:265, 268, 270, 277
"All Heaven Is Blazing Yet" (Rossetti) **50**:314-5
"All in Honour" (Smith) **59**:257
All in the Dark (Le Fanu) **9**:302; **58**:271
All in the Family, or the Married Fiancée (Griboedov)
See *Svoia sem'ia, ili Zamuzhniaia nevesta*
"All in the Family Way" (Moore) **110**:172
"All Men Are Born Free And Equal" (Crawford) **127**:222, 225, 227
All On a Summer's Day (Inchbald) **62**:143, 145, 147
All Religions Are One (Blake) **57**:89; **127**:5, 124
"All Saints" (Rossetti) **50**:312
"All Souls' Day" (Silva)
See "Día de difuntos"
"All the letters I can write" (Dickinson) **77**:145-46
All the World a Mask (Boker)
See *The World a Mask*
"All Things Are Current Found" (Thoreau) **7**:383
"Alla Luna" (Leopardi) **129**:350
"Alla musa" (Foscolo) **8**:280
"Alla primavera o delle favole antiche" (Leopardi) **129**:232, 246, 251, 328, 352-53, 357
"Alla sera" (Foscolo) **8**:279; **97**:67
"Alla sua donna" (Leopardi) **129**:290-91, 293, 295, 297, 350, 357
"Alla sua donna lontana" (Foscolo) **8**:278
"Alla vita abbozzata di Silvio Sarno" (Leopardi) **129**:335
"L'allée" (Verlaine) **2**:628; **51**:378, 380
"Une allée du Luxembourg" (Nerval) **67**:306
"Allégorie" (Baudelaire) **6**:80; **55**:14, 74, 77
Allerton and Dreux; or, the War of Opinion (Ingelow) **39**:263
"An Alley in Flanders" (Desbordes-Valmore)
See "Une Ruelle de Flandres"
"Allez en paix" (Desbordes-Valmore) **97**:13
"Allgegenwart" (Grillparzer) **102**:174
"All'Italia" (Leopardi) **129**:218-20, 316, 328, 330
"Allocution to Poetry" (Bello)
See "Alocución a la Poesia"
"Allouma" (Maupassant) **83**:201-02
"All's Well that Ends Well" (Lamb) **125**:304
"El alma cubana" (Martí) **63**:159-60
"El alma de la rosa" (Silva) **114**:299
"Alma Mater" (Levy) **59**:86
"Al-Mamon" (Gogol) **5**:227
The Almanach-Monger (Pushkin) **3**:434
Almanacks (Emerson) **66**:186-8, 190-5, 197, 221-2
Almansur (Tieck) **5**:523
"Las almas muertas" (Silva) **114**:300
Las almas muertas (Silva) **114**:267
Almeria (Edgeworth) **1**:267; **51**:89-90
"Alnwick Castle" (Halleck) **47**:55-59, 64, 67, 69, 73, 79, 83, 86
Alnwick Castle and other Poems (Halleck) **47**:71
"Alocución a la Poesia" (Bello) **131**:93, 102-7, 109, 111, 113, 119
"Alone" (Poe) **117**:225, 227, 268
"Alone I Go along the Road" (Lermontov) **5**:295; **126**:144
"Alone in the Forest" (Traill) **31**:328
"Alone Upon Zamorna's Plain" (Brontë) **109**:30
"Along the Pasig" (Rizal) **27**:425
"Along the River Rontanka" (Bestuzhev)
See "Vdol' Fontanki-reki"
"Alonzo the Brave and the Fair Imogene" (Lewis) **11**:297, 300, 311
Aloys und Imelde (Brentano) **1**:102
Der Alpenkönig und der Menschenfeind (Raimund) **69**:5, 8-10, 12-13, 18, 22, 25-6, 34-5, 38, 43-6, 48, 50, 53, 58-61
"Alphonso of Castile" (Emerson) **98**:179
"An Alpimalyan Dialogue" (Turgenev) **21**:431
Alpine Roses (Boyesen)
See *Ilka on the Hill-Top*
The Alp-king and the Misanthropist (Raimund)
See *Der Alpenkönig und der Menschenfeind*
"The Alps" (Tyutchev) **34**:381
"The Alps at Daybreak" (Rogers) **69**:67
"Alpuhara" (Mickiewicz)
See "Alpujarra"
"Alpujarra" (Mickiewicz) **3**:398
La Alpujarra (Alarcon) **1**:12, 14
Alroy (Disraeli)
See *The Wondrous Tale of Alroy*

"Als er sein Weib und's Kind an Ihrer Brust Schlafend Fand" (Claudius) **75**:192
"Also on Humor and Style Therein" (Almqvist)
See "Aven om humor och stil däri"
Das alte Buch und die Reise ins Blaue hinein (Tieck) **5**:519
Der alte Leibkutscher Peter des Dritten (Kotzebue) **25**:139-40
Der alte Mann mit der jungen Frau (Nestroy) **42**:230, 233
Das alte Siegal (Stifter) **41**:336, 379
"Der Alte Turmhahn" (Mörike) **10**:447, 453
Der Alte vom Berge (Tieck) **5**:519
Altenglisches Theatre (Tieck) **5**:520; **46**:359
"Although I put away his life-" (Dickinson) **77**:65
Altiora Peto (Oliphant) **47**:278-79, 281, 284-85
Alton Locke, Tailor and Poet (Kingsley) **35**:203-04, 209, 213-15, 220-23, 227, 228, 230-31, 233-34, 235-37, 240-41, 242, 244, 246-48, 249-53, 254-56
Altorf (Wright) **74**:363
"Ałushta at Night" (Mickiewicz)
See "Ałuszta w nocy"
"Ałushta in Daytime" (Mickiewicz)
See "Ałuszta w dzień"
"Ałuszta at Day" (Mickiewicz)
See "Ałuszta w dzień"
"Ałuszta at Night" (Mickiewicz)
See "Ałuszta w nocy"
"Ałuszta w dzień" (Mickiewicz) **3**:403
"Ałuszta w nocy" (Mickiewicz) **3**:403-04
The Alvareda Family (Caballero)
See *La familia de Alvareda: Novela original de costumbres populares*
"Always with You" (Isaacs)
See "Siempre contigo"
Alwin (Fouqué) **2**:267
Alwyn (Holcroft)
See *Alwyn, or The Gentleman Comedian*
Alwyn, or The Gentleman Comedian (Holcroft) **85**:206, 215, 218, 228, 234, 236-37, 239-40, 243
"Am Brunnen vor dem Tore" (Muller) **73**:374, 380-85, 387, 391-92, 394
"Am drei: Sonntag nach Ostern" (Droste-Hülshoff) **3**:196
"Am Feierabend" (Muller) **73**:364, 370
"Am Feste Mariae Lichtmess" (Droste-Hülshoff) **3**:196
"Am Himmelstor" (Meyer) **81**:143, 162
Am Kamin (Storm) **1**:542, 544
"Am Neujahrstag" (Droste-Hülshoff) **3**:202
Am olam (Smolenskin) **30**:186-88, 192-93, 198
"Am Quell der Donau" (Hölderlin) **16**:175, 195
"Am Sylvester" (Meyer) **81**:157
"Am Tage der Freundschaftsfeier" (Hölderlin) **16**:174
"Am Turme" (Droste-Hülshoff) **3**:202
"Am Wassersturz" (Meyer) **81**:142
Amadis (Gobineau) **17**:83
Amadis of Gaul (Southey) **97**:267-68
"Amandar" (Cooke) **110**:43
"Les amants de Kandahar" (Gobineau) **17**:70, 92-3, 103
"Les Amants de Montmorency" (Vigny) **102**:368
Amaryllis (Jefferies)
See *Amaryllis at the Fair*
Amaryllis at the Fair (Jefferies) **47**:91-93, 95, 97, 101-06, 113, 116, 118, 120, 122, 134, 137, 140, 142-43, 145
Amateur Emigrant (Stevenson) **5**:414
The Amateur Poacher (Jefferies) **47**:88, 90, 100-02, 111-12, 114, 121, 126-27, 133-34
"Amatsu otome" (Ueda Akinari) **131**:20-22, 55
Amaury (Dumas) **71**:204
"The Amazon" (Leskov)
See "Voitel' nica"
Ambarvalia (Clough) **27**:41, 43, 76-7, 91, 98, 104-7, 114
The Ambassador's Wife (Gore) **65**:20
The Ambiguities (Melville)
See *Pierre; or, The Ambiguities*
L'ambitieux (Scribe) **16**:388, 414
"Ambition" (Lampman) **25**:201, 208, 220
The Ambitious Ones (Scribe)
See *L'ambitieux*
Ambras Américas (Faustino) **123**:268, 273, 275-77
"Ambrosio, of The Monk" (James)
See *The Monk, a Romance*
"Ambuscades" (Kirkland) **85**:265
"Ambush" (Mickiewicz)
See "Czaty"
"L'ame de la maison ou la vie et la mort d'un grillon" (Gautier) **59**:31
"L'ame du vin" (Baudelaire) **6**:129; **55**:2
"L'âme errante" (Desbordes-Valmore) **97**:29
"Ame et jeunesse" (Desbordes-Valmore) **97**:6
"Amelia" (Patmore) **9**:343
"Amelia Webster" (Austen) **119**:13
Amélie et Germaine (Constant) **6**:223
"Amen!" (Rossetti) **50**:268
"América" (Bello) **131**:109
America: A Prophecy, 1793 (Blake) **13**:159, 163, 167, 183, 214-15, 217, 222, 233, 251-52; **37**:4, 33, 51; **57**:56; **127**:11, 77-8
America libera (Alfieri) **101**:48-50
"America; or, A Poem on the Settlement of the British Colonies" (Dwight) **13**:275, 277
America Revisited (Sala) **46**:234
"America to Great Britain" (Allston) **2**:21
"American civilization" (Emerson) **98**:43-4, 49, 171
"American Claimant" (Hawthorne) **39**:245
The American Crisis (Paine) **62**:247-8, 250, 265, 270, 281, 312, 321-2, 353, 364-71, 391
The American Democrat; or, Hints on the Social and Civil Relations of the United States of America (Cooper) **1**:216-17; **54**:256, 288-90, 300
An American Dictionary of the English Language . . . (Webster) **30**:391, 393-401, 407, 409-14, 419
"The American Drama" (Poe) **55**:172, 182
The American Frugal Housewife (Child) **6**:198-99; **73**:40, 50, 58, 66-7, 75, 86, 96, 129
The American Fugitive in Europe: Sketches of Places and People Abroad (Brown)
See *Three Years in Europe; or, Places I Have Seen and People I Have Met*
The American Gardener (Cobbett) **49**:110, 150, 156
"The American Ideal Woman" (Kirkland) **85**:270, 272
"American Independence" (Freneau) **111**:142
"The American Legend" (Taylor) **89**:302
"American Liberty" (Freneau) **111**:139
"American Literature" (Lazarus) **109**:295, 305
"An American Love Ode" (Warton) **118**:356
American Notebooks (Hawthorne) **17**:153; 95; 105-8, 110-11
American Notes for General Circulation (Dickens) **3**:143-44; **113**:145
"The American Novelist and His Public" (Boyesen) **135**:20, 22
"The American Pantheon" (Cranch) **115**:22, 41
An American Primer (Whitman) **4**:576-77, 580; **31**:374; **81**:286, 309, 311, 326, 347
The American Republic (Brownson) **50**:35, 52-3, 65, 67-8
The American Rushlight (Cobbett)
See *The Rush-Light*
"The American Scholar" (Emerson) **98**:9, 12, 17-19, 21, 26-7, 63, 107, 113, 144, 150, 152-53, 160, 190
American Scholar (Emerson) **1**:285-87, 299, 306-07; **38**:158, 186, 206, 208, 218-22
An American Selection of Lessons in Reading and Speaking (Webster)
See *A Grammatical Institute, of the English Language, Comprising, an Easy, Concise, and Systematic Method of Education, Designed for the Use of English Schools in America*
The American Senator (Trollope) **6**:461, 466, 477, 518; **33**:363; **101**:251, 253, 257, 292, 309, 327
American Silvas (Bello)
See *Silvas Americanas*
"American Slavery" (Emerson) **98**:43, 45
"The American Soldier" (Freneau) **111**:124, 191
The American Spelling Book (Webster)
See *A Grammatical Institute, of the English Language, Comprising, an Easy, Concise, and Systematic Method of Education, Designed for the Use of English Schools in America*
"An American Tale" (Williams) **135**:315
The American Tar (Rowson) **69**:140-41
"The American Village" (Freneau) **1**:320, 324; **111**:100, 108, 139, 143, 146-51, 166
The American Woman's Home; or, Principles of Domestic Science (Beecher) **30**:15, 17, 22-4
American Women: Will You Save Your Country (Beecher)
See *The Duty of American Women to Their Country*
Americans in England (Rowson) **69**:140-41
"America's Mightiest Inheritance" (Whitman) **81**:286-87, 292, 294-95
"Les ames du purgatoire" (Mérimée) **6**:360, 363, 366, 369-70; **65**:48-50, 53-9, 61, 63-4, 102, 105, 121
Les âmes vaillantes (Dumas) **71**:217, 221-22
Améthystes (Banville) **9**:17, 28
"L'ami d'enfance" (Desbordes-Valmore) **97**:28
L'ami des femmes (Dumas) **9**:223-24, 226, 230-31, 245-46, 249, 253
An Amicable Settlement (Turgenev) **21**:432
"Amicus Redivivus" (Lamb) **10**:435-36
Amiel's Journal: The Journal Intime of Henri-Frédéric Amiel (Amiel)
See *Fragments d'un journal intime*
Les amies (Verlaine) **2**:621, 632; **51**:363
"Les amies de pension" (Villiers de l'Isle Adam) **3**:588
"Amigos vellos" (Castro) **3**:101
Amistad funesta (Martí) **63**:85, 92
Ammalat-bek (Bestuzhev) **131**:152, 160-64, 186, 200
"Amnistie" (Desbordes-Valmore) **97**:30
Among Friends One Always Comes to Terms (Ostrovsky)
See *Svoi lyudi—sochtemsya!*
Among My Books (Lowell) **2**:509; **90**:219
"Among the Euganean Hills" (Symonds) **34**:352
"Among the Hills" (Whittier) **8**:521, 525; **59**:361, 371
Among the Hills, and Other Poems (Whittier) **8**:501; **59**:357, 360
Among the Millet, and Other Poems (Lampman) **25**:160-61, 168-69, 176, 178, 180, 183, 192, 194-95, 199, 212
"Among the Multitude" (Whitman) **81**:329
"Among the Orchards" (Lampman) **25**:167
"Among the Timothy" (Lampman) **25**:160, 168, 183, 196, 198-200, 207, 219
"Among the Trees" (Bryant) **6**:168, 174, 187; **46**:15, 19
Amor con Amor se Paga (Martí) **63**:103
Amor de padre (Martínez de la Rosa) **102**:230, 245-47
"Amor en el claustro" (Casal) **131**:264
"Amor eterno" (Isaacs) **70**:307, 311
"Amor mundi" (Rossetti) **2**:562; **50**:272; **66**:305
"Amor Vitae" (Lampman) **25**:218
L'amore delle tre melarance (Gozzi) **23**:107, 113-14, 117-20, 122-25, 127, 129

"Amore e Morte" (Leopardi) **129**:217, 219-20, 357, 360
"Amores catiros" (Castro) **78**:42
"Amores de Soledad" (Isaacs) **70**:306
Amorina (Almqvist) **42**:6, 10, 14, 16-17
Amoroso, King of Little Britain (Planché) **42**:272, 285
"Amos Barton" (Eliot)
See "The Sad Fortunes of the Rev. Amos Barton"
"L'Amour" (Desbordes-Valmore) **97**:5
"Amour" (Maupassant) **83**:174
L'amour (Michelet) **31**:214, 218, 222, 224-25, 260-62
Amour (Verlaine) **2**:618-19, 628, 632; **51**:351-2, 355, 359, 361-2, 266-8, 370, 372
L'Amour Africain (Mérimée) **65**:52, 58, 62, 79, 82
L'amour au 18e siècle (Goncourt and Goncourt) **7**:165
"L'amour de mensonge" (Baudelaire) **29**:101; **55**:23
"L'amour et le crâne" (Baudelaire) **6**:80; **55**:27, 74, 80
L'amour et le grimoire (Nodier) **19**:379
L'amour impossible (Barbey d'Aurevilly) **1**:71
"Amour joie et fléau du monde" (Gautier) **59**:17
"L'amour par terre" (Verlaine) **51**:378, 382
"L'amour suprême" (Villiers de l'Isle Adam) **3**:591
Les amoureuses (Daudet) **1**:238, 243, 248-50
Amours de Gervais et d'Eulalie (Nodier) **19**:402
Les Amours de Philippe (Feuillet) **45**:83, 85, 91
"Les amours de Vienne" (Nerval) **67**:363
Amours de Voyage (Clough) **27**:42-3, 46-9, 52, 56-8, 62, 65-6, 71, 73, 77-82, 92, 97-8, 103, 108-10, 112-16
Les amours forcés (Balzac) **5**:84
Les amours jaunes (Corbière) **43**:2, 4-5, 7, 11, 13, 19, 22, 24, 26-33
Amphitryon (Kleist) **2**:438-39, 442-43, 445, 450, 454, 456, 458; **37**:217, 225, 233, 237, 239, 243, 253, 255, 267, 271-4
"Ample Make This Bed" (Dickinson) **21**:80
The Amulet (Meyer)
See *Das Amulett*
Das Amulett (Meyer) **81**:183, 186-90
"Amusements" (Crabbe) **26**:121
"Amy" (Tennyson) **65**:369
"Amy Cranstoun" (Sedgwick) **19**:444
"Amy Wentworth" (Whittier) **8**:519; **59**:360, 370-1
Amymone, a Romance of the Days of Pericles (Linton) **41**:163, 165
"Amy's Cruelty" (Browning) **61**:7, 45, 76
"An Bodmer" (Klopstock) **11**:237
"An Done" (Klopstock) **11**:237
"An Ebert" (Klopstock) **11**:220, 237
"An Fanny" (Klopstock) **11**:237
"An Giske" (Klopstock) **11**:236
"An Gott" (Klopstock) **11**:237
Anacreon's Grave (Pushkin) **3**:415
Anakreon und die Sogenannten Anakreontischen Lieder (Mörike) **10**:449
Analysis of the Influence of Natural Religion on the Temporal Happiness of Mankind (Bentham) **38**:92, 97-9
Analytical Studies (Balzac)
See *Etudes analytiques*
Ananda math (Chatterji) **19**:204, 211, 213-16, 218-22, 224
Ānandamath (Chatterji)
See *Ananda math*
The Anarchiad: A New England Poem (Trumbull) **30**:352, 375, 379
Anarchichal Fallacies: Being an Examination of the Declaration of Rights Issued During the French Revolution (Bentham) **38**:52
"Anarchism" (Adams) **33**:18, 24
"Anarchy and Authority" (Arnold) **126**:7, 23, 41, 44
The Anas (Jefferson) **11**:171, 173, 199
"Anastasius" (Chivers) **49**:50
"L'anathème" (Leconte de Lisle) **29**:221, 228, 231, 235
"L'Anatomiste" (Borel)
See "Don Andréa Vésalius l'anatomiste"
The Ancestral Footstep (Hawthorne) **2**:324, 333, 335
The Ancestress (Grillparzer)
See *Die Ahnfrau*
"Anchar" (Pushkin) **3**:443
"L'Ancien Régime" (Thomson) **18**:391-92
L'ancien régime (Taine) **15**:425, 430, 432-33, 439, 447, 466, 474
L'ancien régime et la révolution (Tocqueville) **7**:423, 427, 432-35, 445-46, 455, 458; **63**:282, 290, 292-3, 336, 340
"Ancient and Modern Ideas of Purity" (Patmore) **9**:342
Ancient Ballads and Legends of Hindustan (Dutt) **29**:122-23, 125-30
"Ancient Feast" (Shevchenko)
See "Tryzna"
"Ancient Idols" (Horne) **127**:276
"The Ancient Mariner" (Coleridge)
See *The Rime of the Ancient Mariner: A Poet's Reverie*
The Ancient Mariner (Coleridge)
See *The Rime of the Ancient Mariner: A Poet's Reverie*
"The Ancient Poets" (Thoreau)
See "Homer. Ossian. Chaucer."
"An Ancient Proverb" (Blake) **13**:240; **37**:35
"The Ancient Sage" (Tennyson) **30**:226-28, 250, 254, 269-70, 275; **65**:241; **115**:257, 335, 348
Ancient Spanish Ballads, Historical and Romantic (Lockhart) **6**:292-93, 295-97
"An Ancient Tale—Roman and Olda" (Bestuzhev)
See "Starinnaia povest'—Roman i Ol'ga"
"And ar'n't I a woman?" (Truth)
See "Ar'n't I a woman?"
"And Did Those Feet in Ancient Time Walk upon England's Mountains Green?" (Blake) **13**:205
"And If the Branches" (Eminescu) **33**:247, 249
And the Weary Are at Rest (Brontë) **109**:26, 29, 38
"Andenken" (Hölderlin) **16**:176
"¿Cuál es el método o sistema preferible para escribir la historia?" (Martínez de la Rosa) **102**:248, 254
"¿Cuál es la influencia del espíritu del siglo actual sobre la literatura?" (Martínez de la Rosa) **102**:254
André (Dunlap) **2**:210-18
André (Sand) **2**:587; **42**:319-20, 335, 353; **57**:312, 317-20, 332, 367
"André Chénier" (Pushkin) **83**:298-99, 301-06
André del Sarto (Musset) **7**:271, 281
André le Savoyard (Kock) **16**:245
"Andrea del Sarto" (Browning) **19**:117, 127, 132-33, 153; **79**:98, 106, 110-11, 163-64, 170
Andrea of Hungary (Landor) **14**:165
"Andréa Vésalius" (Borel)
See "Don Andréa Vésalius l'anatomiste"
"Andrei Kolosov" (Turgenev) **21**:377, 414, 417, 431, 438; **37**:435; **122**:242, 247, 258, 266
"Andrei Mureşanu" (Eminescu) **33**:245, 264, 266
"Andrej Kolosov" (Turgenev)
See "Andrei Kolosov"
"Andrew Rykman's Prayer" (Whittier) **8**:496, 524; **59**:366
Andrey, knyaz' Pereyaslavskii (Bestuzhev) **131**:147, 151, 182
"Andrey Kolosov" (Turgenev)
See "Andrei Kolosov"
Andrey, Prince of Pereyaslavl' (Bestuzhev)
See *Andrey, knyaz' Pereyaslavskii*
"Andromeda" (Kingsley) **35**:211-212, 219, 232
Andromeda, and Other Poems (Kingsley) **35**:205-06, 249
Andy Blake (Boucicault) **41**:28
Andy Gordon (Alger) **8**:43-44
Andy Grant's Pluck (Alger) **8**:20
Andzhelo (Pushkin) **3**:461
"L'ane" (Banville) **9**:16
"L'ane" (Maupassant) **100**:181
"Anecdote for Fathers" (Wordsworth) **12**:387, 430, 446; **111**:202, 209, 223-25, 227, 251-52, 279-81, 316, 348, 358
"An Anecdote on Byron" (Pushkin) **83**:273
"Anecdotes" (Pushkin) **83**:270
Anecdotes and Egotisms (Mackenzie) **41**:187, 189-90, 190, 192, 195, 210
Anecdotes of Sir Walter Scott (Hogg)
See *Familiar Anecdotes of Sir Walter Scott*
Anecdotes of the Late Samuel Johnson, LL.D., During the Last Twenty Years of His Life (Piozzi) **57**:241-2, 253, 259, 265-7, 270, 275, 285, 287-97, 299, 302-4
Anfangsgründe der Tugendlehre (Huxley) **67**:214
"L'ange exilé" (Beranger) **34**:43
"L'ange, fragment épique" (Lamartine) **11**:273
"L'Ange gardien" (Desbordes-Valmore) **97**:22
"L'ange mélancolique" (Banville) **9**:14
Ange Pitou (Dumas) **71**:232, 242-43
L'ange tutélaire; ou, Le démon femelle (Pixérécourt) **39**:274, 276-77, 279, 286
"The Angel" (Blake) **13**:221; **37**:4, 11, 13, 43, 51, 78, 92
"Angel" (Lermontov) **5**:288, 292-94, 299; **126**:129, 144, 214
"Angel and Daemon" (Eminescu) **33**:245, 247; **131**:295
"Angel and Demon" (Eminescu)
See "Angel and Daemon"
"An Angel in the House" (Hunt) **70**:264
The Angel in the House (Patmore) **9**:335-57, 342-43, 345-49, 351-52, 354-56, 361-62, 364, 366
The Angel in the House, Book I: The Betrothal (Patmore) **9**:329-33, 335-36
The Angel in the House, Book II: The Espousals (Patmore) **9**:330-32
"The Angel of Patience" (Taylor) **89**:306-07
"The Angel of the Odd" (Poe) **117**:192, 195, 217, 221-22, 224, 237-38, 242-43, 260, 280-82, 297, 299, 309, 334, 336
"El ángel y el poeta" (Espronceda) **39**:86
Angela (Dumas)
See *Angèle*
Ángela (Tamayo y Baus) **1**:565-67, 571
Angela Borgia (Meyer) **81**:199
Angèle (Dumas) **11**:43, 48, 57, 67; **71**:193
"Angelic Guidance" (Newman) **38**:345
Angelika (Storm) **1**:536, 539-40
"Angelina" (Edgeworth) **1**:255; **51**:84, 86, 88, 90
Angélique (Nerval) **1**:485; **67**:332, 345-47, 358, 363-64, 366
Angelo (Pushkin) **83**:339
Angelo, Tyran de Padove (Hugo) **3**:256, 269
Angels of the Family (Desbordes-Valmore)
See *Les Anges de la famille*
"The Angel's Whisper" (Chivers) **49**:49
L'angélus (Maupassant) **1**:468; **83**:168, 177-81, 224
"L'Angelus du matin" (Verlaine) **51**:369-70
Les Anges de la famille (Desbordes-Valmore) **97**:12
L'Anglais mangeur d'opium (Musset) **7**:279
"The Angle of a Landscape" (Dickinson) **21**:75
"The Angler" (Irving) **19**:327
"The Angler's Farewell" (Hood) **16**:235
"The Angler's Tent" (Wilson) **5**:545, 567
The Anglo-Irish of the Nineteenth Century (Banim) **13**:141
"Angoisse" (Mallarmé) **41**:241
"Angoisse" (Rimbaud) **4**:487; **35**:296, 313, 323

Anhelli (Slowacki) **15**:348-49, 354-59, 364, 366-69
"Anianpelto" (Kivi) **30**:51
Anima poetae (Coleridge) **9**:157; **99**:77, 87
"Animal Automatism" (Huxley) **67**:16
Animal Magnetism (Inchbald) **62**:143-5, 147-8, 150
"Animal Tranquillity and Decay" (Wordsworth) **111**:227, 276-77
Animi Figura (Symonds) **34**:323
"Ann Lisbeth" (Andersen) **7**:37; **79**:77
"Ann Potter's Lesson" (Cooke) **110**:33
"Ann Withers: The Changeling" (Lamb) **125**:318, 326, 362-63
"Anna" (Hebbel) **43**:253
"Anna Grace" (Ferguson) **33**:293-94
Anna St. Ives (Holcroft) **85**:192-93, 206-07, 228-29, 231, 234, 236-40, 242-44
"Annabel Lee" (Poe) **1**:496, 502-03, 509; **55**:133, 136, 141; **117**:192, 195, 217, 221-22, 224, 237-38, 242-43, 260, 280-82, 297, 299, 309, 334, 336
Annals of a Publishing House: William Blackwood and His Sons, Their Magazine and Friends (Oliphant) **61**:171, 173, 216
Annals of Lacock Abbey (Bowles) **103**:61
Annals of Quodlibet (Kennedy) **2**:429-35
Annals of the Parish; or, The Chronicle of Dalmailing (Galt) **1**:328-37; **110**:76-82, 84-6, 88, 93-4, 96, 98, 101-2
Anne (Woolson) **82**:268-70, 272-73, 277-78, 280-81, 292-93, 308, 314-15, 322, 324-25, 327-28, 330-31, 335
Anne Bäbi Jowäger (Gotthelf)
See *Wie Anne Bäbi Jowäger haushaltet und wie es ihm mit dem Dokterngeht*
Anne Boleyn (Boker) **125**:8, 19-20, 28, 31, 36, 58, 61-62, 64-65, 76
Anne of Geierstein (Scott) **15**:307; **69**:304, 316, 329, 332, 334
Un année dans le sahel (Fromentin) **10**:226-27, 232, 240, 259; **125**:103-4, 106, 108-12, 114-15, 122, 132, 138, 146
"L'année terrible" (Banville) **9**:16
L'année terrible (Hugo) **3**:256
"Annette Delarbre" (Irving) **2**:368, 387, 389
"Annexes" (Whitman) **4**:563
"Annie and Rhoda" (Whittier) **8**:505
"Annie of Tharaw" (Pinkney) **31**:273
"The Annihilation of Aesthetics" (Pisarev)
See "Razrushenie estetiki"
"An Anniversary" (Hayne) **94**:159
"Anno Domini" (Rossetti) **2**:568
"L'annonciateur" (Villiers de l'Isle Adam) **3**:590
Annotations to Lavater (Blake) **57**:63-4
Annotations to Swedenborg (Blake) **57**:63
Annouchka (Turgenev)
See *Asya*
The Annual Register (Crabbe) **121**:73
Annus Domini: A Prayer for Every Day in the Year (Rossetti) **50**:271, 273; **66**:305
"Another Defense of Woman's Great Abilities" (Kierkegaard)
See "Ogsaa et Forsvar for Qvindens hoie Anlæg"
"Another Leaf" (Bestuzhev)
See "Eshche listok"
Another Night with the National Guard (Scribe)
See *Encore une nuit de la Garde Nationale; ou, Le poste de la barrière*
"Another Spring" (Rossetti) **50**:293; **66**:382
"Another View of Hester" (Hawthorne) **10**:289, 297
"Another Way of Love" (Browning) **19**:127; **79**:153
Another's (Dostoevsky) **2**:168
Answer to the Bishop of Llandaff (Paine) **62**:314
"Answer to the Letter from My Beloved" (Petofi)
See "Válasz kedvesem levelére"
"A'n't a Woman?" (Neel)
See "Ar'n't I a woman?"
"The Ant Hills" (Cranch) **115**:47
"The Antagonist's Hymn" (Holmes) **81**:98
"The Antchar" (Turgenev) **21**:401
"Ante el retrato de Juana Samary" (Casal) **131**:256-58
L'antéchrist (Renan) **26**:372, 380, 402, 408
"Antéros" (Nerval) **1**:486; **67**:318, 362
Anthologia Germanica—German Anthology (Mangan) **27**:273-75, 277, 314
Anthologia Hibernica (Mangan) **27**:314
Anthologie auf das Jahr 1782 (Schiller) **39**:339, 354, 357, 386-87
Anthology of Classical Poetry (Mörike) **10**:457
Anthony and Cleopatra (Alfieri)
See *Antonio e Cleopatra*
The Anthropological Principle in Philosophy (Chernyshevsky) **1**:159-60, 167
Anthropologie (Kant) **27**:249, 259-60, 262; **67**:215
Anthropology from a Pragmatic Point of View (Kant)
See *Anthropologie*
Anthropology with a Pragmatic Purpose (Kant)
See *Anthropologie*
Antichrist (Renan)
See *L'antéchrist*
The Antidote (Alfieri)
See *L'antidoto*
L'antidoto (Alfieri) **101**:45, 73
Anti-Dühring (Engels)
See *Herr Eugen Dührings Umwälzung de Wissenschaft: Philosophie; Politische Oekonomie; Sozialismus*
"Antigone" (Arnold) **6**:37
Antigone (Alfieri) **101**:4-5, 11, 12, 32, 42
"The Antigone and Its Moral" (Eliot) **118**:52, 56
"Las antiguedades de Merida" (Larra) **17**:271
"Antiker Form sich nähernd" (Goethe) **4**:193
"The Anti-Marriage League" (Oliphant) **61**:205, 215, 242
Anti-Monarchical Essay (Paine) **62**:271
Anti-Ovid (Wieland) **17**:417-18
"The Antiquarian" (Freneau) **111**:134
The Antiquary (Scott) **15**:259-60, 277, 284, 289, 294-95, 300, 302-03, 309-10, 317; **69**:313, 392
"Antique" (Rimbaud) **35**:322; **82**:232-33
"The Antiquity of Freedom" (Bryant) **6**:168, 189; **46**:7, 47
Anti-Slavery Catechism (Child) **73**:60, 77, 104
The Anti-Slavery Harp: A Collection of Songs for Anti-Slavery Meetings (Brown) **2**:47; **89**:143, 182, 188
"Anti-Slavery in the United States" (Lowell) **90**:213
Anti-Slavery Standard (Child) **73**:51-2, 60, 69-70, 77-80, 87, 96, 105-6
"Anti-Thelyphthora" (Cowper) **94**:110
"Antonia" (Galt) **1**:327
Antonia (Sand) **57**:316
"Antonie" (Villiers de l'Isle Adam) **3**:590
Antoniella (Lamartine) **11**:279, 286
Antonina; or, The Fall of Rome (Collins) **1**:172-73, 177, 181; **93**:19, 64
Antonio e Cleopatra (Alfieri) **101**:57-8
Antony (Dumas) **11**:42-43, 47-48, 57-58, 63, 66-67, 72, 79, 82-83, 89; **71**:184, 187, 193, 204, 209-10, 229-30, 241
"Antony and Octavius" (Landor) **14**:183
Antrag auf Errichtung der Universität Berlin (Humboldt) **134**:204-5
"Antwerp and Bruges" (Rossetti) **4**:521-22
Antwort an Andres auf seinen letzten Brief (Claudius) **75**:193
Der Anverwandten (Nestroy) **42**:233-34
Die Anweisung zum seligen Leben, oder auch die Religionslehre (Fichte) **62**:35
"Any Wife to Any Husband" (Browning) **19**:90, 127, 131, 155; **79**:163
"Aozukin" (Ueda Akinari) **131**:13, 24, 26, 28, 34, 38, 41, 48, 87
Aozukin (Ueda Akinari) **131**:71-72
"La aparición" (Casal) **131**:223, 226, 236, 265-68
"The Ape" (Lamb) **10**:405
"Apel podobo na ogled postavi" (Preseren) **127**:312
Apéndice sobre la tragedia española (Martínez de la Rosa) **102**:246
"The Apennines" (Bryant) **46**:21-2
Aphorismen zur Lebensweisheit (Schopenhauer) **51**:283
"Aphorisms on Man" (Hazlitt) **82**:111
"Aphrodite" (Lazarus) **109**:294
"Apocalypse" (Cowper) **8**:127
"Apollo" (Chivers) **49**:47, 53, 56, 74
"Apollo and the Fates" (Browning) **79**:185
"Apollo in Picardy" (Pater) **7**:303; **90**:245, 272, 276, 290
"An Apologetic Irenicon" (Huxley) **67**:65
Apologia pro Vita Sua: Being a Reply to a Pamphlet Entitled "What, Then, Does Dr Newman Mean?" (Newman) **38**:270-71, 281, 283, 285-86, 290, 292, 295-96, 299, 305, 312-14, 318-20, 322-23, 325-27, 332-42, 344, 346, 348; **99**:212, 218, 241, 243-44, 254, 256, 258-61, 266, 271, 274-76, 278, 282, 285-86, 288, 290-93, 297
"Apologue of Critobulus" (Landor) **14**:187
"The Apology" (Hood) **16**:206
"An Apology for the Hellenics" (Landor) **14**:189
"Apology for the Poor" (Clare) **86**:171
Der Aposte (Ludwig)
See *Der Kandidat*
The Apostles (Renan)
See *Les Apôtres*
"The Apostolical Christian" (Newman) **38**:304
"L'apostrophe" (Balzac) **5**:78
"The Apostrophe to Twilight" (Norton) **47**:239
"L'apothéose de Mouça-al-Kébyr" (Leconte de Lisle) **29**:225-26
"Apotheosis" (Dickinson)
See "Come Slowly, Eden"
Les Apôtres (Renan) **26**:378, 402, 408, 421
"Apparent Failure" (Browning) **19**:112
Apparition (Mallarmé) **41**:277, 279
"The Apparition of the Shade of Samuel" (Lamartine) **11**:249, 277
An Appeal for the Indians (Child) **73**:84
Appeal in Favor of That Class of Americans Called Africans (Child) **6**:199, 203-04, 209; **73**:51, 55, 59, 68, 72, 76-7, 83-4, 86, 97, 102-07, 109, 118
"An Appeal to the Free" (Moodie) **113**:310
Appeal to the Men of Great Britain in Behalf of Women (Hays) **114**:200, 203, 206-7, 210-13, 216, 219, 223-24, 230-33, 240, 247, 254
An Appeal to the People on Behalf of Their Rights as Authorized Interpreters of the Bible (Beecher) **30**:9, 13
Appeal to the Slavs (Bakunin) **25**:45, 63; 58, 97, 106-7, 133
"Appearance is Against Her" (Opie) **65**:172
Appearance is Against Them (Inchbald) **62**:143, 145-7
The Appearance to Mary Magdalen (N-Town Cycle) (Anonymous) **131**:321
Appel au public occidental (Comte) **54**:210
Appel aux conservateurs (Comte) **54**:210
"Appel aux Souverains" (Staël-Holstein) **91**:340, 342
"Appendix" (De Quincey) **4**:87-88
"An Apple Gathering" (Rossetti) **2**:555-6; **50**:295-7, 322; **66**:351-4, 383
"Appledore" (Lowell) **2**:514
"The Apple-Tree Table" (Melville) **3**:380, 382-83

Appreciations (Pater) **90**:241-42, 248, 251, 283, 288, 292, 305, 323-26, 334
Appreciations: With an Essay on Style (Pater) **7**:299-301, 323, 330; **90**:325
"Apprenticed" (Ingelow) **39**:264
Apprenticeship (Goethe)
See *Wilhelm Meisters Lehrjahre*
"l'Appressamento della morte" (Leopardi) **129**:241
"The Approach of Summer" (Bowles) **103**:58
"Approaching Spring" (Dyer) **129**:149
Appropriate Stories (Leskov) (Leskov) **25**:228
"Après" (Maupassant) **83**:182
"Après la pluie" (Corbière) **43**:31
"Après le déluge" (Rimbaud) **4**:462, 466, 473, 487; **35**:322; **82**:230, 233
"Après ma journée faite" (Nerval) **67**:307
L'après-midi d'un faune (Mallarmé) **4**:371, 375-76, 380-81, 387, 389, 395-96; **41**:239, 248-50, 277-80, 294
"April" (Lampman) **25**:165, 183, 188, 198-200
"April 27th, 1865" (Lazarus) **109**:293
"April Gossip" (Jefferies) **47**:138
"April in the Hills" (Lampman) **25**:198
"April Voices" (Lampman) **25**:210
Apuntes biográficos de Emilia Casanova de Villaverde (Villaverde) **121**:335
Apuntes sobre el drama histórico (Martínez de la Rosa) **102**:230
"Aquarelles" (Verlaine) **51**:369, 381-83
"Aquatics" (Thomson) **18**:411
Aquis Submersus (Storm) **1**:536-37, 540-41, 546
"The Arab" (Slowacki) **15**:348-50
"The Arab Horse" (Gordon) **21**:179
"The Arab Steed" (Very) **9**:372
"The Arab Warrior" (Taylor) **89**:302
"Arabella" (Crabbe) **26**:93, 128, 136
"Arabella Hardy; or, The Sea Voyage" (Lamb) **10**:417
"Arabella Stuart" (Hemans) **71**:292
"Arabesque" (Lazarus) **109**:297
Arabesques (Gogol) **5**:209, 216, 219, 240, 253; **15**:85, 94; **31**:101
"Arakoon" (Kendall) **12**:186, 201
"Aralven" (Kendall) **12**:183, 186, 190-91, 199, 201
Aram (Bulwer-Lytton)
See *Eugene Aram*
Araminta May (Almqvist) **42**:4
Arap Petra Velikogo (Pushkin) **3**:435, 456, 462-63; **27**:376; **83**:322-23
Araspes und Panthea (Wieland) **17**:419
"Arbor vitae" (Patmore) **9**:359, 362
L'arbore dri Diana (Da Ponte) **50**:81, 83-4
"Arbutus and Grass" (Rossetti) **50**:275
"Arc de Civa" (Leconte de Lisle) **29**:221
"Arcades Ambo" (Clarke) **19**:249-50
"Archdeacon Hare and Walter Landor" (Landor) **14**:195
Archeology of the Hebrews (Herder) **8**:306
The Archers; or, Mountaineers in Switzerland (Dunlap) **2**:212-13
"Der Archipelagus" (Hölderlin) **16**:162, 174, 181, 187
"The Arctic Voyager" (Timrod) **25**:374
"'Arcturus' Is His Other Name" (Dickinson) **21**:71
"Ardagh" (Le Fanu)
See "The Fortunes of Sir Robert Ardagh"
"Are God and Nature Then at Strife?" (Tennyson) **30**:243
"Are these wild thoughts" (Timrod) **25**:374
"Are Women to Blame?" (Cooke) **110**:54, 63
"Are You the New Person Drawn Toward Me?" (Whitman) **31**:430; **81**:308
"Argemone" (Gordon) **21**:168, 185
L'Argent (Vallès) **71**:358, 378
L'argent des autres (Gaboriau) **14**:19-20
Argirópolis (Faustino) **123**:269-70, 272
Argomenti e abbozzi di poesie (Leopardi) **129**:356
Die Argonauten (Grillparzer) **1**:389; **102**:86-7, 89, 100-03, 163, 186
The Argonauts (Grillparzer)
See *Die Argonauten*
Argow le pirate (Balzac) **5**:58; **53**:23
"Aria Marcella, Souvenir de Pompei" (Gautier) **1**:344-45, 347, 353-54, 356; **59**:6, 11, 13, 32-5, 40, 42
"Ariadne" (Schlegel) **15**:226
"Ariadne Walking" (Hunt) **1**:415
The Arians of the Fourth Century (Newman) **38**:314, 342
"Ariel and Caliban" (Cranch) **115**:35
Ariel and Caliban (Cranch) **115**:18, 23, 35, 37, 39, 42, 55
"Ariel in the Cloven Pine" (Taylor) **89**:300-01
"Ariettes oubliées" (Verlaine) **2**:630; **51**:351, 355, 360, 369, 381-85
"Arion" (Schlegel) **15**:223
Aristipp und einige seiner Zeitgenossen (Wieland) **17**:395-96, 400-01
"Aristocracy" (Emerson) **98**:7, 134
"The Aristocracy of Letters" (Hazlitt) **29**:148
Aristophanes' Apology (Browning) **19**:118, 131; **79**:156, 159, 174-75, 184
Aristotle: a Chapter from the History of Science (Lewes) **25**:288, 295, 310-11
"Arithmetic" (Emerson) **98**:5
"The Ark and the Dove" (Sigourney) **21**:311
L'arlésienne (Daudet) **1**:236, 250, 252
"Armadale" (Dumas) **71**:185
Armadale (Collins) **1**:175, 177, 179-80, 182-83, 185-86; **18**:62, 66, 69, 74, 88; **93**:4, 7-9, 36-40, 44, 46-7, 50, 53, 62, 66
"Armageddon" (Tennyson) **65**:258; **115**:247
Armance; ou, Quelques scènes d'un salon de Paris en 1827 (Stendhal) **23**:349, 362, 367, 370, 374, 378, 392-98, 419; **46**:262, 296
Armand (Mowatt) **74**:216
Der Arme Spielmann (Grillparzer) **1**:385-86, 390-91, 393; **102**:131-32, 139-40, 167-68, 170, 172, 176-79, 184
Der arme Wohltäter (Stifter)
See *Kalkstein*
Armed Neutrality and An Open Letter (Kierkegaard) **125**:265
Das Armenbuch (Arnim) **123**:5, 13-15, 52, 88-89, 92
Die Armennoth (Gotthelf) **117**:4, 32
"Armgart" (Eliot) **4**:107; **13**:334
"Arminius" (Wieland) **17**:396
"L'armoire" (Maupassant) **1**:449; **83**:194, 197, 222
Armuth, Reichtum, Schuld und Busse der Gräfin Dolores: Eine Wahre Geschichte zur lehrreichen Unterhaltung (Arnim) **5**:12-13, 16-17, 21, 23
Armuth und Edelsinn (Kotzebue) **25**:144-47
"The Army Surgeon" (Dobell) **43**:48
Army-Chaplain Schmelzle's Journey to Flaetz (Jean Paul)
See *Des Feldpredigers Schmelzle Reise nach Fätz mit fortgehenden Noten: Nebst der Beichte des Teufels bey einem Staatsmanne*
"Arnold" (Baillie) **71**:16
"Ar'n't I a woman?" (Truth) **94**:302, 311-12, 328, 340
"Arnulph" (Lampman) **25**:183, 220
Arrah-na-Pogue; or, The Wicklow Wedding (Boucicault) **41**:28-31, 33-4, 39, 41, 43, 49-52
Arrest of Five Members by Charles the First: A Chapter of English History Rewritten (Forster) **11**:115
"An Arrogant Bagpiper" (Castro)
See "Un arrogante gaitero"
"Un arrogante gaitero" (Castro) **78**:58
"The Arrow and the Song" (Longfellow) **2**:498; **45**:135, 140, 179
"Ars Longa Vita Brevis" (Cranch) **115**:10
"Ars Longa, Vita Brevis" (Gordon) **21**:160, 164, 181
Ars Poética (Martínez de la Rosa) **102**:226, 228-31, 238-39
"The Ars Poetica of Vojtina" (Arany)
See "Vojtina ars poetikájából"
"The Arsenal at Springfield" (Longfellow) **45**:116, 154-55
"Arsène Guillot" (Mérimée) **6**:354, 359, 362, 364, 368-70; **65**:43, 48-50, 58, 60, 62, 87, 102-3, 113
"A Arsène Houssaye" (Banville) **9**:26
"Art" (Emerson) **1**:280; **38**:173; **98**:114
"L'art" (Gautier) **1**:349; **59**:72
"Art" (Thomson) **18**:403, 420
Art (Reade) **74**:265
"Art and Climate" (Wagner) **119**:249
Art and Revolution (Wagner)
See *Die Kunst und die Revolution*
L'art du dix-huitème siècle (Goncourt and Goncourt) **7**:157, 178-79, 186, 189
Art in Greece (Taine) **15**:419
"L'art moderne" (Gautier) **1**:342
"The Art of Book-Making" (Irving) **2**:368; **19**:328, 347, 350
"The Art of Coquetry" (Lennox) **134**:272, 342
Art of Lying in all its Branches (Opie) **65**:171
"Art of Poetry" (Verlaine)
See "L'Art poètique"
"L'Art poètique" (Verlaine) **2**:621, 624, 629-31; **51**:351, 366, 368-70
L'art pour l'art (Dumas) **9**:233
L'art romantique (Baudelaire) **29**:70, 86; **55**:8
"Art under Plutocracy" (Morris) **4**:445
"Artémis" (Nerval) **1**:476, 481-82, 486; **67**:359-63
"Artemis Prologuises" (Browning) **79**:163
Arthur (Sue) **1**:560
"Arthur Gordon Pym" (Poe)
See *The Narrative of Arthur Gordon Pym, of Nantucket*
Arthur Mervyn; or, Memoirs of the Year 1793 (Brown) **22**:3-5, 7, 11-14, 18-22, 24-5, 27-8, 30-3, 40, 42, 48, 50-5, 57; **74**:4, 9, 11, 13, 15, 17, 19, 21, 36, 41, 47-8, 50-1, 54, 56-7, 61-2, 76, 80, 85, 87, 90, 92, 96-8, 101, 104, 111-14, 117-22, 124, 128-30, 133-36, 143, 161-62, 164, 175, 182; **122**:53-54, 85, 90, 116, 150, 153, 157-58
Arthur O'Leary: His Wanderings and Ponderings in Many Lands (Lever) **23**:300-01
"Arthur Schopenhauer, by A. Zimmern" (Thomson) **18**:400
"The Artic Lover" (Bryant) **6**:169
Articles on the Depreciation of Silver (Bagehot) **10**:26, 31
The Artificial Paradises: On Hashish and Wine as a Means of Expanding Individuality (Baudelaire)
See *Les paradis artificiels: Opium et haschisch*
"The Artilleryman's Vision" (Whitman) **81**:322
"The Artist" (Crampton) **115**:40, 67
The Artist (Shevchenko)
See *Xudoznik*
"The Artist of the Beautiful" (Hawthorne) **2**:303, 329, 332; **39**:223
El artista barquero o los cuatro cinco de junio (Gómez de Avellaneda) **111**:14, 20, 25, 33-5
Artistic Visits or Simple Pilgrimages (Fromentin) **10**:226
"The Artists" (Schiller)
See "Die Künstler"
Artists' Wives (Daudet)
See *Les femmes d'artistes*
The Artwork of the Future (Wagner)
See *Das Kunstwerk der Zukunft*
"As Adam Early in the Morning" (Whitman) **31**:430
"As Consequent, Etc." (Whitman) **31**:388

"As for me, I sing and sing" (Castro)
See "Yo cantar, cantar, canté"
"As I Ebb'd with the Ocean of Life" (Whitman) **4**:582, 600; **31**:388, 405; **81**:249, 364-66
"As I Lay with My Head on Your Lap Camarado" (Whitman) **81**:315, 331
"As I laye a-thinkynge" (Barham) **77**:17
"As I Sat at the Cafe" (Clough) **27**:114
"As I Toilsome Wander'd Virginia Woods" (Whitman) **81**:331
"As I Walkd Forth One May Morning" (Blake) **37**:29
"As If Some Little Arctic Flower" (Dickinson) **21**:8
"As Imperceptibly as Grief" (Dickinson) **21**:67-8
"As Slow Our Ship" (Moore) **110**:190, 192-93
"As the ocean embraces the earthly sphere" (Tyutchev)
See "Kak okean obemlet shar zemnoi"
"As the Starved Maelstrom laps the Navies" (Dickinson) **77**:151
"As You Like It" (Lamb) **125**:306
"Asaji ga yado" (Ueda Akinari) **131**:6-8, 13, 24-25, 29, 34, 38-40, 49, 58, 60, 69-70, 76
"Asathor's Vengeance" (Boyesen) **135**:12, 19
Ascanio (Dumas) **71**:203
"Ascención aerostática" (Larra) **130**:233
Aschenbrödel (Grabbe) **2**:271, 278, 287-88
"Ashaverus" (Andersen) **7**:16
"Ashboughs" (Hopkins) **17**:208, 216
Ashby Manor (Allingham) **25**:11
"Ashes of Soldiers" (Whitman) **4**:543
Ashiwake obune (Motoori) **45**:265-66, 275
Ashmat Shomeron (Mapu) **18**:287-88, 290-93, 295, 298-300
Ashtaroth (Gordon) **21**:149, 151-55, 160, 162, 172-73
"Asia" (Blake) **13**:184
Asia (Turgenev)
See *Asya*
"Eine asiatische Vorlesung" (Claudius) **75**:211, 214-15
Asja (Turgenev)
See *Asya*
Ask Mamma (Surtees) **14**:352-53, 364, 371, 374-75, 377-80
"Ask Me No More" (Tennyson) **30**:239
"Askalonskij zlodej" (Leskov) **25**:229, 245
Aslauga (Fouqué) **2**:265
Asmodeus at Large (Bulwer-Lytton) **45**:19
Asmus, omnia sua secum portans oder Sämtlich Werke des Wandsbecker Boten (Claudius) **75**:183, 192
Asolando (Browning) **19**:110-11, 152; **79**:112-14, 153, 161, 169
Aspasia (Leopardi) **129**:304
"Aspasia; oder Die Platonische Liebe" (Wieland) **17**:427
"Aspects of the Pines" (Hayne) **94**:149, 168
"Aspiration" (Lampman) **25**:161-62, 189, 206, 209, 212
"Aspirations" (Verlaine) **51**:386
Aspirations (Hayne) **94**:134
Aspirations of the World (Child) **6**:203; **73**:54, 72, 84
"The Ass and the Nightingale" (Krylov) **1**:435
"An Assassin" (Adams) **33**:18
"The Assassin of Society" (Cooke) **110**:35-6
"The Assignation" (Poe) **16**:304, 320, 322, 324; **117**:209-10, 281
"Les assis" (Rimbaud) **4**:454, 474; **35**:271, 282, 321
"Assisting at a Negro Night-Meeting" (Harris) **23**:159, 162
The Ass's Burial (Smolenskin)
See *Kevurat hamor*
"Assurance" (Lazarus) **109**:292
"Assyrian Bull" (Tennyson) **30**:215
Asthetische Briefe (Schiller) **69**:257, 260
"Asthetische Erziehung" (Schiller) **39**:380-81; **69**:206, 209-10
Ästhetische Versuche I. Über Göthes Hermann und Dorothea (Humboldt) **134**:193
Astoria (Cooper) **1**:221
Astoria (Irving) **2**:376-77; **95**:254-56, 259
Astraea: The Balance of Illusions (Holmes) **14**:102
Astray on the Path of Life (Smolenskin)
See *ha-To'eh be-darke ha-hayim*
"L'astre rouge" (Leconte de Lisle) **29**:221, 225
Asya (Turgenev) **21**:378, 409, 414, 418, 431, 435, 441; **37**:364; **122**:241-42, 245, 259, 267-68, 277, 348
"At a Dinner of Atheists" (Barbey d'Aurevilly)
See "A un dîner d' athées"
"At a Window" (Allingham) **25**:14
"At Belvoir" (Thomson) **18**:417
At Daggers Drawn (Leskov)
See *Na nožax*
"At Dawn" (Levy) **59**:95, 119
"At Dusk" (Lampman) **25**:185, 210
"At Euroma" (Kendall) **12**:181-82
"At first a thought, embodied" (Baratynsky)
See "Snachala mysl', voploshchena"
"At Half-Past Three a Single Bird" (Dickinson) **21**:33
At His Gates (Oliphant) **61**:173, 206, 211-2, 223
"At Home" (Rossetti) **2**:565; **50**:298; **66**:307
At Home and Abroad (Taylor) **89**:308, 310, 343, 346
At Home and Abroad; or, Things and Thoughts in America (Fuller) **5**:165
"At Last" (Cooke) **110**:3, 9
"At last, beloved Nature" (Timrod) **25**:366, 374
"At Last, To Be Identified!" (Dickinson) **21**:41
"At Ostend" (Bowles)
See "Written at Ostend. July 22, 1787"
"At Pinney's Ranch" (Bellamy) **86**:75
"At Sea" (Lowell) **2**:520
"At Sunset" (Lanier) **6**:238
"At Tarah To-Day" (Mangan) **27**:283
"At the Caberet-Vert" (Rimbaud)
See "Au caberet-vert"
"At the Chateau of Corinne" (Woolson) **82**:276, 308, 310, 341, 345
"At the Door" (Field) **3**:210
"At the Edge of the World" (Leskov)
See "Na kraju sveta"
"At the End of the Year" (Petofi)
See "Az év végén"
"At the Ferry" (Lampman) **25**:169, 188
"At the Foot of the Statue" (Silva)
See "Al pie de la estatua"
"At the Grave of Aron Pumnul" (Eminescu) **131**:294
"At the Grave of Burns" (Wordsworth) **38**:371
"At the Height of the Harvest" (Nekrasov) **11**:417
At the Jubilee in Lund (Tegner) **2**:613
At the Long Sault, and Other New Poems (Lampman) **25**:190, 219-20
"At the Long Sault: May, 1660" (Lampman) **25**:184, 186-87, 189, 199, 201, 219
"At the Mermaid Inn" (Lampman) **25**:177, 179, 208, 218
"At the Mid-Hour of Night When Stars Are Weeping I Fly" (Moore) **6**:391
"At the Pantomine" (Holmes) **14**:109, 128
"At the Polo Ground" (Ferguson) **33**:289
"At the Sun-Rise in 1848" (Rossetti) **77**:292-93, 298
"At the Tea Table" (Pavlova)
See "Za chainym stolom"
"At the Tomb of Leopoldo..." (Isaacs)
See "En la tumba de Leopoldo..."
At the University (Storm)
See *Auf der Universitat*
"At the Water's Edge" (Maupassant)
See "Au bord de l'eau"
"At the West India Docks" (Adams) **33**:16
Atala (Chateaubriand) **134**:3, 15-16, 18-19, 24, 27, 31, 33-36, 39, 46-47, 56-57, 61-63, 70, 78-79, 81, 87, 98, 102-8, 112, 116-23, 127-30, 132, 134, 136-38, 140, 143-49
"Atalanta's Race" (Morris) **4**:416, 427, 447
Atalantis (Simms) **3**:504
L'Atelier d'un peintre (Desbordes-Valmore) **97**:12
Atheismusstreit (Fichte) **62**:47
Athenaeum Fragments (Schlegel) **45**:313, 343-44, 359, 370
Athenaeum-Fragment 51 (Schlegel) **45**:360
Athenaeum-Fragment 77 (Schlegel) **45**:363
Athenaeum-Fragment 116 (Schlegel) **45**:313, 337, 344, 361-62, 366, 369
Athenaeum-Fragment 121 (Schlegel) **45**:381
Athenaeum-Fragment 252 (Schlegel) **45**:364
Athenaeum-Fragment 398 (Schlegel) **45**:382
Athenaeum-Fragment 426 (Schlegel) **45**:366
Athenaeum-Fragment 429 (Schlegel) **45**:315
"An Athenian Reverie" (Lampman) **25**:161, 168, 177-78, 200, 206, 216, 220
Athens, Its Rise and Fall (Bulwer-Lytton) **1**:138, 141, 151-52
Atherton (Mitford) **4**:403
"Atît de frageda" (Eminescu) **33**:249, 251, 265
Atlanta; or, The True Blessed Island of Poesy. A Paul Epic-In Three Lustra (Chivers) **49**:44, 46-7
"The Atlantic Cable" (Ridge) **82**:175
"The Atonement" (Allston) **2**:26
"Atonement" (Taylor) **89**:309
Atta Troll: Ein Sommernachtstraum (Heine) **4**:234, 236, 239-41, 244-46, 252, 265-67; **54**:307, 320, 322
The Attaché; or, Sam Slick in England (Haliburton) **15**:120, 122, 129, 132, 135-36, 144-46
"Attachments of Kindred" (Beattie)
See *Dissertations Moral and Critical: On Memory and Imagination; On Dreaming; The Theory of Language; On Fable and Romance; On the Attachments of Kindred; Illustrations on Sublimity*
"Attack on Fort Sandusky" (Richardson) **55**:342
The Attack upon 'Christendom' (Kierkegaard)
See *Hvad Christus dömmer om officiel Christendom*
"An Attempt of the Author to Estimate His Own Character" (Hunt) **70**:281
"Attempt to Rebut Some Non-Literary Charges" (Pushkin) **83**:317, 320
"An Attempt to Shew the Folly and Danger of Methodism" (Hunt) **1**:406
L'attente (Maupassant) **42**:174; **83**:221
"Attis" (Tennyson) **30**:236
"Au bord de l'eau" (Maupassant) **1**:455
"Au caberet-vert" (Rimbaud) **35**:271, 275, 282,
"Au lecteur" (Baudelaire) **6**:83, 108-09, 114, 122; **29**:95-6, 99; **55**:4, 19, 44-6, 49, 53, 56, 62, 67, 73-4, 78
"Au loisir" (Sainte-Beuve) **5**:347
"Au vieux Roscoff" (Corbière) **43**:14, 32, 34
"Aube" (Rimbaud) **4**:482; **35**:299, 322-25
"L'Aube a l'envers" (Verlaine) **51**:360-61
"L'aube spirituelle" (Baudelaire) **6**:89; **55**:14, 61
L'Auberge rouge (Balzac) **35**:26
Auch ein Beitrag über die neue Politik (Claudius) **75**:194
"Les Audacieux" (Maupassant) **83**:227
"Audley Court" (Tennyson) **30**:238, 279; **65**:258; **115**:335
"Audley End" (Tennyson) **115**:240
Audubon and His Journals (Audubon) **47**:24
"Auerbachs Keller" (Goethe) **4**:215
"Auf dem Canal Grande" (Meyer) **81**:206, 209
"Auf dem Fluße" (Muller) **73**:391, 394
Auf dem Staatshof (Storm) **1**:539, 542
Auf der Universitat (Storm) **1**:535
"Auf der Wanderung" (Meyer) **81**:144

"Auf die Ankunft des Grafen von Falkenstein" (Schiller) **39**:387
"Auf eine Christblume" (Mörike) **10**:454-55
"Auf eine Wanderung" (Mörike) **10**:447
"Auf Goldgrund" (Meyer) **81**:140-41, 150-53, 157, 206
"Auf Wiedersehen" (Longfellow) **45**:132
"Auf Wiedersehen" (Lowell) **2**:511
Der Aufruhr in den Cevennen (Tieck) **5**:514; **46**:397
"Aufsatz, den sichern Weg des Glücks zu finden, und ungestört, auch unter den größten Drangsalen des Lebens, ihn zu genießen1" (Kleist) **37**:218, 235
"Das Auge des Blinden" (Meyer) **81**:209
L'augellin belverde (Gozzi) **23**:112-14, 118-19, 121, 123, 125
"Augure" (Desbordes-Valmore) **97**:14
"Auguries of Innocence" (Blake) **13**:172, 190, 201, 243, 249
"Augury" (Desbordes-Valmore)
See "Augure"
"August" (Clare) **9**:114
"August" (Taylor) **89**:316
"August Moon" (Lazarus) **109**:292, 294-95, 298
"August Night" (Musset)
See "Nuit d' Août"
"An August Pastoral" (Taylor) **89**:315, 317
"August Wilhelm Schlegel" (Lewes) **25**:285, 300
Auguste Comte and Positivism (Mill) **11**:378
"Augustine de Villebranche ou le stratagéme de l'amour" (Sade) **47**:313
"Aul Bastundzi" (Lermontov) **47**:182
"Aulus Persius Flaccus" (Thoreau) **138**:117, 119, 128-30
"Aumône" (Mallarmé) **41**:241, 250, 291
Aunt Carry's Ballads for Children (Norton) **47**:246
Aunt Fanny (Barham) **77**:9
Aunt Jo's Scrap-Bag (Alcott) **6**:15
"Aunt Tabitha" (Holmes) **81**:104
"Auntie Toothache" (Andersen) **79**:66, 73-77
"Auras of Delight" (Patmore) **9**:360
"Aurea dicta" (Patmore) **9**:344, 364
Aurélia (Nerval) **1**:476-78, 480-85, 487; **67**:303-07, 309-14, 322-25, 333-35, 338, 342, 356-58, 360-61, 363-64, 371-76
Aurora (Herder) **8**:307
Aurora Leigh (Browning) **1**:118-25, 128-32; **16**:144, 147, 154; **61**:3-4, 11-2, 14-7, 19, 21, 23-4, 37-9, 44, 49, 52-3, 64, 66, 75-6; **66**:1-118
"L'aurore" (Leconte de Lisle) **29**:224, 244
L'Aurore-Promise (Laforgue) **53**:282
Aus dem Leben eines bekannten Mannes (Hoffmann) **2**:348
"Aus dem Leben eines Taugenichts" (Eichendorff) **8**:210-16, 224, 230-32
Aus dem Regen in die Traufe (Ludwig) **4**:357, 367
Aus den hinterlassenen Papieren (Kotzebue) **25**:133-35
Aus der Chronika eines fahrenden Schülers (Brentano) **1**:96, 100-02, 104-05
"Aus der Vorzeit" (Klopstock) **11**:236
Aus meinen Leben: Dichtung und Wahrheit (Goethe) **4**:168-69, 180, 199
Ausgewählte Werke (Fouqué) **2**:265
"Auspex" (Lowell) **90**:190
"Austin and His Wife" (Opie) **65**:173
Austin Elliott (Kingsley) **107**:188-89, 192, 194, 209, 211, 222-23
"The Austral Months" (Kendall) **12**:200
"Australia Huzza" (Harpur) **114**:144
Australian Essays (Adams) **33**:13, 22, 25
Australian Life (Adams) **33**:13
"An Australian Mining Township" (Clarke)
See "Grumbler's Gully"
"Australian Scenery" (Harpur) **114**:125
The Australians (Adams) **33**:2, 13, 25
"The Austrian Influence on the Romanians in the Principalities" (Eminescu) **131**:325
Authentic Anecdotes of American Slavery (Child) **73**:60, 77
"The Author of 'Saul'" (Taylor) **89**:341
"The Author's Account of Himself" (Irving) **19**:327, 347; **95**:236
"The Authors Address to his Book" (Clare) **86**:173
"The Author's Chamber" (Irving) **2**:372
"An Author's Confession" (Gogol) **5**:227, 230, 238, 254; **15**:85, 92; **31**:127-28
"Author's Introduction" (Lermontov) **5**:304
"An Author's Soliloquy" (Freneau) **111**:161
"Authorship in America" (Taylor) **89**:342
Auto Mariano para recordar la milagrosa aparición de Nuestra Madre y señora de Guadalupe (Lizardi) **30**:68
Autobiografía (Gómez de Avellaneda) **111**:27, 56, 59, 61-2, 65
Autobiographic Sketches (De Quincey) **87**:3, 14, 52, 55
Autobiographical Essays (De Quincey) **4**:65, 70, 79, 83, 85-86
"Autobiographical Fragment" (Froude) **43**:208, 211
Autobiographical fragments (Clare) **86**:171-72, 174
"Autobiographical Memoir" (Newman) **38**:299, 333
"Autobiographical Sketch" (James) **53**:233
Autobiographical Writings (Clare) **86**:109, 151-53, 156-57, 177, 179
Autobiographical Writings (Newman) **38**:299, 333; **99**:286
"Autobiography" (Clare) **86**:108
"Autobiography" (Cranch) **115**:23
"Autobiography" (Huxley) **67**:16, 48, 51-2
"Autobiography" (De Quincey) **87**:48
Autobiography (Adams) **106**:4, 26-31
Autobiography (Alfieri)
See *Vita*
Autobiography (Galt)
See *The Autobiography of John Galt*
Autobiography (Gómez de Avellaneda)
See *Autobiografía*
Autobiography (Madison) **126**:235, 312
Autobiography (Martineau) **137**:236, 242, 245-47, 256, 271-72, 277-79, 281-82, 285, 290, 292-95, 297, 299, 301-3, 315-17, 324-27, 329-36, 356-57, 360
Autobiography (Mill) **11**:351, 353-58, 361, 366-70, 393-94; **58**:319-20, 327, 333, 336-7, 339, 351, 356-9, 361, 375, 378-9
Autobiography (Symonds)
See *The Memoirs*
An Autobiography (Trollope) **6**:467, 475, 478, 483-85, 491-92, 495, 497, 506-07, 510, 514, 519; **33**:364-65, 378; **101**:224, 227, 231, 233, 236, 245-46, 249-51, 253, 261-63, 267-68, 271, 273, 287-88, 290-91, 293, 296, 299, 307-08, 318-22, 330, 332, 335-36, 340-45
The Autobiography and Letters of Mrs. M. O. W. Oliphant (Oliphant) **11**:451-2, 463; **61**:171, 193-4, 196-8, 214-5, 220, 223-4, 234, 237
Autobiography, Letters, and Literary Remains of Mrs. Piozzi (Thrale) (Piozzi) **57**:237, 268, 270, 299
The Autobiography of a Thief (Reade) **2**:546-47; **74**:272, 292
Autobiography of an Actress; or Eight Years on the Stage (Mowatt) **74**:221, 224, 230, 234-35
"Autobiography of an English Opium-Eater" (De Quincey)
See *Confessions of an English Opium-Eater*
"The Autobiography of Author" (Hogg) **109**:274
The Autobiography of Charles Darwin (Darwin) **57**:123, 168
The Autobiography of Christopher Kirkland (Linton) **41**:165, 172-75
The Autobiography of Goethe: Truth and Poetry from My Own Life (Goethe)
See *Aus meinen Leben: Dichtung und Wahrheit*
The Autobiography of James Clarence Mangan (Mangan) **27**:298,301,304
The Autobiography of John Galt (Galt) **1**:334; **110**:86, 88
The Autobiography of Leigh Hunt, with Reminiscences of Friends and Contemporaries (Hunt) **1**:416-18, 424; **70**:259-60, 264, 268, 279-85, 287-88
The Autobiography of Margaret Oliphant: The Complete Text (Oliphant) **61**:238-9
"Autobiography of Mr. Munden" (Lamb) **10**:435
Autobiography of Thomas Jefferson (Jefferson) **11**:173, 196, 199, 205-206; **103**:106, 119, 121, 123, 125, 186-90
"The Autocrat gives a Breakfast to the Public" (Holmes) **81**:98
The Autocrat of the Breakfast-Table (Holmes) **14**:102, 104-06, 110, 112-15, 117, 119-25, 132-33, 139, 143-46; **81**:94-96, 98-99, 104-05
"Autography" (Poe) **55**:170, 188-9; **97**:183-85, 187
"Die Automate" (Hoffmann) **2**:362
"L'automne" (Lamartine) **11**:264, 269, 282
"Autour d'un livre" (Maupassant) **83**:227
L'Autre (Sand) **42**:310
"Autre complainte de Lord Pierrot" (Laforgue) **53**:287, 290
Autre complainte de Lord Pierrot (Laforgue) **53**:265, 279
"Autre eventail de Mademoiselle Mallarmé" (Mallarmé) **4**:380; **41**:260, 262, 265, 291
"Autre Explication" (Verlaine) **51**:361-62
Autres chimères (Nerval) **67**:306-07
"Autumn" (Arany)
See "Ősszel"
"Autumn" (Baratynsky)
See "Osen"
"Autumn" (Clare) **9**:76, 78, 86, 88, 94, 96, 111, 113-14, 123; **86**:113
"Autumn" (Dickinson)
See "The Morns Are Meeker than They Were"
"Autumn" (Dyer) **129**:149
"The Autumn" (Lamartine)
See "L'automne"
"Autumn" (Moodie) **113**:316
"Autumn" (Pushkin) **3**:443
"Autumn" (Rossetti) **2**:575; **50**:289
"Autumn" (Sigourney) **87**:331, 333
"Autumn" (Smith) **59**:333
"Autumn Days in Weimar" (Taylor) **89**:325
"Autumn Flowers" (Very) **9**:378
"Autumn Lament" (Mallarmé)
See "Plainte d'automne"
"Autumn Leaves" (Hugo) **3**:261
"Autumn Leaves" (Very) **9**:388
"Autumn Mood" (Lenau) **16**:275
"An Autumn Morning" (Clare) **9**:111
"Autumn Sadness" (Lazarus) **109**:292
"Autumn Song" (Gordon)
See "A Song of Autumn"
"Autumn Song" (Verlaine)
See "Chanson d'automne"
"An Autumn Thought" (Taylor) **89**:299
"Autumn Violets" (Rossetti) **2**:572
"Autumn Woods" (Bryant) **6**:159-60, 172, 176, 183; **46**:46
"Autumnal Leaves" (Harpur) **114**:100
Autumnal Leaves; Tales and Sketches in prose and rhyme (Child) **73**:62
"Aux Chrétiens" (Lamartine) **11**:279
"Aux modernes" (Leconte de Lisle) **29**:228, 231, 235
"Aux morts" (Leconte de Lisle) **29**:222, 228

"Aux petits enfants" (Daudet) **1**:248
"Avalon" (Chivers) **49**:49, 71
Avant, pendant, et après (Scribe) **16**:382, 390
"Avant-propos" (Silva) **114**:263
Avant-propos (Balzac) **53**:13
"Avarice" (Lampman) **25**:194
The Avaricious Knight (Pushkin)
See *Skupoi rytsar*
Avatar (Gautier) **1**:346; **59**:11-14, 33, 37
"Avatarii faraonului Tlá" (Eminescu) **33**:246; **131**:334
"The Avatars of Pharaoh Tlà" (Eminescu)
See "Avatarii faraonului Tlá"
"The Avatars of the Pharaoh Tlà" (Eminescu)
See "Avatarii faraonului Tlá"
"Ave" (Rossetti) **4**:505, 518-22; **77**:303, 348
"El ave muerta" (Villaverde) **121**:333
"Avec ses vêtements ondoyants et nacrés" (Baudelaire)
See "A une madone"
Avellaneda (Echeverria) **18**:148
"Aven om humor och stil däri" (Almqvist) **42**:11, 16
"The Avenger" (De Quincey) **87**:76
"Avenging and Bright" (Moore) **110**:182
L'avenir de la science (Renan) **26**:394-95, 397-98, 412, 415, 418-19, 423-24
Una aventura de Richelieu (Tamayo y Baus) **1**:571
La aventurera (Gómez de Avellaneda) **111**:28, 49, 53
Les aventures d'Arthur Gordon Pym (Baudelaire) **29**:67
Aventures du dernier Abencérages (Chateaubriand)
See *Aben-Hamet, the Last of the Abencerages*
Aventures prodigieuses de Tartarin de Tarascon (Daudet) **1**:231, 235-36, 240-42, 250-51
L'aventurière (Augier) **31**:2-4, 7-12, 14-16, 19, 23-4, 27
Der Averhahn (Arnim) **5**:19, 21
Averroès et l'Averroïsme (Renan) **26**:377, 379, 389, 415
"Les aveugles" (Baudelaire) **29**:101, 113; **55**:16, 19, 22, 35, 40-2
Avillion and other Tales (Craik) **38**:119
"Avis" (Holmes) **14**:109
"Avis je vous prie" (Laforgue) **5**:277
"Avolio" (Hayne) **94**:144, 158
Avolio and Other Poems (Hayne) **94**:135, 139-40
Le Avventure di Pinocchio (Collodi) **54**:134-42, 147-63
"Awake Ye Muses Nine, Sing Me a Strain Divine" (Dickinson) **21**:62
The Awakening (Hayne) **94**:166
"The Awakening of the Poetic Faculty" (Boker) **125**:82
"Away from You" (Eminescu) **131**:296
"Away, Haunt Thou Not Me" (Clough)
See "In a Lecture-Room"
"An Axe Lay behind God's Door" (Shevchenko)
See "U Boha za dvermy lezhala sokyra"
Axel (Tegner) **2**:611-14
Axël (Villiers de l'Isle Adam) **3**:582-83, 585-92
Axur, re d' Ormus (Da Ponte) **50**:81
Ayala's Angel (Trollope) **6**:470-71, 507; **33**:363; **101**:237, 264
'Ayit zahvu'a (Mapu) **18**:288, 292-301, 303
"Aylmer's Field" (Kendall) **12**:180
"Aylmer's Field" (Tennyson) **30**:220, 236, 249, 254, 280; **65**:248
"The Aylmers of Bally-Aylmer" (Griffin) **7**:198, 206-07, 211, 217
"Aymerillot" (Hugo) **3**:273
The Ayrshire Legatees; or, The Pringle Family (Galt) **1**:328-29, 335, 337; **110**:78, 80, 84-6, 90, 92, 95-6, 113-16
"The Azalea" (Patmore) **9**:349, 358
Azemia (Beckford) **16**:29
Azeth the Egyptian (Linton) **41**:163
"Azrael" (Longfellow) **45**:145, 188
"Azraël" (Villiers de l'Isle Adam)
See "L'annonciateur"
"Azrael, or Destruction's Eve" (Brontë) **109**:30, 48
"La azucena silvestre" (Zorrilla y Moral) **6**:526
"L'azur" (Mallarmé) **4**:378, 395; **41**:250
"The Azure" (Mallarmé)
See "L'azur"
"Bab Ballads" (Muller) **73**:353
"Baby Bertie's Christmas" (O'Brien) **21**:236
"Baby Bloom" (O'Brien) **21**:236, 243-44
"Babylon" (Pixérécourt) **39**:284
"The Babylonian Captivity" (Harpur) **114**:144
"Baby's Age" (Timrod) **25**:360
"The Bacchanals of Euripides" (Pater) **7**:334; **90**:335
"La bacchante" (Beranger) **34**:28, 30
La Bacchante (Thaïs) (Dumas) **71**:218
Bacchanterna eller Fanatismen (Stagnelius) **61**:248, 253, 260, 264-5, 268, 273
The Bacchantes, or Fanaticism (Stagnelius)
See *Bacchanterna eller Fanatismen*
"Bacchus" (Emerson) **38**:183-84, 187; **98**:177
"Bacchus" (O'Brien) **21**:246
"Bacchus and Ariadne" (Hunt) **1**:410
"Bacchus in Tuscany" (Hunt) **70**:248
"Bacco in Toscana" (Hunt) **1**:415
The Bachelor (Stifter)
See *Der Hagestolz*
The Bachelor (Turgenev)
See *Kholostiak*
"Bachelor Housekeeping" (Parton) **86**:348
"A Bachelor's Complaint of the Behaviour of Married People" (Lamb) **10**:403, 409-10, 430, 436; **113**:235, 245
"A Bachelor's Establishment" (Balzac)
See "La rabouilleuse"
Bachelor's Hall; or, All in a Hobble (Bird) **1**:93
The Bachelor's Wife (Galt) **110**:73, 94
"A Backward Glance" (Whitman) **4**:600, 604; **31**:402, 405; **81**:235, 302
"The Backwater" (Turgenev) **21**:415, 431
The Backwoods Boy (Alger) **8**:44
The Backwoods of Canada: Being Letters from the Wife of an Emigrant Officer (Traill) **31**:315-17, 321, 323-24, 327-29
"The Back-Woodsman" (Moodie) **113**:346
The Backwoodsman (Paulding) **2**:525, 528, 530
"Bacon to Beethoven" (Lanier) **118**:243
"Bad Blood" (Rimbaud)
See "Mauvais sang"
"Bad Dreams" (Browning) **19**:96; **79**:112-14
Bad Saint Vitalis (Keller)
See *Der Schlimm-heilige Vitalis*
"Bad Squire" (Kingsley) **35**:206
"Bad Weather" (Hunt) **1**:417
The Baddington Peerage (Sala) **46**:240-42
Die Bäder von Lucca (Heine) **4**:264
"Badger" (Clare) **9**:117, 121; **86**:131
Bádnaya nevésta (Ostrovsky)
See *Bednaya nevesta*
"The Bag" (Krylov) **1**:439
The Bag-Pipers (Sand) **57**:338
"Bahači četvero bolj množnih Slave rodov" (Preseren) **127**:316
"The Bailiff" (Turgenev) **122**:294
Le baiser (Banville) **9**:20
"Le baiser suprême" (Leconte de Lisle) **29**:219
"Bajazeth" (Droste-Hülshoff) **3**:203
"Bajdary" (Mickiewicz) **3**:404
Bajki i przypowieści (Krasicki) **8**:398, 401-02, 404, 406
Bajki nowe (Krasicki) **8**:398, 401-02, 404, 407
"Bajo-Relieve" (Casal) **131**:242
"Bajuški-baju" (Nekrasov) **11**:420
"Bakche-Sarai" (Mickiewicz)
See "Bakczysaraj"
The Bak-Chesarian fountain: A Tale of the Tauride (Pushkin)
See *Bakhchisaraiski Fontan*
"Bakczysaraj" (Mickiewicz) **3**:390, 403
"Baker Farm" (Thoreau) **7**:373, 398
The Bakhchisarai Fontan (Pushkin)
See *Bakhchisaraiski Fontan*
Bakhchisaraiski Fontan (Pushkin) **3**:409, 411, 413-14, 416, 421, 423, 437, 451; **83**:243-44, 248, 299, 332-34, 351, 355, 357, 359
"Bakhchisaray by Night" (Mickiewicz) **101**:190
"Le Bal" (Vigny) **102**:335, 367-68
Bal (Baratynsky) **103**:39-40
Un Bal Masqué (Dumas) **71**:205
"The Balance Between the Esthetic and the Ethical in the Development of the Personality" (Kierkegaard) **125**:235
"La balancelle" (Corbière) **43**:33
Balaustion's Adventure (Browning) **19**:128
"Balcescu and His Followers" (Eminescu) **131**:326
"Le balcon" (Baudelaire) **6**:80, 93, 100, 104; **29**:73, 77, 99; **55**:6-8, 26, 55, 59, 62
"The Balcony" (Baudelaire)
See "Le balcon"
"The Balcony" (Irving) **2**:372
"Balder Dead" (Arnold) **6**:50-51, 67-68, 72; **29**:32; **89**:51, 53
Balder Dead (Arnold) **89**:28
Balder, Part the First (Dobell) **43**:39-40, 42-5, 49-51, 55, 60-2, 65, 68, 74-5
Baldwin (Barham) **77**:5
"Balin and Balan" (Tennyson) **30**:254, 290; **65**:237, 241, 243, 250, 252, 269, 277-8, 281, 290-5, 297-9, 349-51, 374, 376; **115**:335
"Balkis et Solomon" (Nerval) **1**:480
"Der Ball" (Gotthelf) **117**:6
The Ball (Baratynsky)
See *Bal*
"A Ballad" (Turgenev) **21**:376
"Ballad Founded on Fact" (Opie) **65**:160-1
"Ballad Noticing the Difference of Rich and Poor" (Lamb) **10**:389
The Ballad of Abraham Lincoln (Taylor) **89**:342
"Ballad of an Omnibus" (Levy) **59**:88, 102
"A Ballad of Boding" (Rossetti) **2**:558, 575-6
"Ballad of Carmilhan" (Longfellow) **45**:114
Ballad of Delora, or the Passion of Andrea Como (Horne) **127**:255
"Ballad of Fortunatus" (Schlegel) **15**:223
"Ballad of Human Life" (Beddoes) **3**:34
"A Ballad of Religion and Marriage" (Levy) **59**:99, 114
"The Ballad of Sir Brown" (O'Brien) **21**:249
"The Ballad of Sir John Franklin" (Boker) **125**:31
"Ballad of the Barber" (Beardsley) **6**:145-46
"Ballad of the Oysterman" (Holmes) **14**:99, 101
"The Ballad of Trees and the Master" (Lanier) **6**:249, 253-55, 265, 270; **118**:219, 221, 223, 232, 240, 268-9
"Ballade" (Laforgue) **53**:278, 290
"Ballade à la lune" (Musset) **7**:254
"Ballade de Banville aux enfants perdus" (Banville) **9**:16
"Ballade de ses regrets pour l'an 1830" (Banville) **9**:28
"La ballade des pendus" (Baudelaire) **29**:84
"Ballade of Summer's Sleep" (Lampman) **25**:164, 204
Ballades (Hugo) **3**:276
The Ballad-Monger (Banville)
See *Gringoire*
"Ballads" (Kingsley) **35**:218
The Ballads (Banville)
See *Trente-six ballades joyeuses*
Ballads (Stevenson) **5**:410, 428
Ballads (Thackeray) **5**:466
Ballads and Images (Meyer)
See *Romanzen und Bilder*
Ballads and Metrical Tales (Southey) **97**:318

Ballads, and Other Poems (Longfellow) **2**:472; **45**:135, 152, 155, 184, 189
Ballads and Romances (Mickiewicz)
See *Ballady i Romanse*
Ballads and Sonnets (Rossetti) **4**:499, 502; **77**:301
Ballads of New England (Whittier) **8**:506
"Ballads of Wonder" (Baillie) **2**:42
Ballady i Romanse (Mickiewicz) **3**:393, 395-96, 403; **101**:155, 179
Balladyna (Slowacki) **15**:348-50, 352-53, 364-65, 370, 372, 376, 378, 380
Ballantyne Humbug Handled (Lockhart) **6**:305
"Ballast Island" (Woolson) **82**:331-32
"The Balloon" (Cranch) **115**:47
"The Balloon Hoax" (Poe) **16**:300, 313, 323
Baltasar (Gómez de Avellaneda) **111**:28
Balzac: A Critical Study (Taine) **15**:463
Balzac's Contes Drôlatiques: Droll Stories Collected from the Abbeys of Touraine (Balzac) **5**:28, 42, 77-78
"Balzsamcsepp" (Arany) **34**:19
"A bánat? Egy nagy oceán" (Petofi) **21**:279
"Bande Mātaram" (Chatterji)
See "Vande Mataram"
"El bando de Lucifer" (Lizardi) **30**:67
"Bangadesher krishak" (Chatterji) **19**:226
"Banished Man" (Baillie) **2**:42
The Banished Man (Smith) **23**:323, 330, 333, 335; **115**:144, 147, 149-50, 158, 166-68, 207, 211
"Banker's Dream" (Gordon) **21**:160, 180-81
"The Banker's Secret" (Holmes) **14**:128
The Banker's Wife; or, Court and City (Gore) **65**:20, 38
The Bankrupt (Boker) **125**:25, 28, 38, 58
The Bankrupt (Ostrovsky)
See *Svoi lyudi—sochtemsya!*
The Bankruptcy (Gotthelf) **117**:18, 25
"The Banks of the Jordan" (Trollope)
See "A Ride across Palestine"
"The Banner" (Allingham) **25**:6
"The Banner of England" (Moodie) **113**:308-9
"The Banner of the Jew" (Lazarus) **8**:415-17, 419-21, 424, 428; **109**:293, 314-15, 327, 338, 343
The Banner of the Upright Seven (Keller)
See *The Flag of the Seven Upright Ones*
"Banović Strahinja" (Karadzic) **115**:91-2
"The Banquet" (Kierkegaard) **125**:248
"The Banquet's End" (Meyer)
See "Das Ende des Festes"
Banwell Hill (Bowles) **103**:56, 61
"Le baptëme" (Maupassant) **1**:469
"Baptism" (Keble) **87**:203
"The Baptism of Fire" (Longfellow) **2**:487
The Baptism on the Savica (Preseren)
See *Krst pri Svici: Povest v verzih*
Baptiste Montauban (Nodier) **19**:383
"Bar Kochba" (Lazarus) **109**:293
"Los barateros" (Larra) **17**:282; **130**:194
"Barbara Frietchie" (Whittier) **8**:496, 501, 508, 510, 513, 516-17, 522-23, 528, 531; **59**:357-61
"Barbara S——" (Lamb) **10**:436
"Barbara's Courtship" (Alger) **8**:16
"Barbare" (Rimbaud) **4**:455, 473; **35**:269, 308-09, 311-13, 322; **82**:233, 238
"La barbe pointue" (Bertrand) **31**:49
"Barber of Bantry" (Griffin) **7**:201, 215, 218
Barberine (Musset) **7**:270, 276
The Barbers at Court (Mayhew) **31**:159
"Barber-Shop Paradox" (Carroll) **139**:57
"Barbier" (Baudelaire) **29**:70
Barchester Towers (Trollope) **6**:453, 455, 459, 461, 464-66, 468, 470-71, 487, 494, 497, 499-502, 505-06, 510-11, 514, 516-17; **33**:360-426; **101**:232, 235, 253, 265-66, 271, 273-74, 280, 307, 326, 328-30, 332-33, 336-37
"Barclay of Ury" (Whittier) **8**:489, 530
"The Barcoo" (Kendall) **12**:195-96
"Bardale" (Klopstock) **11**:220
"Le barde de Temrah" (Leconte de Lisle) **29**:225
"A Bard's Address to his Youngest Daughter" (Hogg) **109**:202
"Bards of Freedom" (Coleridge) **111**:353
"Bards of Passion" (Keats) **8**:360; **73**:202
"Bards of Passion and of Mirth" (Keats) **73**:257
"The Bards of Wales" (Arany)
See "A walesi bárdok"
"Bard's Song at the Grave of Victorious Slavs" (Zhukovsky) **35**:378-79
"The Barefoot Boy" (Longfellow) **103**:296
"The Barefoot Boy" (Whittier) **8**:510, 525, 531; **59**:356, 358, 371
"Der Barmekiden Untergang" (Droste-Hülshoff) **3**:203
Barnaby Rudge (Dickens) **3**:142, 174; **8**:178, 182; **18**:112, 132; **37**:143, 156; **86**:18, 256-57; **105**:229, 231, 349; **113**:9, 102, 107, 124, 129
The Barnabys in America; or, Adventures of the Widow Wedded (Trollope) **30**:314, 320-21
"Barneti Graven" (Andersen) **79**:76-77
"Barney Brady's Goose" (Carleton) **3**:89
"Barnfloor and Winepress" (Hopkins) **17**:191
Der Barometermacher auf der Zauberinsel (Raimund) **69**:5-7, 12, 21, 29, 36-7, 43-6, 48-9
The Barometer-maker on the Magic Isle (Raimund)
See *Der Barometermacher auf der Zauberinsel*
"La Baronne" (Maupassant) **83**:171, 194-95
Barons (Bulwer-Lytton)
See *The Last of the Barons*
"The Baron's Gloves" (Alcott) **58**:47
Barren Genius (Eminescu)
See *Geniu pustiu*
"Barrenness of the Imaginative Faculty in the Productions of Modern Art" (Lamb) **10**:409; **113**:203, 206, 318
Barrington (Lever) **23**:292, 308
Barry Lyndon (Thackeray)
See *The Memoirs of Barry Lyndon, Esq.*
Barsetshire Chronicle (Trollope) **6**:470-71
"Bart Davis's Dance" (Harris) **23**:141, 159, 163
Barth. Kopitars kleinere Schriften (Kopitar) **117**:91
"Barthli der Korber" (Gotthelf) **117**:6
"Bartleby, the Scrivener: A Story of Wall-Street" (Melville) **3**:331, 354, 362, 368, 380-81, 383; **12**:312; **29**:354; **49**:376-426; **93**:197, 224; **123**:186, 261
"Baryshnia-krest'ianka" (Pushkin) **83**:272, 275-76, 323, 327, 329-30, 337-38, 354
The Bas Bleu; or, Conversation (More) **27**:325, 335-36
"The Base of All Metaphysics" (Whitman) **81**:332
Bases Del Partido Revolucionario Cubano (Martí) **63**:97, 127-9
"The Basic Forms of Motion" (Engels) **85**:38
Basil: A Story of Modern Life (Collins) **1**:172, 174, 177-78, 181, 184-85, 187; **18**:61; **93**:4, 38, 43-4, 46-8, 50, 52-3, 64
Basil Hymen (Sacher-Masoch) **31**:287, 295
"Basil Lee" (Hogg) **4**:283
"Basile Renaud" (Cooke) **110**:9
The Basis of Morality (Schopenhauer)
See *Die beiden Grundprobleme der Ethik*
Basis of Natural Right (Fichte)
See *Grundlage des Naturrechts nach Prinzipen der Wissenshaftslehre*
Basis of the Entire Theory of Science (Fichte)
See *Grundlage der gesamten Wissenschaftslehre*
"A Basket of Sun-Fruit" (Harpur) **114**:101, 139
"The Bastille, A Vision" (Williams) **135**:255, 297, 314, 333
La Bataille (Mérimée) **65**:55
Bataille de dames; ou, Un duel en amour (Scribe) **16**:389, 396-97, 402-03, 405, 407
Le bâtard de Mauléon (Dumas) **11**:51, 68
"bâtard du pape" (Beranger) **34**:38
Le bateau ivre (Rimbaud) **4**:453-57, 459, 463, 468, 471-72, 478-79, 485, 487; **35**:266-67, 270-71, 274-75, 279, 283-88, 299, 320-23, 325; **82**:218, 227, 232, 238, 247, 250, 252, 255-56, 262-63
"Bathed in War's Perfume" (Whitman) **81**:318
The Baths of Lucca (Heine) **54**:317-9, 327
"Bâtons dans les roves" (Hugo) **10**:357
"The Battle Ax" (Leskov)
See "Voitel' nica"
"The Battle of Blenheim" (Southey) **8**:472, 474; **97**:271, 315
"The Battle of Brunanburh" (Tennyson) **30**:236
The Battle of Bunker's Hill (Brackenridge) **7**:43, 47
The Battle of Cheviot (Macaulay) **42**:118
The Battle of Herman (Klopstock)
See *Hermanns Schlacht*
The Battle of Hermann (Kleist)
See *Die Hermannsschlacht*
The Battle of Kings Mountain (Hayne) **94**:167-68
The Battle of Lake Regillus (Macaulay) **42**:111
The Battle of Largs (Galt) **1**:327
Battle of Love (Daudet)
See *La lutte pour la vie*
The Battle of Marathon: A Poem (Browning) **61**:41, 48-9, 61; **66**:44, 71
The Battle of New Orleans (Dunlap) **2**:211, 213
"The Battle of the Baltic" (Campbell) **19**:165, 168-69, 176, 179, 181-82, 185, 188, 190-96
"The Battle of the Bards" (Taylor) **89**:319
"The Battle of the Factions" (Carleton) **3**:89, 92-93, 95
The Battle of the Nile (Bowles) **103**:54, 70
"The Battlefield" (Bryant) **6**:165, 168-69, 172-73; **46**:7, 15
Battle-Pieces and Aspects of War (Melville) **3**:331, 333, 352, 363, 378-79; **29**:315, 360
The Battles of Talavera (Croker) **10**:88-89
"Battle-Song" (Petofi)
See "Csatadal"
Der Bauer als Millionär; oder, Das Mädchen aus der Feenwelt (Raimund) **69**:5, 7-10, 12-13, 23, 26, 30-1, 33-4, 38, 43-6, 49-50, 52-3
"Das Bauernlied" (Claudius) **75**:190
Bauernlieder (Claudius) **75**:190
Der Bauern-Spiegel oder Lebensgeschichte des Jeremias Gotthelf: Von ihm selbst beschrieben (Gotthelf) **117**:4, 7, 14, 17-18, 31-2, 38, 51
"Baugmaree" (Dutt) **29**:122, 127
"The Bay of Glasstown" (Brontë) **109**:35
Bazarov (Pisarev) **25**:330-31, 333-34, 338, 348, 352-54
"Bazarov, Once Again" (Herzen) **61**:109
"Be Good!" (Isaacs)
See "Sed buenos!"
"The Beach of Falesá" (Stevenson) **5**:412, 422, 431, 434; **63**:261
"Beachy Head" (Smith) **115**:118, 126, 129-35, 206, 209
Beachy Head, with Other Poems (Smith) **115**:134, 211, 217
The Beacon (Baillie) **2**:37, 39; **71**:6, 18
"The Beacons" (Baudelaire)
See "Les phares"
"The Beam in Grenley Church" (Barnes) **75**:75
"Beams" (Verlaine) **51**:381-84
"Beanfield" (Clare) **9**:110
"The Bean-Field" (Thoreau) **7**:388, 399, 403-4
"The Bear Hunt" (Lincoln) **18**:273
"The Bear in Charge of the Bees" (Krylov) **1**:435
"The Bear-Hunt" (Nekrasov) **11**:409
"The Beast" (Leskov)
See "Zver'"

"The Beasts in the Tower" (Lamb) **125**:376
"Beata" (Patmore) **9**:357
"Beaten Tracks" (Rimbaud) **35**:269
"The Beating of my own Heart" (Milnes) **61**:152
"La Béatrice" (Baudelaire) **6**:109; **55**:70-1, 74, 77-8
"Beatrice" (Carroll) **139**:30
"Beatrice" (Le Fanu) **58**:276
"Beatrice Cenci" (Landor) **14**:183
Béatrix (Balzac) **5**:84
Beau Austin (Stevenson) **5**:411, 421
Le Beau Laurence (Sand) **57**:316
Le beau Léandre (Banville) **9**:20, 22
Un beau mariage (Augier) **31**:9, 13, 15, 19, 24-5, 27, 31, 34
"Le beau navire" (Baudelaire) **6**:109, 117; **55**:45, 61
Beauchampe; or, The Kentucky Tragedy (Simms) **3**:508-10, 513
"La beauté" (Baudelaire) **6**:123; **29**:97; **55**:58
"Beauté de femmes, leur faiblesse, et ces mains pâles" (Verlaine) **51**:357
"The Beauties of Santa Cruz" (Freneau) **1**:314, 316, 319, 323-24; **111**:80, 82, 100, 140, 143, 146, 148, 151-52, 184
The Beauties of the Court of King Charles II (Jameson)
See *Memoirs of the Beauties of the Court of Charles II*
"A Beautiful Autumn" (Arany)
See "Kies Ősz"
"The Beautiful Aza" (Leskov)
See "Prekrasnaja Aza"
"The beautiful Cassandra" (Austen) **119**:13
"Beautiful City" (Tennyson) **30**:293
"Beautiful Dreamer" (Foster) **26**:291, 296-97, 299
The Beautiful Fiend (Southworth) **26**:434
"The Beautiful One at Night" (Isaacs)
See "La bella de noche"
"The Beautiful Princess and the Fortunate Dwarf" (Karamzin)
See "Prekrasnaja carevna i ščastlivoj karla"
"Beauty" (Lampman) **25**:209
"The Beauty" (O'Brien) **21**:243, 245, 247
"Beauty" (Shaw) **15**:335
"Beauty" (Very) **9**:381
Beauty and the Beast (Lamb) **10**:418
Beauty and the Beast (Planché) **42**:279, 288
Beauty and the Beast; and Tales of Home (Taylor) **89**:314
"Beauty and Truth" (Cranch) **115**:5
"Beauty Cycle" (Baudelaire) **55**:73
"The Beauty of Married Men" (Lewes) **25**:290
"The Beauty—a Fragment" (Pinkney) **31**:277
"Beauty—Be Not Caused—It Is" (Dickinson) **21**:43
Les beaux messieurs de Bois-Doré (Sand) **2**:605; **42**:310; **57**:313
"Beaver Brook" (Lowell) **90**:214-15
"Because I Could Not Stop for Death" (Dickinson) **21**:26, 28, 57; **77**:163, 173
"Der Becher" (Goethe) **4**:193
Becket (Tennyson) **30**:264-66
"Beclouded" (Dickinson)
See "The Sky Is Low, the Clouds Are Mean"
"Becoming Inured" (Martineau) **137**:283
Bedlam-Comödie (Eminescu) **33**:266
"Bednaia Liza" (Bestuzhev) **131**:168
Bednaya nevesta (Ostrovsky) **30**:99, 102, 105, 107, 109-10, 114-15; **57**:218, 220
Bednost ne porok (Ostrovsky) **30**:97-9, 102, 104, 109-10, 113, 115; **57**:195, 198, 201-2, 208-21
Bednye lyudi (Dostoevsky) **2**:156, 160-61, 163, 170, 177, 199; **7**:80; **33**:176, 200; **119**:90, 132
"The Bedouin Song" (Taylor) **89**:302-03, 343
"The Bee" (Lanier) **6**:236, 238, 253; **118**:203
The Bee (Preseren)
See *Čbelica*
The Bee and the Orange Tree (Planché) **42**:288
"A Bee his burnished Carriage/Drove boldly to a Rose-" (Dickinson) **77**:96
The Bee Hunter; or, The Oak Opening (Cooper)
See *The Oak Openings; or, The Bee Hunter*
"The Beech Tree's Petition" (Campbell) **19**:179, 191, 198
The Beer Expedition at Schleusingen (Kivi)
See *Olviretki Schleusingenissä*
"Bees Are Black, with Gilt Surcingles" (Dickinson) **21**:76
"Beethovens Büste" (Lenau) **16**:281
The Beetle (Andersen) **79**:32, 89
"Befordúltam a konyhára" (Petofi) **21**:260, 283
"Before" (Browning) **79**:153
"Before Breakfast" (Allingham) **25**:6
"Before Breakfast" (Cooke) **110**:35
"Before Justice" (Goethe)
See "Vor Gericht"
"Before Sleep" (Lampman) **25**:167
"Before the Battle" (Moore) **110**:187
"Before the Curtain" (Thackeray) **5**:494, 499
"Before the Harvest" (Meyer)
See "Vor der Ernte"
"Before the Ice Is in the Pools" (Dickinson) **21**:55
"Before the Robin" (Lampman) **25**:209
"Before the Storm: A Conversation on Deck" (Herzen) **10**:336-7
Before the Storm: A Novel of the Winter of 1812-13 (Fontane)
See *Vor dem Sturm: Roman aus dem Winter 1812 auf 13*
"Before Vicksburg" (Boker) **125**:81
"Begegnung" (Grillparzer) **102**:174
"Begeisterung ... die Allerschaffende" (Hölderlin) **16**:185
"The Beggar" (Espronceda)
See "El mendigo"
"The Beggars" (Wordsworth) **12**:395
"Beggars' Ballad" (Meyer)
See "Bettlerballade"
"Begger Woman of Locarno" (Kleist)
See "Das Bettelweib von Locarno"
"Beginning and End" (Lazarus) **109**:291
"The Beginning and the End" (Very) **9**:376
"Beginning My Studies" (Whitman) **81**:313
"Beginning of the End" (Storm) **1**:537
Begrebet Angest (Kierkegaard) **78**:122, 125, 157, 159-60, 169, 182, 191, 228; **125**:199, 209, 255-57, 281
"Behavior" (Emerson) **38**:143
"Behind a Mask: Or, A Woman's Power" (Alcott) **58**:3, 38, 46, 59, 67, 75-6, 78-80; **83**:6, 33
Behind a Mask: The Unknown Thrillers of Louisa May Alcott (Alcott) **58**:3
"Behind me dips Eternity" (Dickinson) **77**:140, 143-44
"Behind the Scenes at a Whist Game" (Barbey d'Aurevilly)
See "Le dessous de cartes d'une partie de whist"
"Behind the Veil" (De Mille) **123**:117-18
"Behold this Swarthy Face" (Whitman) **31**:430
Bei und zu Lande auf dem Lande (Droste-Hülshoff) **3**:200
Die beiden Grundprobleme der Ethik (Schopenhauer) **51**:318
Die beiden Herren Söhne (Nestroy) **42**:258
"Die beiden Hunde" (Grillparzer) **102**:174
Die beiden Klingsberg (Kotzebue) **25**:133, 142, 145
Beim Vetter Christian (Storm) **1**:540
"Being Beauteous" (Rimbaud) **4**:455, 487; **35**:294, 296, 308, 311-12, 322; **82**:232-33
"Being the Last Essays of Richard Jefferies, Collected by his Widow" (Jefferies) **47**:133
"Bela" (Lermontov) **5**:291, 295-98, 301-02, 305-06; **126**:147-48, 153-54, 156, 158, 166-67, 169, 173-74, 195-99, 201-2
Bel-Ami (Maupassant) **1**:444, 448, 450, 452-53, 463-64, 467, 469; **42**:169, 189, 201; **83**:171,173,186
Belated Summer (Stifter)
See *Der Nachsommer*
"The Belated Travellers" (Irving) **2**:390
"The Beleaguered City" (Longfellow) **45**:127, 151
A Beleaguered City: Tale of the Seen and Unseen (Oliphant) **11**:439, 445-6, 448-9, 451, 453-4, 459, 463; **61**:174, 216-7
Belford Regis; or, Sketches of a Country Town (Mitford) **4**:401, 407
The Belfry of Bruges (Longfellow) **2**:479; **45**:102, 116, 135, 151, 154, 182, 186; **103**:280
Belgium and Western Germany in 1833 (Trollope) **30**:307, 313
"Belief and Unbelief" (Freneau) **111**:110
"Belief and Unbelief. An Episode from a Poem" (Baratynsky)
See "Vera i neverie. Stsena iz poemy"
"Belief in One God" (Newman) **99**:300
"Belief, whether Voluntary?" (Hazlitt) **29**:173
"Believe: you, my beloved, are dearer than fame to me; ..." (Baratynsky)
See "O ver: ty, nezhnaya, dorozhe slavy mne;..."
Belinda (Edgeworth) **1**:255-56, 261-63, 265-67, 269, 271-72; **51**:79-81, 83, 85, 87-91, 93, 130-31, 135, 136-38, 140
Belkin Tales (Pushkin)
See *Povesti Belkina*
"The Bell" (Andersen) **7**:22-3; **79**:28, 40
"The Bell" (Schiller)
See "The Song of the Bell"
"The Bell Bird" (Ingelow) **39**:258
"Bell of the Wreck" (Sigourney) **21**:301
"Bell Songs" (Cooke) **110**:9
"La bella de noche" (Isaacs) **70**:311
"Belladonna" (O'Brien) **21**:236, 242-43
Bellah (Feuillet) **45**:84-5, 87
"Bellambi's Maid" (Kendall) **12**:193
"Bell-Birds" (Kendall) **12**:182, 186, 191, 194, 197-99, 201
Belle au Bois Dormant (Feuillet) **45**:89
"La belle dame sans merci" (Keats) **8**:341, 347-48, 351, 357, 360, 375, 380-81; **73**:154, 188-93, 200, 202, 218, 224, 226-30, 232, 243, 261, 271, 282, 303-04, 307, 329; **121**:144, 205
"La belle Dorothée" (Baudelaire) **6**:87
La Belle Jenny (Gautier) **1**:346; **59**:12
"La belle Juive" (Timrod) **25**:374, 384
"La belle Véronique" (Banville) **9**:16
"Bellerophon at Argos" (Morris) **4**:447
"Bellerophon in Lycia" (Morris) **4**:420, 447
"The Bell-Founder of Breslau" (Muller)
See "Der Glockenguss zu Breslau"
"Bellini" (Wagner) **119**:190
"Bellona" (Gordon) **21**:154, 163, 172, 181
"The Bells" (Poe) **1**:496, 502, 519; **55**:141, 149, 154, 213; **117**:192, 195, 231, 242-43, 280, 283, 287-88, 309
"The Bells" (Southey) **8**:472
The Bells (Hayne) **94**:162
Bells and Pomegranates (Browning) **19**:75, 78
Bells and Pomegrantes (Browning) **79**:93, 147, 152, 181
"The Bells of Lynn" (Longfellow) **45**:190
"The Bells of San Blas" (Longfellow) **2**:484; **45**:139, 141, 151, 163-64
Les bells poupées (Banville) **9**:31
"Bell's Trouble" (Cooke) **110**:58
"The Bell-Tower" (Melville) **3**:331, 380, 382
"Beloved Tune" (Child) **6**:201; **73**:90
The Belton Estate (Trollope) **6**:470-71, 499, 501-02, 515-16; **101**:264, 310, 319

Le belvéder; ou, La vallée de l'Etna (Pixérécourt) **39**:274, 277, 279, 282
"Belyj orel" (Leskov) **25**:240, 242, 244
"Bema pamięci żałobny rapsod" (Norwid) **17**:365, 367, 375-77, 379
Bemerkungen und Ansichten (Chamisso) **82**:25
Ben Jonson (Symonds) **34**:342
Ben, the Luggage Boy; or, Among the Wharves (Alger) **8**:37, 39, 44; **83**:112
"Benbow" (Crabbe) **26**:121
"Beneath the Cards of a Game of Whist" (Barbey d'Aurevilly)
See "Le dessous de cartes d'une partie de whist"
"Bénédiction" (Baudelaire) **6**:82, 92, 97, 114, 117, 123; **29**:77, 102; **55**:12, 48-50, 53, 56, 62-5
"Benediction de Dieu dans la solitude" (Lamartine) **11**:265, 270, 279
"Beneict Arnold's Departure" (Freneau) **111**:81
"The Benevolent Protector, or Bartholomew as Alphonse" (Norwid) **17**:370
"The Benighted Sportsman" (Surtees) **14**:349
Beniowski (Slowacki) **15**:348-49, 354, 358-59, 365, 368, 371, 374-76, 378, 380-81
"Benito Cereno" (Melville) **3**:331, 344, 347, 354, 361-62, 368, 380-84; **29**:362-63; **93**:188-93, 197, 201-07, 210-19, 222-24, 226-27, 229-37, 240-41, 243-45, 248-49; **123**:186, 226, 254-55, 261
Benito Cereno (Melville) **91**:204
"Benjamin the Waggoner" (Wordsworth) **111**:204, 370
Ben's Nugget (Alger) **8**:44
"Bentham" (Mill) **11**:361, 370; **58**:327, 333, 351
Beobachtungen über das Gefühl des Schönen und Erhabenen (Kant) **67**:214
"Beowulf" (Morris) **4**:441
Beppo: A Venetian Story (Byron) **2**:64, 72, 92-94, 97; **12**:70-71, 80, 84, 87, 103, 106, 125, 127; **109**:67
"Béranger" (Bagehot) **10**:62
"Bereavement" (Bowles) **103**:55
"Bereavement" (Keble) **87**:134
"Berenice" (Poe) **1**:500, 514; **16**:291, 297, 300, 304-05, 308, 314, 331, 334-35; **55**:148, 187, 194, 206; **94**:202; **97**:180, 208-09; **117**:299-300, 322-23; **117**:299-300, 322-23
Berenice, Ein erotischer Spaziergang (Muller) **73**:366
Bergkristall (Stifter) **41**:344, 351
Bergmilch (Stifter) **41**:372
"Die Bergwerke zu Falun" (Hoffmann) **2**:360
"Berkeley the Banker" (Martineau) **26**:314, 330
Berkeley the Banker (Martineau) **137**:267
Bernard Brooks' Adventures (Alger) **8**:43, 45
"Bernardine du Born" (Sigourney) **21**:298
"Le Bernica" (Leconte de Lisle) **29**:216, 244
Berta (Droste-Hülshoff) **3**:196-97
"Bertha" (Alcott) **83**:5
"Bertha" (Lazarus) **8**:411, 417; **109**:297, 321, 342
"Bertha in the Lane" (Browning) **1**:112, 115, 117-8; **61**:65-6
Bertha's Christmas Vision: An Autumn Sheaf (Alger) **83**:96
"Berthe" (Maupassant) **83**:219
Bertoldo (Da Ponte) **50**:80
Bertram; or, The Castle of St. Aldobrand (Maturin) **6**:317-24, 328, 332-33, 339-40, 342-44
"Bertram to the Lady Geraldine" (Thomson) **18**:396, 407
The Bertrams (Trollope) **6**:463, 470, 484, 499-500, 512, 514-15; **101**:253, 290, 307, 312
Bertrand et Raton; ou, L'art de conspirer (Scribe) **16**:388, 414
"The Beryl Stone" (Browning) **1**:124
Beschluss, über das Ideal der Sprache (Herder) **8**:317
De beschriebene Tännling (Stifter) **41**:354
"Besenok" (Baratynsky)
See "Besyonok"
Beshenye dengi (Ostrovsky) **30**:105, 111; **57**:213-4, 220
"El beso" (Bécquer) **106**:98, 108, 121
Bespridannitsa (Ostrovsky) **30**:100, 104, 110, 115; **57**:213, 220
"Der Bessenbinder von Rychiswyl" (Gotthelf) **117**:6
"Bessey of the Glen" (Clare) **86**:89
"Bessonnitsa" (Tyutchev) **34**:389, 391, 393, 395, 399
"Bessy's Troubles at Home" (Gaskell) **70**:185
"The Best Man in the Vield" (Barnes) **75**:77
"Best Things" (Parton) **86**:352
Die Bestimmung des Menschen (Fichte) **62**:29, 31, 34, 54
"Der Besuch auf dem Lande" (Gotthelf) **117**:6
"Besuch des Eros" (Mörike) **10**:450
*Der Besuch in St. Hiob zu*** (Claudius) **75**:190
"Besuch in Urach" (Mörike) **10**:448
"Besy" (Pushkin) **83**:279
Besy (Dostoevsky) **2**:158, 161-62, 167-68, 170-72, 175, 179-80, 184-86, 190, 197, 202-04; **7**:80, 102; **21**:88-146; **33**:165, 173, 177-79, 182, 234; **43**:91-92, 99, 122, 130, 134, 143, 148, 151, 155, 160; **119**:81-2, 87-9, 91, 150, 154
"Besyonok" (Baratynsky) **103**:9-10, 16, 22
"Beszel a fákkal..." (Petofi) **21**:285
"La bête à Maître Belhomme" (Maupassant) **1**:463
"Betrachtungen über den Weltlauf" (Kleist) **37**:249
Betrachtungen und Gedanken uber verschiedene Gegonstande der Welt und der Litteratur (Klinger) **1**:432
"Betrayal" (Lanier) **118**:202
The Betrothal (Boker) **125**:8, 19-20, 31, 36, 58
The Betrothal (Kivi)
See *Kihlaus*
The Betrothed (Manzoni)
See *I promessi sposi*
The Betrothed (Scott) **15**:313; **69**:313-14, 319, 331
The Betrothed (Tieck) **5**:513
"Das Betrübte Madchen" (Claudius) **75**:191
"Das Bettelweib von Locarno" (Kleist) **2**:448; **37**:246, 248, 254-5
"The Better Day" (Lampman) **25**:217
"The Better Land" (Hemans) **29**:207
"Better Late Than Never" (Goncharov)
See "Luchshe pozdno, chem nikogda"
"A Better Resurrection" (Rossetti) **2**:575; **50**:322; **66**:330
Bettina von Arnims Sätliche Werke (Arnim) **38**:13
Bettinas Briefwechsel mit Goethe (Arnim)
See *Goethes Briefwechsel mit einem Kinde: Seinem Denkmal*
Bettine (Musset) **7**:271
"Bettlerballade" (Meyer) **81**:207
"Betty Foy" (Wordsworth) **12**:430
Between Heaven and Earth (Ludwig)
See *Zwischen Himmel und Erde*
"Between the Rapids" (Lampman) **25**:160-61, 167-68, 190, 205-06
"Between the Wind and the Rain" (Crawford) **12**:156, 162
"Between Two Stools" (Levy) **59**:95, 107-9, 111, 120
Bevis (Jefferies)
See *Bevis, The Story of a Boy*
Bevis, The Story of a Boy (Jefferies) **47**:91, 93, 101, 111-12, 120, 124, 126-29, 131-32, 142
"Bevis's Zodiac" (Jefferies) **47**:113
"Bewitched" (Shevchenko)
See "Prycynna"
Bewitched (Barbey d'Aurevilly)
See *L'ensorcelée*
"A Bewitched Place" (Gogol)
See "Zakoldovannoe mesto"
"The Bewitched Spot" (Gogol)
See "Zakoldovannoe mesto"
"Beyond Kerguelen" (Kendall) **12**:190-91, 199-200
"Beyond the Ravine Another Ravine" (Shevchenko)
See "Za bairakom bairak"
Beyträge zur geheimen Geschichte des menschlichen Verstandes und Herzens (Wieland) **17**:407
Bez viný vinovátye (Ostrovsky) **57**:220
"Bezhin Lea" (Turgenev) **21**:413, 418, 422; **122**:260, 337, 343, 348-49
"Bežin Meadow" (Turgenev)
See "Bezhin Lea"
"Beznadeznost'" (Baratynsky) **103**:26
Bezpridńnitsa (Ostrovsky)
See *Bespridannitsa*
"Beztalanny" (Shevchenko)
See "Tryzna"
"Bezumnykh let vgasshee vesel'e" (Pushkin) **83**:304
"Bhagavat" (Leconte de Lisle) **29**:221-23, 234, 242, 245
"Bharat kalanka" (Chatterji) **19**:225
"Bharatvarsher swadhinata ebang paradhinata" (Chatterji) **19**:225
Białe kwiaty (Norwid) **17**:371
"Bianca among the Nightingales" (Browning) **61**:7, 45
Bianca, or The Young Spanish Maiden (Dutt) **29**:129
"Bianca's Dream" (Hood) **16**:235
" Ein biBchen Freude" (Meyer) **81**:145
Bible de l'humanité (Michelet) **31**:210, 216, 218, 232, 248, 258
The Bible in Spain; or, The Journeys, Adventures, and Imprisonments of an Englishman, in an Attempt to Circulate the Scriptures in the Peninsula (Borrow) **9**:37-40, 42, 47-8, 50-1, 53, 55-6, 59, 65-6
Bible of Hell (Blake) **57**:44, 53, 55, 82, 92-3
The Bible of Humanity (Michelet)
See *Bible de l'humanité*
The Bible of Mankind (Michelet)
See *Bible de l'humanité*
Biblical Dialogues Between a Father and His Family (Rowson) **69**:109, 116-17
"Bibliographical Notes" (Eminescu) **131**:325
Bibliomanie (Flaubert) **62**:101
"Le bibliophile" (Bertrand) **31**:48
Biblioteca Americana (Bello) **131**:92, 101-2, 107, 109, 116, 118, 129-30
"A bid for an Editorship" (Parton) **86**:318
Die bieden Nachtwandler (Nestroy) **42**:231
"Les bienfaits de la lune" (Baudelaire) **6**:87
"The Bienfilâtre Sisters" (Villiers de l'Isle Adam)
See "Les demoiselles de Bienfilâtre"
"La bienveillance universelle" (Joubert) **9**:292
"Bifurcation" (Browning) **19**:88
"Big Claus and Little Claus" (Andersen)
See "Lille Claus og Store Claus"
The Biglow Papers (Lowell) **2**:504, 508-09, 511, 513-14, 516-17, 519-20, 522-23; **90**:188-90, 193, 198, 210, 215, 217-19, 221, 225
"Les bijoux" (Baudelaire) **29**:73; **55**:7-9, 56, 59, 76
"Les bijoux" (Maupassant) **1**:463
"Das Bild des Bathyllos" (Mörike) **10**:450
Bilder aus der deutschen Vergangenheit (Freytag) **109**:158, 165-67, 171-72, 177, 180-81
Bilder aus Westphalen (Droste-Hülshoff) **3**:193, 197, 200
"Bilder und Balladen" (Meyer) **81**:150, 152
"Bilder und Sagen aus der Schweiz" (Gotthelf) **117**:33
"Das Bildnes der Geliebten" (Mörike) **10**:450
"Bill Ainsworth's Quarter Race" (Harris) **23**:140, 142

Bill for Religious Freedom (Jefferson) **103**:157
"Bill Jones on Prayer" (Thomson) **18**:403
"Bill the Bullock-Driver" (Kendall) **12**:190, 192, 195
"Le Billet" (Desbordes-Valmore) **97**:12
Billet à Lily (Verlaine) **51**:363
"A Billet Doux" (Horton) **87**:96
"Billiards" (Shaw) **15**:335
"Billingsgate Music" (Maginn) **8**:441
The Billiten in the Parsonage (Arnim)
See *Die Einquartierung im Pfarrhause*
"Bills of Mortality" (Cowper) **8**:103
Billy Budd, Sailor: An Inside Narrative (Melville) **3**:336, 345, 347, 358-59, 363-64, 366-68, 370-73, 375, 384-85; **29**:314-83; **45**:213, 233, 242, 244, 248; **49**:379; **91**:53, 193; **93**:214; **123**:186, 197, 212
"Billy Vickers" (Kendall) **12**:190-91
"Bimini" (Heine) **4**:238; **54**:330-3, 337
"Binsey Poplars" (Hopkins) **17**:186, 204, 223, 256
Biographia (Coleridge)
See *Biographia Borealis*
Biographia Borealis (Coleridge) **90**:15, 24, 32
Biographia Literaria; or, Biographical Sketches of My Literary Life and Opinions (Coleridge) **9**:136-37, 152, 155, 157, 159-61, 163-65, 169, 173-74, 178-79, 184, 199-200, 205-07; **54**:80, 83, 101, 107, 114-5; **99**:4, 6, 13, 34-5, 38-40, 42, 53-4, 77-9, 86-7, 92, 95, 99, 104, 106, 115; **111**:201, 245, 290-91, 295, 311-13
Biographical Essays (De Quincey) **4**:61-62
A Biographical History of Philosophy (Lewes) **25**:274, 276, 287-88, 293, 295-96, 299-300, 304, 307, 320
"Biographical Memoir of Mr. Liston" (Lamb) **10**:435
Biographical Memoirs of Extraordinary Painters (Beckford) **16**:15, 17-22, 29, 36-7
Biographical Recreations under the Cranium of a Giantess (Jean Paul) **7**:227
Biographical Sketches (Martineau) **26**:348-49
Biographical Studies (Bagehot) **10**:23, 43
Biographies of Good Wives (Child) **73**:47, 59, 64, 72, 75, 97
The Biographies of Madame de Staël and Madame Roland, Married Women; or, Biographies of Good Wives (Child) **6**:197-98, 203; **73**:59, 72
"Biography and Writings of A. M. Hyde" (Sigourney) **87**:321
"Biography of Females" (Sigourney) **87**:321
"Biography of Pious Persons" (Sigourney) **87**:321
Birāngana̅ Kabya (Dutt) **118**:30
"The Birch Grove Near Endermay" (Muller) **73**:352
"The Birch-Tree at Loschwitz" (Levy) **59**:90, 119
The Bird (Michelet) **31**:215, 219, 242-44, 247, 259-60, 263
"The Bird and the Bell" (Cranch) **115**:15, 17, 22, 27, 35
The Bird and the Bell, with Other Poems (Cranch) **115**:17, 22-3, 26, 40, 55
"The Bird and the Hour" (Lampman) **25**:169
"The Bird and the Ship" (Muller) **73**:350, 352
The Bird in the Pear-Tree (Andersen) **79**:11
"Bird Language" (Cranch) **115**:41, 43
"The Bird Mediæval" (Cooper) **129**:71
"Bird of Paradise" (Ueda Akinari)
See *Bupposo*
"The Bird Primeval" (Cooper) **129**:71
"Birds Climbing the Air" (Jefferies) **47**:136
"A Bird's Eye View" (Rossetti) **2**:556; **50**:289
"Birds in the High Hall-Garden" (Tennyson) **30**:242
"Birds in the Night" (Verlaine) **2**:632; **51**:381, 383-84
"The Bird's Nest" (Hale) **75**:284-85, 289
"The Bird's Nest" (Keble) **87**:134
"Birds' Nests" (Clare) **9**:108, 110-11; **86**:144
Birds of America (Audubon) **47**:3, 11, 13-15, 18, 20, 23, 27-30, 32-3, 36-8, 40, 45-7, 50-3
The Birds of Aristophanes (Planché) **42**:273-75, 277, 281-82, 284-86, 291, 293
"The Birds of Killingworth" (Longfellow) **2**:481; **45**:130, 137, 145, 149, 180, 188, 191
"The Birds of Passage" (Hemans) **71**:263
"Birds of Passage" (Longfellow) **45**:116, 133, 137
"The Birds on the Wires" (Cranch) **115**:43
"The Bird's Release" (Hemans) **71**:264
The Birds' Rivalry (Da Ponte)
See *La gara degli uccelli*
"Birds Then and Now" (Cooper) **129**:71
"Birjuk" (Turgenev) **122**:264
Birth (Robertson) **35**:335, 361, 363-65, 369
"The Birth of Flattery" (Crabbe) **26**:78-9, 81; **121**:9
"Birth of the Duke of Bordeaux" (Hugo) **3**:234
"The Birth of the Horse" (Taylor) **89**:302-03
"A Birthday" (Rossetti) **2**:559; **50**:289; **66**:311, 342, 344, 382
"Birthday of Longfellow" 2 (Sigourney) **87**:326
"The Birthday of the Soul" (Very) **9**:387
"Birthday Song" (Lanier) **6**:237
Birth-Day Song of Liberty (Chivers) **49**:45
"A Birthday Song to S. G." (Lanier) **118**:260
"A Birthday Wish" (Lamb) **125**:372
"The Birthmark" (Hawthorne) **2**:311, 319, 322, 324; **17**:145, 151; **23**:218; **79**:308; **95**:105, 110, 207
"Bishop Berkeley on the Metaphysics of Sensation" (Huxley) **67**:86-7
"Bishop Blougram's Apology" (Browning) **19**:79, 100, 117, 120-23, 131, 136-38; **79**:163, 171
"The Bishop Orders His Tomb at San Praxed's" (Browning) **19**:77, 114, 117, 119, 133, 136-37
"The Bishop Orders His Tomb at St. Praxed's" (Browning) **79**:94, 98-99, 103
Bishop Percy's Folio Manuscript (Percy) **95**:309, 314, 331
"The Bishop: The Philosopher" (Arnold) **126**:89
"A Bit O' Sly Coorten" (Barnes) **75**:78, 82, 93
"A Bit of Injustice" (Parton) **86**:320
The Bit o'Writing (Banim and Banim) **13**:130-31
"Bite deep and wide, O Axe, the tree!" (Crawford) **127**:151
"The Biter Bit" (Collins) **1**:187
Bits of Travel (Jackson) **90**:144, 167
Bitter Drops (Silva)
See *Gotas amargas*
"Bitter for Sweet" (Rossetti) **2**:558, 575
"Bitter Fruits from Chance-Sown Seeds" (Kirkland) **85**:265, 301
"Bitter Potions" (Silva)
See "Gotas Amargas"
"The Bivouac of the Dead" (Bryant) **6**:172
"Blaavin" (Smith) **59**:333
Black (Dumas) **71**:204
"Black and White" (Barnes) **75**:98
"The Black and White Question" (Hood) **16**:239
The Black Arrow: A Tale of Two Roses (Stevenson) **5**:405, 409, 415, 430-31; **63**:222, 228, 255-6, 261
The Black Baronet (Carleton) **3**:89-90
"The Black Birds and Yellow Hammers" (Griffin) **7**:218
The Black Cabinet (Sacher-Masoch) **31**:295
"The Black Cat" (Poe) **1**:495, 521; **16**:294-95, 301, 303, 309, 314-15, 325-27, 329-32, 334; **55**:148; **78**:281-87, 298-99; **117**:320, 322-23
"Black Cats" (Coleridge) **90**:9
The Black Domino (Scribe)
See *Le domino noir*
The Black Dwarf (Scott) **15**:259-60; **69**:308
"The Black Fox" (Whittier) **8**:526
Black Giles the Poacher: Containing Some Account of a Family Who Had Rather Live by Their Wits than Their Work (More) **27**:346
"The Black Jack" (Maginn) **8**:438
"A Black Job" (Hood) **16**:238-39
"Black Kate" (Kendall) **12**:192
"Black Lizzie" (Kendall) **12**:192
Black Man (Brown)
See *The Black Man: His Antecedents, His Genius, and His Achievements*
The Black Man: His Antecedents, His Genius, and His Achievements (Brown) **2**:48, 50; **89**:143-44, 163, 178-79
The Black Man's Lament (Opie) **65**:175
The Black Prophet: A Tale of Irish Famine (Carleton) **3**:85-86, 90, 94-96
"Black Regiment" (Boker) **125**:25, 33, 39
The Black Robe (Collins) **1**:184
"The Black Shawl" (Pushkin)
See "Chornaya shal"
"Black Sonnets" (Silva)
See "Sonetos negros"
"The Black Spider" (Gotthelf)
See "Die Schwarze Spinne"
"Black Stories" (Silva)
See "Los cuentos negros"
The Black Tulip (Dumas)
See *La tulipe noire*
"Black, White, and Brown" (Hood) **16**:206
The Blackamoor of Peter the Great (Pushkin)
See *Povesti Belkina*
Blackberries Picked off Many Bushes (Allingham) **25**:22
"Blackbirds" (Ketcham) **118**:242
Black-Eyed Susan; or, All in the Downs (Jerrold) **2**:395, 401, 403-05, 408
Black-Jewel Scroll (Ueda Akinari)
See *Nubatama no Maki*
"Blackmwore Maidens" (Barnes) **75**:4, 101
"Blackwood" (Tennyson) **115**:235
Blagonamerennyya rechi (Saltykov) **16**:359, 373
Blake (Delany)
See *Blake; or, The Huts of America: A Tale of the Mississippi Valley, the Southern United States, and Cuba*
Blake, Coleridge, Wordsworth, Lamb, Etc.: Being Selections from the Remains of H. C. Robinson (Robinson) **15**:185
Blake: Complete Writings with Variant Readings (Blake) **127**:93-100
"Blake or the Huts of America" (Delany) **93**:104
Blake; or, The Huts of America: A Tale of the Mississippi Valley, the Southern United States, and Cuba (Delany) **93**:104, 107-09, 112, 153-56, 160-64, 166-67, 169-75
"Blakesmoor in H—shire" (Lamb) **10**:435-36
Le blanc et le noir (Grillparzer) **102**:113
"Blanco y negro" (Casal) **131**:256-57
Les Blancs et les bleus (Dumas) **71**:192
"Blandois' Song" (Dickens) **113**:131
"Blanduzia's Fountain" (Eminescu)
See "Fântâna Blanduziei"
"Blaney" (Crabbe) **26**:121
"Blank Misgivings of a Creature Moving about in Worlds Not Realized" (Clough) **27**:106-7, 114
The Blank Paper (Sacher-Masoch) **31**:298
Blank Verse, by Charles Lloyd and Charles Lamb (Lamb) **113**:161, 181, 269, 274, 277-78
Blanka von Kastilien (Grillparzer) **1**:386; **102**:78-9, 148, 189
Blanks and Prizes (Gore) **65**:21
"The Blasphemy of Gasconade and Self-Dependence in a Certain General" (Brackenridge) **7**:44
Blätter für Deutsche Art und Kunst (Herder) **8**:299
Bleak House (Dickens) **3**:151-52, 159, 166, 169-72, 174, 178, 186-87; **8**:159-205;

18:100, 127, 132-34; **26**:157, 171, 177, 202, 205; **37**:164, 174, 192, 202, 204; **86**:18, 197, 201, 222, 255-56, 260; **105**:201, 211, 213-14, 228, 244, 256, 288, 290, 292, 294, 311, 317, 320, 330, 334, 336, 354; **113**:29, 34, 42, 48, 51, 63, 69, 91-3, 98, 106-07
The Bleeding Rock (More) **27**:336
Blenda (Stagnelius) **61**:253-6
"Bless God, He Went as Soldiers" (Dickinson) **21**:55
"Blessed Are They Who Have No Talent:' Emerson's Unwritten Life of Amos Bronson Alcott" (Emerson) **98**:74-5
"Blessed Damozel" (Rossetti) **66**:304
"The Blessed Damozel" (Rossetti) **4**:491-93, 495, 501-02, 504-05, 508, 510-14, 516-19, 522, 526-27, 529-30; **77**:301-06, 338, 340, 344-46, 348-54
"The Blessed Virgin, Compared to the Air We Breathe" (Hopkins) **17**:188, 205, 208, 247
"Blick auf die slavischen Mundarten, ihre Literatur und die Hülfsmittel sie zu studieren" (Kopitar) **117**:73, 115
"The Blind" (Baudelaire)
See "Les aveugles"
"Blind Bartimeus" (Longfellow) **2**:472; **45**:99, 128
"Blind Girl" (Shevchenko)
See "Slepaya"
Blind Love (Collins) **93**:19, 66
"The Blind Man" (Shevchenko)
See "Slipyi"
"Blind One" (Shevchenko)
See "Slepaya"
"The Blind Seer" (Cranch) **115**:9, 40
"A Blind Woman" (Shevchenko)
See "Slepaya"
"The Blindman's World" (Bellamy) **4**:31; **86**:7, 9, 17, 75, 79
The Blindman's World and Other Stories (Bellamy) **86**:70, 75
"Blindness" (Martineau) **26**:349
"The Blissful" (Kivi)
See "Onnelliset"
The Blithedale Romance (Hawthorne) **2**:300-03, 306, 313-14, 326, 329-30, 332; **10**:295; **17**:108-59; **23**:169, 183, 205, 208-09, 213-14; **39**:177, 180, 186, 188, 224, 227, 229; **79**:295-96, 304; **95**:104, 106, 125, 150, 205
"The Blizzard" (Aksakov)
See "Buran"
"The Blizzard" (Pushkin)
See "Metel"
"Blliz stana yunosha prekrasnyy . . ." (Bestuzhev) **131**:182
"Das Blockhaus" (Lenau) **16**:269, 283
The Blockheads; or, The Affrighted Officers (Warren) **13**:419, 428, 436
"The Blockhouse" (Traill) **31**:325
Der blonde Eckbert (Tieck) **5**:514, 517, 519, 523-25, 529-31; **46**:332-3, 337-45, 348-52, 355-56, 364-65, 374-75, 377, 381-87, 391-92, 414
"The Bloodstained Robe" (Ueda Akinari)
See "Chi katabira"
The Bloody Buoy (Cobbett) **49**:107, 109
"The Bloody Vestiges of Tyranny" (Brackenridge) **7**:44
"The Blossom" (Blake) **37**:3, 11, 14, 36, 39, 41, 57, 65, 72, 75, 83, 85-7, 92
The Blossom of Happiness (Andersen) **79**:13-14
A Blot in the 'Scutcheon (Browning) **19**:76, 95, 102, 113-14; **79**:147, 188-89
Bloudie Jacke of Shresberrie (Barham) **77**:9
"Blown Up with Soda" (Harris) **23**:140, 143, 153, 159, 163
"The Blue and the Gray" (Alcott) **83**:7
"The Blue and the Gray" (Bryant) **6**:172
Blue Beard (Dunlap) **2**:211
Blue Beard (Planché) **42**:279, 288, 292, 299
The Blue Belles of England (Trollope) **30**:327-29
"The Blue Bower" (Morris) **4**:425
"The Blue Closet" (Morris) **4**:411, 419, 421, 423, 425-26, 431
"The Blue Evening" (Isaacs)
See "La tarde azul"
"Blue Flower" (Eminescu)
See "Floare albastra"
"The Blue Hood" (Ueda Akinari)
See *Aozukin*
"A Blue Love Song" (Moore) **110**:172
The Blue Monster (Gozzi)
See *Il mostro turchino*
"The Blue Room" (Mérimée)
See "La chambre bleue"
Bluebeard the Knight (Tieck)
See *Ritter Blaubart*
"Blue-Beard's Closet" (Cooke) **110**:51
"The Bluebell" (Brontë) **71**:165
"Blue-Stocking Reveals" (Hunt) **70**:271
Blumen-, Frucht-, und Dornenstücke; oder, Ehestand Tod, und Hochzeit des Armena dvocaten Firmian Stanislaus Siebenkäs (Jean Paul) **7**:232, 236, 238-40
"Blümlein Vergißmein" (Muller) **73**:365, 373-74
Blütenstaub (Novalis) **13**:365, 376, 379
"Der Blutstropfen" (Meyer) **81**:199, 205, 209
Der Blutsuger (Polidori)
See *The Vampyre: A Tale*
Blyzniata (Shevchenko) **54**:392, 396
"Boädicea" (Tennyson) **30**:230, 233, 236
"Boadicea. An Ode" (Cowper) **8**:107, 111, 120; **94**:32
The Boarder (Turgenev)
See *Nakhlebnik*
Boarding Out; or, Domestic Life (Hale) **75**:341
The Boarding School, or Lessons of a Preceptress to Her Pupils, The (Foster) **99**:122, 126, 138-42, 144, 167, 197, 199-204
"Boarding Schools" (Hale) **75**:345
"The Boar's Head Tavern, Eastcheap" (Irving) **2**:381; **19**:327, 347
The Boatman Artist (Gómez de Avellaneda)
See *El artista barquero o los cuatro cinco de junio*
"The Boatman of Whitehall" (O'Brien) **21**:248
"Bob Burke's Duel with Ensign Brady" (Maginn) **8**:438-40
Bob Burton; or, The Young Ranchman of the Missouri (Alger) **8**:43
"Bob the Fiddler" (Barnes) **75**:77, 81
"Bobolinks" (Cranch) **115**:41, 43
"Boccaccio and Petrarca" (Landor) **14**:195
"Bocetos antiguos" (Casal) **131**:269
"Bochsa" (Chivers) **49**:73
"Un bock" (Maupassant) **1**:450
La boda y el duelo (Martínez de la Rosa) **102**:253
"The Boding Dream" (Beddoes) **3**:34
"Body's Beauty" (Rossetti) **4**:520; **77**:326, 330, 345, 355-56, 358
"The Bog King's Daughter" (Andersen)
See "Dynd-Kongens Datter"
Bogdan Chmielnicki (Mérimée) **65**:85
Bogdan the Blind (Eminescu) **131**:292
Bogdan-Dragoş (Eminescu) **33**:265-66; **131**:291
"Bogdanovicu" (Baratynsky) **103**:25
Bogle Corbet (Galt) **110**:88-9
"Bog-Wood" (Ichiyō)
See "Umoregi"
"Bohater" (Norwid) **17**:375
La bohème galante (Nerval) **67**:303, 306, 357
"The Bohemian" (O'Brien) **21**:236-37, 239, 243-45, 252
"Bohemian Hymn" (Emerson) **1**:297
La Bohémienne; ou, L'Amérique en 1775 (Scribe) **16**:388
"Bohémiens en voyage" (Baudelaire) **55**:53, 58
"Bohemios" (Casal) **131**:243
"Bojarin Orša" (Lermontov) **126**:184
Bojarin Orša (Lermontov) **5**:294; **126**:128
"Le Bol de punch" (Gautier) **59**:10, 27
La bola de nieve (Tamayo y Baus) **1**:570
Boland Istók (Arany) **34**:16, 21
"The Bold Dragoon" (Irving) **19**:345
"Bold Words by a Bachelor" (Collins) **93**:61
"Bolond Istók" (Petofi) **21**:264, 267-69
"Bolts of Melody" (Dickinson) **77**:107
Bolts of Melody (Dickinson) **77**:128
"Bolyashchiy dukh vrachuet pesnopenie..." (Baratynsky) **103**:5
"Le bon Dieu" (Beranger) **34**:42
Le Bon Disciple (Verlaine) **51**:363, 367, 372
Un bon enfant (Kock) **16**:247-48
"Bon-Bon" (Poe) **16**:312
Boncourt Castle (Chamisso) **82**:4
"A Bond of Two Generations" (Ueda Akinari)
See "Nise no en"
"Bonden Pavo" (Runeberg) **41**:317
"The Bone Setter" (Le Fanu)
See "The Ghost and the Bone Setter"
Bone to Gnaw for the Democrats (Cobbett) **49**:109
"The Bones of Columbus" (Freneau) **111**:122
"Le bonheur" (Rimbaud) **4**:484
Bonheur (Verlaine) **2**:618-19; **51**:352, 356
"Le bonheur dans le crime" (Barbey d'Aurevilly) **1**:74-75
La bonne chanson (Verlaine) **2**:617, 621-23, 627, 629-30; **51**:350, 356, 359, 361, 363, 376, 382, 384, 387
"Une bonne fortune" (Musset) **7**:264, 267, 275
"La bonne nourrice" (Banville) **9**:16
"Bonne Pensée du Matin" (Rimbaud) **82**:231-32, 248, 251
"La bonne vieille" (Beranger) **34**:28-9, 39
Bonneybell Vane (Cooke) **5**:126
"Bonnie Dundee" (Scott) **15**:318
"Bonnie Prince Charlie" (Hogg) **4**:284
"The Bonny Brown Hand" (Hayne) **94**:159-60
The Bonny Brown Hand (Hayne) **94**:134, 160
"Bons Bourgeois" (Verlaine) **51**:386
"Bonsoir" (Corbière) **43**:25, 27, 33
"A Book" (Mickiewicz) **3**:390
Book for Children (Martínez de la Rosa)
See *El libro de los niños*
The Book of Ahania (Blake) **13**:184, 221-22, 225-26, 252; **127**:111
"Book of Aphorisms" (Thomson) **18**:429
The Book of Fallacies (Bentham) **38**:37, 90
The Book of Los (Blake) **13**:184, 221-22, 226; **127**:111
Book of Memoranda (Dickens) **86**:221-22
The Book of Mormon (Smith) **53**:348, 355-63, 366, 368, 374-8, 380-2, 384-7
The Book of Moses (Smith) **53**:380
The Book of Mothers and Children (Desbordes-Valmore)
See *Le Livre des mères et des enfants*
Book of Nonsense (Lear) **3**:295, 297-99, 306
"The Book of Odes" (Freneau) **111**:129
"The Book of Revelation" (Engels) **85**:44, 48
A Book of Romances, Lyrics, and Songs (Taylor) **89**:300, 307, 346
The Book of Roses (Parkman) **12**:347
The Book of Snobs (Thackeray) **5**:446, 453, 465-66, 468, 478, 486-87, 500, 502; **14**:395-96, 402, 409, 422, 451; **43**:362, 388, 391
Book of Sparrows: Collection of Projects, Plots, Ideas, and Plans for Different Things that Might or Might not Be Finished in Accordance with how the Wind Blows (Bécquer)
See *Libro de los gorriones: colección de proyectos, argumentos, ideas y planes de cosas diferentes que se concluirán o no según sople el viento*
The Book of the Church (Southey) **8**:463, 467; **97**:265-66, 268, 283, 330, 337
"Book of the Dead" (Boker) **125**:33
The Book of the Dead (Boker) **125**:18, 41, 78-80, 82
"The Book of the Poets" (Browning) **61**:58, 66; **66**:44

The Book of the Wild Rose (Almqvist)
See *Törnrosens bok*
The Book of Thel (Blake) **13**:172, 177, 183-84, 218, 220-21, 234, 250-51; **37**:15, 20, 22, 42, 72, 96; **127**:79-80, 82
The Book of Urizen (Blake) **13**:184, 194, 205, 221-29, 243, 252; **37**:53, 56; **57**:44, 91-2; **127**:11, 34, 66, 71, 87, 111
The Book of Verses (Silva)
See *El libro de versos*
The Book on Adler (Kierkegaard) **78**:247
"Book on Logic" (Bentham) **38**:92
"The Book to the Reader" (Fuller) **50**:237-8
"Books" (Emerson) **1**:280; **38**:175; **98**:7-8
"The Books" (Eminescu)
See "Carţile"
"Books and Gardens" (Smith) **59**:303, 309
The Books of the Polish Nation and the Polish Pilgrimage (Mickiewicz)
See *Księgi narodu polskiego i pielgrzymastwa polskiego*
"Books Which Have Incluenced Me" (Stevenson) **63**:239
"The Boon Which I Last Crave" (Eminescu) **33**:267, 273; **131**:294, 297-98
"Bor vitéz" (Arany) **34**:15
"Bor'ba za suščestvovanie" (Pisarev) **25**:342, 344
"Bor'ba za žizn" (Pisarev) **25**:344, 346-47, 355-56
Border Beagles (Simms) **3**:502, 508-09, 514
The Border States (Kennedy) **2**:432
"A Border Tradition" (Bryant) **6**:180
The Borderers (Wordsworth) **38**:421, 425-26; **111**:223, 239, 254, 263, 346-47
The Borderers; or, The Wept of Wish-ton-Wish (Cooper)
See *The Wept of Wish-ton-Wish*
"Borderland" (Levy) **59**:119
"Boredom" (Kivi)
See "Ikävyys"
"A borigines" (Whitman) **81**:353
Boris Godunov (Pushkin) **27**:379; **83**:246, 248, 250, 256, 264, 303, 305-06, 309, 332-35, 338-40, 342-43, 347, 353, 355, 361-65, 367, 369, 372-73
"A Born Chieftain" (Boyesen) **135**:15
"Borne Along by the Tide" (Eliot) **4**:134
"Borodinó" (Lermontov) **5**:295, 300; **126**:144, 223
The Borough (Crabbe) **26**:86, 89, 93, 102, 111, 115-16, 118-19, 122-25, 127, 132-34, 138, 141, 151; **121**:4-5, 10-11, 24, 28-9, 31, 34, 36, 58-9, 62-3, 66, 72, 74, 76-7, 83-6, 88-90
"A borozó" (Petofi) **21**:276
"Borrowed Plumes" (Gordon) **21**:164
"Borrowed Spectacles" (Silva)
See "Lentes ajenos"
"Bos amores" (Castro) **78**:42
Boscobel; or, The Royal Oak: A Tale of the Year 1651 (Ainsworth) **13**:36
"Die böse Farbe" (Muller) **73**:363, 365, 372-73
Der böse Geist Lumpazivagabundus oder Das liederliche Kleeblett (Nestroy) **42**:231-32, 236, 238-40, 254-57, 263
"Böse Stunde" (Grillparzer) **102**:174
"The Bosom Serpent" (Hawthorne) **2**:296, 305, 311; **95**:105
Bosquejo histórico de la política de España (Martínez de la Rosa) **102**:252
"Le bossu Bitord" (Corbière) **43**:3, 5, 7-8, 10, 21, 23, 29, 33
"A Boston Ballad" (Whitman)
See "Poem of Apparitions in Boston in the 73rd Year of These States"
"The Boston Hymn" (Emerson) **1**:279, 284-85, 289, 296; **98**:39, 41, 45, 49-50, 182-83
Boswell (Macaulay) **42**:86
"Boswell's Life of Johnson" (Carlyle) **70**:7, 9
The Botanic Garden (Darwin) **106**:181, 186-87, 191-94, 198-200, 203, 207-09, 214, 218-19, 221, 225, 228, 230, 232, 235-37, 241-42, 244-45, 248, 251-52, 259, 261, 265, 273-77
Botany Bay Eclogues (Southey) **97**:260, 314-15
Both Americas (Faustino)
See *Ambras Américas*
The Bothie of Toper-na-Fuosich: A Long-Vacation Pastoral (Clough) **27**:37-8, 40-1, 43, 45, 49, 52, 56-60, 65-6, 71, 74, 77, 79-80, 82, 91-2, 95-8, 103-04, 111, 113-15
Bötjer Basch (Storm) **1**:540, 544
"The Bottle Imp" (Stevenson) **5**:412, 415, 419
"The Bottle in the Sea" (Vigny)
See "La bouteille à la mer"
"The Bottleneck" (Andersen) **79**:69
"Bottom" (Rimbaud) **4**:484-85
"Boule de suif" (Maupassant) **1**:442, 447, 449, 454, 459, 462, 465-66; **83**:168, 190, 193-94, 229
Bound to Rise; or, Harry Walton's Motto (Alger) **8**:42; **83**:124, 134
Bouquets and Prayers (Desbordes-Valmore)
See *Bouquets et prières*
Bouquets et prières (Desbordes-Valmore) **97**:13
"Le bourget" (Lamartine) **11**:264
"The Bourne" (Rossetti) **2**:572
"Bournemouth" (Verlaine) **2**:628; **51**:355, 370-71
"La bouteille à la mer" (Vigny) **7**:472, 474, 483-84, 486
Bouvard et Pécuchet (Flaubert) **2**:232-3, 236, 238, 243, 256; **19**:274, 319; **62**:69, 72-3, 79, 82, 91, 98; **66**:256, 263
Bouvard et Pécuchet, oeuvre posthume (Flaubert) **135**:93-95, 126, 174, 177
Bowden Hill (Bowles) **103**:54
"The Bower by Moonlight" (Harpur) **114**:144
"A Box of Novels" (Thackeray) **43**:350, 383, 385
"The Boy and the Angel" (Browning) **19**:77; **79**:94, 101
The Boy in Grey (Kingsley) **107**:192, 211, 223
A Boy Suffers (Meyer)
See *Das Leiden eines Knaben*
The Boyar Orsha (Lermontov)
See *Bojarin Orša*
"Boyarinya Marfa Andreyevna" (Leskov) **25**:246
Boyhood in Norway: Stories of Boy-life in the Land of the Midnight Sun (Boyesen) **135**:8
Boyhood in Norway: Stories of Boylife in the Land of the Midnight Sun (Boyesen)
See *Boyhood in Norway: Stories of Boy-life in the Land of the Midnight Sun*
The Boyne Water (Banim and Banim) **13**:127, 129-32, 134-36, 143-52
The Boy's Froissart (Lanier) **118**:267
The Boy's King Arthur (Lanier) **118**:267
The Boy's Mabinogion (Lanier) **118**:267
Boys of Other Countries (Taylor) **89**:326, 342
"The Boys of Venus" (Landor) **14**:181
The Boy's Percy (Lanier) **118**:267
"A Boy's Poem" (Smith) **59**:318, 321, 329, 332, 336
"Boys' Reading Book" (Sigourney) **87**:321
Bracebridge Hall (Irving) **2**:368-69, 371, 374, 377-78, 381-82, 384, 387, 390; **19**:331, 333-34, 339, 344; **95**:236-38, 280
"The Braggarts" (Petofi)
See "A szájhösök"
"Brahma" (Emerson) **1**:293-97, 302, 304; **98**:177, 184
The Bramleighs of Bishop's Folly (Lever) **23**:292
"A Branch from Palestine" (Lermontov) **126**:145
"La branche d'amandier" (Lamartine) **11**:254
"The Branded Hand" (Whittier) **8**:510
"Brandons Both" (Rossetti) **2**:558; **66**:352
"Bransoletka" (Norwid) **17**:369-70
"Brat, stolko let soputstvovavshiy mne" (Tyutchev) **34**:399
Brat'ya Karamazovy (Dostoevsky) **2**:161-2, 164, 167, 169-73, 175-8, 180-1, 186, 188, 190-1, 193-5, 204-5; **7**:86, 101-2, 115; **21**:102, 118, 124, 128, 141, 146; **33**:165, 171, 177, 180, 183, 194, 212, 227, 239; **43**:76-173; **119**:71-2, 78, 82, 85, 88, 91, 130-2, 134-6, 153
Bratya Razboiniki (Pushkin) **3**:411, 417, 423, 451; **83**:243, 247, 357
"Die Braut" (Muller) **73**:360
Braut und Bräutigam in einer Person (Kotzebue) **25**:145
"Braut von Korinth" (Goethe) **4**:192
Die Braut von Messina (Schiller) **39**:320-21, 346, 361, 375; **69**:169-71, 181-82, 244-45, 255, 263-64, 267
Die Brautfahrt oder Kunst von der Rose: Lustspiel in fünf Akten (Freytag) **109**:139
"Bräutigamswahl" (Muller) **73**:360
"Die Brautnacht" (Muller) **73**:366
Brave and Bold; or, The Fortunes of a Factory Boy (Alger) **18**:25, 27, 43; **83**:148
The Bravo (Cooper) **1**:200, 214, 218-22, 224; **54**:255-6, 263, 278, 288
The Bravo of Venice (Lewis) **11**:297
A Breach of Promise (Robertson) **35**:333
"Bread and the Newspaper" (Holmes) **81**:102
"Bread and Wine" (Hölderlin)
See "Brot und Wein"
"Break, Break, Break" (Tennyson) **30**:222, 248, 280
"Breakfast" (Sigourney) **87**:326
"Breakfast ato the Paxes" (Parton) **86**:366
"Breakfast in Sunshine" (Corbière) **43**:15
The Breakfast Table Series (Holmes) **81**:107
"Breathe Not His Name" (Moore) **110**:185
"Breathings of Spring" (Hemans) **71**:263
"The Breeze on Beachy Head" (Jefferies) **47**:134, 136
"Brennende Liebe" (Droste-Hülshoff) **3**:200-01
"Bretter" (Turgenev) **122**:268
"Brev om den skandinaviska Nordens betydelse för Europas fornhistoria" (Almqvist) **42**:18
"Brevet Brigadier-General Frank Winthrop" (Lazarus) **109**:292
"Brewing of Soma" (Whittier) **8**:516, 520; **59**:360
"Brian the Still Hunter" (Moodie) **14**:231
"The Bridal Ballad" (Poe) **117**:237-38, 280
"Bridal Birth" (Rossetti) **77**:338
The Bridal Journey, or Kunz von der Rosen (Freytag)
See *Die Brautfahrt oder Kunst von der Rose: Lustspiel in fünf Akten*
The Bridal of Carrigvarah (Le Fanu) **58**:253
"The Bridal of Malahide" (Griffin) **7**:196
"Bridal of Pennacook" (Whittier) **8**:489, 510, 519, 521; **59**:355
"The Bridal of Polmood" (Hogg) **4**:283
The Bride (Baillie) **2**:40; **71**:6
"The Bride of Abydos: A Turkish Tale" (Byron) **2**:61, 71-73, 81, 86, 95, 103; **109**:64
The Bride of Lammermoor (Scott) **15**:287, 289, 300, 304, 309, 311, 317, 322; **69**:371
The Bride of Ludgate (Jerrold) **2**:401, 408
The Bride of Messina (Schiller)
See *Die Braut von Messina*
"The Bride of the Greek Isle" (Hemans) **71**:292, 304, 306
"The Bride of Torrisdale" (Boyesen) **135**:5
"Bride Song" (Rossetti) **50**:264
The Bridegroom (Pushkin) **3**:417
"Bridegroom's Park" (Allingham) **25**:30-1
"The Bride's Chamber" (Rossetti) **4**:528
The Bride's Fate (Southworth) **26**:433
"The Brides of Venice" (Rogers) **69**:80
The Bride's Ordeal (Southworth) **26**:434
"The Bride's Prelude" (Rossetti) **4**:505, 508, 513, 518-20, 523, 527-29, 531-32; **77**:293, 326, 329, 348

The Brides' Tragedy (Beddoes) **3**:24-29, 31-36, 39
"The Bridge" (Longfellow) **45**:115, 135, 148; **103**:293, 297
"The Bridge of Sighs" (Hood) **16**:205-07, 209, 212, 215, 220-21, 224-26, 228, 231, 233-34, 237-38
"A Brief Appraisal of the Greek Literature" (De Quincey) **87**:77
"Brief eines Dichters an einem Andern" (Kleist) **37**:251
A Brief History of Epidemic and Pestilential Diseases; with the Principal Phenomena of the Physical World, Which Precede and Accompany Them, and Observations Deduced from the Facts Stated . . . (Webster) **30**:406, 426
Brief Outline of Theological Study in the Form of Introductory Lectures (Schleiermacher) **107**:267, 359, 377-78, 399
"Brief über den Durchgang der Venus" (Claudius) **75**:201-03
"Brief über den Roman" (Schlegel) **45**:309, 322, 344, 365, 368, 370-71
"Ein Brief, von C. an D." (Claudius) **75**:202
"Briefe" (Grillparzer) **102**:118
"Briefe an Andres" (Claudius) **75**:210-12, 216-18
Briefe an eine Freundin (Humboldt) **134**:158-59, 162, 167, 209-10
Briefe an Lina (La Roche) **121**:271, 279
Briefe aus Berlin (Heine) **54**:306, 316, 336
"Briefe aus dem Wuppertal" (Engels) **85**:75
Briefe aus dem Wuppertal (Engels) **85**:75, 108
"Briefe über die ästhetische Erziehung des Menschen" (Schiller) **39**:336, 352, 362, 367, 373, 389; **69**:250, 273
Briefe über die Französische Bühne (Heine) **54**:308
Briefe über Mannheim (La Roche) **121**:242, 250-51
Briefe von Verstorbenen an hinterlassene Freunde (Wieland) **17**:418
Briefe zur Beförderung der Humanität (Herder) **8**:313-14
Briefwechsel (Varnhagen von Ense) **130**:340-41, 343
Briery Creek (Martineau) **137**:269, 331
"The Brigadier" (Turgenev)
See "Brigadir"
"Brigadir" (Turgenev) **21**:414-15, 441; **37**:373; **122**:242, 264, 268, 348
The Brigand Brothers (Pushkin)
See *Bratya Razboiniki*
"The Brigand of Askalon" (Leskov)
See "Askalonskij zlodej"
"The Brigands" (Villiers de l'Isle Adam)
See "Les brigands"
"Les brigands" (Villiers de l'Isle Adam) **3**:590
"Bright Broken Maginn" (Lockhart) **6**:296
"Bright Star! Would I Were Steadfast as Thou Art" (Keats) **73**:154; **121**:123-24
Brigitta (Stifter) **41**:343, 366, 375, 379
"Bring Flowers" (Hemans) **71**:264
"Brise marine" (Mallarmé) **4**:395; **41**:250, 289
"A Brisk Wind" (Barnes) **75**:37, 97
The Bristles of the Neck of the Aged Sparrow (Dutt)
See *Buro Sāliker Ghāre Ro*
"Britannia's Wreath" (Moodie) **113**:309
The British Novelists (Barbauld)
See *British Novelists with an Essay and Prefaces Biographical and Critical*
British Novelists with an Essay and Prefaces Biographical and Critical (Barbauld) **50**:16, 17-20
The British Prison-Ship (Freneau) **1**:319; **111**:80, 139-40, 143, 146
"British Senate" (Hazlitt) **29**:161
British Synonymy; or, an Attempt at Regulating the Choice of Words in Familiar Conversation (Piozzi) **57**:242, 252-3, 271, 293, 298, 301
"Britons, Guard Your Own" (Tennyson) **30**:294
"Bro" (Woolson) **82**:303
"A Broadway Pageant" (Whitman) **31**:393; **81**:313
Broke (Turgenev)
See *Lack of Funds*
"The Broken Doll" (Lamb) **125**:330, 337
"The Broken Heart" (Barnes) **75**:7
"The Broken Heart" (Irving) **2**:366, 377; **19**:327, 350; **95**:238, 277
The Broken Jug (Kleist)
See *Der Zerbrochene Krug*
"Broken Love" (Blake) **13**:172
"The Broken Oar" (Longfellow) **45**:146
"The Broken Oath" (Carleton) **3**:92
"Broken Pane" (Corbière) **43**:15
"The Broken Toy" (Lazarus) **109**:291
"A Broken-Hearted Lay" (Mangan) **27**:280, 283, 298
The Broker of Bogotá (Bird) **1**:87-90, 93
The Bronze Horseman (Pushkin)
See *Medny Vsadnik*
"The Bronze Pig" (Andersen) **7**:37
"The Bronze Trumpet" (Kendall) **12**:200, 202
"The Brook" (Krylov) **1**:435
"The Brook" (Tennyson) **30**:215, 223; **115**:358
"The Brook" (Wordsworth) **111**:245
Brooke and Brooke Farm (Martineau) **137**:251-52, 260, 268, 270, 272
"Brooklyniana" (Whitman) **81**:343
"Brookside" (Milnes) **61**:136
"The Broomstick Train; or, The Return of the Witches" (Holmes) **14**:121, 125, 132
"Brot und Wein" (Hölderlin) **16**:162, 176, 187, 191-92, 194-95
"Brother and Sister" (Carroll) **139**:32-33
"Brother and Sister" (Eliot) **4**:107, 115; **13**:334
"Brother and Sister" (Grimm and Grimm)
See "Brüderchen und Schwesterchen"
"The Brother and Sister" (Opie) **65**:158, 180
"The Brother and Sister" (Solomos) **15**:389, 396
"Brother Where Dost Thou Dwell" (Thoreau) **7**:383
"Brother, who accompanied me for so many years" (Tyutchev)
See "Brat, stolko let soputstvovavshiy mne"
"Brotherhood" (Muller)
See "Brüderschaft"
"The Brothers" (Crabbe) **26**:93, 120, 130-31; **121**:11, 40
"The Brothers" (Runeberg) **41**:312
"The Brothers" (Wordsworth) **12**:396, 402; **111**:212-13, 228-29, 236, 243-44, 254, 294
The Brothers (Macha) **46**:201
"Brothers, and a Sermon" (Ingelow) **39**:257, 263
Brothers and Sisters: A Tale of Domestic Life (Bremer)
See *Syskonlif*
"Brothers from Far-Away Lands" (Kendall) **12**:183
The Brothers Highwaymen (Pushkin)
See *Bratya Razboiniki*
The Brothers Karamazov (Dostoevsky)
See *Brat'ya Karamazovy*
The Brothers; or Consequences. A Story of what happens Every day (Hays) **114**:186
"The Brothers, or The Influence of Example" (Child) **73**:131-32,134
"Brough Bells" (Southey) **8**:474
Brouillon (Novalis) **13**:405
"Brown Eyes" (Isaacs)
See "Los ojos pardos"
Brown, Jones, and Robinson (Trollope) **6**:460, 514
"The Brown Man" (Griffin) **7**:198, 211
"Brown of Ossawatomie" (Whittier) **8**:495
The Brownie of Bodsbeck, and Other Tales (Hogg) **4**:276, 285, 287-88; **109**:190-91, 209, 230-31, 269
"The Brownie of the Black Haggs" (Hogg) **4**:283; **109**:270, 280
The Browning's Correspondence (Browning) **61**:64, 66-7, 70-1, 74-5
Browning's Essay on Chatterton (Browning)
See "Essay on Tasso and Chatterton"
Brownson's Quarterly Review (Brownson) **50**:28, 32-5, 49-55, 61-4, 66, 68
Bruder Moritz der Sonderling, oder Die Colonie für die Pelew-Inseln (Kotzebue) **25**:143, 145-46
"Brüderchen und Schwesterchen" (Grimm and Grimm) **3**:228-29, 231
"Brudermord" (Hebbel) **43**:237, 253
"Brüderschaft" (Muller) **73**:352, 379
Bruderzwist (Grillparzer)
See *Ein Bruderzwist in Habsburg*
Ein Bruderzwist im Hause Habsburg (Grillparzer)
See *Ein Bruderzwist in Habsburg*
Ein Bruderzwist in Habsburg (Grillparzer) **1**:385, 389, 395-96; **102**:106, 110, 113, 131, 166, 169, 172, 183, 186-87, 191-92, 195, 203, 205, 214-15
"A Bruised Reed Shall He Not Break" (Rossetti) **50**:314; **66**:330
"Brumes et pluies" (Baudelaire) **6**:79; **29**:101; **55**:23, 61
Brunehilde; or, The Last Act of Norma (Alarcon)
See *El final de Norma*
Bruno and Sylvie (Carroll)
See *Sylvie and Bruno*
"Bruno Bauer and Early Christianity" (Engels) **85**:44-46, 48
Bruno oder über das göttliche und natürliche Prinzip der Dinge (Schelling) **30**:128, 160-62, 167, 174, 179
Bruno; or, On the Divine and Natural Principle of Things (Schelling)
See *Bruno oder über das göttliche und natürliche Prinzip der Dinge*
"Brussels: Merry-Go-Round" (Verlaine) **51**:368, 374
"Brute Neighbours" (Thoreau) **7**:388, 398
Bruto I (Alfieri)
See *Bruto primo*
"Bruto Minore" (Leopardi) **129**:306
Bruto primo (Alfieri) **101**:17-18, 42-3, 50
Bruto secondo (Alfieri) **101**:18-19, 42-3
Brutus the Younger (Alfieri)
See *Bruto secondo*
"Bruxelles" (Rimbaud) **4**:483
"Bruxelles: Simple fesques" (Verlaine) **51**:382
Bryan Perdue (Holcroft)
See *The Memoirs of Bryan Perdue*
Brytan bryś (Fredro) **8**:285
The Bubbles of Canada (Haliburton) **15**:117-19, 128
Bubbles of the Day (Jerrold) **2**:395, 402-03
"The Buccaneer" (Dana) **53**:157, 168-9
The Buccaneer and Other Poems (Dana) **53**:157
Buch der Lieder (Heine) **4**:232, 239, 248-50, 253-54, 259, 261, 268; **54**:308, 335, 348
Buch des Richters (Kierkegaard) **78**:235
Buch über Shakespeare (Tieck) **5**:520; **46**:359
"La bûche" (Maupassant) **83**:230
"Die Bücher der Zeiten" (Hölderlin) **16**:174, 185
Buckstone's Adventures with a Polish Princess (Lewes) **25**:291
The Bucktails; or, Americans in England (Paulding) **2**:527
"Buckthorne" (Irving) **2**:369
"Buckthorne and His Friends" (Irving) **2**:390
"The Buckwheat" (Andersen) **6**:33; **79**:23
Bucolique (Mallarmé) **41**:281
Buda halála (Arany) **34**:5, 8, 10-12, 15, 18-20

Buda's Death (Arany)
See *Buda halála*
Le budget d'un jeune ménage (Scribe) **16**:393
"Budničnye storony žizni" (Pisarev) **25**:344
"Buds and Bird Voices" (Hawthorne) **2**:296, 298
"Le buffet" (Rimbaud) **35**:271; **82**:247-48
Bug-Jargal (Hugo) **3**:234, 236-37, 239, 254; **21**:198, 201
"The Bugler's First Communion" (Hopkins) **17**:194
Ein Bühnenfestpiel für drei Tage und einen Vorabend (Wagner) **9**:469
"The Builders" (Longfellow) **45**:127, 131
"The Building of the Ship" (Longfellow) **2**:493; **45**:116, 147, 153-54; **101**:92
Bulemanns Haus (Storm) **1**:542
"The Bull" (Allingham) **25**:6
"Bullocktown" (Clarke) **19**:231, 250-51
"Bull-Thomas" (Kivi)
See "Härka-Tuomo"
The Bulwark of Art (Andersen) **79**:16
"Bunch Poem" (Whitman) **81**:360
Bunte Steine (Stifter) **41**:337, 351, 359, 362-64, 368-69, 391, 396
"Buonaparte" (Hölderlin) **16**:174
"Buonaparte" (Tennyson) **30**:293
De Buonaparte et des Bourbons (Chateaubriand) **134**:5
"Bupposo" (Ueda Akinari) **131**:6, 8-9, 13, 24, 26, 32-33, 38, 40, 57
Bupposo (Ueda Akinari) **131**:65
"Buran" (Aksakov) **2**:13, 15
"The Burden of Egypt" (Milnes) **61**:130
"The Burden of Nineveh" (Rossetti) **4**:491, 502, 511, 517-18, 523-24, 527, 529; **77**:291-97, 299, 340, 348, 352-54
"Burger of St Gall" (Gore) **65**:21
Der Bürgergeneral (Goethe) **4**:222
Les burgraves (Hugo) **3**:256, 268-69, 276
"Die Bürgschaft" (Schiller) **39**:388
"The Burial of King Cormac" (Ferguson) **33**:278, 301, 303
The Burial of the Donkey (Smolenskin)
See *Kevurat hamor*
"Burial of Two Young Sisters" (Sigourney) **87**:337
"A Burial Place" (Allingham) **25**:24
"The Burial-Place of a Favourite Bird" (Collins) **93**:63
Buried Alive; or, Two Years of Penal Servitude in Siberia (Dostoevsky)
See *Zapiski iz mertvogo doma*
"The Buried Life" (Arnold) **29**:27, 31, 34-6; **89**:14, 18, 20-6, 53, 83, 88
"A Buried Life" (Ichiyō)
See "Umoregi"
"Burley-bones" (Cranch) **115**:57-8
"Burncombe Hollow" (Barnes) **75**:15
"The Burning of Fairfield" (Dwight) **13**:270, 272, 278
"The Burning of the Caroline" (Moodie) **113**:308
"Burns" (Carlyle) **70**:7, 9
Buro Sāliker Ghāre Ro (Dutt) **118**:5
"Burya" (Baratynsky) **103**:10, 14, 17
"Burza" (Mickiewicz) **3**:390, 403
"Buschlieder" (Ludwig) **4**:353
Die Buschnovelle (Ludwig) **4**:356
Bush Ballads and Galloping Rhymes (Gordon) **21**:149-52, 155, 159, 163-64, 167, 170-71, 173, 175-76, 181, 183-84, 187-88
"A Bush Girl" (Adams) **33**:13
"The Bush Trembles" (Petofi)
See "Reszket a bokor..."
"The Bushfire" (Harpur) **114**:99, 115, 125-26, 158
"The Bushrangers" (Harpur) **114**:94, 114-15
The Bushrangers: A Play in Five Acts and Other Poems (Harpur) **114**:109, 114-15, 120, 122, 127
"The Business Man" (Poe) **16**:312, 324
"Busque Vd. quien cargue el saco, que yo no he de ser el loco" (Lizardi) **30**:67
"The Bustle in a House" (Dickinson) **77**:129, 133
"But, However—" (Mayhew) **31**:158
"Buttercup, Poppy, Forget-Me-Not" (Field) **3**:206
"A Butterfly" (Pavlova)
See "Motylek"
"The Butterfly" (Andersen)
See "Sommerfuglen"
"The Butterfly" (Brontë) **16**:103
"The Butterfly" (Crawford)
See "The Mother's Soul"
"The Butterfly" (Lamb) **125**:347
"The Butterfly" (Sigourney) **87**:330
"The Butterfly Obtains" (Dickinson) **21**:29
"Buttoo" (Dutt) **29**:121, 124, 128, 130-31
"Buvaly voiny" (Shevchenko) **54**:390
"Buvard, bavard" (Hugo) **10**:357
"A buzzard has risen from the glade" (Tyutchev)
See "S polyany korshun podnyalsya"
"The Bwoate" (Barnes) **75**:58, 90
"By a River" (Kendall) **12**:183
"By Blue Ontario's Shore" (Whitman) **4**:579; **31**:388, 444; **81**:293, 313, 350
"By Flood and Field" (Gordon) **21**:154, 159
"By the Alders" (O'Brien) **21**:245
"By the Bivouac's Fitful Flame" (Whitman) **4**:543
"By the Exe" (Jefferies) **47**:136
"By the Fireside" (Browning) **19**:105, 127, 153; **79**:157
By the Fireside (Eminescu) **33**:266
"By the Goddess of Plain Truth A Manifesto and Proclamation" (Paine) **62**:325
"By the Grave of Henry Timrod" (Hayne) **94**:149
"By the Passaic" (O'Brien) **21**:246
"By the Sea" (Lampman) **25**:193
"By the Sea" (Rossetti) **50**:297
"By the Seaside" (Longfellow) **2**:493
By the Waters of Babylon (Lazarus) **109**:296-97, 311, 332
"By the Waters of Babylon: Little Poems in Prose" (Lazarus) **8**:421-23, 426-28
By the Way: Verses, Fragments, and Notes (Allingham) **25**:18, 21
"By Thomas Gage...A Proclamation" (Trumbull) **30**:351, 374
"By Wood and Wold" (Gordon) **21**:159
"Byezhin Prairie" (Turgenev)
See "Bezhin Lea"
"By-Gone Days" (Tonna) **135**:204
Byloe i dumy (Herzen) **61**:83, 88, 90, 93, 95-8, 100, 103-4, 106, 122-3
The By-Passed (Leskov)
See *Obojdennye*
"Byron" (Tyutchev) **34**:393
The Byrth, Lyf and Actes of King Arthur (Southey) **97**:263
"Byvalo, otrok, zvonkim klikom..." (Baratynsky) **103**:4, 14, 19-20, 47
By-Ways of Europe (Taylor) **89**:312, 351
"Ça?" (Corbière) **43**:13, 15, 31
"Ça Ira" (Maupassant) **83**:194, 198, 200-01
El caballero de las botas azules (Castro) **3**:106-07; **78**:45-47, 52
El Caballo del Rey Don Sancho (Zorrilla y Moral) **6**:525
"Cabbage Soup" (Turgenev)
See "Shchi"
The Cabinet Minister (Gore) **65**:20
"El cabo Muñoz" (Isaacs) **70**:305
"Cache-cache" (Tyutchev) **34**:389
"Cäcilie" (Kleist)
See *Die heilige Cäcilie; oder, die Gewalt der Musik*
El cacique de Tumerqué (Gómez de Avellaneda) **111**:28
"Cacka" (Norwid) **17**:374
"Cacoethes Scribendi" (Sedgwick) **98**:302-04
"Cada vez que recuerda tanto oprobio" (Castro) **78**:42
"La cadène" (Hugo) **10**:357
Cadio (Sand) **57**:316
"Le Cadre" (Baudelaire) **55**:10
"Caelicola" (Chivers) **49**:56
Caesar, a Sketch (Froude) **43**:175, 177
Caesar Borgia; or, the King of Crimee: Verses on the Exile of the Prince (Jefferies) **47**:121
"Caesareanism As It Now Exists" (Bagehot) **10**:46
"Caesaris" (Wergeland) **5**:540
"The Caesars" (De Quincey) **4**:61, 74-75
"Caesar's Wife" (Crawford) **12**:155
"El café" (Larra) **17**:267-70, 279
A Café (Ostrovsky) **30**:96
"La Cafetière" (Gautier) **1**:355; **59**:9, 25-6, 29, 32-3, 36, 38
"The Cage at Cranford" (Gaskell) **97**:168
"The Caged Skylark" (Hopkins) **17**:185, 221, 257
Le cahier rouge de Benjamin Constant (Constant) **6**:222-23
Cahier staëlien (Staël-Holstein) **91**:359-60
Cahiers de jeunesse (Renan) **26**:413, 415
"Cain" (Coleridge)
See "The Wanderings of Cain"
Cain (Byron) **2**:66-67, 72, 76, 81, 91, 94, 97, 99; **12**:102, 109, 139; **109**:99-106, 123, 126
Cakes and Ale (Jerrold) **2**:397-98, 400-02
"Cal Culver and the Devil" (Cooke) **110**:8-20, 24, 33
"Calamus" (Whitman) **4**:546, 554, 557-58, 565, 575, 581-82, 584, 592, 599, 603-04; **81**:249, 258, 268, 271, 299, 301-02, 307-08, 312, 326, 328-33, 364
"The Calash" (Gogol) **5**:219
Calavar; or, The Knight of the Conquest (Bird) **1**:81-84, 86-87, 90
"Los Calaveras, Artículo segundo y conclusión" (Larra) **130**:226
Calaynos (Boker) **125**:8, 18-20, 25, 28, 30-31, 35-36, 58-59, 62, 64-65, 76
"Caldas" (Isaacs) **70**:313
Calderon the Courtier (Bulwer-Lytton) **45**:58
"The Caldron of Kibitsu" (Ueda Akinari)
See *Kibitsu no Kama*
Caleb Field: A Tale of the Puritans (Oliphant) **11**:429; **61**:219
Caleb Williams (Godwin)
See *Things As They Are; or, The Adventures of Caleb Williams*
Caleb Williams (Radcliffe) **55**:275, 278, 280
"Calef in Boston" (Whittier) **8**:509
Calendrier positiviste (Comte) **54**:199
Caliban (Renan) **26**:377, 387, 389, 408
"Caliban upon Setebos" (Browning) **19**:130, 153; **79**:150, 164, 185
"Caliban upon Setebos" (Emerson) **1**:289
"Calico Pie" (Lear) **3**:301
"Calidore" (Keats) **73**:151, 214, 311, 321; **121**:162
The California and Oregon Trail: Being Sketches of Prairie and Rocky Mountain Life (Parkman)
See *The Oregon Trail*
Caligula (Dumas) **11**:45, 47, 51; **71**:187
"Calin Nebunul" (Eminescu) **33**:260; **131**:299-300, 302-4
"Calin the Fool" (Eminescu)
See "Calin Nebunul"
"Calin the Madcap" (Eminescu)
See "Calin Nebunul"
"Calin—file din poveste" (Eminescu) **33**:247, 249, 262-63; **131**:299-300, 302-3, 305, 332
"Calin—Leaves from a Fairy Tale" (Eminescu)
See "Calin—file din poveste"
"Calin—Leaves from a Folktale" (Eminescu)
See "Calin—file din poveste"

Caliste; or, the Sequel to Letters Written from Lausanne (Charriere)
See *Caliste; ou, Suite des lettres écrites de Lausanne*
Caliste; ou, Suite des lettres écrites de Lausanne (Charriere) **66**:121, 123-6, 128, 135, 138, 142-3, 145-6, 160-1, 163-7, 169
"The Call" (Very) **9**:375, 378
"A Call to Be a Husband" (Parton) **86**:367
"A Call to Husbands" (Parton) **86**:363, 366
"Call to the Ordeal" (Arany) **34**:9
Called to Be Saints (Rossetti) **66**:344
Callista: A Sketch of the Third Century (Newman) **38**:290, 292-93, 342; **99**:218, 252-56
"The Callousness Produced by Care" (Brontë) **109**:30
La calomnie (Scribe) **16**:388, 412-13
"El calor" (Bécquer) **106**:113
"The Calpe Obessa; or, Siege of Gibraltar" (Bowles) **103**:53, 56
"Calpurnia" (Boyesen) **135**:4
"Le calumet du Sachem" (Leconte de Lisle) **29**:225
La camaraderie; ou, La courte échelle (Scribe) **16**:384-85, 388-89, 402-03, 407
"The Cambridge Churchyard" (Holmes) **14**:128
"Cambridge Thirty Years Ago" (Lowell) **2**:507, 520
"Cambyses and the Macrobian Bow" (Hayne) **94**:149, 154, 156-59, 169
"The Cameronian Preacher's Tale" (Hogg) **4**:283
Camilla; or, A Picture of Youth (Burney) **12**:18-19, 21-3, 25, 28-30, 32-4, 43, 46, 50-1, 57-9, 62; **54**:18, 25, 27-31, 33-4, 36, 51-63; **107**:12-13, 15-16
Camilla; or, Rome Delivered (Zhukovsky) **35**:377
Camille, ou le nouveau roman (Charriere) **66**:180
Camors; or, Life under the New Empire (Feuillet)
See *Monsieur de Camors*
The Camp (Sheridan) **91**:242
The Camp at the Olympic (Planché) **42**:276, 291, 294
"The Camp of Souls" (Crawford) **12**:156, 162; **127**:202
Campaign of the Great Army (Faustino)
See *Campaña en el Ejército Grande*
Campaña en el Ejército Grande (Faustino) **123**:268, 272-73, 346, 351-52
"Campanas de Bastabales" (Castro) **78**:41
Campaner Thal (Jean Paul) **7**:234
"Campaspe" (Kendall) **12**:190, 193
"El campo americano" (Bello) **131**:109
"Campo Vaccino" (Grillparzer) **102**:175
"Camptown Races" (Foster) **26**:291, 294-95, 298
"Can a Life hide Itself?" (Taylor) **89**:315
Can You Forgive Her? (Trollope) **6**:457, 461-63, 467, 470, 477, 484, 491, 495, 499-500, 504, 508, 515-16; **33**:363, 416; **101**:216, 235, 262, 266-68, 292, 301, 307-08, 319-20, 326-27
"Canada" (Moodie) **113**:349
"Canada to England" (Crawford) **12**:159; **127**:153
"Canadian Boat Song" (Moore) **6**:390
The Canadian Brothers; or, The Prophecy Fulfilled. A Tale of the Late American War (Richardson) **55**:290, 292-3, 299-300, 304, 311, 313, 316, 318-21, 323-4, 326-7, 330-49, 356-7, 362, 364-6, 368
"A Canadian Campaign" (Richardson) **55**:329-31, 333-4, 344
The Canadian Crusoes: A Tale of the Rice Lake Plains (Traill) **31**:316, 324-25, 327-29
"The Canadian Herd Boy" (Moodie) **14**:218
"The Canadian Hunter's Song" (Moodie) **113**:348
"Canadian Life" (Moodie) **113**:325, 332
Canadian Life (Moodie) **113**:326, 333, 370
"A Canadian Scene" (Traill) **31**:324
The Canadian Settler's Guide (Traill)
See *The Female Emigrant's Guide, and Hints on Canadian Housekeeping*
"Canadian Sketches" (Moodie) **14**:231
"A Canadian Song" (Moodie) **14**:227; **113**:344, 348
Canadian Wild Flowers (Traill) **31**:328
"Canadians Will You Join the Band. A Loyal Song" (Moodie) **113**:308-9
"La canción de la morfina" (Casal) **131**:250
"Canción del pirata" (Espronceda) **39**:100, 113-14, 118
"La canción del torero" (Casal) **131**:236
"Canción patriótica" (Espronceda) **39**:105
"Candente esta la atmosfera" (Castro) **78**:41
The Candidate (Crabbe) **26**:76; **121**:10, 18
Candidates for Confirmation (Tegner) **2**:612
"The Candle Indoors" (Hopkins) **17**:195, 245
The Candle's Out (Fredro)
See *Świeczka zgasta*
"Cando penso que te fuches" (Castro) **78**:41
The Cannibal's Progress (Cobbett) **49**:107, 109
"The Canoe" (Crawford) **12**:163-65, 168
Canolles; or, The Fortunes of a Partisan of '81 (Cooke) **5**:125, 131-32, 135
"Cantan os galos" (Castro) **78**:7
"Cantares 8" (Castro)
See "Un arrogante gaitero"
Cantares gallegos (Castro) **3**:98, 100, 104-05, 107; **78**:2-7, 27-33, 37-38, 54-60
Cantata (Lanier) **118**:203, 208-10, 278
"Cantate pour la première communion" (Mallarmé) **41**:289
"Cantate pour les enfants d'une maison de Charité" (Lamartine) **11**:279
"The Canterbury Pilgrims" (Hawthorne) **79**:296
Canti (Leopardi) **129**:245, 304, 310-11, 327-28, 330, 332, 335, 339, 347-49, 351-57, 360
Cantico del gallo silvestre (Leopardi) **129**:230
Cantique de Saint-Jean (Mallarmé) **41**:280
"Cantique des mères" (Desbordes-Valmore) **97**:30
"Cantique sur la mort de la duchesse de Broglie" (Lamartine) **11**:271
"Cantiques des bannis" (Desbordes-Valmore) **97**:30
"Canto a Teresa" (Espronceda) **39**:85, 90-1, 102-04, 117
"Canto al glorioso protomártir San Felipe de Jesús" (Lizardi) **30**:68
"Canto de Maria Clara" (Rizal) **27**:425
"El canto del cosaco" (Espronceda) **39**:100, 120
"Canto del viajero" (Rizal) **27**:425
"Canto notturno di un pastore errante dell'Asia" (Leopardi) **129**:220, 223, 247, 307, 311, 339, 341, 347-48, 350-51, 359
Cantos del trovador (Zorrilla y Moral) **6**:523-24
Canzio (Kivi) **30**:50, 65
"Canzone per nozze" (Leopardi) **129**:327
Canzoni (Leopardi) **129**:348, 352
"The Cap and Bells" (Keats) **8**:341, 359; **73**:155, 208, 295, 299
Cape Cod (Thoreau) **7**:355-6, 361, 390, 411; **61**:348; **138**:167
Caper-Sauce (Parton) **86**:375
Le Capitaine Pamphile (Dumas) **71**:204
Le capitaine Paul (Dumas) **11**:58
Capital: A Critical Analysis of Capitalist Production (Marx)
See *Das Kapital: Kritik der politischen Ökonomie*
"Capital—the Mother of Labor: An Economical Problem Discussed from a Physiological Point of View" (Huxley) **67**:68
El capitán Veneno (Alarcon) **1**:15-16
Le capitane Fracasse (Gautier) **1**:344-46, 348; **59**:5-8, 12
Capitola (Southworth)
See *The Hidden Hand*
Un caprice (Musset) **7**:268, 270-72, 275
Les caprices de Marianne (Musset) **7**:262, 267, 269, 271-72, 276-78, 281, 283
Caprices et zigzags (Gautier) **1**:341, 344, 352
"Cápsulas" (Silva) **114**:317
Cápsulas (Silva) **114**:263, 273
"Capsules" (Silva)
See "Cápsulas"
Captain Bonneville (Irving)
See *Albert and Emily*
Captain Fracasse (Gautier)
See *Le capitane Fracasse*
"Captain Jackson" (Lamb) **10**:392, 404, 409, 436
"Captain Jones' Invitation" (Freneau) **1**:317
"Captain Jones's Invitation" (Freneau)
See "The Invitation"
"Captain Leka's Sister" (Karadzic) **115**:92
"Captain Paton's Lament" (Lockhart) **6**:295-96
Captain Rock (Moore)
See *Memoirs of Captain Rock*
Captain Spike; or, The Islets of the Gulf (Cooper)
See *Jack Tier; or, The Florida Reefs*
Captain Spitfire and the Unlucky Treasure (Alarcon)
See *El capitán Veneno*
Captain Sword and Captain Pen (Hunt) **70**:270-71
The Captain's Daughter; or, the Generosity of the Russian Usurper Pugatscheff (Pushkin)
See *Kapitanskaya-dochka*
"The Captain's Dream" (Brontë) **4**:44
The Captain's Mistress (Shevchenko)
See *Kapitansha*
"The Captain's Well" (Whittier) **8**:516
"The Captain's Wife" (Dobell) **43**:46
The Captive Ladie (Dutt) **118**:31
"The Captive of Castile; or, The Moorish Maiden's Vow" (Alcott) **83**:4
The Captive of the Caucasus (Pushkin)
See *Kavkazsky plennik*
"The Captive Stork" (Arany)
See "A rab gólya"
The Captive Woman (Echeverria)
See *La cautiva*
"Captivity" (Rogers) **69**:68, 74
The Capture of Murány (Arany)
See *Murány ostroma*
"The Captured Wild Horse" (Fuller) **5**:169
"Cara-Ali" (Mérimée) **65**:58
Caractacus (Brontë) **109**:14
La caractère estérieur de magistrat (Maistre) **37**:312
"The Caravan" (Hugo) **3**:262
"Card Drawing" (Griffin) **7**:197, 201, 211-12, 217
"The Card-Dealer" (Rossetti) **4**:506, 509, 518, 521-22, 524-25, 528
"Cardinal Newman" (Rossetti) **50**:309
"The Careless Nurse Mayde" (Hood) **16**:237
"Careless Rambles" (Clare) **86**:142
"The Cares of the World" (Baratynsky)
See "Les Soucis matériels"
"Les Caresses" (Maupassant) **83**:176-77, 223
Les cariatides (Banville) **9**:14, 17-19, 25-26, 28
Caridorf (Bird) **1**:87, 89
Carita (Oliphant) **61**:173
Carl Werner (Simms) **3**:510
"Carlota y Welster" (Lizardi) **30**:71
"Carlsbad" (Field) **3**:206
Carmagnola (Manzoni)
See *Il conte di Carmagnola*
Carme (Foscolo)
See *Le grazie, carme*
Carmen (Mérimée) **6**:353-7, 360, 362-5, 367, 369, 371-3; **65**:42-3, 48, 52, 54, 56, 58, 62,

64, 66, 79, 82, 85, 87-8, 102, 104, 114, 119-22, 132-3, 137, 140
"Carmen Triumphale" (Timrod) **25**:362, 376
Carmen Triumphale for the Commencement of the Year 1814 (Southey) **97**:262
"Carmilla" (Le Fanu) **9**:312, 318, 321-23; **58**:251, 257-61, 274, 302-3
Carmosine (Musset) **7**:268, 271, 276
"Carnaval" (Banville) **9**:30
Les carnets de Joseph Joubert (Joubert) **9**:290-92, 295
Carnets de voyage: Notes sur la province, 1863-1865 (Taine) **15**:452
The Carniolan Bee (Preseren)
See *Kranjska čbelica*
Carnioli (Feuillet) **45**:88
"Carolina" (Hayne) **94**:161
"Carolina" (Timrod) **25**:360, 362-63, 367, 372, 375-76, 384, 388
"Caroline" (Brontë) **109**:4-6, 30, 33
"Caroline Vernon" (Brontë) **3**:80; **105**:31
"Caroline's Prayer" (Brontë) **109**:4
"A Carp in a Dream" (Ueda Akinari)
See *Muo no Rigyo*
"The Carp that Came to My Dream" (Ueda Akinari)
See *Muo no Rigyo*
"The Carpenter's Wife" (Clare) **86**:90
"The Carriage" (Gogol) **5**:235, 254, 257; **15**:94, 97
"A Carrion" (Baudelaire)
See "Une charogne"
"Carrion Comfort" (Hopkins) **17**:204, 243, 249, 256, 261-62
"Le carrosse du Saint Sacrement" (Mérimée) **6**:362-3; **65**:59, 79, 81-2
Carsten Curator (Storm) **1**:540, 546
"Carta" (Bello) **131**:106
Carta (Bécquer) **106**:119
Carta desde mi celda (Bécquer)
See *Cartas literarias desde mi celda*
"Carta Escrita de Londres a París por un Americano a Otro" (Bello) **131**:133
"Carta I" (Bécquer) **106**:112-13, 153, 156
"Carta II" (Bécquer) **106**:113-14, 116
Cartas desde mi celda (Bécquer)
See *Cartas literarias desde mi celda*
Cartas inéditas (Gómez de Avellaneda) **111**:57, 62
Cartas literarias a una mujer (Bécquer) **106**:102-03, 105, 109, 112, 114, 116, 118-19, 142, 167-69, 172
Cartas literarias desde mi celda (Bécquer) **106**:93-4, 96, 106, 108-9, 112-13, 118-21, 153, 155, 162
"Carțile" (Eminescu) **33**:251
"The Cartusians" (Meyer)
See "Die Kartäuser"
Carwin, the Biloquist (Brown)
See *Memoirs of Carwin the Biloquist*
"Cary O'Kean'" (Hogg) **109**:250
The Caryatids (Banville)
See *Les cariatides*
"Un cas de divorce" (Maupassant) **83**:176
Casa Guidi Windows: A Poem (Browning) **1**:118-9, 122, 125, 127, 130; **61**:12, 14-6, 22-4, 37, 43-4; **66**:44-5, 52, 90-1, 95
"La casa paterna" (Isaacs) **70**:303
"Casabianca" (Hemans) **29**:204-06; **71**:270, 272, 279, 283
"Casar Borgias Ohnmacht" (Meyer) **81**:199, 207
"El casarse pronto y mal" (Larra) **17**:275, 278-80; **130**:275
"The Cascade of Melsingah" (Bryant) **6**:180
A Case of Conscience (Inchbald) **62**:144, 147, 149
"The Case of the Officers of the Excise" (Paine) **62**:278
"A Case That Was Dropped" (Leskov)
See "Pogassee delo"
"Casey's Tabble Dote" (Field) **3**:209
"Casey's Table d'Hôte" (Field) **3**:205
"Cashel of Munster" (Ferguson) **33**:294
"Casino des trépassés" (Corbière) **43**:32
"The Cask of Amontillado" (Poe) **1**:500, 506; **16**:303, 309, 329, 332; **55**:148; **78**:265-66; **97**:180; **117**:260
"Caso de ablativo" (Bécquer) **106**:146
"Cassandra Southwick" (Whittier) **8**:489, 505, 509-11, 513, 515, 527, 530; **59**:358
La Casse-Noisette (Dumas) **71**:242
Cassiodor (Eminescu) **33**:266
The Cassique of Accabee (Simms) **3**:504
The Cassique of Kiawah (Simms) **3**:503, 508, 514
"The Castaway" (Cowper) **8**:108, 113, 119, 122, 125, 133, 137-38; **94**:24, 32, 38-9, 123
Caste (Robertson) **35**:330, 332-34, 336, 338, 340-41, 343-47, 349, 351-52, 355-56, 358, 359-60, 362, 364-65, 367, 369-71, 372-73
"El Castellano viejo" (Larra) **17**:278; **130**:230
"Castellanos de Castilla!" (Castro) **78**:40
"Castillo" (Martí) **63**:157-8
El castillo de Balsain (Tamayo y Baus) **1**:571
"El castillo real de Olite" (Bécquer) **106**:106
"The Castle Builder" (Longfellow) **45**:127
"Castle Carnal" (Harpur) **114**:144
Castle-Croquet (Carroll) **139**:57
Castle Dangerous (Scott) **15**:308; **69**:332, 334
Castle Dismal (Simms) **3**:510
"Castle in the Air" (Paine) **62**:324-5
Castle Nowhere: Lake Country Sketches (Woolson) **82**:269, 272, 277, 283, 286-87, 292-94, 299, 305, 322, 330, 333, 335, 338-40
The Castle of Balsain (Tamayo y Baus)
See *El castillo de Balsain*
The Castle of Loch-Leuven (Pixérécourt)
See *Le chateau de Loch-Leven; ou, L'évasion de Marie Stuart*
"The Castle of Smalholm" (Zhukovsky) **35**:388, 393
Castle Rackrent (Edgeworth) **1**:255, 261-67, 269, 271-73; **51**:75, 77, 79-82, 88-9, 91-3, 95-100, 102, 104-05, 107-08, 113, 135
Castle Richmond (Trollope) **6**:470-71, 499, 514; **101**:245-46, 248-53, 262-64, 271, 276, 293-96, 298, 312
The Castle Spectre (Lewis) **11**:294-95, 302, 304-05
Castles in the Air (Gore) **65**:21
The Castles of Athlin and Dunbayne: A Highland Story (Radcliffe) **6**:403, 405, 409, 410, 413, 415, 418, 424, 426, 429, 435, 442; **55**:224-5, 229, 241, 274
"The Castles of the Gleichen" (Taylor) **89**:308, 310
Castruccio Castracani (Landon) **15**:164
"A Casual Observation" (Kleist)
See "Unmaßgebliche Betrachtung"
"Casuisty of Roman Meals" (De Quincey) **4**:69
"Časy" (Turgenev) **122**:242-44, 246, 266
"Cat and Cook" (Krylov) **1**:439
"The Catalogue Raisonné of the British Institution" (Hazlitt) **29**:144
"The Cataract" (Hayne) **94**:134, 153
"The Cataract of Lodore" (Southey) **8**:472, 474
"Catarina to Camoens" (Browning) **1**:125; **61**:66
Catechism of a Revolutionary (Bakunin) **25**:53, 72, 74
Catéchisme Positiviste ou Sommaire exposition de la religion universelle en onze entretiens systématiques entre une femme et un pretre de l'Humanité (Comte) **54**:210
"Catecismo democratico" (Martí) **63**:122
"Catharina" (Cowper) **8**:119
"Catharine" (Austen) **1**:66; **119**:13
Catharine, or the Bower (Austen) **95**:4; **119**:11
"The Cathedral" (Lowell) **90**:190, 193-94, 207-10
The Cathedral Folk (Leskov)
See *Soborjane*
"Cathedral Walk" (Crabbe) **26**:109
"Catherine" (Shevchenko)
See "Kateryna"
Catherine (Arany)
See *Katalin*
Catherine (Thackeray) **5**:452, 465, 470, 482, 490, 492, 497; **14**:400, 402, 411, 420, 433; **43**:348, 351, 358-59, 364, 375-76, 381, 383, 389-91
Catherine Blum (Dumas) **71**:204
"Catherine Lloyd" (Crabbe) **26**:135; **121**:43, 45, 47-9
"The Catholic Convert" (Hale) **75**:357-61
The Catholic Reaction (Symonds) **34**:331, 346, 360, 368
"Catholicism" (Mallarmé) **41**:254-55
Catiline (Dumas) **11**:53-54
"Cato's Tragedy" (Warren) **13**:414
Catriona, a Sequel to "Kidnapped": Being Memoirs of the Further Adventures of David Balfour at Home and Abroad (Stevenson) **5**:415, 417, 426-27, 437-39; **63**:274
The Catspaw (Jerrold) **2**:402-03
"Catterskill Falls" (Bryant) **6**:172; **46**:19-20, 28, 38
"El Cauca" (Isaacs) **70**:310
The Caucasian Captive (Pushkin)
See *Kavkazsky plennik*
"The Caucasus" (Shevchenko)
See "Kavkaz"
"Cauchemar" (Banville) **9**:16
"El caudillo de las manos rojas" (Bécquer) **106**:108-10, 113, 130, 133
Cause in the Decline of Taste in Different Nations (Herder) **8**:307
"Causerie" (Baudelaire) **55**:3, 55, 61
Les causeries du lundi (Sainte-Beuve) **5**:325-26, 329-31, 339-40
"The Causes of Methodism" (Hazlitt) **29**:162
La cautiva (Echeverria) **18**:147-54, 156-57
"Cava lixeiro, cava" (Castro) **78**:42
"Cavalry Crossing a Ford" (Whitman) **81**:312
"Cavalry Raids" (Bestuzhev)
See "Nayezdy"
"The Cave" (Taylor)
See "Cave of Trophonius"
"Cave of Trophonius" (Taylor) **89**:311
"The Caves of Dahra" (Patmore) **9**:329
Caxtoniana (Bulwer-Lytton) **1**:155; **45**:23
The Caxtons, a Family Picture (Bulwer-Lytton) **1**:144-45, 148, 150, 155; **45**:19, 21-2, 69-70
Čbelica (Preseren) **127**:294
"Ce poème homérique et sans ègal au monde" (Gautier) **59**:18
"Ce que dit la bouche d'ombre" (Hugo) **3**:273
Ce qui est arrivéà la France en 1870 (Gobineau) **17**:95
"Ce qu'on dit au poète à propos de fleurs" (Rimbaud) **4**:472, 475, 486; **35**:282-83, 308, 321
"Ce te legeni codrule" (Eminescu) **33**:253
Cecil, a Peer (Gore) **65**:22
Cecil; or, the Adventures of a Coxcomb (Gore) **65**:15, 17, 21, 28, 36
Cécile (Constant) **6**:223-24
Cécile (Dumas) **71**:203
Cécile (Fontane) **26**:236, 252, 255, 259, 270-71
Cecilia; or, Memoirs of an Heiress (Burney) **12**:16-18, 21-2, 25, 27-37, 41-6, 48, 50, 57-64; **54**:3, 6-8, 12-14, 17, 29, 36-7, 50, 52-3, 61; **107**:12, 16
Cecilia Valdés (Villaverde) **121**:330-40, 344, 349, 352, 356, 359, 361, 366, 368
Cedarcroft Pastoral (Taylor) **89**:315
Ceinture dorée (Augier) **31**:5, 13, 15, 19, 25, 27, 30, 34
Celebrated Crimes (Dumas)
See *Crimes célèbres*
"The Celebration of Intellect" (Emerson) **98**:48
"Celestial Love" (Emerson) **98**:91, 93

"The Celestial Maidens" (Ueda Akinari)
See "Amatsu otome"
"Celestial Publicity" (Villiers de l'Isle Adam)
See "L'affichage céleste"
"The Celestial Railroad" (Hawthorne) **2**:298, 302-03, 305, 333; **23**:205; **95**:116, 125-26, 137, 156
Celestina (Smith) **23**:316, 322, 327-29; **115**:123, 146, 157-58, 160, 222-23
Les célibataires (Balzac)
See *Le curé de Tours*
"Celle-ci et Celle-là ou la Jeune-France passionnée" (Gautier) **59**:27-8, 31, 63-4
"Celles qui osent" (Maupassant) **83**:228
"The Cell-Theory" (Huxley) **67**:80, 83
Cellulairement (Verlaine) **2**:632
Celtic Bards, Chiefs, and Kings (Borrow) **9**:57
"Celtic Literature" (Arnold) **6**:41
"The Cemetery" (Very) **9**:386
The Cenci (Shelley) **18**:314, 316-17, 320, 336, 341, 344, 360, 362, 365-69, 375, 382; **93**:266-67, 269-72, 275-80, 351-56, 358
"Cenciaja" (Browning) **19**:88
Les 120 journées de Sodome; ou, L'école du libertinage (Sade) **3**:479, 481, 488-89, 492, 494-96; **47**:301, 305-06, 310-12, 315, 318-19, 323, 326-32, 334, 336, 339, 342, 345, 350, 352, 364-65
Le centénaire (Balzac) **5**:58
"The Centenarian's Story" (Whitman) **81**:317, 320
"Centennial Cantata" (Lanier) **6**:233-34, 236, 254, 260, 262; **118**:210, 238
The Centennial Edition of the Works of Sidney Lanier (Lanier) **6**:268; **118**:227, 251
"The Centennial Meditation of Columbia" (Lanier) **118**:237, 275
Centennial Meditation of Columbia (Lanier) **6**:232; **118**:261, 278-79
A Century of Dishonor (Jackson) **90**:135, 143-46, 148-50, 153-54, 157, 159, 169
Cenuşotca (Eminescu) **33**:266
"Cerep" (Baratynsky) **103**:6-7, 27
"Čertogon" (Leskov) **25**:234
"Certopxanov and Nedopjuskin" (Turgenev)
See "Chertopkhanov and Nedopyuskin"
Cervantes (Oliphant) **11**:439
Ces passions qu'eux seuls nomment encore amours (Verlaine) **51**:363
César Birotteau (Balzac) **53**:11
"César Borgia" (Verlaine) **2**:622, 624; **51**:356
Césarine Dietrich (Sand) **57**:313
"C'est l'extase langoureuse..." (Verlaine) **51**:355, 381-82, 384
"Cezara" (Eminescu) **131**:297
"The Chace" (Patmore) **9**:351
El Chacho (Faustino) **123**:274
"Chactas or the Lament of the Harmonious Voice" (Chivers) **49**:73
"Chacun sa chimère" (Baudelaire) **55**:78
"The Chaffinch" (Jefferies) **47**:139
A Chain (Scribe)
See *Une chaîne*
A Chain of Events (Lewes) **25**:291
The Chainbearer; or, The Littlepage Manuscripts (Cooper) **1**:217, 219-21, 224; **54**:258, 280, 288
Une chaîne (Scribe) **16**:384, 387-89, 400, 402-03, 405
"La chaîne d'or" (Gautier) **1**:347-48; **59**:32
The Chained Fantasy (Raimund)
See *Die gesfesselte Phantasie*
Chair (Verlaine) **51**:352, 372
"The Chaldee Manuscript" (Hogg) **109**:261, 275
"Chaldee Manuscript" (Wilson) **5**:561
Chaldee Manuscript (Hogg) **109**:258
Chaldee Manuscript (Lockhart) **6**:296
"Châli" (Maupassant) **83**:201-02
"The Challenge" (Longfellow) **45**:161
"The Chamber over the Gate" (Longfellow) **45**:132, 162, 166
"The Chambered Nautilus" (Holmes) **14**:109-10, 118-19, 125-26, 129, 133, 140; **81**:97, 107
"La chambre 11" (Maupassant) **83**:171
"La chambre bleue" (Mérimée) **6**:360, 364, 369, 371; **65**:47-50, 52, 56, 62, 64-5, 85, 96, 98, 104, 140-3
"La chambre double" (Baudelaire) **29**:107; **55**:12
"La chambre gothique" (Bertrand) **31**:46, 51
Le Champ d'Oliviers (Maupassant) **1**:459, 464, 468; **42**:170; **83**:175, 179
Champavert, contes immoraux (Borel) **41**:3-6, 8, 10, 12-14, 19
"Champavert le lycanthrope" (Borel)
See "Testament de Champavert"
Champavert: Seven Bitter Tales (Borel)
See *Champavert, contes immoraux*
"The Champion" (Fouqué) **2**:266
The Champion of Virtue (Reeve)
See *The Old English Baron*
Le chandelier (Musset) **7**:262, 264, 267, 270-71, 276
Chandrasekhar (Chatterji) **19**:206, 210, 212, 214-15, 217-21, 224-25
Chandrashekhar (Chatterji)
See *Chandrasekhar*
"The Change" (Smith) **59**:331-2
"Change" (Very) **9**:383
"The Changed Allegiance" (Patmore) **9**:347-48, 351
The Changed Brides (Southworth) **26**:433
"The Changeling" (Lamb) **10**:402
"The Changeling" (Lamb)
See "Ann Withers: The Changeling"
"The Changeling" (Lowell) **90**:214
"The Changes of Home" (Dana) **53**:157-8, 178
"Chanson d'automne" (Verlaine) **2**:624; **51**:351, 355
"La chanson de fortunio" (Musset) **7**:275
"Chanson de la plus haute tour" (Rimbaud) **82**:226, 230-31, 233, 247, 249, 259
"La chanson des ingénues" (Verlaine) **2**:629-30; **51**:356, 369
"Chanson du petit hypertrophique" (Laforgue) **5**:275
Chansons bas (Mallarmé) **41**:249
Chansons des rues et des bois (Hugo) **3**:264
"Chansons et légendes du Valois" (Nerval) **1**:485; **67**:371
Chansons inédites (Beranger) **34**:44
Chansons pour elle (Verlaine) **2**:621-22; **51**:352
"Chant alterné" (Leconte de Lisle) **29**:223, 239-40
"Chant d'amour" (Lamartine) **11**:283
"Chant d'automne" (Baudelaire) **6**:115; **55**:3, 6, 64
"Chant de guerre parisien" (Rimbaud) **4**:465; **35**:271; **82**:238
Le chant du sacre (Lamartine) **11**:246
"Chant lyrique du jugement dernier" (Lamartine) **11**:273
"Chanting the Square Deific" (Whitman) **4**:544, 587; **31**:390; **81**:314
Les chants de Maldoror: Chant premier (Lautréamont) **12**:206-09, 211-12, 214-19, 222-44
Les chants de Maldoror: Chants I, II, III, IV, V, VI (Lautréamont) **12**:209-44
Chants Democratic and Native American (Whitman) **81**:349
"Les chants du Crépuscule" (Hugo) **3**:270-71, 273
Chants for Socialists (Morris) **4**:445
"Les chants lyriques de Saül" (Lamartine) **11**:269
The Chapel (Almqvist)
See *Kapellet*
"The Chapel in Lyoness" (Morris) **4**:411, 421, 431
"The Chapel of the Hermits" (Whittier) **8**:492, 495, 500-01; **59**:370
La chapelle des bois; ou, Le témoin invisible (Pixérécourt) **39**:287
"The Chaplet of Cypress" (Chivers) **49**:72
"A Chapter in the History of a Tyrone Family" (Le Fanu) **58**:253
"Chapter on Autography" (Poe)
See "Autography"
"A Chapter on Dreams" (Stevenson) **14**:333, 338
"A Chapter on Ears" (Lamb) **10**:409, 411; **113**:200, 235
"A Chapter on Literary Women" (Parton) **86**:348
Chapters on Flowers (Tonna) **135**:203
"Chapters on Ghostcraft" (Mangan) **27**:291, 303
"Character" (Emerson) **98**:55, 61-2, 75
"A Character" (Tennyson) **30**:280
"Character and Intelligence of the Britons" (Barnes) **75**:64
"The Character and Poetry of Keats" (Lampman) **25**:203, 214-15
"The Character and Scope of the Sonnet" (Timrod) **25**:380
"A Character in the Antithetical Manner" (Wordsworth) **111**:235, 300
"The Character of Dramatic Poetry" (Wagner) **9**:467
"Character of Lord Chatham" (Hazlitt) **82**:109
"The Character of Milton's Eve" (Hazlitt) **29**:148
"Character of Mr. Burke" (Hazlitt) **82**:110
"The Character of Sir Robert Peel" (Bagehot) **10**:62
"The Character of the Happy Warrior" (Wordsworth) **12**:395
"A Character of the Later Elia. By a Friend" (Lamb) **10**:408; **113**:199, 234
"Characteristics" (Carlyle) **70**:7, 42-44, 57
"Characteristics" (Hazlitt) **82**:98
Characteristics: In the Manner of Rouchefoucauld's Maxims (Hazlitt) **29**:151, 170, 183; **82**:126
Characteristics of Shakespeare's Women (Jameson)
See *Characteristics of Women*
Characteristics of the Eighteenth Century (Humboldt) **134**:186, 188
"Characteristics of the Genius of Scott" (Martineau) **26**:350
The Characteristics of the Presnt Age (Fichte)
See *Die Grundzüge der Gegenwärtigun Zeitalters*
Characteristics of Women (Jameson) **43**:305, 312, 314-17, 319, 323
"Characters" (Trumbull) **30**:348
"Characters of Dramatic Writers Contemporary with Shakespeare" (Lamb) **10**:387, 412; **113**:256
Characters of Shakespeare's Plays (Hazlitt) **29**:134, 138, 146-48, 163, 174-76, 186-87; **82**:93
Characters of Worldly Mistresses (Ueda Akinari)
See *Seken tekake katagi*
"The Charge of the Heavy Brigade at Balaclava" (Tennyson) **30**:295
"The Charge of the Light Brigade" (Tennyson) **30**:223, 280, 286, 294, 296, 298-99
"Chariceteristic Descriptive Pastorals in prose on rural life and manners" (Clare) **86**:173
"The Chariot" (Dickinson)
See "Because I Could Not Stop for Death"
"Charity" (Boyesen) **135**:13
"Charity" (Carroll) **139**:61
"Charity" (Cowper) **94**:27-8, 115, 124, 126
"Charity" (Harpur) **114**:154
Charity (Cowper) **94**:10
"Charity Bowery" (Child) **73**:80
"A Charity Sermon" (Hood) **16**:235
"The Charivari" (Moodie) **14**:231
Le charlatanisme (Scribe) **16**:384

Charlemont; or, The Pride of the Village (Simms) **3**:508-09
"Charleroi" (Verlaine) **51**:370, 382-83
Charles VII. à Naples (Augier) **31**:11
Charles Chesterfield; or, The Adventures of a Youth of Genius (Trollope) **30**:309, 327-29
"Charles Darwin" (Huxley) **67**:48
"Charles Dickens's Readings" (Faustino) **123**:383
Charles I (Shelley) **18**:327
"Charles Lamb" (Pater) **7**:306
"Charles Lamb" (De Quincey) **87**:31
Charles O'Malley, the Irish Dragoon (Lever) **23**:270-73, 275, 281, 283-87, 290-92, 294-96, 300, 303-04, 306, 309-10
Charles Stuart (Chivers) **49**:79
Charles the Bold (Pixérécourt)
See *Charles-le-téméraire; ou, Le Siège de Nancy*
Charles VII chez ses grands vassaux (Dumas) **11**:42, 47-48, 57, 71; **71**:241, 243, 244
Charles-le-téméraire; ou, Le Siège de Nancy (Pixérécourt) **39**:274-75, 278, 282, 284, 295-96
"Charleston" (Timrod) **25**:362-63, 376, 385-86
Charlotte: A Tale of Truth (Rowson) **5**:309-23; **69**:98-100, 102-06, 108-09, 111-14, 117, 122, 129-36, 140-41, 158
"Charlotte Smith" (Scott) **110**:277-78
Charlotte Temple: A Tale of Truth (Rowson)
See *Charlotte: A Tale of Truth*
"Charlotte Wilmot: The Merchant's Daughter" (Lamb) **125**:317
Charlotte's Daughter; or, The Three Orphans (Rowson) **5**:310, 312-13, 315-17; **69**:103, 105-06, 114, 130
"The Charm of Days Gone By" (Zhukovsky) **35**:403
"Charmed Picture" (Hemans) **29**:206; **71**:303
"The Charmed Sea" (Martineau) **26**:313
"The Charmed Spot" (Gogol)
See "Zakoldovannoe mesto"
"Une charogne" (Baudelaire) **6**:93, 115; **29**:83-4, 103; **55**:6, 10, 31-2, 44, 55, 59, 76
"The Charter; Addressed to My Nephew Athanase C. L. Coquerel, on His Wedding Day, 1819" (Williams) **135**:315, 335
The Charterhouse of Parma (Stendhal)
See *La chartreuse de Parme*
"Chartism" (Carlyle) **70**:46-47, 53, 71, 73, 93, 105-111
La chartreuse de Parme (Stendhal) **23**:345-56, 358-59, 361-63, 365, 368-71, 374, 376, 378, 383-85, 389, 391, 393, 397, 400-02, 404-05, 408-17, 424-26; **46**:262-63, 279-80, 310, 316, 318, 323, 325
Charts de la patrie (Chateaubriand) **3**:126
"La chasse" (Bertrand) **31**:49
"La chasse au caribou" (Gobineau) **17**:80, 92-3, 103
La Chasse au Chastre (Dumas) **71**:204
"Le chasse de l'aigle" (Leconte de Lisle) **29**:216, 225
"La chasse spirituelle" (Rimbaud) **4**:484
Le Chasseur de Sauvagine (Dumas) **71**:204
"Chasy i zerkalo" (Bestuzhev) **131**:154, 186
"Le Chat" (Baudelaire) **55**:9, 61
Le château de Combourg (Chateaubriand) **3**:133
Le château de la misère (Gautier) **1**:346
Le chateau de Loch-Leven; ou, L'évasion de Marie Stuart (Pixérécourt) **39**:277, 279, 285, 294
"Le château de Robert le diable" (Nodier) **19**:378
Le Château des Désertes (Sand) **42**:310-11, 313-14
Chateaubriand (Dumas) **71**:218
Chateaubriand et son groupe littéraire sous l'empire (Sainte-Beuve) **5**:338, 342, 349
"La Châtelaine de Langeville ou la femme vengée" (Sade) **47**:313
De Chatillon (Hemans) **29**:201; **71**:276
"Châtiment de l'orgueil" (Baudelaire) **55**:58
"Le châtiment de Tartuff" (Rimbaud) **4**:471
Les Châtiments (Hugo) **3**:256, 262-64, 271, 273; **21**:214
"Le chat-qui-pelote" (Balzac)
See "La maison du chat-qui-pelote"
Chatterton (Vigny) **7**:471, 473-74, 479; **102**:336, 341-44, 358, 360-65, 378
"Chatterton to His Sister" (Polidori) **51**:242
Chaturdaspadi Kavitāvali (Dutt) **118**:5
"Chaucer" (Longfellow) **45**:161, 186
"Chaucer and Shakspere" (Lanier) **118**:246
"The Chaunt of Cholera" (Banim and Banim) **13**:129
The Chaunt of the Cholera: Songs for Ireland (Banim and Banim) **13**:129
"Che stai?" (Foscolo) **8**:278-79
Cheap Clothes and Nasty (Kingsley) **35**:205, 227-28
Cheap Repository Tracts (More) **27**:350-51
Checkmate (Le Fanu) **9**:301, 304, 312, 317; **58**:251, 273-5, 295
Cheerfulness Taught by Reason (Browning) **66**:44
The Cheese Factory (Schuecking)
See *Die Käserei in der Vehfreude*
"Le Chef d'oeuvre inconnu" (Balzac) **5**:53, 67, 79-80; **53**:25
Les chefs écossais (Pixérécourt) **39**:284
"Le chêne" (Lamartine) **11**:255, 270, 279
"Cher petit oreillet" (Desbordes-Valmore) **97**:16
"Cheramour" (Leskov) **25**:239
"Les chercheuses de poux" (Rimbaud) **35**:271; **4**:454, 458
"Cherep" (Bestuzhev) **131**:150
Chérie (Goncourt) **7**:173-74, 183, 188
"Cherkesy" (Lermontov) **126**:167
"Chernets" (Shevchenko) **54**:387
"The Cherokee Love Song" (Ridge) **82**:175, 181
"Cherry Blossoms in a Moonless Night" (Ichiyō)
See "Yamizakura"
"Chertopkhanov and Nedopyuskin" (Turgenev) **21**:453; **122**:293-94
"The Cherub" (Hogg) **109**:248
"Cherubin" (Grillparzer) **102**:78
"Cherwell" (Bowles)
See "To the River Cherwell, Oxford"
"The Chest and the Ghost" (Stendhal)
See "Le coffre et le revenant"
Chester Rand (Alger) **8**:44, 46; **83**:91
The Chestnut Tree (Tyler) **3**:574
"Chesuncook" (Thoreau) **7**:368
The Chevalier (Dumas) **71**:219
Le chevalier de Maison-Rouge (Dumas) **11**:53, 68, 76-7; **71**:193-94, 209, 232
Le chevalier des touches (Barbey d'Aurevilly) **1**:70-73
Le chevalier d'Harmental (Dumas) **11**:51-52, 60, 63, 68-69, 74; **71**:194, 203-04, 228
"Le Chevalier double" (Gautier) **59**:13, 31, 37
Les chevaliers (Lamartine) **11**:289
"Chevaux de bois" (Verlaine) **51**:383
"La chevelure" (Baudelaire) **6**:79, 117-18, 128; **29**:73, 103, 109; **55**:5-6, 9, 25-6, 50, 55, 64, 67-8
"La Chevelure" (Maupassant) **1**:449; **83**:228
Le Cheveu Blanc (Feuillet) **45**:77, 79-80, 88-90
"Chevy Chase" (Maginn) **8**:439
"Chez le ministre" (Maupassant) **83**:227-28
"Chi katabira" (Ueda Akinari) **131**:20-22, 52-53
Chicot the Jester; or, The Lady of Monsareua (Dumas)
See *La dame de Monsoreau*
Chidiock Tichbourne; or, The Catholic Conspiracy (Clarke) **19**:240
"Chief Justice Harbottle" (Le Fanu)
See "Mr. Justice Hartbottle"
Le chien de Montargis; ou, La forêt de Bondy (Pixérécourt) **39**:273, 277, 279, 281, 284, 286, 288-89
"Chiens" (Verlaine) **51**:363
"The Child" (Kivi)
See "Lapsi"
"Child and Boatman" (Ingelow) **39**:268
"Child and Hind" (Campbell) **19**:190
"The Child and the Profligate" (Whitman) **81**:327
"The Child Angel: A Dream" (Lamb) **10**:404, 435-36; **113**:217
Child from the Sea (Castro)
See *La hija del mar*
"Child Harold" (Clare) **9**:108, 112; **86**:89-90, 99, 102, 114, 117-23, 153, 162
"The Child in the House" (Pater)
See "Imaginary Portrait. The Child in the House"
The Child in the House (Pater)
See *An Imaginary Portrait*
"Child Left in a Storm" (Sigourney) **21**:293
Child Life in Prose (Whittier) **59**:349
The Child of Love (Kotzebue)
See *Das Kind der Liebe*
The Child of Nature (Inchbald) **62**:143-3, 147-8
"A Child of the Age" (Boyesen) **135**:13, 20-21, 29
A Child of the Age (Adams) **33**:4, 10, 14, 16-17, 19-20
The Child of the Island (Norton) **47**:246, 254, 260
"The Child that Loved a Grave" (O'Brien) **21**:236
"Child Wife" (Verlaine) **2**:632; **51**:381, 383-84
"Childe Christopher" (Cranch) **115**:13, 38, 54
Childe Harold (Byron)
See *Childe Harold's Pilgrimage: A Romaunt*
"Childe Harold's Last Pilgrimage" (Bowles) **103**:55
Childe Harold's Pilgrimage: A Romaunt (Byron) **2**:59, 62, 69, 71-72, 74-75, 81-82, 85-86, 91-92, 94-95, 103; **12**:73, 76, 88, 92, 95, 102, 103, 104, 109, 112, 113, 114, 122, 128, 129, 138, 143; **109**:62, 66-8, 70, 72, 83, 87-8, 118
Childe Harold's Pilgrimage: Canto the Second (Byron) **2**:96, 99, 95
"Childe Roland to the Dark Tower Came" (Browning) **19**:99, 106, 117, 141, 153-54; **79**:106-07, 110-11, 113-15, 164, 174
"Childhood II" (Rimbaud) **35**:269
Childhood Years (Leskov)
See *Detskie gody*
"The Children" (Very) **9**:383
"Children like Parents" (Keble) **87**:153
"Children of Adam" (Whitman) **4**:551-52, 557, 568-69, 577, 593, 599-601, 603-04; **81**:271, 279, 329-30
"The Children of Mount Ida" (Child) **6**:201; **73**:77
"Children of the Snow" (Bryant) **46**:8
"The Children of Venus" (Landor) **14**:181
Children's Book (Martínez de la Rosa)
See *El libro de los niños*
Children's Book (Piozzi) **57**:281, 283, 299
"The Children's Crusade" (Longfellow) **45**:128, 137
"The Children's Dance" (Wilson) **5**:567
"The Children's Hour" (Longfellow) **2**:490, 499; **45**:179, 187
"The Children's Joke" (Alcott) **6**:16
"The Child's Answer" (Very) **9**:387
"Child's Book" (Sigourney) **87**:321
"The Child's Champion" (Whitman) **81**:301, 327
"A Child's Funeral" (Bryant) **46**:3
A Child's Garden of Verses (Stevenson) **5**:395-96, 402, 404, 413, 428
A Child's History of England (Dickens) **18**:117, 134

"Child's Play" (Stevenson) **5**:389, 395
"The Child's Purchase" (Patmore) **9**:352, 357, 360
"A Child's Thought of God" (Browning) **1**:127
"Chillawassee Mountain" (Woolson) **82**:273
The Chimeras (Nerval)
See *Les Chimères*
Les Chimères (Nerval) **1**:480, 483-88; **67**:306-07, 311-12, 314-18, 320, 356-57, 359, 363
The Chimes (Dickens) **3**:145, 149 165
"The Chimney Sweeper" (Blake) **13**:219-21, 242; **37**:3, 6, 9, 34, 39, 42, 47, 50, 57, 62-5, 67, 70-2, 76, 79, 91-2, 94
Chinese Miscellanies (Percy)
See *Miscellaneous Pieces Relating to the Chinese*
"Chinese Serenade" (Chivers) **49**:54
"A Chinese Story" (Cranch) **115**:57
Ching-hua yuan (Li Ju-chen) **137**:182, 186-87, 189-97, 200-210, 212-13, 217, 220-21, 225-26
"Chione" (Lampman) **25**:169
"A Chippewa Legend" (Lowell) **90**:193
"Chiron" (Hölderlin) **16**:191
"The Choice" (Allingham) **25**:14
"The Choice" (Lazarus) **8**:421; **109**:304, 335
"The Choice" (Rossetti) **4**:514, 529
The Choice: A Poem on Shelley's Death (Shelley) **14**:272
"Choice and Chance" (Hayne) **94**:166
The Choleric Fathers (Holcroft) **85**:216-17
"Chor der Toten" (Meyer) **81**:205
"Chor' i Kalinyč" (Turgenev) **122**:277
"Choral Song of the Temperance Legions" (Chivers) **49**:49-50
"Chornaya shal" (Pushkin) **83**:247, 350-51, 355
"A Chorus of Ghosts" (Bryant) **46**:21
"Chorus of the Dead" (Meyer)
See "Chor der Toten"
Choses vues (Hugo) **3**:265
Les Chouans (Balzac) **53**:11, 15, 22
Chrestomathia (Bentham) **38**:88
"Le Chretien Mourant" (Lamartine) **11**:245
"Le Christ aux Oliviers" (Nerval) **1**:478, 486; **67**:07, 315, 318, 339, 362
"Christ Crucified" (Emerson) **98**:162
"Christ Our All in All" (Rossetti) **50**:285
"Christ Stilling the Tempest" (Hemans) **29**:206
"Christ upon the Waters" (Newman) **38**:304, 310
"Christabel" (Rossetti) **4**:510
Christabel (Coleridge) **9**:133-34, 138-40, 142-44, 146, 148-50, 152, 156, 179-81, 183, 187, 192-94; **54**:79-81, 89, 98, 100, 106, 127-9; **99**:2, 5, 23, 65-6, 101; **111**:201, 232-34, 292, 295-97, 300-1, 303, 308, 322, 332
Christabel. Kubla Khan. The Pains of Sleep (Coleridge) **9**:133-34
Die Christenheit oder Europa (Novalis) **13**:386, 388, 402
"The Christian Church as an Imperial Power" (Newman) **38**:308
Christian Discourses (Kierkegaard) **34**:224, 264; **78**:238
The Christian Faith (Schleiermacher)
See *Der christliche Glaube nach den Grundsäzen der evengelischen Kirche im Zusammenhange dargestellt*
Christian Life: Its Course, Its Hindrances, and Its Helps (Arnold) **18**:7, 10, 15
Christian Life: Its Hopes, Its Fears, and Its Close (Arnold) **18**:15
Christian Melville (Oliphant) **61**:219
Christian Morals (More) **27**:334
"The Christian Mysteries" (Newman) **38**:305
The Christian Physiologist: Tales Illustrative of the Five Senses (Griffin) **7**:201, 204, 214, 218
"Christian Politics" (Brownson) **50**:51
"The Christian Slave!" (Whittier) **8**:489, 510
"Christian Sympathy" (Newman) **38**:306
"Christian Worship" (Channing) **17**:47
"The Christian Year" (Keble) **87**:122-23, 126-32, 134-38, 140-41
The Christian Year (Keble) **87**:116-19, 121, 149-51, 153-54, 156-57, 159-60, 164, 166-67, 169-78, 181-82, 185-86, 188, 190, 194-95, 198-205
"Christianity and Progress" (Patmore) **9**:342
Christianity or Europe (Novalis)
See *Die Christenheit oder Europa*
Christianity, the Logic of Creation (James) **53**:204, 208-9
Christianity Unveiled (Godwin) **14**:56
Christian's Mistake (Craik) **38**:108-09, 113, 116, 126-27
Christie Johnstone (Reade) **2**:532-34, 536, 539-41, 543, 545, 548; **74**:243, 255, 264-65, 268, 271-72, 278, 281, 293, 319
"Christine" (Leconte de Lisle) **29**:220
Christine; ou, Stockholm, Fountainebleau, et Rome (Dumas) **11**:42, 47, 57, 63; **71**:193, 241, 248, 250
Der christliche Glaube nach den Grundsäzen der evengelischen Kirche im Zusammenhange dargestellt (Schleiermacher) **107**:268, 304, 313, 319-21, 323, 325, 347-48, 351-52, 355, 357-59, 361-63, d65, 382, 397, 399-403, 405
"Ein christliches Sprüchlein" (Meyer) **81**:156
"Christmas" (Irving) **19**:351
"Christmas" (Smith) **59**:303, 309, 315-6, 318-9
"Christmas" (Timrod) **25**:362, 364, 372, 382-83, 386, 388
"Christmas" (Very) **9**:383
"The Christmas Banquet" (Hawthorne) **2**:296; **95**:134, 148
Christmas Books (Dickens) **105**:348
Christmas Books (Thackeray) **5**:469
"A Christmas Carol" (Rossetti) **50**:314, 318
A Christmas Carol (Dickens)
See *A Christmas Carol. In Prose. Being a Ghost Story of Christmas*
A Christmas Carol. In Prose. Being a Ghost Story of Christmas (Dickens) **3**:144-45, 152, 165, 173; **26**:222; **37**:144-45; **86**:256; **105**:244, 330, 335; **113**:102-3, 107
Christmas Chimes (Dickens)
See *The Chimes*
"Christmas Creek" (Kendall) **12**:194, 199
"Christmas Day" (Irving) **19**:328
"Christmas Day" (Martineau) **26**:313
"The Christmas Dinner" (Irving) **19**:328
"Christmas Eve" (Browning) **19**:132; **79**:152, 184
"Christmas Eve" (Gogol)
See "Noč pered roždestvom"
"Christmas Eve" (Wergeland) **5**:537
Christmas Eve (Runeberg)
See *Julqvällen*
Christmas Eve: A Dialogue on the Celebration of Christmas (Schleiermacher)
See *Die Weihnachtsfeier: Ein Gespräch*
Christmas Eve: Dialogue on the Incarnation (Schleiermacher)
See *Die Weihnachtsfeier: Ein Gespräch*
Christmas Greetings (From a Fairy to a Child) (Carroll) **139**:147
"Christmas Hymm" (Hale) **75**:284
"A Christmas Party" (Woolson) **82**:290
Christmas Stories (Leskov) **25**:228
"Christmas Storms and Sunshine" (Gaskell) **137**:4, 41
"The Christmas Tree" (Lazarus) **109**:297
Christmas-Eve and Easter Day (Browning) **19**:130, 132; **79**:148, 150
Christophe Colomb; ou, La découverte du nouveau monde (Pixérécourt) **39**:277-79, 282-83, 286
"Christopher at the Lakes" (Wilson) **5**:568
"Christopher Found" (Levy) **59**:96
"Christopher in His Aviary" (Wilson) **5**:563
Christopher Kirkland (Linton)
See *The Autobiography of Christopher Kirkland*
"Christopher North in His Sporting Jacket" (Wilson) **5**:560
"Christopher on Colonsay" (Wilson) **5**:568
"Christ's Hospital Five and Thirty Years Ago" (Lamb) **10**:407-08, 435-36; **113**:154, 177, 214, 226, 234, 240, 266
"Christ's Night" (Saltykov) **16**:369
Christus (Hebbel) **43**:234
Christus: A Mystery (Longfellow) **2**:484, 495, 497-98; **45**:113, 124, 127-28, 133, 138-39,142-44, 150-51, 159, 165
"The Chronicle of Ladislas Kun" (Petofi)
See "Kun László Krónikája"
The Chronicle of the Cid (Southey) **97**:267, 336
The Chronicle of the Conquest of Granada (Irving) **2**:380, 384, 387; **95**:231, 280
Chronicles of Carlingford (Oliphant) **11**:429, 432, 438-40, 445, 449, 453-4, 459; **61**:171-2, 187, 195, 198, 216
Chronicles of Golden Friars (Le Fanu) **58**:285
Chronicles of the Canongate (Scott) **15**:269, 277, 322; **110**:293
Chronicles of the Clovernook (Jerrold) **2**:400, 402, 404-05
"Chronik von Lutzelflüh" (Gotthelf) **117**:30
Chronique du temps de Charles IX (Mérimée) **6**:352-3, 356-8, 360, 362-3, 365-6, 369; **65**:46-8, 52, 54-6, 59-62, 79, 86-7, 90-5, 99-101, 103-05, 111
Chroniques (Maupassant) **83**:184-85, 188, 190, 227
Chroniques italiennes (Stendhal) **23**:381, 409; **46**:307
"Chrysanthemum Tryst" (Ueda Akinari)
See "Kikuka no chigiri"
"Chrysanthos" (Runeberg) **41**:318
"Chrysaor" (Landor) **14**:181, 183-84, 190
"Chrysaor" (Longfellow) **45**:116, 154
Chto delat'? (Chernyshevsky) **1**:159-68
"Chto za zvuki?" (Baratynsky) **103**:16, 22
"Chudny grad" (Baratynsky)
See "Chudnyy grad poroy solyotsya..."
"Chudnyy grad poroy solyotsya..." (Baratynsky) **103**:3, 10, 16, 22
An Chúirt (Merriman)
See *Cúirt an Mheadhon Oidhche*
"The Church" (Runeberg)
See "Kyrkan"
"The Church a Home for the Lonely" (Newman) **38**:306
The Church against No Church (Brownson) **50**:26
"Church and State" (Moore) **110**:172
"Church Going" (Rogers) **69**:80
"The Church of Brou" (Arnold) **6**:42, 44, 66-67, 72; **29**:36; **89**:7
"The Church, our Zoar" (Keble) **87**:174
"Church Sectarianism" (Coleridge) **90**:9
Church-of-Englandism and its Catechism Examined (Bentham) **38**:34, 92, 96, 98
La chute d'un ange (Lamartine) **11**:252-53, 255, 268, 271, 273-76, 278, 283-85, 287, 289
The Cicerone: A Guide to the Enjoyment of the Artworks of Italy (Burckhardt)
See *Der Cicerone: Eine Einleitung zum Genuss der Kunstwerke Italiens*
Der Cicerone: Eine Einleitung zum Genuss der Kunstwerke Italiens (Burckhardt) **49**:10, 27
"The Cid" (Bowles) **103**:61
"Ciel brouillé" (Baudelaire) **6**:80; **55**:61
"Le ciel est, par-dessus le toit" (Verlaine) **51**:352, 355
"Le ciel et l'enfer" (Mérimée) **6**:351, 362-3; **65**:44, 55, 79, 83
"Ciemność" (Mickiewicz) **101**:159-64
Las ciento y una (Faustino) **123**:338, 352
La cifra (Da Ponte) **50**:82
Cigáni (Macha) **46**:201-02, 204, 212-14

Čigiriaski Kobzar' i Gaydamaki (Shevchenko) **54**:379
La ciguë (Augier) **31**:4, 8, 10-11, 14-15, 23, 29, 34
El cinco de Agosto (Tamayo y Baus) **1**:565-66, 571
Cinderella (Grabbe)
See *Aschenbrödel*
"Cinnamon and Pearls" (Martineau) **137**:251
Cinq Lettres sur l'Éducation Publique en Russie (Maistre) **37**:314
"Le cinq Mai" (Beranger) **34**:28-9
Cinq-Mars; ou, Une conjuration sous Louis XIII (Vigny) **7**:467-71, 473, 477; **102**:335, 337, 345-47, 350, 352-53, 369-70, 378-80, 382-84
The Circassian (Lermontov)
See "Cherkesy"
The Circassian Boy (Lermontov)
See *Mtsyri*
"Circles" (Emerson) **38**:143, 169-71, 205-06, 224, 229-30; **98**:18-19, 22, 24, 26, 35-6, 58, 65, 89, 101, 109, 116, 145, 147-48, 162, 190-91
"Circumference Thou Bride of Awe" (Dickinson) **21**:82
Circumstances (Staël-Holstein)
See *Des circonstances actuelles qui peuvent terminer la Révolution et des principles qui dolvent fonder la répuldique en France*
The Circumvented (Leskov)
See *Obojdennye*
"Las circunstancias" (Larra) **130**:194
"Cis-Alpine" (Pater) **90**:276
"Cisza morska" (Mickiewicz) **3**:403-04
Citation and Examination of William Shakespeare (Landor) **14**:165, 173, 178-79
La citerne (Pixérécourt) **39**:272, 274, 277-79, 284
"La cithare" (Banville) **9**:16
"The Citizen of the World" (Dyer) **129**:105
"The Citizen's Resolve" (Freneau) **1**:314; **111**:150
"Cito Pede Preterit Ætas" (Gordon) **21**:159
"The City" (Lampman) **25**:172, 189, 192, 199-200, 204
"City Burying Places" (Freneau) **111**:81
"The City in the Sea" (Poe) **1**:512; **55**:150; **117**:216-17, 221, 227, 229, 232-34, 236, 244, 264, 274-75, 281-82, 306, 316
The City Looking Glass (Bird) **1**:87-90, 93
"The City of Dreadful Night" (Levy) **59**:91
"The City of Dreadful Night" (Thomson) **18**:388-92, 394-401, 403-12, 415-32
The City of Dreadful Night and Other Poems (Thomson) **18**:390-91
"The City of Sin" (Poe) **117**:274
"The City of the End of Things" (Lampman) **25**:169, 172, 177-78, 180-81, 184, 187, 190, 192-95, 198-99, 204
"The City of the Plague" (Wilson) **5**:546, 550
The City of the Plague, and Other Poems (Wilson) **5**:546, 553, 561
City of the Saints (Burton) **42**:58
The City of the Silent (Simms) **3**:505
City Poems (Smith) **59**:285, 288, 293-4, 297-8, 302, 312, 316, 318-9, 321, 326, 329-33, 336-7
"The City Poet" (Freneau) **111**:132
"City Scenes and City Life" (Parton) **86**:351
"The City Tree" (Crawford) **12**:156, 169
"City Visions" (Lazarus) **109**:294
"Civil and Religious Freedom" (Brownson) **50**:51
"Civil Disobedience" (Thoreau) **7**:375, 381, 385-6, 400, 406; **21**:318-72; **61**:368, 370, 373; **138**:130-31
"Civil Rights" (Lanier) **118**:227-28, 231
The Civil War in France (Marx) **114**:8, 39, 41, 46-7
"Civilisation in the United States" (Arnold) **89**:100
Civilización i barbarie: La vida de Juan Facundo Quiroga i aspecto fisico, costumbres, i ábitos de la República Arjentina (Faustino) **123**:269-70, 272, 274, 279-82, 291-99, 302, 304-9, 318-20, 322, 329-35, 337-38, 341, 345, 347-52, 357, 360-61, 364-70, 373-81, 383-84
"Civilization" (Emerson) **38**:209
Civilization (Burckhardt)
See *Die Kultur der Renaissance in Italien*
Civilization and Barbarism (Faustino)
See *Civilización i barbarie: La vida de Juan Facundo Quiroga i aspecto fisico, costumbres, i ábitos de la República Arjentina*
The Civilization of the Renaissance in Italy (Burckhardt)
See *Die Kultur der Renaissance in Italien*
"Civilization—Signs of the Times" (Mill) **58**:329
A civilizátor (Madach) **19**:370-74
The Claims of Labour (Mill) **58**:349
"Claims of the Negro Ethnologically Considered" (Douglass) **7**:124
"Clair de lune" (Verlaine) **2**:628, 631; **51**:352, 373-74, 377, 381
"Claire de Lune" (Maupassant) **83**:168, 182
Claire Lenoir (Villiers de l'Isle Adam) **3**:581, 588
"Clara" (Meyer) **81**:151
Clara Howard (Brown) **22**:7, 12, 14, 18-19, 23, 27, 30, 48-52; **74**:15, 19, 21, 49, 57, 77, 92, 94, 98-9, 102-03, 105, 134, 138-39, 155, 164-66, 176, 179-82, 184; **122**:54-55
"Clara Milich" (Turgenev)
See "Klara Milich"
"Clara's Question" (Cooke) **110**:18
Clarel: A Poem and Pilgrimage in the Holy Land (Melville) **3**:330, 333, 335, 344-45, 352, 363, 366-68, 378, 385; **29**:318, 328-29, 334-35, 361; **45**:228; **91**:9, 184; **93**:205; **123**:252, 256-57, 260
Clarence; or, A Tale of Our Own Times (Sedgwick) **19**:429-33, 443-45, 447-49, 453; **98**:298-99, 321, 334
"Claret and Tokay" (Browning) **19**:77; **79**:94, 101, 103
"Clari" (Kendall) **12**:193
"Claribel" (Tennyson) **30**:211, 223-24, 238; **65**:369
"Clary's Trial" (Cooke) **110**:34-6, 51
Class Poem (Lowell) **90**:221-21
"The Class Struggle in France" (Marx) **114**:70
The Class Struggles in France (Engels) **85**:136
The Class Struggles in France, 1848-1850 (Marx) **17**:321, 334-35; **114**:8, 37, 39
Classical Dialogues (Landor) **14**:189
Claude Duval: A Tale of the Days of Charles the Second (Ainsworth) **13**:28
"Claude Gueux" (Hugo) **10**:367, 369, 381
Claudie (Sand) **42**:309
Claudine von Villabella (Goethe) **4**:164
The Claverings (Trollope) **6**:457-58, 470, 499-500
Clavigo (Goethe) **4**:164, 174, 211, 219; **34**:69
Clavis Fichtiana (Jean Paul) **7**:226
"El clavo" (Alarcon) **1**:14
"The Clay" (Very) **9**:381
Le Clé d'Or (Feuillet) **45**:77, 80, 90
"Cleanliness" (Lamb) **10**:418
"The Clearer Self" (Lampman) **25**:193, 203, 217
Cœlebs in Search of a Wife: Comprehending Observations on Domestic Habits and Manners, Religion and Morals (More) **27**:325, 328-30, 333-35, 338-39, 349-53, 355
"Clef Poem" (Whitman) **81**:367
"Clelia" (Crabbe) **26**:121
Clelia und Sinibald (Wieland) **17**:410
"Clematis Lane" (Jefferies) **47**:136
Clemencia: Novela de costumbres (Caballero) **10**:71, 76, 84-85
Clemens Brentanos Frühlingskranz aus Jugendbriefen ihm geflochten, wie er selbst schriftlich verlangte (Arnim) **38**:15; **123**:5, 31-32, 34-36, 38, 42, 47-49, 52, 59
"Clementina" (Isaacs) **70**:304, 309
Clementina von Porretta (Wieland) **17**:419
"Cleon" (Browning) **19**:79, 117, 130-31, 137, 152; **79**:106-07, 110, 163-64
Cléontine (Sade) **47**:361-62
Cleopatra Prima (Alfieri) **101**:67
Cleopatra Tragedia (Alfieri) **101**:71
Cleopatrassa (Alfieri) **101**:4, 16, 18, 31-32, 36
"The Clergyman's Advice to the Villagers" (Dwight) **13**:270, 272, 278
"The Clergyman's First Tale" (Clough) **27**:60
Clergymen of the Church of England (Trollope) **33**:394; **101**:294
"Clerical Oppressors" (Whittier) **8**:525; **59**:361
"Clever Elsie" (Grimm and Grimm) **3**:227
"The Cliff" (Lermontov) **126**:144
Clifford (Bulwer-Lytton)
See *Paul Clifford*
"The Cliffs and Springs" (Thoreau) **7**:384
"Clifton and a Lad's Love" (Symonds) **34**:352
"Climat, faune, et flore de la lune" (Laforgue) **5**:277
The Clique (Scribe)
See *La camaraderie; ou, La courte échelle*
"Clive" (Browning) **79**:164
Clive (Macaulay) **42**:87
"The Cloak" (Gogol)
See "Shinel"
"La cloche fêlée" (Baudelaire) **6**:129; **29**:94; **55**:43, 51, 61
"Les Cloches et les larmes" (Desbordes-Valmore) **97**:13
"Clochette" (Maupassant) **83**:174
"The Clock" (Baudelaire)
See "L'horloge"
"The Clock and the Mirror" (Bestuzhev)
See "Chasy i zerkalo"
"Clock-a-Clay" (Clare) **9**:85, 105, 117
The Clockmaker; or, The Sayings and Doings of Samuel Slick of Slickville (Haliburton) **15**:117, 119, 124-26, 128-33, 135, 137-39, 143-47
"The Clod and the Pebble" (Blake) **13**:221, 247; **37**:4, 15, 25, 42, 47, 50, 56, 80, 92
"Clodpoll" (Andersen) **79**:64
The Cloister and the Hearth: A Tale of the Middle Ages (Reade) **2**:533-35, 537-41, 543-45, 548-52; **74**:243, 245-46, 250, 253-54, 257-59, 261-65, 298-99, 311-15, 323-24, 326-27, 329
"The Cloister Berry. In reminiscence of the Frankfurt Jewish Ghetto" (Arnim)
See "Die Klosterbeere. Zum Andenken an die Frankfurter Judengasse"
"Clopton House" (Gaskell) **137**:4
"The Close of Autumn" (Bryant) **46**:3
"Close to the Sky" (Meyer)
See "Himmelsnähe"
The Closed Commercial State (Fichte)
See *Der geschlossene Handelsstaat*
"The Closed Industrial State" (Fichte) **62**:17
"Closing In" (Hayne) **94**:166
"The Clote" (Barnes) **75**:23
Clotel; or, The President's Daughter: A Narrative of Slave Life in the United States (Brown) **2**:46-48, 50-52, 54-55; **89**:143, 149, 154-55, 157-61, 170-82, 184-85, 187, 189-91
Clotelle: A Tale of the Southern States (Brown)
See *Clotel; or, The President's Daughter: A Narrative of Slave Life in the United States*

Clotelle; or, The Colored Heroine (Brown)
See *Clotel; or, The President's Daughter: A Narrative of Slave Life in the United States*
"The Cloud" (Lanier) **118**:239, 248, 268
"The Cloud" (Shelley) **18**:329, 355-56
"Cloud and Wind" (Rossetti) **77**:314
"The Cloud Confines" (Rossetti) **4**:499, 509, 518; **77**:314
"The Cloud on the Way" (Bryant) **6**:165
Cloud Pictures (Hayne) **94**:136
"Cloudbreak" (Lampman) **25**:169
"The Clouded Morning" (Very) **9**:383
Cloudesly: A Tale (Godwin) **14**:44-8, 50, 68, 70, 81, 83, 89; **130**:36
"Clouds" (Barnes) **75**:94
Clouds (Petofi)
See *Felhök*
Clouds and Sunshine (Reade) **74**:254, 260, 262-65
"The Cloud's Brother" (Runeberg)
See "Molnets broder"
"Clover" (Lanier) **6**:247-48, 253, 255, 258; **118**:203, 220
"The Clown Chastized" (Mallarmé)
See "Le pitre châtié"
"Le club des hachichins" (Gautier) **1**:355; **59**:22, 32, 36
"A Clump of Daisies" (Dana) **53**:158
"The Clydesdale Yeoman's Return" (Lockhart) **6**:293
"A Clymene" (Verlaine) **51**:379-80, 384, 386
"Clytie" (Lazarus) **109**:294
"Cmyk . . . Cmyk . . . Cmyk!" (Turgenev)
See "Stuk...stuk...stuk"
"Coach" (Barnes) **75**:8
"The Coal-Imp" (Cranch) **115**:58
"A Coast View" (Harpur) **114**:105, 126, 142-44, 158, 166-67
Cobbett's Corn (Cobbett)
See *A Treatise on Cobbett's Corn*
Cobbett's Poor Man's Friend (Cobbett) **49**:148, 154, 156, 160
Cobbett's Sermons (Cobbett)
See *Twelve Sermons*
Cobbett's Tour in Scotland (Cobbett) **49**:133, 160
Cobbett's Twopenny Trash (Cobbett) **49**:94, 111, 120, 135, 160
Cobbett's Weekly Political Register (Cobbett) **49**:87, 89, 94-5, 97-8, 107, 109-11, 113-14, 116, 118-19, 130-32, 134-35, 141-42, 147, 149, 151-52, 153, 155, 160, 162-64, 168, 170, 178, 181
"The Cobbler of Hagenau" (Longfellow) **45**:162, 188
Cobblers on the Heath (Kivi)
See *Nummisuutarit*
"Cobwebs" (Rossetti) **66**:341
"La coccinelle" (Hugo) **3**:263
Le Cocher de Cabriolet (Dumas) **71**:205
"The Cock" (Barnes) **75**:54
The Cock and Anchor, Being a Chronicle of Old Dublin City (Le Fanu) **9**:301, 316-17; **58**:273, 275
"The Cock Is Crowing" (Wordsworth) **12**:447
"Cock-a-Doodle-Doo!" (Melville) **3**:355; **49**:391-92
"Coco" (Maupassant) **83**:181
"Cocoon" (Dickinson)
See "Drab Habitation of Whom?"
"Cocoons" (Silva)
See "Crisálidas"
Le cocu (Kock) **16**:248, 251
"Le Cocu de lui-même ou le raccommodement imprévu" (Sade) **47**:313
Le code des gens honnêtes (Balzac) **35**:25
Codification Proposal Addressed by Jeremy Bentham to All Nations Professing Liberal Opinions (Bentham) **38**:55, 57
Código Civil (Bello) **131**:116, 124-25
"Codlingsby" (Thackeray) **14**:433, 451
Coelina; ou, L'enfant du mystère (Pixérécourt) **39**:272, 275, 277-79, 289-90
Un coeur simple (Flaubert) **2**:227, 232-3, 236, 253, 257-9; **62**:91-2, 97, 105, 107; **66**:281; **135**:83, 109, 145, 169-70
"Le coeur supplicié" (Rimbaud) **4**:478; **82**:224, 227
"La coeur volé" (Rimbaud) **4**:485; **35**:275, 279, 281-82
"The Coffer and the Ghost" (Stendhal)
See "Le coffre et le revenant"
"The Coffin" (Ainsworth) **13**:19
The Coffin-Maker (Pushkin)
See "Grobovshchik"
"Le coffre et le revenant" (Stendhal) **46**:307
"Cohen of Trinity" (Levy) **59**:97-8, 105, 112-3, 115
"Cold in the Earth" (Brontë)
See "Remembrance"
"The Cold Snap" (Bellamy) **86**:75
The Cold Water Man (Dunlap) **2**:210
"The Cold Wedding" (Allingham) **25**:8
"La colère de Samson" (Vigny) **7**:469, 474, 479, 484-85; **102**:376-77
"Coleridge" (Mill) **11**:361, 370
"Coleridge" (Pater) **7**:321; **90**:241
"Coleridge as a Theologican" (Pater) **90**:276
"Coleridge's Writings" (Pater) **90**:296, 298
"The Coliseum" (Poe) **117**:264, 270-71, 276-71
"Coll'alto" (Rogers) **69**:84
"The Collar" (Andersen) **7**:28; **79**:40
Collected Letters (Dickinson) **21**:46-7
The Collected Letters of Samuel Taylor Coleridge (Coleridge) **99**:6, 25-6, 40, 52, 55, 57, 59, 61, 66, 101, 106; **111**:232-33, 243, 290, 293-95, 310-13, 364-66
The Collected Notebooks of Samuel Taylor Coleridge (Coleridge) **54**:107, 109; **99**:3-4, 22, 57, 64, 106
Collected Poems (Dickinson) **21**:46
Collected Poems (Rossetti)
See *The Poetical Works of Christina Georgina Rossetti*
The Collected Poems of Isabella Valancy Crawford (Crawford) **12**:155, 175
Collected Works (Claudius) **75**:207, 210-11, 215, 218, 220
Collected Works (Herder) **8**:313
Collected Works (Rossetti) **77**:317
Collected Works (Rossetti)
See *The Poetical Works of Christina Georgina Rossetti*
Collected Works (Stagnelius)
See *Samlade skrifter*
Collected Works (Varnhagen von Ense)
See *Rahel-Bibliothek: Gesammelte Werke*
The Collected Works of Edgar Allan Poe (Poe) **94**:229, 245; **97**:228-9; **117**:209, 225, 235, 260, 262, 268, 271-72, 275-6, 293, 304-5, 309-13, 330-3, 335-6.
The Collected Works of John Galt (Galt) **110**:76-81, 90, 93, 104
The Collected Works of Ralph Waldo Emerson (Emerson) **98**:33-7, 57, 63, 66, 68-73, 75-6, 90, 92, 94-101, 107-17, 129, 132-33, 135, 159, 162, 177
"Collected Writings of Edgar Alan Poe" (Poe) **94**:229-35, 244, 267
The Collected Writings of Thomas De Quincey (De Quincey) **87**:52-7, 61-2, 64-5, 69-70
"Collection of Letters" (Austen) **119**:13
A Collection of Papers on Political, Literary, and Moral Subjects (Webster) **30**:408
A Collection of Poems, Chiefly Manuscript, and from Living Authors (Baillie) **71**:2
Collection of Poems on American Affairs (Freneau) **111**:160-61
The Colleen Bawn; or, The Brides of Garryowen (Boucicault) **41**:28-32, 39, 41, 43, 49-50, 53
"College Breakfast Party" (Eliot) **4**:115
"College Lyfe" (Cranch) **115**:3, 6
The Collegians (Griffin) **7**:193-209, 212-19
Le collier de la reine (Dumas) **11**:68-69; **71**:232, 234
"A Colloguy" (Rossetti) **50**:311
"Colloque sentimental" (Verlaine) **2**:628, 631; **51**:355, 374, 377-78, 384, 388
Colloquies on the Progress and Prospects of Society (Southey) **97**:252, 264, 266, 270, 284, 287, 291, 293
"The Colloquy of Monos and Una" (Poe) **1**:519-20; **16**:295, 308, 331; **78**:259
Colomba (Mérimée) **6**:352, 354-5, 357-8, 360, 363, 365-70; **65**:43, 46-7, 50, 54-8, 60-2, 64, 66, 79, 85, 87, 90, 100-05, 123-9, 137
La Colombe (Dumas) **71**:218-19
"Colombine" (Verlaine) **51**:351, 378-80
Colombine (Almqvist) **42**:4, 16, 19
Colon and Spondee (Tyler) **3**:575
Le Colonel Chabert (Balzac) **35**:27
Colored Stones (Stifter)
See *Bunte Steine*
"The Colubriad" (Cowper) **94**:34, 122
Columbe's Birthday (Browning) **19**:95, 102; **79**:93-94, 100, 147, 189
"Columbia libre" (Isaacs) **70**:313
The Columbiad (Barlow) **23**:3-8, 10-20, 22-6, 29, 32, 36-9
"Columbian War Hymn" (Isaacs)
See "Himno de guerra columbiano"
"Columbia's Ships" (Sigourney) **21**:299
"The Columbine" (Very) **9**:372, 376, 380, 385, 391, 396-97
"Columbus" (Lowell) **90**:219, 221
"Columbus to Ferdinand" (Freneau) **111**:143, 147
Le combe de l'homme mort (Nodier) **19**:379
Combination (Tonna) **135**:208-10, 215-17
"Come Back Again My Olden Heart" (Clough) **27**:105
"Come Down, O Maid" (Tennyson) **30**:280
"Come Send Round the Wine" (Moore) **110**:185
"Come Slowly, Eden" (Dickinson) **21**:8
"Come Up from the Fields Father" (Whitman) **4**:592; **81**:320-21
"Come Where My Love Lies Dreaming" (Foster) **26**:285, 287, 291, 298
La comédie de la mort (Gautier) **1**:340-42; **59**:19, 33-4
"Comédie de la soif" (Rimbaud) **4**:472-73, 487; **35**:321
La Comédie humaine (Balzac) **5**:29-32, 37, 39-42, 44-57, 59-64, 67-73, 76-81, 83-8; **53**:10, 22, 26, 31, 35
Comédies (Banville) **9**:22
Comédies et proverbes (Musset) **7**:268, 275-77
"The Comedy of Errors" (Lamb) **125**:305
"Comet" (Holmes) **14**:101
"Comfort" (Browning) **1**:112
"Comfort" (Lampman) **25**:209
"Comfort of the Fields" (Lampman) **25**:189
Comic Dramas (Edgeworth) **1**:257
Comic Tales and Sketches (Thackeray) **5**:444
Comic Tragedies (Alcott) **83**:4, 9
"Coming Days" (Crawford) **127**:217-19, 226
"The Coming of Age of The Origin of Species" (Huxley) **67**:4, 61
"The Coming of Arthur" (Tennyson) **30**:249, 253, 279, 287; **65**:236, 239, 243, 249, 252-3, 257, 277-8, 280-1, 288-9, 292, 298, 300-1, 312, 314-5, 319-20, 349, 352, 369, 372
"The Coming of the Lord" (Very) **9**:378, 385
"The Coming of Winter" (Lampman) **25**:204
The Coming P (Vallès) **71**:372
The Coming Race (Bulwer-Lytton) **1**:150-51, 154; **45**:22, 32, 38-40, 42-6, 71
"The Coming Woman" (Parton) **86**:366
Comische Erzählungen (Wieland) **17**:394, 413, 418, 426-28
"Commands" (Preseren)
See "Ukazi"
Comme il vous plaira (Sand) **42**:310, 346-49

Commémoration Générale (Comte) **54**:213
"Commemoration Ode" (Lowell) **2**:509, 514, 516, 519, 522; **90**:188, 193
"Commemorative of the Genius of Shakespeare" (Rowson) **5**:322
"Commemorative Sonnets" (Clough) **27**:104
Comment je devins auteur dramatique (Dumas) **71**:217
The Commentaries of Caesar (Trollope) **101**:321
"Commentaries sur les mœurs de mon temps et document pour l'histoire" (Vigny) **102**:380
Commentary on Luke (Schleiermacher)
See *Über die Schriften des Lukas: Ein kritischer Versuch*
A Commentary on the Writings of Henrik Ibsen (Boyesen) **135**:46
"Commerce" (Freneau) **111**:101
A Commercial Crisis (Boker) **125**:28
"Commercial Speculation Offering a Net Profit of 300 Percent in Six Months" (Fourier) **51**:185
"The Commissary Driver" (Runeberg) **41**:314
"A Commission of Inquiry on Royalty" (Thomson) **18**:425
"Commodity" (Thoreau) **7**:396
Commodus (Madach) **19**:362, 368, 370
"The Common A-Took In" (Barnes) **75**:43, 48, 57, 93, 101
Common Sense (Paine) **62**:246-8, 251, 257, 263-5, 268, 270-1, 274, 276-7, 279, 281, 285, 293, 295, 298, 309, 312, 319, 322, 334-5, 337-8, 340, 343, 345-50, 352-3, 364-71, 373, 378, 380, 391-3
Common Sense Applied to Religion; or, The Bible and the People (Beecher) **30**:9-10, 12-13
"Common Sense to the Public on Mr Deane's Affairs" (Paine) **62**:249
A Common Story (Goncharov)
See *Obyknovennaya istoriya*
"The Commonplace" (Whitman) **31**:434
Commonplace, and Other Short Tales (Rossetti) **2**:557; **50**:271; **66**:328, 330
"Commonplace Book" (Cranch) **115**:68
Commonplace Book (Southey) **8**:472
A Commonplace Book of Thoughts, Memories, and Fancies, Original and Selected (Jameson) **43**:306, 327
"Commonplace Critics" (Hazlitt) **29**:148
La Commune de Paris (Vallès) **71**:332-39
A Communication to My Friends (Wagner) **9**:425, 437, 444; **119**:248
The Communion of Labour (Jameson) **43**:327
Communist Manifesto (Engels)
See *Manifest der kommunistischen Partei*
The Communist Manifesto (Marx)
See *Manifest der Kommunistischen*
"Cómo llovía, suaviño" (Castro) **78**:59
Le compagnon du tour de France (Sand) **2**:589, 608; **57**:365
"A Companion Fairy" (Pavlova)
See "Sputnica feia"
Companion to the Most Celebrated Private Galleries of Art in London (Jameson) **43**:306, 321
The Companion Tour of France (Sand)
See *Le compagnon du tour de France*
A Comparative Statement of the Two Bills for the Better Government of the British Possessions in India (Sheridan) **91**:273
Comparing Heights (Ichiyō)
See *Takekurabe*
Comparison (Hayne) **94**:138
The Compassionate Beneficence of the Deity (Blair) **75**:116
A Compendious Dictionary of the English Language (Webster) **30**:388, 396, 398, 409
Compendium (Schleiermacher) **107**:370, 382
"Compensation" (Emerson) **1**:280; **38**:170-71, 178, 224; **98**:109-14, 131, 190
"Compensation" (Ingelow) **39**:267
"The Complaint" (Wordsworth)
See "The Complaint of the Forsaken Indian Woman"
"The Complaint of the Forsaken Indian Woman" (Wordsworth) **12**:387; **111**:202, 208, 210-11, 314-15
"Complaint of the Poor Knight Errant" (Laforgue)
See "Complainte du pauvre chevalier-errant"
"A Complaint on the Decay of Beggars in the Metropolis" (Lamb) **10**:403, 409, 426, 430, 436; **113**:218, 235, 252, 263
Complainte de la bonne défunte (Laforgue) **53**:283
"Complainte de Lord Pierrot" (Laforgue) **53**:287
"Complainte des complaintes" (Laforgue) **5**:277
"Complainte des Noces de Pierrot" (Laforgue) **53**:287
"Complainte des pianos qu'on entend dans les quertiersaisés" (Laforgue) **5**:272; **53**:292
"Complainte des printemps" (Laforgue) **53**:294
"Complainte du pauvre chevalier-errant" (Laforgue) **5**:275
"Complainte du Temps et de sa commère l'Espace" (Laforgue) **53**:267
"Complainte du vent qui s'ennuie la nuit" (Laforgue) **53**:294
Les complaintes (Laforgue) **5**:275, 277, 280-2; **53**:278-9, 281, 287-90
The Complaints of the Poor People of England (Dyer) **129**:98, 103, 112, 115, 125, 128-29, 136-37, 142, 145
The Complete Andersen (Andersen) **7**:37
Complete Edition (Hayne) **94**:138
The Complete Nonsense of Edward Lear (Lear) **3**:305
The Complete Poems (Dickinson) **21**:71
Complete Poems (Hayne) **94**:134
Complete Poetic Works (Coleridge) **90**:32-3
Complete Poetical Works (Longfellow) **103**:295, 305
The Complete Poetical Works and Letters of John Keats (Keats) **121**:126-27, 192
Complete Poetical Works of Samuel Taylor Coleridge (Coleridge) **99**:3, 106
The Complete Poetry and Prose of William Blake (Blake) **127**:32-33, 36, 56-57, 59-60, 63-73, 75, 77-82, 101, 105-7, 112, 123-25, 127-40
The Complete Prose Works of Matthew Arnold (Arnold) **89**:31-40, 64-7, 80, 89, 91-3, 98, 100-07, 109-13; **126**:36-38, 42-44, 46, 48-50, 52, 59-60, 87-88, 90-91, 93-95, 100, 102-9, 111-17, 119-22
Complete Prose Works of Matthew Arnold, Volume I (Arnold) **126**:111-12, 114
Complete Prose Works of Matthew Arnold, Volume II (Arnold) **126**:112-13
Complete Prose Works of Matthew Arnold, Volume III (Arnold) **126**:38, 94, 102-7, 109, 114, 122
Complete Prose Works of Matthew Arnold, Volume IV (Arnold) **126**:88, 115-16
Complete Prose Works of Matthew Arnold, Volume IX (Arnold) **126**:104, 114
Complete Prose Works of Matthew Arnold, Volume V (Arnold) **126**:36-38, 44, 100, 103, 108-9, 119-22
Complete Prose Works of Matthew Arnold, Volume VI (Arnold) **126**:90, 93, 108-9
Complete Prose Works of Matthew Arnold, Volume VIII (Arnold) **126**:37, 91, 104
Complete Prose Works of Matthew Arnold, Volume X (Arnold) **126**:36, 43, 59, 95, 106, 116-17
Complete Prose Works of Matthew Arnold, Volume XI (Arnold) **126**:37, 59-60
The Complete Sermons of Ralph Waldo Emerson (Emerson) **98**:61, 91, 93-5
The Complete Short Stories of Guy de Maupassant (Maupassant) **83**:189-202
"The Complete Work of Edgar Allan Poe" (Poe) **94**:228-29, 245
Complete Works (Bécquer)
See *Obras completas*
Complete Works (Browning) **79**:189-90
Complete Works (Freytag)
See *Gesammelte Werke*
Complete Works (Gómez de Avellaneda)
See *Obras de doña Gertrudis de Avellaneda*
Complete Works (Paine) **62**:374-6, 380-1
Complete Works (Tonna)
See *The Works of Charlotte Elizabeth*
The Complete Works of Edgar Allen Poe (Poe) **117**:225, 235, 260, 262, 268, 275-76, 304-5, 309-13, 330-33, 335-36
The Complete Works of Elizabeth Barrett Browning (Browning) **61**:22, 49, 51, 53, 56-8, 66, 76
The Complete Works of Nathaniel Hawthrone (Hawthorne) **95**:91
The Complete Works of Ralph Waldo Emerson (Emerson) **98**:33, 40-50, 54-63, 66, 68, 72-3, 75-6, 91-2, 96, 101, 109, 113, 127, 130-31, 133-35, 166, 185
The Complete Works of William Hazlitt (Hazlitt) **82**:128
Complete Writings (Whitman) **81**:235, 267
The Complete Writings of William Blake (Blake) **127**:56-57, 59-60, 63-73, 75, 77-82
"Composed during a walk on the Downs, in November 1787" (Smith)
See "Sonnet 42"
"Composed upon Westminster Bridge, Sept. 3, 1802" (Wordsworth) **12**:417
"Compromise" (Tennyson) **30**:295
"Comrades, Fill No Glass for Me" (Foster) **26**:286
Comradeship (Scribe)
See *La camaraderie; ou, La courte échelle*
Le comte de Monte-Cristo (Dumas) **11**:52, 59, 61, 63, 65, 68-9, 71, 74, 76, 83, 86; **71**:184-85, 193,209
Le comte de Moret (Dumas) **71**:217-220
Le Comte Hermann (Dumas) **71**:193
Comte's Philosophy of the Sciences (Lewes) **25**:295
La Comtesse de Charney (Dumas) **71**:232, 242
La comtesse de Rudolstadt (Sand) **2**:589, 598; **42**:314, 338, 358; **42**:372; **57**:360
Con Cregan (Lever)
See *Confessions of Con Cregan, the Irish Gil Blas*
"Conaire" (Ferguson)
See "Conary"
"Conary" (Ferguson) **33**:279, 281, 285, 290, 294, 298, 303-04, 306
The Concept of Anxiety (Kierkegaard)
See *Begrebet Angest*
"A Concept of Diabolical Possession" (Lamb) **10**:404
The Concept of Dread (Kierkegaard) **34**:200, 204, 223-24, 226-29, 231; **78**:138, 236, 238-39
The Concept of Irony, with Special Reference to Socrates (Kierkegaard)
See *Om Begrebet Ironi med stadigt Hensyn til Socrates*
"Concerning Actors and Singers" (Wagner) **9**:414
"Concerning Geffray, Teste Noire" (Morris) **4**:431, 444
"Concerning Illusions and Truth" (Baratynsky)
See "O zabluzhdeniyakh i istine"
Concerning the Aesthetic Education of the Human Being (Schiller)
See "Briefe über die ästhetische Erziehung des Menschen"

"Concerning the Art of Conducting" (Wagner) **9**:414, 475
Concerning the Concept of the Wissenschaftslehre, or, of So-Called Philosophy (Fichte)
See *Über den Begriff der Wissenschaftslehre*
Concerning the Influence of the Passions upon the Happiness of Individuals and of Nations (Staël-Holstein)
See *De l'influence des passions sur le bonheur des individus et des nations*
Concerning the Shakespeare Madness (Grabbe) **2**:280
The Conchologist's First Book (Poe) **1**:497; **16**:297
Le concierge de la rue du Bac (Kock) **16**:259
Le concile féerique (Laforgue) **5**:270, 276, 281-82
"Concluding Address" (Brontë) **109**:35
Concluding Unscientific Postscript to the Philosophical Fragments (Kierkegaard)
See *Afsluttende uvidenskabelig Efterskrift*
"Conclusion" (Grillparzer)
See "Schlußwort"
"Conclusion" (Hawthorne) **10**:286-87
"Conclusion" (Pater) **7**:288, 314-15, 327, 332-33, 338-39; **90**:336
"Conclusion" (Tennyson) **65**:368
"Conclusion" (Thoreau) **7**:389, 399
"Conclusion of the Mirror" (Mackenzie) **41**:187
Concord and Merrimac Rivers (Thoreau)
See *A Week on the Concord and Merrimack Rivers*
Concord Days (Alcott) **1**:21, 24-26
"Concord Ode" (Emerson) **1**:289, 296, 299, 305
The Concubine (Baratynsky)
See *Nalozhnitsa*
El conde de Moret (Dumas)
See *Le comte de Moret*
El Conde Fernán González (Larra) **17**:279
Condensation of Determinants (Carroll) **139**:4
Condition (Delany)
See *The Condition, Elevation, Emigration, and Destiny of the Colored People of the United States, Politically Considered*
The Condition (Engels)
See *Die Lage der arbeitenden Klasse in England*
Condition and Elevation (Delany)
See *The Condition, Elevation, Emigration, and Destiny of the Colored People of the United States, Politically Considered*
The Condition, Elevation, Emigration, and Destiny of the Colored People of the United States, Politically Considered (Delany) **93**:99, 105, 107, 120, 122, 125, 143, 153-4, 159, 161-63, 166-67, 169
Condition of England (Engels)
See *Die Lage der arbeitenden Klasse in England*
"Condition of the Members of the Christian Empire" (Newman) **38**:308
Condition of the Working Class (Engels)
See *Die Lage der arbeitenden Klasse in England*
The Condition of the Working class in England in 1844 (Engels)
See *Die Lage der arbeitenden Klasse in England*
Condition of Working Class in England (Engels)
See *Die Lage der arbeitenden Klasse in England*
"The Conditions and Prospects of Protestantism" (Froude) **43**:213
The Condor (Stifter)
See *Der Condor*
Der Condor (Stifter) **41**:335, 339,341, 366, 376, 380-81
"The Conduct of Life" (Emerson) **98**:8-9
The Conduct of Life (Emerson) **1**:290, 300; **38**:154, 157; **98**:8, 19, 72, 89, 130-33, 151, 186
"Conductor Bradley" (Whittier) **8**:517, 523
"The Confederate Memorial Address" (Lanier) **3**:245; **118**:258
"Confession" (Baudelaire) **55**:14, 60
"The Confession" (Lermontov)
See "Ispoved"
"La Confession" (Maupassant) **83**:228
Confession (Bakunin) **25**:40-4, 58, 60, 63, 72, 75; **58**:102, 107-8, 114
"La Confession de Théodule Sabot" (Maupassant) **83**:171
La confession d'un enfant du siècle (Musset) **7**:259, 266, 273-74, 280
La confession d'une jeune fille (Sand) **42**:311
"Confession of Faith" (Engels) **85**:127
Confession; or, The Blind Heart (Simms) **3**:506, 509-10, 512, 514
"The Confessional" (Browning) **79**:99, 164
"Confessions" (Browning) **1**:125; **66**:42
"Confessions" (Browning) **19**:115
Confessions (Bomans) **51**:371
Confessions (Heine) **4**:240-41, 244-45
Confessions (De Quincey)
See *Confessions of an English Opium-Eater*
Confessions (Verlaine) **51**:371
"Confessions d'une femme" (Maupassant) **83**:213
"Confessions of a Drunkard" (Lamb) **10**:409, 414-15, 435; **113**:261-63
The Confessions of a Justified Sinner (Hogg)
See *The Private Memoirs and Confessions of a Justified Sinner*
"The Confessions of a Medium" (Taylor) **89**:308
"Confessions of a Reformed Ribbonman" (Carleton) **3**:92
"Confessions of a Second-Rate, Sensitive Mind" (Tennyson) **30**:204
Confessions of a Sinner (Hogg)
See *The Private Memoirs and Confessions of a Justified Sinner*
Confessions of an English Opium Eater (Musset)
See *L'Anglais mangeur d'opium*
Confessions of an English Opium-Eater (De Quincey) **87**:3-5, 11, 16, 29, 36, 40-2, 48, 52, 55-6, 60-1, 70, 75, 78
"The Confessions of an odd-tempered Man" (Opie) **65**:163
"The Confessions of an Office-Holder" (Kennedy) **2**:432
"Confessions of an Opium Eater" (De Quincey) **4**:59-61, 63, 66, 77, 79, 83-85, 87-89
Confessions of Con Cregan, the Irish Gil Blas (Lever) **23**:304, 311
"Confessions of Fitzboodle" (Thackeray) **5**:451; **43**:387
The Confessions of Harry Lorrequer (Lever) **23**:268-73, 281-85, 287, 290-94, 297, 299-300, 302-03, 306, 309
"The Confidant" (Crabbe) **26**:93, 102, 130-32, 136; **121**:6, 67, 69
The Confidantes of a King: The Mistresses of Louis XV (Goncourt and Goncourt)
See *Les maîtresses de Louis XV*
La Confidence (Maupassant) **83**:230
The Confidence-Man: His Masquerade (Melville) **3**:331, 334, 337, 344, 347, 354-55, 362, 364, 368-70, 372, 384-85; **12**:269, 271, 274, 293; **29**:327-28, 334, 355, 362; **45**:199, 235; **49**:391, 402, 408, 417; **91**:84, 121, 175, 177, 180, 204; **93**:197, 220, 244-45, 249; **123**:179, 201, 204, 219, 241
Les confidences (Lamartine) **11**:265, 266, 278
Confidential Letters on Lucinde (Schleiermacher)
See *Vertraute Briefe über Friedrich Schlegels Lucinde*
Confidential Letters on Schlegel's Lucinda (Schleiermacher)
See *Vertraute Briefe über Friedrich Schlegels Lucinde*
"Confiteor" (Gordon) **21**:150, 164
"Le confitéor de l'artiste" (Baudelaire) **29**:97
"The Conflict" (Schiller)
See "Kampf"
"The Conflict of Convictions" (Melville) **3**:352
Conflit (Mallarmé) **41**:280
"Conflits pour rire" (Maupassant) **83**:169, 227-28
The Conformists (Banim and Banim) **13**:121, 129-30, 135-37, 149-50
Confrontation (Mallarmé) **41**:280
Congal (Ferguson) **33**:283, 285-86, 289-91, 293-94, 296-99, 302-03, 306-09
Congiura de'Pazzi (Alfieri) **101**:32, 42
"Congratulations" (Rizal) **27**:425
Coningsby; or, The New Generation (Disraeli) **2**:139-40, 144-45, 147-54; **39**:2-4, 6-11, 15-17, 19-24, 27-9, 34-5, 40-1, 43-51, 56, 64-6, 69, 73, 75-6, 80; **79**:195, 198-99, 212-14, 216-19, 221-22, 234-35, 239, 245, 248, 250, 257-60, 263, 269-71, 273, 278-79, 281-82
Conjectural Beginning of the Human Race (Kant) **27**:236
Conjugalia (Reade) **2**:549
La conjuración de Venecia (Martínez de la Rosa) **102**:226, 230, 238-47
La Conjuration de Catilina (Mérimée) **65**:85
Une Conjuration sous Louis XIII (Vigny)
See *Cinq-Mars; ou, Une conjuration sous Louis XIII*
"Connecticut" (Halleck) **47**:57
"Connecticut River" (Sigourney) **21**:301, 310; **87**:331
"The Connection and the Mutual Assistance of the Arts and Sciences, and the Relation of Poetry to Them All" (Dyer) **129**:110
"Connel of Dee" (Hogg) **109**:243-44
El conocido sabio Cornelius (Silva) **114**:263
"The Conqueror Worm" (Poe) **1**:512; **97**:181; **117**:192, 242-45, 281, 287, 301
"The Conqueror's Grave" (Bryant) **6**:165, 168; **46**:3
The Conquest of Canaän: A Poem in Eleven Books (Dwight) **13**:259, 261-63, 265, 269-71, 273-78
Conquest of Granada (Irving)
See *The Chronicle of the Conquest of Granada*
Conrad and Eudora (Chivers)
See *Conrad and Eudora; or; The Death of Alonzo*
Conrad and Eudora; or; The Death of Alonzo (Chivers) **49**:50, 52, 57, 61-2, 79, 81, 83
Conrad Wallenrod (Mickiewicz)
See *Konrad Wallenrod*
"Conscience" (Patmore) **9**:342
"Conscience l'Innocent" (Dumas) **71**:185, 187, 204
"Conscience-Stricken Daniel" (Leskov)
See "Legenda o sovestnom Danile"
"Conscious Am I in My Chamber" (Dickinson) **21**:53, 74
"The Conscript" (Balzac) **5**:52-3
"Consequences of Happy Marriages" (Horton) **87**:110
"The Conservative" (Emerson) **1**:287; **38**:227
"Consider the Lilies of the Field" (Rossetti) **66**:301
A Consideration of Objections against the Retrenchment Association at Oxford during the Irish Famine in 1847 (Clough) **27**:82-3

Considerations (Staël-Holstein)
See *Considérations sur la Révolution française*
"Considerations By the Way" (Emerson) **98**:131
Considerations on France (Maistre)
See *Considérations sur la France*
Considerations on Lord Grenville's and Mr. Pitt's Bill Concerning Treasonable and Seditious Practices, and Unlawful Assemblies (Godwin) **130**:88, 95, 166
Considerations on Representative Government (Mill) **58**:330-1, 350, 376, 379
Considerations on Spiritual Power (Comte)
See *Considérations sur le pouvoir spirituel*
Considérations philosophiques sur les sciences et les savants (Comte) **54**:210, 237
Considérations sur la France (Maistre) **37**:278-80, 291-92, 295, 299, 300-06, 313, 315-17, 320, 322-23
Considérations sur la Révolution française (Staël-Holstein) **91**:323, 360
Considérations sur le pouvoir spirituel (Comte) **54**:203, 210, 238
"Consolatio" (Herzen) **10**:336, 338
Les consolations (Sainte-Beuve) **5**:325, 333, 335, 341, 346, 348, 351
Conspectus of Useful and Harmful Plants that Grow Wild or Cultivated in Northern Germany (Chamisso) **82**:5
"The Conspiracy of Catiline" (Mérimée) **6**:353
The Conspiracy of Fiesco at Genoa (Schiller)
See *Die Verschwörung des Fiesco zu Genua*
The Conspiracy of Kings (Barlow) **23**:14, 27
Conspiracy of the Pazzi (Alfieri)
See *Congiura de'Pazzi*
"The Conspirators" (Mérimée) **6**:353
The Conspirators (Dumas)
See *Le chevalier d'Harmental*
The Constable de Bourbon (Ainsworth) **13**:41
The Constable of the Tower (Ainsworth) **13**:42
Constance Verrier (Sand) **2**:598; **42**:312; **57**:316
"The Constant Tin Solider" (Andersen)
See "Den standhaftige Tinsoldat"
Constantine (Burckhardt)
See *Die Zeit Constantins des Grossen*
Constantine Paleologus; or, The Last of the Caesars (Baillie) **2**:34-35, 37, 39-40; **71**:5, 12-13
Constantinople (Gautier) **1**:344; **59**:5
Constantinople of Today (Gautier)
See *Constantinople*
"The Constellations" (Bryant) **6**:165, 168
Constitución del Colegio de Señoritas de la Advocación de Santa Rosa de América (Faustino) **123**:354
Constitution for the School for Young Ladies of the Appellation of Saint Rose of America (Faustino)
See *Constitución del Colegio de Señoritas de la Advocación de Santa Rosa de América*
Constitution Lost (Arany)
See *Az elveszett alkomány*
Constitutional Code (Bentham) **38**:44-5, 87-8
Consuelo (Sand) **2**:588-89, 593-96, 603-04; **42**:314, 320, 330-32, 337-38, 343, 372; **57**:310, 313, 316-7, 359-61
Los consuelos (Echeverria) **18**:147-49, 152
Les consultations du Docteur Noir: Stello; ou, les diables bleus, première consultation (Vigny) **7**:467-71, 473-75, 479, 485-86; **102**:335-40, 342-44, 360-61, 378, 380
"Consummatum Est" (Hayne) **94**:165-66
La contagion (Augier) **31**:7-10, 13, 16, 19-24, 27-8, 31
"The Contagiousness of Puerperal Fever" (Holmes) **81**:101-02
"Containing Observations" (Brackenridge) **7**:51, 58, 65
"Containing Reflections" (Brackenridge) **7**:51, 58, 65
Contarini Fleming: The Psychological Romance (Disraeli) **2**:137-38, 143, 145-49, 153; **39**:3, 22, 24, 31, 33, 39-42, 52, 54-6, 66-7, 74; **79**:201-02, 206, 209, 211, 214-15, 217-18, 226-27, 239, 271-73, 282
"Conte" (Rimbaud) **4**:466, 470, 473, 477, 482-83; **35**:290, 294-96, 322, 324-25; **82**:230, 232
"Conte de Noël" (Maupassant) **83**:182
Conte di Carmagnola (Manzoni)
See *Il conte di Carmagnola*
Il conte di Carmagnola (Manzoni) **29**:250-51, 254, 261, 275, 300; **98**:201, 204-05, 208-09, 213, 220-21, 223-25, 230, 241
"Contemplation" (Blake) **13**:181
"The Contemplation of God" (Klopstock) **11**:223
Les contemplations (Hugo) **3**:242, 253, 263, 271, 273; **10**:369, 373, 375
"The Contemporary" (Turgenev) **122**:343
"Contemporary" (Tyutchev)
See "Sovremennoe"
"The Contemporary God" (Isaacs)
See "El Dios del siglo"
"Contempt of Court—Almost" (Harris) **23**:159
"Contentment" (Field) **3**:208
"Contentment" (Holmes) **14**:109
"Contentment, or If You Please Confession" (Paine) **62**:324
Contes bourgeois (Banville) **9**:31
Contes choisis (Daudet) **1**:243
Contes cruels (Villiers de l'Isle Adam) **3**:581-82, 584, 586, 589-90
Contes de la bécasse (Maupassant) **1**:442
Les contes de la reine de Navarre (Scribe) **16**:412
Contes de la veillée (Nodier) **19**:384
Contes d'Espagne et d'Italie (Musset) **7**:254-56, 259, 263, 265, 278
Les contes d'Hoffman (Hoffmann) **2**:341
Contes drolatiques (Balzac) **53**:25
Les contes du Lundi (Daudet) **1**:231, 234, 239, 243
Contes en prose (Desbordes-Valmore) **97**:12
Contes en vers (Desbordes-Valmore) **97**:12
Contes et facétites (Nerval) **67**:357
"Contes et nouvelles" (Maupassant) **42**:203; **83**:189-202
Contes et nouvelles (Musset) **7**:259
Contes fantastiques (Banville)
See *Contes féeriques*
Contes fantastiques (Gautier) **59**:33-6, 38, 40
Contes fantastiques (Nodier) **19**:395
Contes féeriques (Banville) **9**:31-32
Contes héroïques (Banville) **9**:31
Contes immoraux (Borel)
See *Champavert, contes immoraux*
Contes pour les femmes (Banville) **9**:31-32
La contesse romani (Dumas) **9**:230
A Contest of Faculties (Kant) **27**:237
The Continent (Cooke) **110**:39
The Continentalist (Hamilton) **49**:295, 325
Continental Journal (Wordsworth)
See *Journal of a Tour on the Continent*
Continuation and Conclusion of Dead Souls (Gogol) **5**:218
Continuation of Early Tales (Edgeworth) **51**:81, 110
"Continued" (Arnold) **29**:34
"The Contract" (Patmore) **9**:352, 359
"Contracted Views in Religion" (Newman) **38**:306
"Contralto" (Gautier) **59**:19
"The Contrast" (Edgeworth) **51**:82, 88-9
The Contrast (Tyler) **3**:571-79
"Contrasted Songs" (Ingelow) **39**:264
Contribution to the Correction of the Public Verdict on the French Revolution (Fichte) **62**:34
"A Contribution to the Critique of Hegel's Philosophy of Right: An Introduction" (Marx) **114**:69, 83
A Contribution to the Critique of Political Economy (Marx)
See *Zur kritik der politischen Ökonomie*
"A Contribution to the History of Early Christianity" (Engels) **85**:44, 48
Contributions Designed to Correct the Judgment of the Public on the French Revolution (Fichte)
See *Contribution to the Correction of the Public Verdict on the French Revolution*
Contributions to the Edinburgh Review (Jeffrey) **33**:314, 322, 332, 348, 354-55
"The Contrite Heart" (Cowper) **8**:130-31; **94**:71-2
The Controversy of the Faculties (Kant) **67**:227
"The Convalescent" (Lamb) **10**:410, 419, 436
"The Convent Threshold" (Rossetti) **2**:562, 564-5, 568, 575-6; **50**:266, 322; **66**:304-5, 308, 311-2, 341
Convention of Cintra (Wordsworth) **12**:461
"Conversation" (Cowper) **8**:106, 125-26; **94**:14, 23, 26-8, 51, 115
"Conversation" (Mickiewicz)
See "Rozmowa"
"Conversation" (Thoreau) **138**:129
"A Conversation" (Turgenev) **21**:377, 431
Conversation (Schlegel)
See *Gespräch über die Poesie*
Conversation entre onze heures et minuit (Balzac) **5**:73
"The Conversation of Eiros and Charmion" (Poe) **1**:496, 519-20; **16**:297, 331; **97**:179-83
A Conversation in the Kremlin (Pavlova)
See *Razgovor v Kremle*
A Conversation in the Trianon (Pavlova)
See *Razgovor v Trianone*
A Conversation on the Highway (Turgenev) **21**:428, 432; **122**:247
"Conversations as Good as Real III" (Hazlitt) **82**:98
Conversations for the Use of Children and Young Persons (Smith) **115**:119
Conversations of James Northcote, Esq., R. A. (Hazlitt) **29**:148
Conversations on Liberalism and the Church (Brownson) **50**:63, 65, 67-8
Conversations on Some of the Old Poets (Lowell) **2**:504; **90**:195-97, 212-13
Conversations with Children on the Gospels (Alcott) **1**:19-20
Conversations with Demons (Arnim)
See *Gespräche mit Dämonen. Des Königsbuchs zweiter Band*
"The Conversazióne" (Hale) **75**:347-8
"The Conversazzhyony" (Field) **3**:211
"The Convert" (Crabbe) **26**:93, 129
The Convert (Brownson) **50**:48, 50
"The Convict" (Shevchenko)
See *Varnak*
"The Convict" (Wilson) **5**:547
"The Convict" (Wordsworth) **12**:386, 388; **111**:202, 313, 315, 357
"The Convict's Dream" (Crabbe) **26**:100
"Le convive des dernières fêtes" (Villiers de l'Isle Adam) **3**:590
"Le convive inconnu" (Villiers de l'Isle Adam)
See "Le convive des dernières fêtes"
"Coogee" (Kendall) **12**:181, 199
"The Coolun" (Ferguson) **33**:294
Coombe-Ellen (Bowles) **103**:54-5, 60, 70
Cooper Union Speech (Lincoln) **18**:212, 226, 240, 245-47, 253, 257, 264, 280
"The Cooper's Ward, or the Waif of the New Year" (Alger) **83**:96
"Cooranbean" (Kendall) **12**:182
"The Copperhead" (Boker) **125**:81
The Copperhead (Frederic) **10**:183-84, 188, 192-94, 203-04
"The Copse" (Mitford) **4**:408
Coquette (Norton) **47**:248

The Coquette; or the History of a Eliza Wharton. A Novel Founded on Fact, By a Lady of Massachusetts (Foster) **99**:121-22, 126-27, 130-31, 133-35, 137-42, 144, 146-48, 150, 152, 154-57, 161, 163-65, 167-69, 171-72, 176-83, 185-89, 191-92, 197-200, 202-04
The Coquette: Or, the History of Eliza Wharton (Foster)
See *The Coquette; or the History of a Eliza Wharton. A Novel Founded on Fact, By a Lady of Massachusetts*
The Coquette or, the History of Elizabeth Wharton (Foster)
See *The Coquette; or the History of a Eliza Wharton. A Novel Founded on Fact, By a Lady of Massachusetts*
"Les coquillages" (Verlaine) **2**:624; **51**:378-79
"Le cor" (Vigny) **7**:470, 474, 481, 484-85; **102**:335, 366
"Coral Insect" (Sigourney) **21**:296
"The Coral Insect" (Sigourney) **87**:334
Les corbeaux (Becque) **3**:13-19, 21-22
Cord and Creese (De Mille) **123**:121, 130
"La corde" (Baudelaire) **29**:109-10
La corde au cou (Gaboriau) **14**:18, 20, 22-3, 25
"La corde roide" (Banville) **9**:27
Corilla (Nerval) **1**:485; **67**:363
"Corinne at the Capitol" (Hemans) **71**:297
Corinne ou l'Italie (Staël-Holstein) **91**:291-92, 303, 314-15, 318, 320, 327-31, 337-38, 340-42, 344-56, 359-60, 365
"Coriolanus" (Hazlitt) **82**:164
"Corn" (Lanier) **6**:235-38, 246, 248, 252, 254, 259-60, 269, 278-79, 281; **118**:202-3, 205-6, 215, 218, 230, 233, 235-36, 238, 240, 262, 265, 270
"Corn Shucking Song" (Chivers) **49**:55
Cornelius O'Dowd upon Men and Women and Other Things in General (Lever) **23**:303
Corner of the Woods (Storm)
See *Waldwinkel*
"The Cornflower" (Krylov) **1**:435
"Corn-husking" (Arany)
See "Tengerihántás"
"Coro dei morti" (Leopardi) **129**:349
The Coronal (Child) **6**:198; **73**:42, 59
"The Coronation" (Barham) **77**:19, 26
"Coronation Soliloquy" (Hunt) **1**:423; **70**:258
"Corporal Munoz" (Isaacs)
See "El cabo Muñoz"
Corpus Inscriptionum Semitacarum (Renan) **26**:399
Correspondance (Flaubert) **2**:255; **10**:150; **62**:101, 105-6, 114-5, 123; **66**:289; **135**:137
Correspondance (Sand) **42**:329-31, 370, 372-73
Correspondance (Stendhal) **23**:365
Correspondance avec Hector Malot: 1862-1884 (Vallès) **71**:357-58, 372-73, 376
Correspondance de C. A. Sainte-Beuve, 1822-69 (Sainte-Beuve) **5**:336
Correspondance de George Sand et d'Alfred de Musset (Musset) **7**:266
Correspondance de H. de Balzac, 1819-1850 (Balzac) **5**:44
Correspondance intime (Desbordes-Valmore) **97**:32, 35-6
"Correspondances" (Baudelaire) **6**:114-15; **29**:74, 82, 97; **55**:49
"A Correspondence" (Turgenev)
See "Peripiska"
Correspondence (Cowper)
See *The Correspondence of William Cowper*
Correspondence (Emerson) **98**:66
Correspondence (Melville) **91**:218, 220, 222
Correspondence (Mill) **102**:304, 306, 311-12
Correspondence (Southey) **97**:291
A Correspondence (Turgenev) **21**:397, 401, 414, 418
Correspondence (Vigny) **102**:378, 384
Correspondence (Whitman) **81**:308
Correspondence (Williams) **135**:308
The Correspondence and Diaries of the Right Hon. John Wilson Croker (Croker) **10**:96-97
Correspondence of Fräulein Günderode and Bettina von Arnim (Arnim)
See *Die Günderode: Den Studenten*
The Correspondence of Henry Crabb Robinson with the Wordsworth Circle, 1808-1866 (Robinson) **15**:189
The Correspondence of Henry David Thoreau (Thoreau) **138**:117, 120-21, 124, 126-28, 130
The Correspondence of Sammuel Richardson (Barbauld) **50**:17, 19
The Correspondence of William Cowper (Cowper) **8**:105, 128; **94**:23-5, 28-9
Correspondence with a Child (Arnim)
See *Goethes Briefwechsel mit einem Kinde: Seinem Denkmal*
Correspondence with John Keble (Newman) **38**:314
"Correspondences" (Cranch) **115**:9, 22, 35-6, 54, 67
"Correspondencia de 'El Duende'" (Larra) **17**:269
"Corridas de torros" (Larra) **17**:269
"Corrupt Youth" (Eminescu) **33**:245
Corruption (Moore) **110**:171
The Corsair (Byron) **2**:61-62, 70, 86, 89-90, 95, 99; **12**:110; **109**:102, 118
"Corsica" (Barbauld) **50**:9
The Corsican Brothers (Boucicault) **41**:30, 32
"Cortege" (Verlaine) **51**:378
"La corza blanca" (Bécquer) **106**:88-90, 108, 156
"Corza blanca" (Bécquer)
See "La corza blanca"
Una cosa rara o sia bellezza ed onestá (Da Ponte) **50**:83
Cosas que fueron (Alarcon) **1**:15
Cosette (Hugo) **3**:246
Cosi fan tutte o la scoula delle amanti (Da Ponte) **50**:82, 84-5, 92, 94-6, 98
"Cosi gl'interi giorni" (Foscolo) **8**:278
Cosima (Sand) **42**:309
Cosmo de' Medici, an Historical Tragedy (Horne) **127**:236, 238, 241, 253-54, 256, 258, 270
"Cossack Cradlesong" (Lermontov) **5**:300
"The Cossacks" (Mérimée) **6**:353
"The Cost of Improvement" (Barnes) **75**:103
"Cost of Production" (Bagehot) **10**:20
A Cosy Couple (Lewes) **25**:291
Cot and Cradle Stories (Traill) **31**:323
"The Cottage" (Very) **9**:378
Cottage Economy: Containing Information Relating to the Brewing of Beer, Making of Bread, Keeping of Cows (Cobbett) **49**:110, 114-15, 130, 138, 140, 146, 152, 156-57, 175-78, 181-82
"The Cottage Girl" (Child) **73**:128, 132-34
"A Cottage in Kolonna" (Pushkin) **83**:272
"The Cottage Maiden" (Runeberg) **41**:312, 321
"The Cottage on the Hill" (Hayne) **94**:161
"A Cottage Scene" (Sigourney) **21**:310
"The Cottager to Her Infant" (Wordsworth) **25**:421; **138**:311
"The Cotton Boll" (Timrod) **25**:360, 363, 368, 370, 372, 374-77, 384, 387-88
"Coucher de soleil" (Leconte de Lisle) **29**:216
"Le coucher du soleil romantique" (Baudelaire) **29**:88
"Le Coucher d'un petit garçon" (Desbordes-Valmore) **97**:29, 38
"Could That Sweet Darkness Where They Dwell" (Dickinson) **21**:69
"Councillor Krespel" (Hoffmann)
See "Rat Krespel"
"Counsel to an Unknown Young Man" (Vigny) **7**:483
"The Counsels of Old Men Despised, or, the Revolt and Division of Empire" (Webster) **30**:424
"The Count Arnaldos" (Lockhart) **6**:297
Count Basil (Baillie) **2**:31, 34, 39-40, 43; **71**:4, 6, 12-13, 16, 28-30, 32, 35-38, 43, 45, 47-48, 51, 66
Count Benyowsky; or, The Conspiracy of Kamtschatka (Kotzebue)
See *Graf Benyowsky, oder die Verschwörung auf Kamschatka*
Count Donski (Sacher-Masoch) **31**:289
Count Frontenac and New France under Louis XIV (Parkman) **12**:336, 341, 372, 375
"Count Gismond" (Browning) **19**:129; **79**:164
Count Julian (Landor) **14**:157-58, 161, 176, 182, 192-94
Count Julian (Simms) **3**:507-08
Count Nulin (Pushkin)
See *Graf Nulin*
"The Count of Gleichen" (Taylor) **89**:310
The Count of Monte Cristo (Dumas)
See *Le comte de Monte-Cristo*
The Count of Morian, The Count of Morion, Woman's Revenge (Dumas)
See *Le comte de Moret*
Count Robert of Paris (Scott) **15**:309, 314; **69**:313-14, 319-20, 333-34
Count Waldemar (Freytag)
See *Graf Waldemar: Schauspiel in fünf Akten*
"Countess" (Le Fanu)
See "A Passage in the Secret History of an Irish Countess"
"The Countess" (Whittier) **8**:516, 519; **59**:360, 371
"Countess Laura" (Boker) **125**:77
The Countess of Rudolstadt (Sand)
See *La comtesse de Rudolstadt*
"The Counting-House" (Turgenev) **21**:377
"A Country Apothecary" (Mitford) **4**:408
"A Country Barber" (Mitford) **4**:408
"Country Boys" (Mitford) **4**:401
"A Country Christmas" (Alcott) **58**:47
"The Country Church" (Irving) **19**:327-28
"The Country Doctor" (Turgenev) **21**:451-52; **37**:435; **122**:293
Country Doctor (Balzac)
See *Le Médecin de Campagne*
A Country Gentleman and His Family (Oliphant) **11**:460, 462; **61**:210-1, 241
"The Country Girl" (Clare) **9**:75
"The Country Girl" (Hogg) **109**:203
"The Country Inn" (Turgenev)
See "The Inn"
The Country Inn (Baillie) **2**:34-35; **71**:2, 13, 64
"The Country Justice" (Crabbe) **26**:133
The Country Seat (Barham) **77**:6
Country Stories (Mitford) **4**:401
"The Country Sunday" (Jefferies) **47**:112-13, 138
The Country Waif (Sand)
See *François le Champi*
"The Countryman" (Martí)
See "Hombre del campo"
"The Countryside" (Pushkin)
See "Derevnya"
"The County Mayo" (Ferguson) **33**:287
Un coup de dés jamais n'abolira le hasard (Mallarmé) **4**:379, 383-86, 392, 395-96; **41**:248-51, 267, 277, 280, 285-88, 301
"Un coup d'etat" (Maupassant) **1**:469
La coupe et les lèvres (Musset) **7**:256, 258, 260, 264, 274
La cour d'Assises (Scribe) **16**:394
"Courage" (Arnold) **29**:23, 27
Courage and Caution (Ueda Akinari)
See *Tandai shoshin roku*
"La Couronne effeuillé" (Desbordes-Valmore) **97**:13
Cours de philosophie positive (Comte) **54**:166-88, 190, 205, 209-12, 217-39, 241, 244

Cours familier de littérature: Un entretien par mois (Lamartine) **11**:262, 272-73
A Course of Lectures on Dramatic Art and Literature (Schlegel)
See *Ueber dramatische Kunst und Litteratur*
Course of Lectures on Positive Philosophy (Comte)
See *Cours de philosophie positive*
Court Circular (Carroll) **139**:57
"A Courteous Explanation" (Arnold) **6**:62
"The Courtin'" (Lowell) **2**:511, 513-14, 522; **90**:193
Court-intriguing and Love (Schiller)
See *Kabale und Liebe*
The Courtship of Miles Standish (Longfellow) **2**:478-80, 483-84, 487, 495, 498; **45**:103, 106, 109-10, 113-14, 124, 128, 134, 137, 139, 142, 144-45, 147, 149-50, 159, 187; **103**:283
"The Courtship of Susan Bell" (Trollope) **101**:235
"The Courtship of the Yonghy Bonghy Bo" (Lear) **3**:297-98, 301, 309
Cousin Bette (Balzac)
See *La cousine Bette*
Cousin Henry (Trollope) **6**:470; **101**:251, 309, 311
"Cousin Kate" (Rossetti) **2**:575; **50**:270; **66**:329, 331, 350-3, 355
"Cousin Marshall" (Martineau) **26**:305, 351
Cousin Marshall (Martineau) **137**:264, 267, 315
Cousin Mary (Oliphant) **11**:462
"Cousin Phillis" (Carlyle) **70**:224-25, 227-28, 230, 232
Cousin Phillis (Gaskell)
See *Cousin Phyllis*
Cousin Phyllis (Gaskell) **5**:185, 190-92, 197-98, 201-03, 205; **70**:185, 198, 227; **97**:110
Le cousin Pons (Balzac) **5**:51-52, 55, 76-77, 81-82
"La Cousine" (Nerval) **1**:478; **67**:306
La cousine Bette (Balzac) **53**:35
A Cousin's Conspiracy (Alger) **8**:42; **83**:117
"The Covenanters" (Landon) **15**:161
The Covenanters (Galt) **110**:107
The Covetous Knight (Pushkin)
See *Skupoi rytsar*
The Cowled Lover (Bird) **1**:87, 89
"Cowper Hill" (Clare) **9**:78, 108
"Cowper's Grave" (Browning) **1**:124-6; **66**:44
"The Cracked Bell" (Baudelaire)
See "La cloche fêlée"
"A Cradle and a Grave" (Lazarus) **109**:291
"A Cradle Song" (Blake) **13**:220; **37**:3, 24, 31, 38, 40, 61, 69, 71-2, 74-5, 92
"The Craft of History" (Bello) **131**:123
"The Crane" (Lenau) **16**:276
"The Cranes of Ibycus" (Lazarus) **109**:294
"The Cranes of Ibycus" (Schiller)
See "Die Kraniche des Ibykus"
Cranford (Gaskell) **5**:185-87, 189-91, 193, 197-201, 203, 205; **70**:119, 185, 188, 193, 197, 199, 216-23; **97**:103-76; **137**:41, 167
"Le crapaud" (Corbière) **43**:10
Le crapaud (Hugo) **3**:271
The Crater; or, Vulcan's Peak (Cooper) **1**:220-21; **27**:144; **54**:263, 276
The Crayfish: An Introduction to the Study of Zoology (Huxley) **67**:9, 11, 95
A Crayon Miscellany (Irving)
See *The Crayon Miscellany*
The Crayon Miscellany (Irving) **2**:373; **95**:253
Crayonné au théâtre (Mallarmé) **4**:373; **41**:269-71, 301
"La creación" (Bécquer) **106**:97
"The Created" (Very) **9**:378, 383-84
"Creation" (Emerson) **1**:282
"Credat Judaeus Apella" (Gordon) **21**:160, 180
"Creed en Dios" (Bécquer) **106**:97, 130, 136
"The Creek of the Four Graves" (Harpur) **114**:92, 96-99, 101, 104-5, 115-17, 121, 123-27, 131, 134, 144, 147, 151-53, 158, 167
"Crépuscule de dimanche d'été" (Laforgue) **53**:270
"Le crépuscule du matin" (Baudelaire) **29**:101, 113; **55**:15, 24, 62
"Le crépuscule du soir" (Baudelaire) **6**:129-30; **29**:101, 109, 113; **55**:15, 22, 24-5
"Crepuscule du soir mystique" (Verlaine) **51**:361
"Crepúsculo" (Silva) **114**:294, 299, 301-2, 313
"The Crescent Moon Shines in the Sky" (Grillparzer)
See "Der Halbmond glänzet am Himmel"
"Crest and Gulf" (Patmore) **9**:358, 362
"The Cretan" (Solomos) **15**:398, 404-05
"Crete" (Lampman) **25**:190
"Le cri de l'âme" (Lamartine) **11**:270
Le Cri du Peuple (Vallès) **71**:377
Crichton (Ainsworth) **13**:17-18, 21-22, 34, 36, 42
"The Cricket on the Hearth" (Dickens) **3**:165; **113**:51
"The Crickets Sang" (Dickinson) **21**:67-9
"Cries of the Blindman" (Corbière)
See "Cris d'aveugle"
"Crime and Automatism" (Holmes) **14**:117, 132, 137
Crime and Punishment (Dostoevsky)
See *Prestuplenie i nakazanie*
Le crime d'Orcival (Gaboriau) **14**:16, 19, 21-7, 29, 33
"Crime of Love" (Verlaine)
See *Crimen Amoris*
"Crimean Sonnets" (Mickiewicz) **101**:157
Crimean Sonnets (Mickiewicz)
See *Sonety Krymskie*
Crimen Amoris (Verlaine) **51**:368-69, 372, 375
Crimes célèbres (Dumas) **11**:46
Les crimes de l'amour (Sade) **3**:468-70, 478, 481; **47**:309, 361
The Crimes of Passion (Sade)
See *Les crimes de l'amour*
Criminal Out of Infamy (Schiller) **69**:275
The Criminal Prisons of London and Scenes of London Life (Mayhew)
See *The Great World of London*
"The Crimson Curtain" (Barbey d'Aurevilly)
See "Le rideau cramoisi"
"The Cripple" (Andersen)
See "Krøblingen"
"Crippled Jane" (Norton) **47**:252
"The cripple's wife" (Lonnrot) **53**:339
"Cris d'aveugle" (Corbière) **43**:11, 13, 17-18, 28-9, 32, 34
"Crisálidas" (Silva) **114**:299
Le Crise (Feuillet) **45**:77, 79, 88, 90
"Crise de vers" (Mallarmé) **41**:240, 267, 273-74, 284-85, 294
"The Crisis" (Mérimée) **6**:353
The Crisis and A Crisis in the Life of an Actress (Kierkegaard) **34**:204, 252
"The Crisis and the Cuban Revolutionary Party" (Martí) **63**:168
Crisis Extraordinary (Paine) **62**:370
"Crisis política de España en el siglo XVI" (Martínez de la Rosa) **102**:252
"Cristina" (Browning) **19**:129
"El Cristo de la calavera" (Bécquer) **106**:99, 120, 130, 135
"El Cristo de la Luz" (Bécquer) **106**:147, 158
The Critic; or, Tragedy Rehearsed (Sheridan) **5**:357-58, 361-63, 367, 369-73, 378, 383; **91**:242, 244-45, 255-58, 260, 262-64
"Crítica ligera" (Silva) **114**:296
Critical and Historical Essays (Taine)
See *Essais de critique et d'histoire*
Critical and Historical Essays Contributed to the Edinburgh Review (Macaulay) **42**:65, 72, 76, 84, 87-88, 92-3, 103, 124, 152
Critical and Miscellaneous Essays (Macaulay)
See *Critical and Historical Essays Contributed to the Edinburgh Review*
A Critical Dissertation on the Poems of Ossian (Blair) **75**:115, 117-18, 125-26, 136
Critical Essay of Political Economy (Engels) **85**:8
Critical Essay on the Gospel of St. Luke (Schleiermacher)
See *Über die Schriften des Lukas: Ein kritischer Versuch*
Critical Essays and Literary Notes (Taylor) **89**:324, 341
Critical Essays on the Performers of the London Theatres, Including General Observations on the Practise (Hunt) **1**:406
"Critical Fancy" (Horne) **127**:257
"The Critical Historians of Jesus" (Renan) **26**:368
"A Critical Letter" (Eminescu) **131**:310
"Critical Notice" (Brown) **74**:37
Critical Remarks on Dr Dorn's Chrestomathy of Pushtu (Burton) **42**:53
"Critical Words" (Eminescu) **33**:272
"Critics" (Parton) **86**:352
"Critique des Poemes saturniens" (Verlaine) **51**:388
Critique of Hegel's Doctrine of the State (Marx) **114**:69-70
Critique of Judgment (Kant)
See *Kritik der Urtheilskraft*
Critique of Practical Reason (Kant)
See *Kritik der praktischen Vernunft*
Critique of Pure Reason (Kant)
See *Kritik der reinen Vernunft*
"Critique of the Gotha Program" (Marx) **114**:70
Critique of the Power of Judgment (Kant)
See *Kritik der Urtheilskraft*
Critique of the so-called First Epistle of Paul to Timothy (Schleiermacher) **107**:268
"A Critique of Walter Scott's New Novel Kenilworth" (Bestuzhev)
See "Kritika na novyi roman Val'ter Skotta—Kenil'vort"
Critiques and Addresses (Huxley) **67**:44
"Črkarska pravda" (Preseren) **127**:314-15
"The Crofton Boys" (Martineau) **26**:310, 323, 349
The Crofton Boys (Martineau) **137**:256-59, 262, 277, 281-83, 335
Crohoore of the Bill-Hook (Banim and Banim) **13**:115-17, 122-23, 125-30, 132-34, 139-41
The Croker Papers (Croker)
See *The Correspondence and Diaries of the Right Hon. John Wilson Croker*
Cromwell (Balzac) **5**:51
Cromwell (Hugo) **3**:233, 236, 241, 261, 268-69, 275; **21**:197, 201, 222-23, 226
Cromwell (Mérimée) **65**:44, 80, 86-7
Cromwell et Charles 1er (Dumas) **71**:222
"The Crone" (Pavlova) **138**:33
"The Crooked Branch" (Gaskell) **5**:190, 201; **70**:189
"Crooked John" (Boyesen) **135**:13
"Crop Rotation" (Kierkegaard)
See "Rotation Method"
The Croppy (Banim and Banim) **13**:121, 125-27, 129, 134-35, 137-38, 147, 151
"Croquis femenino" (Casal) **131**:258-60, 265
"The Cross of Snow" (Longfellow) **45**:116, 125, 132, 137
"Cross-Examination" (Allingham) **25**:4
"Crossing Brooklyn Ferry" (Whitman) **4**:569, 571, 582, 600; **31**:389, 391, 405, 407, 431, 443, 445; **81**:260, 359, 362-68
"Crossing the Bar" (Tennyson) **30**:223, 280, 282; **115**:239
"A Cross-Road Epitaph" (Levy) **59**:98
"Le croup" (Daudet) **1**:248
The Crow (Gozzi)
See *Il corvo*
"Crow and Fox" (Krylov) **1**:439

"The Crowd" (Turgenev) **122**:243, 247
"Crowds" (Baudelaire)
See "Les foules"
"The Crowing of the Red Cock" (Lazarus) **8**:415-17, 419; **109**:293, 304, 327, 337, 343
"Crowland Abbey" (Clare) **86**:108, 110, 112
"Crowley Castle" (Gaskell) **5**:206; **70**:189
Crown Bride (Tegner) **2**:613
Crowned and Buried (Browning) **66**:44
"A Crowned King" (Blake) **37**:29
"The Crowning of the Cock" (Lazarus)
See "The Crowing of the Red Cock"
The Crows (Becque)
See *Les corbeaux*
"Le crucifix" (Lamartine) **11**:255, 268, 270-72, 278, 283
"Un Crucifix" (Verlaine) **51**:359
Cruelty and Despair or the Black Cave and the Wretched Incense Burners (Eminescu) **33**:266
"La cruz del diablo" (Bécquer) **106**:97, 110, 121
"The Cry at Midnight" (Patmore) **9**:359
"A Cry for Ireland" (Mangan) **27**:311
"The Cry of Hungary" (Chivers) **49**:50
"The Cry of the Children" (Browning) **1**:115-7, 121, 123-5; **61**:5, 9, 42; **66**:25, 42, 44
"The Cry of the Human" (Browning) **1**:113, 115, 117
"A Cry to Arms" (Timrod) **25**:360, 367, 372, 384
The Cryptogram (De Mille) **123**:119, 121
"The Crystal" (Lanier) **6**:245, 248; **118**:219-21, 234, 239, 268
"The Crystal Bell" (O'Brien) **21**:236, 245-46
"The Crystal Cabinet" (Blake) **13**:172, 243
Csák végnapjai (Madach) **19**:370
"Csaladi kör" (Arany) **34**:16
"A csárda romjai" (Petofi) **21**:285
"Császár Ferenc őnagyságához" (Petofi) **21**:278
"Csatadal" (Petofi) **21**:286
"Csokonai" (Petofi) **21**:283
Cuauhtemoc, The Last Aztec Emperor (Gómez de Avellaneda)
See *Guatimozín, último emperador de México*
The Cuban Album of the Good and the Beautiful (Gómez de Avellaneda)
See *Album cubano de lo bueno y lo bello*
"The Cuban Soul" (Martí)
See "El alma cubana"
"Cuckoo" (Wordsworth) **12**:431, 436
The Cuckoo in the Nest (Oliphant) **11**:461
"Čudni dihur" (Preseren) **127**:315
Cudzoziemszczyzna; czyli, Nauka zbawlenia (Fredro) **8**:285
Cuento (Espronceda)
See *El estudiante de Salamanca*
Cuentos amartorios (Alarcon)
See *Novelas cortas: Cuentos amartorios*
"Los cuentos negros" (Silva) **114**:300
Cuentos negros (Silva) **114**:267
"Cuerpo y alma" (Casal) **131**:240, 245, 256, 271
"La cueva de la mora" (Bécquer) **106**:99, 130, 133
"La cueva de Taganana" (Villaverde) **121**:333
"Cui Bono?" (Gordon) **21**:154, 156, 160, 164
"The Cuirassier: A Partisan Officer's Story" (Bestuzhev)
See "Latnik: Rasskaz partizanskogo ofitsera"
Cúirt an Mheadhon Oidhche (Merriman) **70**:348-88
"Cúirt an Mheán Oíche" (Merriman) **70**:364-69
Cúirt an Mheán Oíche (Merriman)
See *Cúirt an Mheadhon Oidhche*
The Cultural History of Greece (Burckhardt)
See *Griechische Kulturgeschichte*
"Culture" (Emerson) **38**:174, 209; **98**:9, 68
Culture and Anarchy: An Essay in Political and Social Criticism (Arnold) **6**:53, 60, 62; **29**:10, 19-20, 42, 45; **89**:54, 59-66, 81, 84, 101, 104, 110-11, 121-22, 127, 132; **126**:1-125
Culture and its Enemies (Arnold) **29**:19-21; **126**:7, 16, 23, 40-41, 44
Culture's Garland (Field) **3**:209, 211-12
"Culver Dell and the Squire" (Barnes) **75**:57, 104
"The Cumberbund" (Lear) **3**:296, 307
"Cumberland" (Longfellow) **45**:189
"Çunacépa" (Leconte de Lisle) **29**:219-20, 223, 234
The Cup (Tennyson) **30**:265-66
"The Cup of Life" (Lampman) **25**:189, 198, 206, 218
"The Cup of Life" (Lermontov) **5**:299; **126**:223
"Cupid and Psyche" (Morris) **4**:416, 427-28, 445, 447
"Cupid and Psyche" (Patmore) **9**:338
"Cupido" (Taylor) **89**:317
Cupid's Arrow Poisoned (Beddoes) **3**:37-39
The Curate in Charge (Oliphant) **11**:439, 461-2
Curator Carsten (Storm)
See *Carsten Curator*
Le curé de Tours (Balzac) **53**:25
A Cure for Melancholy (Shewing the Way to Do Much Good with Little Money) (More) **27**:346
The Curé of Tours (Balzac)
See *Le curé de Tours*
"The Cure on the Banks of the Rhone" (Barbauld) **50**:14
"Curfew" (Longfellow) **45**:151; **103**:293
Curiosa Mathematica, Part I: A New Theory of Parallels (Carroll) **2**:111
Curiosa Mathematica. Part II: Pillow Problems Thought Out during Wakeful Hours (Carroll) **139**:11
Curiosés estheétiques (Baudelaire) **29**:86
"Curiosités déplacées" (Laforgue) **53**:270
"The Curious Man" (Pushkin) **83**:272
"A Curious Man's Dream" (Baudelaire)
See "Le rêve d'un curieux"
"The Curlew Song" (Kendall) **12**:191
"The Current Has Thickened and Grown Opaque" (Tyutchev) **34**:393
"Curse" (Grillparzer)
See "Verwünschung"
"A Curse for a Nation" (Browning) **61**:6, 44
The Curse of Clifton: A Tale of Expiation and Redemption (Southworth) **26**:432-34, 438, 442
The Curse of Kehama (Southey) **8**:453, 456, 459, 461, 468, 470, 474, 476-77; **97**:261, 278-79, 291, 293-94, 297-98, 307, 322, 329, 336
"The Curse of Love" (Petofi)
See "Szerelem átka"
"The Curse of Mother Flood" (Kendall) **12**:182
"The Curse of the Joyces" (Ferguson) **33**:289
"Curse of the Laureate" (Hogg) **109**:248
"The Cursed Mountain" (Gómez de Avellaneda)
See "La montaña maldita"
Cursory Reflections on Political and Commercial Topics (Galt) **110**:76, 92, 94
Cursory Remarks on an Enquiry into the Expediency and Propriety of Public or Social Worship (Hays) **114**:177-78, 185, 194
"Cursory Remarks on Readers, and the Nature of Poetry; on Dreams and Visions" (Dyer) **129**:94
Cursory Strictures on Chief Justice Eyre's Charge to the Grand Jury (Godwin)
See *Cursory Strictures on the Charge delivered by Lord Chief Justice Eyre to the Grand Jury, October 2, 1794*
Cursory Strictures on the Charge delivered by Lord Chief Justice Eyre to the Grand Jury, October 2, 1794 (Godwin) **14**:67; **130**:5, 47, 88
"Curtius" (Crawford) **12**:155
"Custom House" (Hawthorne) **2**:298, 311; **10**:271, 314; **39**:222, 234, 237, 240; **79**:331
The Cyclopaedia of Medieval Costume (Planché) **42**:274
Cyclopaedia of Modern Travel (Taylor) **89**:354
"Cyclopeedy" (Field) **3**:211
Les cydalises (Nerval) **1**:478; **67**:306
Cydippe (Stagnelius) **61**:248, 265
"Le cygne" (Baudelaire) **6**:80, 115-16; **29**:81, 100, 107, 115; **55**:3, 16, 19, 26, 29, 36-7, 41-2, 64, 67
"Cyhyryne Cyhyryne" (Shevchenko) **54**:364, 378-9, 388
"Cymbeline" (Lamb) **125**:306
Cymon and Iphigenia (Planché) **42**:277
Cynthio and Bugboo (Beddoes) **3**:33
Cyprus Leaves from the Grave of Dear Ethel (Petofi)
See *Czipruslombok Etelke sírjáról*
"Cythere" (Verlaine) **51**:378, 380
"Cywilizacja" (Norwid) **17**:378-79, 383
"Czar Alexander the Second (13th of March 1881)" (Rossetti) **77**:298
"Czar Nikita" (Pushkin)
See "Tsar Nikita"
Czarne kwiaty (Norwid) **17**:371, 373
"Czas i prawda" (Norwid) **17**:374
"Czaty" (Mickiewicz) **101**:164
"Czatyr Dagh" (Mickiewicz)
See "Czatyrdah"
"Czatyrdah" (Mickiewicz) **3**:403; **101**:188-90
Czipruslombok Etelke sírjáról (Petofi) **21**:279, 285
"Da ich ein Knabe war ..." (Hölderlin) **16**:174, 176
"A Dacian's Prayer" (Eminescu) **131**:286-87, 296-98, 346
Daddy Goriot; or, Unrequited Affection (Balzac)
See *Le père Goriot: Histoire Parisienne*
Daddy O'Dowd (Boucicault) **41**:28-9, 34
Daddy's Gogu (Eminescu) **33**:266
Dad's Always Right (Andersen) **79**:25
"Dad's Dog School" (Harris) **23**:140, 159-60, 162-63
"Daffodils" (Wordsworth) **12**:420, 427, 431
"Dagestan Theme" (Bestuzhev) **131**:203
"The Dagger" (Pushkin) **83**:253-54
"Un dahlia" (Verlaine) **2**:630
"The Daisy" (Tennyson) **30**:215, 234, 236
"The Daisy Follows Soft the Sun" (Dickinson) **21**:79; **77**:147-48
"Dalaim" (Petofi) **21**:264, 284
"The Dale" (Lamartine)
See "Le vallon"
"Dalforrás" (Madach) **19**:369
Dalila (Feuillet) **45**:74-5, 78-81, 88
"The Dalliance of the Eagles" (Whitman) **4**:572, 592, 602-03
The Daltons; or, Three Roads in Life (Lever) **23**:289, 292, 297, 304-05
"Da, mnogo bylo nas . . ." (Pavlova) **138**:20
"La dama de Amboto" (Gómez de Avellaneda) **111**:65
"Dama i fefela" (Leskov) **25**:229
La dame aux camélias (Dumas) **9**:219-20, 223-25, 227, 229, 231-32, 234-37, 239-41, 245-47, 250, 252-55
La dame aux perles (Dumas) **9**:219
La dame blanche (Scribe) **16**:401, 408
La dame de Monsoreau (Dumas) **11**:52, 68, 74; **71**:190-91, 193-94, 205, 242
Dames et demoiselles (Banville) **9**:31-32
The Damnation of Theron Ware (Frederic) **10**:184-86, 189-99, 202-06, 208-17, 219-20
"Damned Women" (Baudelaire)
See "Femmes damnées"
"Les damnés" (Leconte de Lisle) **29**:223, 228
Damokles (Klinger) **1**:427
Damon and Pythias (Banim) **13**:128
The Damsel of Darien (Simms) **3**:508

"The Damsel of Peru" (Bryant) **6**:162, 169, 172
Damy i huzary (Fredro) **8**:289-92
"The Dance" (Browning) **1**:121
"The dance" (Lonnrot) **53**:339
"Dance of Death" (Beddoes) **3**:34
The Dance of Death (Lazarus)
See *The Dance to Death*
"The Dance to Death" (Lazarus) **8**:415-17, 420-24, 426, 428; **109**:289, 294, 296, 302, 304, 311-12, 337, 343-44
The Dance to Death (Lazarus) **109**:297, 326
"The Dance to the Death" (Lazarus)
See "The Dance to Death"
The Dance to the Death (Lazarus)
See *The Dance to Death*
"The Dancing Girl of Shamakha" (Gobineau)
See "La danseuse de Shamakha"
The Dandie's Rout (Norton) **47**:246, 248, 250
"Danger of Praise" (Keble) **87**:119
"Danger of Regulating Our Conduct by the Rules of Romantic Sentiment" (Mackenzie) **41**:190
Dangerous Acquaintances (Laclos)
See *Les liaisons dangereuses; ou, Lettres recueillies dans une société et publiées pour l'instruction de quelques autres*
Dangerous Connections; or, Letters Collected in a Society, and Published for the Instruction of Other Societies (Laclos)
See *Les liaisons dangereuses; ou, Lettres recueillies dans une société et publiées pour l'instruction de quelques autres*
"A Dangerous Virtue" (Boyesen) **135**:13, 21, 28
"Les dangers de l'inconduite" (Balzac) **35**:26-7
The Dangers of Coquetry (Opie) **65**:174, 178-9
"The Dangers of Immigration" (Boyesen) **135**:16, 30
"Daniel and the Devil" (Field) **3**:206
Daniel Deronda (Eliot) **4**:108-09, 112-14, 121-26, 128-29, 133, 135-37, 144, 152; **13**:295, 317-18, 320, 322, 344; **23**:49-100; **41**:68, 70, 72, 77, 79, 121, 129, 133-34; **49**:237, 243; **89**:204; **118**:49, 51, 57, 60, 62, 76, 82, 102, 105, 107-10, 136, 164, 173, 182
"Daniel Jovard ou la Conversion d'un classique" (Gautier) **59**:10, 27-8
La Daniella (Sand) **2**:592; **42**:311, 338; **57**:316
Danischmend (Wieland) **17**:407
"The Danish Boy" (Wordsworth) **111**:212, 227
"Danksagung an den Bach" (Muller) **73**:363-64, 370
Dans la fournaise (Banville) **9**:30-31
"Dans la grotte" (Verlaine) **51**:378-80
"Dans la sierra" (Gautier) **59**:19
"Dans le ciel clair" (Leconte de Lisle) **29**:224
"Dans le rue, par un jour funèbre de Lyon" (Desbordes-Valmore) **97**:30
"Dans les rues" (Desbordes-Valmore) **97**:30
"Dans l'interminable..." (Verlaine) **51**:382
Danse des Morts (Flaubert) **62**:28
"Danse des Moucherons" (Lanier) **118**:242
"Danse macabre" (Baudelaire) **55**:23
"La danseuse de Shamakha" (Gobineau) **17**:69, 92, 103
"Dante" (Arany) **34**:19
Dante (Macaulay) **42**:116
Dante (Oliphant) **11**:439
"Dante and Beatrice" (Arnold) **126**:42
Dante and His Circle: With the Italian Poets Preceding Him, 1100/1200/1300 (Rossetti) **4**:497
"Dante at Verona" (Rossetti) **4**:493, 497, 518-19, 522, 525, 529-30; **77**:297, 337
"Dante Gabriel Rossetti" (Pater) **7**:306
Danton's Death (Büchner)
See *Dantons Tod*
Dantons Tod (Büchner) **26**:3-5, 7-11, 14-17, 20, 23-8, 32-3, 35-48, 49, 51, 56, 62-6, 69-71
Danylo Reva (Shevchenko) **54**:367
"Daphles" (Hayne) **94**:153-58
"Daphne" (Kendall) **12**:181, 192
"Daphne" (Lazarus) **109**:294
Daphné-Deuxième consultation du Docteur Noir (Vigny) **7**:473-74, 485-86; **102**:380
Darby's Return (Dunlap) **2**:208, 210-11, 213, 215, 217
"Dare You See a Soul at the White Heat?" (Dickinson) **21**:21; **77**:67
"Darest Thou Now O Soul" (Whitman) **4**:586
"Dark Ages" (Thoreau) **138**:120
"A Dark Day" (Rossetti) **4**:491
"Dark Days" (Parton) **86**:347
"The Dark Days of Autumn" (Clare) **9**:111
"Dark House By Which Once More I Stand" (Tennyson) **30**:273
"The Dark Interpreter" (De Quincey) **4**:88-89; **87**:9
"Dark Night, Clear Night" (Macha) **46**:201
"A Dark Night's Work" (Gaskell) **5**:192, 201-02, 205; **70**:185, 187-90, 198; **137**:40
"Dark Rosaleen" (Mangan) **27**:279, 281-84, 287-90, 293-95, 297-99, 304-11, 313-14, 318-19
"Dark Shadowing Chestnut Tree" (Meyer)
See "Schwarzschattende Kastanie"
"The Dark Stag" (Crawford) **12**:166; **127**:171-73, 223, 228
"Darkness" (Byron) **2**:94
"Darkness and the Poet" (Eminescu) **131**:287
"Darling Room" (Tennyson) **30**:210
"The Darning Needle" (Andersen) **79**:23, 34, 69, 89
Darstellung der Wissenschaftslehre aus dem Jahre 1801 (Fichte) **62**:13
Darstellung meines Systems der Philosophie (Schelling) **30**:127, 167, 174
Dartmoor (Hemans) **29**:202; **71**:261
"Darwin's Critics" (Huxley) **67**:86-7
"Darwin's Thoughts about God" (Symonds) **34**:336
"Dary Tereka" (Lermontov) **5**:287
Dastanbuy (Ghalib) **39**:149-51
Daughter and Mother (Tamayo y Baus)
See *Hija y madre*
A Daughter of the Philistines (Boyesen) **135**:14, 37, 42-43, 67
Daughters of Fire (Nerval)
See *Les filles du feu*
Davenport Dunn: A Man of Our Day (Lever) **23**:288-89, 292, 296, 301, 305
"David and Abigail" (Lampman) **25**:167, 201, 220
David Balfour: Being Memoirs of His Adventures at Home and Abroad (Stevenson)
See *Kidnapped: Being Memoirs of the Adventures of David Balfour in the Year 1751*
David Copperfield (Dickens)
See *The Personal History of David Copperfield*
David Garrick (Robertson) **35**:335, 355
"David Swan" (Hawthorne) **2**:298
Davila (Adams)
See *Discourses on Davila*
"Dawn" (Isaacs)
See "Albor"
The Dawn (Krasiński)
See *Przedświt*
"Dawn and Sunrise in the Snowy Mountains" (Harpur) **114**:158
Dawn Island (Martineau) **137**:250
"A Dawn on the Lievre" (Lampman) **25**:190, 205, 210
"Dawnings of Genius" (Clare) **9**:72, 74, 105, 120; **86**:173
"The Day after To-Morrow" (Patmore) **9**:349, 358
"The Day After Tomorrow" (Stevenson) **63**:239
"Day and Night" (Tyutchev)
See "Den i noch"
Day and Night Songs (Allingham) **25**:7, 16, 22
"The Day Before the St. Petersburg Flood of 1824" (Mickiewicz)
See "The Day Preceding the St. Petersburg Flood of 1824"
"The Day Dream" (Coleridge) **99**:104
"A Day! Help! Help! Another Day!" (Dickinson) **77**:161
"A Day in an English Village Tavern" (Bestuzhev)
See "Den' v traktire Angliiskogo gorodka"
"A Day in Surrey with William Morris" (Lazarus) **8**:423
"A Day in the Wilderness" (Frederic) **10**:203
"The Day is Done" (Longfellow) **45**:116, 135, 151-52, 187; **103**:293
"The Day Is Gone" (Keats) **73**:155
"The Day of Dead Soldiers" (Lazarus) **8**:413
"Day of the Dead" (Silva)
See "Día de difuntos"
"The Day of the Lord is at Hand, at Hand!" (Kingsley) **35**:206, 219
"The Day of Tomorrow" (Eminescu)
See "Ziua de mâine"
"The Day of Trial" (Griffin) **7**:214
"The Day Preceding the St. Petersburg Flood of 1824" (Mickiewicz) **3**:401
"A Day with the Surrey" (Surtees) **14**:376
"Daybreak" (Dana) **53**:158, 178
"Day-Dream" (Bryant) **6**:165, 168
"The Day-dream" (Tennyson) **65**:232
"a Day-dream at Tintagel" (Poe) **94**:229
"A Daydream in Summer" (Clare) **86**:90
"Daydreams" (Lonnrot) **53**:339
"Day-Dreams" (Rossetti) **50**:293
"Daylight and Moonlight" (Longfellow) **45**:160
"Days" (Emerson) **1**:290, 296, 299-300; **98**:177, 184, 191
Days Departed (Bowles) **103**:54
The Days of My Life (Oliphant) **11**:462; **61**:206, 209
A Day's Ride: A Life's Romance (Lever) **23**:286, 292, 302, 304
"Las de l'amer repos" (Mallarmé) **41**:250
"The Deacon and His Daughter" (Crawford) **12**:151, 172
Deacon Brodie; or, The Double Life: A Melodrama Founded on Facts (Stevenson) **5**:411, 421
"Deacons' Daughters and Ministers' Sons" (Parton) **86**:376
"The Deacon's Masterpiece; or, The Wonderful 'One-Hoss' Shay" (Holmes) **14**:109-10, 115-16, 119, 121, 125-26, 128, 143; **81**:98-99, 107
"The Deacon's Week" (Cooke) **110**:14, 18, 43
"The Dead" (Silva)
See "Muertos"
"The Dead" (Very) **9**:373, 378, 397
"Dead Achilles" (Meyer)
See "Der tote Achill"
"The Dead Are in the Silent Graves" (Hood) **16**:222
"The Dead Babe" (Field) **3**:208
"Dead before Death" (Rossetti) **2**:557; **50**:310; **66**:341
"Dead Cities" (Lampman) **25**:210
"The Dead City" (Rossetti) **66**:306
"The Dead Drummer Boy" (Barham) **77**:35
"The Dead Eagle" (Campbell) **19**:183
"The Dead Feast of the Kol-Folk" (Whittier) **8**:516; **59**:360
"Dead Friends" (Meyer)
See "Die toten Freunde"
"The Dead Horse" (Bertrand) **31**:54
"Dead Language" (Patmore) **9**:361
"The Dead Leman" (Gautier) **1**:347
"The Dead Man: A Folktale from Funen" (Andersen) **79**:86
"The Dead Man's Dream" (Darley) **2**:127, 130
"The Dead Man's Grave" (Moodie) **14**:231
"A Dead Man's Love" (Lermontov) **5**:299
"The Dead Pan" (Browning) **1**:124, 128; **66**:44

"The Dead Princess and the Seven Heroes" (Pushkin)
See "Skazka o Mertvoy Tsarevne"
"The Dead Prophet" (Tennyson) **65**:380-1
"A Dead Secret" (O'Brien) **21**:242
The Dead Secret (Collins) **1**:174, 178-79, 182, 184-85; **93**:46-7, 53, 64
"Dead Souls" (Silva)
See "Las almas muertas"
Dead Souls (Gogol)
See *Tchitchikoff's Journey; or Dead Souls*
"The Dead Stone-Breaker" (Crabbe) **26**:103
"The Dead Year" (Thomson) **18**:394, 406, 414
Deaf and Dumb (Holcroft)
See *Deaf and Dumb; or, the Orphan Protected*
Deaf and Dumb; or, the Orphan Protected (Holcroft) **85**:199, 212, 223
"Deákpályám" (Petofi) **21**:279
Dealings with the Firm of Dombey and Son (Dickens) **3**:145, 147, 151, 156, 161, 172-73, 175, 178-79, 181; **8**:169, 171-72, 175-76, 178, 195, 199; **18**:119; **26**:175; **37**:168, 199; **86**:189, 221; **105**:228, 231, 330; **113**:29, 42, 68, 97, 107, 144
Dean Dunham (Alger) **8**:43
The Dean's Doughter; or, The Days We Live In (Gore) **65**:22, 30
"Dear is my little Native Vale" (Rogers) **69**:66
"Dear Lord and Father of Mankind" (Whittier) **8**:520, 525
"Death" (Lampman) **25**:187
"Death" (Turgenev) **21**:413, 454
"Death among the Trees" (Sigourney) **87**:337
"Death and Love" (Rossetti) **77**:313, 339
"Death and the Fear of Dying" (Smith) **59**:303, 307, 309, 315, 322
"A Death at Sea" (Adams) **33**:4
"A Death in the Bush" (Kendall) **12**:179-80, 186, 189-90, 192, 201-02
"A Death in the Desert" (Browning) **19**:117, 130, 138, 153; **79**:133-34
"Death in the Kitchen" (Hood) **16**:235-36
"Death is the supple Suitor" (Dickinson) **77**:163, 173
"The Death of a Devotee" (Carleton) **3**:92
"The Death of A. G. A." (Brontë) **16**:123
"Death of a Son of the Late Honorable Fisher Ames" (Sigourney) **87**:337
"Death of a Youn Musician" (Sigourney) **87**:337
"Death of a Young Lady at the Retreat for the Insane" (Sigourney) **87**:337
"Death of a Young Wife" (Sigourney) **87**:337
"The Death of Adaline" (Chivers) **49**:48
The Death of Adam (Klopstock) **11**:218, 231
"The Death of an Infant" (Sigourney) **21**:299, 310; **87**:326
"The Death of Artemidora" (Landor) **14**:181-82, 190-91
"The Death of Artists" (Baudelaire)
See "La mort des artistes"
Death of Buda (Arany)
See *Buda halála*
"The Death of Byrhtnoth" (Lanier) **118**:216, 218
"The Death of Cicero" (Brown) **122**:119
"The Death of Dermid" (Ferguson) **33**:293
"The Death of Don Pedro" (Lockhart) **6**:297
"Death of General Brock" (Richardson) **55**:342
The Death of General Montgomery in Storming the City of Quebec (Brackenridge) **7**:44, 47, 50
"The Death of Jonathan" (Lamartine) **11**:249
The Death of King Buda (Arany)
See *Buda halála*
"The Death of Lovers" (Baudelaire)
See "La mort des amants"
The Death of Marlowe: a Tragedy in One Act (Horne) **127**:236, 238, 256-57, 263, 269-71
"Death of Mrs. Harriet W. L. Winslow" (Sigourney) **87**:337
"The Death of Oenone" (Tennyson) **30**:233; **115**:337
"The Death of Paris" (Morris) **4**:447-48
"The Death of Prince Frederick" (Darwin) **106**:181
"The Death of Raschi" (Lazarus) **109**:325, 337, 342
The Death of Richelieu (Dumas) **71**:219
"The Death of Slavery" (Bryant) **6**:169, 174
"Death of Socrates" (Lamartine)
See *La morte de Socrate*
"Death of the Dauphin" (Daudet) **1**:238
"The Death of the Devil" (Chivers) **49**:78
"The Death of the Flowers" (Bryant) **6**:168-69, 171-72, 177, 183; **46**:3, 9, 26
"Death of the Orphan" (Solomos) **15**:389
"Death of the Poet" (Lermontov)
See "Smert' poeta"
The Death of the Poet (Tieck)
See *Der Tod des Dichters*
"The Death of the Poor" (Baudelaire)
See "La mort des pauvres"
"Death of the Rev. Alfred Mitchell" (Sigourney) **87**:337
"Death of the Rev. Gordon Hall" (Sigourney) **87**:337
"Death of the Rev. W. C. Walton" (Sigourney) **87**:337
"The Death of the Sergeant" (Isaacs)
See "La muerte del sargento"
"Death of the Shepherd" (Solomos) **15**:389
"Death of the Wife of a Clergyman, during the Sickness of Her Husband" (Sigourney) **87**:337
"The Death of the Wolf" (Vigny)
See "La mort du loup"
"The Death of Time" (Chivers) **49**:57
"The Death of Wind-Foot" (Whitman) **81**:343
"Death opens her sweet white arms" (Fuller) **50**:243
"The Death Raven" (Borrow) **9**:54
"Death Ride" (Meyer)
See "Der Ritt in den Tod"
"The Death Song of a Gaelic Warrior of the Sixth Century" (Leconte de Lisle) **29**:236
"The Death Song of the Cherokee" (Freneau) **111**:166
"Death, That Struck when I Was Most Confiding" (Brontë) **16**:87, 122
"Death to the Invalid" (Martineau) **137**:283, 295
"The Death-Bed" (Hood) **16**:216, 219
"The Death-Bed" (Opie) **65**:159, 179
Death's Jest Book; or, The Fool's Tragedy (Beddoes) **6**:26-37, 39-41
"Death's Ramble" (Hood) **16**:224, 237
"The Debate" (Lermontov) **126**:142, 144
"The Debate in the Sennit" (Lowell) **90**:219
"The Debate over the Election of Mr. Maiorescu" (Eminescu) **131**:325
"La débauche" (Gautier) **1**:348
Debit and Credit (Freytag)
See *Soll und Haben*
"Deborah's Book" (Ingelow) **107**:162
"The Debtor" (Freneau) **111**:132
Debutante; or, the London Season (Gore) **65**:21
"Les débuts d'un aventurier" (Mérimée) **6**:353-4, 356; **65**:79-80, 83, 88
"Decay A Ballad" (Clare) **86**:169
A Decayed Family (Leskov)
See *Zaxudalyj rod*
Decebalus (Eminescu) **33**:264
"Deceived" (Lonnrot) **53**:339
"December Night" (Musset)
See "Nuit de Décembre"
"December XXXI." (Cooke) **110**:3
"Deception" (Leskov)
See "Obman"
Declaration of American Independence (Jefferson)
See *In Congress, July 4, 1776: A Declaration by the Representatives of the United States of America, in General Congress Assembled*
Declaration of Independence (Jefferson)
See *In Congress, July 4, 1776: A Declaration by the Representatives of the United States of America, in General Congress Assembled*
"Déclin" (Corbière) **43**:25, 27
The Decline and Fall of the English System of Finance (Paine) **62**:262, 368
"The Decline of Faith" (Hayne) **94**:167
Decline of the Heroic Age (Grundtvig) **1**:401
"Décourageux" (Corbière) **43**:11, 31-4
"Découverte" (Maupassant) **42**:174
A Decrepit Clan (Leskov)
See *Zaxudalyj rod*
"Le dedans du désespoir" (Hugo) **10**:357
Dédicaces (Verlaine) **2**:622; **51**:351, 362, 372
"Dedication" (Crabbe) **121**:85
"A Dedication" (Gordon) **21**:150, 163-64, 167, 175-76, 184-87
"Dedication" (Keble) **87**:199
"Dedication" (Lamartine) **11**:246
"Dedication" (Lamb) **113**:202
"Dedication" (Tennyson) **65**:349
"A Dedication" (Timrod) **25**:361, 372, 375
"Dedication" (Whittier) **8**:520
Dedication (Goethe) **4**:163
Dedications (Verlaine)
See *Dédicaces*
"Dedicatory Sonnet: To S. T. Coleridge" (Coleridge) **90**:32
"Dedikation" (Claudius) **75**:207
"Deeds" (Lampman) **25**:199, 210
"The Deep" (Sigourney) **87**:332-33
The Deep, Deep Sea; or, Perseus and Andromeda (Planché) **42**:273, 286, 302
"Deep in Earth" (Poe) **55**:214
Deerbrook (Martineau) **26**:310-11, 315, 317, 319, 322-23, 329-33, 349, 357; **137**:253-55, 259-62, 304, 309-13, 329, 331-32
The Deerslayer; or, The First War-Path (Cooper) **1**:205, 207-11, 214, 221-24; **27**:126, 129-30, 132-35, 138-41, 143, 151-54, 158, 186-88; **54**:258-9, 262, 269, 276
The Defeat (Warren) **13**:425-26
"Defects in the English Constitution" (Dyer) **129**:110
"Ein defekter locus communis" (Claudius) **75**:213
"The Defence" (Adams)
See "A Defence of the Constitutions of Government of the United States, Against the Attack of Mr Turgot"
"Defence" (Longfellow) **103**:295
"The Defence of Guenevere" (Morris) **4**:412, 420-22, 424, 429-31, 441-44
"The Defence of Lucknow" (Tennyson) **30**:295
"A Defence of Poetry" (Shelley) **93**:258, 295, 310, 312-13
A Defence of Poetry (Shelley) **18**:333, 337, 347, 349-51, 353-55, 357, 363, 371, 384; **93**:266-67, 275, 278, 327, 344-46, 357
"A Defence of the Constitutions of Government of the United States, Against the Attack of Mr Turgot" (Adams) **106**:11-13, 35-40, 44-7, 54, 66, 79-80
A Defence of the Rockingham Party (Godwin) **130**:49
Défense du Génie du christianisme (Chateaubriand) **134**:24, 26-30
The Defense of Guenevere, and Other Poems (Morris) **4**:412, 418-19, 425-26, 434, 441, 444
Defense of Usury (Bentham) **38**:37, 44
"A Defense of Whigs" (Kennedy) **2**:430, 432
"The Definition of Poetry" (Bestuzhev)
See "Opredelenie poezii"
The Deformed Transformed (Byron) **2**:68, 72, 80; **109**:123

"The Degree to Which Popular Tradition Has Participated in the Development of Russian Literature" (Dobrolyubov) **5**:141
La dégringolade (Gaboriau) **14**:20
Dei Sepolcri (Foscolo)
See *I sepolcri*
Déidamie (Banville) **9**:22
"Deirdre" (Ferguson) **33**:279-80, 285, 290, 298
"Dejaneira" (Arnold) **6**:37
"Dejection" (Baratynsky) **103**:7
"Dejection: An Ode" (Coleridge) **54**:66, 70; **99**:5, 19, 81-3; 111;226
"Dekletam" (Preseren) **127**:329
Del dicho al hecho (Tamayo y Baus) **1**:569
Del dramma storico (Manzoni) **98**:216
"Del influjo de la religión cristiana en la literatura" (Martínez de la Rosa) **102**:254
Del principe e delle lettere (Alfieri) **101**:14, 41, 51-2, 58, 62, 69, 76-8, 84, 86
Del romanzo storico (Manzoni) **29**:276, 305, 308-09
"Delay Has Danger" (Crabbe) **26**:100, 110, 130-31; **121**:55, 84-6, 88
"The Delectable Ballad of the Waller Lot" (Field) **3**:211
"Delfica" (Nerval) **1**:478, 486-87; **67**:307, 316, 363
"Deliciae sapientiae de amore" (Patmore) **9**:335, 339, 347, 359, 361
"Delilah" (Gordon) **21**:164, 166
Delineations of American Scenery and Character (Audubon) **47**:14-15, 18
Les Deliquescences (Verlaine) **51**:361-62
"Délires" (Rimbaud) **4**:466; **82**:222, 226, 229, 231, 234, 238-39, 241, 245
"Délires I" (Rimbaud) **4**:481; **35**:291-94, 302, 310, 317, 319; **82**:230-31, 241-42, 245-46, 255, 257
"Délires II" (Rimbaud) **4**:481; **35**:302, 311-12, 317, 319, 324; **82**:232-33, 240-41, 245, 247, 250, 255, 257-58, 260-61
"The Dell" (Mitford) **4**:408
"Della poesia moderna" (Foscolo) **97**:89
Della tirannide (Alfieri) **101**:41-2, 45, 51-2, 62, 69, 73, 76, 79, 83-5
"Dell'educare la gioventú italiana" (Leopardi) **129**:329, 332
Dell'indipendenza dell'Italia (Manzoni) **98**:279
Dell'invenzione (Manzoni) **29**:276
"Dell'origine e dell'ufficio della letteratura: Orazione" (Foscolo) **8**:261
"Delora" (Horne) **127**:256, 271
Deloraine (Godwin) **14**:68, 70, 81-3
Delphine (Staël-Holstein) **3**:517, 523-25, 527, 529-30, 534; **91**:291-92, 297-98, 304-05, 308-10, 312, 3253-55, 359-60, 365
"Delphine et Hippolyte" (Baudelaire)
See "Femmes damnées"
"The Deluge" (Moodie) **113**:317
"Le déluge" (Vigny) **7**:472-73, 480-81; **102**:335, 367
"The Deluge" (Vigny)
See "Le déluge"
"Delusion" (Lenau) **16**:276
"Dely's Cow" (Cooke) **110**:44, 47
"Dem Allgegenwärtigen" (Klopstock) **11**:237
Dem Andenken des k. k. Lyceal-Bibliothekars in Laibach, Mathia Zhop (Preseren) **127**:305
"Dem Erlöser" (Klopstock) **11**:237
"Dem Unendlichen" (Klopstock) **11**:238
"Demagogues" (Kennedy) **2**:432
"Demarara" (Martineau) **26**:304
Demerara (Martineau) **137**:250-51, 260-61, 304, 324-25
"Demeter" (Isaacs) **70**:313
"Demeter and Persephone" (Tennyson) **30**:245; **65**:300
Demetrius (Schiller) **39**:335, 368, 371-72, 375, 380, 385; **69**:169, 243-45, 250
Demetrius: Eine Tragödie (Hebbel) **43**:230, 234, 238, 240, 246, 261-62, 283, 300
Demetrius Zaar von Moscou (Kotzebue) **25**:136, 140
Le demi-monde (Dumas) **9**:219-24, 227, 229, 231-32, 236-37, 240-41, 245-47, 250
The "Demi-Monde" (Dumas)
See *Le demi-monde*
"Democracy" (Arnold) **6**:46; **89**:36-7, 40, 62, 101-02; **126**:77, 88, 112-13
"Democracy" (Lowell) **2**:510
"Democracy" (Whitman) **4**:564
Democracy, and Other Addresses (Lowell) **2**:510
Democracy in America (Tocqueville)
See *De la démocratie en Amérique*
"Democratic Art" (Symonds) **34**:327
"Democratic Catechism" (Martí)
See "Catecismo democratico"
Democratic Legends of the North (Michelet) **31**:258
Democratic Vistas (Whitman) **4**:551, 566, 575, 581, 590, 594-95, 597, 601; **31**:397, 441-42; **81**:255, 295-96, 300, 332
"Démocratie" (Rimbaud) **35**:324; **82**:232-33, 238
"Democritus Junior; or, the Laughing Philosopher" (Dyer) **129**:114
La demoiselle à marier; ou, La première entrevue (Scribe) **16**:384, 393
"Les demoiselles de Bienfilâtre" (Villiers de l'Isle Adam) **3**:581
Les demoiselles de Saint-Cyr (Dumas) **71**:209
"Les demoiselles Malfilatre" (Villiers de l'Isle Adam) **3**:588
"The Demon" (Lermontov) **126**:215, 217, 223-24
"The Demon" (Pushkin) **83**:248, 253, 299
The Demon (Lermontov) **5**:289, 291, 293, 295, 300; **47**:160, 188; **126**:128, 130-32, 138, 140, 144-45
"Le démon de l'analogie" (Mallarmé) **4**:371; **41**:251, 280
Le démon du foyer (Sand) **42**:314
"The Demon of Perversity" (Poe)
See "The Imp of the Perverse"
"Demonism" (Eminescu) **33**:261, 263; **131**:287
"The Demon's Cave" (Darley) **2**:133
"The Demon's Cave" (Whittier) **59**:363
"The Demon-Ship" (Hood) **16**:224, 235
"Demyàn's Fish Soup" (Krylov) **1**:435
An den erwarteten Sohn (Humboldt) **134**:167
"An den Frühling" (Hölderlin) **16**:181
"Den' v traktire Angliiskogo gorodka" (Bestuzhev) **131**:165
"Deniehy's Grave" (Kendall) **12**:194
Denis Duval (Thackeray) **5**:463, 474, 490; **14**:452; **43**:357
"Denis Haggerty's Wife" (Thackeray) **43**:381
"Denis O'Shaughnessy Going to Maynooth" (Carleton) **3**:88-89, 91, 93, 95
Denise (Dumas) **9**:228, 231-32, 243, 247, 250
"Dennis Delany" (Hogg) **109**:201
The Denounced (Banim and Banim) **13**:121, 147, 149
"Une dentelle s'abolit" (Mallarmé) **4**:393; **41**:274, 281, 294, 297-98, 300-01, 304-05
"Denys l'Auxerrois" (Pater) **7**:298, 307, 312; **90**:245, 272, 288, 333, 336
Deontology (Bentham) **38**:40, 44, 48-51, 80, 84, 87
"Départ" (Rimbaud) **35**:322-23
"Depart de Lyon" (Desbordes-Valmore) **97**:23
"Départ pour le sabbat" (Bertrand) **31**:48
"The Departed" (Hemans) **71**:264
"Departure" (Patmore) **9**:343
The Departure from the Theatre (Gogol)
See *Teatral'nyi raz'ezd posle predstavleniia novoi komedii*
"The Departure of Hannah More from Barley Wood, at the Age of Eighty-Three" (Sigourney) **21**:293
"Derevnia" (Turgenev) **122**:308
"Derevnya" (Pushkin) **83**:305
Le Dernier amour (Sand) **57**:316
"Le dernier chant de pèlerinage de Childe Harold" (Lamartine) **11**:245-47, 268, 270
"Le dernier des Maourys" (Leconte de Lisle) **29**:226-27
Le dernier jour d'un condamné (Hugo) **3**:235, 239-40; **10**:367; **21**:192, 225
"Dernier mot" (Amiel) **4**:14
"Le dernier souvenir" (Leconte de Lisle) **29**:228
La Dernière Aldini (Sand) **57**:312, 316
La dernière fée (Balzac) **5**:58
La Derniere Fete galante (Verlaine) **51**:362
Le dernière idole (Daudet) **1**:231, 249
La dernière incarnation de Vautrien (Balzac) **5**:46
La Dernière mode (Mallarmé) **41**:249, 294
"La Dernière nuit de travail" (Vigny) **102**:361-62
"La dernière vision" (Leconte de Lisle) **29**:222, 228
Dernières nouvelles (Mérimée) **6**:355
Derniéres Poésites (de Navarre)
See *Essays*
"Dernières Reflexions" (Pixérécourt) **39**:280-81
Derniers poèmes (Leconte de Lisle) **29**:221, 235
"Derniers vers" (Rimbaud) **4**:472; **35**:321, 323; **82**:240, 263
Les derniers vers de Jules Laforgue (Laforgue) **5**:270-1, 273, 276-80, 282-3; **53**:258-9, 261-5, 272, 278, 280-2, 289-92, 294-5, 297-300
"La derrochadora" (Casal) **131**:258-60, 264-65
Derry: A Tale of the Revolution in 1688 (Tonna) **135**:203
"Des Arztes Vermächtnis" (Droste-Hülshoff) **3**:196, 199, 201-02
"Des Baches Wiegenlied" (Muller) **73**:363, 365, 374, 376
"Des bells chalonnaises" (Banville) **9**:16
Des circonstances actuelles qui peuvent terminer la Révolution et des principles qui dolvent fonder la répuldique en France (Staël-Holstein) **91**:291
Des Dichters Leben (Tieck) **5**:514, 526; **46**:397
Des Feldpredigers Schmelzle Reise nach Fätz mit fortgehenden Noten: Nebst der Beichte des Teufels bey einem Staatsmanne (Jean Paul) **7**:339, 241
Des Fleurs de bonne volonté (Laforgue) **5**:276, 281-2; **53**:256-7, 272, 278, 290, 298-301
"Des Hallucinations et des songes en matiére criminelle" (Nodier) **19**:400
"Des Kaisers Bildsäule" (Grillparzer) **102**:175
Des Knaben Wunderhorn (Arnim) **5**:12, 19
Des Knaben Wunderhorn: Alte deutsche Lieder (Brentano) **1**:95, 98-99
Des Lebens Überfluss (Tieck) **5**:532
Des Meeres und der Liebe Wellen (Grillparzer) **1**:384-85, 390; **102**:83, 88, 90, 93, 95, 111, 118, 149, 165-66, 170, 187
"Des Morgens" (Hölderlin) **16**:181, 184
"Des Müllers Blumen" (Muller) **73**:363-64
"Des Négociations relatives à la Grèce" (Chateaubriand) **134**:8
Des Oeuvres Complètes de M. Paul de Kock (Kock) **16**:251
"Des Sängers Klage" (Preseren) **127**:315
Des types en littérature (Nodier) **19**:379, 392
Des vers (Maupassant) **1**:455
El desafío del diablo (Zorrilla y Moral) **6**:523
"Descartes" (Huxley) **67**:87
"A Descent into the Maelström" (Poe) **1**:500, 514, 518; **16**:294-96, 301, 303, 306, 315, 331-34; **78**:258; **117**:224, 264, 269, 320
The Descent of Liberty (Hunt) **1**:412, 423; **70**:292
The Descent of Man, and Selection in Relation to Sex (Darwin) **57**:142-3, 147-52, 163, 165, 172, 174
"La descente aux enfers" (Beranger) **34**:41

"Description of Bethlehem; in the State of Pennsylvania" (Murray) **63**:181
"Description of New-York one-hundred and fifty years hence" (Freneau) **111**:124
"Description of Recently Founded Communist colonies Still in Existence" (Engels) **85**:124, 180
"A Description of Spinoza's System" (Schleiermacher) **107**:328
A Description of the Ride to Hulne Abbey (Percy) **95**:313, 328
A Descriptive Catalogue (Blake) **13**:159; **127**:64
Descriptive Sketches (Wordsworth) **12**:385-86; **38**:363; **111**:214, 262
Desde mi celda (Bécquer)
See *Cartas literarias desde mi celda*
"El Desdichado" (Nerval) **1**:476, 478, 480-82, 485, 488; **67**:305-07, 316-17, 356, 359-60
"Le désert" (Leconte de Lisle) **29**:223, 225
"The Desert-Born" (Hood) **16**:222, 235-36
"Deserted" (Bellamy) **86**:75
The Deserted Daughter (Holcroft) **85**:192, 206, 222-23, 225
"The Deserted Farm-House" (Freneau) **111**:141, 148, 151
"The Deserted Garden" (Browning) **1**:117
"The Deserted House" (Tennyson) **30**:222
Deserted Village (Dickens) **113**:147
The Deserted Wife (Southworth) **26**:431-32, 437, 443, 445-46
"The Deserter" (Frederic) **10**:203
"The Deserter" (Landon) **15**:161
"Les déserts de l'amour" (Rimbaud) **4**:484, 486; **35**:290-91; **82**:226, 253
"Le désespoir" (Lamartine) **11**:245, 254, 264, 272, 279, 282
"The Desire" (Eminescu) **131**:296
"Desire" (Lermontov) **126**:223
"Desire" (Zhukovsky)
See "Zhelanie"
"Desire for Travel" (Grillparzer)
See "Reiselust"
"The Desire to Be a Man" (Zorrilla y Moral) **3**:590
Desmond: A Novel (Smith) **23**:317, 319, 322, 325-29, 333, 335-36, 338, 340; **115**:126, 134, 136, 140, 142, 144-47, 158-64, 167-68, 207, 210-11, 223-26
"Desolation" (Baratynsky)
See "Zapustenie"
"Despair" (Lamartine)
See "Le désespoir"
"Despair" (Tennyson) **30**:245, 254
"The Despairing Wanderer" (Opie) **65**:155
"La despedida del patriota griego" (Espronceda) **39**:106, 108
"The Desperado" (Turgenev)
See "Otchayanny"
"A Desperate Character" (Turgenev)
See "Otchayanny"
"Despised and Rejected" (Rossetti) **2**:559
"Despondency" (Arnold) **29**:27
"Despondency" (Lampman) **25**:187, 194, 196-97, 209, 219
"Despondency and Aspiration" (Hemans) **71**:270
Despot Voda (Eminescu) **131**:292
"Después da la victoria" (Isaacs) **70**:311
"Le dessous de cartes d'une partie de whist" (Barbey d'Aurevilly) **1**:74-75
Les Destinees (Vigny)
See *Les destinées: Poèmes philosophiques*
Les destinées de la poésie (Lamartine) **11**:276
Les destinées: Poèmes philosophiques (Vigny) **7**:469-71, 474, 478-86; **102**:353
The Destinies: Philosophical Poems (Vigny)
See *Les destinées: Poèmes philosophiques*
"Destiny" (Byron) **109**:293
"Destiny" (Emerson) **38**:189
"The Destiny of Nations" (Coleridge) **54**:68-9; **99**:105
Destiny; or, The Chief's Daughter (Ferrier) **8**:238, 240, 242-44, 246-52, 255-56
"The Destiny that Spanned Two Lifetimes" (Ueda Akinari)
See "Nise no en"
"La destruction" (Baudelaire) **6**:123; **55**:48, 74-5, 79-80
"The Destruction of Aesthetics" (Pisarev)
See "Razrushenie estetiki"
"The Destruction of Babylon" (Moodie) **113**:317
"The Destruction of Babylon" (Trumbull) **30**:345
"The Destruction of Psara" (Solomos) **15**:386
"The Destruction of Sennacherib" (Byron) **2**:88
"The Destruction of the Pequods" (Dwight) **13**:270, 272, 278
"Desultory Thoughts upon the Utility of Encouraging a Degree of Self-Complacency, Especially in Female Bosoms" (Murray) **63**:184, 206, 210
"Detached Pieces" (Austen) **119**:13
"Detached Thoughts on Books and Reading" (Lamb) **10**:440
"Details of Episcopal Life" (Leskov)
See "Meloči arxierejskoj žizni"
Determination of the Concept of a Race of Men (Kant) **67**:215
Detraction Displayed (Opie) **65**:171, 203-4
Detskie gody (Leskov) **25**:253, 258
Deukalion (Taylor)
See "The Eye and the Ear"
Der deutsche Bauernkrieg (Engels) **85**:117, 132, 144, 185
Die Deutsche Gelehrtenrepublik (Klopstock) **11**:227, 234-36, 238
Deutsche Grammatik (Grimm and Grimm) **3**:216-17, 219-20
Die deutsche Hausfrau (Kotzebue) **25**:141
Die deutsche Ideologie (Engels) **85**:44, 93,97, 109-10, 115-17, 120, 126-28, 157; **114**:52-4, 69-70, 83-6
Der deutsche Mann und die vornehmen Leute (Kotzebue) **25**:145
Deutsche Mythologie (Grimm and Grimm) **3**:216-17, 220
Deutsche Rechtsalterthümer (Grimm and Grimm) **3**:216-17
Deutsche Sagen (Grimm and Grimm) **3**:219
Die deutschen Kleinstädter (Kotzebue) **25**:143
Deutsches Wörterbuch (Grimm and Grimm) **3**:216-17
Deutschland: Ein Wintermärchen (Heine) **4**:236, 240, 243, 245-46, 252, 265-67; **54**:312, 337-8, 340, 347
"Deutschland und seine Fürsten" (Schiller) **39**:388
"Deux amis" (Maupassant) **83**:181
"Deux augures" (Villiers de l'Isle Adam) **3**:589-90
Les deux aveugles de Chamouny (Nodier) **19**:381, 384
"Les Deux Bonnes Soeurs" (Baudelaire) **55**:74, 77
"Deux chiens" (Desbordes-Valmore) **97**:5
"Les deux héritages" (Mérimée) **6**:362; **65**:79-84
"Les Deux mères" (Desbordes-Valmore) **97**:23
"Le deux mîtresses" (Musset) **7**:264
"Les Deux peupliers" (Desbordes-Valmore) **97**:5, 15
"Les deux pigeons" (Laforgue) **5**:278, 281
"Les Deux ramiers" (Desbordes-Valmore) **97**:5
"Development" (Newman) **99**:297, 300
Development of Christian Doctrine (Newman)
See *An Essay on the Development of Christian Doctrine*
Development of Doctrine (Newman)
See *An Essay on the Development of Christian Doctrine*
"The Development of English Literature" (Clough) **27**:101-2
The Development of Socialism from a Utopia to a Science (Engels)
See *Die Entwicklung des Sozialismus von der Uopie zur Wissenschaft*
Devereux (Bulwer-Lytton) **1**:145-46, 150, 155; **45**:13, 21, 24, 32, 34, 55, 68-70
"The Devil and the Lady" (Tennyson) **30**:282; **65**:248-9
"The Devil and Tom Walker" (Irving) **2**:391; **19**:336
"The Devil in Manuscript" (Hawthorne) **2**:332; **95**:176, 184
"The Devil in the Belfry" (Poe) **16**:301, 323
"The Devil of Jóka" (Arany)
See "Jóka ördöge"
"The Devil-Drive" (Leskov)
See "Čertogon"
"The Devils" (Pushkin)
See "Besy"
The Devils (Dostoevsky)
See *Besy*
The Devil's Elixir (Hoffmann)
See *Die Elixiere des Teufels*
"The Devil's Putty and Varnish" (Shaw) **15**:341
"The Devil's Sooty Brother" (Grimm and Grimm) **3**:227
Devocionario (Gómez de Avellaneda) **111**:29
"Dévotion" (Rimbaud) **35**:293, 323-24; **82**:233
"Devotion: An Epistle" (Brown) **122**:91, 96
Devotional Exercises (Martineau) **26**:310, 312; **137**:326, 329, 335-36
The Dewy Morn (Jefferies) **47**:93, 98, 101-03, 112-13, 117-19, 137
"Dezvoltarea istorica a României" (Eminescu) **131**:326
Dharmatattwa (Chatterji) **19**:216, 222, 225
"Día de difuntos" (Silva) **114**:294, 301-2, 313
Día de difuntos (Silva) **114**:262, 272
"Día de difuntos de 1836" (Larra) **130**:209, 224, 238, 274
"El día de difuntos de 1836" (Larra) **17**:273, 276, 284-85
"Le diable" (Maupassant) **83**:182
Le diable aux champs (Sand) **42**:314, 346-49
El diablo mundo (Espronceda) **39**:84-7, 90-1, 94, 97-8, 101, 108-10, 112-13, 118-21
Les diaboliques (Barbey d'Aurevilly) **1**:70-1, 73-9
Dialectic (Schleiermacher)
See *Dialektik*
"Dialectics" (Engels) **85**:38
Dialectics of Nature (Engels)
See *Dialektik der Natur*
Dialektik (Schleiermacher) **107**:285, 323, 325, 382
Dialektik der Natur (Engels) **85**:10, 12, 24, 36-44, 95, 105-06
"Dialog om sättet att sluta stycken" (Almqvist) **42**:9, 11, 16
Dialogo della natura e di un islandese (Leopardi) **129**:247, 255, 259
Dialogo di Federico Ruysch e delle sue mummie (Leopardi) **129**:232, 344, 350
"Dialogo di Plotino e di Porfirio" (Leopardi) **129**:250, 257-58
"Dialogo di Torquato Tasso e del suo genio familiare" (Leopardi) **129**:267
"Dialogo di un venditore d'almanacchi e di un passaggero" (Leopardi) **129**:243
"Dialogos" (Solomos) **15**:389, 402, 405
"A Dialogue" (Shelley) **18**:342
"Dialogue" (Solomos)
See "Dialogos"
"A Dialogue between Cadmus and Hercules" (Montagu) **117**:182
"A Dialogue between the Head and Heart of an Irish Protestant" (Ferguson) **33**:295
"Dialogue for Three Young Ladies" (Rowson) **69**:117
"A Dialogue in the Reading Room" (Hogg) **109**:262
"Dialogue in the Shades" (Barbauld) **50**:14

"Dialogue on How to Conclude Pieces" (Almqvist)
See "Dialog om sättet att sluta stycken"
Dialogue on Poetry (Schlegel)
See *Gespräch über die Poesie*
The Dialogue upon the Gardens at Stow (Gilpin) **30**:36, 43
"Dialogues" (Brown) **74**:170, 174
Dialogues between a Pair of Tongues (Wieland) **17**:393
Dialogues et fragments philosophiques (Renan) **26**:374-75, 380, 394-95, 397, 408, 413
Dialogues of the Dead (Montagu) **117**:135, 141, 152, 158, 178-79, 182
"Dialogues of the Living" (Brown) **74**:40
Der Diamant des Geisterkönigs (Raimund) **69**:5, 7, 10, 21, 23, 31-3, 37, 43, 47
Der Diamant: Eine Komödie in fünf Acten (Hebbel) **43**:255, 297
Les diamants de la couronne (Scribe) **16**:384
"Diamantul Nordului" (Eminescu) **131**:348
The Diamond (Hebbel)
See *Der Diamant: Eine Komödie in fünf Acten*
The Diamond and the Pearl (Gore) **65**:32
"The Diamond Lens" (O'Brien) **21**:234-38, 240, 242, 244-51, 253-55
"The Diamond Necklace" (Maupassant)
See "La parure"
The Diamond of the King of Spirits (Raimund)
See *Der Diamant des Geisterkönigs*
"The Diamond of the North" (Eminescu)
See "Diamantul Nordului"
The Diamond of the Spirit-king (Raimund)
See *Der Diamant des Geisterkönigs*
Diana (Warner) **31**:349-51
Diana and Persis (Alcott) **58**:69
Diana Trelawny (Oliphant) **61**:202, 207
Diana's Tree (Da Ponte)
See *L'arbore dri Diana*
Diane (Augier) **31**:4, 8, 11, 14, 23, 34
Diane au Bois (Banville) **9**:18, 20, 22
Diane de Lys (Dumas) **9**:219, 224, 228, 230, 239, 240, 247, 249
"Diaphaneité" (Pater) **7**:304, 312, 333-34; **90**:260, 272-73, 287, 295-90, 298, 305
"Diapsalmata" (Kierkegaard) **125**:230, 248
Diario de un testigo de la guerra de Africa (Alarcon) **1**:12, 14
Diario íntimo (Gómez de Avellaneda) **111**:54
Diary (Allingham) **25**:18-21, 23, 26
Diary (Macha) **46**:215
Diary (De Quincey)
See *A Diary of Thomas De Quincy, 1803*
Diary (Shevchenko) **54**:386-7
Diary and Autobiography of John Adams (Adams) **106**:66
Diary and Letters of Madame d'Arblay (Burney) **12**:26-34, 36-7, 61; **107**:40
A Diary in America, with Remarks on Its Institutions (Marryat) **3**:312-15, 319-20
The Diary of a Cosmopolitan (Sacher-Masoch) **31**:292
The Diary of a Desennuyee (Gore) **65**:26
"Diary of a Madman" (Gogol) **31**:95, 110; **5**:219-20, 227, 232, 236, 241, 252
"The Diary of a Plain Girl" (Levy) **59**:108
The Diary of a Scoundrel (Ostrovsky)
See *Na vsyakogo mudretsa dovolno prostoty*
"The Diary of a Superfluous Man" (Turgenev)
See "Dnevnik lišnego čeloveka"
The Diary of a Writer (Dostoevsky)
See *Dnevnik pisatelya*
Diary of an Ennuyée (Jameson) **43**:304, 319, 322, 333-38
"The Diary of Anne Rodway" (Collins) **1**:187
The Diary of Dr. John William Polidori (Polidori) **51**:206
Diary of EBB: The Unpublished Diary of Elizabeth Barrett Browning (Browning) **61**:50
Diary of Marie Bashkirtseff (Bashkirtseff)
See *Le journal de Marie Bashkirtseff*
"Diary of the Seducer" (Kierkegaard) **125**:182, 189-90, 198-200, 202-3, 206-8, 210-12, 214, 229-30, 232, 248, 250, 269, 279
Diary of the Voyage of H.M.S. Beagle (Darwin) **57**:113, 116, 143, 152
A Diary of Thomas De Quincy, 1803 (De Quincey) **87**:60, 75-7, 72
Diary, Reminiscences, and Correspondence of Henry Crabb Robinson (Robinson) **15**:172-73, 176-83, 185-87
Diaries (Carroll) **139**:62, 65
Der Dichter und der Komponist (Hoffmann) **2**:347, 350
Dichter und ihre Gesellen (Eichendorff) **8**:222
"Dichters Blumenstrauss" (Brentano) **1**:95
"Dichters Naturgelfül" (Droste-Hülshoff) **3**:202
Dichtung und Wahrheit (Goethe) **34**:58, 69, 122
"Dickens in Relation to Criticism" (Lewes) **25**:280, 286, 306, 308, 317, 322
Dickinson (Dickinson)
See *Poems, second series*
"Dickon the Devil" (Le Fanu) **9**:320
Dictionary of Poetical Quotations (Hale) **75**:284, 341
Dictionary of Received Ideas (Flaubert)
See *Dictionnaire des idées recues*
A Dictionary of the English Language, Compiled for the Use of Common Schools in the United States (Webster) **30**:396
Dictionnaire des idées recues (Flaubert) **2**:167; **62**:69-70, 72-3, 94; **66**:263, 274
"Did I?" (Cooke) **110**:4
"Did the Harebell Loose Her Girdle" (Dickinson) **21**:41
"Diddling Considered as One of the Exact Sciences" (Poe) **16**:312, 323
"Diderot" (Carlyle) **70**:57
Diderot à Pétersbourg (Sacher-Masoch) **31**:288
Didymus the Clerk (Foscolo) **8**:262-63
"An die aufgelöste Preußische Nationalversammlung" (Arnim) **123**:8
"An die Deutschen" (Hölderlin) **16**:194
An die Freude (Schiller)
See *Lied an die Freude*
"An die Geliebte" (Mörike) **10**:449
"An die Hofnung" (Hölderlin) **16**:181
"An die jungen Dichter" (Hölderlin) **16**:190
"An Die Natur im Spätsommer" (Meyer) **81**:140-41, 145-48, 151, 151
"An die Sammlung" (Grillparzer) **102**:170
"An die Schriftstellerinnen in Deutschland und Frankreich" (Droste-Hülshoff) **3**:202
An die Slowenen die in deutscher Sprache dichten (Preseren) **127**:306
"An die Sonne" (Schiller) **39**:338, 355
"An die Vollendung" (Hölderlin) **16**:174
Dies Buch Gehört dem König (Arnim) **38**:9, 16; **123**:5, 9, 11-12, 31, 42, 47-51, 62, 65, 69-70, 88-89, 92
"Dies Irae" (Leconte de Lisle) **29**:216, 235-36, 242-45
Dies Irae (Macaulay) **42**:116
Dietegen (Keller) **2**:415, 423
"Dieu" (Lamartine) **11**:269
Dieu (Hugo) **3**:273
"Le Dieu des bonnes gens" (Beranger) **34**:28
Le Dieu et la bayadère (Scribe) **16**:382, 409-10
Dieu et l'état (Bakunin) **25**:39, 50, 72; **58**:99
"Dieu et ma dame" (Patmore) **9**:341
Les Dieux antiques (Mallarmé) **41**:249, 277
"The Difference between History and Romance" (Brown) **74**:110, 192
Difficulties (Newman)
See *Lectures on Certain Difficulties Felt by Anglicans in submitting to the Catholic Church*
Difficulties of Anglicans (Newman)
See *Lectures on Certain Difficulties Felt by Anglicans in submitting to the Catholic Church*
Digging for Gold (Alger) **83**:114
"The Dignity of Woman" (Schiller) **39**:306
The Digression (Mickiewicz) **3**:401
Digte, første ring (Wergeland) **5**:536, 539-40
Dikter (Runeberg) **41**:313, 317, 325
"The Dilemma" (Holmes) **14**:109
Dilettantism in Science (Herzen) **10**:346; **61**:98
"La diligencia" (Larra) **17**:279
Dílo (Macha)
See *Dílo Karla Hynka Mácha*
Dílo Karla Hynka Mácha (Macha) **46**:202-3, 212, 218
"Dimanches" (Laforgue) **5**:280; **53**:292, 299
Dimitri Roudine (Turgenev)
See *Rudin*
"Dina la belle juive" (Borel) **41**:4, 6-7, 13
"The Dinkey Bird" (Field) **3**:210
"Dinner Real and Reputed" (De Quincey) **4**:61
Dinorah (Andersen) **79**:9
"Dion" (Wordsworth) **12**:427
"El Dios del siglo" (Isaacs) **70**:309
"Dios nos asista" (Larra) **17**:282; **130**:223
The Diplomatic Blunderbuss (Cobbett) **49**:109
Dipsychus (Clough) **27**:45, 53, 56, 69, 74, 76-80, 84-6, 97-101, 103, 105, 112-16, 119
"Dirce" (Landor) **14**:176, 183, 199
"Directions for Courtship" (Freneau) **111**:132
"Dirge" (Emerson) **98**:93, 179, 182
"A Dirge" (Levy) **59**:90
"A Dirge" (Rossetti) **2**:557
"A Dirge" (Tennyson) **30**:211, 223
"Dirge for a Soldier" (Boker) **125**:25, 31, 33, 39
"Dirge for Two Veterans" (Whitman) **31**:391
"The Dirty Old Man" (Allingham) **25**:8, 23
"Dîs Aliter Visum" (Browning) **19**:112
"Dis Aliter Visum" (Browning) **79**:165-66
The Disagreeable Woman: A Social Mystery (Alger) **83**:99, 116, 145
"Disappointment" (Coleridge) **31**:62
"A Disastrous Partnership" (Boyesen) **135**:14, 20-21, 30
The Discarded Daughter (Southworth) **26**:437
"The Discarded Son" (Alger) **83**:96
"The Discharged Soldier" (Wordsworth) **111**:347-48
"The Disciple" (Very) **9**:383, 393
The Disciples at Saïs (Novalis)
See *Die Lehrlinge zu Saïs*
"The Discontented Poet" (Emerson) **38**:193
Discorso di un italiano intorno alla poesia romantica (Leopardi) **129**:256, 264-65, 314
Discorso sopra alcuni punti della storia longobardica in Italia (Manzoni) **98**:213, 215, 217, 241
"Discorso storico sul testo del 'Decamerone'" (Foscolo) **8**:263
Discorso sul testo e su le opinioni diverse prevalenti intorno alla storio e alla emendazione critica della "Commedia" di Dante (Foscolo) **8**:263
Discours Préliminaire (Comte) **54**:210, 214
Discours sur la Vertu (Maistre) **37**:302
Discours sur l'ensemble du positivisme (Comte) **54**:203
Discours sur l'esprit positif (Comte) **54**:236
Discours sur Victor Hugo (Leconte de Lisle) **29**:233
"Discourse for the Congress of Lyons" (Foscolo)
See "Orazione a Bonaparte pel congresso di Lione"
"Discourse on Poetry" (Harpur) **114**:102, 164
A Discourse on the Constitution and Government of the United States (Calhoun) **15**:22-3, 35, 44, 53, 55, 73

"A Discourse on the Manners of the Antient Greeks" (Shelley) **18**:354
Discourse on the Text of Dante, and on the Various Opinions concerning the History and the Corrections of the "Divina Commedia" (Foscolo)
See *Discorso sul testo e su le opinioni diverse prevalenti intorno alla storio e alla emendazione critica della "Commedia" di Dante*
"A Discourse upon Beards" (Freneau) **111**:134
Discourse upon Certain Points of the History of the Longobards (Manzoni) **29**:251
Discourses (Schleiermacher)
See *Über die Religion: Reden an die Gebildeten unter ihren Verächtern*
Discourses Addressed to Mixed Congregations (Newman) **38**:303, 308-10, 315; **99**:233-34, 266-67
Discourses in America (Arnold) **6**:40-41, 46; **126**:43
Discourses on Davila (Adams) **106**:11-13, 18, 40, 44-5, 51-4
Discourses on Religion (Schleiermacher)
See *Über die Religion: Reden an die Gebildeten unter ihren Verächtern*
Discourses on Religion, addressed to the educated, among those who despise it (Schleiermacher)
See *Über die Religion: Reden an die Gebildeten unter ihren Verächtern*
Discourses on University Education (Newman) **99**:212
Discourses, Reviews, and Miscellanies (Channing) **17**:7, 46
Discourses to Mixed Congregations (Newman)
See *Discourses Addressed to Mixed Congregations*
"The Discoverer of the North Cape" (Longfellow) **45**:160
The Discovery of the Great West (Parkman)
See *La Salle and the Discovery of the Great West*
The Discreet Princess (Planché) **42**:274, 279, 292
Discussions and Arguments on Various Subjects (Newman) **38**:311-12
"The Dish of Tea" (Freneau) **111**:142
"The Disinherited" (Nerval)
See "El Desdichado"
"The Disinterred Warrior" (Bryant) **6**:172; **46**:3
The Disowned (Bulwer-Lytton) **1**:138, 145, 150; **45**:10, 13, 21, 24, 34, 68-9
"Dispostions for Faith" (Newman) **38**:305, 310
"Disputation" (Heine) **4**:255
A Disquisition on Government (Calhoun) **15**:22-3, 28, 34, 44, 50-1, 53, 55, 59, 64, 67, 69-71, 73
Dissertation (Feuerbach)
See *De ratione, una, universali, inifinita*
Dissertation (Kant) **27**:220-21; **67**:214, 219
"Dissertation on Didactic Poetry" (Warton) **118**:338
Dissertation on First Principles of Government (Paine) **62**:261, 267, 271, 300, 302
"Dissertation on Language" (Beattie)
See *Dissertations Moral and Critical: On Memory and Imagination; On Dreaming; The Theory of Language; On Fable and Romance; On the Attachments of Kindred; Illustrations on Sublimity*
"Dissertation on Pastoral Poetry" (Warton) **118**:338, 342
"A Dissertation on Poetry and Music, as They Affect the Mind" (Beattie)
See *Essays: On Poetry and Music, as They Affect the Mind; On Laughter, and Ludicrous Composition; On the Utility of Classical Learning*
Dissertation on the Canon and Feudal Law (Adams) **106**:4, 14, 28, 47
A Dissertation on the Theory and Practice of Benevolence (Dyer) **129**:98, 103, 112, 115, 125, 130-31, 136-37, 143
"A Dissertation upon Roast Pig" (Lamb) **10**:392, 404, 415, 435; **113**:159, 162, 200, 238
Dissertations Moral and Critical: On Memory and Imagination; On Dreaming; The Theory of Language; On Fable and Romance; On the Attachments of Kindred; Illustrations on Sublimity (Beattie) **25**:98-100, 114-15
Dissertations on Government, the Affairs of the Bank, and Paper Money (Paine) **62**:270, 294, 368
Dissertations on the English Language; with Notes, Historical and Critical (Webster) **30**:403, 408, 410, 413-16
Dissertazione sopra l'anima delle bestie (Leopardi) **129**:324
"A Dissolving View" (Cooper) **129**:51, 67, 73-74, 77-80
"Distant Correspondents" (Lamb) **10**:436; **113**:245, 249
"Distant View of England from the Sea" (Bowles) **103**:55
"Distiches" (Taylor) **89**:318
"Distinction" (Patmore) **9**:342, 344
"La Diva" (Gautier) **59**:18
Divagations (Mallarmé) **4**:373, 377, 396; **41**:252
Dīvān (Ghalib)
See *Diwan-E-Ghalib*
"The Divell's Chrystmasse" (Field) **3**:205, 211
"The Diver" (Schiller) **39**:330
"Divers Worlds. Time and Eternity" (Rossetti) **50**:285
Diversity of Human Language Structure and Its Influence on the Mental Development of Mankind (Humboldt)
See *On Language*
The Diverting History of John Bull and Brother Jonathan (Paulding) **2**:528
"The Diverting History of John Gilpin" (Cowper) **8**:98, 105, 108, 118-19, 122-23, 133, 137; **94**:26, 36-7, 84
"Divided" (Ingelow) **39**:257, 262-63, 268; **107**:119-20, 122-23
"The Divine Image" (Blake) **13**:240-41, 243; **37**:3, 5, 9, 18, 23, 25, 31-3, 38, 40, 44-5, 52-3, 57, 71-2, 79; **127**:31
The Divine Tragedy (Longfellow) **2**:484, 495-98; **45**:113, 127, 129, 150, 159, 164-65
"Divinia Commedia" (Longfellow) **45**:186
"The Divining Cauldron of Kibitsu" (Ueda Akinari)
See *Kibitsu no Kama*
"The Divinity School Address" (Emerson) **1**:303, 306-07; **38**:147, 198, 202, 204-05, 207-08; **98**:4, 7, 9, 18-19, 27, 43, 61, 124, 159-65, 176, 181, 190
"The Division" (Krylov) **1**:435
"Division of an Estate" (Horton) **87**:102
The Divorced Woman (Sacher-Masoch)
See *The Separated Wife*
Diwan-E-Ghalib (Ghalib) **39**:126, 129, 156; **78**:65, 69, 77
Dix années d'exil (Staël-Holstein) **3**:521, 527; **91**:325, 350-1, 360, 363, 365
Dix ans de la vie d'une femme; ou, Les Mauvais Conseils (Scribe) **16**:412
"Les djinns" (Hugo) **3**:261
"Djoûmane" (Mérimée) **6**:369-71; **65**:51-2, 56, 58-9, 63, 98
Dmitri Kalinin (Belinski) **5**:101
Dmitry Samozvanets i Vasily Shuysky (Ostrovsky) **30**:101; **57**:206-7
"Dnevnik lišnego čeloveka" (Turgenev) **21**:388, 401, 414, 418, 433, 439; **37**:438; **122**:247, 258, 266, 342-43
Dnevnik pisatelya (Dostoevsky) **2**:162, 185-86; **21**:106, 109; **33**:163, 170-71, 175, 179; **43**:87, 92, 157, 159, 167; **119**:74, 90
Dnevnik provintsiala v Peterburge (Saltykov) **16**:343, 359, 373-74
Do and Dare; or, A Brave Boy's Fight for Fortune (Alger) **8**:19, 25, 44, 46
"Do czytelnika" (Norwid) **17**:371
"Do I Love Thee?" (Ridge) **82**:182
"Do króla" (Krasicki) **8**:407
"Do no imitate: genius is original..." (Baratynsky)
See "Ne podrazhay: svoeobrazen genity..."
"Do not believe the poet, maiden" (Tyutchev)
See "Ne ver, ne ver poetu, deva"
Do Not Live As You Want To (Ostrovsky)
See *Ne tak zhiví kak khóchetsya*
"Do Osnovjanenka" (Shevchenko) **54**:373-4
"Do przyjaciól Moskali" (Mickiewicz) **3**:401
"Do You Know Why I Love Her?" (Isaacs)
See "¿Sabéis por qué la amo?"
"Do You Want Me to Settle Down?" (Grillparzer)
See "Willst du, ich soll Hütten bauen?"
"Dobbin Dead" (Barnes) **75**:35
"Döbeln at Juutas" (Runeberg)
See "Döbeln vid Juutas"
"Döbeln vid Juutas" (Runeberg) **41**:312-15, 323
"The Doctor" (Maginn) **8**:435
The Doctor, & c; (Southey) **8**:467-68, 470-73; **97**:264-65, 267, 271, 276, 288-92, 320-24, 329, 331
"Dr. Bullivant" (Hawthorne) **95**:130
"Dr Frühlingsfeier" (Klopstock) **11**:234, 236, 238, 240-41
Doctor Grimshawe's Secret (Hawthorne) **2**:315, 324, 333-35; **95**:106
"Dr. Heidegger's Experiment" (Hawthorne) **2**:291-92, 298, 311, 328; **95**:105
The Doctor in Spite of Himself (Tyler) **3**:573
Doctor Jekyll and Mr. Hyde (Stevenson)
See *The Strange Case of Dr. Jekyll and Mr. Hyde*
"Doctor Krupov" (Herzen) **61**:108
"Doctor Marigold" (Dickens) **3**:163
"Doctor Parker's Patty" (Cooke) **110**:34
"El Doctor Rafael Núñez" (Silva) **114**:296
"Doctor Tarr and Professor Fether" (Poe)
See "The System of Doctor Tarr and Professor Fether"
"Doctor Theophilus" (Cranch)
See "The Legend of Doctor Theophilus: or, The Enchanted Clothes"
Doctor Thorne (Trollope) **6**:453, 459, 463, 470, 480-81, 491, 499-501, 512, 516-17; **101**:235, 251, 253, 264, 272-74, 321, 333
"Doctor Tristan's Treatment" (Villiers de l'Isle Adam)
See "Le traitement du docteur Tristan"
Doctor Vandyke (Cooke) **5**:124, 130, 132
Doctrine (Heine)
See *Doktrin*
"The Doctrine of the Soul" (Emerson) **38**:177
The Dodd Family Abroad (Lever) **23**:288-89, 292, 296-97, 301-02, 305, 307
The Dodge Club (De Mille) **123**:130
"Det døende Barn" (Andersen) **79**:76
"The Dog" (Turgenev)
See "Sobaka"
"The Dog and the Water-Lily: No Fable" (Cowper) **8**:119; **94**:122, 124
Dogma socialista (Echeverria) **18**:150
Dogmatic (Schleiermacher)
See *Der christliche Glaube nach den Grundsäzen der evengelischen Kirche im Zusammenhange dargestellt*
"The Dogs" (Hunt) **1**:423
"Dog-Scratcher" (Petofi)
See "Kutyakaparó"
"Doings of the Sun Beam" (Holmes) **81**:102, 125-26

Dokhodnoye mesto (Ostrovsky) **30**:91, 101, 105, 111, 115; **57**:198, 202, 209-10, 218, 220
Doktor Luther: Eine Schilderung (Freytag) **109**:148
Doktrin (Heine) **54**:345-6, 350
Dolce far Niente (Hayne) **94**:136
"Dolefully" (Bestuzhev)
See "Zaunno"
The Dolliver Romance, and Other Pieces (Hawthorne) **2**:324, 326, 335
"Dolly's Mistake" (Clare) **9**:74-75; **86**:155-56
Dolores, Pages from a Family Chronicle (Gómez de Avellaneda)
See *Dolores, páginas de una crónica de familia*
Dolores, páginas de una crónica de familia (Gómez de Avellaneda) **111**:13, 24, 30
"Dolorida" (Vigny) **7**:470, 473; **102**:335, 367-68
"Dolorosa" (Casal) **131**:259, 267, 269
"Dolph Heyliger" (Irving) **2**:368, 390; **19**:336-37, 341, 345
Dom Gigadas (Balzac) **5**:58
"The Domain of Arnheim" (Poe) **16**:304, 336; **55**:147; **94**:240; **117**:265, 290, 310
"Dombey and Son" (Crawford) **127**:196
Dombey and Son (Dickens)
See *Dealings with the Firm of Dombey and Son*
"The Domestic Affections" (Hemans) **71**:278, 289-91
"The Domestic Affections" and Other Poems (Hemans) **71**:272-73, 278, 289
"Domestic Asides" (Hood) **16**:235
"Domestic Economy" (Delany) **93**:162
"Domestic Education of Children" (Murray) **63**:181
"Domestic Fame" (Milnes) **61**:136
"Domestic Happiness" (Halleck) **47**:57
"Domestic Life" (Emerson) **1**:280; **38**:212; **98**:82
The Domestic Manners and Private Life of Sir Walter Scott (Hogg) **4**:278
Domestic Manners of the Americans (Trollope) **30**:304, 310, 312, 314-15, 320-24, 326
"Domestic Peace" (Coleridge) **99**:48
A Domestic Picture (Ostrovsky)
See *Semeynaya kartina*
"A Domestic Tale" (Hemans) **71**:289
Domik v Kolomne (Pushkin) **3**:444, 456; **27**:367, 386; **83**:275, 338
"Dominion" (Ingelow) **39**:266
Dominique (Fromentin) **10**:227-28, 230-31, 233, 236-42, 245-46, 248-60, 262; **125**:95-98, 101, 104-15, 121-26, 128-32, 134-36, 138-42, 146-49, 155, 159, 161-63, 165, 167, 169-70
Le domino noir (Scribe) **16**:384, 401
"Don Andréa Vésalius l'anatomiste" (Borel) **41**:4, 6, 13
Don Caesar de Bazan (Boucicault) **41**:30
Don Carlos (Schiller) **39**:312, 314, 324, 330, 334-36, 343, 360, 362, 371, 375-76, 380-81, 389-90; **69**:169, 242-44
Don Catrín de la fachenda (Lizardi)
See *Vida y hechos del famoso caballero Don Catrín de la fachenda*
"Don du poème" (Mallarmé) **41**:250, 274-75, 281
Don Garzia (Alfieri) **101**:4, 8, 32, 38, 42
"Don Giovanni" (Kierkegaard) **125**:212
Don Giovanni (Byron) **12**:82-83
Don Giovanni (Da Ponte)
See *Il dissoluto punito o sia il Don Giovanni*
Don John: A Story (Ingelow) **39**:261, 264; **107**:118, 124, 151
"Don Juan" (Clare) **9**:107-08, 124; **86**:90
"Don Juan" (Pushkin) **83**:275
Don Juan (Byron) **2**:65, 68-72, 75-7, 80-2, 85-7, 90-4, 97-8; **12**:70-147; **109**:62, 67-8, 73, 85, 93, 99, 102-03, 118, 120, 127
Don Juan (Hoffmann) **2**:345-47
Don Juan (Lenau) **16**:268-69, 274, 279, 281-82
Don Juan and Faust (Grabbe)
See *Don Juan und Faust*
"Don Juan aux enfers" (Baudelaire) **6**:83, 89; **55**:58
Don Juan de Covadonga (Silva) **114**:262
Don Juan de Marana (Dumas) **11**:45, 47; **71**:211, 214
"Don Juan Duped" (Verlaine) **51**:372
"Don Juan in Hades" (Baudelaire)
See "Don Juan aux enfers"
Don Juan of Kolomea (Sacher-Masoch) **31**:286-87, 290-93
Don Juan Tenorio (Zorrilla y Moral) **6**:523-27
Don Juan und Faust (Grabbe) **2**:272-75, 281, 283-85, 287
"Don Juanito Marques Verdugo do los Leganes" (Chamisso) **82**:6
"Don Paez" (Musset) **7**:256, 265, 267, 277-78
"Don Pedrillo" (Lazarus) **8**:425; **109**:324
Don Pedro of Castile (Boker) **125**:58
Don Quixote (Percy) **95**:338
Don Simplicio Bobadilla (Tamayo y Baus) **1**:571
Don Sylvio von Rosalva (Wieland) **17**:390, 397, 404-06, 412, 424
Don the Newsboy (Alger) **8**:43
Doña Juana the Magnate (Tamayo y Baus)
See *La ricahembra*
"Donald Caird" (Scott) **15**:318
"Donald MacDonald" (Hogg) **4**:284
Das Donauweib (Tieck) **5**:519
El doncel de don Enrique el Doliente (Larra) **17**:270, 279; **130**:197-98, 200, 228, 274
"Done For" (Cooke) **110**:9
"Dong, Sounds the Brass in the East" (Thoreau) **7**:384
"Dong with a Luminous Nose" (Lear) **3**:299-300, 307-09
"Donkey Cabbages" (Grimm and Grimm) **3**:227
Donna de Solis (Martínez de la Rosa) **102**:228
Donna Florida (Simms) **3**:501
La donna serpente (Gozzi) **23**:108, 119, 121, 123, 125
"Donoso-Cortés, Marqués de Valdegamas, and Julian, Roman Emperor" (Herzen) **10**:339
"Don't Ceäre" (Barnes) **75**:9
Don't Get Into Another's Sleigh (Ostrovsky)
See *Ne v svoi sani ne sadis!*
"Don't propose on a Sunday" (Lonnrot) **53**:339
Don't Sit in Another's Sleigh (Ostrovsky)
See *Ne v svoi sani ne sadis!*
"Doom and Dan" (Cooke) **110**:28
"The Doom of a City" (Thomson) **18**:397, 406-07, 409, 412-14, 421, 424-25, 431
"The Doom of King Acrisius" (Morris) **4**:442, 447-48
"The Doom of the Griffiths" (Gaskell) **5**:192, 201; **70**:191, 193
"The Doom of the Sirens" (Rossetti) **4**:510
A Door Must Be Either Open or Shut (Musset)
See *Il faut qu'une porte soit ouvertr ou fermée*
The Doorkeeper at the Mansion (Stifter)
See *Tourmaline*
"Doors and Windows" (Corbière)
See "Portes et fenêtres"
Ein Doppelgänger (Storm) **1**:541, 550
"Doppelheimweh" (Lenau) **16**:281
"Die Doppeltgänger" (Hoffmann) **2**:360
"Dora" (Ingelow) **39**:258
"Dora" (Kendall) **12**:180
"Dora" (Tennyson) **30**:233, 241
"Dora Dee" (O'Brien) **21**:243, 246-47
"Dora Greenwell" (Whittier) **59**:365
"Dorchester Giant" (Holmes) **14**:101
Dorfweisthümer (Grimm and Grimm) **3**:216
"A Dorio ad Phrygium" (Norwid) **17**:368
"Le dormeur du val" (Rimbaud) **4**:465; **35**:271, 321; **82**:230, 233, 247
"Doroga ot stantsii Almaly do posta Mugansy" (Bestuzhev) **131**:160
Dorotheas Blumenkörbchen (Keller) **2**:412, 416
"Dorothée" (Baudelaire)
See "La belle Dorothée"
Dorothy and Other Italian Stories (Woolson) **82**:275, 283, 293, 299, 308, 338, 341, 344
Dorothy Chance (Moodie) **14**:226
"Dorothy Q" (Holmes) **14**:109, 118, 128; **81**:103
"Dorset Folk and Dorset" (Barnes) **75**:57
Dos amores (Villaverde) **121**:333-34
"El dos de mayo" (Espronceda) **39**:120
Dos mujeres (Gómez de Avellaneda) **111**:8, 13-14, 18-22, 25, 28-29, 33-35, 56-57, 61, 64
"Las dos olas" (Bécquer) **106**:126
Le dossier no. 113 (Gaboriau) **14**:14-16, 18-19, 22-4, 26, 29, 32-3
Dot (Boucicault) **41**:34
"Doth true Love lonely grow?" (Crawford) **127**:151-52
"Le douanier" (Corbière) **43**:21
"Les douaniers" (Daudet) **1**:252
The Double (Dostoevsky)
See *Dvoynik*
"The Double Chamber" (Baudelaire)
See "La chambre double"
"La double conversion" (Daudet) **1**:249
"Double Knock" (Hood) **16**:236
The Double Marriage (Reade) **2**:541, 547
La double méprise (Mérimée) **6**:352-4, 357, 360, 366, 368-70; **65**:54-7, 62-4, 100-01, 117, 128
"The Double Mistake" (Mérimée)
See *La double méprise*
"Double Quatuor" (Hugo) **10**:361
"A Double Thanksgiving" (Cooke) **110**:50
"Double Triangle Serpent and Rays" (Fuller) **50**:247-8
"The Double-Headed Snake" (Whittier) **59**:360
Doublets (Carroll) **139**:57
"Doubt" (Cooke) **110**:9
"Doubt and Prayer" (Tennyson) **65**:248, 267
"Doubt Me! My Dim Companion" (Dickinson) **21**:54, 57
"Doubtful Dreams" (Gordon) **21**:155-57, 159-61, 176, 183
"Douces larmes" (Banville) **9**:30
The Dough Face (Brown) **89**:182
"Doust Thou Not Care?" (Rossetti) **50**:263
"Dover Beach" (Arnold) **6**:37, 44, 48, 64, 66, 73; **29**:33, 35; **89**:14, 20, 22, 25-8, 46, 51-2, 62, 88, 119, 121; **126**:6, 75, 83
"Dover Cliffs" (Bowles)
See "On Dover Cliffs. July 20, 1787"
The Doves (Cowper) **94**:108
"The Doves and the Crows" (Hood) **16**:239
Dovol'no (Turgenev) **37**:443
The Dowager; or, the New School for Scandal (Gore) **65**:20
Dowerless (Ostrovsky)
See *Bespridannitsa*
The Dowerless Girl (Ostrovsky)
See *Bespridannitsa*
"Down Stream" (Rossetti) **4**:511, 518
"Down the Dardanelles" (Darley) **2**:128
"Down Whitechapel Way" (Sala) **46**:246
"Down with the Tide" (Dickens) **105**:217
"Downs" (Jefferies) **47**:130
"Downtrodden People" (Dobrolyubov) **5**:147
Dożywocie (Fredro) **8**:285-86, 290, 292
dq1Stanzas Written at the Island of Madeira" (Freneau) **111**:105
Dr. Bahrdt (Kotzebue) **25**:134, 142
Dr. Birch's School (Thackeray) **5**:459
"Dr. Farmer's 'Essay on the Learning of Shakespeare' Considered" (Maginn) **8**:435, 438, 442
"Dr. Francia" (Carlyle) **70**:93

Dr. Heidenhoff's Process (Bellamy) **4**:23, 26-27, 29, 31, 34; **86**:6, 10, 17, 29, 64, 66
Dr Katzenbergers Badereise: Nebst einer Auswahl verbesserter Werkchen (Jean Paul) **7**:239, 241
Dr Luther (Freytag)
See *Doktor Luther: Eine Schilderung*
Dr. Stanley's Lectures on the Irish Church (Arnold) **126**:89
"Dr. Stanley's Lectures on the Jewish Church" (Arnold) **29**:14
"Dr. Tarr and Prof. Fether" (Poe) **78**:278
Dr. Wortle's School (Trollope) **6**:470; **101**:291, 307, 311, 315
"Drab Habitation of Whom?" (Dickinson) **21**:18
"Drachenfels" (Fuller) **50**:248
"Draft of a Communist Confession of Faith" (Engels) **85**:27
"The Dragon Fang Possessed by the Conjurer Piou-Lu" (O'Brien) **21**:235-36, 252
Dragoş's Wedding (Eminescu) **33**:265
The Drama at Home; or, An Evening with Puff (Planché) **42**:273, 276, 290
"Drama del alma" (Zorrilla y Moral) **6**:524
Drama Indio (Martí) **63**:104
Un drama nuevo (Tamayo y Baus) **1**:565-66, 568-70
"A Drama of Exile" (Browning) **1**:112-3, 115-7, 122, 129; **61**:4; **66**:3, 44, 71
The Drama of Exile, and Other Poems (Browning) **1**:114, 116, 126-7; **61**:43, 45
Dramas (Baillie) **2**:39-40; **71**:2
The Drama's Levëe (Planché) **42**:273, 299
Dramatic Essays (Lewes) **25**:325
"The Dramatic Fragment" (Wordsworth) **12**:387
Dramatic Idylls, Second Series (Browning) **79**:153, 163-64
Dramatic Lyrics (Browning) **19**:109; **79**:93-94, 103, 146, 148, 163, 166, 190
Dramatic Romances and Lyrics (Browning) **79**:93-94, 103, 146, 148, 163
Dramatic Scenes from Real Life (Morgan) **29**:390, 394
The Dramatic Works of Mary Russell Mitford (Mitford) **4**:404
Dramatic Works of Wycherley, Congreve, Vanbrugh, and Farquhar (Hunt) **70**:260, 265
Dramatis Personae (Browning) **19**:116, 130; **79**:149, 152, 163, 165, 182
"Un drame au bord de la mer" (Balzac) **5**:53
Drames philosophiques (Renan) **26**:395, 397, 408, 413
"The Draughts" (Mickiewicz) **3**:398
Drauszen im Heidedorf (Storm) **1**:540
"A Drawing-Room Drama" (O'Brien) **21**:236, 243, 247
"A Dream" (Allingham) **25**:6, 8, 20, 23-4
"A Dream" (Bertrand)
See "Un rêve"
"A Dream" (Blake) **13**:182; **37**:3, 14, 41, 65, 71-2, 92
"A Dream" (Bryant) **46**:3, 20
"The Dream" (Chivers) **49**:68
"The Dream" (Clare) **9**:84
"Dream" (Lermontov) **126**:227
"The Dream" (Mickiewicz)
See "Sen"
"The Dream" (Norton) **47**:236, 238-39, 243, 248, 259
"A Dream" (Poe) **117**:214-15, 280
"Dream" (Shevchenko)
See "Son"
"The Dream" (Solomos) **15**:393
"The Dream" (Turgenev)
See "Son"
"A Dream" (Turgenev)
See "Son"
The Dream (Baillie) **2**:36, 39; **71**:12-14, 16
Dream (Leopardi) **129**:304
"A Dream, after Reading Dante's Episode of Paolo and Francesca" (Keats) **73**:228, 230
The Dream and Other Poems (Norton) **47**:239-40, 244-46, 248, 253-54, 259-60
"Dream and Waking" (Chamisso) **82**:5
"Dream at Sea" (Tyutchev)
See "Son na more"
"The Dream by the Fountain" (Harpur) **114**:92, 94, 97, 106-7, 116, 144
A Dream Is Life (Grillparzer)
See *Der Traum ein Leben*
"The Dream of a Queer Fellow" (Dostoevsky)
See "The Dream of a Ridiculous Man"
"The Dream of a Ridiculous Man" (Dostoevsky) **2**:202; **33**:227, 229; **43**:139
"A Dream of Antiquity" (Moore) **110**:178
"The Dream of Boccaccio" (Landor) **14**:187
"The Dream of Cesara" (Krasiński)
See "Sen Cezary"
The Dream of Eugene Aram (Hood) **16**:202, 206-07, 209, 211, 215, 220-21, 225-28, 231, 233-35, 238
"A Dream of Fair Women" (Tennyson) **30**:209, 223-24, 264; **65**:235
Dream of Gerontius (Newman) **38**:324, 342, 345-46, 348; **99**:256
"A Dream of John Ball" (Morris) **4**:425, 436-39, 441, 445
"The Dream of John Macdonnell" (Mangan) **27**:308
"A Dream of My Mother" (Foster) **26**:286
"The Dream of Petrarca" (Landor) **14**:187
Dream on the Volga (Ostrovsky)
See *Voevoda: Son na Volge*
"A Dream within a Dream" (Poe) **117**:215
"Dream-Children: A Reverie" (Lamb) **10**:404, 407, 410, 415, 421, 430, 435-37; **113**:157, 165, 173, 200, 244
"The Dreamer and the Worker" (Horne) **127**:266
"Dream-Fugue, Founded on the Preceding Theme of Sudden Death" (De Quincey) **4**:82, 86, 89
"Dreaming" (Beattie)
See *Dissertations Moral and Critical: On Memory and Imagination; On Dreaming; The Theory of Language; On Fable and Romance; On the Attachments of Kindred; Illustrations on Sublimity*
"Dream-Land" (Poe) **1**:526-27; **55**:150; **117**:227, 232-35, 242-44, 264, 280-83, 316-18, 330
"Dreamland" (Rossetti) **2**:563
"Dream-Love" (Rossetti) **50**:324; **66**:311
"Dream-Pedlary" (Beddoes) **3**:32, 34, 39
"Dreams" (Brontë) **71**:91
"Dreams" (Cranch) **115**:50
"Dreams" (Heine)
See "Traumbilder"
"Dreams" (Lazarus) **8**:413, 420
"Dreams" (Poe) **1**:514; **117**:214
"Dreams" (Sigourney) **21**:299
"Dreams" (Timrod) **25**:363, 366, 382
Dreams (Robertson) **35**:333, 335, 354, 363, 369
Dreams and Sounds (Nekrasov) **11**:399
"Dreams Awake" (Wieland) **17**:394
Dreams of a Spirit-Seer (Kant) **27**:200; **67**:219
Dreams of Love (Scribe)
See *Rêves d'amour*
Dreams of the King (Andersen) **79**:13, 17
Dreams, Waking Thoughts, and Incidents (Beckford) **16**:25
"Dreamthorp" (Smith) **59**:309, 315-7
Dreamthrop (Smith) **59**:295, 299, 302-4, 306, 308-9, 311, 314-6, 319, 322-4, 326, 337
"Dreary Hour" (Arany)
See "Meddőórán"
Dred: A Tale of the Great Dismal Swamp (Stowe) **3**:550-52, 559-61, 567
"Die drei" (Lenau) **16**:265
"Die Drei Brüder" (Gotthelf) **117**:44, 49, 51, 55-8
Die drei gerechten Kammacher (Keller) **2**:412, 414-15, 424-25
"Die drei Indianer" (Lenau) **16**:269, 278, 283-84
Drei Schmiede ihres Schicksals (Stifter) **41**:366
Drei Väter auf einmal (Kotzebue) **25**:136
"Die drei Zigeuner" (Lenau) **16**:285
Dresden Forefathers' Eve Wilno Forefathers' Eve (Mickiewicz)
See *Dziady III*
"The Dresser" (Whitman) **81**:330
The Dressmaker (Martineau) **26**:322
"Drifting Away" (Eliot) **4**:140
Drink (Reade) **2**:544, 551
"Drink of This Cup" (Moore) **110**:190
"Drinking Song" (Smith) **59**:331
Driven from Home (Alger) **8**:43
"Droga nad przepascic w Czufut-Kale" (Mickiewicz) **3**:403; **101**:188-89
Droll Stories (Balzac)
See *Contes drolatiques*
Dronningen paa 16 Aar (Andersen) **79**:9
Dronningen Skibet (Andersen) **79**:9
"A Drop of Balm" (Arany)
See "Balzsamcsepp"
"A Drop of Blood" (Meyer)
See "Der Blutstropfen"
"A Drop of Water" (Andersen)
See "Vanddraaben"
Drottningens juvelsmycke (Almqvist) **42**:4, 6, 9-14, 17
The Drowned (Pushkin) **3**:423
"The Drowned Girl" (Gogol)
See "Majskaja noč, ili Vtoplennica"
"The Drowned Girl" (Shevchenko)
See "Utoplena"
"Drowne's Wooden Image" (Hawthorne) **2**:298; **39**:222
Drüben am Markt (Storm) **1**:540, 544
"Drumlanrig" (Hogg) **109**:270
Drum-Taps (Whitman) **4**:542-43, 569, 571, 578, 580, 582, 586, 592, 595; **81**:258, 311-21, 326, 330-31
"The Drunkard" (Harpur) **114**:141
The Drunken Boat (Rimbaud)
See *Le bateau ivre*
"The Drunken God" (Meyer)
See "Der trunkene Gott"
"Drunkenness" (Krasicki)
See "Pijaństwo"
"Druses et Maronites" (Nerval) **67**:333
"Dry Be That Tear" (Sheridan) **91**:232
Dry Sticks, Fagoted by W. S. L. (Landor) **14**:170, 177
"The Dryad" (Andersen) **7**:24
"Le Dryade et Symeta" (Vigny) **102**:335
"La dryade: Idyll in the Manner of Theocritus" (Vigny) **7**:468-69
"Dryden and His Times" (Clough) **27**:103
"Dryden and Pope" (Hazlitt) **29**:166
Du dandysme et de Georges Brummel (Barbey d'Aurevilly) **1**:71
Du fantastic dans la littérature (Nodier) **19**:378
Du Pape (Maistre) **37**:288, 290-92, 294, 299-300, 302, 304, 306-09, 314-15
"Du style" (Joubert) **9**:293
"The Dual Existence" (Clarke) **19**:231
Dubrovsky (Pushkin) **3**:429, 435-36, 442, 459; **27**:375; **83**:276, 316
"The Duc De L'Omellette" (Poe) **16**:304, 313
The Duchess of la Vallière (Bulwer-Lytton) **1**:147; **45**:62
The Duchesse de Langeais (Balzac) **5**:45; **35**:2
"The Duck and the Kangaroo" (Lear) **3**:297, 307, 309
"The Duckling" (Andersen)
See "Den grimme Ælling"
"The Duel" (Kleist)
See *Der Zweikampf*
"The Duel" (O'Brien) **21**:243, 245, 247
"Duel at Midnight" (Arany)
See "Éjféli párbaj"
"Duel aux camélias" (Corbière) **43**:27
"The Duelist" (Turgenev) **21**:417

"The Duellist" (Turgenev)
See "The Duelist"
"Duellum" (Baudelaire) **29**:99
Duels of Honor (Tamayo y Baus)
See *Lances de honor*
El duende satírico del día (Larra) **130**:247
The Duenna; or, The Doubling Elopement (Sheridan) **5**:358-59, 361-62, 365, 369, 380-83; **91**:241-42, 251
"Duets" (Woolson) **82**:322
"Duke Carl of Rosenmold" (Pater) **7**:299; **90**:245, 345-46, 348-49
"Duke Humphrey's Dinner" (O'Brien) **21**:243-44
The Duke of Monmouth (Griffin) **7**:193, 196, 198, 200-01, 204, 216, 219
"Duke of Portland" (Villiers de l'Isle Adam) **3**:590
The Duke of Stockbridge: A Romance of Shay's Rebellion (Bellamy) **4**:26, 30; **86**:11
"Duke Richelieu, Sir Firebrace Cotes, Lady G——, and Mr. Normanby" (Landor) **14**:178
The Duke's Children (Trollope) **6**:461, 466-67, 471, 490, 495, 497, 500, 519; **101**:264-65, 268, 288, 291, 311, 318, 324
"Duló Zebedeus kalandjai" (Madach) **19**:369, 371
"Duma" (Lermontov) **5**:286, 295; **126**:144, 216
"Duma" (Pavlova) **138**:4, 51
"The Dumb Cake" (Clare) **86**:108
"The Dumb Orators" (Crabbe) **26**:93, 129, 135; **121**:11-12, 61
"Dumka" (Shevchenko) **54**:373
"Dumy moji dumy moji" (Shevchenko) **54**:373
The Dun (Edgeworth) **1**:267; **51**:89-90, 140
"Dunbar" (Smith) **59**:309
"The Duncaid of Today" (Disraeli) **39**:52-3, 55
"The Dungeon" (Coleridge) **9**:131; **111**:197, 315, 357
"The Dungeon" (Wordsworth) **12**:386-87
"Dungog" (Kendall) **12**:180, 187
"Duns Scotus's Oxford" (Hopkins) **17**:185, 211, 219
Duplicity (Holcroft) **85**:191, 205, 214-16, 218, 225, 234, 239, 246
"Durandarte and Belerma" (Lewis) **11**:297
"Durchwachte Nacht" (Droste-Hülshoff) **3**:196, 200
"Dursli der Branntweinsäufer" (Gotthelf) **117**:51, 58
"A Dutch Picture" (Longfellow) **45**:144
Dutch Pictures (Sala) **46**:237
The Dutchman's Fireside (Paulding) **2**:526-30
"Duties and Responsibilities of Unitarian Christians" (Cranch) **115**:47
"The Duties of Man" (Mazzini) **34**:281-282
"Duty" (Clough) **27**:52, 91, 103, 105
"Duty" (Solomos) **15**:399
Duty before All (Herzen) **61**:97
"The Duty of a Brother" (Lamb) **125**:331
The Duty of American Women to Their Country (Beecher) **30**:15
The Duty of Disobedience to the Fugitive Slave Law (Child) **73**:63
"The Duty of the Free States" (Channing) **17**:25, 32-3
"Dva chetverostishiia" (Turgenev) **122**:312
"Dve byli i esche odna" (Zhukovsky) **35**:398
"Dve doli" (Baratynsky) **103**:6-8, 11, 26-7
Dvoinaia zhizn' (Pavlova) **138**:3, 5, 7-10, 13, 20, 22, 31, 36, 38-43, 47, 56-57, 59
Dvoinik (Dostoevsky)
See *Dvoynik*
Dvorianskoe gnezdo (Turgenev)
See *Dvoryanskoe gnezdo*
Dvoryanskoe gnezdo (Turgenev) **21**:393-94, 397, 399-400, 409-10, 413, 417-19, 421-22, 427, 430-31, 434-35, 437-39, 442-44, 446-48, 452; **37**:335, 367, 379, 382, 402, 436, 444; **122**:248-52, 256, 267-68, 270-72, 278-79, 288, 292, 315, 317, 324-26
Dvoynaya zhizn' (Pavlova)
See *Dvoinaia zhizn'*
Dvoynik (Dostoevsky) **2**:157, 177, 179, 199; **33**:167, 171-73, 200, 203-04; **43**:92, 130
The Dwarf (Tieck) **5**:517
Dwie blizny (Fredro) **8**:285
"The Dying Beauty" (Chivers) **49**:49, 56
"The Dying Child" (Clare) **9**:85, 102
"The Dying Crow" (Bryant) **46**:13
"The Dying Daughter to her Mother" (Opie) **65**:155, 182
"Dying! Dying in the Night!" (Dickinson) **21**:55
"The Dying Elm" (Freneau) **111**:142-43
"The Dying Enthusiast" (Mangan) **27**:280, 298
Dying Gladiator (Lermontov) **47**:151
"The Dying Indian" (Warton) **118**:335, 356
"The Dying Indian: Tomo-Chequi" (Freneau) **1**:315, 317, 322; **111**:102, 145, 147-50, 152, 166, 190
"The Dying need but little, Dear,/ A Glass of Water's all" (Dickinson) **77**:163
"The Dying Philosopher" (Sigourney) **87**:331-32
"The Dying Raven" (Dana) **53**:158, 168
"The Dying Seneca" (Holmes) **14**:100
"The Dying Soldier" (Runeberg) **41**:312-15, 321, 323
"The Dying Speech of an Old Philosopher" (Landor) **14**:201-02
"The Dying Swan" (Chivers) **49**:71
"The Dying Swan" (Tennyson) **30**:211, 223, 231-32
"A Dying Tiger moaned for Drink" (Dickinson) **77**:162-63
"The Dying Warrior" (Runeberg)
See "The Dying Soldier"
Dym (Turgenev) **21**:389-90, 392-93, 396, 400-01, 406, 409, 411, 413, 419, 421-22, 426-27, 431, 435-39, 441, 444-45; **37**:367-68, 391, 424, 436, 444, 447; **122**:248-49, 261, 269, 271, 279, 282-87, 320, 325-27, 341, 364
The Dynamics of a Particle (Carroll) **2**:117
"The Dynamiter" (Stevenson)
See *The New Arabian Nights*
"Dynd-Kongens Datter" (Andersen) **7**:28, 30, 32; **79**:7, 28, 58, 70-1
Dziady III (Mickiewicz) **3**:389, 391-93, 395-97, 399-403; **101**:156-58, 171, 197, 208, 210
"E. B. B." (Thomson) **18**:392
"E. I. Bulgarinoy" (Bestuzhev) **131**:150
"Each and All" (Emerson) **1**:285, 296; **38**:184, 190; **98**:177, 179
"The Eagle" (Tennyson) **30**:280
"The Eagle and Fowls" (Krylov) **1**:435
"The Eagle as Maecenas" (Saltykov) **16**:358
"The Eagle Hunter" (Taylor) **89**:299
"The Eagles" (Very) **9**:383
"Eäriné" (Allingham) **25**:14
"Earl Sigurd's Christmas Eve" (Boyesen) **135**:4
"Early Adieux" (Gordon) **21**:154, 173
"Early American Verse" (Bryant) **46**:32, 51
"Early Death and Fame" (Arnold) **29**:26, 28
The Early Diary of Frances Burney, 1768-1778 (Burney) **12**:33; **54**:18, 24; **107**:12, 14, 38, 40
Early England and the Saxon-English (Barnes) **75**:40, 103
The Early English Church: A Paper Read before the Church of England Institute (De Mille) **123**:120, 125
Early Essays and Miscellanies (Thoreau) **61**:339, 376; **138**:127
"Early Graves" (Klopstock) **11**:220
The Early Italian Poets (Rossetti) **77**:335
The Early Italian Poets from Ciullo to Dante Alighieri, 1100/1200/1300 in the Original Metres, Together with Dante's "Vita Nuova" (Rossetti) **4**:490
The Early Lectures of Ralph Waldo Emerson (Emerson) **98**:66-8, 70, 81, 94-9, 96
Early Lessons (Edgeworth) **51**:81, 85, 89, 102, 110, 114
"The Early Life of Sut Lovingood, Written by His Dad" (Harris) **23**:150, 152
Early Notebooks (Darwin) **57**:145-6
Early Poems of John Clare (Clare) **86**:130-31, 160
Early Polemical Writings (Kierkegaard) **125**:271
"The Early Spring Book" (Dana) **53**:178
Early Theological Writings (Hegel)
See *Hegels theologische Jungendschriften*
"Earth" (Bryant) **6**:168, 172; **46**:7, 22, 28, 39
"The Earth" (Very) **9**:378, 381
"Earth Has Not Anything to Show More Fair" (Wordsworth) **12**:466
"The Earth Is Too Much with Us" (Wordsworth) **12**:466
"Earth, my Likeness" (Whitman) **31**:430; **81**:258
The Earthly Paradise (Morris) **4**:414-16, 419-22, 424-25, 427-35, 442-43, 446-48
"The Earthquake" (Moodie) **113**:317
The Earthquake (Galt) **1**:328, 335
"The Earthquake in Chile" (Kleist)
See "Das Erdbeben in Chili"
"Earth's Answer" (Blake) **13**:191, 221, 226; **37**:32, 42, 47-9
"Earth's Children Cleave to Earth" (Bryant) **46**:21
"Earth's Holocaust" (Hawthorne) **2**:296, 298, 305; **10**:290, 311; **17**:129; **23**:205; **39**:229; **79**:296; **95**:156
"Earth's Immortalities" (Browning) **79**:94, 101
"Earth—the Stoic" (Lampman) **25**:167
"The Easiest Mode of Learning the Greek and Latin Languages" (Dyer) **129**:110
East Angels (Woolson) **82**:268-71, 274-75, 279, 293, 299, 315-19
"East Wind" (Hunt) **1**:417
"Easter Day" (Clough) **27**:55, 87-8, 100
Easter Day (Browning) **19**:132
"Easter Day: Naples, 1849" (Clough) **27**:76
"Easter Eve" (Lampman) **25**:160, 167, 199, 201
"An Easter Greeting to Every Child Who Loves Alice" (Carroll) **139**:12, 52
"An Easter Hymn" (Kendall) **12**:192
The Easter Recess (Morgan) **29**:390
"Easter Zunday" (Barnes) **75**:77
"An Eastern Legend" (Turgenev)
See "Vostochnaia Legenda"
Eastern Life Past and Present (Martineau) **137**:285, 324, 343
Eastern Life, Present and Past (Martineau) **26**:311, 319, 326, 328-29, 359
Eastern Lyrics (Hugo)
See *Les orientales*
Easy Money (Ostrovsky)
See *Beshenye dengi*
"Eathlina's Lament" (Moore) **110**:194
L'eau de Jouvence (Renan) **26**:386, 389, 408, 417
"L'eau douce" (Desbordes-Valmore) **97**:27
"Eaves-Dropping a Lodge of Free-Masons" (Harris) **23**:139, 161
The Ebb-Tide: A Trio and Quartette (Stevenson) **5**:412, 415, 419, 427; **63**:261
Ecarté; or, The Salons of Paris (Richardson) **55**:293-4, 304, 312-3, 321, 327, 329, 339, 344-6
"Az ecce homo" (Madach) **19**:369
"Eccentricity" (Allston) **2**:19, 21
Ecclesiastical Sketches (Wordsworth) **12**:409, 466; **38**:368, 371
Ecclesiastical Sonnets (Wordsworth)
See *Ecclesiastical Sketches*
"Echa-czasu" (Norwid) **17**:373
"L'echelonnement des hais" (Verlaine) **51**:355, 370
"Echo and the Fairy" (Ingelow) **39**:264

The Echo Club and Other Literary Diversions (Taylor) **89**:319, 337, 339, 343, 351
"An Echo of Antietam" (Bellamy) **86**:10-11, 75, 78
"Echoes" (Lazarus) **8**:423; **109**:294, 301-02, 321
"Echoes in the City of the Angels" (Jackson) **90**:149
"Echoes of the Week" (Sala) **46**:245
"The Echoing Green" (Blake) **13**:181; **37**:3, 14, 25, 35, 37-8, 57, 65-6, 68, 71-2, 80, 92; **127**:81
Der Echte und der falsche Waldemar (Arnim) **5**:21
"L'eclair" (Rimbaud) **4**:466; **82**:222, 224, 229, 236, 241, 251, 255, 261-62
"Les Éclairs" (Desbordes-Valmore) **97**:27
"L'eclatante victoire de Saarebrück" (Rimbaud) **4**:465; **35**:271
"Eclipse in Italy" (Wordsworth) **38**:363
"Eclogue" (Lear) **3**:298
"Eclogues" (Barnes) **75**:95
El eco del Torrente (Zorrilla y Moral) **6**:525
L'ecole des ménages (Balzac) **5**:74
"L'ecole païenne" (Baudelaire) **29**:70
"L'Écolier" (Desbordes-Valmore) **97**:38
"L'écolier de Leyde" (Bertrand) **31**:46
Economic and Philosophic Manuscripts of 1844 (Marx) **17**:329-30, 350, 352, 360; **114**:69
Economic Studies (Bagehot) **10**:20-22, 25-26, 32, 34, 48
"Economics" (Thoreau) **7**:389
"Economy" (Thoreau) **7**:387-8, 398-9, 402-3; **138**:78, 125, 129, 192
The Economy of Happiness (Bellamy) **4**:27
The Economy of Vegetation (Darwin) **106**:187, 189-90, 192-93, 195-97, 203, 205, 208-09, 212, 220, 225, 232, 236-38, 241-42, 245, 248-49, 256, 263-64, 266, 273-77
L'Ecossais (Dumas) **71**:217
Eda (Baratynsky) **103**:10, 39-40
La Edad de Oro (Martí) **63**:104
"Edax on Appetite" (Lamb) **10**:409, 411; **113**:236-39, 263
"Eden Bower" (Rossetti) **66**:305
"Eden Bower" (Rossetti) **4**:492, 496, 498, 505, 511, 518, 527, 530; **77**:326, 328-30, 361-62
"Edgar and Emma" (Austen) **119**:13, 16
Edgar Huntly; or, Memoirs of a Sleep-Walker (Brown) **22**:3, 5, 7-9, 12-13, 18-22, 24, 27-31, 40-2, 48-9, 52-4, 56-7; **74**:4, 9-12, 15, 19, 24, 36, 41, 49-50, 52-7, 61, 63, 65, 80-2, 84, 86-7, 89, 92-6, 98-9, 101-02, 104-05, 111-12, 117-20, 122, 124-27, 129-30, 133, 135, 139, 141, 143, 147-50, 161, 164; **122**:53-54, 82-84, 90, 93, 95-96, 116
Edgar Poe and His Critics (Whitman) **19**:456-60
"The Edge of the Swamp" (Simms) **3**:507
Edifying Discourses (Kierkegaard) **34**:203, 227, 238; **78**:197, 239
Edifying Discourses in a Different Vein: Three Godly Discourses (Kierkegaard) **34**:224, 246, 252, 254
"Edinburgh" (Smith) **59**:299, 333-4
Edinburgh: Picturesque Notes (Stevenson) **5**:387
Edipo (Martínez de la Rosa) **102**:230, 232, 246
"Edith and Nora" (Wilson) **5**:550
"Edith May" (Parton) **86**:349-50
"The Editor and the Schoolma'am" (Frederic) **10**:193, 212
"Editors" (Parton) **86**:348
"Editor's Table" (Hale) **75**:317
"A Edmond et Jules de Goncourt" (Banville) **9**:26
"La educación de entonces" (Larra) **130**:194
"Education" (Emerson) **98**:66
L'éducation sentimentale: Histoire d'un jeune homme (Flaubert) **2**:225-33, 235-40, 242-3, 245-9, 256; **10**:119, 122, 124-5, 130, 135, 159, 161, 164, 170, 174; **19**:264-322; **62**:69, 74, 76, 83, 88, 90-1, 95-9, 102, 105, 111, 115, 119-21, 123; **66**:256, 270, 293; **135**:78, 89, 93-95, 103, 107-9, 133, 174, 176-77, 180
Educational Reminiscences and Suggestions (Beecher) **30**:16, 25
Der Edukationsrat (Kotzebue) **25**:136
"Edward Fane's Rose-Bud" (Hawthorne) **2**:305
"Edward Gray" (Tennyson) **30**:222
"Edward III" (Blake)
See "King Edward the Third"
"Edward Randolph's Portrait" (Hawthorne) **95**:105
"Edward Shore" (Crabbe) **26**:93, 100
Edwin (Hays) **114**:177
Edwin and Eltruda: A Legendary Tale (Williams) **135**:315, 333
Edwin Drood (Dickens)
See *The Mystery of Edwin Drood*
Edwin of Deira (Smith) **59**:294, 298, 305, 312, 318-21, 326, 333, 337
"Edwy" (Radcliffe) **6**:412
Edwy and Elgiva (Burney) **12**:17, 46-47; **54**:59
Eekenhof (Storm) **1**:540
"Les effarés" (Rimbaud) **4**:455, 465, 485; **35**:271; **82**:226, 230, 251
"The Effects of Religion on Minds of Sensibility. Story of La Roche" (Mackenzie) **41**:180, 188
"Effects of Rural Objects on the Mind" (Mackenzie) **41**:190-91
Effects of Slavery on Morals and Industry (Webster) **30**:404
Effi Briest (Fontane) **26**:235-36, 239, 241, 243-44, 246, 248, 251-52, 258-59, 264-65, 267-72, 276, 278
Les éffrontés (Augier) **31**:5, 7, 9-10, 12-13, 15, 19-20, 24-7, 31-2, 34, 38-9
"Effusion on the Death of James Hogg" (Wordsworth) **12**:431
Egalité (Silva) **114**:263
"L'égalité chrétienne" (Renan) **26**:377
L'Egarement de l'infortune (Sade) **47**:361-62
Egilona (Gómez de Avellaneda) **111**:28
L'église chrétienne (Renan) **26**:402
"L'Église d'Aroma" (Desbordes-Valmore) **97**:6
Egmont (Goethe) **4**:162-64, 167, 172, 190, 194-96, 204, 211-12, 218-22; **34**:71
"Ego" (Whittier) **59**:364
"The Egoist" (Turgenev) **21**:454
"Egos of the Week" (Sala) **46**:245
"Egy nyíri temetõn" (Madach) **19**:369
"Egyptian Maid" (Wordsworth) **111**:213
The Egyptian Nights (Pushkin) **3**:435; **83**:273, 275-76
Die Ehenschmiede (Arnim) **5**:22
"Eidólons" (Whitman) **31**:390
"Eifersucht und Stolz" (Muller) **73**:364
The Eight Commandment (Reade) **74**:269, 315
Eight Cousins (Alcott) **58**:41, 46, 48-50; **83**:44, 47
Eight Cousins; or, The Aunt Hill (Alcott) **6**:16-17, 21
815 (Dickinson) **77**:151
892 (Dickinson) **77**:97
801 (Dickinson) **77**:131
875 (Dickinson) **77**:120
872 (Dickinson) **77**:151
864 (Dickinson) **77**:150
838 (Dickinson) **77**:89
822 (Dickinson) **77**:93
Eight Women (Desbordes-Valmore)
See *Huit Femmes*
Eight Years in Canada (Richardson) **55**:294, 298-9, 303, 311, 314, 317, 320, 329, 334-7, 343-4
"1867" (Patmore) **9**:334, 337-38, 340, 358, 362
"1880-85" (Patmore) **9**:339-40, 358, 362
1811 (Barbauld)
See *Eighteen Hundred and Eleven*
1844 Sketch (Darwin)
See *On the Origin of Species by Means of Natural Selection or the Preservation of Favoured Races in the Struggle for Life*
1842 Sketch (Darwin)
See *On the Origin of Species by Means of Natural Selection or the Preservation of Favoured Races in the Struggle for Life*
Eighteen Hundred and Eleven (Barbauld) **50**:5, 17
Eighteen Upbuilding Discourses (Kierkegaard)
See *Edifying Discourses*
"The Eighteenth Brumaire of Louis Bonaparte" (Marx) **114**:70
The Eighteenth Brumaire of Louis Bonaparte (Marx) **17**:315, 322, 328, 335, 353, 355; **114**:8, 11, 37, 41, 46
"Eighty-five Model Farms and Eighty-five Follies" (Fourier) **51**:180
"Eileen a Ruin" (Griffin) **7**:204
"Eileen Aroon" (Mangan) **27**:283
"An einem Wintermorgen vor Sonnenaufgang" (Mörike) **10**:448, 453-55
An einen ehemaligen Goetheaner (Heine) **54**:344
"Einer Toten" (Meyer) **81**:205, 209
Einfältiger Hausvater-Bericht uber die christlich Religion (Claudius) **75**:193, 210, 214-16, 220
"Eingelegte Ruder" (Meyer) **81**:199, 201, 203
Einleitung zu Don Quixote (Heine) **54**:329
Einleitung zur Kawi-Sprache, Ueber die Verschiedenheit des menschlichen Sprachbaues und ihren Einfluss auf die geistige Entwicklung des Menschengeschlects (Humboldt) **134**:206
Die Einquartierung im Pfarrhause (Arnim) **5**:21
"Einsamkeit" (Lenau) **16**:281
"Einsamkeit" (Muller) **73**:366, 384, 386, 391
"Der Einzige" (Hölderlin) **16**:166-9, 175-6, 191
"Eiros and Charmion" (Poe)
See "The Conversation of Eiros and Charmion"
"Eisen Castle" (Bestuzhev)
See "Zamok Eyzen"
"Eislauf" (Klopstock) **11**:233
Either/Or: A Fragment of a Life (Kierkegaard)
See *Enten/Eller*
"Éjféli párbaj" (Arany) **34**:5, 15
"Ekalavya" (Dutt) **29**:124
Ekei Ki Bale Sabhyatā (Dutt) **118**:5
"Ekhidna" (Leconte de Lisle) **29**:221-22
"Èksprompt" (Pavlova) **138**:52
"Él y Ella" (Echeverria) **18**:147
"Elaine" (Tennyson) **30**:279; **65**:307, 310, 315, 318, 359
"Elden-Tree" (Baillie) **2**:42
"The Elder Brother" (Crabbe) **26**:111, 129
Elder Edda (Grimm and Grimm) **3**:220
"Eldorado" (Poe) **94**:229; **117**:196, 235, 237-38, 242-43, 281, 283
Eldorado (Taylor) **89**:300, 343, 346, 355
"Eldorado at Islington" (Levy) **59**:92
"Eleanore" (Tennyson) **30**:207
The Election: A Comedy on Hatred (Baillie) **2**:31, 33; **71**:12, 64
"The Elections to the Hebdomadal Council" (Carroll) **139**:35
Elective Affinities (Goethe)
See *Die Wahlverwandtschaften*
"The Electric Telegraph" (Bryant) **46**:9
"Oi eleftheroi poliorkimenoi" (Solomos) **15**:386, 391-92, 397-401, 405
"Elegant Tom Dillar" (O'Brien) **21**:249
Elegiac Sonnets, and Other Essays (Smith) **23**:314-15; **115**:120, 122-23, 125, 135, 152, 154-56, 165-66, 174-75, 199-204, 207, 209-12, 215, 217, 223
Elegiac Sonnets, and Other Poems (Blake) **115**:180
"Elegiac Stanzas" (Wordsworth) **12**:458-60; **38**:360, 398

"Elegiac Verses" (Longfellow) **45**:129, 161
"Elegiacs" (Tennyson) **30**:211
"Elégie" (Desbordes-Valmore) **97**:7
"Elégie" (Lamartine) **11**:254
"Elegie auf den Tod eines Jünglings" (Schiller) **39**:339-40, 386
"Elegies" (Tennyson) **115**:236
"Elegija" (Pushkin) **83**:259, 304
"An Elegy" (Chivers) **49**:70
"Elegy" (Cowper) **94**:36
"Elegy" (Darwin) **106**:182
"Elegy" (Pushkin)
See "Elegija"
"Elegy" (Thoreau)
See "Sympathy"
"Elegy for Sulieman the Magnificent" (Mangan) **27**:285
"Elegy of Rome" (Schlegel) **15**:223
"Elegy on Our Lost Princess" (Hunt) **70**:257
"Elegy on the Death of a British Officer" (Sheridan) **91**:233
"Elegy on the Death of a Young Man" (Schiller)
See "Elegie auf den Tod eines Jünglings"
"Elegy on the Death of Dr. Channing" (Lowell) **2**:507
"An Elegy on the Death of Mr. Buckingham St. John" (Trumbull) **30**:348
"An Elegy on the Times" (Trumbull) **30**:346, 350, 353, 374
"An Elegy on the Tironian and Tirconnellian Princes Buried at Rome" (Mangan)
See "Lament for the Princes of Tyrone and Tyrconnell"
"Elegy to Dr. Small" (Darwin) **106**:182
Elegy to the Memory of the Late Duke of Bedford (Opie) **65**:175-7
"Elegy, written at the Hotwells, Bristol" (Bowles) **103**:79
"Elemental Drifts" (Whitman) **4**:544
"Elementargeister" (Heine) **4**:268
"Elementary Education" (Arnold) **89**:110
Elementary Lessons in Physiology (Huxley) **67**:95
The Elementary Spelling Book (Webster)
See *A Grammatical Institute, of the English Language, Comprising, an Easy, Concise, and Systematic Method of Education, Designed for the Use of English Schools in America*
"Elementary Studies" (Newman) **99**:214, 297
"The Elements" (Newman) **38**:345
"Elements of Critical Jurisprudence" (Bentham) **38**:94
The Elements of Mental and Moral Philosophy, Founded upon Reason, Experience, and the Bible (Beecher) **30**:11, 23, 25
Elements of Moral Science (Beattie) **25**:101, 121
The Elements of Rhetoric (De Mille) **123**:161, 163-64
Elën (Villiers de l'Isle Adam) **3**:581, 583-84
"Elena" (Casal) **131**:224-26, 235, 266, 268
"Elena" (Herzen) **10**:347-48; **61**:108
"Elena" (Isaacs) **70**:307-08
"Eleonora" (Poe) **1**:497-98; **16**:305-06, 308, 324, 336; **55**:148, 151; **117**:300, 302
"Les eléphants" (Leconte de Lisle) **29**:210, 216-17, 221, 223-24, 230-31
"Elet vagy halál" (Petofi) **21**:286
"The Eleusinian Feast" (Schiller)
See "Das Eleusische Fest"
"The Eleusinian Festival" (Schiller)
See "Das Eleusische Fest"
"Das Eleusische Fest" (Schiller) **39**:305, 337
"Elévation" (Baudelaire) **6**:82-83, 97, 114, 128; **29**:89-90; **55**:27
Elévation sur Paris (Vigny) **7**:469
1126 (Dickinson) **77**:63, 92, 95
"Eleven Tales of the Arabesque" (Poe) **94**:239
"The Eleventh Hour" (Lazarus) **109**:298, 301, 323
"The Eleventh-Hour Guest" (Villiers de l'Isle Adam)
See "Le convive des dernières fêtes"
"Elfen, Die" (Tieck) **46**:350
"Elfenlied" (Mörike) **10**:446, 455
"Les elfes" (Leconte de Lisle) **29**:220
Elfide (Klinger) **1**:429
"The Elfin Mound" (Andersen) **7**:23; **79**:23, 28
"Elfrida" (Lazarus) **8**:411, 417
Elfrida (Eminescu)
See *The King and the Knight*
"Elfsong" (Mörike)
See "Elfenlied"
"The Elgin Marbles" (Hazlitt) **82**:160
Elgskyttarne (Runeberg) **41**:309-10, 313, 317, 331
Elia: Essays Which Have Appeared under That Signature in the "London Magazine" (Lamb) **10**:389, 391, 393, 395, 403, 406-07, 410-11, 414-16, 420-21, 434; **113**:159, 163, 167, 169-70, 202, 221, 228, 230, 234-35, 240-48, 265-67, 281-83
Elia; o, La España de treinta años ha (Caballero) **10**:77
"Elia to Robert Southey" (Lamb) **10**:408
"Elias Wildmanstadius ou l'Homme moyenage" (Gautier) **59**:26-7
"Elijah" (Kendall) **12**:192
"Elijah's Wagon knew no thill" (Dickinson) **77**:68
"Elinor" (Southey) **97**:314
Elinor and Marianne (Austen) **1**:53; **81**:74; **119**:17, 37, 45
"Elinor Forester: The Father's Wedding" (Lamb) **125**:318, 324-25
Elinor Wyllys; or, The Young Folk of Longbridge. A Tale (Cooper) **129**:9-12, 14, 16-18, 20, 49, 57, 61, 65
"Eliot Carson" (Bellamy) **86**:16-17
Elisa (Goncourt)
See *La fille Élisa*
"Eliveria" (Isaacs) **70**:310
Die Elixiere des Teufels (Hoffmann) **2**:339, 341, 343-44, 348, 358, 360, 362
The Elixir of Long Life (Balzac) **53**:25
"Elizabeth" (Longfellow) **45**:128
Elizabeth Barrett Browning: Hitherto Unpublished Poems and Stories with an Inedited Autobiography (Browning) **61**:48, 50
Elizabeth Barrett to Mr. Boyd: Unpublished Letters of Elizabeth Barrett Browning to Hugh Stuart Boyd (Browning) **61**:14, 28, 50
Elizabeth Bennet; or, Pride and Prejudice (Austen)
See *Pride and Prejudice*
"Elizabeth Hastings" (Brontë) **109**:42
"Elizabeth Villiers: The Sailor Uncle" (Lamb) **125**:312, 317, 324-25, 368-70
"Elizabeth Wilson" (Child) **73**:80
"Elizir d'amor" (Corbière) **43**:13
"The Elk" (Poe) **16**:336
The Elk Hunters (Runeberg)
See *Elgskyttarne*
"Ella duerme!" (Isaacs) **70**:310
"Ella of Garveloch" (Martineau) **26**:304, 306, 351
Ella of Garveloch (Martineau) **137**:243
Elle et lui (Sand) **2**:597, 604; **42**:312; **57**:317
"Ellen Aeyre" (Chivers) **49**:40, 49
"Ellen Bawn" (Mangan) **27**:314
"Ellen Brine ov Allenburn" (Barnes) **75**:8, 46
"Ellen Dare o'Lindenore" (Barnes) **75**:58
Ellen Gray (Bowles) **103**:54
"Ellen Irwin, or the Braes of Kirtle" (Wordsworth) **111**:323
"Ellen Orford" (Crabbe) **26**:149; **121**:36, 88-9
Ellernklipp (Fontane) **26**:237, 243-44, 250-53, 255, 272
Ellie; or, The Human Comedy (Cooke) **5**:121-22, 129
"The Elliotts" (Austen) **1**:53
"The Elm Tree, a Dream in the Woods" (Hood) **16**:210, 220, 222, 224-25, 228-29, 233, 235
"The Elm Trees" (Sigourney) **21**:301
Éloa (Vigny) **102**:335-36, 348, 350, 367-68, 379
Eloge de Victor-Amédée III (Maistre) **37**:302, 311
"Eloquence" (Emerson) **1**:280; **98**:7
"Elsi, die seltsame Magd" (Gotthelf) **117**:6
Elsie Venner: A Romance of Destiny (Holmes) **14**:103, 105-06, 110, 113-15, 117, 119-20, 123-26, 130-41, 143, 148-49, 151; **81**:102, 107-09, 111, 113
"Az első halott" (Madach) **19**:369
"Elverhøi" (Andersen) **79**:76
"The Elves" (Leconte de Lisle)
See "Les elfes"
Az elveszett alkomány (Arany) **34**:16, 21-2
Elvira and Her Desperate Love for a Ludicrous King (Eminescu) **33**:266
Elvira; o, La novia del Plata (Echeverria) **18**:147-49, 152
"Elvira Silva" (Isaacs) **70**:310, 312
"Elysium Is as Far as To" (Dickinson) **21**:10
"The Emancipated Slaveholders" (Child) **73**:80
"The Emancipated Woman at last Found" (Fourier) **51**:180
Emancipation (Channing) **17**:25, 32
"Emancipation in the British West Indies" (Emerson)
See "Emancipation of the British West Indies"
"Emancipation of the British West Indies" (Emerson) **98**:43, 45, 48, 167, 171
"Emancipation Proclamation" (Emerson) **98**:43
Emancipation Proclamation (Lincoln) **18**:219, 231-35, 268-71
Die Emanzipation der Domestiken (Ludwig) **4**:367
Emaux et camées (Gautier) **1**:342-43, 347-48, 350; **59**:3, 17-20, 43
"The Embalmer" (Maginn) **8**:438
The Embargo; or, Sketches of the Times (Bryant) **6**:157; **46**:25
"Az ember" (Petofi) **21**:264
Az ember tragédiája (Madach) **19**:354-57, 360-62, 364-74
"Emblem" (Harpur) **114**:116
"Emerald Uthwart" (Pater) **7**:303, 324
"Emerson" (Arnold) **126**:43
Emerson: Collected Poems and Translations (Emerson) **98**:177
Emerson in His Journals (Emerson) **98**:134
"Emerson the Lecturer" (Lowell) **90**:219-21
"Emerson's Limitations as a Poet" (Cranch) **115**:33
"Emerson's Personality" (Lazarus) **109**:305-06
"Emerson's 'Thoreau'" (Emerson) **98**:73-4
"L'Emeute" (Baudelaire) **55**:36
"The Emigrant Mother" (Sigourney) **21**:298
"The Emigrants" (Smith) **115**:121
The Emigrants (Smith) **115**:126, 129, 133-34, 158, 164, 166, 168, 195-97, 199, 204, 206-11, 218
"Emigrant's Farewell" (Allingham) **25**:15
The Emigrant's Guide (Cobbett) **49**:152-53
The Emigrants of Ahadarra (Carleton) **3**:90, 94, 96
"The Emigrant's Unhappy Predicament" (Boyesen) **135**:32
L'émigré (Charriere) **66**:136
Les Émigrés (Charriere) **66**:124
Emilie (Nerval) **1**:485; **67**:304, 363, 365
"Emilie De Coulanges" (Edgeworth) **51**:89
"Emilie de Tourville ou la cruauté fraternelle" (Sade) **47**:313
The Emissary (Sacher-Masoch) **31**:285, 289
Emma (Austen) **1**:30, 32-4, 36-40, 44-6, 48, 50-2, 54-5, 60-1, 63-4; **13**:66, 93-4, 96, 104; **19**:1-70; **33**:39, 57-9, 62-5, 69, 71, 74, 76,

80, 84, 88-90, 92-3, 96-7, 99; **51**:15, 41; **81**:5, 12-3, 18, 35, 68, 78-9, 83; **95**:13, 18, 21, 25, 39, 55-6, 58, 73, 86; **119**:14-18, 21-8, 33, 39-43, 48, 57
"Emma and Ermingard" (Longfellow) **45**:145
Emmeline, the Orphan of the Castle (Smith) **23**:314-15, 319-24, 327-29, 332-33, 335; **115**:136-42, 144-46, 150, 153, 187-90, 192, 210, 221-24
"Emotional Art" (Patmore) **9**:342
Empedocles (Hölderlin)
See *Empedokles*
"Empedocles on Etna" (Arnold) **6**:31, 38, 42, 48, 51-52, 54, 56, 59, 66-67, 70-72; **29**:5-6, 26-7, 29, 31, 36-7, 53; **89**:14, 49-51, 53, 82, 120
Empedocles on Etna, and Other Poems (Arnold) **6**:28, 30, 73-74; **29**:27, 35; **89**:88, 91-2
Empedokles (Hölderlin) **16**:159, 164-65, 187-88, 190-91
"Emperor and Proletarian" (Eminescu)
See "Împarat şi proletar"
"The Emperor of China and Tsing-ti" (Landor) **14**:165, 167, 178
"The Emperor's New Clothes" (Andersen)
See "Keiserens nye Klæder"
"The Emperor's Nightingale" (Andersen) **7**:37
"The Emperor's Son without a Star" (Eminescu) **131**:347
"The Emperor's Statue" (Grillparzer)
See "Des Kaisers Bildsäule"
"L'Empire Knouto-Germanique et la Révolution Sociale" (Bakunin) **25**:46, 48-9, 59; **58**:99, 140
"The Empire of the Chimilas" (Isaacs)
See "El imperio chimila"
Empires of the World (Fouqué) **2**:267
Les employés (Balzac) **35**:3
En 18.. (Goncourt and Goncourt) **7**:161, 167, 186-87, 189
"En balde" (Castro) **78**:40
"En bateau" (Verlaine) **2**:630; **51**:378-79
En Comedie i det Gronne (Andersen) **79**:9
"En la tortura" (Isaacs) **70**:310
"En la tumba de Leopoldo..." (Isaacs) **70**:306
"En las cumbres de Chisacá" (Isaacs) **70**:310
"En las orillas del Sar" (Castro) **3**:103; **78**:10, 12-13, 16-17, 21, 23, 25, 29-30, 32, 38, 41, 54
"En lisant" (Maupassant) **83**:185
En literair Anmeldelse. To Tidsaldre (Kierkegaard) **125**:203, 231
"En loor de la Reina gobernadora" (Larra) **130**:202
"En los ecos de los organos o en el rumor del viento" (Castro) **78**:41
"En los ecos del Organo o en el rumor del viento" (Castro) **78**:21
"En masse" (Whitman) **4**:564
Una en otra (Caballero) **10**:72
"En patinant" (Verlaine) **51**:378-79
"En Route" (Browning) **61**:15
"En sourdine" (Verlaine) **2**:624; **51**:351, 378-81
"En Suenos te di un beso, vida mia" (Castro) **78**:23
En Suisse (Dumas) **71**:205
"En voyage" (Maupassant) **83**:158-62, 194, 228
Enamels and Cameos (Gautier)
See *Emaux et camées*
"The Encantadas; or, The Enchanted Isles" (Melville) **3**:331, 344, 347, 354, 361-62, 368, 380-81, 383-84; **45**:233; **123**:254
"The Enchanted Knight" (Taylor) **89**:298
"The Enchanted Lyre" (Darley) **2**:127, 132
"The Enchanted Pilgrim" (Leskov)
See "Očarovannyj strannik"
"The Enchanted Spot" (Gogol)
See "Zakoldovannoe mesto"
"The Enchanted Titan" (O'Brien) **21**:238
"The Enchanted Wanderer" (Leskov)
See "Očarovannyj strannik"
Encore une nuit de la Garde Nationale; ou, Le poste de la barrière (Scribe) **16**:391, 393, 400
Encyclopedia of the Philosophical Sciences in Outline. Part 1. The Logic (Hegel)
See *Enzyklopädie der philosophischen Wissenshaften im Grundrisse. Theil 1. Die Logik*
Encyclopedia of the Philosophical Sciences in Outline. Part 2. Philosophy of Nature (Hegel)
See *Enzyklopädie der philosophischen Wissenshaften im Grundrisse. Theil 2. Naturphilosophie*
"The End" (Corbière)
See "La fin"
"An End in Paris" (Wagner)
See "Ein Ende in Paris"
"The End of All" (Brontë) **109**:4, 30
"The End of the World" (Turgenev) **21**:431, 453
"Das Ende des Festes" (Meyer) **81**:143, 169, 200
"Ein Ende in Paris" (Wagner) **9**:475
"Endicott of the Red Cross" (Hawthorne) **2**:329-31; **10**:308
"The Ending of 'The Government Inspector'" (Gogol)
See "Razviazka 'Révizor'"
"Ends of the Church" (Arnold) **18**:47
"Endymion" (Cranch) **115**:5
"Endymion" (Wieland) **17**:426
Endymion (Disraeli) **2**:145-46, 150; **39**:3-4, 21-4, 31, 36-7, 43-4, 49, 51, 66, 71-81; **79**:212, 222, 234, 257, 269
Endymion (Keats)
See *Endymion: A Poetic Romance*
Endymion: A Poetic Romance (Keats) **8**:323-28, 330-37, 340-42, 344-50, 353-61, 364-66, 368-70, 372, 385-86; **73**:142, 144, 152-53, 158, 170-72, 177, 192, 198, 201-04, 208-09, 211, 233-34, 246, 248, 254, 258, 260, 268-71, 290-91, 310-11, 314, 322-25, 332-36, 338-39, 341-42; **121**:98, 102, 104, 109, 122, 125, 136, 139, 141, 147-48, 151, 162-69, 173, 175, 187, 206, 209, 225, 228-29, 233
"Enfance" (Rimbaud) **4**:466, 473, 484; **35**:297, 299, 304-07, 322-23; **82**:232-33, 253
"Les enfans de la France" (Beranger) **34**:28
"L'Enfant" (Maupassant) **83**:213-16, 223
"L'enfant aux souliers de pain" (Gautier) **1**:348; **59**:32, 36
L'enfant prodigue (Becque) **3**:13, 15-16
L'Enfant prodigue (Mallarmé) **41**:278
"Enfer et diable" (Beranger) **34**:41
"The Enfranchisement of Women" (Mill) **102**:282-83, 285-87, 297-302, 315-16, 320, 330
The Enfranchisement of Women (Mill) **11**:393
The Engagement (Kivi)
See *Kihlaus*
Der Engel Von Augsburg (Ludwig) **4**:350
"Engelberg" (Meyer) **81**:155
"Den Engelske lods" (Wergeland) **5**:536, 538, 541
"England" (Emerson) **98**:7
England and Spain; or Valour and Patriotism (Hemans) **71**:271, 278
England and the English (Bulwer-Lytton) **1**:151-53; **45**:32, 36-8, 47-8, 71
"England in Egypt" (Adams) **33**:12
England in Time of War (Dobell) **43**:40, 44, 60, 62
England, the Civilizer (Wright) **74**:375, 377-78
"England's Day" (Dobell) **43**:45
"England's Dead" (Hemans) **71**:278
"England's Forgotten Worthies" (Froude) **43**:184
"England's Glory: A Loyal Song" (Moodie) **113**:310
English Bards and Scotch Reviewers (Byron) **2**:58, 62, 70, 85, 92, 95, 103; **12**:88, 103, 105-06, 129
"The English Boy" (Hemans) **71**:277
The English Constitution (Bagehot) **10**:15, 19, 22-23, 32, 34-35, 40, 45, 48, 50-54, 59, 63-66
English Ecologues (Southey) **97**:315, 318
"The English Factory" (Tonna) **135**:196
The English Gardener (Cobbett) **49**:108, 110, 113-14, 140, 150-51
English Grammar (Cobbett)
See *Grammar of the English Language*
The English Humourists of the Eighteenth Century (Thackeray) **5**:457, 466, 490; **43**:376
"English Idylls" (Tennyson) **30**:249
The English in Ireland in the Eighteenth Century (Froude) **43**:193-96
The English in Little (Jerrold) **2**:406-08
The English in the West Indies (Froude) **43**:192
English Laws of Custom and Marriage for Women of the Nineteenth Century (Norton) **47**:248, 254, 261-63
"English Literature" (Pater) **90**:333, 337
"The English Mail-Coach" (De Quincey) **87**:22-4, 30, 43-4, 47
The English Mail-coach (De Quincey) **4**:67, 74, 77, 82, 86-89; **87**:3, 15
English Notebooks (Hawthorne)
See *Passages from the English Notebooks of Nathaniel Hawthorne*
The English Novel and the Principle of Its Development (Lanier) **6**:245, 252, 265-66; **118**:204, 218, 248, 283
"The English Pilot" (Wergeland)
See "Den Engelske lods"
"An English Poet" (Pater) **90**:290, 340
"An English Prologue and Epilogue to the Latin Comedy of Ignoramus with a Preface and Notes relative to modern Times and Manners" (Dyer) **129**:105, 116
"The English Revolution of 1848" (Rossetti) **77**:291-92, 294
"English Slavery" (Tonna) **135**:204, 211
An English Tragedy (Kemble) **18**:191
English Traits (Emerson) **1**:278, 281, 284, 286, 288, 299; **38**:173, 213-18; **98**:5, 55, 72, 76, 130
"The English View of Internal Crises" (Engels) **85**:121
"English Writers on America" (Irving) **19**:327-28, 347, 350; **95**:293-94
"The Englishman in Italy" (Browning) **19**:98; **79**:94, 97
"Englyn" (Barnes) **75**:54
"Enid" (Tennyson) **30**:249, 279; **65**:226, 359, 381
"An Enigma" (Poe) **117**:242
L'Enlèvement (Becque) **3**:13, 16
"L'enlèvement de la rédoute" (Mérimée) **6**:353-4, 358, 363-4, 366-7, 369, 371; **65**:57, 60, 87, 103-4
"L'ennemi" (Baudelaire) **6**:117; **55**:58
Ennui (Edgeworth) **1**:257, 262, 264, 267-68, 270; **51**:86-90, 93, 104, 137
Ennuyée (Jameson)
See *Diary of an Ennuyée*
"Enoch" (Very) **9**:378
"Enoch Arden" (Crabbe) **26**:135, 150
Enoch Arden (Tennyson) **30**:218-20, 233, 238, 249, 276, 282
"Enosis" (Cranch) **115**:5, 13-14, 22, 27-9, 32, 35, 54, 67
"Enough" (Turgenev) **21**:420, 435, 440; **122**:241, 243, 247, 337, 343
Enough Silliness in Every Wise Man (Ostrovsky)
See *Na vsyakogo mudretsa dovolno prostoty*
The Enquirer: Reflections on Education,

Manners, and Literature (Godwin) **14**:75, 79-80, 84, 86-7; **130**:7, 40, 113, 115, 125
Enquiry concerning Political Justice and Its Influence on General Virtue and Happiness (Godwin) **14**:37-8, 40-3, 47, 50-1, 54-76, 78, 80-3, 85, 87-8, 90, 92-3; **130**:5, 7-9, 14, 20-21, 23-25, 27, 30, 32-33, 36-37, 47-49, 52-55, 58, 60-62, 64, 70-72, 74-76, 81, 88-98, 100, 107-11, 113-14, 122-23, 129-30, 142-45, 150-52, 154, 156-57, 161, 164, 169-73, 182-83
Enquiry concerning Political Justice and Its Influence on Morals and Happiness (Godwin)
See *Enquiry concerning Political Justice and Its Influence on General Virtue and Happiness*
"An Enquiry Whether the Fine Arts are Promoted by Academies" (Hazlitt) **29**:144
"Enragée" (Maupassant) **83**:223, 230
Ensayos (Bécquer) **106**:96
"The Ensign at the Fair" (Runeberg)
See "Fänrikens marknadsminne"
Ensign Stål (Runeberg)
See *Fänrik Ståls sägner*
"The Ensign's Greeting" (Runeberg) **41**:312, 314
"Ensimmäinen lempi" (Kivi)
See "Nuori Karhunampuja"
L'ensorcelée (Barbey d'Aurevilly) **1**:70-73
The Entail (Hoffmann)
See *Der Majorat*
The Entail; or, The Lairds of Grippy (Galt) **1**:329, 331-32, 335, 337; **110**:78-9, 82, 93, 96, 98-9, 101-2, 105-7, 114
Enten/Eller (Kierkegaard) **34**:178, 192, 201, 203, 205, 222, 236, 238, 240, 248-54, 258, 268; **78**:166-68, 173-74, 176, 178, 181-82, 187, 198, 215, 227, 238, 242-43, 248, 252; **125**:173-287
Enten/Eller Vol. I (Kierkegaard) **125**:177-79, 182, 191, 198, 200-215, 230, 232-33, 247-57, 278-80
Enten/Eller Vol. II (Kierkegaard) **125**:179-80, 200, 202, 204, 209-10, 213-14, 218-26, 231, 234, 250, 259-64, 282-84
"Entends comme brame" (Rimbaud) **35**:321; **82**:238
"L'enterrement" (Verlaine) **2**:630
"L'enthousiasme" (Lamartine) **11**:245
"Enthusiasm" (Moodie) **113**:317-21
Enthusiasm (Baillie) **71**:6
Enthusiasm, and other Poems (Moodie) **113**:313-17, 321, 324, 368
"Enthusiasmus und Schwärmerei" (Wieland) **17**:411
"The Enthusiast: A Daydream in Summer" (Clare) **86**:113
The Enthusiast; or the Lover of Nature (Warton) **118**:297-98, 300-301, 304, 331-33, 335-36, 350, 354, 356
"La entrada del invierno en Londres" (Espronceda) **39**:87, 105
Entre quatre murs (Mallarmé) **41**:248-49
"Entre sueños" (Bécquer) **106**:115, 157
Entretiens journaliers avec le très docte et très habile docteur Piffoël (Sand) **57**:380
"L'entrevue au ruisseau" (Desbordes-Valmore) **97**:27
"Entsagung" (Grillparzer) **102**:117
Die Entwicklung des Sozialismus von der Uopie zur Wissenschaft (Marx) **85**:6, 24, 59, 105, 181; **114**:4, 39, 44
"L'Envoi" (Taylor) **89**:359
"L'Envoy" (Irving) **95**:265
"The Envoy" (Mangan) **27**:300
Enzyklopädie der philosophischen Wissenshaften im Grundrisse. Theil 1. Die Logik (Hegel) **46**:60-2, 70, 78, 89-91, 108, 112-13, 124-25, 150, 153, 155, 159, 162, 164-65, 181-83, 186, 189
Enzyklopädie der philosophischen Wissenshaften im Grundrisse. Theil 2. Naturphilosophie (Hegel) **46**:70, 89-90, 108, 112, 124-25, 150, 153, 155, 159, 162, 164-65, 181-83, 186, 189
"The Eolian Harp" (Coleridge)
See "The Aeolian Harp"
"Eolova arfa" (Zhukovsky) **35**:398
Eonchs of Ruby (Chivers) **49**:42-3, 47, 49, 52, 70, 72-3
Eonchs of Ruby: A Gift of Love (Chivers)
See *Eonchs of Ruby*
"L'épée" (Banville) **9**:16
"Epée d'Angantyr" (Leconte de Lisle) **29**:215
Epen Erskine; or, The Traveller (Galt) **1**:334
"The Ephemeral Life" (Ichiyō)
See "Utsusemi"
Ephesus Widow (Eminescu) **33**:266
"The Epic" (Tennyson) **30**:279; **65**:348, 354, 368
"Epic Poetry" (Very) **9**:370, 379, 387
"Epic-in three Lustra" (Chivers) **49**:43
The Epicurean (Moore) **6**:384-85; **110**:167-68, 188-89
"The Epicurean's Song" (Brontë) **109**:5
"Epicurius, Leontium, and Ternissa" (Landor) **14**:178
Die Epigonen: Familienmemoiren in neun Büchern (Immermann) **4**:292-97; **49**:365-66, 369, 371-72
"Epigones" (Eminescu) **33**:245, 255; **131**:338
The Epigram (Keller)
See *Das Sinngedicht*
"Epigram on a Long-Nosed Friend" (Paine) **62**:325
Das Epigramm (Kotzebue) **25**:137, 141
"Epigramma na Zhukovskogo" (Bestuzhev) **131**:148
"Epigramme" (Goethe) **4**:193
Epigrammes (Verlaine) **51**:351
"Epilog" (Heine) **4**:257
"Epilogue" (Arany) **34**:5
"Epilogue" (Browning) **79**:169
"Epilogue" (Crawford) **127**:178
"Epilogue" (Lamartine) **11**:286-87, 289
"Epilogue" (Pater) **7**:323
"Epilogue" (Preseren) **127**:293
"Epilogue" (Tennyson) **30**:295
"Epilogue" (Verlaine) **2**:631
"Epilogue à la ville de Paris" (Baudelaire) **29**:79
"Epilogue to the Breakfast-Table Series" (Holmes) **14**:109
"Epimetheus; or, The Poet's Afterthought" (Longfellow) **2**:492
"Les epingles" (Maupassant) **1**:458; **83**:194, 201
"Epiphany" (Leconte de Lisle) **29**:218
Epipsychidion (Shelley) **18**:340, 346, 349-51, 354, 362-64, 369-70, 373, 383; **93**:275, 277, 279-81, 343-46, 348
"Les épis" (Leconte de Lisle) **29**:246
"Episcopal Justice" (Leskov)
See "Vladyčnyj sud"
Épisode (Lamartine) **11**:274
"Épisode de l'histoire de la Russie" (Mérimée) **6**:356; **65**:79
An Episode under the Terror (Balzac) **5**:52-53
Episodes in a Life of Adventure (Oliphant) **47**:286, 289
The Episodes of Vathek (Beckford) **16**:29, 50
"Episteln" (Goethe) **4**:193
"Epistle" (Shevchenko)
See "Poslaniie"
"Epistle IV" (Eminescu) **33**:245, 247, 265; **131**:288, 332
"Epistle from a Father to a Child in her Grave" (Brontë) **109**:6
"Epistle from Henry of Exeter to John of Tehume" (Moore) **6**:388
"An Epistle from Joshua Ibn Vives of Allorqui" (Lazarus) **109**:297
"An Epistle from the Maid of Corinth to Her Lover" (Opie) **65**:174
"Epistle John Hamilton to Reynolds" (Keats) **8**:362, 389; **73**:162, 201, 203, 209, 259, 266
"Epistle of Condolence from a Slave-Lord to a Cotton-Lord" (Moore) **110**:172
"An Epistle of Karshish the Arab Physician" (Browning) **19**:79, 115, 117, 129-30, 137; **79**:140, 142, 164, 185
"Epistle on Miracles" (Very) **9**:395
"Epistle to ..." (Halleck) **47**:77
Epistle to a Friend (Rogers) **69**:73, 78
"An Epistle to a Friend on New-Year's Day" (Opie) **65**:154
"Epistle to Charles Cowden Clarke" (Keats) **8**:359; **73**:152,193
"An Epistle to Dr. Moore" (Williams) **135**:255, 333-34
"Epistle to George Felton Mathew" (Keats) **8**:364; **73**:224, 311
"Epistle to Mr. Hill" (Cowper) **8**:97, 103
"Epistle to My Brother George" (Keats) **73**:152, 257, 323
Epistle to Ovid (Pushkin) **3**:415
"Epistle to Sir Walter Scott" (Brackenridge) **7**:57
"Epistle to the Author of 'Festus'" (Landor) **14**:198
"Epistle to the Duke de Frias" (Martínez de la Rosa) **102**:228-29
"An Epistle to the Hebrews" (Lazarus) **109**:338
An Epistle to the Hebrews (Lazarus) **8**:424; **109**:289, 303, 312, 320, 322, 330, 337-39, 346-48
"Epistle to the Recorder by Thomas Castaly Edq" (Halleck) **47**:68, 71-72, 77-78, 81, 86
"The Epistles" (Eminescu)
See "Scrisorile"
"Epistles" (Keats) **8**:359-60
Epistles (Eminescu) **131**:297
Epistles (Very) **9**:393-96
"Epistles V" (Eminescu) **33**:245, 247, 249
Epistles, Odes, and Other Poems (Moore) **6**:377, 387, 390, 395; **110**:177-78
Epistles of the Fudge Family (Moore) **6**:382
Epistolario Rizalino (Rizal) **27**:417
"Epi-Strauss-Ium" (Clough) **27**:89, 100
"Epitalamio" (Lizardi) **30**:68
"Epitaph" (Cowper)
See "Epitaph on a Hare"
"Epitaph (On a commonplace person who died in bed)" (Levy) **59**:105, 110
"Epitaph on a Hare" (Cowper) **94**:32-4, 36
"Epitaph on Brooks" (Sheridan) **91**:233
Epitaph on Henry Martyn (Macaulay) **42**:116
"Epitaph on King John" (Southey) **97**:318
"Épitaphe" (Nerval) **67**:306-07
"Epitaphe pour Tristan Joachim-Edouard Corbière, Philosophe" (Corbière) **43**:11, 17-18, 22, 25-7, 31,34
"Epithalamion" (Hopkins) **17**:255
"Epithalamium" (Trumbull) **30**:349, 366
"L'Epître au malheur" (Staël-Holstein) **91**:335, 358
"Die Epochen der Dichkunst" (Schlegel) **45**:306, 308, 320, 324, 360, 370
"Epochs" (Lazarus) **8**:413, 418-20; **109**:292, 297-98
"Epochs of Poetry" (Schlegel)
See "Die Epochen der Dichkunst"
"L'Epoux Corrigé" (Sade) **47**:313
"L'Époux infernal" (Rimbaud) **82**:222, 241-42, 245
"Eppich" (Meyer) **81**:200
The Epping Hunt (Hood) **16**:224, 233-35
"Equality" (Arnold) **6**:45, 46; **89**:101, 104; **126**:37, 81
Equality (Bellamy) **4**:25-27, 29-31, 33; **86**:3-4, 12, 22-23, 28, 30, 32, 55, 62, 64-6, 68
"The Equality of the Sexes" (Murray) **63**:180
"Equilibrium" (Eminescu) **33**:272

"Equilibrium between the Aesthetic and Ethical" (Kierkegaard) **125**:282
Gli equivoci (Da Ponte) **50**:80
" Er schuf sie ein Männlein und Fräulein" (Claudius) **75**:192
"Era" (Gaskell) **137**:61-62
"Era apacible el dia" (Castro) **78**:17, 20-22
"Erbauliche Betrachtung" (Mörike) **10**:447
Die Erbförster (Ludwig) **4**:347-52, 354, 364-66
"Erbvetter Joggeli" (Gotthelf) **117**:25
"Das Erdbeben in Chili" (Kleist) **2**:445, 452, 456-57; **37**:237, 239, 242-3, 245-9, 253-5
"Das Erdbeeri Mareili" (Gotthelf) **117**:6, 32-3, 43, 51-5, 57-8
Eremit auf Formentera (Kotzebue) **25**:141
The Erie Train Boy (Alger) **8**:30, 44
"Erin, Oh Erin" (Moore) **110**:182
"Erin, the Tear and the Smile in Thine Eye" (Moore) **6**:390
"Erinna" (Landon) **15**:156-57, 166, 168
"Erinna an Sappho" (Mörike) **10**:457, 459
"Erinna to Sappho" (Mörike)
See "Erinna an Sappho"
"Die Erinnerung" (Klopstock) **11**:237
Erinnerungen aus meinem Leben (Freytag) **109**:177
Erinnerungen meiner dritten Schweizerreise (La Roche) **121**:242, 251
Erinnerungern aus Rubens (Burckhardt) **49**:14
"Erin's Warning" (Crawford) **127**:217
Erkenne dich selb (Wagner) **9**:475; **119**:291
Erklärung (Heine) **4**:248
Die Erlebnisse eines Schuldenbauers (Gotthelf) **117**:6-7, 15, 17-18, 22-3, 25, 32, 38
Erlebtes (Eichendorff) **8**:220-21
Erlkönig (Goethe) **4**:192
"Erlösung" (Muller) **73**:366
"L'Ermite" (Maupassant) **83**:228
"Ermolai and the Miller's Wife" (Turgenev)
See "Yermolai and the Miller's Wife"
"Ermolaj and the Miller's Wife" (Turgenev)
See "Yermolai and the Miller's Wife"
"Ermolaj i mel'ničicha" (Turgenev) **122**:264
"Ermunterung" (Hölderlin) **16**:187-9
Ernest Maltravers (Bulwer-Lytton) **1**:138, 140, 148-49, 155; **45**:21, 23, 28-9, 68
Ernestus Berchtold; or, The Modern Oedipus (Polidori) **51**:193-94, 201-02, 206-07, 231-34, 237-39, 241-42
Ernst und Kurzweil, von meinem Vetter an mich (Claudius) **75**:197
"Ernteabend" (Meyer) **81**:152-53, 155-56
"Erntegewitter" (Meyer) **81**:141, 153-57, 206
"Erntelied" (Brentano) **1**:105
"Erntelied" (Meyer) **81**:152-54
"Erntenacht" (Meyer) **81**:152-54, 156
"Der Erntewagen" (Meyer) **81**:140-41, 144, 150-52, 154-55
"Der Eroberer" (Schiller) **39**:338, 355, 386-88
"Eros and Psyche" (Patmore) **9**:339, 365
Les Errinyes (Leconte de Lisle) **29**:222, 225
"The Errors and Abuses of English Criticism" (Lewes) **25**:285, 304
The Errors of Ecstasie (Darley) **2**:124-25, 127, 129, 133-34
Erscheinungen am See Oneida (La Roche) **121**:291, 326
"Erstarrung" (Muller) **73**:385, 394
"Die erste nacht" (Meyer) **81**:155
"Erster Schmerz, letzter Scherz" (Muller) **73**:364, 373
"Erstes Liebeslied eines Mädchens" (Mörike) **10**:448, 455
"Erwin and Linda" (Barnes) **75**:76
Erwin und Elmire (Goethe) **4**:164
Erzählprosa (Gotthelf) **117**:43
"Die Erzdes Heckebeutels" (Arnim)
See "Der Heckebeutel"
Es en el siglo XXIV (Silva) **114**:263
"Es ist eine alte Geschichte" (Heine) **4**:249
El escándalo (Alarcon) **1**:12-13, 16-17
The Escape; or, A Leap for Freedom (Brown) **2**:48-52; **89**:143, 153, 163, 182, 187
The Escapes (Holcroft) **85**:199
Escenas norteamericanas (Martí) **63**:74, 81-2, 88, 167
Les esclaves de Paris (Gaboriau) **14**:15
"Les esclaves gaulois" (Beranger) **34**:29
"El esclavo Pedro" (Isaacs) **70**:304
Escorial (Symonds) **34**:335
"Escuela normal de mujeres" (Faustino) **123**:360
Las escuelas, base de la prosperidad y de la república en los Estados Unidas (Faustino) **123**:275
"Eshche listok" (Bestuzhev) **131**:165, 171
"La Esmeralda" (Hugo) **3**:261
"Les Espagnols en Danemark" (Mérimée) **6**:354, 362; **65**:44, 46, 51, 60, 62, 79, 82, 86
España (Gautier) **59**:5, 18
El español en Venecia (Martínez de la Rosa) **102**:230
Espatolino (Gómez de Avellaneda) **111**:21, 23
La esperanza de la patria (Tamayo y Baus) **1**:571
El espetón de oro (Villaverde) **121**:333, 361
Espíritu del siglo (Martínez de la Rosa) **102**:228, 248-49, 253
L'esprit pur (Vigny) **7**:472, 478, 483, 485-86
"L'esprit saint" (Lamartine) **11**:270, 279
"Esquivez" (Casal) **131**:239
"Essa on the Muel, bi Josh Billings" (Shaw) **15**:339, 341
Essai historique, politique, et moral sur les révolutions anciennes et modernet considérées dans leurs rapports avec la révolution Française (Chateaubriand) **3**:114
Essai sur la Guerre Sociale (Mérimée) **65**:85
Essai sur la littérature Anglaise et considérations sur le génie des hommes, des temps et, des révolutions (Chateaubriand) **3**:119-20, 128, 132; **134**:12-13, 15-17, 19, 43
"Essai sur le drame fantastique: Goethe, Byron, Mickciewicz" (Sand) **42**:314, 369
Essai sur le principe générateur des constitutions politiques et des autres institutions humaines (Maistre) **37**:292, 295, 297, 299, 303-04, 306, 311, 314
Essai sur les fables de La Fontaine (Taine) **15**:410, 430, 463, 468, 472
Essai sur les fictions (Staël-Holstein) **3**:523-4, 532; **91**:299-301, 303-4, 311, 332, 339-40
Essai sur les forces humaines (Balzac) **5**:28
Essai sur les révolutions anciennes et modernes (Chateaubriand) **3**:112; **134**:3, 17, 19, 27, 30, 83, 102-5, 107
Essai sur l'inégalité des races humaines (Gobineau) **17**:60, 62-3, 70-4, 76-7, 79-81, 83-4, 86, 88, 90-2, 94-5, 97-104
Essai sur Tite-Live (Taine) **15**:412, 430-31
Essais de critique et d'histoire (Taine) **15**:410, 438, 468, 473
Essais de morale et de critique (Renan) **26**:364, 379, 414-15, 417
Essay (Staël-Holstein)
See *Essai sur les fictions*
An Essay in Aid of a Grammar of Assent (Newman) **38**:272, 288, 305, 307, 311-12, 314, 317, 321, 324; **99**:217, 237-45, 254, 297-98, 300-01
An Essay in Political and Social Criticism (Arnold) **126**:75
Essay in Refutation of Atheism (Brownson) **50**:53
Essay of 1844 (Darwin) **57**:159
Essay on Aesthetic Poetry (Pater) **90**:326
"Essay on American Literature" (Fuller) **5**:159
"An Essay on an Old Subject" (Smith) **59**:308, 315, 317, 322
Essay on Anglo-Saxon (Jefferson) **11**:199; **103**:106
"An Essay on Anglo-Saxon and Modern Dialects of the English Language" (Jefferson) **103**:106
"Essay on Blake" (Robinson) **15**:183
"Essay on Chivalry" (Scott) **69**:329, 341
Essay on Christianity (Shelley) **18**:354, 375, 377; **93**:352
"Essay on Commercial Policy" (Galt) **110**:92
"Essay on Critics" (Fuller) **50**:226-7
Essay on Development (Newman)
See *An Essay on the Development of Christian Doctrine*
Essay on Dramatic Compostion (Holcroft) **85**:218
"Essay on Elegiac Poetry" (Dyer) **129**:94
"Essay on English Poetry" (Campbell) **19**:171-73, 175, 184, 191
"Essay on Epitaphs" (Wordsworth) **12**:472; **38**:400
Essay on Fiction (Staël-Holstein)
See *Essai sur les fictions*
Essay on Human Forces (Balzac)
See *Essai sur les forces humaines*
"Essay on Interpretation" (Arnold) **18**:24
"Essay on Irish Bulls" (Edgeworth) **1**:267; **51**:97-9
"Essay on Landscape" (Clare) **9**:110; **86**:96-7
"Essay on Language" (Bentham) **38**:92
"Essay on Life" (Shelley) **93**:338
"Essay on Logic" (Bentham) **38**:56, 92, 94-5, 99
"Essay on Method" (Coleridge) **9**:208
"Essay on Mind" (Browning) **16**:141; **66**:44
An Essay on Mind, with other Poems (Browning) **61**:4, 41, 48-50, 61
An Essay on Percy Bysshe Shelley (Browning) **19**:132-33, 155; **79**:107, 111, 167-68, 186
"An Essay on Poetry" (Beattie)
See *Essays: On Poetry and Music, as They Affect the Mind; On Laughter, and Ludicrous Composition; On the Utility of Classical Learning*
Essay on Political Tactics (Bentham) **38**:91
Essay on Ranke (Macaulay) **42**:80, 96
Essay on Revolutions (Chateaubriand)
See *Essai sur les révolutions anciennes et modernes*
"Essay on Romance" (Scott) **69**:340
"Essay on Self-Justification" (Edgeworth) **1**:262
Essay on Sepulchres; or, A Proposal for Erecting Some Memorial of the Illustrious Dead in All Ages on the Spot Where Their Remains Have Been Interred (Godwin) **14**:40, 53
An Essay on Slavery and Abolitionism with Reference to the Duty of American Females (Beecher) **30**:23-4
"Essay on Tasso and Chatterton" (Browning) **19**:140; **79**:186
"An Essay on the Ancient English Minstrels" (Percy) **95**:323, 327, 329-30, 332, 345, 364-65
An Essay on the Development of Christian Doctrine (Newman) **38**:263, 283, 307, 311, 322, 326; **99**:217, 244
Essay on the Development of Doctrine (Newman)
See *An Essay on the Development of Christian Doctrine*
"Essay on the Different Styles of Goethe's Early and Late Works" (Schlegel)
See "Versuch über den verschiedenen Styl in Goethe's früheren und späteren Werken"
An Essay on the Education of Female Teachers (Beecher) **30**:15
Essay on the Fables of La Fontaine (Taine)
See *Essai sur les fables de La Fontaine*

Essay on the Genius and Writing of Shakespeare (Montagu) **117**:135, 139-40, 149, 152, 158, 160, 179, 184-87
Essay on the Inequality of the Human Races (Gobineau)
See *Essai sur l'inégalité des races humaines*
Essay on the Life and Character of William III (Macaulay) **42**:144
An Essay on the Nature and Immutability of Truth (Beattie) **25**:80-7, 94, 96, 101, 103-05, 112-13, 120-23
An Essay on the Principles of Human Action (Hazlitt) **29**:133, 159-60, 162, 168-69, 171-72, 183, 185-86; **82**:74, 121, 131-32, 137
Essay on the Punishment of Death (Shelley) **93**:324
"Essay on the Social Progress of States" (Arnold) **18**:53
Essay on the Source of Positive Pleasure (Polidori) **51**:201, 207
"An Essay on the Uses and Advantages of the Fine Arts" (Trumbull) **30**:359
Essay on the Writings and Genius of Pope (Warton) **118**:301, 350, 352-53, 356, 358, 361, 364, 304, 307-14, 322, 324-27, 329, 334-37, 341, 343, 345-48
An Essay on the Writings and Genius of Shakespeare, Compared with the Greek and French Dramatic Poets: with Some Remarks upon the Misrepresentations of M. de Voltaire (Montagu) **7**:250-51
"Essay on Tragic Influences" (Horne) **127**:258
Essay on Truth (Beattie)
See *An Essay on the Nature and Immutability of Truth*
"Essay on Woman" (Browning) **61**:40-1
"Essay, Supplementary to the Preface" (Wordsworth) **111**:238-39, 309, 315, 366
Essay Towards a Critique of All Revelation (Fichte)
See *Versuch einer Kritik aller Offenbarung*
"Essayists Old and New" (Smith) **59**:323
Essays (Coleridge)
See *Essays and Marginalia*
Essays (Eliot) **89**:260; **118**:56, 187, 189, 194
Essays (Emerson) **1**:276, 286, 290, 292; **38**:170, 173, 194, 199, 204 223-24; **98**:4-5, 96, 122, 153, 171
Essays (Huxley) **67**:81-8, 92
Essays (Irving)
See *Salmagundian Essays*
Essays (Macaulay)
See *Critical and Historical Essays Contributed to the Edinburgh Review*
Essays (Smolenskin) **30**:196-98
Essays (Southey) **97**:250-51
Essays (Wordsworth) **12**:436
Essays Addressed to Volunteers (Engels) **85**:83
Essays and Lectures (Emerson) **98**:149-55, 163, 176, 181, 186
Essays and Marginalia (Coleridge) **90**:9-10
Essays and Phantasies (Thomson) **18**:393, 395, 415
Essays and Poems (Very) **9**:370, 373, 381
Essays and Reviews (Poe) **94**:269-71, 274, 276
Essays and Reviews (Southey) **8**:461
Essays and Sketches (Newman) **99**:301
Essays Critical and Historical (Newman) **99**:222, 224, 253
Essays Critical and Imaginative (Wilson) **5**:559-60, 562-63
Essays: First Series (Emerson)
See *Essays*
"Essays from "The Guardians"" (Pater) **90**:333, 337
Essays in Criticism (Arnold) **6**:33, 36, 46-48, 53, 56-57, 69, 72; **29**:10, 55-6, 58-60; **89**:30, 36, 112; **126**:3, 6, 19, 22, 42-43, 78-79, 82-83
Essays in Modernity: Criticisms and Dialogues (Adams) **33**:9
Essays Moral and Political (Southey) **97**:286
Essays Never Before Published (Godwin) **14**:55
Essays on Bacon (Macaulay) **42**:80, 121-22
Essays on Chivalry (Scott) **69**:338
Essays on Petrarch (Foscolo) **8**:263, 271
Essays: On Poetry and Music, as They Affect the Mind; On Laughter, and Ludicrous Composition; On the Utility of Classical Learning (Beattie) **25**:97, 114-15, 117-19, 122
Essays on Prints (Gilpin) **30**:36
Essays on Religious History (Renan)
See *Etudes d'histoire religieuse*
Essays on Scandinavian Literature (Boyesen) **135**:8, 22
Essays on Some Controverted Questions (Huxley) **67**:21, 23
"Essays on the Art of Thinking" (Martineau) **26**:309; **137**:350-51
"Essays on the English Stage" (Percy) **95**:323-24
Essays on Various Subjects, Principally Designed for Young Ladies (More) **27**:337
Essays: Second Series (Emerson) **1**:276, 286, 290, 292; **38**:169, 171; **98**:161
Essays, Speculative and Suggestive (Symonds) **34**:323, 326, 331-32, 336
"Essays, Tales, and Poems" (Freneau) **111**:132
"Essays, upon Epitaphs" (Wordsworth) **111**:238
The Essence of Christianity (Feuerbach)
See *Das Wesen des Christentums*
Essence of Criticism (Schlegel) **45**:366
The Essence of Religion (Feuerbach)
See *Das Wesen der Religion*
"Essor empirique du républicanisme français" (Comte) **54**:205
"Est, Est" (Muller) **73**:353
Estatutos secretos (Martí) **63**:128-9
"Este vaise i aquel vaise" (Williams) **78**:40
Esteticheskie otnosheniia iskusstva k deistvitel'nosti (Chernyshevsky) **1**:158, 161-62
Esther (Grillparzer) **102**:172
L'esthétique de la laideur suivi de Diderot à Pétersbourg (Sacher-Masoch) **31**:288
An Estimate of the Religion of the Fashionable World (More) **27**:333, 338
Estimates of Some Englishmen and Scotchmen (Bagehot) **10**:66
"Estrellas que entre lo sombrío" (Silva) **114**:296
"Estrofas libres" (Isaacs) **70**:313
El estudiante de Salamanca (Espronceda) **39**:85-8, 90, 94, 97-9, 101, 108-10
"Est' liubimtsy vdokhnovenii" (Pavlova) **138**:14, 20, 50
"Estudio sobre Virgilio, por P. F. Tissot" (Bello) **131**:112
"Et ego in Arcadia" (Hoffmann) **2**:356
"Et godt Humeur" (Andersen) **79**:76
"Et la tigresse epouvantable d'Hyrcanie" (Verlaine) **51**:351
Et la-ta'at (Smolenskin) **30**:187, 192-93
"L'Etat des Esprits en 1849" (Renan) **26**:377
Un été dans le Sahara (Fromentin) **10**:224-27, 232, 240, 252, 259; **125**:103, 105-7, 110-12, 114-16, 132, 138, 146
"The Eternal Goodness" (Whittier) **8**:517, 524; **59**:361, 365
The Eternal Husband (Dostoevsky)
See *Vechny muzh*
"The Eternal Jew" (Arany)
See "Az örök zsidó"
"Eternal Love" (Bryant) **46**:15
"Eternal Love" (Isaacs)
See "Amor eterno"
The Eternal People (Smolenskin)
See *Am olam*
"L'eternité" (Rimbaud) **4**:456; **35**:321; **82**:230-31, 233, 247, 249-50
"Eternity in Time" (Lanier) **118**:224
"The Eternity of Nature" (Clare) **9**:80; **86**:90, 113
"Eth Laasoth" (Smolenskin) **30**:189
"Ethan Brand" (Hawthorne) **2**:318, 322, 327; **95**:110, 116, 137
Ethel Churchill; or, The Two Brides (Landon) **15**:159, 161
Ethelinde; or, The Recluse of the Lake (Smith) **23**:319, 322-24, 327-29, 333; **115**:149
"Etheline" (Kendall) **12**:193
Ethelstan; or, The Battle of Brunanburh (Darley) **2**:125, 128, 130-31, 134
"Ethnogenesis" (Timrod) **25**:360, 363, 367, 372, 374-77, 383-84, 387-88
Ethwald (Baillie) **2**:31-34, 39, 43; **71**:4, 6, 12
"Eto bylo blestiashchee more" (Pavlova) **138**:4, 16
"L'étoile a pleuré rose" (Rimbaud) **4**:485
"Les étoiles" (Lamartine) **11**:245, 268, 270
Les Étoiles du monde (Dumas) **71**:247
L'étrangère (Dumas) **9**:222, 224-25, 228, 230-32, 238, 242-43, 245, 249
"Les étrennes des orphelins" (Rimbaud) **4**:465, 484; **35**:282; **82**:226
L'Etruria vendicata (Alfieri) **101**:43
"Etude de femme" (Balzac) **35**:27
Étude sur la soveraineté (Maistre) **37**:302-04, 312
Etude sur le roman (Maupassant) **1**:467; **42**:163, 169, 179, 183, 188, 198-99, 203
Etudes analytiques (Balzac) **5**:28, 32
Etudes anglo-americaines (Mérimée) **65**:90
Études de moeurs au XIXe siècle (Balzac) **5**:28-29
Etudes d'histoire religieuse (Renan) **26**:364, 368, 370, 413, 415, 421
Etudes historiques (Chateaubriand) **3**:114; **134**:16, 19
Études philosophiques (Balzac) **5**:28-29, 32, 53
Etudes philosophiques (Balzac) **53**:31
"Etwas über William Shakespeare bei Gelegenheit Wilhelm Meisters" (Schlegel) **15**:227
Euclid and His Modern Rivals (Carroll) **2**:108, 111
"Eugene and Julia" (Karamzin) **3**:290
Eugene Aram (Bulwer-Lytton) **1**:135, 140, 145, 150, 155; **45**:7, 9, 11-13, 19, 24-7, 34, 68-70
Eugene Onegin (Pushkin)
See *Yevgeny Onegin*
Eugenia (Keller) **2**:416
Eugénie de Franval (Sade) **3**:470, 492
Eugénie Grandet (Balzac) **5**:29, 32-4, 36, 46, 52, 57, 62-4, 66, 73-5; **35**:2, 6, 7, 13, 55, 60; **53**:1-36
"Eulalie— A Song " (Poe) **117**:233, 242-44, 280-82
"Eulogium" (Murray) **63**:179
"Eulogy" (Horton) **87**:95, 100
"Eulogy, George Washington" (Rowson) **5**:322
Eulogy on King Philip (Apess) **73**:3, 7, 10, 13-14, 16, 27-28
"The Eulogy to the Memory of My Grandfather" (Krylov) **1**:438
Euphemia (Lennox) **23**:229, 233-35, 253
"Euphemia, A Sketch" (Levy) **59**:98
Euphémie de Melun (Sade) **47**:361
"Euphorion" (Taylor) **89**:309-10
Euphranor: A Dialogue on Youth (FitzGerald) **9**:265, 270-71
"Euphrasia" (Shelley) **14**:271
"Euphuism" (Pater) **7**:343
"Eureka" (Poe) **117**:193
Eureka: A Prose Poem (Poe) **1**:502, 510, 515, 517, 519-20, 522, 526; **16**:300, 330-31, 335; **55**:149, 151-5, 209; **78**:260; **94**:195-200, 212, 217-21, 248; **97**:180-81, 183, 206, 222; **117**:199, 230, 234, 247, 262, 270, 275, 287-91, 304-5, 307-13, 319-24
Ta euriskomena (Solomos) **15**:390
"Euroclydon" (Kendall) **12**:183

"Európa csendes, újra csendes" (Petofi) **21**:264, 286
"Europe" (Whitman) **31**:419, 425
Europe: A Prophecy, 1794 (Blake) **13**:159, 174, 176, 183-85, 214, 216-17, 221-22, 224-25, 232, 251-52; **37**:33, 77, 80; **127**:11, 77, 79-82, 139
"Europe Is Still, Still Again" (Petofi)
See "Európa csendes, újra csendes"
"The European Revolution" and Correspondence with Gobineau (Tocqueville) **7**:456-58; **63**:283
Europeiska missnöjets grunder (Almqvist) **42**:19
"Eurycome" (Solomos) **15**:389
"Eurydice" (Lowell) **90**:214
"Eurydice" (Patmore) **9**:343
The Eustace Diamonds (Trollope) **6**:503-04, 511-13; **101**:235, 256, 264, 275, 285, 306, 313, 324-25, 327
Eutaw: A Sequel to The Forayers (Simms) **3**:507-08, 513
"Eutaw Springs" (Freneau) **111**:83, 179
"Euterpe" (Kendall) **12**:199
"Euthanasia" (Mickiewicz) **101**:160
"Az év végén" (Petofi) **21**:286
"A Eva" (Espronceda) **39**:105
"Evangelical Teaching: Dr. Cumming" (Eliot) **118**:75
Evangeline: A Tale of Acadie (Longfellow) **2**:473-74, 476-78, 480, 483-84, 488, 490, 493, 495; **45**:102-03, 105-06, 109-10, 113, 119, 124, 128, 134, 137, 139, 142, 144-45, 147, 149-50, 157, 159, 163, 166, 179, 180, 187, 190; **101**:92, 149; **103**:270-316
L'évangéliste (Daudet) **1**:233-35, 243-44, 251
Les évangiles (Renan) **26**:402
"Eve" (Rossetti) **66**:330
L'eve future (Villiers de l'Isle Adam) **3**:581, 583-84, 588
"The Eve of Crecy" (Morris) **4**:423, 426
"The Eve of St. Agnes" (Keats) **8**:328, 333, 340, 347, 351, 355-56, 362, 372-73, 375, 380-81; **73**:142-43, 154-55, 159, 163-65, 170-72, 182, 186, 188-89, 199-200,228, 233, 255, 259-60, 294-96, 299, 304, 307, 328; **121**:105-6, 110-11, 138, 144, 162, 165
"The Eve of St. John" (Scott) **15**:317
"Eve of St. Mark" (Keats)
See "The Eve of St. Mark"
"The Eve of St. Mark" (Keats) **8**:340, 347, 357, 375; **73**:154, 298-99, 307; **121**:162
The Eve of the Fourth (Frederic) **10**:188
The Eve of toldi (Arany)
See *Toldi estéje*
"Evek, ti még jövendőévek" (Arany) **34**:19
"Eveleen's Bower" (Moore) **110**:185
Evelina; or, A Young Lady's Entrance into the World (Burney) **12**:15-17, 19, 21-2, 24-34, 37, 39-40, 42-6, 49-52, 56-7, 60-3; **54**:3, 8, 14-19, 21-4, 26-31, 33-8, 41-52, 61; **107**:1-115
"Evelyn" (Austen) **119**:13
Evelyn (Mowatt) **74**:211, 228
"Evelyn Hope" (Browning) **19**:129
Even a Cat Has Lean Times (Ostrovsky)
See *Ne vse kotu maslenitsa*
"Even beyond Music" (Lampman) **25**:216
Even the Wise Stumble (Ostrovsky)
See *Na vsyakogo mudretsa dovolno prostoty*
"Evenen in the Village" (Barnes) **75**:83, 88-9, 95
"Evenen Twilight" (Barnes) **75**:95
"An Evening" (Allingham) **25**:18
"Evening" (Bowles) **103**:88-9, 92, 95
"Evening" (Chivers) **49**:72
"Evening" (Clare) **9**:111
"Evening" (Grillparzer)
See "Der Abend"
"Evening" (Keble) **87**:169-70, 175, 200
"Evening" (Lampman) **25**:173, 210
"Evening" (Tyutchev) **34**:389
"Evening" (Zhukovsky) **35**:386, 393, 402-05
An Evening: An Epistle in Verse (Wordsworth) **12**:385, 386, 445
"An Evening at a Caucasian Spa in 1824" (Bestuzhev)
See "Vecher na kavkazskikh vodakh v 1824 godu"
"The Evening at Bezdz" (Macha) **46**:205, 208
"An Evening at Home" (Smith) **59**:320, 333, 335-6
"Evening, by a Tailor" (Holmes) **14**:100
"Evening Discourse" (Mickiewicz) **3**:399-400
"Evening Hymn" (Moodie) **113**:317
"Evening Hymn in the Hovels" (Adams) **33**:12
An Evening in Sorrento (Turgenev) **21**:428
"Evening in the Bush" (Kendall) **12**:185
"An Evening Lull" (Whitman) **31**:434
"Evening on a Bivouac" (Bestuzhev)
See "Vecher na bivuake"
"Evening Prayer at a Girls' School" (Hemans) **71**:290
"Evening Readings in History" (Sigourney) **87**:321
Evening Readings in History (Sigourney) **87**:339
"An Evening Revery" (Bryant) **6**:168, 183; **46**:38
"Evening Song" (Lanier) **6**:249, 254; **118**:238, 240
"The Evening Star" (Eminescu)
See "Luceafarul"
"The Evening Star" (Longfellow) **45**:116; **103**:295
"Evening Star" (Poe) **117**:260, 277
"The Evening Sun Was Sinking Down" (Brontë) **16**:86
An Evening Thought: Salvation by Christ with Penetential Cries (Hammon) **5**:261-65
"Evening Twilight" (Baudelaire)
See "Le crépuscule du soir"
An Evening Walk (Wordsworth) **111**:261-64
"An Evening with Spenser" (Thomson) **18**:402
"Evening—A Close View" (Allingham) **25**:5
An Evening's Improvement: Shewing the Necessity of Beholding the Lamb of God (Hammon) **5**:265
"Evenings in Greece" (Moore) **110**:167
Evenings in New England (Child) **73**:123-27
Evenings in the Antilles (Desbordes-Valmore)
See *Veillées des Antilles*
Evenings on a Farm near Dikanka (Gogol)
See *Vechera ná khutore bliz Dikanki*
"The Event Was Directly Behind Him" (Dickinson) **21**:55
"Eventail" (Mallarmé)
See "Autre eventail de Mademoiselle Mallarmé"
The Events of 1848 (Milnes) **61**:138, 146
Eventyr, fortalte for bøorn (Andersen) **7**:16, 18, 20; **79**:3, 7-8, 65, 76, 80
Eventyr og historier (Andersen) **7**:28; **79**:23, 25-26, 37, 80
"Ever Let the Fancy Roam" (Keats) **8**:360
"Evergreens" (Pinkney) **31**:276, 281
"The Everlasting Gospel" (Blake) **13**:181, 209, 211
Every Evil Hath Its Good (Tamayo y Baus)
See *No hay mal que por bien no venga*
Every One Has His Fault (Inchbald) **62**:142, 144, 146-9, 184
Every One in His Own Place (Ostrovsky)
See *Ne v svoi sani ne sadis!*
Every Wise Man Can Be a Fool (Ostrovsky)
See *Na vsyakogo mudretsa dovolno prostoty*
"Everybody's Vacation Except Editors" (Parton) **86**:348
"Every-day Aspects of Life" (Pisarev)
See "Budničnye storony žizni"
"Everything in Its Right Place" (Andersen) **79**:30, 54
"Everywhere and Always" (Pavlova)
See "Vezde i vsegda"
Evgeni Onegin (Pushkin)
See *Yevgeny Onegin*
"The Evidences of Revealed Religion: Discourse before the University in Cambridge" (Channing) **17**:3
"The Evil" (Rimbaud)
See "Le mal"
The Evil Eye (Carleton) **3**:86
The Evil Genius (Collins) **93**:66
"The Evil Guest" (Le Fanu) **9**:302, 314; **58**:272
"Evil Hour" (Grillparzer)
See "Böse Stunde"
"Evil Landscape" (Corbière)
See "Paysage mauvais"
"Evil May-Day" (Allingham) **25**:11, 30
Evil May-Day (Allingham) **25**:18
The Evils of Slavery and the Cure of Slavery (Child) **73**:60, 77
"Eviradnus" (Hugo) **3**:264
"Evolution" (Boyesen) **135**:6, 9, 45-47
"Evolution" (Symonds)
See "Philosophy of Evolution"
"Evolution and Ethics" (Huxley) **67**:10, 29, 62, 64-6, 68-9, 90, 103, 105-08, 111
Evolution and Ethics (Huxley) **67**:44, 90-3, 101, 103-11
"Evolution: Application to Literature and Art" (Symonds) **34**:336
Evrei v Rossii (Leskov) **25**:265, 267-69
"Ewig jung ist nur die Sonne" (Meyer) **81**:140, 143-44, 146-48, 155
"Ex Fumo Dare Lucem" (Gordon) **21**:160
"Examen de conscience philosophique" (Renan) **26**:414, 417
Examen de la philosophie de Bacon (Maistre) **37**:286, 300, 313, 316
An Examination into the Leading Principles of the Federal Constitution Proposed by the Late Convention Held at Philadelphia (Webster) **30**:408
An Examination of Sir William Hamilton's Philosophy and of the Principal Philosophical Questions Discussed in His Writings (Mill) **11**:358, 390; **58**:337
Examination of the Philosophy of Bacon (Maistre)
See *Examen de la philosophie de Bacon*
The Examiner (Hunt) **70**:266
"An Excellent Scotch Parody" (Hunt) **70**:257
"Excelsior" (Longfellow) **2**:473, 493, 498; **45**:100, 102, 111-12, 115-16, 127, 135, 140, 148, 152, 155, 164, 165, 179; **103**:293, 305
"Excerpts from the Biography of Nashchokin" (Pushkin) **83**:273
"Excerpts from the Poem 'Mother'" (Nekrasov)
See "Otryvki iz poèmy 'Mat'"
L'excommunié (Balzac) **5**:58
Excursion (Wordsworth)
See *The Excursion, Being a Portion of "The Recluse"*
Excursión a Vueltabajo (Villaverde) **121**:334, 361-62, 365
The Excursion, Being a Portion of "The Recluse" (Wordsworth) **12**:397-99, 404, 411-12, 414, 416, 420-23, 425-26, 436, 438, 442-45, 447, 450, 458-60, 468, 472; **38**:362, 364, 367, 371, 373, 376-77, 379, 388, 395, 405, 412, 421; **111**:240, 243, 245
Excursion (Futile Enough) to Paris; Autumn 1851 (Carlyle) **70**:91
Excursion on Concord & Merrimack Rivers (Thoreau)
See *A Week on the Concord and Merrimack Rivers*
"Excursions" (Thoreau) **7**:356; **61**:339; **138**:160
"Excuse macabre" (Laforgue) **53**:272
"The Execution" (Galt) **110**:86
The Execution (Barham) **77**:4

"The Execution Bell" (Bestuzhev)
See "Kolokol kazni"
"The Execution of Troppmann" (Turgenev) **21**:420
"The Executor" (Oliphant) **11**:454, 459; **61**:174
"The Exemplary Key" (Martí) **63**:166
Exercises in History, Chronology, and Biography (Rowson) **69**:116
Exhibition of My System of Philosophy (Schelling)
See *Darstellung meines Systems der Philosophie*
"Exhilaration—Is Within" (Dickinson) **21**:53
"Exhortation" (Hölderlin)
See "Ermunterung"
"Exil" (Banville) **9**:29
"Exile" (Lewis) **11**:297-98
"The Exile" (Mackenzie) **41**:190
"An Exile from Paradise" (Lermontov) **5**:292
"The Exile of Erin" (Campbell) **19**:179, 181, 190, 194, 198
"The Exiles" (Whittier) **8**:510, 526-28; **59**:358
The Exiles (Banville)
See *Les exilés*
Les exilés (Banville) **9**:17, 19, 27, 30
"An Exile's Farewell" (Gordon) **21**:154, 173
The Exiles; or, Memoirs of the Count de Cronstadt (Reeve) **19**:408, 412
"The Exile's Secret" (Holmes) **14**:128
The Existence of God (Brownson) **50**:27
"The Exodus (August 3, 1492)" (Lazarus) **109**:332, 335
"Exorcism" (Taylor) **89**:309
"An Exotic" (Timrod) **25**:365-66, 372, 375
The Expedition of Orsua and the Crimes of Aguirre (Southey) **97**:283
"Experience" (Emerson) **1**:301, 307; **38**:143, 169-71, 173-74, 207, 209, 226, 230; **98**:19-24, 27, 55, 59, 61, 63, 89-90, 93, 95-6, 100, 107, 110, 114, 136, 145-46, 153, 180-82, 189
"The Experience of the Adolescent" (Hoffmann) **2**:356
Experience, or How to Give a Northern Man a Backbone (Brown) **89**:153-54, 1182
The Experiences of Five Christian Indians of the Pequod Tribe (Apess)
See *The Experiences of Five Christian Indians: Or the Indian's Looking Glass for the White Man*
The Experiences of Five Christian Indians: Or the Indian's Looking Glass for the White Man (Apess) **73**:5-7, 9-11, 15, 29-31
"The Experiences of the A.C." (Taylor) **89**:315
"The Experiments of an Adventurer" (Mérimée)
See "Les débuts d'un aventurier"
L'expiation (Hugo) **3**:270; **10**:373, 375
"Explanation" (Verlaine) **51**:372
"Explanatory Notes" (Wright) **74**:348-49
Explication (Verlaine) **51**:362
"Exploit of Ovechkin and Shcherbina in the Caucasus" (Bestuzhev)
See "Podvig Ovechkina i Shcherbiny za Kavkazom"
"The Exposition Ode" (Hayne) **94**:145
Exposition of the False Medium and Barriers excluding Men of Genius from the Public (Horne) **127**:236, 238-40, 251-52, 263, 270, 273
"Expostulation" (Cowper) **8**:106, 110, 112, 120; **94**:28, 30, 58, 111-12, 124
"Expostulation" (Whittier) **8**:512
Expostulation (Cowper) **94**:52
"Expostulation and Reply" (Wordsworth) **12**:387, 436; **111**:202, 209, 225, 255, 259, 281-83
"Expression" (Clare) **9**:121
The Expression of the Emotions in Man and Animals (Darwin) **57**:142
Exspriella (Southey) **97**:289
"Extempore Effusion upon the Death of James Hogg" (Wordsworth) **111**:370
"The Extinguishers" (Moore) **110**:172
An Extract from the Life of Lorenzo Da Ponte (Da Ponte) **50**:97
"Extract of a Letter from Geneva" (Polidori) **51**:218-19
"Extradited" (Crawford) **12**:169-70
"Extra-Hazardous" (Bellamy) **4**:30
"An Extraordinary Adventure in the Shades" (Mangan) **27**:291
Extraordinary Tales (Poe) **1**:499
"Extravagantes hijos de mi fantasía" (Bécquer) **106**:118
Extravaganzas (Planché) **42**:273, 299
"Exultation" (Ingelow) **39**:264
"Exultation is the going" (Dickinson) **77**:75
"The Eye and Ear" (Emerson) **38**:195, 197
"The Eye and the Ear" (Very) **9**:394
An Eye for an Eye (Trollope) **6**:470, 501; **101**:245-47, 251-52, 264, 276, 293-94, 296-97
"The Eye of the Blind" (Meyer)
See "Das Auge des Blinden"
"Eyes" (Ridge) **82**:185
"Eyes and Noses" (Collodi)
See *Occhi e Nasi*
"Eyre's March" (Kingsley) **107**:208
"Ez az élet" (Arany) **34**:21
"Ezrivel terem" (Petofi) **21**:283
The Fabians (Freytag)
See *Die Fabier: Trauerspiel in fünf Acten*
Die Fabier: Trauerspiel in fünf Acten (Freytag) **109**:139
"A Fable" (Cowper) **94**:121
"Fable" (Emerson) **98**:179
Fable (Lowell)
See *A Fable for Critics: A Glance at a Few of Our Literary Progenies*
"Fable and Romance" (Beattie)
See *Dissertations Moral and Critical: On Memory and Imagination; On Dreaming; The Theory of Language; On Fable and Romance; On the Attachments of Kindred; Illustrations on Sublimity*
A Fable for Critics: A Glance at a Few of Our Literary Progenies (Lowell) **2**:504-07, 510, 513, 516, 519-22; **90**:188, 190, 198, 202, 207, 215-16, 220-22, 225
Fables (Saltykov)
See *Skazki*
Fables and Parables (Krasicki)
See *Bajki i przypowieści*
"Fables choises mises en prose" (Banville) **9**:32
Fables for the Holy Alliance (Moore) **6**:388, 395; **110**:172
"The face I carry with me-last" (Dickinson) **77**:147
The Face of the Deep: A Devotional Commentary on the Apocalypse (Rossetti) **2**:559, 570, 572; **50**:275, 277-9, 285-7, 321, 342-5; **66**:306-9, 376
"Face to Face" (Hayne) **94**:149, 153, 167-68, 170
"Faces" (Whitman) **31**:372, 425
"Faces in the Fire" (Carroll) **139**:30
Facing the World; or, The Haps and Mishaps of Harry Vane (Alger) **8**:40, 43
Facino Cane (Balzac) **35**:44
Fact and Fiction (Child) **6**:201; **73**:61
"Factitious Life" (Dana) **53**:158, 178
The Factory Controversy: A Warning against Meddling Legislation (Martineau) **137**:268
"The Facts in the Case of M. Valdemar" (Poe) **16**:308-09, 314, 331; **117**:300
Facts of Consciousness (Fichte)
See *Tatsachen des Bewusstseins*
Facundo: Civilización y barbarie (Faustino)
See *Civilización i barbarie: La vida de Juan Facundo Quiroga i aspecto fisico, costumbres, i ábitos de la República Arjentina*
"The faded joy of heedless years" (Pushkin)
See "Bezumnykh let vgasshee vesel'e"
"Faded Leaves" (Arnold) **89**:14, 49
Fader och dotter: En skildring ur lifvet (Bremer) **11**:34
"Failure" (Ingelow) **39**:267; **107**:119
"Faim" (Rimbaud) **82**:231, 247, 249
Faint Heart Never Won Fair Lady (Planché) **42**:292
"Faint yet Pursuing" (Patmore) **9**:358, 365
"Fainting by the Way" (Kendall) **12**:178, 199
"The Fair at Sorotchintsy" (Gogol)
See "Soročinskaja jamarka"
"The Fair Azra" (Leskov)
See "Prekrasnaja Aza"
The Fair Egbert (Tieck)
See *Der blonde Eckbert*
"Fair Elenor" (Blake) **18**:181
"The Fair Hills of Ireland" (Mangan) **27**:275, 283, 295
"Fair Ines" (Hood) **16**:218, 222, 231, 233
The Fair Maid of Perth (Scott)
See *St. Valentine's Day; or, The Fair Maid of Perth*
"The Fair Morning" (Very) **9**:384
The Fair of May Fair (Gore) **65**:20
The Fair One with the Golden Locks (Planché) **42**:273, 288, 294, 301, 303
Fair Play (Southworth) **26**:434, 446
"Fairest, Sweetest, Dearest, A Song" (Opie) **65**:168
Fairfax; or, The Master of Greenway Court: A Chronicle of the Valley of the Shenandoah (Cooke) **5**:124, 126, 128, 132, 134-35
"The Fairies" (Allingham) **25**:6, 8, 18, 20, 22-3, 25, 30
The Fairies (Wagner)
See *Die Feen*
"The Fairies of Pesth" (Field) **3**:205
"A Fairy Companion" (Pavlova)
See "Sputnica feia"
"The Fairy" (Baratynsky)
See "Feya"
"The Fairy" (Lamb) **125**:354
"Fairy" (Rimbaud) **4**:455; **35**:290
"Fairy Dialogue" (Allingham) **25**:6
Fairy Fingers (Mowatt) **74**:215-16, 218-19
"The Fairy Fountain" (Lampman) **25**:205, 219
"Fairy Hill, or The Poet's Wedding" (Allingham) **25**:30
"The Fairy Island" (Woolson) **82**:272
"Fairy Land" (Poe) **117**:264, 272, 281, 305-6, 316-18
Fairy Tale (Goethe)
See *Märchen*
The Fairy Tale of My Life (Andersen) **79**:19, 22, 48, 59, 64
"The Fairy Tale Queen" (Eminescu) **33**:247
Fairy Tales (Andersen)
See *Eventyr, fortalte for bøorn*
Fairy Tales (Pushkin)
See *Skazki*
Fairy Tales (Saltykov) **16**:358-59
Fairy Tales of Isabella Valancy Crawford (Crawford) **12**:172; **127**:181
"The Fairy Thorn" (Ferguson) **33**:287, 303
"Fairy-Tale Dream" (Petofi)
See "Tündérálom"
"A Fairy-Tale for Children" (Lermontov)
See *Skazka dlya detey*
A Fairytale for Children (Lermontov)
See *Skazka dlya detey*
Le faiseur (Balzac) **5**:52, 74
"Faith" (Lamartine)
See "La foi"
"Faith" (Tennyson) **65**:267
Faith (Robertson) **35**:335
"Faith and Doubt" (Newman) **38**:310
"Faith and Experience" (Newman) **38**:304
"Faith and Knowledge" (Hegel)
See "Glauben und Wissen"

"Faith and Private Judgement" (Newman) **38**:310
"Faith and Reason Contrasted as Habits of Mind" (Newman) **38**:307; **99**:298
"Faith and Sight" (Newman) **38**:304
"Faith and Sight" (Very) **9**:385
"Faith and the World" (Newman) **38**:305
"Faith, Hope and Charity" (Crawford) **127**:202
"Faith without Sight" (Newman) **38**:305
Faithful for Ever (Patmore) **9**:332
The Faithful Friend (Cowper) **94**:123
"The Faithful Mountains Stand Guard" (Eichendorff) **8**:210
"A Faithful Servant of His Master" (Grillparzer)
See *Ein Treuer Diener Seines Herrn*
"Faithless Nellie Gray" (Hood) **16**:224, 228, 234
"Faithless Sally Brown" (Hood) **16**:224, 227-28, 234
The Falcon (Tennyson) **30**:265
"The Falcon of Ser Federigo" (Longfellow) **2**:492; **45**:145, 149
Falconberg (Boyesen) **135**:7-8, 12, 16, 20-21, 26-27, 51
Falconet (Disraeli) **2**:148; **39**:36, 43-4, 70-2
Falconry in the Valley of the Indus (Burton) **42**:36, 38
"Falkland" (Arnold) **89**:101
Falkland (Bulwer-Lytton) **1**:139, 148, 150; **45**:21, 23, 40, 68-71
Falkner (Shelley) **14**:260-61, 265, 267, 270, 274-75; **59**:155, 189-90, 192-3
"Fall" (Keats)
See *The Fall of Hyperion: A Dream*
The Fall (Keats)
See *The Fall of Hyperion: A Dream*
The Fall of an Angel (Lamartine)
See *La chute d'un ange*
"The Fall of d'Assas" (Hemans) **29**:204
"The Fall of Hebe. A Dithyrambic Ode" (Moore) **110**:178
The Fall of Hyperion: A Dream (Keats) **8**:347, 349, 353, 358-59, 361-62, 365-66, 368, 379, 381; **73**:153, 155, 162-63, 170-71, 198, 202, 207-209, 212-218, 264, 266-67, 294-95, 299, 301, 306, 328-29,339; **121**:100-113, 116-22, 130-32, 140-49, 154, 160, 169-79, 192, 194-202, 205-6, 208-19, 226, 228-29, 231, 233
The Fall of Robespierre (Coleridge) **9**:159
The Fall of Robespierre (Southey) **97**:260, 293, 314-16
The Fall of the Angels (Polidori) **51**:201
Fall of the Free City-States of Greece (Humboldt) **134**:186
"The Fall of the House of Usher" (Eminescu) **131**:335
"The Fall of the House of Usher" (Poe) **1**:492-93, 496, 504-05, 513, 522-23; **16**:294-95, 300, 303-07, 309-10, 316-19, 321-22, 324, 326, 332, 334, 336; **55**:133, 148, 151, 153, 155, 169, 194, 198-9, 206; **78**:257, 266; **94**:215; **97**:177-246; **117**:193, 200, 235, 257, 277, 281, 299, 303, 320
"The Fall of the Leaf" (Mitford) **4**:408
"The Fall of the Pequod" (Sigourney) **87**:339
"The Fall of the Usher" (Chivers) **49**:74
"Fall Time" (Barnes) **75**:32
"The Fallen Elm" (Clare) **9**:86
The Fallen Leaves (Collins) **1**:180, 184; **93**:4
Fallen Pride (Southworth)
See *The Curse of Clifton: A Tale of Expiation and Redemption*
"Das fallende Laub" (Meyer) **81**:141, 145-46, 148-49, 155
"Falling Asleep" (Lampman) **25**:208
Falling in with Fortune (Alger) **83**:119
"Le falot" (Bertrand) **31**:48
Falsche Scham (Kotzebue) **25**:145, 155
"False but Beautiful" (Ridge) **82**:182
"The False Collar" (Andersen) **7**:23
"The False Demetrius" (Mérimée) **6**:353
"The False Knights Tragedy" (Clare) **86**:98
False Medium (Horne)
See *Exposition of the False Medium and Barriers excluding Men of Genius from the Public*
False Shame; or, The American Orphan in Germany (Dunlap) **2**:214
False Shame, or The White Hypocrite (Mackenzie) **41**:184, 207, 213-14, 216-17, 226
"Fältmarskalken" (Runeberg) **41**:324
A falu bolondja (Arany) **34**:19
"A faluban utcahosszat" (Petofi) **21**:283
"Fame" (Moodie) **113**:315
Fame and Fortune; or, The Progress of Richard Hunter (Alger) **8**:30, 37; **83**:127, 130-31, 139, 140, 144
La familia de Alvareda: Novela original de costumbres populares (Caballero) **10**:72, 76, 81-84
"The Familiar" (Le Fanu) **9**:302, 317, 319-22; **58**:302
Familiar Anecdotes of Sir Walter Scott (Hogg) **4**:278; **109**:200, 204, 208, 258
"A Familiar Epistle" (Sheridan) **91**:231
"Familiar Epistle to a Friend" (Clare) **9**:74
"Familiar Epistle to a Little Boy" (Allingham) **25**:26
Familiar Epistles to Frederick E. Jones, Esq., on the Present State of the Irish Stage (Croker) **10**:88, 91
"A Familiar Letter" (Holmes) **14**:109
"A Familiar Letter to the Reader" (Taylor) **89**:312
The Familiar Letters of John Adams and His wife Abigail during the Revolution (Adams) **106**:4-5
Familiar Studies of Men and Books (Stevenson) **5**:390, 415, 425
Die Familie Schroffenstein (Kleist) **2**:438, 443, 445-46, 449-50, 454-57; **37**:217, 223, 225-26, 229, 236-37, 253, 255, 266-69, 272-74
Die Familien Zwiern, Knieriem und Liem (Nestroy) **42**:231, 251, 255-56
The Families of Plants (Darwin) **106**:226, 232, 274
Familjen H. (Bremer) **11**:17-19, 24, 30, 35
La famille de Carvajal (Mérimée) **6**:351, 362; **65**:54, 58, 60, 79, 81, 87
La Famille de Germandre (Sand) **57**:316
Family Annals, or the Sisters (Hays) **114**:186, 208
A Family Charge (Turgenev)
See *Nakhlebnik*
"Family Circle" (Arany)
See "Csaladi kör"
"A Family Court" (Saltykov) **16**:341
Family Distress; or, Self-immolation (Kotzebue)
See *Der Opfertod*
A Family in Decline (Leskov)
See *Zaxudalyj rod*
The Family Legend (Baillie) **2**:35; **71**:5-6, 12-14, 18
Family Nurse (Child) **73**:60
The Family of Carvajal (Mérimée)
See *La famille de Carvajal*
The Family Picture (Holcroft) **85**:192, 234
A Family Picture (Ostrovsky)
See *Semeynaya kartina*
"Family Portraits" (Sigourney) **21**:290
The Family Robinson Crusoe; or, Journal of a Father Shipwrecked, with His Wife and Children, on an Uninhabitated Island (Wyss)
See *Der Schweizerische Robinson; oder, Der schiffbrüchige Schweizerprediger und seine Familie*
"Family Stories, by Thomas Ingoldsby" (Barham) **77**:4
Family Strife in Habsburg (Grillparzer)
See *Ein Bruderzwist in Habsburg*
Fanchon the Cricket (Sand) **57**:338
"A fanciful nickname..." (Baratynsky)
See "Svoenravnoe prozvanie..."
"Le fanciulle nella tempesta" (Leopardi) **129**:340
"The Fancy" (Hazlitt) **82**:128
A Fancy of Hers (Alger) **83**:99, 116, 145
"Fancy's Ramble" (Freneau) **111**:151
"Fancy's Show-Box" (Hawthorne) **2**:291, 298, 305; **95**:91, 128, 134, 136
La Fanfarlo (Baudelaire) **29**:106
Fanferlieschen (Brentano) **1**:102
Fanni ou les effects du désespoir (Sade) **47**:361-62
Fanny (Halleck) **47**:64, 68, 70, 72-73, 76-77, 83, 85, 99
"Fanny Ford" (Parton) **86**:338-39
"Fanny Ford: A Story of Everyday Life" (Parton) **86**:337
Fänrik Ståls sägner (Runeberg) **41**:308-21, 323, 325-29, 331
"Fänrikens marknadsminne" (Runeberg) **41**:314, 325
Fanshawe (Hawthorne) **2**:326; **79**:296, 314
"Fantaisie" (Nerval) **1**:486
Fantasmagorii (Pavlova) **138**:10-11, 16-17, 22, 34-35, 49, 53
"Fântâna Blanduziei" (Eminescu) **131**:361
"Fantasia" (Cooke) **110**:51
Fantasiestüeke in Callots Manier (Hoffmann) **2**:340-41, 348, 361
Fantasio (Musset) **7**:258, 260, 262, 264, 269, 272, 276, 282-83
Fantazy (Slowacki) **15**:349, 352, 354, 365, 368, 378, 380-82
"Fantine" (Hugo) **3**:244-46; **10**:355, 361, 364
"Fantoches" (Verlaine) **2**:629; **51**:378-79
"Un fantôme" (Baudelaire) **29**:99; **55**:10
Far Away and Long Ago (Kemble) **18**:191
"Far Edgerley" (Woolson) **82**:273
"Far, Far Away" (Tennyson) **30**:226
"The Far Future" (Kendall) **12**:200
"The Faraway Forest" (Kivi)
See "Kaukametsä"
"Farce éphémère" (Laforgue) **53**:270
Fardorougha the Miser; or, The Convicts of Lisnamona (Carleton) **3**:83, 85, 87, 94
"A Farewell" (Arnold) **89**:95
"The Farewell" (Lamartine)
See "L'adieu"
"A Farewell" (Levy) **59**:109
"A Farewell" (Patmore) **9**:343, 358
"Farewell" (Pushkin) **83**:259
"Farewell" (Rogers) **69**:82
"Farewell" (Thoreau) **7**:383
"Farewell Address at Springfield" (Lincoln) **18**:213, 254, 259, 264, 280-81
A Farewell, for Two Years, to England (Williams) **135**:334, 355
"Farewell Life" (Hood) **16**:219, 228, 233
"Farewell of a Missionary to Africa, at the Grave of his Wife and Child" (Sigourney) **87**:337
"The Farewell of a Virginia Slave Mother to Her Daughters Sold into Foreign Bondage" (Whittier) **8**:508-10, 512-13; **59**:354
"Farewell Old Cottage" (Foster) **26**:295
"Farewell, Sweet Mother" (Foster) **26**:286
"Farewell to Deirdre" (Ferguson) **33**:278
"Farewell to Essay-Writing" (Hazlitt) **29**:147-49, 165; **82**:99, 127
"Farewell to Frances" (Horton) **87**:102
"Farewell to Gastein" (Grillparzer)
See "Abschied von Gastein"
"Farewell to Patrick Sarsfield" (Mangan) **27**:297-98, 311, 314
"Farewell to the Caspian" (Bestuzhev)
See "Proshchanie s Kaspiem"

"Farewell to the Market: 'Susannah and Mary Jane'" (Adams) **33**:18
"A Farewell to the South" (Hallam) **110**:119
"Farewell to Tobacco" (Lamb) **10**:389, 404
"A Farewell to Wales" (Hemans) **71**:277
"Farewell to Youth" (Preseren)
See "Slovo od mladosti"
La Farisea (Caballero) **10**:83
"A farkasok dala" (Petofi) **21**:264
The Farm House; or, The Female Duellists (Tyler) **3**:573
The Farm Lease (Almqvist)
See *Ladugårdsarrebnet*
"Farmer Hayden's Thanksgiving-Day" (Alger) **8**:44
"The Farmer of Tilsbury Vale: A Character" (Wordsworth) **111**:235
The Farmer Refuted (Hamilton) **49**:293, 325
"Farmer Stebbin's Opinions" (Crawford) **12**:151, 161
"The Farmer's Advice to the Villagers" (Dwight) **13**:270, 272, 278
"Farmer's Sons" (Barnes) **75**:101
"The Farmer's Winter Evening" (Freneau) **111**:143, 150-51
"Farmer's Winter Evening" (Freneau) **111**:149
"The Farmer's Woldest Da'ter" (Barnes) **75**:6, 101
"The Farrers of Budge Row" (Martineau) **26**:352
Farys (Mickiewicz) **3**:389, 392, 397
"Fashion" (Madison) **126**:329
Fashion; or Life in New York (Mowatt) **74**:211, 215-15, 219, 221-24, 227-30, 223-33
Fashionable Life; or, Paris and London (Trollope) **30**:332
"The Fashionable Preacher" (Parton) **86**:352
"The Fashionable Wife" (Krasicki)
See "Żona modna"
"The Fashionable Wife" (Opie) **65**:159
"A Fast Keeper" (Mangan) **27**:301
"Fata în gradina de aur" (Eminescu) **131**:287, 299
Fata morgana (Fouqué) **2**:267
The Fatal Deception; or, The Progress of Guilt (Dunlap)
See *Leicester*
The Fatal Falsehood: A Tragedy (More) **27**:332, 337
Fatal Revenge; or, The Family of Montorio (Maturin) **6**:316-17, 320-24, 328-31, 340-42, 346
The Fatal Secret (Southworth) **26**:434
"The Fatalist" (Lermontov) **5**:291, 295, 298-99, 301, 303, 306; **126**:151, 153, 195, 201-3, 217
"Fate" (Emerson) **1**:296; **38**:154-55, 157; **98**:19-20, 59, 61, 109, 151-55, 181, 185
"The Fate of Adelaide" (Landon) **15**:165
"The Fate of Cathleen" (Griffin) **7**:194-95
"The Fate of Genius" (Clare) **86**:109
"The Fate of the Explorers" (Kendall) **12**:199
"The Fate of Tyranny and Toryism" (Brackenridge) **7**:44
Fated to be Free (Ingelow) **39**:260-61, 264; **107**:118-19, 124-25
"The Father" (Sigourney) **21**:290, 306, 311-13
"Father Aleksej" (Turgenev)
See "Rasskaz ottsa Aleksaya"
"Father Alexey's Story" (Turgenev)
See "Rasskaz ottsa Aleksaya"
Father and Daughter: A Portraiture from the Life (Bremer)
See *Fader och dotter: En skildring ur lifvet*
The Father and Daughter: A Tale in Prose (Opie) **65**:152-3, 155, 163, 168, 171-2, 174, 178-9, 184-5, 192-5, 197-8
Father Bombo's Pilgrimage to Mecca (Brackenridge) **7**:54, 62-63
"Father Butler: The Lough Dearg Pilgrim" (Carleton) **3**:88, 90, 92
"Father Come Hwome" (Barnes) **75**:101
Father Connell (Banim and Banim) **13**:122, 128-31
"Father Gerasim's Lion" (Leskov)
See "Lev starca Gerasima"
"Father Giles of Ballymoy" (Trollope) **101**:234, 245, 262, 267, 273
Father Goriot (Balzac)
See *Le père Goriot: Histoire Parisienne*
Father Marek (Slowacki)
See *Ksiądz Marek*
"Father Nicholas" (Mackenzie) **41**:189
The Father of an Only Child (Dunlap)
See *The Father; or, American Shandyism*
The Father of the Plague-Stricken at El-Arish (Slowacki)
See *Ojciec zadżumionych*
The Father; or, American Shandyism (Dunlap) **2**:207-08, 210-11, 213-15, 217
"A Father to His Motherless Children" (Sigourney) **21**:309
"Fatherhood" (Barnes) **75**:7
"Fatherland" (Grundtvig) **1**:402
Fathers and Children (Turgenev)
See *Ottsy i deti*
Fathers and Sons (Turgenev)
See *Ottsy i deti*
"Father's Letter" (Field) **3**:210
"Father's Return" (Mickiewicz) **3**:398
"The Father's Wedding" (Lamb)
See "Elinor Forester: The Father's Wedding"
"The Father's Wedding-Day" (Lamb) **10**:406
"Fatima and Urganda: An Eastern Tale" (Rowson) **69**:112, 129
"Fatum" (Norwid) **17**:373-74
"Fauconshawe" (Gordon) **21**:160, 166, 181
"Le Faune" (Verlaine) **51**:378-80, 382
La Fausse Industrie (Fourier) **51**:161, 174
La fausse maîtresse (Balzac) **5**:84
Faust (Chamisso) **82**:18
Faust (Lenau) **16**:263-64, 266-75, 278-80, 282, 285
Faust (Turgenev) **21**:414, 417-18, 431, 451-52; **122**:243-44, 246-47, 261, 266, 268, 298, 300-304, 324, 337, 348, 364
Faust: A Tragedy (Goethe)
See *Faust: Eine Tragödie*
Faust. Der Tragödie zweiter Teil (Goethe) **4**:181, 191, 222; **34**:48-138; **90**:106
Faust. Die Erster Teil (Goethe) **34**:48-138
Faust: Ein Fragment (Goethe) **4**:162, 164, 167-69, 172-77, 179, 181, 183-84, 187-88, 194-95, 199, 201, 205, 210-21; **34**:68, 85-6, 95, 123-24, 127
Faust: Eine Tragödie (Goethe) **34**:48-138
Faust I (Goethe)
See *Faust. Die Erster Teil*
Faust II (Goethe)
See *Faust. Der Tragödie zweiter Teil*
The Faust of the Orient (Klinger) **1**:433
Faust Overture (Wagner) **119**:189, 279
La faustin (Goncourt) **7**:162-63, 167, 170, 174, 183, 188
"Faustina" (Jacobsen) **34**:168
Faustina (Goncourt)
See *La faustin*
Faust's Leben, Thaten, und Hollenfahrt (Klinger) **1**:430
Faustus: His Life, Death, and Descent into Hell (Klinger)
See *Faust's Leben, Thaten, und Hollenfahrt*
Une faute (Scribe) **16**:394
Les Faux Demetrius (Mérimée) **65**:85
"Favorites of Pan" (Lampman) **25**:217
"Feäir Ellen Dare" (Barnes) **75**:58
"Fear" (Shaw) **15**:335
Fear and Trembling (Kierkegaard)
See *Frygt og Baeven*
"Fears and Scruples" (Browning) **19**:88, 96
Fears in Solitude (Coleridge) **9**:146, 149, 158; **99**:48-9; **111**:310
The Feast during the Plague (Pushkin)
See *Pir vo vremiachumy*
A Feast in Time of the Plague (Pushkin)
See *Pir vo vremiachumy*
"Feast of Brougham Castle" (Wordsworth) **12**:393
"The Feast of Famine" (Stevenson) **5**:410, 428
"The Feast of Lights" (Lazarus) **8**:421; **109**:335, 338
"The Feast of the Poets" (Hunt) **1**:412; **70**:271
The Feast of the Poets, with Notes, and Other Pieces in Verse (Hunt) **1**:407, 412, 414; **70**:253, 292-93
"Feasts" (Baratynsky) **103**:8-9
Feats on the Fiord (Martineau) **137**:255-57, 259, 261
"Feats on the Fjord" (Martineau) **26**:317, 323
"Features for the Characterization of the Russian Common People" (Dobrolyubov) **5**:140
"February: A Thaw" (Clare) **9**:107, 116; **86**:95, 98, 104, 165
"Federal Catechism" (Webster) **30**:405
The Federalist (Hamilton) **49**:297-9, 303-04, 306-07, 311-19, 322-25, 327
Federalist "Number 1" (Madison) **126**:265
Federalist "Number 10" (Madison) **126**:234, 252, 254, 260-62, 269-71, 276-87, 297-98, 304, 309, 311, 314
Federalist "Number 14" (Madison) **126**:282-83, 295, 305, 309
Federalist "Number 18" (Madison) **126**:278, 296
Federalist "Number 19" (Madison) **126**:278, 296, 309
Federalist "Number 20" (Madison) **126**:278, 296
Federalist "Number 37" (Madison) **126**:309, 316
Federalist "Number 38" (Madison) **126**:309
Federalist "Number 39" (Madison) **126**:233, 243, 298
Federalist "Number 40" (Madison) **126**:316
Federalist "Number 41" (Madison) **126**:310
Federalist "Number 43" (Madison) **126**:278, 282
Federalist "Number 45" (Madison) **126**:309
Federalist "Number 47" (Madison) **126**:278, 282
Federalist "Number 48" (Madison) **126**:298, 316
Federalist "Number 49" (Madison) **126**:309
Federalist "Number 50" (Madison) **126**:309
Federalist "Number 51" (Madison) **126**:252, 254, 261, 269, 304, 314
Federalist "Number 52" (Madison) **126**:233
Federalist "Number 54" (Madison) **126**:311
Federalist "Number 57" (Madison) **126**:263
Federalist "Number 63" (Madison) **126**:278
"Federigo" (Mérimée) **6**:366; **65**:111-13
"La fédor" (Daudet) **1**:251-52
"Fedor and Abram" (Leskov)
See "Skazanie o Fyodore—Khristianine i o druge ego Abrame—zhidovine"
"Fedya" (Turgenev) **21**:376
Fée (Feuillet) **45**:88
La fée aux miettes (Nodier) **19**:377, 381, 383-86, 388, 391-92, 396-98, 400
"Feelings of an Enthusiast Upon the Commencement of the French Revolution" (Wordsworth) **38**:424
Die Feen (Wagner) **9**:435-36, 473; **119**:189, 268
"Feet in the Fire" (Meyer)
See "Die Füsse im Feuer"
Feldblumen (Stifter) **41**:335, 366, 375-81
Felhök (Petofi) **21**:284
"Félice and Petit Poulain" (Field) **3**:206
"Felicia Hemans" (Browning) **61**:51
"Felicitations" (Krasicki)
See "Powinszowania"
"Felipa" (Woolson) **82**:273, 299, 307
"Felisa" (Isaacs) **70**:304, 307, 309

Felix Holt the Radical (Eliot) **4**:101-03, 111, 114, 121, 123, 127, 133, 137, 144; **13**:318, 325; **23**:51, 55, 57, 63, 80; **41**:68, 72, 82, 84-5, 91, 96-7, 99; **89**:278; **118**:34-194
"Felix Randal" (Hopkins) **17**:194, 254
"La Fellah-sur une aquarelle de la Princesse M" (Gautier) **59**:19
"The Fellow Traveller" (Andersen) **7**:32
"Fellowship" (Barnes) **75**:109
"Felo de Se" (Levy) **59**:90, 107-8
"The Female Convict" (Landon) **15**:161
"The Female Convict" (Southey) **97**:314
"Female Education" (Beecher) **30**:14
"Female Education" (Martineau) **26**:320
Female Education (Darwin)
See *Plan for the Conduct of Female Education in Boarding Schools*
The Female Emigrant's Guide, and Hints on Canadian Housekeeping (Traill) **31**:316, 327, 329
The Female Patriot (Rowson) **69**:141
The Female Quixote; or, The Adventures of Arabella (Lennox) **23**:226-30, 232-40, 242-44, 246-56, 261-65; **134**:217-350
Female Quixotism: Exhibited in the Romantic Opinions and Extravagant Adventures of Dorcasina Sheldon (Tenney) **122**:170, 172, 177, 181, 184, 186-87, 193-97, 199-200, 202, 205-10, 212-19, 221-24, 227, 229
"The Female Sovereigns of England When Young" (Hunt) **70**:258
"Female Suffrage: A Letter to the Christian Women of America" (Cooper) **129**:70, 87-89
A Female Sultan (Sacher-Masoch) **31**:294
"Female Trials in the Bush" (Traill) **31**:327
"Female Types" (Pisarev) **25**:338
"The Female Vagrant" (Wordsworth) **111**:201-2, 234, 253, 265, 268, 306-7, 310-11, 315, 317, 356-57
"Female Writers on Practical Divinity" (Martineau) **26**:312, 319; **137**:236
"Femme" (Corbière) **43**:9-10, 12, 18, 32,34
La femme à deux maris (Pixérécourt) **39**:272-73, 277, 279, 282, 284, 286
La femme abandonnée (Balzac) **5**:37; **35**:24, 26
"La Femme adultere" (Vigny) **102**:335, 367
La femme au 18e siècle (Goncourt and Goncourt) **7**:165, 176
La femme de Claude (Dumas) **9**:225-26, 228-30, 234, 240-43, 245, 248-49
"La femme de Paul" (Maupassant) **83**:182, 194-95, 198-200, 203
"Une femme de Rubens" (Banville) **9**:19
La femme de trente ans (Balzac) **5**:37, 49, 83, **35**:2, 26
"Une femme est l'amour" (Nerval) **67**:307
"Une femme est un diable" (Mérimée) **6**:362-3; **65**:50, 54, 57, 79, 82-3
"Femme et chatte" (Verlaine) **2**:630; **51**:356
La femme, la famille, et le prêtre (Michelet) **31**:214, 218, 222, 224-25, 244, 260-62
La femme, le mari, et l'amant (Kock) **16**:245-46
"Femme Passée" (Linton) **41**:164
Femmes (Verlaine) **51**:352, 363
"Femmes damnées" (Baudelaire) **6**:89, 109; **29**:74, 99; **55**:4-6, 26, 32-3, 45, 73-4, 76
Les femmes d'artistes (Daudet) **1**:239, 249
"Les femmes du Caire" (Nerval) **67**:334, 363
"Den femte juli" (Runeberg) **41**:312, 326-27
La Fenêtre (Maupassant) **83**:230
"Les fenêtres" (Baudelaire) **29**:110; **55**:41
"Les fenêtres" (Mallarmé) **4**:378, 395; **41**:241-42, 250
Feodore (Kotzebue) **25**:139-40
"Ferdinand and Ottilie" (Goethe) **4**:197
A férfi és nő (Madach) **19**:362, 370
"Fergus Wry-Mouth" (Ferguson) **33**:285, 301, 304
Ferishtah's Fancies (Browning) **19**:96
Fermo e Lucia (Manzoni) **29**:307; **98**:213, 217, 219-20, 240, 250, 258, 263-65, 267, 273, 284-88, 290
Fern Leaves (Parton)
See *Fern Leaves, Second Series*
Fern Leaves from Fanny's Port-Folio (Parton)
See *Fern Leaves, Second Series*
Fern Leaves, Second Series (Parton) **86**:318, 346-52
"The Fern Owls Nest" (Clare) **86**:144
"A Fern Soliloquy" (Parton) **86**:347
A Fernand Longlois (Verlaine) **51**:361-62
Fernande (Dumas) **71**:204, 228
Fernere Darstellungen (Schelling) **30**:128, 174
"Ferragus" (Balzac) **5**:77; **35**:43; **53**:28
Ein Fest auf Haderslevhuus (Storm) **1**:540-41, 547
"The Festal Hour" (Hemans) **29**:207
"A Festival of Life" (Thomson) **18**:409
"Festival of Love" (Lenau) **16**:276, 278
"Festus" (Fuller) **50**:227
The Fetches (Banim and Banim) **13**:116, 119, 126, 132, 139-41
"La fête chez Thérèse" (Hugo) **3**:270
"Fêtes de la faim" (Rimbaud) **4**:472-73; **82**:247
"Fêtes de la patience" (Rimbaud) **35**:309, 311; **82**:251
Fêtes galantes (Verlaine) **2**:617-18, 623-24, 628-31; **51**:351-2, 355-6, 359, 361, 365, 368-69, 373-74, 376-78, 380-87
"Le feu du ciel" (Hugo) **3**:234, 261
The Feud (Gordon) **21**:160, 173, 183
The Feud of the Schroffensteins (Kleist)
See *Die Familie Schroffenstein*
Feudal Tyrants; or, The Counts of Carlsheim and Sargans (Lewis) **11**:297
Feuerbach (Engels)
See *Ludwig Feuerbach und der Aus gang der klassischen deutschen Philosophie*
"Der Feuerreiter" (Mörike) **10**:451, 453, 455
Les feuilles d'automne (Hugo) **3**:236, 261, 266, 270; **21**:196, 214, 222, 225
"Feuilles mortes" (Banville) **9**:30
Le feuilleton d'Aristophane (Banville) **9**:19
The Few (Alfieri)
See *I pochi*
"A Few Biographical and Bibliographical Notes on Pushkin" (Dobrolyubov) **5**:140
A Few Days in Athens (Wright) **74**:363, 372, 376-77
"A Few Words on Dueling" (Freneau) **111**:135
"A few Words on Ostrovsky's New Play 'The Poor Bride'" (Turgenev) **37**:381
"Feya" (Baratynsky) **103**:10, 16-18, 21-2
"FF" (Parton) **86**:338
Le Fiabe di Carlo Gozzi (Gozzi) **23**:113
"Fiamnak" (Arany) **34**:19
Fiancée (Scribe) **16**:382
Les fiancés (Nodier) **19**:384
"Fiat nox" (Leconte de Lisle) **29**:228, 234-35
"La ficelle" (Maupassant) **1**:447, 457; **83**:188
"Fiction and Matter of Fact" (Hunt) **1**:421
"The Fiddler" (Melville) **3**:354, 381
"The Fiddler" (O'Brien) **21**:243, 249-50
"Fiddler Bob" (Barnes)
See "Bob the Fiddler"
"Fidelity" (Wordsworth) **12**:404
"Fidelity Till Death" (Hemans) **71**:291
Field and Hedgerow; Being the last Essays of Richard Jefferies, Collected by his Widow (Jefferies) **47**:102, 111-12, 133, 138-39
"The Field Marshall" (Runeberg)
See "Fältmarskalken"
"Field Notes" (Cranch) **115**:66
"The Field of the Grounded Arms" (Halleck) **47**:57, 62, 74, 79
"Field Play" (Jefferies) **47**:136
"Field Words and Ways" (Jefferies) **47**:138
"Fieldlarks and Blackbirds" (Lanier) **118**:241
"The Fields of Coleraine" (Gordon) **21**:160
The Fields of Fancy (Shelley)
See *Mathilda*
"The Fiends" (Pushkin) **3**:443
Fiesco (Schiller)
See *Die Verschwörung des Fiesco zu Genua*
Fiesques de Lavagna (Dumas) **71**:217, 241, 244
Fifine at the Fair (Browning) **19**:121-22, 136; **79**:154, 186
1572: A Chronicle of the Times of Charles the Ninth (Mérimée)
See *Chronique du temps de Charles IX*
Fifteen Days of Sinai (Dumas) **11**:48
1593 (Dickinson) **77**:97
1528 (Dickinson) **77**:121
1525 (Dickinson) **77**:184
Fifteen Sermons (Newman)
See *Fifteen Sermons Preached before the University of Oxford*
Fifteen Sermons Preached before the University of Oxford (Newman) **99**:219, 224, 297-98, 300-02
Fifteen Years of a Drunkard's Life (Jerrold) **2**:403
"Fifth Canto" (Lamartine) **11**:247
"Fifth Epistle" (Eminescu) **131**:331
The Fifth of August (Tamayo y Baus)
See *El cinco de Agosto*
"The Fifth of July" (Cumbaa)
See "Den femte juli"
"The Fifth of May" (Manzoni)
See "Il cinque maggio"
Fifty Suggestions (Poe) **117**:320
"Fifty Years" (Bryant) **6**:175
Figaro (Holcroft)
See *The Follies of a Day; or, The Marriage of Figaro*
"Fígaro en el cementario" (Larra) **17**:277-78
"The Fight" (Hazlitt) **29**:151, 153, 167, 169; **82**:127
"The Fight for Life" (Pisarev)
See "Bor'ba za žizn"
"Fight for Status" (Grillparzer)
See "Rangstreit"
"The Fight for Survival" (Pisarev)
See "Bor'ba za suščestvovanie"
"Fight of Ronscevalles" (Lewis) **11**:298
"The Fight of the Forlorn" (Darley) **2**:133
"The Fight with the Dragon" (Schiller) **39**:330
"Figura" (Leskov) **25**:258-60
File No. 113 (Gaboriau)
See *Le dossier no. 113*
"La Fileuse et l'enfant" (Desbordes-Valmore) **97**:20, 28
El filibusterismo (Rizal) **27**:407-09, 412, 416, 418-25, 427-29
Filippo (Alfieri) **101**:4, 8, 10-11, 15, 18-19, 38, 58-61, 63, 67
"Filisa's Picture" (Isaacs)
See "El retrato de Felisa"
"Fill the Bumper Fair" (Moore) **110**:190
"Une Fille" (Maupassant) **83**:227
La fille aux yeux d'ors (Balzac) **5**:46; **35**:22, 24, 26; **53**:29
"Fille de Fille" (Maupassant) **83**:227
"La Fille de Jephte" (Vigny) **7**:472, 481; **102**:335, 367
La fille de l'exilé; ou, Huit mois en deux heures (Pixérécourt) **39**:274-75, 278-79, 282, 284, 294
Une fille d'Eve (Balzac) **5**:83-84; **35**:26
La fille du marquis (Dumas) **71**:218
Une fille du régent (Dumas) **11**:51
La fille Élisa (Goncourt) **7**:152-53, 155, 161, 170, 182, 188-90
Filles (Verlaine) **2**:632; **51**:363
"Les filles de Milton" (Villiers de l'Isle Adam) **3**:586, 588
Les filles du feu (Nerval) **1**:476-77, 485; 304, 309, 313, 325, 332, 334, 344, 347, 357-58, 360, 363-65, 370
Filles, Lorettes, et Courtisanes (Dumas) **71**:228
La Filleule (Sand) **57**:316
Filosofia del entendimiento (Bello) **131**:94-97, 131

"Filosofías" (Silva) **114**:264, 319
Filosofías (Silva) **114**:262
"Les Filous" (Sade) **47**:314
"Un fils" (Maupassant) **1**:449
Le fils de Cromwell; ou, Une Restauration (Scribe) **16**:388
Le fils de Giboyer (Augier) **31**:3, 5, 7-10, 13, 16, 19-21, 25, 27-8, 31-2, 34, 38-9
"Le fils de Lamartine et de Graziella" (Corbière) **43**:30
Le Fils du Forçat (Dumas) **71**:204
Le fils du Titien (Musset) **7**:264
Les fils naturel (Dumas) **9**:224, 232, 236-37, 241-42, 245, 247, 249-51, 253
Le Fils naturel (Sade) **47**:362-63
"La fin" (Corbière) **43**:7, 9, 14, 23, 29-30
La fin de Don Juan (Baudelaire) **6**:119
"El fin de la fiesta" (Larra) **130**:194
"La fin de la fin" (Banville) **9**:32
"La fin de la journée" (Baudelaire) **55**:12, 73
"Fin de l'homme" (Leconte de Lisle) **29**:217
La fin de Satan (Hugo) **3**:273; **10**:377; **21**:201
"A Final Appeal to the Public relative to Pope" (Bowles) **103**:54
The Final Cause of Poetry (Coleridge) **90**:15
"Final Chorus" (Darley) **2**:133
El final de Norma (Alarcon) **1**:13, 15
"The Final Death" (Baratynsky)
See "Poslednyaya smert'"
"Final Impenitence" (Verlaine) **51**:372
"Der Findling" (Kleist) **2**:463; **37**:245, 247, 253-55
"The Fine Arts" (Hazlitt) **29**:144
Fine Arts (Symonds) **34**:318-19, 346-48, 357, 368, 370-71, 374-75
"The Finest Diner in the World" (Villiers de l'Isle Adam)
See "Le plus beau dîner du monde"
"Finis Exoptatus" (Gordon) **21**:159-60
"The Finishing School" (O'Brien) **21**:234, 250
"Finland" (Baratynsky) **103**:10
Fior d'Aliza (Lamartine) **11**:266, 278, 286, 288
"Fire" (Pavlova)
See "Ogon"
"Fire, Famine, and Slaughter" (Coleridge) **9**:146
"The Fire of Drift-Wood" (Longfellow) **2**:475; **45**:154, 162, 166, 187; **101**:92
"Fire Pictures" (Hayne) **94**:149, 161-64
"The Fire That Filled My Heart of Old" (Thomson) **18**:403
"Fire Worship" (Hawthorne) **2**:296, 298
"The Fire Worshippers" (Moore) **6**:380, 387-88, 393; **110**:166, 203, 210, 212-14, 216-20, 222-25
"The Fireplace" (Cranch) **115**:42
"The Fires" (Tyutchev) **34**:393
Fireside Travels (Lowell) **2**:507; **90**:202, 206
"The Firmament" (Bryant) **6**:178, 190; **46**:6
"Firmly I Believe and Truly" (Newman) **38**:346
"Firnelicht" (Meyer) **81**:142
"First Attempts in Rhyme" (Hood) **16**:236
First Book of Odes (Brontë) **109**:17
The First Book of Urizen (Blake)
See *The Book of Urizen*
First Brutus (Alfieri)
See *Bruto primo*
The First Communion (Tegner)
See *Nattvardsbarnen*
"The First Day" (Longfellow) **45**:137-38
"The First Death in the Clearing" (Traill) **31**:328
"First Edinburgh Reviewers" (Bagehot) **10**:18, 27, 62, 65
"The First English Poet" (Allingham) **25**:11
"The First Epistle" (Eminescu) **33**:245-46, 264; **131**:286, 297, 344
"The First Extra" (Levy) **59**:92, 120
"The First Fan" (Holmes) **14**:109
First Footsteps in East Africa (Burton) **42**:40, 42, 58
"First Going to Church" (Lamb) **10**:402, 417
First Impressions (Austen) **1**:52; **13**:97, 107; **119**:17-18, 37
"First Impressions—Quebec" (Moodie) **14**:243
First Inaugural Address (Lincoln) **18**:214-15, 235, 242, 254, 257
First Introduction to the Theory of Science (Fichte) **62**:36
"The First Kiss" (Isaacs)
See "El primer beso"
"The First Love" (Kierkegaard) **125**:203, 207-8, 248, 254, 280
"First Love" (Kivi)
See "Nuori Karhunampuja"
"First Love" (Lazarus) **109**:292
"First Love" (Sedgwick) **98**:302
First Love (Turgenev)
See *Pervaya lyubov'*
The First Madman (Castro)
See *El primer loco*
"First O Songs for a Prelude" (Whitman) **31**:393; **81**:330
"The First of January" (Lermontov) **5**:295
"First Paper" (De Quincey) **87**:77
The First Printer (Reade) **74**:331
The First Settlers of New England (Child) **73**:75, 97
"The First Snowfall" (Lowell) **2**:511; **90**:193, 214
"The First Spring Day" (Rossetti) **2**:575
"The First Sunday after Advent" (Keble) **87**:200
"First Sunday after Christmas" (Keble) **87**:160
"First Sunday after Epiphany" (Keble) **87**:159, 174
"First Sunday after Trinity" (Droste-Hülshoff) **3**:201
The First Temptation of Saint Anthony (Flaubert)
See *La tentation de Saint Antoine*
"First Vision" (Lamartine) **11**:273
"The Fir-Tree" (Andersen) **7**:22, 28, 34; **79**:23, 32-33, 62, 67
"Fischer" (Goethe) **4**:192
"Ein Fischer sass im Kahne" (Brentano) **1**:104
"Fish Soup without Fish" (Leskov)
See "Uxa bez ryby"
"The Fish, the Man, and the Spirit" (Hunt) **1**:415
The Fisher of Souls (Sacher-Masoch) **31**:298, 301
"The Fisherman" (Goethe) **4**:165
"The Fisherman" (Preseren)
See "Ribič"
"The Fisherman" (Whittier) **8**:520
"The Fisherman and the Fish" (Pushkin)
See "Skazka o Rybake i Rybke"
The Fisherman Thorsten (Stagnelius) **61**:260
"The Fisher's Son" (Thoreau) **7**:408
"A Fisher-Wife" (Rossetti) **50**:288, 313
"Fishing Song" (Cooke) **110**:9
"Fitter to See Him, I May Be" (Dickinson) **21**:57
"Fitz Adam's Story" (Lowell) **2**:520; **90**:190
The Fitzboodle Papers (Thackeray) **5**:507
5 (Dickinson) **77**:120
"The Five Ages" (Freneau) **111**:146
500 (Dickinson) **77**:121
The Five Hundred Dollar Check (Alger) **83**:114
"Five Hundred Dollars" (Alger) **83**:96
508 (Dickinson) **77**:72, 153
585 (Dickinson) **77**:129
584 (Dickinson) **77**:132
582 (Dickinson) **77**:68, 75
553 (Dickinson) **77**:83
505 (Dickinson) **77**:104-05, 139
540 (Dickinson) **77**:153
547 (Dickinson) **77**:162-64
519 (Cantor) **77**:162-64
593 (Dickinson) **77**:147
579 (Dickinson) **77**:148
577 (Dickinson) **77**:111, 147
506 (Dickinson) **77**:184
564 (Dickinson) **77**:77
566 (Dickinson) **77**:49, 162-63
510 (Dickinson) **77**:88
539 (Dickinson) **77**:94
536 (Dickinson) **77**:88, 163-64
512 (Dickinson) **77**:97
520 (Dickinson) **77**:148
528 (Dickinson) **77**:67, 83
525 (Dickinson) **77**:67
526 (Dickinson) **77**:109-10
"The Five Indispensable Authors" (Lowell) **90**:196
Five Novelettes: Passing Events. Julia. Mina Laury. Henry Hastings. Caroline Vernon (Brontë) **3**:80
"Five Peas from One Pod" (Andersen) **7**:36
Five Pieces of Runic Poetry Translated from the Islandic Language (Percy) **95**:313, 321, 358, 360-61
"Five Scenes" (Landor) **14**:170
"A Five-O'Clock Tea" (Crawford) **12**:169-70
The Fixed Period (Trollope) **6**:500; **101**:321
"Le flacon" (Baudelaire) **6**:80, 129; **55**:61
The Flag of the Seven Upright Ones (Keller) **2**:412
Flamarande (Sand) **2**:596; **57**:316
"Le flambeau vivant" (Baudelaire) **55**:14, 59-60
Flaminio (Sand) **42**:310
Flavio (Castro) **3**:106-07
"The Fleece of Gold" (Gautier)
See "La chaîne d'or"
"The Fleet" (Tennyson) **30**:295
Fleetwood; or, The New Man of Feeling (Godwin) **14**:40, 44, 48, 50, 59-60, 68-71, 73-4, 78, 80-1, 83, 90; **130**:37, 60, 99-101, 105, 115, 122
Flegeljahre: Eine Biographie (Jean Paul) **7**:232, 234, 236, 238, 240, 242
"Flegeljahretraum" (Jean Paul) **7**:239-40
Flesh (Verlaine)
See *Chair*
"Fleur" (Banville) **9**:30
"Fleur d'art" (Corbière) **43**:27
"Les Fleurs" (Mallarmé) **41**:250
"Fleurs" (Rimbaud) **4**:484; **35**:269, 311, 322; **82**:233
Les fleurs du mal (Baudelaire) **6**:79-87, 89-91, 93, 100-05, 108, 110-11, 114, 116-23, 128; **29**:64-72, 75, 77-84, 86-91, 93, 95-109, 111-12; **55**:1-83
Der fliegende Holländer (Wagner) **9**:401, 403, 406, 414-17, 421, 437, 440, 446, 448, 461, 463, 469, 473; **119**:176, 189, 192, 198, 240, 274
"The Flight of the Duchess" (Browning) **19**:77, 88, 126, 131; **79**:94, 100-01, 164
"The Flight of the Heather" (Stevenson) **5**:404
"A Flight of Wild Ducks" (Harpur) **114**:125
"The Flight of Youth" (Milnes) **61**:136, 139, 145
"Fling out the Flag" (Adams) **33**:12
"The Flitting" (Clare) **9**:97, 105; **86**:113, 141-42, 145, 169
"Floare albastra" (Eminescu) **33**:251; **131**:304, 331
"Floating Island at Hawkshead, an Incident in the Schemes of Nature" (Wordsworth) **138**:227-28, 355
"The Flood" (Clare) **9**:122
"The Flood of Years" (Bryant) **6**:168, 172, 175, 179, 182, 189, 193; **46**:21-3, 38-9
The Floods in Emmental (Gotthelf) **117**:22, 25
La flor (Castro) **3**:103-04; **78**:6, 12, 25, 28-29, 32, 37
"Flor entre flores" (Rizal) **27**:425
"Flora" (Smith) **115**:119
Flora Lyndsay; or, Passages in an Eventful Life (Moodie) **14**:217, 226, 237; **113**:295-96, 323, 325, 335, 358, 362
Floral Biography; or Chapters on Flowers (Tonna)
See *Chapters on Flowers*
Flora's Interpreter; or, The American Book of Flowers and Sentiments (Hale) **75**:349
"Flora's Party" (Sigourney) **21**:311

Florence Macarthy (Morgan) **29**:389-90, 393
"A Florentine Joke" (Eliot) **4**:111
"Florentinische Nächte" (Heine) **4**:262, 267
Florida: Its Scenery, Climate, and History (Lanier) **6**:264; **118**:212-15, 233, 286
"A Florida Sunday" (Lanier) **118**:275
Florio: A Tale for Fine Gentlemen and Fine Ladies (More) **27**:335, 337
Florise (Banville) **9**:18, 22
Florville et Courval (Sade) **3**:470
"Das flotte Herz" (Muller) **73**:361
"The Flourishing Village" (Dwight) **13**:270, 272, 278-79
Flower Dust (Novalis)
See *Blütenstaub*
Flower Fables (Alcott) **58**:46; **83**:4
Flower, Fruit, and Thorn Pieces; or, The Married Life, Death, and Wedding of the Advocate of the Poor Firmian Stanislaus Siebankäs (Jean Paul)
See *Blumen-, Frucht-, und Dornenstücke; oder, Ehestand Tod, und Hochzeit des Armena dvocaten Firmian Stanislaus Siebenkäs*
The Flower Garden; or Chapters on Flowers (Tonna)
See *Chapters on Flowers*
"A Flower in a Letter" (Browning) **1**:117
"Flower in the Crannied Wall" (Tennyson) **30**:222, 280
"A Flower (in Time of War)" (Allingham) **25**:11
"Flower Life" (Timrod) **25**:362, 367
"A Flower of the Snow" (Woolson) **82**:272, 334
Flower Pieces and Other Poems (Allingham) **25**:14
"The Flower Sower" (Cooke) **110**:9
"The Flower That Smiles Today" (Shelley) **93**:303
Flower-De-Luce (Longfellow) **45**:138
"The Flowers" (Crabbe) **26**:138-39
"Flowers" (Longfellow) **45**:129
"Flowers at Dusk" (Ichiyō)
See "Yamizakura"
Flowers for Children (Child) **73**:61, 66
"Flowers for the Dead" (Adams) **33**:13
"The Flower's Name" (Browning) **79**:94, 99
The Flowers of Evil (Baudelaire)
See *Les fleurs du mal*
Flowers of Exile (Martí) **63**:109
"Fluctuations" (Brontë) **4**:45, 50; **71**:91
"Die Flüsse" (Schiller) **39**:388
"La flûte" (Vigny) **7**:472-73, 482-83; **102**:336, 339
Flute Player (Augier)
See *Joueur de flûte*
"Flute-Music" (Browning) **19**:153
"The Fly" (Blake) **13**:220, 229, 241-42, 247; **37**:4, 12, 43, 50-1, 93
"The Fly and the Bee" (Krylov) **1**:435
"The Fly and the Bullock" (Moore) **110**:172
The Flying Dutchman (Wagner)
See *Der fliegende Holländer*
The Flying Scud (Boucicault) **41**:28
"The Flying Tailor: Being a Further Extract from the Recluse" (Hogg) **4**:282, 284; **109**:247
"The Flying Trunk" (Andersen)
See "Den flyvende Kuffert"
"Den flyvende Kuffert" (Andersen) **7**:24; **79**:23, 26, 30, 73, 75-76, 82
Fodrejse (Andersen) **79**:80
"Fog" (Lazarus) **8**:420; **109**:297
"La foi" (Lamartine) **11**:245, 269, 282
"Föl a szentháborúra" (Petofi) **21**:286
"Foliage" (Hunt) **1**:411; **70**:263, 283, 293
The Folk Tribunal (Sacher-Masoch) **31**:287
"The Folk-Mote by the River" (Morris) **4**:423
Follas novas (Castro) **3**:100-01, 104-05, 107; **78**:2-9, 29-30, 32-33, 38, 40-41, 54
Folle (Staël-Holstein) **91**:360
"Follen" (Whittier) **8**:486, 491
Follies of a Day (Holcroft)
See *The Follies of a Day; or, The Marriage of Figaro*
The Follies of a Day; or, The Marriage of Figaro (Holcroft) **85**:192, 195, 209, 234
The Follies of Marianne (Musset)
See *Les caprices de Marianne*
"The Folly of Atheism" (Darwin) **106**:185-86
"Föltámadott a tenger" (Petofi) **21**:286
La Fondateur de la Société positiviste a quiconque désire s'y incorporer (Comte) **54**:210
"La Fontaine and de La Rochefoucault" (Landor) **14**:165
"La fontaine aux lianes" (Leconte de Lisle) **29**:212, 217, 221, 234, 245
"La fontaine de sang" (Baudelaire) **55**:27, 74, 77
"Fontan" (Tyutchev) **34**:397-98, 400
"Fonthill Abbey" (Hazlitt) **82**:154, 159
Foolish Steve (Arany)
See *Boland Istók*
The Fool's Tragedy (Beddoes)
See *Death's Jest Book; or, The Fool's Tragedy*
"Footpaths" (Jefferies) **47**:134
"Footsteps" (Coutinho)
See "Stapfen"
"The Footsteps of Angels" (Longfellow) **2**:479, 493; **45**:132, 155
"For a Venetian Pastoral by Giorgione" (Rossetti) **4**:499
"For an Album" (Clarke) **19**:233
"For an Urn in Thoresby Park" (Landor) **14**:200
"For Annie" (Poe) **1**:509; **117**:211-12, 227, 237-38, 242-43, 281, 283, 309
"For Each and For All" (Martineau) **26**:351
"For Exmoor" (Ingelow) **39**:264
For Love and Life (Oliphant) **61**:204
For Love; or, The Two Heroes (Robertson) **35**:333, 335, 356, 369
"For Me" (Lampman)
See "Ambition"
"For our Happiness" (Grillparzer)
See "Für unser Glück"
For Self-Examination (Kierkegaard) **34**:224-25, 261, 266; **78**:238
"For the Dear Old Flag I'll Die" (Foster) **26**:288
For the Honor of God (Sacher-Masoch) **31**:294
For the Major (Woolson) **82**:269-70, 273-74, 278, 293, 297-99, 315-16
"For the Monument of the Rev. W. Mason" (Darwin) **106**:182
"For the Penny-Wise" (Tennyson) **30**:294
"For the Power to whom we bow" (Fuller) **50**:249, 251
For the Term of His Natural Life (Clarke)
See *His Natural Life*
"For Though the Caves Were Rabitted" (Thoreau) **7**:384
"For You O Democracy" (Whitman) **31**:430; **81**:328
The Forayers; or, The Raid of the Dog-Days (Simms) **3**:507-09, 513
Force and Freedom (Burckhardt)
See *Weltgeschichtliche Bertrachtungen*
The Force of Fashion (Mackenzie)
See *False Shame, or The White Hypocrite*
The Force of Ridicule (Holcroft) **85**:198, 223
"Foreboding" (Pushkin) **83**:257
Forefathers' Eve (Mickiewicz)
See *Dziady III*
"Foreign Influence" (Madison) **126**:326
"Forerunners" (Emerson) **1**:296
The Forest (Ostrovsky)
See *Les*
Forest and Game Law Tales (Martineau) **26**:311; **137**:250
"The Forest Hymn" (Bryant) **6**:159, 164-65, 168-72, 177, 187, 192-93; **46**:6, 8, 16, 20, 23, 25, 28, 41, 43, 47, 55
Forest Life (Kirkland) **85**:260-61, 263-65, 270, 282-86, 298, 301
The Forest Minstrel: A Selection of Songs, Adapted to the Most Favourite Scottish Airs (Hogg) **4**:274, 281
"Forest, Oh My Forest" (Eminescu) **33**:247
"A Forest Path in Winter" (Lampman) **25**:209
"Forest Pictures" (Hayne) **94**:144, 149, 165
"The Forest Pool" (Eminescu) **131**:293
"Forest Quiet (In the South)" (Hayne) **94**:166
"The Forest Sanctuary" (Hemans) **71**:261, 268-69
The Forest Sanctuary, and Other Poems (Hemans) **29**:196-97, 199, 201-02, 205, 207; **71**:274, 284, 305, 307
The Forest Wanderer (Stifter)
See *Der Waldgänger*
The Forest Warden (Ludwig)
See *Die Erbförster*
"Forest, Why D'You Swing So Low?" (Eminescu)
See "Ce te legeni codrule"
"Forester" (Edgeworth) **51**:84-90, 135
The Foresters (Wilson) **5**:549, 558, 561, 567, 569
The Forester's Letters (Paine) **62**:270
The Foresters—Robin Hood and Maid Marian (Tennyson) **30**:265
"La forêt" (Banville) **9**:30
"La forêt vierge" (Leconte de Lisle) **29**:216-17, 231
"Forever at His side to walk-" (Dickinson) **77**:65
"Le forgeron" (Rimbaud) **4**:465; **82**:238
"The Forger's Bride" (Cooke) **110**:36-7
"Forget and Forgive" (Edgeworth) **1**:265
"Forget-Me-Not Song" (Crawford) **127**:150-52
"The Forging of the Anchor" (Ferguson) **33**:287
"The Forgiven Dead" (Ridge) **82**:182
"A Forgiveness" (Browning) **19**:88; **79**:157
"Forgotten Arietta" (Verlaine)
See "Ariettes oubliées"
"The Forgotten Village" (Nekrasov) **11**:409
"The Forgotten Wedding Day" (Mangan) **27**:275
"The Formation of Coal" (Huxley) **67**:83
"A Former Life" (Baudelaire)
See "La Vie antérieure"
Formerly and Not So Long Ago (Verlaine)
See *Jadis et naguère*
Formosa (Boucicault) **41**:31
"The Forms of Nature and the Unity of Their Origin" (Very) **9**:386-87
Forord (Kierkegaard) **125**:231, 260
"The Forsaken" (Turgenev) **21**:401
"Forsaken Child" (Norton) **47**:246
"The Forsaken Girl" (Mörike) **10**:446
"The Forsaken Home" (Tonna) **135**:194, 198-99, 209, 213-16, 220-22
"The Forsaken Merman" (Arnold) **6**:37, 44, 54, 66; **29**:35; **89**:6
Fort comme la mort (Maupassant) **1**:446, 450, 459, 464, 467, 470; **42**:169; **83**:175, 180-82
"Fortepjan Szopena" (Norwid) **17**:367, 372
La forteresse du Danube (Pixérécourt) **39**:277, 279, 281, 286
Fortnight in the Wilderness (Tocqueville) **7**:424
Fortunat (Tieck) **5**:514, 525
The Fortunate Beggars (Gozzi)
See *I pitocchi fortunati*
"The Fortunate Fisher-maiden" (Muller)
See "Die Glückliche Fischerin"
"Fortune and the Begger" (Krylov) **1**:435
The Fortune Hunter; or the Adventurers of a Man about Town (Mowatt) **74**:210-11, 228, 230
Fortune; or, The Art of Success (Jefferies) **47**:121
The Fortunes of Colonel Torlogh O'Brien (Le Fanu) **9**:309
The Fortunes of Glencore (Lever) **23**:286, 292, 301

The Fortunes of Nigel (Scott) **15**:306, 309; **69**:304-05, 308, 313; **110**:264
The Fortunes of Perkin Warbeck (Shelley) **14**:255-56, 262, 265, 267, 270-71; **59**:144, 190, 192; **103**:342, 347
"The Fortunes of Sir Robert Ardagh" (Le Fanu) **9**:322; **58**:253, 263
"Fortunio" (Hayne) **94**:156
Fortunio (Gautier) **1**:346-47, 349-50, 352; **59**:5, 7, 12, 30
Fortunio and his Seven Gifted Servants (Planché) **42**:273, 280, 292, 295
49 (Dickinson) **77**:80, 184
The Forty-Five Guardsmen (Dumas)
See *Les quarante-cinq*
"The Foster Mother's Tale" (Wordsworth) **111**:358
"The Fostering of Aslaug" (Morris) **4**:447
The Fosterling (Fredro)
See *Wychowanka*
"The Foster-Mother's Tale" (Coleridge) **9**:131
"Le fou" (Bertrand) **31**:46-8
"Un fou" (Maupassant) **1**:449; **83**:176, 181
Foul Play (Reade) **2**:540-41, 547-48, 551; **74**:248, 258, 263-65, 284, 318
"Les foules" (Baudelaire) **29**:111; **55**:40
"Les Foules" (Maupassant) **83**:188
"Found" (Rossetti) **4**:508
The Found Remains (Solomos)
See *Ta euriskomena*
Foundations (Kant) **27**:220, 243; **67**:259-60, 262-63, 265
The Foundations of a Creed (Lewes)
See *The Problems of Life and Mind*
The Foundations of European Discontent (Almqvist)
See *Europeiska missnöjets grunder*
Foundations of Natural Right According to the Principles of Wissenschaftslehre (Fichte)
See *Grundlage des Naturrechts nach Prinzipen der Wissenshaftslehre*
Foundations of the entire Wissenschaftslehre (Fichte)
See *Grundlage der gesamten Wissenschaftslehre*
"The Foundling" (Kleist)
See "Der Findling"
"The Fountain" (Bryant) **6**:168, 188, 191; **46**:26, 39
"The Fountain" (Lowell) **2**:507
"The Fountain" (Tyutchev)
See "Fontan"
"The Fountain" (Wordsworth) **12**:427, 450; **111**:326
"The Fountain of Blood" (Baudelaire)
See "La fontaine de sang"
"The Fountain of Oblivion" (Hemans) **71**:304
The Fountain of Youth (Sacher-Masoch) **31**:298, 301
Fountainville Abbey (Dunlap) **2**:212-13
4 (Dickinson) **77**:120
"Four Beasts in One; or, The Homo-Cameleopard" (Poe) **16**:324
"The Four Bridges" (Ingelow) **107**:122
"Four Charades" (Cranch) **115**:58
"Four Ducks on a Pond" (Allingham) **25**:20
The Four Georges (Thackeray) **5**:490; **14**:438, 451; **14**:451
481 (Dickinson) **77**:173
486 (Dickinson) **77**:131
458 (Dickinson) **77**:139
452 (Dickinson) **77**:152
449 (Dickinson) **77**:119, 129
441 (Dickinson) **77**:71, 110, 112
443 (Dickinson) **77**:103
414 (Dickinson) **77**:114
497 (Dickinson) **77**:82
493 (Dickinson) **77**:64
401 (Dickinson) **77**:180
416 (Dickinson) **77**:110, 112
465 (Dickinson) **77**:49, 163
461 (Dickinson) **77**:145
413 (Cantor) **77**:80
430 (Dickinson) **77**:92, 132-34, 139
429 (Dickinson) **77**:93
Four Letters (Paine) **62**:369, 371
Four Letters on the English Constitution (Dyer) **129**:106, 110, 132, 137
"The Four Ox-Cart" (Petofi)
See "A négy ökrös szekér"
Four Stories High (Clarke) **19**:251
"Four to Four" (Hugo) **10**:361
The Four Zoas: The Torments of Love and Jealousy in the Death and Judgement of Albion the Ancient Man (Blake) **13**:173, 177, 183-85, 192-93, 195, 197, 199, 205, 208-10, 213, 220-21, 224-26, 228-29, 231, 233-38, 244; **37**:24-5, 27, 35, 64, 77; **57**:29, 46, 48, 63, 82; **127**:15, 17-18, 24, 29, 50, 53, 57, 67, 87, 89, 93, 97, 124, 132, 134
Les Fourberies de Nérine (Banville) **9**:20, 22
Les Fourchambault (Augier) **31**:2-3, 8-10, 13, 16, 26, 28, 31, 34
14 (Dickinson) **77**:149
"1492" (Lazarus) **8**:422, 427; **109**:335-36
1481 (Dickinson) **77**:125
1452 (Dickinson) **77**:92
1445 (Dickinson) **77**:96, 163, 173
1461 (Dickinson) **77**:82
1463 (Dickinson) **77**:95, 118, 121
Fourteen Sonnets, written chiefly on Picturesque Spots during a Journey, 1789 (Bowles) **103**:56, 65, 78, 85-7, 93-4
"Fourth Epistle" (Eminescu)
See "Epistle IV"
"Fourth of July Ode" (Emerson) **1**:284
"Fourth Sunday after Advent" (Keble) **87**:173
"The Fourth Sunday after Trinity" (Keble) **87**:202
"Fourth Sunday in Advent" (Keble) **87**:160, 173-74
"The Fox and the Bird" (Very) **9**:385
"The Fox and the Marmot" (Krylov) **1**:435
"The Fox and the Wolf" (Krasicki)
See "Lis i wilk"
"The Fox-Hunters" (Irving) **2**:369
Fra Diavolo; ou, L'hôtellerie de Terraine (Scribe) **16**:401
"Fra Lippo Lippi" (Browning) **19**:79, 132, 152; **79**:163, 171
"Fra Pedro" (Lazarus) **8**:425; **109**:324
Fra Rupert (Landor) **14**:165
Fragen zu Denkübungen für Wilhelmine (Kleist) **37**:219
"Fragment" (Allston) **2**:26
"A Fragment" (Baratynsky)
See "Otryvok"
"A Fragment" (Bryant)
See "Inscription for the Entrance into a Wood"
"Fragment" (Clare) **86**:114-15, 166-67
"A Fragment" (Crawford) **127**:217
"A Fragment" (Gilpin) **30**:40
"A Fragment" (Pushkin) **83**:320
A Fragment (Keats)
See *Hyperion: A Fragment*
"A Fragment for a System" (Schelling) **30**:155-56
"A Fragment from Fourier on Trade" (Marx) **114**:57
"Fragment: Notes for a Lecture" (Lincoln) **18**:240
"Fragment: Notes for Law Lecture—July 1, 1850" (Lincoln) **18**:240
Fragment of 1790 (Goethe)
See *Faust: Ein Fragment*
"Fragment of a Journal. To G.M. Esq" (Moore) **110**:178
"Fragment of a Mythological Hymn to Love" (Moore) **110**:178-80
"Fragment of an 'Antigone'" (Arnold) **29**:34-5
"Fragment of an Epistle" (Dana) **53**:158
"A Fragment of Bion" (Freneau) **111**:141
A Fragment on Government (Bentham) **38**:37, 44, 49, 58, 84, 88-9, 93
"A Fragment on Ontology" (Bentham) **38**:92-5
"Fragment on Religious Ideas" (Hölderlin) **16**:166-68, 171
Fragment on the Church (Arnold) **18**:24
Fragmentarium (Eminescu) **33**:255-57
Fragmente über die neuere deutsche Literatur (Herder) **8**:299, 303, 305-07, 309, 313-15
Fragmente uber Recensenten-Unfug (Kotzebue) **25**:152
Fragmentos (Martí) **63**:124
Fragments (Martí)
See *Fragmentos*
Fragments d'un journal intime (Amiel) **4**:12-15, 17, 19-21
"Fragments from a Writing Desk" (Melville) **123**:175, 251
Fragments of a Roman Tale (Macaulay) **42**:154
Fragments of Philosophy (Kierkegaard)
See *Philosophiske Smuler*
Fragments on the New German Literature (Herder)
See *Fragmente über die neuere deutsche Literatur*
"Fragments on Universal Grammar" (Bentham) **38**:92
Fragments Relating to Language and Poetry (Klopstock)
See *Über Sprach und Dichtkunst*
"Fragments Upon the Nymphs" (Hunt) **70**:248
"Le frais matin dorait" (Leconte de Lisle) **29**:224
Framley Parsonage (Trollope) **6**:455, 464, 467, 470, 491, 499-502, 516-17; **33**:363, 365; **101**:234-35, 266, 273, 319, 321, 333
"France" (Dutt) **29**:128
"France" (Whitman) **4**:544
France (Morgan) **29**:386
"France: An Ode" (Coleridge)
See "Ode to France"
France and England in North America (Parkman) **12**:336, 351-52, 359, 365, 369, 371-77
"France and Spain" (Browning) **79**:94, 99
France before the Eyes of Europe (Michelet) **31**:219, 258
France depuis vingt-cinq ans (Gautier) **1**:349
Francesca Carrara (Landon) **15**:158-59, 161, 164
Francesca da Rimini (Boker) **125**:20, 22-25, 28-29, 31-34, 36-38, 41-43, 45, 48-50, 52, 55-56, 58, 66-67, 70-72, 75-77
Franchise et trahison (Sade) **47**:361
Francia (Sand) **57**:316
Francillon (Dumas) **9**:228, 231, 235, 243, 246, 249-50
Francis of Assisi (Oliphant) **11**:433, 445
Francis the First (Kemble) **18**:160-62, 164, 167, 178
"Franciscae meae laudes" (Baudelaire) **55**:61
François le Champi (Sand) **42**:309, 323-24, 326-28, 338, 340, 365, 366-68, 374; **57**:317, 338, 358, 365-6, 368
Frank, A Tale (Edgeworth) **1**:262; **51**:78, 81-2
Frank and Fearless; or, The Fortunes of Jasper Kent (Alger) **8**:24, 45
"The Frank Courtship" (Crabbe) **26**:93, 116, 129, 131, 135, 147; **121**:65-7, 69, 71-2, 77
Frankenstein; or, The Modern Prometheus (Shelley) **14**:247-56, 258-72, 274-77, 279-81, 283-90, 292-93, 295-307; **59**:138-251; **103**:322, 329-31, 338, 349, 358, 360, 363-66
"Franklin" (Landor) **14**:166
Franklin Evans (Whitman) **4**:582-83; **81**:327, 343, 347
Frank's Campaign; or, What Boys Can Do on the Farm for the Camp (Alger) **8**:40; **83**:104, 139, 144
"Frank's Sealed Letter" (Morris) **4**:430
Franz Sternbald's Travels (Tieck)
See *Franz Sternbalds Wanderungen*

Franz Sternbalds Wanderungen (Tieck) **5**:521, 525, 527-28, 531; **46**:375-76, 393, 395-98, 401, 405
Französische Maler (Heine) **4**:259, 264; **54**:339
Französische Zustände (Heine) **4**:246
Frascati's; or, Scenes in Paris (Richardson) **55**:329, 350
"Fraser Papers" (Maginn) **8**:435, 437
Fratricide (Macha) **46**:202
Frau Jenny Treibel (Fontane) **26**:235-36, 239-40, 245, 252, 257, 270-72, 278
"Die Frau Pfarrerin" (Gotthelf) **117**:44, 51
"Frau Rebekka mit den Kindern, an einem Maimorgen" (Claudius) **75**:190
Frau Regel Amrain und ihr Jüngster (Keller) **2**:415
"Frau Susanne" (Goethe) **4**:189
Frauenliebe und Leben (Chamisso) **82**:3
Die Fräulein von Scuderi (Ludwig) **4**:349, 351
"Frederic" (Southey) **97**:314
"Frederic and Elfrida" (Austen) **1**:67; **119**:13
Frederick (Macaulay) **42**:87
"Frederick and Catherine" (Grimm and Grimm) **3**:227
Frederick Engels on Russia (Engels) **85**:9
Fredolfo (Maturin) **6**:322-23, 332, 343-44, 347
"The Free Besieged" (Solomos)
See "Oi eleftheroi poliorkimenoi"
"Free C." (Isaacs)
See "Columbia libre"
Free Labour (Reade) **2**:551
"Free Strophes" (Isaacs)
See "Estrofas libres"
Free Thoughts on Public Affairs (Hazlitt) **29**:169
Freedmen's Book (Child) **73**:63, 71, 84
"Freedom" (Emerson) **98**:182-83
"Freedom" (Lampman) **25**:182, 188, 192, 198, 217, 219
"Freedom" (Lowell) **90**:215
"Freedom" (Tennyson) **65**:285
Freedom Comes to Krähwinkel (Nestroy)
See *Freiheit in Krähwinkel*
"Freedom of the Press" (Whittier) **59**:364
"Freedom Wheeler's Controversy" (Cooke)
See "Freedom Wheeler's Controversy with Providence"
"Freedom Wheeler's Controversy with Providence" (Cooke) **110**:10, 14, 20, 24-5, 28, 34, 44, 46, 48, 50, 57, 65, 68
"Freedon Wheeler's Controversy with God" (Cooke)
See "Freedom Wheeler's Controversy with Providence"
"The Freeholder Ovsyanikov" (Turgenev) **21**:377; **122**:294
Fregat Nadezhda (Bestuzhev) **131**:154-55, 168, 175-76, 187, 210
"La frégate 'La Sérieuse'" (Vigny) **7**:473, 485; **102**:368
"Freigeisterei der Leidenschaft" (Schiller) **39**:387
Freiheit in Krähwinkel (Nestroy) **42**:233, 235, 237, 244, 249, 252-53, 263-64, 266
"Der Freischütz" (Wagner) **119**:190
"Fremont's Ride" (Cooke) **110**:9
French Affairs: Letters from Paris (Heine)
See *Französische Zustände*
French and Italian Notebooks (Hawthorne)
See *Passages from the French and Italian Notebooks of Nathaniel Hawthorne*
"A French Critic on Goethe" (Arnold) **6**:45
"A French Critic on Gray" (Arnold) **6**:58
"A French Critic on Heine" (Arnold) **6**:58
"A French Critic on Keats" (Arnold) **6**:58
"A French Critic on Milton" (Arnold) **6**:45, 58
"A French Critic on Shelley" (Arnold) **6**:58
"The French Drama: Racine and Victor Hugo" (Lewes) **25**:285
"A French Eton" (Arnold) **89**:102
A French Eton, or middle-class education and the state (Arnold) **126**:3, 6, 12
French Grammar (Cobbett) **49**:160
"French Life" (Gaskell) **70**:186, 188-89
The French Philosophers of the Nineteenth Century (Taine)
See *Les philosophes Français du XIXme siècle*
The French Revolution (Blake) **13**:184, 221, 242, 251-52, 254; **37**:35; **57**:20,57,106
The French Revolution (Carlyle) **70**:12, 17, 44-45, 56-61, 70-71, 76-77, 89, 98, 105, 107-108, 111
French XVIII Century Painters (Goncourt and Goncourt)
See *L'art du dix-huitème siècle*
Le frère aîné (Daudet) **1**:249
Frère Jacques (Kock) **16**:245, 247-49, 258
Les frères invisibles (Scribe) **16**:412, 414
Les frères Zemganno (Goncourt) **7**:155-57, 162, 166-67, 170, 174-76, 183-84, 188-89
"Fresca, lozana, pura y olorosa" (Espronceda) **39**:94, 102
"Fresh from the Dewy Hill" (Blake) **13**:182; **37**:35
Fresh Leaves (Parton) **86**:337
"Freude" (Hölderlin) **16**:185
Der Freund (Hoffmann) **2**:347
Die Freunde (Tieck) **5**:523
"Freundeswort" (Grillparzer) **102**:175
"Die Freundschaft" (Schiller) **39**:357
"The Friar of Orders Gray" (Percy) **95**:323
"Friede auf Erden" (Meyer) **81**:155
"Der Frieden" (Hölderlin) **16**:181
"Friedensfeier" (Hölderlin) **16**:175, 192, 196
"Friedrich Rückert" (Taylor) **89**:325
"The Friend" (Coleridge) **9**:155, 205, 207; **54**:107; **111**:291
"A Friend" (Cranch) **115**:26
"A Friend in Need" (Harpur) **114**:139
"The Friend in Need" (Hood) **16**:221
The Friend of the Family (Dostoevsky) **21**:121; **33**:191, 195; **43**:92
"A Friendly Address to Mrs. Fry" (Hood) **16**:235
"Friends" (Krasicki)
See "Przyjaciele"
"Friends" (Rossetti) **66**:307
"The Friends of Man" (Sigourney) **21**:293
"Friendship" (Cowper) **94**:23, 117
"Friendship" (Emerson) **98**:90, 96-7, 99-101
"Friendship" (Lampman) **25**:196
"Friendship with Nature" (Sigourney) **21**:301
Friendship's Garland: Being the Conversations, Letters, and Opinions of the Late Arminus, Baron von Thunder-Ten-Tronckh (Arnold) **6**:37, 53, 61; **89**:109; **126**:7, 42, 83, 103
The Frigate Hope (Bestuzhev)
See *Fregat Nadezhda*
Frinko Balaban (Sacher-Masoch) **31**:303
"Frisson d'hiver" (Mallarmé) **4**:371, 373, 377
Frithiof's Saga (Tegner) **2**:610-14
"The Frogs" (Lampman) **25**:161, 168, 182, 184, 200, 209
"From All the Jails the Boys and Girls" (Dickinson) **21**:18
"From Bacon to Beethoven" (Lanier) **6**:245
From Canal Boy to President; or, The Boyhood and Manhood of James A. Garfield (Alger) **8**:24, 45
From Farm to Fortune (Alger) **8**:30
"From Goethe" (Lermontov) **126**:223
"From Hand to Mouth" (O'Brien) **21**:248, 250, 252-53
"From Hezekiah Salem's Last Basket" (Freneau) **111**:136
"From House to Home" (Rossetti) **2**:556, 566, 572; **66**:301, 304, 306-9, 312, 320-1, 329, 356, 382
"From Lightning and Tempest" (Gordon) **21**:160, 165, 167, 188
"From Montauk Point" (Whitman) **31**:389
"From Moscow to Leipzig" (Dobrolyubov) **5**:140
"From One of the Society of Friends to Her Kinswoman" (Haliburton) **15**:129
From Paris to Cadiz (Dumas)
See *Impressions de voyage*
"From Paumanok Starting I Fly like a Bird" (Whitman) **81**:313
"From Pent-Up Aching Rivers" (Whitman) **31**:400, 405; **81**:329
"From Perugia" (Whittier) **8**:493, 512; **59**:373
"From Pindemonte" (Pushkin) **83**:261
"From Roman Scenes" (Herzen) **10**:348
"From Sunset to Star Rise" (Rossetti) **66**:341, 372
"From the bosom of ocean I seek thee" (Taylor) **89**:300
"From the Castle in the Air to the Little Corner of the World" (Paine) **62**:324
"From the Flats" (Lanier) **6**:255
"From the German" (Beddoes) **3**:34
"From the High Priest of Apollo" (Moore) **110**:178
"From the Italian" (Halleck) **47**:57
"From the life, that once raged here" (Tyutchev)
See "Ot zhizni toy, chto bushevala zdes"
From the Other Shore (Herzen)
See *Vom andern Ufer*
From the Papers of the Still Living (Kierkegaard)
See *Af en endnu Levendes Papirer*
"From the Sketchbook" (Jacobsen) **34**:170
"From the Upland to the Sea" (Morris) **4**:421
"From the Waves of Time" (Eminescu) **33**:246
"From the Woods" (Hayne) **94**:159-60, 165
"From the Work of Dr. Krupov on Mental Ailments in General and Their Epidemic Development in Particular" (Herzen) **10**:323, 350
"From the Wreck" (Gordon) **21**:149, 155-56, 159, 163-65, 170, 172, 176, 178, 183, 187-88
"From Yule to Yule" (Crawford) **127**:193-96
Fromont jeune et Risler aîné (Daudet) **1**:231-34, 239, 241, 248, 250-51
Fromont the Younger and Risler the Elder (Daudet)
See *Fromont jeune et Risler aîné*
"The Front Yard" (Woolson) **82**:275, 290-91, 293, 296-97, 343
The Front Yard and Other Italian Stories (Woolson) **82**:275, 283, 293, 299, 338, 341, 343
"Frontier Ballads" (Cooke) **110**:3
"Frost at Midnight" (Coleridge) **9**:150, 158; **54**:69; **99**:2, 5, 19, 61, 73, 104-05; **111**:310
"Frost in the Holidays" (Allingham) **25**:6
"The Frost Spirit" (Whittier) **59**:375
The Frozen Deep (Collins) **1**:183; **93**:38, 40
"Frozen Tears" (Muller)
See "Gefror'ne Tränen"
"Fru Fønss" (Jacobsen) **34**:158, 160, 171
Fru Marie Grubbe: Interieurer fra det syttende Asrhundreded (Jacobsen) **34**:140-44, 151-60, 162, 164, 167, 169
The Frugal Housewife (Child)
See *The American Frugal Housewife*
"Die frühen Gräber" (Klopstock) **11**:236, 240
"Frühlingseinzug" (Muller) **73**:366
Der Frühlingskranz (Arnim)
See *Clemens Brentanos Frühlingskranz aus Jugendbriefen ihm geflochten, wie er selbst schriftlich verlangte*
"Frühlingskranz aus dem Plauenschen Grunde bei Dresden" (Muller) **73**:366, 373, 380
"Frühlingslieder aus dem Plauenscen Grunde" (Muller) **73**:366
"Das Frühlingsmahl" (Muller) **73**:366
"Frühlingsschrei eines Knechtes aus der Tiefe" (Brentano) **1**:102, 105
"Frühlingstraum" (Muller) **73**:366, 391-92, 397
Le Fruit Défendu (Feuillet) **45**:79, 89
"Fruit of Travel Long Ago" (Melville) **3**:351

"Frustrating a Funeral" (Harris) **23**:156, 159-60
Frygt og Baeven (Kierkegaard) **34**:201, 223, 227, 239, 241, 246-47, 259, 260, 262, 263-66; **78**:119, 147, 154, 157-66, 168-69, 173, 178-82, 197, 238, 242, 244, 252; **125**:177, 201, 213, 233, 236, 238
The Fudge Family (Moore) **110**:190
The Fudge Family in England (Moore) **110**:172
The Fudge Family in Paris (Moore) **6**:384, 388, 395; **110**:173, 188
Fugitive Verses (Baillie) **2**:41-42
The Fugitives (Kivi)
See *Karkurit*
"Fuillet's La Morte" (Pater) **90**:326
A Full Vindication of the Measures of Congress (Hamilton) **49**:293, 296, 325
"Fülle" (Meyer) **81**:155, 169, 208
"The Function of Criticism at the Present Time" (Arnold) **6**:34, 47, 57, 69; **29**:9, 38-44, 48, 51, 55-6; 139; **89**:30, 33-4, 38-9, 62, 72, 76, 81-2, 85-6, 101, 109; **126**:6, 38, 52, 73, 78, 83, 88, 94, 114, 122
"The Function of the Poet" (Lowell) **2**:521
Fundamental Principles (Kant)
See *Grundlegung*
"Der Fundator" (Droste-Hülshoff) **3**:200
"De fundersamme" (Almqvist) **42**:19
"Funeral" (Arnold) **6**:67
"The Funeral" (Nekrasov) **11**:409
"A Funeral" (Rogers) **69**:81
"The Funeral and Party Fight" (Carleton) **3**:92
"The Funeral at Sea" (Sigourney) **21**:293
"Funeral Feast" (Shevchenko)
See "Tryzna"
"Funeral of Dr. Mason F. Cogswell" (Sigourney) **87**:337
"Funeral of Louis XVII" (Hugo) **3**:234
"Funeral Song for the Princess Charlotte of Wales" (Southey) **8**:474
Der funfzehnte November (Tieck) **46**:412-14
"Für die Mouche" (Heine) **4**:247, 269
El Fureidis (Cummins) **139**:165-66, 185, 194-96
"Für unser Glück" (Grillparzer) **102**:175
"Furlow College Address" (Lanier) **118**:230
"Fürst Ganzgott und Sänger Halbogott" (Arnim) **5**:13, 18
Further Exhibitions from the System of Philosophy (Schelling)
See *Fernere Darstellungen*
"Further in Summer Than the Birds" (Dickinson) **21**:19, 59, 67-9; **77**:95
Further Notes of a Young Man (Herzen) **61**:108
Further Records: 1848-1883 (Kemble) **18**:189-90
"Fusées" (Baudelaire) **29**:71, 98; **55**:8, 11, 40, 43, 45-6
"Die Füsse im Feuer" (Meyer) **81**:207
"Fussreise" (Mörike) **10**:448
"The Fust Baby" (Shaw) **15**:335
"Fut-il jamais douceur de coeur pareille" (Musset) **7**:275
"Futura" (Silva) **114**:316
Futura (Silva) **114**:262
"Future" (Silva)
See *Futura*
The Future Australian Race (Clarke) **19**:236
"The Future Glory of America" (Trumbull) **30**:349-50
"The Future Home" (Macha) **46**:202
"The Future Life" (Bryant) **6**:168
"The Future of Liberalism" (Arnold) **89**:111
"The Future of Protestantism and Catholicity" (Brownson) **50**:54
The Future of Science (Renan)
See *L'avenir de la science*
"Fyrtøjet" (Andersen) **7**:21, 26, 34; **79**:23, 49-50, 52, 58-9, 64-5, 68, 76, 80-1
Gabriel (Sand) **2**:587; **42**:359; **57**:312
Gabriel Lambert (Dumas) **71**:194, 204
Gabrièle Mimanso (Almqvist) **42**:5
"The Gabrieliad" (Pushkin) **83**:332
Gabrielle (Augier) **31**:4-5, 7, 9-11, 14, 18-19, 23-4, 29
Gabrielle de Belle-Isle (Dumas)
See *Mademoiselle de Belle-Isle*
"Gadki" (Norwid) **17**:373
"The Gagging Bill" (Kendall) **12**:200, 202
Gahagan (Thackeray) **5**:470
"Gaia, or Willy Rhymer's Address to his London Landladies" (Dyer) **129**:148
Galanterie macabre (Mallarmé) **41**:278
"Galatea" (Casal) **131**:223-25, 228, 235, 266, 268
"Galatea" (Kendall) **12**:192
Galician Songs (Castro)
See *Cantares gallegos*
A Galician Tale (Sacher-Masoch) **31**:289, 303
"Galileo" (Landor) **14**:166
Gallant Festivals (Verlaine)
See *Fêtes galantes*
"The Gallant Lads in Green" (Crawford) **127**:220
A Gallery of Illustrious Literary Characters, 1830-1838 (Maginn) **8**:434, 439-40
"A Gallery of Portraits" (Bestuzhev)
See "Portretnaia Gallereia"
Gallician songs (Castro)
See *Cantares gallegos*
Gallomania (Disraeli) **79**:269
"The Gallows" (Whittier) **8**:512, 525; **59**:361
"Gambara" (Balzac) **5**:79
"The Gambler" (Krasicki)
See "Gracz"
"The Gambler" (Pushkin)
See *Skazhi, Kakoi sud'boi*
The Gambler (Dostoevsky)
See *Igrok*
The Gamblers (Gogol)
See *Igroki*
Gambler's Fate (Dumas) **11**:42
"Gambler's Fortune" (Hoffmann) **2**:342
"The Gambrel-Roofed House and Its Outlook" (Holmes) **81**:103
"The Game of Backgammon" (Mérimée) **6**:354, 367-9
"A Game of Lawn Tennis" (Levy) **59**:92, 119
The Game of Logic (Carroll) **2**:108; **139**:57
The Game of Speculation (Lewes) **25**:284
The Game-keeper at Home; or, Sketches of Natural History and Rural Life (Jefferies) **47**:88, 90, 97, 103, 107, 111, 114, 121, 133, 137, 141-42
"The Gaming Table" (Baudelaire)
See "Le jeu"
"Det gamle Egetræes sidste Drøm" (Andersen) **79**:77
Den gamle trädgårdsmästarens brev (Runeberg) **41**:318
"Gamlet i Don Kikhot" (Turgenev) **21**:412, 431, 438, 442; **37**:403; **122**:325, 345-46
"Gamlet ščigrovskogo uezda" (Turgenev) **21**:378; **37**:402; **122**:264, 342
Ganar perdiendo (Zorrilla y Moral) **6**:525
"Der Gang nach dem Eisenhammer" (Schiller) **39**:388
"Der Gang von Wittow nach Jasmund" (Muller) **73**:360
"Ganymed" (Hölderlin) **16**:191
"Ganymede" (Chivers) **49**:74
Det går an (Almqvist) **42**:4-8, 14, 18, 20
La gara degli uccelli (Da Ponte) **50**:77
"Garafelia" (Child) **73**:128
"Garcon un bock" (Maupassant) **42**:200; **83**:228
"The Garden" (Cowper) **8**:111, 123, 128; **94**:10, 23, 26-7, 29-30, 120, 128-29
"The Garden" (Cranch) **115**:9-10, 31, 35
"The Garden" (Very) **9**:377, 383-84
"A Garden by the Sea" (Morris) **4**:421
"Garden Fancies" (Browning) **19**:77; **79**:94, 99
"The Garden of Adonis" (Lazarus) **8**:420; **109**:294
"The Garden of Eden" (Andersen) **79**:23-24, 59, 76, 82
"The Garden of Irem" (Taylor) **89**:304
"Garden of Love" (Blake) **13**:181-82, 220-21; **37**:4, 15-16, 25, 33, 43, 47-8, 52, 57-8, 92
"Garden of Paradise" (Andersen) **7**:24
"The Garden of the World" (Andersen) **7**:29
"The Gardener and His Master" (Andersen) **7**:37; **79**:55
The Gardener and the Squire (Andersen) **79**:36
"The Gardener's Daughter" (Tennyson) **30**:213, 267
"Gareth and Lynette" (Tennyson) **30**:283, 287-88; **65**:236, 241, 243-5, 278, 281, 284, 287-8, 293, 300-1, 307, 311, 349, 367, 369-76, 382
Les Garibaldiens (Dumas) **71**:205
Garland for Girls (Alcott) **58**:51
"Garland of Sonnets" (Preseren)
See "Sonetni venec"
Garrick Fever (Planché) **42**:294
"The Garrison of Cape Ann" (Whittier) **8**:492; **59**:375
Garzia (Alfieri)
See *Don Garzia*
Gaslight and Daylight (Sala) **46**:237, 246
"Gaspar Becerra" (Longfellow) **45**:131
Gaspard de la nuit: fantaisies à la manière de Rembrandt et de Callot (Bertrand) **31**:43-7, 49-55
"Gasparo Bandollo" (Mangan) **27**:301
Der Gastfreund (Grillparzer) **102**:86, 100-03, 163
Gaston de Blondeville; or, The Court of Henry III Keeping Festival in Ardenne, St. Alban's Abbey: A Metrical Tale, with Some Poetical Pieces (Radcliffe) **6**:416-17, 421, 425, 427; **55**:223-5, 274, 281-2
Gaston de Latour (Pater) **7**:308, 323, 340; **90**:242, 288, 290, 338, 340
The Gates of Paradise (Blake) **37**:4
The Gathering of the West (Galt) **110**:79, 114, 116
El gaucho Martín Fierro (Hernández) **17**:162-69, 171-73, 175-79
"Gaudissart" (Balzac)
See "L'illustre Gaudissart"
Gaule et France (Dumas) **71**:203
La gaviota: Novela de costumbres (Caballero) **10**:72-73, 76-81, 83-84
Gavriiliada (Pushkin) **3**:427-28, 451
The Gavriiliada (Pushkin)
See *Gavriiliada*
"The Gay Day Still Sounded" (Tyutchev) **34**:389
"Gay Grimaces" (Collodi) **54**:137
Gazette Publications (Brackenridge) **7**:56
Gazzettino del Del Mundo (Foscolo) **97**:88
"Gde sladkiy shyopot..." (Baratynsky) **103**:10
Le géant Yéocis (Sand) **42**:314
"La géante" (Baudelaire) **6**:80, 115, 123; **55**:30, 59
"The Geäte A-Vallen To" (Barnes) **75**:14, 64, 97, 99
"Gebet" (Mörike) **10**:455
"Gebir" (Arnold) **6**:54
Gebir (Landor) **14**:155-57, 161, 164, 168, 176, 180-81, 183-84, 188-89, 192-94, 199-200, 203-06
Gebirus (Landor) **14**:203-04
"Geburt und Wiedergeburt" (Claudius) **75**:210, 214, 216
Gedanken über Tod und Unsterblichkeit, aus den Papieren eines Denkers, nebst einem Anhang theologischsatyrischer Xenien, herausgegeben von einem seiner Freunde (Feuerbach) **139**:241, 294-95, 297-99, 318, 330, 343-48
"Gedichte" (Grillparzer) **102**:106, 117
Gedichte (Droste-Hülshoff) **3**:200
Gedichte (Keller) **2**:421
Gedichte (Meyer) **81**:140, 146, 148, 153-57, 199, 208-09
Gedichte (Mörike) **10**:444-45, 447

Gedichte, 1853 und 1854 (Heine) **4**:256-57, 260
Gedichte aus den hinterlassenen Papieren eines reisenden Waldhornisten, Band II (Muller) **73**:383, 391
"Gedichte vermischten Inhalts" (Droste-Hülshoff) **3**:200
"The 'Gees" (Melville) **93**:201
"Der Gefangene" (Eichendorff) **8**:218
"Der gefesselte Strom" (Hölderlin) **16**:162, 176
"Gefror'ne Tränen" (Muller) **73**:385, 390
Der gefühlvolle Kerkermeister (Nestroy) **42**:224-25
"Die gegeisselte Psyche" (Meyer) **81**:206, 209
Gegen Torheit gebt es kein Mittel (Nestroy) **42**:247, 251
"Das Gegenwärtige" (Klopstock) **11**:237
"Gehazi" (Kendall) **12**:192
"Das Geheimnis der Reminiszenz" (Schiller) **39**:357
Geist und Vernunft und Verstand (Herder) **8**:306
"Die Geister am Mummelsee" (Mörike) **10**:453
"Das Geisterross" (Meyer) **81**:207
"Die Geisterstunde" (Pavlova) **138**:11-12
Das Geistliche Jahr in Liedern auf alle Sonn-und Festtage (Droste-Hülshoff) **3**:196, 199-201, 203
Geistliche Lieder (Novalis) **13**:376-77, 385, 392, 397, 400, 402, 405
Geld und Geist oder die Versöhnung (Gotthelf) **117**:5, 8, 20-1, 32-3, 35, 38, 43, 51
Die Gelehrte (Freytag) **109**:138
Der Gelstag (Gotthelf) **117**:5, 7, 32-3, 35, 38
"Das Gelübde" (Hoffmann) **2**:360
"Das Gemälde" (Meyer) **81**:143
Le gendre de Monsieur Poirier (Augier) **31**:3, 5, 8-20, 24-31, 33, 35-6, 38-40
A General Description of Nova Scotia (Haliburton) **15**:144
"General Gage's Soliloquy" (Freneau) **1**:315
General History and Comparative System of the Semitic Languages (Renan)
See *Histoire général et système comparé des langues Sémitiques*
General Lopez, the Cuban Patriot (Villaverde) **121**:335
"General Taylor and the Veto" (Lincoln) **18**:250
"General Toptýgin" (Nekrasov) **11**:407, 421
A General View of Positivism (Comte) **54**:203, 210
"La genèse Polynésienne" (Leconte de Lisle) **29**:228
The Genesis of the Spirit (Slowacki)
See *Genezis z ducha*
"Geneva's Double Strike" (Bakunin) **58**:131
"Genevieve" (Coleridge) **9**:144, 146
Geneviève de Brabant (Staël-Holstein) **91**:359
Genevieve; or, The Reign of Terror (Boucicault) **41**:32
Genezis z ducha (Slowacki) **15**:360-61, 366, 374
"Gengulphus" (Barham) **77**:19-20, 26-27
"Génie" (Rimbaud) **35**:294-96, 309, 311, 313, 324; **82**:230, 232-33, 251
Le génie bonhomme (Nodier) **19**:384-85
"Le génie dans l'obsurité" (Lamartine) **11**:289
Génie du christianisme (Staël-Holstein) **91**:332, 359
Le génie du Christianisme; ou, Beautés de la religion Chrétienne (Chateaubriand) **3**:110-17, 124, 126, 128-29, 131-32; **134**:4, 10-19, 24-30, 34, 37, 40, 42-45, 61, 63, 65, 70, 73, 84, 88, 90, 92, 102-7, 118, 120, 132, 140, 143-44
Geniu pustiu (Eminescu) **33**:245, 247, 254, 264; **131**:294
"Genius" (Emerson) **98**:65
"Genius" (Mangan) **27**:298
"Genius Lost" (Harpur) **114**:100, 105, 125, 137, 144-46
"The Genius of America: An Ode" (Trumbull) **30**:350
"The Genius of America Weeping the Absurd Follies of the Day" (Warren) **13**:431, 433
The Genius of Christianity; or, The Spirit and Beauties of the Christian Religion (Chateaubriand)
See *Le génie du Christianisme; ou, Beautés de la religion Chrétienne*
"The Genius of Harmony. An Irregular Ode" (Moore) **110**:177
"The Genius of Plato" (Pater) **90**:334
Genoveva: Tragödie in fünf Acten (Hebbel) **43**:230, 233-34, 238-39, 243-44, 247, 254-57, 259, 262, 271, 273-74
"Le Genre" (Mallarmé) **41**:239
The Genteel Style in Writing (Lamb) **10**:412
Le Gentilhomme de la montagne (Dumas) **71**:194
Gentle and Simple (Martineau) **137**:271
"Gentle Armour" (Hunt) **70**:252-53
"The Gentle Boy" (Hawthorne) **2**:319, 327; **79**:318, 322; **95**:128, 132, 137, 196
"The Gentle Giantess" (Lamb) **10**:436
"A Gentle Hint to Writing Women" (Lewes) **25**:290
"The Gentle Look" (Coleridge) **99**:22
"The Gentleman Farmer" (Crabbe) **26**:93; **121**:11-12
A Gentleman from Ireland (O'Brien) **21**:250
Gentleman Jews (Jerrold) **2**:408
The Gentleman of the Blue Boots (Castro) **3**:106-07
"Gentleness" (Lampman) **25**:209-10
"Geoffrey Chaucer" (Smith) **59**:309
Geoffrey Hamlyn (Kingsley)
See *The Recollections of Geoffry Hamlyn*
Geoffrey Moncton (Moodie) **113**:295-97, 324-25
Geographical Dictionary of England and Wales (Cobbett) **49**:160
"The Geography of an Irish Oath" (Carleton) **3**:93
"Geologia" (Harpur) **114**:124-25
George and Sarah Green: A Narrative (Wordsworth) **138**:225, 227, 229, 233-37
George Crabbe: The Complete Poetical Works (Crabbe) **121**:84-8, 90-1
George Eliot Letters (Eliot) **89**:266; **118**:88, 90-91, 164-66, 181
George Eliot—A Writer's Notebook 1854-1879 (Eliot) **118**:111-13
"George Levison; or, the School Fellows" (Allingham) **25**:7
George Sand in Her Own Words (Sand) **42**:332-33
"George Silverman's Explanation" (Dickens) **3**:164
"George the Third's Soliloquy" (Freneau) **111**:140
"George Washington" (Harpur) **114**:140
Georges (Dumas) **71**:204, 229, 242, 244
Georgette; ou, La nièce du tabellion (Kock) **16**:245-46
A Georgia Spec; or, Land in the Moon (Tyler) **3**:573-74
"Georgia Waters" (Chivers) **49**:43
"Geraint and Enid" (Tennyson) **30**:253, 288-90; **65**:237, 241, 278, 324, 328-9, 331, 351, 353, 381
"Geraldine" (Brontë) **16**:121
"The Geraldine's Daughter" (Mangan) **27**:293
"Ein Gerichtstag auf Huahine" (Chamisso) **82**:21, 27-29
"The German Constitution" (Hegel) **46**:111
German Dictionary (Grimm and Grimm) **3**:216
German Folk Tales (Grimm and Grimm) **3**:226
German Grammar (Grimm and Grimm)
See *Deutsche Grammatik*
"A German Home" (Taylor) **89**:308
The German Ideology (Engels)
See *Die deutsche Ideologie*
The German Ideology (Marx) **17**:326, 332-34, 349-52, 360; **114**:52-4, 69-70, 83-6
"A German Idyl" (Taylor) **89**:308
"A German Poet" (Mangan) **27**:291
German Romance (Carlyle) **70**:94, 108
"Germanien" (Hölderlin) **16**:174-75, 189, 195
Germany (Heine)
See *De l'Allemagne*
Germany (Staël-Holstein)
See *De l'Allemagne*
Germany: A Winter's Tale (Heine)
See *Deutschland: Ein Wintermärchen*
Germany: Revolution and Counter-Revolution (Engels)
See *Revolution and Counter-revolution in Germany*
Germinie Lacerteux (Goncourt and Goncourt) **7**:155-58, 162-65, 167, 170, 174, 176-80, 182, 184, 187-90
Geroi nashego vremeni (Lermontov) **5**:286-87, 291-92, 294-95, 297-99, 301-02, 304-06; **47**:149-230; **126**:128, 132-33, 139, 145, 147-48, 151, 153-58, 160-62, 164-66, 170, 172, 174, 192, 195-200, 203, 205, 214, 216-17, 223-26
Gerolstein (Sue) **1**:555
Gerontius (Newman)
See *Dream of Gerontius*
"Gertha's Lovers" (Morris) **4**:429
"Gertrude of Wyoming: A Pennsylvanian Tale" (Campbell) **19**:164-66, 168-71, 174-75, 178-79, 181, 183-85, 188-89, 193, 195-96, 198
Gertrude of Wyoming: A Pennsylvanian Tale, and Other Poems (Campbell) **19**:164-65, 176
Gertrude; or, Family Pride (Trollope) **30**:332
Gertrude's Cherries (Jerrold) **2**:403
Gesammelte Gedichte (Keller) **2**:421
Gesammelte Novellen (Tieck) **5**:516
Gesammelte Schriften (Humboldt) **134**:158, 199-200
Gesammelte Schriften und Dichtungen (Wagner) **119**:189
Gesammelte Werke (Freytag) **109**:147
Gesamtkunstwerk (Goethe) **34**:127
"Der Gesang der Klio" (Meyer) **81**:152
"Gesang der Räuber" (Mörike) **10**:453
"Der Gesang des Meeres" (Meyer) **81**:155, 199
"Gesang Weylas" (Mörike) **10**:446, 448
"Gesang zu Zweien in der Nacht" (Mörike) **10**:448-49
Die Geschichte der Abderiten (Wieland) **17**:397, 399, 424
Geschichte der alten und neuen Literatur (Schlegel) **45**:294, 299, 305, 317, 323-28
Geschichte der deutschen Sprache (Grimm and Grimm) **3**:216-17
"Die Geschichte der Jungfrau von Orleans" (Hebbel) **43**:255
Geschichte der neueren Philosophie von Bacon von Verulam bis Benedict Spinoza (Feuerbach) **139**:283, 303, 344, 347-48
Geschichte der poetischen Literatur Deutschlands (Eichendorff) **8**:219-20, 233
Die Geschichte der Renaissnce in Italien (Burckhardt)
See *Die Kultur der Renaissance in Italien*
Geschichte des Abfalls der vereinigten Niederlande von der spanischen Regierung (Schiller) **69**:169
Geschichte des Agathon (Wieland) **17**:391, 396-97, 399-400, 405, 408, 413, 420-30
Geschichte des Dreissigjährigen Kriegs (Schiller) **69**:188
Geschichte des Fräuleins von Sternheim (La Roche) **121**:242-44, 246-51, 256, 258, 262, 265-66, 268-72, 274-76, 279-85, 291, 298, 302, 304, 308-12, 315, 318-19, 322, 325-26
Geschichte des Romans (Eichendorff) **8**:217
Die Geschichte meines Vaters (Kotzebue) **25**:138

"Geschichte vom braven Kasperl und dem schönen Annerl" (Brentano) **1**:95, 99-101, 105
Geschischte des Herrn William Lovell (Tieck) **46**:398
Der geschlossene Handelsstaat (Fichte) **62**:34, 48
Die gesfesselte Phantasie (Raimund) **69**:7-8, 12, 24, 35-6, 44-5, 47-9, 52
"Gespräch der Reformatoren im Himmel" (Gotthelf) **117**:30, 35
"Gespräch des Socrates mit Timoclea von der scheinbaren und wahren Schönheit" (Wieland) **17**:418
Gespräch über die Poesie (Schlegel) **45**:306-10, 314-16, 320-24, 328, 344, 348, 358-60, 362-65, 367-68, 370, 372, 375, 382
Gespräche, die Freiheit betreffend (Claudius) **75**:194
Gespräche mit Dämonen. Des Königsbuchs zweiter Band (Arnim) **38**:12, 16; **123**:9-10, 12, 15, 60, 62-63, 65-67, 69-70
Geständnisse (Heine) **4**:248
Der gestiefelte Kater (Tieck) **5**:516-17, 521-24, 529-30, 532; **46**:406-09
"Die Gestirne" (Klopstock) **11**:241
"Gethsemane" (Droste-Hülshoff) **3**:196
"Getreue Eckart und der Tannen häuser, Der" (Tieck) **46**:350
"Gettin' On" (Field) **3**:210
"Getting Up a Pantomime" (Mayhew) **31**:179
"Gettsyburg Address" (Lincoln) **18**:220-21, 227, 235, 238, 241-42, 246-48, 250-51, 254, 257, 264-65, 267, 271, 274, 277, 280-82
"Ghaselle" (Emerson) **98**:179
"Ghasta; or, The Avenging Demon" (Shelley) **18**:342
"The Ghetto at Florence" (Levy) **59**:111
"The Ghost" (Andersen) **79**:24
"A Ghost" (Barnes) **75**:75
"A Ghost" (Baudelaire)
See "Un fantôme"
The Ghost, a Canterbury Tale (Barham) **77**:5, 36
"The Ghost and the Bone Setter" (Le Fanu) **9**:321, 323
"Ghost Glen" (Kendall) **12**:181, 183
"The Ghost in the Garden Room" (Gaskell)
See "The Crooked Branch"
The Ghost of Abel (Blake) **57**:14
Ghost Stories and Tales of Mystery (Le Fanu) **9**:302-03, 314
"The Ghosts" (Eminescu) **33**:246; **131**:286, 291, 295-96, 335, 347
"Ghosts" (Turgenev) **122**:337
"The Ghost's Moonshine" (Beddoes) **3**:34
"The Ghost's Petition" (Rossetti) **2**:558, 565; **50**:288
Giannettino (Collodi) **54**:140
"Giannettino's Trip through Italy" (Collodi)
See *Minnuzolo; Il Viaggio per l'Italia de Giannettino*
"The Giantess" (Baudelaire)
See "La géante"
"The Giant's Coffin" (Simms) **3**:506
The Giaour: A Fragment of a Turkish Tale (Byron) **2**:60, 72-73, 76, 81, 86, 103; **12**:82; **109**:102, 118
Giboyer (Augier)
See *Le fils de Giboyer*
Giboyer's Son (Augier)
See *Le fils de Giboyer*
"The Gift of Righteousness" (Newman) **99**:232
"Die Giftmischerin" (Chamisso) **82**:27
"Gifts" (Karamzin) **3**:284
"Gifts" (Lazarus) **8**:420-21; **109**:335-36
"Gifts and Graces" (Rossetti) **50**:285
"The Gifts of the Terek" (Lermontov)
See "Dary Tereka"
"Gilbert" (Brontë) **105**:54
The Gilded Clique (Gaboriau) **14**:31-2
Giles Corey of the Salem Farms (Longfellow) **2**:496-97; **45**:128, 165
"The Gilliflower of Gold" (Morris) **4**:432
Der Gimpel auf der Messe (Kotzebue) **25**:133
"La ginestra" (Leopardi) **129**:218, 220, 222-23, 225-26, 244, 250, 253, 260, 273, 304, 307-8
"Ginevra" (Shelley) **18**:327
Giovanna of Naples (Landor) **14**:165
The Gipsies (Macha)
See *Cigáni*
Gipsies (Pushkin)
See *Tsygany*
The Gipsy (Runeberg) **41**:309
"The Gipsy Nurse, or Marked for Life" (Alger) **83**:96
"The Gipsy's Evening Blaze" (Clare) **9**:72
The Gipsy's Prophecy (Southworth) **26**:433-34
"The Girl from Abroad" (Schiller) **39**:306
"The Girl in the Golden Garden" (Eminescu)
See "Fata în gradina de aur"
"The Girl of the Period" (Linton) **41**:160, 163, 169
The Girl of the Period and Other Social Essays (Linton) **41**:163
"The Girl Who Trod on the Loaf" (Andersen) **7**:31, 32, 37
The Girl Without a Dowry (Ostrovsky)
See *Bespridannitsa*
"The Girl without Hands" (Grimm and Grimm) **3**:227
The Girl's Book (Child) **6**:198; **73**:41, 50, 59, 75, 96
"The Girl's Lamentation" (Allingham) **25**:7-8, 16-17, 22, 29
"Girls' Reading Book" (Sigourney) **87**:321
"The Girt Woak Tree That's in the Dell" (Barnes) **75**:36, 108
"Girt Wold House o'Mossy Stwone" (Barnes) **75**:6, 103
Gisela (Kotzebue) **25**:136
"Giselle" (Gautier) **59**:34, 39
Gisippus (Griffin) **7**:194-95, 198-99, 202-03, 209, 216
"Gisli the Chieftain" (Crawford) **12**:156, 161, 172; **127**:159-61, 163-64, 174-75, 178, 192, 195-97, 199
"Giulia" (Barnes) **75**:30
Give a Dog a Bad Name (Lewes) **25**:291
"Give All to Love" (Emerson) **1**:296; **98**:92, 179
"Give Me the Splendid Silent Sun" (Whitman) **31**:391, 393-94; **81**:314
"Give me women wine and snuff" (Keats) **73**:322
"Giver of Glowing Light" (Hood) **16**:222
"Gjentagelsen" (Kierkegaard) **125**:272, 281
Gjentagelsen (Kierkegaard) **34**:200, 223, 260, 262; **78**:119, 157-66, 168-69, 173, 238; **125**:198, 208
"Gladesmure" (Landon) **15**:161
The Gladiator (Bird) **1**:83, 86-88, 90, 92
"The Gladness of Nature" (Bryant) **6**:161
"Gladys and Her Island" (Ingelow) **39**:265
Gladys and Her Island: On the Advantages of a Poetical Temperament (Ingelow) **107**:137-41, 155, 159
Glagolita Clozianus (Kopitar) **117**:64, 68, 117
"A Glance behind the Curtain" (Lowell) **90**:219, 221
"A Glance within the Forest" (Traill) **31**:327
Glanes (Mallarmé) **41**:248
"Glanvil on Witches" (Lamb) **10**:402
"Glasgow" (Smith) **59**:312, 316, 321, 330, 332-4, 336
The Glass of Water (Robertson) **35**:354
The Glass of Water; or, Causes and Effects (Scribe)
See *Le Verre d'eau; ou, Les Effets et les causes*
"Glauben und Wissen" (Hegel) **46**:165
Glaubenslehre (Schleiermacher)
See *Die praktische Theologie nach den Grundsätzen der evangelischen Kirche im Zusammenhang dargestellt*
"Glauben—Wissen—Handeln" (Lenau) **16**:272, 278
"Glaucé" (Leconte de Lisle) **29**:239, 245-46
Glaucus (Boker) **125**:25, 28, 41, 76-78
Glaucus; or, The Wonders of the Shore (Kingsley) **35**:232, 254-55
"The Gleam" (Tyutchev)
See "Problesk"
"A Gleam of Sunshine" (Longfellow) **2**:473, **45**:116
The Gleaner: A Miscellanous Production in Three Volumes (Murray) **63**:174-82, 184-5, 188, 193, 195, 197-201, 203-4, 207-12, 214-5
"The Gleaner Unmasked" (Murray) **63**:201
Gleanings (Sigourney) **87**:326
Gleanings in Europe (Cooper) **1**:201; **54**:256
"Glee—The Great Storm Is Over" (Dickinson) **21**:43
Die Gleichen (Arnim) **5**:21
"The Glen of Arrawatta" (Kendall) **12**:180, 186, 190, 192, 201
"The Glen of the Whiteman's Grave" (Harpur) **114**:121, 144, 148, 150, 152
"Glenara" (Campbell) **19**:169, 181
Glenarvon (Lamb) **38**:234-46, 248, 250-60
"Gleneden's Dream" (Brontë) **16**:79-80
"Glenfinlas" (Scott) **15**:317
"Glimmerings" (Cranch) **115**:51
"The Glimpse of the Coming Day" (Morris) **4**:438
Glimpses Into My Own Life and Literary Character (Browning) **61**:48
"The Gloamin" (Hogg) **109**:203
"Der Glockenguss zu Breslau" (Muller) **73**:351, 355
"Das Glöcklein" (Meyer) **81**:143-44, 147
"Le gloire" (Lamartine) **11**:269
"La gloria de México en María Santísima de Guadalupe" (Lizardi) **30**:68
"Gloria mundi" (Allston) **2**:26
Gloria mundi (Frederic) **10**:189, 192, 194, 201, 205, 211-13, 215-17
"The Glories of Mary for the Sake of Her Son" (Newman) **38**:303, 310
"Glorified Mists" (Hayne) **94**:144
"Gloriola" (Meyer) **81**:156
"The Glory Machine" (Villiers de l'Isle Adam)
See "La machine à gloire"
The Glory of Columbia: Her Yeomanry! (Dunlap) **2**:208, 211-14, 217
"The Glory of Motion" (De Quincey) **4**:82
"The Glory of Poetry" (Ueda Akinari)
See "Uta no homare"
"Glosa" (Preseren) **127**:308
"The Gloss" (Eminescu)
See "Glossa"
"Glossa" (Eminescu) **33**:250; **131**:287, 298
"The Glove" (Browning) **19**:126; **79**:94, 102-03, 164
"The Glove" (Schiller)
See "Der Handschuh"
"The Glove and the Lions" (Hunt) **1**:416; **70**:264
"Glowing is her Bonnet" (Dickinson) **77**:121
Glück, Mißbrauch und Rückkehr (Nestroy) **42**:250-51, 256
"Die Glückliche Fischerin" (Muller) **73**:353, 361
"Die Glückseligkeit Aller" (Klopstock) **11**:241
Die Glücksritter (Eichendorff) **8**:222
"The Gnat and the Shepherd" (Krylov) **1**:435
"El gnomo" (Bécquer) **106**:98, 108, 130, 134-35
"Gnosis" (Cranch) **115**:8
"Go Not, Happy Day" (Tennyson) **30**:242
"Go Slow My Soul, to Feed Thyself" (Dickinson) **21**:66
"Go, Thought!" (Isaacs)
See "Ve, pensamiento!"

"Go Where Glory Waits Thee" (Moore) **110**:182, 185
Goa (Burton) **42**:38
"The Goblet of Life" (Longfellow) **2**:472; **45**:99, 116, 152
"The Goblin and the Hukster" (Andersen)
See "Nissen hos Spekhøkeren"
"The Goblin at the Grocer's" (Andersen)
See "Nissen hos Spekhøkeren"
"Goblin Market" (Rossetti) **2**:555, 558, 560, 563, 565-7, 569-73, 575, 577-8; **50**:266, 270, 288, 291-7 , 321-2, 324; **66**:297-390
Goblin Market, and Other Poems (Rossetti) **2**:555-7, 563, 573-4, 576-7; **66**:312-3
"Gobseck" (Balzac) **53**:22-3
Gockel, Hinkel, und Gackeleia (Brentano) **1**:95, 100, 102, 105-06, 108
God and the Bible: A Review of Objections to "Literature and Dogma" (Arnold) **6**:40, 48, 53, 66; **29**:15, 50, 52; **126**:63-64, 90
God and the State (Bakunin)
See *Dieu et l'état*
"God Be with You" (Clough) **27**:106-7
"God moves in a mysterious way" (Cowper) **94**:69-70
"God of the Living" (Cowper) **8**:116
"God of the Meridian" (Keats) **73**:269
"God Preserve the King" (Moodie) **113**:310
"God Save the Queen" (Moodie) **113**:371
"Godiva" (Hunt) **1**:414; **70**:264
"Godiva" (Tennyson) **65**:231
Godolphin (Bulwer-Lytton) **45**:26-7, 29-32, 35-8, 68
"God's Commandments Not Grievous" (Newman) **38**:305
"God's Grandeur" (Hopkins) **17**:191-92, 212, 218-19, 229, 243-44
Gods in Exile (Heine)
See *Die Götter im Exil*
"God's Judgement on a Wicked Bishop" (Southey) **97**:271
"The Gods of Greece" (Schiller)
See "Die Götter Griechenlands"
Godwi; oder, Das steinerne Bild der Mutter (Brentano) **1**:96, 97-99, 102, 104-07
Godzien litości (Fredro) **8**:286
Godzina myśli (Slowacki) **15**:363-64, 373
"Goethe" (Carlyle) **70**:9, 96
"An Goethe" (Schiller) **39**:389
Goethe (Lewes)
See *The Life and Works of Goethe*
"Goethe and Byron" (Mickiewicz) **101**:175-76
"Goethe and his Time" (Tieck)
See "Goethe und seine Zeit"
Goethe and Schiller (Boyesen) **135**:45, 49
Goethe and Schiller's Xenions (Goethe)
See *Xenien*
"Goethe as a Man of Science" (Lewes) **25**:312
"Goethe und seine Zeit" (Tieck) **46**:356-57, 359, 403
Goethe-Book (Arnim) **123**:42-43
"Goethe's Botany: The Metamorphosis of Plants" (Goethe) **4**:207-08, 210
"Goethes Briefe, Hamburger Ausgabe in 4 Bänden" (Goethe)
See "Werke: Hamburger Ausgabe"
Goethes Briefwechsel mit einem Kinde: Seinem Denkmal (Arnim) **38**:3-4, 8, 10, 13-16; **123**:7, 9, 22, 24-26, 28, 42, 59, 64, 94-95, 98-100
"Goethe's Colour Theory" (Goethe)
See "Theory of Colours"
Goethe's Correspondence with a Child: For His Monument (Arnim)
See *Goethes Briefwechsel mit einem Kinde: Seinem Denkmal*
Goethe's Roman Elegies (Goethe)
See *Römische Elegien*
Goethe's Works (Goethe) **4**:173
"Goetz of Berlichingen with the Iron Hand" (Goethe)
See *Götz von Berlichingen mit der eisernen Hand*
"Going to Heaven" (Dickinson) **21**:56
Going to See a Man Hanged (Thackeray) **5**:507
Gold (Reade) **2**:551; **74**:244, 277-79, 281, 291-92, 319, 330-31, 342
"The Gold Bug" (Poe) **1**:500, 506, 524; **16**:293, 295-96, 298, 300-01, 303, 312-13, 315, 332, 334; **55**:133, 135, 141, 148-9, 153
Gold Coast for Gold (Burton) **42**:40
"The Gold Pen-A Poem, Inscribed to the Gentleman Who Presented the Gift" (Hale) **75**:284
The Golden Age (Martí)
See *La Edad de Oro*
The Golden Branch (Planché) **42**:288-89, 293
"Golden Brown" (Jefferies) **47**:143
The Golden Calf (Boyesen) **135**:14, 22, 31, 37, 59, 61-63, 65, 67-68
"Golden Chain" (Moore) **110**:177
"The Golden Cockerel" (Reisman)
See "Skazka o Zolotom Petushke"
"Golden Dreams" (Irving) **2**:390
The Golden Fleece (Grillparzer)
See *Das goldene Vließ*
The Golden Fleece (Planché) **42**:273, 275, 286-87
"The Golden Ingot" (O'Brien) **21**:238-39, 242, 244-45, 248, 252
"The Golden Island" (Clarke) **19**:231
"A Golden Key on the Tongue" (Clough) **27**:107
The Golden Legend (Longfellow) **2**:475-76, 479-80, 484, 486-87, 496, 498; **45**:113-14, 119, 127-28, 130-31, 133, 143, 147, 150, 157, 163-65, 178, 190; **101**:93
The Golden Lion of Granpère (Trollope) **101**:235, 310, 313
"Golden Milestone" (Longfellow) **45**:116, 161
"The Golden Net" (Blake) **13**:243
The Golden Pot: Fairy Tale of Our Times (Hoffmann)
See "Der goldene Topf"
The Golden Skull (Slowacki)
See *Złota czaszka*
The Golden Violet with Its Tales of Romance and Chivalry, and Other Poems (Landon) **15**:158, 161, 166, 168
"Golden Wings" (Morris) **4**:411, 419, 425, 432, 444
"The Golden Year" (Tennyson) **65**:285; **115**:240
Der goldene Spiegel (Wieland) **17**:397, 408-09
"Der goldene Topf" (Hoffmann) **2**:341, 345, 349-50, 352-56, 361-62
Das goldene Vließ (Grillparzer) **1**:383-85, 387, 389, 397; **102**:86, 95, 100, 107, 117, 149, 163, 165-66, 174, 180, 186-88
"Goldenrod" (Lampman) **25**:210
"Goldilocks and Goldilocks" (Morris) **4**:423, 434
"Der goldne Tag ist heimgegangen" (Brentano) **1**:105
"Goldoni and Italian Comedy" (Lewes) **25**:285
"Le golfe de Baïa" (Lamartine) **11**:245, 269, 282
The Golovlyov Family (Saltykov)
See *Gospoda Golovlyovy*
The Goncourt Journals, 1851-1870 (Goncourt and Goncourt) **7**:160-63
"The Gondola" (Pavlova) **138**:16-17
"Egy gondolat bánt engémet" (Petofi) **21**:284
"Gondolatok" (Arany) **34**:18
"The Gondolier's Wedding" (Symonds) **34**:364
"Gone" (Gordon) **21**:154, 159, 163-64, 168, 181
"Gone" (Whittier) **8**:491
"Gone in the Wind" (Mangan) **27**:298
"The Good Aunt" (Edgeworth) **51**:82-4, 87
"The Good Clerk" (Lamb) **113**:199
"The Good Clerk, a Character; With Some Account of 'The Complete English Tradesman'" (Lamb) **10**:436
"The Good Disciple" (Verlaine)
See *Le Bon Disciple*
A Good Fight (Reade) **2**:540
"Good for Nothing" (Boyesen) **135**:12, 19, 21, 26
"The Good French Governess" (Edgeworth) **51**:82-3, 85, 87, 89-90
"Good Friday" (Rossetti) **50**:268
The Good Genius That Turned Everything into Gold (Mayhew) **31**:161
"The Good Governess" (Edgeworth) **1**:255
"A Good Knight in Prison" (Morris) **4**:431, 444
Good Lord! What the Devil Is This! (Fredro)
See *Gwałltu, co sie dzieje*
"Good Measter Collins" (Barnes) **75**:73
"Good Night" (Barnes) **75**:33
"Good Night" (Muller)
See "Gute Nacht"
"Good Old Gvadányi" (Petofi)
See "A régi jó Gvadányi"
"The Good Old Rule" (Thomson) **18**:392
"The Good Part" (Longfellow) **103**:290
"The Good Part of Mary" (Newman) **38**:306
Good People and Their Adventures (Sacher-Masoch) **31**:295
The Good Song (Verlaine)
See *La bonne chanson*
"A Good Time Going" (Holmes) **81**:95
Good Wives (Alcott) **6**:16, 21; **83**:34, 79, 82
The Good Woman in the Wood (Planché) **42**:279, 298, 301
"A Good Word for Winter" (Lowell) **2**:510, 517; **90**:196
"Good-bye" (Emerson) **38**:186; **98**:177
"Good-Bye My Fancy!" (Whitman) **4**:563; **31**:434-35
"Goodbye, Unwashed Russia" (Lermontov) **5**:295
"Goodbye's the Word" (Crawford) **12**:156
"Good-for-Nothing" (Andersen)
See "Hun duede ikke"
"Good-Nature" (Hazlitt) **29**:150
The Good-Natured Bear (Blake) **127**:264-66
"Goody Blake and Harry Gill" (Wordsworth) **12**:387, 402, 445; **111**:199-200, 202-3, 209, 225, 251, 276, 306, 349-50, 356, 359-60
"Googly-Goo" (Field) **3**:210
"Gora" (Leskov) **25**:229, 239, 245-46
"Góra Kikineis" (Mickiewicz) **3**:403; **101**:188-89
Gordon: A Tale (Lamb) **38**:258-59
Gore ot Uma (Griboedov) **129**:152-54, 161-66, 168-73, 175-81, 186, 192-94, 197-98, 206-10
"Gorodok" (Pushkin) **83**:331
"El gorrión" (Isaacs) **70**:304, 308
"Gospel according to Walt Whitman" (Stevenson) **5**:390
"The Gospel of Love" (Chivers) **49**:72
The Gospel of Suffering (Kierkegaard) **78**:239
The Gospel of the Pentateuch and David (Kingsley) **35**:253
The Gospels (Renan)
See *Les évangiles*
Gospoda Golovlyovy (Saltykov) **16**:342-43, 346-47, 349, 351-57, 359, 361-67, 369-76
Gospoda Tashkentsy (Saltykov) **16**:343, 345, 357, 365, 369, 373
"A Gossip on a Novel of Dumas's" (Stevenson) **5**:430; **63**:240
"A Gossip on Romance" (Stevenson) **63**:239-41, 258, 260, 274
"Gotas Amargas" (Silva) **114**:276, 300
Gotas amargas (Silva) **114**:264, 316-17, 319, 321-22
"The Gothic Room" (Bertrand)
See "La chambre gothique"
"Der Gott und die Bajadere" (Goethe) **4**:192
"Die Götter" (Hölderlin) **16**:181

"Die Götter Griechenlands" (Schiller) **39**:305, 331, 349, 387
Die Götter im Exil (Heine) **4**:235, 239-40, 267-68
Götterdämmerung (Heine) **4**:252
Die Götterdämmerung (Wagner) **9**:409, 417, 441, 446, 449-51, 454, 460, 463, 467, 469-70; **119**:175, 186, 19 234-35, 277, 283, 310, 318, 322, 346-56
"Gottfried Wolfgang" (Borel) **41**:5, 20-3
Die Göttin Diana (Heine) **4**:267
"Das Göttliche" (Goethe) **4**:193
Götz von Berlichingen mit der eisernen Hand (Goethe) **4**:162-63, 165, 167, 174, 190, 194-96, 198-99, 211-12, 218-19, 221-22; **34**:69-70, 120-21
"Le goût du néant" (Baudelaire) **55**:65, 67
"L'gov" (Turgenev) **122**:294
"Government: Anarchy or Regimentation" (Huxley) **67**:68, 111
"The Government Inspector" (Gogol)
See *Révizor*
"A Government-Man" (Hazlitt) **29**:152
"Governor Manco" (Irving) **2**:372
Gr. A. K. Tolstomu (Pavlova) **138**:4
"Das Grab" (Klopstock) **11**:239
"Grabež" (Leskov) **25**:228
"Grace" (Verlaine) **51**:367, 372
"Grace before Meat" (Lamb) **10**:408-09, 424; **113**:173, 175-76, 219, 243
"Grace Greenwood" (Hale) **75**:353
"Grace O'Malley" (Ferguson)
See "Grana Uaile"
"The Graceful and the Exalted" (Schiller) **39**:367
"Les grâces" (Banville) **9**:30
The Graces (Foscolo)
See *Le grazie, carme*
The Graces (Wieland) **17**:399
La Graceta de las Mujeres (Gómez de Avellaneda) **111**:7, 27
Graciosa and Percinct (Planché) **42**:280, 288-89
Les Gracques (Dumas) **71**:217
"Gracz" (Krasicki) **8**:407
Graf Benyowsky, oder die Verschwörung auf Kamschatka (Kotzebue) **25**:134, 136-37, 139-40, 145, 147
"Graf Eberhard der Greiner von Wirtemberg" (Schiller) **39**:387
Graf Nulin (Pushkin) **3**:414, 443, 445, 451; **27**:367, 386; **83**:272, 275, 332, 334-38, 357-58
Graf Petöfy (Fontane) **26**:241, 244, 253-54, 258
"Der Graf von Habsburg" (Schiller) **39**:389
"Der Graf von Thal" (Droste-Hülshoff) **3**:195, 200, 202
Graf Waldemar: Schauspiel in fünf Akten (Freytag) **109**:138
"Grafven i Perrho" (Runeberg) **41**:309, 313, 317, 325
Graham Hamilton (Lamb) **38**:237, 251
Grains de mil (Amiel) **4**:13, 15
Gramática de la Lengua Castellana destinada al uso de los Americanos (Bello) **131**:94, 116, 120
A Grammar and Glossary of the Dorset Dialect (Barnes) **75**:27, 40, 53, 65, 79
Grammar of Assent (Newman)
See *An Essay in Aid of a Grammar of Assent*
Grammar of the English Language (Cobbett) **49**:93, 108, 120, 134, 140, 148, 160
Grammar of the Serbian Language (Karadzic)
See *Pismenica serbskoga iezika*
"A Grammarian's Funeral" (Browning) **19**:89, 117; **79**:164
A Grammatical Institute, of the English Language, Comprising, an Easy, Concise, and Systematic Method of Education, Designed for the Use of English Schools in America (Webster) **30**:388, 392-93, 395, 403-04, 414, 417-21
Grammatik der slavischen Sprache in Krain, Kärnten und Steyermark (Kopitar) **117**:65-6, 78, 82-3, 87, 91, 101, 116
"Grammer A-Crippled" (Barnes) **75**:48, 67
"Grammer's Shoes" (Barnes) **75**:77
"Grana Uaile" (Ferguson) **33**:278, 283
"Granada" (Zorrilla y Moral) **6**:523, 525, 527
Grand dictionnaire de cuisine (Dumas) **71**:210, 218
"The Grand Inquisitor" (Dostoevsky)
See "The Legend of the Grand Inquisitor"
"Grand March of Intellect" (Keats) **121**:124
Un grand mariage (Balzac) **5**:59
"Grand Master of Alcantara" (Irving) **2**:388
"Grand opéra" (Corbière) **43**:31
"Grandad Mazáy" (Nekrasov) **11**:421
"La grande bretèche" (Balzac) **5**:52-3, 78
"Une grande dame" (Verlaine) **2**:629-30
"Grandfather Glen" (Parton) **86**:349
Grandfather's Chair (Hawthorne) **95**:140
"Grandfather's Spectacles" (Cranch) **115**:51
"La grand'mère" (Beranger) **34**:28
"The Grandmother and the Granddaughter" (Silva)
See "La abulea y la nieta"
"The Grandmother's Shoe" (Ingelow) **107**:162
"Grandmother's Story of Bunker-Hill Battle" (Holmes) **14**:116
"The Grandsire" (Field) **3**:210
The Grange Garden (Kingsley) **107**:192
Grannarne (Bremer) **11**:15, 17-20, 25, 27-28, 30, 33-35
Gran'ther Baldwin's Thanksgiving, with Other Ballads and Poems (Alger) **8**:16
"Grantræ et" (Andersen) **79**:76
"Grasmere—A Fragment" (Wordsworth) **138**:230, 284
"Grasmere and Rydal Water" (Sigourney) **21**:301
Grasmere Journal (Wordsworth) **25**:392, 396, 400, 403, 405-06, 409, 412, 415, 417, 422, 424, 428-30
Grasmere Journals (Wordsworth)
See *Journals of Dorothy Wordsworth: The Alfoxden Journal, 1798; The Grasmere Journals, 1800-1803*
"The Grasshopper Papers" (Crawford) **12**:169-70
"The Grateful Negro" (Edgeworth) **51**:89
"Gratitude" (Horton) **87**:92, 100
"The Grave" (Chivers) **49**:47
"The Grave at Perrho" (Runeberg)
See "Grafven i Perrho"
"Grave Comedy" (Sheridan) **91**:245
"The Grave of a Family" (Hemans) **71**:279
"The Grave of a Poetess" (Hemans) **71**:297
"The Grave of a Suicide" (Campbell) **19**:181
"The Grave of Manuel" (Beranger) **34**:46
"The Grave of Miyagi" (Ueda Akinari) **131**:58, 88
"The Grave of the Countess Potocka" (Mickiewicz)
See "Grób Potockiej"
The Grave of the Last Saxon (Bowles) **103**:54, 61
The Grave of the Reichstal Family (Krasiński)
See *Grób Reichstalów*
"The Gravedigger" (Pushkin) **83**:272, 275
"The Graves of a Household" (Hemans) **29**:198, 204, 206; **71**:279
"Graves of Infants" (Clare) **86**:110
"Graves of the Harem" (Mickiewicz)
See "Mogiły haremu"
"Graves on the Coast" (Storm) **1**:547
"The Gray Champion" (Hawthorne) **2**:311, 329-30, 333; **79**:308
"Grayling; or, Murder Will Out" (Simms) **3**:502, 506, 508
Grazie (Foscolo)
See *Le grazie, carme*
Le Grazie (Foscolo)
See *Le grazie, carme*
Le grazie, carme (Foscolo) **8**:266-69, 271, 273-74; **97**:51-3, 57, 49-60, 62, 68, 78, 83-4, 87-8, 93
Graziella (Lamartine) **11**:266, 278, 286, 289
"Grażyna" (Mickiewicz) **3**:391-93, 397, 399, 401
"Great Are the Myths" (Whitman) **31**:419, 425
"The Great Carbuncle" (Hawthorne) **2**:305, 311, 322
The Great Exile (Lermontov) **5**:292
"Great Expectations" (Irving) **2**:390
Great Expectations (Dickens) **3**:156, 170-71, 173, 176, 179, 186; **8**:194-96; **18**:111, 114, 119, 121, 127-28, 132-33; **26**:154-230; **37**:153-54, 164, 172; **86**:186, 189, 207, 222, 256, 258; **105**:227-28, 244, 248, 311, 317, 334, 351; **113**:6, 20, 39, 51, 54, 89, 97, 102-3, 111, 115, 118-19, 127, 137
A Great Fight (Reade) **74**:245
The Great Hoggarty Diamond (Thackeray) **5**:459, 464-65, 470, 482; **14**:402, 420; **43**:355, 359, 368, 381
"The Great House" (Griffin) **7**:215
"The Great Lawsuit" (Fuller) **5**:163
"A Great Lord" (Krylov) **1**:439
A Great Man for Little Affairs (Fredro)
See *Wielki cztowiek do matych interesbw*
"Great Poets and Small" (Hayne) **94**:160
"A Great Sorrow" (Andersen) **7**:21, 23
"Great spirits now" (Keats) **73**:147
"The Great Stone Face" (Hawthorne) **2**:322; **95**:105
"The Great Unrepresented" (Oliphant) **61**:238
"The Great Vault" (Shevchenko)
See "Velykyj l'ox"
The Great World of London (Mayhew) **31**:186-87, 189-93
"The Great Wrath of the Tyrant and the Cause of It" (Brackenridge) **7**:44
"The Greatcoat" (Gogol)
See "Shinel"
"The Greatest Love of Don Juan" (Barbey d'Aurevilly)
See "Le plus bel amour de Don Juan"
The Greatest Plague of Life; or, The Adventures of a Lady in Search of a Good Servant (Mayhew) **31**:160-61, 178
"Great-grandfather" (Andersen) **79**:84
"The Greatness and Littleness of Human Life" (Newman) **38**:303
"The Grecian Girl's Dream of the Blessed Islands" (Moore) **110**:178
"Greek Architecture" (Melville) **29**:370
"Greek Boy" (Bryant) **6**:172, 181
Greek Cultural History (Burckhardt)
See *Griechische Kulturgeschichte*
The Greek Drama (Lockhart)
See *Greek Tragedy*
"A Greek Girl" (Levy) **59**:96
"The Greek Minstrel" (Arany) **34**:23
"The Greek Partisan" (Bryant) **6**:172; **46**:7
"A Greek Pastoral" (Hogg) **109**:200
Greek Studies (Pater) **7**:303, 312, 323-24, 330-32; **90**:242, 245-46, 248, 283, 286, 335, 338
Greek Tragedy (Lockhart) **6**:293, 295-96
"Green" (Barnes) **75**:46, 68
"Green" (Verlaine) **51**:381, 383
Green Henry (Keller)
See *Der Grüne Heinrich*
A Green Leaf (Storm) **1**:536
"Green River" (Bryant) **6**:158, 169, 171, 176-77, 182-83; **46**:19, 23, 34, 38-9, 45, 47
"The Green Rustle" (Nekrasov)
See "Zelyóny shum"
"Green Tea" (Le Fanu) **9**:302, 308, 312, 317, 319-22; **58**:251, 254-7, 302
"Green Wood Will Last Longer than Dry" (Webster) **30**:423
Greene Ferne Farm (Jefferies) **47**:93, 113, 116, 142

Greenfield Hill (Dwight) **13**:266, 269-70, 272-73, 276-79
Greenway Court (Cooke) **5**:133
Gregory VII: A Tragedy in One Act (Horne) **127**:236, 238, 241, 257-58, 263, 274-75
"Der greise Kopf" (Muller) **73**:366,394
Grekh da beda na kogo ne zhivyot (Ostrovsky) **30**:98, 101, 104, 112
La grenadière (Balzac) **5**:37; **35**:26
"Grenzen der Menschheit" (Goethe) **4**:193; **34**:98
Grete Minde (Fontane) **26**:236-37, 243, 250-51, 258, 272
"Gretna Green" (Crabbe) **26**:100
Greville (Bulwer-Lytton) **45**:32, 34-5, 38, 71
Greville; or, a Season in Paris (Gore) **65**:8-9, 20
Grey Dolphin (Barham) **77**:4, 36
"The Grey Woman" (Gaskell) **5**:187, 193, 202; C **0**:185, 188; **97**:127
Griechen und Roemer (Schlegel)
See *Poesie der Griechen und Roemer*
Griechenlieder (Muller)
See *Lieder der Griechen*
Die Griechensklavin (Humboldt) **134**:162
Der griechische Kaiser (Tieck) **5**:519
Griechische Kulturgeschichte (Burckhardt) **49**:5, 15-16, 32
"Grief" (Browning) **16**:133
"Grief" (Lazarus) **8**:419
"Grief an' Gladness" (Barnes) **75**:32
"The Grievances of Women" (Oliphant) **61**:240
Griffith Gaunt; or, Jealousy (Reade) **2**:537-39, 541-42, 546, 548-53; **74**:246, 249-50, 253, 255, 257-58, 263-65, 298-300, 309-10
"Grigore Ghicavoevod" (Eminescu) **131**:325
Grillparzers Gespräche und die Charakteristiken seiner Persönlichkeit durch die (Grillparzer) **102**:106, 108-09, 111
"Grim, King of the Ghosts; or, The Dance of Death" (Lewis) **11**:303
"Grimaldi" (Hood) **16**:200
"Grimm" (Sainte-Beuve) **5**:330
"Den grimme Ælling" (Andersen) **7**:22, 25, 30; **79**:4, 11, 21, 23, 30, 34, 51-2, 62, 64, 70-1, 73-4, 81
Grimm's Fairy Tales (Grimm and Grimm)
See *Kinder-und Hausmärchen*
"Grimm's Law" (Grimm and Grimm) **3**:220
Grimstahamn's New Settlement (Almqvist)
See *Grimstahamns nybygge*
Grimstahamns nybygge (Almqvist) **42**:4
"Grinding song" (Lonnrot) **53**:339
Gringoire (Banville) **9**:18-19, 21, 24
"Griselda" (Levy) **59**:112-3
"La Grisette" (Holmes) **14**:100-01
"Grit" (Cooke) **110**:24, 43
Grit, The Young Boatman (Alger) **83**:91, 93
"The Groans of the Tankard" (Barbauld) **50**:4
Grób Agamemnona (Slowacki) **15**:365, 376
"Grób Potockiej" (Mickiewicz) **3**:390, 403; **101**:188-89
Grób Reichstalów (Krasiński) **4**:312
"Grobovshchik" (Pushkin) **3**:435, 452; **83**:295, 323, 327, 337, 354
"The Grocers Dethroned" (Fourier) **51**:180
Der Groß-Cophta (Goethe) **4**:222
"Die Grösse der Welt" (Schiller) **39**:357
Les grostesques (Gautier) **1**:351
"The Grotto" (Sheridan) **91**:232
Groundwork of the Metaphysics of Morals (Kant)
See *Grundlegung zur Metaphysik der Sitten*
The Group (Warren) **13**:411-14, 416-19, 425-26, 428-29
"The Growth of Love" (Lampman) **25**:201
"The Growth of Words" (Whitman) **81**:287, 290-91, 293-94
Groza (Ostrovsky) **30**:93, 96, 100, 102, 104, 109-11, 113, 115, 119; **57**:209-10, 212-3, 219, 221-5, 227, 229
"Gruffmoody Grim" (Barnes) **75**:79
Gruie sînger (Eminescu) **33**:265
"Grumbler's Gully" (Clarke) **19**:250-51
Grumbling and Contradiction (Fredro)
See *Zrzędnosc i przecora*
"Grund zum Empedokles" (Hölderlin) **16**:165, 178
Grundlage der gesamten Wissenschaftslehre (Fichte) **62**:11, 13, 34, 39-47
Grundlage des Naturrechts nach Prinzipen der Wissenshaftslehre (Fichte) **62**:34, 48, 58-9
Grundlegung (Kant) **67**:216, 220, 222, 225, 237, 288-94
Grundlegung zur Metaphysik der Sitten (Kant) **27**:194, 217, 259, 261; **67**:214, 216, 222, 260-62, 271, 273-74, 278, 285, 288, 291
Grundlinien der Philosophie des Rechts, order Naturrech und Staatwissenschaft im Grundrisse (Hegel) **46**:111, 113, 140, 147, 151, 157, 171, 175-79, 191-94
Grundrisse (Marx) **114**:70, 85-6
Grundsätze der Philosophie der Zukunft (Feuerbach) **139**:283, 290, 293, 343
Die Gründung Prags (Brentano) **1**:101-02
Die Grundzüge der Gegenwärtigun Zeitalters (Fichte) **62**:35
Der Grüne Heinrich (Keller) **2**:411-12, 414-25
Ein Grünes Blatt (Storm) **1**:539
"Grustno veter voet" (Pavlova) **138**:15
"La gruta del ensueño" (Casal) **131**:256
El guajiro (Villaverde) **121**:334
"The Guardian Angel" (Browning) **19**:116, 127
"Guardian Angel" (Eminescu) **131**:331
The Guardian Angel (Holmes) **14**:104-06, 110, 113, 115, 117, 124, 131, 133-38, 140-43; **81**:102, 107
"The Guardian of the Red Disk" (Lazarus) **109**:338
The Guardians of the Crown (Arnim)
See *Die Kronenwächter*
The Guards in Canada; or, The Point of Honor (Richardson) **55**:303, 358
Guatimozín, último emperador de México (Gómez de Avellaneda) **111**:23-4, 71
Gubernskie ocherki (Saltykov) **16**:342-45, 347, 357, 368, 372, 374-75
"The Gude Greye Katt" (Hogg) **109**:248-49
Gudhataren (Almqvist) **42**:17
"The Guerilla" (Hogg) **4**:282; **109**:246
"The Guerilla Chief" (Landon) **15**:161
"La Guerre" (Maupassant) **83**:189
"Guerre" (Rimbaud) **4**:473; **35**:322; **82**:232
"La guerre des Turcomans" (Gobineau) **17**:69-70, 103-04
La Guerre Sociale (Mérimée) **65**:85
"The Guests Were Arriving at the Dacha" (Pushkin) **83**:313-17, 319
"Les gueux" (Beranger) **34**:30
"Le gueux" (Maupassant) **1**:448
Guide to the Lakes (Martineau) **26**:311
"Le guignon" (Baudelaire) **29**:103; **55**:58
"Le Guignon" (Mallarmé) **4**:376; **41**:241, 250, 280, 290
Guilt and Sorrow (Wordsworth) **38**:426; **111**:201, 253
"'Guilty?'/'Not Guilty?'" (Kierkegaard) **125**:198-99, 201
Guilty Without Guilt (Ostrovsky)
See *Bez viný vinovátye*
"Guinevere" (Tennyson) **30**:279, 292; **65**:228-9, 239, 243-6, 251, 277, 279, 282, 285, 292-3, 296-301, 305, 307, 312, 314, 318-9, 324, 335, 340, 342, 350, 357, 359, 365, 374, 381, 383-6
Guiskard (Kleist)
See *Robert Guiskard, Herzog der Normänner*
"Guitare" (Corbière) **43**:14, 34
"Guitare" (Laforgue) **53**:272
"Gulistan" (Taylor) **89**:302
Gulliver (Dumas) **71**:217
Gulzara; or the Persian Slave (Mowatt) **74**:227
The Günderode (Arnim)
See *Die Günderode: Den Studenten*
Die Günderode: Den Studenten (Arnim) **38**:7, 10, 15; **123**:9, 25-26, 28, 30-31, 38, 42-47, 50, 59, 70, 95
Gunlog (Stagnelius) **61**:253, 255-6
Gunnar: A Tale of Norse Life (Boyesen) **135**:3, 5-6, 10-11, 18-19, 24, 30, 32-33, 36-37, 50
"Gunnar's Howe" (Morris) **4**:434
"Gunpowder Treason" (Keble) **87**:204
"Gurresange" (Jacobsen) **34**:163, 165
Gustav Adolfs Page (Meyer) **81**:139, 155, 162-63, 166, 184, 212-13, 217, 220, 227
Gustave; ou, Le mauvais sujet (Kock) **16**:245-46, 260
"Gustavo Moreau" (Casal) **131**:236, 268-69
"Gute Lehre" (Mörike) **10**:453
"Gute Nacht" (Muller) **73**:382, 384-85, 390-93
"An Gutenstein" (Raimund) **69**:10-12, 14-19
Der gutmütig Teufel (Nestroy) **42**:242, 246
"Guy Faux's Night" (Barnes) **75**:77
Guy Fawkes; or, The Gunpowder Treason (Ainsworth) **13**:39-40, 47
Guy Mannering (Scott) **15**:259-60, 272, 280, 289, 300, 302, 309, 324; **69**:303, 391; **110**:299, 325
Guy Rivers (Simms) **3**:499-500, 508-10
"Guys" (Baudelaire) **29**:70
La guzla; ou, Choix de poésies illyriques (Mérimée) **6**:350-2, 362; **65**:44, 46, 58, 87, 115
"Guzman's Family" (Maturin) **6**:333, 335
"Gwain Down the Steps vor Water" (Barnes) **75**:6
"Gwain to Brookwell" (Barnes) **75**:4
Gwałltu, co sie dzieje (Fredro) **8**:292
"Gwin, King of Norway" (Blake) **13**:182, 219, 239
"Gyalázatos világ" (Petofi) **21**:278
Gyges and His Ring (Hebbel)
See *Gyges und sein Ring: Eine Tragödie in fünf Acten*
Gyges und sein Ring: Eine Tragödie in fünf Acten (Hebbel) **43**:230, 238-40, 246, 249, 259-62, 278, 283-85, 288-89, 291, 293, 296-300
The Gypsies (Pushkin)
See *Tsygany*
The Gypsies of Nagy Ida (Arany)
See *A nagyidai czigányok*
The Gypsy Girl (Baratynsky)
See *Nalozhnitsa*
"The Gypsy King" (Norton) **47**:252
"H" (Rimbaud) **4**:484; **35**:308, 322
The H— Family (Bremer)
See *Familjen H.*
H. Taine: Sa vie et sa correspondance (Taine) **15**:453
"Habeas Corpus" (Jackson) **90**:159
"The Habit of Perfection" (Hopkins) **17**:191
"Habits of Grate Men" (Shaw) **15**:335
"Hacen las cosas tan claras que hasta los ciegos ven" (Lizardi) **30**:67
"Had a man's fair form" (Keats) **73**:148
Hadlaub (Keller) **2**:414
"Hadst Thou Liv'd in Days of Old" (Keats) **73**:259
"Hafbur and Signy" (Morris) **4**:423
"Hafiz" (Emerson) **98**:179
"The Hag" (Turgenev) **21**:431
ha-Gemul (Smolenskin) **30**:190, 195
Der Hagestolz (Stifter) **41**:343, 357, 359-62, 364, 391
Haidamaky (Shevchenko) **54**:358, 360, 367, 369, 375-6, 379, 381, 386, 388-90
Das Haidedorf (Stifter) **41**:335, 341, 366, 376, 380-81, 385
"Hail Briton!" (Tennyson) **30**:293
"Hail Great Republic" (Paine) **62**:324
"Hail, humble Helpstone" (Clare) **86**:93
"Hail Matrimony" (Blake) **37**:29

"Haine du pauvre" (Mallarmé)
See "Aumône"
"Der Halbmond glänzet am Himmel" (Grillparzer) **102**:174
"Half a Lifetime Ago" (Gaskell) **5**:191, 201-02, 205; **70**:185
"The Half of Life Gone" (Morris) **4**:434
The Half-Breed: A Tale of the Western Frontier (Whitman) **81**:344
"The Half-Brothers" (Gaskell) **70**:186
The Half-Brothers; or, The Head and the Hand (Dumas)
See *Le bâtard de Mauléon*
A Half-Century of Conflict (Parkman) **12**:341, 346, 351, 353, 366, 370-72, 377
"Half-Sir" (Griffin) **7**:201, 211-12, 217
"Hälfte des Lebens" (Hölderlin) **16**:174-6, 192
"The Hall" (Crabbe) **26**:129
"The Hall and the Wood" (Morris) **4**:434
"The Hall of Cynddylan" (Hemans) **29**:205
"The Hall of Justice" (Crabbe) **26**:78-9, 82, 118; **121**:9, 34
"Hall of the Muses" (Meyer)
See "Der Musensaal"
Halle und Jerusalem (Arnim) **5**:19-22, 24
Eine Halligfahrt (Storm) **1**:540, 542, 544
"Hallowed Ground" (Campbell) **19**:179, 183
"Hallowed Pleäces" (Barnes) **75**:7, 59
"Halt" (Muller) **73**:364, 370
"Halte là!—le chant de victoire des Ottomans" (Beranger) **34**:28
The Halton Boys (Crawford) **12**:170, 172-74; **127**:193, 196
"The Hamadryad" (Hayne) **94**:158
"The Hamadryad" (Landor) **14**:168, 190
"Hamalija" (Shevchenko) **54**:358, 367, 377, 379
"Hamatreya" (Emerson) **1**:293, 295-97; **38**:187; **98**:177, 179-80
The Hamiltons; or, Official in Life in 1830 (Gore) **65**:16, 18-19, 28, 31
"Hamlet" (Lamb) **125**:304
"Hamlet" (Very) **9**:370, 379
"Hamlet and Don Quixote" (Turgenev)
See "Gamlet i Don Kikhot"
"A Hamlet of the Scigry District" (Turgenev)
See "Gamlet ščigrovskogo uezda"
"Hamlet of the Shchigrovsky District" (Turgenev)
See "Gamlet ščigrovskogo uezda"
"Hamlet of the Shchigry District" (Turgenev)
See "Gamlet ščigrovskogo uezda"
"Hamlet; or, The Consequences of Filial Piety" (Laforgue)
See "Hamlet; ou, les suites de piété filiale"
"Hamlet; or, The Results of Filial Devotion" (Laforgue)
See "Hamlet; ou, les suites de piété filiale"
"Hamlet; ou, les suites de piété filiale" (Laforgue) **5**:271, 274, 281-2; **53**:273, 293
"The Hamlets" (Martineau) **137**:251
The Hamlets (Martineau) **137**:271
The Hammer of the Village (Petofi)
See *A helység kalapácsa*
Han d'Islande (Hugo) **3**:233-34, 236-37, 239, 254, 258; **21**:195, 198, 201, 205
"The Hand and Foot" (Very) **9**:382-84, 397
"Hand and Heart" (Gaskell) **70**:185-86
"Hand and Soul" (Ingelow) **39**:267
"Hand and Soul" (Rossetti) **4**:504, 510; **77**:331, 333-34, 339, 341
"Hand and Word" (Griffin) **7**:198, 212, 217
"Der Hand der Jezerte" (Mörike) **10**:456-57
"A Hand Mirror" (Whitman) **81**:364
The Hand of Glory (Barham) **77**:9, 33-34
"The Hand of Jezerte" (Mörike)
See "Der Hand der Jezerte"
The Hand of the Arch-Sinner (Brontë) **109**:52
A Handbook to the Courts of Modern Sculpture (Jameson) **43**:327
A Handbook to the Public Galleries of Art in and near London (Jameson) **43**:306, 317, 321-22
Handley Cross (Surtees) **14**:343, 346-49, 353-54, 357, 361-63, 366, 369-70, 372-75, 377, 380-81
"Hands All Round!" (Tennyson) **30**:294-95
"Der Handschuh" (Schiller) **39**:337, 388
The Handy Cook Book (Beecher) **30**:15
"Hanging of the Crane" (Longfellow) **45**:139
"The Hangman" (Espronceda)
See "El verdugo"
The Hangman's Rope (Petofi)
See *A hóhér kötele*
Hangover from Another's Feast (Ostrovsky)
See *V chuzhom piru pokhmelye*
"Hankai" (Ueda Akinari) **131**:21-23, 52-53, 58-60
Hanna (Runeberg) **41**:309-10, 317
Hannah Thurston (Taylor) **89**:310, 343, 347
"Hannan laulu" (Kivi) **30**:51
"Hanna's Song" (Kivi)
See "Hannan laulu"
Hannibal (Grabbe) **2**:272-73, 276, 282, 284-85, 287-88
Hanns Frei (Ludwig) **4**:349
Hans Christian Andersen's Correspondence (Andersen) **7**:24
Hans Christian Andersen's Fairy Tales (Andersen) **7**:26, 29-33
"Hans Fingerhut's Frog Lesson" (Lampman) **25**:205-06, 219
"Hans Joggeli der Erbvetter" (Gotthelf) **117**:6, 18
Hans Max Giesbrecht (Kotzebue) **25**:136
Hans of Iceland (Hugo)
See *Han d'Islande*
"Hans Pfaal" (Poe)
See "The Unparalleled Adventure of One Hans Pfaall"
Hans und Heinz Kirch (Storm) **1**:537, 540, 550
Hanswursts Hochzeit (Goethe) **4**:213
"Hanz Kuechelgarten" (Gogol) **31**:115
"Hapless Dionis" (Eminescu)
See "Sarmanul Dionis"
"Happier Dead" (Baudelaire)
See "Le mort joyeux"
The Happiest Day of My Life (Scribe) **16**:382
"Happiness" (Milnes) **61**:136
"Happiness in Crime" (Barbey d'Aurevilly)
See "Le bonheur dans le crime"
"The Happiness of the Jokers" (Krasicki)
See "Szczęsacliwość filutów"
The Happy Age (Undset)
See *Den lykkelige alder*
"The Happy Daes When I Wer Young" (Barnes) **75**:22, 56
Happy Dodd; Or, "She Hath Done What She Counld" (Cooke) **110**:12, 21, 39, 50, 55, 58
"A Happy Evening" (Wagner) **119**:192, 197
"The Happy Family" (Andersen) **7**:33; **79**:23, 31
"Happy is England" (Keats) **73**:147
"A Happy Poet" (Thomson) **18**:413
"Happy Sundays for Children" (Hale) **75**:282
"The Happy Valley" (Woolson) **82**:272
"Happy Warrior" (Wordsworth) **38**:360
"Happy Women" (Alcott) **83**:34, 36
Hard Cash: A Matter-of-Fact Romance (Reade) **2**:533-37, 539-41, 545, 548-51; **74**:245-48, 250, 253, 255, 257-58, 262-65, 284, 287-89, 298, 318-19
"A Hard Lesson" (Cooke) **110**:39
Hard Times for These Times (Dickens) **3**:150, 155-56, 158, 166, 172, 174, 184-85, 188; **8**:171, 176; **18**:114, 121-22, 134; **26**:168, 171, 177; **37**:175, 200, 202; **50**:105-215; **86**:249, 260; **105**:231, 244, 254, 256, 258-59, 261, 274, 330-31, 336, 340, 354; **113**:97
"Hard Up" (O'Brien) **21**:249
Hardscrabble; or, The Fall of Chicago. A Tale of Indian Warfare (Richardson) **55**:303-4, 313-4, 321, 344, 346
"The Hardy Tin Soldier" (Andersen)
See "Den standhaftige Tinsoldat"
"The Hare Chase" (Leskov)
See "Zajačij remiz"
"The Hare Park" (Leskov)
See "Zajačij remiz"
"Hareem" (Milnes) **61**:130
"Harem's Graves" (Mickiewicz)
See "Mogiły haremu"
"Hark, My Soul! It Is the Lord" (Cowper) **8**:127; **94**:73
"Hark to the Shouting Wind" (Timrod) **25**:364, 373
"Härka-Tuomo" (Kivi) **30**:64
"Harlem" (Bertrand) **31**:49, 54
"The Harlequin of Dreams" (Lanier) **118**:240
"Harmonie du soir" (Baudelaire) **29**:77; **55**:14, 28
Harmonies poétiques et religieuses (Lamartine) **11**:248, 250, 252-53, 255, 265, 268-74, 278-80, 283, 286
Harold (Southey) **97**:312
Harold (Tennyson) **30**:263-64, 293
"Harold and Tosti" (Sigourney) **21**:298-99
Harold, the Last of the Saxon Kings (Bulwer-Lytton) **1**:146, 150-52; **45**:13-15, 21-2, 60-2
"The Harp" (Lonnrot) **53**:327
"The Harp of Broken Strings" (Ridge) **82**:174, 180-81
"The Harp that once" (Moore) **110**:194
"The Harp That Once through Tara's Halls" (Moore) **6**:391, 398
"Harpagus' Ballad" (Beddoes) **3**:34
"The Harper" (Campbell) **19**:188, 190, 198
The Harper's Daughter (Lewis) **11**:305
"Harriet" (Brontë) **109**:30
"Harriet II" (Brontë) **109**:29
Harriet Martineau's Autobiography (Martineau) **26**:311, 315-16, 318, 322-23, 327-28, 330, 338, 341-47, 349, 352, 357
Harriet Martineau's Letters to Fannie Wedgewood (Martineau) **137**:323, 335
"Harrington" (Edgeworth) **1**:258; **51**:88-90, 117-29
Harriot and Sophia (Lennox)
See *Sophia*
Harry and Lucy Continued, Being the Last Part of Early Lessons (Edgeworth) **51**:81
Harry Clinton; a Tale of Youth (Hays) **114**:186
"Harry Gill" (Wordsworth)
See "Goody Blake and Harry Gill"
Harry Heathcote of Gangoil (Trollope) **101**:241
Harry Joscelyn (Oliphant) **11**:446, 449
Harry Lorrequer (Lever)
See *The Confessions of Harry Lorrequer*
Harry Muir (Oliphant) **11**:432
"Harry Ploughman" (Hopkins) **17**:189, 225, 256
"Hartleap Well" (Wordsworth) **12**:434; **111**:236, 348
"Hart-Leap Well" (Wordsworth)
See "Hartleap Well"
Hartlebury (Disraeli) **79**:269, 274-75
"Hartley Coleridge" (Bagehot) **10**:18, 31, 40-41, 55
"The Hartz Journey" (Heine)
See *Die Harzreise*
The Hartz Journey (Heine)
See *Die Harzreise*
"Harun's Sons" (Meyer)
See "Die Söhne Haruns"
Harusame Monogatari (Ueda Akinari) **131**:20-22, 40-41, 45, 51-53, 55-56, 60, 86, 88
"Harvest Hwome" (Barnes) **75**:78
"The Harvest Moon" (Longfellow) **45**:161
"Harvest Morning" (Clare) **9**:74
"A Harvest of Tares" (Boyesen) **135**:33
"Harvest Song" (Meyer)
See "Schnitterlied"
"Harvest Storm" (Meyer)
See "Erntegewitter"
The Harveys (Kingsley) **107**:192-93

"Harzer Hans" (Gotthelf) **117**:43, 58
Die Harzreise (Heine) **4**:253; **54**:316, 327-8, 336
"Has the Frog a Soul, and of What Nature is That Soul, Supposing It to Exist" (Huxley) **67**:86
Hasara Raba (Sacher-Masoch) **31**:287, 294
"The Haschish" (Whittier) **8**:531
Hastings (Macaulay) **42**:87
The Hasty-Pudding (Barlow) **23**:14-15, 19, 29, 32-4, 36, 39-44
ha-To'eh be-darke ha-hayim (Smolenskin) **30**:186, 189-92, 195
"Hatteras" (Freneau) **111**:105
Hau Kiou Choaan (Percy) **95**:313
"Haunted and the Haunters" (Bulwer-Lytton) **1**:151; **45**:71
"The Haunted Baronet" (Le Fanu) **9**:312; **58**:286, 295, 302-4
Haunted Hearts (Cummins) **139**:166, 185
The Haunted Hotel: A Mystery of Modern Venice (Collins) **1**:180, 183; **93**:36-7, 42-4
"The Haunted House" (Hood) **16**:205, 208, 210, 216, 220-22, 224-29, 231-36
"Haunted House" (Whittier) **8**:485
"Haunted Houses" (Longfellow) **45**:116-17
Haunted Lives (Le Fanu) **9**:312; **58**:272-5
The Haunted Man and the Ghost's Bargain (Dickens) **113**:51
The Haunted Marsh (Sand)
See *La mare au diable*
"The Haunted Mind" (Hawthorne) **2**:305; **39**:224;
"The Haunted Palace" (Poe) **1**:508, 512; **16**:295; **55**:169, 181, 212; **97**:181-82, 191-93, 195-96, 199, 204-05, 210; **117**:192, 242-44, 278, 281, 303
The Haunted Pool (Sand)
See *La mare au diable*
"Haunted Tower" (Irving) **2**:372
"The Haunting of the Tiled House" (Le Fanu) **9**:315
"Haunts of the Lapwing" (Jefferies) **47**:137
Häuptlingabendwind (Nestroy) **42**:232
Das Haus der Temperamente (Nestroy) **42**:227, 232, 238, 240, 243
"Häusliche Szene" (Mörike) **10**:453
"Hautot père et fils" (Maupassant) **83**:227
"Have Compassion on Me" (Isaacs)
See "Ten piedad de mi"
"Have Faith" (Harpur) **114**:147
"Have I Not Striven, My God, and Watched and Prayed?" (Rossetti) **50**:317
"Have We Any Men Among Us?" (Parton) **86**:352
"Haverhill" (Whittier) **8**:532
Hawbuck Grange (Surtees) **14**:349, 353, 369, 374, 377, 379
The Hawks of Hawk Hollow: A Tradition of Pennsylvania (Bird) **1**:83-84, 86, 88, 90-91
"Haworth Churchyard" (Arnold) **6**:72; **29**:26, 28, 32-3, 37
"Hawthorne and his Mosses" (Melville) **91**:33-4, 140, 209, 212, 219
"Hay muertos que no hacen ruido" (Lizardi) **30**:67
"Hay-Carren" (Barnes) **75**:77
"Hay-Meaken" (Barnes) **75**:77
"The Haystack in the Floods" (Morris) **4**:422, 425-26, 432, 441, 444
"The Hayswater Boat" (Arnold) **29**:36
"He and I" (Rossetti) **4**:491; **77**:339
"He and She" (Rossetti) **66**:341
"He fumbles at your Soul" (Dickinson) **77**:76-77, 88
"He Heard Her Sing" (Thomson) **18**:417, 419
He is not well-born (Andersen) **79**:16
He Knew He was Right (Trollope) **6**:459, 477, 491, 493, 497, 504, 513; **33**:363; **101**:241, 289, 291, 321
"He put the Belt around my life" (Dickinson) **77**:156
"He Saw My Heart's Woe" (Brontë) **3**:62
"He scanned it—staggered—/Dropped the Loop" (Dickinson) **77**:162
"He strained my faith" (Dickinson) **77**:82
"He Was Killed" (Bestuzhev)
See "On bly ubit"
"He Was Weak, and I Was Strong—Then" (Dickinson) **21**:79
He Who Hated God (Almqvist)
See *Gudhataren*
He Who Will Not When He May (Oliphant) **11**:446
The Head of the Family (Craik) **38**:110, 120, 126-27
Head of the Family (Oliphant) **11**:428
The Headsman of Berne (Cooper) **1**:200, 218-19; **54**:256, 262, 288
"The Headstwone" (Barnes) **75**:8
"The Healing of Conall Carnach" (Ferguson) **33**:278-79, 283, 289
"A Health" (Pinkney) **31**:269, 272-76, 280
Health, Husbandry and Handicraft (Martineau) **26**:346
Hear Both Sides (Holcroft) **85**:199, 218
"The Heare" (Barnes) **75**:35
"The Heart" (Emerson) **38**:211; **98**:94-100
Heart and Cross (Oliphant) **61**:203
Heart and Science: A Story of the Present Times (Collins) **1**:176, 180; **93**:12, 66
"The Heart asks Pleasure—first" (Dickinson) **77**:163-64
"The Heart Healed and Changed by Mercy" (Cowper) **94**:72
The Heart of Gold (Jerrold) **2**:402
"The Heart of John Middleton" (Gaskell) **5**:205; **70**:188-90; **137**:59
The Heart of Mid-Lothian (Scott) **15**:277, 289, 294, 300-01, 304, 317-18, 321-24; **69**:303, 310-13, 368
"Heart's Hope" (Rossetti) **77**:312
Hearts of Oak (Rowson) **69**:140-41
"Heat" (Lampman) **25**:162, 166, 168, 171-72, 180, 182, 184-85, 192-94, 197-200, 202, 210
"Heat Lightning" (Meyer)
See "Wetterleuchten"
The Heath Cobblers (Kivi)
See *Nummisuutarit*
The Heathcock (Arnim)
See *Der Averhahn*
"Heathlands" (Jefferies) **47**:134
"L'héautontimorouménos" (Baudelaire) **6**:115; **55**:24, 61, 71
Heaven and Earth (Byron) **2**:67, 80, 91; **12**:139; **109**:102-03, 106
"'Heaven'—is what I cannot reach!" (Dickinson) **77**:96
"Heavenly Love" (Horton) **87**:110
"The Heavenly Vision" (Chivers) **49**:50
"Heaven's Mourning" (Lenau) **16**:275
"A Heavy Heart" (Rossetti) **50**:313
"Hebräische Melodien" (Heine) **4**:253-55, 269
"Hebraism and Hellenism" (Arnold) **89**:60
"Hebrew Dirge" (Sigourney) **21**:309
"Hebrew Melodies" (Heine)
See "Hebräische Melodien"
Hebrew Melodies (Byron) **2**:63, 90, 103
"The Hebrew Mother" (Hemans) **29**:196; **71**:275
"Der Heckebeutel" (Arnim) **123**:15, 88-92
"Hector in the Garden" (Browning) **1**:117; **61**:43
Hector's Inheritance; or, The Boys of Smith Institute (Alger) **8**:16, 35, 43-44
Hector-Vadh (Dutt) **118**:5
"Hedge School" (Carleton) **3**:86, 89, 93
"The Hedgehog" (Clare) **9**:107
"Hegel" (Marx) **17**:295
"Hegel's Aesthetics: The Philosophy of Art" (Lewes) **25**:288, 299-300
Hegels theologische Jungendschriften (Hegel) **46**:139, 163
Heidebilder (Droste-Hülshoff) **3**:193, 196, 200, 203
"Heidelberg" (Hölderlin) **16**:161
"Die Heidelberger Ruine" (Lenau) **16**:278
"Der Heidemann" (Droste-Hülshoff) **3**:197
The Heidenmauer (Cooper) **1**:218-19, 224; **54**:256, 264, 288
"Heidenröslein" (Goethe) **34**:122
"Die Heideschenke" (Lenau) **16**:285
"Ein heidnisches Sprüchlein" (Meyer) **81**:156
"The Height of the Ridiculous" (Holmes) **14**:98-9, 101
Der Heilige (Meyer) **81**:164, 171-74, 193, 196, 198
Die heilige Cäcilie; oder, die Gewalt der Musik (Kleist) **2**:461; **37**:245, 247, 249, 254-55
Die heilige Familie, oder Kritik der kritischen Kritik: Gegen Bruno Bauer und Consorten (Engels) **85**:6, 8, 13, 57, 109, 114, 120; **114**:69, 83
Die heilige Familie, oder Kritik der kritischen Kritik: Gegen Bruno Bauer und Consorten (Marx) **17**:328, 331-34, 352; **114**:69, 83
"Das heilige Feuer" (Meyer) **81**:208
"Die Heimat" (Eichendorff) **8**:221
"Die Heimkehr" (Meyer) **81**:141-45, 147-48, 150-51, 155
Die Heimkehr (Heine) **4**:248-49, 252, 258-59; **54**:326, 348
"Heimkunft" (Hölderlin) **16**:187, 193, 195
Heine on Shakespeare: A Translation of His Notes on Shakespeare's Heroines (Heine)
See *Shakespeares Mädchen und Frauen*
"Heine's Grave" (Arnold) **6**:54, 72; **29**:38
"Heinrich Heine" (Arnold) **89**:32, 38, 121; **126**:100, 114, 120
"Heinrich Heine" (Eliot) **41**:65
"Heinrich Heine" (Pisarev) **25**:339
Heinrich Heine's Book of Songs (Heine)
See *Buch der Lieder*
Heinrich von Offerdingen (Novalis) **13**:360, 362-68, 371, 374, 377-78, 381-82, 386, 394-97, 400-02
"The Heir of Dremore" (Crawford) **127**:193, 195-96
The Heir of Gaymount (Cooke) **5**:124, 130, 132, 134-35
The Heir of Selwood (Gore) **65**:20
The Heir Presumptive and the Heir Apparent (Oliphant) **61**:204-5
The Heirs in Tail (Arnim)
See *Die Majoratsherren*
Die Heiterethei und ihr Widerspiel (Ludwig) **4**:347-48, 354-57, 362, 367
"Helavalkea" (Kivi) **30**:51
Heldenthum und Christenthum (Wagner) **9**:475
Hélé ena (Vigny) **102**:335, 379
"Helen" (Lamb) **125**:374
"Helen" (Lamb) **10**:385
Helen (Edgeworth) **1**:259, 261, 263, 266, 269; **51**:88, 90-1, 93, 95, 113
Helen Fleetwood: A Tale of the Factories (Tonna) **135**:193, 195-201, 203-4, 207-13, 220-21, 236, 238-39, 241, 243, 245-46
Helen Ford (Alger) **8**:42; **83**:139, 142, 145
"Helen Lee" (O'Brien) **21**:246
"Helen of Tyre" (Longfellow) **45**:132
"Helena" (Heine) **4**:257
"Helena" (Taylor) **89**:310
Helena (Goethe) **4**:179, 207, 216
Helena's Household: A Tale of Rome in the First Century (De Mille) **123**:117-21, 123-26
"Hélène" (Leconte de Lisle) **29**:222, 224, 238
Hélène Gillet (Nodier) **19**:383-84
"Helen's Rock" (Crawford) **127**:189, 193-94
Hellas (Shelley) **18**:332, 344, 353, 362, 368, 377; **93**:271, 333

The Hellenics (Landor) **14**:168, 177, 181, 189-91, 196-97
"The Helot" (Crawford) **12**:153, 155-56, 161, 169, 174; **127**:178, 218
"Help" (Whittier) **8**:509
Helping Himself (Alger) **8**:44
"Helpstone" (Clare) **9**:73, 96, 106, 112-13; **86**:128-29, 155
A helység kalapácsa (Petofi) **21**:265-66, 276-78, 283
"Un hemisferio en una cabellera" (Casal) **131**:264
"Un hemisphère dans une chevelure" (Baudelaire) **6**:87
Hemmen i den nya verlden: En dagbok i bref, skrifna under tvenne års resor i Norra Amerika och på Cuba (Bremer) **11**:26, 30, 32-33
Hemmet; eller, Familje-sorger och fröjder (Bremer) **11**:17-21, 24, 34-36
"Hen Baily's Reformation" (Harris) **23**:159, 162
"The Henchman" (Whittier) **8**:513, 517, 529; **59**:360
"Hendecasyllables" (Coleridge) **9**:143
Henri III et sa cour (Dumas) **71**:184, 193, 209, 231, 241, 248-52
"A Henri Murger" (Banville) **9**:26
Henrietta (Lennox) **23**:228-29, 232-35
Henrietta Temple (Disraeli) **2**:138-39, 143-44, 146-47; **39**:3-4, 20, 22, 24, 26-31, 40, 46, 52, 65, 67-8, 74-6; **79**:205-07, 209-12, 214-15, 218-19, 223-31, 233, 239, 269, 273, 276-77, 279
Henriette et Saint-Clair (Sade) **47**:361-63
Henriette Maréchal (Goncourt and Goncourt) **7**:170-71
"A Henrique. Ora y espera!" (Isaacs) **70**:304, 309
Henriquez (Baillie) **2**:39-41; **71**:4-6
"Henry and Eliza" (Austen) **119**:13
Henry Crabb Robinson on Books and Their Writers (Robinson) **15**:194
Henry Esmond (Thackeray)
See *The History of Henry Esmond, Esq., a Colonel in the Service of Her Majesty Q. Anne*
"Henry George" (Adams) **33**:25
"Henry Purcell" (Hopkins) **17**:225
Henry St. John, Gentleman, of "Flower of Hundreds" in the County of Prince George, Virginia: A Tale of 1774-'75 (Cooke) **5**:122-24, 127-29, 131, 135-36
"Hepzibah's Story" (Woolson) **82**:333
"Her cheeks are like roses" (Clare) **86**:119
Her Country's Hope (Tamayo y Baus)
See *La esperanza de la patria*
"Her Ladyship's Private Office" (Turgenev) **21**:441
"Her Little Parasol to Lift" (Dickinson) **21**:56
Her Majesty the Queen (Cooke) **5**:130, 132
"Her Majesty's Name" (Hunt) **70**:258
"Her Name" (Hugo) **3**:234
"Her Seed, It Shall Bruise Thy Head" (Rossetti) **50**:315
"Hèraklès au Taureau" (Leconte de Lisle) **29**:217
"Herald of Freedom" (Thoreau) **138**:128-29
"The Heraldic Blazon of Foss the Cat" (Lear) **3**:298
Herbert Carter's Legacy; or, The Inventor's Son (Alger) **8**:46; **83**:92-4, 129
"Herbert Selden, the Poor Lawyer's Son" (Alger) **83**:96
"Herbstfeier" (Hölderlin) **16**:162
"Herbsttag" (Meyer) **81**:148
"Hércules ante la Hidra" (Casal) **131**:223, 225-26, 236
"Hércules y las Estinfálides" (Casal) **131**:236
"Here comes the night" (Fuller) **50**:249
"Here is a faithful list of impressions" (Baratynsky)
See "Vot vernyi spisok vpechatlenii"
"Here, where the vault of heaven so inertly" (Tyutchev)
See "Zdes, gde tak vyalo svod nebesnyy"
"Hereafter" (Clare) **9**:78
"Hérésies artistiques: L'art pour tous" (Mallarmé) **41**:254, 256, 258, 282
"The Heretic" (Shevchenko)
See "Jeretyk"
"The Heretic's Tragedy" (Browning) **19**:117, 153
Hereward the Wake, "Last of the English" (Kingsley) **35**:208, 220, 226, 230-31, 241, 243-44, 249
"L'héritage" (Maupassant) **83**:229
L'héritière de Birague (Balzac) **5**:58
"Herman and Dorothea" (Goethe)
See *Hermann und Dorothea*
Die Hermann sschlacht (Grabbe) **2**:272, 276, 282-85, 287-88
Hermann und Dorothea (Goethe) **4**:161-62, 167, 172, 191, 193, 205-07, 222
Hermann und Thusnelde (Kotzebue) **25**:141
Hermanns Schlacht (Klopstock) **11**:226, 228
Die Hermannsschlacht (Kleist) **2**:440, 442, 446-47, 450; **37**:217, 225, 228, 231-32, 236, 253-55, 267, 269, 270, 272, 274
Hermeneutics: The Handwritten Manuscripts (Schleiermacher)
See *Hermeneutik: Nach den Handshriften neu herausgegeben*
Hermeneutik: Nach den Handshriften neu herausgegeben (Schleiermacher) **107**:370, 378-86
Hermes Britannicus (Bowles) **103**:54
"The Hermit" (Beattie) **25**:104, 106-07
"The Hermit and the Bear" (Krylov) **1**:435
"Hermit of Warkworth" (Percy) **95**:343
The Hermit of Warkworth (Percy) **95**:365
Hernán Pérez del Pulgar (Martínez de la Rosa) **102**:227-28, 252
Hernani (Hugo) **3**:236-37, 248-49, 261, 264, 268, 273; **10**:362, 373; **21**:194, 197
"Hero and Leander" (Hood) **16**:200-01, 208, 215, 218, 221, 225, 227, 229-30
"Hero and Leander" (Hunt) **1**:410
Hero and Leander (Grillparzer)
See *Des Meeres und der Liebe Wellen*
Hero and Leander (Hunt) **70**:251, 253
"Hero Bor" (Arany)
See "Bor vitéz"
A Hero of Our Time (Lermontov)
See *Geroi nashego vremeni*
Hero of the North (Fouqué) **2**:265-66, 268
Herod (Hebbel)
See *Herodes und Mariamne: Eine Tragödie in fünf Acten*
Herodes und Mariamne: Eine Tragödie in fünf Acten (Hebbel) **43**:230, 234, 238-39, 243, 245, 248, 250, 257-59, 262, 267, 277-79, 282-84, 287, 289, 296-300
"Herodiade" (Flaubert) **135**:171
Hérodiade (Mallarmé) **4**:371, 375, 377, 380-81, 386-87, 394-96; **41**:233, 236, 239, 245-46, 249-50, 267, 269-72, 274-75, 278-81, 289
"Hérodias" (Flaubert) **2**:227, 233, 236, 246, 256-8; **135**:109
Herodias (Mallarmé)
See *Hérodiade*
"Heroes" (Lazarus) **8**:411, 413, 420; **109**:293
The Heroes (Kingsley) **35**:220, 232, 249
Heroic Idylls (Landor) **14**:189-91
The Heroic Slave (Douglass) **7**:130, 146-47; **55**:123-4
Heroic Songs of the Recent Times of the War for Freedom (Karadzic)
See *Pjesme junaĉke srednjijeh vrema*
"Heroism" (Cowper) **8**:139; **94**:41-4, 48
"Heroism" (Emerson) **1**:307; **98**:65, 176
Heroism and Christianity (Wagner)
See *Heldenthum und Christenthum*
"Der Herr Esau" (Gotthelf) **117**:6, 15, 27, 32
Der Herr Etatsrat (Storm) **1**:540
Herr Eugen Dühring's Revolution in Science; or Anti-Dühring (Engels)
See *Herr Eugen Dührings Umwälzung de Wissenschaft: Philosophie; Politische Oekonomie; Sozialismus*
Herr Eugen Dührings Umwälzung de Wissenschaft: Philosophie; Politische Oekonomie; Sozialismus (Engels) **85**:6, 24-25, 31-34, 37-42, 59, 69, 104-06, 121, 128; **114**:41
Herr Rassmussen (Andersen) **79**:16
"El herrador y el zapatero" (Lizardi) **30**:68
"Herrenston" (Barnes) **75**:104-05
"Die Herrlichkeit der Schöpfung" (Schiller) **39**:339
"Hershey and the Incarnation" (Brownson) **50**:53
Hertha (Bremer) **11**:30-31, 34-36
Herz und Gemüth (Herder) **8**:306
Herzog Theodor von Gothland (Grabbe) **2**:271-76, 280, 283-84, 286-88
He's Much to Blame (Holcroft) **85**:198, 212, 223
"The Hesperides" (Tennyson) **30**:208, 280; **65**:357-8
Hesperus; or, Forty-Five Dog-Post-Days (Jean Paul) **7**:226-27, 230, 232, 238-40
The Hessian Courier (Büchner)
See *Der Hessische Landbote*
The Hessian Messenger (Büchner)
See *Der Hessische Landbote*
Der Hessische Landbote (Büchner) **26**:4-5, 14, 27-8, 64, 68, 70
"Hester" (Crabbe) **121**:24-6
"Hester" (Lamb) **10**:407
Hester (Oliphant) **11**:441, 446, 461; **61**:187-90, 223, 226, 231-3, 235
"Hétköznapi történet" (Madach) **19**:369
Hetty (Kingsley) **107**:192
Hetty's Strange History (Jackson) **90**:144, 164-69
"L'heure du sabbat" (Bertrand) **31**:46
"Heures" (Corbière) **43**:34
"L'Heureuse Feinte" (Sade) **47**:313
Hexameron vom Rosenhain (Wieland) **17**:410
"Hexenküche" (Goethe) **4**:215
Der Hexensabbath (Tieck) **5**:514
"Hiawatha" (Longfellow)
See *The Song of Hiawatha*
Hiawatha (Longfellow)
See *The Song of Hiawatha*
"Hiawatha's Photographing" (Carroll) **139**:35
The Hibernian Nights' Entertainments (Ferguson) **3**:290
"Les Hiboux" (Baudelaire) **55**:43
The Hidden Hand (Southworth) **26**:433, 438, 441-49
"Hidden Love" (Clough) **27**:55, 77
Hide and Seek (Collins) **1**:178-79, 181, 186-87; **93**:46-7, 53, 64
"Hièronymus" (Leconte de Lisle) **29**:225
"High and Low Life in Italy" (Landor) **14**:165
The High Jumpers (Andersen) **79**:31
High, Low, Jack and the Game (Planché) **42**:295
High Profession and Negligent Practice (More) **27**:342
"The High Tide on the Coast of Lincolnshire, 1571" (Ingelow) **39**:257, 262-63, 266, 268; **107**:119-20, 122-23
High Times and Hard Times (Harris)
See *Sut Lovingood: Yarns Spun by a "Nat'ral Born Durn'd Fool"*
"Higher Laws" (Thoreau) **7**:352, 376, 388, 392, 407
"The Higher Pantheism" (Tennyson) **30**:254, 269-70; **65**:265, 274
"The Highland Reaper" (Wordsworth) **12**:427
"The Highland Widow" (Scott) **15**:312; **110**:305

"A Highway for Freedom" (Mangan) **27**:296
Hihon tamakushige (Motoori) **45**:275-76
La hija de las flores (Gómez de Avellaneda) **111**:47
La hija del mar (Castro) **3**:105-06; **78**:45-47, 49, 52
Hija y madre (Tamayo y Baus) **1**:571
El hijo pródigo (Alarcon) **1**:15
Hilary St. Ives (Ainsworth) **13**:45
"Hilda Silfverling" (Child) **6**:201
"The Hill and the Valley" (Martineau) **26**:304
The Hill and the Valley (Martineau) **137**:266, 268-70
"Hill in Kikineis" (Mickiewicz)
See "Góra Kikineis"
"The Hill of Venus" (Lazarus) **109**:290
"The Hill of Venus" (Morris) **4**:447-48
"Hill or Dell" (Barnes) **75**:87
"The Hill Summit" (Rossetti) **4**:515
Hillingdon Hall (Surtees) **14**:343, 345, 349, 353, 362, 364-65, 375, 377, 380
The Hills of the Shatemuc (Warner) **31**:337, 343
Hillyars (Kingsley)
See *The Hillyars and the Burtons*
The Hillyars and the Burtons (Kingsley) **107**:183-86, 188-89, 191-92, 194-95, 206, 209, 211, 213, 216-21, 223-24, 228, 231-32, 250-56
Hilt to Hilt; or, Days and Nights in the Shenandoah in the Autumn of 1864 (Cooke) **5**:127-28, 132, 134
"Himmelsnähe" (Meyer) **81**:206
"Himmelstrauer" (Lenau) **16**:278
"Himno a la divina providencia" (Lizardi) **30**:69
"Himno a Talisay" (Rizal) **27**:425
"Himno al sol" (Espronceda) **39**:100, 106, 109
"Himno al trabajo" (Rizal) **27**:425
"Himno de guerra columbiano" (Isaacs) **70**:313
"Himpukuron" (Ueda Akinari) **131**:13, 15, 24, 26, 28, 32, 39
Himpukuron (Ueda Akinari) **131**:66
"Hints for a History of Highwaymen" (Thackeray) **43**:381
Hints from Horace (Byron) **2**:85; **12**:145
"Hints on European Travel" (Jefferson) **103**:114-17
Hints towards Forming the Character of a Young Princess (More) **27**:333, 341
"Hippodromania" (Gordon) **21**:154, 159-60, 164-65, 177, 180
"Hiram Powers' Greek Slave" (Browning) **16**:130
"His Clay" (Crawford) **12**:156, 159, 172
"His Departed Love to Prince Leopold" (Hunt) **70**:257
"His mind alone is kingly ..." (Harpur) **114**:115
His Natural Life (Clarke) **19**:230-46, 248, 251-52, 255-61
"Hisbrien om en Moder" (Andersen) **7**:23, 31-5; **79**:26-7, 76, 81, 89
Histoire de XIXème siècle (Michelet) **31**:211, 213, 238, 247
Histoire de Don Pédre Ier, roi de Castille (Mérimée) **6**:353, 356; **65**:85
Histoire de France (Michelet) **31**:207, 210-11, 220, 225, 238, 242, 247-48, 253, 257
"Histoire de Gambèr-Aly" (Gobineau) **17**:69, 103
Histoire de Juliette on les Prosperites du vice (Sade)
See *Juliette; ou, Les prospérités du vice*
Histoire de la grandeur et de la décadence de César Birotteau, parfumeur (Balzac) **5**:31-33, 47, 57; **35**:26, 34
Histoire de la littérature Anglaise (Taine) **15**:414-15, 418-19, 432, 435, 442-45, 447, 449, 451-52, 454, 456, 459, 462-63, 468, 473
Histoire de la peinture en Italie (Stendhal) **23**:352, 367, 391
"L'histoire de la reine du matin et de Soliman, prince Génies" (Nerval) **1**:480, 484; **67**:315
Histoire de la révolution de 1848 (Lamartine) **11**:258, 260
Histoire de la Révolution Française (Michelet) **31**:211, 213, 217, 231, 234-35, 237, 239, 246-47, 249-51, 255-56, 259
Histoire de la société Française pendant la révolution (Goncourt and Goncourt) **7**:153, 186
"Histoire de l'Abbé de Bucquoy" (Nerval) **67**:332
"Histoire de ma vie" (Bakunin) **25**:49
Histoire de ma vie (Sand) **2**:604, 607; **42**:311, 324, 328, 331-32, 337, 340, 354, 356-57, 379-81, 385-86; **42**:332, 364-66, 368, 370; **57**:309-10, 312, 326, 333, 336, 359-61, 366-7, 370
Histoire de mes Bêtes (Dumas) **71**:204, 210
Histoire de Pauline (Staël-Holstein) **91**:324, 339-40, 358, 360
Histoire de Sybille (Feuillet) **45**:78-9, 81, 83, 85-7, 91
Histoire des constituents (Lamartine) **11**:257, 261
Histoire des girondins (Lamartine) **11**:256-57, 259-61, 266-67, 274
Histoire des origines du christianisme (Renan) **26**:373, 377-79, 381, 390, 393, 395, 398, 400, 407-08, 410-11, 419-21
Histoire des perses (Gobineau) **17**:71, 81
Histoire des treize (Balzac) **5**:36
L'histoire d'Ottar Jarl, pirate norvégien, conquérant du pays de Bray, en Normandie, et de sa descendance (Gobineau) **17**:81, 88, 101
L'histoire du Calife Hakem (Nerval) **1**:475, 480, 483; **67**:335-36, 365
Histoire du chien de Brisquet (Nodier) **19**:381, 402
Histoire du peuple d'Israël (Renan) **26**:390, 395, 400, 407-08, 414, 417, 419, 421
Histoire du rêveur (Sand) **42**:378; **57**:368
L'histoire du roi de Bohême et de ses sept châteaux (Nodier) **19**:377, 380-82, 387-88, 392, 400-04
L'histoire d'un crime (Hugo) **3**:257, 262
Histoire d'une Colombe (Dumas)
See *La Colombe*
"L'histoire d'une fille de ferme" (Maupassant) **1**:448, 466; **83**:208, 210, 212-14, 222-24
Histoire général et système comparé des langues Sémitiques (Renan) **26**:365, 370, 421
Histoire populaire du Christianisme (Leconte de Lisle) **29**:212
Histoires comme ça (Verlaine) **51**:387
Histoires extraordinaires (Baudelaire) **29**:65-7
Histoires extraordinaires (Poe) **16**:298-99
Historia (Bécquer)
See *Historia de los Templos de España*
Historia de los Templos de España (Bécquer) **106**:97, 101, 108, 146, 158
"Historic Notes of Life and Letters in New England" (Emerson) **98**:91
An Historical and Statistical Account of Nova Scotia (Haliburton) **15**:116, 125, 127-28, 133, 144
"Historical Anecdotes" (Pushkin) **83**:273
"Historical deduction of seats" (Cowper) **94**:120
Historical Dialogues for Young Persons (Hays) **114**:186
"Historical Discourse at Concord" (Emerson) **38**:173
"Historical Discourse on the Text of 'Decamerone'" (Foscolo)
See "Discorso storico sul testo del 'Decamerone'"
An Historical, Political and Moral Essay on Revolutions, ancient and modern (Chateaubriand)
See *Essai sur les révolutions anciennes et modernes*
"Historical Romance: Alexandre Dumas" (Lewes) **25**:286
"Historical Sketch" (Bello) **131**:123
Historical Sketches (Newman) **38**:312, 314; **99**:212, 220
Historical Sketches of the Reign of George Second (Oliphant) **11**:433
"Historien" (Heine) **4**:254-56
"History" (Emerson) **38**:176-78; **98**:40, 65-6, 75, 111, 151, 153-55, 185
History (Macaulay)
See *The History of England from the Accession of James II*
History from the Commencement (Martineau) **26**:339-40
History of a Crime (Hugo)
See *L'histoire d'un crime*
History of a Six Weeks' Tour through a Part of France, Switzerland, Germany, and Holland (Shelley) **14**:251, 276; **59**:234; **103**:358-59
History of Ancient and Modern Literature (Schlegel)
See *Geschichte der alten und neuen Literatur*
History of Brazil (Southey) **8**:452-53, 459, 469; **97**:259, 262, 265, 268-69, 273-75, 283, 303, 305-06, 308-09, 330
History of British Costume (Planché) **42**:273, 281
The History of Caroline Evelyn (Burney) **54**:15
History of Costume (Planché) **42**:274
"History of Don Raymond" (Lewis) **11**:311
The History of Eliza Wharton, A Novel; Founded on Fact (Foster)
See *The Coquette; or the History of a Eliza Wharton. A Novel Founded on Fact, By a Lady of Massachusetts*
History of England (Froude) **43**:177-78, 181-82, 185, 187-91, 193, 203, 210-13
History of England (Macaulay)
See *The History of England from the Accession of James II*
The History of England during the Thirty Years' Peace, 1816-46 (Martineau) **26**:311, 323, 338-40, 354, 359
History of England during the Thirty Years' Peace 1816-1846 (Martineau) **137**:236, 262-63, 265, 270, 273-74, 285
The History of England from the Accession of James II (Macaulay) **42**:72, 76, 78, 82-3, 85-8, 92, 94-103, 106-07, 113, 116, 118-20, 122, 124-29, 131-33, 135, 138-43, 149, 151-2, 155-9
History of English Literature (Taine)
See *Histoire de la littérature Anglaise*
The History of English Philosophy (Hazlitt) **29**:163
History of France (Michelet)
See *Histoire de France*
History of Friedrich II. of Prussia, Called Frederick the Great (Carlyle) **70**:7, 92-93
History of Greece: From the Earliest Records of that Country to the Time in which it was reduced into a Roman Province (Godwin) **130**:161
The History of Henry Esmond, Esq., a Colonel in the Service of Her Majesty Q. Anne (Thackeray) **5**:450-51, 453, 459, 461-62, 464, 466-68, 471-72, 474, 478, 480-81, 484, 486, 488-89, 492, 497, 503-04; **14**:397, 406, 412, 434, 451-52; **43**:349-50, 356, 389
The History of Hester Wilmot (More) **27**:345
"The History of His Own Time" (Hawthorne) **95**:137
History of Ireland (Allingham) **25**:20-1
History of Lacock Abbey (Bowles) **103**:54

"The History of Lieutenant Ergunov" (Turgenev)
See "Istoriya leytenanta Ergunova"
"History of Marcus Aurelius" (Sigourney) **87**:321
History of Marie Antoinette (Goncourt and Goncourt) **7**:153
The History of Matthew Wald (Lockhart) **6**:289-90, 292, 294, 296, 302-03, 307, 310-12
History of Modern Philosophy (Feuerbach)
See *Geschichte der neueren Philosophie von Bacon von Verulam bis Benedict Spinoza*
History of Mr. Fantom the New-Fashioned Philosopher (More) **27**:342, 344
"History of My Botanical Studies" (Goethe) **4**:208
History of My Religious Opinions (Newman)
See *Apologia pro Vita Sua: Being a Reply to a Pamphlet Entitled "What, Then, Does Dr Newman Mean?"*
History of Napolean (Blake) **127**:264
A History of New York, for Schools (Dunlap) **2**:210
A History of New York, from the Beginning of the World to the End of the Dutch Dynasty (Irving) **2**:367, 369, 373, 375-81, 385, 388-92; **19**:348-49; **95**:225-26, 230, 274-75, 278
The History of Ottar Jarl, Norwegian Pirate (Gobineau)
See *L'histoire d'Ottar Jarl, pirate norvégien, conquérant du pays de Bray, en Normandie, et de sa descendance*
The History of Our Lord (Jameson) **43**:324, 327
History of Painting (Stendhal)
See *Histoire de la peinture en Italie*
The History of Pendennis: His Fortunes and Misfortunes, His Friends and His Greatest Enemy (Thackeray) **5**:449-50, 453-54, 459-61, 464, 471-72, 474, 477-78, 464, 471, 472, 474, 477, 478, 483-84, 486-90, 492, 497-98, 500, 503-05; **14**:418, 422; **43**:349, 356, 359, 389
History of Perez del Pilgar (Martínez de la Rosa)
See *Hernán Pérez del Pulgar*
"The History of Perourou; or, The Bellows-Mender; Written by Himself" (Williams) **135**:260, 303, 335
History of Peter the Cruel (Mérimée)
See *Histoire de Don Pédre Ier, roi de Castille*
The History of Philosophy (Lewes)
See *A Biographical History of Philosophy*
History of Philosophy from Bacon to Spinoza (Feuerbach)
See *Geschichte der neueren Philosophie von Bacon von Verulam bis Benedict Spinoza*
History of Portugal (Southey) **8**:469; **97**:283, 289
"The History of Primitive Christianity" (Engels) **85**:6
A History of Pugačev (Pushkin) **83**:295
History of Rome (Arnold) **18**:37, 54
The History of Samuel Titmarsh and the Great Hoggarty Diamond (Thackeray)
See *The Great Hoggarty Diamond*
The History of Scotland (Scott) **15**:277; **110**:288, 305
History of South Carolina (Simms) **3**:504
A History of the American Theatre (Dunlap) **2**:208, 210-11, 213-15, 217-18
The History of the Carrils and Ormes (Brown) **74**:7, 50
History of the Commonwealth of England (Godwin) **14**:48
History of the Condition of Women in Various Ages and Nations (Child) **6**:204; **73**:50, 59, 72, 76, 97
History of the Conspiracy of Pontiac, and the War of the North American Tribes against the English Colonies after the Conquest of Canada (Parkman) **12**:330-31, 333, 336, 338-39, 341-42, 348, 351-52, 369
History of the Constituent Assembly (Lamartine)
See *Histoire des constituents*
"History of the English Language" (Whitman) **81**:292
History of the Four Movements (Fourier)
See *Théorie des quatre mouvements*
History of the French Revolution (Michelet)
See *Histoire de la Révolution Française*
History of the French Revolution of 1848 (Lamartine)
See *Histoire de la révolution de 1848*
History of the German Language (Grimm and Grimm) **3**:217, 220
History of the Girondists; or, Personal Memoirs of the Patriots of the French Revolution (Lamartine)
See *Histoire des girondins*
History of the Grandeur and Downfall of César Birotteau (Balzac)
See *Histoire de la grandeur et de la décadence de César Birotteau, parfumeur*
History of the Italian Revolution (Fuller) **5**:165
A History of the Life and Voyages of Christopher Columbus (Irving) **2**:371, 387; **95**:223, 225, 228-34, 255, 259
History of the Manor of Goryukhino (Pushkin) **3**:435
History of the Middle Ages (Michelet) **31**:259
History of the Monastic Orders (Southey) **8**:469
History of the Navy of the United States of America (Cooper) **1**:202
History of the Nineteenth Century (Michelet)
See *Histoire de XIXème siècle*
History of the Peace (Martineau)
See *The History of England during the Thirty Years' Peace, 1816-46*
History of the Peninsular War (Southey) **8**:459, 463; **97**:250, 264, 269, 283, 299, 332
History of the People of Israel (Renan)
See *Histoire du peuple d'Israël*
History of the Persians (Gobineau)
See *Histoire des perses*
A History of the Protestant "Reformation"in England and Ireland (Cobbett) **49**:110, 114, 116, 154-55, 157
The History of the Pugachev Rebellion (Pushkin) **3**:436; **83**:275
History of the Renaissance (Michelet) **31**:211, 245-47
The History of the Revolt of the Netherlands (Schiller) **39**:378
A History of the Rise and Progress of the Arts of Design in the United States (Dunlap) **2**:209-10, 214-15
History of the Rise, Progress, and Termination of the American Revolution: Interspersed with Biographical and Moral Observations (Warren) **13**:411-13, 415, 419-20, 422-27, 431-37
History of the Russian State (Karamzin) **3**:279-83, 287, 291-92
History of the Thirty Years' Peace (Martineau)
See *The History of England during the Thirty Years' Peace, 1816-46*
History of the United States, to Which is Prefixed a Brief Historical Account of Our English Ancestors, from the Dispersion at Babel, to Their Migration to America, and of the Conquest of South America, by the Spaniards (Webster) **30**:421
History of the University and Colleges of Cambridge (Dyer) **129**:115-16
A History of the Village Goryukhino (Pushkin)
See *Istoriia sela Goriukhino*
History of the War (Richardson)
See *War of 1812*
"The History of the Young Men" (Brontë) **109**:34-5, 44, 47
History of Turkey (Lamartine) **11**:260
"Historyk" (Norwid) **17**:373
"Hit és tudás" (Madach) **19**:369
"L'Hiver qui vient" (Laforgue) **5**:279; **53**:299-300, 302
"Hjertesorg" (Andersen) **79**:76
Hobart the Hired Boy (Alger) **8**:24
Hobomok: A Tale of Early Times (Child) **6**:196-97, 199-200, 204-05, 207-08; **73**:39, 50, 57-8, 64-5, 74-5, 111-16, 118, 123, 126
Der Hochwald (Stifter) **41**:336, 342, 356, 379, 385
Die Hochzeit des Mönchs (Meyer) **81**:164, 181-82, 193-94, 198-99
Hodge and his Masters (Jefferies) **47**:98, 109-12, 121, 133, 137, 142
"Hohenlinden" (Campbell) **19**:165, 168-69, 171, 178-79, 181, 185, 187-90, 192-96
Hohenstaufen I: Kaiser Friedrich Barbarossa (Grabbe) **2**:272, 275-76, 281, 284-85
Hohenstaufen II: Kaiser Heinrich der Sechste (Grabbe) **2**:275-76, 281, 284-85
A hóhér kötele (Petofi) **21**:284
"Die Höheren Stufen" (Klopstock) **11**:239
Hojas al viento (Casal) **131**:236
"Hojas Secas" (Bécquer) **106**:129
Hokousaï (Goncourt) **7**:163
Hold Your Tongue (Planché) **42**:293
"Holger Danske" (Andersen) **7**:29
"A Holiday at Gwerndovennant" (Wordsworth) **138**:229
A Holiday Dream—Before Dinner (Ostrovsky)
See *Prazdnichny son—do obeda*
Holiday Peak, and Other Tales (Clarke) **19**:236, 249-51
"Holiness" (Emerson) **98**:160
"Holion" (Hebbel) **43**:237, 252
"Holland" (Fromentin) **10**:232
Holland-Tide; or, Munster Popular Tales (Griffin) **7**:194, 201, 211-12, 216-17
Höllenangst (Nestroy) **42**:231, 235, 246, 260
"The Hollow Land" (Morris) **4**:424, 430
"The Hollow of the Three Hills" (Hawthorne) **2**:327; **23**:204; **95**:95
"Hollow-Sounding and Mysterious" (Rossetti) **2**:576
"The Holly Tree" (Southey) **8**:472, 474; **97**:271
"L'holocauste" (Leconte de Lisle) **29**:225
"Holy Baptism" (Keble) **87**:153
The Holy Cross, and Other Tales (Field) **3**:206-08
"Holy Cross Day" (Browning) **19**:79, 98, 116
The Holy Family (Engels)
See *Die heilige Familie, oder Kritik der kritischen Kritik: Gegen Bruno Bauer und Consorten*
The Holy Family (Marx)
See *Die heilige Familie, oder Kritik der kritischen Kritik: Gegen Bruno Bauer und Consorten*
The Holy Genofeva (Tieck)
See *Leben und Tod der heiligen Genoveva*
"The Holy Grail" (Tennyson) **30**:228, 249, 254, 279, 282, 284, 292; **65**:237, 241-2, 245, 247, 250, 256, 270, 280-2, 284, 287, 295-6, 299, 314-5, 317-8, 320, 323, 333, 352, 361-2, 376, 385
"The Holy Night Has Risen into the Firmament" (Tyutchev)
See "Svyataya noch na nebosklon vzoshla"
"Holy Russia" (Adams) **33**:18
"Holy Thursday" (Blake) **13**:182, 219-21, 241; **37**:3-4, 7, 11, 14, 25, 30-1, 36-7, 40, 42, 46-7, 49-50, 57, 62-4, 66, 69-72, 76, 78, 82, 92, 94
"El hombre de las muletas de níquel" (Casal) **131**:264
"Hombre del campo" (Martí) **63**:88

"El hombre menguado" (Larra) **130**:193-94
"El hombre propone y Dios dispone, o lo que ha de ser el periodista" (Larra) **130**:194, 201
"Un hombre y una musa" (Castro) **3**:106
"El hombre-globo" (Larra) **17**:282
Hombres (Verlaine) **51**:352, 363
Los hombres de bien (Tamayo y Baus) **1**:569
"Home" (Nekrasov) **11**:407, 421
Home (Robertson) **35**:335, 369
Home (Sedgwick) **19**:435, 440, 443, 447
Home as Found (Cooper) **1**:216-17, 220; **54**:255-6, 275, 288
"Home at Grasmere" (Wordsworth) **111**:243, 370
Home Ballads and Poems (Whittier) **8**:492, 495-96; **59**:356, 371
"Home in Grasmere" (Wordsworth) **38**:362
"Home in War Time" (Dobell) **43**:48
"Home of an Early Friend" (Sigourney) **87**:320
The Home; or, Family Cares and Family Joys (Bremer)
See *Hemmet; eller, Familje-sorger och fröjder*
Home Pastorals, Ballads and Lyrics (Taylor) **89**:315
"Home-Rule Mystery" (Carroll) **139**:67
"Home Sweet Home" (Castro)
See "Miña casiña"
"Home Thoughts, From Abroad" (Browning) **79**:94, 98, 163
Homecoming (Heine)
See *Die Heimkehr*
Homegoing from the Theatre (Gogol)
See *Teatral'nyi raz'ezd posle predstavleniia novoi komedii*
"Homeland" (Nekrasov)
See "Rodina"
"Homeopathy and Its Kindred Delusions" (Holmes) **81**:101, 108
"Homeopathy vs. Allopathy" (Holmes) **14**:111
"Homer. Ossian. Chaucer." (Thoreau) **138**:121, 126
Homeric Ballads (Maginn) **8**:434-35, 439-40
Homer's Iliad and Odyssey (Cowper) **8**:119, 121
Homes Abroad (Martineau) **137**:273
The Homes of England (Hemans) **29**:204-05; **71**:278
The Homes of the New World: Impressions of America (Bremer)
See *Hemmen i den nya verlden: En dagbok i bref, skrifna under tvenne års resor i Norra Amerika och på Cuba*
"Homesick in Heaven" (Holmes) **81**:104
"Homesickness" (Mörike) **10**:446
"The Homestead" (Lanier) **6**:260; **118**:218, 230, 235
"Homeward bound on Easter Eve. . ." (Pushkin) **83**:272
Homeward Bound; or, The Chase (Cooper) **1**:201, 208, 217, 221; **54**:256, 276, 288
Homicide (Baillie) **2**:40-41
Hommage à Wagner (Mallarmé) **41**:280
"L'homme" (Lamartine) **11**:245, 264, 269, 273, 282
"L'homme à la cervelle d'or" (Daudet) **1**:249
L'homme à trois visages; ou, Le proscrit de Venise (Pixérécourt) **39**:272-74, 276-77, 279, 284, 286, 293-94
L'homme de bien (Augier) **31**:4, 10, 12, 14, 18, 23
L'homme de neige (Sand) **42**:312; **57**:313, 316
"L'Homme et la mer" (Baudelaire) **55**:53, 58, 62, 65
"L'homme juste" (Rimbaud) **4**:465, 485
L'homme qui rit (Hugo) **3**:249-50, 252-53, 260, 267
L'homme-femme: Résponse à M. Henri d'Ideville (Dumas) **9**:221, 234, 244
"L'Homme-fille" (Maupassant) **83**:189, 193, 195
Les hommes de lettres (Goncourt and Goncourt) **7**:162, 165-67, 181-82, 186, 188-89
"Homo" (Patmore) **9**:363
"The Honest Man" (Shaw) **15**:335
"Honeysuckle" (Allingham) **25**:14
"The Honeysuckle" (Rossetti) **4**:491
Les honnêtes femmes (Becque) **3**:15-16
Honneur d'Artiste (Feuillet) **45**:92-93
Honorine (Balzac) **5**:83-84
"Honours" (Ingelow) **39**:255-57
"Hood's Isle and the Hermit Oberlus" (Melville) **3**:362
Hood's Own (Hood) **16**:204, 214, 217, 219, 229, 231
"Hooking Watermelons" (Bellamy) **4**:30; **86**:75
"Hope" (Clare) **86**:160
"Hope" (Cowper) **8**:105, 115, 120; **94**:26, 29-30
Hope (Bowles) **103**:56, 69
Hope (Cowper) **94**:55-60
"Hope against Hope" (Patmore) **9**:328
"Hope A-Left Behind" (Barnes) **75**:7
"Hope Dieth: Love Liveth" (Morris) **4**:421
Hope Leslie; or, Early Times in the Massachusetts (Sedgwick) **19**:427-29, 433, 439, 442-43, 447-53; **98**:296-301, 306-11, 321-22, 326-30, 334, 339=51, 355-57, 359-60, 363-65, 367-72, 374-77, 381
The Hope of a Family (Daudet)
See *Soutien de famille*
"Hope of Liberty" (Horton)
See "The Hope of Liberty. Containing a Number of Poetical Pieces."
"The Hope of Liberty. Containing a Number of Poetical Pieces." (Horton) **87**:83-6
Hope of Liberty. Containing a Number of Poetical Pieces. (Horton) **87**:94, 99-101, 104, 108-11
"Hopelessness" (Baratynsky)
See "Beznadeznost'"
"Hop-Frog" (Poe) **16**:312, 324; **117**:300
"Hoping Against Hope" (Rossetti) **50**:288
"Hora tras hora, dia, tras dia" (Castro) **78**:41
Horace (Sand) **2**:589; **57**:361
Horace and Petrarch (Coleridge) **90**:25,
Horace Chase (Woolson) **82**:275, 277, 280, 293, 299, 319-20, 324
Horace Walpoe (Macaulay) **42**:87
"Horae Germanicae" (Lockhart) **6**:293
"Horas de invierno" (Larra) **17**:276, 283-84; **130**:209, 238, 278
Horatius (Macaulay) **42**:111, 154
"Horia" (Eminescu) **33**:245
"Le horla" (Maupassant) **1**:449, 453-55, 57, 462-63, 471-72; **83**:218-19, 222
"L'horloge" (Baudelaire) **29**:104; **55**:28, 67
"The Horn" (Vigny)
See "Le cor"
"The Horn of Egremont Castle" (Wordsworth) **12**:395
Horn of Oberon: Jean Paul Richter's School for Aesthetics (Jean Paul)
See *Vorschule der Aesthetik: Nebst einigen Vorlesungen in Leipzig über die Parte ien der Zeit*
Hornby Mills (Kingsley) **107**:192
"Horologe of the Fields, addressed to a Young Lady, on seeing at the house of an acquaintance a magnificent French Time-piece" (Smith) **115**:119
"L'horreur sympathique" (Baudelaire) **29**:85; **55**:13, 65
"A Horse Ride at Dawn" (Eminescu) **131**:330
The Horseman's Manual (Surtees) **14**:350
The Horses of Lysippus (Coleridge) **90**:14
Horse-Shoe Robinson: A Tale of the Tory Ascendancy (Kennedy) **2**:428-33, 435
Horsztyński (Slowacki) **15**:352, 364, 371, 378, 380
"Hortensia Antomarchi" (Isaacs) **70**:308
"Horton" (Smith) **59**:321, 332, 336
"Horus" (Nerval) **1**:480, 484, 486; **67**:307
"Hospita on Immoderate Indulgence of the Pleasures of the Palate" (Lamb) **10**:409, 411; **113**:236-39
"The Hospital" (Lermontov) **126**:223
"A Hospital Christmas" (Alcott) **83**:7
Hospital Sketches (Alcott) **6**:12-13; **58**:17, 46, 48-9, 67; **83**:8, 34, 78
"Das Hospiz auf dem Groszen Sankt Bernhard" (Droste-Hülshoff) **3**:195-96, 199, 201
The Host (Grillparzer)
See *Der Gastfreund*
"Hot and Cold" (Hazlitt) **29**:156
"An Hour" (Alcott) **83**:7
"The Hour and the Ghost" (Rossetti) **2**:557, 563
The Hour and the Man (Martineau) **26**:310-11, 314, 323, 329; **137**:252, 259
"The Hour of Death" (Le Fanu) **9**:302
"The Hour of Death" (Hemans) **29**:205-06
"The Hour of Feeling" (Bryant) **46**:55
"An Hour of Romance" (Hemans) **29**:194
An Hour of Thought (Slowacki)
See *Godzina myśli*
"Hours Continuing Long" (Whitman) **81**:332
"An Hour's Musings on the Atlantic" (Brontë) **109**:30
Hours of Idleness (Byron) **2**:58, 62, 77, 88, 103; **12**:138
Hours of Life, and Other Poems (Whitman) **19**:455, 457
"Hours of Spring" (Jefferies) **47**:102, 138, 143
"An Hour's Talk on Poetry" (Wilson) **5**:552, 558
"House" (Browning) **19**:87, 96, 110
"The House Amidst the Thickets" (Ueda Akinari)
See "Asaji ga yado"
"The House and the Vineyard" (Lamartine)
See "La vigne et la maison"
The House at Kolomna (Pushkin) **83**:277
"The House Beautiful" (Stevenson) **5**:401
The House by the Churchyard (Le Fanu) **9**:300-03, 308-12, 315-17; **58**:251, 256, 266-8, 278, 281, 283, 285
A House Divided against Itself (Oliphant) **11**:460, 462; **61**:204-5, 211
"House Divided" Speech (Lincoln) **18**:208, 238, 280
"A House in the Blue Ridge" (Cooke) **5**:133
"The House in the Reeds" (Ueda Akinari)
See "Asaji ga yado"
The House Maid (Martineau) **26**:322
"The House of Clouds" (Browning) **1**:115
A House of Gentlefolk (Turgenev)
See *Dvoryanskoe gnezdo*
"The House of Heine Brothers, in Munich" (Trollope) **101**:235
"The House of Life" (Rossetti) **4**:490, 496-97, 499-503, 507-10, 512, 514-18, 526-29, 531; **77**:308, 312, 326, 329, 333, 337-40, 348, 353, 355, 358, 361
"The House of Night" (Freneau) **1**:314, 316, 318-19, 323; **111**:80, 82, 107, 140, 143, 151-52, 184
The House of the Dead; or, Prison Life in Siberia (Dostoevsky)
See *Zapiski iz mertvogo doma*
The House of the Seven Gables (Hawthorne) **2**:298-99, 302-03, 305-06, 309-10, 312, 314-17, 320-21, 324-27, 329, 332; **17**:112, 114, 116-17, 130-32, 147, 149, 150; **23**:168-69, 183, 192, 202, 205, 209, 213; **39**:165-252; **79**:295, 304; **95**:109-10, 116
"The House of the Wolfings" (Morris) **4**:435-38, 440
"The House of Titian" (Jameson) **43**:323
"The House of Usher" (Poe)
See "The Fall of the House of Usher"
The House on the Moor (Oliphant) **11**:432
"The House upon the Hearth" (Lewis) **11**:303

"The House with the Green Blinds" (Stevenson) **5**:393
Household Book of the Earl of Northumberland in 1512 (Percy) **95**:313, 327-28
Household Education (Martineau) **26**:311, 329, 331, 342-43, 346-48; **137**:237, 247, 277, 282, 285, 321, 333, 349-52
Household Tales (Grimm and Grimm)
See *Kinder-und Hausmärchen*
"The Household Wreck" (De Quincey) **4**:83
"The Householder" (Browning) **19**:96
The Housekeeper (Jerrold) **2**:401
"Housekeeping in Belgravia" (Mayhew) **31**:181
"House-Martins" (Jefferies) **47**:138
"House-Warming" (Thoreau) **7**:398
"The Houstonia" (Very) **9**:372
"The How and the Why" (Tennyson) **30**:204
"How Are You?" (Foscolo)
See "Che stai?"
"How Celia Changed Her Mind" (Cooke) **110**:33-4, 36, 44, 46, 50-1, 65
"How Celia Changed Her Mind" and Other Stories (Cooke) **110**:50-1, 62
"How gently it rained" (Castro)
See "Cómo llovía, suaviño"
How He Won Her (Southworth) **26**:434, 446
"How Husbands May Rule" (Parton) **86**:349
"How I Learned to Celebrate" (Leskov) **25**:247
"How I Look" (Parton) **86**:376
"How I Overcame My Gravity" (O'Brien) **21**:236, 252-53
"How I Read the Morning Papers" (Parton) **86**:366
"How I Went Out to Service" (Alcott) **58**:11
"How Is It?" (Parton) **86**:351
"How It Happened" (O'Brien) **21**:245
"How It Strikes a Contemporary" (Browning) **19**:79, 132, 139; **79**:175-76
"How Lisa Loved the King" (Eliot) **4**:108; **13**:334
"How Long?" (Lazarus) **8**:413, 417, 420; **109**:295
"How Long?" (Very) **9**:386
"How Love Looked for Hell" (Lanier) **6**:249; **118**:217, 267
"How Many a Time, Beloved . . ." (Eminescu) **131**:332
"How Many Bards" (Keats) **73**:256
"How Many Times These Low Feet Staggered" (Dickinson) **21**:9, 38, 41
"How Mr. Storm Met His Destiny" (Boyesen) **135**:12-13, 27
"How Nellie Lee Was Pawned" (O'Brien) **21**:245
"How Off Has the Banshee Cried" (Moore) **6**:391; **110**:184
"How One Muzhik Fed Two Generals" (Saltykov)
See "Povest' o tom, kak odin muzhik dvukh generalov prokormil"
"How She Found Out" (Cooke) **110**:35
"How Solemn as One by One" (Whitman) **81**:314
"How sweetly slumbers the dark green garden" (Tyutchev)
See "Kak sladko dremlet sad temnozelenyi"
"How the Bell Rang, July 4, 1776" (O'Brien) **21**:247
"How the Change Came" (Morris) **4**:440
"How the Melbourne Cup Was Won" (Kendall) **12**:183
"How the Nightingale and the Parrot Wooed the Rose" (Crawford) **127**:181-84, 186, 188
"How the Old Horse Won the Bet" (Holmes) **14**:109, 115, 128
"How the Women Went from Dover" (Whittier) **8**:529
"How They Brought the Good News from Ghent to Aix" (Browning) **19**:88; **79**:94, 164
"How to be Happy" (Sigourney) **87**:321
"How to Cook Soup upon a Sausage Pin" (Andersen) **7**:28, 37
How to Observe Morals and Manners (Martineau) **26**:322, 333-34; **137**:241, 302, 317, 331, 343, 348-49, 351, 353, 358
"How to Pick Out a Dog" (Shaw) **15**:335
"How to Pick Out a Horse" (Shaw) **15**:335
"How to Read Chaucer" (Lanier) **118**:218
"How to Think in Love of Those Who Passed Away" (Kierkegaard) **34**:198
"How to Write a Blackwood Article" (Poe) **16**:322-23; **55**:134; **117**:322
"How unexpectedly and brightly" (Tyutchev)
See "Kak neozhidanno i yarko"
"How We Beat the Favourite" (Gordon) **21**:149, 151, 154-59, 161, 165, 170, 175-76, 181, 188
"How We Come to Give Ourselves False Testimonials and Believe in Them" (Eliot) **118**:118
"How Weary! How Mournful!" (Lermontov)
See *I skuchno! I grustno!*
"How Willie Coasted by Moonlight" (Cranch) **115**:58
"How Woman Loves" (Parton) **86**:349
"Howe's Masquerade" (Hawthorne) **2**:292-93
"However heavy the final hour may be" (Tyutchev)
See "Kak ni tyazhel posledniy chas"
"Howling Song of Al-Mohara" (Mangan) **27**:285, 292, 295, 298
Hoze hezyonot (Mapu) **18**:292, 301
"Hubert" (Patmore) **9**:326
Huckleberries Gathered from New England Hills (Cooke) **110**:19, 33-7, 39, 43-4, 50
The Hue and Cry (Inchbald) **62**:144-6
Hugh and Ion (Crawford) **12**:169, 174; **127**:161, 163-67, 169, 218, 222-28
Hugh Trevor (Holcroft)
See *The Adventures of Hugh Trevor*
"Hugo" (Slowacki) **15**:348-49
Hugo, the Deformed (Alger) **8**:42; **83**:96
Les Huguenots (Scribe) **16**:390, 398, 401, 408-09
Huit Femmes (Desbordes-Valmore) **97**:12
"The Human Abstract" (Blake) **13**:221, 224, 226, 240, 242-43; **37**:4, 25, 33, 44-5, 47, 49, 52-3, 92
"Human Applause" (Hölderlin)
See "Menschenbeifall"
The Human Comedy (Balzac)
See *La Comédie humaine*
"Human Frailty" (Cowper) **94**:102
Human Happiness (Holcroft) **85**:192, 215, 234
"The Human Lad" (Field) **3**:210
"Human Life" (Arnold) **6**:50; **89**:88, 98
Human Life (Rogers) **69**:69-70, 74
"Human Repetends" (Clarke) **19**:251
"Human Responsibility as Independent of Circumstances" (Newman) **38**:307
"Human Sacrifice" (Whittier) **8**:485, 512
"The Human Wheel" (Holmes) **81**:124-30
"Human Work" (Silva)
See "Obra humana"
"L'humanitè" (Lamartine) **11**:255, 270, 279
"Humble drame" (Maupassant) **83**:209
"A Humble Remonstrance" (Stevenson) **63**:239, 258, 260
"The Humble-Bee" (Emerson) **1**:289, 296
"The Humboldt Desert" (Ridge) **82**:185
"Humboldt River" (Ridge) **82**:185
"Humboldt's Birthday" (Holmes) **81**:102
Hume, With Helps to the Study of Berkeley (Huxley) **67**:13, 27, 93-5
The Humiliated and the Wronged (Dostoevsky)
See *The Insulted and Injured*
"The Humiliation of the Eternal Son" (Newman) **38**:305
Humilis Domus: Some Thoughts on the Abodes, Life and Social Conditions of the Poor, Especially in Dorsetshire (Barnes) **75**:57-8, 102, 106
"The Humming Bird" (Cranch) **115**:40
"Humphrey and William" (Southey) **97**:314-15
"Hun duede ikke" (Andersen) **79**:72
The Hunchback of Notre-Dame (Hugo)
See *Notre-Dame de Paris*
The Hundred and One (Faustino) **123**:268
"The Hungarian Nation" (Petofi)
See "A magyar nemzet"
"The Hungarian Nobleman" (Petofi)
See "A magyar nemes"
Hungary's Decline and Maria of Austria (Sacher-Masoch) **31**:290
"A Hungry Day" (Crawford) **127**:217
"Hunt after my Captain" (Holmes) **14**:118
The Hunt for Happiness (Adams) **33**:19
"The Hunt of Eildon" (Hogg) **4**:283, 285
Hunt of Eildon (Hogg) **109**:233
"Hunter of Comar" (Hogg) **109**:203
"The Hunter of the Prairies" (Bryant) **6**:169, 172
"The Hunters of Men" (Whittier) **8**:489, 510, 526
"The Hunter's Serenade" (Bryant) **6**:169; **46**:20
Hunter's Sketches (Turgenev)
See *Zapiski okhotnika*
"The Hunter's Twain" (Crawford) **127**:164
The Hunters Twain (Crawford)
See *Hugh and Ion*
"Hunter's Vision" (Bryant) **46**:4, 28
The Hunting of the Snark: An Agony in Eight Fits (Carroll) **2**:106, 117; **53**:40-2, 55-6, 84-5, 107, 109-10, 112, 116; **139**:5-15, 19, 29, 31-32, 35, 38, 40-41, 50, 65, 80, 120, 123-25, 128, 139
Hunting Seat (Almqvist) **42**:17
"Les hurleurs" (Leconte de Lisle) **29**:210, 215, 217, 230
"Hurrahing in Harvest" (Hopkins) **17**:208, 211, 217
"The Hurricane" (Bryant) **6**:159, 161, 176; **46**:6, 20, 28, 47
"The Hurricane" (Freneau) **1**:323; **111**:105, 147-48, 150, 154, 178-81
Husband and Wife (Fredro)
See *Mąż i żona*
"The Husbandman" (Rossetti) **77**:353
"The Husband's and Wife's Grave" (Dana) **53**:158, 168
"Hushaby Song" (Field) **3**:212
"Hussens Kerker" (Meyer) **81**:140-41, 143, 149-50, 155
"The Hut by the Black Swamp" (Kendall) **12**:181-83, 194, 201
"The Hut by the Tanks" (Adams) **33**:13
"Huttens letze Tage" (Meyer) **81**:140-41, 146, 148-49, 152, 156, 164
Hvad Christus dömmer om officiel Christendom (Kierkegaard) **34**:196, 200, 225, 266; **78**:226, 238; **125**:234
"Hvad gamle Johanne fotalte" (Andersen) **79**:74
Hwomely Rhymes. A Second Collection of Poems in the Dorset Dialect (Barnes) **75**:18, 40, 69, 79
"The Hwomestead a-Vell Into Hand" (Barnes) **75**:102
"Hyazinth and Rosenblüte" (Novalis) **13**:393
"Hy-Brasil" (Kendall) **12**:183, 187, 199
Hydrozoa (Huxley) **67**:4
The Hyena of the Poussta (Sacher-Masoch) **31**:298, 301
"Hylas" (Taylor) **89**:358
"Hymen and Hirco: A Vision" (Sheridan) **91**:230
"Hymn" (Emerson) **98**:177, 182
"Hymn" (Lanier) **118**:259
"Hymn before Sunrise in the Vale of Chamouni" (Coleridge) **9**:148; **99**:36, 81
"Hymn by T.P. at school" (Percy) **95**:337

"Hymn for Pentecost" (Mangan) **27**:296
"Hymn II" (Barbauld) **50**:8
Hymn in Honor of the Plague (Pushkin) **3**:434, 449
Hymn No. VIII (Cowper)
See "O Lord, I Will Praise Thee"
Hymn No. IX (Cowper)
See "The Contrite Heart"
Hymn No. 11 (Cowper)
See "Jehovah Our Righteousness"
Hymn No. V8 (Cowper)
See "The New Convert"
Hymn No. VI7 (Cowper)
See "I will praise the Lord at all times"
"Hymn of Apollo" (Shelley) **18**:345, 360, 362
"Hymn of Death" (Lamartine)
See "Hymne de la mort"
"Hymn of Evening in the Temples" (Lamartine) **11**:248
"Hymn of Pan" (Shelley) **18**:327
"Hymn of Praise" (Kendall) **12**:183, 192
"Hymn of the Fishermen" (Ferguson) **33**:290
"Hymn of the Morning" (Lamartine)
See "L'hymne du matin"
"A Hymn of the Sea" (Bryant) **6**:168; **46**:6, 9
"Hymn of the Waldenses" (Bryant) **6**:159
"Hymn of Trust" (Holmes) **81**:100
"Hymn on Prosperity" (Darwin) **106**:185
"Hymn to Air" (Taylor) **89**:304
"Hymn to Beauty" (Baudelaire)
See "Hymne à la beauté"
"Hymn to Charity" (Hale) **75**:343
"Hymn to Death" (Bryant) **6**:159-60, 168, 170, 172, 177, 183; **46**:3, 9, 15, 21, 23
"Hymn to Death" (Whitman) **31**:432
"Hymn to Intellectual Beauty" (Shelley) **18**:331, 341, 361, 364, 376; **93**:262
"Hymn to Intllectual Beauty" (Browning) **79**:113
"Hymn to Liberty" (Solomos)
See "Hymnos eis ten Eleutherian"
"Hymn to Mercury" (Shelley) **18**:363
"Hymn to Mont Blanc" (Coleridge) **9**:144
"Hymn to Pan" (Keats) **8**:344; **73**:198, 204, 218, 280; **121**:141-42, 146-47
"Hymn to the Earth" (Coleridge) **99**:4
"Hymn to the Moon" (Hogg) **109**:248
"Hymn to the Mother of God" (Slowacki) **15**:349
"Hymn to the Night" (Longfellow) **2**:492; **45**:115, 146, 151, 184
Hymn to the Ship of the Muses (Foscolo) **97**:52
"Hymn to the Sun" (Darley) **2**:131
"Hymn to the Sun" (Hood) **16**:208, 221
"A Hymn Yet Not a Hymn" (Clough) **27**:46
"Hymne à la beauté" (Baudelaire) **6**:123, 128; **29**:97-8; **55**:64-6, 73
"L'hymne à la douleur" (Lamartine) **11**:265, 270, 279
"Hymne an den Genius Griechenlands" (Hölderlin) **16**:174
"Die Hymne an den Unendlichen" (Schiller) **39**:339
"Hymne an die Göttin der Harmonie" (Hölderlin) **16**:173
"Hymne au Christ" (Lamartine) **11**:279
"L'hymne au soleil" (Lamartine) **11**:269
"Hymne de la mort" (Lamartine) **11**:248, 279
"L'hymne de la nuit" (Lamartine) **11**:270
"Hymne de l'enfant" (Lamartine) **11**:279
"L'hymne du matin" (Lamartine) **11**:248, 270, 283
"La hymne du soir dans les temples" (Lamartine) **11**:265, 270, 279
Hymnen an die Nacht (Novalis) **13**:360, 362-63, 365, 367, 374, 376-79, 390-92, 394, 397, 401-02, 405
"Hymnos eis ten Eleutherian" (Solomos) **15**:386-90, 392, 403-04
"Hymns for the Kirk" (Baillie) **2**:41
Hymns in Prose for Children (Barbauld) **50**:6-9
"Hymns of the City" (Bryant) **6**:161; **46**:55
"Hymns of the Marshes" (Lanier) **6**:238, 240, 247, 249, 264, 273; **118**:204, 240
Hymns to the Night (Novalis)
See *Hymnen an die Nacht*
Hynde (Hogg)
See *Queen Hynde*
Hypatia; or, New Foes with Old Faces (Kingsley) **35**:209, 215-16, 218-20, 222, 224, 226, 228-36, 241-44, 249, 252, 255-56
"Hypatie" (Leconte de Lisle) **29**:213, 223, 238, 240
"Hypatie et Cyrille" (Leconte de Lisle) **29**:240
Hyperboräische Esel (Kotzebue) **25**:138
"Hyperion" (Eminescu)
See "Luceafarul"
Hyperion (Hölderlin) **16**:158, 161, 164-65, 172-74, 176-77, 182-83, 185-87, 190-91
Hyperion (Keats) **8**:328-29, 331, 333-34, 336, 340-41, 345-47, 350, 352-53, 355-56, 358-59, 361-63, 365-68, 381-83, 385-86; **73**:144, 153-54, 159-61, 170-72, 177-78, 181-82, 192, 204, 209, 254-55, 259, 261, 263, 294-95, 328-30, 337-39; **121**:95-239
Hyperion (Longfellow) **2**:469-70, 474, 480, 489-90, 494; **45**:103, 181, 183-84; **103**:284-86
Hyperion: A Fragment (Keats) **121**:173, 205, 212
"Hyperions Schicksalslied" (Hölderlin) **16**:173-74, 176, 181, 184
"The Hypnotizers" (Bakunin) **58**:131
Hypochondria (Tegner)
See *Mjältsjukan*
"Hypochondriacus" (Lamb) **10**:389
"Hypocrite lecteur" (Baudelaire)
See "Au lecteur"
"Hyrdinden og Skorsteensfeieren" (Andersen) **79**:70-1
"i a probina qu'esta xorda" (Castro) **78**:2, 7
"I Am" (Clare) **9**:90, 100, 103, 105; **86**:87, 114, 153, 170
"I Am a Parcel of Vain Strivings Tied" (Thoreau) **7**:383
"I Am Ashamed—I Hide" (Dickinson) **21**:57
"I Am Here Again under Protection of the Roof" (Pavlova)
See "La snova zdes' pod sen'iu krova"
"I Am Not the Man I Used to Be" (Foscolo)
See "Non son chi fui"
"I Am Pleading for My People" (Truth) **94**:332
"I Am the Autumnal Sun" (Thoreau) **7**:384
"I Am the Little Irish Boy" (Thoreau) **7**:384
"I Am Weary, Let Me Go" (Gordon) **21**:160-61
"I and My Chimney" (Melville) **3**:354, 380-81, 383; **12**:303; **93**:188
"I and the Dog" (Barnes) **75**:36
"I Can Wade Grief" (Dickinson) **21**:64
"I Cannot Dance upon My Toes" (Dickinson) **21**:82; **77**:130
"I Cannot Forget with What Fervid Devotion" (Bryant) **6**:177; **46**:38
"I cannot live with You" (Dickinson) **77**:96
"I cannot love thee" (Norton) **47**:238
"I Commend You" (Rossetti) **66**:307
"I Could Not Be up to You" (Eminescu) **33**:265
"I det grø onne" (Wergeland) **5**:541
"I Died for Beauty" (Dickinson) **21**:43; **77**:119
"I Dream of Bloody Days" (Petofi)
See "Véres napokról álmodom"
"I Dream'd in a Dream" (Whitman) **31**:394; **81**:328, 331
"I Dreamed a Dream" (Clough) **27**:103
"I Dreamt Last Night" (Brontë) **4**:45
"I drink alone" (Pushkin) **83**:373
"I Felt a Funeral in My Brain" (Dickinson) **21**:64; **77**:76
"I Give Thee Joy! O Worthy Word" (Clough) **27**:103
"I Got So I Could Take His Name" (Dickinson) **21**:64
"I Got Two Vields" (Barnes) **75**:101
"I Grew up in a Foreign Land" (Shevchenko)
See "I vyris ya na chyzhyni"
"I gynaika tis Zakynthos" (Solomos) **15**:393, 396-97
"I Had a Dove" (Keats) **8**:360
"I Had a Guinea Golden" (Dickinson) **21**:15
"I had been hungry, all the Years" (Dickinson) **77**:148
"I Had No Time to Hate" (Dickinson) **21**:42
"I have a Cottage" (Boker) **125**:7
"I Have No Need of the Hoarfrost" (Arany)
See "Nem kell dér"
"I Hear It Was Charged against Me" (Whitman) **31**:430
"I heard a Fly buzz—when I died—" (Dickinson) **77**:156, 163
"I Heard an Angel Singing" (Blake) **37**:38
"I Held a Jewel in My Fingers" (Dickinson) **21**:64
"I Hide Myself within My Flower" (Dickinson) **21**:8, 69
"I Knew a Man by Sight" (Thoreau) **7**:383
"I know not why, but all this weary day" (Timrod) **25**:366
"I know that He exists" (Dickinson) **77**:77
"I Laid Me Down upon a Bank" (Blake) **13**:181
"I Lay the Lute Down" (Arany)
See "Leteszem a lantot"
"I like a look of Agony" (Dickinson) **21**:9, 42; **77**:162
"I like to see it lap the Miles—" (Dickinson) **21**:49; **77**:129
"I Lost the Love of Heaven" (Clare) **9**:101
"I Love the Jocund Dance" (Blake) **37**:35
"I love you, goddesses of song" (Baratynsky)
See "Liubliu ia vas, bogini pen'ia"
"I Love You, My Sweet" (Petofi)
See "Szeretlek, kedvesem"
"I Loving Freedom for Herself" (Tennyson) **30**:294
"I mertvym i zyvym i nenarodzenym zemljakam mojim v Ukrajini i ne v Ukrajini moje druznjeje poslanije" (Shevchenko)
See "Poslaniie"
"I Never Lost as Much but Twice" (Dickinson) **21**:63
"I Never Told the Buried Gold" (Dickinson) **21**:54
"Den i noch" (Tyutchev) **34**:396-97
I pitocchi fortunati (Gozzi) **23**:107, 113, 119, 121, 123, 125-26
I pochi (Alfieri) **101**:45,73
"I Poetic" (Alfieri) **101**:32
I Racconti delle fate (Collodi) **54**:143, 144-7
"I Remember, I Remember" (Hood) **16**:219, 233, 237
"I Rose Because He Sank" (Dickinson) **21**:43, 67
"I Saw A Boy" (Barnes) **75**:70
"I Saw a Monk of Charlemaine" (Blake) **13**:243
"I Saw from the Beach" (Moore) **6**:389, 396
"I Saw Her Once" (Mangan) **27**:298
"I Saw in Louisiana a Live-Oak Growing" (Whitman) **31**:379, 392; **81**:364
"I Saw No Way—The Heavens Were Stitched" (Dickinson) **21**:76, 83
"I Saw Old General at Bay" (Whitman) **81**:319
"I Saw Thee on Thy Bridal Day" (Poe)
See "Song"
I Say No (Collins) **1**:188, 191
"I See around Me Tombstones Grey" (Brontë) **16**:98
"I should have been to glad, I see-" (Cantor) **77**:84
"I Sing the Body Electric" (Whitman) **4**:571-72; **31**:372, 404, 425, 430; **81**:311, 342, 358-59
"I sit thoughtful and alone" (Tyutchev)
See "Sizhu zadumchiv i odin"
I skuchno! I grustno! (Lermontov) **5**:287
"I Sonnet" (Corbière) **43**:32

"I Started Early—Took My Dog" (Dickinson) **21**:79; **77**:148
"Les i step" (Turgenev) **122**:264
"I Stood on Tiptoe" (Keats)
See "I Stood Tip-Toe"
"I Stood Tip-Toe" (Keats) **8**:343, 364; **73**:158, 213, 225-26, 259, 267, 322
"I Taste a Liquor Never Brewed" (Dickinson) **21**:37, 41, 65; **77**:93
"I thank my God because my hairs are grey!" (Coleridge) **90**:27
"I think the Hemlock likes to stand" (Dickinson) **77**:67
"I Think to Live May Be a Bliss" (Dickinson) **21**:80
"I Thought of Thee, My Partner and My Guide" (Wordsworth) **12**:466
"I Thought That Knowledge Alone Would Suffice" (Whitman) **81**:332
"I tie my Hat" (Dickinson) **77**:103, 105
"I traduttori e le traduzioni" (Collodi) **54**:143
"I travelled among unknown men" (Wordsworth) **111**:323
I troppi (Alfieri) **101**:45, 73
"I Visited Thy Tomb" (Nekrasov) **11**:404
"I vyris ya na chyzhyni" (Shevchenko) **54**:394
"I Wake and Feel the Fell of Dark, Not Day" (Hopkins) **17**:242, 261-62
"I Wandered Lonely as a Cloud" (Wordsworth) **12**:456, 463; **111**:323
"I watched the Moon around the House" (Dickinson) **77**:121
"I will praise the Lord at all times" (Cowper) **94**:69, 75
"I wish I were where Helen lies" (Fuller) **50**:243, 245
"I Would I Knew the Lady of Thy Heart" (Kemble) **18**:181
"Ib and Little Christine" (Andersen) **7**:29, 32; **79**:82
"Ibo" (Hugo) **3**:263
"Icarus" (Taylor) **89**:310
"The Ice Maiden" (Andersen)
See "Iisjomfruen"
The Ice-Island (Bird) **1**:87
"Ich schnitt' es gern in alle Rinden ein" (Muller) **73**:381
"Ich strafe die Bosheit" (Gotthelf) **117**:58
"Ich wandle wieder durch die Waldesspitze" (Meyer) **81**:147
"Ichabod" (Whittier) **8**:490, 495, 500, 509-10, 513, 515, 520-22, 526, 530-31; **59**:357, 360, 368-73
"Ichneumon" (Taylor) **89**:311
"The Icon in its Frame" (Eminescu) **131**:286
Icons Old and New (Eminescu) **131**:313
"Ida Grey" (Levy) **59**:106
"Idea for a Rational Catechism for Noble Ladies" (Schleiermacher) **107**:395
Idea for a Universal History with a Cosmopolitan Purpose (Kant) **27**:237; **67**:222
The Idea of a University, Defined and Illustrated (Newman) **38**:286, 294, 296, 302, 307, 323, 342, 344-45; **99**:210-17, 248, 266, 278, 296, 298
"Idea of the Human Soul" (Freneau) **111**:132
"L'idéal" (Baudelaire) **6**:123; **29**:97-8; **55**:31, 58
"The Ideal" (Baudelaire)
See "L'idéal"
"The Ideal and Life" (Schiller)
See "Das Ideal und das Leben"
The Ideal in Art (Taine) **15**:469
"Das Ideal und das Leben" (Schiller) **39**:332, 337, 370
"Ideal Women" (Linton) **41**:164
"Ideale" (Schiller)
See "Das Ideal und das Leben"
"Ideale der Menschheit" (Hölderlin) **16**:175
"An Idealistic Flounder" (Saltykov) **16**:358
Ideas (Kierkegaard) **78**:122
Ideas (Schlegel)
See *Ideen*
Ideas, 129a (Schlegel) **45**:343
Ideas, 135 (Schlegel) **45**:343
Ideas for a Philosophy of Nature (Schelling)
See *Ideen zu einer Philosophie der Natur*
Idée sur les romans (Sade) **3**:468-69; **47**:312, 346
Ideen (Schlegel) **45**:342-43, 363, 382
Ideen, Das Buch Le Grand (Heine) **4**:250-1, 259, 266, 317; **54**:317, 331, 336, 338-9
Ideen zu einem Versuch, die Grenzen der Wirksamkeit des Staats zu bestimmen (Humboldt) **134**:164, 170, 177, 184, 192, 202
Ideen zu einer Philosophie der Natur (Schelling) **30**:125, 165, 171-75
Ideen zur Geschichte und Kritik der Poesie und bildenden Künste (Herder) **8**:307, 313
Ideen zur Philosophie der Geschichte der Menschheit (Herder) **8**:299-301, 303, 309-12
Ideen zur Philosophie der Geschichte der Menschheit (Humboldt) **134**:208
Les idées de Madame Aubray (Dumas) **9**:220, 225, 228, 235, 241-43, 249-51
"Les Idées du Colonel" (Maupassant) **83**:181, 194
Idées et sensations (Goncourt and Goncourt) **7**:152
"The Identity of Thought with Nature" (Emerson) **98**:7
"Ideological Analysis of the Tenses of the Spanish Conjugation" (Bello) **131**:120
Ideolus (Baudelaire) **6**:119
"Idilio" (Silva) **114**:263
The Idiot (Dostoevsky) **2**:162, 164, 167-69, 171, 175, 180, 187, 199, 202-04; **7**:103; **21**:90, 94, 102, 108-09, 112-13, 115, 121, 140, 142, 144; **33**:165, 179, 199, 212; **43**:91, 98, 134, 167; **119**:64-167
"The Idiot Boy" (Wordsworth) **12**:386-87, 402, 445-46, 451; **111**:200, 202-3, 223, 225-26, 245, 248, 293, 305-7, 313, 316, 348, 367-68
"Idiots Again" (Martineau) **26**:349
The Idle Man (Dana) **53**:160, 167, 174, 177
"The Idle Shepherd-boys" (Wordsworth) **111**:235
"The Idler" (Very) **9**:383
"L'idole: sonnet du trou du cul" (Rimbaud) **35**:291
Idris und Zenide (Wieland) **17**:410-12
"Idyl from Lake Constance" (Mörike) **10**:456
Idyll och epigram (Runeberg) **41**:309, 317, 320-21
"Idylle" (Chamisso) **82**:27-29
"Idylle coupée" (Corbière) **43**:33
L'idylle rue Plumet (Hugo) **3**:246
Idylle von Bodensee; oder, Fischer Martin und die Glockendiebe (Mörike) **10**:447, 449-50, 452
Idylles Prussiennes (Banville) **9**:16, 24, 30
Idyllia heroica (Landor) **14**:181, 190, 204
"Idylls of the King" (Tennyson) **115**:235
Idylls of the King (Tennyson) **30**:216-18, 220, 233, 242, 249, 252-54, 258, 265, 267, 269-70, 274, 276, 279-82, 287, 292-93, 295; **65**:223-390; **115**:269, 275, 309, 341
Idyls and Epigrams (Runeberg)
See *Idyll och epigram*
Idyls of Norway and Other Poems (Boyesen) **135**:8-10, 47
"If Ever I See" (Hale) **75**:279, 286
"If I Can Stop One Heart from Breaking" (Dickinson) **21**:37
"If I Drive at Night through the Dark Street" (Nekrasov) **11**:409
"If I Had" (Eminescu) **131**:330-32
"If I Were Dead" (Patmore) **9**:343, 349, 358
"If Life Be Final" (Cranch) **115**:18
"If Thou Sayest, Behold, We Knew It Not" (Rossetti) **2**:577
"If Thou Wilt Ease Thine Heart" (Beddoes) **3**:34
"If You Come to My Field" (Isaacs)
See "Si vienes a mi campo"
"If You Only Knew Lords" (Shevchenko)
See "Yak by vy znaly panychi"
"If You Speak, I'll Pretend Deafness . . ." (Eminescu) **33**:257
"If You Were Coming in the Fall" (Dickinson) **21**:7, 75
Igitur (Mallarmé) **4**:383, 385-86, 392; **41**:232-34, 237-39, 249, 271, 275, 286, 300
Igrok (Dostoevsky) **2**:188; **43**:92; **119**:147, 156
Igroki (Gogol) **5**:231, 239, 256; **15**:84, 98, 104
"Ihr hörtet von dem Zwerge argem Sinnen" (Preseren) **127**:313
"Iisjomfruen" (Andersen) **7**:29, 32; **79**:28, 32, 58, 70-71, 82-84, 88-89
"Ikävyys" (Kivi) **30**:51
"Il Balen" (Lanier) **118**:243
Il burbero di buon cuore (Da Ponte) **50**:78
Il Cinque di Maggio (Manzoni)
See *Il cinque maggio*
"Il cinque maggio" (Manzoni) **98**:204, 211, 220, 223, 245
Il cinque maggio (Manzoni) **29**:263, 299; **98**:201, 213
"Il Copernico" (Leopardi) **129**:320, 351
Il corvo (Gozzi) **23**:107, 112-13, 119, 121, 123, 125
Il dissoluto punito o sia il Don Giovanni (Da Ponte) **50**:76, 80-6, 88-94, 96, 98
Il faut qu'une porte soit ouvertr ou fermée (Musset) **7**:259, 262, 268, 271-72, 275
Il filosofo punito (Da Ponte) **50**:80
Il mostro turchino (Gozzi) **23**:108, 119, 121, 123, 125-26
Il ne faut jurer de rien (Musset) **7**:259, 268, 270-72, 275
"Il nome di Maria" (Manzoni) **29**:253
"Il Parini" (Leopardi) **129**:305
"Il Passero Solitario" (Leopardi) **129**:220, 229, 249, 339, 341
Il pasticcio (Da Ponte) **50**:82
Il pastor fido (Da Ponte) **50**:82
Il penseroso (Amiel) **4**:15, 19
"Il pleure dans mon coeur" (Verlaine) **2**:631; **51**:351, 355, 384
"Il Ponte del Paradiso" (Symonds) **34**:355
Il re cervo (Gozzi) **23**:107, 112-14, 119, 123, 125-26
Il ricco d' un qiorno (Da Ponte) **50**:77-8
"Il Risorgimento" (Leopardi) **129**:218, 330, 358
"Il sabato del villaggio" (Leopardi) **129**:219, 229, 243, 339, 341
Il tramonto della luna (Leopardi) **129**:220
"Il viccolo di Madama Lucrezia" (Mérimée) **6**:366, 369-70; **65**:47, 52, 57-61, 98, 118, 133, 135
The Ilau (Sacher-Masoch) **31**:295
Ildikó (Arany) **34**:8
The Iliad (Hunt) **1**:411
The Iliad of Homer (Bryant) **6**:166
Ilius Goethes Briefwechsel mit einem Kinde: Seinem Denkmal (Arnim)
See *Goethes Briefwechsel mit einem Kinde: Seinem Denkmal*
Ilius Pamphilius und die Ambrosia (Arnim) **38**:15; **123**:5, 8
Ilka on the Hill-Top (Boyesen) **135**:13
Ilka on the Hill-Top and Other Stories (Boyesen) **135**:13, 27, 30
"I'll Tell Thee All—How Blank It Grew" (Dickinson) **21**:38
I'll Tell You What (Inchbald) **62**:143, 146, 148
"Illa Creek" (Kendall) **12**:179, 181, 186
"The Illuminated City" (Hemans) **71**:277
Illumination (Frederic)
See *The Damnation of Theron Ware*
Les illuminations (Rimbaud) **4**:453-55, 457, 459-63, 465-66, 468, 470-74, 476-77, 479-80, 482-83, 487; **35**:269-72, 275, 278,291, 293-94, 304, 310-312, 320, 321-26; **82**:218-

19, 223-27, 23 0-33, 237, 240-43, 247-48, 250-51, 253, 255, 262-63
Illuminations (Rimbaud)
See *Les illuminations*
"Les illuminés; ou, Les précurseurs de socialisme" (Nerval) **1**:476, 485; **67**:357, 371
The Ill-Used Giant, Being a new and true version of "Jack and the Beanstalk" (Horne) **127**:266
"L'illusion suprême" (Leconte de Lisle) **29**:214, 217-18, 224, 234-36
"Illusions" (Emerson) **1**:295, 300; **98**:89, 101, 186, 191
Illusions perdues (Balzac) **5**:39, 43, 45, 49, 63, 72, 75, 80; **35**:20, 51, 60; **53**:8
Illustrated Excursions in Italy (Lear) **3**:295
Illustrated Poems (Sigourney) **21**:297; **87**:321
Illustrations of Lying (Opie) **65**:204
Illustrations of Political Economy (Martineau) **26**:303, 309-10, 329-30, 334-35, 337-39, 341, 348, 351, 355; **137**:236, 239-40, 245, 250-51, 256, 259-60, 262-63, 266, 270, 272, 276, 280, 302, 304, 309, 315, 324, 330, 336, 356-58
Illustrations of Taxation (Martineau) **137**:250
"Illustrations on Sublimity" (Beattie)
See *Dissertations Moral and Critical: On Memory and Imagination; On Dreaming; The Theory of Language; On Fable and Romance; On the Attachments of Kindred; Illustrations on Sublimity*
"L'illustre Gaudissart" (Balzac) **35**:11
"L'illustre magicien" (Gobineau) **17**:69, 92, 104
"The Illustrious Gaudissart" (Balzac)
See "L'illustre Gaudissart"
"The Illustrious Magician" (Gobineau)
See "L'illustre magicien"
"I'm ceded, I've stopped being theirs" (Dickinson) **77**:143, 153
"Im Dorfe" (Muller) **73**:390-92
"Im Grase" (Droste-Hülshoff) **3**:200
"Im Krug zum grünen Kranze" (Muller) **73**:379-81, 383
"Im Mai" (Heine) **4**:256
"Im Moose" (Droste-Hülshoff) **3**:196
Im Nachbarhause links (Storm) **1**:540
"I'm Nobody! Who Are You?" (Dickinson) **21**:71
Im Saal (Storm) **1**:539
Im Schloss (Storm) **1**:540
Im Sonnenschein (Storm) **1**:539
"Im Spätboot" (Meyer) **81**:199, 201-02
"Im Veltlin" (Meyer) **81**:150
"I'm 'Wife'—I've Finished That" (Dickinson) **21**:64
"L'Image dans l'eau" (Desbordes-Valmore) **97**:27
"The Image in Lava" (Hemans) **71**:276, 304-05, 307
"The Image in the Heart" (Hemans) **71**:303
L'imagier de Harlem (Nerval) **67**:340
Imaginary Conversations (Landor) **14**:158-59, 162, 165-66, 168, 170-73, 176, 180, 184, 186, 191-95, 201-02, 206-08, 210
An Imaginary Portrait (Pater) **7**:296, 298-99, 303-04, 307, 312, 317, 323-24, 341; **90**:242, 248, 336, 338, 340
"Imaginary Portrait. The Child in the House" (Pater) **90**:263-4, 272, 276, 290-4, 333, 336-8, 340, 345
Imaginary Portraits (Pater)
See *An Imaginary Portrait*
"Imagination" (Beattie)
See *Dissertations Moral and Critical: On Memory and Imagination; On Dreaming; The Theory of Language; On Fable and Romance; On the Attachments of Kindred; Illustrations on Sublimity*
"Imagination" (Emerson) **1**:282
Imagination and Fancy; or, Selections from the English Poets...and an Essay in Answer to the Question "What Is Poetry?" (Hunt) **1**:417-20
"Imelda of Bologna" (Sedgwick) **19**:445
L'imitation de Notre-Dame la lune (Laforgue) **5**:275-8, 283; **53**:256-7, 259, 263, 278-9, 287-8, 290-1
Imitation Ermine (Sacher-Masoch) **31**:290
"Imitation of boileau's First Satire" (Bestuzhev)
See "Podrazhaniye pervoy satire Bualo"
"An Imitation of Dr. Watts" (Field) **3**:211
"Imitation of Spenser" (Keats) **8**:342; **73**:151, 158, 328
"Imitations from the German" (Harpur) **114**:144
Imitations of the Koran (Pushkin) **83**:282
"The Immediate Erotic Stages" (Kierkegaard) **125**:182, 185, 187, 193, 198, 201, 203, 205-8, 210, 212-13, 247-48, 255-56
Immensee (Storm) **1**:535-39, 545-46, 550
"The Immortal" (Very) **9**:385
"The Immortal Golovan" (Leskov)
See "Nesmertel' nyj Golovan"
"Immortal Ode" (Wordsworth) **38**:368
"The Immortal Ones" (Isaacs)
See "Los immortales"
"Immortale jecur" (Hugo) **10**:357
"Los immortales" (Isaacs) **70**:313
"L'immortalité" (Lamartine) **11**:269-70, 272, 278, 282
"Immortality" (Allston) **2**:26
"Immortality" (Lamartine)
See "L'immortalité"
"Immortality Ode" (Wordsworth)
See "Ode: Intimations of Immortality from Recollections of Early Childhood"
"The Immortality of the Soul" (Newman) **38**:304-05
L'immortel (Daudet) **1**:237, 239, 244, 249, 251
"The Imp" (Baratynsky)
See "Besyonok"
"The Imp of the Perverse" (Poe) **1**:500-01, 518; **16**:301, 331-32; **78**:260, 278, 281, 284-86, 298-99
"Împarat şi proletar" (Eminescu) **33**:245, 250
The Impasse (Leskov)
See *Nekuda*
"Imperfect Sympathies" (Lamb) **10**:410-11, 413, 424-25, 435; **113**:164, 199, 202, 217, 219, 235, 243, 247, 250
"Imperfect Thoughts" (Fuller) **5**:169
"El imperio chimila" (Isaacs) **70**:311
The Impertinents (Augier)
See *Les éffrontés*
Impetus philosophicus (Claudius) **75**:190
"Implicit and Explicit Reason" (Newman) **38**:307
"Implora Pace" (Cooke) **110**:9
"Implora Pace" (Taylor) **89**:294
"The Importance of a Man to Himself" (Smith) **59**:303, 309, 316, 322-3
Important Considerations (Cobbett) **49**:164
"L'Impossible" (Desbordes-Valmore) **97**:5-6, 22
"L'Impossible" (Laforgue) **53**:270, 289
"L'impossible" (Rimbaud) **4**:466; **35**:271, 303-04, 313, 319; **82**:229, 235, 237-38, 241, 250, 253, 260, 262
"Impotens" (Levy) **59**:96, 98
Impressions de voyage (Dumas) **11**:48, 52, 62-64, 90; **71**:185
Impressions de voyage: De Paris à Cadix (Dumas)
See *Impressions de voyage*
Impressions de voyage: Suisse (Dumas)
See *Impressions de voyage*
Impressions of Theophrastus Such (Eliot) **4**:110, 152; **23**:73
"L'imprévu" (Baudelaire) **6**:109; **55**:2
"Impromptu" (Pavlova)
See "Ékspromt"
"Impromptu, upon Leaving Some Friends" (Moore) **110**:177
"Improvements Suggested in Female Education" (Hays) **114**:256
"Improvisation" (Taylor) **89**:319
"Improvisation V" (Taylor) **89**:319
"Improvisation VIII" (Taylor) **89**:318
Improvisations (Taylor) **89**:318
"The Improvisatore" (Beddoes) **3**:33
The Improvisatore, in Three Fyttes, with Other Poems (Beddoes) **3**:28, 32, 36, 38
The Improvisatore; or, Life in Italy (Andersen) **7**:14-16, 19, 24; **79**:48, 79-80
The Improvisatrice, and Other Poems (Landon) **15**:154-56, 158, 160-61, 165, 168
"In a Balcony" (Browning) **19**:79, 131
"In a Battle" (Schiller) **39**:336
"In a Bye-Canal" (Melville) **3**:352, 363
"In a Drear-Nighted December" (Keats) **8**:360
"In a Garden" (Allingham) **25**:14
In a Glass Darkly (Le Fanu) **9**:302, 308, 312, 315, 317, 320-21, 323; **58**:252, 254-7, 264, 301-2
"In a Gondola" (Browning) **19**:93, 130-31
"In a Lecture-Room" (Clough) **27**:105
"In a Minor Key" (Levy) **59**:96
"In a Neat Cottage" (Crabbe) **26**:139; **121**:12
In a New World; or, Among the Gold-Fields of Australia (Alger) **8**:17, 40, 44-45
"In a Swedish Graveyard" (Lazarus) **109**:294
"In a World of Darkness" (Eminescu) **131**:287
"In a Year" (Browning) **19**:127
"In Absence" (Lanier) **118**:215, 259
"In an Artist's Studio" (Rossetti) **66**:350
"In Behalf of My Country" (Isaacs)
See "Pro patria"
"In Cabin'd Ships at Sea" (Whitman) **31**:387-88
"In Carey's Footsteps" (Ferguson) **33**:289
In Congress, July 4, 1776: A Declaration by the Representatives of the United States of America, in General Congress Assembled (Jefferson) **11**:137, 139-57, 159, 162-66, 169-70, 172-79, 184-85, 189, 193-96, 198-203, 205, 207, 209-10; **103**:103-04, 106, 108, 115, 122, 125-29, 144, 163, 168-72, 183, 189, 193, 201, 206, 209-10, 241, 249-50, 252-53, 255, 259-63
"In Crowds of People, in the Hurly-burly of the Day" (Tyutchev) **34**:389
"In das Femdenbuch de Thalhofes zu Reichenau" (Raimund) **69**:13
"In days of boundless enthusiasms..." (Baratynsky)
See "V dni bezgranichnykh uvlecheniy..."
"In deserto" (Gautier) **1**:350
"In Ev'ry Dream Thy Lovely Features Rise" (Barnes) **75**:70
"In excelsis" (Leconte de Lisle) **29**:228, 235
"In Exile" (Lazarus) **109**:335, 338
"In Falling Timbers Buried" (Dickinson) **21**:43
"In Gastein again" (Grillparzer)
See "Noch einmal in Gastein"
"In Harbor" (Hayne) **94**:149 167-68
"In Harmony with Nature" (Arnold) **6**:55; **29**:34
"In Him We Live" (Very) **9**:378, 381, 384-85
"In Love with a Marble" (Eminescu) **131**:330-31
In malayischer Form (Chamisso) **82**:27
"In May" (Lampman) **25**:172
"In Memoriam" (Lazarus) **8**:413, 417
"In Memoriam" (Tennyson) **115**:235-41, 313, 318
In Memoriam (Tennyson) **30**:213, 220, 223-24, 226-28, 230, 233, 235-36, 238-43, 245-46, 255-62, 267, 269, 271-77, 279-80, 282-83, 287, 293; **65**:231, 234-5, 240-1, 248-9, 257, 267, 271, 277, 279-80, 282, 334, 348, 358, 375; **115**:231-381
"In Memory of a Happy Day in February" (Brontë) **4**:46; **71**:165-66
"In Memory of A. I. Odoevsky" (Lermontov) **126**:143-44
"In Memory of My Mother" (Opie) **65**:182

"In Memory of Széchenyi" (Arany)
See "Széchenyi emlékezete"
"In Memory of V.A. Zhukovsky" (Tyutchev)
See "Pamyati V.A. Zhukovskogo"
In morte del Carlo Imbonati (Manzoni) **98**:247
In morte del fratello Giovanni (Foscolo) **97**:62, 67
"In My Own Album" (Lamb) **10**:405
"In November" (Lampman) **25**:171, 193-94, 199, 210
"In October" (Lampman) **25**:171, 192, 204
"In Our Abode in Arby Wood" (Barnes) **75**:54
"In Our Forest of the Past" (Thomson) **18**:394, 427
In Parallel (Verlaine)
See *Parallèlement*
"In Paths Untrodden" (Whitman) **31**:393; **81**:328
"In Praise of Poetry" (Ueda Akinari) **131**:52
"In Prison" (Morris) **4**:423, 444
"In Progress" (Rossetti) **2**:573; **50**:286, 293
"In School-Days" (Whittier) **8**:513, 517, 522
"In Search of the Earth's Peace" (Eminescu) **33**:264
In Search of Treasure (Alger) **8**:43
"In September" (Levy) **59**:90
"In shades obscure and gloomy warmd to sing" (Clare) **86**:173
In Spain (Andersen) **7**:19; **79**:79
In St. Jürgen (Storm) **1**:536, 540, 543
"In Summer-Time" (Jefferies) **47**:93
In Sweden (Andersen) **79**:80
In Switzerland (Slowacki) **15**:348-49, 353-54, 358-59, 364
"In Tenderness To Me Whom Thou Didst Spurn" (Barnes) **75**:70
"In the Bazaar at Smyrna" (Taylor) **89**:357
"In the Beginning of 1812" (Pushkin) **83**:320
"In the Black Forest" (Levy) **59**:93
"In the Bleak Mid-Winter" (Rossetti) **50**:312
"In the Breast of a Maple" (Crawford) **12**:169-70
"In the Canadian Woods" (Traill) **31**:329
"In the cathedral" (Castro)
See "N'a catredal"
"In the Churchyard at Cambridge" (Longfellow) **45**:125
"In the Corner of a Small Sqaaure" (Pushkin) **83**:315-18
"In the Cotton Country" (Woolson) **82**:273, 302, 305, 339-40, 343
"In the Desert" (Melville) **29**:375
"In the Duckyard" (Andersen) **7**:37
"In the Dumps" (Parton) **86**:366
"In the Foam" (Lanier) **118**:215
"In the Garden" (Arany)
See "Kertben"
"In the Garden at Swainston" (Tennyson) **115**:341
"In the Glooming Light" (Tennyson) **30**:211
"In the Great Metropolis" (Clough) **27**:103, 114
"In the Hammock" (Cooke) **110**:51
"In the Hedge I pass a little nest" (Clare) **86**:145
"In the Hospital" (Cooke) **110**:9
"In the Jewish Synagogue at Newport" (Lazarus) **8**:417, 422, 424-25; **109**:296, 302, 324, 332, 336, 342
In the Key of Blue (Symonds) **34**:343, 352-53
"In the Market" (Arany)
See "Vásárban"
"In the Meadows" (Taylor) **89**:307
"In the Mile End Road" (Levy) **59**:96, 119
"In the Pine Groves" (Lampman) **25**:209
"In the Room" (Thomson) **18**:397, 403, 405, 407, 418, 420, 423
"In the Round Tower at Jhansi, June 8, 1857" (Rossetti) **66**:371, 377
"In the Same Old Lane" (Eminescu) **131**:296
In the Sixties (Frederic) **10**:187-88
"In the Spring" (Barnes) **75**:21
"In the Stillness o'Night" (Barnes) **75**:71
"In the Teutoburger Forest" (Taylor) **89**:313
In the Valley (Frederic) **10**:183-84, 187-88, 190, 192-93, 201, 203-04, 207, 210-11, 213
"In the Valley of Cauteretz" (Tennyson) **30**:280; **115**:341
"In the Valley of Humiliation" (Thomson) **18**:425
"In the Valley of the Elwy" (Hopkins) **17**:220
"In the village" (Tyutchev)
See "V derevne"
"In the Wilds" (Lampman) **25**:172, 190, 218
"In Three Days" (Browning) **19**:127
"In Torture" (Isaacs)
See "En la tortura"
"In Trafalgar Square" (Adams) **33**:4
In Trust (Oliphant) **61**:203
"In Utrumque Paratus" (Gordon) **21**:159, 164
"In Venice" (Woolson) **82**:289-91, 341
"In Vino Veritas" (Kierkegaard) **125**:184, 267
In War Time, and Other Poems (Whittier) **8**:493-94
"In Winter" (Taylor) **89**:309
"In Winter in my Room" (Dickinson) **77**:148
"In winter, when the fields are white" (Carroll) **139**:39
"Inaugural Lecture on the Study of Modern History" (Arnold) **18**:54
"L'incantation du loup" (Leconte de Lisle) **29**:225, 230, 237
"The Incarnate Son, a Sufferer and Sacrifice" (Newman) **38**:305
"The Inca's Daughter" (Whitman) **81**:343, 345
"The Incendiary" (Rowson) **69**:129
"The Inch Cape Rock" (Southey) **8**:474
"An Incident in a Railroad Car" (Lowell) **2**:522; **90**:194
"Incident of the French Comp" (Browning) **79**:164
Incidents in the Life of a Slave Girl, Written by Herself (Jacobs) **67**:119-22, 124-27, 130, 135-36, 138-41, 143, 145-48, 150-51, 153, 159, 163-64, 166, 170-76, 178-80, 183, 187-88, 191-93, 196-97
Incidents of the Insurrection in the Western Parts of Pennsylvania in the Year 1794 (Brackenridge) **7**:48, 55-56
"Inclusions" (Browning) **16**:135-6
"L'Inconnue" (Maupassant) **83**:182, 201
"L'inconnue" (Villiers de l'Isle Adam) **3**:590
"Inconstancy of the Populace" (Webster) **30**:424
Les Inconvénients de la vie de Paris (Staël-Holstein) **91**:358
"Incubus" (Grillparzer) **102**:174
"Independence" (Parton) **86**:353
"Independence Bell—July 4, 1776" (O'Brien)
See "How the Bell Rang, July 4, 1776"
"Independence of the Church" (Brownson) **50**:54
India, China, and Japan (Taylor) **89**:302, 355
"The Indian Bride" (Pinkney) **31**:268, 276, 281
"The Indian Burying-Ground" (Freneau)
See "Lines Occasioned by a Visit to an Old Indian Burying Ground"
"The Indian, City" (Hemans) **71**:275, 293
"The Indian Convert" (Freneau) **111**:104
"The Indian Fisherman's Light" (Moodie) **113**:347
"The Indian Girl's Lament" (Bryant) **6**:182; **46**:22
"The Indian Jugglers" (Hazlitt) **29**:167; **82**:90, 95, 97, 101
Indian Nullification of the Unconstitutional Laws of Massachusetts Relative to the Marshpee Tribe; or, the Pretended Riot Explained (Apess) **73**:7, 10, 12-14, 16, 27
"The Indian Spring" (Bryant) **6**:181
"Indian Story" (Bryant) **6**:161, 186; **46**:42
"Indian Student, or, Force of Nature" (Freneau) **1**:315; **111**:103
"Indian Summer" (Lampman) **25**:210
Indian Summer (Stifter)
See *Der Nachsommer*
"An Indian Summer Reverie" (Lowell) **2**:507; **90**:215
"The Indian With His Dead Child" (Hemans) **71**:279
"Indian Woman's Death-Song" (Hemans) **71**:274, 294
Indiana (Sand) **2**:581-85, 589, 598, 603, 605-07; **42**:306-09, 315-17, 320, 324, 328-29, 333, 337-42, 349, 351-54, 356-58, 364, 378-81, 383-89; **57**:308-11, 316, 318-20, 322-5, 327-30, 332-3, 335-9, 344, 348-50, 359, 363-7, 371, 374-81
Die Indianer in England (Kotzebue) **25**:145-47
"Der Indianerzug" (Lenau) **16**:269, 278, 284
"Indian's Tale" (Whittier) **8**:485
The Indians: The Ten Lost Tribes (Apess) **73**:15
"Indicaciones sobre la Conveniencia de Simplificar y Uniformar la Ortografía en América" (Bello) **131**:130
"Indications of Immortality" (Channing) **17**:54
The Indicator and the Companion: A Miscellany for the Fields and the Fireside (Hunt) **1**:412
Indira (Chatterji) **19**:209, 213, 217-19, 221-22, 224
"Individuality" (Lanier) **6**:238, 242; **118**:219-20
"The Individuality of the Soul" (Newman) **38**:304
"Indolence" (Keats)
See "Ode on Indolence"
"Indolence" (Thomson) **18**:401
"The Indolence of the Filipinos" (Rizal)
See "Sobre la indolencia de los Filipinos"
"The Indolent Monk" (Baudelaire)
See "Le mauvais moine"
"Les indolents" (Verlaine) **2**:624; **51**:379-80
"Indroducción" (Casal) **131**:269
"Indulgence in Religious Privileges" (Newman) **38**:304
"The Industrious Family" (Child) **73**:130-31,134
"Inebriety" (Crabbe) **121**:10
Inebriety (Crabbe) **26**:110-11, 146; **121**:81
"Ines de Castro" (Landor) **14**:161
Inès de las Sierras (Nodier) **19**:377, 384
Ines Mendo (Mérimée) **65**:46-7, 54, 59-60, 63, 79, 83
"The Inevitable Trial" (Holmes) **81**:102
"The Inexpressible" (Zhukovsky)
See "Nevyrazimoe"
The Infamy (Eminescu) **33**:266
"Infancy" (Crabbe) **121**:79
"Infant Joy" (Blake) **13**:182; **37**:6, 9, 13, 39, 41, 44, 57, 65, 71-2, 78, 84, 92, 95-6
"Infant Sorrow" (Blake) **13**:219-20, 242; **37**:11-12, 24, 33, 44, 53, 57, 75, 84, 96
The Infant with the Globe (Alarcon)
See *El niño de la bola*
"The Infant's Prayer" (Sigourney) **21**:299
The Infernal Marriage (Disraeli) **39**:3, 33, 52, 54-5, 75
Infernaliana (Nodier) **19**:378, 383
The Infidel; or, The Fall of Mexico (Bird) **1**:82-84, 86-87, 90
"L'infini dans les cieux" (Lamartine) **11**:265, 270
L'Infinito (Leopardi) **129**:217, 228, 232, 246, 263-64, 268-72, 305, 352-55, 357
The Inflexible Captive: A Tragedy (More) **27**:336
"Influence of Academies" (Arnold) **6**:47
"Influence of Time and Grief" (Bowles) **103**:58
Les Infortunes de la vertu (Sade)
See *Justine ou les malheurs de la vertu*
"Les ingénus" (Verlaine) **2**:624; **51**:378
The Ingoldsby Legends (Barham) **77**:4, 6, 8-12, 16-23, 25, 28-30, 32-34, 36-37, 39-41, 43-44
The Ingoldsby Lyrics (Barham) **77**:21, 28
The Ingoldsby Penance (Barham) **77**:10
"Ingvi and Alf" (Lampman) **25**:201

The Inheritance (Ferrier) **8**:236-40, 242-44, 246-56
The Inheritance (Smolenskin) **30**:189-90
The Inhibited Imaginatin (Raimund)
See *Die gesfesselte Phantasie*
"The Iniquity of the Fathers upon the Children" (Rossetti) **66**:329
"The Injured Tree" (Meyer)
See "Der verwundete Baum"
Injury and Insult (Dostoevsky)
See *The Insulted and Injured*
"The Inkpot" (Petofi)
See "A tintásüveg"
An Inland Voyage (Stevenson) **5**:386, 388, 390, 405, 410
"The Inn" (Turgenev) **21**:415, 418, 441, 453; **122**:241
The Inn Album (Browning) **19**:85-6, 106, 112
"The Inner Life of Art" (Lewes) **25**:294
"Inner Voices" (Hugo) **3**:261
Inni Sacri (Manzoni) **98**:203-04, 220, 228-29
Inno ai patriarchi (Leopardi) **129**:347
"Innocence" (Isaacs)
See "Inocencia"
"Innocent Child and Snow-White Flower" (Bryant) **46**:38
"Innocent Prudencij" (Leskov)
See "Nevinnyj Prudencij"
"Inns" (Crabbe) **26**:121
"Inocencia" (Isaacs) **70**:306
Inquiry (Kant) **27**:220-21
An Inquiry into the Nature of Subscription to the Thirty-Nine Articles (Dyer) **129**:100, 102, 106, 112, 115, 125-28, 136
The Inquisitor (Holcroft) **85**:198
The Inquisitor; or, Invisible Ramble (Rowson) **5**:309-10, 315-16, 321-22; **69**:103, 112, 122-28, 132, 141
"Insanity: A Fragment" (Brown) **74**:108
The Inscribed Firtree (Stifter)
See *De beschriebene Tännling*
"Inscription" (Whitman) **4**:589, 603
"Inscription for a Fountain on the Heath" (Coleridge) **99**:104
"Inscription for the Entrance into a Wood" (Bryant) **6**:158, 168-69, 176, 182-83, 187; **46**:22, 34, 45, 47, 55
"Inscription for the Monument of Dr. Small" (Darwin) **106**:183
"Inscription Written at the Request of Sir George Beaumont, Bart., and in His Name, for an Urn, Placed by Him at the Termination of a Newly-Planted Avenue, in the Same Grounds" (Wordsworth) **12**:445
"Inscriptions" (Mackenzie) **41**:184
Inscriptions (Southey) **8**:468; **97**:318
"The Insect" (Turgenev) **21**:451
The Insect (Michelet) **31**:215, 219, 242, 244-45, 247-48, 260-61, 263-64
"Insects" (Clare) **9**:85
"Insight" (Lampman) **25**:163
"Insomnia" (Isaacs)
See "Insomnio"
"Insomnia" (Thomson) **18**:394, 397, 400, 403, 405, 407, 409, 415, 417-20
"Insomnia" (Tyutchev)
See "Bessonnitsa"
"Insomnie" (Corbière) **43**:13, 34
"Insomnio" (Isaacs) **70**:313
"The Inspector General" (Gogol)
See *Révizor*
"Inspiration" (Emerson) **38**:149
"Inspiration" (Thoreau) **7**:383
"Inspiration Has Her Favorites" (Pavlova)
See "Est' liubimtsy vdokhnovenii"
"The Inspiration of Song" (Crawford) **12**:154, 161; **127**:202
The Inspired Version (Smith) **53**:391
"Instans Tyrannus" (Browning) **19**:115
The Instant (Kierkegaard)
See *Hvad Christus dömmer om officiel Christendom*
"Instinct and Inspiration" (Emerson) **98**:7-8
"Instinkt" (Droste-Hülshoff) **3**:193, 201
The Insulted and Injured (Dostoevsky) **2**:161; **7**:70, 75, 80, 82, 107; **33**:161-62, 165, 195, 203; **43**:92
"Intellect" (Emerson) **38**:173; **98**:20, 25, 144-47
"Intellect, the Instrument of Religious Training" (Newman) **38**:305
The Intellectual and Moral Reform of France (Renan)
See *La réforme intellectuelle et morale*
"Intellectual Wants of Greece" (Sigourney) **21**:311
"The Intelligence Officer" (Hawthorne) **2**:298
"The Intemperate" (Sigourney) **21**:290
"Inter Vias" (Lampman) **25**:204
"An Intercepted Letter to Dickens" (Kirkland) **85**:270
Intercepted Letters; or, The Two penny Post-Bag (Moore) **6**:382, 384, 388, 392, 395; **110**:171, 190
"L'interdiction" (Balzac) **35**:4
"The Interior of a Heart" (Hawthorne) **2**:327; **10**:297
"Intermède" (Banville) **9**:32
Das Intermezzo, oder Der Landjunker zum ersten Male in der Residenz (Kotzebue) **25**:147
"The International Working-Men's Movement" (Bakunin) **58**:134
"Interpreting Nature" (Very) **9**:388, 390
"An Interregnum" (Crawford) **127**:159, 163
"L'intersigne" (Villiers de l'Isle Adam) **3**:581
"The Interview" (Hawthorne) **10**:297
"Interviews with German Authors" (Taylor) **89**:308
Intimate Journal (Sand)
See *Le secrétaire intime*
Intimate Journals (Baudelaire)
See *Journaux intimes*
"The Intimations Ode" (Wordsworth)
See "Ode: Intimations of Immortality from Recollections of Early Childhood"
"Intimations of Immortality" (Wordsworth)
See "Ode: Intimations of Immortality from Recollections of Early Childhood"
Intimidades (Silva) **114**:310-11, 315-17, 319
"Into the Kitchen Door I Strolled" (Petofi)
See "Befordúltam a konyhára"
Intolerance (Moore) **110**:171
Intrigue and Love (Schiller)
See *Kabale und Liebe*
An Intrigue in a Hurry (Fredro)
See *Intryga na predce; czyli, Niema złego bez dobrego*
"Introducción a los elementos de física del dr. N. Arnott" (Bello) **131**:109
"Introducción sinfónica" (Bécquer) **106**:109, 113-14, 118, 120, 147-48, 167-69
"Introduction" (Blake) **13**:182, 191, 241-42; **37**:10, 13, 18, 20, 24, 31, 38, 41-2, 45, 47-9, 57, 65, 73, 92
Introduction à l'histoire universelle (Michelet) **31**:227, 246, 258
Introduction to the Dialectics of Nature (Engels) **85**:10
Introduction to the Principles of Morals and Legislation (Bentham) **38**:24-5, 38, 44, 48-56, 81-9
An Introduction to the Study of Dante (Symonds) **34**:351
Introduction to Universal History (Michelet)
See *Introduction à l'histoire universelle*
"Introductions to Wissenschaftslehre" (Fichte) **62**:4, 34
"Introductory Discourse" (Baillie) **71**:9, 28-29, 31-32, 65
Introductory Lectures Delivered at Queen's College, London (Kingsley) **35**:250
Introductory Lectures on Modern History (Arnold) **18**:12, 14, 29
"Introductory Sonnet" (Rossetti) **77**:359
Intryga na predce; czyli, Niema złego bez dobrego (Fredro) **8**:289
"The Intuitions of the Soul" (Very) **9**:388
"L'inutile beauté" (Maupassant) **1**:448, 459, 464, 468; **83**:177, 179, 223-24
Invariable Principles of Poetry (Bowles) **103**:63-4
The Invasion (Griffin) **7**:194, 197-201, 204, 212, 214, 218
Invectives (Verlaine) **2**:621; **51**:351
"Inventory of the Moon" (Zhukovsky)
See "Podrobnyi otchet o lune"
"Inversnaid" (Hopkins) **17**:191, 195
"Investigations" (Bello) **131**:123
The Invisible Brothers (Scribe)
See *Les frères invisibles*
The Invisible Lodge (Jean Paul)
See *Die Unsichtbare Loge*
The Invisible Man (Andersen) **79**:11, 17
The Invisible Prince (Planché) **42**:273, 288, 301
"The Invisible World" (Newman) **38**:282, 303-04
"The Invitation" (Clare) **86**:87
"The Invitation" (Freneau) **111**:105, 154-55
"The Invitation" (Shelley)
See "To Jane: The Invitation"
"Invitation and Reply" (Pinkney) **31**:279, 281
"L'invitation au voyage" (Baudelaire) **6**:87, 115, 118, 128; **29**:109; **55**:29, 61, 69
"Invitation to a Painter" (Allingham) **25**:21, 29
"An Invitation to the Country" (Bryant) **6**:165
"Invite to Eternity" (Clare) **9**:103; **86**:87-91
"Invocation" (Boker) **125**:81
"Invocation" (Hemans) **29**:205
"L'invocation" (Lamartine) **11**:269-70, 273, 277
"Invocation" (Lamartine)
See "L'invocation"
"Invocation to Misery" (Shelley) **18**:372
"The Inward Morning" (Thoreau) **7**:383
"Inward Morning" (Very) **9**:391
"Inward Pose" (Rossetti) **50**:298
"Inworld" (Cranch) **115**:35
"Ioan Eliad" (Eminescu) **131**:325
"Ion" (Alcott) **1**:25
Iphigenia in Tauris (Goethe)
See *Iphigenie auf Tauris*
Iphigenie auf Tauris (Goethe) **34**:90-119
"Ippolito di Este" (Landor) **14**:162
"¡Qué hace en Portugal su Majestad?" (Larra) **130**:201, 241, 243-44
"Ireland" (Lanier) **118**:218
"Ireland" (Martineau) **26**:305, 307, 309, 352
"Irené" (Lowell) **2**:502, 507
"Irenens Wiederkehr" (Grillparzer) **102**:192
Iridion (Krasiński) **4**:303-05, 307-14, 319
"Iris" (Holmes) **14**:109
Irish Anthology (Mangan) **27**:279
"The Irish Beneficed Clergyman" (Trollope) **101**:293-95
"Irish Catholicism and British Liberalism" (Arnold) **89**:101, 103; **126**:104
Irish Essays, and Others (Arnold) **6**:40
"The Irish Heart" (Child) **73**:80
The Irish Heiress (Boucicault) **41**:28, 40-1, 49
The Irish Melodies (Moore) **6**:383-84, 386-92, 394, 396-400; **110**:166, 168, 171, 181-87, 190-93, 195-96, 198, 203
"Irish National Hymn" (Mangan) **27**:296, 316
The Irish Post (Planché) **42**:278
"The Irish Schoolmaster" (Hood) **16**:234
The Irish Sketch Book (Thackeray) **5**:452, 482; **43**:349, 360, 380, 383, 386
Irish Songs and Poems (Allingham) **25**:12, 15, 16
"Irishman and the Lady" (Maginn) **8**:441
"The Iron Gate" (Holmes) **14**:116
"An Iron Will" (Leskov)
See "Železnaja volja"
"Iron World" (Smith) **59**:330

"Ironia" (Norwid) **17**:374
Irregular Stanzas (Wordsworth)
See "Irregular Verses"
"Irregular Verses" (Wordsworth) **25**:421; **138**:226-27, 229, 285
"L'irrémédiable" (Baudelaire) **6**:109, 115; **55**:13, 24, 29, 61, 72
"L'Irréparable" (Baudelaire) **6**:115; **55**:29, 61
"The irresistible" (Lonnrot) **53**:339
"Irrlicht" (Muller) **73**:392
Irrungen, Wirrungen (Fontane) **26**:235-36, 240, 243-45, 248, 258, 262, 264, 270-71
"Irtóztató csalódás" (Petofi) **21**:278
Is He Popenjoy? (Trollope) **6**:470, 477, 483; **33**:363; **101**:249, 251, 271-72, 318, 325, 327
"Is Housekeeping a Failure?" (Cooke) **110**:63
"Is it not great—this feat of Fate" (Fuller) **50**:249
"Is It True, Ye Gods, Who Treat Us" (Clough)
See "Wen Gott betrügt, ist wohl betrogen"
"Is Music the Type or Measure of All Art?" (Symonds) **34**:351
Is She His Wife? (Dickens) **37**:153, 210
Is This What You Call Civilization? (Dutt)
See *Ekei Ki Bale Sabhyatā*
"Isaac Laquedem" (Dumas) **71**:185
Isaac T. Hopper: A True Life (Child) **6**:204; **73**:61,79
"Isabel" (Dobell) **43**:48
"Isabel" (Tennyson) **30**:271; **65**:369
"Isabel" (Whittier) **8**:513
Isabel de Bavière (Dumas) **11**:49, 58
Isabel of Bavaria (Dumas)
See *Isabel de Bavière*
"Isabella" (Keats) **8**:340, 347, 351-52, 355-56, 362; **73**:144-45, 153, 162, 171-72, 174, 183, 189, 208, 233, 255, 259, 323, 328, 336
Isabella of Egypt (Arnim)
See *Isabella von Ägypten, Kaiser Karl des Fünften erste Jugendliebe*
"Isabella; or, The Pot of Basil" (Keats)
See "Isabella"
Isabella von Ägypten, Kaiser Karl des Fünften erste Jugendliebe (Arnim) **5**:12-13, 17-18, 20-21
"Isabelle" (Hogg) **109**:248
Isabelle de Bavière (Sade) **47**:335
"Isadore" (Chivers) **49**:72
Ishmael; or, In the Depths (Southworth) **26**:433-36, 439, 447
Isidora (Sand) **2**:588-89; **42**:322; **57**:312, 315-6, 368
Isis (Nerval) **1**:485; **67**:363, 371
Isis (Villiers de l'Isle Adam) **3**:581
"An Island" (Browning) **61**:42
The Island (Byron) **109**:99, 102
An Island in the Moon (Blake) **37**:28-9, 31, 62-3; **57**:80
Island Nights' Entertainments (Stevenson) **5**:412, 422
The Island of Barrataria (Tyler) **3**:572-73
"The Island of Bornholm" (Karamzin)
See "Ostrov Borngol'm"
The Island of Jewels (Planché) **42**:273, 289
"The Island of Maddalena: witha Distant View of Caprera" (Taylor) **89**:313
"The Island of the Fay" (Poe) **16**:331, 335; **117**:273
The Islanders (Leskov)
See *Ostrovitjane*
"L'Isle de Feu" (Dumas) **71**:185
"The Isle of Devils" (Lewis) **11**:300
"The Isle of Palms" (Wilson) **5**:545-46, 550
The Isle of Palms, and Other Poems (Wilson) **5**:544-46, 556, 561, 566
Ismael: an Oriental Tale: with Other Poems (Bulwer-Lytton) **45**:68
Ismaelillo (Martí) **63**:63, 90, 104-6, 109-10, 126
"Ismaïl Bey" (Lermontov) **5**:289
"Isobel's Child" (Browning) **1**:112, 126-7; **61**:53, 55-6
"Isolation: To Marguerite" (Arnold) **29**:31; **89**:16, 18-19, 22
"Ispoved" (Lermontov) **126**:128
"Ispytaniye" (Bestuzhev) **131**:154, 175-76, 186-87, 192, 210-13
Israel Potter: His Fifty Years in Exile (Melville) **3**:330, 334, 344, 354-55, 384; **29**:315, 334; **123**:192-93, 261
L'Israëlite (Balzac) **5**:58
"Israfel" (Poe) **1**:527; **16**:330; **117**:221, 227, 232-34, 237, 243-44, 257-62, 281
"Istina" (Baratynsky) **103**:6-7, 15, 21, 25-6
Istoriia sela Goriukhino (Pushkin) **3**:447-48, 459; **83**:275, 330
"Istorija lejtenanta Ergunova" (Turgenev)
See "Istoriya leytenanta Ergunova"
"Istoriya leytenanta Ergunova" (Turgenev) **21**:399, 415, 440-41; **122**:267
Istoriya moega znakomstva s Gogolem (Aksakov) **2**:13
Istoriya odnogo goroda (Saltykov) **16**:340-41, 343, 345, 357, 359, 361, 364, 368, 372-73, 375-76, 378
"It bloomed and dropt, a Single Noon—" (Dickinson) **77**:121
"It Can't Be 'Summer'" (Dickinson) **21**:55
"It Fortifies My Soul to Know" (Clough)
See "With Whom Is No Variableness, Neither Shadow of Turning"
"It Is Easy to Work When the Soul Is at Play" (Dickinson) **21**:64
It Is Never Too Late to Mend (Reade) **2**:533-34, 539-42, 544-45, 548-49, 551; **74**:244, 246, 251, 255, 262-65, 269, 271-72, 277-79, 281, 284-89, 297-98, 311-12, 315, 318-22, 330-33, 336-37, 339
"It Is Not Always May" (Longfellow) **45**:116, 135; **103**:304
"It Is Not Beauty I Demand" (Darley) **2**:129, 131-33
"It Is Not Time" (Pavlova) **138**:34
"It Is Quite True" (Andersen) **7**:35
"It Is the Evening Hour" (Clare) **9**:103
"It Is the First Mild Day of March" (Wordsworth)
See "Lines on the First Mild Day of March"
"It Sifts from Leaden Sieves" (Dickinson) **21**:49; **77**:93
"It Snows" (Hale) **75**:279, 283, 285, 293
"It Was a Glittering Sea" (Pavlova)
See "Eto bylo blestiashchee more"
It Was a Lover and His Lass (Oliphant) **11**:439-41
"It Was an April morning" (Wordsworth) **111**:218
"It was not Death" (Dickinson) **77**:88
"It Was Not in the Winter" (Hood) **16**:218, 228
"It would have starved a Gnat—" (Dickinson) **77**:131
"Itak, opyat uvidelsya ya s vami" (Tyutchev) **34**:399
Italia (Gautier) **1**:339, 341, 344; **59**:5
"The Italian Banditti" (Irving) **2**:390
Italian By-Ways (Symonds) **34**:323, 364
Italian Chronicles (Stendhal)
See *Chroniques italiennes*
The Italian Father (Dunlap) **2**:211, 213-15, 217
Italian Letters (Godwin) **130**:102
Italian Literature (Symonds) **34**:321, 340, 346, 348, 357, 368
Italian Notebooks (Hawthorne)
See *Passages from the French and Italian Notebooks of Nathaniel Hawthorne*
The Italian; or, The Confessional of the Black Penitents (Radcliffe) **6**:405-06, 409-21, 425, 427, 429-30, 435, 437, 442-47; **55**:225, 228-31, 233, 249-52, 255-6, 259, 261-5, 267-70, 273-6, 278-81; **106**:295, 300, 341, 343-45, 349, 351, 364
Italian Renaissance (Symonds)
See *Renaissance in Italy*
"Italian Villa" (Tyutchev)
See "Italyanskaya villa"
"The Italians" (Pisarev)
See "Italjancy"
"The Italian's Daughter" (Craik) **38**:119
Italienische Reise (Grillparzer) **102**:189
"Italjancy" (Pisarev) **25**:347
"Italy" (Bryant) **46**:7
"Italy" (Petofi)
See "Olaszország"
"Italy" (Pinkney) **31**:267, 273, 276
Italy (Gautier)
See *Italia*
Italy (Rogers) **69**:70-2, 74, 80-1, 84
Italy: Florence and Venice (Taine)
See *Voyage en Italie*
Italy in 1859 (De Mille)
See *The Dodge Club*
"Italy in England" (Browning) **79**:94, 96-97, 104, 164
Italy: With Sketches of Spain and Portugal (Beckford) **16**:18-19, 21, 25
"Italyanskaya villa" (Tyutchev) **34**:379, 397
The Itching Parrot (Lizardi)
See *El periquillo sarniento*
"Ite Domum Saturæ, Venit Hesperus" (Clough) **27**:72
"Az ítélet" (Petofi) **21**:286
Itinéraire de Paris à Jérusalem et de Jérusalem à Paris, en allant par la Grèce, et revenant par l'Egypte, a Barbarie, et l'Espagne (Chateaubriand) **3**:110, 113, 118; **134**:4-5, 8, 12, 16, 18-19
It's a Family Affair—We'll Settle It Ourselves (Ostrovsky)
See *Svoi lyudi—sochtemsya!*
"It's Hour with itself" (Dickinson) **77**:75
"It's Jean de Nivelle's Dog" (Verlaine) **51**:368
It's Perfectly True (Andersen) **79**:31
"Ivan FederovičŠpon'ka and His Aunt" (Gogol)
See "Ivan FederovičŠpon'ka i ego tetsuška"
"Ivan FederovičŠpon'ka i ego tetsuška" (Gogol) **5**:218, 231, 239, 249, 254, 256; **31**:88, 108
"Ivan Kolosov" (Turgenev) **122**:264, 266
"Ivan Pidkova" (Shevchenko) **54**:373-4, 389
"Ivan Savich Podzhabrin" (Goncharov) **63**:3, 43-4
Ivanhoe (Dumas) **71**:217
Ivanhoe (Scott) **15**:272, 277, 281, 283-84, 288-89, 304, 308, 313, 317-18; **69**:286-394
"I've dropped my Brain—My Soul is numb" (Dickinson) **77**:163
"I've heard an organ talk sometimes" (Dickinson) **77**:158
"I've Known a Heaven Like a Tent" (Dickinson) **21**:62
"I've seen a Dying Eye" (Dickinson) **77**:162-64
"The Ivory Carver" (Boker) **125**:7, 31, 38
L'ivrogne (Baudelaire) **6**:119-20
"The Ivy" (Barnes) **75**:8
"Ivy" (Meyer)
See "Eppich"
Ixion (Sheridan) **91**:257
Ixion in Heaven (Disraeli) **39**:3, 33, 52, 54-5, 75
"Iz Gafiza, Iz Gete" (Bestuzhev) **131**:150
"Iz Gete" (Bestuzhev) **131**:150
"Iz odnogo doroznogo dnevnika" (Leskov) **25**:259
"Iz pis!ma k S. V. Savitskoy" (Bestuzhev) **131**:148
"Izmail-Bej" (Lermontov) **126**:181
"Izmennik" (Bestuzhev) **131**:156, 171, 182, 185
"A J. Y. Colonna" (Nerval) **67**:307
"Jabberwocky" (Carroll) **2**:120; **53**:41, 59, 74, 85, 93, 108-9, 113, 124, 144; **139**:13, 29, 33-34, 37-39, 51, 84, 94-95, 137, 153

Jack (Daudet) **1**:231-34, 236, 243-44, 247-50
"Jack and Alice" (Austen) **119**:13
Jack and Jill: A Village Story (Alcott) **6**:17-18, 20-21; **58**:41, 49; **83**:68
"Jack Brag in Spain" (Richardson) **55**:301
"Jack Brass, Emperor of England" (Jefferies) **47**:141
"Jack Hall" (Hood) **16**:235
Jack Hatch (Mitford) **4**:404, 406
Jack Hinton, the Guardsman (Lever) **23**:272, 285, 292, 295, 300, 303, 306-07, 309
Jack of All Trades (Reade) **2**:547; **74**:265
Jack Sheppard (Ainsworth) **13**:22-5, 27-31, 33-40
"Jack Tar" (Tennyson) **30**:294
Jack Tier; or, The Florida Reefs (Cooper) **1**:208, 221, 227; **54**:258, 276-7
"The Jackdaw of Rheims" (Barham) **77**:37
Jack-o'-Lantern (Cooper) **1**:208
Jack's Ward (Alger) **8**:43, 45
"Jackson of Paul's" (Kingsley) **107**:211, 216
Jacob Faithful (Marryat) **3**:315, 318-19, 321-22
Jacob Pasinkov (Turgenev)
See *Yakov Pasynkov*
"Jacob Pasynkov" (Turgenev)
See "Stepnoy Korol 'Lir"
Jacob the Journeyman's Travels through Switzerland (Gotthelf)
See *Jakobs, des Handwerksgesellen Wanderungen durch die Schweiz*
"A Jacobin" (Hazlitt) **29**:152
The Jacobite Relics of Scotland; Being the Songs, Airs, and Legends of the Adherents of the House of Stuart (Hogg) **4**:276
Jacobite's Epitaph (Macaulay) **42**:88
"Jacobo e Irene" (Lizardi) **30**:71
Jacopo Ortis (Foscolo)
See *Ultime lettere di Jacopo Ortis*
Jacopo Ortis' Last Letters (Foscolo)
See *Ultime lettere di Jacopo Ortis*
Jacqueline (Rogers) **69**:68, 71, 73, 82
"The Jacquerie" (Lanier) **6**:236-37, 244, 269, 276; **118**:202, 206, 217, 230, 236, 257-62
La jacquerie (Mérimée) **6**:351, 360, 362; **65**:47, 49, 54-5, 58-61, 79, 81-3, 86, 90-2, 94
Jacques (Sand) **2**:582, 587-89, 597-98, 603; **42**:316, 320, 335; **57**:313, 316, 318-20
Jacques Ortis (Dumas) **11**:58
Jacques Vingtras (Vallès) **71**:311, 314-17, 325, 330-31, 357
Jacques Vingtras IV: Le Proscrit: Correspondance avec Arthur Arnould (Vallès) **71**:358, 365, 372, 375, 377
Jacques Vingtras: Le Bachelier (Vallès) **71**:312, 314-18, 321-23, 326-27, 330, 340-42, 345-46, 350-52, 355, 363, 365, 370, 384-85
Jacques Vingtras: L'Enfant (Vallès) **71**:311, 314-15, 320-21, 327, 330, 340, 345, 352, 357-58, 362-70, 372, 384-85
Jacques Vingtras: L'Insurgé: 1871 (Vallès) **71**:313-17, 322-23, 330-31, 340-42, 345, 350, 378, 380, 382, 384-86
"Jadis" (Rimbaud) **82**:245
Jadis et naguère (Verlaine) **2**:623, 631-32; **51**:355, 357, 359-61, 366, 369, 371-72, 387-88
"Jaffaar" (Hunt) **1**:414
"Die Jagd" (Droste-Hülshoff) **3**:193
"Jagd im Winter" (Grillparzer) **102**:175
"Das Jagdrecht" (Ludwig) **4**:365
"Der Jäger" (Mörike) **10**:451
"Der Jäger" (Muller) **73**:364, 368, 372
"Le jaguar" (Leconte de Lisle) **29**:222, 231
Jahrbücher der Medicin (Schelling) **30**:125
Der Jahrmarkt (Tieck) **5**:514
"J'ai dit à mon coeur, à mon faible coeur" (Musset) **7**:275
"J'aime le souvenir de ces époques nues" (Baudelaire) **29**:80, 115; **55**:48, 57-8, 67
Jakobs, des Handwerksgesellen Wanderungen durch die Schweiz (Gotthelf) **117**:6, 14-15, 32, 34, 40
"The Jamaica Funeral" (Freneau) **1**:314, 316; **111**:80, 171
James Clarence Mangan: His Selected Poems (Mangan) **27**:287
"James Lee" (Browning) **19**:131-32
"James Lee's Wife" (Browning)
See "James Lee"
"James Rigg: Another Extract from the Recluse" (Hogg) **4**:282, 284-85; **109**:192, 247
"James Thomson BV A Minor Poet" (Levy) **59**:107
Jan Bielecki (Slowacki) **15**:348-49
"Jan Van Hunks" (Rossetti) **4**:532
"Jan van Huysums blomsterstykke" (Wergeland) **5**:536, 538
"Jan van Huysum's Flower-Piece" (Wergeland)
See "Jan van Huysums blomsterstykke"
Jane Austen's Letters to Her Sister Cassandra and Others (Austen) **1**:52; **19**:29
Jane Eyre (Dumas) **71**:217
Jane Eyre: An Autobiography (Brontë) **3**:43-7, 49-50, 52-6, 58-80; **8**:51-93; **33**:103, 105, 107, 109, 111-12, 117-22, 131, 140, 144, 148, 151; **58**:155-6, 160, 171-3, 178-9, 184, 187, 189-90, 194-200, 203-4, 210, 213, 219-22, 224; **105**:2, 4, 6-7, 11-21, 45-6, 53, 64, 67, 70, 73, 75
Jane Gray (Staël-Holstein) **91**:323, 326, 335, 340, 358
Jane la pâle (Balzac) **5**:58, 65
"Jane Redgrave" (Moodie) **14**:238
Jane Sinclair (Carleton) **3**:91
Jane Talbot (Brown) **22**:5, 7, 12, 14, 23, 27, 30, 48-52; **74**:11, 15, 19-21, 49, 56, 77-8, 92-6, 98-9, 102-03, 105, 134, 138, 154-55, 164-66, 176, 179, 182-84; **122**:53-54
"Janet's Repentance" (Eliot) **4**:92, 98, 119; **13**:291; **41**:101; **118**:48, 103
János vitéz (Petofi) **21**:258-59, 261, 264, 266-67, 270-71, 273-75, 277, 283-84, 286
"January" (Clare) **9**:107; **86**:102
"January in the Sussex Woods" (Jefferies) **47**:136
"A January Morning" (Lampman) **25**:210
Japhet in Search of a Father (Marryat) **3**:318-19
"Jaquez Barraou, le charpentier" (Borel) **41**:4, 6, 13
"Los jardines" (Bello) **131**:112
"Jardines públicos" (Larra) **17**:282
"A Jarifa en una orgía" (Espronceda) **39**:85, 94, 100, 102-04, 108-09, 113, 117-20
"Jasei no in" (Ueda Akinari) **131**:6, 13-14, 23-24, 26-27, 34-35, 38-40, 60, 87
Jasei no In (Ueda Akinari) **131**:76-77
"Játszik öreg földünk" (Petofi) **21**:279
"Javert déraillé" (Hugo) **10**:378-80
"The Jay His Castanet Has Struck" (Dickinson) **21**:67
"Jazvitel' nyj" (Leskov) **25**:230
"Je devine..." (Verlaine) **51**:384
"Je n'ai pas oublié voisine de la ville" (Baudelaire) **55**:23, 61, 65
"Je ne sais pourquoi" (Verlaine) **2**:631
"Je t'adore a l'égal" (Baudelaire) **55**:60
"Je te donne ces vers" (Baudelaire) **55**:11, 56, 59, 62
The Jealousies (Keats) **73**:299-300; **121**:173, 228
"Jealousy" (Eminescu) **33**:265
Jean (Kock) **16**:244
Jean de la Roche (Sand) **42**:312
Jean de Thommeray (Augier) **31**:5, 8, 10, 13, 15-16, 24, 26, 28, 31
Jean de Witt (Staël-Holstein) **91**:358
"A Jean Duseigneur Sculpteur" (Gautier) **59**:19
Jean et Jeannette (Gautier) **1**:348; **59**:12
Jean Louis (Balzac) **5**:58
"Jean Paul Richter" (Carlyle) **70**:96
Jean Sbogar (Nodier) **19**:376, 380, 383-84
Jean Valjean (Hugo) **3**:246
"Jeäne" (Barnes) **75**:6, 7, 30, 71
Jean-François les bas-bleus (Nodier) **19**:383, 391
"Jeanie with the Light Brown Hair" (Foster) **26**:291, 293, 297
Jeanne (Sand) **2**:588-89, 594, 601, 605; **42**:322, 340, 365; **57**:338, 365-6
Jeanne d'Arc (Pavlova) **138**:13
Jeanne Eyre (Dumas)
See *Jane Eyre*
Jeanne Laisné (Sade) **47**:361
"Jeannette" (Woolson) **82**:284, 305, 307, 333
Jed, the Poorhouse Boy (Alger) **8**:21, 33-34, 42, 44; **83**:114, 127
"Jehovah Our Righteousness" (Cowper) **8**:131; **94**:72
Jehovah-Rophi, I am the Lord That healeth thee (Cowper) **94**:74
Jemmy (Nerval) **1**:485; **67**:363
"Jenny" (Rossetti) **4**:492-93, 495-97, 506-08, 510-12, 514, 517-20, 523-24, 526-27, 529, 531; **77**:308-11, 316-22, 336-37, 339, 348
"Jenny Away from Home" (Barnes) **75**:58
"Jenny Kissed Me" (Hunt) **1**:415; **70**:269
Jenseit des Tweed (Fontane) **26**:233
"Jephthah's Daughter" (Vigny)
See "La Fille de Jephte"
"Jeremiah Desborough" (Richardson) **55**:299
"Jeretyk" (Shevchenko) **54**:381
"Jérôme Chasseboeuf" (Borel) **41**:13
Jerry the Buckwoods Boy (Alger) **83**:119
The Jerseymen Meeting (Martineau) **137**:268
The Jerseymen Parting (Martineau) **137**:264, 268
Jerusalem: The Emanation of the Giant Albion (Blake) **13**:158, 166-67, 172, 177, 179, 183-84, 191-92, 205, 210-14, 220-21, 227, 229, 231, 233-39, 246-49, 252-53; **37**:8, 20, 46, 48, 66, 69, 80, 85; **57**:46, 60, 89, 92-3, 97-8; **127**:1-145
"Jesse and Colin" (Crabbe) **26**:93, 128
"Jessica" (Brown) **74**:133-34, 138
"Jessie Lee" (Barnes) **75**:58, 89-90
Jest, Satire, Irony and Deeper Significance (Grabbe)
See *Scherz, Satire, Ironie und tiefere Bedeutung*
Les Jésuites (Michelet) **31**:225, 241
"Jesuitisme" (Verlaine) **51**:356
The Jesuits in North America in the Seventeenth Century (Parkman) **12**:333, 336, 341, 352, 355, 366, 371
"Jesus Christ in Flanders" (Balzac)
See "Jésus-Christ en Flandre"
"Jesus! Thy Crucifix" (Dickinson) **21**:63
Jesus von Nazareth (Wagner) **9**:474
"Jésus-Christ en Flandre" (Balzac) **5**:46; **53**:25
"Le jet d'eau" (Baudelaire) **29**:77
Jettatura (Gautier) **1**:346; **59**:11-13, 33, 39
"Jetzt rede du" (Meyer) **81**:144, 205
"Le jeu" (Baudelaire) **29**:81, 101; **55**:23
"La Jeune Fille et le ramier" (Desbordes-Valmore) **97**:27
"La Jeune fille et sa mère" (Desbordes-Valmore) **97**:8
Un jeune homme charmant (Kock) **16**:253
Le Jeune Homme Pauvre (Feuillet)
See *Le Roman d'un Jeune Homme Pauvre*
"Jeune ménage" (Rimbaud) **4**:475
Jeunes Têtes et jeunes coeurs (Desbordes-Valmore) **97**:12
Les jeunes-France, romans goguenards (Gautier) **1**:339, 349; **59**:12, 27, 29, 63-5
"Jeunesse" (Rimbaud) **4**:473; **35**:322; **82**:242, 251
La jeunesse (Augier) **31**:7-8, 13, 15, 24, 27, 30, 33, 35
La jeunesse à vingt ans (Dumas) **9**:219
Le jeunesse de Louis XIV (Dumas) **71**:210

"The Jew" (Turgenev) **21**:399, 414, 417; **122**:243
"The Jew" (Very) **9**:383
"The Jew in Fiction" (Levy) **59**:98, 111, 127
"The Jew, Nine Blooming Branches from a Thornbush" (Wergeland) **5**:537-38
The Jew, the Gypsy, and El-Islam (Burton) **42**:61
The Jeweled Comb-Box (Motoori)
See *Tamakushige*
The Jewess (Planché) **42**:292
The Jewess (Scribe)
See *La Juive*
"The Jewess, Eleven Blooming Branches" (Wergeland) **5**:537-38
The Jewess of Toledo (Grillparzer)
See *Die Jüdin von Toledo*
"The Jewish Cemetery at Newport" (Longfellow) **45**:132, 163, 167, 186
"Jewish Children, By a Maiden Aunt" (Levy) **59**:98, 112, 133
"Jewish Humour" (Levy) **59**:111
"The Jewish Lamentation at Euphrates" (Freneau) **111**:110
"The Jewish Problem" (Lazarus) **8**:424; **109**:293, 303, 313, 331, 337-39
"The Jewish Question" (Marx) **114**:69-70, 74, 76
Jewish Tales (Sacher-Masoch) **31**:285
"Jewishness in Music" (Wagner)
See "Das Judentum in der Musik"
"The Jews" (Marx) **17**:295
The Jews in Russia (Leskov)
See *Evrei v Rossii*
"Język-ojczysty" (Norwid) **17**:373
The Jilt; or, Thundercloud's Year (Boucicault) **41**:27-8
"Jim Is Poetical Rarely" (Kendall) **12**:195
"Jim the Splitter" (Kendall) **12**:190, 192
"Jimmy Rose" (Melville) **3**:354, 380-81
"Jimmy's Cruise in the Pinafore" (Alcott) **58**:49
"The Jinx" (Baudelaire)
See "Le guignon"
Jó név és erény (Madach) **19**:370
"Joachim Du Bellay" (Pater) **7**:338
Joan (Oliphant) **11**:447
"Joan of Arc" (De Quincey) **87**:15
Joan of Arc (Southey) **8**:447, 459, 461, 473-74, 476-79; **97**:260, 268, 273, 278-79, 281, 293, 307, 312-18, 332
Joan of Arc (Tamayo y Baus)
See *Juana de Arco*
"Joan of Arc, in Rheims" (Hemans) **71**:295
Joanna von Montfaucon (Kotzebue) **25**:136, 145
Joaquìn Murieta (Ridge)
See *The Life and Adventures of Joaquìn Murieta, the Celebrated California Bandit*
"Job Warner's Christmas" (Alger) **83**:97
Jocelyn: Épisode; Journal trouvé chez un curé de village (Lamartine) **11**:251-53, 255, 262, 271-75, 278, 281, 283-89
"Jochonan in the City of Demons" (Maginn) **8**:440
"Joe's Courtship" (Cooke) **110**:33
Joe's Luck (Alger) **83**:100, 104-05
"Jogadhya Uma" (Dutt) **29**:120-21, 124, 128, 130
Johannes Climacus or De Omnibus Dubitandum Est (Kierkegaard) **78**:217
Johannes und Esther (Muller) **73**:365
"John Barbour's Bruce" (Lanier) **118**:218
"John Bloom in Lon'on" (Barnes) **75**:101
"John Brown" (Douglass) **7**:126, 129-30
"John Bull" (Irving) **2**:381; **19**:328; **95**:265, 268, 279, 294
John Bull in America; or, The New Munchausen (Paulding) **2**:528
"John Bull on the Guadalquivir" (Trollope) **101**:234
John Caldigate (Trollope) **6**:466, 470; **101**:312
"John Carter's Sin" (Cooke) **110**:18
John Clare (Clare) **86**:110, 113, 130-32, 179
John Clare: Poems Chiefly from Manuscript (Clare) **9**:86-87, 89-91, 93, 97, 102
John Doe; or, Peep o'Day (Banim and Banim) **13**:116-17, 119, 122, 126, 129, 131, 133-34, 141
John Endicott (Longfellow) **2**:486, 496-97; **45**:128, 165
"John Ferncliff" (Horne) **127**:260
"John Gilpin" (Cowper)
See "The Diverting History of John Gilpin"
John Gilpin (Cowper)
See "The Diverting History of John Gilpin"
John Godfrey's Fortunes (Taylor) **89**:310-11, 347, 363
John Halifax, Gentleman (Craik) **38**:106-11, 113, 116-25, 127-28, 131-39
"John Huss" (Shevchenko) **54**:383
"John Inglefield's Thanksgiving" (Hawthorne) **95**:148
John Jerome: His Thoughts and Ways (Ingelow) **39**:264
"John Jones" (Hood) **16**:234
John Marr, and Other Sailors (Melville) **3**:363, 379-80; **29**:318, 320, 322, 360
"John Maynard, A Ballad of Lake Erie" (Alger) **8**:16; **83**:138-39
"John Milton" (Emerson) **98**:67
John Riew' (Storm) **1**:540
John Rintoul (Oliphant) **11**:447; **61**:203
"John Samuel and Richard" (Southey) **97**:314
"John Smith's Shanty" (Jefferies) **47**:137, 141
John the Hero (Petofi)
See *János vitéz*
"John Trot" (Hood) **16**:234
"John Underhill" (Whittier) **8**:509
John Woodvil: A Tragedy (Lamb) **10**:385, 387-89, 397-98, 400-01, 404, 407, 409, 411; **113**:163, 180-82, 184, 278, 283
Johnson (Macaulay) **42**:87
"Johnson and Horne Tooke" (Landor) **14**:166
Johnsonian Anecdotes (Piozzi)
See *Anecdotes of the Late Samuel Johnson, LL.D., During the Last Twenty Years of His Life*
"La joie de Siva" (Leconte de Lisle) **29**:221
"Jóka ördöge" (Arany) **34**:16
La jolie fille du faubourg (Kock) **16**:254
"Jon of Iceland" (Taylor) **89**:342
"Jonathan to John" (Lowell) **2**:516
"Jones' Private Argument" (Lanier)
See "Jones's Private Argyment"
"Jones's Private Argyment" (Lanier) **118**:227-28
Jorrocks's Jaunts and Jollities (Surtees) **14**:343, 349, 352, 355, 358, 360, 362, 365-66, 369
Jo's Boys and How They Turned Out (Alcott) **6**:20; **58**:3, 31, 35, 41-3, 47, 50-1, 72; **83**:17, 33-34, 39, 42-43, 47, 62
Joseph (Maupassant) **83**:229
Joseph and His Brethren (Tyler) **3**:572-73
Joseph and His Friend (Taylor) **89**:311, 348, 357, 359
Joseph Balsamo (Dumas) **71**:232, 234
"Joseph de Maistre on Russia" (Arnold) **126**:104
"Joseph Priestley" (Huxley) **67**:48
Joseph Rushbrook; or, The Poacher (Marryat) **3**:320-21
"Josephine de Montmorenci" (Trollope) **101**:235
Josh Billings' Farmer's Allminax (Shaw) **15**:332-33, 338-39
Josh Billings, Hiz Sayings (Shaw) **15**:339
"Josh Billings Insures His Life" (Shaw) **15**:338
Josh Billings' Spice Box (Shaw) **15**:338, 342
Joshua Davidson (Linton)
See *The True History of Joshua Davidson, Christian and Communist*
"Joubert" (Arnold) **89**:39, 83
Joueur de flûte (Augier) **31**:4, 11, 14, 23, 27
Jour à jour (Amiel) **4**:13, 15
Le jour des rois (Hugo) **3**:270-71
Journal (Clare) **86**:112
Journal (Longfellow) **2**:491; **103**:301
Journal (Macaulay) **42**:130
Journal (Michelet) **31**:258, 264
Journal (Percy) **95**:315-17
Journal (Scott)
See *The Journal of Sir Walter Scott*
Journal (Thoreau) **7**:369, 372, 376-8, 385-6, 388-91, 397; **21**:321, 328, 331-2, 337-40; **61**:300, 305-6, 311, 316, 331-7, 339, 341-2, 347-8, 352-7, 361-2, 364, 367, 375-7, 382-6; **138**:106, 116-24, 126, 128-29, 134-36, 146-49, 151, 160, 162, 170, 185-89, 192
Journal abrégé (Constant) **6**:223
Journal C (Emerson) **98**:78
Le journal de Mademoiselle d'Arvers (Dutt) **29**:120, 129
Le journal de Marie Bashkirtseff (Bashkirtseff) **27**:1-35
Journal des Goncourt: Mémoires de la vie littéraire (Goncourt and Goncourt) **7**:157-59, 165-66, 168, 171-77, 180, 183-86, 189-90
Le journal d'un poète (Vigny) **7**:469, 471-72, 475, 483; **102**:356, 364, 368, 379-80, 383
Le Journal d'une Femme (Feuillet) **45**:91
Journal einer Reise durch Frankreich (La Roche) **121**:242, 298, 301-2, 305
Journal intime de Benjamin Constant et lettres à sa famille et à ses amis (Constant) **6**:214-15, 223
"Journal of a Frenchman" (Brontë) **109**:35
Journal of a Residence in America (Kemble) **18**:164-67, 169-70, 172-74, 179-80, 182, 186, 191, 199, 201-02
Journal of a Residence on a Georgian Plantation in 1838-1839 (Kemble) **18**:185-86, 190-91, 193-99, 202-03
"The Journal of a Superfluous Man" (Turgenev)
See "Dnevnik lišnego čeloveka"
Journal of a tour and residence in Great Britain (Irving) **95**:277
Journal of a Tour in the Isle of Man (Wordsworth) **25**:421
Journal of a Tour on the Continent (Wordsworth) **25**:411, 421; **138**:257, 260, 293
Journal of a West Indian Proprietor, Kept during a Residence in the Island of Jamaica (Lewis) **11**:299-300
A Journal of a Year's Residence in the United States (Cobbett) **49**:110, 113, 120, 153
"Journal of an Actress" (Haliburton) **15**:118, 125, 129
The Journal of an Author (Dostoevsky)
See *Dnevnik pisatelya*
Journals of Dorothy Wordsworth (Wordsworth) **138**:203-4, 206-11, 214, 216, 241-46, 248, 251-57, 259-61, 266-79, 282-83, 290-91, 293, 319-21, 334, 340-45, 348-49
Journals of Dorothy Wordsworth: The Alfoxden Journal, 1798; The Grasmere Journals, 1800-1803 (Wordsworth) **138**:200-203, 205, 214-21, 241-44, 246-48, 252, 254-55, 257-58, 260, 263, 273-74, 279, 282-84, 300-301, 304, 308-9, 311, 315-16, 318-19, 321, 329, 332-34, 337, 340-42, 344-45, 348, 351-52, 354
Journal of F. A. Butler (Kemble)
See *Journal of a Residence in America*
The Journal of Julius Rodman (Poe) **16**:313; **94**:180-86
The Journal of Marie Bashkirtseff (Bashkirtseff)
See *Le journal de Marie Bashkirtseff*
Journal of My Second Tour of Scotland (Wordsworth) **25**:421; **138**:254, 256, 258
Journal of Researches into the Geology and Natural History of the Various Countries

Visited by H. M. S. Beagle (Darwin) **57**:113, 117, 119, 123, 125
The Journal of Sir Walter Scott (Scott) **69**:332; **110**:307, 313-14
Journal of the Movements of the British Legion (Richardson) **55**:296-7, 329
Journal of Visit to Hamburgh and of Journey from Hamburgh to Goslar (Wordsworth) **25**:402, 419
"Journal sans date" (Chateaubriand) **134**:47-49, 51-52
Journal through France and Italy (Hazlitt) See *Notes of a Journey through France and Italy*
Journal trouvé chez un curé de village (Lamartine) **11**:274
Journalisten (Freytag) **109**:141
The Journalists (Freytag) See *Journalisten*
Journals (Hazlitt) **82**:100
Journals (Kierkegaard) See *Papirer*
The Journals and Letters of Fanny Burney-Madame D'Arblay (Burney) **12**:55; **54**:3, 11
The Journals and Miscellaneous Notebooks of Ralph Waldo Emerson (Emerson) **98**:34, 37, 47-8, 55-6, 60-2, 64-8, 72, 74-6, 79-80, 83-4, 86, 89, 92, 94-8, 1089-09, 112, 116-17, 162, 185
Journals of a Residence in Portugal (Southey) **97**:271
The Journals of Bronson Alcott (Alcott) **1**:25
Journals of Dorothy Wordsworth (Wordsworth) **25**:396, 426
The Journals of Francis Parkman (Parkman) **12**:352
The Journals of Ralph Waldo Emerson (Emerson) **1**:292-93, 296; **38**:142
"Journals of Tours" (Robinson) **15**:181
Journaux intimes (Baudelaire) **6**:99-100, 105; **29**:70, 77, 97-9; **55**:14
Journaux intimes (Constant) **6**:223
Journées de Florbelle (Sade) **47**:365
"Journey" (Irving) **2**:372
"The Journey" (Very) **9**:383-85
A Journey Due North (Sala) **46**:238-40, 244, 246, 249
Journey from Cornhill to Cairo (Thackeray) **5**:452, 482
"A Journey from Philadelphia to New-York" (Freneau) **111**:131
Journey into Northern Pennsylvania and the State of New York (Crèvecoeur) **105**:91, 94
"A Journey into Poles'e" (Turgenev) See *Liebe-Hütten*
A Journey Made in the Summer of 1794 through Holland and the Western Frontier of Germany (Radcliffe) **6**:414, 417; **55**:222, 233
"Journey of Despair" (Eliot) **4**:124
"The Journey of Life" (Bryant) **46**:38, 42
Journey on foot from Holmens Canal to the east pount of Amager (Andersen) **79**:79-80
Journey out of Essex (Clare) **86**:117, 175, 177-78
Journey to America (Tocqueville) **63**:281
A Journey to Central Africa (Taylor) **89**:346
Journey to Germany (Carlyle) **70**:92
"The Journey to Panama" (Trollope) **101**:235
"Journey to Polessie" (Turgenev) **21**:431
Journey to Reveal (Bestuzhev) See *Poezdka v Revel'*
"Journey to the Dead" (Arnold) **6**:67
"Journey to the Harz" (Heine) See *Die Harzreise*
Journey to the Pyrenees (Taine) See *Voyage aux eaux des Pyrénées*
Journeys in Italy (Gautier) See *Italia*
"Jours d'été" (Desbordes-Valmore) **97**:20
"Joust First Being the Right Pleasant Joust betwixt Heart and Brain" (Lanier) **118**:238, 259-60
"Joust Second Being the Rare Joust of Love and Hate" (Lanier) **118**:259, 261
La joven de la flecha de oro (Villaverde) **121**:334-35
"Jövendöles" (Petofi) **21**:264
"Joy and Peace in Believing" (Cowper) **94**:75
The Joy of the Wicked (Smolenskin) See *Simhat hanef*
"Joy Passing By" (Barnes) **75**:59
"Joy, Shipmate, Joy" (Whitman) **31**:388-89
Joyce (Oliphant) **61**:202, 206
"Joyeuse vie" (Hugo) **3**:262
"Ju. F. Abaze" (Tyutchev) **34**:413
Juan Dandolo (Zorrilla y Moral) **6**:523
"Juan Ruiz" (al-Mutanabbi) See "Morcia Funebre"
Juana de Arco (Tamayo y Baus) **1**:565, 567, 570-71
"Jubal" (Eliot) **4**:107-08; **13**:334
"Jubal, the Ringer" (O'Brien) **21**:252
"'Jubilate': Lecture for Poetical Persons" (Jean Paul) **7**:234
"Jubilation of Sergeant Major M'Turk in Witnessing The Highland Games" (Smith) **59**:331
Judae Capta (Tonna) **135**:207
Judah's Lion (Tonna) **135**:203, 207, 211
"Judaism" (Newman) **38**:345
"Judaism in Music" (Wagner) See "Das Judentum in der Musik"
Judas Iscariot (Horne) **127**:263
Judas Maccabaeus (Longfellow) **2**:496-97; **45**:127-28, 155
Die Juden in Breslau (Freytag) **109**:167, 180
Die Judenbuche: Ein Sittengemalde aus dem gebirgichten Westfalen (Droste-Hülshoff) **3**:191-92, 196-200
"Das Judentum in der Musik" (Wagner) **119**:248-49, 253, 291, 305
Judge for Yourselves! (Kierkegaard) **34**:225; **78**:238
"Judge Nothing before the Time" (Rossetti) **50**:309
"Judged" (Cooke) **110**:16, 20
"Judgement" (Petofi) See "Az ítélet"
The Judgement of Solomon (Tyler) **3**:572-73
"Judgment of God" (Morris) **4**:422, 431, 444
The Judgment of Paris (Beattie) **25**:109-12
Die Jüdin von Toledo (Grillparzer) **102**:85, 87, 110-11, 131, 170-71, 177, 192-93, 195, 203, 205-07, 212
Judith: Eine Tragödie in fünf Acten (Hebbel) **43**:230, 233-34, 239, 242-44, 253-58, 262, 271, 277-80, 283-87, 296-97, 299
The Judith of Bialopol (Sacher-Masoch) **31**:298
Judith und Holofernes (Nestroy) **42**:225, 227-28, 231, 234
"Judol'" (Leskov) **25**:239
"Le jugement de Komor" (Leconte de Lisle) **29**:226
Jugenderinnerungen im Grünen (Grillparzer) **102**:175
"Jugendsehnen" (Eichendorff) **8**:213
"The Juggler Pamphalon" (Leskov) See "Skomorox Pamfalon"
"Jugurtha" (Longfellow) **2**:492; **45**:146
"Jugurtha" (Rimbaud) **4**:465
La Juive (Scribe) **16**:390, 398, 408-10
Julia (Brontë) **3**:80
Julia (Hebbel) **43**:230, 237, 239, 257
Julia: A Novel; Interspersed with Some Poetical Pieces (Williams) **135**:255-56, 296-99, 301, 333, 343, 346, 349-50, 352
Julia de Roubigné (Mackenzie) **41**:181-82, 184, 203, 209, 212, 222, 224-26, 228
Julia de Trécoeur (Feuillet) **45**:77-9, 85-7, 89, 93
"Julia; or the Convent of St. Clair, a Tale, founded on Fact" (Opie) **65**:160-1
Julian (Mitford) **4**:400, 404
"Julian and Maddalo" (Shelley) **18**:326, 331, 338, 356-57, 359
Julian and Maddalo (Shelley) **93**:277, 315-17, 320, 351
"Julian M. and A. G. Rochelle" (Brontë) **16**:73, 75, 86-7
Juliette; ou, Les prospérités du vice (Sade) **3**:495-96; **47**:304, 309, 311, 313, 324-25, 328, 334-36, 341-42, 346, 350, 364-65
Julius (Stifter) **41**:376-77
Julius; or, The Street Boy Out West (Alger) **7**:43; **83**:100
Julqvällen (Runeberg) **41**:309-10, 314, 317-18, 328-32
"July" (Clare) **86**:96-7, 101, 104
"July Fourth 1844" (Fuller) **50**:248
"The Jumblies" (Lear) **3**:309
"June" (Bryant) **6**:165, 168, 172; **46**:3, 19, 22-3
"June" (Clare) **86**:99-101
"June" (Lampman) **25**:172, 183
"A June Morning" (Ridge) **82**:185
"A June Night" (Lazarus) **109**:294
"A June-Tide Echo (After a Richter Concert)" (Levy) **59**:92, 94
"Jung Tirel" (Meyer) **81**:207
"Jung Volkers Lied" (Mörike) **10**:453
Der junge Tischlermeister (Tieck) **5**:520, 532; **46**:397
"Die Jungfrau" (Meyer) **81**:206
Die Jungfrau als Ritter (Keller) **2**:416
Die Jungfrau und der Teufel (Keller) **2**:416
Die Jungfrau und die Nonne (Keller) **2**:416
Die Jungfräu von Orleans (Schiller) **39**:319-20, 322, 325, 329-30, 335, 345-46, 350, 360-61, 365, 371-72, 376-80; **69**:175, 181-82, 185, 188, 255, 261, 263-64, 266, 269
"Les jungles" (Leconte de Lisle) **29**:212, 217, 224, 231-32
Die jüngsten Kinder meiner Laune (Kotzebue) **25**:139
"The Juniper-Tree" (Grimm and Grimm) **3**:225
"La junta de Castel-o-Branco" (Larra) **130**:194
Jupiter Lights (Woolson) **82**:275, 280, 293, 299, 318-19, 329, 335
"Júpiter y Europa" (Casal) **131**:236
Jürg Jenatsch (Meyer) **81**:135-36
Jusan'ya (Ichiyō) **49**:331, 336-37, 341, 345, 348, 353
"Just Lost, When I Was Saved!" (Dickinson) **21**:64
"The Just Man" (Rimbaud) See "L'homme juste"
"The Just Men" (Leskov) See "Spravedlivyj čelovek"
"Justice and Expediency" (Whittier) **59**:364
"Justice as a Principle of Divine Governance" (Newman) **99**:298
"Justice for Ireland" (Allingham) **25**:3
"Justifiable Homicide in Southern California" (Jackson) **90**:153
A Justified Sinner (Hogg) See *The Private Memoirs and Confessions of a Justified Sinner*
The Justified Sinner (Hogg) See *The Private Memoirs and Confessions of a Justified Sinner*
Justin Harley (Cooke) **5**:131, 135
Justine or the misfortunes of virtue (Sade) See *Justine ou les malheurs de la vertu*
Justine ou les malheurs de la vertu (Sade) **47**:47; 306, 309, 311, 314, 328, 333-36, 340-43, 350, 355, 364-65, 367, 370-72
Juvenile Journal (Burney) **54**:16
Juvenile Miscellany (Child) **73**:40, 50, 56, 58, 61, 66, 68, 74-6, 101-02, 121-22, 124-25, 127-32, 134-35
Juvenile Poems (Coleridge) **9**:146
Juvenilia (Austen) **13**:96; **51**:13, 15;
Juvenilia 1829-1835 (Brontë) **105**:77

Juvenilia; or, A Collection of Poems Written between the Ages of Twelve and Sixteen (Hunt) **1**:405, 411, 416; **70**:263, 264
Einen Jux will er sich machen (Nestroy) **42**:239-40, 243, 245, 249, 264
"K ***" (Pavlova) **138**:53
"K chemu nevol'niku" (Baratynsky)
See "K chemu nevolniku mechtania svobody?..."
"K chemu nevolniku mechtania svobody?..." (Baratynsky) **103**:10, 16-17, 21
"K Konsinu" (Baratynsky) **103**:3, 27-9
"K mesyatsu" (Zhukovsky) **35**:403-04, 407
"K moriu" (Pushkin) **83**:254-55, 261, 304, 351, 366
"K nekotorym poetam" (Bestuzhev) **131**:148
"K oblaku" (Bestuzhev) **131**:151
"K slovesu" (Preseren) **127**:323
"K.A. Sverbeevoy" (Baratynsky)
See "To K.A. Sverbeevaya"
"Kaadt ukrudt" (Wergeland) **5**:541
Kabale und Liebe (Schiller) **39**:310-11, 327, 334, 342, 350, 375, 389-90, 393-94; **69**:169, 171, 196, 242, 277
Kadril' (Pavlova) **138**:5, 13-14, 20, 35-36, 47, 49-50, 56-57, 59-62
"Kaiphas, Kaiphas, Sanchedrin" (Grillparzer) **102**:174
"Kairail Fish" (Brontë) **109**:34
"Kaiser Heinrich" (Klopstock) **11**:236
Kaiser Octavianus (Tieck) **5**:514, 519, 521, 525, 529, 532
"Kaizoku" (Ueda Akinari) **131**:20-22, 52, 56
"Kak idyot kuznets da iz kuznitsy . . ." (Bestuzhev) **131**:181
"Kak neozhidanno i yarko" (Tyutchev) **34**:400
"Kak ni tyazhel posledniy chas" (Tyutchev) **34**:399
"Kak okean obemlet shar zemnoi" (Tyutchev) **34**:389, 404-07, 409-10
"Kak ptichka, ranneyu zarey" (Tyutchev) **34**:399
"Kak sladko dremlet sad temnozelenyi" (Tyutchev) **34**:405
Kakaika (Ueda Akinari) **131**:20
"Kakemono" (Casal) **131**:257
Kakizome kigenkai (Ueda Akinari) **131**:19, 51
"Kaleidoscope" (Verlaine) **51**:355, 364, 371
The Kalevala (Lonnrot) **53**:307-10, 312-40
Kalkstein (Stifter) **41**:357, 360, 362-64, 373, 375
Kalligone (Herder) **8**:313
"Kallundborg Church" (Whittier) **8**:513, 529
"Kám?" (Preseren) **127**:318, 325
Kamalakanta (Chatterji) **19**:216, 225-26
Kamalakanter daptar (Chatterji) **19**:216, 220, 226
"Kamalakanter jabanbandi" (Chatterji) **19**:226
"Kamalakanter patra" (Chatterji) **19**:226
"Kambaleu" (Longfellow) **45**:145
Kamennyi gost' (Pushkin) **3**:424, 433-34, 447, 452; **83**:263-65, 285-86, 288-90, 327, 338-39, 351-543, 355-36
"Kampf" (Schiller) **39**:331, 387
Kampl (Nestroy) **42**:221, 249-51
Kan ej (Runeberg) **41**:310
Der Kandidat (Ludwig) **4**:356
"Kane" (O'Brien) **21**:234, 246
Kanervala (Kivi) **30**:51
"The Kangaroo Hunt" (Harpur) **114**:99, 125, 144, 158, 166
"The Kansas Immigrants" (Child) **73**:83, 106
"'Kantate': Lecture on Poetical Poetry" (Jean Paul) **7**:234
Kanteletar (Lonnrot) **53**:321-2, 338-40
Kapalkundala (Chatterji) **19**:204, 206, 208-10, 212, 214-15, 217-19, 222, 224
Kapellet (Almqvist) **42**:4, 16, 19
Das Kapital: Kritik der politischen Ökonomie (Marx) **17**:289, 291, 293, 295-97, 302-03, 308, 310-16, 326-27, 331, 333, 335-39, 344, 354-55, 359; **114**:8, 11, 36-7, 54, 70, 73, 82, 85
Kapitansha (Shevchenko) **54**:363, 392, 395
Kapitanskaya-dochka (Pushkin) **3**:428-29, 436, 442, 452, 460, 464; **83**:268, 275, 291, 293, 295-96, 337, 354-56
"Der Kapwein und der Johannesberger" (Klopstock) **11**:238
"The Karamanian Exile" (Mangan) **27**:278, 286-87, 292, 295, 298
Karkurit (Kivi) **30**:50-1, 53, 64-5
Karl I (Heine) **54**:347
Karl von Berneck (Tieck) **5**:519, 523, 527; **46**:374-75
"Karluv tejn" (Macha) **46**:201
"Die Kartäuser" (Meyer) **81**:206
Kartofa (Mickiewicz)
See "Kartofel"
"Kartofel" (Mickiewicz) **3**:396-98
Kartofla (Mickiewicz)
See "Kartofel"
Die Käserei in der Vehfreude (Gotthelf) **117**:6, 15, 22-5, 32, 35
Kashoden (Ueda Akinari) **131**:20
Kasidah (Burton) **42**:42-44, 53
"Kastraten und Männer" (Schiller) **39**:356, 386
Katalin (Arany) **34**:16, 23-4
Das Kätchen von Heilbronn; oder, Die Feuerprobe (Kleist) **2**:437, 440, 443, 446, 450, 457-58; **37**:217, 225-28, 230, 233, 237, 253-55, 257, 260, 262, 270, 272, 274
"Kate O'Belashanny" (Allingham) **25**:16
Kate of Heilbronn (Kleist)
See *Das Kätchen von Heilbronn; oder, Die Feuerprobe*
"Kateryna" (Shevchenko) **54**:371, 373-5, 389
"Kathaleen-Ny-Houlahan" (Mangan) **27**:297-98, 310
Katharine Walton; or, The Rebel of Dorchester (Simms) **3**:503, 507-08, 513-14
Käthi die Großmutter (Gotthelf) **117**:5, 18, 25, 32
"Kathleen" (Whittier) **8**:516, 528; **59**:360, 371
"Katie" (Timrod) **25**:361, 367, 372, 375, 384
"Katie Cheyne" (Hogg) **4**:283
Katie Stewart (Oliphant) **11**:439, 446-7; **61**:173
Katzensilber (Stifter) **41**:391
"Kaukametsä" (Kivi) **30**:51-2
"Kaunisnummella" (Kivi) **30**:51
Kaunitz (Sacher-Masoch) **31**:291
Kavanagh (Longfellow) **2**:480-81, 489-90, 494; **45**:158, 168, 184; **101**:92
"Kavkaz" (Shevchenko) **54**:383, 389
Kavkazsky plennik (Pushkin) **3**:409-11, 413, 415-16, 421, 423, 437, 445, 451; **27**:392; **83**:242-44, 246-48, 251, 299, 309, 332, 357, 359
The Kawi Language of the Island of Java (Humboldt) **134**:186
"Kdor ne zna napisa brati" (Preseren) **127**:315
Kean, on désordre et genie (Dumas) **11**:46-7; **71**:209-10, 230, 242
"Keats" (Lampman)
See "The Character and Poetry of Keats"
"Keepen Up O' Christmas" (Barnes) **75**:77
"Keeping Fast and Festival" (Newman) **38**:304
Keeping House and Housekeeping (Hale) **75**:341
"Keinu" (Kivi) **30**:51
"Keiserens nye Klæder" (Andersen) **7**:25, 28, 34; **79**:21, 23, 25-6, 52, 64, 68, 72, 76, 81, 88
"Keith of Ravelston" (Dobell) **43**:47-8
"Die Kellnerin von Bacharach und ihre Gäste" (Muller) **73**:366,380
The Kellys and the O'Kellys; or, Landlords and Tenants (Trollope) **6**:452, 458, 500, 514; **101**:245-51, 253, 263-67, 269, 271, 273, 276, 293, 295, 299, 321
"The Kelp Gatherer" (Griffin) **7**:214
Kenelm Chillingly, His Adventures and Opinions (Bulwer-Lytton) **1**:147, 149, 151, 155; **45**:68-9
Kenilworth (Scott) **15**:277, 289, 309, 313, 317; **69**:303-04, 308, 313
Kensington Gardens in 1830: A Satirical Trifle (Richardson) **55**:329
Kept in the Dark (Trollope) **6**:500-01; **101**:309
"Kéramos" (Longfellow) **45**:130, 139, 147, 157; **103**:295
Kerry (Boucicault) **41**:28
"Kertben" (Arany) **34**:18-19
"Kesäyö" (Kivi) **30**:51-2
Kevurat hamor (Smolenskin) **30**:189-90, 192, 195
"Kew Gardens" (Symonds) **34**:355
"The Key of the Street" (Sala) **46**:245-46, 248, 250
"The Key to My Book" (Rossetti) **50**:274
A Key to the New Testament (Percy) **95**:313, 336, 338
A Key to Uncle Tom's Cabin: Presenting the Original Facts and Documents upon Which the Story Is Founded (Stowe) **3**:543-44, 547, 559
"Khadji Abrek" (Lermontov) **47**:182
"Khirôn" (Leconte de Lisle) **29**:222-23, 238, 245-46
Kholostiak (Turgenev) **21**:428, 432
"Khor and Kalinych" (Turgenev)
See "Chor' i Kalinyč"
"Khozyaika" (Dostoevsky) **2**:156, 179; **21**:94; **33**:177; **43**:92
Khudozhnik (Shevchenko)
See *Xudoznik*
"Kiama" (Kendall) **12**:178
"Kibitsu no kama" (Ueda Akinari) **131**:3-4, 6, 13, 24, 26-27, 38-40, 48, 87
Kibitsu no Kama (Ueda Akinari) **131**:75-76
A Kick for a Bite (Cobbett) **49**:109
Kicklebury's on the Rhine (Thackeray) **5**:459, 506
Kidnapped (Stevenson)
See *Kidnapped: Being Memoirs of the Adventures of David Balfour in the Year 1751*
Kidnapped: Being Memoirs of the Adventures of David Balfour in the Year 1751 (Stevenson) **5**:400, 402-05, 409, 414-15, 417, 424-27, 429, 433-35, 438-39; **63**:257, 261, 269, 274
Kierkegaard: Letters and Documents (Kierkegaard)
See *Papirer*
Kierkegaard's Attack upon 'Christendom' (Kierkegaard)
See *Hvad Christus dömmer om officiel Christendom*
"Kies Ősz" (Arany) **34**:19
Kihlaus (Kivi) **30**:48, 50, 53, 64
"Kikuka no chigiri" (Ueda Akinari) **131**:5-7, 13-15, 24-25, 27, 32, 34, 38, 40-41, 48, 60
Kikuka no Chigiri (Ueda Akinari) **131**:64-65, 69, 74-75
"Kilmeny" (Hogg) **4**:274, 279-80, 282-83, 285; **109**:209, 243, 248, 270-72
Das Kind der Liebe (Kotzebue) **25**:130, 134, 136, 141, 144-46, 151
"The Kind Master and Dutiful Servant" (Hammon) **5**:262, 264-65
"Kinderfrühling" (Muller) **73**:366
Kindergeschichten (Stifter)
See *Bunte Steine*
"Kinderlust" (Muller) **73**:366
Kinder-und Hausmärchen (Grimm and Grimm) **3**:216, 218-20, 226-27, 230; **77**:189-284
"Die Kindesmörderin" (Ludwig) **4**:353
The King and Queen of Hearts (Lamb) **10**:417
The King and the Knight (Eminescu) **33**:264
King Arthur (Bulwer-Lytton) **1**:143-44; **45**:15-18, 22
"King Arthur's Tomb" (Morris) **4**:426, 431, 444

King Charles, the Young Hero (Tegner) **2**:613
King Charles's Beauties (Jameson)
See *Memoirs of the Beauties of the Court of Charles II*
King Charming (Planché) **42**:300
"King Cophetua the First" (Patmore) **9**:335
"King David" (Woolson) **82**:273, 294-95, 300
"King Edward the Third" (Blake) **13**:171, 181, 184, 239; **127**:13
"King Etzel's Sword" (Meyer)
See "König Etzels Schwert"
King Fjalar (Runeberg)
See *Kung Fjalar*
"King Harold on the Eve of the Battle of Hastings" (Brontë) **16**:104
"King Lear" (Lamb) **125**:306-7
"A King Lear of the Steppes" (Turgenev)
See "Stepnoy Korol 'Lir"
"The King of Achen's Daughter" (Maginn) **8**:437
"The King of Clubs" (Alcott) **83**:8
"The King of Hukapetapank" (Muller) **73**:353
The King of the Peacocks (Planché) **42**:273, 288, 293-94
King Otakar's Rise and Fall (Grillparzer)
See *König Ottokars Glück und Ende*
King Ottocar: His Rise and Fall (Grillparzer)
See *König Ottokars Glück und Ende*
"King Penguin" (Horne) **127**:263, 266, 268
"King Pest" (Poe) **1**:500; **16**:308, 313
"King Robert of Sicily" (Longfellow) **45**:114, 128, 137, 145, 149, 188
"King Saul at Gilboa" (Kendall) **12**:190-92, 199-202
King Solomon's Mines (Stevenson) **63**:257
King Spirit (Slowacki)
See *Król Duch*
King Stephen (Keats) **8**:341, 360; **73**:155, 306
"King Ulysses" (Isaacs)
See "El rey Ulises"
King Victor and King Charles (Browning) **19**:102, 113
"King Volmer and Elsie" (Whittier) **8**:529
"King Wine" (Muller) **73**:353
"King Witlaf's Drinking-Horn" (Longfellow) **45**:116
"The Kingdom of Darkness" (Dobrolyubov) **5**:140-41, 151
"The Kingdom of the Saints" (Newman) **38**:305
The King's Book (Arnim)
See *Dies Buch Gehört dem König*
"The King's Dream" (Andersen) **7**:23
The King's Edict (Hugo)
See *Marion de Lorme*
The King's Fool (Hugo)
See *Le roi s'amuse*
"The King's Garments" (Crawford) **12**:156
Kings in Exile (Daudet)
See *Les rois en exil*
The King's Judgement (Eminescu) **33**:266
"A King's Lesson" (Morris) **4**:439
The Kings on Salamis (Runeberg)
See *Kungarne på Salamis*
The King's Own (Marryat) **3**:317, 319
"The King's Scholar's Story" (Barham) **77**:9
"The King's Tragedy" (Rossetti) **4**:499-500, 502-04, 506, 508, 513, 518, 525-27, 529, 532; **77**:298
"The King's Vow" (Petofi)
See "A király esküje"
The Kingsmen; or, The Black Riders of Congaree (Simms)
See *The Scout*
Kinsa (Ueda Akinari) **131**:20
Kinsa jogen (Ueda Akinari) **131**:20
"A király esküje" (Petofi) **21**:264
Kirjali (Pushkin) **3**:436; **83**:325
Kirsteen: A Story of a Scottish Family Seventy Years Ago (Oliphant) **11**:449-51, 457-8; **61**:173, 195, 202, 216, 223, 226, 233-5, 241
"Kismet" (Ingelow) **39**:258
"The Kiss" (Rossetti) **77**:338-39
"Kitty Tyrrell" (Ferguson) **33**:301
Kjerlighedens Gjerninger (Kierkegaard) **125**:250, 257, 262, 265
Klage und Trost (Tieck) **5**:519
"Klänge aus dem Orient" (Droste-Hülshoff) **3**:195, 203
"Klara Hebert" (Lenau) **16**:286
"Klara Milič" (Turgenev)
See "Klara Milich"
"Klara Milich" (Turgenev) **21**:408, 415, 420, 431, 438, 441, 451-52; **122**:242, 244, 246-47, 265-68, 365, 374-75, 378
"Klára Zách" (Arany) **34**:20
"Klaskaniem mając obrzękłe prawice" (Norwid) **17**:374
Klassische Blumenlese (Mörike) **10**:449, 452, 456
Klaus und Klajus: Ein Roman von einem Schulmeister leben (Ludwig) **4**:356
Kleider machen Leute (Keller) **2**:415, 423
Klein Zaches gennant Zinnober (Hoffmann) **2**:341, 351, 361-62
Die kleine Zigeunerin (Kotzebue) **25**:147
Kleinere Schriften (Kopitar)
See *Barth. Kopitars kleinere Schriften*
Kleopatria i Cezar (Norwid) **17**:367, 369, 379
"Klods-Hans" (Andersen) **79**:72, 81
"Klokken" (Andersen)
See "The Bell"
Das Kloster bei Sendomir (Grillparzer) **102**:176-77
"Die Klosterbeere. Zum Andenken an die Frankfurter Judengasse" (Arnim) **123**:60, 62-63, 65, 69
Klosterheim; or, The Masque (De Quincey) **4**:65, 81; **87**:76, 79
"Klosterszene" (Grillparzer) **102**:175
"Klytie" (Leconte de Lisle) **29**:239
"Der Knabe im Moor" (Droste-Hülshoff) **3**:193, 200
Knave or Not? (Holcroft) **85**:198-99, 223
"Kniazhna" (Shevchenko) **54**:387, 389, 394
Kniazhna (Shevchenko) **54**:369, 390-4, 397-8
Knickerbocker (Irving)
See *Knickerbocker Stories from the Old Dutch Days of New York*
Knickerbocker Stories from the Old Dutch Days of New York (Irving) **2**:365-66, 368-69, 371, 373, 385-87; **95**:226-27, **3**:1817-18
Knickerbocker's History (Irving)
See *A History of New York, from the Beginning of the World to the End of the Dutch Dynasty*
"Knight Aagen and Maiden Else" (Morris) **4**:423
"The Knight and the Dragon" (Hood) **16**:233
The Knight and the Lady (Barham) **77**:10
"The Knight for an Hour" (Nekrasov)
See "Rycar' na čas"
"A Knight of Dannebrog" (Boyesen) **135**:13, 21, 27
The Knight of Guadalquiver (Dunlap) **2**:213, 215
The Knight of Gwynne: A Tale of the Time of the Union (Lever) **23**:292, 305-07, 310-11
"A Knight of Our Times" (Karamzin) **3**:281, 287
"Knight Pázmán" (Arany)
See "Pázmán lovag"
"The Knight's Epitaph" (Bryant) **46**:3
The Knights of the Round Table (Planché) **42**:292
Knjaginja (Shevchenko)
See *Kniazhna*
"The Knob Dance" (Harris) **23**:141, 147
"Knocking" (De Quincey) **87**:77
"Knock...Knock...Knock" (Turgenev)
See "Stuk...stuk...stuk"
"A Knot of Roses" (Kivi)
See "Ruususolmu"
"The Knouto-Germanic Empire and the Social Revolution" (Bakunin)
See "L'Empire Knouto-Germanique et la Révolution Sociale"
The Knouto-Germanic Empire and the Social Revolution (Bakunin) **25**:46, 48-9, 59
Know Your Place (Ostrovsky)
See *Ne v svoi sani ne sadis!*
Know Yourself (Wagner)
See *Erkenne dich selb*
"Knoware" (Cooke) **110**:21
"Knowledge" (Lampman) **25**:194, 209
"Knowlwood" (Barnes) **75**:58
"Known in Vain" (Rossetti) **4**:491
"Knyagine Z.A. Volkonskoy" (Baratynsky) **103**:10
Kobboltozo: A Sequel to The Last of the Huggermuggers (Cranch) **115**:16-17, 54-9
Kobzar (Shevchenko) **54**:358-9, 364, 372-5, 379, 384, 386
"Kogda drjaxlejušcie sily" (Tyutchev) **34**:415
"Kogda ischeznet omrachenie" (Baratynsky) **103**:5, 9-10
"Kogda karateliam velikim" (Pavlova) **138**:13
Kohlhaas (Kleist)
See *Michael Kohlhaas*
Kojiki den (Motoori) **45**:268, 274-77
"Kolebka pieśni" (Norwid) **17**:374
"Kółko" (Norwid) **17**:373
"Kolokol kazni" (Bestuzhev) **131**:172
"A Kolozsiak" (Madach) **19**:369
"Kőltőés szabadság" (Madach) **19**:368
Der Komet; oder, Nikolaus Marggraf: Eine komische Geschichte (Jean Paul) **7**:238-39, 242
"Komu na Rusi zhit khorosho" (Nekrasov) **11**:405-09, 413-15, 418-21
"The Kondem Phool" (Shaw) **15**:335
"Konec" (Turgenev) **122**:264-65
König (Arnim)
See *Königsbuch*
"König Etzels Schwert" (Meyer) **81**:207
"Der König in Thule" (Goethe) **34**:122
König Ottokars Glück und Ende (Grillparzer) **1**:383-84, 387, 395, 397; **102**:105, 107-08, 111, 115, 117, 165-66, 168, 180
"Die Königin Luise" (Klopstock) **11**:237
Königsbuch (Arnim) **123**:9-15
Königsmark, the Legend of the Hounds, and other Poems (Boker) **125**:25, 33, 38, 58, 70, 76-78
"Königsmark the Robber; or, The Terror of Bohemia" (Lewis) **11**:302
Koningsmarke, the Long Finne: A Story of the New World (Paulding) **2**:527, 529-31
Konrad Wallenrod (Mickiewicz) **3**:389-92, 394-95, 398-99, 401; **101**:157, 171, 183-84, 197-201
Konradin (Klinger) **1**:429
"Konyága" (Saltykov) **16**:346, 373-74
"Kooroora" (Kendall) **12**:192, 201
Kopala kundala (Chatterji)
See *Kapalkundala*
Kordian (Slowacki) **15**:348, 352-53, 364-65, 369, 373, 375-76, 378-80
"Körner and His Sister" (Hemans) **71**:275
"Korobeyniki" (Nekrasov) **11**:407, 411, 413, 420-21
"Korrespondent" (Turgenev)
See "Peripiska"
"Eine Korrespondent mit mir selbst" (Claudius) **75**:209
"Korrespondenz zwischen mir und meinem Vetter, die Bibelübersetzungen betreffend" (Claudius) **75**:209-10
Der Kosak und der Freiwillige (Kotzebue) **25**:140
"Kossuth" (Whittier) **59**:371
"Kotin and Platonida" (Leskov)
See "Kotin doilec"
"Kotin doilec" (Leskov) **25**:239
"Koto no Ne" (Ichiyō) **49**:335, 353

"Kotterii" (Baratynsky) **103**:11, 49
Koz'ma Zakhar'ich Minin Sukoruk (Ostrovsky) **57**:206-7
Kozma Zakharich Minin the One-Armed (Ostrovsky)
See *Koz'ma Zakhar'ich Minin Sukoruk*
"Die Krähe" (Muller) **73**:394
Krak (Slowacki) **15**:353, 371
"The Kraken" (Tennyson) **30**:211, 233; **65**:280
Krakus (Norwid) **17**:366-67, 369, 376, 379
"Die Kraniche des Ibykus" (Schiller) **39**:330, 332, 337, 350
Kranjska čbelica (Preseren) **127**:304, 311-12, 315, 320, 329, 333
"Krasnoe polryvalo" (Bestuzhev) **131**:161
Krates und Hipparchia (Wieland) **17**:400-01
Kreisleriana, Kreislers musikalische Leiden (Hoffmann) **2**:346-47, 358-59
Kreislers Lehrbrief (Hoffmann) **2**:346
"Kreislers musikalisch-poetischer Klub" (Hoffmann) **2**:347
"Krempeljnu" (Preseren) **127**:314
"Krestyánskie déti" (Nekrasov) **11**:403, 421
"Das Kreuz" (Lenau) **16**:275, 281
Kreuzfahrer (Kotzebue) **25**:136
"Kriegslied" (Claudius) **75**:183, 194
Kriemhilds Rache (Hebbel) **43**:261
Krigssåang för skånska lantvärnet (Tegner) **2**:612
"Krinken" (Field) **3**:211
Krishna charitra (Chatterji) **19**:204-05, 216, 222, 225
Krishna Kumāri (Dutt) **118**:5, 21, 23
Krishnakanter will (Chatterji) **19**:205, 209-10, 213, 215, 217-19, 221-22
Kritik der praktischen Vernunft (Kant) **27**:196, 203-05, 208, 224, 229, 231, 246, 248, 251, 255, 257, 264; **67**:214, 216, 219-22, 252, 261, 264, 271, 288, 294-95
Kritik der reinen Vernunft (Kant) **27**:194-201, 203-05, 208-09, 220-26, 229, 231, 233, 246-48, 250-51, 253-57, 259-61, 263-64, 266-68, 270; **67**:212, 214, 216, 218-19, 222, 264, 287, 294
Kritik der Urtheilskraft (Kant) **27**:196, 203, 205, 210, 228, 231, 237, 248, 251, 255, 267; **67**:214
Kritik der Verfassung Deutschlands (Hegel) **46**:150
"Kritika na novyi roman Val'ter Skotta—Kenil'vort" (Bestuzhev) **131**:165
"Kritische Fragments" (Schlegel) **45**:358-59
Kritische Friedrich Schlegel Ausgabe (Schlegel) **45**:355, 357
Kritische Wälder (Herder) **8**:305, 307-08, 313-14
"Krivoklad" (Macha) **46**:201, 214
"The Krkonoe Pilgrimage" (Macha) **46**:210-12
"Krøblingen" (Andersen) **7**:28; **79**:77
Król Duch (Slowacki) **15**:349-50, 354, 356, 360-62, 365-66, 374-77
Die Kronenwächter (Arnim) **5**:13, 16-18, 20, 23
"Krónika két pénzdarab sorśaról" (Madach) **19**:369
"Kronos; To Coachman Kronos" (Goethe)
See "An Schwager Kronos"
Krösus (Grillparzer) **102**:105
"Krotkaya" (Dostoevsky) **2**:162; **33**:179-80
Krsnacaritra (Chatterji)
See *Krishna charitra*
Krsnakānter Uil (Chatterji)
See *Krishnakanter will*
Krst pri Svici: Povest v verzih (Preseren) **127**:293, 297, 308-10, 329-32
Kruglyi god (Saltykov) **16**:374
"Das Kruzifix" (Chamisso) **82**:27
"Krytyka" (Norwid) **17**:374
K. S. Aksakovu (Pavlova) **138**:5
Ksiądz Marek (Slowacki) **15**:348, 352, 360, 365, 371, 378
Księgi narodu polskiego i pielgrzymastwa polskiego (Mickiewicz) **3**:388-89, 395, 397-98, 401; **101**:183-84
"Ktaadn, and the Maine Woods" (Thoreau) **138**:72, 115, 128-30, 148
Kto vinovat? (Herzen) **10**:321-3, 326-7, 331, 333-4, 348; **61**:97, 106-9, 113-5
Kuang fang-yen (Li Ju-chen) **137**:206
"Kubla Khan" (Coleridge) **9**:133-34, 140-42, 149, 151, 155, 158, 179-80, 182-83, 192-96, 204; **54**:82, 87, 89, 98-9, 106, 115; **99**:1-118; **111**:250, 258, 308
Kullervo (Kivi) **30**:48, 54-6, 58-62, 64
"Kulneff" (Runeberg) **41**:312, 323
Die Kultur der Renaissance in Italien (Burckhardt) **49**:3, 11, 16-6, 20-1, 23-4, 27, 29-30, 32
Kulturgeschichte (Burckhardt)
See *Griechische Kulturgeschichte*
Kun en spillemand (Andersen) **7**:15-16, 21, 26, 33; **79**:18-19, 21
"Kun László Krónikája" (Petofi) **21**:264
"Kundiman" (Rizal) **27**:425
"Die Künftiege Geliebte" (Klopstock) **11**:236
Kung Fjalar (Runeberg) **41**:310, 317-18, 325
Kungarne på Salamis (Runeberg) **41**:310, 318
Die Kunst und die Revolution (Wagner) **9**:404, 425-26, 432, 452; **119**:238, 248-53, 256-58
"Die Künstler" (Schiller) **39**:336, 389
Das Kunstwerk der Zukunft (Wagner) **9**:405, 425, 432-33, 452; **119**:238, 248-53, 257-60, 274, 294, 323
"Kurze Freude" (Meyer) **81**:147
Kurze Ubersicht der Manufakturen in Russland (Kotzebue) **25**:141
Kuse monogatari (Ueda Akinari) **131**:19, 36, 40, 51
"A kutyák dala" (Petofi) **21**:264
"Kutyakaparó" (Petofi) **21**:260, 277, 285
Kuzubana (Motoori) **45**:275-76
"The Kyffhäuser and its Legends" (Taylor) **89**:312
"Kyozukue" (Ichiyō) **49**:352
"Kyrkan" (Runeberg) **41**:318
"L. E. L.'s Last Question" (Browning) **16**:133; **61**:51
"A la Belleza" (Casal) **131**:270-71
"De la bonne doctrine" (Banville) **9**:16
"A la castidad" (Casal) **131**:255, 267
"De la Cause des Hellènes" (Chateaubriand) **134**:8
"De la Clôture de la session de la Chambre des Pairs" (Chateaubriand) **134**:8
De la démocratie en Amérique (Tocqueville) **7**:417-25, 427, 429, 432-34, 440, 443-46, 448-53, 455-56, 458-59, 461; **63**:279, 281-4, 287-8, 290-3, 297-302, 304, 306, 308, 316-23, 326, 328, 332-3, 336, 342, 352-4, 357-60, 366-8, 371-2, 379, 388, 391
De la educación popular (Faustino) **123**:288, 330, 360
A la Feuille de Rose (Maupassant) **83**:199-201, 203
"A la juventud Filipina" (Rizal) **27**:425
De la littérature considérée dans ses rapports avec les institutions sociales (Staël-Holstein) **3**:519, 524, 527-8, 530-3; **91**:298, 304-6, 310-12, 323-4, 326, 332, 340, 359
"De la littérature dans ses raports avec la liberté" (Constant) **6**:224
"A la luna" (Espronceda) **39**:105-06
"De la misère en Allemagne" (Arnim) **123**:5
"De la monarchie constitutionelle en France" (Renan) **26**:377
De la monarchie selon la charte (Chateaubriand) **3**:110, 112; **134**:5
"A la muerte de Don Joaquín de Pablo (Chapalangarra)" (Espronceda) **39**:105
"A la nue accablante tu" (Mallarmé) **41**:250, 294
"A la patria" (Espronceda) **39**:100, 105
"A la poesía" (Gómez de Avellaneda) **111**:28
De la religion considérée dans sa source, ses formes, et ses développements (Constant) **6**:213, 221
La Salle and the Discovery of the Great West (Parkman) **12**:336, 341, 372, 378-79
"La Salle Painted by Himself" (Parkman) **12**:378
"De la sátira y los satíricos" (Larra) **130**:238, 241, 276
"A la Srta. C. O. Y. R." (Rizal) **27**:425
"A la traslación de las cenizas de Napoleón" (Espronceda) **39**:120
El Laberinto (Gómez de Avellaneda) **111**:21
"The Laboratory" (Browning) **19**:77, 96; **79**:94, 99
"The Laboring Classes" (Brownson) **50**:31, 42, 48
"The Laboring Skeleton" (Baudelaire)
See "Le squelette laboureur"
"The Labourer's Daily Life" (Jefferies) **47**:141
The Labourers of the Ten Little Hard Parishes to Alexander Baring, Loan-Monger (Cobbett) **49**:113
"Les laboureurs" (Lamartine) **11**:274, 284
Labours of Idleness; or, Seven Night's Entertainments (Darley) **2**:127, 129-30
"Le lac" (Lamartine) **11**:245, 248, 263-64, 268-70, 277-78, 280-82
Le lac des fées (Scribe) **16**:410
"A l'Académie de Marseille, Gethsémani" (Lamartine) **11**:271
"The Lace Runners" (Tonna) **135**:199-200, 209-10, 213, 216, 220-23
"Lacinularia Socialis" (Huxley) **67**:79-80
Lack of Caution (Turgenev) **21**:428
Lack of Funds (Turgenev) **21**:428, 432
"Lacordaire and Catholic Progress" (Brownson) **50**:51
"Ladder of St. Augustine" (Longfellow) **45**:116, 127
Ladies and Hussars (Fredro)
See *Damy i huzary*
The Ladies' Battle (Reade) **74**:331
The Ladies' Battle (Robertson) **35**:354
The Ladies' Battle; or, A Duel of Love (Scribe)
See *Bataille de dames; ou, Un duel en amour*
The Ladies' Family Library (Child) **6**:198; **73**:97, 100
The Ladies Lindores (Oliphant) **11**:439, 441, 445-7; **61**:204, 206, 208-9, 240
The Ladies of Castile (Warren) **13**:412-14, 418-19, 429-30, 436
"The Ladies of the Sacred Heart" (Sedgwick) **19**:446
The Ladies' Wreath (Hale) **75**:337, 341, 349
"Ladislaus the Fifth" (Arany)
See "László V"
"Ladraban contra min" (Castro) **78**:42
Ladugårdsarrebnet (Almqvist) **42**:4
"Lady Alice" (Allingham) **25**:18
"The Lady and the Slut" (Leskov)
See "Dama i fefela"
Lady Anna (Trollope) **6**:470, 475; **101**:249, 251, 253, 310, 313
"Lady Anne and Lady Jane" (Opie) **65**:171-2
"Lady Barbara" (Crabbe) **26**:129
"Lady Barbara" (Smith) **59**:320, 331, 333
Lady Byron Vindicated: A History of the Byron Controversy, from Its Beginning in 1816 to the Present Time (Stowe) **3**:556, 562
Lady Car (Oliphant) **61**:208
"Lady Geraldine's Courtship" (Browning) **1**:114-8, 125-7; **61**:4, 42, 65-7, 75; **66**:44-5, 56, 71, 74, 87-91, 93, 101
Lady Johanna Gray (Wieland) **17**:419-20
"The Lady Lisle and Elizabeth Gaunt" (Landor) **14**:185
"Lady Macbeth" (Galt) **1**:327
"Lady Macbeth" (Maginn) **8**:439, 442

"A Lady Macbeth of the Mtsensk District" (Leskov)
See "Ledi Makbet Mcenskogo uezda"
Lady Mary and Her Nurse; or, A Peep into the Canadian Forest (Traill) **31**:316, 327
"Lady Moon, Lady Moon" (Milnes) **61**:154
Lady Morgan's Memoirs (Morgan) **29**:394
"The Lady of Amboto" (Gómez de Avellaneda)
See "La dama de Amboto"
The Lady of La Garaye (Norton) **47**:245-46, 248, 252
"The Lady of Little Fishing" (Woolson) **82**:272, 286, 293-94, 306, 322, 334
The Lady of Lyons; or, Love and Pride (Bulwer-Lytton) **1**:140; **45**:18, 62, 69
"The Lady of Shalott" (Tennyson) **30**:206, 211-12, 222-23, 231, 241, 258, 267, 279; **65**:234, 240, 337, 357; **115**:335, 358
"A Lady of Sorrow" (Thomson) **18**:393, 400-01, 412-13, 421, 424-25, 427
The Lady of the Camelias (Dumas)
See *La dame aux camélias*
"The Lady of the Castle" (Hemans) **29**:198; **71**:288
The Lady of the Ice (De Mille) **123**:119
The Lady of the Lake (Scott) **15**:256, 273, 283, 292-93, 318-19; **69**:304, 361
"The Lady of the Land" (Morris) **4**:442, 448
The Lady of the Rock (Holcroft) **85**:199, 212, 218, 224-25
"The Lady of the Sea" (Allingham) **25**:12
Lady Susan (Austen) **1**:35-36, 39, 51-52; **33**:86; **119**:17, 26, 30, 44-5
"The Lady Turned Peasant" (Pushkin)
See "Baryshnia-krest'ianka"
Lady und Schnieder (Nestroy) **42**:233-35, 237, 249-50
Lady William (Oliphant) **61**:202
"The Lady-Peasant" (Pushkin)
See "Baryshnia-krest'ianka"
A Lady's Diary (Jameson)
See *Diary of an Ennuyée*
"The Lady's Dream" (Hood) **16**:209, 220, 235
The Lady's Maid (Martineau) **26**:322
"Laeti et Errabundi" (Verlaine) **51**:356, 363, 372
"Lafayette en Amérique" (Beranger) **34**:29
Die Lage der arbeitenden Klasse in England (Engels) **85**:3-6, 8, 13, 31, 110-11, 113-15, 121, 125, 165, 171-72, 177, 179-81, 184; **114**:4, 35, 41, 73
Lágrimas: Novela de costumbres contemporáneas (Caballero) **10**:76
"Laida" (Echeverria) **18**:148
The Laird of Norlaw (Oliphant) **11**:432
"The Laird of Peatstacknowe's Tale" (Hogg) **4**:287
Laïs (Eminescu) **33**:267
"Laisser-courre" (Corbière) **43**:31
La laitière de Montfermeil (Kock) **16**:245, 249
"The Lake" (Eminescu) **131**:296
"The Lake" (Lamartine)
See "Le lac"
"The Lake" (Melville) **3**:352
The Lake Regions of Central Africa (Burton) **42**:41, 58
"Lake Zurich" (Klopstock) **11**:220
"The Lake—To—" (Poe) **117**:266, 271-72, 281, 283
Lalla Rookh (Moore) **6**:378-81, 386-88, 391, 393, 396, 399; **110**:165-68, 171, 175-76, 189, 202-3, 211-13, 216, 219-25
De l'Allemagne (Heine) **4**:232
De l'Allemagne (Staël-Holstein) **3**:520, 526-8, 530, 532-4; **91**:338, 340, 350-1, 359-60, 365
"The Lamb" (Blake) **13**:180-82, 221, 241-45; **37**:3, 6, 9, 12, 39, 54, 57, 65, 69, 76, 91-2
"The Lamb" (Krylov) **1**:435
Lambro (Slowacki) **15**:348, 358, 363-64, 376
"O Lambros" (Solomos) **15**:386, 389, 393-94, 396-97, 405
"Lame Jervas" (Edgeworth) **51**:87, 89
"The Lament for Captain Paton" (Lockhart) **6**:293
"A Lament for Kilcash" (Mangan) **27**:315
"Lament for Sarsfield" (Mangan) **27**:279
"A Lament for the Birds" (Cooper) **129**:35, 72
"Lament for the Decline of Chivalry" (Hood) **16**:219
"Lament for the Princes of Tyrone and Tyrconnell" (Mangan) **27**:296-98, 310-12, 319
"The Lament of a Canadian Emigrant" (Moodie) **113**:345
"The Lament of King Cormac" (Mangan) **27**:314
"The Lament of Swordy Well" (Clare) **9**:108, 110, 118; **86**:131-32, 178
The Lament of Tasso (Byron) **2**:64, 96; **12**:106
"Lament of the Winds" (Lampman) **25**:204
"The Lament of Youth" (Chivers) **49**:48, 69-70
"Lament on the Death of My Mother" (Chivers) **49**:39
"Lament over the Ruins of the Abbey of Teach Molaga" (Mangan) **27**:319
"Lamentation for the Death of Sir Maurice Fitzgerald" (Mangan) **27**:290, 310-11
"Lamentation of Mac Liag for Kincora" (Mangan) **27**:297, 310-12
"Lamentationen" (Heine) **4**:254-55
"The Lamentations of Round Oak Waters" (Clare) **9**:119
"Lamia" (Keats) **8**:333-34, 340-41, 345, 347, 350, 356-57, 360-61, 366, 370, 375, 383, 385-86; **73**:154-55, 171-73, 190, 198, 202, 208-09, 212-13, 218, 228, 232-34, 255, 261-62, 277, 285, 304, 306-07, 322, 325, 328
Lamia (Hood) **16**:229
Lamia, Isabella, The Eve of St. Agnes, and Other Poems (Keats) **8**:326-28, 331-32, 340, 350; **73**:155, 197, 233; **121**:108, 112, 154, 165, 173, 162
Lamiel (Stendhal) **23**:384, 395, 397, 409, 418-19; **46**:318
De l'amour (Stendhal) **23**:347, 368, 374, 423; **46**:262, 273, 276, 323-24, 327-28
"La lampe du temple" (Lamartine) **11**:279
The Lamplighter (Cummins) **139**:161-64, 166-68, 170-76, 178, 180-87, 190-94, 198-201, 204-5, 207-9, 213-14, 216, 220, 222, 224, 226-28
The Lamplighter Picture Book, or the Story of Uncle True and Little Gerty, Written for the Little Folks (Cummins) **139**:183
"The Lamp's Shrine" (Rossetti) **77**:339
Lancashire Collier Girl (More) **27**:358
The Lancashire Witches: A Romance of Pendle Forest (Ainsworth) **13**:37, 40-1, 47-8
"Lancelot and Elaine" (Tennyson) **30**:249, 291-92; **65**:227, 237, 241, 243, 246, 250, 252-4, 278-9, 282, 284, 294-5, 297, 299-301, 312, 335-7, 342, 352, 357-60, 364, 366, 385
"Lancelot and Guinevere" (Tennyson) **65**:376
Lances de honor (Tamayo y Baus) **1**:565, 569
"Land East of the Sun and West of the Moon" (Morris) **4**:416-17, 447
"The Land of Dreams" (Blake) **13**:181, 243
"The Land of Dreams" (Bryant) **46**:39
"The Land of Dreams" (Hemans) **29**:205
Land of Midian Revisited (Burton) **42**:41, 56
"The Land of Pallas" (Lampman) **25**:184, 193-94, 196, 201, 204, 211, 220
"The Land of Paoli" (Taylor) **89**:313
The Land of Upside Down (Tieck)
See *Die Verkehrte Welt*
"The Landing of the Pilgrim Fathers" (Hemans) **71**:271, 283
"The Landlady" (Dostoevsky)
See "Khozyaika"
The Landleaguers (Trollope) **6**:471, 495, 500; **101**:245-46, 250-53, 262, 264, 267, 276, 293-94, 296, 298-99, 319
Ländliche Lieder (Muller) **73**:352, 362, 366-67, 387
"The Landlord" (Thoreau) **138**:121
"Landor, English Visiter and Florentine Visiter" (Landor) **14**:195
"Landor's Cottage" (Poe) **16**:304, 336; **55**:147, 153; **97**:184, 187; **117**:310
"The Landowner" (Turgenev) **122**:293
The Lands of the Saracen (Taylor) **89**:346
"The Landscape Garden" (Poe)
See "Landscape Gardening"
"Landscape Gardening" (Poe) **16**:304; **97**:186
"Landscapes" (Baudelaire)
See "Paysages"
"Landscapes" (Crèvecoeur) **105**:102, 125, 177-94
"Landshövdingen" (Runeberg) **41**:325-27
"The Lane" (Barnes)
See "The Leane"
"Lánggal égo" (Petofi) **21**:283
"Language" (Emerson) **38**:178
"The Language of Religion" (Patmore) **9**:341
"Langueur" (Verlaine) **51**:360
Lanrick (Carroll) **139**:57
"The Lantern Out of Doors" (Hopkins) **17**:185, 220, 244
"The Lantern-Bearers" (Stevenson) **5**:410; **63**:239
La lanterne magique (Banville) **9**:21
Lant-virágok (Madach) **19**:368
"The Laocoön" (Blake) **127**:53-54, 124
"Laodamia" (Wordsworth) **12**:414, 427, 459; **38**:356
Laon and Cythna, or the Revolution in the Golden City (Shelley) **18**:308, 311, 313-14, 319, 332, 334, 336, 338, 342, 344, 347, 379-81, 384; **93**:267, 270, 292-96, 298, 300, 331-32, 334, 336, 338, 340-41, 355
"Lappen og Professoren" (Andersen)
See "The Professor and the Flea"
"The Lapse of Time" (Bryant) **6**:159-60, 172
"Lapsi" (Kivi) **30**:51
"Laquelle des deux? Histoire perplexe" (Gautier) **59**:29
"Laquelle est la vraie?" (Baudelaire) **29**:110
Lara (Byron) **2**:62, 70, 73, 81, 86, 89, 95, 99; **12**:82; **109**:102
"The Largest Life" (Lampman) **25**:163, 190, 217
"A Lark's Flight" (Smith) **59**:303, 309, 311, 315, 317, 319, 323
"The Lark's Nest" (Clare) **9**:108, 110
"Larme" (Rimbaud) **4**:472, 478; **82**:231-33, 247-48
"Une larme du diable" (Gautier) **1**:339, 345
"Les larmes de l'ours" (Leconte de Lisle) **29**:230
"Larmes de Racine" (Sainte-Beuve) **5**:342
"Larry M'Farland's Wake" (Carleton) **3**:89, 92
"Lars" (Taylor) **89**:315
Lars: A Pastoral of Norway (Taylor) **89**:315, 349
"A las cubanas" (Gómez de Avellaneda) **111**:30, 65
The Las Essays of Elia. Being a Sequel to Essays Published under that Name (Lamb) **113**:198, 217-218, 221, 228, 247, 252-53, 261, 265, 281, 282-84
"A las flores de Heidelberg" (Rizal) **27**:425
De las Monarchie selon la Charte (Chateaubriand) **134**:5
"Lass die heilgen Parabolen" (Heine) **4**:257
"The Lass of Carrick" (Mangan) **27**:314
The Last (Krasiński)
See *Ostatni*
"A Last Adieu" (Hogg) **109**:202
"The Last Banquet of Antony and Cleopatra" (Hemans) **71**:295
The Last Baron of Crana (Banim and Banim) **13**:121, 129-31, 135-37, 147, 149-51
"The Last Buccaneer" (Kingsley) **35**:227
The Last Buccaneer (Macaulay) **42**:88

"Last Canto of Childe Harold" (Lamartine)
See "Le dernier chant de pèlerinage de Childe Harold"
"Last Child" (Lampman) **25**:216
The Last Chronicle of Barset (Trollope) **6**:458, 461, 467, 470-71, 479, 484, 491-92, 494, 497-98, 507, 509, 516-17; **33**:363, 417-18, 422; **101**:235, 265-66, 272-74, 279, 285, 289, 320-21, 326, 333, 342-43
"A Last Confession" (Rossetti) **4**:495-97, 500-03, 507-08, 510-12, 518-19, 523-24, 526-27; **77**:286-7, 293, 304, 317, 337
The Last Constantine, with Other Poems (Hemans) **29**:202
The Last Day of a Condemned (Hugo)
See *Le dernier jour d'un condamné*
"The Last Day of Castle Connor" (Le Fanu) **9**:320
"The Last Days of a Criminal" (Hood) **16**:203
"The Last Days of John Brown" (Thoreau) **7**:406
The Last Days of Pompeii (Bulwer-Lytton) **1**:136-38, 140, 146, 149-53; **45**:3, 5, 13, 22, 27, 29, 32-3, 55-7, 62, 68-70
"The Last Dream of the Old Oak" (Andersen) **79**:62
The Last Essays of Elia (Lamb) **10**:392, 435-37
Last Essays on Church and Religion (Arnold) **6**:53; **29**:21; **89**:65, 131; **126**:90-91
Last Foray in Lithuania (Mickiewicz)
See *Pan Tadeusz; czyli, Ostatni zajazd na Litwie*
"The Last Frost of Spring" (Ichiyō)
See "Wakerejimo"
The Last Fruit off an Old Tree (Landor) **14**:169-70
"The Last Generation in England" (Gaskell) **97**:110, 121, 127, 167-68
"The Last Judgement" (Macha)
See "Poslednì soud"
"The Last Judgment" (Levy) **59**:93
"The Last Lamp of the Alley" (Maginn) **8**:441
"The Last Leaf" (Holmes) **14**:100-01, 109, 120-21, 125, 129, 132; **81**:107
"The Last Leap" (Gordon) **21**:159, 181, 186
Last Leaves (Smith) **59**:298-9, 306, 308, 311, 314, 317, 319-23, 333, 337, 340
Last Letters (Foscolo)
See *Ultime lettere di Jacopo Ortis*
The Last Letters of Aubrey Beardsley (Beardsley) **6**:138
The Last Letters of Jacopo Ortis (Foscolo)
See *Ultime lettere di Jacopo Ortis*
Last Letters of Ortis (Foscolo)
See *Ultime lettere di Jacopo Ortis*
"Last Love" (Tyutchev) **34**:403
"The Last Man" (Campbell) **19**:176, 179, 181, 187, 190, 192, 196, 198
"The Last Man" (Hood) **16**:202, 231-34
The Last Man (Beddoes) **3**:37-39
The Last Man (Shelley) **14**:253-54, 256, 262, 265, 267, 269-71, 274-76, 290, 292-93, 299; **59**:144, 155, 177, 195; **103**:329, 331-33, 338-40, 348
"The Last National Revolt of the Jews" (Lazarus) **8**:424
"The Last Night that She Lived" (Dickinson) **21**:35
"Last Norridgewock" (Whittier) **8**:485
"The Last of His Tribe" (Kendall) **12**:190-92, 196, 201
"The Last of Macquarie Harbour" (Clarke) **19**:257
The Last of the Barons (Bulwer-Lytton) **1**:140-41, 146, 150-52; **45**:14-15, 21, 58-60, 62, 70
"The Last of the Flock" (Wordsworth) **12**:386-87; **111**:202-3, 208, 210, 224, 234, 253, 307, 311, 315, 359
The Last of the Foresters; or, Humors on the Border: A Story of the Old Virginia Frontier (Cooke) **5**:122, 128-29, 131, 133-34, 136
The Last of the Huggermuggers (Cranch) **115**:16-17, 54-9
The Last of the Lairds; or, The Life and Opinions of Malachi Mailings, Esq. of Auldbiggings (Galt) **1**:332, 334-35, 337; **110**:76-7, 96
The Last of the Mohicans: A Narrative of 1757 (Cooper) **1**:197-200, 202-03, 205, 207, 212, 217, 221, 225; **27**:124, 127-36, 138, 140-44, 147, 150, 153-54, 157, 160-67, 172-73, 175-79, 181, 183-85, 187; **54**:254, 267, 269, 271, 283-4, 286-7, 299, 301
The Last of the Mortimers (Oliphant) **11**:446
The Last of the Mușat Kin (Eminescu) **33**:264
"The Last of the War Cases" (Whitman) **4**:554
"The Last of Ulysses" (Landor) **14**:181
Last Poems (Browning) **1**:121; **61**:44
Last Poems (Heine) **4**:238
Last Poems (Lowell) **2**:512; **90**:188
The Last Poems of Philip Freneau (Freneau) **111**:162, 190
"The Last Poet" (Baratynsky)
See "Posledny poet"
"Last Public Address" (Lincoln) **18**:225
"The Last Reader" (Holmes) **14**:98-100
"The Last Ride Together" (Browning) **19**:127, 131
"The Last Song of Sappho" (Hemans) **71**:296
"Last Songs" (Nekrasov) **11**:407
"The Last Sunset" (Isaacs)
See "El último arrebol"
"The Last Tournament" (Tennyson) **30**:254; **65**:238-9, 241, 246, 251-3, 269, 279, 282, 285, 291-3, 296-8, 300, 352-3, 363, 369, 372-4, 376, 383
"The Last Walk in Autumn" (Whittier) **8**:517; **59**:360, 366, 368
Last Words (Arnold) **29**:54
"The Last Words of Al-Hassan" (Mangan) **27**:287, 290
"The Last Words of Charles Edwards" (Maginn) **8**:438
"The Last Words of Stonewall Jackson" (Lanier) **6**:237
"László V" (Arany) **34**:15, 20
"Late November" (Lampman) **25**:182
The Late Summer (Stifter)
See *Der Nachsommer*
Later Letters of Edward Lear (Lear) **3**:299
"Later Life" (Rossetti) **2**:563, 566, 570, 575; **50**:272, 284, 292
"Laterna Magica" (Pavlova) **138**:51
Later Poems (Whittier) **8**:495
The Later Poems of John Clare 1837-1864 (Clare) **86**:198, 111, 113-15, 117-22, 162, 166, 170, 180
"The Latest Decalogue" (Clough) **27**:83-4, 91, 103, 114
"Latnik: Rasskaz partizanskogo ofitsera" (Bestuzhev) **131**:156-59, 175-76
"The Latter Rain" (Very) **9**:380, 385
Latter-Day Pamphlets (Carlyle) **70**:72, 82, 91
Latter-Day Pamphlets (Froude) **43**:218
"Der Laudachsee" (Lenau) **16**:283
"Laudamus" (Gordon) **21**:160, 164, 175
Laughable Lyrics (Lear) **3**:296-97, 309
"Laughing Life Cries at the Feast" (Rossetti) **66**:307
"The Laughing Song" (Blake) **37**:3, 9, 13, 40, 61, 65, 71-2, 78-9, 91-2
"Laughter" (Crawford) **12**:156
Die Launen des Glückes (Nestroy) **42**:238, 257
"Launfal" (Lowell) **90**:198
Laura (Sand) **42**:359, 363
"Laurance" (Ingelow) **107**:148
"Laurette; ou, Le cachet rouge" (Vigny) **7**:478
"Laus Deo" (Whittier) **8**:515, 531; **59**:360-1, 385
"Laus Mariae" (Lanier) **118**:215
Lautréamont's Preface to His Unwritten Volume of Poems (Lautréamont)
See *Poésies I, II*
Lavengro: The Scholar—The Gypsy—The Priest (Borrow) **9**:40-56, 60-9
The Law and the Lady (Collins) **1**:188, 191
"Law as Suited to Man" (Dana) **53**:180-1
Lawrence Bloomfield in Ireland (Allingham) **25**:10-11, 13, 16, 18-19, 21-3, 26-7, 29, 31-4
Lawrie Todd; or, The Settlers in the Woods (Galt) **1**:330-31
The Lawton Girl (Frederic) **10**:183-84, 187-88, 192-93, 201, 203-04, 209, 211, 213-14
The Lawyers (Lewes) **25**:291
"The Lawyer's First Tale" (Clough) **27**:81
"The Lay of a Golden Goose" (Alcott) **58**:6
The Lay of Maldoror (Lautréamont)
See *Les chants de Maldoror: Chants I, II, III, IV, V, VI*
The lay of St. Cuthbert (Barham) **77**:9
"A Lay of St. Dunstan" (Barham) **77**:41-42
The Lay of St. Gengulphus (Barham) **77**:9, 43
"The Lay of the Bell" (Schiller)
See "The Song of the Bell"
"The Lay of the Brown Rosary" (Browning) **1**:115, 117, 126; **61**:31-2, 43, 65-7, 74-5; **66**:44
"A Lay of the Early Rose" (Browning) **1**:117; **61**:43
"The Lay of the Humble" (Milnes) **61**:130, 145
"The Lay of the Laborer" (Hood) **16**:209, 220, 228, 233, 237-38
The Lay of the Last Minstrel (Scott) **15**:249-52, 267, 273, 286, 293, 318-19; **69**:298, 302, 304
The Lay of the Laureate: Carmen Nuptiale (Southey) **8**:462; **97**:263
The Lay of the Scottish Fiddle (Paulding) **2**:525
"A Lay Preacher" (Cooke) **110**:37
Lay Sermons (Huxley) **67**:4, 44
"Lay this Laurel on the One" (Dickinson) **77**:118
Lays (Macaulay)
See *Lays of Ancient Rome*
Lays and Legends of the Rhine (Planché) **42**:274
Lays for the Dead (Opie) **65**:182
Lays of Ancient Rome (Macaulay) **42**:84, 86, 88, 111, 113, 151
Lays of Many Lands (Hemans) **29**:202-03; **71**:261, 295
Lays of My Home, and Other Poems (Whittier) **8**:485-86; **59**:353, 370
Lays of the Red Branch (Ferguson) **33**:293-94
Lays of the Western Gael (Ferguson) **33**:279, 281, 285, 287, 289-91, 293-94, 297-99
"Lázaro" (Silva) **114**:301
Lázaro (Silva) **114**:273
"Lazarus" (Silva)
See *Lázaro*
Lazarus (Heine) **4**:248, 254, 257
"The Lazy Crow" (Simms) **3**:509
The Lazy Tour of Two Idle Apprentices (Collins) **1**:185
The Lazy Tour of Two Idle Apprentices (Dickens) **86**:188
Lea (Kivi) **30**:48, 50, 53, 65
"Lead, Kindly Light" (Newman) **38**:282, 315, 336
"Lead lunar ray" (Fuller) **50**:249, 250
"The Leaden Echo and the Golden Echo" (Hopkins) **17**:186-87, 193, 200, 205, 210-12, 225
"Leady-Day an' Ridden House" (Barnes) **75**:77, 81, 83
"The Leady's Tower" (Barnes) **75**:72-3
"A Leaf from King Alfred's Orosius" (Longfellow) **45**:160
"A Leaf from the Diary of a Guard Officer" (Bestuzhev)
See "Listok iz dnevnika gvardeyskogo ofitsera"

"A Leaf From the Sky" (Andersen) **7**:22
"The Leaf Glancing Boughs" (Harpur) **114**:116
"Leander" (Keats) **8**:361
"The Leane" (Barnes) **75**:15-16, 55, 68, 101, 104
"The Leap Frog" (Andersen) **7**:23, 25
"A Lear of the Steppes" (Turgenev)
See "Stepnoy Korol 'Lir"
"The Learned Boy" (Crabbe) **26**:93, 130; **121**:40
"Learned Lady" (Irving) **95**:239
"The Leather Bottell" (Maginn) **8**:438
Leather Stocking and Silk; or, Hunter John Myers and His Times: A Story of the Valley of Virginia (Cooke) **5**:127-29, 131-32, 136
The Leatherstocking Tales (Cooper) **1**:205-06, 211-12, 215, 217, 221-28; **54**:284
"Leave, O leave Me to My Sorrows" (Blake) **37**:29
"Leaves" (Barnes) **75**:15
Leaves (Parton)
See *Fern Leaves, Second Series*
"The Leaves Are Falling—So Am I" (Landor) **14**:199
"Leaves from a Note-Book" (Eliot) **118**:187
Leaves from Australian Forests (Kendall) **12**:180-81, 184, 186, 192-93, 196, 200
Leaves From Margaret Smith's Journal (Whittier) **59**:362, 380-1, 384
"Leaves from My Omnibus Book" (Cranch) **115**:50
Leaves of Grass (Whitman) **4**:535-37, 539-47, 551, 553-55, 558, 561-63, 566-67, 574-76, 579, 581, 583-89, 591-96, 600-01, 603-04; **31**:357-448; **81**:237, 241-42, 244, 254-71, 275, 281, 286-87, 293, 295, 299, 302, 309-10, 312-18, 325-30, 332, 336, 340-43, 345-47, 350-51, 353-54, 361, 363-64, 369
"Leaving Fishkill for New York" (Fuller) **50**:249
"Leaving the Theater after the Performance of a New Comedy" (Gogol)
See *Teatral'nyi raz'ezd posle predstavleniia novoi komedii*
"Lebed" (Tyutchev) **34**:410
Das Leben der Hochgräfin Gritta von Rattenzuhausbeiuns (Arnim) **123**:74, 77, 81-82
"Leben des vergnügten Schulmeisterleins Maria Wuz in Aventhal" (Jean Paul) **7**:235-36, 238, 242
Leben Fibels, des Verfassers der Bienrodischen Fibel (Jean Paul) **7**:235, 239, 241, 242
Leben und Tod der heiligen Genoveva (Tieck) **5**:511, 514, 521, 525, 529, 532
Leben und Tod des kleinen Rothkäppchens (Tieck) **5**:523
Lebens-Ansichten des Katers Murr nebst fragmentarischer Biographie des Kapellmeisters Johannes Kreisler in züfalligen Makulaturblättern (Hoffmann) **2**:340-41, 346-47, 353, 356-58, 360, 362-63
Lebenselemente (Tieck) **5**:518
Lebens-Lieder und Bilder (Chamisso) **82**:6
Lecoq the Detective (Gaboriau)
See *Monsieur Lecoq*
"A Lecture Delivered before the Female Anti-Slavery Society of Salem" (Brown) **2**:47, 53
"Lecture I" (Keble) **87**:154
Lecture IV (Keble) **87**:151
"Lecture on 'Discoveries; Inventions; and Improvements'" (Lincoln) **18**:240
"Lecture on Slavery" (Emerson) **98**:169, 171
"Lecture on the Anti-Slavery Movement" (Douglass) **7**:124
"Lecture on the 'Nature of Poetry'" (Dobell)
See "The Nature of Poetry"
"Lecture on the Poetry of Wordsworth" (Clough) **27**:59, 101-03, 106
"Lecture on the Poets of America" (Poe) **55**:177
"Lecture on the Times" (Emerson) **1**:301; **38**:209
Lecture XL (Keble) **87**:151
Lecture XVI (Keble) **87**:154
Lecture XXII (Keble) **87**:150, 154
Lecture XXVIII (Keble) **87**:154
Lecture XXX (Keble) **87**:154
"Lecture XXXIX" (Keble) **87**:153
Lecturers on the French and Belgian Revolutions (Cobbett) **49**:160
Lectures and Biographical Sketches (Emerson) **98**:65
Lectures and Essays on University Subjects (Newman) **38**:324, 327; **99**:212
Lectures and Miscellanies (James) **53**:209, 217
Lectures Chiefly on the Dramatic Literature of the Age of Elizabeth (Hazlitt) **29**:146-47, 163, 174
Lectures for Working Men (Huxley) **67**:85
Lectures on Aesthetics (Hegel)
See *Vorlesungen über die Aesthetik*
Lectures on Ancient and Modern Literature (Schlegel)
See *Geschichte der alten und neuen Literatur*
Lectures on Art (Taine) **15**:469
Lectures on Art, and Poems (Allston) **2**:23-25, 27
Lectures on Certain Difficulties Felt by Anglicans in submitting to the Catholic Church (Newman) **38**:291, 310-11, 328; **99**:263
"Lectures on English Philosophy" (Hazlitt) **82**:108
Lectures on Ethics (Kant) **27**:248, 262
Lectures on Justification (Newman)
See *Lectures on the Doctrine of Justification*
"Lectures on Murder Considered as One of the Fine Arts" (De Quincey) **4**:61, 68, 73-74, 78, 85; **87**:76-7, 79
Lectures on Philosophical Theology (Kant) **27**:244
"Lectures on Poetry" (Bryant) **6**:190; **46**:10, 12, 16, 27, 29, 43, 48, 52
Lectures on Poetry (Keble) **87**:152, 154, 156-57, 161, 175, 183-84, 193, 199
Lectures on Recent Philosophy (Schelling) **30**:163
"Lectures on Revealed Religion" (Coleridge) **99**:41
Lectures on Rhetoric and Belles Lettres (Blair) **75**:115-19, 123, 127, 131, 133, 136-37, 141-44, 146-47, 149-50, 157, 160, 164-65, 177
Lectures on Shakespeare and Milton (Coleridge) **99**:105
Lectures on the Doctrine of Justification (Newman) **38**:315; **99**:223, 229-34, 278
Lectures on the Elevation of the Laboring Portion of the Community (Channing) **17**:26, 41
Lectures on the English Comic Writers (Hazlitt) **29**:145-47, 163, 165, 167, 174
Lectures on the English Poets (Hazlitt) **29**:134, 138, 145-48, 163-65, 174, 176-77, 183; **82**:123
Lectures on the Essence of Religion (Feuerbach)
See *Vorlesung über das Wesen der Religion: Nebst Zusätzen und Anmerkungen*
Lectures on the History of Literature (Schlegel) **45**:288
Lectures on the Life of Christ (Schleiermacher) **107**:268
Lectures on the Philosophy of History (Hegel)
See *Vorlesungen über die Philosophie der Geschichte*
Lectures on the Philosophy of History (Schlegel) **45**:300
Lectures on the Philosophy of Religion: Together with a Work on the Proofs of the Existance of God (Hegel)
See *Vorlesungen über die Philosophie der Religion, nebst iener Schrift über die Beweise vom Dasein Gottes*
Lectures on the Present Position of Catholics in England: Addressed to the Brothers of the Oratory (Newman) **38**:294, 310, 328; **99**:211, 264
Lectures on the Prophetical Office of the Church (Newman) **38**:315; **99**:220-21, 225
Led Astray (Feuillet)
See *Tentation*
"Ledi Makbet Mcenskogo uezda" (Leskov) **25**:228, 233-34, 245-48, 264-65
"De l'Education" (Laclos)
See *De l'Education des femmes*
De l'Education des femmes (Laclos) **4**:325, 340, 342; **87**:239-40, 246, 274
"Ledwina" (Droste-Hülshoff) **3**:196, 203
Lee and His Lieutenants (Cooke) **5**:124
"Lee Shore" (Melville) **49**:414, 416
"The Leech of Folkestone" (Barham) **77**:33, 35
"The Left-handed Craftsman" (Leskov)
See "Levša"
"The Left-Handed Smith and the Steel Flea" (Leskov)
See "Levša"
"The Lefthander" (Leskov)
See "Levša"
Legacies to Labourers; or, What is the Right Which Lords, Baronets and Squires Have to the Lands of England? (Cobbett) **49**:155
"The Legacy" (Moore) **6**:399; **110**:185
Legacy to Parsons; or, Have the Clergy of the Established Church and Equitable Right to the Tithes (Cobbett) **49**:114
Legacy to Peel (Cobbett) **49**:114
"The Legal Codes of Lycurgus and Solon" (Schiller)
See "The Legislation of Lycurgus and Solon"
"Legem tuam dilexi" (Patmore) **9**:359, 361
"The Legend" (Herzen) **10**:346-47; **61**:108
"A Legend" (Krasiński)
See "Legenda"
Legend (Longfellow)
See *The Golden Legend*
Legend (Pushkin) **3**:445, 448
"The Legend Beautiful" (Longfellow) **45**:188
"The Legend of Bottle Hill" (Maginn) **8**:440
"The Legend of Brittany" (Lowell) **2**:505, 515
"The Legend of Dhruva" (Dutt) **29**:123, 126
"The Legend of Doctor Theophilus: or, The Enchanted Clothes" (Cranch) **115**:54, 57-9
The Legend of Florence (Hunt) **1**:412, 415, 423; **70**:263
Legend of Hamilton Tighe (Barham) **77**:4, 19, 26, 36
The Legend of Jubal, and Other Poems (Eliot) **4**:107, 115
"Legend of Khalif Hakem" (Nerval)
See *L'histoire du Calife Hakem*
"The Legend of Knockgrafton" (Maginn) **8**:440
"The Legend of Knocksheogowna" (Maginn) **8**:440
"Legend of Lake Switez" (Mickiewicz) **3**:393
"Legend of Maryland" (Kennedy) **2**:431-33
A Legend of Montrose (Scott) **15**:300, 304, 309; **69**:303, 308, 313, 322
"Legend of Oxford" (Sigourney) **21**:290
"Legend of Pennsylvania" (Sigourney) **87**:342
"The Legend of Rabbi Ben Levi" (Longfellow) **45**:137
The Legend of Saint Julien Hospitaller (Flaubert)
See *La légende de Saint-Julien l'Hospitalier*

The Legend of Saint Julien the Hospitator (Flaubert)
See *La légende de Saint-Julien l'Hospitalier*
"A Legend of Sheppey" (Barham) **77**:44
"The Legend of Sleepy Hollow" (Irving) **2**:367, 376, 379, 381-84, 389-90, 392-93; **19**:327-29, 331-37, 339-41, 343-45, 347-49; **95**:227, 240, 242-44, 249, 265, 268, 283-86, 296
"The Legend of St. Leonor" (Lanier) **118**:218-19
"Legend of St. Lucas" (Schlegel) **15**:223
"A Legend of the Apostle John" (Child) **6**:201
"The Legend of the Brown Rosarie" (Browning)
See "The Lay of the Brown Rosary"
The Legend of the Centuries (Hugo)
See *La légende des siècles*
"Legend of the Delewares" (Bryant) **46**:4
A Legend of the Devil's Dyke (Boucicault) **41**:40
"The Legend of the Devil's Pulpit" (Bryant) **6**:181
"Legend of the Enchanted Soldier" (Irving) **2**:388
"The Legend of the Grand Inquisitor" (Dostoevsky) **2**:181, 185, 188, 191-92; **21**:112; **33**:177, 230; **43**:92, 95-96, 98, 103, 107, 120, 122-23, 127, 137-38, 149-53, 157, 169-72
"The Legend of the Hounds" (Boker) **125**:34, 38, 77
"The Legend of the Morning Star" (Eminescu) **131**:288
The Legend of the Rhine (Thackeray) **5**:464
"Legend of the Sheep Fold" (Harpur) **114**:150
"Legenda" (Krasiński) **4**:306, 313
"Legenda o sovestnom Danile" (Leskov) **25**:245
"Lègende" (Laforgue) **5**:280; **53**:294
La Légende de Saint Julien Hospitalier (Flaubert)
See *La légende de Saint-Julien l'Hospitalier*
La légende de Saint-Julien l'Hospitalier (Flaubert) **2**:227, 232-3, 236, 246, 257-8; **62**:93, 108; **135**:109, 134
La légende de Soeur Béatrix (Nodier) **19**:385
"La légende des Nornes" (Leconte de Lisle) **29**:226-28
La légende des siècles (Hugo) **3**:253, 255, 262, 264, 270-72, 276; **10**:375; **21**:196
Légendes démocratiques (Michelet) **31**:232
"Légendes rustiques" (Sand) **42**:314
Legends and Lyrics (Hayne) **94**:136, 141-42, 144, 148, 151, 154-57, 159, 164, 169
Legends of New England in Prose and Verse (Whittier) **8**:484-85, 526; **59**:363
Legends of the Madonna (Jameson) **43**:306, 324, 326
Legends of the Monastic Orders (Jameson) **43**:306, 324-25
"The Legends of the Province House" (Hawthorne) **2**:293, 322; **95**:140
"The Legislation of Lycurgus and Solon" (Schiller) **39**:363
De l'Église gallicane (Maistre) **37**:295, 299
Lehrjahre (Goethe)
See *Wilhelm Meisters Lehrjahre*
Die Lehrlinge zu Saïs (Novalis) **13**:366, 368, 370-71, 374-77, 381, 384-86, 401, 403
"Leib und Seele" (Heine) **4**:257
Leicester (Dunlap) **2**:210-13, 215, 217
Leicester, an Autobiography (Adams)
See *A Child of the Age*
"Leichhardt" (Kendall) **12**:182, 194, 199
"Leiden" (Hölderlin) **16**:185
Die Leiden des jungen Werthers (Goethe) **34**:94, 120
Das Leiden eines Knaben (Meyer) **81**:175-76, 180, 182, 215
Leiden und Freuden eines Schulmeisters (Gotthelf) **117**:4, 7, 14, 17, 19, 25, 27, 32, 35, 38, 46, 51
Das Leidende Weib (Klinger) **1**:428
Der Leiermann (Muller) **73**:386, 390, 393, 395-97
Leighton Court (Kingsley) **107**:188, 192-93, 197, 209, 228-29
"Leila: A Tale" (Browning) **61**:36
"Leila in the Arabian zone" (Fuller) **50**:247, 250
Leila; or, The Siege of Granada (Bulwer-Lytton) **45**:58
"Leisure" (Lamb) **10**:405
"The Leisure of a Dramatic Critic" (Lewes) **25**:291
"Leitenant Belozor" (Bestuzhev) **131**:154
"A Lejtőn" (Arany) **34**:19
Lélia (Sand) **2**:581-85, 587-89, 595-98, 603-04, 606-08; **42**:316, 318, 320, 322, 338, 349-57, 360, 362-6, 379; **57**:313, 318-22, 324-5, 327-37, 339, 360, 367, 370
"Lenardos Tagebuch" (Goethe) **4**:189
"Lenore" (Poe) **55**:133; **117**:192, 195, 217, 221, 226-27, 236-38, 242, 295-96, 299
"Lentes ajenos" (Silva) **114**:317
Lenz (Büchner) **26**:4, 18, 20, 27-8, 36, 41-2, 46-8, 50-5, 59, 67
Leo and Liina (Kivi)
See *Leo ja Liina*
Leo Burckart (Nerval) **1**:475; **67**:303
Leo ja Liina (Kivi) **30**:64
"Leofric and Godiva" (Landor) **14**:185-86
"Leonard and Susan" (Coleridge) **90**:7, 25
Leonard and Susan (Coleridge) **90**:16, 20
"Leonardo da Vinci" (Pater) **7**:305, 311; **90**:296, 298, 305
Leonce und Lena (Büchner) **26**:4, 9, 20, 25-8, 30, 32-3, 38-9, 43, 45, 55, 62, 64
Leoncia (Gómez de Avellaneda) **111**:12, 15, 55
Leone Leoni (Sand) **2**:587; **57**:312, 316, 341, 360
Leoni or the Orphan of Venice (Chivers) **49**:52, 61-3
Leoni the Orphan of Venice (Chivers)
See *Leoni or the Orphan of Venice*
Leonor de Guzman (Boker) **125**:8-9, 17, 20-22, 24, 31, 36, 55, 58, 64-66, 76
Leonora (Edgeworth) **1**:256; **51**:87-90
"Leopold" (Beddoes) **3**:33
The Leper of the City of Aoste: A Narrative (Williams) **135**:312, 314
"Leper-House of Janval" (Gore) **65**:21
"Les lépreux" (Bertrand) **31**:47
"Der Lerche" (Droste-Hülshoff) **3**:193, 202
Les (Ostrovsky) **30**:100, 104, 111, 113, 115, 119; **57**:220
The Lesbians (Baudelaire)
See *Les fleurs du mal*
Les Lesbiennes (Baudelaire)
See *Les fleurs du mal*
"Lesbos" (Baudelaire) **29**:66, 72-4; **55**:6-8, 33, 61, 73-4
LesForestiers (Dumas) **71**:193
"Lesley Castle" (Austen) **13**:72; **119**:13, 15
De l'espit de conquête et de l'usurpation dans leurs rapports avec la civilisation Européenne (Constant) **6**:222, 225
De l'esprit des traductions (Staël-Holstein) **91**:340
"De l'Essence du rire" (Baudelaire) **55**:68, 72
"Lessing" (Lewes) **25**:286
"Lessing" (Lowell) **2**:509
"A Lesson for Kings" (Hunt) **70**:258
The Lesson of Life, and Other Poems (Boker) **125**:18, 30, 35, 57
"A Lesson on Sensibility" (Brown) **74**:108
Lessons for Children (Barbauld) **50**:2, 7
"Lessons in Criticism to William Roscoe, and Farther Lessons to a Quarterly Reviewer" (Bowles) **103**:54
"Let Be!" (Patmore) **9**:339, 358, 365
"Let Down the Bars, O Death" (Dickinson) **21**:20
"Let Erin Remember the Days of Old" (Moore) **6**:397, 399; **110**:185, 194, 198
"Let My Name Survive" (Chivers) **49**:70
Let Off with a Scare (Vigny)
See *Quitte pour la peur*
"Let Pure Hate Still Underprop" (Thoreau) **7**:382
"Let the Brothels of Paris Be Opened" (Blake) **13**:243
"Let There Be Light" (Wergeland)
See "Vord lys!"
"Let Us Gather in Congress" (Eminescu) **33**:272
"Leteszem a lantot" (Arany) **34**:13, 19
"Léthé" (Baudelaire) **29**:73
"Le lethe" (Baudelaire)
See "Léthé"
"Lethe" (Meyer) **81**:199, 204, 209
"Letnij vecer" (Tyutchev) **34**:389, 411
"A Letter" (Lermontov)
See "Pis'mo"
"Letter" (Martineau) **137**:308
"Letter" (Melville) **93**:210
Letter (Pavlova)
See "Pis'mo v redakcïiu Sovremennika"
"Letter" (Whitman) **81**:287
Letter (Crèvecoeur)
See *Lettres d'un Cultivateur Américain*
"Letter about Censorship in Russia" (Tyutchev) **34**:384
A Letter, Addressed to the People of Piedmont (Barlow) **23**:27-8
Letter and Spirit: Notes on the Commandments (Rossetti) **50**:271, 276-7, 324; **66**:306-7, 342, 375
"Letter: From a Missionary of the Methodist Episcopal Church South in Kansas to a Distinguished Politician" (Whittier) **8**:525, 531; **59**:361, 369-71
"Letter from George Henry Boker to Bayard Taylor" (Boker) **125**:87-88
"Letter from George Henry Boker to Elizabeth Stoddard" (Boker) **125**:83
"Letter from George Henry Boker to John Seely Hart" (Boker) **125**:84
"Letter from George Henry Boker to Richard Henry Stoddard" (Boker) **125**:82, 85-87
"A Letter from London to Paris from one American to Another" (Bello)
See "Carta Escrita de Londres a París por un Americano a Otro"
"Letter from Mexico" (Corbière) **43**:14
Letter from Noah Webster, Esq., of New Haven, Connecticut, to a Friend in Explanation and Defense of the Distinguishing Doctrines of the Gospel (Webster) **30**:408
"A Letter from St. Petersburg" (Turgenev) **122**:294
"A Letter from the Pope to the Bishop of Rochester Prior to his Exile" (Bestuzhev)
See "Pis'mo Popa k episkopu Rochester-skomu pered ego izgnaniem"
"The Letter L" (Ingelow) **39**:264
"Letter of Advice to a Young American" (Godwin) **130**:37
"Letter of Elia to Robert Southey" (Lamb) **113**:178
"Letter of John Bull" (Barbauld) **50**:14
"Letter of the Seer" (Rimbaud)
See "Lettre du voyant"
"Letter on Music" (Moore) **110**:192
Letter on the Novel (Schlegel)
See "Brief über den Roman"
"Letter on travelling, & c" (Cranch) **115**:48
"Letter on Watering-places" (Barbauld) **50**:14
Letter ot Old George Rose (Cobbett) **49**:113
"Letter to a Friend in London" (Shelley) **18**:327
Letter to a Friend of Robert Burns (Wordsworth) **111**:370
"Letter to a newly elected Young Member of the Lower House" (Freneau) **111**:124
"Letter to a Young Gentleman" (Stevenson) **5**:420

"Letter to a Young Gentleman Commencing His Education" (Webster) **30**:408
"Letter to B—" (Poe) **55**:142, 162, 170; **117**:304
"Letter to Balzac" (Stendhal) **46**:325
"Letter to Beethoven" (Fuller) **5**:167
"Letter to Doctor Erman" (Bestuzhev)
See "Pis'mo k doktoru Ermanu"
Letter to Dorothea (Schlegel) **45**:363, 365
A Letter to Dr. David Ramsay, Of Charleston, (S. C.) Respecting the Errors in Johnson's Dictionary, and Other Lexicons (Webster) **30**:398
"Letter to Dumas" (Nerval) **67**:357
Letter to Emerson (Landor) **14**:207
Letter to Governor Hamilton on the Subject of State Interposition (Calhoun) **15**:28, 59
A Letter to his Countrymen (Cooper) **54**:256
"Letter to his Son" (Hazlitt) **82**:88
Letter to Jack Harrow an English Labourer on the New Cheat of Savings Banks (Cobbett) **49**:113
"Letter to Lamartine" (Musset)
See "Lettre à M. de Lamartine"
"Letter to Maria Gisborne" (Shelley) **18**:356
"A Letter to Mary Ann" (Cooke) **110**:39, 41-2, 67-8
"Letter to Mathetes" (Wordsworth) **111**:255, 257
"Letter to Mr.—" (Poe) **55**:138
"Letter to Mrs. Bixby" (Lincoln) **18**:257
Letter to the Abbé Raynal (Paine) **62**:322, 359
"Letter to the Bishop fo Llandaff" (Wordsworth) **38**:422, 426; **111**:253, 263, 345
"Letter to the Deaf" (Martineau) **26**:349-50
"Letter to the Editor of the Literary Gazette" (Pushkin) **83**:320
"Letter to the Editors of Sovremennik" (Pavlova)
See "Pis'mo v redakcïiu Sovremennika"
A Letter to the Governors, Instructors, and Trustees of the Universities, and Other Seminaries of Learning, in the United States, on the Errors of English Grammar (Webster) **30**:414
A Letter to the Hon. Henry Clay, on the Annexation of Texas to the United States (Channing) **17**:22, 32-3, 35
A Letter to the Marquis of Lansdowne (Milnes) **61**:145
A Letter to the National Convention of France (Barlow) **23**:18, 27-8
"Letter to the Queen on Lord Chancellor Cranworth's Marriage and Divorce Bill" (Norton) **47**:248, 250, 254, 261, 263
"Letter to the Young Women of Malolos" (Rizal) **27**:417
"A Letter to Thomas Campbell" (Bowles) **103**:54
Letter to W. Windham (Holcroft)
See *Letter to William Windham, on the Intemperance and Dangerous Tendency of His Conduct*
Letter to William Gifford, Esq. (Hazlitt) **29**:167, 169-70; **82**:98
A Letter to William Smith, Esq. M.P. (Southey) **97**:263, 312
Letter to William Windham, on the Intemperance and Dangerous Tendency of His Conduct (Holcroft) **85**:194-95, 199, 209, 227-28, 235
Lettera sul romanticismo (Manzoni) **98**:215
The Letter-Bag of the Great Western; or, Life in a Steamer (Haliburton) **15**:118-19, 125-26, 129, 135, 145
"The Letter-Bell" (Hazlitt) **29**:153
Lettere (Leopardi) **129**:278
Lettere scritte dall'Inghilterra (Foscolo) **97**:88-93
"Letters" (Emerson) **1**:296
"Letters" (Kirkland) **85**:296, 299, 301
"Letters" (Rossetti) **77**:296, 301
"Letters" (Schiller) **39**:337
Letters (Austen) **95**:30
Letters (Byron)
See *Letters and Journals*
Letters (Carroll) **139**:63-66
Letters (Coleridge) **90**:32
Letters (Cowper) **94**:94-5, 119-25
Letters (Dickens) **113**:15, 107, 127, 130
Letters (Dickinson) **21**:21-2, 30
Letters (Eliot)
See *George Eliot Letters*
Letters (Emerson)
See *The Letters of Ralph Waldo Emerson*
Letters (Eminescu) **131**:333
Letters (Freneau)
See *Letters on Various Interesting and Important Subjects*
Letters (Gaskell) **97**:127, 130, 142, 170, 173
Letters (Ghalib) **39**:154-55
Letters (Hayne) **94**:154
Letters (Keats) **121**:108, 110-11, 124, 126, 129-30, 132, 172, 174, 177-81, 185-88, 192-94, 197, 202
Letters (Krasicki)
See *Listy*
Letters (Lamb) **113**:182, 202-3, 230
Letters (Longfellow)
See *The Letters of Henry Wadsworth Longfellow*
Letters (Mill) **58**:321
Letters (Moore) **110**:182, 184
Letters (Newman)
See *The Letters and Diaries of John Henry Newman*
Letters (Poe) **117**:321
Letters (Scott) **110**:240, 260-61, 263-64, 313, 315
Letters (Sigourney) **87**:337
Letters (Symonds) **34**:331-32, 336-37
Letters (Tennyson) **65**:378; **115**:360
Letters (Trelawny)
See *Letters of Edward John Trelawny*
Letters (Webster) **30**:397
Letters and Correspondence (Newman) **38**:296, 312-13
The Letters and Diaries of John Henry Newman (Newman) **99**:218-25, 252-53, 283, 285, 291
Letters and Essays, Moral and Miscellaneous (Hays) **114**:177-78, 185, 188, 190, 194, 200, 206-7, 210, 216, 219-20, 229-30
Letters and Journals (Byron) **2**:87; **109**:122, 126
Letters and Journals of Lord Byron, with Notices of His Life (Moore) **6**:385, 393; **110**:175
Letters and Literary Remains of Edward FitzGerald (FitzGerald) **9**:268-70
The Letters and Private Papers of William Makepeace Thackeray (Thackeray) **5**:485
Letters and Remains (Clough) **27**:53
Letters and Social Aims (Emerson) **1**:282
"Letters by Robert Slender, O. S. M." (Freneau) **1**:315
Letters containing a Sketch of the Politics of France (Williams) **135**:258, 260-61, 268, 282-83, 291-92, 312, 334, 338-41, 343
Letters containing a Sketch of the Scenes which passed in various Departments of France during the Tyranny of Robespierre and of the Events which took place in Paris on the Tenth of Thermidor (Williams) **135**:258, 260-61, 283, 291-92, 312, 338, 341
Letters for Literary Ladies (Edgeworth) **1**:267; **51**:81, 83
Letters from a Dead House (Dostoevsky)
See *Zapiski iz mertvogo doma*
"Letters from Abroad" (Hunt) **1**:416; **70**:279
Letters from Abroad to Kindred at Home (Sedgwick) **19**:441, 445-47
Letters from an American Farmer; describing certain provincial situations, manners and customs (Crèvecoeur) **105**:90, 93-108, 110-12, 114-28, 130-33, 135-39, 144-47, 149-50, 152-59, 162-65, 168-69, 172-73, 177-83, 185-91, 193-94
The Letters from Avenue Marigny (Herzen) **61**:86
Letters from Berlin (Heine)
See *Briefe aus Berlin*
"Letters from Dagestan" (Bestuzhev)
See "Pis'ma iz Dagestana"
Letters from England (Southey) **8**:475-76; **97**:266, 268, 270-71, 278-79, 281, 284-87, 291, 322
Letters from France (Williams) **135**:256-58, 261, 267-77, 281-83, 285-93, 296-97, 299, 302, 308, 312, 321-23, 326-28, 333-34, 336-44, 353-55, 358-59
Letters from France, containing a Great Variety of Interesting and Original Information Concerning the most Important Events that have lately occurred in that Country and particularly respecting the Campaign of 1792 (Williams) **135**:258, 267-68, 276, 282-83, 338-39, 341
Letters from France, containing Many New Anecdotes Relative to the French Revolution and the Present State of French Manners (Williams) **135**:257-58, 267, 284, 288-89, 321, 323, 327-28, 334, 342-43
Letters from My Mill (Daudet)
See *Lettres de mon moulin*
Letters from New York (Child) **6**:200-03, 206-07, 209; **73**:51, 56, 59-61, 67, 80-81, 87
Letters from Paris (Barlow) **23**:28
Letters from Phocian (Hamilton) **49**:325
Letters from the Levant (Galt) **110**:76, 92, 96
Letters from the South (Paulding) **2**:525, 531
Letters from the Underworld (Dostoevsky)
See *Zapiski iz podpol'ya*
Letters from the Wuppertal (Engels)
See *Briefe aus dem Wuppertal*
The Letters of A. Bronson Alcott (Alcott) **1**:27
Letters of a Lifetime (Moodie) **113**:324, 369
Letters of a Russian Traveler, 1789-1790 (Karamzin) **3**:280, 282-83, 286-87
The Letters of a Solitary Wanderer (Smith) **115**:124, 221-22
Letters of a Traveller (Sand)
See *Lettres d'un voyageur*
Letters of a Traveller; or, Notes of Things Seen in Europe and America (Bryant) **6**:171; **46**:5, 25
Letters of a Traveller, second series (Bryant) **6**:171
The Letters of Alexander Pushkin (Pushkin) **3**:457; **83**:247-49
Letters of an American Farmer (Crèvecoeur)
See *Letters from an American Farmer; describing certain provincial situations, manners and customs*
"Letters of an Englishman" (Brontë) **109**:44
Letters of an Englishman (Brontë) **109**:27, 37, 50
The Letters of Anthony Trollope (Trollope) **101**:320
The Letters of Charles and Mary Lamb (Lamb) **125**:317, 333-34, 343, 347-48
Letters of Dorothy Wordsworth (Wordsworth) **138**:227, 236
Letters of Dupuis and Cotonet (Musset)
See *Lettres de Dupuis et Cotonet*
The Letters of Edgar Allen Poe (Poe) **117**:304
Letters of Edward John Trelawny (Trelawny) **85**:322, 324, 330
The Letters of Elizabeth Barrett Browning (Browning) **61**:13-17, 29, 48, 51, 61, 67; **66**:50-1, 70

Letters of Elizabeth Barrett Browning to Mary Russell Mitford 1836-1854 (Browning) **61**:29-32, 49, 51-2, 66-7, 73; **66**:74
Letters of Emily Dickinson, 2 vols. (Dickinson) **77**:75
The Letters of Francis Parkman (Parkman) **12**:364
The Letters of Gerard Manley Hopkins to Robert Bridges (Hopkins) **17**:214, 223
The Letters of Gustave Flaubert (Flaubert)
See *Correspondance*
Letters of Hannah More (More) **27**:338
The Letters of Henry Wadsworth Longfellow (Longfellow) **2**:498
The Letters of Herman Melville (Melville) **91**:30, 32-3; **123**:192, 194-95, 232, 235
Letters of James Russell Lowell (Lowell) **90**:222
Letters of Jane Austen (Austen) **119**:54
The Letters of John Clare (Clare) **86**:99, 103, 155-56, 159, 172
Letters of John Keats to Fanny Brawne (Keats) **8**:334, 374
Letters of John Keats to His Family and Friends (Keats) **8**:374, 390-91; **73**:158, 254-58, 264-70, 328-29, 331-32, 335-42
Letters of Julia and Caroline (Edgeworth) **1**:272; **51**:86-7
The Letters of Karl Marx (Marx) **17**:355-56
Letters of Life (Sigourney) **21**:300, 302, 307, 311, 314; **87**:323, 325, 343
The Letters of Lydia Maria Child (Child) **73**:50, 73
Letters of Matthew Arnold, 1848-1888 (Arnold) **6**:43-45; **89**:46
The Letters of Matthew Arnold to Arthur Hugh Clough (Arnold) **89**:52; **126**:112
The Letters of Mrs. Elizabeth Montagu (Montagu) **117**:141, 178
The Letters of Mrs. Elizabeth Montague: With Some of the Letters of Her Correspondents (Montagu) **7**:248-49
Letters of Mrs. Gaskell (Gaskell) **137**:46, 53-54, 64, 90, 95, 99-101, 112, 124, 162-63, 166-67, 169
Letters of Mrs. Henley (Charriere)
See *Lettres de Mistriss Henley publiées par son amie*
"Letters of Parepidemus II" (Clough) **27**:98
The Letters of Ralph Waldo Emerson (Emerson) **98**:81-4, 91-2, 95, 97
The Letters of Robert Browning and Elizabeth Barrett 1845-1846 (Browning) **61**:27, 32-5, 49, 58, 72; **66**:69, 74, 76-7
The Letters of Robert Louis Stevenson (Stevenson) **5**:422, 430; **63**:234
"Letters of Runnymede" (Disraeli) **79**:205, 211, 269, 279-80
The Letters of William and Dorothy Wordsworth (Wordsworth) **138**:214, 227, 236, 251-52, 255, 259, 273-74, 276-79, 291, 329-31, 333, 343-44
The Letters of William and Dorothy Wordsworth: The Early Years 1787-1805 (Wordsworth) **111**:233, 236, 239, 243-44, 294, 315-16
The Letters of William and Dorothy Wordsworth: The Later Years (Wordsworth) **111**:239, 242
The Letters of William and Dorothy Wordsworth: The Middle Years (Wordsworth) **111**:243
Letters of William Hazlitt (Hazlitt) **82**:86-7, 90
Letters on Demonology and Witchcraft (Scott) **15**:277
Letters on Don Carlos (Schiller) **69**:241
Letters on Lucinda (Schleiermacher)
See *Vertraute Briefe über Friedrich Schlegels Lucinde*
Letters on Old England by a New England Man (Paulding) **2**:525
Letters on Shakespeare (Tieck) **5**:526; **46**:403
"Letters on the Church of the Fathers" (Newman) **99**:260
"Letters on the Coup d'état of 1851" (Bagehot) **10**:25-26, 58, 63
Letters on the Difficulties of Religion (Beecher) **30**:3, 7, 11
Letters on the Events which Have Passed in France since the Restoration in 1815 (Williams) **135**:261, 312, 314, 335
Letters on the Laws of Man's Nature and Development (Martineau) **26**:311, 327, 329, 336; **137**:236, 327, 332, 335, 360
"Letters on the Oxford Counter-Reformation" (Froude) **43**:178
"Letters on the Significance of the Scandinavian North for Prehistorical Europe" (Almqvist)
See "Brev om den skandinaviska Nordens betydelse för Europas fornhistoria"
Letters on the Spanish Inquisition (Maistre)
See *Lettres à un gentilhomme russe sur l'Inquisition espagnole*
Letters on the Study of Nature (Herzen) **10**:326; **61**:98
Letters on the Works and Character of J. J. Rousseau (Staël-Holstein) **3**:523
Letters on Theron and Aspasio: Addressed to the Author (James) **53**:239
Letters on Various Interesting and Important Subjects (Freneau) **111**:111, 136, 138
Letters Relating to the Study of Theology (Herder) **8**:297, 306
Letters to a Frenchman about the Present Crisis (Bakunin) **25**:48-9, 74; **58**:114
"Letters to a Young Man whose Education has been Neglected" (De Quincey) **87**:33
Letters to Addington on the Peace of Amiens (Cobbett) **49**:113
Letters to an Aunt (Saltykov)
See *Pisma k tyotenke*
Letters to an Englishman (Brontë)
See *Letters of an Englishman*
Letters to an Old Comrade (Herzen) **10**:329
Letters to and from the Late Samuel Johnson, LL.D. (Piozzi) **57**:241-2, 253, 271, 298
Letters to Elizabeth Barrett Browning Addressed to Richard Hengist Horne (Browning) **61**:34
Letters to Fanny Kemble (FitzGerald) **9**:269
"Letters to Henrietta G." (Brown) **74**:134
Letters to Kugelmann (Marx) **114**:41
"Letters to Landlords, No. 2" (Kingsley) **35**:255
Letters to Marcie (Sand)
See *Lettres à Marcie*
"Letters to Mothers" (Sigourney) **87**:321-22
Letters to Mothers (Sigourney) **87**:338
"Letters to My Pupils" (Sigourney) **87**:321-22
Letters to Persons Who are Engaged in Domestic Service (Beecher) **30**:15, 17
Letters to the Chopsticks (Cobbett) **49**:160
Letters to the Mob (Norton) **47**:248, 254
Letters to the People on Health and Happiness (Beecher) **30**:8, 16-17
Letters to William Pitt (Cobbett) **49**:113
"Letters to Young Ladies" (Sigourney) **87**:321-22
Letters to Young Ladies (Sigourney) **21**:295; **87**:338
Letters Written During a Short Residence in Spain and Portugal (Southey) **97**:284
Letters written from Lausanne (Charriere)
See *Lettres écrites de Lausanne*
Letters Written in France in the Summer of 1790, to a Friend in England. Containing Various Anecdotes Relative to the French Revolution and the Memoirs of Mons. and Madame du F— (Williams) **135**:256-57, 267-69, 271-77, 282-83, 285-90, 296-97, 321, 323, 327-28, 333, 336-37, 340, 342-43, 353-54
Lettre à Fontanes sur la campagne romaine (Chateaubriand) **134**:18
"Lettre à Lord ***" (Vigny) **7**:476
"Lettre à M. Berthelot" (Renan) **26**:380
Lettre à M. Chauvet sur l'unité de temps et de lieu dans la tragédie (Manzoni) **29**:275, 289; **98**:213, 220, 241, 287
Lettre à M. de Fontanes (Chateaubriand) **134**:27, 116, 123
"Lettre à M. de Lamartine" (Musset) **7**:261-62, 266, 273, 275
Lettre à une Dame Russe (Maistre) **37**:314
Lettre de Cachet (Gore) **65**:20
Une Lettre de femme (Desbordes-Valmore) **97**:2, 10, 22, 26-7
Lettre de Junius (Vallès) **71**:357-58
"Lettre du voyant" (Rimbaud) **4**:457, 471, 473, 475, 481, 486; **35**:274, 282, 295, 297, 302, 307-08, 310-12; **82**:221, 223, 235, 238-40, 246-47, 249
"Lettre sur l'art du dessin dans les paysages" (Chateaubriand) **134**:15
Lettres (Staël-Holstein)
See *Lettres sur les ouvrages et le caractère de Jean-Jacques Rousseau*
Lettres à Marcie (Sand) **42**:330, 358-60; **57**:337
Lettres à un absent (Daudet) **1**:231
Lettres à un gentilhomme russe sur l'Inquisition espagnole (Maistre) **37**:323, 325
Lettres à une inconnue (Mérimée) **6**:355-6, 356, 359, 361, 364-5; **65**:45
Lettres de Benjamin Constant à Madame de Récamier, 1807-1830 (Constant) **6**:214
Lettres de Dupuis et Cotonet (Musset) **7**:258
Lettres de jeunesse (Fromentin) **125**:100, 139-41
Lettres de Mistriss Henley publiées par son amie (Charriere) **66**:121-3, 125, 128-9, 138-43, 146-54, 156-7, 176
Lettres de mon moulin (Daudet) **1**:231, 234-35, 239, 243, 245, 249-52
Lettres d'un Cultivateur Américain (Crèvecoeur) **105**:101, 114, 153, 180
Lettres d'un Royaliste Savoisien (Maistre) **37**:312
Lettres d'un voyageur (Sand) **2**:582, 588, 599; **42**:319, 336-37, 340, 386; **57**:315, 360-1
Lettres écrites de Lausanne (Charriere) **66**:121, 123-5, 135, 138, 142-3, 145, 161, 165, 168-9, 172, 176
Lettres inedites (Laclos)
See *Lettres inedites de Choderlos de Laclos*
Lettres inedites de Choderlos de Laclos (Laclos) **87**:273
Lettres neuchâteloises (Charriere) **66**:122-6, 136, 138, 160, 165, 168, 176
Lettres sur les ouvrages et le caractère de Jean-Jacques Rousseau (Staël-Holstein) **91**:339, 358
Lettres sur Rousseau (Staël-Holstein)
See *Lettres sur les ouvrages et le caractère de Jean-Jacques Rousseau*
Lettres trouvées dans des porte-feuilles d'émigrés (Charriere) **66**:125, 136, 172, 174-7
Lettres trouvées dans des porte-feuilles d'émigrés, suite (Charriere) **66**:175-7
Letzte Gaben (Droste-Hülshoff) **3**:193, 200
Letzte Gedichte und Gedanken (Heine) **4**:248, 250, 252
"Letzte Hoffnung" (Muller) **73**:389
Der Letzte König von Orplid (Mörike) **10**:445
"Das letzte Lied" (Raimund) **69**:10, 18-19
"Leucas" (Milnes) **61**:128-9
Die Leute von Seldwyla (Keller) **2**:411, 413-15, 423-24
"Lev starca Gerasima" (Leskov) **25**:245
Levana; or, The Doctrine of Education (Jean Paul) **7**:226
"Levavi Oculos" (Allingham) **25**:8
"Le lever" (Musset) **7**:267
"An Levin Schücking" (Droste-Hülshoff) **3**:200

"Le lévrier de Magnus" (Leconte de Lisle) **29**:223, 225
"Levša" (Leskov) **25**:228, 233, 238
"The Lew O' the Rick" (Barnes) **75**:79
"Lewti" (Coleridge) **9**:149, 151, 158
"Lex Talionis" (Gordon) **21**:159
Leyendas (Bécquer) **106**:86, 96, 99, 107-10, 118-20, 122, 129-31, 142
"Leyendo a María" (Isaacs) **70**:303
"Liab's First Christmas" (Cooke) **110**:37
Liaisons (Laclos)
See *Les liaisons dangereuses; ou, Lettres recueillies dans une société et publiées pour l'instruction de quelques autres*
Les Liaisons (Laclos)
See *Les liaisons dangereuses; ou, Lettres recueillies dans une société et publiées pour l'instruction de quelques autres*
Liaisons dangereuses (Laclos)
See *Les liaisons dangereuses; ou, Lettres recueillies dans une société et publiées pour l'instruction de quelques autres*
Les liaisons dangereuses; ou, Lettres recueillies dans une société et publiées pour l'instruction de quelques autres (Laclos) **4**:324-38, 340-43; **87**:207-315
"The Lianhan Shee" (Carleton) **3**:96
"The Liar" (Krylov) **1**:438-39
"Libbie Marsh's Three Eras" (Gaskell) **5**:205; **70**:185; **137**:4, 38, 41, 61-62
Liber Amoris; or The New Pygmalion (Hazlitt) **29**:157, 170; **82**:74-8, 81, 85-91, 97-8, 101-06, 122, 125-26, 141-46
"Liberal" (Saltykov) **16**:374
"Liberal Education and Where to Find It" (Huxley) **67**:10, 26, 28, 40, 53, 56, 85, 92, 97
The Liberal Preacher (Martineau) **137**:315
Liberalism and the Church (Brownson)
See *Conversations on Liberalism and the Church*
Liberia, or Mr. Peyton's Experiments (Hale) **75**:317, 321, 326, 328, 330-1, 339-341
Liberté, Egalité, Fraternité (Silva) **114**:263
"Liberty" (Horton)
See "On Liberty and Slavery"
"Liberty" (Pushkin)
See "Vol'nost': Oda"
Liberty (Coleridge) **90**:16
"Liberty. An Ode" (Pushkin)
See "Vol'nost': Oda"
"Liberty and Love" (Petofi)
See "Szabadság, szerelem"
"Liberty and Necessity" (Thomson) **18**:395
"Liberty and Slavery" (Horton)
See "On Liberty and Slavery"
"Liberty Tree" (Paine) **62**:320, 366, 379
"Liberty's Victim" (Boyesen) **135**:14, 20, 29
"The Library" (Crabbe) **121**:52, 83-4
The Library (Crabbe) **26**:77-9, 81, 110; **121**:18, 26-7, 83-4, 88-9
Library of Poetry and Song (Bryant) **6**:176
Libres méditations d'un solitaire inconnu sur le détachement du monde et sur d'autres objets de la morale reliqieuse (Senancour) **16**:433, 436
Libro de gorriones (Bécquer)
See *Libro de los gorriones: colección de proyectos, argumentos, ideas y planes de cosas diferentes que se concluirán o no según sople el viento*
Libro de los gorriones: colección de proyectos, argumentos, ideas y planes de cosas diferentes que se concluirán o no según sople el viento (Bécquer) **106**:127, 129, 167, 169
El libro de los niños (Martínez de la Rosa) **102**:229, 254
Libro de versos (Silva) **114**:310-11, 313, 316-18, 321-22
El libro de versos (Silva) **114**:300
Libussa (Grillparzer) **1**:385, 389; **102**:100, 117-18, 131, 170, 192, 196, 198-203, 208, 213
"An Lida" (Goethe) **4**:193
"Lide" (Bestuzhev) **131**:150
"Die Liebe" (Claudius) **75**:193
"Die Liebe" (Hölderlin) **16**:181, 185
"Die liebe Farbe" (Muller) **73**:364,372-73
Liebe, Mißverständnis und Freundschaft (La Roche) **121**:326
Liebegeschichten und Heiratsachen (Nestroy) **42**:220, 223, 241
Liebe-Hütten (La Roche) **121**:250
"Liebesfrühling" (Lenau) **16**:281
"Liebesjahr" (Meyer) **81**:154
Das Liebesverbot; oder, Die Novize von Palermo (Wagner) **9**:414, 436, 473-74
"Liebeszauber" (Tieck) **46**:350
Das Liebhaber-Theater vor dem Parlament (Kotzebue) **25**:147
"Lied" (Gautier) **59**:19
Lied an die Freude (Schiller) **39**:331, 336, 358, 388
"Lied der Auswanderer nach Amerika" (Ludwig) **4**:353
"Das Lied der Toten" (Novalis) **13**:374, 401-02
"Lied des Lynkeus" (Goethe) **34**:98
"Das Lied von der Bernauerin" (Ludwig) **4**:353
"Lied von der Glocke" (Schiller) **39**:347
Lieder aus dem Meerbusen von Salerno (Muller) **73**:352-53, 358, 360, 362, 366-67
Lieder aus Franzensbad bei Eger (Muller) **73**:366
Lieder der Griechen (Muller) **73**:354, 387, 389
"Liederseelen" (Meyer) **81**:149, 201
"Lieutenant Yergunov's Story" (Turgenev)
See "Istoriya leytenanta Ergunova"
"Lieutenant Zidén" (Runeberg) **41**:321-22
"The Lieutenant's Daughter" (Froude) **43**:192
"Life" (Barbauld) **50**:3
"Life" (Bryant) **6**:168
"Life" (Crawford) **127**:202
"Life" (Rossetti) **50**:311
"Life" (Very) **9**:381
Life (Barham) **77**:21, 28
Life among the Piutes: Their Wrongs and Claims (Winnemucca) **79**:336, 342-52, 354, 358, 361-7
Life and Adventures (Sala) **46**:237
The Life and Adventures of Joaquìn Murieta, the Celebrated California Bandit (Ridge) **82**:176-77, 186, 188, 190-95, 198-209
The Life and Adventures of Jonathan Jefferson Whitlaw; or, Scenes on the Mississippi (Trollope) **30**:314, 319, 322
The Life and Adventures of Martin Chuzzlewit (Dickens) **3**:144-45, 151-52, 161, 163, 172, 178; **8**:165; **18**:100, 112, 116, 132; **26**:157, 184; **37**:145; **86**:189, 256; **105**:227, 229, 311; **113**:29, 98, 106-7
The Life and Adventures of Michael Armstrong, the Factory Boy (Trollope) **30**:316-18
The Life and Adventures of Nicholas Nickleby (Dickens) **3**:138-41, 152, 154, 179, 182, 184; **8**:183; **18**:100, 121; **26**:164, 167, 177, 200; **26**:164, 167, 177, 200; **37**:143, 149, 164, 168, 186, 194, 202; **86**:256; **105**:204-05, 214; **113**:88, 92, 103, 106
The Life and Adventures of Oliver Goldsmith (Forster) **11**:95-96, 99, 101, 115, 128-29
The Life and Adventures of Peter Porcupine (Cobbett) **49**:153
"Life and Art" (Lazarus) **109**:295
The Life and Correspondence of Robert Southey (Southey) **8**:479; **97**:269-70, 282-83, 336
"Life and Death" (Rossetti) **2**:575; **50**:264, 289; **66**:341
The Life and Death of Jason (Morris) **4**:412-16, 418-21, 425-27, 431-36, 442
Life and Letters (Huxley) **67**:27, 86-7
The Life and Letters of Charles Darwin (Darwin) **57**:124, 142, 174
"Life and Manners" (De Quincey) **4**:61
The Life and Morals of Jesus of Nazareth, extracted textually from the Gospels in Greek, Latin, French, and English (Jefferson) **11**:199; **103**:106, 163
"Life and Nature" (Lampman) **25**:189, 196, 198, 207
The Life and Opinions of Kater Murr: With the Fragmentary Biography of Kapellmeister Johannes Kreisler on Random Sheets of Scrap Paper (Hoffmann)
See *Lebens-Ansichten des Katers Murr nebst fragmentarischer Biographie des Kapellmeisters Johannes Kreisler in züfalligen Makulaturblättern*
The Life and Poetical Works of George Crabbe (Crabbe) **26**:113
Life and Recollections (Planché) **42**:274-75, 299
Life and Selected Writings of Thomas Jefferson (Jefferson) **103**:119
"Life and Song" (Lanier) **6**:249, 270; **118**:217, 235, 240
Life and Times of Frederick Douglass, Written by Himself (Douglass) **7**:130-31, 134, 136-37, 145; **55**:107-8, 110-1, 113, 122-3, 128
The Life and Times of Salvator Rosa (Morgan) **29**:391
"Life and Times of Thomas Becket" (Froude) **43**:178
The Life and Works of Goethe (Lewes) **25**:274-75, 287, 294, 296-98, 301-04, 306, 308, 320-21, 325
"The Life and Works of Leopardi" (Lewes) **25**:286
The Life and Writings of Joseph Mazzini (Mazzini) **34**:275
Life and Writings of Nancy Maria Hyde (Sigourney) **87**:325
The Life Annuity (Fredro)
See *Dożywocie*
"Life calls us" (Pavlova) **138**:33-34, 37
A Life Drama (Smith) **59**:261-2, 264-5, 267, 269, 272, 288, 291, 296-8, 301, 305, 312-3, 318-21, 326, 328-33, 335-42
A Life for a Life (Craik) **38**:110, 113, 122, 126, 133
"Life for Life" (Boyesen) **135**:15
"A Life Fragment" (Smith) **59**:254, 256-7
"Life in a Love" (Browning) **19**:127; **79**:153
"Life in London" (Mayhew) **31**:181
Life in Manchester (Gaskell) **137**:4
Life in the Clearings versus the Bush (Moodie) **14**:217, 220-27, 234-36, 239-41; **113**:295, 307-9, 318, 323-26, 331, 333, 353, 355, 358, 361, 373
Life in the Sick-Room (Martineau) **26**:310, 323, 325, 349-50; **137**:277, 283, 334-35
"Life in the Thüringian Forest" (Taylor) **89**:308
"Life in the Wilds" (Martineau) **26**:303
Life in the Wilds (Martineau) **137**:260
"Life Is the Desert and the Solitude" (Mangan) **27**:299
The Life, Letters, and Literary Remains of Edward Bulwer, Lord Lytton (Bulwer-Lytton) **1**:148
Life, Letters, and Literary Remains of John Keats (Keats) **8**:374
The Life, Letters, and Literary Remains of John Keats (Milnes) **61**:138, 140, 143-9
Life North and South: Showing the True Character of Both (Hale) **75**:315, 339
"The Life of a Well-Known Character" (Hoffmann) **2**:342
"The Life of Alexander Percy" (Brontë) **109**:29
"The Life of an Edinburgh Baillie" (Hogg) **4**:283
Life of Andrew Jackson (Cobbett) **49**:160
The Life of Benvenuto Cellini (Symonds) **34**:331, 334, 350

The Life of Bernard Gilpin (Gilpin) **30**:33
Life of Bishop Ken (Bowles) **103**:54
Life of Byrn (Moore) **110**:189
Life of Byron (Galt) **110**:91
Life of Carlyle (Froude)
See *Thomas Carlyle*
The Life of Charles Brockden Brown (Dunlap) **2**:208, 215
The Life of Charles Dickens (Forster) **11**:103-04, 106, 108-12, 115-27, 131-32
The Life of Charlotte Brontë (Gaskell) **5**:183-86, 188-89, 198, 201, 205; **70**:116, 119, 176-77, 182, 196, 199, 205, 213, 234-35, 237-41
Life of Charlotte Elizabeth, as Contained in her Personal Recollections (Tonna)
See *Personal Recollections of Charlotte Elizabeth, Continued to the Close of her Life*
Life of Christopher Columbus (Irving)
See *A History of the Life and Voyages of Christopher Columbus*
The Life of Cicero (Trollope) **101**:321, 344
Life of Columbus (Irving)
See *A History of the Life and Voyages of Christopher Columbus*
Life of Cromwell (Southey) **8**:472
The Life of Edward Irving, Minister of the National Scottish Church (Oliphant) **11**:429-30, 433, 439, 446-7; **61**:216
Life of Franklin Pierce (Hawthorne) **2**:303, 314; **39**:229
The Life of Friedrich Schiller (Carlyle) **70**:38-39
A Life of General Robert E. Lee (Cooke) **5**:130
Life of Geoffrey Chaucer (Godwin) **14**:53
The Life of George Washington (Irving) **2**:374-75, 377-78
"Life of Goldsmith" (Irving) **2**:376
The Life of Harriot Stuart (Lennox) **23**:226, 231-35, 252-53, 263; **134**:219, 229, 238, 342, 347
The Life of Henri Brulard (Stendhal)
See *Vie de Henri Brulard*
The Life of Hugh Latimer, Bishop of Worcester (Gilpin) **30**:33-4
The Life of Jesus (Renan)
See *La vie de Jésus*
The Life of Jesus (Schleiermacher) **107**:363, 400
Life of John Bunyan (Southey) **8**:465, 472
"The Life of John Smith" (Ingelow)
See "The Life of Mr. John Smith"
The Life of John Sterling (Carlyle) **70**:54
The Life of Jonathan Swift (Forster) **11**:110, 115, 120
"Life of Life" (Shelley) **18**:340, 345; **93**:305-07
Life of Lord George Bentinck (Disraeli) **2**:147; **39**:44; **79**:239, 269
The Life of Maximilen Robespierre with Extracts from His Unpublished Correspondence (Lewes) **25**:320
The Life of Michelangelo Buonarroti (Symonds) **34**:328-29, 331, 334, 350-51, 356
"The Life of Mr. John Smith" (Ingelow) **107**:161-64, 175
The Life of Napolean (Horne) **127**:236
The Life of Napoleon Bonaparte (Hazlitt) **29**:173; **82**:105, 144, 146, 163, 165
The Life of Napoleon Bonaparte (Scott) **15**:271, 277; **69**:303
The Life of Nelson (Southey) **8**:453-54, 459, 463, 467, 471-72, 474; **97**:250, 259, 262, 265-66, 268-71, 283, 290-93, 306, 328, 330
The Life of ... Northangerland (Brontë) **109**:42, 45-6, 52
Life of Perez del Pulgar (Martínez de la Rosa)
See *Hernán Pérez del Pulgar*
Life of Quintus Fixlein (Jean Paul) **7**:223
Life of Robert Burns (Lockhart) **6**:292, 297, 300, 308-10
The Life of Samuel Johnson, LL.D., Including a Journal of a Tour to the Hebrides, by James Boswell, Esq. (Croker) **10**:90-93, 95-97
"Life of Scott" (Keble) **87**:135
Life of Stonewall Jackson (Cooke) **5**:130
"The Life of Strafford" (Forster) **11**:120
"Life of the Blessed" (Bryant) **6**:159
The Life of the Countess Gritta von Ratsatourhouse (Arnim)
See *Das Leben der Hochgräfin Gritta von Rattenzuhausbeiuns*
The Life of the Fields (Jefferies) **47**:95-7, 102, 112, 122, 133, 136-37
The Life of Thomas Cranmer, Archbishop of Canterbury (Gilpin) **30**:34
"Life of Warner Howard Warner" (Brontë) **109**:34
A Life of Washington (Paulding) **2**:526
The Life of Wesley and the Rise and Progress of Methodism (Southey) **8**:459, 463, 467, 471-72; **97**:259, 263-66, 268, 283, 306
Life of West (Galt) **110**:90, 93
Life of Wolsey (Galt) **110**:76, 96
"Life or Death" (Petofi)
See "Elet vagy halál"
"The Life That Is" (Bryant) **6**:165
"Life Without Principle" (Thoreau) **7**:381, 385, 398; **21**:322, 328, 347-8
"Life-in Love" (Rossetti) **77**:339
"Life's Hebe" (Thomson) **18**:391-92
"A Life's Parallels" (Rossetti) **66**:343
"A Lifetime" (Bryant) **6**:175, 182
"The Lifted Veil" (Eliot) **41**:102-03, 108; **118**:59
"Ligeia" (Poe) **1**:504-05, 513-14, 518-19; **16**:295, 303-06, 308, 314, 322, 324, 328, 331, 335; **55**:133, 151, 197, 201; **78**:285; **94**:202; **97**:180, 182, 208-09, 211; **117**:193, 222, 237, 245, 281, 299, 301, 303
"The Light" (Allingham) **25**:6
"Light" (Hugo) **3**:262
"Light!" (Petofi)
See "Világosságot!"
"The Light and Glory of the Word" (Cowper) **94**:70
"Light and Shade" (Ingelow) **39**:256
"A Light Exists in Spring" (Dickinson) **21**:59, 75
"The Light Has Dawned" (Zhukovsky)
See "Vzoshla zaria..."
"Light Love" (Rossetti) **2**:557; **50**:298; **66**:329, 331, 352
The Light of Her Countenance (Boyesen) **135**:14, 37, 41
"Light of Shadow" (Isaacs)
See "Lumbre de sombra"
"The Light of Stars" (Longfellow) **2**:479, 492; **45**:112, 116, 127, 148, 152; **103**:295
"The Light of the Haram" (Moore) **6**:380-81, 388; **110**:217, 222, 224-25
"Light shining out of darkness" (Cowper) **94**:70
"Light Summer Reading" (Freneau) **111**:33
"Light Up Thy Halls" (Brontë) **16**:80
"A Light Woman" (Browning) **79**:163
"The Lighthouse" (Longfellow) **45**:161; **101**:92
"The Light-House" (Poe) **117**:310
The Lighthouse (Collins) **93**:38, 64
"The Lighthouses" (Baudelaire)
See "Les phares"
"The Lightning and the Lantern" (Cranch) **115**:49
"The Lightning-Rod Man" (Melville) **3**:331, 354, 381-82
Lights and Shadows of Scottish Life: A Selection from the Papers of the Late Arthur Austin (Wilson) **5**:547-49, 554-55, 558, 567, 569
"Den liile Idas Blomster" (Andersen) **7**:22; **79**:23, 32-3, 50, 65, 76, 87
"Den liile pige med Svovlstikkerne" (Andersen) **79**:76
"Like a little bird at early dawn" (Tyutchev)
See "Kak ptichka, ranneyu zarey"
"Like Clouds Have Passed the Years . . ." (Eminescu) **33**:246
Die Likedeeler (Fontane) **26**:244
"Likeness to God: Discourse at the Ordination of the Rev. F. A. Farley" (Channing) **17**:46, 53
"The Lilac" (Barnes) **75**:38
"Lilian" (Patmore) **9**:326, 328
"Lilian" (Tennyson) **30**:223; **65**:368
"Lilian of the Vale" (Darley) **2**:127, 130
"The Lilies" (Mickiewicz)
See "Lilje"
Lilies in Sharon and The Martyrs (Stagnelius)
See *Liljor i Saron och Martyrerna*
"The Lilies of the Field and the Birds of the Air" (Kierkegaard) **78**:239
"Lilith" (Kendall) **12**:199
"Lilith" (Rossetti) **4**:506
"Lilje" (Mickiewicz) **3**:398
Liljor i Saron och Martyrerna (Stagnelius) **61**:248, 251, 253, 260
Lilla Weneda (Slowacki) **15**:348-49, 352-53, 361, 365, 371, 373, 378, 380
"Lille Claus og Store Claus" (Andersen) **7**:21, 25; **79**:23-4, 50, 59, 64-5, 68, 72, 76
"Den Lille Havfrue" (Andersen) **7**:23, 26, 28-9, 34, 36; **79**:19, 21, 23, 26, 51, 58, 62-63, 66, 70, 76, 82, 87-88
Lilliesleaf: Being a Concluding Series of Passages in the Life of Mrs. Margaret Maitland (Oliphant) **11**:432; **61**:163, 203
"The Lilly" (Blake) **37**:43, 51, 80
"Lily Adair" (Chivers) **49**:38, 42, 49, 72, 74
"A Lily and a Lute" (Ingelow) **39**:264
"The Lily Bed" (Crawford) **12**:162, 166-67, 172; **127**:167-72, 228
"The Lily Confidante" (Timrod) **25**:361, 365-66, 372, 375
"The Lily of Liddesdale" (Wilson) **5**:558, 564
The Lily of the Valley (Balzac)
See *Le lys dans la valée*
"Lily Song" (Crawford) **127**:151-52
"The Lily's Quest" (Hawthorne) **2**:305
Les Limbes (Baudelaire)
See *Les fleurs du mal*
"Limbo" (Verlaine) **51**:371
"The Limerick Gloves" (Edgeworth) **51**:87, 89, 137
Limestone (Stifter)
See *Kalkstein*
"Limits of Knowledge" (Symonds) **34**:336
The Limits of State Action (Humboldt)
See *Ideen zu einem Versuch, die Grenzen der Wirksamkeit des Staats zu bestimmen*
"Lincoln Ode" (Lowell) **2**:511
"Lincoln-Douglas Debates" (Lincoln) **18**:210-11, 234, 243, 245, 247-48, 253, 255, 259, 267, 280
Lincoln's Life (Faustino)
See *Vida de Abrán Lincoln*
Linda Tressel (Trollope) **101**:334
"Linden Lea" (Barnes) **75**:33
"Der Lindenbaum" (Muller)
See "Am Brunnen vor dem Tore"
"Lindenborg Fool" (Morris) **4**:430, 440
"Lines" (Cowper)
See "Lines Written during a Period of Insanity"
"Lines" (Horton)
See "Lines to My —"
"Lines Above Tintern Abbey" (Wordsworth)
See "Lines Composed a Few Miles Above Tintern Abbey"
"Lines Addressed to Mr. Jefferson, On his retirement from the presidency of the United States.—1809" (Freneau) **111**:160
"Lines Attributed to Alexander Selkirk" (Cowper) **8**:107
"Lines by A. G. A. to A. S." (Brontë) **16**:79

"Lines By a Lady on the Loss of Her Trunk" (Sheridan) **91**:233
"Lines by Claudia" (Brontë) **16**:80
"Lines Composed a Few Miles Above Tintern Abbey" (Wordsworth) **12**:386, 388, 407, 431, 436, 441, 449, 455, 464, 467-70; **38**:360, 366-67; **111**:198-200, 202, 225, 236, 243, 248, 251, 256-59, 284, 286-87, 294, 307, 310-11, 314-15
"Lines Composed in a Wood on a Windy Day" (Brontë) **4**:49; **71**:85
"Lines Extempore by Thomas Paine July 1803" (Paine) **62**:325
"Lines from the Port-Folio of H——" (Pinkney) **31**:276, 279
"Lines Intended for Edith Southey's Album" (Wordsworth) **138**:285
"Lines Intended for My Niece's Album" (Wordsworth) **138**:226
"Lines Left upon a Seat in a Yew-Tree, Which Stands near the Lake of Esthwaite, on a Desolate Part of the Shore, Commanding a Beautiful Prospect" (Wordsworth) **12**:386-87, 345, 464; **111**:200, 202, 306, 313-14, 316, 349, 359
"Lines Occasioned by a Visit to an Old Indian Burying Ground" (Freneau) **1**:315, 317, 319, 323; **111**:81, 140, 164-71, 173-74, 190
"Lines Occasioned by reading Mr. Paine's Rights of Man" (Freneau) **111**:108, 124
"Lines Occasioned by the Death of an Infant" (Murray) **63**:208
"Lines on a Friend" (Coleridge) **99**:22
"Lines on a Humming Bird Seen at a Lady's Window" (Ridge) **82**:181
"Lines on Alexandria" (Campbell) **19**:181
"Lines on an Autumnal Evening" (Coleridge) **99**:17
"Lines on Constantinople" (Opie) **65**:160
"Lines on Poland" (Campbell) **19**:183
"Lines on Revisiting the Country" (Bryant) **46**:39
"Lines on the Birth of Her Majesty's Third Child" (Hunt) **70**:260
"Lines on the Death of an Aged Relative" (Cranch) **115**:8
"The Lines on the Death of Joseph Rodman Drake" (Halleck) **47**:57, 65
"Lines on the Death of Lucy Hooper" (Whittier) **8**:486, 520
"Lines on the First Mild Day of March" (Wordsworth) **12**:387; **111**:200, 281
"Lines on the Loss of the Royal George" (Cowper) **8**:111, 116, 118, 120; **94**:32-3, 38
"Lines on the Opening of a Spring Campaign" (Opie) **65**:160
"Lines on the Place de Concorde, at Paris" (Opie) **65**:160
"Lines on the Portrait of a Celebrated Publisher" (Whittier) **8**:525; **59**:361
"Lines on the Receipt of My Mother's Picture" (Cowper) **8**:108, 112, 135-37; **94**:20, 33-4
"Lines Suggested by Reading a State Poper" (Whittier) **59**:371
"Lines Tangled about the Round Table" (Lanier) **118**:260
"Lines: The Soft Unclouded Blue of Air" (Brontë) **16**:111
"Lines to Dora H." (Wordsworth) **138**:284
"Lines to a Friend on His Marriage" (Bryant) **6**:177
"Lines to a Friend on the Death of His Sister" (Whittier) **8**:491
"Lines to a Lady on the Death of her Lover" (Rogers) **69**:67
"Lines to a Reviewer" (Shelley) **18**:327
"Lines to a Young Ass" (Coleridge) **9**:149
Lines to Agnes Ballie on Her Birthday (Baillie) **71**:2-3
"Lines to Hartley Coleridge" (Wordsworth) **12**:431
"Lines to Louisa" (Poe) **1**:514
"Lines to Melrose Abbey" (Wilson) **5**:545
"Lines to My ——" (Horton) **87**:109-110
"Lines to —— On the Death of His Friend" (Very) **9**:376
"Lines to the Planet Mars" (Longfellow) **2**:473; **45**:116
"The Lines upon the Yew-Tree Seat" (Coleridge) **9**:131
"Lines: When the Lamp is Shattered" (Shelley) **18**:362, 371
"Lines written a few miles above Tintern Abbey" (Wordsworth)
See "Lines Composed a Few Miles Above Tintern Abbey"
"Lines Written among the Euganean Hills" (Shelley) **18**:329, 371-73
"Lines Written at a Small Distance from My House, and Sent by My Little Boy to the Person to Whom They Are Addressed" (Wordsworth) **12**:445; **111**:202
"Lines written at Norwich on the First News of Peace" (Opie) **65**:175
"Lines, Written at Seventeen" (Mangan) **27**:298
"Lines Written at the Foot of Brother's Bridge" (Wordsworth) **12**:393
"Lines written at the Pallisades, newar Port-Royal, in the Island of Jamaica—September 1784" (Freneau) **111**:148
"Lines Written at Thorp Green" (Brontë) **71**:165
"Lines Written during a Period of Insanity" (Cowper) **8**:137; **94**:24, 32, 38
"Lines Written in 1799" (Opie) **65**:160
"Lines Written in a Burial-Ground" (Wilson) **5**:567
"Lines Written in Early Spring" (Wordsworth) **12**:387, 436, 450, 466; **111**:200, 202, 224, 281-82, 284, 317
"Lines Written in Kensington Gardens" (Arnold) **29**:34
"Lines Written in the Bay of Lerici" (Shelley) **18**:362, 369, 373
"Lines written in the Highlands" (Keats) **73**:176, 201, 209, 226
"Lines Written near Richmond" (Wordsworth) **12**:387; **111**:202, 350
"Lines Written on 29 May, the Anniversary of Charles's Restoration" (Keats) **73**:331
"Lines Written on a Summer Evening" (Clare) **9**:75, 117, 122
"Lines Written on Hearing the News of the Death of Napoleon" (Shelley) **18**:362
"Lines Written on Leaving a Scene in Bavaria" (Campbell) **19**:179, 193
"Lines Written on Revisiting a Scene in Argyleshire" (Campbell) **19**:181, 193
"Lines—Now heavily in clouds" (Brontë) **109**:30
De l'influence des passions sur le bonheur des individus et des nations (Staël-Holstein) **3**:524; **91**:298-305, 311, 332-6, 340
"Les linges, le cygne" (Laforgue) **5**:277
"The Linnet in the Rocky Dells" (Brontë) **109**:27
De l'intelligence (Taine) **15**:465, 467
"Lintukoto" (Kivi) **30**:51-2
The Linwoods; or, "Sixty Years Since" in America (Sedgwick) **19**:433-34, 436, 439, 442, 445, 447-49, 453; **98**:296, 299-301, 334, 351
"Le lion du cirque" (Gautier) **1**:342
The Lion of the West (Paulding) **2**:527
"The Lion, the Chamois, and the Fox" (Krylov) **1**:435
Lionel Lincoln; or, The Leagues of Boston (Cooper) **1**:197, 200, 221; **54**:254, 299, 301
"Lionizing" (Poe) **16**:295, 313, 321-22
Les lionnes pauvres (Augier) **31**:2, 5-7, 9-10, 12-13, 15, 19, 24, 27, 30
Lions and Foxes (Augier)
See *Lions et renards*
Lions et renards (Augier) **31**:8-9, 13, 16, 19, 25-8, 31, 34, 38
"The Lions in Trafalgar Square" (Jefferies) **47**:141
"Lis i wilk" (Krasicki) **8**:403
"Lise" (Hugo) **3**:263
"Listening" (Rossetti) **50**:310; **66**:307
"Listok iz dnevnika gvardeyskogo ofitsera" (Bestuzhev) **131**:148, 165, 182
Listy (Krasicki) **8**:398
"Le lit 29" (Maupassant) **83**:169
"La litanie du sommeil" (Corbière) **43**:17, 24, 31, 34
"Litanies de misère" (Laforgue) **53**:270
"Les litanies de satan" (Baudelaire) **6**:80, 83, 89, 94, 116
"The Litanies of Satan" (Baudelaire)
See "Les litanies de satan"
"Litany of Sleep" (Corbière)
See "La litanie du sommeil"
"Literärische Scherze" (Preseren) **127**:315
"Literarischer Reichsanzeiger; oder, Archiv der Zeit und ihres Geschmacks" (Schlegel) **15**:229
Literary and General Lectures and Essays (Kingsley) **35**:250
Literary and Social Silhouettes (Boyesen) **135**:23, 38, 51
Literary and Theatrical Reminiscences (Aksakov)
See *Literaturnye i teatralnya vospominaniya*
"Literary Aspects of the Romantic School" (Boyesen) **135**:6
Literary Commonplace Book (Jefferson) **103**:241
"Literary Ethics" (Emerson) **38**:209; **98**:176
The Literary History of England in the End of the Eighteenth and Beginning of the Nineteenth Century (Oliphant) **61**:171
"Literary Importation" (Freneau) **111**:111
"The Literary Influence of Academies" (Arnold) **6**:57, 69; **29**:55, 57; **89**:35-6
Literary Letters to a Woman (Bécquer)
See *Cartas literarias a una mujer*
The Literary Life and Miscellanies of John Galt (Galt) **1**:330, 334-35; **110**:115
Literary Note-Book (Thoreau) **21**:338, 340
Literary Recreations (Whittier) **59**:365
The Literary Remains of Samuel Taylor Coleridge (Coleridge) **9**:157
The Literary Remains of the Late Henry James (James) **53**:193, 199, 201-2, 204, 209-13, 215, 219-21, 223, 225, 227, 232-3, 235, 242, 250
"Literary Reminiscences" (Hood) **16**:206, 229, 240
"Literary Reminiscences" (De Quincey) **4**:61-62
Literary Reminiscences (De Quincey) **87**:62
Literary Reminiscences (Turgenev) **122**:256, 262
The Literary Republic of the Germans (Klopstock)
See *Die Deutsche Gelehrtenrepublik*
"Literary Reveries" (Belinski) **5**:96, 102, 108
Literary Studies (Bagehot) **10**:18-19, 25, 31, 43
"Literary Work" (Smith) **59**:306
Literary Works (Gómez de Avellaneda) **111**:57
The Literati: Some Honest Opinions about Authorial Merits and Demerits, with Occasional Works of Personality (Poe) **55**:133, 138, 164, 182, 189
"Literatura. Rápida ojeada sobre la historia e índole de la nuestra" (Larra) **17**:280-84; **130**:217-18, 278
"Literature" (Emerson) **1**:278
"Literature" (Newman) **38**:296, 327
"Literature and Dogma" (Arnold) **89**:66-7
Literature and Dogma: An Essay towards a Better Apprehension of the Bible (Arnold)

6:39-40, 48, 53-54, 61, 66; **29**:11, 15, 18, 20-1, 45, 50-2; **89**:82, 112; **126**:3, 28, 90, 93, 108
"Literature and Science" (Arnold) **6**:46, 72; **29**:46, 49; **126**:36, 114-17
"Literature at the South: The Fungous School" (Hayne) **94**:143
"Literature from Botoşani" (Eminescu) **131**:311
"Literature in the South" (Timrod) **25**:384
Literaturnye i teatralnya vospominaniya (Aksakov) **2**:13, 15
"The Litigation" (Gogol) **5**:224
"Litość" (Norwid) **17**:373
Littérature et philosophie mêlées (Hugo) **3**:247, 273; **21**:203
"Little Annie's Ramble" (Hawthorne) **2**:291
A Little Bacchante (Crawford) **127**:192
"The Little Beach-Bird" (Dana) **53**:158
The Little Bee from Kranj (Preseren)
See *Kranjska čbelica*
"Little Benny" (Parton) **86**:377
The Little Bird Fair Green (Gozzi)
See *L'augellin belverde*
"The Little Black Boy" (Blake) **13**:220; **37**:3, 6, 39, 67-8, 71-2, 78, 82-3, 91-2, 94
A Little Boat Breaking a Path Through the Reeds (Motoori)
See *Ashiwake obune*
"Little Book, in Green and Gold" (Southey) **8**:474
A Little Book of Profitable Tales (Field) **3**:205, 208
A Little Book of Western Verse (Field) **3**:205-06, 211
"The Little Boy Blue" (Chivers) **49**:41, 54-5
"Little Boy Blue" (Field) **3**:205, 208, 210, 212
"The Little Boy Found" (Blake) **37**:3, 31, 67, 72, 77, 92
"A Little Boy Lost" (Blake) **13**:220-21, 242; **37**:3-4, 31, 40, 44, 57, 65, 67, 72, 92
"Little Britain" (Irving) **19**:327-28, 351
"A Little Bunker Hill" (Parton) **86**:350
"The Little Chap" (Boyesen) **135**:15
The Little Children of the Snow (Bryant)
See "The Little People of the Snow"
"Little Claus and Big Claus" (Andersen)
See "Lille Claus og Store Claus"
"Little Death for a Laugh" (Corbière) **43**:18
Little Dorrit (Dickens) **3**:151, 159, 166, 169, 173-74, 186-87; **8**:195; **18**:100, 116, 121-22, 127, 132, 134, 139; **26**:157, 168, 171, 177-78, 228; **37**:164, 174, 177, 192, 204-06; **86**:197, 201, 233, 265; **105**:201, 214, 228, 244, 248, 258, 261, 311, 318, 330; **113**:3-149
"A Little East of Jordan" (Dickinson) **21**:63; **77**:161
"Little Ella" (Lanier) **118**:243
Little Fadette (Sand)
See *La petite Fadette*
"The Little Fir Tree" (Andersen)
See "The Fir-Tree"
Little Foxes (Cooke) **110**:21
"The Little Girl Found" (Blake) **37**:4, 40, 42, 55, 57, 71-3, 77, 92
"The Little Girl Lost" (Blake)
See "A Little Girl Lost"
"A Little Girl Lost" (Blake) **13**:220; **37**:4, 11, 13, 19, 44, 49, 55, 57, 71-3, 77, 92; **127**:82;
The Little Girl's Own Book (Child)
See *The Girl's Book*
"The Little Girl's Song" (Dobell) **43**:48
Little Green Bird (Gozzi)
See *L'augellin belverde*
"The Little Handmaiden" (Lampman) **25**:199
"Little Homer's Slate" (Field) **3**:210
The Little House of Kolomna (Pushkin)
See *Domik v Kolomne*
"Little Ida's Flowers" (Andersen)
See "Den liile Idas Blomster"
Little Kirsten (Andersen) **79**:17
"Little Klaus and Big Criticism" (Andersen)
See "Lille Claus og Store Claus"
The Little Lame Prince (Craik) **38**:122
"The Little Land of Appenzell" (Taylor) **89**:312
"The Little Lost Sister" (Barnes) **75**:58
"The Little Maid I Lost Long Ago" (O'Brien) **21**:246
"The Little Match Girl" (Andersen) **7**:33-4; 23, 63, 66
"The Little Match Seller" (Andersen)
See "The Little Match Girl"
Little Men: Life at Plumfield with Jo's Boys (Alcott) **6**:15, 20; **58**:41, 43, 47, 69; **83**:31, 34-35, 39, 44, 47, 61
"The Little Mermaid" (Andersen)
See "Den Lille Havfrue"
"A Little More about Irish Snobs" (Thackeray) **43**:388
"The Little Old Women" (Baudelaire)
See "Les petites vielles"
The Little Parish Church (Daudet)
See *La petite paroisse*
"The Little Peach" (Field) **3**:211
"The Little People of the Snow" (Bryant) **6**:165, 169, 171; **46**:4, 21
A Little Pilgrim in the Unseen (Oliphant) **11**:448, 452
"The Little Pin Headers" (Tonna) **135**:199-200, 209, 213, 215-16, 220-22
"Little Plays For Children" (Edgeworth) **51**:81
Little Poems in Prose (Baudelaire)
See *Petits poèmes en prose: Le spleen de Paris*
"The Little Post-Boy" (Taylor) **89**:342
The Little Reader's Assistant (Webster) **30**:418
"Little Rie and the Rosebuds" (Ingelow) **107**:150
"The Little Sea-Maid" (Andersen)
See "Den Lille Havfrue"
A Little Slaveno-Serbian Songbook (Karadzic)
See *Mala prostonarodnja slaveno-serbska pjesnarica*
Little Slaveno-Serbian Songbook for the Common Folk (Karadzic)
See *Mala prostonarodnja slaveno-serbska pjesnarica*
Little Snowdrop (Ostrovsky)
See *Snegurochka*
"Little Soul" (Meyer)
See "Das Seelchen"
The Little Stepmother (Storm)
See *Viola tricolor*
"The Little Tower" (Morris) **4**:423, 444
Little Tragedies (Pushkin) **3**:433-34, 446-47, 454-55, 461
"Little Travels and Roadside Sketches" (Thackeray) **14**:452
"Little Trotty Wigtail" (Clare) **9**:85
"Little Tuk" (Andersen) **7**:29
"The Little Vagabond" (Blake) **13**:182, 219-21, 242; **37**:15, 34, 43, 46-7, 52
"A Little While" (Rossetti) **4**:492
"A Little While, a Little While" (Brontë) **16**:87
Little Women; or, Meg, Jo, Beth, and Amy (Alcott) **6**:15-25; **58**:3-9, 17-23, 25, 31-2, 35, 39-41, 46-7, 49-53, 55-7, 59, 61, 64-73, 75, 78-9, 88; **83**:1-87
"The Little Yaller Baby" (Field) **3**:208, 211
Little Zack (Hoffmann)
See *Klein Zaches gennant Zinnober*
"Little-Oh-Dear" (Field) **3**:210
"Liubliu ia vas, bogini pen'ia" (Baratynsky) **103**:48
Live and Let Live; or, Domestic Service Illustrated (Sedgwick) **19**:438, 447, 449; **98**:330, 334
"Live Oak With Moss" (Whitman) **81**:328, 364
"Live Poetry" (Silva)
See "Poesía viva"
A Lively Spot (Ostrovsky)
See *Na bóikom méste*
Lives (Coleridge)
See *Lives of the Northern Worthies*
Lives of Celebrated Female Sovereigns (Jameson)
See *Memoirs of Celebrated Female Sovereigns*
Lives of E. and J. Philips, Nephews and Pupils of Milton (Godwin) **14**:53
Lives of the British Admirals (Southey) **97**:265, 269, 283
"Lives of the Great Composers" (Fuller) **50**:227
Lives of the Most Eminent Literary and Scientific Men of Italy, Spain, and Portugal (Shelley) **14**:263, 271
Lives of the Necromancers; or, An Account of the Most Eminent Persons Who Have Claimed or to Whom Has Been Imputed the Exercise of Magical Power (Godwin) **14**:50-1
Lives of the Northern Worthies (Coleridge) **90**:8, 21, 23-4
Lives of the Saints (Froude) **43**:177
"Living Alone" (Ichiyō) **49**:348
"A Living and a Dead Faith" (Cowper) **94**:72
"The Living Lost" (Bryant) **6**:162
"A Living Relic" (Turgenev) **21**:416, 441; **122**:244, 294, 337, 343
"Living Relics" (Turgenev)
See "A Living Relic"
"The Living Temple" (Holmes) **14**:109-10; **81**:98
"Living Without God in the World" (Lamb) **113**:268-75
"Livre Antique" (Vigny) **102**:335
Livre d'amour (Sainte-Beuve) **5**:331, 351-52
Le Livre des mères et des enfants (Desbordes-Valmore) **97**:12
"Livre Moderne" (Vigny) **102**:335
"Livre Mystique" (Vigny) **102**:335
Le livre posthume (Boulter) **51**:356, 364
Le livre posthume (Verlaine) **51**:356, 364
"Lizzie" (Field) **3**:210
"Lizzie Griswold's Thanksgiving" (Cooke) **110**:33
"Lizzie Leigh" (Gaskell) **5**:187, 201-02, 205; **70**:150, 171-72, 176-78, 182-186, 190, 193; **97**:127
Lizzie Lorton of Gregrigg (Linton) **41**:159, 166, 167
"The Lloyds" (Hale) **75**:298
"Lo, Here Is God, and There Is God!" (Clough)
See "The New Sinai"
"Lo, Victress on the Peaks" (Whitman) **81**:318
The Loan of a Lover (Planché) **42**:272
"A Lobster: Or, the Study of Zoology" (Huxley) **67**:16, 82-3
"Lochiel's Warning" (Campbell) **19**:165, 168-69, 179, 181, 193, 196
"Lochleven Castle" (Sigourney) **21**:309
"Lock the Door, Lariston" (Hogg) **4**:284
"Locksley Hall" (Tennyson) **30**:213, 221, 223, 233, 236, 243, 245, 260, 280, 283, 296; **65**:232, 363; **115**:252, 359
Locksley Hall (Tennyson) **115**:263
"Locksley Hall Sixty Years After" (Tennyson) **30**:233, 254, 269, 296; **65**:241, 285, 381
"El loco y la Venus" (Casal) **131**:263
La locura de amor (Tamayo y Baus) **1**:565, 570-71
"Locutions de Pierrot" (Laforgue) **5**:277; **53**:287-8
"The Lodge House" (Clare) **86**:172
"The Lodge in the Wilderness" (Traill) **31**:325
"A Lodging amidst Shallow Reeds" (Ueda Akinari) **131**:6
"A Lodging for the Night: A Story of François Villon" (Stevenson) **5**:391, 394, 407, 415, 431
Lodore (Shelley) **14**:259-60, 265, 267, 269-71, 275; **59**:192, 195; **103**:329, 347

"A Lofty Beauty from her Poor Kinsman" (Coleridge)
See "To a Lofty Beauty Edith Southey, from her Poor Kinsman"
"Logic of Political Economy" (De Quincey) **4**:78
"Logical Arrangements or Instruments of Inventions and Discovery Employed by Jeremy Bentham" (Bentham) **38**:92
"Lohengrin" (Lazarus) **8**:413-14; **109**:292, 294, 319
"Lohengrin" (Levy) **59**:92, 120
Lohengrin (Nestroy) **42**:225
Lohengrin (Wagner) **9**:403, 406, 410, 415-16, 418-19, 421, 437, 441-42, 444, 446, 448-50, 452, 462-63, 469, 473-74; **119**:171, 180, 192, 198, 241, 248, 259, 268-72, 274, 328
"Lohengrin, fils de Parsifal" (Laforgue) **5**:269, 271, 274, 278, 281; **53**:294
"Lohengrin, Son of Parsifal" (Laforgue)
See "Lohengrin, fils de Parsifal"
Lohn der Wahrheit (Kotzebue) **25**:141, 147
"Lois the Witch" (Gaskell) **5**:202-03, 205; **70**:176, 182-83, 188, 189, 194
Lois the Witch (Carlyle) **70**:200, 213
Les Loisirs de la poste (Mallarmé)
See *Vers de circonstance*
"Lokis" (Mérimée) **6**:355-6, 360, 364, 366, 369-71; **65**:48, 52, 54, 56-9, 61, 63, 98, 101-03, 114, 117, 140
"Lola Montez" (Grillparzer) **102**:171
Lombard Street: A Description of the Money Market (Bagehot) **10**:19-22, 26, 30-31, 34-35, 40, 45, 48, 50, 58, 64
"London" (Adams) **33**:17
"London" (Blake) **13**:240, 242; **37**:17, 26, 33-5, 43, 49, 52, 57-8, 82, 84-6, 89, 92
London (Blake) **127**:30
"London: A National Song" (Moodie) **113**:310
London Assurance (Boucicault) **41**:26-9, 32, 40-1, 44-6, 48-9
London Characters (Mayhew) **31**:181
"London in July" (Levy) **59**:89, 102
London Labour and the London Poor (Mayhew) **31**:156, 161-62, 165, 167-69, 173, 176-82, 186-87, 189, 193-98, 200-03
"A London Plane-Tree" (Levy) **59**:88, 119
A London Plane-Tree and Other Verse (Levy) **59**:86, 88-9, 93-4, 99, 102-3, 114, 118, 120
"London Poets" (Levy) **59**:119
"The London Road" (Jefferies) **47**:95
"A London Trout" (Jefferies) **47**:134
London up to Date (Sala) **46**:247-48
"Lone Enthroned" (Rossetti) **4**:507
Lone Genius (Eminescu)
See *Geniu pustiu*
"Lone I Walk at Night" (Lermontov) **5**:301
"Loneliness" (Lazarus) **8**:419
"Loneliness" (Lenau) **16**:277
"Loneliness" (Muller)
See "Einsamkeit"
"Lonely lady tell me why" (Fuller) **50**:249
Long Ago and A Short While Ago (Verlaine)
See *Jadis et naguère*
Long Ago and Not So Long Ago (Verlaine)
See *Jadis et naguère*
"Long Branch, Saratoga, and Lake George" (Shaw) **15**:338
"Long, Long Hence" (Whitman) **31**:434
Long Odds (Clarke) **19**:234
"The Long Path" (Holmes) **81**:97
The Long Strike (Boucicault) **41**:31
"The Long-Ago" (Milnes) **61**:130, 136, 145
"Longbow's Horse" (Cooke) **5**:130
"The Longest Hour of My Life" (Hood) **16**:217
"Longfellow and Other Plagiarists" (Poe) **1**:507
"Longing" (Eminescu) **131**:293
"Longing" (Lanier) **118**:242
"A Look at Old and New Literature in Russia" (Bestuzhev) **131**:178-79
"A Look at Russian Literature during 1823" (Bestuzhev) **131**:178
"Look at Russian Literature during 1824 and the Beginning of 1825" (Bestuzhev) **131**:179
"Look at the Clock" (Barham) **77**:34
"Look Down Fair Moon" (Whitman) **31**:392
"Look, how on the river expanse" (Tyutchev)
See "Smotri kak na rechnom prostore"
"Look You, My Simple Friend, 'Tis One of Those" (Clough) **27**:103, 107
"Looking at a Bust" (Meyer)
See "Vor einer Büste"
Looking at Life (Sala) **46**:237
"Looking Back" (Arany)
See "Visszatekintés"
"Looking Back" (Muller) **73**:385-86
"Looking Backward" (Eliot) **118**:36
Looking Backward, 2000-1887 (Bellamy) **4**:23-29, 31-34; **86**:3-4, 6-7, 9-14, 17-20, 22, 25, 27, 30, 32, 36, 38, 43-55, 58, 60-71, 75, 77, 79-82
Looking Glass (Carroll)
See *Through the Looking-Glass, and What Alice Found There*
Looking towards sunset (Child) **73**:63,71
"Looking Westward" (Keble) **87**:134
The Loom and the Lugger (Martineau) **137**:267
"Lord Alcohol" (Beddoes) **3**:32, 34
Lord Byron and Some of His Contemporaries: With Recollections of the Author's Life and of His Visit to Italy (Hunt) **1**:412, 424; **70**:261, 279-88, 2
"Lord Coleraine, Rev. Mr. Bloombury, and Rev. Mr. Swan" (Landor) **14**:178
"'Lord Erlistoun'" (Craik) **38**:113
"Lord John of the East" (Baillie) **2**:42
Lord Kilgobbin: A Tale of Ireland in Our Own Time (Lever) **23**:291-92, 297, 299, 306, 308, 311-12
"The Lord of the Castle of Indolence" (Thomson) **18**:391-92, 397, 402
The Lord of the Isles (Scott) **15**:273, 283, 319-20
The Lord of Thoulouse (Barham) **77**:9
Lord Ruthwen; ou, Les Vampires (Nodier) **19**:378
Lord Ruthwen ou les Vampires (Polidori)
See *The Vampyre: A Tale*
"Lord Ullin's Daughter" (Campbell) **19**:169, 179, 181, 186, 188, 190, 193, 195-96
"Lord Walter's Wife" (Browning) **61**:8, 45, 76; **66**:90
"Loreley" (Brentano) **1**:95, 104
Lorely: Souvenirs d'Allemagne (Nerval) **1**:475; **67**:303, 357
Lorenzaccio (Musset) **7**:258-59, 261-62, 264-65, 268-69, 271, 274, 276
La lorette (Goncourt and Goncourt) **7**:153
De l'origine des Hindous (Schlegel) **15**:224
De l'origine du langage (Renan) **26**:377
The Los Pleiad and Other Poems (Chivers) **49**:38-40, 42-4, 47
"A los terremotos occurridos en España en el presente año de 1829" (Larra) **17**:270
"Lose Ware" (Mörike) **10**:450
"The Losing of the Child" (Tennyson) **65**:373, 376
Loss and Gain: The Story of a Convert (Newman) **38**:290-93, 324, 326, 342; **99**:250-54, 262, 286, 296-98, 300
"Loss of Breath" (Poe) **16**:312; **117**:322
"The Loss of Conscience" (Saltykov) **16**:352
"The Loss of the Eurydice" (Hopkins) **17**:183-85, 194, 203-04, 220, 255
"Lost" (Bellamy) **4**:31
"Lost" (Silva)
See "Perdida"
"The Lost" (Very) **9**:378, 384-85, 391, 393-94
"The Lost Adventurer" (Freneau) **111**:149, 153
Lost and Saved (Norton) **47**:248, 256, 258
"The Lost and the Living" (Parton) **86**:349
"The Lost Bird" (Bryant) **6**:165
"The Lost Bower" (Browning) **1**:115, 117; **61**:43
"The Lost Charter" (Gogol) **5**:231
Lost Constitution (Arany)
See *Az elveszett alkomány*
"Lost Days" (Rossetti) **4**:491, 498-99
"The Lost Diamond of St. Dalmas" (Crawford) **127**:193-94
The Lost Eden (Rizal)
See *Noli me tangere*
"A Lost Evening" (Musset) **7**:256
"Lost Faith" (Preseren)
See "Zgubljena vera"
"Lost for Me, Smiling You Walk By" (Eminescu) **33**:265
"Lost for Me, You Move Smilingly in the World" (Eminescu) **131**:297
"The Lost Heir" (Hood) **16**:207
The Lost Heiress (Southworth) **26**:434, 440
The Lost Husband (Reade) **74**:263
Lost Illusions (Balzac)
See *Illusions perdues*
Lost in the Backwoods (Traill) **31**:314
"Lost in the Bush" (Harpur) **114**:99, 102
"The Lost Leader" (Browning) **19**:78; **79**:94, 97
"The Lost Letter" (Gogol)
See "Propavšaja gramotax"
Lost Love—Lost Life (Eminescu) **33**:264
"The Lost Mistress" (Browning) **19**:115; **79**:94, 97-98
A Lost Name (Le Fanu) **9**:302; **58**:272, 301-2
"Lost Notes" (Silva)
See "Notas perdidas"
"The Lost Occasion" (Whittier) **8**:509-10
"Lost on the Color" (Allingham) **25**:6
"Lost on the Prairie" (Cooke) **110**:9
"The Lost Pleiad" (Hemans) **71**:264
"The Lost Pleiad" (Simms) **3**:507
The Lost Pleiad (Chivers)
See *The Los Pleiad and Other Poems*
"The Lost Room" (O'Brien) **21**:234, 236-37, 239, 245, 248-50, 252-53
Lost Sheep (Ostrovsky) **30**:96
The Lost Smile (Keller)
See *Das Verlorene Lachen*
"The Lost Sword" (Meyer)
See "Das verlorene Schwert"
"The Lost Titian" (Rossetti) **66**:328
"A Lot o' Maidens A-Runnèn the Vields" (Barnes) **75**:67
"Lota" (Allingham) **25**:6
Lothair (Disraeli) **2**:141-47, 149-50; **39**:4-5, 19-20, 23-5, 29-31, 36-7, 39-44, 46, 51-2, 71, 75-80; **79**:212, 222, 269, 276
"The 'Lotments" (Barnes) **75**:18, 43-4, 93, 101, 104
"The Lotos-Eaters" (Tennyson) **30**:209, 211, 222-24, 241, 258, 279-80, 283, 298; **65**:357; **115**:235-36, 275, 305
"Lotta Svärd" (Runeberg) **41**:326, 328
"The Lottery" (Edgeworth) **51**:87, 89
"The Lottery Ticket" (Hale) **75**:298
"The Lotus" (Dutt) **29**:127
"The Lotus Garland of Antinous" (Symonds) **34**:342
"Louis XI" (Beranger) **34**:28
Louis Lambert (Balzac) **5**:49, 67, 77, 79-81; **53**:22, 28
Louis XI (Boucicault) **41**:30, 32
"Louisa" (Wordsworth) **12**:395; **111**:323
"Louisa Preston" (Child) **73**:131-32, 134
"Louisa Venoni" (Mackenzie) **41**:189
Louison (Musset) **7**:260
"Le loup criait" (Rimbaud) **82**:231, 247, 249
Les Louves de Machecoul (Dumas) **71**:219
"Love" (Alger) **8**:44
"Love" (Coleridge) **9**:140, 149, 151; **54**:81
"Love" (Cooke) **110**:33
"Love" (Emerson) **98**:90, 96-101
"Love" (Halleck) **47**:57
"Love" (Horton) **87**:89

"Love" (Shaw) **15**:335
"Love" (Tennyson) **65**:248
"Love" (Very) **9**:381
Love (Michelet)
See *L'amour*
Love (Sacher-Masoch) **31**:287, 291, 295
Love (Verlaine)
See *Amour*
Love Abused: The Thought Suggested by 'Thelyphthora' (Cowper) **94**:109
Love Affairs and Wedding Bells (Nestroy)
See *Liebegeschichten und Heiratsachen*
Love Affairs of a Bibliomaniac (Field) **3**:207, 210-12
"Love Affairs of Soledad" (Isaacs)
See "Amores de Soledad"
"Love among the Ruins" (Browning) **19**:105, 127, 153; **79**:161-62
"Love and Death" (Leopardi)
See "Amore e Morte"
"Love and Death: A Symphony" (Symonds) **34**:354
"Love and Duty" (Opie) **65**:181
"Love and Duty" (Tennyson) **65**:248
Love and Fortune (Planché) **42**:277, 285, 291, 293, 295
Love and Freindship (Austen) **51**:7, 24-25, 30, 59; **119**:13, 16, 30-1
"Love and Friendship" (Austen) **1**:41-42, 46, 58-59, 65-66; **13**:74, 107, **95**:30,
Love and Friendship (Austen)
See *Love and Freindship*
"Love and Harmony Combine" (Blake) **13**:182; **37**:35
Love and Intrigue (Schiller)
See *Kabale und Liebe*
Love and Money (Reade) **2**:551
"Love and Self-Love" (Alcott) **83**:6
"Love Can Do All but Raise the Dead" (Dickinson) **21**:55
"The Love Child" (Barnes) **75**:7, 57
"Love Dreams and Death" (Levy) **59**:119
"Love from the North" (Rossetti) **2**:555; **66**:328
"Love, Hope, and Patience Supporting Education" (Coleridge) **9**:159
"Love, Hope, Desire, and Fear" (Shelley) **18**:373
"Love in a Dairy" (Crawford) **127**:170
"Love in a Life" (Browning) **19**:127; **79**:153
"Love in Idleness" (Beddoes) **3**:34
Love in the Phalanstery (James) **53**:245-7, 249
Love Is Enough; or, The Feeling of Pharamond (Morris) **4**:420-22, 424, 433-34, 442-43
"Love Is Strong as Death" (Rossetti) **50**:317
"Love Letter" (Hogg) **109**:200
Love Letters of Mrs. Piozzi written when she was eighty to William Augustus Conway (Piozzi) **57**:243
"Love, Love" (Petofi)
See "A szerelem, a szerelem"
Love Me Little, Love Me Long (Reade) **2**:534, 537, 539, 542, 548-49; **74**:245, 251, 253-54, 258, 262, 264-65
"Love, Mystery and Superstition" (Opie) **65**:172
"The Love of a Marble" (Eminescu) **33**:267; **131**:286
"The Love of Alcestis" (Lazarus) **109**:290
"The Love of Alcestis" (Morris) **4**:447-48
"The Love of Christ which Passeth Knowledge" (Rossetti) **50**:268; **66**:330
"Love of Flowers" (Traill) **31**:327
"The Love of Plato" (Sacher-Masoch)
See "Platonic Love"
"Love of the Fatherland" (Smolenskin) **30**:198
"The Love of the Lie" (Baudelaire)
See "L'amour de mensonge"
"The Love of the World Reproved; or, Hypocrisy Detected" (Cowper) **94**:117
The Love of Three Oranges (Gozzi)
See *L'amore delle tre melarance*
The Love of Toldi (Arany)
See *Toldi szerelme*
Love on St. Nicholas Tower, or What Says the Pit (Andersen) **79**:10
Love Poems (Coleridge) **9**:146
"The Love Poet" (Dyer) **129**:94
"Love Song" (Beddoes) **3**:34
"The Love Song of the Conquering Lovers" (Turgenev)
See "Pesn' torzhestvuyushchey lyubvi"
Love Stories from Several Centuries (Sacher-Masoch) **31**:295
"A Love Story Reversed" (Bellamy) **4**:30; **86**:70, 74-5
"Love Thou Thy Land" (Tennyson) **30**:293
"The Love-Charm" (Tieck) **5**:511
"Loved Once" (Browning) **1**:117, 125
"Love-Doubt" (Lampman) **25**:209
Lovel the Widower (Thackeray) **14**:411
"Love-Lily" (Rossetti) **4**:512; **77**:310
"Lovely Mary Donnelly" (Allingham) **25**:8, 13, 16-17, 20, 22-3
"The Lovely Sisters" (Sigourney) **87**:321
"The Lover and Birds" (Allingham) **25**:8
A Lover by Proxy (Boucicault) **41**:40, 44
"The Lovers" (Andersen) **7**:23
"Lovers' Death" (Baudelaire)
See "La mort des amants"
"The Lover's Farewell" (Horton) **87**:110
"Lovers' Farewels" (Baillie) **2**:42
"The Lover's Journey" (Crabbe) **26**:93, 122, 129-30, 139; **121**:11, 54, 78
"The Lovers of Gudrun" (Morris) **4**:416-17, 420, 427, 442-43, 447
"The Lovers of Kandahar" (Gobineau)
See "Les amants de Kandahar"
"A Lovers' Quarrel" (Browning) **19**:127
"The Lover's Secret" (Holmes) **14**:128
"The Lovers' Tale" (Maturin) **6**:333, 335
Lover's Vows (Dunlap) **2**:211
Lovers' Vows (Inchbald) **62**:142, 144, 146-8, 150, 154, 183, 185
Lovers' Vows (Kotzebue)
See *Das Kind der Liebe*
"Lovers' Wine" (Baudelaire)
See "Le vin des amants"
Loves (Darwin)
See *The Loves of the Plants*
"Love's Delay" (Crabbe) **26**:129
"Love's Farewell" (Brontë) **16**:86
"Love's Forget-Me-Not" (Crawford) **12**:155
Love's Frailties (Holcroft) **85**:198, 212, 221-23, 235
"Love's Gleaning Tide" (Morris) **4**:434
"Love's like a Dizziness" (Hogg) **109**:201
"Love's Logic" (Timrod) **25**:372
"Love's Natural Death" (Crabbe)
See "The Natural Death of Love"
"Love's Nocturn" (Rossetti) **4**:492, 501, 510-13, 518; **77**:358-59, 361
Loves of Plants (Darwin)
See *The Loves of the Plants*
The Loves of the Angels (Moore) **6**:382-83, 387-88, 393; **110**:167-68
"The Loves of the Plants" (Crabbe) **26**:103
Loves of the Plants (Darwin)
See *The Loves of the Plants*
The Loves of the Plants (Darwin) **106**:183, 187-92, 194-95, 197, 199, 205, 209, 216, 225-27, 230, 232, 234, 236, 238-39, 241-42, 245, 247-48, 251-52, 259-60, 266, 269, 273-76
The Loves of the Poets (Jameson)
See *Memoirs of the Loves of the Poets*
"Love's Philosophy" (Shelley) **18**:345, 358
"Love's Rebuke" (Brontë) **16**:80
"Love-Sight" (Rossetti) **4**:498
Love-Songs of Childhood (Field) **3**:209
"Love-Sweetness" (Rossetti) **4**:491, 496, 498
"Love-Wonder" (Lampman) **25**:208
"A Loving Epistle to Mr William Cobbett of North Hempstead Long Island" (Halleck) **47**:76
"Low Life" (Thomson) **18**:411-12
Low Wages: Their Causes, Consequences and Remedies (Mayhew) **31**:176
"Lower Bohemia Series" (Clarke) **19**:234, 256-58
"The Lowest Place" (Rossetti) **2**:563, 566; **50**:272; **66**:330-1, 352
"The Lowest Room" (Rossetti)
See "The Lowest Place"
"Lucca della Robbia" (Pater) **7**:338
"Luceafarul" (Eminescu) **33**:245-47, 249-50, 252, 259; **131**:286-88, 290, 293, 297, 332, 348
"Luchshe pozdno, chem nikogda" (Goncharov) **1**:367, 375; **63**:3-4, 32, 47, 53
"Lucia to Edgardo" (Lazarus) **109**:294
"Lucian and Timotheus" (Landor) **14**:165, 167
Lucianic Comediettas (Maginn) **8**:439
"Lucien Létinois" (Verlaine) **51**:367
Lucien Leuwen (Stendhal) **23**:370, 374, 376, 378, 384, 392-93, 395-97, 404-06, 410, 412-13, 416; **46**:263, 275, 285, 294, 310, 316, 318, 325
"Lucifer" (Brontë) **109**:30
"Lucifer" (Eminescu) **131**:332
Lucinde (Schlegel) **45**:283, 287, 289-92, 302-03, 305, 321-22, 339-48, 350-56, 358-59, 365, 373, 375, 380-81
Lucinde (Schleiermacher)
See *Vertraute Briefe über Friedrich Schlegels Lucinde*
Luck and Pluck Series (Alger) **8**:43-44; **83**:140
The Luck of Barry Lyndon (Thackeray)
See *The Memoirs of Barry Lyndon, Esq.*
The Lucky Beggars (Gozzi)
See *I pitocchi fortunati*
A Lucrative Job (Ostrovsky)
See *Dokhodnoye mesto*
Lucrèce Borgia (Hugo) **3**:236, 239, 248, 261, 264, 269
Lucretia Borgia (Hugo)
See *Lucrèce Borgia*
Lucretia; or, The Children of the Night (Bulwer-Lytton) **1**:153, 155; **45**:19, 69
"Lucretius" (Tennyson) **30**:222, 254, 280; **115**:335
Lucrezia Floriani (Sand) **2**:597, 599; **57**:311, 314, 316-7
Lucy Crofton (Oliphant) **11**:445
"Lucy Gray" (Wordsworth) **12**:426, 446; **111**:218, 226-27, 324, 326
Lucy Temple; or, The Three Orphans (Rowson)
See *Charlotte's Daughter; or, The Three Orphans*
Ludwig Börne: Recollections of a Revolutionist (Heine) **4**:260-61, 264, 266; **54**:322
Ludwig Feuerbach (Engels)
See *Ludwig Feuerbach und der Aus gang der klassischen deutschen Philosophie*
Ludwig Feuerbach und der Aus gang der klassischen deutschen Philosophie (Engels) **85**:6, 9, 24, 37, 40, 105-06, 109
Ludwig Marcus. Words in his Memory (Heine) **54**:321
Ludwig Tieck's Schriften (Tieck) **5**:524
"Lui?" (Maupassant) **1**:457
Luigia Pallavicini, Thrown from her Horse (Foscolo) **97**:50
Luise Millerin (Schiller)
See *Kabale und Liebe*
"An Luise Nast" (Hölderlin) **16**:174
Luke Walton or The Chicago Newsboy (Alger) **83**:112-13
"Lullabies" (Lonnrot) **53**:339
Lullabies (Nekrasov) **11**:411
"Lullaby" (Mangan) **27**:292
"Lullaby" (Nekrasov)
See "Bajuški-baju"
Lullaby-Land (Field) **3**:209

"Lulling D. to Sleep" (Isaacs)
See "Adormeciendo a David"
Lulu's Library (Alcott) **58**:51
"Lumbre de sombra" (Isaacs) **70**:313
"The Lumley Autograph" (Cooper) **129**:66
Lumpazivagabundus (Nestroy)
See *Der böse Geist Lumpazivagabundus oder Das liederliche Kleeblett*
"Luna Through a Lorgnette" (Cranch) **115**:41
Lunch with the Marshal of the Nobility (Turgenev) **21**:428
Les lundis (Sainte-Beuve) **5**:342-43
"La lune blanche" (Verlaine) **2**:631; **51**:352, 355
"Lurelay" (Mangan) **27**:282
Luria (Browning) **19**:103, 113; **79**:159-60
"The Lusiad" (Chivers) **49**:71
"The Lust of the Serpent's Spirit" (Ueda Akinari)
See *Jasei no In*
"The Lust of the White Serpent" (Ueda Akinari)
See *Jasei no In*
"Lusts" (Verlaine)
See "Luxures"
"Das Lustspiel" (Meyer) **81**:154
Lutezia (Heine) **4**:265, 268; **54**:309
La lutte pour la vie (Daudet) **1**:236
Luttrell of Arran (Lever) **23**:292, 295, 305
"Luxures" (Verlaine) **51**:372
"La luz" (Bello) **131**:112
"Luz de la luna" (Silva) **114**:301-2
Luz de luna (Silva) **114**:262, 271
Lyceum 26 (Schlegel) **45**:364
Lyceum 42 (Schlegel) **45**:363
Lyceum Fragment 57 (Schlegel) **45**:312
Lyceum Fragment 60 (Schlegel) **45**:314
Lyceum Fragments (Schlegel) **45**:343, 359
Lycidas (Tennyson) **115**:258
"Lycus the Centaur" (Hood) **16**:199-201, 208, 210, 218, 221, 225-27, 229-32, 236
"Lydia and Marian" (Rowson) **69**:128
Den lykkelige alder (Undset) **3**:516, 522
"Lyra Apostolica" (Keble) **87**:131-32
Lyra Apostolica (Keble) **87**:160
Lyra Apostolica (Newman) **38**:282, 336, 343-44
"Lyra Innocentium" (Keble) **87**:134
—Lyra Innocentium (Keble)
See *Lyra Innocentium: Thoughts in Verse on Christian Children, Their Ways, and Their Privileges*
Lyra Innocentium: Thoughts in Verse on Christian Children, Their Ways, and Their Privileges (Keble) **87**:119, 152-53, 159-60, 195
The Lyre (Sand)
See *Les sept cordes de la lyre*
"Lyric Intermezzo" (Heine)
See *Lyrisches Intermezzo*
"The Lyric Muse" (Allingham) **25**:6
Lyrical and Other Poems Selected from the Writings of Jean Ingelow (Ingelow) **39**:264
Lyrical Ballads (Coleridge) **9**:130-31, 137, 163, 165; **54**:80, 99-100, 103, 114, 120-1, 127; **99**:22; **111**:195-374
Lyrical Ballads, with a Few Other Poems (Wordsworth) **12**:386, 390, 394, 398, 400, 410-11, 413, 444, 450, 463; **38**:359, 364, 420; **111**:195-374
"Lyrical Poem on the Death of Lord Byron" (Solomos)
See "Poiema lyriko eis ton thanato tou Lord Byron"
Lyrics of Earth (Lampman) **25**:162, 169, 178, 183, 199, 212, 220
Lyrics of Earth: Sonnets and Ballads (Lampman) **25**:170, 174, 194-96
Lyrisches Intermezzo (Heine) **4**:248-49, 252, 254, 258-59
Le lys dans la valée (Balzac) **35**:2, 34; **53**:28
"Lysene" (Andersen) **79**:76
"Lyudmila" (Zhukovsky) **35**:378-79, 388-89, 398-99, 400-01
M. Dupont; ou, La jeune fille et sa bonne (Kock) **16**:245
"M. Renan and the Jews" (Lazarus) **109**:337
"Ma bohème" (Rimbaud) **4**:484; **35**:266, 271-72, 275, 282, 289; **82**:226
"À M.A. de L" (Desbordes-Valmore)
See "À Monsieur Alphonse de Lamartine"
"Ma Fille" (Verlaine) **51**:386
Ma soeur Jeanne (Sand) **57**:322, 325-6
"Ma vocation" (Beranger) **34**:28
"Mabel Martin" (Whittier) **8**:516; **59**:351, 360
Mabel Parker: or The Hidden Treasure. A Tale of the Frontier Settlements (Alger) **83**:98, 119, 145
"Mabel's May Day" (Alcott) **83**:5
Mabel Vaughan (Cummins) **139**:164-66, 185-86
An Macalla (Merriman) **70**:372
"Macbeth" (Lamb) **125**:304
The Maccabees (Ludwig)
See *Die Makkabäer*
The Macdermots of Ballycloran (Trollope) **6**:452, 500, 509, 514; **33**:364; **101**:222-29, 245-48, 251-53, 262-64, 271, 293-94, 296-300, 312
"La machine à gloire" (Villiers de l'Isle Adam) **3**:581
"Die Macht des Gesanges" (Schiller) **39**:388
"Macht des Weibes" (Schiller) **39**:388
Macías (Larra) **17**:277, 279; **130**:217, 228, 251, 253, 274
"Mackery End, in Hertfordshire" (Lamb) **10**:408, 435-36; **113**:155-56, 235
Mackintosh (Macaulay)
See *Sir James Mackintosh*
"Le maçon" (Bertrand) **31**:47-8
"The Macrobian Bow" (Hayne)
See "Cambyses and the Macrobian Bow"
"MacSwiggen" (Freneau) **1**:315
"The Mad Banker of Amsterdam" (Lockhart) **6**:293, 295
"The Mad Convalescent at Fort Rattonneau" (Arnim)
See "Der Tolle Invalide auf dem Fort Ratonneau"
Mad Monkton (Collins) **1**:185
"The Mad Mother" (Coleridge) **9**:131
"The Mad Mother" (Solomos) **15**:389, 396
"The Mad Mother" (Wordsworth) **12**:387, 402; **111**:200, 202-3, 208, 211, 248, 261, 314-15
"Mad Song" (Blake) **13**:181-82; **37**:72
Mad Song (Blake) **127**:27
"The Mad Wanderer, a Ballad" (Opie) **65**:160
Madam (Oliphant) **11**:450; **61**:216
"A Madame A. Tastu" (Desbordes-Valmore) **97**:5
Madame Bovary; moeurs de province (Flaubert) **2**:220-44, 246-54, 256-7; **10**:115-78; **19**:271, 273, 276-8, 280-1, 286, 290, 294, 296, 300-2, 304, 306-9, 313, 315; **62**:69, 82, 91-3, 96-8, 103, 109-12, 121; **66**:233-96; **135**:78, 80-81, 83, 85, 89, 93, 95, 102-3, 107-8, 115, 125, 133-34, 139, 167, 170-72, 174, 183
Madame Caverlet (Augier) **31**:8, 10, 13, 16, 26, 28, 31, 34-5
"Madame Crowl's Ghost" (Le Fanu) **9**:317
Madame Crowl's Ghost, and Other Tales of Mystery (Le Fanu) **9**:301
Madame de Chamblay (Dumas) **71**:194
"Madame De Fleury" (Edgeworth) **51**:87, 89
"Madame de Soubise" (Vigny) **7**:473; **102**:366-67
"Madame Emile de Girardin" (Desbordes-Valmore) **97**:30
Madame Gervaisais (Goncourt and Goncourt) **7**:157, 159-60, 166-67, 174, 182, 188-89
"Madame Hermet" (Maupassant) **83**:176, 216, 218-19
"A Madame Ida Dumas" (Nerval) **67**:307, 316
"Madame la marquise" (Musset) **7**:267
Madame Putiphar (Borel) **41**:3, 5, 8-10, 12, 14-20
Madame Robert (Banville) **9**:31
"Madame Tellier's Girls" (Maupassant) **1**:461
Madame Valentine (Freytag)
See *Die Valentine: Schauspiel in fünf Aufzügen*
"Madamoiselle Agathe" (Banville) **9**:32
"Das Mädchen von Orleans" (Schiller) **39**:376
Madeleine (Kock) **16**:246
"Madeline: A Domestic Tale" (Hemans) **71**:288, 303, 307
Madeline: A Tale (Opie) **65**:172, 174, 178, 180, 182-3, 198
"Madeline, the Temptress" (Alger) **83**:96
"Mademoiselle" (Oliphant) **61**:204
"Mademoiselle Bistouri" (Baudelaire) **29**:79
Mademoiselle de Belle-Isle (Dumas) **11**:57, 71; **71**:193, 209-10, 242
Mademoiselle de Marsan (Nodier) **19**:384-85
Mademoiselle de Maupin (Gautier) **1**:339, 342-43, 346, 348-56; **59**:3, 5-6, 12, 21-2, 25, 28, 30, 41-5, 59, 63-8
Mademoiselle de Scudéry (Hoffmann) **2**:342, 344-45, 356, 360
Mademoiselle Irnois (Gobineau) **17**:91-2, 103
Mademoiselle La Quintinie (Sand) **57**:313
Mademoiselle Mathilde (Kingsley) **107**:187-88, 190, 192, 224-28
Mademoiselle Merquem (Sand) **57**:316
"Mademoisselle Fifi" (Maupassant) **1**:442; **83**:190, 200
"Los maderos de San Juan" (Silva) **114**:299, 301-3, 310, 313
Los maderos de San Juan (Silva) **114**:269-70
"Madhouses Prisons Wh-re shops" (Clare) **86**:118
Das Mädl aus der Vorstadt (Nestroy) **42**:248-49
"The Madman" (Petofi)
See "Az örült"
"A Madman's Diary" (Gogol)
See "Diary of a Madman"
The Madness of Love (Tamayo y Baus)
See *La locura de amor*
"Madness of Orestes" (Landor) **14**:168
Madoc (Southey) **8**:450-51, 453, 456, 459, 461, 469-70, 474, 476, 478-79; **97**:260-62, 268, 273, 278-79, 293-94, 296-97, 322
"The Madonna" (Baratynsky) **103**:8
"Madonna" (Pushkin) **83**:259
"The Madonna" (Tennyson) **30**:209
Madonna Mary (Oliphant) **11**:447-8, 450; **61**:173, 206, 209, 239
"Mador of the Moor" (Hogg) **4**:275, 280, 282
Mador of the Moor (Hogg) **109**:204-07, 240-41, 244, 250
De Madrid à Nápoles (Alarcon) **1**:12
"Madrigal" (Silva) **114**:263
"Madrigal" (Verlaine) **51**:360-61
Madrigals and Chronicles: Being Newly Founded Poems Written by John Clare (Clare) **9**:91, 93-94
"Maese Pérez el organista" (Bécquer) **106**:95-7, 120, 161
"Magdalen" (Halleck) **47**:57, 69
"Magdalen" (Levy) **59**:98, 110
Magdalen Hepburn: The Story of the Reformation (Oliphant) **11**:448; **61**:163, 219
"A Magdalena" (Gómez de Avellaneda) **111**:30
Magelone (Tieck) **5**:525
"Les mages" (Hugo) **3**:273
"Maggie, a Lady" (Rossetti) **66**:302, 331
"The Magic Mirror" (Wilson) **5**:567
The Magic of Kindness (Mayhew) **31**:161
The Magic Ring (Fouqué)
See *Der Zauberring*
The Magic Skin (Balzac) **5**:32
"The Magic Slippers" (Allston) **2**:26
"The Magician" (Emerson) **1**:307-09
"Magistrale" (Preseren) **127**:295-96

"The Magistrate" (Petofi)
See "A táblabíro"
"Magna est vernitas" (Patmore) **9**:358
"Magna moralia" (Patmore) **9**:344
"The Magnetic Lady to her Patient" (Shelley) **18**:369
"Der Magnetiseur" (Hoffmann) **2**:345, 360
"Magnetism" (Lazarus) **109**:294
"Magnit" (Bestuzhev) **131**:150
"Magnolia Cemetery Ode" (Timrod)
See "Ode Sung on the Occasion of Decorating the Graves of the Confederate Dead at Magnolia Cemetery"
"Magnolia Gardens (Near Charleston, S.C.)" (Hayne) **94**:138
"Magus Wandering among the Stars" (Eminescu) **131**:348
"A magyar ifjakhoz" (Petofi) **21**:280
"A magyar nemes" (Petofi) **21**:264
"A magyar nemzet" (Petofi) **21**:279
"Mahmoud" (Hunt) **1**:416
"Mahomets Gesang" (Goethe) **4**:212
"Mahommed and the Assassin" (Milnes) **61**:130
"Mahommedanism" (Milnes) **61**:130
Maid Marian (Planché) **42**:273
"The Maid Martyr" (Ingelow) **39**:258
"The Maid o' Newton" (Barnes) **75**:58, 89
The Maid of All Work (Martineau) **26**:322
"Maid of Astolat" (Tennyson) **65**:227
The Maid of Orleans (Schiller)
See *Die Jungfräu von Orleans*
"The Maid Vor My Bride" (Barnes) **75**:71
The Maiden from the Fairy-world or the Peasant as Millionaire (Raimund)
See *Der Bauer als Millionär; oder, Das Mädchen aus der Feenwelt*
"Maiden Song" (Rossetti) **2**:563, 571; **50**:264; **66**:302, 328
"Maidenhood" (Longfellow) **2**:493; **45**:100, 135, 140, 155
"The Maiden's Complaint" (Schiller) **39**:306
"Maiden's Sorrow" (Bryant) **46**:20
Maidens' Vows; or, The Magnetism of the Heart (Fredro)
See *Śluby panieńskie; czyli, Magnetyzm serca*
"The Maids of Elfin-Mere" (Allingham) **25**:18, 20, 23
"The Maid's Story" (Crabbe) **26**:129
"Maid's Tragedy" (Tennyson) **65**:228
"Mail from Tunis" (Dickinson) **77**:118
"La Main du Major Muller" (Verlaine) **51**:387
"La main enchantée" (Nerval) **1**:483; **67**:332
"Main Street" (Hawthorne) **2**:329-30; **10**:315; **17**:152; **39**:212; **95**:95, 128, 139
"The Main-Chance" (Hazlitt) **82**:126
The Maine Woods (Thoreau) **7**:361, 368, 378, 390; **21**:372; **61**:348; **138**:124, 134, 148, 155, 159, 167
"Mais ve que o meu corazon" (Castro) **78**:42
La maison blanche (Kock) **16**:245
La maison claes (Balzac) **5**:33
"La Maison de ma mère" (Desbordes-Valmore) **97**:23, 28
"La maison du Berger" (Vigny) **7**:469, 472, 478-79, 481-82, 484-86; **102**:354-55, 357-58
"La maison du chat-qui-pelote" (Balzac) **5**:74, 83
La maison d'un artiste (Goncourt) **7**:175
La maison nucingen (Balzac) **5**:46; **35**:43
"La maison Tellier" (Maupassant) **1**:459, 463, 466; **83**:169, 171, 190, 193, 200
Maison Turque (Maupassant) **83**:199-201, 203
Maître Cornélius (Balzac) **53**:23
Maître Guérin (Augier) **31**:2, 8-10, 13, 15-16, 25, 28, 31, 34
"Maitre Pied" (Villiers de l'Isle Adam) **3**:588
Les maîtres d'autrefois: Belgigue, Hollande (Fromentin) **10**:226-35, 251; **125**:97, 103-16, 124, 134-35, 148, 169
Les maîtres mosaïstes (Sand) **42**:319
"Les maitres sonneurs" (Maupassant) **1**:448
Les maîtres sonneurs (Sand) **2**:601, 603, 606; **42**:240, 370; **57**:313, 317, 338
Les maîtresses de Louis XV (Goncourt and Goncourt) **7**:164-65
Máj (Macha) **46**:198-207, 213-26, 228-30
The Majolo (Galt) **1**:327-28
Der Majorat (Hoffmann) **2**:340, 346, 361
Die Majoratsherren (Arnim) **5**:13, 18, 20, 23
"Majskaja noč, ili Vtoplennica" (Gogol) **5**:218, 224, 231, 251
The Maker of His Fortune (Keller)
See *Der Schmied seines Glückes*
"The Maker to Posterity" (Stevenson) **5**:401
The Makers of Florence (Oliphant) **11**:439, 445
The Makers of Modern Rome (Oliphant) **61**:215
"The Make-Up Artist" (Leskov)
See "Tupejnyi xudožnik"
Making His Way (Alger) **8**:25
"The Making of Man" (Tennyson) **30**:274
Die Makkabäer (Ludwig) **4**:347-48, 350
"Maksim Maksimovich" (Lermontov) **5**:291, 295-96, 298, 301-02, 304-05; **126**:148-49, 153, 156-57, 195-96, 199
"Le mal" (Rimbaud) **35**:271, 321
Mal' chik v shtanakh i mal' chik bez shtanov (Saltykov) **16**:375
"Le Mal d'André" (Maupassant) **83**:221
"El mal del siglo" (Silva) **114**:316
El mal del siglo (Silva) **114**:272
"Le Mal du pays" (Desbordes-Valmore) **97**:29
"Mal du siécle" (Silva) **114**:316
Mala prostonarodnja slaveno-serbska pjesnarica (Karadzic) **115**:77, 82, 100-1, 105, 110
"Målaren" (Almqvist) **42**:16
"Mal'aria" (Tyutchev) **34**:397
"Malavolti" (Chivers) **49**:47
"The Malay—took the Pearl" (Dickinson) **77**:152
"Malcolm's Katie" (Crawford) **12**:151, 153, 155-59, 161-62, 166, 168-69, 171-72; **127**:148-53, 155-56, 158-59, 161, 163-67, 169-76, 178, 181-82, 192, 194-95, 197-201, 203-4, 212, 217-18, 223-24, 228
"The Maldive Shark" (Melville) **3**:352
Maldoror (Lautréamont)
See *Les chants de Maldoror: Chants I, II, III, IV, V, VI*
"Malédiction de Cypris" (Banville) **9**:20
"La malédiction de Vénus" (Banville) **9**:14
"Malen' kaja ošibka" (Leskov) **25**:234
Maler Nolten (Mörike) **10**:444-47, 450-51, 454-55
"Le maline" (Rimbaud) **35**:271
"Malines" (Verlaine) **51**:383
Die Maltheser (Schiller)
See *Demetrius*
Maltravers (Bulwer-Lytton)
See *Ernest Maltravers*
Malvino; ou, Le mariage d'inclination (Scribe) **16**:382, 393
The Mammon of Unrighteousness (Boyesen) **135**:14, 22-23, 31-32, 37, 48, 54-57, 59, 61, 63, 67-68
"Man" (Allston) **2**:26
"The Man" (Kivi)
See "Mies"
"Man" (Lamartine)
See "L'homme"
"A Man and a Muse" (Castro)
See "Un hombre y una musa"
"The Man and His Shadow" (Krylov) **1**:435
"Man and Nature" (Lampman) **25**:217
The Man and the Hour (Martineau) **137**:329
Man and Wife (Collins) **1**:180, 182; **18**:63-4, 66; **93**:5, 12, 19, 34
The Man at Home (Brown) **74**:47, 173, 196; **122**:60, 119
"Man Born to Be King" (Morris) **4**:417, 420, 427
A Man Full of Nothing (Nestroy)
See *Der Zerrissene*
"The Man in Business" (Freneau) **111**:132
"Man in Harmony with Nature" (Very) **9**:387, 389-90
"Man in the Bell" (Maginn) **8**:436, 438, 440
"The Man in the Cloak" (Mangan) **27**:302
The Man in the Iron Mask (Dumas) **71**:242-43
"A Man Like Many Others" (Turgenev) **21**:376
"A Man Made of Money" (Jerrold) **2**:396-99, 401-06
"The Man of Adamant" (Hawthorne) **79**:316; **95**:131
The Man of Feeling (Mackenzie) **41**:180-86, 188-89, 194-96, 198-204, 207, 214, 217-220, 222-28
The Man of Fortitude; or, The Knights Adventure (Dunlap) **2**:213
"The Man of Ninety" (Freneau) **1**:320; **111**:101
"The Man of Snow" (Horne) **127**:264
The Man of Surrenders (Sacher-Masoch) **31**:291
The Man of Ten Thousand (Holcroft) **85**:198, 222-23
"The Man of the Crowd" (Poe) **1**:500, 518; **16**:295, 297, 303, 316, 331, 336; **78**:281
The Man of the World (Mackenzie) **41**:181, 184, 195-96, 199, 200, 202-03, 208-09, 214, 222-26, 228
The Man out of Business (Freneau) **111**:132
"The Man That Was Used Up" (Poe) **16**:292, 308, 312
"Man the Reformer" (Emerson) **98**:26, 110, 112-13, 116
"Man Thinking" (Emerson) **98**:18
"Man to April" (Freneau) **1**:317
The Man Who Laughs (Hugo)
See *L'homme qui rit*
"The Man Who Lost His Name" (Boyesen) **135**:12, 20, 25-26
"The Man Who Never Laughed Again" (Morris) **4**:417, 447-48
The Man with Three Faces (Pixérécourt)
See *L'homme à trois visages; ou, Le proscrit de Venise*
"Manasseh" (Kendall) **12**:192
Manchester Lectures (Cobbett) **49**:160
"The Manchester Marriage" (Gaskell) **5**:202; **70**:185
"Manchester Strike" (Martineau) **26**:305
A Manchester Strike (Martineau) **137**:250-51, 265-66, 304
"Le manchy" (Leconte de Lisle) **29**:210, 212, 214, 217-18, 224
Mandeville: A Tale of the Seventeenth Century in England (Godwin) **14**:40-2, 44, 49-51, 57, 68-71, 81, 83; **130**:52
"Mandoline" (Verlaine) **2**:628; **51**:351, 374, 378, 380
Mandrivka z pryemnistiu ta y ne bez morali (Shevchenko)
See *Matros*
Manette Salomon (Goncourt and Goncourt) **7**:155, 157-58, 162, 167, 175-76, 180, 182, 187
Manfred (Byron) **2**:64, 66, 70, 72, 79-81, 84, 87, 90, 93, 97, 99-101, 103; **12**:88, 100, 102; **109**:55-134
The Manhaters and the Poet (Fredro)
See *Odluki i poeta*
"Manhood" (Thoreau) **7**:383
The Mania for Things Foreign (Fredro)
See *Cudzoziemszczyzna; czyli, Nauka zbawlenia*
Manifest der Kommunistischen (Marx) **17**:293-94, 296, 303, 309-10, 314, 316, 319, 321-23, 333-34, 336, 357, 359; **114**:3, 8-24, 28-41, 43-57, 59-80, 82-7
Manifest der kommunistischen Partei (Engels) **85**:6, 8, 13, 21, 32, 53, 65, 68, 105, 117, 120, 127-28, 132, 136-38, 140-41, 147-49, 151, 157, 161-62, 170, 181-82; **114**:3, 8-24, 28-41, 43-57, 59-80, 82-7
"Manifest Destiny" (Shaw) **15**:341

"Manifeste du Comité central des 20 arrondissements" (Vallès) **71**:330
Manifesto (Engels)
See *Manifest der kommunistischen Partei*
Manifesto of the Communist Party (Engels)
See *Manifest der kommunistischen Partei*
"The manifold Hills forsaken by the sun" (Harpur) **114**:115-16
The Manikins (Cooper) **1**:216, 220, 223
"Manly Amusement" (Pater) **7**:342
"Der Mann von fünfzig Jahren" (Goethe) **4**:193, 197
"The Manna Gatherers" (Keble) **87**:134
"Mannahatta" (Whitman) **31**:393-94
The Mannequin (Staël-Holstein)
See *Le Mannequin*
Le Mannequin (Staël-Holstein) **91**:326, 360
Mannering (Scott)
See *Guy Mannering*
"Manners" (Emerson) **38**:211; **98**:101
Manners; or, Happy Homes and Good Society All the Year Round (Hale) **75**:283
Männerwürde (Schiller) **39**:331, 339
Människosläkets saga (Almqvist) **42**:18
Manoeuvering (Edgeworth) **1**:267; **51**:89-90
"The Man-of-War Bird" (Whitman) **31**:363
Manon Lescaut (Daudet) **1**:237
Manor Sackville (Morgan) **29**:390, 394-95
"Man's Future" (Lampman) **25**:217
A Man's Life (Trelawny) **85**:347
Man's Place in Nature (Huxley) **67**:4, 9-10, 46, 72, 81-2, 96, 98, 105-06
"A Man's Requirements" (Browning) **61**:43
"Man's Three Guests" (Sigourney) **21**:299
Mansfield Park (Austen) **1**:32-34, 36, 38-40, 44-45, 47, 49-54, 59-62, 64; **13**:54, 60-1, 84, 93, 97, 101, 106; **19**:2, 5-6, 14, 32, 39, 42, 55, 64; **33**:35, 37, 41, 55, 57, 63-4, 66, 69-70, 74-5, 85-6, 88-93, 96, 99; **51**:8, 25-6; **81**:5, 18, 52, 61, 69, 77; **95**:2-7, 9-18, 20-6, 28-36, 38-40, 42-6, 48-50, 52-6, 58-60, 62, 65, 67-80, 83-4; **119**:12, 14, 18, 20-1,
"Mansion of Many Apartments" (Keats) **121**:207
Manson the Miser, or Life and Its Vicissitudes (Alger) **8**:42; **83**:96
Manthorn (Holcroft)
See *Manthorn the Enthusiast*
Manthorn the Enthusiast (Holcroft) **85**:228, 230, 236-39, 243
A Manual of Parliamentary Practice (Jefferson) **11**:148, 199
A Manual of Political Economy (Bentham) **38**:45, 92
A Manual of Useful Studies: For the Instruction of Young Persons of Both Sexes, in Families and Schools (Webster) **30**:420
Manuel (Maturin) **6**:320, 322, 328, 331-32
"The Manufacturers" (Edgeworth) **51**:87, 89-90
Manuscripts (Whitman) **81**:364
Le manuscrit de ma mère (Lamartine) **11**:265
Man-Woman; or, The Temple, the Hearth, the Street (Dumas)
See *L'homme-femme: Résponse à M. Henri d'Ideville*
"Many a pilgrim goes to Rome, to Compostella" (Preseren) **127**:293
Many Moods (Symonds) **34**:323, 325
"The Maple Tree" (Clare) **86**:180
"The Maple Tree" (Moodie) **113**:348-49, 371
Die Mappe meines Urgrossvaters (Stifter) **41**:335-37, 343-44, 358, 380
Les marana (Balzac) **35**:25
La marâtre (Balzac) **5**:52
The Marble Faun; or, The Romance of Monte Beni (Hawthorne) **2**:305-07, 310, 313-14, 317, 320-21, 324-25, 328, 333; **10**:296; **17**:116, 124; **23**:168-221; **39**:170, 177, 222, 224, 231; **79**:302, 304, 314; **95**:205
"The Marble Statue" (Eichendorff)
See "Das Marmorbild"
"A Marble Woman; or, The Mysterious Model" (Alcott) **58**:46, 75-6; **83**:6
"The Marble Youth" (Meyer)
See "Der Marmorknabe"
"The Marbles of Aegina" (Pater) **7**:330
"Marbre de Paros" (Gautier) **59**:19
Marc-Aurèle et la fin du monde antique (Renan) **26**:402, 408, 410, 420-21
Marcelle Rabe (Banville) **9**:31
"Marcellus and Hannibal" (Landor) **14**:189
"March" (Bryant) **46**:9, 38
"March" (Clare) **9**:106; **86**:94, 102, 104, 165-67
"March" (Crawford) **12**:155
"March" (Lampman) **25**:160
"March" (Taylor) **89**:300
"A March Day in London" (Levy) **59**:89
"The March Hare" (Leskov)
See "Zajačij remiz"
March Hares (Frederic) **10**:186, 188, 192, 194, 201-02, 208, 212
"A March in the Ranks Hard-Prest, and the Road Unknown" (Whitman) **81**:321-23, 331
"The March into Virginia" (Melville) **3**:352
"The March of Winter" (Lampman) **25**:210
"The March to Moscow" (Southey) **8**:474
"Le marchand de tulipes" (Bertrand) **31**:48
"Marche de funèbre pour la mort de la terre" (Laforgue) **5**:275
Märchen (Goethe) **34**:122; **90**:107
"Märchen vom Murmeltier" (Brentano) **1**:100
"Märchen vom Schneider Siebentot auf einen Schlag" (Brentano) **1**:100, 104
Das Märchen von blonden Eckbert (Tieck)
See *Der blonde Eckbert*
"Das Märchen von dem Hause Starenberg" (Brentano) **1**:104
Marchmont (Smith) **23**:323, 335; **115**:148
"Marco Bozzaris" (Halleck) **47**:56, 66-67, 69-70, 78-, 81, 83-84
"Marcus Aurelius" (Arnold) **89**:36
Marcus Aurelius (Sigourney) **87**:339
Marcus Aurelius and the End of the Ancient World (Renan)
See *Marc-Aurèle et la fin du monde antique*
Mardi: And a Voyage Thither (Melville) **3**:327, 332-33, 335, 337-39, 341-42, 348-49, 352, 355-56, 359-60, 363-65, 367, 370, 380, 383; **12**:252, 262, 274, 317; **29**:317, 324, 329, 354; **45**:197, 210, 229, 247, 251-54; **49**:376, 391, 407; **91**:4, 7, 10, 18, 30-2, 42-3, 45-6, 55, 88, 121, 204, 212; **93**:188, 193, 205; **123**:193-94, 203-4, 211, 231, 241, 243, 251-52
"Mardoche" (Musset) **7**:254, 267, 275, 278-79
La mare au diable (Sand) **2**:599-601, 603-06, 608; **42**:314, 327, 338, 340, 363, 367; **57**:317, 338, 359, 361, 366
"Mare Rubrum" (Holmes) **81**:98
La maréchale d'ancre (Vigny) **7**:473; **102**:336
"The Maremma" (Hemans) **71**:291
"Marenghi" (Shelley) **18**:345
"Marfa posadnica" (Karamzin) **3**:285-86
"Marfa the Mayoress" (Karamzin)
See "Marfa posadnica"
"Marfeast" (Arany)
See "Ünneprontók"
"Marfiles viejos" (Casal) **131**:267-68
La marfisa bizzarra (Gozzi) **23**:110
"Margaret" (Wordsworth) **12**:429
"Margaret: A Pearl" (Field) **3**:205
"Margaret Fuller and Mary Wollstonecraft" (Eliot) **118**:134
"Margaret Green: The Young Mahometan" (Lamb) **125**:302, 312, 319, 323, 343, 349
"Margaret in the Xebec" (Ingelow) **39**:264
Margaret of Navarre; or, The Massacre of Saint Bartholome's Ev e (Dumas)
See *La reine Margot*
Margaret Smith's Journal (Whittier) **8**:509, 512
"Margareta" (Ludwig) **4**:353
Margareta (Kivi) **30**:65
"Margaretta Story" (Murray) **63**:174, 176-8, 190
"Margarita" (Castro) **3**:102
Margarita (Hugo) **3**:264
"Marginalia" (Poe) **94**:178; **117**:202, 285, 320, 330, 337
Marginalia (Coleridge) **99**:113
Marginalia (Poe) **55**:134, 136, 138, 160, 171, 182
Marginalia (Stendhal) **46**:324
"Margret" (Browning) **1**:126
"Marguerite" (Arnold) **89**:14, 48, 88
"Marguerite" (Whittier) **8**:509, 519; **59**:371
Marguerite d'Anjou (Pixérécourt) **39**:276, 284
Marguerite de Valois (Dumas) **71**:205-06
"Marguerite Schneider" (Banville) **9**:16
Mari Magno; or, Tales on Board (Clough) **27**:52-3, 57, 59-60, 62, 65, 69, 74, 77-81, 90, 114-19
María (Isaacs) **70**:302-04, 311-12, 317-29, 331-45
Maria (Ludwig) **4**:356, 367
"Maria, A Highland Legend" (Hogg) **109**:203
Maria Antoinette (Heine) **54**:347
"Maria Howe" (Lamb) **10**:417
Mária királynő (Madach) **19**:370
Maria Magdalen: Ein bürgerliches Trauerspiel in drei Acten, nebst einem Vorwort (Hebbel) **43**:230, 234, 237, 239, 242-43, 248, 251, 255, 257-59, 261-62, 266-67, 269-71, 277, 279-80, 283, 286-87, 296-97, 299-301
Maria Stuarda (Alfieri) **101**:8, 18, 21, 32
Maria Stuart (Schiller) **39**:318-19, 330, 345-46, 368, 372, 375-76, 378-80, 383-84; **69**:169, 175, 194, 239, 244, 246, 277
"Maria Szécsi" (Petofi)
See "Szécsi Mária"
Un Mariage dans le Monde (Feuillet) **45**:83, 85
Le mariage d'argent (Scribe) **16**:382, 384, 386-88, 393
Le mariage de raison (Scribe) **16**:382, 393
Le mariage de Victorine (Sand) **42**:310
Le mariage d'Olympe (Augier) **31**:2-3, 5-8, 12, 15, 19, 23-5, 27, 29-31, 35
"Le Mariage du lieutenant Laré" (Maupassant) **83**:172, 181, 195
Le Mariage du siècle (Sade) **47**:361-62
Un mariage sous Louis XV (Dumas) **11**:71; **71**:209
Marian and Lydia (Rowson) **5**:312
"Marian Hume" (Brontë) **109**:42
"Mariana" (Tennyson) **30**:211, 223, 237, 276, 279, 286; **115**:358
"Mariana and Oenone" (Tennyson) **30**:245
"Mariana in the South" (Tennyson) **30**:207
"Mariana's Grove" (Zhukovsky)
See "Mar'ina roshcha"
Marianna (Dumas) **71**:205
Marianne (Sand) **42**:370
"Marianne's Dream" (Shelley) **18**:326
"Maria's Tale" (Hogg) **109**:203
Marie Antoinette; or, The Chevalier of the Red House: A Tale o f the French Revolution (Dumas)
See *Le chevalier de Maison-Rouge*
"Marie Bertrand, or the Felon's Daughter" (Alger) **83**:96, 143
Marie Grubbe: Interiors from the Seventeenth Century (Jacobsen)
See *Fru Marie Grubbe: Interieurer fra det syttende Asrhundreded*
"Marie Rogêt" (Poe)
See "The Mystery of Marie Rogêt"
Marie Tudor (Hugo) **3**:240, 256, 268-69
Marienbader Elegie (Goethe) **4**:193
"Mariia" (Shevchenko) **54**:389
"Mar'ina roshcha" (Zhukovsky) **35**:379, 384, 398
"Marine" (Rimbaud) **35**:269, 309; **4**:475

Mariner (Coleridge)
See *The Rime of the Ancient Mariner: A Poet's Reverie*
"The Mariner's Cave" (Ingelow) **39**:267
"Marinka" (Macha) **46**:198, 204, 208-09, 214-15
Marino Caboga (Arnim) **5**:21
Marino Faliero: Doge of Venice (Byron) **2**:65-66, 70, 79-80, 90, 99
Marion de Lorme (Hugo) **3**:236, 238-39, 261, 268-69; **10**:369; **21**:197
"Marion Delorme" (Dumas) **71**:189
Marion Fay (Trollope) **6**:470, 475, 484; **101**:311-13, 315, 322, 325
"Marionettentheater" (Kleist)
See "Über das Marionettentheater"
Marius (Hugo) **3**:246; **10**:359, 375
Marius the Epicurean: His Sensations and Ideas (Pater) **7**:293-96, 298, 301, 306-12, 314-15, 317-19, 322-23, 325, 327, 329, 335-36, 340-42; **90**:239-42, 248, 251-54, 257-58, 264, 268-69, 272-76, 280-81, 283-91, 314, 318, 325-32, 340-41
Marius und Sulla (Grabbe) **2**:272, 274-75, 280-82, 284, 287-88
Marja Stuart (Slowacki) **15**:348-50, 353, 362-63, 369, 373, 378
Marjam (Almqvist) **42**:19
Mark Hurdlestone (Moodie) **113**:295, 297, 324, 334, 370, 372-73
Mark Hurdlestone, the Gold Worshipper (Moodie) **14**:217, 226, 237
Mark, the Match Boy; or, Richard Hunter's Ward (Alger) **8**:37, 39; **83**:105, 131
"Mark the Nihilist" (Goncharov) **63**:3
"The Market Man" (Freneau) **111**:132
The Market-Place (Frederic) **10**:189-92, 194, 202, 206-08, 213, 215, 217
Markgraf Carl Philipp von Brandenburg (Arnim) **5**:21
"Markheim" (Stevenson) **5**:415, 418, 424, 429
"Marko Kraljević and Demo of the Mountain" (Karadzic) **115**:91
"Marko Kraljević and Lujutica Bogdan" (Karadzic) **115**:91
"Marko Kraljević and Musa Kesedžij" (Karadzic) **115**:91
"Marko Kraljević and the Daughter of the Arab King" (Karadzic) **115**:91
"Marko Kraljević Knows His Father's Sword" (Karadzic) **115**:91
Mark's Peak; or The Crater (Cooper)
See *The Crater; or, Vulcan's Peak*
Marmion (Scott) **15**:252, 254-56, 267, 273, 283, 285, 292-93, 318-20; **69**:304
"Das Marmorbild" (Eichendorff) **8**:216, 225, 233
"Der Marmorknabe" (Meyer) **81**:207
"Le Marquis de Carabas" (Beranger) **34**:29
"Le Marquis de Fumerol" (Maupassant) **83**:171
Marquis de Grandvin (Melville) **3**:379-80
Le marquis de Villemer (Sand) **2**:604-05; **42**:310, 312-13; **57**:317
Le marquis du Ier Houzards (Baudelaire) **6**:119-20
The Marquis of Villemer (Sand)
See *Le marquis de Villemer*
La marquise (Sand) **2**:594, 598-99
La Marquise de Ganges (Sade) **47**:314, 326
"Die Marquise von O..." (Kleist) **37**:217, 230, 237, 245-9, 253-5
La Marraine (Sand) **57**:367
Marriage (Ferrier) **8**:236-56
Marriage (Gogol)
See *Zhenit'ba; Sovershenno neveroyatnoye sobitye*
The Marriage: An Utterly Incredible Occurence (Gogol)
See *Zhenit'ba; Sovershenno neveroyatnoye sobitye*
"Marriage Bells" (Lazarus) **109**:292
The Marriage of Elinor (Oliphant) **61**:202-3, 205, 210-1, 242
The Marriage of Figaro (Da Ponte)
See *Le nozze di Figaro*
"The Marriage of Geraint" (Tennyson) **30**:288; **65**:226, 236, 241, 249, 255, 278, 297, 324, 328-9, 350, 381
The Marriage of Heaven and Hell (Blake) **13**:167, 170, 174, 176, 178-79, 184, 187, 192-93, 195, 200, 208, 210-11, 218, 222, 229-30, 246; **37**:18, 40, 42, 44-5, 48-9, 56, 59, 79; **57**:1-110; **127**:17, 23, 25, 33, 39, 46, 73, 77, 82-83, 88, 90, 112, 123-25, 128-29
The Marriage of the Monk (Meyer)
See *Die Hochzeit des Mönchs*
"Marriage Service" (Carroll) **139**:65
"Marriages" (Crabbe) **121**:89
The Married Man (Inchbald) **62**:143, 146
Married or Single? (Sedgwick) **19**:445-47, 453; **98**:300, 334
"Married Peäir's Love Walk" (Barnes) **75**:7
"Married with an Opal" (Crawford) **127**:193, 195
"Marroca" (Maupassant) **83**:201
"Les marrons du feu" (Musset) **7**:254, 256, 264, 277-79
"Marrying in haste" (Lonnrot) **53**:339
"Mars of Florence" (Meyer)
See "Der Mars von Florenz"
"Der Mars von Florenz" (Meyer) **81**:199
"Marseillaise" (Whittier) **8**:504
"La marseillaise de la paix" (Lamartine) **11**:271, 276
"Marseilles Harbor" (Pavlova)
See "Port marsel'skii"
Marsena, and Other Stories of Wartime (Frederic) **10**:188, 192, 203-04
"The Marsh King's Daughter" (Andersen)
See "Dynd-Kongens Datter"
"Marsh Song at Sunset" (Lanier) **6**:246, 249, 258; **118**:240
"The Marshes of Glynn" (Lanier) **6**:236-38, 240, 243, 246-47, 253-54, 256, 265, 268-73, 280-81; **118**:204, 223-24, 232, 238-40, 260, 263, 265, 267-71, 274-75, 287
"Martha Wyatt's Life" (Cooke) **110**:35
Marthe und ihre Uhr (Storm) **1**:537, 546
"Marthy's Younkit" (Field) **3**:211
The Martian (Du Maurier) **86**:278-82, 286-87
Martin Chuzzlewit (Dickens)
See *The Life and Adventures of Martin Chuzzlewit*
Martin Faber (Simms) **3**:499, 502, 504, 510, 514
Martin Fierro (Hernández)
See *El gaucho Martín Fierro*
"Martin Luther" (Emerson) **98**:67
"Martin Relph" (Browning) **79**:163
Martin Salander (Keller) **2**:413, 415-16, 419-20, 423
"Martina y Jacinto" (Isaacs) **70**:306
"La Martine" (Maupassant) **83**:223
The Martins of Cro' Martin (Lever) **23**:292, 297, 306, 308
The Martyr (Baillie) **2**:39, 41
The Martyr Age of the United States (Martineau) **137**:317, 327-28, 331
The Martyr of the Catacombs: A Tale of Ancient Rome (De Mille) **123**:117, 123
"Martyrdom of Saint Maura" (Kingsley) **35**:206, 211, 222
"Une martyre" (Baudelaire) **6**:87; **29**:104; **55**:5, 74-5, 79
"The Martyrs" (Lampman) **25**:160, 199
Les martyrs; ou, Le triomphe de la religion Chrétienne (Chateaubriand) **3**:110-12, 117, 124-26, 128-29, 132; **134**:4, 15-16, 18-20, 37, 70, 73, 80, 87
"Marvel and Parker" (Landor) **14**:165, 167
"Marvel of Marvels" (Rossetti) **2**:570
The Marvellous Adventures of Pinocchio (Collodi)
See *Le Avventure di Pinocchio*
The Marvellous Tale of Peter Schlemihl (Chamisso)
See *Peter Schlemihls Wundersame Geschichte*
"Mary" (Blake) **13**:243
"Mary and Her Little Lamb" (Hale)
See "Mary's Lamb"
"Mary Ann" (Cooke)
See "A Letter to Mary Ann"
"Mary Ann's Mind" (Cooke) **110**:35, 51
"Mary Ann's New Year" (Cooke) **110**:56
Mary Barton: A Tale of Manchester Life (Gaskell) **5**:177-80, 182-85, 187, 189-92, 196-200, 203-06; **70**:119-24, 126, 129-33, 135-36, 140, 144, 146, 149-50, 152-58, 161-65, 170-71, 173, 175-78, 185-87, 189, 190, 193, 196, 198, 200, 206-07, 214, 218, 221; **97**:110, 112, 173; **137**:3-180
"Mary Burnie of the Mill" (O'Brien) **21**:243, 245-46
"Mary Garvin" (Whittier) **8**:509; **59**:371
"Mary Gresley" (Trollope) **101**:233, 265
"Mary Had a Little Lamb" (Hale)
See "Mary's Lamb"
"Mary Lee" (Parton) **86**:337, 349-50
"Mary Magdalene" (Bryant) **6**:159, 161
"Mary Magdalene" (Rossetti) **4**:498
Mary; or The Test of Honor (Rowson) **5**:321; **69**:112, 114, 122, 125-28, 134, 141-42
"Mary Rivers" (Kendall) **12**:183, 199
"Mary Scott" (Hogg) **4**:284
Mary Stewart (Alfieri)
See *Maria Stuarda*
Mary Stuart (Schiller)
See *Maria Stuart*
Mary Stuart (Slowacki)
See *Marja Stuart*
"Maryelle" (Villiers de l'Isle Adam) **3**:589-90
"Mary's Dream" (Hood) **16**:203
"Mary's Ghost" (Hood) **16**:237
"Mary's Lamb" (Hale) **75**:279, 284-294, 323, 349
"Mary's Little Lamb" (Hale)
See "Mary's Lamb"
Marzella; or, The Fairy Tale of Love (Sacher-Masoch) **31**:287, 292
"Marzo 1821" (Manzoni) **98**:220
Marzo 1821 (Manzoni) **98**:213, 219, 279
Masaniello; or, The Dumb Girl of Portici (Scribe)
See *La muette de Portici*
"Masha" (Turgenev) **21**:454
"The Mask" (Baudelaire)
See "Le masque"
"The Mask" (Browning) **1**:125
The Mask of Anarchy (Shelley)
See *The Masque of Anarchy*
Maskarad (Lermontov) **5**:294; **47**:160; **126**:154, 192, 216-17
Die Masken (Kotzebue) **25**:147
"Der Maskenball" (Lenau) **16**:278
Masks and Faces (Reade) **2**:534, 544; **74**:243, 277-78, 319, 331
"Le masque" (Baudelaire) **6**:79, 123; **55**:67, 73
"Le masque" (Maupassant) **1**:469
The Masque of Anarchy (Shelley) **18**:328, 336, 338, 362, 368; **93**:272, 334
The Masque of Pandora (Longfellow) **2**:497; **45**:113
The Masque of the Devils; or, The Canterbury Clock (Bird) **1**:93
The Masque of the Gods (Taylor) **89**:313-14
"The Masque of the Red Death" (Poe) **1**:500, 513, 521; **16**:306, 324, 331, 335; **55**:151
"A Masque of Venice" (Lazarus) **8**:411, 420
"Masquerade" (Lermontov)
See *Maskarad*
"The Mass of Christ" (Adams) **33**:18

"Massachusetts to Virginia" (Whittier) **8**:486, 526, 530-31; **59**:349, 364, 368
The Massacre (Inchbald) **62**:144
"The Massacre at Scio" (Bryant) **46**:3, 7
"Le massacre de Mona" (Leconte de Lisle) **29**:226, 228
"Massa's in de Cold Ground" (Foster) **26**:283, 285, 291, 295, 298
"Massimilla doni" (Balzac) **5**:65, 67
"The Master and the Dog" (Krasicki)
See "Pan i pies"
Master Flea (Hoffmann)
See *Meister Floh: Ein Märchen in seiben Abenteuern zweier Freunde*
"Master Hugues of Saxe-Gotha" (Browning) **19**:97, 153; **79**:106, 108, 164
The Master of Ballantrae: A Winter's Tale (Stevenson) **5**:405-09, 415, 418, 422, 425, 429-37; **63**:243, 261, 274
"The Master of Masters" (Mickiewicz) **3**:399-400
"'Master of St. Bede's'" (Craik) **38**:113
"Master Pinty" (Petofi)
See "Pinty úrfi"
Master Thaddeus; or, The Last Foray in Lithuania (Mickiewicz)
See *Pan Tadeusz; czyli, Ostatni zajazd na Litwie*
"Master Theme" (Preseren)
See "Magistrale"
Masterman Ready; or, The Wreck of the Pacific (Marryat) **3**:316, 320, 322-23
The Mastersingers of Nuremberg (Wagner)
See *Die Meistersinger von Nürnberg*
Masurao monogatari (Ueda Akinari) **131**:57
"Mat" (Nekrasov) **11**:419
"El matadero" (Echeverria) **18**:148-54
The Match (Baillie) **71**:6, 64
"Match-Making" (Cooke) **110**:35
"Matelots" (Corbière) **43**:7, 30-1, 33
"Mater Pulchrae Delections" (Rossetti) **77**:301, 344
"Mater Tenebrarum" (Thomson) **18**:403, 418
Materiali estetici (Manzoni) **98**:215
Mathilda (Shelley) **59**:154, 190, 192; **103**:320-85
Mathilde Möhring (Fontane) **26**:240, 244, 258, 271
Matiju Čopu (Preseren) **127**:330
Matilda Montgomerie (Richardson)
See *The Canadian Brothers; or, The Prophecy Fulfilled. A Tale of the Late American War*
"Matilda Muffin" (Cooke)
See "The Memorial of A.B., or Matilda Muffin"
"Matin" (Rimbaud) **4**:466; **35**:292, 304; **82**:222, 225, 229, 236-37, 240-41, 243, 251-53, 255, 2 61-62
"Matinée d'ivresse" (Rimbaud) **4**:474; **35**:269, 272, 295-96, 311-12, 322; **82**:233, 235
"Matins" (Lazarus) **8**:418
Matrimonial Speculations (Moodie) **14**:226, 236; **113**:295, 297
The Matrons (Percy) **95**:313, 336, 338
"The Matron's Tale" (Wordsworth) **111**:233, 237
Matros (Shevchenko) **54**:391-3, 397-8
"Matt Hyland" (Griffin) **7**:194, 198, 201-02
Matteo Falcone (Mérimée) **6**:354, 358-60, 362-6, 368-70; **65**:54-5, 57, 66, 100, 102, 106-7, 109-10, 113, 124
"Mátyás anyja" (Arany) **34**:20
"Mátyás's Mother" (Arany)
See "Mátyás anyja"
"Maud" (Tennyson) **115**:237
Maud, and Other Poems (Tennyson) **30**:213-14, 218-19, 221, 231-33, 236, 241-42, 245, 254, 258, 266-67, 276-85, 287, 294-95, 297-99; **65**:234, 267-9, 285, 348, 369, 372, 380, 384, 386; **115**:252, 269, 275, 341, 359
"Maud Miller" (Whittier) **8**:496, 501, 509-11, 513, 515, 521-24; **59**:358, 361, 371
"Maude Clare" (Rossetti) **2**:555, 575; **66**:330-1, 352-3, 355
Maude: Prose and Verse (Rossetti) **50**:301; **66**:317, 320-1, 331
Mauprat (Sand) **2**:586, 588-89, 599-600, 603, 605, 608; **42**:310, 319-20, 324, 327-28, 332, 338, 340, 363-64, 366; **57**:316-7, 320-1, 341, 360, 366, 375, 381
Les maures d'espagne; ou, Le pouvoir de l'enfance (Pixérécourt) **39**:273-74, 277-79, 281, 293
"Maurice de Guerin" (Arnold) **89**:81-2
The Maurice Mystery (Cooke) **5**:132
Maurice Tiernay, the Soldier of Fortune (Lever) **23**:292, 294, 304
"Mausfallen-Sprüchlein" (Mörike) **10**:455
"Le mauvais moine" (Baudelaire) **6**:120, 130; **55**:49, 58
"Mauvais sang" (Rimbaud) **4**:476, 481; **35**:290-91, 302, 313-15, 319, 325; **82**:218, 222, 224, 229, 234-35, 237-38, 240-45, 251, 255, 257, 262
"Maxim Maximych" (Lermontov)
See "Maksim Maksimovich"
"Maximes" (Pushkin) **83**:270
Maxims of Sir Morgan O'Doherty, Bart. (Maginn) **8**:436, 438, 440-42
"May" (Barnes) **75**:6
"May" (Clare) **86**:100-02
May (Macha)
See *Máj*
May (Oliphant) **11**:434, 446; **61**:173
"May Day 1837" (Norton) **47**:238, 241
May Day in Town; or, New York in an Uproar (Tyler) **3**:573-74
"May Evening" (Bryant) **6**:176
"The May Flower" (Very) **9**:372
"The May Magnificat" (Hopkins) **17**:202, 216
"May Night" (Musset)
See "Nuit de Mai"
"A May Night; or, The Drowned Maiden" (Gogol)
See "Majskaja noč, ili Vtoplennica"
The May Queen (Tennyson) **30**:223
Māyā Kānan (Dutt) **118**:5
"Maya, the Princess" (Cooke) **110**:3, 45-6
"May-Day" (Emerson) **1**:279, 284, 296, 299-300; **38**:184; **98**:182-84
May-Day and Other Pieces (Emerson) **1**:279; **38**:192-93; **98**:177, 179, 182-84
The Mayfair Set (Frederic)
See *Mrs. Albert Grundy: Observations in Philistia*
The Mayflower; or, Sketches of Scenes and Characters among the Descendants of the Puritans (Stowe) **3**:549, 564
"Mayo" (Isaacs) **70**:303-04
The Mayor of Wind Gap (Banim and Banim) **13**:129-30
Mayor of Zalamca (FitzGerald) **9**:258-59
"The Maypole of Merry Mount" (Hawthorne) **2**:329-31; **10**:300, 302, 307; **17**:157; **79**:296; **95**:131, 137, 213
"May-Time" (Taylor) **89**:316
"The May-Tree" (Barnes) **75**:32
Mąż i żona (Fredro) **8**:285, 289-92
Mazépa (Pushkin) **3**:422
Mazepa (Slowacki) **15**:348-49, 351-53, 364, 371, 378
Mazeppa (Byron) **2**:65, 96; **12**:110, 139; **109**:103
"Mazzini on Music" (Lanier) **118**:243
"Mcyri" (Lermontov)
See *Mtsyri*
"Me, Change! Me, Alter!" (Dickinson) **21**:65
"Me hitotsu no kami" (Ueda Akinari) **131**:21-22, 57
"Me imperturbe" (Whitman) **4**:568, 569
"Me piden versos" (Rizal) **27**:425
"Mea Culpa" (Allingham) **25**:7
"The Meadow Lake" (Clare) **9**:117
Meadow Saffron (Arany)
See *Őszikék*
"Meadow Thoughts" (Jefferies) **47**:101, 136
The Meadows in Spring (FitzGerald) **9**:275
"Meaning of Swedish Poverty" (Almqvist)
See "Svenska fattigdomens betydelse"
Means and Ends; or, Self-Training (Sedgwick) **19**:441, 446; **98**:330, 333, 335-38
"Meäry Wedded" (Barnes) **75**:58, 71
"Measure for Measure" (Lamb) **125**:304, 306
Mechanism in Thought and Morals (Holmes) **14**:130, 132, 135-37, 150
"Les mécontents" (Mérimée) **6**:362; **65**:58, 63, 79, 81-3
"Le médaillon" (Villiers de l'Isle Adam)
See "Antonie"
Médaillons et portraits (Mallarmé)
See *Quelques médaillons et portraits en pied*
"Meddőórán" (Arany) **34**:21
Medea (Grillparzer) **1**:387; **102**:86-8, 90-1, 93-104, 110, 164, 186-87
"Medea, a Fragment of Drama after Euripides" (Levy) **59**:91, 102, 109-10
Medea auf dem Kaukasos (Klinger) **1**:426-27
Medea in Korinth (Klinger) **4**:426-27
Le Médecin de Campagne (Balzac) **5**:31, 33; **35**:25; **53**:9, 28
"Medfield" (Bryant) **6**:178, 181
"The Median Supper" (Beddoes) **3**:33
"The Mediatorial Life of Jesus" (Brownson) **50**:48
Medical Essays (Holmes) **81**:108
"El médico y su mula" (Lizardi) **30**:67
"A Meditation" (Pavlova)
See "Duma"
"Meditation" (Baudelaire)
See "Recueillement"
"Meditation" (Lermontov)
See "Duma"
"Meditation of a Thirsty Man" (Petofi)
See "Szomjas ember tünödése"
"Meditations" (Pavlova) **138**:33-34
"Meditations in Verse" (Emerson) **1**:285
"Meditations on Rhode Island Coal" (Bryant) **6**:161
Méditations poétiques (Lamartine) **11**:244-46, 248-50, 252-55, 263, 265, 268-69, 271-73, 275-77, 279, 281-82, 284
Meditative Poems (Coleridge) **9**:146
The Medium; or Happy Tea Party (Murray)
See *The Medium; or Virtue Triumphant*
The Medium; or Virtue Triumphant (Murray) **63**:184-5, 189, 193, 195, 199, 201, 214
"A Medley" (Coleridge) **90**:27
Medny Vsadnik (Pushkin) **27**:386; **83**:251, 312-13, 350, 352-53, 358
"Medusa Dying" (Meyer)
See "Die sterbende Meduse"
"A Meek One" (Dostoevsky)
See "Krotkaya"
"Meeresstille" (Lenau) **16**:283
Eine Meerfahrt (Eichendorff) **8**:215, 217
"Meeting" (Arnold) **89**:15-16, 19, 95
"The Meeting" (Clare) **9**:74
"Meeting" (Grillparzer)
See "Begegnung"
"Meeting" (Rossetti) **66**:311
"The Meeting" (Turgenev)
See "Svidanie"
"The Meeting of the Dryads" (Holmes) **14**:109, 128
"Még ez egyszer" (Arany) **34**:21
"Meg Merrilies" (Keats) **8**:360
Meghnādbadh Kābya (Dutt) **118**:2, 5-9, 11-15, 25-31
"Mehr Unterricht" (Klopstock) **11**:238
Die Mehreren Wehmüller und die ungarischen Nationalgesichter (Brentano) **1**:100-01
Mehri-Nimroze (Ghalib) **39**:152

"Le meilleur amour" (Villiers de l'Isle Adam) **3**:588
"Mein!" (Muller) **73**:351, 364, 368, 370-72
"Mein Beruf" (Droste-Hülshoff) **3**:193
"Mein Eigentum" (Hölderlin) **16**:173
"Mein Fluss" (Mörike) **10**:448
Mein Freund (Nestroy) **42**:221, 243, 248, 250
"Mein Jahr" (Meyer) **81**:141, 153, 155-56
Mein Leben (Stifter) **41**:375
Mein Leben (Wagner) **119**:187, 189, 192-94, 288
"Mein Stern" (Lenau) **16**:269
"Mein Stern" (Meyer) **81**:146
"Mein Vaterland" (Klopstock) **11**:236
"Mein Wort über das Drama" (Hebbel) **43**:264, 267, 280, 283
"Meine Göttin" (Goethe) **4**:193
Meine Kinderjahre (Fontane) **26**:234, 247, 258-64, 271-72
"An Meinen Sohn Johannes 1799" (Claudius) **75**:210
Meister Floh: Ein Märchen in seiben Abenteuern zweier Freunde (Hoffmann) **2**:359, 362
Meister Martin (Hoffmann) **2**:340
Meisters Wanderjahre (Goethe)
See *Wilhelm Meisters Wanderjahre; oder, Die Entsagenden*
Die Meistersinger von Nürnberg (Wagner) **9**:408-10, 412-13, 415-16, 419, 421, 425, 443, 446-47, 452-56, 465, 468; **119**:176, 180, 182, 198, 210, 228, 241, 268-69, 290-91, 293, 349
"The Melamed of Osterreich" (Leskov)
See "Rakušanskij melamed"
"Melancholia" (Gautier) **1**:350
"Melancholy" (Coleridge) **90**:9
"Melancholy" (Eminescu) **33**:264; **131**:332, 334-35
"Melancholy" (Lenau) **16**:276
"Melancholy" (Macha)
See "Tezkomyslnot"
"A Melancholy Moon" (Baudelaire)
See "Les tristesses de la lune"
"Melancthon and Calvin" (Landor) **14**:165, 167
Mélanges de littérature et de politique (Constant) **6**:224
Mélanges posthumes (Laforgue) **53**:291, 294
The Melbournians (Adams) **33**:15, 18
"Melhill Feast" (Barnes) **75**:20, 26, 30, 68, 94
Mellichampe (Simms) **3**:503, 507-08
"Mellonta Tauta" (Poe) **55**:152; **94**:212, 215, 217
Melmoth the Wanderer (Maturin) **6**:323-30, 332-42, 344-47
Melochi zhizni (Saltykov) **16**:369, 375
"Meloči arxierejskoj žizni" (Leskov) **25**:228
Melodies (Moore)
See *The Irish Melodies*
Melusina (Grillparzer) **102**:113, 149, 189-90
Melville's Marquesas (Melville) **45**:194
The Member (Galt) **110**:76, 79, 94
"Member of the Haouse" (Holmes) **81**:103
"Memento mori" (Eminescu) **33**:250, 259, 261; **131**:286, 288, 290
"Memoir" (Trumbull) **30**:346
Memoir (Jefferson)
See *Autobiography of Thomas Jefferson*
Memoir (Southey) **97**:288
Memoir (Tennyson) **65**:249
Memoir and Correspondence of Susan Ferrier, 1782-1854 (Ferrier) **8**:245
Memoir, Letters, and Remains Alexis de Tocqueville (Tocqueville) **7**:424; **63**:282
Memoir of Count de Montalembert (Oliphant) **11**:434
A Memoir of Maria Edgeworth (Edgeworth) **51**:108, 114, 117
"Memoir of the Cats of Greta Hall" (Southey) **97**:274
Memoir of the Early Life of William Cowper, Esq. (Cowper) **8**:124, 129, 133-35; **94**:19-20, 27, 57-8
Memoir on Ancient and Modern Russia (Karamzin) **3**:283
"A Memoir on the Discovery of Certain Bones of a Quadruped of the Clawed Kind in the Western Parts of Virginia" (Jefferson) **103**:106
"Mémoire" (Rimbaud) **4**:475, 478-79, 484, 486; **35**:297, 299, 301-02, 304, 307; **82**:218, 255
Memoire de Lorenzo Da Ponte da Ceneda (Da Ponte) **50**:76- 82, 84-7, 96, 99-101
Mémoire sur la captivitéde madame la duchesse de Berry (Chateaubriand) **134**:97
Mémoire sur l'Orient (Chateaubriand) **134**:8
Memoiren (Heine) **54**:329
"Die Memoiren des Herren von Schnabelewopski" (Heine) **4**:262, 268
Memoires (Flaubert)
See *Les mémoires d'un fou*
Mémoires de deux jeunes mariées (Balzac) **5**:40, 83-84
Mémoires de Marquis de Calvière (Goncourt and Goncourt) **7**:164
Mémoires de Sophie Arnoud (Goncourt and Goncourt) **7**:164
Mémoires d'outre-tombe (Chateaubriand) **3**:118-21, 127, 129, 134-35; **134**:7, 12, 14-20, 25, 51, 63-64, 66-69, 77, 80, 86-87, 91, 93-95, 102-7, 109-10, 112-14, 129, 147
Les mémoires d'un fou (Flaubert) **2**:249, 255-6; **10**:170; **19**:288, 299, 304; **62**:83-91, 95; **66**:269-72
Mémoires d'un médecin: Joseph Balsamo (Dumas) **11**:51, 76
Mémoires d'un touriste (Stendhal) **23**:355, 359, 409-10; **46**:269, 325
Mémoires inédites (Lamartine) **11**:265
Memoires of a Physician (Dumas)
See *Mémoires d'un médecin: Joseph Balsamo*
Mémoires sur le Duc de Berry (Chateaubriand) **134**:84
"Memoirs" (Hogg) **109**:268
Memoirs (Alfieri)
See *Vita*
Memoirs (Bashkirtseff)
See *Le journal de Marie Bashkirtseff*
Memoirs (Holcroft)
See *Memoirs of the Late Thomas Holcroft, Written by Himself and Continued by William Hazlitt to the Time of His Death from His Diary, Notes and Other Papers*
Memoirs (Huxley) **67**:79-80
Memoirs (Moore) **110**:202
The Memoirs (Symonds) **34**:331-32, 335-37, 374-75
Memoirs and Essays Illustrative of Art, Literature, and Social Morals (Jameson) **43**:323
Les Memoirs d'un veuf (Verlaine) **51**:363, 386
Memoirs from Underground (Dostoevsky)
See *Zapiski iz podpol'ya*
"Memoirs of a Good-for-Nothing" (Eichendorff)
See "Aus dem Leben eines Taugenichts"
The Memoirs of a Nihilist (Turgenev)
See *Ottsy i deti*
The Memoirs of a Sportsman (Turgenev)
See *Zapiski okhotnika*
Memoirs of Alexander Herzen (Herzen)
See *Byloe i dumy*
The Memoirs of Barry Lyndon, Esq. (Thackeray) **5**:452, 459-60, 465, 470-71, 482, 490, 492, 497; **14**:400, 402, 451; **43**:346-97
The Memoirs of Bryan Perdue (Holcroft) **85**:193, 199-200, 207, 228, 231, 236, 238, 244-46
Memoirs of Captain Rock (Moore) **6**:395; **110**:193
Memoirs of Carwin the Biloquist (Brown) **74**:5, 17-18, 48, 54, 76, 133, 142-43, 161-62, 164, 199-200, 202-03; **122**:30, 33, 36, 53, 91, 94, 157-58, 163
Memoirs of Celebrated Characters (Lamartine) **11**:259-60, 262
Memoirs of Celebrated Female Sovereigns (Jameson) **43**:305-06, 309, 319
Memoirs of Chateaubriand, written by himself (Chateaubriand)
See *Mémoires d'outre-tombe*
Memoirs of Dr. Burney: Arranged from His Own Manuscripts, from Family Papers, and from Personal Recollections (Burney) **12**:23-6, 28, 32-3, 47-8; **54**:15-16, 18
Memoirs of Dr. Richard Gilpin, of Scaleby Castle in Cumberland; and of His Posterity in the Two Succeeding Generations (Gilpin) **30**:35
The Memoirs of Emma Courtney (Hays) **114**:172, 175, 178-80, 182-83, 185-86, 188-89, 191-92, 194, 197, 200, 207-8, 210-16, 219, 223, 229-30, 232, 240-44, 247-49, 251
Memoirs of François René, Vicomte de Chateaubriand, Sometime Ambassador to England (Chateaubriand)
See *Mémoires d'outre-tombe*
Memoirs of Josias Rogers, Esq., Commander of His Majesty's Ship Quebec (Gilpin) **30**:35
"Memoirs of Literature and Life" (Turgenev) **122**:242
Memoirs of Lorenzo Da Ponte (Da Ponte)
See *Memoire de Lorenzo Da Ponte da Ceneda*
Memoirs of Margaret Fuller Ossoli (Fuller) **5**:162, 170; **50**:223, 236, 253
Memoirs of Mary Wollstonecraft (Godwin) **130**:37, 115
Memoirs of Mme. de Stael and Mme. Roland (Child)
See *The Biographies of Madame de Staël and Madame Roland, Married Women; or, Biographies of Good Wives*
Memoirs of Morgan O'Doherty (Maginn) **8**:438
"Memoirs of Phebe Hammond" (Sigourney) **87**:321
Memoirs of Queens Illustrious and Celebrated (Hays) **114**:187, 200
Memoirs of Richard Lovell Edgeworth (Edgeworth) **51**:81
Memoirs of Sir Roger de Clarendon, the Natural Son of Edward Prince of Wales, Commonly Called the Black Prince (Reeve) **19**:408, 412
Memoirs of Stephen Calvert (Brown) **74**:15, 51, 133-34, 161, 164
Memoirs of the Author of "A Vindication of the Rights of Women" (Godwin) **14**:53, 88-91
Memoirs of the Author's Life (Hogg) **109**:200, 258-63, 267
Memoirs of the Beauties of the Court of Charles II (Jameson) **43**:308-09
Memoirs of the Duke of Sully (Lennox) **134**:219
Memoirs of the Early Italian Painters (Jameson) **43**:323, 333, 335-38
Memoirs of the Late Thomas Holcroft, Written by Himself and Continued by William Hazlitt to the Time of His Death from His Diary, Notes and Other Papers (Holcroft) **85**:190, 192, 195, 199-200, 205, 209-10, 212, 221, 237
Memoirs of the Life and Writings of Robert Robinson (Dyer) **129**:97, 104, 112, 115, 126, 145
Memoirs of the Life of George Frederick Cooke (Dunlap) **2**:208
Memoirs of the Life of Sir Walter Scott, Bart. (Lockhart) **6**:290-95, 297-98, 300, 305, 307, 309-10

Memoirs of the Life of William Collins, Esq., R.A. (Collins) **1**:184-85; **93**:46
Memoirs of the Life of William Wirt, Attorney General of the United States (Kennedy) **2**:429, 432, 435
Memoirs of the London Doll (Blake) **127**:262-69
Memoirs of the Loves of the Poets (Jameson) **43**:305-09, 315, 319
"Memoirs of the Right Honourable James Wilson" (Bagehot) **10**:31
Memoirs of Two Young Married Women (Balzac)
See *Mémoires de deux jeunes mariées*
Memorabilien (Immermann) **49**:368
"The Memorable Victory of Paul Jones" (Freneau)
See "Poem on the memorable victory obtained by the gallant capt. Paul Jones, or the Good Man Richard, over the Seraphis, etc. under the command of capt. Pearson"
Memoralia; or Phials of Amber Full of the Tears of Love: A Gift for the Beautiful (Chivers) **49**:40, 42-4, 73
"Memoranda during the War" (Whitman) **4**:551
"A Memorandum at a Venture" (Whitman) **81**:276
Memoria sobre Ortografía Americana (Faustino) **123**:325, 377
"Memorial and Remonstrance" (Madison) **126**:312-13, 315
A Memorial and Remonstrance against Religious Assessments (Madison) **126**:291-92, 296
Memorial Edition of Jefferson's Works (Jefferson) **103**:106
"The Memorial of A.B., or Matilda Muffin" (Cooke) **110**:51, 67
"Memorial Thresholds" (Rossetti) **77**:359-61
"Memorial to Robert Browning" (Cranch) **115**:22
"Memorial Verses" (Arnold) **29**:4, 31; **89**:22-3, 47
Memorialia (Chivers)
See *Memoralia; or Phials of Amber Full of the Tears of Love: A Gift for the Beautiful*
The Memorials of a Residence on the Continent, and Historical Poems (Milnes) **61**:137, 144
Memorials of a Tour in Greece (Milnes) **61**:137, 145
"Memorials of a Tour in Italy, 1837" (Wordsworth) **12**:465
Memorials of a Tour on the Continent (Wordsworth) **12**:409
Memorials of Many Scenes (Milnes) **61**:145
Memorias (Faustino)
See *Memoria sobre Ortografía Americana*
Memorias de un estudiante de Manila (Rizal) **27**:424
Memorie inutili della vita di Carlo Gozzi (Gozzi) **23**:115, 123
"Memories" (Whittier) **8**:486, 505, 511, 513
Memories (Renan)
See *Souvenirs d'enfance et de jeunesse*
Memories and Portraits (Sheridan) **5**:416, 421, 530
Memories of a Tourist (Stendhal)
See *Mémoires d'un touriste*
"Memories of Youth in the Countryside" (Grillparzer)
See *Jugenderinnerungen im Grünen*
"Memory" (Brontë) **109**:27
"Memory" (Lamb) **125**:371
"Memory" (Rossetti) **2**:575
"Memory and Imagination" (Beattie)
See *Dissertations Moral and Critical: On Memory and Imagination; On Dreaming; The Theory of Language; On Fable and Romance; On the Attachments of Kindred; Illustrations on Sublimity*
"Memory and Want of Memory" (Hunt) **70**:257
"A Memory Picture" (Arnold) **29**:35; **89**:20
Men (Verlaine)
See *Hombres*
Men and Women (Browning) **19**:79, 89, 110, 116, 118, 126-27, 130, 133, 154-56; **79**:140-42, 148-49, 151-52, 163-64, 175, 182, 184
Men of Capital (Gore) **65**:36
Men of Character (Jerrold) **2**:395, 397-98, 401-03
Men of Color, to Arms! (Douglass) **7**:132
"Men of England" (Campbell) **19**:176, 183, 191
"Men of Letters" (Smith) **59**:322
Men of Letters (Goncourt and Goncourt)
See *Les hommes de lettres*
"The Men of Old" (Milnes) **61**:136
Un ménage de garçon en province (Balzac) **5**:32-33
Menander und Glycerion (Wieland) **17**:400
"El mendigo" (Espronceda) **39**:85, 100, 108, 113-14, 118
"Menego" (Norwid) **17**:370, 381-83
Le Meneur de Loups (Dumas) **71**:204
Mennesket (Wergeland)
See *Skabelsen, mennesket, og messias*
"Menons Klagen um Diotima" (Hölderlin) **16**:187
Men's Wives (Thackeray) **43**:381
"Der Mensch" (Hölderlin) **16**:181, 185-86
"Der Mensch und das Leben" (Ludwig) **4**:353
"Menschenbeifall" (Hölderlin) **16**:190
Menschenhass und Reue (Kotzebue) **25**:129-31, 133-34, 136-37, 140-41, 144-46, 148-51
"The Mental Condition of Babies" (Lewes) **25**:287
"Mental Disorder" (Silva)
See "Psicopatía"
"The Mental Sufferings of Our Lord in His Passion" (Newman) **38**:303, 309
"The Mental Traveller" (Blake) **13**:172, 244; **37**:71, 96
Mentoria; or, The Young Lady's Friend (Rowson) **3**:310, 312-13, 315-16; **69**:103, 105, 112, 114, 128-30, 134-35, 141
"Menzel, Critic of Gogol" (Belinski) **5**:96, 115
La mer (Michelet) **31**:215, 242, 245-47, 260, 262-63
Mercadet (Balzac)
See *Le faiseur*
Mercedes of Castile; or, The Voyage to Cathay (Cooper) **1**:220; **54**:258, 262, 264
"The Merchant" (Krylov) **1**:435
"Merchant and his Wife" (Froude) **43**:178
"The Merchant of Venice" (Lamb) **125**:304
"Merchant Sailor Nikitin" (Bestuzhev)
See "Morekhod Nikitin"
"The Merchant's Daughter" (Lamb)
See "Charlotte Wilmot: The Merchant's Daughter"
The Merchant's Wedding (Planché) **42**:273
"Mercury and a Modern Fine Lady" (Montagu) **117**:182
Mercy Philbrick's Choice (Jackson) **90**:144, 164-65, 168
"La Mère aux monstres" (Maupassant) **83**:181, 208, 223
"La Mère qui pleure" (Desbordes-Valmore) **97**:8
"La mère sauvage" (Maupassant) **83**:181, 210-11, 219, 222
Merkland: A Story of Scottish Life (Oliphant) **11**:428-9, 432, 454; **61**:238
Das merkwürdigste Jahr meines Lebens (Kotzebue) **25**:138
"Merlin" (Emerson) **1**:296; **38**:170, 184; **98**:179-81
Merlin (Immermann) **4**:292; **49**:358
"Merlin and the Gleam" (Tennyson) **30**:254, 282
"Merlin and Vivien" (Tennyson) **30**:254, 279, 290; **65**:227, 237, 241, 255, 278, 281-2, 284, 290-3, 297, 299-300, 302, 331-3, 335-6, 338, 351, 371-4, 376, 378-81, 383, 386
"The Mermaid" (Hogg) **4**:284
"The Mermaid" (Lermontov) **126**:144-45
"Mermaid of Margate" (Hood) **16**:224
"The Mermaidens Vesper Hymn" (Darley) **2**:131
"Merope" (Kendall) **12**:183, 192
Merope (Alfieri) **101**:18-19, 42
Merope (Arnold) **6**:33, 37, 44, 49-51; **29**:2, 54 ; **89**:14, 28, 51, 53
"Merriment and Grief" (Baratynsky)
See "Veselie i gore"
"Merry England" (Hazlitt) **29**:148, 153
The Merry Men and Other Tales and Fables (Stevenson) **5**:403, 415, 418, 429, 431
The Merry Tales of the Three Wise Men of Gotham (Paulding) **2**:528
The Merry-Go-Round (Becque)
See *La navette*
Mervyn Clitheroe (Ainsworth) **13**:40, 45
Mes hôpitaux (Verlaine) **2**:625
"Mes Memoirs" (Dumas) **71**:186, 188, 204-05, 211, 214, 217, 228, 237-38, 240-41
"Mes petites amoureuses" (Rimbaud) **4**:455; **35**:282, 290-91, 294, 321
Mes souvenirs (Banville) **9**:18, 20-21
"Meses do inverno frios" (Castro) **78**:41
"Mesgedra" (Ferguson) **33**:279-80, 285, 304
"Mesmeric Revelation" (Poe) **1**:496; **16**:295, 297, 335; **78**:258; **117**:310
"Mesmerism" (Browning) **19**:131
"The Message" (Very) **9**:375
"Message of a Friend" (Grillparzer)
See "Freundeswort"
"A Message of Remembrance to My Home Town" (Rizal) **27**:425
"The Message of the March Wind" (Morris) **4**:434, 443
"Message to Siberia" (Pushkin) **83**:256
The Messalinas of Vienna (Sacher-Masoch) **31**:294
The Messenger of Europe (Pushkin) **3**:414
Mesyats v derevne (Turgenev) **21**:428-29, 432-33; **122**:257, 261, 275
"Metacom" (Whittier) **8**:485
"The Metallic Pig" (Andersen) **79**:89
"Les métamorphoses du vampire" (Baudelaire) **29**:73, 99; **55**:10, 29-30, 33-4, 70, 73, 76
"The Metamorphoses of the Vampire" (Baudelaire)
See "Les métamorphoses du vampire"
"Metamorphosis of Animals" (Goethe) **4**:172
"Metamorphosis of Plants" (Goethe) **34**:70
Metaphysical Elements of Justice (Kant) **67**:267
Metaphysical Principles of Doctrine of Virtue (Kant)
See *Grundlegung zur Metaphysik der Sitten*
Metaphysical Principles of Right (Kant)
See *Grundlegung zur Metaphysik der Sitten*
Metaphysics of Morals (Kant)
See *Grundlegung zur Metaphysik der Sitten*
"La métaphysique et son avenir" (Renan) **26**:380, 426
"Metel" (Pushkin) **3**:452; **83**:272, 276, 323, 326-27, 329, 337, 354; **3**:435
"Metellus and Marius" (Landor) **14**:189
"Metempsychosis" (Cooke) **110**:3, 10
"The Metempsychosis" (Mangan) **27**:301
"The Method of Nature" (Emerson) **38**:158, 169; **98**:65-6, 72, 108, 113-14, 176, 191
"Methuselah" (Field) **3**:206
Metrical Legends of Exalted Characters (Baillie) **2**:37-38; **71**:2
"Metrical Romances" (Percy)
See "On the Ancient Metrical Romances"
"Métropolitain" (Rimbaud) **35**:322-24; **82**:233
"The Metropolitan Museum of Art" (Martí) **63**:112
"Metzengerstein" (Poe) **1**:514; **16**:320-21, 324, 335; **55**:185; **117**:193, 300

Le meunier d'Angibault (Sand) **2**:589, 601; **42**:322-23, 340, 378
"Die Mewe" (Muller) **73**:358-59
"Mexican Sketches" (Horne) **127**:256
The Mexican Thinker (Lizardi)
See *El pensador Mexicano*
"Mezzo Cammin" (Longfellow) **45**:131, 142, 181-82, 186
M'Fingal: A Modern Epic Poem in Four Cantos (Trumbull) **30**:339-44, 346-47, 349, 351-58, 360, 362-65, 373-79, 382-82
"A mi" (Rizal) **27**:425
Mi defensa (Faustino) **123**:283, 309, 312, 321-22, 324-25, 351, 373
"Mi ensueño" (Casal) **131**:240
"A mi hija Clementina" (Isaacs) **70**:311
"Mi lárma ez megént?" (Petofi) **21**:278
"A mi madre" (Casal) **131**:255
A mi madre (Castro) **3**:104; **78**:23-25, 37
"Mi museo ideal" (Casal) **131**:219-20, 222-23, 227-29, 235-37, 244, 252, 265-70, 281
"Mi nombre y mis propósitos" (Larra) **130**:248
"Mi raza" (Martí) **63**:91
"Mi retiro" (Rizal) **27**:425
"Mi ultimo adios" (Rizal) **27**:425
"The Mice in Council" (Krylov) **1**:435
"Michael" (Wordsworth) **12**:396, 402, 427, 429, 436, 444, 447, 451; **38**:389; **111**:212, 219-20, 226, 228-29, 232-34, 236, 241, 243-45, 254, 294-301, 303, 322, 350, 367
Michael Angelo (Longfellow) **2**:486; **45**:113, 127, 130-32, 138-39, 150, 162
Michael Bonham; or, The Fall of Bexar (Simms) **3**:505, 514
Michael Kohlhaas (Kleist) **2**:438, 442, 446-48, 450, 455, 458, 463; **37**:217, 230, 241, 243, 245, 247-49, 253-55
Michael O'Dowd (Boucicault)
See *Daddy O'Dowd*
"Michael Scott's Wooing" (Rossetti) **4**:510
Michel Angelo: Ein Drama in zwei Akten (Hebbel) **43**:230, 234, 239, 259
"Michel et Christine" (Rimbaud) **4**:475; **82**:232, 255
Michel Pauper (Becque) **3**:13, 15-16
"Michelangelo and His Statues" (Meyer)
See "Michelangelo und seine Statuen"
"Michelangelo und seine Statuen" (Meyer) **81**:204
"Michelangelo's Kiss" (Rossetti) **77**:314
"Michels Brautschau" (Gotthelf) **117**:6, 18, 25
Midas (Shelley) **14**:268, 272
"Middle of Life" (Hölderlin)
See "Hälfte des Lebens"
"Middle-Class Jewish Women of To-Day" (Levy) **59**:111
Middlemarch: A Study of Provincial Life (Eliot) **4**:106-07, 109-12, 114, 116-18, 120-23, 125, 127, 129-31, 133-39, 144, 147, 152-54, 154; **13**:282-355; **23**:49-51, 53-4, 57, 60, 64-5, 67-8, 75, 80; **41**:68, 72, 76, 80, 82-3, 85, 91, 93, 96-7, 99, 103-04, 107-09, 126, 133-34; **49**:188, 215, 222, 227, 265; **89**:221, 261; **118**:36, 41, 48, 51-4, 62, 70, 78, 80, 102-10, 121, 125, 130-31, 134, 136, 1
"Middleton Sonnet" (Smith)
See "Sonnet 44"
"Midi" (Leconte de Lisle) **29**:213, 222-24, 236, 242-43
"Midnight" (Cooke) **110**:3
"Midnight" (Crabbe) **26**:139, 143, 146; **121**:10
"Midnight" (Lampman) **25**:168, 180, 194, 204
"Midnight" (Mörike) **10**:445-46
"Midnight Attack" (Whittier) **8**:485
"The Midnight Court" (Merriman)
See "Cúirt an Mheán Oíche"
The Midnight Court (Merriman)
See *Cúirt an Mheadhon Oidhche*
"A Mid-Night Drama" (Bellamy) **4**:30
"Midnight Duel" (Arany)
See "Éjféli párbaj"
The Midnight Hour (Inchbald) **62**:142-3, 145-7, 150
"A Midnight Landscape" (Lampman) **25**:217
"The Midnight Mass" (Carleton) **3**:89, 96
"Midnight Mass for the Dying Year" (Longfellow) **2**:471, 474, 479
"A Midnight Storm in the Gulph Stream" (Freneau) **111**:105
"Midsummer" (Bryant) **46**:48
The Midsummer Cushion (Clare) **86**:94-5, 132-33, 160, 166-69
"Midsummer in the South" (Hayne) **94**:149
"A Midsummer Night's Dream" (Lamb) **125**:303, 305, 353, 355-58
"A Midsummer Noon in the Australian Forest" (Harpur) **114**:101, 103-4, 110-11, 125, 144, 156, 158, 164
"A Mien to Move a Queen" (Dickinson) **21**:61-2, 65; **77**:66
"Mies" (Kivi) **30**:51
"Might versus Right" (Sedgwick) **19**:446
"The Mighty Dead" (Chivers) **49**:71
The Mighty Magician (FitzGerald) **9**:264
"Mighty Maker" (Moodie) **113**:348
Mignons (Goethe) **4**:173
"Mikhail Tverskoy" (Bestuzhev) **131**:147-48, 182
Mikkel's Parisian Love Stories (Andersen) **79**:11
Mikołaja Doświadczyńskiego przypadki (Krasicki) **8**:398-99, 404
"Mikyagi ga tsuka" (Ueda Akinari) **131**:22
"Milczenie" (Norwid) **17**:371
Miles Standish (Longfellow)
See *The Courtship of Miles Standish*
Miles Wallingford (Cooper) **1**:221; **54**:258, 266
The Milesian Chief (Maturin) **6**:322, 328, 331-32, 335, 342-43, 346-47
The Military Necessity (Vigny)
See *Servitude et grandeur militaires*
"Militona" (Gautier) **1**:345, 347-48; **59**:12
"The Milkmaid" (Allingham) **25**:8, 16
"The Milk-maid o' the Farm" (Barnes) **75**:58, 77
"The Mill of the Rapids: A Canadian Sketch" (Traill) **31**:324
The Mill on the Floss (Eliot) **118**:40, 43, 49, 57, 59, 104, 108, 164
"Mille ans après" (Leconte de Lisle) **29**:228, 235
"La Mille et deuxieme nuit" (Gautier) **59**:31
"The Millennium" (Freneau) **111**:112
The Miller of Angibault (Sand)
See *Le meunier d'Angibault*
"The Miller's Daughter" (Tennyson) **30**:207, 279; **65**:248
"Milliners and Dressmakers" (Tonna) **135**:199, 208-9, 212-17, 220-23
"Milly Dove" (O'Brien) **21**:235, 239, 243
"Milly; ou, La terre natale" (Lamartine) **11**:248, 270, 289
Miłość czysta u kąpieli morskich (Norwid) **17**:379
"Milton" (Landor) **14**:166
"Milton" (Longfellow) **45**:186
Milton (Blake) **13**:174, 176, 183-84, 186, 192-93, 195, 205-07, 211-13, 221, 231, 234-35, 245, 247-48, 251-54; **37**:20, 66, 88; **57**:56-64, 89-90, 93; **127**:15-16, 20, 22-24, 28-29, 50-51, 65-67, 78, 80, 87-88, 90, 96-97, 124-27, 132, 134
Milton (Macaulay) **42**:116
"Mimi Pinson" (Musset) **7**:264, 275
Mimic Life; or Before and Behind the Curtain (Mowatt) **74**:219, 221, 233-38
"Mimie's Grass Net" (Ingelow) **107**:161
"Miña casiña" (Castro) **78**:2
"Mind and Motive" (Hazlitt) **82**:75, 103
"The Mind the Greatest Mystery" (Very) **9**:396
"Mind under Water" (Jefferies) **47**:136
"Minden House" (Barnes) **75**:78
Mindowe (Slowacki) **15**:348-49, 353, 369, 373
"The Mind-Reader's Curse" (Clarke) **19**:240
"Mindvégig" (Arany) **34**:21
"Mine!" (Muller)
See "Mein!"
"Mine by the Right of the White Election" (Dickinson) **21**:57; **77**:67-68
"Minek nevezzelek" (Petofi) **21**:285
"The Miner" (Pavlova)
See *"Rudokop"*
"Mines and Miners" (Hugo) **10**:377
Les mines de Pologne (Pixérécourt) **39**:277-79, 292
Minin (Ostrovsky)
See *Koz'ma Zakhar'ich Minin Sukoruk*
"The Minister in a Maze" (Hawthorne) **10**:269
"El ministerial" (Larra) **130**:194, 197, 201, 204
"The Minister-Painter" (Smith) **59**:316-7
"The Minister's Black Veil" (Hawthorne) **2**:291-92, 317, 320, 322, 324, 331; **79**:288-90, 294-96, 299, 301-04, 307-11, 313, 315-18, 322, 324, 327, 330, 332-33; **95**:105, 140, 148, 187
"The Minister's Vigil" (Hawthorne) **10**:269, 297
The Minister's Wife (Oliphant) **11**:432, 446, 448-9; **61**:162-4, 166, 173, 205, 209, 211, 238
The Minister's Wooing (Stowe) **3**:553, 555, 558-59, 563, 567
Minnesota; or, The Far West (Oliphant) **47**:288
Minnuzolo; Il Viaggio per l'Italia de Giannettino (Collodi) **54**:140
"The Minor Festivals Devotionally Studied" (Rossetti) **2**:568, 572; **50**:271, 274-5, 285, 294, 321
Minor Morals, interspersed with sketchs of natural history, historical anecdotes, and original stories (Smith) **115**:129
"The Minor Peace of the Church" (Pater) **7**:337
"A Minor Poet" (Levy) **59**:90, 94, 108, 110, 119
A Minor Poet and Other Verse (Levy) **59**:81, 86, 91, 93, 98, 102, 107-9
"A Minor Prophet" (Eliot) **4**:107; **41**:65
Minor Works (Austen) **51**:59; **95**:77-8,; **119**:55
"The Minotaur" (Hawthorne) **79**:309
"The Minstrel" (Lampman) **25**:201, 216
The Minstrel (Shevchenko)
See *Kobzar*
"The minstrel boy" (Moore) **110**:198
Minstrel Love (Fouqué) **2**:263
The Minstrel; or, the Progress of Genius (Beattie) **25**:81-2, 103, 105-09, 111-12, 117-20, 122-23, 126
"Minstrel's Song, on the Restoration of Lord Clifford the Shepherd" (Wordsworth) **12**:395
"The Minstrel's Valedictory" (Chivers) **49**:69
The Minstrelsy of the Scottish Border (Scott) **15**:273-74, 318, 320, 322; **69**:377
"M'introduire dans ton histoire" (Mallarmé) **41**:243-44, 250, 280
Miorita (Eminescu) **33**:252, 267
Mira (Eminescu) **33**:254, 264; **131**:289, 333
"Le Miracle des roses" (Laforgue) **5**:271, 281; **53**:256-7, 294
"The Miracle of Our Being" (Emerson) **38**:148
"The Miracle of the Roses" (Laforgue)
See "Le Miracle des roses"
"Miracles" (Emerson) **38**:148
"Miradoniz" (Eminescu) **33**:261, 263; **131**:290
Miralda; or, The Beautiful Quadroon (Brown)
See *Clotel; or, The President's Daughter: A Narrative of Slave Life in the United States*
"Mirandola" (Hebbel) **43**:237
Mirgorod (Gogol) **5**:209, 216, 218, 231, 235, 242, 248-49, 256-57; **15**:94-5; **31**:106, 118
Miriam, and Other Poems (Whittier) **8**:501
"Miron and the Beautiful Girl without a Body" (Eminescu)
See "Miron şi frumoasa fara corp"

"Miron şi frumoasa fara corp" (Eminescu) **131**:299
Mirra (Alfieri)
See *Myrrha*
"The Mirror" (Rossetti) **77**:358, 360
"The Mirror" (Whittier) **59**:361
The Mirror of Peasants (Gotthelf)
See *Der Bauern-Spiegel oder Lebensgeschichte des Jeremias Gotthelf: Von ihm selbst beschrieben*
Mirza, ou lettre d'un voyageur (Staël-Holstein) **91**:339-42, 358, 360
Le Misanthrope par amour (Sade) **47**:361-63
Misanthropy and Repentance (Kotzebue)
See *Menschenhass und Reue*
Misc C (Coleridge) **99**:63
Misc. Essays (Lamb) **113**:230
Miscellaneous and Uncollected Writings of Charlotte and Patrick Branwell Brontë (Brontë) **109**:26, 51
Miscellaneous and Unpublished (Brontë)
See *Miscellaneous and Uncollected Writings of Charlotte and Patrick Branwell Brontë*
Miscellaneous Pieces in Prose (Barbauld) **50**:3
Miscellaneous Pieces Relating to the Chinese (Percy) **95**:313, 315, 336
Miscellaneous Plays (Baillie) **2**:34-35; **71**:6, 64
Miscellaneous Poems (Mitford) **4**:400
Miscellaneous Poems (Paine) **62**:322, 325
Miscellaneous Poems (Rowson) **69**:129
Miscellaneous Poems (Silva)
See *Poesías varias*
Miscellaneous Prose Works (Scott) **110**:277
Miscellaneous Studies (Pater) **7**:303; **90**:248, 250, 261, 276, 287, 289-90, 333, 335-37
The Miscellaneous Works of Mr. Philip Freneau, Containing His Essays and Additional Poems (Freneau) **111**:130-32, 134, 139, 149, 159, 161
Miscellaneous Writings (Macaulay)
See *Critical and Historical Essays Contributed to the Edinburgh Review*
Miscellanies (Martineau) **137**:316, 335
Miscellanies (Thackeray) **43**:367, 373, 378, 381, 387
Miscellanies: Prose and Verse (Maginn) **8**:436-37, 442
The Mischief-Making Crown (Raimund)
See *Die unheilbringende Zauberkrone*
"Mischka" (Lenau) **16**:265
Mischmasch (Carroll) **139**:32-33, 57
"Misconceptions" (Browning) **19**:127
"The Miser" (Krylov) **1**:435, 439
Les misérables (Hugo) **3**:243-50, 252-53, 255, 259, 263-65, 267, 270, 272, 274; **10**:354-83; **21**:195
Misere (Bécquer) **106**:162-63
Misère de la philosophie: Réponse à la philosophie de la misère de M. Proudhon (Marx) **17**:332-34, 336, 339, 357; **114**:3, 43, 69, 86
"El miserere" (Bécquer)
See *Cartas literarias desde mi celda*
"Miserere" (Heine) **4**:257
"'Miserikordia': Lecture for Stylists" (Jean Paul) **7**:234
The Miser's Daughter (Ainsworth) **13**:28, 35, 40
"Misery" (Brontë) **109**:36
"Misery I" (Brontë)
See "Misery, Part I"
"Misery II" (Brontë)
See "Misery, Part II"
"Misery Landing" (Woolson) **82**:272, 285, 333
"Misery, Part I" (Brontë) **109**:30, 33
"Misery, Part II" (Brontë) **109**:30, 33
"A Misfortunate Girl" (Turgenev)
See "Neschastnaya"
"The Misfortunes of Frederick Pickering" (Trollope)
See "The Adventures of Frederick Pickering"
Misogallo (Alfieri) **101**:79
"Miss Austen and Miss Mitford" (Oliphant) **61**:234
"Miss B—" (Clare) **86**:89
Miss Beecher's Housekeeper and Healthkeeper (Beecher) **30**:15, 22
"Miss Beulah's Bonnet" (Cooke) **110**:33, 40, 47, 51
Miss Brooke (Eliot) **4**:133; **13**:282
Miss Eden's Letters (Eden) **10**:104
"The Miss Greens" (Moodie) **14**:237
"Miss Grief" (Woolson) **82**:275, 295-96, 308, 310, 324
"Miss Harriet" (Maupassant) **83**:228
Miss Kilmansegg and Her Precious Leg: The Golden Legend (Hood) **16**:207, 217, 219-20, 222, 225-27, 229, 231, 233-36, 238
"Miss Lucinda" (Cooke) **110**:20, 35, 43, 47, 51, 57
Miss Ludington's Sister: A Romance of Immortality (Bellamy) **4**:23, 26-27, 31, 34; **86**:6, 9, 11, 17
Miss Mackenzie (Trollope) **6**:457, 470-71, 499, 515-16; **101**:237-38, 241, 274, 307, 309, 313
Miss Marjoribanks (Oliphant) **11**:442, 446, 449, 452, 454, 456-61, 463; **61**:174-5, 180-1, 188, 196, 198, 201, 212, 221-2, 226-9, 239
Miss Meredith (Levy) **59**:86-7, 98, 112, 115-6
Miss Oona McQuarrie (Smith) **59**:314, 319
"Miss Ophelia Gledd" (Trollope) **101**:234
Die Missbrauchten Liebesbriefe (Keller) **2**:415, 423
"Mission Endeavor" (Woolson) **82**:333-34
"The Mission of America" (Brownson) **50**:50
"The Mission of St. Philip" (Newman) **38**:310
"The Mission of the War" (Douglass) **7**:126
The Missionary of the Andes (Bowles) **103**:54-5, 71
"Les missionnaires" (Beranger) **34**:29
"Missions to the Oneidas" (Cooper) **129**:72
"Mist" (Lenau) **16**:277
"Mr. Higginbotham's Catastrophe" (Hawthorne) **2**:292, 298, 305, 324, 333
"Mistress Agnes" (Arany)
See "Agnes asszony"
Mistress and Maid (Craik) **38**:109, 113
"Mistress and Maid on Dress and Undress" (Linton) **41**:164
"Mistress into Maid" (Pushkin)
See "Baryshnia-krest'ianka"
Mistress Lee (Arnim) **5**:13, 18, 21
Mistriss Henley (Charriere)
See *Lettres de Mistriss Henley publiées par son amie*
"Mists and Fogs" (Hunt) **1**:417
"Mists and Rain" (Baudelaire)
See "Brumes et pluies"
"Mit dem grünen Lautenbande" (Muller) **73**:368,372
Mit Livs Eventyr (Andersen) **79**:26
" Mit zwei Worten" (Meyer) **81**:199
"Mithridates" (Emerson) **1**:299
Die Mitschuldigen (Goethe) **4**:211
"Mixed Days of May and December" (Jefferies) **47**:138
Mixed Essays (Arnold) **6**:58; **89**:101, 103, 113
"Miyagi ga tsuka" (Ueda Akinari) **131**:21-22, 58
"Mizpah" (Bryant) **46**:3
Mjältsjukan (Tegner) **2**:614
"M'Kinnon" (Hogg) **4**:275
"M.L." (Alcott) **83**:7
"Mlle. Luther and the Art of Acting" (Lewes) **25**:291
"Mnemosyne" (Hölderlin) **16**:192
"Mnich" (Slowacki) **15**:348-49
Mnich (Macha) **46**:200, 202-03, 206
Moby-Dick; or, The Whale (Melville) **3**:329, 332-55, 357, 359-64, 366-71, 373-8, 380-5; **12**:249-322; **29**:315-17, 324-27, 329, 331-32, 334, 337-38, 340, 343, 349, 354-57, 362, 364-65, 367, 369, 371-72, 378-79; **45**:197, 204, 206, 210, 212-13, 228-9, 231, 235, 243-7, 251-2, 254; **49**:376-8, 391, 402, 407, 409-10, 414, 416, 421; **91**:3-6, 9-10, 18, 21, 24, 28-34, 41-7, 50-1, 53-6, 68, 74, 81, 88-90, 93, 111, 113, 115, 121, 134, 180-81, 193, 198, 204, 206, 212-13, 217-20; **93**:187-88, 203, 222; **123**:186-87, 190, 192, 196, 200, 204, 211-12, 230, 232, 241, 251-52, 256
"The Mocking Bird" (Lanier) **6**:236, 238-39, 248
"The Mocking-Bird" (Hayne) **94**:149, 166
"The Model Husband" (Parton) **86**:376
"A Model Husband" (Parton) **86**:351
"The Model Man" (Shaw) **15**:335
"The Model Minister" (Parton) **86**:376
"The Model Step-Mother" (Parton) **86**:349
"The Model Wife" (Parton) **86**:376
"Modern" (Wagner) **119**:291
The Modern Abraham (Polidori) **51**:233
"Modern Antiques" (Mitford) **4**:401
The Modern Aria (Klinger)
See *Die neue Arria*
"The Modern Chevalier" (Brackenridge) **7**:54
Modern Chivalry: Containing the Adventures of Captain John Farrago and Teague O'Regan, His Servant (Brackenridge) **7**:42-61, 63-5
"A Modern Cinderella" (Alcott) **83**:8-9
"A Modern Classic" (Patmore) **9**:345
"Modern Gallantry" (Lamb) **10**:404, 408, 420-21, 436
Modern Greece (Hemans) **29**:202; **71**:261, 274
The Modern Griselda (Edgeworth) **1**:262, 272; **51**:90
The Modern Job (Sacher-Masoch)
See *Der neue Hiob*
A Modern Man's Confession (Musset)
See *La confession d'un enfant du siècle*
A Modern Mephistopheles (Alcott) **6**:20-21
"A Modern Mephistopheles or The Fatal Love Chase" (Alcott) **58**:46, 66, 69; **83**:35
"Modern Metaphysics and Moral Philosophy in France" (Lewes) **25**:314
"The Modern Migration of Nations" (Boyesen) **135**:31
"Modern Mothers" (Linton) **41**:164
Modern Novel Writing; or, The Elegant Enthusiast, and Interesting Emotions of Arabella Bloomville (Beckford) **16**:29, 36-7, 41
The Modern Oedipus (Polidori)
See *Ernestus Berchtold; or, The Modern Oedipus*
"The Modern Philosophy of France" (Lewes) **25**:288
"The Modern Politician" (Lampman) **25**:194, 209
"A Modern Sappho" (Arnold) **6**:44
"The Modern School of Poetry in England" (Lampman) **25**:203, 211-13, 215
"The Modern Thames" (Jefferies) **47**:143
The Modern Vikings: Stories of Life and Sport in the Norseland (Boyesen) **135**:8, 13
"Modern Women" (Linton) **41**:160
Modern Women and What is Said of Them (Linton) **41**:163, 170
"A Modern Workshop" (Silva)
See "Taller moderno"
The Modest Soldier; or, Love in New York (Dunlap) **2**:211, 213
Modeste Mignon (Balzac) **5**:39
"Modjesky as Cameel" (Field) **3**:206
"Modos de vivir que no dan de vivir" (Larra) **17**:282
Mogens (Jacobsen) **34**:152, 155-56, 159-60, 163, 165-68

Mogg Megone (Whittier) **8**:489, 492, 501, 510, 517; **59**:353, 355
"Mogiły haremu" (Mickiewicz) **3**:403-04; **101**:188-89
The Mogul Tale (Inchbald) **62**:142, 145-6, 148
Les Mohicans de Paris (Dumas) **71**:192-94
Mohun; or, The Last Days of Lee and His Paladins: Final Memoirs of a Staff-Officer in Virginia (Cooke) **5**:128, 130, 132-35
"Moia napast.' Moe bogatstvo, moe sviatoe remeslo" (Pavlova) **138**:11
"Moiron" (Maupassant) **1**:449; **83**:176
Moisasur's Magic Curse (Raimund)
See *Moisasur's Zauberfluch*
Moisasur's Zauberfluch (Raimund) **69**:8, 15, 18-19, 24, 27, 45, 47-8, 52
"Moïse" (Vigny) **7**:469, 479, 481, 484; **102**:335, 340, 372
Moïse (Chateaubriand) **134**:15, 97
"Moja ispoved" (Karamzin) **3**:290
"Moja piosnka" (Norwid) **17**:365, 367
Molière (Oliphant) **11**:439
Moll Pitcher and The Minstrel Girl (Whittier) **59**:353
"Molly Astore" (Ferguson) **33**:301
"Molnets broder" (Runeberg) **41**:311-13, 315, 318, 321
"Moloch" (Crawford) **127**:213-14
Moloch (Hebbel) **43**:234, 240, 258, 262
Molodye suprugi (Griboedov) **129**:162-63, 172
"Mon coeur mis à nu" (Baudelaire) **6**:100, 112; **29**:70-1, 97; **55**:68
"Mon Dieu m'a dit" (Verlaine) **51**:351-2
"Mon files, après l'avoir conduit au collège" (Desbordes-Valmore) **97**:29
"À mon fils, avant le collège" (Desbordes-Valmore) **97**:9, 29
"Mon rêve familier" (Verlaine) **51**:351-52, 355-56
Mon voisin Raymond (Kock) **16**:245
"Monadnoc" (Emerson) **1**:299; **38**:169
"Monadnock from Wachuset" (Whittier) **8**:531
Monakh (Pavlova) **138**:4
Monaldi (Allston) **2**:20-22, 24-28
The Monarchy according to the Charter (Chateaubriand)
See *De la monarchie selon la charte*
Le monastère abandonné; ou, La malédiction paternelle (Pixérécourt) **39**:278, 289-90
The Monastery (Scott) **15**:263, 289; **69**:313; **110**:233
The Monastery of Sendomir (Grillparzer)
See *Das Kloster bei Sendomir*
"Monastery Scene" (Grillparzer)
See "Klosterszene"
Die Monate (Muller) **73**:366
"Der Mönch von Bonifazio" (Meyer) **81**:143
"Monday in Holy Week" (Droste-Hülshoff) **3**:202
Monday Tales (Daudet)
See *Les contes du Lundi*
"Mondesaufgang" (Droste-Hülshoff) **3**:200
"Mondesnacht" (Droste-Hülshoff) **3**:193
"Mondnacht" (Eichendorff) **8**:230
Der Mondsüchtige (Tieck) **5**:519
Money (Bulwer-Lytton) **1**:140, 147, 153; **45**:18, 69
Money and Spirit (Gotthelf)
See *Geld und Geist oder die Versöhnung*
"The Money Diggers" (Irving) **2**:390; **95**:227
The Money Question (Dumas)
See *La question d'argent*
The Money-Lender (Gore) **65**:37-8
De Monfort (Baillie) **2**:31, 34, 38-40, 43; **71**:4, 6-7, 9-12, 16-17, 19, 26-27, 31-32, 35-36, 38, 44-45, 48, 51, 53, 66
Monikins (Cooper) **54**:256
"The Monitions of the Unseen" (Ingelow) **39**:267
"The Monitors" (Hogg) **109**:202
"The Monk" (Lampman) **25**:168, 176, 192, 199, 206, 220
"The Monk" (Shevchenko)
See "Chernets"
"The Monk" (Slowacki)
See "Mnich"
The Monk (Macha)
See *Mnich*
The Monk, a Romance (Lewis) **11**:292-303, 306-15, 317-25
"Monk and the Face" (Eminescu) **33**:264
The Monk Knight of St. John: A Tale of the Crusades (Richardson) **55**:304, 313, 319, 322-7, 350-3, 366
"Monk Tellenbach's Exile" (Boyesen) **135**:13, 29
"The Monks of Casal-Maggiore" (Longfellow) **45**:138, 149, 162, 180, 188, 191
The Monk's Wedding (Meyer) **81**:136
"Monna Innominata" (Rossetti) **2**:561, 563, 565, 571, 575, 577; **50**:272, 282, 284, 288, 290, 299, 321-4
"The Monochord" (Rossetti) **4**:491; **77**:314
"Monodies II" (Harpur) **114**:144
Monody at Matlock (Bowles)
See *Monody Written at Matlock*
"Monody on the Death of a Friend" (Dyer) **129**:137
"Monody on the Death of Chatterton" (Coleridge) **99**:58
"Monody on the Death of Dr. Warton" (Bowles) **103**:53, 78-9, 83
"Monody on the Death of Robert Robinson A celebrated Dissenting Preacher, formerly of Cambridge" (Dyer) **129**:149
Monody Written at Matlock (Bowles) **103**:55, 60, 72, 87
Monographs (Milnes) **61**:136, 138
Monologen: Eine Neujahrsgabe (Schleiermacher) **107**:266-68, 335-36, 376, 378, 384, 397-98, 407
Monologues (Schleiermacher)
See *Monologen: Eine Neujahrsgabe*
"Monos and Daimonos" (Bulwer-Lytton) **45**:19
"À Monsieur A.L." (Desbordes-Valmore)
See "À Monsieur Alphonse de Lamartine"
Monsieur Alphonse (Dumas) **9**:224-25, 228, 230, 232, 242, 247, 250
"À Monsieur Alphonse de Lamartine" (Desbordes-Valmore) **97**:3, 17, 26
M. Antoine (Sand)
See *Le péché de M. Antoine*
"M. Augustin Thierry" (Renan) **26**:417
M. Cazotte (Nodier) **19**:384
Monsieur de Camors (Feuillet) **45**:75, 77-80, 85-6, 90
"M. de Lamennais" (Renan) **26**:417
"Monsieur de l'Argentière, l'accusateur" (Borel) **41**:4, 6, 12
"Monsieur de Miroir" (Hawthorne) **2**:298; **95**:105
Monsieur Jean (Sainte-Beuve) **5**:341
Monsieur Lecoq (Gaboriau) **14**:17-20, 23-9, 31-2
M. P.; or, The Blue-Stocking (Moore) **6**:378, 392, 395
"Monsieur Parent" (Maupassant) **83**:201
"Monsieur Phoebus" (Crawford) **127**:193, 216
Monsieur Sylvestre (Sand) **57**:313
"The Monstre Balloon" (Barham) **77**:19, 26
"Monstrous World" (Petofi)
See "Gyalázatos világ"
"Mont Blanc" (Shelley) **18**:327, 338, 361, 363-64, 378; **93**:256-60, 264, 333
"Le mont des Oliviers" (Vigny) **7**:469, 472-74, 479, 481-82, 484; **102**:372-73
La Montagne "and Mr. Coullery" (Bakunin) **58**:131
"Montaigne; or, the Skeptic" (Emerson) **38**:169, 171, 227; **98**:22, 25-6, 33, 68, 76
Montalbert (Smith) **23**:323, 330, 336; **115**:145
"La montaña maldita" (Gómez de Avellaneda) **111**:65
La montaña maldita (Gómez de Avellaneda) **111**:28
"La montañero" (Isaacs) **70**:305
Montcalm and Wolfe (Parkman) **12**:335-36, 341, 343, 345, 348, 359-60, 370-71, 375, 377-79
"El monte de las ánimas" (Bécquer) **106**:99, 108, 112, 120
"Les monténégrins" (Nerval) **67**:340
A Month in the Country (Turgenev)
See *Mesyats v derevne*
"The Months of Apprenticeship" (Hoffmann) **2**:356
"Months of Youth" (Hoffmann) **2**:356
Montjoie (Feuillet) **45**:75, 79, 89
Montmorency (Staël-Holstein) **91**:358
Mont-Oriol (Maupassant) **1**:450, 467-69; **42**:167, 169, 174, 189; **83**:173-75, 186, 200
"Montreurs" (Leconte de Lisle) **29**:214
"Monument" (Pushkin)
See "Pamjatnik"
"The Monument and the Bridge" (Lowell) **2**:516
"A Monument I Reared" (Pushkin) **3**:451
"Monument Moors des Räubers" (Schiller) **39**:386
"Monument Mountain" (Bryant) **6**:183, 186-87; **46**:6, 19, 28
"The Monument of Phaon" (Freneau) **111**:148, 150
"The Monument to I. Heliade Radulescu" (Eminescu) **131**:311
"The Monument to Peter the Great" (Mickiewicz) **3**:401
"Moods" (Longfellow) **45**:139
Moods (Alcott) **6**:12-14; **58**:24-5, 28-33, 37, 47-9, 69, 75; **83**:9, 52
"Moods and Thoughts" (Levy) **59**:119
"Moods of My Own Mind" (Wordsworth) **12**:393
"The Moon and the Comet, a Fable" (Opie) **65**:160
"The Moon is distant from the Sea" (Dickinson) **77**:93
"The Moon of Mobile" (Chivers) **49**:49
"The Moon Path" (Lampman) **25**:204
"The Moon upon her fluent Route" (Dickinson) **77**:121
"The Moon was a-Waning" (Hogg) **109**:268
"Mooni" (Kendall) **12**:182-83, 187, 190, 197, 199
"Moonlight" (Eichendorff)
See "Mondnacht"
"Moonlight" (Silva)
See "Luz de la luna"
"Moonlight" (Verlaine)
See "Clair de lune"
A Moonlight Adventure (Mitford) **4**:406
A Moonlight Night (Sacher-Masoch) **31**:287, 291, 302
"Moonshiners" (Cooke) **5**:133
The Moonstone: A Romance (Collins) **1**:175, 177, 180-84, 187-91; **18**:60-93; **93**:7, 12, 19, 42, 44, 46-7, 50, 53, 61-2, 66-74, 76-83
The Moor of Peter the Great (Pushkin)
See *Arap Petra Velikogo*
The Moorish Girl (Andersen) **79**:12-13
"Moorish Melodies" (Maginn) **8**:441
Moorland Cottage (Gaskell) **5**:183, 198, 202, 205; **70**:185, 188, 190
"The Moors" (Wilson) **5**:560-61
"Moors and Christians" (Alarcon)
See "Moros y cristianos"
"The Moor's Legacy" (Irving) **2**:372
"A Moosehead Journal" (Lowell) **2**:520; **90**:202-06
Mopsa the Fairy (Ingelow) **39**:259, 264, 266-68; **107**:118, 129, 134-37, 143, 151, 164-77
"The Morai" (Williams) **135**:315
"The Moral Argument against Calvinism" (Channing) **17**:9, 52-3
"The Moral Bully" (Holmes) **14**:126

"La moral del juguete" (Casal) **131**:263
"The Moral Effect of Works of Satire" (Clough) **27**:104
Moral Epistle, Respectfully Submitted to Earl Stanhope (Landor) **14**:175
"Moral Independence" (Martineau) **137**:316
The Moral of Many Fables (Martineau) **137**:250, 265, 270
Moral Pieces (Sigourney)
See *Moral Pieces, in Prose and Verse*
"Moral Pieces in Prose and Verse" (Sigourney) **87**:320-21
Moral Pieces, in Prose and Verse (Sigourney) **21**:289; **87**:325, 337
"A Moral Poem" (Lermontov) **126**:133
"Moral Reflection on the Cross of Saint Paul's" (Hood) **16**:235
"The Moral Satires" (Cowper) **8**:113
Moral Sketches of Prevailing Opinions and Manners, Foreign and Domestic: With Reflections on Prayer (More) **27**:334
Moral Tales (Laforgue)
See *Moralités légendaires*
Moral Tales for Young People (Edgeworth) **1**:255-56, 267; **51**:81-7, 89, 102, 119
The Moral Teaching of Jesus Christ (Shelley) **93**:352
"A Moral Thought" (Freneau) **111**:144-45, 150, 154
Moralism and Christianity; or, Man's Experience and Destiny (James) **53**:216, 236
"Moralitas" (Hogg) **109**:203
Moralités légendaires (Laforgue) **5**:268-9, 271, 274, 276, 278, 280-2; **53**:256-7, 272, 287, 290-1, 293-5, 298-9
"Morality" (Arnold) **6**:56
"The Morality of Wilhelm Meister" (Eliot) **89**:227
"Morals" (Emerson) **1**:282
Morayma (Martínez de la Rosa) **102**:245-46
"Morbid Appetite for Money" (Whitman) **81**:238
"De Morbo Oneirodynia" (Polidori) **51**:223
"Morcia Funebre" (Chivers) **49**:75
Le more de Venise (Vigny) **7**:476
More Letters of Charles Darwin (Darwin) **57**:147, 151
More Letters of Edward FitzGerald (FitzGerald) **9**:269
"The More Mature Months" (Hoffmann) **2**:356
More Nonsense, Pictures, Rhymes, Botany, Etc. (Lear) **3**:295, 297
More Sinned Against Than Sinning (Ostrovsky)
See *Bez viný vinovátye*
More Than Pearls and Gold (Andersen) **79**:14
"The Morehens Nest" (Clare) **86**:141
"Morekhod Nikitin" (Bestuzhev) **131**:154-55, 159
"Morella" (Eminescu) **131**:334
"Morella" (Poe) **1**:492, 514; **16**:304, 316, 331, 335-36; **55**:151, 197, 201; **97**:180, 208-09; **117**:299-301, 303
"The Mores" (Clare) **9**:114; **86**:140-41, 145
Morgane (Villiers de l'Isle Adam) **3**:581, 583-84
"Morgengesang am Schöpfungsfeste" (Klopstock) **11**:238
Morgengespräch zwischen A. und dem Kandidaten Bertram (Claudius) **75**:197, 210-11, 217
"Morgengruß" (Muller) **73**:364
"Morgenlied" (Meyer) **81**:141, 151, 155
"Morgenlied" (Muller) **73**:366
"Moria el sol, y las marchitas hojas" (Castro) **78**:41
Morituri salutamus (Longfellow) **2**:486; **45**:130-31, 146
Morley Court (Le Fanu) **9**:301
"The Mormon's Wife" (Cooke) **110**:4, 9, 33, 36
"A Morn of May" (Ingelow) **39**:264
"Morning" (Browning) **79**:94, 101, 153
"Morning" (Cranch) **115**:5
"Morning" (Harpur) **114**:115
"Morning" (Keble) **87**:169, 174, 200
"Morning" (Lazarus) **8**:420
"Morning" (Rimbaud)
See "Matin"
"Morning" (Very) **9**:383
"A Morning After Storm" (Hayne) **94**:166
"Morning and Evening" (Arany)
See "Reg és Est"
"The Morning Angelus" (Verlaine)
See "L'Angelus du matin"
"Morning Bells" (Bowles) **103**:55
"Morning Hymn" (Keble) **87**:153
"Morning Hymn" (Moodie) **113**:317
"Morning in the Bush" (Kendall) **12**:185
"Morning in the Mountains" (Tyutchev) **34**:389
"The Morning Moon" (Barnes) **75**:72
The Morning of a Man of Business (Gogol) **15**:94
"Morning on the Lievre" (Lampman) **25**:172, 190
"The Morning Star" (Eminescu)
See "Luceafarul"
"The Morning Star" (Hogg) **109**:249
"Morning Twilight" (Baudelaire)
See "Le crépuscule du matin"
"Morning Walk" (Clare) **9**:122
"The Morning Watch" (Very) **9**:378, 383
"The Morning Wind" (Clare) **9**:104
Morning-Glories and Other Stories (Alcott) **58**:50
"The Morning's Hinges" (Ferguson) **33**:290
"The Morns Are Meeker than They Were" (Dickinson) **21**:7
"The Moro River" (Isaacs)
See "Río Moro"
"Moros y cristianos" (Alarcon) **1**:14
Moroz krasni nos (Nekrasov) **11**:402, 404-05, 407-09, 412-14, 416, 420-21
"Mort!" (Verlaine) **51**:266
La mort (Baudelaire) **6**:116, 122; **55**:5, 53, 62-3, 66, 73-4
"La mort de l'exilé" (Nerval) **67**:307
"La mort de Philippe II" (Verlaine) **2**:622, 624; **51**:356
"La Mort de S.M. le Roi Louis II de Bavière" (Verlaine) **51**:359
"La mort de Valmiki" (Leconte de Lisle) **29**:215, 223, 234, 241
"La mort des amants" (Baudelaire) **6**:116; **29**:105; **55**:12, 73
"La mort des artistes" (Baudelaire) **55**:12, 29, 62, 66, 73
"La mort des pauvres" (Baudelaire) **29**:80, 112-13; **55**:73
"La mort des petits poux" (Rimbaud) **35**:266
"La mort du diable" (Beranger) **34**:42
"La mort du loup" (Vigny) **7**:469, 472-73, 478-79, 481-82; **102**:336, 373-75
"Le mort joyeux" (Baudelaire) **55**:12, 44
"Une mort trop travaillée" (Corbière) **43**:31
"Mortal, Angel AND Demon" (Verlaine) **51**:372
A Mortal Antipathy: First Opening of the New Portfolio (Holmes) **14**:113, 115, 131, 133-34, 136-39, 143; **81**:107, 118
"The Mortal Immortal" (Shelley) **14**:264, 267, 272, 299; **59**:155
La Morte (Feuillet) **45**:90-1
"La morte amoureuse" (Gautier) **1**:341, 346, 348, 350, 353, 355; **59**:8-13, 29, 33-6, 39-40
"Morte d'Arthur" (Tennyson) **30**:212-13, 222, 224, 230, 242, 249, 253, 269, 279-80; **65**:240, 245-7, 278-82, 285, 297-8, 300-1, 305, 311, 315, 318-20, 324, 339, 349, 368, 376; **115**:235
La morte de Socrate (Lamartine) **11**:245, 268-70, 289
"Morton Hall" (Gaskell) **5**:201, 205; **70**:188-89
"Morts de quatre-vingt-douze et de quatre-vingt-treize" (Rimbaud) **4**:465
"Mortua est" (Eminescu) **33**:249, 257, 264; **131**:294, 297, 331
Mosaïque (Mérimée) **65**:79, 113
"Moscow" (Pavlova)
See "Moskva"
"Moses" (Vigny) **7**:474
"Moses on the Mountain" (Wergeland) **5**:537
"Moskaleva Krynycja" (Shevchenko) **54**:368, 389
"Moskva" (Pavlova) **138**:50, 54
"Mosque" (Milnes) **61**:130
"Moss on a Wall" (Kendall) **12**:179-80, 186, 194, 199, 201
"The Moss Supplicateth for the Poet" (Dana) **53**:178
"Mosses" (Melville)
See "Hawthorne and his Mosses"
Mosses from an Old Manse (Hawthorne) **2**:294, 298; **39**:233; **95**:104, 110
"Motes in the Sun-Beans" (Lamb) **125**:348
"The Moth" (Pavlova)
See "Motylek"
"The Moth and the Flowers" (Zhukovsky)
See "Motylyok i tsvety"
"The Mother" (Andersen) **79**:66
"The Mother" (Crabbe) **26**:93, 128-30; **121**:11, 36
"Mother" (Nekrasov)
See "Mat"
"Mother and Eliza" (Child) **73**:129
"Mother and Poet" (Browning) **61**:10, 14, 44-5, 66
"Mother and Son" (Morris) **4**:434
"The Mother and the Child" (Kivi)
See "Äiti ja lapsi"
"Mother Earth" (Isaacs)
See "La tierra madre"
Mother Elder (Andersen) **79**:15
The Mother of God (Sacher-Masoch) **31**:295, 298, 302
"Mother of God I Shall Pray in Humility" (Lermontov) **126**:143
"Mother of Pearl" (O'Brien) **21**:239-40, 244-45, 252
"Mother, Thou'rt Faithful to Me" (Foster) **26**:295
The Mother-in-Law (Southworth) **26**:431-32, 446-47
"Motherland" (Lermontov)
See "Rodina"
"The Motherless Child" (Barnes) **75**:58
Mothers and Daughters (Gore) **65**:16, 20, 30-1
The Mother's Book (Child) **6**:198-99; **73**:41, 50, 59, 67, 73, 75, 96, 101, 130
"The Mother's Dream" (Barnes) **75**:17
"The Mother's Heart" (Norton) **47**:241-42
"The Mother's Hymn" (Bryant) **6**:165
"Mother's Name" (Grundtvig) **1**:402
"The Mother's Prayer" (Lazarus) **109**:293
"Mother's Revenge" (Whittier) **8**:485
"The Mother's Secret" (Holmes) **14**:128
"The Mother's Soul" (Crawford) **12**:156, 171; **127**:160
"A Mother's Wail" (Timrod) **25**:372, 382, 384
The Motley Assembly (Warren) **13**:419, 428-29, 436
Les Mots anglaise (Mallarmé) **41**:249
Motsart i Sal'eri (Pushkin) **3**:424, 433-34, 444, 447, 452; **83**:263-64, 275, 285-88, 324, 338-39, 351, 353
"Motylek" (Pavlova) **138**:3-4, 14, 48
"Motylyok i tsvety" (Zhukovsky) **35**:393, 403
"Mouche" (Maupassant) **1**:464, 468-69; **83**:194, 198
"Le mouchoir rouge" (Gobineau) **17**:80, 92-3, 103
"Mount Kikineis" (Mickiewicz)
See "Góra Kikineis"
"The Mount of Olives" (Vigny)
See "Le mont des Oliviers"
"Mount Orient" (Griffin) **7**:215

"Mount Shasta, Seen from a Distance" (Ridge) **82**:174, 184, 195, 197, 210
Mount Vernon, a Letter to the Children of America (Cooper) **129**:4
"The Mountain" (Leskov)
See "Gora"
The Mountain (Michelet) **31**:215, 242, 247-48, 257-58, 260, 262-63
The Mountain Bard: Consisting of Ballads and Songs, Founded on Facts and Legendary Tales (Hogg) **4**:277, 281-82; **109**:268-69, 276
"The Mountain Fires" (Hemans) **71**:277
The Mountain Forest (Stifter)
See *Der Hochwald*
"The Mountain Girl" (Isaacs)
See "La montañero"
The Mountain King and the Misanthrope (Raimund)
See *Der Alpenkönig und der Menschenfeind*
"Mountain Lyre" (Hogg) **109**:270
"Mountain Moss" (Kendall) **12**:179, 186
The Mountain of the Lovers: With Poems of Nature and Tradition (Hayne) **94**:137-38, 141, 148, 151, 168-69
"A Mountain Spring" (Kendall) **12**:183
"The Mountain Village of Bastundzhi" (Lermontov)
See "Aul Bastundzi"
"The Mountain's Face" (Boyesen) **135**:13
"Le mourant" (Banville) **9**:16
"The Mourner" (Opie) **65**:155
"The Mourner" (Shelley) **14**:264, 272; **59**:155; **103**:343, 345-47
"The Mourning Daughter" (Sigourney) **21**:299
"The Mouse" (Shaw) **15**:335
"The Mouse's Nest" (Clare) **9**:101
Le Mousqetaire (Dumas) **71**:204
"Le mousse" (Corbière) **43**:28
"Mouvement" (Rimbaud) **4**:475; **35**:269; **82**:232
"Movables Credit" (Eminescu) **33**:273
Movements of the British Legion with Strictures on the Course of Conduct (Richardson)
See *Journal of the Movements of the British Legion*
"Möwenflug" (Meyer) **81**:199-200, 208
"Moy dar ubog, i golos moy ne gromok..." (Baratynsky) **103**:9
"Moy Eliziy" (Baratynsky) **103**:8
Moya Rodoslovnaya (Pushkin) **83**:317
Mozart and Salieri (Pushkin)
See *Motsart i Sal'eri*
Mozart auf der Reise nach Prag (Mörike) **10**:445, 448-49, 458
Mozart on the Way to Prague (Mörike)
See *Mozart auf der Reise nach Prag*
Mózes (Madach) **19**:362, 368, 371
The M.P. (Robertson) **35**:333-34, 336, 340, 351, 357, 360-62, 364-65, 369
Mr. Ambrose's Letters on the Rebellion (Kennedy) **2**:432
"Mr. and Mrs. Discobbolos" (Lear) **3**:308
Mr. Benet (Fredro)
See *Pan Benet*
Mr. Buckstone's Ascent of Mount Parnassus (Planché) **42**:273, 276, 291
Mr. Buckstone's Voyage Round the World (Planché) **42**:273, 291
"Mr. Clifford" (Austen) **119**:13
"Mr. Dana of the New York Sun" (Field) **3**:211
"Mr. Darwin's Hypothesis" (Lewes) **25**:287, 311
"Mr. Deucease at Paris" (Thackeray) **43**:367
"Mr. Emerson's New Course of Lectures" (Lowell) **90**:220
Mr. Facey Romford's Hounds (Surtees) **14**:347, 349-50, 353, 355, 364, 366, 369-72, 374-75, 380-81
"Mr. Gilfil's Love Story" (Eliot) **4**:92-93, 98; **41**:101; **118**:103
Mr. H. or Beware A Bad Name (Lamb) **10**:401; **113**:158, 202, 256, 278, 280, 286
"Mr. Harley" (Austen) **119**:13
"Mr. Harrison's Confessions" (Gaskell) **5**:187, 190, 193, 201-03, 205; **97**:127, 168, 171; **137**:54
"Mr. Hosea Biglow to the Editor of the Atlantic Monthly" (Lowell) **2**:516
Mr. Joviality (Fredro)
See *Pan Jowialski*
"Mr. Justice Hartbottle" (Le Fanu) **9**:302, 317, 320-22; **58**:272, 301-2; **58**:256
"Mr. Kean's Iago" (Hazlitt) **82**:75
"Mr. Lowe as Chancellor of the Exchequer" (Bagehot) **10**:31
Mr. Midshipman Easy (Marryat) **3**:316-19, 322
Mr. Moneyful (Fredro)
See *Pan Geldhab*
"Mr. Paul Pató" (Petofi)
See "Pató Pál úr"
Mr. Scarborough's Family (Trollope) **6**:471, 501, 503; **101**:249, 267, 292, 318, 321
"Mr Shuffleton's Allegorical Survey" (Hogg) **109**:248
"Mr. Sludge, 'The Medium'" (Browning) **19**:98, 131; **79**:150, 163-64, 171
Mr. Sponge's Sporting Tour (Surtees) **14**:345-47, 349-50, 353, 355-56, 358, 361, 363, 365, 369-72, 374, 377-78, 380-83
Mrinalini (Chatterji) **19**:204, 209-10, 212-13, 215, 217-21, 224
Mrnālinī (Chatterji)
See *Mrinalini*
"Mrs. Adolphus Smith Sporting the 'Blue Stocking'" (Parton) **86**:352
Mrs. Albert Grundy: Observations in Philistia (Frederic) **10**:194, 201-02, 214
Mrs Armytage; or, Female Domination (Gore) **65**:19-20, 30
Mrs. Arthur (Oliphant) **61**:203-4, 209-10
"Mrs. Battle's Opinions on Whist!" (Lamb) **10**:390, 428, 436; **113**:155-56, 200, 227, 244
"Mrs. Brumby" (Trollope) **101**:234
"Mrs. Caudle's Breakfast Talk" (Jerrold) **2**:407
Mrs. Caudle's Curtain Lectures (Jerrold) **2**:395-96, 398, 402-03, 405-08
"Mrs. Caudle's Papers" (Jerrold) **2**:407
"Mrs. Flint's Married Experience" (Cooke) **110**:19-20, 24, 33-4, 37, 44, 46, 50, 56, 58, 66
"Mrs. Fønss" (Jacobsen)
See "Fru Fønss"
"Mrs. General Talboys" (Trollope) **101**:234-35
"Mrs. Jaypher" (Lear) **3**:301
Mrs. Leicester's School (Lamb) **10**:402-03, 406, 417; **113**:278, 286
Mrs. Leicester's School (Lamb) **125**:302, 312, 314, 316-17, 320, 322-23, 325-26, 332, 349, 360, 362-63, 365, 368-71, 375
"Mrs. Macsimmum's Bill" (O'Brien) **21**:243
Mrs. Mathews; or, Family Mysteries (Trollope) **30**:331-32
Mrs. Perkins' Ball (Thackeray) **5**:445
"Mrs. Philip Schuyler" (Cooper) **129**:71
"Mrs Pierrepoint" (Levy) **59**:106
"Mrs. Rozgonye" (Arany)
See "Roz goniné"
"Mrs. Throckmorton's Bulfinch" (Cowper)
See "On the Death of Mrs. Throckmorton's Bulfinch"
"Mrs. Twardowski" (Mickiewicz) **3**:398
"Mrs. Weasel's Husband" (Parton) **86**:350
"Mrs. Yardley's Quilting" (Harris) **23**:140, 159
MS 1 (An Enquiry Concerning Political Justice and Its Influence on General Virtue and Happiness) (Godwin)
See *Enquiry concerning Political Justice and Its Influence on General Virtue and Happiness*
MS 2 (An Enquiry Concerning Political Justice and Its Influence on General Virtue and Happiness (Godwin)
See *Enquiry concerning Political Justice and Its Influence on General Virtue and Happiness*
"MS. Found in a Bottle" (Poe) **1**:492, 514; **16**:292, 299, 301, 315, 330-34; **55**:185, 202, 205-6; **94**:223-25
MS I (An Enquiry Concerning Political Justice and Its Influence on General Virtue and Happiness) (Godwin)
See *Enquiry concerning Political Justice and Its Influence on General Virtue and Happiness*
MS I (Things as They Are; or, The Adventures of Caleb Williams) (Godwin)
See *Things As They Are; or, The Adventures of Caleb Williams*
MS II (An Enquiry Concerning Political Justice and Its Influence on General Virtue and Happiness) (Godwin)
See *Enquiry concerning Political Justice and Its Influence on General Virtue and Happiness*
MS II (Things as They Are; or, The Adventures of Caleb Williams) (Godwin)
See *Things As They Are; or, The Adventures of Caleb Williams*
MS III (An Enquiry Concerning Political Justice and Its Influence on General Virtue and Happiness) (Godwin)
See *Enquiry concerning Political Justice and Its Influence on General Virtue and Happiness*
MS III (Things as They Are; or, The Adventures of Caleb Williams) (Godwin)
See *Things As They Are; or, The Adventures of Caleb Williams*
MS IV (An Enquiry Concerning Political Justice and Its Influence on General Virtue and Happiness) (Godwin)
See *Enquiry concerning Political Justice and Its Influence on General Virtue and Happiness*
MS V (An Enquiry Concerning Political Justice and Its Influence on General Virtue and Happiness) (Godwin)
See *Enquiry concerning Political Justice and Its Influence on General Virtue and Happiness*
"Mtsiri" (Lermontov)
See *Mtsyri*
"Mtsyri" (Lermontov)
See *Mtsyri*
Mtsyri (Lermontov) **5**:289, 293, 295; **126**:128-29, 131, 145, 181-83, 185-87, 217, 224
"Much Ado about Nothing" (Lamb) **125**:304, 306
The Muddy Bay (Ichiyō)
See *Nigorie*
"Mudrecu" (Baratynsky) **103**:27
"La muerte del sargento" (Isaacs) **70**:306
"Muertos" (Silva) **114**:301, 303
Los muertos (Silva) **114**:269-70
La muette de Portici (Scribe) **16**:382, 386, 398, 401, 408-11
Muhganni Nama (Ghalib) **39**:153
"Das Mühlenleben" (Muller) **73**:364,370
"La mujer" (Gómez de Avellaneda) **111**:30, 33, 56-7, 64-7
"La mujer alta" (Alarcon) **1**:14
"La mujer de piedra" (Bécquer) **106**:146, 149, 167-69
"La mula y el macho" (Lizardi) **30**:68
The Mulatto (Andersen) **79**:12-13, 17
Mulla Nur (Bestuzhev) **131**:152, 161, 186, 200
Müller Kohlenbrenner und Sesseltrager (Nestroy) **42**:240, 256
"Müller Radlauf" (Brentano) **1**:104
"Der Müller und der Bach" (Muller) **73**:365, 373

The Mummy's Tale (Gautier)
See *Le Roman de la momie*
"Mumu" (Turgenev) **21**:399, 415, 418, 457, 459; **122**:241, 244, 265, 294-97, 344, 348-49
Münchhausen: Eine Geschichte in arabesken (Immermann) **4**:290-95, 297; **49**:358, 361-62, 366-67
De mundi sensibilis et intelligibilis forma ac principiis (Kant) **67**:210
"Un mundo por un soneto" (Isaacs) **70**:306
"El mundo todo es máscaras, todo el año es carnaval" (Larra) **130**:230-31
Munio Alfonso (Gómez de Avellaneda) **111**:4, 12, 24, 28
"Munter" (Runeberg) **41**:312, 314, 327
"Muo no rigyo" (Ueda Akinari) **131**:9, 13-14, 16, 24-25, 28, 32, 34, 38, 40-41, 48, 60
Muo no Rigyo (Ueda Akinari) **131**:70-72
"Murad the Unlucky" (Edgeworth) **51**:88-9
"La muralla de México en la protección de María Santísima Nuestra Señora" (Lizardi) **30**:68
Murány ostroma (Arany) **34**:4, 16
"Murder" (De Quincey)
See "Lectures on Murder Considered as One of the Fine Arts"
"Murder Considered" (De Quincey)
See "Lectures on Murder Considered as One of the Fine Arts"
"The Murder of the Lamb" (Harpur) **114**:148, 150
"Murder Will Out" (Opie) **65**:159
"The Murdered Cousin" (Le Fanu)
See "A Passage in the Secret History of an Irish Countess"
"Murdered Lady" (Whittier) **8**:485
"The Murdered Traveller" (Bryant) **46**:3, 42
"The Murders in the Rue Morgue" (Poe) **1**:506, 521, 530-31; **16**:293, 295-96, 298, 300-01, 303, 306, 312, 315, 332; **55**:135, 141, 149; **78**:281-82; **94**:245; **97**:208, 211-12
"Mureşanu" (Eminescu) **131**:287
"The Murmuring of Bees Has Ceased" (Dickinson) **21**:68-9
Murnis (Almqvist) **42**:10
"Musa" (Holmes) **14**:133
Musarion (Wieland) **17**:394, 396, 398-400, 411-16, 426-27, 429
"Muşat and the Weirds" (Eminescu) **33**:269
"Muscadines" (Hayne) **94**:149, 167, 169
"Muscheln" (Muller) **73**:360, 371
Muscheln von der Insel Rügen (Muller) **73**:352, 356, 358-60, 367, 371
"The Muse" (Baratynsky)
See "Muza"
The Muse (Pushkin) **3**:423
La muse du département (Balzac) **5**:84
"La Muse malade" (Baudelaire) **55**:48, 58
"The Muse of Australia" (Kendall) **12**:184, 195-96
"The Muse of the Coming Age" (Andersen) **7**:23; **79**:84
"Muse, un nommé ségur" (Hugo) **3**:256
"La Muse vénale" (Baudelaire) **55**:46-7, 58, 62
"Musée secret" (Gautier) **1**:348
"Der Musensaal" (Meyer) **81**:140, 154-56, 199, 209
"Music" (Emerson) **38**:193
"Music" (Halleck) **47**:57
"Music" (Lampman) **25**:167, 187, 208, 210, 216
"Music" (Thoreau) **7**:384
"The Music Grinders" (Holmes) **14**:99
"The Music Master" (Allingham) **25**:3, 5, 7, 9, 12, 16, 18, 23, 25, 27
"The Music of Nature" (Cranch) **115**:67
"Music of the Future" (Wagner)
See "Zukunftsmusik"
"Music, when soft voices die" (Shelley) **18**:373
"A Musical Instrument" (Browning) **1**:124; **66**:85
"A Musical Reminiscence" (Harpur) **114**:144
The Musician (Shevchenko)
See *Muzykant*
"Musician's Tale" (Longfellow) **45**:148
"Musings" (Dana) **53**:173-5
"Musings" (Thoreau) **138**:106
"Musings of a Recluse" (Cranch) **115**:32, 51
"La Musique" (Baudelaire) **55**:29, 61
La Musique et les lettres (Mallarmé) **41**:277, 280-81, 298
"The Musk Ox" (Leskov)
See "Ovcebyk"
The Musk-Ox, and Other Tales (Leskov) **25**:230-31
Musterkarte (Muller) **73**:366
"Mut" (Muller) **73**:390
"Mutability" (Shelley) **18**:340, 344
"The Mutability of Literature" (Irving) **19**:328, 347
"Mutation" (Bryant) **46**:46
The Mute from Portici (Scribe)
See *La muette de Portici*
"Mute Thy Coronation" (Dickinson) **21**:56
"Muth" (Muller) **73**:366
The Mutiny at the Nore (Jerrold) **2**:401
"Der Mutter Erde" (Hölderlin) **16**:174
"Die Mutter und die Tochter" (Klopstock) **11**:238
Mutter und Kind (Hebbel) **43**:238
"The Mutual Interdependence of Things" (Hoffmann) **2**:342
"Művészeti értekezés" (Madach) **19**:370
"Muza" (Baratynsky) **103**:9, 11
Muzykant (Shevchenko) **54**:387, 390, 392, 394
"My Aged Uncle Arly" (Lear) **3**:300-01
"My Ancient Ship upon My Ancient Sea" (Brontë) **109**:28
"My Aunt" (Holmes) **14**:109, 128
"My Aunt Margaret's Adventure" (Le Fanu) **9**:323
My Aunt Margaret's Mirror (Galt) **1**:334
My Aunt Susan (Frederic) **10**:188
"My Biography" (Beranger) **34**:37
"My Birth-day" (Lamb) **125**:364
"My Birthplace" (Nekrasov) **11**:403
"My Bohemian Life" (Rimbaud)
See "Ma bohème"
My Bondage and My Freedom (Douglass) **7**:124-25, 128-29, 131, 134, 143; **55**:106-7, 113, 117, 120-8
"My Books" (Longfellow) **45**:121
"My Boots" (Thoreau) **7**:384
My Brother Jack; or, The Story of What-D'ye-Call'em (Daudet)
See *Le petit chose*
"My Bugle and How I Blow It" (Mangan) **27**:302
"My Castle" (Alger) **8**:16
"My Childhood's Home I See Again" (Lincoln) **18**:240, 272
My Cid (Southey) **8**:459
"My Coat" (Beranger) **34**:46
"My Companions" (Holmes) **14**:100
"My Confession" (Karamzin)
See "Moja ispoved"
"My Contraband" (Alcott) **58**:47; **83**:7
"My Country" (Hale) **75**:286
"My Countrymen" (Arnold) **89**:102; **126**:7, 15
My Cousin Nicholas (Barham) **77**:6
"My Cricket" (Dickinson)
See "Further in Summer Than the Birds"
"My Darling Julia" (Barnes)
See "My Dearest Julia"
"My Days among the Dead Are Passed" (Southey) **8**:474
"My Dearest Julia" (Barnes) **75**:72-3
"My Depature" (Whitman) **81**:237
"My Elysium" (Baratynsky)
See "Moy Eliziy"
"My Emma, my darling" (Hogg) **109**:250
"My Fairy" (Carroll) **139**:61
"My Fate is Sealed: I Am Getting Married" (Pushkin) **83**:320
"My First Acquaintance with Poets" (Hazlitt) **29**:148-49, 165-66; **82**:107, 123, 126, 144
"My First Book" (Stevenson) **63**:229, 240, 243, 269
"My First Play" (Lamb) **113**:153-54, 177, 200, 202, 218
"My French Master" (Gaskell) **5**:190, 201
"My Friend, My Guardian Angel" (Zhukovsky) **35**:376, 403
"My Garden" (Very) **9**:388
"My Garden Acquaintance" (Lowell) **2**:517
My Geneology (Pushkin)
See *Moya Rodoslovnaya*
"My gift is mean and my voice is low..." (Baratynsky)
See "Moy dar ubog, i golos moy ne gromok..."
My Great-Grandfather's Papers (Stifter)
See *Die Mappe meines Urgrossvaters*
My Great-Grandfather's Portfolio (Stifter)
See *Die Mappe meines Urgrossvaters*
"My Heart Laid Bare" (Baudelaire)
See "Mon coeur mis à nu"
"My Heart Leaps Up" (Wordsworth) **12**:431
My Heart's Idol (Planché) **42**:293
"My Hope" (Arany)
See "Reménvem"
"My Hopes Have Departed Forever" (Foster) **26**:295
"My Hunt After 'The Captain'" (Holmes) **81**:102
"My Ideal Museum" (Casal)
See "Mi museo ideal"
"My Kingdom" (Alcott) **58**:37
"My Kinsman, Major Molineux" (Hawthorne) **2**:329-31; **17**:137; **23**:201, 217; **39**:180; **79**:299, 304; **95**:105, 112, 114-16, 125, 196
My Lady Ludlow (Gaskell) **5**:191, 201-03, 205; **70**:185-86
My Lady Pokahontas (Cooke) **5**:126, 132, 135
My Lady's Money (Collins) **1**:188
"My Landlady and Her Lodgers" (Galt) **110**:79
"My Last Duchess" (Browning) **19**:114, 117, 119, 126, 133, 135-37; **79**:95-96, 100, 164, 169-70, 185
My Life (Sand)
See *Histoire de ma vie*
My Life (Wagner)
See *Mein Leben*
"My Life Closed Twice before Its Close" (Dickinson) **21**:19, 23
"My Life Had Stood—A Loaded Gun" (Dickinson) **21**:48, 71; **77**:88, 143, 161
"My Life Is like a Stroll upon the Beach" (Thoreau) **7**:355
My Literary Life (Linton) **41**:165
"My Little Lovers" (Rimbaud)
See "Mes petites amoureuses"
"My Little Rabbit" (Wergeland) **5**:539
My Little Song Book (Hale)
See *School Song Book*
"My Lost Self" (Boyesen) **135**:20, 32
"My Lost Youth" (Longfellow) **45**:116, 131, 137, 142, 160, 186-87, 189
"My Love is Good" (Barnes) **75**:6, 8, 58
"My Love's Guardian Angel" (Barnes) **75**:17, 21
"My Mary" (Clare) **9**:74-75
"My Mary of the Curling Hair" (Griffin) **7**:198, 201
My Miscellanies (Collins) **1**:185
"My Misfortune. My Riches, My Holy Craft" (Pavlova)
See "Moia napast.' Moe bogatstvo, moe sviatoe remeslo"
"My Native Land" (Lermontov)
See "Rodina"
My Novel; or, Varieties in English Life (Bulwer-Lytton) **1**:145-46, 148-51, 155; **45**:22, 69-70

"My Old Kentucky Home, Good Night" (Foster) **26**:283-87, 289-91, 297-98
"My Old Village" (Jefferies) **47**:102, 138-39, 143
"My Orcha'd in Linden Lea" (Barnes) **75**:20, 29, 46, 60, 69, 87-8, 96, 101
"My Own Heart Let Me More Have Pity On" (Hopkins) **17**:245, 261
My Past and Thoughts (Herzen)
See *Byloe i dumy*
"My period had come for Prayer" (Dickinson) **77**:564
"My Playmate" (Whittier) **8**:505-06, 508-09, 520; **59**:349, 356, 371
"My Pretty Rose Tree" (Blake) **37**:43, 45, 48, 51, 92
My Prisons (Verlaine) **51**:372
"My Psalm" (Whittier) **8**:496
"My Race" (Martí)
See "Mi raza"
"My Relations" (Lamb) **10**:436; **113**:236, 248
My Relations with Carlyle (Froude) **43**:191, 202, 210, 220
"My Remarks on the Russian Theater" (Pushkin) **83**:331
"My River Runs to Thee" (Dickinson) **21**:8
"My School Career" (Petofi)
See "Deákpályám"
"My seal ring" (Fuller) **50**:247-8
"My 71st Year" (Whitman) **31**:434
"My Sister's Sleep" (Rossetti) **4**:517-19, 521-22, 525-26; **77**:303, 306, 344
"My Son, Sir" (O'Brien) **21**:237, 243, 247
"My Song" (Norwid)
See "Moja piosnka"
"My Songs" (Petofi)
See "Dalaim"
"My Soul and I" (Whittier) **8**:491; **59**:348, 361, 375, 377
"My Soul Is Dark" (Byron) **2**:103
My Southern Home; or, The South and Its People (Brown) **2**:48-51, 53; **89**:144, 160
"My Springs" (Lanier) **6**:238, 242; **118**:202, 215
"My Star" (Browning) **19**:96; **79**:140-41
"My stranno soshlis' . . ." (Pavlova) **138**:4
"My Study Windows" (Lowell) **2**:510
My Study Windows (Lowell) **90**:197, 220
"My Stuffed Owl" (Sigourney) **87**:326
"My Style of Drawing Birds" (Audubon) **47**:24
"My sweet Ann Foot, my bonny Ann" (Clare) **86**:89
"My Tale" (Clough) **27**:115-16, 118
"My Tenants" (Cooke) **110**:4
"My Testament" (Slowacki) **15**:365
"My Thoughts" (Cranch) **115**:15
"My Thoughts on Shakhovskoy" (Pushkin) **83**:332
"My Tract" (Hood) **16**:216
"My Triumph" (Whittier) **59**:361
"My Two Springs" (Lanier) **118**:231, 235
"My Valentine" (O'Brien) **21**:246
"My Visitation" (Cooke) **110**:36, 45
"My Vocation" (Dutt) **29**:127
"My Wheel Is in the Dark" (Dickinson) **21**:63
My Wife and I (Stowe) **3**:561-62, 567
"My Wife's Tempter" (O'Brien) **21**:234, 239, 243, 245, 247
My Years of Childhood (Fontane)
See *Meine Kinderjahre*
"Mycerinus" (Arnold) **6**:34, 44; **29**:32, 34
Mykyta Hajday (Shevchenko)
See *Nikita Hayday*
Myrrha (Alfieri) **101**:13, 19, 22, 39, 41, 50, 59
"Myrtho" (Nerval) **1**:476, 480, 486; **67**:307, 363
Myrtis, with Other Etchings and Sketchings (Sigourney) **21**:301; **87**:321
"Mysli iz raznykh avtorov" (Bestuzhev) **131**:168
Le Mystère dans les lettres (Mallarmé) **41**:272, 282
"Le mystère des trois cors" (Laforgue) **5**:279-80
Les mystères de Paris (Sue) **1**:553-55, 557-63
Les mystères du peuple (Sue) **1**:558-59
Les mystères du théâtre (Goncourt and Goncourt) **7**:153
"The Mysteries of Nature and of Grace" (Newman) **38**:304, 310
The Mysteries of Paris (Sue)
See *Les mystères de Paris*
The Mysteries of Udolpho (Radcliffe) **6**:404-06, 408-11, 413-23, 425, 427, 429-31, 433-39, 441-44, 446-47; **55**:216-22, 224, 226-31, 235-41, 252-4, 256-7, 259-60, 263, 265-6, 270-8; **106**:281-373
"The Mysterious Bride" (Hogg) **109**:233, 281
"The Mysterious Lodger" (Le Fanu) **9**:319
The Mysterious Monk (Dunlap) **2**:214
"The Mysterious Stanger" (Opie) **65**:172-3
"The Mysterious Visitor" (Holmes) **14**:99, 121, 128
"The Mystery" (Austen) **119**:13
The Mystery of Edwin Drood (Dickens) **3**:160, 177; **18**:96-143; **26**:228; **37**:164, 172-73; **86**:257; **105**:244, 290
"The Mystery of Major Molineux" (Clarke) **19**:251
The Mystery of Major Molineux, and Human Repetends (Clarke) **19**:251
"The Mystery of Marie Rogêt" (Poe) **1**:530-31; **16**:293, 295-96, 300, 303, 306, 315; **97**:208, 211-12
The Mystery of Mrs. Blencarrow (Oliphant) **61**:208
The Mystery of Orcival (Gaboriau)
See *Le crime d'Orcival*
"The Mystery of Pain" (Dickinson)
See "Pain Has an Element of Blank"
"The Mystery of Reminiscence" (Schiller) **39**:339
The Mystery of the Fall (Clough)
See *Adam and Eve*
"The Mystic" (Tennyson) **30**:283
"Mystic Trumpeter" (Whitman) **4**:579, 586
"Mystification" (Poe) **16**:322
"Mystification of the Sirens of Progress" (Fourier) **51**:185
"Mystique" (Rimbaud) **4**:487; **35**:269, 309; **82**:232-33, 243
"The Myth of Demeter and Persephone" (Pater) **90**:245, 247, 263
"Mythological Hymn" (Moore)
See "Fragment of a Mythological Hymn to Love"
N. M. Yazykovu: Otvet na otvet (Pavlova) **138**:4
"N. M. Yzykovu" (Baratynsky)
See "To N. M. Yazykov"
"N:o femton, Stolt" (Runeberg) **41**:325
Na bóikom méste (Ostrovsky) **57**:220
"N'a catredal" (Castro) **3**:101; **78**:5
"Na chto vy, dni" (Baratynsky) **103**:22
"Na kraju sveta" (Leskov) **25**:228, 231, 239, 255, 259
Na nožax (Leskov) **25**:225, 237, 248, 252-53
"Na pokoj grecki w eomu księżnej Zeneidy Wołkońskiej w Moskwie" (Mickiewicz) **101**:204-06, 208-09
"Na posev lesa" (Baratynsky) **103**:45, 48
"Na rodine" (Goncharov) **63**:18
"Na smert Gyote" (Baratynsky) **103**:8, 10
"Na śmierćś.p. Jana Gajewskiego" (Norwid) **17**:368
"Na vicnu pamjat' Kotljarevs' komu" (Shevchenko) **54**:371-2
Na vsyakogo mudretsa dovolno prostoty (Ostrovsky) **30**:100, 105, 112-13, 116, 118; **57**:219
Le nabab (Daudet) **1**:232-35, 237, 240-41, 243-48, 250
"Nabby" (Freneau) **111**:124
The Nabob (Daudet)
See *Le nabab*
"Nach der Lese" (Meyer) **81**:146
"Nach einem Niederländer" (Meyer) **81**:206
"Nachgelassene Werke" (Fichte) **62**:7
"Nachklänge Beethovenscher Musik" (Brentano) **1**:102
Nachkommenschaften (Stifter) **41**:375, 377
Nachlass (Fichte) **62**:39
"Nachricht von Fossilen Colossalen Knochen eines Raubthieres in Virginien Gefunden" (Jefferson)
See "A Memoir on the Discovery of Certain Bones of a Quadruped of the Clawed Kind in the Western Parts of Virginia"
Nachricht von meiner Aidienz beim Kaiser von Japan (Claudius) **75**:183, 194
Der Nachsommer (Stifter) **41**:334, 337-39, 343-46, 348, 351, 354, 357-60, 363, 369, 374-75, 378, 380, 384-85, 387-400
Nachstücke (Hoffmann) **2**:341-42
"Nacht in der Ernte" (Meyer) **81**:151
"Nachtgeräusche" (Meyer) **81**:201, 203
Nachtgesänge (Hölderlin) **16**:191
Nachtgeschichten (Hoffmann) **2**:348
"Die nächtliche Fahrt" (Lenau) **16**:286
"Nachträge Zu den Reisebildern" (Heine) **4**:231
"Nachts, Im Walde" (Eichendorff) **8**:213
Nachtwachen (Bonaventura) **35**:77-106
Nachtwachen des Bonaventura, Die (Tieck) **46**:384
Nacoochee (Chivers) **49**:42-5, 47-8, 52, 57
Nadeschda (Runeberg) **41**:310, 317, 328
"Nadie pase sin hablar al portero o los viajeros en Vitoria" (Larra) **130**:193, 221
"Nadorvannye" (Saltykov) **16**:372
"Nadpis' nad mogiloy Mikhalevykh v Yakutskom monastyre" (Bestuzhev) **131**:150
Nagerl und Handschuh (Nestroy) **42**:225, 242
Några ord om nejderna, folklynnet och levnadssättet i Saarijärvi socken (Runeberg) **41**:316
A nagyidai czigányok (Arany) **34**:5, 16, 23
"The Nail" (Alarcon)
See "El clavo"
Naimychka (Shevchenko) **54**:383, 387, 392
"Le Nain de Beauvoisine" (Desbordes-Valmore) **97**:14
Nakanune (Turgenev) **21**:382-83, 385-86, 393-94, 396-97, 399-400, 409-10, 413, 418-19, 426, 432, 434-39, 442-45, 448-49, 452-54; **37**:372, 379, 382, 384-85, 402-03, 407, 411, 428, 442, 444; **122**:249, 251-52, 256, 261, 267, 270-72, 276-77, 288, 292, 315, 320, 343
"Nakanune godovščiny avgusta 1864 g." (Tyutchev) **34**:412
Naked Genius (Horton) **87**:86, 101-02
"The Naked Goddess" (Thomson) **18**:391-92
Nakhlebnik (Turgenev) **21**:428
"Nala and Damayanti" (Zhukovsky) **35**:379
Nalozhnitsa (Baratynsky) **103**:8, 10, 39-44, 46
"Nameless Grave" (Landon) **15**:166
"A Nameless Grave" (Longfellow) **45**:121
"The Nameless Grave" (Moodie) **113**:316
"The Nameless One" (Mangan) **27**:276, 280-81, 287-89, 292, 297-98, 305
"Names upon a Stone" (Kendall) **12**:187, 189
"The Naming of Cuchullin" (Ferguson) **33**:279, 285
"Namouna" (Musset) **7**:255, 259, 264, 267, 275
"Nancy Chisholm" (Hogg) **109**:203
"Nancy Collins" (Mackenzie) **41**:189
Nannette und Maria (Grabbe) **2**:275-76, 287
"Nanny" (Freneau) **111**:124
"Nanny's Sailor Lad" (Allingham) **25**:8, 17
Naobi no mitama (Motoori) **45**:275-76
"Naomi" (Moodie) **14**:231
"Naples" (Pavlova)
See "Neapol"
"Napolean's Grave" (Tyutchev) **34**:389
"Napolean's Midnight Review" (Hood) **16**:235
"Napoleón" (Gómez de Avellaneda) **111**:6

"Napoleon" (Lockhart) **6**:309
"Napoleon" (Wergeland) **5**:539
"Napoleon and the British Sailor" (Campbell) **19**:187, 190
"Napoleon at Gotha" (Taylor) **89**:319
"Napoleon at Helena" (Sigourney) **21**:299
Napoléon Bonaparte; ou, Trente ans de l'histoire de France (Dumas) **11**:42, 57, 71; **71**:193
"Napoleon III in Italy" (Browning) **61**:12
Napoléon le petit (Hugo) **3**:262
Napoleon oder die hundert Tage (Grabbe) **2**:276-77, 281-82, 284-85, 287-88
Nápolyi Endre (Madach) **19**:370
Narbonne (Schiller) **69**:169
Narcisse (Sand) **42**:311
Narcissus (Stagnelius) **61**:248, 265
"The Nard" (Meyer)
See "Die Narde"
"Die Narde" (Meyer) **81**:206
"Narobe Katon" (Preseren) **127**:316
Narodna srbska pjesnarica (Karadzic) **115**:77, 110-11
"Narodnyye knizhki" (Pisarev) **25**:348
Der Narr auf Manegg (Keller) **2**:414
"Narrara Creek" (Kendall) **12**:187, 199
Narrative (Truth)
See *The Narrative of Sojourner Truth*
Narrative (Wordsworth)
See *George and Sarah Green: A Narrative*
"A Narrative of American Slavery" (Brown) **2**:52
Narrative of ARthur Gordon Pym (Poe)
See *The Narrative of Arthur Gordon Pym, of Nantucket*
The Narrative of Arthur Gordon Pym, of Nantucket (Poe) **1**:499-501, 518, 526, 529; **16**:300, 302, 312-13, 315, 324, 334; **55**:133, 149, 202; **78**:258; **94**:174, 176-88, 192, 195-206, 209-21, 225-28, 230-35, 239-49, 251-53, 255-58, 260-63, 266-76; **117**:197, 205, 224, 335
*Narrative of Events Which Have Taken Place in France from the Landing of Napoleon Bonaparte, on the 1st of March, 1815, till the Restoration of Louis XVIII, with an account of the Present State of Society and Public Opinion**** (Williams) **135**:261, 310-13, 335
A Narrative of Facts (Holcroft)
See *A Narrative of Facts relating to a Prosecution for High Treason*
A Narrative of Facts relating to a Prosecution for High Treason (Holcroft) **85**:194-95, 199, 209, 227, 235
The Narrative of Sojourner Truth (Truth) **94**:288-90, 292, 297-305, 308, 310, 312, 314, 316-24, 330, 333, 337
The Narrative of Sojourner Truth, A Northern Slave Emancipated Frodily Servitude By The State of New York in 1828 (Truth) **94**:301
Narrative of the Earl of Elgin's Mission to China and Japan . . . (Oliphant) **47**:287
"Narrative of the Life and Escape of William Wells Brown" (Brown)
See *Narrative of William W. Brown, a Fugitive Slave, Written by Himself*
Narrative of the Life and Escape of William Wells Brown (Brown)
See *Narrative of William W. Brown, a Fugitive Slave, Written by Himself*
A Narrative of the Life of David Crockett of the State of Tennessee (Crockett) **8**:144-49, 151-55
Narrative of the Life of Frederick Douglass, an American Slave, Written by Himself (Douglass) **7**:120-21, 125, 128-31, 133-39, 141-42, 144-45; **55**:87, 95-119, 121-6, 128
Narrative of the Operations of the Right Division of the Army in Upper Canada (Richardson) **55**:344
Narrative of William W. Brown, a Fugitive Slave, Written by Himself (Brown) **2**:46-9, 55; **89**:156, 160-68, 184
"Narrative Two" (Crawford) **127**:164
Die Narrenburg (Stifter) **41**:335, 366, 379
"A narrow Fellow in the Grass" (Dickinson) **77**:129
"A Narrow Girdle of Rough Stones and Crags" (Wordsworth) **111**:348
"The Narrow Way" (Brontë) **4**:46
"Nashi poslali" (Turgenev) **122**:256-57
"Naslazhdaytes: vsyo pokhodit!..." (Baratynsky) **103**:11
Les Natchez (Chateaubriand) **134**:12, 16, 19, 23-25, 27, 47, 76, 81-83, 95, 102, 112, 143
National Airs (Moore) **110**:186
National Anti-Slavery Standard (Child)
See *Anti-Slavery Standard*
"National Apostasy" (Keble) **87**:131, 199
"The National Capital, Abraham Lincoln" (Douglass) **7**:126
"National Literature" (Paulding) **2**:531
"National Ode" (Taylor) **89**:296, 326
"National Song" (Petofi)
See "Nemzeti dal—Talpra magyar"
"A National Song. The Wind That Sweeps Our Native Sea" (Moodie) **113**:308, 311
"Nationality in Drinks" (Browning) **19**:96
A Nation's Duty in a War for Freedrom (Schleiermacher) **107**:364
"The Nation's First Number" (Mangan) **27**:315
"Native Moments" (Whitman) **31**:430; **81**:329
"The Nativity" (Manzoni) **29**:253
"Nattergalen" (Andersen) **7**:37; **79**:23, 35, 40, 42, 51-2, 59, 62, 65, 73-4, 76
Nattvardsbarnen (Tegner) **2**:611-14
Die Natur der Dinge (Wieland) **17**:416-18
"Natur und Kunst oder Saturn und Jupiter" (Hölderlin) **16**:162, 173
"De natura decorum" (Patmore) **9**:338-39, 360, 365
"Natura Naturans" (Clough) **27**:106-7, 113
The Natural Daughter (Dunlap) **2**:213
Natural Daughter (Goethe)
See *Die Natürliche Tochter*
"The Natural Death of Love" (Crabbe) **26**:100, 109, 111, 147
"The Natural History" (Thoreau) **7**:396
"Natural History Letters" (Clare) **9**:116
The Natural History of Birds (Smith) **115**:126, 211
"The Natural History of German Life" (Eliot) **89**:212, 234, 260, 266; **118**:53-4, 189
Natural History of Intellect and Other Papers (Emerson) **38**:172; **98**:55-60
"Natural History of Massachusetts" (Thoreau) **138**:83, 119, 127, 154
"Natural History of the Intellect" (Emerson) **1**:302; **38**:142, 147, 180; **98**:7-8, 190
"The Natural History of the Vale of Belvoir" (Crabbe) **121**:44
The Natural History Prose Writings of John Clare (Clare) **86**:129, 172
"Natural Science and Spirit World" (Engels) **85**:40
Natural Selection (Darwin)
See *On the Origin of Species by Means of Natural Selection or the Preservation of Favoured Races in the Struggle for Life*
"Naturam furca expellas" (Arany) **34**:21
"Nature" (Alcott) **1**:23
"Nature" (Emerson) **98**:109, 143-46
"Nature" (Longfellow) **2**:488
"Nature" (Mill) **11**:359, 379
"Nature" (Turgenev) **21**:431
"Nature" (Very) **9**:376, 380, 387
Nature (Emerson) **1**:275, 285, 287, 293, 300-01, 305-06, 309; **38**:143, 146, 169, 171, 173-74, 176-78, 180-81, 183, 186, 194-200, 202, 208-10; **98**:3, 7, 9, 17, 21, 24-7, 32, 35, 47, 57-9, 63, 65, 99, 107, 109, 111-12, 115-16, 126, 131-33, 160, 189
"Nature II" (Emerson) **38**:184
"Nature and Art" (Newman) **38**:343
Nature and Art (Inchbald) **62**:132-6, 139-40, 144, 161, 180
"The Nature and Artifice of Toryism" (Brackenridge) **7**:44
"Nature and Books" (Jefferies) **47**:143
Nature and Eternity (Jefferies) **47**:114
Nature and Human Nature (Haliburton) **15**:124-27, 131, 136, 145
"Nature as Discipline" (Emerson) **1**:295, 309
La Nature et l'art (Charriere) **66**:126
"Nature in the Louvre" (Jefferies) **47**:94, 101, 138
"Nature Intelligible" (Very) **9**:390
"Nature is not what you think" (Tyutchev)
See "Ne to, chto mnite vy, priroda"
"Nature morte" (Corbière) **43**:28
"Nature Myths" (Symonds) **34**:336
Nature near London (Jefferies) **47**:112, 133-36, 138
The Nature of Evil, Considered in a Letter to the Reverend Edward Beecher, D.D., Author of "The Conflict of the Ages" (James) **53**:184, 235
"The Nature of Faith in Relation to Reason" (Newman) **38**:307; **99**:300
"The Nature of Poetry" (Dobell) **43**:60-1, 66-7
"Nature on the Roof" (Jefferies) **47**:137
"Nature Teaches Us of Time and Its Duration" (Very) **9**:388
Nature, the Utility of Religion, and Theism (Mill) **11**:358, 365; **58**:338
"Nature-Notes 1877-'81" (Whitman) **81**:369-70
"Nature's Beauty" (Sigourney) **21**:293
"Nature's Help for the Soul" (Very) **9**:387
Die Natürliche Tochter (Goethe) **4**:167, 222
Natur-Philosophie (Schelling) **30**:122, 124
"The Naughty Boy" (Andersen) **79**:25, 88
Naval History of the United States (Cooper) **54**:256
La navette (Becque) **3**:15-16
"La navicella Greca" (Solomos) **15**:405
"Navigation" (Mickiewicz)
See "Żegluga"
"Nay Tell Me Not Today the Publish'd Shame" (Whitman) **31**:435
"Nayezdy" (Bestuzhev) **131**:167, 176, 208
Nazar Stodolja (Shevchenko) **54**:365, 367-8, 381, 391
"Le Nazaréen" (Leconte de Lisle) **29**:231
"Ne bod'mo šalobarde! Moskvičanov" (Preseren) **127**:314
"N'e de morte" (Castro) **78**:8
"Ne podrazhay: svoeobrazen genity..." (Baratynsky) **103**:3
"Ne raz seba ia voproshaiu strogo" (Pavlova) **138**:15
Ne tak zhiví kak khóchetsya (Ostrovsky) **30**:102; **57**:197-8, 201-2, 220
"Ne to, chto mnite vy, priroda" (Tyutchev) **34**:398
Ne v svoi sani ne sadis! (Ostrovsky) **30**:96, 101, 110, 113; **57**:198, 201, 208-9
"Ne ver, ne ver poetu, deva" (Tyutchev) **34**:400, 404
Ne vse kotu maslenitsa (Ostrovsky) **30**:104, 112
"Neal Malone" (Carleton) **3**:89, 93
"Neapol" (Pavlova) **138**:53-54
"Near Hastings" (Dutt) **29**:122
"Near the camp stood a handsome youth" (Bestuzhev)
See "Blliz stana yunosha prekrasnyy . . ."
"A Nearness to Tremendousness" (Dickinson) **21**:77
"Die Nebensonnen" (Muller) **73**:366, 393, 396
'Nebo bleshchet biryuzoyu' (Pavlova) **138**:4
"Nebuchadnezzar's Dream" (Keats) **73**:333
"Necedad yanqui" (Silva) **114**:263-64

The Necessity of Atheism (Shelley) **18**:374
"Necessity of Religion, Especially in Adversity" (Murray) **63**:207
"Nechto o gluptsakh" (Bestuzhev) **131**:168
"The Neckan" (Arnold) **6**:66
"The Necklace" (Maupassant)
See "La parure"
"Necrologia. Exequias del Conde de Campo Alange" (Larra) **130**:238, 278
"Nečto o naukax, iskusstvax, i proveščenii" (Karamzin) **3**:284, 289
"Ned Bratts" (Browning) **19**:117
"Ned Connor" (Harpur) **114**:102, 150
"Ned M'Keown" (Carleton) **3**:92
Ned Myers (Cooper) **54**:274
"Nedonosok" (Baratynsky) **103**:16, 21
"Needlework" (Tonna) **135**:217
"Néférou-Ra" (Leconte de Lisle) **29**:215
Die Negersklaven (Kotzebue) **25**:141, 143, 145
"Neglect of Divine Calls and Warnings" (Newman) **38**:304, 309
"Negra Sombra" (Castro) **78**:24
"Une négresse par le démon secouée" (Mallarmé) **41**:241, 250, 280
"The Negro Boy's Lament" (Opie) **65**:175
"The Negro Boy's Tale" (Opie) **65**:156
The Negro in the American Rebellion: His Heroism and His Fidelity (Brown) **2**:48, 51-53; **89**:143
The Negro in the Rebellion (Brown)
See *The Negro in the American Rebellion: His Heroism and His Fidelity*
The Negro of Peter the Great (Pushkin)
See *Arap Petra Velikogo*
Negro Slavery Described By a Negro: Being the Narrative of Ashton Warner, a Native of St. Vincent's (Moodie) **113**:310
The Negro Slaves (Kotzebue)
See *Die Negersklaven*
"Negro Speculation" (Horton) **87**:102
"A négy ökrös szekér" (Petofi) **21**:264
"La neige" (Vigny) **7**:474; **102**:335, 366-67
"The Neighbour-in-Law" (Child) **6**:201
The Neighbours: A Story of Every-Day Life (Bremer)
See *Grannarne*
"Neighbours on the Green" (Oliphant) **61**:217
"Neihausen Castle" (Bestuzhev)
See "Zamok Neigauzen"
"Neiztrohnjeno srce" (Preseren) **127**:298
Nekam berit (Smolenskin) **30**:192, 195
Nekuda (Leskov) **25**:225, 237, 250-53
"Nell and I" (Foster) **26**:285
Nell Cook (Barham) **77**:9, 36
Nell Gwynne (Jerrold) **2**:401
"Nelle nozze della sorella Paolina" (Leopardi) **129**:219, 327-32, 334-35
"Nelly Bly" (Foster) **26**:287, 291
"Nelly Was a Lady" (Foster) **26**:286, 291
"Nem kell dér" (Arany) **34**:21
Nemesis of Faith (Froude) **43**:177, 192-93, 195, 202, 204, 208-09, 217
"A nemzetgyüléshez" (Petofi) **21**:279
"A nemzethez" (Petofi) **21**:280
"Nemzeti dal—Talpra magyar" (Petofi) **21**:280, 286
"Le nénuphar blanc" (Mallarmé) **4**:376; **41**:279-80
"Nénuphar blanc" (Mallarmé)
See "Le nénuphar blanc"
"Neobyknovennaya istoriya" (Goncharov) **1**:367
"The Neophytes" (Shevchenko) **54**:390, 397
"Neostorožnost" (Turgenev) **122**:268
Nepenthe (Darley) **2**:125-29, 131-34
"Neptune's Shore" (Woolson) **82**:276, 291
Nerina (Leopardi) **129**:304
"The Nervous Man" (Whittier) **59**:367
"Nerwy" (Norwid) **17**:372, 374
"Nesčastnaja" (Turgenev)
See "Neschastnaya"
"Neschastnaia" (Turgenev)
See "Neschastnaya"
"Neschastnaya" (Turgenev) **21**:415, 437, 440-41, 451; **122**:243, 245, 265, 267, 279, 364
"Nesmertel' nyj Golovan" (Leskov) **25**:239
The Nest of Gentlefolk (Turgenev)
See *Dvoryanskoe gnezdo*
A Nest of Gentlefolk (Turgenev)
See *Dvoryanskoe gnezdo*
"The Nest of Nightingales" (Gautier) **1**:347
"A Nest of Nightingales" (O'Brien) **21**:236
Nest of Noblemen (Turgenev)
See *Dvoryanskoe gnezdo*
Nest of the Gentry (Turgenev)
See *Dvoryanskoe gnezdo*
"Nesting Time" (Lampman) **25**:210
"Nests" (Silva)
See "Nidos"
"Neszastnye" (Nekrasov) **11**:418
"Nešzataja polosa" (Nekrasov) **11**:412-13
Netherlands (Schiller)
See *The History of the Revolt of the Netherlands*
Netley Abbey (Barham) **77**:9, 37
Der neue Amadis (Wieland) **17**:396, 399, 424
Die neue Arria (Klinger) **1**:429
Der Neue Don Quixote (Ludwig) **4**:356
Neue Erfindung (Claudius) **75**:193
Neue Gedichte (Heine) **4**:249; **54**:345
Der neue Hiob (Sacher-Masoch) **31**:287
Das neue Jahrhundert (Kotzebue) **25**:147
"Neue Liebe" (Mörike) **10**:455
Die Neue Undine (Ludwig) **4**:356
Neuer Frühling (Heine) **4**:259
"Der Neugierige" (Muller) **73**:364,370-71, 374
"Neurosis" (Casal) **131**:274
La neuvaine de la chandeleur (Nodier) **19**:378, 380, 384
"Die Neve Melusine" (Goethe) **4**:194
"Never Bet the Devil Your Head" (Poe) **16**:323-24
"Never Mind" (Harpur) **114**:101
"Never Return" (Milnes) **61**:136
"The 'Nevers' of Poetry" (Harpur) **114**:105, 117, 144
Nevinnye razskazy (Saltykov) **16**:343, 368
"Nevinnyj Prudencij" (Leskov) **25**:245
"Nevskij Avenue" (Gogol) **5**:209, 219, 227, 232, 241, 250, 252, 255; **31**:122
"Nevsky Prospect" (Gogol) **5**:209, 219, 227, 232, 241, 250, 252, 255; **31**:122
"Nevyrazimoe" (Zhukovsky) **35**:403
The New Adam and Eve (Hawthorne) **2**:325; **10**:290
"The New Age" (Arnold) **6**:51
"The New Age; or, Truth Triumphant" (Freneau) **1**:320; **111**:110
New and Old (Symonds) **34**:323
"The New and the Old" (Bryant) **6**:165; **46**:48
The New Arabian Nights (Stevenson) **5**:391, 393-94, 397, 399, 402-04, 407-08, 415, 430-31, 433; **14**:312, 335
The New Belfry of Christ Church, Oxford (Carroll) **139**:35
"The New Birth" (Very) **9**:375, 378, 390
"The New Body" (Very) **9**:394
A New Canto (Lamb) **38**:258-60
"The New Colossus" (Lazarus) **8**:416, 420, 427; **109**:289, 300, 306-07, 310, 318, 334-35, 337-40, 345, 347, 349
"The New Convert" (Cowper) **8**:132; **94**:72-3
"The New Covenant" (Paine) **62**:324
A New Drama (Tamayo y Baus)
See *Un drama nuevo*
The New Egypt (Adams) **33**:8, 18
"A New England Legend" (Whittier) **59**:360
The New England Primer, Amended and Improved . . . (Webster) **30**:409
"New England Reformers" (Emerson) **38**:157; **98**:112, 115, 117
"A New England Sketch" (Stowe) **3**:562
New England Tragedies (Longfellow) **2**:484, 487, 496-98; **45**:113, 142, 149-50, 159, 165
"New England Two Centuries Ago" (Lowell) **2**:509; **90**:195
"The New Ezekiel" (Lazarus) **8**:428; **109**:312, 338, 343
"New Fables" (Krasicki)
See *Bajki nowe*
"A New Forest Ballad" (Kingsley) **35**:218
A New French and English Dictionary (Cobbett) **49**:160
"New Guinea Converts" (Adams) **33**:18
The New Haymarket Spring Meeting (Planché) **42**:291
A New Home (Kirkland)
See *A New Home—Who'll Follow?*
A New Home—Who'll Follow? (Kirkland) **85**:251, 255-56, 259-61, 263, 265, 267-70, 274-89, 291, 293, 295-301
The New Housekeeper's Manual (Beecher) **30**:15
The New Industrial World (Fourier)
See *Le Nouveau Monde industriel et sociétaire*
"New Jerusalem and Its Citizens" (Rossetti) **50**:285
The New Justine (Sade)
See *La nouvelle Justine*
"The New Kite" (Horne) **127**:264
"The New Laocoon" (Arnold) **6**:51
New Leaves (Castro)
See *Follas novas*
New Letters (Southey) **97**:270, 276, 278-79, 290
New Letters of James Russell Lowell (Lowell) **90**:222
"The New Locksley Hall: 'Forty Years After'" (Adams) **33**:18
"New Love New Life" (Levy) **59**:96
The New Magdalen (Collins) **1**:176, 180, 182-83; **93**:5, 38
"The New Man" (Very) **9**:378, 382, 397
The New Maternity Ward (Andersen) **79**:15-17
"A New Method of Evaluation of p" (Carroll) **139**:6
"New Moon" (Cooke) **110**:9
"New Morality" (Coleridge) **111**:353
"New Morality" (Keats) **73**:316
A New Path to Fortune (Alger) **83**:91
"New Philosophy Scrapbook" (Cranch) **115**:54
New Pilgrim's Progress; or, A Christian's Painful Passage from theTown of Middle Class to the Golden City (Jefferies) **47**:93
The New Planet; or, Harlequin out of Place (Planché) **42**:290
The New Pleasing Instructor (Tenney) **122**:210
New Poems (Arnold) **6**:37; **29**:26; **89**:46, 51
New Poems (Coleridge) **90**:32
New Poems (Heine)
See *Neue Gedichte*
New Poems (Rossetti) **2**:563-4
New Poems and Variant Readings (Stevenson) **5**:427
New Poems by George Crabbe (Crabbe) **26**:139; **121**:13
New Poetical Meditations (Lamartine) **11**:245, 283
"The New Poor Laws" (Barnes) **75**:43-4, 101, 103
"New School" (Cranch) **115**:40
"The New School of American Fiction" (Levy) **59**:110
The New Schoolma'am (Alger) **83**:116, 142
"The New Sinai" (Clough) **27**:77
"The New Sirens" (Arnold) **6**:71; **126**:111
"The New South" (Lanier) **6**:245, 256, 260, 263; **118**:206, 218, 230
A New Spirit of the Age (Horne) **127**:238, 263, 285, 287
New Stories (Andersen)
See *Eventyr, fortalte for bøorn*
New Tales (Opie) **65**:171, 174, 179, 197-8

The New Timon (Bulwer-Lytton) **1**:141-42
"New Variations on an Old Theme" (Herzen) **61**:102
New Views of Christianity Socity and the Church (Brownson) **50**:47
"New Wife and the Old" (Whittier) **8**:487, 508-09, 528; **59**:350
The New Woman: In Haste and at Leisure (Linton) **41**:161, 164
"The New World" (Very) **9**:378, 397
"The New Writing" (Preseren)
See "Nova pisarija"
"The New Year" (Whittier) **8**:524
"The New Year—Rosh Hashanah, 5643" (Lazarus) **8**:420, 427; **109**:338
"A New Year's Blessing" (Alcott) **83**:5
"A New Year's Burden" (Rossetti) **4**:491
"New Year's Day" (Sedgwick) **19**:428, 444-45
"New Year's Eve" (Lamb) **10**:415; **113**:217, 235-36, 248-49, 251-52
"New Year's Eve" (Lampman) **25**:199, 201, 209
"New Year's Eve" (Landon) **15**:166
"A New Year's Lay" (Mangan) **27**:296
"The New Zealot to the Sun" (Melville) **29**:380
"Newborn Death" (Rossetti) **4**:491
The Newcomes: Memoirs of a Most Respectable Family (Thackeray) **5**:454-57, 459-61, 465-66, 472, 476, 478, 484, 488, 497-505; **14**:397, 406, 434; **43**:356, 389
A New-England Tale; or, Sketches of New-England Character and Manners (Sedgwick) **19**:424-25, 427, 430, 439, 442, 447, 450; **98**:296, 307, 321, 326, 334, 342
"News from Nowhere" (Morris) **4**:425, 436, 439-41, 445-46
"News from Pannonia" (Allingham) **25**:11
News of the Night; or, A Trip to Niagara (Bird) **1**:89, 90, 92-93
"Newscarrier's Address" (Trumbull) **30**:375
The News-paper (Crabbe) **26**:78-9, 81, 110, 132; **121**:15, 18, 21, 23, 26, 83, 89
Newstead Abbey (Irving) **2**:373
Newton Forster (Marryat) **3**:317
Next Door Neighbours (Inchbald) **62**:144-6, 149
"Nezakonska mati" (Preseren) **127**:292, 298
"N'hay peor meiga qu'un-ha gran pena" (Castro) **78**:7
Ni jamais ni toujours (Kock) **16**:246-47
"Niagara" (Lenau) **16**:269, 283
"Niagara" (Sigourney) **21**:296, 299; **87**:326, 333-34
"A Niagara Landscape" (Lampman) **25**:210
Die Nibelungen (Hebbel) **43**:230, 234-35, 240, 242-44, 246, 261, 276, 278, 297, 300
Nibelungen-Lied (Fouqué) **2**:265
The Nibelungs (Hebbel)
See *Die Nibelungen*
The Nibelung's Ring (Wagner)
See *Der Ring des Nibelungen*
Nicholas Nickleby (Dickens)
See *The Life and Adventures of Nicholas Nickleby*
Nick of the Woods; or, The Jobbenainosay (Bird) **1**:85-86, 88-89, 91-92
"Nicolas Flamel" (Nerval) **1**:484
"Le Nid d'hirondelles" (Desbordes-Valmore) **97**:12
"Le Nid solitaire" (Desbordes-Valmore) **97**:28
"Nidos" (Silva) **114**:316
Nieboska komedyia (Krasiński) **4**:301
Niels Lyhne (Jacobsen) **34**:142-47, 150-58, 160-62, 166-68
Niera Baranoff (Sacher-Masoch) **31**:302
Nieve (Casal) **131**:235-36, 255-58, 264-65, 268-70
Niewola (Norwid) **17**:369, 377
"Nigger Book" (Rimbaud) **4**:456
The Nigger of Peter the Great (Pushkin)
See *Arap Petra Velikogo*
"Night" (Blake) **13**:181, 220-21; **37**:3, 6, 9, 13-14, 37, 40, 54, 62, 64, 66, 69, 82, 84, 92
"Night" (Brontë) **71**:106
"Night" (Browning) **79**:94, 101, 153
"Night" (Hugo) **3**:262
"Night" (Lampman) **25**:175, 209, 217
"Night" (Lanier) **6**:237
"Night" (Thomson) **18**:418
"Night" (Very) **9**:393
"Night and Day" (Lanier) **6**:237; **118**:234, 240
Night and Day (Kivi)
See *Yö ja päivä*
"Night and Morning" (Browning) **79**:94, 101
Night and Morning (Bulwer-Lytton) **1**:140, 145, 150; **45**:19, 22, 69
"Night and the Merry Man" (Browning) **1**:126
"Night and the Soul" (Cranch) **115**:5
"A Night at Sea" (Griffin) **7**:215
A Night in Roskilde (Andersen) **79**:14
"The Night Journey of a River" (Bryant) **6**:165; **46**:38-9
"The Night Mare or Superstitions Dream" (Clare) **86**:113
"Night of Hell" (Rimbaud)
See "Nuit de l'enfer"
"A Night of Storm" (Lampman) **25**:188, 209-10
"The Night of Taras" (Shevchenko)
See "Tarasova nic"
"A Night of Terror" (Maginn) **8**:440
"Night on Board Ship" (Bestuzhev)
See "Noch' na korable"
"A Night on Salisbury Plain" (Wordsworth) **111**:265-68
"Night on the Prairies" (Whitman) **4**:577
"Night Owls" (Leskov)
See "Polunoščniki"
"A Night Scene" (Ridge) **82**:182, 184
"Night Sketches" (Hawthorne) **23**:204; **39**:229
"Night Sounds" (Meyer)
See "Nachtgeräusche"
The Night Watches (Bonaventura)
See *Nachtwachen*
A Night with the National Guard (Scribe)
See *Encore une nuit de la Garde Nationale; ou, Le poste de la barrière*
"The Nightingale" (Andersen)
See "Nattergalen"
"The Nightingale" (Coleridge) **9**:131, 132, 150; **99**:2, 66; **111**:200, 307, 317, 358
"Nightingale" (Keats)
See "Ode to a Nightingale"
"The Nightingale" (Wordsworth) **12**:387
The Nightingale (Robertson) **35**:333, 335, 354, 356, 361, 363, 369
"The Nightingale and Glow-worm" (Cowper) **94**:121
"The nightingale and the cuckoo" (Pushkin)
See "Solovei i Kukushka"
"The Nightingale and the Rose" (Crawford) **127**:187-88
"The Nightingales" (Krylov) **1**:435
"The Nightingales Nest" (Clare) **9**:105; **86**:144
"A Night-Piece" (Wordsworth) **12**:446, 451
"The Nights" (Musset)
See "Les nuits"
A Night's Adventure (Robertson) **35**:354
"Nights at Home" (Silva)
See "Las noches del hogar"
"The Nights in the Mountains" (Isaacs)
See "Las noches en la montaña"
"A Night's Lodging" (Hugo) **3**:262
"Nights of Jealousy" (Runeberg)
See "Svartsjukans nätter"
"The Nights of Ramazan" (Nerval)
See "Les nuits de Ramazan"
"A Night's Work" (Gaskell)
See "A Dark Night's Work"
Nigorie (Ichiyō) **49**:331, 336-37, 345-48, 351, 353-54
"Nihilismo" (Casal) **131**:274
Nikita Gaidai (Shevchenko)
See *Nikita Hayday*
Nikita Hayday (Shevchenko) **54**:367, 386, 391
"The Nile" (Hunt) **70**:263
The Nile Basin (Burton) **42**:41
"Nima" (Isaacs) **70**:304, 308
"Nimuë" (Tennyson) **30**:249; **65**:378
Nina (Bremer) **11**:20, 34-35
Nina Balatka (Trollope) **101**:313, 334
La Nina de Guatemala (Martí) **63**:104
"Nina Replies" (Rimbaud)
See "Les reparties de Nina"
"9 from 8" (Lanier) **118**:227-28
986 (Dickinson) **77**:129, 173
978 (Dickinson) **77**:121
960 (Dickinson) **77**:118
930 (Dickinson) **77**:122-24
922 (Dickinson) **77**:68
1962 (Dickinson) **77**:162
"Nineteenth Century Scholastics" (Pisarev)
See "Sxolastiki xix veka"
"19th March 1823" (Zhukovsky) **35**:381
"A XIX század koltöi" (Petofi) **21**:264
"Nineteenth-Century Poets" (Petofi)
See "A XIX század koltöi"
98 (Dickinson) **77**:120, 163
Ninety-Three (Hugo)
See *Quatre-vingt treize*
"Ninguna diga queén es, que sus obras lo dirán" (Lizardi) **30**:67
El niño de la bola (Alarcon) **1**:12-15
"Niobé" (Leconte de Lisle) **29**:222, 224-25, 238, 245-46
"Nirvâna" (Lanier) **6**:236, 238, 270; **118**:235
"Nise no en" (Ueda Akinari) **131**:20-22, 52-53, 56
"Nissen hos Spekhøkeren" (Andersen) **79**:28, 55, 63, 73
"Die Nixe" (Pavlova) **138**:12
"Nixe Binsefuss" (Mörike) **10**:455
"The Nixy's Chord" (Boyesen) **135**:15, 33-34
No (Cooke) **110**:50, 66
"No Coward Soul Is Mine" (Brontë) **16**:70, 74, 86, 88; **35**:147
"No doubt 'twere Heresy, or something worse" (Coleridge) **90**:33
No hay mal que por bien no venga (Tamayo y Baus) **1**:569
"No Man Saw Awe, Nor to His House" (Dickinson) **21**:83
No más mostrador (Larra) **17**:267, 273-74, 279; **130**:228
No más mostrator (Larra)
See *No más mostrador*
"No Name" (Gordon) **21**:161, 164, 166, 176
No Name (Collins) **1**:174-75, 180, 182, 185, 187; **18**:63-6; **93**:5, 7, 11-12, 19-23, 34, 36-8, 44, 46, 50-3, 61-3, 65-6
"No Poet Is Bill" (Kendall) **12**:194
"A nő teremtése" (Madach) **19**:369
"No, Thank You, John!" (Rossetti) **66**:331
No Thoroughfare (Collins) **1**:185
No Trifling with Love (Musset)
See *On ne badine pas avec l'amour*
No Way Out (Leskov)
See *Nekuda*
"No Worst, There Is None" (Hopkins) **17**:261
"Noah's Ark" (Muller) **73**:353
Noah's Warning over Methuselah's Grave (Brontë) **109**:4, 14
Le Noble (Charriere) **66**:121-2, 172-6, 178
The Noble Heart (Lewes) **25**:284, 298-99
The Noble Jilt (Trollope) **101**:266
A Noble Life (Craik) **38**:107, 116
The Noble Peasant (Holcroft) **85**:192
"Noble Sisters" (Rossetti) **2**:575; **66**:302, 312, 352
The Nobleman (Charriere)
See *Le Noble*
A Nobleman's Nest (Turgenev)
See *Dvoryanskoe gnezdo*
"The Nobleman's Wedding" (Allingham) **25**:7-8, 17

Noblemen's Home (Turgenev)
See *Dvoryanskoe gnezdo*
"The Nobler Lover" (Lowell) **2**:512
Nobody (Warner) **31**:338
"Noč pered roždestvom" (Gogol) **5**:217, 231
Noc tysiączna druga (Norwid) **17**:367
Les Noces d'Hérodiade (Mallarmé)
See *Hérodiade*
"Noch einmal" (Meyer) **81**:206
"Noch einmal in Gastein" (Grillparzer) **102**:175
"Noch' na korable" (Bestuzhev) **131**:185
"La Noche de difuntos" (Bécquer) **106**:96
"La Nochebuena de 1836" (Larra) **17**:276-78, 285; **130**:209, 211, 213, 237-38, 257-65, 274-75, 278-79, 281-86
"Las noches del hogar" (Silva) **114**:316
"Las noches en la montaña" (Isaacs) **70**:309
Noches tristes y día alegre (Lizardi) **30**:67, 70-73
"Nochnoi smotr" (Zhukovsky) **35**:398
Noctes Ambrosianae (Wilson) **5**:553-57, 559-60, 562-63, 565-69
Noctes Ambrosiannae (Lockhart) **6**:305
"Nocturnal Boat" (Meyer)
See "Im Spätboot"
"Nocturnal Sketch" (Hood) **16**:236
"Nocturnal Song of a Wandering Shepherd in Asia" (Leopardi)
See "Canto notturno di un pastore errante dell'Asia"
"Nocturne" (Silva)
See "Nocturno III"
"Nocturne II" (Desbordes-Valmore) **97**:5
"Nocturne of a Wandering Shepherd in Asia" (Leopardi)
See "Canto notturno di un pastore errante dell'Asia"
"Nocturne Parisien" (Verlaine) **2**:624
"Nocturne vulgaire" (Rimbaud) **4**:487; **35**:323; **82**:232-33, 248
"Nocturno III" (Silva) **114**:261-62, 267, 270, 294-97, 299-304
"Noget" (Andersen) **79**:75, 77
"A Noiseless Patient Spider" (Whitman) **31**:379, 442; **81**:309
"Nola" (Isaacs) **70**:310
Noli me tangere (Rizal) **27**:407-09, 411, 415-16, 419-29, 431-32
"Nominalist" (Emerson) **98**:143-45
"Nominalist and Realist" (Emerson) **38**:173, 208; **98**:65, 69, 71, 151
"Nomography" (Bentham) **38**:92
"Non son chi fui" (Foscolo) **8**:278
Nonsense Songs, Stories, Botany, and Alphabets (Lear) **3**:295, 297, 304
"Noon" (Tyutchev)
See "Polden"
"Nora of the Amber Hair" (Ferguson) **33**:301
"Nora or Records of a Poet's Love" (Harpur) **114**:138
Nordens mytologi (Grundtvig) **1**:403
Das Nordlicht: Proben er neuen russichen Literatur (Pavlova) **138**:11-12, 30
"Die Nordsee" (Heine) **4**:248-49, 254-55, 266
Die Nordsee (Heine) **4**:258-59, 266, 269; **54**:318
"Normal School for Women" (Faustino)
See "Escuela normal de mujeres"
Norman Maurice: The Man of the People (Simms) **3**:502, 505, 514
"Un normand" (Maupassant) **83**:171-72
"Norna; or, The Witch's Curse" (Alcott) **83**:4
"A Norse Atlantis" (Boyesen) **135**:15, 20, 33
"The Norse Emigrant" (Boyesen) **135**:5, 25
"A Norse Stev" (Boyesen) **135**:5, 10, 18, 36
Norseland Tales (Boyesen) **135**:8, 15
A Norseman's Pilgrimage (Boyesen) **135**:6, 11, 24-25
"The Norseman's Ride" (Taylor) **89**:306
"Norsemen" (Whittier) **8**:486
"The North American Indian" (Richardson) **55**:313
North American Men (Martí) **63**:74
North American Scenes (Martí)
See *Escenas norteamericanas*
North and South (Gaskell) **5**:183, 187, 189-92, 196-97, 201, 204-05; **70**:119-20, 123, 129, 133, 152, 154, 187, 189, 193, 196, 198-99, 205-06, 219-20; **97**:110, 127, 134; **137**:9, 17, 20, 33, 40, 42, 64, 101, 104, 124, 129, 146-47, 163, 167, 170-71, 173-77
"The North and the South" (Browning) **61**:24
North Sea (Heine)
See *Die Nordsee*
"The North Wind" (Brontë) **4**:44
Northanger Abbey (Austen) **1**:30-1, 33-4, 36-41, 44, 49-51, 53, 58-61, 64; **13**:68, 73, 76, 104; **19**:8, 14, 17, 38, 44, 62; **33**:68, 75-6, 79-80, 96; **51**:1-73; **81**:3-5, 12, 18, 70, 77-78; **95**:12, 30, 49; **119**:14, 17-18, 25-6, 28, 31-5, 37-8, 47, 51-3
"Northangerland's Name" (Brontë) **109**:30
Northern Antiquities (Percy) **95**:313, 321, 364
"The Northern Farmer" (Tennyson) **30**:222, 226, 233
"The Northern Farmer—New Style" (Tennyson) **30**:280
"The Northern Farmer—Old Style" (Tennyson) **30**:280
Northern Lights (Pavlova)
See *Das Nordlicht: Proben er neuen russichen Literatur*
Northern Tour (Cobbett) **49**:159
Northern Travel (Taylor) **89**:346
Northern Worthies (Coleridge)
See *Lives of the Northern Worthies*
The Northern Worthies (Coleridge)
See *Lives of the Northern Worthies*
Northumberland Houshold Book (Percy)
See *Household Book of the Earl of Northumberland in 1512*
Northwood: A Tale of New England (Hale) **75**:280, 295, 301, 311-315, 317-319, 321,326, 328-330, 336-7, 339, 341, 343-4, 349, 357
"Norway and the Norwegians" (Boyesen) **135**:15
"Norwegian Painters" (Boyesen) **135**:32
"Nos Anglais" (Maupassant) **83**:176
Nos fils (Michelet) **31**:214, 218, 226, 248, 260
"The Nose" (Gogol) **5**:219, 226-29, 232, 234, 254-56; **31**:103, 111, 117, 144
"Nostalgias" (Casal) **131**:248
"Not as These" (Rossetti) **77**:353
Not Paul but Jesus (Bentham) **38**:92, 98-9
"Not Sing at Night" (Barnes) **75**:22
Not So Bad As We Seem (Bulwer-Lytton) **45**:22
"Not That From Life, and All Its Woes" (Bryant) **46**:21
"Not Yet" (Bryant) **46**:7
"Not Youth Pertains to Me" (Whitman) **81**:316
"Notas perdidas" (Silva) **114**:300
"Note on George Meredith" (Thomson) **18**:402
"A Note on Realism" (Stevenson) **63**:229, 234
"Note on the Projected Gathering at Stephen the Great's Tomb at Putna" (Eminescu) **33**:272
"Note sur la Grèce" (Chateaubriand) **134**:7
The Note-Book of William Blake (Blake) **13**:240, 242-43
"Notebooks" (Dostoevsky) **119**:130
Notebooks (Whitman) **81**:358-60
Notebooks and Journals of Dorothy and Mary Wordsworth (Wordsworth) **138**:252, 254, 257-58
Notebooks for "The Idiot" (Dostoevsky) **119**:71, 81-4, 86-9, 98-9, 140, 143, 146, 159-60
Notebooks on Transmutations of Species (Darwin) **57**:141, 144-6, 153
"Notes" (Gogol) **5**:224
Notes and Journal of Travel in Europe, 1804-05 (Irving) **2**:385
Notes de voyage (Flaubert)
See *Voyages*
Notes de Voyage (Mérimée) **65**:87
"Notes for the Biography of a Distinguée" (Kirkland) **85**:270-72
Notes from the Underground (Dostoevsky)
See *Zapiski iz podpol'ya*
Notes from Underground (Dostoevsky)
See *Zapiski iz podpol'ya*
Notes littéraires (Sade) **47**:333
Notes of a Hunter (Turgenev)
See *Zapiski okhotnika*
Notes of a Journey through France and Italy (Hazlitt) **29**:153; **82**:154, 161
"Notes of a Madman" (Gogol)
See "Diary of a Madman"
"Notes of a Three-Days' Tour to the Netherlands" (Carlyle) **70**:89-90, 93
The Notes of a Young Man (Herzen) **10**:348; **61**:108
Notes of an Old Man (Fredro)
See *Zapiski starucha*
Notes of an Orenburg Province Rifle Hunter (Aksakov)
See *Zapiski ruzheynago okhotnika*
"Notes of Archeological Rambles" (Mérimée) **6**:352
Notes on a Journey (Petofi)
See *Úti jegyzetek*
"Notes on Ancient and Modern Confederacies" (Madison) **126**:297
Notes on Ancient Britain and the Britons (Barnes) **75**:40, 46, 107
"Notes on Eighteenth-Century Russian History" (Pushkin) **83**:309
Notes on England (Taine)
See *Notes sur l'Angleterre*
Notes on Fishing (Aksakov)
See *Zapiski ob uzhenyi ryby*
"Notes on Form in Art" (Eliot) **4**:153; **13**:334-35, 342
Notes on Paris (Taine)
See *Notes sur Paris: Vie et opinions de M. Frédéric-Thomas Graindorge*
"Notes on Reynolds" (Blake) **13**:179
"Notes on Style" (Symonds) **34**:336
"Notes on the Advisability of Simplifying and Standardizing Orthography in America" (Bello)
See "Indicaciones sobre la Conveniencia de Simplificar y Uniformar la Ortografía en América"
"Notes on the Religious Tradition" (Clough) **27**:85
Notes on the State of Virginia (Jefferson) **11**:148, 166, 172-73, 192, 199, 203, 205-10; **103**:105, 110-11 121, 124, 128-36, 144-6, 157, 159, 186, 194, 203, 207, 221, 227-29, 231-36, 240-47, 250-51
"Notes on Theism" (Symonds) **34**:336
Notes on Virginia (Jefferson)
See *Notes on the State of Virginia*
Notes sur l'Angleterre (Taine) **15**:427-28, 431, 437, 441, 452, 462-63
Notes sur Paris: Vie et opinions de M. Frédéric-Thomas Graindorge (Taine) **15**:424, 436-37, 440, 449-50, 452
Notes upon Some of Shakespeare's Plays (Kemble) **18**:192
Notice (Gautier) **1**:351
Notions élémentaires de linguistique (Nodier) **19**:401
Notions of the Americans (Cooper) **1**:218; **27**:153; **54**:254-6, 283
"Notizia intorno a Didimo Chierico" (Foscolo) **97**:90-1
Notre coeur (Maupassant) **1**:447-48, 450, 452, 459, 464, 468, 470; **42**:169, 201; **83**:180-81
Notre Dame des Soirs (Laforgue) **53**:281
Notre-Dame de Paris (Hugo) **3**:236-40, 245, 251, 253-55, 257-59, 261, 263, 267, 274, 276; **10**:367, 369, 371, 373, 377; **21**:190-231
"Notus Ignoto" (Taylor) **89**:317-18

Nous ne sommes pas le troupeau (Verlaine) **51**:363
Nous n'irons plus au bois (Banville) **9**:18
Nous tour (Banville) **9**:20, 30
"Le nouveau Diogène" (Beranger) **34**:30
Le nouveau monde (Villiers de l'Isle Adam) **3**:582
Le Nouveau Monde industriel et sociétaire (Fourier) **51**:156, 161
Le nouveau Pourceaugnac (Scribe) **16**:388
"Un nouveau-né" (Desbordes-Valmore) **97**:6, 9, 13, 22, 24
Nouveaux contes cruels (Villiers de l'Isle Adam) **3**:582, 586
Les nouveaux jeux de l'amour et du hasard (Scribe) **16**:388
Nouveaux lundis (Sainte-Beuve) **5**:328, 331, 339, 341
Nouvelle confidences (Lamartine) **11**:265
La Nouvelle Justine (Leopardi) **129**:304
La nouvelle Justine (Sade) **3**:480; **47**:309-12, 334, 336, 350, 365
Nouvelles asiatiques (Gobineau) **17**:68-9, 92-3, 96, 103
Nouvelles histoires extraordinaires (Baudelaire) **29**:67, 92
Nouvelles lettres d'un voyageur (Sand) **57**:366, 368
Nouvelles méditations poétiques (Lamartine) **11**:245, 248, 254, 269-70, 273, 275-77, 283
"Nouvelles Variations sur le Point-du-Jour" (Verlaine) **51**:361
Nov' (Turgenev) **21**:402, 412, 414, 419, 421, 432, 435, 437-39, 441, 445; **37**:394, 404, 417, 443; **122**:249, 257, 286-89, 292, 337, 341, 376
"Nova pisarija" (Preseren) **127**:293, 298, 312-13
"Novalis and the Blue Flower" (Boyesen) **135**:6
A Novel in Letters (Pushkin)
See *Roman v pismakh*
A Novel in Seven Letters (Bestuzhev)
See *Roman v semi pis'makh*
Novel of the War of 1808 (Runeberg) **41**:314
Novelas cortas: Cuentos amartorios (Alarcon) **1**:14-15
Novelas cortas: Historietas nacionales (Alarcon) **1**:14-15
Novelas cortas: Narraciones inverosimiles (Alarcon) **1**:14-15
Novellas and Sketches (Jacobsen)
See *Noveller of Skitser*
Novellen (Tieck) **5**:514
Noveller of Skitser (Jacobsen) **34**:171
The Novels of Charles Brockden Brown (Brown) **22**:8
"November" (Clare) **9**:114; **86**:97, 103-04, 110, 168
"November" (Coleridge) **90**:26
"November" (Taylor) **89**:316
November Boughs (Whitman) **4**:551, 576
"Novembersonne" (Meyer) **81**:146-48, 155
Novembre: Fragments de style quelconque (Flaubert) **2**:249, 255-6; **10**:139, 160, 170; **19**:282, 288-91, 299, 304, 309; **62**:83, 85-91, 95; **66**:269-72; **135**:107
The Novice (Lermontov)
See *Mtsyri*
The Novice of St. Dominick (Morgan) **29**:389-90
"El novillo y el toro viejo" (Lizardi) **30**:68
"Novissima verba" (Lamartine) **11**:270, 278-79
"Now" (Browning) **79**:161
"Now Finalè to the Shore" (Whitman) **31**:389
"Now Precedent Songs, Farewell" (Whitman) **31**:434
"Now Sleeps the Crimson Petal" (Tennyson) **30**:279-80
"Now You Shall Speak" (Meyer)
See "Jetzt rede du"
Nowa dejanira (Slowacki)
See *Fantazy*
"Now—But One Moment, Let Me Stay" (Brontë) **109**:31
The Nowlans (Banim and Banim) **13**:117, 119-22, 124, 128-31, 133-35, 141-43
"Nox" (Leconte de Lisle) **29**:243
Le nozze di Figaro (Da Ponte) **50**:76, 79-82, 85, 92-3, 96, 98
Le nuage rose (Sand) **42**:314
Nubatama no Maki (Ueda Akinari) **131**:63, 68
"Nuesta America" (Martí) **63**:131, 153
"Nuestro pecado de los folletines" (Faustino) **123**:378
"La nuit" (Banville) **9**:30
"Nuit d' Août" (Musset) **7**:255, 261-62, 274
"Une nuit de Clèopâtre" (Gautier) **1**:341, 344-45, 348, 350; **59**:10-11, 13-14, 30, 33, 42
"Nuit de Décembre" (Musset) **7**:255, 262, 274, 280
"Une nuit de Don Juan" (Flaubert) **10**:176
"Nuit de l'enfer" (Rimbaud) **4**:452, 474, 481-82; **35**:289, 292, 302-03, 310, 317; **82**:218, 222-23, 225, 229, 235-36, 238, 240-45, 249, 252, 255, 257, 262
"Nuit de Mai" (Musset) **7**:255, 261-62, 274, 280-81
"Une nuit de mon âme" (Desbordes-Valmore) **97**:13, 23-4
"Nuit de Noël" (Maupassant) **83**:172, 194, 197, 223
La nuit de Noël (Sand) **42**:313
"Nuit d'hiver" (Sand) **57**:368
"Nuit d'Octobre" (Musset) **7**:255, 261
"Une Nuit que j'étais" (Baudelaire) **55**:6
La nuit Vénitienne; ou, Les noces de laurette (Musset) **7**:259-60, 267, 275-76, 280-81
"Les nuits" (Musset) **7**:255-58, 262-63, 266, 272, 274-75
"Nuits de juin" (Hugo) **3**:273
"Les nuits de Ramazan" (Nerval) **1**:475, **67**:311, 333
Les nuits d'Octobre (Nerval) **1**:482; **67**:313, 324, 332-33, 336, 357
Numa Roumsetan (Daudet) **1**:233-35, 237, 239, 241, 243, 246, 250-51
Number 91 (Alger) **83**:112
"Number Fifteen, Stolt" (Runeberg)
See "N:o femton, Stolt"
Number Seventeen (Kingsley) **107**:192
"Number Two" (Cooke) **110**:35-6
"Numbers; on the Majority and the Remnant" (Arnold) **6**:41, 46; **126**:106
"Numbness" (Muller)
See "Erstarrung"
Nummisuutarit (Kivi) **30**:48, 50-1, 53, 55, 64
"Numpholeptos" (Browning) **19**:88, 153
"The Nun" (Rogers) **69**:80
"Nuori Karhunampuja" (Kivi) **30**:51
"Nuptial Sleep" (Rossetti) **4**:494, 496-97; **77**:326, 338-41
"Nuremberg" (Longfellow) **2**:473, 479; **45**:116
"Nurse Green" (Lamb) **125**:362
"Nurse Miller" (Crawford) **127**:220
The Nursery Alice (Carroll) **139**:120, 147
Nursery and Household Tales (Grimm and Grimm)
See *Kinder-und Hausmärchen*
Nursery Reminiscences (Barham) **77**:6, 9
"Nurse's Song" (Blake) **13**:220; **37**:3, 9, 24, 31, 41-2, 50, 57, 61, 66, 71-2, 92
"The Nurse's Story" (Barham) **77**:33
"Nursing" (Lamb) **125**:332
"Nutcracker" (Hoffmann) **2**:351-52
"Nutting" (Wordsworth) **38**:370; **111**:227, 250
Nydia (Boker) **125**:25-26, 28, 41, 58, 76-78
"The Nymphs" (Hunt) **70**:291
The Nymphs (Hunt) **1**:412, 415, 421
"O Blest Unfabled Incense Tree" (Darley) **2**:133
"O Breathe Not His Name" (Moore) **6**:391, 398-99
"O bylom, o pogibshem . . ." (Pavlova) **138**:20
"O Captain! My Captain!" (Whitman) **4**:602; **31**:438; **81**:319, 321
"O chem ty voesh, vetr nochnoy?" (Tyutchev) **34**:398
"O Dearest Friend! Now Thou Art Joyful" (Zhukovsky) **35**:403
"O God! While I in Pleasure's Wiles" (Brontë) **109**:37
"O Jeannie There's Naethin tae Fear Ye" (Hogg) **4**:284
"O Krytykach i Recenzentach" (Mickiewicz) **101**:191-92
"O kühler Wald" (Brentano) **1**:105
"O Land of Empire, Art and Love!" (Clough) **27**:103
"O Let the Solid Ground" (Tennyson) **30**:242
"O light canoe, where dost thou glide?" (Crawford) **127**:151, 155
"O Living Always, Always Dying" (Whitman) **81**:308-09
"O Lord, I Will Praise Thee" (Cowper) **8**:131
"O Love builds on the azure sea" (Crawford) **127**:151
"O May, Thou Art a Merry Time" (Darley) **2**:133
"O Me! O Life!" (Whitman) **81**:315
"O, Mother" (Eminescu) **131**:297
"O my prophetic soul!" (Tyutchev)
See "O veschaya dusha moya!"
"O My Thoughts My Thoughts" (Shevchenko)
See "Dumy moji dumy moji"
"O mysl! tebe udel tsvetka:..." (Baratynsky) **103**:11
"O Nightingale!" (Wordsworth) **111**:323
"O Qui Me" (Clough) **27**:103
"O saisons, ô châteaux!" (Rimbaud) **82**:231, 233, 247
"O stanowisku Polski z Bożych i ludzkich względów" (Krasiński) **4**:313
"O Stern und Blume, Geist und Kleid" (Brentano) **1**:105
"O Strength and Stay, Upholding All Creation" (Cowper) **8**:116
O. T. (Andersen) **7**:16; **79**:18
"O Tell Me, Friends" (Clough) **27**:52
"O tend my flowers" (Dickinson) **77**:148
"O Thou Whose Image" (Clough) **27**:53
"O thought! the flower's fate is yours:..." (Baratynsky)
See "O mysl! tebe udel tsvetka:..."
"O triste..." (Verlaine) **51**:384
"O ver: ty, nezhnaya, dorozhe slavy mne;..." (Baratynsky) **103**:11
"O veschaya dusha moya!" (Tyutchev) **34**:397
"O, Wand'ring is the Miller's Joy" (Muller)
See "Das Wandern ist des Müllers Lust"
"O Welt, du schöne Welt, du" (Eichendorff) **8**:233
"O Wind, Why Do You Never Rest" (Rossetti) **50**:306
"O World, O Life, O Time" (Shelley) **93**:303-04
"O! would that Fortune might bestow on me" (Boker) **125**:82
"O zabluzhdeniyakh i istine" (Baratynsky) **103**:19
"O zemście" (Norwid)
See "Z pamiętnika"
"The Oak and the Broom, A Pastoral" (Wordsworth) **111**:242
"The Oak and the Poplar" (Very) **9**:372
"Oak in Autumn" (Sigourney) **87**:332
The Oak Openings; or, The Bee Hunter (Cooper) **1**:221; **27**:139, 141-42, 145; **54**:259, 263
"The Oak Tree and the Ivy" (Field) **3**:208
"Oaks" (Castro)
See "Los robles"
Oakshott Castle, Being the Memoir of an Eccentric Nobleman (Kingsley) **107**:192-93, 195, 209
"Oars at Rest" (Meyer)
See "Eingelegte Ruder"
Oasis (Child) **73**:60, 77
The Oath (Macha) **46**:212

"The Oath of the Canadian Volunteers. A Loyal Song for Canada" (Moodie) **14**:222; **113**:308
"Ob slovesu" (Preseren) **127**:292, 298
"Der Oberamtmann und der Amtsrichter" (Gotthelf) **117**:6
Der Oberhof (Immermann) **4**:291, 293, 295, 297
Der Oberhof: A Tale of Westphalian Life (Immermann)
See *Der Oberhof*
Obermann (Senancour) **16**:423, 425, 427-28, 431-38, 441-50, 454-55
"Obermann Once More" (Arnold) **6**:51, 72; **29**:11; **89**:82, 132
"Die Obermedicinalräthin" (Hebbel) **43**:238
Oberon (Planché) **42**:273, 292
Oberon (Wieland) **17**:392-93, 396-98, 400, 402-04, 410-11
Oblomov (Goncharov) **1**:359, 361-66, 368-69, 371-80; **63**:3-5, 10, 17, 20-4, 26-30, 35-6, 41, 46
"Oblomov's Dream" (Goncharov) **1**:369, 372, 377-78; **63**:45-6
"The Oblong Box" (Poe) **55**:148
"Obman" (Leskov) **25**:265-67
Obojdennye (Leskov) **25**:232, 251-52
"Obra humana" (Silva) **114**:303
Obras completas (Bécquer) **106**:126, 168-69
Obras completas (Bello) **131**:102, 107, 109-10
Obras Completas (Faustino) **123**:319-23, 325, 346
Obras completas (Martí) **63**:122, 167
Obras Completas (Silva) **114**:296
Obras completas (Williams) **78**:23, 29, 58-59
Obras completas de D. Esteban Echeverría (Echeverria) **18**:154
Obras de doña Gertrudis de Avellaneda (Gómez de Avellaneda) **111**:3-4, 6, 9, 17, 19-25, 27-9, 75
Obras de Mariano José de Larra (Larra) **130**:193-99, 201, 203-6, 209-16, 218-20, 226, 228-29, 231, 233, 241-46, 269-76
Obras de Mariano José de Larra, Vol. 1 (Larra)
See *Obras de Mariano José de Larra*
Obras de Mariano José de Larra, Vol. 127 (Larra)
See *Obras de Mariano José de Larra*
Obras de Mariano José de Larra, Vol. 128 (Larra)
See *Obras de Mariano José de Larra*
Obras de Mariano José de Larra, Vol. I (Larra)
See *Obras de Mariano José de Larra*
Obras de Mariano José de Larra, Vol. II (Larra)
See *Obras de Mariano José de Larra*
Obras de Mariano José de Larra, Vol. III (Larra)
See *Obras de Mariano José de Larra*
Obras de Mariano José de Larra, Vol. IV (Larra)
See *Obras de Mariano José de Larra*
Obras de Martínex de la Rosa (Martínez de la Rosa) **102**:248-51, 252-54
Obras literatias (Martínez de la Rosa) **102**:231-32, 246
The O'Briens and the O'Flahertys (Morgan) **29**:389-90, 393
Obryv (Goncharov) **1**:362-66, 368-69, 371, 373-75, 378-79; **63**:3-4, 15-6, 26, 29-30, 32, 50
"Observation on the Tragedies of Mrs. Warner" (Murray) **63**:196
"Observation on the Tragedies of Mrs. Warren" (Murray) **63**:180
"Observations" (Bowles) **103**:64
Observations and Reflections Made in the Course of a Journey through France, Italy, and Germany (Piozzi) **57**:242, 251, 253-4, 257, 259, 266, 271, 298
"Observations on Female Abilities" (Murray) **63**:211-2
"Observations on Female Attitudes" (Murray) **63**:184
Observations on the Feeling of the Beautiful and the Sublime (Kant) **27**:200, 262
Observations on the New Constitution and on the Federal Convention by a Columbian Patriot, Sic Transit Gloria Americana (Warren) **13**:420, 422, 436
Observations on the River Wye (Gilpin) **30**:41
Observations, Relative Chiefly to Picturesque Beauty, Made in the Year 1772 (Gilpin) **30**:31-2, 42
"Obsession" (Baudelaire) **55**:46, 55, 65, 68
"The Obstructions of Genius" (Horton) **87**:102
Obyknovennaya istoriya (Goncharov) **1**:359, 361-62, 364-69, 367, 373-74, 377-79; **63**:3-5, 9, 17-8, 20-22, 24, 26-7, 29, 32, 34-5, 42-3, 45-53
"Očarovannyj strannik" (Leskov) **25**:227-28, 233, 238-39
L'occasion (Mérimée) **6**:362-63; **65**:47, 49-50, 55, 58, 60, 63-4, 79, 82-3
"Occasional Discourse on the Nigger Question" (Carlyle) **70**:72, 91
Occasional Papers (Keble) **87**:188-91, 195
Occasional Sermons (Newman)
See *Sermons Preached on Various Occasions*
Occasional Services (Keble) **87**:116
"Occasioned by a Legislation Bill proposing a Taxation upon Newspapers" (Freneau) **111**:124
Occhi e Nasi (Collodi) **54**:137, 140
"L'occident" (Lamartine) **11**:270, 279
Les occidentales (Banville) **9**:19, 22
"Occult Memories" (Villiers de l'Isle Adam)
See "Souvenirs occulte"
"The Occultation of Orion" (Longfellow) **45**:154-55
"The Ocean" (Cranch) **115**:5, 67
Oceana (Froude) **43**:186
"Oceano" (Foscolo) **8**:266
"Oceano nox" (Herzen) **10**:327
"O'Connor's Child" (Campbell) **19**:169, 181, 193
"The O'Conors of Castle Conor, County Mayo" (Trollope) **101**:234, 245, 262, 264, 271
Octavia (Kotzebue)
See *Oktavia*
"Octavie" (Beranger) **34**:28
Octavie: L'illusion (Nerval) **1**:477-78, 485-86; **67**:357-58, 363-64
"October" (Bryant) **6**:183; **46**:4
"October" (Clare) **86**:93, 98, 101, 168
"October 10!" (Martí) **63**:130
"October Hills" (Ridge) **82**:185
"October Night" (Musset)
See "Nuit d'Octobre"
October Nights (Nerval)
See *Les nuits d'Octobre*
"October Sunset" (Lampman) **25**:204
"Octogenary Reflections" (Barbauld) **50**:5
The Octoroon; or, Life in Louisiana (Boucicault) **41**:29, 31-3, 35-6, 49
"Oda a la exposición de la industria española del año 1827" (Larra) **17**:266
"Oda în metru antic" (Eminescu) **33**:250
"Oda o Mlodości" (Mickiewicz) **3**:392-93, 398; **101**:155
"Odd Characters" (Hogg) **109**:281
"Odd Miss Todd" (Cooke) **110**:35, 37, 44
The Odd Number: Thirteen Tales (Maupassant) **1**:447
"Odds and Ends" (Levy) **59**:119-20
"An Odd-tempered Man" (Opie) **65**:172
"Ode" (Boyesen) **135**:47
"Ode" (Emerson) **38**:189
"Ode" (Freneau) **111**:140
"Ode" (Lamartine) **11**:264
"An Ode" (Lowell) **2**:507
"Ode" (Taylor) **89**:349
"Ode" (Tennyson) **30**:215
"Ode: 1815" (Wordsworth) **38**:427
"Ode à Bonaparte" (Lamartine) **11**:245, 268, 270
"Ode against Capital Punishment" (Lamartine)
See "Ode contre la peine de mort"
Ode all'amica risanata (Foscolo) **97**:50, 72
"Ode auf die glückliche Wiederkunft unseres gnädigsten Fürsten" (Schiller) **39**:338, 387
"Ode Concerning Revolutions" (Lamartine)
See "Ode sur les révolutions"
"Ode contre la peine de mort" (Lamartine) **11**:276, 283
"Ode for a Celebration" (Bryant) **6**:172
"Ode for a Social Meeting/With slight alterations by a teet.taler" (Holmes) **81**:97-98
"Ode for Saint Cecilia's Eve" (Hood) **16**:234
"Ode for the Charleston Centennial Celebration" (Hayne) **94**:145
"Ode III" (Moore) **6**:392
"Ode in Ancient Metre" (Eminescu)
See "Oda în metru antic"
"Ode in Saphic Metre" (Eminescu)
See "Ode (In Sapphic Metre)"
"Ode (In Sapphic Metre)" (Eminescu) **33**:262; **131**:298
"Ode Inscribed to W. H. Channing" (Emerson) **38**:184, 191; **98**:179-80, 183
"Ode: Intimations of Immortality from Recollections of Early Childhood" (Wordsworth) **12**:395, 416, 423, 425, 427, 429-31, 436, 440-49, 451-52, 460, 462, 467, 471, 473; **38**:359-60, 367, 396, 398; **111**:219, 226, 235
"Ode on a Distant Prospect of Clapham Academy" (Hood) **16**:234
"Ode on a Grecian Urn" (Keats) **8**:351-52, 355, 365, 368, 382, 386-90; **73**:154, 158-60, 165, 198-99, 202-04, 209, 230, 246, 258, 262, 268, 270, 282, 309; **121**:106, 144
"Ode on a Jar of Pickles" (Taylor) **89**:338
"Ode on Dejection" (Coleridge) **9**:147-49, 158, 181, 193
"Ode on Indolence" (Keats) **8**:387, 391; **73**:154, 158, 198, 211, 289, 328
"Ode on Liberty" (Dyer) **129**:103, 107, 112, 137, 140
"Ode on Lord Hay's Birth-day" (Beattie) **25**:106
"Ode on Melancholy" (Keats) **8**:351, 361, 375, 378-79; **73**:159-60, 165, 198, 201, 206, 244, 259-60, 271, 308-09; **121**:111, 144
"Ode on Occasion of the Meeting of the Southern Congress" (Timrod) **25**:387
"Ode on Peace, written in Jesus College Garden" (Dyer) **129**:103, 112
"Ode on Pity" (Dyer) **129**:137
"Ode on the Death of the Duchess de Frias" (Martínez de la Rosa) **102**:226
"Ode on the Death of the Duke of Wellington" (Tennyson) **30**:294
An Ode on the Peace (Williams) **135**:305, 333
"Ode on the Spring" (Dyer) **129**:137
"Ode prima: Accenna le cagioni della guerra" (Alfieri) **101**:48
"Ode quarta: Commenda il Generale Washington" (Alfieri) **101**:48
"Ode Recited at the Harvard Commemoration" (Lowell) **90**:190
"Ode seconda: Annovera i popoli belligeranti" (Alfieri) **101**:48
"Ode Sung at the Opening of the International Exhibition" (Tennyson) **30**:295
"Ode Sung in the Town Hall, Concord, July 4, 1857" (Emerson) **98**:182-83
"Ode Sung on the Occasion of Decorating the Graves of the Confederate Dead at Magnolia Cemetery" (Timrod) **25**:368-69, 372, 376, 382, 386, 388-89

"Ode sur les révolutions" (Lamartine) **11**:271, 279, 283
"Ode terza: Parla del Sig. de La Fayette" (Alfieri) **101**:48
"Ode to a Mountain Oak" (Boker) **125**:78
"Ode to a Nightingale" (Keats) **8**:328, 332, 351, 355, 365, 368-69, 376-78, 380, 386-88, 390-91; **73**:143, 154, 159, 165-66, 174, 184, 198-201, 203, 209, 212-13, 244, 261-62, 294, 309, 312; **121**:110-12, 123, 144
"Ode to America" (Boker) **125**:39
"Ode to Apollo" (Cowper) **94**:34
"Ode to Apollo" (Keats) **73**:151, 257, 328
"Ode to Autumn" (Hood) **16**:225, 227-28, 231, 233
"Ode to Autumn" (Keats) **8**:348-49, 368, 379-83; **73**:155, 158, 163, 165, 193, 198, 213-14, 218, 233-37,248, 285, 308-09, 327, 329, 339-42; **121**:113, 145-46, 149, 211
"Ode to Beauty" (Emerson) **1**:296-97; **38**:192
"Ode to Corinth" (Landor) **14**:161, 187, 196
"Ode to David the Sculptor" (Sainte-Beuve) **5**:340
"Ode to Diana" (Mill) **58**:319
"Ode to Duty" (Wordsworth) **12**:395, 444, 451, 458, 459, 460; **38**:360, 368, 398; **111**:228
"Ode to Evening" (Warton) **118**:298
"The Ode to Fancy" (Freneau) **1**:314; **111**:151
"Ode to Fancy" (Warton) **118**:298, 349-51, 353-57, 359
"Ode to Fortune" (Halleck) **47**:76
"Ode to France" (Coleridge) **9**:149; **54**:85; **111**:310
"Ode to Freedom" (Pushkin)
See "Vol'nost': Oda"
"Ode to Freedom" (Slowacki) **15**:349
"Ode to Genius" (Hunt) **1**:406
"Ode to Health" (Warton) **118**:298
"Ode to Heaven" (Shelley) **18**:332
Ode to His Lady on Her Recovery (Foscolo)
See *Ode all'amica risanata*
"Ode to Hope" (Beattie) **25**:106
Ode to Joy (Schiller)
See *Lied an die Freude*
"Ode to Liberty" (Horton) **87**:101
"Ode to Liberty" (Pushkin)
See "Vol'nost': Oda"
"Ode to Liberty" (Shelley) **18**:319, 327, 361-62; **93**:271, 359
"Ode to Maia" (Keats) **8**:348
"Ode to Melancholy" (Hood) **16**:206, 219, 224, 236
"Ode to Memory" (Tennyson) **30**:204, 211, 223, 233; **65**:358; **115**:358
"Ode to Naples" (Shelley) **18**:338; **93**:359, 367
"Ode to Napoleon Buonaparte" (Byron) **2**:62
"Ode to Peace" (Beattie) **25**:112
"Ode to Peace" (Williams) **135**:300, 305-7, 314, 334
"Ode to Pity" (Austen) **119**:13
"Ode to Psyche" (Keats) **8**:363, 368-71, 376, 379, 389, 391; **73**:154, 158-59, 165, 198-200, 211, 215, 231, 233, 243, 270; **121**:100, 102-3, 106, 123, 128
"Ode to Rae Wilson, Esquire" (Hood) **16**:205, 216, 219, 226, 229, 233, 235
Ode to Sappho (Grillparzer)
See *Sappho*
"Ode to Sir Andrew Agnew, Bart." (Hood) **16**:235
"Ode to Sleep" (Trumbull) **30**:348-49, 352
"Ode to Solitude" (Warton) **118**:298, 350
"Ode to Sorrow" (Keats) **8**:348; **73**:198
"Ode to Spring" (Timrod) **25**:362
Ode to Superstition (Rogers) **69**:66-7, 73
"Ode to the Confederate Dead" (Timrod)
See "Ode Sung on the Occasion of Decorating the Graves of the Confederate Dead at Magnolia Cemetery"
"Ode to the Departing Year" (Coleridge) **99**:66
"Ode to the Great Unknown" (Hood) **16**:200
"Ode to The Happy Life" (Warton) **118**:349, 359
"An Ode to the Hills" (Lampman) **25**:186, 189, 193, 204, 219
"Ode to the Moon" (Hood) **16**:219, 221
"Ode to the Nightingale" (Keats)
See "Ode to a Nightingale"
"Ode to the Polar Star" (Brontë) **109**:27
"Ode to the River Derwent" (Darwin) **106**:182
"Ode to the Surveyor-General" (Halleck) **47**:76
"The Ode to the West Wind" (Morris) **4**:431
"Ode to the West Wind" (Shelley) **18**:319, 345, 361, 372; **93**:305
"Ode to Twilight" (Opie) **65**:156
"Ode to West" (Warton) **118**:298
"Ode to Winter" (Campbell) **19**:188
"Ode to Youth" (Mickiewicz)
See "Oda o Mlodości"
Les odelettes (Banville) **9**:19, 26
Odelettes (Nerval) **1**:486; **67**:303, 306
"Oden an Laura" (Schiller) **39**:339
"Odes" (Patmore) **9**:345
Odes (Foscolo) **97**:62
Odes and Addresses to Great People (Hood) **16**:200, 202, 219, 223, 233
Odes et ballades (Hugo) **3**:234, 236; **21**:202, 214
Odes et poésies diverses (Hugo) **3**:236
Odes et poesies sacrées (Hugo) **3**:233, 236
Odes funambulesques (Banville) **9**:16-17, 19, 23-25, 27, 30
Odes of Anacreon (Moore) **6**:376-77, 382, 392, 399; **110**:183-84, 189
Odes of Klopstock from 1747 to 1780 (Klopstock) **11**:228
Odes on Various Subjects (Warton) **118**:300, 304, 308, 335-37, 349-51, 358-60
Odes to Free America (Alfieri)
See *Odi per l'America libera*
Odes to His Royal Highness the Prince Regent, and His Imperial Majesty the Emperor of Russia (Southey) **97**:262
Odi per l'America libera (Alfieri) **101**:41, 51-2
"Odin" (Boker) **125**:35
Odluki i poeta (Fredro) **8**:284
O'Donnel (Morgan) **29**:387, 389, 393
The O'Donoghue: A Tale of Ireland Fifty Years Ago (Lever) **23**:292, 294, 300, 305, 307
The O'Dowd (Boucicault)
See *Daddy O'Dowd*
"Odyn and the Poet" (Eminescu) **131**:287
"L'Odyssée d'une fille" (Maupassant) **83**:194, 197, 200
Odyssey (Zhukovsky) **35**:379-81, 391-93
The Odyssey of Homer (Morris) **4**:420-21, 441
Oedipus Tyrannus; Or Swellfoot the Tyrant (Shelley) **93**:271, 359-61, 363-65, 367
L'oeillet blanc (Daudet) **1**:231, 249
"Oenone" (Tennyson) **30**:212, 223, 245, 258, 280; **65**:227, 267; **115**:235, 258
"O'er the Tree Tops" (Eminescu) **33**:265
"Ó-és újkor" (Madach) **19**:369
Oeuvre (Rimbaud) **4**:476
L'oeuvre de Watteau (Goncourt and Goncourt) **7**:165
Oeuvres (Leopardi) **129**:247
Oeuvres (Sand) **2**:586
Oeuvres autobiographiques (Sand) **42**:332
Oeuvres complémentaires (Nerval) **67**:315
Oeuvres complètes (Charriere) **66**:134-5, 137, 141-2, 146, 161, 172
Oeuvres complètes (Chateaubriand) **3**:114; **134**:37
Oeuvres complètes (Flaubert) **135**:104
Oeuvres complètes (Maupassant) **83**:163
Oeuvres complètes (Sade) **47**:349
Oeuvres complètes (Staël-Holstein) **91**:332-36
Oeuvres complètes (Verlaine) **51**:365
Oeuvres Completes d'Alexis de Tocqueville (Tocqueville) **63**:280
Oeuvres complètes de George Sand (Sand) **42**:323, 357; **57**:337
Oeuvres de jeunesse (Balzac) **5**:58
Oeuvres de jeunesse inédites (Flaubert) **2**:255; **135**:93
Oeuvres dramatiques du comte Alfieri (Alfieri) **101**:75
Oeuvres philosophiques (Balzac)
See *Études philosophiques*
Oeuvres poétiques: La volupté et pièces diverses (Bertrand) **31**:54-5
Oeuvres posthumes (Verlaine) **51**:365
Oeuvres posthurnes (Maupassant) **83**:178-79, 181
"Of All the Souls That Stand Create" (Dickinson) **21**:74
"Of Bronze—and Blaze" (Dickinson) **21**:64-5
"Of Choice in Reading" (Godwin) **130**:115
Of Dandyism and of George Brummel (Barbey d'Aurevilly)
See *Du dandysme et de Georges Brummel*
"Of Difference of Opinion" (Godwin) **130**:113
"Of History and Romance" (Godwin) **130**:170
Of Laws in Gerneral (Bentham) **38**:94
"Of Love and Friendship" (Godwin) **130**:136
"Of Many a Smutch'd Deed Reminiscent" (Whitman) **31**:435
"Of Old Sat Freedom on the Heights" (Tennyson) **30**:294
"Of Pacchiarotto, and How He Worked in Distemper" (Browning) **19**:86-8, 98
"Of Paradise' Existence" (Dickinson) **21**:65
Of Population (Godwin) **14**:50
"Of That Blithe Throat of Mine..." (Whitman) **31**:434
Of The Difference Between a Genius and an Apostle (Kierkegaard) **78**:197
"Of the disease of the woe in dreams" (Polidori)
See "De Morbo Oneirodynia"
"Of the Terrible Doublt of Appearances" (Whitman) **81**:314, 363
Of Tombs (Foscolo)
See *I sepolcri*
"Of Tradition" (Sainte-Beuve) **5**:350
"Of Tribulation These Are They" (Dickinson) **21**:31, 38, 55
Of Tyranny (Alfieri)
See *Della tirannide*
"Of what do you wail, wind of the night?" (Tyutchev)
See "O chem ty voesh, vetr nochnoy?"
"Of what use are the dreams of freedom to a slave?..." (Baratynsky)
See "K chemu nevolniku mechtania svobody?..."
"Of Yore" (Hugo) **3**:253
"Off Rough Point" (Lazarus) **8**:426
Off the Skelligs (Ingelow) **39**:259-60, 264; **107**:118, 124-25
Offices (Mallarmé) **41**:254, 259
"Official Piety" (Whittier) **8**:525-26; **59**:361
Official Report of the Niger Valley Exploring Party (Delany) **93**:158-61, 167, 170, 173
"Oft in the Stilly Night" (Moore) **6**:389; **110**:194, 196
"Often I Question Myself Severely" (Pavlova)
See "Ne raz sebia ia voproshaiu strogo"
"Ogier the Dane" (Morris) **4**:417, 442, 447
The Ogilvies (Craik) **38**:109, 120, 122
Ogilvies (Oliphant) **11**:428
"Ogon" (Pavlova) **138**:4, 12
"Ogorodnik" (Nekrasov) **11**:412
"Ogsaa et Forsvar for Qvindens hoie Anlæg" (Kierkegaard) **125**:265
"Ogyges" (Kendall) **12**:190-92, 201
"Oh! Blame Not the Bard" (Moore) **6**:390; **110**:185
"Oh Canada! Thy Gloomy Woods" (Moodie) **113**:345-46
"Oh, Clear Up Cold Dark . . ." (Eminescu) **33**:263
"Oh, Do Not Look at Me" (Arany)
See "Oh! ne rézz rám"

"Oh Fairest of the Rural Maids" (Bryant) **6**:171-72, 179, 182, 186
"Oh! For a Closer Walk with God" (Cowper) **8**:127
"Oh! Had We Some Bright Little Isle of Our Own" (Moore) **6**:396
"Oh love, art thou a silver deer?" (Crawford) **127**:202
"Oh Mother of a Mighty Race" (Bryant) **46**:7
"Oh! ne rézz rám" (Arany) **34**:19
"Oh, Stay with Me" (Eminescu) **131**:296, 340
"Oh! Susanna" (Foster) **26**:282, 285, 291-92, 294, 298
"Oh, to be in England" (Browning) **79**:98
"Oh, to the Dead Be Faithful" (Storm) **1**:537
"Oh!Can You Leave Your Native Land?" (Moodie) **113**:344
"O'Hussey's Ode to the Maguire" (Mangan) **27**:283, 289, 292, 296-98, 311, 313-14
"Oinea" (O'Brien) **21**:244
"L'oiseau bleu" (Daudet) **1**:249
Ojciec zadżumionych (Slowacki) **15**:348-50, 354, 358, 364
"Los ojos pardos" (Isaacs) **70**:307
"Los ojos verdes" (Bécquer) **106**:86-8, 97-8, 108, 120-21, 124, 130, 132, 134
"Okatootáia" (Petofi) **21**:280
Oktavia (Kotzebue) **25**:134, 141
Olalla (Stevenson) **5**:429, 431; **14**:334, 339
"Olaszország" (Petofi) **21**:286
The Old Adam (Boyesen) **135**:13
"Old Adam, the Carrion Crow" (Beddoes) **3**:32
"Old Age" (Emerson) **1**:280
Old age of Toldi (Arany)
See *Toldi estéje*
"The Old Agency" (Woolson) **82**:272, 284
Old and Modern Poems (Vigny)
See *Poèmes antiques et modernes*
"Old and New Art" (Rossetti) **4**:529; **77**:348
"Old and New Year Ditty" (Rossetti) **50**:272
"The Old and the New Schoolmaster" (Lamb) **10**:408, 410, 436; **113**:162, 190, 192-93, 217, 236
"The Old and the Young" (Eminescu) **131**:325
"The Old Apple Dealer" (Hawthorne) **2**:296
"The Old Ash Tree" (Moodie) **113**:316-17
"The Old Bachelor" (Crabbe) **26**:110
"An Old Bachelor" (Mitford) **4**:408
"The Old Bardic Poetry" (Barnes) **75**:46, 53-4
"The Old Benchers of the Inner Temple" (Lamb) **10**:407, 416, 435-36; **113**:162, 177, 218, 236
"Old Billowy Hawksb'ry" (Harpur) **114**:144
"Old Black Joe" (Foster) **26**:285-86, 289, 291, 295, 298-99
"Old Burns's Bull-Ride" (Harris) **23**:159, 163
The Old Castellan (Sacher-Masoch) **31**:295
"Old China" (Lamb) **10**:407-08, 410, 428, 435-37; **113**:157, 163, 173, 200, 252, 265-66
Old Christmas (Irving) **19**:351
The Old Clothesman (Holcroft) **85**:198
The Old Continental; or, The Price of Liberty (Paulding) **2**:527-28, 530
"Old Coppees" (Verlaine) **51**:372
Old Court (Ainsworth) **13**:42
"The Old Cumberland Beggar" (Wordsworth) **12**:470; **111**:228, 236, 279, 347-48
The Old Curiosity Shop (Dickens) **3**:141, 142, 152, 156, 166, 167, 173, 181, 182, 183, 184; **8**:174, 182; **18**:100, 112, 121; **26**:167; **86**:256; **105**:227, 231; **113**:91, 107, 110, 124, 127, 129
Old Days in Plodomasovo (Leskov)
See *Starye gody v sele Plodomasove*
"Old Dog Tray" (Foster) **26**:283, 291
The Old English Baron (Reeve) **19**:407-13, 415-16, 418-21
Old English Theatre (Tieck) **5**:511
"Old Familiar Faces" (Lamb) **10**:404, 407; **113**:161
"Old Folks at Home" (Foster) **26**:281-87, 289-91, 294, 297-99
"The Old Folks' Party" (Bellamy) **4**:31; **86**:75
"Old Gardiston" (Woolson) **82**:273, 294-95, 297, 300-03, 322, 339
The Old Gardner's Letters (Runeberg)
See *Den gamle trädgårdsmästarens brev*
"Old General de Berir—Untitled story about" (Crawford) **127**:193
Old Goriot (Balzac)
See *Le père Goriot: Histoire Parisienne*
"Old Hannah; or, The Charm" (Moodie) **14**:231
Old Heads and Young Hearts (Boucicault) **41**:28
"The Old House" (Andersen) **79**:89
"The Old House" (Levy) **59**:80, 93, 119
The Old House at Coate (Jefferies) **47**:129
"Old Icons and New Icons" (Eminescu) **131**:326
"Old Ironsides" (Holmes) **14**:98, 109, 125, 128
The Old Judge; or, Life in a Colony (Haliburton) **15**:125-26, 129, 132, 145, 147-48, 151
Old Lady Mary (Oliphant) **11**:446
"The Old Landowner" (Turgenev) **21**:376-77
"Old Leaven" (Gordon) **21**:160
"An Old Lesson from the Fields" (Lampman) **25**:194
"Old Love" (Morris) **4**:431, 444
"Old Maids" (Sedgwick) **19**:440
"The Old Man Dreams" (Holmes) **81**:96
The Old Man of the Mountain, The Love-Charm, and Pietro of Abano (Tieck) **5**:512
"The Old Man Travelling" (Wordsworth) **12**:387; **111**:202, 273-77, 279-83, 286-87, 306, 310, 315, 348, 357, 367
The Old Manor House (Smith) **23**:318, 320, 322-31, 333, 336; **115**:133, 145, 147-50, 166, 174, 207, 211, 222-24
"The Old Man's Comforts" (Southey) **97**:291
"The Old Man's Counsel" (Bryant) **6**:187; **46**:25, 49
"The Old Man's Funeral" (Bryant) **6**:159, 162; **46**:3
An Old Man's Love (Trollope) **6**:467, 500, 518
"The Old Manse" (Hawthorne) **39**:181; **79**:311; **95**:106, 137
Old Margaret (Kingsley) **107**:192, 211
"The Old Margate Hoy" (Lamb) **10**:411, 435-36; **113**:217, 219, 251
The Old Masters of Belguim and Holland (Fromentin)
See *Les maîtres d'autrefois: Belgigue, Hollande*
"Old Mat and His Man" (Krylov) **1**:439
"Old Memories" (Foster) **26**:295
"Old Mortality" (Stevenson) **5**:416
Old Mortality (Scott) **15**:260-61, 272, 283, 285, 289, 292, 300, 303-04, 309, 313-15, 321-22; **69**:304-05, 308, 366, 371; **110**:233, 313-14
Old Mr. Tredgold (Oliphant) **11**:449; **61**:215
"Old News" (Hawthorne) **2**:329
"The Old Nurse's Story" (Gaskell) **5**:206; **70**:186, 189, 193, 196-97; **97**:127
"Old Oak of Summer Chace" (Tennyson) **30**:215
"Old Oak Tree's Last Dream" (Andersen)
See "The Last Dream of the Old Oak"
"The Old Oak Tree's Last Thoughts" (Andersen) **7**:35
"Old Pictures in Florence" (Browning) **19**:131-32, 154; **79**:161
"The Old Poet" (Levy) **59**:89
"Old Portraits" (Turgenev)
See "Starye portrety"
Old Portraits and Modern Sketches (Whittier) **59**:365
The Old Regime and the Revolution (Tocqueville)
See *L'ancien régime et la révolution*
The Old Régime in Canada (Parkman) **12**:333-34, 336, 341-44, 348, 351, 370-71, 374
Old Saint Paul's: A Tale of the Plague and the Fire (Ainsworth) **13**:28, 31-4, 36-7, 39-40, 43, 45, 47
"Old Sári" (Petofi)
See "Sári néni"
Old Sir Douglas (Norton) **47**:248, 257-58
"Old Skissim's Middle Boy" (Harris) **23**:156-57, 159
"An Old Song Ended" (Rossetti) **77**:337
"Old Spense" (Crawford) **12**:151-52, 172
"Old Spookses' Pass" (Crawford) **12**:151-54, 156-58, 160-63, 171-72; **127**:178, 195, 197, 199-200, 203, 224-25
Old Spookses' Pass, Malcolm's Katie, and Other Poems (Crawford) **12**:151-53, 158; **127**:148, 161, 203, 218
"Old St. David's at Radnor" (Longfellow) **45**:130
"The Old Stoic" (Brontë) **16**:70
The Old Stone House (Woolson) **82**:272, 325
Old Tales of a Young Country (Clarke) **19**:256-59
"Old Things" (Silva)
See "Vejeces"
"Old Times" (Dana) **53**:178
Old Times in Poshekhouie (Saltykov)
See *Poshekhonskaya starina*
"Old Uncle Ned" (Foster) **26**:281-82, 285-86, 289, 291
"Old War-Dreams" (Whitman) **31**:392
"The Old Washerwoman" (Chamisso) **82**:6
"The Old Woman" (Pavlova)
See "Starukha"
"The Old Woman" (Turgenev) **21**:452
"The Old Woman Clothed in Grey" (Barham) **77**:36
"The Old Woman of Berkeley" (Southey) **8**:472, 474
"Old Woman's Gossip" (Kemble)
See *Record of a Girlhood*
The Old World and Russia (Herzen) **10**:329
The Old World and the New (Trollope) **30**:315
"An Old World Thicket" (Rossetti) **50**:293; **66**:342
Old Years in Plodomasovo (Leskov)
See *Starye gody v sele Plodomasove*
"The Olden Warrior" (Harpur) **114**:144
Oldest Heroic Songs (Karadzic)
See *Pjesme junačke najstarije*
An Old-Fashioned Girl (Alcott) **6**:14-16, 20-21; **58**:48, 69; **83**:30, 47
"Old-Fashioned Landowners" (Gogol)
See "Starosvetskie Pomeščiki"
"Old-Testament Gospel" (Cowper) **94**:74
Oldtown Fireside Stories (Stowe) **3**:563
Oldtown Folks (Stowe) **3**:553-56, 561-63, 568
"Old-World Landowners" (Gogol)
See "Starosvetskie Pomeščiki"
"Ole luck-oin" (Andersen) **7**:16
"Ole Luköie" (Andersen) **79**:15, 17
"Ole Shut-Eye" (Andersen)
See "Ole luck-oin"
"Oleszkiewicz" (Mickiewicz) **3**:401
Olive (Craik) **38**:110, 119, 120, 130
"Olive Buds" (Sigourney) **87**:321
Oliver Twist (Dickens) **3**:138-41, 153-54, 168-69, 175-77, 182, 184; **8**:182, 199; **18**:122-23, 132, 139; **26**:156, 159, 167, 172; **37**:133-214; **86**:255-56; **105**:214, 226, 337; **113**:28, 89, 96, 98, 102-3, 106, 118, 120, 124
Olney Hymns (Cowper) **8**:140; **94**:68-9, 72, 102, 116
Olviretki Schleusingenissä (Kivi) **30**:50, 65
Olympic Devils (Planché) **42**:286, 298, 300
Olympic Revels; or, Prometheus and Pandora (Planché) **42**:272, 285-86, 295, 297, 299
"Om Bacchanterna" (Stagnelius) **61**:266
Om Begrebet Ironi med stadigt Hensyn til Socrates (Kierkegaard) **34**:222-23, 236, 268; **78**:250; **125**:184, 186, 189-90, 192-93, 202-3, 209, 232,
Om brottsliges behandling (Almqvist) **42**:17

"Om poesi i sak" (Almqvist) **42**:18-19
O'Malley (Lever)
See *Charles O'Malley, the Irish Dragoon*
"Ombra adorata" (Hoffmann) **2**:346-47
"L'ombre des arbres" (Verlaine) **51**:384
The Omen (Galt) **1**:330, 334
"Omens" (Baratynsky)
See "Primety"
Omne animal (Silva) **114**:263
Omniana (Southey) **8**:468, 472; **97**:271, 288, 330
"Omnipotence in Bonds" (Newman) **38**:305, 310
"Omnipresence" (Grillparzer)
See "Allgegenwart"
Omoo: A Narrative of Adventures in the South Seas (Melville) **3**:326-28, 330, 333-34, 337, 339-41, 347, 355-56, 360, 363-64, 370; **12**:255, 257; **29**:331, 354; **45**:194-95, 206, 210, 212, 244, 248-49, 251, 253; **91**:10, 42, 45, 55, 212; **123**:187, 192, 211, 231-32, 236-39, 251-52
"Omphale ou la Tapisserie amoureuse, histoire rococo" (Gautier) **1**:355; **59**:10, 29, 32, 37-8, 42
"On a Cattle Track" (Kendall) **12**:181, 191
"On a Certain Condescension in Foreigners" (Lowell) **2**:517
"On a Dream" (Keats) **73**:191-94
"On a Dutch Landscape" (Lenau) **16**:276
"On a Goldfinch Starved to Death in His Cage" (Cowper) **94**:123
"On a Lady's Singing Bird" (Freneau) **111**:145
"On a Landscape of Nicholas Poussin" (Hazlitt) **82**:157
"On a Lock of My Mother's Hair" (Lazarus) **8**:417; **109**:290
"On a Lost Greyhound" (Clare) **9**:105
"On a Panegyric of Theocracy and Mortmain" (Fourier) **51**:184
"On a Picture of the Corpse of Napoleon lying in State" (Coleridge) **90**:27
"On a Piece of Chalk" (Huxley) **67**:16, 48, 58, 80, 83, 90
"On a Piece of Music" (Hopkins) **17**:194
"On a Prayer-Book: With Its Frontispiece, Ary Scheffer's 'Christus Consolator,' Americanized by the Omission of the Black Man" (Whittier) **8**:525, 531; **59**:361
"On a Rock" (O'Brien) **21**:249
"On a Street" (Kendall) **12**:198
"On a Sunday" (Meyer)
See "Sonntags"
"On a Sun-Dial" (Hazlitt) **82**:95-6
"On a Target at Drakelow" (Darwin) **106**:182
"On a Tear" (Rogers) **69**:73
"On a Text Heard in the Street" (Crawford) **127**:220
"On a Tuft of Grass" (Lazarus) **8**:413
On Actors and the Art of Acting (Lewes) **25**:284-85, 290, 308, 315-17, 319, 325
"On Amanda's Singing Bird" (Freneau) **111**:133
On an Ancient Hymn to the Graces (Foscolo) **97**:53
"On an Infant Dying as Soon as Born" (Lamb) **10**:405
"On an Infant's Grave" (Clare) **9**:74
"On Another's Sorrow" (Blake) **13**:220; **37**:3, 5, 23, 41, 72, 92
"On Application to Study" (Hazlitt) **29**:147
"On Art in Fiction" (Bulwer-Lytton) **45**:23, 69
On Authority and Revelation: The Book on Adler (Kierkegaard) **34**:238; **78**:152, 154, 197
"On Awakening the Mind" (Godwin) **14**:75
"On Becoming Sober" (Kierkegaard) **34**:225
"On Being a Good Hater" (Hazlitt) **82**:90
"On being cautioned against walking on an headland overlooking the sea, because it was frequented by a lunatic" (Smith)
See "Sonnet 70"
"On Blending Spirit with Matter" (Murray) **63**:207
"On bly ubit" (Bestuzhev) **131**:161
On Board "The Emma" (Dumas)
See *Les Garibaldiens*
"On Burial Societies and the Character of the Undertaker" (Lamb) **10**:436
"On Calais Sands" (Wordsworth) **38**:413
"On Caroline" (Brontë) **109**:4
"On Catullus" (Landor) **14**:199
"On Certain Political Measures Proposed to Their Consideration" (Barlow) **23**:28
"On Chapman's Homer" (Keats) **73**:342
"On City Burying Places" (Freneau) **111**:134
"On Classical Learning" (Brown) **74**:192
"On Consistency of Opinion" (Hazlitt) **82**:108, 110
"On Courting" (Shaw) **15**:335
"On Criticism" (Hazlitt) **29**:148, 167
"On Death" (Clare) **86**:160
"On Death" (Horton) **87**:110
"On Depth and Superficiality" (Hazlitt) **82**:108, 123-24
"On Descartes' 'Discourse on Method'" (Huxley) **67**:86
"On Descartes' 'Discourse Touching the Method of Using One's Reason Rightly and of Seeking Scientific Trush'" (Huxley) **67**:65
"On Diotima" (Schlegel)
See "Über die Diotima"
"On Dover Cliffs. July 20, 1787" (Bowles) **103**:68, 72
"On Dreams" (Hazlitt) **82**:142
"On Dreams and Dreaming" (Smith) **59**:315
"On Duelling" (Mackenzie) **41**:190
"On Effeminacy of Character" (Hazlitt) **29**:148
"On Elgin Marbles" (Keats) **73**:152
"On English Prose Fiction as a Rational Amusement" (Trollope) **6**:508; **33**:364; **101**:333
"On Envy" (Hazlitt) **29**:147, 156
"On Epic Poetry" (Freneau) **111**:160
"On Fame" (Keats) **73**:194-95, 197
"On Familiar Style" (Hazlitt) **29**:148, 167; **82**:97-101, 115, 125
"On Female Education" (Martineau) **137**:237
"On First Looking into Chapman's Homer" (Keats) **8**:343, 349, 354, 361; **73**:152, 173, 258, 278, 279, 323, 339-40
"On Genius" (Mill) **58**:326
"On Genius and Common Sense" (Hazlitt) **29**:147, 162, 179
"On Genius. On taking leave of Dr. Priestley, when preparing to go to America" (Dyer) **129**:149
"On Gentleness" (Blair) **75**:154
"On German Opera" (Wagner) **119**:190
On Germany (Staël-Holstein) **91**:326-27
"On Going a Journey" (Hazlitt) **29**:153, 166; **82**:95
"On Going a Walk" (Hazlitt) **82**:90
"On Golden Ground" (Meyer)
See "Auf Goldgrund"
"On Good-Nature" 1 (Hazlitt) **82**:115
"On Great and Little Things" (Hazlitt) **82**:76, 89, 97
"On Greatness" (Irving) **2**:391
"On Growing Old" (Arnold) **6**:52
"On Gusto" (Hazlitt) **82**:117
"On hearing of the intention of a gentleman to purchase the Poet's freedom" (Horton) **87**:101, 109
"On Hearing the 'Messiah'" (Bowles) **103**:55
On Heroes, Hero-Worship, and the Heroic in History (Carlyle) **70**:20, 23, 26, 43, 46-55, 71
"On History" (Carlyle) **70**:39, 73
"On Howells' Work" (Boyesen) **135**:39
"On Idleness" (Musset) **7**:256
"On Imprisonment for Debt" (Freneau) **111**:129
"On Improving Natural Knowledge" (Huxley) **67**:20
"On Incomprehensibility" (Schlegel)
See "Über die Ünverständlichkeit"
"On Kaunisnummi" (Kivi)
See "Kaunisnummella"
"On Lake Temiscamingue" (Lampman) **25**:186, 210
"On Landing at Ostend" (Bowles) **103**:85
On Language (Humboldt) **134**:198-200
"On Latmos" (Clough) **27**:107
"On Leaving California" (Taylor) **89**:357
On Liberty (Mill) **11**:343, 352, 360, 363, 368, 374-75, 377, 383-84, 389; **58**:327, 330-1, 342, 349-51, 359, 375-80
"On Liberty and Necessity" (Hazlitt) **82**:108, 112
"On Liberty and Slavery" (Horton) **87**:99, 101-102, 105, 109
"On Life" (Shelley) **93**:294-95, 311, 326
"On Living to One's-self" (Hazlitt) **29**:142
"On Love" (Shelley) **18**:354; **93**:286, 289, 295
On Love (Stendhal)
See *De l'amour*
"On Luculle's Recovery" (Pushkin) **83**:272
"On Madan's Answer to Newton's Comments on Thelyohthora" (Cowper) **94**:110
"On Milton's Lycidas" (Hazlitt) **82**:117-18
"On Milton's Sonnets" (Hazlitt) **29**:148
"On Modern Revolutions" (Carlyle) **70**:47
"On Monastic Institutions" (Barbauld) **50**:3
"On Mrs. Kemble's Readings from Shakespeare" (Longfellow) **45**:125
"On Murder Considered as a Fine Art" (De Quincey)
See "Lectures on Murder Considered as One of the Fine Arts"
"On Murder Considered as One of the Fine Arts" (De Quincey)
See "Lectures on Murder Considered as One of the Fine Arts"
"On Music" (Brown) **74**:174
"On Music" (Moore) **6**:399
"On My Bad Poems" (Petofi)
See "Rosz verseimröl"
"On My Volcano Grows the Grass" (Dickinson) **21**:80
On My Work as an Author (Kierkegaard) **34**:205
"On Naive and Sentimental Poetry" (Schiller)
See "Über naïve und sentimtalische Dichtung"
On ne badine pas avec l'amour (Musset) **7**:258-60, 267-72, 276-78, 282-83
"On Needle-Work" (Lamb) **125**:290, 293-95, 297-98, 313, 325, 327, 361, 371
"On Novel Writing" (Hays) **114**:217-18
"On Novelty and Familiarity" (Hazlitt) **82**:97, 99, 101, 110
"On November 10th, 1840" (Pavlova) **138**:18
"On Observing Some Names of Little Note in the Biographia Britannica" (Cowper) **94**:121
"On, on the Same Ye Jocund Twain" (Whitman) **4**:586
"On Originality and Imitation" (Bryant) **46**:11, 32, 34, 53
"On Our European Literature" (Mazzini) **34**:277
"On Our Knowledge of the Causes of the Phenomena of Organic Nature" (Huxley) **67**:60
On Our Own Ground: The Complete Writings of William Apess, A Pequot (Apess) **73**:14-16
"On Oysters and the Oyster Question" (Huxley) **67**:87
"On Painting" (Brown) **74**:174
"On Paradox and Commonplace" (Hazlitt) **29**:147; **82**:99
"On Parliamentary Reform" (Southey) **97**:263
"On Pathos" (Schiller) **39**:349, 367
"On Peace" (Keats) **73**:145, 332

"On Pedantry" (Hazlitt)
See "Pedantry"
"On Personal Character" (Hazlitt) **29**:184
"On Personal Identity" (Hazlitt) **82**:81, 101
On Picket Duty, and Other Tales (Alcott) **58**:49
"On Picturesque Beauty" (Gilpin) **30**:36
"On Planting a Forest" (Baratynsky)
See "Na posev lesa"
"On Poesy or Art" (Coleridge) **99**:6, 87
"On Poetry and Its Relation of Our Age and Country" (Bryant) **46**:33
"On Poetry and Music" (Horton)
See "On Poetry and Musick"
"On Poetry and Musick" (Horton) **87**:91, 99
"On Poetry in General" (Hazlitt) **29**:160-61, 165, 174, 176, 179; **82**:93
"On Ponkawtasset, Since We Took Our Way" (Thoreau) **7**:383
"On Ponkawtasset, since, with such delay" (Thoreau)
See "On Ponkawtasset, Since We Took Our Way"
On Popular Education (Faustino)
See *De la educación popular*
"On Pressing Some Flowers" (Timrod) **25**:372
"On Rationalism" (Coleridge) **31**:63
"On Reading New Books" (Hazlitt) **29**:148
"On Reading Old Books" (Hazlitt) **29**:147
"On Reading the Proclamation Delivered by William Lyon Mackenzie, On Navy Island" (Moodie) **113**:308, 310-11
"On Reason and Imagination" (Hazlitt) **29**:185
"On receiving a curious Shell" (Keats) **73**:311
"On Receiving a Laurel Crown from Leigh Hunt" (Keats) **73**:332
On Religion (Schleiermacher)
See *Über die Religion: Reden an die Gebildeten unter ihren Verächtern*
On Religion (Schopenhauer) **51**:271, 340
On Religion: Speeches to its Cultured Despisers (Schleiermacher)
See *Über die Religion: Reden an die Gebildeten unter ihren Verächtern*
"On Retirement" (Freneau) **111**:100
"On Satirical Productions" (Trumbull) **30**:365
"On Science and Art in Relation to Education" (Huxley) **67**:33, 72
"On Seeing a Lock of Milton's Hair" (Keats) **73**:257
"On Seeing a Skull on Cowper Green" (Clare) **9**:76, 80, 108, 119
"On Self-Delusion" (Adams) **106**:4
"On Sensation and the Unity of Structure of Sensiferous Organs" (Huxley) **67**:95
"On Sensibility" (Blair) **75**:155
"On Shakespeare and Milton" (Hazlitt) **29**:146, 161
"On Sitting Down to Read King Lear Once Again" (Keats) **8**:344; **73**:259, 323
"On Social Freedom" (Mill) **58**:378
"On Some Fossil Remains of Man" (Huxley) **67**:83
"On Some of the Characteristics of Modern Poetry, and on the Lyrical Poems of Alfred Tennyson" (Hallam) **110**:128, 158
"On Some of the Old Actors" (Lamb) **10**:423; **113**:206
"On Spring" (Horton) **87**:110
"On Standards of Taste" (Brown) **74**:192, 194
"On Summer" (Horton) **87**:110
"On Superstition" (Freneau) **1**:320; **111**:110
"On Taste" (Hazlitt) **29**:148
"On Teaching the Children of the Poor to Read" (Cobbett) **49**:97
"On the Advisableness of Improving Natural Knowledge" (Huxley) **67**:16, 26, 48, 56, 83-4, 87
"On the Aesthetic Education of Man" (Schiller)
See "Briefe über die ästhetische Erziehung des Menschen"
"On the Agency" (Martineau) **137**:350
"On the Alliterative Metre of Pierce Plowman's Visions" (Percy) **95**:313, 324
"On the Altar-Piece by Tiepolo" (Symonds) **34**:352
"On the Anatomy and the Affinities of the Family of the Medusae" (Huxley) **67**:79
"On the Ancient Metrical Romances" (Percy) **95**:323-24
"On the Application of Evolutionary Principles to Art and Literature" (Symonds) **34**:326
"On the Approaching Revolution in Great Britain" (De Quincey) **87**:40
"On the Artificial Comedy of the Last Century" (Lamb) **10**:392, 409, 411, 413, 419, 422-24, 427, 432; **113**:167, 202, 286
On the Athenian Orators (Macaulay) **42**:118, 120
"On the Banks of the Torrent" (Isaacs)
See "A orillas del torrente"
On the Basis of Aesthetics (Schlegel) **45**:332
"On the Beach at Midnight" (Whitman) **4**:592
"On the Beach at Night" (Whitman) **31**:391, 431
"On the boundless plain careering" (Fuller) **50**:246-7
On the Brink (Feuillet) **45**:88
"On the British Constitution" (Paine) **62**:325
"On the Canal Grande" (Meyer)
See "Auf dem Canal Grande"
"On the Capture of Fugitive Slaves Near Washington" (Lowell) **90**:215, 219
"On the Catholic Claims" (Dyer) **129**:110
"On the Character of Rousseau" (Hazlitt) **82**:164
"On the Civilization of the Western Aboriginal Country" (Freneau) **111**:190
"On the Clerical Character" (Hazlitt) **29**:152
On the Concept of Irony, with Special Reference to Socrates (Kierkegaard)
See *Om Begrebet Ironi med stadigt Hensyn til Socrates*
"On the Conduct of Life" (Hazlitt) **29**:150, 156; **82**:75, 122
On the Connection between the Animal and the Spiritual Nature of Man (Schiller)
See *Über den Zusammenhang der tierischen Natur des Menschen mit seiner geistigen*
"On the Connexion between Mythology and Philosophy" (Hopkins and Hugo) **17**:229
On the Constitution of the Church and State (Coleridge) **99**:115
"On the Conversation of Authors" (Hazlitt) **29**:147
"On the Conversation of Poets" (Hazlitt) **29**:165
On the Cracow-Vienna Line (Fredro) **8**:286
"On the Cranial Nerves" (Büchner) **26**:50, 68
"On the Custom of Hissing at the Theatres" (Lamb) **10**:409-11
"On the Death of Adaline" (Chivers) **49**:68
"On the Death of an Infant" (Horton) **87**:110
"On the Death of Captain Biddle" (Freneau) **1**:317; **111**:143
"On the Death of Dr. Adam Clarke" (Sigourney) **21**:309
"On the Death of Elizabeth Linley" (Sheridan) **91**:232
"On the Death of General Wolf" (Darwin) **106**:182
"On the Death of Goethe" (Baratynsky)
See "Na smert Gyote"
"On the Death of Lieut William Howard Allen" (Halleck) **47**:57
"On the Death of Mrs. Throckmorton's Bulfinch" (Cowper) **94**:33-8, 120, 123-24
"On the Death of My Parents" (Petofi)
See "Szüleim halálára"
On the Death of Pushkin (Lermontov)
See "Smert' poeta"
"On the Death of Rebecca" (Horton) **87**:94, 101, 110
"On the Death of Sir W. Russell" (Cowper) **94**:24
"On the Defects and Abuses in Public Institutions" (Dyer) **129**:110
"On the Definition of Political Economy" (Mill) **58**:338
On the Development of Revolutionary Ideas in Russia (Herzen) **10**:324; **61**:109
"On the Development of the Teeth" (Huxley) **67**:52-3, 81-3
"On the Devil, and Devils" (Shelley) **18**:367, 375
"On the Disadvantages of Intellectual Superiority" (Hazlitt) **29**:150
"On the Dove's Leaving the Ark" (Sigourney) **21**:289
"On the Dread and Dislike of Science" (Lewes) **25**:314
"On the Dual Form" (Humboldt)
See "Über den Dualis"
"On the Duties of Children" (Channing) **17**:4
"On the Educational Value of the Natural History Sciences" (Huxley) **67**:52-3, 81-3
On the Ego (Schelling) **30**:152-53
"On the Emigration to America" (Freneau) **111**:166
"On the Equality of the Sexes" (Murray) **63**:184, 188, 193, 206, 208-9, 212
"On the Essence of Religion" (Schleiermacher) **107**:340
On the Eve (Turgenev)
See *Nakanune*
"On the Eve of the First Anniversary of August 4, 1864" (Tyutchev)
See "Nakanune godovščiny avgusta 1864 g."
"On the Evening and Morning" (Horton) **87**:92
"On the Evening, Meditated on the Welsh Coast" (Dyer) **129**:148
"On the Evils of Human Life" (Freneau) **111**:111
"On the Extinction of the Venetian Republic" (Wordsworth) **12**:395, 431
"On the Fear of Death" (Hazlitt) **29**:152, 170-71; **82**:96, 106
"On the Feeling of Immortality in Youth" (Hazlitt) **29**:152; **82**:96
"On the Field of Waterloo" (Rossetti) **77**:296, 363, 365
"On the Formation of Coal" (Huxley) **67**:27
"On the Foundation of Our Belief in a Divine Government of the Universe" (Fichte) **62**:62
On the Fourfold Root of the Law of Sufficient Reason (Schopenhauer)
See *Über die vierfache Wurzel des Satzes vom zureichenden Grunde*
On the Fourfold Root of the Thesis of Adequate Ground (Schopenhauer)
See *Über die vierfache Wurzel des Satzes vom zureichenden Grunde*
"On the Future Extinction of Blue Eyes" (Lewes) **25**:310
"On the Genius and Character of Hogarth" (Lamb) **10**:387, 408, 411, 420; **113**:203
On the Gods of Samothrace (Schelling) **30**:143
"On the Gradual Formation of Thought during Speech" (Kleist)
See "Über die allmähliche Verfertigung der Gedanken beim Reden"
"On the Grasshopper and the Cricket" (Keats) **73**:218, 324
"On the Grecian Room in Princess Zeneida Volkonskaia's House i n Moscow" (Mickiewicz)
See "Na pokoj grecki w eomu księżnej Zeneidy Wołkońskiej w Moskwie"
On the Ground of our Belief in a Divine World-Order (Fichte)
See *Ueber den Grund unseres Glaubens an eine göttliche Weltregierung*
"On the Headland" (Taylor) **89**:309

On the Historical (Manzoni)
See *Del romanzo storico*
"On the Historical Progress of Free Thought in Russia" (Bestuzhev) **131**:178, 184
"On the Honourable Emanuel Swedenborg's Universal Theology" (Freneau) **111**:110
"On the Hypothesis that Animals Are Automata and Its History" (Huxley) **67**:86-7, 95, 100
"On the Ideal in Art" (Cranch) **115**:68
"On the Ignorance of the Learned" (Hazlitt) **29**:150
"On the Importance of Educating Hindu Females" (Dutt) **118**:30
"On the Inconveniency of Being Hanged" (Lamb) **10**:387
"On the Independence of Judges" (Dyer) **129**:110
"On the Indestructibility of Our True Being through Death" (Schopenhauer) **51**:333
"On the Inevitable Crisis" (Holmes) **14**:111
"On the Influence of Authority and Custom on the Female Mind and Manners" (Hays) **114**:206
"On the Ingratitude of Republics" (Freneau) **111**:160, 162
"On the Introduction of Rationalistic Principles into Revealed Religion" (Newman) **99**:266
"On the Judging of Pictures" (Hazlitt) **29**:144
"On the Knocking at the Gate in 'Macbeth'" (De Quincey) **4**:78, 85; **87**:74
"On the Knocking on the Door in Macbeth" (De Quincey)
See "On the Knocking at the Gate in 'Macbeth'"
"On the Knowledge of Character" (Hazlitt) **29**:186; **82**:76
"On the Last Day of the Year" (Ichiyō)
See "Otsugomori"
On the Late Persecution of the Protestants in the South of France (Williams) **135**:311, 335
"On the Literary Character" (Hazlitt) **29**:148
"On the Literary Criticism and Views of the 'Moscow Observer'" (Belinski) **5**:96
"On the Living Poets" (Hazlitt) **29**:161, 166
"On the Loss of the Royal George" (Cowper)
See "Lines on the Loss of the Royal George"
"On the Love of Life" (Hazlitt) **82**:115
"On the Memorable Victory" (Freneau)
See "Poem on the memorable victory obtained by the gallant capt. Paul Jones, or the Good Man Richard, over the Seraphis, etc. under the command of capt. Pearson"
"On the Method of Zadig" (Huxley) **67**:48, 63
"On the Methods and Results of Ethnology" (Huxley) **67**:97
"On the Metre of Pierce Plowman's Visions" (Percy)
See "On the Alliterative Metre of Pierce Plowman's Visions"
"On the Modern Element in Literature" (Arnold) **29**:11, 53; **89**:32, 38, 40, 42, 44, 118, 121
On the Modern Spirit in Literature (Arnold) **29**:23
"On the Monument of Dante to be erected in Florence" (Leopardi)
See "Sopra il monumento di Dante"
"On the Morphology of the Cephalous Mollusca" (Huxley) **67**:53
"On the Mysticism Attributed to the Early Fathers of the Church" (Keble) **87**:191
"On the Natural History of the Man-like Apes" (Huxley) **67**:83
"On the Natural Inequality of Men" (Huxley) **67**:67
"On the Nature of Poetry" (Bryant) **6**:182; **46**:31, 33, 33
On the Nature of the Scholar (Fichte)
See *Ueber das Wesen des Gelehrten*
On the New Dramatic School in Italy (Foscolo) **8**:270
"On the New Year, 1816" (Tyutchev) **34**:387
"On the Oldest Myths" (Schelling) **30**:150, 152
"On the Origin and Progress of Novel-Writing" (Barbauld) **50**:17
On the Origin of Species by Means of Natural Selection or the Preservation of Favoured Races in the Struggle for Life (Darwin) **57**:113-25, 127, 131, 133-7, 139-40, 142, 145, 149-52, 154-5, 158-9, 161-2, 164-70, 173-5, 181-2, 189, 192
"On the Paroo" (Kendall) **12**:192
"On the Past and Future" (Hazlitt) **29**:142; **82**:157
"On the Periodical Essayists" (Hazlitt) **82**:93
"On the Physical Basis of Life" (Huxley) **67**:37, 40-2, 58, 78, 80, 84-6, 95
"On the Place of Man in Nature" (Herzen) **10**:347-8
"On the Pleasure of Hating" (Hazlitt) **29**:147, 152, 182; **82**:98, 106, 129
"On the Pleasure of Painting" (Hazlitt) **29**:182, 184; **82**:154-55, 161, 165
"On the Poet and His Contemporary Significance" (Zhukovsky) **35**:397
"On the Poetic Muse" (Horton) **87**:94, 111
"On the Poetry of Essence" (Almqvist)
See "Om poesi i sak"
"On the Position and Incomes of the Cathedral Clergy" (Bowles) **103**:54
On the Possibility of a Form for Philosophy in General (Schelling) **30**:151-52
On the Power of the Spirit to Control Its Morbid Feelings by Mere Resolution (Kant) **27**:227
"On the Present State of Literature" (Mill) **11**:384; **58**:332
"On the Proposal to Erect a Monument in England to Lord Byron" (Lazarus) **109**:294
"On the Proposed System of State Consolidation" (Freneau) **111**:191
"On the Prose Style of Poets" (Hazlitt) **29**:147, 167; **82**:123-24
"On the Prospect of Establishing a Pantisocracy in America" (Coleridge) **99**:48
"On the Punishment of Death" (Wilson) **5**:568
"On the Puppet Theater" (Kleist)
See "Über das Marionettentheater"
"On the Qualifications Necessary to Success in Life" (Hazlitt) **29**:147
"On the Realities of the Imagination" (Hunt) **1**:421
"On the Receipt of My Mother's Picture out of Norfolk" (Cowper)
See "Lines on the Receipt of My Mother's Picture"
"On the Receipt of My Mothers's Picture from Norfolk" (Cowper)
See "Lines on the Receipt of My Mother's Picture"
On the Relative Social Position of Mothers and Governesses (Jameson) **43**:323
"On the Religion of Nature" (Freneau) **1**:321; **111**:141
"On the Removal of an Ancient Mansion" (Sigourney) **87**:320
On the Report of a Monument to Be Erected in Westminster Abbey, to the Memory of a Late Author (Beattie)
See *Verses on the Death of the Revd Mr Charles Churchill*
"On the Rise and Progress of Popular Disaffection" (Southey) **97**:263
"On the Rising Glory of America" (Freneau)
See *A Poem, on the Rising Glory of America*
"On the Road" (Nekrasov)
See "V doroge"
"On the Ryne" (Bowles)
See "Sonnet on the Ryne"
"On the Sanity of True Genius" (Lamb) **10**:410
"On the Sea" (Keats) **73**:259
"On the Sending of 'The Ball' to S.E." (Baratynsky) **103**:5
"On the Separate Existence of the Soul" (Hogg) **109**:231
"On the Sleep of Plants" (Freneau) **1**:320; **111**:101
"On the Slops" (Arany)
See "A Lejtőn"
"On the Spirit of Monarchy" (Hazlitt) **82**:103
"On the Spirit of Obligations" (Hazlitt) **82**:74
"On the Stage" (Kemble) **18**:192
On the State of the Poor (Southey) **97**:250
"On the State of Women in the French Republic" (Williams) **135**:304, 335
"On the Study of Biology" (Huxley) **67**:83, 87
On the Study of Celtic Literature (Arnold) **6**:42, 46-47, 69; **29**:11, 58; **126**:44, 101-8
"On the Study of Greek Poetry" (Schlegel)
See "Über das Studium der griechischen Poesie"
"On the Style and Imitation of Models" (Lewes) **25**:325
"On the Sublime" (Schiller)
See "Über das Erhabene"
"On the Summits of Chisacá" (Isaacs)
See "En las cumbres de Chisacá"
"On the Supernatural in Poetry" (Radcliffe) **55**:223-4
"On the System of Policy Hitherto Pursued by Their Government" (Barlow) **23**:28
On the Thirteenth Night (Ichiyō)
See *Jusan'ya*
"On the Threshold" (Levy) **59**:96, 105, 119
"On the Too Remote Extension of American Commerce" (Freneau) **111**:101
"On the Tragedies of Shakespeare Considered with Reference to Their Fitness for Stage Representation" (Lamb) **10**:387, 409, 411-13, 420, 427, 432; **113**:202, 204, 206, 218, 280
"On the Translation of the Odyssey" (Zhukovsky) **35**:391
On the Treatment of the Criminal (Almqvist)
See *Om brottsliges behandling*
"On The True Religion" (Brownson) **50**:39
"On the Truth of the Savior" (Horton) **87**:110
"On the Uniformity and Perfection of Nature" (Freneau) **1**:324; **111**:109, 141
"On the Unity of Epism and Dramatism: A Conception of the Poetic Fugue" (Almqvist) **42**:10
"On the Universality and Other Attributes of the God of Nature" (Freneau) **111**:109, 141
"On the Vanity of Youthful Expectations" (Trumbull) **30**:348
On the Various Races of Mankind (Kant) **27**:215
"On the Vicissitudes of Things" (Freneau) **111**:107, 113
"On the Volga" (Nekrasov) **11**:400, 420
"On the Want of Money" (Hazlitt) **29**:183
"On the Wing" (Rossetti) **2**:561
On the World Soul (Schelling) **30**:171
"On the Writing of Essays" (Smith) **59**:314, 322
"On the Wye in May" (Levy) **59**:89
"On the Zoological Relations of Man with the Lower Animals" (Huxley) **67**:81-2
"On Translating Homer" (Arnold) **89**:82; **126**:46, 114
On Translating Homer (Arnold) **6**:46-47, 59; **29**:9, 41, 54; **126**:28
On Tyranny (Alfieri)
See *Della tirannide*
"On Vagabonds" (Smith) **59**:303, 309, 315-6

"On Violet's Wafers, Sent Me When I Was Ill" (Lanier) **118**:219
"On Visiting a Favourite Place" (Clare) **9**:120, 124
"On Visiting the Graves of Hawthorne and Thoreau" (Very) **9**:397
"On Visiting the Tomb of David Hume" (Dyer) **129**:105
"On Vulgarity and Affectation" (Hazlitt) **82**:99-100
"On Warsaw Critics and Reviewers" (Mickiewicz)
See "O Krytykach i Recenzentach"
"On Winter" (Horton) **87**:110
"On Women Who Cultivate Letters" (Staël-Holstein) **91**:311
"On Wordsworth" (Pater) **90**:323
"Ona" (Baratynsky) **103**:28
"Once Again" (Meyer)
See "Noch einmal"
"Once, as a lad, with a ringing call" (Baratynsky)
See "Byvalo, otrok, zvonkim klikom..."
"Once I Passed through a Populous City" (Whitman) **31**:378
"Once More This Time" (Arany)
See "Még ez egyszer"
Once Upon a Time There Were Two Kings (Planché) **42**:288-89, 295, 298
"L'onde et l'ombre" (Hugo) **10**:357
"Den onde Fryste" (Andersen) **79**:77
"Ondine à l'école" (Desbordes-Valmore) **97**:29
"L'Ondine et le pêcheur" (Gautier) **59**:34
1 (Dickinson) **77**:120
The One (Alfieri)
See *L'uno*
"One Among So Many" (Adams) **33**:4
"One Bumper at Parting" (Moore) **110**:190
"The One Called Dead" (Muller) **73**:352
"One Crucifixion is recorded only" (Dickinson) **77**:83
"One Day" (Rossetti) **66**:307
"One Dignity Delays for All" (Dickinson) **21**:62; **77**:163
"One Foot in Sea and One on Shore" (Rossetti) **66**:341
"The One Hope" (Rossetti) **4**:491, 518
188 (Dickinson) **77**:113
140 (Dickinson) **77**:84
144 (Dickinson) **77**:162-63
196 (Dickinson) **77**:93
106 (Dickinson) **77**:147
164 (Dickinson) **77**:83
130 (Dickinson) **77**:122-24
The 120 Days of Sodom; or, The Romance of the School for Libertinage (Sade)
See *Les 120 journées de Sodome; ou, L'école du libertinage*
124 (Dickinson) **77**:173
102 (Dickinson) **77**:173
"One Identity" (Whitman) **4**:564
"One Life" (Shelley) **93**:327-28
"One More Letter to Mary Ann" (Cooke) **110**:39, 67-8
"The One Mystery" (Mangan) **27**:280-81, 298
"One Need Not Be a Chamber to Be Haunted" (Dickinson) **77**:97
"One of Cleopatra's Nights" (Gautier)
See "Une nuit de Clèopâtre"
One of the "Forty" (Daudet)
See *L'immortel*
"One of the New Voters" (Jefferies) **47**:112, 137, 139, 143
"One of Them" (Cooke) **110**:35, 56
One of Them (Lever) **23**:289, 292-93
"One Thought Keeps Tormenting Me" (Petofi)
See "Egy gondolat bánt engèmet"
1084 (Dickinson) **77**:50
1082 (Dickinson) **77**:94
1058 (Dickinson) **77**:94
1053 (Dickinson) **77**:183
1046 (Dickinson) **77**:130, 163
1099 (Dickinson) **77**:84
1078 (Dickinson) **77**:129
1071 (Dickinson) **77**:89
1076 (Dickinson) **77**:80
1032 (Dickinson) **77**:49
1026 (Dickinson) **77**:163
The One Too Many (Linton) **41**:164
One Tract More (Milnes) **61**:129, 137-8
"One Versus Two" (Woolson) **82**:272
"One Way of Love" (Browning) **19**:127; **79**:153
"One Word More" (Browning) **19**:110, 127, 131; **79**:163
One Word More (Browning) **66**:52
"One Year Ago—Jots What?" (Dickinson) **21**:64; **77**:63, 147
"The One-Eyed God" (Ueda Akinari)
See "Me hitotsu no kami"
The Ones Passed-By (Leskov)
See *Obojdennye*
"One's-Self I Sing" (Whitman)
See "Song of Myself"
Onestá (Feuillet) **45**:87
"Only a Curl" (Browning) **61**:9
Only a Fiddler (Andersen)
See *Kun en spillemand*
Only a Girl (Jefferies) **47**:92-93, 121
Only an Irish Boy (Alger) **8**:40; **83**:143
"Only Friendship" (Isaacs)
See "¿Solo amistad?"
"The Only One" (Hölderlin)
See "Der Einzige"
"Onnelliset" (Kivi) **30**:51
"Onuphrius ou les Vexations fantastiques d'un admirateur d'Hoffmann" (Gautier) **1**:356; **59**:9, 26-7
"Onward to the Holy War" (Petofi)
See "Föl a szenthháborúra"
The Open Air (Jefferies) **47**:95, 102, 107, 122, 130, 133, 137
The Open Door (Oliphant) **11**:454
"Open Letter to a French Friend (Frederic Villot)" (Wagner) **119**:198
"The Open Question" (Hood) **16**:235
"Open Secret Societies" (Thomson) **18**:401
"Open Thy Lattice Love" (Foster) **26**:285
"Open Vields" (Barnes) **75**:101
"Opening Discourse" (Sainte-Beuve) **5**:349
"The Opening of the Piano" (Holmes) **81**:99
Oper und Drama (Wagner) **9**:405-06, 414, 426, 452-56, 467, 475; **119**:202, 248, 250, 253, 256, 258-63, 274-75, 291, 294
Opera and Drama (Wagner)
See *Oper und Drama*
The Opera of "The Prophet" (Scribe)
See *Le prophète*
Opere (Leopardi) **129**:246-53
Opere inedite o rare (Manzoni) **98**:214
Operette morali (Leopardi) **129**:222, 226, 241-44, 255, 257, 259, 265, 267, 276, 302, 304, 307, 339, 343-44, 350-51, 353
Der Opfertod (Kotzebue) **25**:144, 154-55
"Ophélie" (Rimbaud) **4**:458, 484, 486; **82**:247
"Opinions of Mansfield Park" (Austen) **95**:18
Opium Confessions (De Quincey)
See *Confessions of an English Opium-Eater*
Opium-Eater (De Quincey)
See *Confessions of an English Opium-Eater*
"The Opossum Hunters" (Kendall) **12**:191
"The Opposite Neighbour" (Opie) **65**:168, 172
"The Opposite Page" (Eminescu) **33**:254
"Opposition" (Lanier) **6**:254; **118**:239, 265
"Opravdanie" (Baratynsky) **103**:28
"Opredelenie poezii" (Bestuzhev) **131**:165
"The Optimist" (Bestuzhev)
See "Otryvok iz Komedii 'Optimist'"
Opus Maximum (Coleridge) **54**:109
Opus Postumum (Kant) **27**:239, 245, 248
"Oración" (Casal) **131**:243
"La oración" (Isaacs) **70**:303-04
"Les oracles" (Vigny) **7**:480
Oráculos de Talía (Gómez de Avellaneda) **111**:51, 53
"Oraison du soir" (Rimbaud) **4**:454, 484; **35**:282
Oralloossa, Son of the Incas (Bird) **1**:87, 90
"The Orange and Green" (Griffin) **7**:195-96
"Orara" (Kendall) **12**:182, 186-87, 190-92, 195, 198-99, 201
An Oration Delivered before the Phi Beta Kappa Society at Cambridge, August 31, 1837 (Emerson)
See *American Scholar*
An Oration, Pronounced before the Knox and Warren Branches of the Washington Benevolent Society, at Amherst . . . (Webster) **30**:414-16
"Oration upon Rum" (Freneau) **111**:81
Orations and Addresses (Bryant) **46**:5
"Orator" (Bestuzhev) **131**:165, 183
"Orazione a Bonaparte pel congresso di Lione" (Foscolo) **8**:261
"The Orchard Harvest" (Mitford) **4**:401
"The Orchard Pit" (Rossetti) **4**:504, 510, 516; **77**:355-56
"The Orchestra of Today" (Lanier) **6**:276; **118**:243
"Ordeal of the Bier" (Arany)
See "Tetemrehívás"
The Order of Nature (Bryant) **46**:16, 25
The Order of St. Vladimir (Gogol) **15**:84-5; **78**:258
The Oregon Trail (Parkman) **12**:328, 336, 338, 341, 346, 351-52, 354, 358, 377
"L'Oreiller d'une petite fille" (Desbordes-Valmore) **97**:29, 38
Oreste (Alfieri) **101**:4, 8, 32, 42
"The Organic Development of Man in Connection with His Mental and Spiritual Activities" (Dobrolyubov) **5**:140
"The Organist" (Lampman) **25**:160, 192, 199, 216
"The Organization of the International" (Bakunin) **58**:136
"L'orgie Parisienne; ou, Paris se Repeuple" (Rimbaud) **4**:458, 466; **35**:271; **82**:238
"Oriana" (Sigourney) **21**:290
"Oriana" (Tennyson) **30**:223, 245
Les orientales (Hugo) **3**:234, 236, 261-62, 265, 270; **10**:362; **21**:194, 202
Origin and Objects of Ancient Freemasonry (Delany) **93**:159, 163
"The Origin and Progress of the Art of Writing" (Bello) **131**:120, 130
"Origin and the Duties of Literature" (Foscolo)
See "Dell'origine e dell'ufficio della letteratura: Orazione"
Origin of Masonry (Paine) **62**:314
"Origin of Poe's 'Raven'" (Chivers) **49**:38
"The Origin of Species" (Huxley) **67**:83
The Origin of Species (Darwin)
See *On the Origin of Species by Means of Natural Selection or the Preservation of Favoured Races in the Struggle for Life*
"The Origin of the English Stage" (Percy) **95**:313, 323-24, 327
Origin of the Family, Private Property and the State (Engels)
See *Der Ursprung der Familie, des Privateigenthums und des Staats*
The Origin of the Feast of Purim; or, The Destinies of Haman and Mordecai (Tyler) **3**:572-73
The Origin of the Hindoos (Schlegel)
See *De l'origine des Hindous*
"The Origin of the Sail" (Opie) **65**:160
Original Letters, etc., of Sir John Falstaff and his Friends (Lamb) **113**:277
Original Panoramic Views (Brown) **89**:184, 188
Original Poetry by Victor and Cazire (Shelley) **18**:307, 342
Les origines de la France contemporaine (Taine) **15**:424-25, 429, 432, 437, 440-42, 445-46, 453-56, 466, 471, 473-77

Origines du droit française cherchées dans les symboles et formules du droit universel (Michelet) **31**:228-29
The Origins of Christianity (Renan)
See *Histoire des origines du christianisme*
The Origins of Contemporary France (Taine)
See *Les origines de la France contemporaine*
Origins of the Family, Private Property and the State (Engels)
See *Der Ursprung der Familie, des Privateigenthums und des Staats*
"A orillas del torrente" (Isaacs) **70**:310
"Orina, the Soldier's Mother" (Nekrasov) **11**:404-05, 421
Orion (Horne) **127**:236, 238, 242, 245-48, 259, 263, 268-69, 277-81
"Oriska" (Sigourney) **21**:299
"Orlando Innamorato" (Bello) **131**:92
Orley Farm (Trollope) **6**:455-56, 463, 470, 492-94, 499, 514-15; **33**:363; **101**:269, 279, 285, 301-02, 306, 308, 310, 319
Ormond (Edgeworth) **1**:258, 262-64, 266-68, 270-71; **51**:77, 79-80, 88, 90-1, 104-05
Ormond Grosvenor (Hale) **75**:320
Ormond; or, The Secret Witness (Brown) **22**:3-4, 7-8, 12, 14, 17-18, 20-1, 25, 27, 30, 45, 47-52, 54-5; **74**:4, 9-10, 15, 17, 19, 21, 36, 47-8, 51, 54, 56, 61, 68, 73, 76, 80, 82-3, 92-4, 96-7, 101, 103-04, 109-12, 117-21, 124, 126, 129-30, 133-35, 137-39, 142-43, 153, 156, 159-61, 164; **122**:53-54, 118-19, 150, 153, 159
Ormus och Ariman (Almqvist) **42**:15-16
"Ormuzd and Ahriman" (Cranch) **115**:23
"Ornières" (Rimbaud) **4**:473
Ornithological Biography (Audubon) **47**:11, 13-14, 24, 32-3, 38, 40, 42, 44, 51
"Az örök zsidó" (Arany) **34**:18-19
"The Orphan" (Opie) **65**:158
"The Orphan Boy's Tale" (Opie) **65**:156, 175
The Orphan of the Castle (Smith)
See *Emmeline, the Orphan of the Castle*
"Orpheus" (Lazarus) **8**:412-14, 418, 420, 425; **109**:292, 294, 319
Orpheus in der Unterwelt (Nestroy) **42**:232
Orpheus in the Haymarket (Planché) **42**:275, 287, 294
Orphic Sayings (Alcott) **1**:21-22, 24-26
"Orphisch" (Hölderlin) **16**:176
Orra (Baillie) **71**:6-7, 12
Orra: A Lapland Tale (Barnes) **75**:14-15, 18, 22, 26, 69-70, 92
Ortis (Foscolo)
See *Ultime lettere di Jacopo Ortis*
"Az örült" (Petofi) **21**:264
Oscar; ou, Le mari qui trompe sa femme (Scribe) **16**:389, 412
"Oscar y Malvina" (Espronceda) **39**:106
"Osen" (Baratynsky) **103**:25, 28, 39
Osorio (Coleridge)
See *Remorse*
Osservazioni sulla morale cattolica (Manzoni) **29**:269, 289, 294-95, 299, 301-03; **98**:238
"Őszzel" (Arany) **34**:19, 24
Ostatni (Krasiński) **4**:307, 311
"Der Ostermorgen" (Ludwig) **4**:353
"Ostrov Borngol'm" (Karamzin) **3**:285-89, 291
Ostrovitjane (Leskov) **25**:232, 252
Őszikék (Arany) **34**:16
"Ot zhizni toy, chto bushevala zdes" (Tyutchev) **34**:398, 409
"Otchayanny" (Turgenev) **21**:441; **122**:242
Otcy i deti (Turgenev)
See *Ottsy i deti*
Other People's Money (Gaboriau)
See *L'argent des autres*
The Other Side of the Tweed (Fontane)
See *Jenseit des Tweed*
Otho the Great (Keats) **8**:341, 348, 360; **73**:154, 173, 208, 234, 306; **121**:108, 177-78
"The Otonabee" (Moodie) **113**:347
"Otryvki iz poèmy 'Mat'" (Nekrasov) **11**:419-20
"Otryvki iz vospominanij svoich i čužich" (Turgenev) **122**:267
"Otryvok" (Baratynsky) **103**:8-9
"Otryvok iz Komedii 'Optimist'" (Bestuzhev) **131**:181
"Otsego Leaves" (Cooper) **129**:71-72
"Otsugomori" (Ichiyō) **49**:336-37, 343-44, 353
Ottavia (Alfieri) **101**:8, 38, 50
Otto (Klinger) **1**:428
Otto of Wittelsbach (Mitford) **4**:404
"Otto von Fieandt" (Runeberg) **41**:314
Ottokar (Grillparzer)
See *König Ottokars Glück und Ende*
Ottsy i deti (Turgenev) **21**:388-89, 391-92, 394, 396, 400-01, 405, 409-10, 413, 418-20, 422-23, 425-26, 432, 434, 436-37, 439, 442-49, 452; **37**:353-452; **122**:248-49, 251-52, 254, 256-57, 262, 265, 268, 275, 277-80, 282-83, 287, 292, 306, 315-17, 320, 325, 336
"Our America" (Martí)
See "Nuesta America"
"Our Be'th Place" (Barnes) **75**:59
"Our Casuarina Tree" (Dutt) **29**:121-22, 125, 127, 129
"Our Countrymen in Chains!" (Whittier) **8**:489, 510
"Our Country's Call" (Bryant) **46**:7
"Our Dead Singer" (Holmes) **14**:129
"Our Dramatic Repertoire" (Eminescu)
See "Our Theatrical Repertory"
"Our Father in Heaven" (Hale) **75**:279, 286
"Our Father's Works" (Barnes) **75**:79
"Our Granite Hills" (Hale) **75**:284
"Our Hatty" (Parton) **86**:348
"Our Heroic Themes" (Boker) **125**:33, 39
Our Hundred Days in Europe (Holmes) **81**:107
"Our Jack" (Kendall) **12**:192
"Our Lady of Sorrow" (Thomson) **18**:407
"Our Land" (Runeberg) **41**:312, 315-16, 319-20, 326-27
"Our Language and Literature" (Whitman) **81**:287, 289, 292
"Our Liberal Practitioners" (Arnold) **126**:10, 29, 61, 81
"Our Love Is Gone" (Eminescu) **131**:287
"Our Master" (Whittier) **8**:524; **59**:361
Our Mutual Friend (Dickens) **3**:159, 163, 166, 169-70, 173-74, 181, 188; **8**:194; **18**:111-12, 114, 116, 119-22, 132-34; **26**:170, 174, 184, 225; **37**:164, 173-4, 192, 206; **86**:198, 201, 204, 207, 214, 222, 224; **105**:199-357; **113**:20, 39, 42, 97, 118-19, 124, 127, 135, 142-44
"Our Nelly" (Parton) **86**:351
Our Nig; or, Sketches from the Life of a Free Black (Wilson) **78**:311-13, 315-20, 322-25, 327-31, 334-35, 338-41, 343, 345, 348-58, 360-63
"Our Old Earth Is Playing" (Petofi)
See "Játszik öreg földünk"
"Our Old Feuillage" (Whitman) **31**:387, 392; **81**:312
Our Old Home (Hawthorne) **2**:306-07, 314; **39**:179, 245
"Our Own" (Lowell) **90**:198
Our Own Folks—We'll Settle It Among Ourselves (Ostrovsky)
See *Svoi lyudi—sochtemsya!*
"Our Parish" (Dickens) **105**:353
"Our People Sent Me" (Turgenev)
See "Nashi poslali"
"Our Sin, the Feuilletons" (Faustino)
See "Nuestro pecado de los folletines"
"Our Slave" (Cooke) **110**:57-8
"Our Society at Cranford" (Gaskell) **5**:205; **70**:216
Our Sons (Michelet)
See *Nos fils*
"Our Theatrical Repertory" (Eminescu) **33**:272; **131**:310-11
"Our Tsar is a Russian (Prussian) German" (Bestuzhev)
See "Tsar, nash, nemets russkiy . . ."
"Our Village Post Office" (Sedgwick) **19**:444
Our Village: Sketches of Rural Character and Scenery (Mitford) **4**:400-01, 403-05, 407-08
"Our Village—By a Villager" (Hood) **16**:235-36
"Our Willie" (Timrod) **25**:372
Ours (Robertson) **35**:330, 333-34, 336, 338, 340-41, 345, 349, 351-56, 358, 360, 362, 363-65, 369-72
L'ours et le pacha (Scribe) **16**:382, 400
Out for Business (Alger) **83**:118, 119
"Out of Debt, Out of Danger" (Edgeworth) **51**:89
"Out of Doors in February" (Jefferies) **47**:137, 143
"Out of Prison" (Lampman)
See "Freedom"
"Out of the Cradle Endlessly Rocking" (Whitman) **4**:544, 551, 561, 567, 571, 579, 582, 592, 594-96, 602; **31**:368, 370, 379, 388-92, 403-04, 418, 421-22, 431, 437; **81**:249, 255, 257-58, 264, 271, 281-83, 366-70
"Out of the Deep I Have Called Unto Thee, O Lord" (Rossetti) **50**:285
"Out of the Depths I Cried to Thee" (Baudelaire)
See "De Profundis clamavi"
Out of the Foam (Cooke) **5**:130, 132
Out of the Frying Pan (Tamayo y Baus) **1**:571
"Out of the Rolling Ocean, the Crowd" (Whitman) **4**:544, 601
"Out of Town" (Levy) **59**:89, 119
Outamaro (Goncourt) **7**:163
"The Outer from the Inner" (Dickinson) **21**:65
"The Outlaw" (Kingsley) **35**:219
"The Outlet" (Dickinson)
See "My River Runs to Thee"
"Outline" (Bello) **131**:105
An Outline of English Speech-Craft (Barnes) **75**:27, 40, 65
An Outline of Rede-Craft (Barnes) **75**:27, 40
"Outline of Universal History" (Rowson) **69**:115-16
"Outlines for a Tomb" (Whitman) **31**:432; **81**:290
"Outlines of a Critique of Political Economy" (Engels) **85**:110, 125
Outlines of a Critique of Political Economy (Engels) **85**:110, 114, 167
Outlines of a Philosophy of the History of Man (Herder)
See *Ideen zur Philosophie der Geschichte der Menschheit*
"Outlook" (Lampman) **25**:209
"Outoplena" (Shevchenko)
See "Utoplena"
"Outre-Mer" (Kendall) **12**:183, 189
Outre-Mer: A Pilgrimage beyond the Sea (Longfellow) **2**:469, 475, 478, 489, 494; **45**:181, 183
"Outside London" (Jefferies) **47**:137
"Outside the Church" (Lazarus) **109**:298, 322
"Outsiders of Society and Their Homes in London" (Mayhew) **31**:181
"Outworld" (Cranch) **115**:35
"Ouverture ancienne d'Hérodiade" (Mallarmé) **41**:242, 277
"Ouvriers" (Rimbaud) **4**:465, 485; **35**:323
"The Oval Portrait" (Poe) **1**:500; **16**:331, 336; **117**:293-94
"Ovcebyk" (Leskov) **25**:230, 239
"Over the Carnage Rose Prophetic a Voice" (Whitman) **81**:313, 331
Over the Teacups (Holmes) **14**:115, 124, 133, 143, 146; **81**:118
"The Overcoat" (Gogol)
See "Shinel"

"Over-Soul" (Emerson) **1**:295, 298, 300, 307; **38**:154, 168-71, 176-77; **98**:92, 100, 190
"An Ovid" (Grillparzer) **102**:174
Ovingdean Grange: A Tale of the South Downs (Ainsworth) **13**:36, 41-3
"Ovsianko the Freeholder" (Turgenev)
See "The Freeholder Ovsyanikov"
"Ovskyanikov the Freeholder" (Turgenev)
See "The Freeholder Ovsyanikov"
Owen Tudor (Arnim) **5**:22
The Owl and the Pussycat (Lear) **3**:297, 307-09
"The Owl and the Sparrow" (Trumbull) **30**:345, 349
"Owlet" (Cooke) **5**:133
The Owners of the Entail (Arnim)
See *Die Majoratsherren*
"Owney and Owney Napeak" (Griffin) **7**:198
"Oxford in the Vacation" (Lamb) **10**:407, 436-37; **113**:192, 194, 199, 225, 236, 248, 253
"The Oxford Malignants and Dr Hampden" (Arnold) **18**:53
Oxford University Sermons (Newman) **38**:289, 304, 307, 309, 312
Oxtiern (Sade) **47**:361
"Ozero Valen" (Pavlova) **138**:54
"Ozorniki" (Saltykov) **16**:372
"Paa Sygeleiet" (Wergeland) **5**:541
Pacchiarotto, and Other Poems (Browning) **19**:86
Pacific Series (Alger) **8**:43
"Pacsirtaszót hallok megint" (Petofi) **21**:286
"The Padlocked Lady" (Dyer) **129**:94, 105
Padmā vati (Dutt) **118**:5
"A Paean" (Poe) **117**:238
"Pagan and Mediaeval Religious Sentiment" (Arnold) **29**:55; **89**:34, 39
"Paganini" (Hunt) **1**:415
"Page and the Lady" (Smith) **59**:257
"A Page from A Woman's Heart" (Parton) **86**:347
"Page from the Diary of a Guards Officer" (Bestuzhev)
See "Listok iz dnevnika gvardeyskogo ofitsera"
The Page of Gustavus Adolphus (Meyer)
See *Gustav Adolfs Page*
"A Pageant" (Rossetti) **2**:558-9, 571, 576
A Pageant, and Other Poems (Rossetti) **2**:558, 563, 575; **50**:271
"The Pageant of Summer" (Jefferies) **47**:97, 101, 114, 136-37
Pages (Mallarmé) **4**:376-77
"The Pah-Utes" (Winnemucca) **79**:340
"Paimentyttö" (Kivi) **30**:51
"Pain" (Coleridge) **99**:22
"Pain" (Patmore) **9**:347, 360, 363, 365
"Pain and Time Strive Not" (Morris) **4**:434
"Pain Has an Element of Blank" (Dickinson) **21**:8, 77
"The Pains of Sleep" (Coleridge) **9**:133-34, 155, 177, 194; **54**:87; **99**:67, 74, 91, 93
"The Paint King" (Allston) **2**:20
"The Painted Columbine" (Very) **9**:380
"The Painted Cup" (Bryant) **46**:7
"The Painter" (Almqvist)
See "Målaren"
"The Painter" (Crabbe) **26**:102
"The Painter of Modern Life" (Baudelaire)
See "Le Peintre de la vie moderne"
A Painter's Atelier (Desbordes-Valmore)
See *L'Atelier d'un peintre*
"The Painter's Scarecrow" (Cranch) **115**:57
"Pairing Time Anticipated" (Cowper) **94**:121
"Paisaje espiritual" (Casal) **131**:239, 242, 267
"Paisaje tropical" (Silva) **114**:301
"La paix des dieux" (Leconte de Lisle) **29**:221, 229, 231, 234
"Las palabras" (Larra) **17**:275; **130**:204-5
The Palace (Almqvist)
See *Palatset*
"The Palace of Art" (Tennyson) **30**:209, 211, 223-24, 233, 258, 266-67; **65**:248, 258, 261, 270, 357-8; **115**:237, 274, 335
"The Palace of Humbug" (Carroll) **139**:33
"Palace of Pleasure" (Hunt) **1**:406
"The Palace of Ruin" (Darley) **2**:128
Palatset (Almqvist) **42**:20
"Palinodia al marchese Gino Capponi" (Leopardi) **129**:248
The Palliser Novels (Trollope) **6**:506
"The Palm and the Pine" (Taylor) **89**:310
Palm Leaves (Milnes) **61**:130, 137
"Palm Sunday" (Keble) **87**:177, 201
Palma, ou la nuit du Vendredi-Saint (Feuillet) **45**:89
"La paloma celosa" (Lizardi) **30**:68
"The Palsy of the Heart" (Milnes) **61**:136
Paméla Giraud (Balzac) **5**:51-52
"Pamfalon the Clown" (Leskov)
See "Skomorox Pamfalon"
"Pamiati Iu. P. Vrevskoi" (Turgenev) **122**:313
"Pamiatnik" (Pushkin)
See "Pamjatnik"
"Pamjatnik" (Pushkin) **83**:261
A Pamphlet to the Journeymen and Labourers of England, Scotland, and Ireland (Cobbett) **49**:110
"Pamyati V.A. Zhukovskogo" (Tyutchev) **34**:398
"Pan" (Emerson) **1**:297
"Pan" (Leconte de Lisle) **29**:224
"Pan and Luna" (Browning) **19**:153; **79**:153
"Pan and the Syrinx" (Laforgue)
See "Pan et la Syrinx"
Pan Benet (Fredro) **8**:285
"Pan et la Syrinx" (Laforgue) **5**:271, 274, 278, 281; **53**:293
Pan Geldhab (Fredro) **8**:285-86, 289-90, 292
"Pan i pies" (Krasicki) **8**:403, 407
"Pan Is Dead" (Browning) **1**:123
Pan Jowialski (Fredro) **8**:285-87, 290, 292-93
Pan Podstoli (Krasicki) **8**:398-401, 405-06
Pan Tadeusz; czyli, Ostatni zajazd na Litwie (Mickiewicz) **3**:389-92, 394-95, 397, 400-03; **101**:158, 167, 169, 171, 183-86, 193-94, 196-97, 210
Pandora (Nerval) **67**:312-13, 363-64
Panegirico do Plinio a Traiano (Alfieri) **101**:41-2
Panegyric of Pliny to Trahan (Alfieri)
See *Panegirico do Plinio a Traiano*
"Panegyric on the Drama" (Murray) **63**:184
Panegyric. ... to Trajan (Alfieri)
See *Panegirico do Plinio a Traiano*
"The Panjandrum" (Trollope) **101**:234-35
Pankraz, der Schmoller (Keller) **2**:415
"Panni Panyó" (Petofi) **21**:285
"Panorama" (Whittier) **8**:496, 531
The Panorama, and Other Poems (Whittier) **8**:495; **59**:371
"Panorama matritense. Cuadros de costumbres de la capital observados y descritos por un Curioso Parlante" (Larra) **130**:228, 255
"The Panorama of Lausanne" (Jameson) **43**:337
"The Panorama of Vanities" (Eminescu) **131**:287, 343
"Pan's Pipes" (Stevenson) **5**:388
"A Pansy from the Grave of Keats" (Whitman) **19**:457
"Panthère noire" (Leconte de Lisle) **29**:216-17, 224
"Pantisocracy" (Coleridge) **99**:48
"Pantomime" (Verlaine) **2**:629; **51**:378-80
"Le papa de Simon" (Maupassant) **1**:462
Papa Gobseck (Balzac) **35**:9, 26-7
"The Papacy and the Roman Question" (Tyutchev) **34**:383
Der Papagei (Kotzebue) **25**:146-47
"Papal Benediction" (Milnes) **61**:129
Paper Against Gold and Glory Against Prosperity (Cobbett) **49**:110
The Papers of James Madison (Madison) **126**:247, 278
The Papers of Thomas Jefferson (Jefferson) **103**:127
Papers on Literature and Art (Fuller) **5**:159-60, 164
The Paphian Bower (Planché) **42**:286, 299
Die Papiere des Teufels (Nestroy) **42**:260
Papirer (Kierkegaard) **34**:200, 207, 222, 238-40; **78**:136, 158, 160, 162-63, 166, 189, 197-98, 21 7, 225-29, 238-39, 242-43, 251; **125**:184, 193, 207, 260, 262, 265-67
Pappenheim Cuirassier (Fouqué) **2**:267
La pâques dramatique (Nerval) **67**:324
Par les champs et par les grèves (Flaubert) **62**:73
"The Parable" (Pushkin) **83**:272
"Les paraboles de Dom Guy" (Leconte de Lisle) **29**:225
Paracelsus (Browning) **19**:74-5, 78, 99, 103, 105, 109, 116, 120, 139-40; **79**:98, 140, 146, 149, 159, 168, 181, 185, 190
"Parade" (Rimbaud) **35**:308, 312, 322; **82**:232
Les paradis artificiels: Opium et haschisch (Baudelaire) **6**:80, 84, 119, 124; **29**:67, 71, 96; **55**:68-9
"Paradise" (Rossetti) **2**:563; **50**:272
"The Paradise and the Peri" (Moore) **6**:380-81, 387-88; **110**:213, 217, 221
"Paradise Lost" (Browning) **1**:128
"The Paradise of Bachelors" (Melville) **3**:354, 380
Paradise on the Dniester (Sacher-Masoch) **31**:287, 295, 310
"Paradise (to Be) Regained" (Thoreau) **21**:347
"Paradox of Achilles and the Tortoise" (Carroll) **139**:57
Parallèlement (Verlaine) **2**:618, 620-21, 625, 632; **51**:352, 359, 361-63, 366, 368, 371-72, 388
Parasha (Turgenev) **21**:376; **122**:247, 276
The Parasite (Turgenev)
See *Nakhlebnik*
"Pardon of Sainte-Anne" (Corbière)
See "La rapsode foraine et le pardon de Saint-Anne"
"Parental Indulgence" (Webster) **30**:424
Parentation uber Anselmo (Claudius) **75**:191
The Parent's Assistant (Edgeworth) **1**:261-63, 266-67; **51**:78-9, 81, 87, 89, 102, 110
Les parents pauvres (Balzac) **5**:35, 37, 63
Parere sulle tragedie (Alfieri) **101**:73
Parerga and Paralipomena (Schopenhauer)
See *Parerga und Paralipomena*
Parerga und Paralipomena (Schopenhauer) **51**:246, 271, 275, 278, 296-97, 326-27, 333-34, 336, 345-47
Un parfum à sentir (Flaubert) **2**:256
"Parfum de Hélios-Apollon" (Leconte de Lisle) **29**:246
"Parfum exotique" (Baudelaire) **6**:79, 128; **29**:103; **55**:9, 26, 69-70
"Le parfum impérissable" (Leconte de Lisle) **29**:218
"Paria" (Corbière) **43**:26-7, 31, 34
"Paris" (Vigny) **102**:368
"Paris at Daybreak" (Baudelaire)
See "Le crépuscule du matin"
"Paris at Nightfall" (Baudelaire)
See "Le crépuscule du soir"
"Paris diurne" (Corbière) **43**:31
"Paris Manuscripts" (Marx) **114**:69
"Paris nocturne" (Corbière) **43**:15, 31, 34
The Paris Sketch Book (Thackeray) **5**:444, 507; **43**:359, 392
Paris Spleen (Baudelaire)
See *Petits poèmes en prose: Le spleen de Paris*
Paris under Siege, 1870-1871: From the Goncourt Journal (Goncourt and Goncourt) **7**:185
"The Parish" (Clare) **9**:96-97
The Parish (Martineau) **137**:269-72
"The Parish Register" (Crabbe) **26**:78, 81-2, 86,

111, 118-19, 122, 124, 127, 132-33, 141; **121**:9-11, 26-7, 31, 48-9, 59-60, 66, 73-7, 83-5, 88-90
"The Parish Register: Burials" (Crabbe) **121**:43, 49
"The Parish-Clerk" (Crabbe) **26**:79, 134, 136
"A Parisian Dream" (Baudelaire)
See "Rêve parisien"
The Parisian Prowler (Baudelaire)
See *Petits poèmes en prose: Le spleen de Paris*
The Parisians (Bulwer-Lytton) **1**:150
La Parisienne (Becque) **3**:12-18
"Parisina" (Byron) **2**:63, 72, 96, 99
Parkman Reader (Parkman) **12**:368
"Parleying with Charles Avison" (Browning) **19**:149
"Parleying with Francis Furini" (Browning) **19**:126, 128-29
"Parleying with Gerard de Lairesse" (Browning) **19**:104, 108; **79**:174
Parleyings with Certain People of Importance in Their Day (Browning) **19**:99
Parliamentary History (Cobbett) **49**:163
Parochial and Plain Sermons (Newman) **38**:282, 302-06, 309-10, 314, 336; **99**:219, 221-25
The Parochial History of Bremhill (Bowles) **103**:54
Parochial Sermons (Newman)
See *Parochial and Plain Sermons*
Le parole dopo la musica (Da Ponte) **50**:79
El parricida (Martínez de la Rosa) **102**:247
"The Parrock" (Barnes) **75**:70
"Parrot" (Baillie) **2**:42
"The Parrot of Mull: A Domestic Anecdote" (Campbell) **19**:186-87, 190
Parsifal (Wagner) **9**:414-15, 418-19, 421, 423, 433-35, 440, 443, 446-47, 450-51, 454, 456, 461, 465, 470-71; **119**:171-78, 183, 185, 188, 193, 195, 228, 241, 243-44, 264-73, 291, 293, 300-07, 311, 328-45
"Parson Avery" (Whittier) **8**:509
"Parson Field's Experience" (Cooke) **110**:33, 36
"Parson John Bullen's Lizards" (Harris) **23**:159, 161, 163
"Parson Turell's Legacy; or, The President's Old Arm-Chair" (Holmes) **14**:109, 115, 126, 128
"The Parson's Daughter of Oxney Colne" (Trollope) **101**:235
La part du rêve (Amiel) **4**:13
"The Part Played by Labor in the Transition from Ape to Man" (Engels)
See "The Role Played by Labor in the Transition from Ape to Man"
"A Particular Providence as Revealed in the Gospel" (Newman) **38**:306
"Une partie de campagne" (Maupassant) **83**:228
"La partie de tric-trac" (Mérimée) **6**:353, 366, 369-71; **65**:49, 52, 54, 56-7, 61, 63, 66, 102
"Parting" (Arnold) **89**:17-19, 48, 95
"The Parting" (Brontë) **4**:44, 46
"Parting" (Dickinson)
See "My Life Closed Twice before Its Close"
"Parting After Parting" (Rossetti) **66**:311
Parting and Meeting (Andersen) **79**:10-11, 16-17
"The Parting Hour" (Crabbe) **26**:93, 100, 124, 126, 135, 149; **121**:11, 56
"Parting Lovers" (Browning) **61**:44-5
"The Parting of Friends" (Keble) **87**:125
"The Parting of Friends" (Newman) **38**:306, 308-09
"The Parting of the Ways" (Ichiyō)
See "Wakare-Michi"
"The Parting of the Ways" (Lowell) **90**:214
"Parting Words" (Preseren)
See "Ob slovesu"
The Partisan (Simms) **3**:500-02, 506-10, 513
"The Partition of the Earth" (Schiller) **39**:333, 337
"The Partridges" (Turgenev) **122**:293
"The Party of Cats" (Craik) **38**:119
"A Party of Travellers" (Oliphant) **61**:217-8
"Party Politics" (Froude) **43**:187, 215
"La parure" (Maupassant) **1**:447, 463
"Parus" (Lermontov) **47**:215
"The Parvenue" (Shelley) **14**:264
"Pas d'Extase" (Chivers) **49**:74-5
"Pascal" (Pater) **7**:308
Pascal Bruno (Dumas) **71**:204
"Paseo" (Silva) **114**:263
The Pasha of Many Tales (Marryat) **3**:319
"The Pasha's Son" (Taylor) **89**:342
"La pasionaria" (Zorrilla y Moral) **6**:526
Passage Birds (Tegner) **2**:612
"A Passage in the Secret History of an Irish Countess" (Le Fanu) **9**:304, 314, 316; **58**:253-4, 261, 307, 313
"Passage on Oxford Studies" (Clough) **27**:70
"Passage to India" (Whitman) **4**:551, 567-68, 579, 582, 586-87, 590; **31**:388, 404, 432-33, 442; **81**:310
Passages from the American Notebooks of Nathaniel Hawthorne (Hawthorne) **2**:307, 310, 314
Passages from the English Notebooks of Nathaniel Hawthorne (Hawthorne) **2**:306-07, 310, 314; **39**:245
Passages from the French and Italian Notebooks of Nathaniel Hawthorne (Hawthorne) **2**:310, 314; **23**:196-97
Passages in the Life of Mrs. Margaret Maitland of Sunnyside (Oliphant) **11**:427-8, 431-2, 445-6, 448-9; **61**:163, 216
"Le passé" (Lamartine) **11**:281
"Passereau l'élier" (Borel) **41**:4, 6-7, 13
"Passe-Temps" (Claudius) **75**:212, 218
"Passing Away, Saith the World, Passing Away" (Rossetti) **2**:559, 567, 570, 572
"Passing by the Odd Number of Poplars" (Eminescu) **33**:246
"Passing Clouds" (Ichiyō)
See "Yuku Kumo"
"The Passing of Arthur" (Tennyson)
See "Morte d'Arthur"
"The Passing of Spring" (Lampman) **25**:185, 210
"Passing of the Sires" (Taylor) **89**:310
"The Passing of the Spirit" (Lampman) **25**:207, 210
"Passion" (Lampman) **25**:184
"The Passion" (Manzoni) **29**:253
"Une passion" (Maupassant) **83**:173
"Une passion dans le désert" (Balzac) **5**:46
Passion et vertu (Flaubert) **62**:102
Passion Flower (Robertson) **35**:335
"A Passion for Questions" (Bestuzhev)
See "Strast' sprosit"
"A Passion in the Desert" (Balzac)
See "Une passion dans le désert"
"The Passionate Father" (Parton) **86**:349
Passions (Staël-Holstein)
See *De l'influence des passions sur le bonheur des individus et des nations*
The Passions of the Human Soul (Fourier) **51**:161
"Passive Imagination and Insanity" (Coleridge) **90**:9
"The Past" (Bryant) **6**:168-69, 172, 174, 182, 189; **46**:38
"The Past" (Timrod) **25**:366-68
Past and Present (Carlyle) **70**:16-20, 46, 71, 90-91, 93
"The Past Condition of Organic Nature" (Huxley) **67**:59
Past Meridian (Sigourney) **21**:301; **87**:326
"Pasticcio" (Wagner) **119**:190
Paston Carew, Millionaire and Miser (Linton) **41**:165
"El Pastor Clasiquino" (Espronceda) **39**:101
"Pastor Cum" (Gordon) **21**:181
"A Pastoral Ballad, by John Bull" (Moore) **110**:172
"Pastoral Fancies" (Clare) **9**:123
"The Pastoral of Bowman" (Wordsworth) **111**:236
"Pastoral Poesy" (Clare) **86**:132
Pastoral Poesy (Clare) **9**:100, 120-21
"La pastorale de Conlie" (Corbière) **43**:28
"Pastoral-Erfahrung" (Mörike) **10**:453
Pastorals (Hogg)
See *Scottish Pastorals*
"Pastorals in Prose" (Clare) **86**:173
Pater Brey (Goethe) **4**:213
"The Paternal Home" (Isaacs)
See "La casa paterna"
"A Paternal Ode to My Son" (Hood) **16**:235
"The Path" (Bryant) **46**:49
The Path of Sorrow (Chivers)
See *The Path of Sorrow; or the Lament of Youth: A Poem*
The Path of Sorrow; or the Lament of Youth: A Poem (Chivers) **49**:43-4, 46-8, 51-2, 57, 68-70
The Path through the Woods (Stifter)
See *Der Waldsteig*
The Pathfinder; or, The Inland Sea (Cooper) **27**:127, 129-35, 138, 140, 150-51, 153-54, 156, 158-59, 185-88; **1**:202, 204-07, 211; **54**:258-59, 265
"Patience, Hard Thing!" (Hopkins) **17**:261
"Patmos" (Hölderlin) **16**:166-72, 174-76, 180-81, 189, 191-92
"Pató Pál úr" (Petofi) **21**:264
"The Patriarch" (Sigourney) **21**:290
The Patriarchal Institution (Child) **73**:63
Patricia Kemball (Linton) **41**:166
"The Patriot" (Browning) **19**:96
Patriotic Sketches of Ireland, Written in Connaught (Morgan) **29**:391
Patriotic Songs (Moodie) **113**:309
"Patriotische Phantasien eines Slaven" (Kopitar) **117**:107, 117-18
"The Patron" (Crabbe) **26**:93; **121**:11, 61, 78, 83-5
"Patronage" (Edgeworth) **1**:268; **51**:81, 87-90, 93, 104, 136
"La patronne" (Maupassant) **1**:469
"Pauca meae" (Hugo) **10**:373
"Paucity of Original Writers. Passages which Pope has borrowed pointed out" (Warton) **118**:337
Paul and Virginia (Williams) **135**:334
Paul and Virginia (Zhukovsky) **35**:377
Paul Clifford (Bulwer-Lytton) **1**:140, 145, 148, 150; **45**:7, 11-13, 19, 23-4, 27, 30, 34, 69-70
Paul Erdmanns Fest (Claudius) **75**:182-83, 186-87
"Paul Felton" (Dana) **53**:160, 174, 176, 178-9
Paul Forestier (Augier) **31**:7-8, 10, 13, 16, 23, 28, 31, 35
"Paul H. Hayne's Poetry" (Lanier) **6**:252
Paul; ou, La ressemblance (Nodier) **19**:384
Paul Prescott's Charge (Alger) **8**:43; **83**:139, 142, 144-45
"Paul Revere's Ride" (Longfellow) **2**:490, 498; **45**:114, 124, 137, 139, 179-80, 188, 191
Paul the Peddlar; or, The Adventures of a Young Street Merchant (Alger) **8**:44; **83**:112, 133
"Pauline" (Hemans) **71**:292
Pauline (Browning) **19**:73, 102, 105, 110, 116, 120, 126, 133; **79**:107, 146-47, 151, 166, 174, 176, 188, 190
Pauline (Dumas) **11**:49; **71**:204
Pauline (Sand) **42**:373; **57**:316
Pauline (Staël-Holstein)
See *Histoire de Pauline*
"Pauline's Passion and Punishment" (Alcott) **58**:39, 46, 59; **83**:6
"A Paumanok Picture" (Whitman) **81**:319
"The Pauper's Christmas Carol" (Hood) **16**:235

Pausanias the Spartan (Bulwer-Lytton) **1**:151-52; **45**:61-2
"Pause" (Muller) **73**:351, 368, 372
"A Pause" (Rossetti) **2**:574; **50**:289
"Le pauvre énfant pâle" (Mallarmé) **4**:371
"Pauvre garçon" (Corbière) **43**:25, 27, 34
"Les pauvres à l'église" (Rimbaud) **4**:454-55, 458, 466; **82**:230
Pauvres fleurs (Desbordes-Valmore) **97**:12, 18, 28, 30
"Les pauvres gens" (Hugo) **3**:273
Les pauvres Saltimbanques (Banville) **9**:19
"The Pavilion on the Links" (Stevenson) **5**:391, 394, 397, 403, 408, 413, 426, 431, 434; **63**:243, 274
"Le Pavillon sur l'eau" (Gautier) **59**:32
"Pax animae" (Casal) **131**:267
"Paysage mauvais" (Corbière) **43**:15, 28, 31
"Paysage polaire" (Leconte de Lisle) **29**:230
"Paysages" (Baudelaire) **29**:100; **55**:24, 35-6, 65
"Paysages belges" (Verlaine) **51**:381-82
"Paysages tristes" (Verlaine) **51**:355
Les paysans (Balzac) **5**:40, 66-69, 73
"Pázmán lovag" (Arany) **34**:5
Pazukhin's Death (Saltykov) **16**:368
"Peace" (Clare) **9**:78; **86**:160
"Peace" (Crawford) **127**:221
"Peace" (Hopkins) **17**:255
"Peace" (Lampman) **25**:219
"Peace" (Patmore) **9**:334, 358
"Peace in Believing" (Newman) **38**:305
"Peace in Life and Art" (Patmore) **9**:342, 346
"Peaceful Death and Painful Life" (Brontë) **109**:31, 38
"The Peal of Another Trumpet" (Mangan) **27**:296
"A Peal of Bells" (Rossetti) **66**:307
"The Pearl Divers" (Krylov) **1**:438
"The Pearl of Good Fortune" (Andersen) **7**:23
Pearl of Great Price (Smith) **53**:381
The Pearl of Orr's Island: A Story of the Coast of Maine (Stowe) **3**:555-56, 559, 561, 563, 567
Pearls and Pebbles; or, The Notes of an Old Naturalist (Traill) **31**:314-15, 317, 323, 328-29
The Pearls of Love (Petofi)
  See *Szerelem Gyöngyei*
The Peasant and the Prince (Martineau) **137**:256-57
"The Peasant and the Sheep" (Krylov) **1**:435, 439
"The Peasant and the Workman" (Krylov) **1**:435
The Peasant as Millionaire, or The Maiden from the Fairy World (Raimund)
  See *Der Bauer als Millionär; oder, Das Mädchen aus der Feenwelt*
"The Peasant Children" (Nekrasov)
  See "Krestyánskie déti"
"The Peasant Gentlewoman" (Pushkin) **3**:435
The Peasant in Debt (Gotthelf)
  See *Die Erlebnisse eines Schuldenbauers*
"The Peasant in Distress" (Krylov) **1**:435
Peasant Justice (Sacher-Masoch) **31**:294
"The Peasant Pavo" (Runeberg)
  See "Bonden Pavo"
The Peasant War (Engels)
  See *Der deutsche Bauernkrieg*
The Peasant War in Germany (Engels)
  See *Der deutsche Bauernkrieg*
"A Peasant Woman" (Nekrasov) **11**:416
The Peasantry (Balzac)
  See *Les paysans*
"The Peasants and the River" (Krylov) **1**:435
The Peasants' Mirror (Gotthelf)
  See *Der Bauern-Spiegel oder Lebensgeschichte des Jeremias Gotthelf: Von ihm selbst beschrieben*
Peasants' War (Engels)
  See *Der deutsche Bauernkrieg*
La peau de chagrin (Balzac) **5**:29, 32, 49, 58, 79-80; **53**:8, 22, 25, 35
"Peccavi, Domine" (Lampman) **25**:193
"Pečerskie antiki" (Leskov) **25**:258-59
Le péché de M. Antoine (Sand) **2**:589; **42**:322; **57**:375
"Le péché véniel" (Balzac) **5**:78
Pechorin's Journal (Lermontov) **5**:295-98, 301-02, 304
"Der Pechvogel" (Lenau) **16**:265
A Peculiar Position (Scribe) **16**:405
"Pedantry" (Hazlitt) **29**:148; **82**:115
"Pedantry" (Mackenzie) **41**:188
"The Pedlar" (Hogg) **4**:282; **109**:280
"The Pedlars" (Nekrasov)
  See "Korobeyniki"
"Pedro Ladron; or, The Shepherd of Toppledown Hill" (Darley) **2**:129
"Pedro the Slave" (Isaacs)
  See "El esclavo Pedro"
"Peele Castle" (Wordsworth)
  See "Stanzas on Peele Castle"
Peers and Parvenus (Gore) **65**:21
Peg Woffington (Reade) **2**:533-34, 536, 539-40, 544-45, 548, 552; **74**:243-44, 253, 255-56, 262-65, 268, 277, 281, 299, 319
"Pegasus in Harness" (Schiller) **39**:337
"Pegasus in Pound" (Longfellow) **103**:284
"Le Peintre de la vie moderne" (Baudelaire) **55**:8, 33-4
Le peintre de Salztbourg (Nodier) **19**:378-79, 384-85
Pelayo (Espronceda) **39**:84, 100
Pelayo: A Story of the Goth (Simms) **3**:507-08
Le pèlerin blanc; ou, Les orphelins du hameau (Pixérécourt) **39**:277, 284, 289, 291
Pélérinage a Ermenonville (Pilgrimage to Ermenonville) (Dumas) **71**:241
Pelham; or, The Adventures of a Gentleman (Bulwer-Lytton) **1**:135, 140, 145, 148-50, 153-55; **45**:11, 18-19, 21, 23, 32-5, 37-8, 68-71
"The Pelican Chorus" (Lear) **3**:307
"Le Pélican ou les deaux mères" (Desbordes-Valmore) **97**:5
"Pelleas and Ettarre" (Tennyson) **30**:249, 254; **65**:238, 254, 279, 282, 285, 288, 291, 300, 315, 318, 320, 323, 352, 361, 374, 376
Pelopidas (Bird) **1**:88, 90
The Pen and the Album (Thackeray) **5**:485
"La peña blanca" (Villaverde) **121**:333
Pendennis (Thackeray)
  See *The History of Pendennis: His Fortunes and Misfortunes, His Friends and His Greatest Enemy*
Pénélope (Charriere) **66**:127
"Penelope's Choice" (Lazarus) **109**:294
The Peninsular War (Southey) **97**:265
El penitente (Villaverde) **121**:333-34
"Penn and Peterborough" (Landor) **14**:178
"A Pennsylvania Legend" (Bryant) **6**:180
"The Pennsylvania Pilgrim" (Whittier) **8**:511, 521-23
The Pennsylvania Pilgrim, and Other Poems (Whittier) **8**:501, 516; **59**:366
"A Penny Plain and Twopence Colored" (Stevenson) **5**:421; **63**:237-8, 242
El pensador Mexicano (Lizardi) **30**:67, 77, 85
"Pensar, dudar" (Hugo) **3**:271
"Pensée de Byron" (Nerval) **67**:307
"Pensées" (Amiel) **4**:14-15
Pensées d'aôut (Sainte-Beuve) **5**:331, 335, 341
Pensées de Joseph Joubert (Joubert) **9**:290
"Pensées de minuit" (Gautier) **59**:18
"Pensées des morts" (Lamartine) **11**:255, 265, 279
Pensées, essais, maxmimes, et correspondance de Joseph Joubert (Joubert) **9**:281, 283-86
Pensées, réflexions et maximes (Chateaubriand) **134**:116
Pensieri (Leopardi) **129**:276-77, 302
"Pensiero dominante" (Leopardi) **129**:341
Pensiero XVIII (Manzoni) **98**:214
La pension bourgeoise (Scribe) **16**:394
"Pensive on Her Dead Gazing" (Whitman) **31**:370
La Pentacoste (Manzoni) **29**:253; **98**:213
The Pentameron and Pentalogia (Landor) **14**:164-65, 175, 178, 191, 193-95, 202, 207
"La pente de la rêverie" (Hugo) **21**:223
"The Pentecost" (Manzoni)
  See *La Pentacoste*
"La Pentecoste" (Manzoni) **98**:220
Penthesilea (Kleist) **2**:437-38, 440-42, 444, 446-47, 450, 452, 454-57, 461, 463; **37**:217, 219, 223, 225-26, 228, 230-34, 237, 253, 255, 263, 266-72, 274
"Pentheus" (Meyer) **81**:207
"Pentridge by the River" (Barnes) **75**:59
"Pentucket" (Whittier) **8**:520
"Penumbra" (Rossetti) **4**:491
The People (Michelet)
  See *Le peuple*
The People of Seldwyla (Keller)
  See *Die Leute von Seldwyla*
The People's Cause or Pugachov, Romanov, or Pestel (Bakunin) **25**:64
"The People's Hands Were Swollen with Applause" (Norwid) **17**:364
"The peperman's nightcap" (Andersen) **79**:83-84
"Per Contra: The Poet, High Art, Genius" (Thomson) **18**:412, 421
"Per prima Messa" (Solomos) **15**:385-86
"Perambulatory Musings, from Blenheim House, at Woodstock, in Oxfordshire, the Seat of the Duke of Marlborough, to Titley House, in Herefordshire, the Seat of William Greenly" (Dyer) **129**:138-39
"Perchatka" (Zhukovsky) **35**:398
"Perchè Pensa? Pensando S'Invecchia" (Clough) **27**:72
Percival Keene (Marryat) **3**:319-20
Percy: A Tragedy (More) **27**:324-25, 332, 337
"Percy Hall" (Brontë) **109**:4-5, 30
"Percy's Musings upon the Battle of Edwardston" (Brontë) **109**:30
"Perdida" (Silva) **114**:311
Perdu (Droste-Hülshoff) **3**:197
"Le père amable" (Maupassant) **1**:448, 469; **83**:171
"Le Père Canet" (Balzac)
  See *Facino Cane*
Le père Goriot: Histoire Parisienne (Balzac) **5**:29, 32, 34, 43-6, 52-3, 67, 76, 85-7; **35**:1-76; **53**:9, 13, 21-2, 28-9
"Le Père Judas" (Maupassant) **83**:176
Le Père la Ruine (Dumas) **71**:204
Un père prodigue (Dumas) **9**:224, 229, 231, 237, 241, 245-46, 248-50, 253
"Perebendja" (Shevchenko) **54**:373
"Peregrina" (Mörike) **10**:449, 451, 454-55
"Père-la-Chaise" (Adams) **33**:17
"Perepiska" (Turgenev)
  See "Peripiska"
"La pereza" (Bécquer) **106**:93, 96
The Perfect Life (Channing) **17**:46
"Perfect Love" (Lampman) **25**:209
"Una peri" (Casal) **131**:226, 236, 267
"La Péri" (Gautier) **59**:34-6
"Perichole" (Mérimée) **6**:353
Pericles (Lamb) **125**:304
Pericles and Aspasia (Landor) **14**:165, 176, 178, 187, 189, 194
"A Perilous Incognito" (Boyesen) **135**:13, 29
A Perilous Secret (Reade) **74**:257, 263-64, 289
The Perils of the Nation: An Appeal to the Legislature, the Clergy, and the Higher and Middle Classes (Tonna) **135**:193, 200, 205, 207-9, 211-13, 215-17
"The Periodical Essayists" (Hazlitt) **29**:165, 167
"Das Peripatetiker" (Muller) **73**:366
"Peripiska" (Turgenev) **122**:243-45, 247, 266, 268, 312

El periquillo sarniento (Lizardi) **30**:67, 69-80, 82-3, 85-8
"El perjurio" (Villaverde) **121**:333
"Perkin Warbeck" (Schiller) **39**:368
Perkin Warbeck (Shelley)
See *The Fortunes of Perkin Warbeck*
Perourou, the Bellows-Mender (Williams)
See "The History of Perourou; or, The Bellows-Mender; Written by Himself"
The Perpetual Curate (Oliphant) **11**:439, 446-9, 454-7, 459-60; **61**:166, 174, 177-8, 180, 198, 202, 206-8, 218, 220, 222, 226-7
"Perpetual Forces" (Emerson) **98**:61
Perpetual Peace: A Philosophical Sketch (Kant)
See *Zum ewigen Frieden: Ein philosophischer Entwurf*
"The Perpetuation of Our Political Institutions" (Lincoln) **18**:240, 248, 278-79
"Perplexed Music" (Browning) **16**:133
"Perplexities" (Clare) **86**:166-67
"El perro en barrio ageno" (Lizardi) **30**:68
The Persecuted (Fouqué)
See *Der Verfolgte*
"Persée et Andromède" (Laforgue) **5**:269, 271, 281; **53**:294, 298-9, 301
"Persephone" (Ingelow) **39**:263
"Persia" (Kendall) **12**:198
"Persian Poetry" (Emerson) **1**:295
The Personal History of David Copperfield (Dickens) **3**:146-47, 149, 151, 156-57, 162, 171-72, 180, 172, 186; **8**:165, 173, 176, 182; **18**:99, 111, 121; **26**:156-57, 163, 168-69, 171, 174-75, 177, 201; **37**:145, 164, 168, 171, 197; **86**:186, 201, 256, 258; **105**:231, 311, 338; **113**:29, 41, 56, 70, 80-1, 88, 97, 102-3, 110, 113-14, 118-19, 124, 127
"Personal Influence: the Means of Propagating the Truth" (Newman) **99**:301
Personal Memoirs of Major Richardson; As Connected with the Singular Oppression of that Officer While in Spain (Richardson) **55**:297, 299, 336
A Personal Narrative of Travels to the Equinoctial Regions of the New Continent, During the Years 1799-1804, by Alexander de Humboldt and Aimé Bonpland; with maps, plans, etc. (Williams) **135**:309
Personal Recollections (Tonna) **135**:194-95, 207, 228
Personal Recollections of Charlotte Elizabeth, Continued to the Close of her Life (Tonna) **135**:194
"Personal Reminiscences" (Cranch) **115**:27
"Personal Talk" (Wordsworth) **12**:431; **111**:286
"Persten'" (Baratynsky) **103**:2, 30-3, 47
Persuasion (Austen) **1**:30-1, 33-5, 37-41, 44-6, 50, 53, 60-4; **13**:61, 84, 93-4; **19**:8, 52, 55; **33**:27-101; **51**:33, 41; **81**:48, 52; **95**:11, 15, 84, 86; **119**:12, 14, 17-18, 20-1, 23-8, 36-41, 48, 55, 57
Peru, A Poem. In Six Cantos (Williams) **135**:286, 300, 314-15, 333, 341
Pervaia liubov (Turgenev)
See *Pervaya lyubov'*
Pervaja ljubov (Turgenev)
See *Pervaya lyubov'*
Pervaya lyubov' (Turgenev) **21**:393, 415, 418-20, 422, 431, 435, 439, 441, 449-51; **37**:382; **122**:241, 243, 245, 247, 259-60, 265, 267-68, 280, 306, 333-36, 342, 346, 348, 358, 360-62
Pescara'a Temptation (Meyer)
See *Die Versuchung des Pescara*
"Peschiera" (Clough) **27**:79
"Pesn skandinavskix voinov" (Tyutchev) **34**:412
"Pesn' toržestvujuščej liubvi" (Turgenev)
See "Pesn' torzhestvuyushchey lyubvi"
"Pesn' torzhestvennoi liubvi" (Turgenev)
See "Pesn' torzhestvuyushchey lyubvi"
"Pesn' torzhestvuyushchey lyubvi" (Turgenev) **21**:408, 415, 420, 441, 452; **37**:449; **122**:241, 267, 306, 337, 350, 365, 371, 373-74, 376, 378
Pesnja pro kuptsa Kalashinikova (Lermontov)
See *Pesnya pro tsarya Ivana Vasilievicha, molodogo oprichnika i undalogo kuptsa Kalashnikova*
Pesnya pro tsarya Ivana Vasilievicha, molodogo oprichnika i undalogo kuptsa Kalashnikova (Lermontov) **5**:288, 294, 300; **126**:136-38, 215, 224
"Pessimism" (Symonds) **34**:337
"Pessimisme" (Banville) **9**:31
"The Pessimist" (Crawford) **12**:174-75; **127**:222-23
"Pest-Nests" (Mayhew) **31**:179
"The Pet Name" (Browning) **1**:117
Peter Bell (Wordsworth) **12**:408-09, 421-22, 445; **111**:202-3, 222, 226, 245, 267
Peter Bell the Third (Shelley) **18**:351, 358, 368
"Peter Connell" (Carleton) **3**:85
"Peter Goldthwaite's Treasure" (Hawthorne) **39**:190
"Peter Grimes" (Crabbe) **26**:111, 113, 116, 119, 124-26, 128, 134-35, 141, 147; **121**:5, 10, 24-5, 52, 56, 62, 83, 87
Peter Ibbetson (Du Maurier) **86**:278-80, 285, 287-88, 290, 292
Peter Leberecht, eine Geschichte ohne Abeuteuerlichheiten (Tieck) **5**:515, 519-21
Peter Leberechts Volks mährchen (Tieck) **5**:515
"Peter of Barnet" (Hogg) **109**:248
Peter of the Castle (Banim and Banim) **13**:117-18, 129, 131
Peter Pilgrim (Bird) **1**:86
Peter Schlemihls Wundersame Geschichte (Chamisso) **82**:6, 9-12, 15-16, 18, 20-22, 27, 30, 32, 35, 38, 40-41, 48-49, 51, 53, 56-57, 60, 62-65, 67-69
Peter Simple (Marryat) **3**:315, 317-19, 321-22
Peter the Great (Dunlap) **2**:215
"Peter the Parson" (Woolson) **82**:284, 286, 293, 330, 333, 3367
"Peter the Piccaninny" (Kendall) **12**:192
Peter's Letters to His Kinsfolk (Lockhart) **6**:285, 293, 295-97, 300, 305, 308
"The Petersburg Stage" (Gogol) **31**:94
"Le Petit Bègue" (Desbordes-Valmore) **97**:14
Le petit chose (Daudet) **1**:231, 234-36, 243, 249-51
"Petit Gervais" (Hugo) **10**:357
"Le Petit Incendiaire" (Desbordes-Valmore) **97**:14
"Le Petit Peureux" (Desbordes-Valmore) **97**:38
Le petit Picpus (Hugo) **10**:373-74
Petit traité de poésie Française (Banville) **9**:20-21, 23-25, 27-28
Le petit vieux des Batignolles (Gaboriau) **14**:17-18, 22, 29
La Petite Comtesse (Feuillet) **45**:85-7
"La petite Fadette" (Maupassant) **1**:448
La petite Fadette (Sand) **2**:599, 601, 603, 605; **42**:323, 340, 363-65, 367, 373-75, 377; **57**:317, 338
La petite paroisse (Daudet) **1**:237, 251
Petite prière sans prétentions (Laforgue) **53**:265
"La petite rogue" (Maupassant) **1**:454; **83**:197, 199, 201
"Les petites vielles" (Baudelaire) **6**:79, 85, 91-2, 109, 116; **29**:80, 100, 114; **55**:2-4, 16, 19, 21-2, 28, 35, 39-42, 67, 73
"Pétition" (Laforgue) **5**:280
Petits châteaux de bohème (Nerval) **67**:305, 331
"Les petits coups" (Beranger) **34**:29
Petits poèmes en prose: Le spleen de Paris (Baudelaire) **6**:84, 86-87, 90, 103, 111; **29**:68, 75, 79, 108, 110-11; **55**:43, 46-8, 52
"Les Petits Sauvages" (Desbordes-Valmore) **97**:14
"The Pet-Lamb: A Pastoral" (Wordsworth) **111**:235
"Petöfi dem Sonnengott" (Arnim) **123**:8
"Petr Petrovič Karataev" (Turgenev) **122**:264
Petru rareş (Eminescu) **33**:264-65; **131**:292
"Pettichap's Nest" (Clare) **9**:85; **86**:144-45
Petticoat Government (Trollope) **30**:331
Le peuple (Michelet) **31**:207, 214, 217-18, 229-32, 234, 239-42, 248, 250-51, 257, 260-61
Le peuple russe et le Socialisme (Herzen) **10**:332, 335-6
"Pevcu" (Preseren) **127**:298
Peveril of the Peak (Scott) **15**:313
"Pevuchest est v morskikh volnakh" (Tyutchev) **34**:398
"Pewit's Nest" (Clare) **9**:85; **86**:133
"The Pewter Quart" (Maginn) **8**:438, 441
La Peyrouse (Kotzebue) **25**:141, 145, 147
Die Pfarrose (Ludwig) **4**:349, 351
Pfingstbetrachtung (Freytag) **109**:180
Der Pförtner im Herrenhause (Stifter)
See *Tourmaline*
"Phadrig's Dilemma" (Griffin) **7**:198
"Phaeton" (Cranch) **115**:58
Phaeton (Kingsley) **35**:249
"Phantasie an Laura" (Schiller) **39**:338
"Phantasies" (Lazarus) **8**:418-19; **109**:291
Phantasmagoria (Pavlova)
See *Fantasmagorii*
Phantasmagoria and Other Poems (Carroll) **139**:29, 35, 124, 127, 129
Phantasmion (Coleridge) **31**:58-63
"Phantasms" (Turgenev)
See "Prizraki. Fantaziya"
"Phantasus" (Tieck) **46**:333
Phantasus (Tieck) **5**:515, 517, 527; **46**:332-3, 348-50
"A Phantasy" (Taylor) **89**:307
"The Phantom" (Taylor) **89**:307
The Phantom (Baillie) **2**:40-41; **71**:6
"The Phantom Horse" (Meyer)
See "Das Geisterross"
"The Phantom Hour" (Pavlova) **138**:31
The Phantom Ship (Marryat) **3**:317, 320
The Phantom Wedding; or, The Fall of the House of Flint (Southworth) **26**:434
"Phantoms" (Turgenev)
See "Prizraki. Fantaziya"
Le phare des Sanguinaires (Daudet) **1**:247
"Les phares" (Baudelaire) **6**:98, 114, 123; **29**:97; **55**:4, 58
"Pharoah Tla's Avatars" (Eminescu)
See "Avatarii faraonului Tlá"
"Phaudhrig Crohoore" (Le Fanu) **9**:299
"Phelim O'Toole's Courtship" (Carleton) **3**:86, 91
"Phenomena" (Hoffmann) **2**:342
"Le phénomène futur" (Mallarmé) **4**:371; **41**:281
The Phenomenology of Mind (Hegel) **46**:114-15, 126, 133-34, 136, 138-39
The Phenomenology of the Spirit (Hegel)
See *System der Wissenschaft: 1. Theil. Der Phänomenologies des Geistes*
"Phidylé" (Leconte de Lisle) **29**:224
Phil Fogarty: A Tale of the Fighting Onety-Oneth (Thackeray) **14**:450; **43**:384
"Phil Purcel, the Pig-Driver" (Carleton) **3**:86
Phil, the Fiddler; or, The Story of a Young Street Musician (Alger) **8**:21, 24, 33-34, 43; **83**:127
"Philander" (Arnim) **5**:13
"The Philanthropist" (Griffin) **7**:215
"Philanthropy" (Thoreau) **7**:351
Philiberte (Augier) **31**:2, 4, 10, 12, 14, 23-4, 27
Philip (Alfieri)
See *Filippo*
Philip II (Alfieri) **101**:18
"Philip, my King" (Craik) **38**:120
"Philip of Pokanoket" (Irving) **19**:328; **95**:265-66, 268-69

Philological Grammar (Barnes) **75**:19, 26, 40, 64-5
"Philomela" (Arnold) **89**:7, 19
"The Philosopher" (Brontë) **16**:68, 74
"Philosopher" (Emerson) **98**:93
"The Philosopher's Conclusion" (Brontë) **35**:147
Les philosophes Français du XIXme siècle (Taine) **15**:409, 412, 431, 458
"Philosophic Humbugs" (Clarke) **19**:234
Philosophic Studies (Balzac)
See *Etudes philosophiques*
A Philosophical and Practical Grammar of the English Language (Webster) **30**:413
"Philosophical Considerations on the General Science of Mathematics" (Comte) **54**:180-3
Philosophical Considerations on the Physical Sciences (Comte) **54**:172, 180-3
Philosophical Dialogues and Fragments (Renan)
See *Dialogues et fragments philosophiques*
Philosophical Fragments (Kierkegaard)
See *Philosophiske Smuler*
Philosophical Fragments; or, A Fragment of Philosophy (Kierkegaard)
See *Philosophiske Smuler*
Philosophical Lectures (Coleridge) **9**:208
Philosophical Letters (Schelling)
See *Philosophische Briefe über Dogmatismus und Kriticismus*
Philosophical Notebooks (Newman) **99**:244
"Philosophical Reflections" (Freneau) **111**:146
"A Philosophical Satire" (Moore) **110**:171
A Philosophical View of Reform (Shelley) **18**:338
La philosophie dans le boudoir (Sade) **3**:492-93, 495; **47**:304, 310, 318, 327, 334-35, 339, 341, 346, 350-53, 355-59, 364
Philosophie de l'art (Taine) **15**:452
Philosophie der Mythologie (Schelling) **30**:142, 144
Philosophie der Mythologie und Offenbarung (Schelling) **30**:138
Philosophie des Lebens (Schlegel) **45**:294, 298
Philosophische Briefe über Dogmatismus und Kriticismus (Schelling) **30**:128, 153-55
Philosophische Untersuchungen über das Wesen der menschlichen Freiheit und die damit zusammenhängende Gegenstände (Schelling) **30**:135, 168
Philosophiske Smuler (Kierkegaard) **34**:200-01, 204, 223-224, 237; **78**:119, 131, 134, 144, 148, 152, 154, 161-62, 189, 199, 201, 204, 211, 214-18, 227, 237-38, 240-41; **125**:250
"Philosophy" (Levy) **59**:102, 120
"Philosophy" (Silva)
See "Filosofías"
"Philosophy" (Thomson) **18**:390, 418
Philosophy and Common Sense (Brownson) **50**:27
"Philosophy and Religion" (Very) **9**:386
"Philosophy as an Element of Culture" (Lewes) **25**:288
Philosophy in the Bedroom (Sade)
See *La philosophie dans le boudoir*
Philosophy in the Boudoir (Sade)
See *La philosophie dans le boudoir*
Philosophy of Art (Schelling) **30**:175-77, 181
The Philosophy of Composition (Poe) **1**:512, 516-18, 523, 526, 528; **55**:138-9, 141, 147-8, 161, 208-9, 211-2; **97**:213; **117**:203, 205, 241, 245, 275-76, 282, 286-88, 290, 294, 296, 312, 315-16, 318, 327, 333-38
"Philosophy of Evolution" (Symonds) **34**:336
"The Philosophy of Furniture" (Poe) **16**:304; **55**:147
"The Philosophy of History" (Lanier) **118**:283
The Philosophy of History (Emerson) **98**:66
Philosophy of History (Hegel) **46**:119, 125, 128-30, 156-57
Philosophy of Mythology (Schelling)
See *Philosophie der Mythologie*
Philosophy of Nature (Hegel) **46**:171
Philosophy of Nature (Schelling)
See *Natur-Philosophie*
Philosophy of Revelation (Schelling) **30**:157, 159
"The Philosophy of the Obvious" (Pisarev) **25**:332
"The Philosophy of the Supernatural" (Brownson) **50**:52
"Philosophy of War" (Horne) **127**:253
Philothea: A Grecian Romance (Child) **6**:199-201, 203-05, 208-09; **73**:51, 60, 68, 77-8
"A Philoxène Boyer" (Banville) **9**:26
"The Philter" (Stendhal)
See "Le Phitre"
"The Philtre" (Rossetti) **4**:510
Phineas Finn (Trollope) **101**:253, 262, 267-70, 276, 307, 312-13
Phineas Finn, the Irish Member (Trollope) **6**:461, 463, 466, 470, 472, 495; **33**:364; **101**:276
Phineas Redux (Trollope) **6**:463, 466, 472-73, 495, 513, 519; **33**:424; **101**:251, 253, 267-68, 271, 274, 302, 306-08
"Le Phitre" (Stendhal) **46**:294, 307
"The Phocaeans" (Landor) **14**:164, 181, 184
"Phoebe Dawson" (Crabbe) **26**:100, 102, 116, 133
Phoebe, Junior: A Last Chronicle of Carlingford (Oliphant) **11**:446-8, 454, 456-7, 459, 462; **61**:162-3, 165-8, 174, 182, 198, 216, 229-30
Phoebus (Kleist) **2**:437
"The Phoenix" (Andersen) **79**:84
"Phokaia" (Lampman) **25**:203
"Phosphorous and Civilization" (Lewes) **25**:310
"Photography Extraordinary" (Carroll) **139**:125
"Phrases" (Rimbaud) **35**:297; **82**:232-33
The Physical Basis of Mind (Lewes)
See *The Problems of Life and Mind*
The Physician, the Dying, and the Dead (Herzen) **10**:329
Physics and Politics; or, Thoughts on the Application of the Principles of "Natural Selection" and "Inheritance" to Political Society (Bagehot) **10**:16, 19, 24-26, 34-36, 39, 44-46, 48, 65-66
"The Physics of Music" (Lanier) **118**:215, 242
Physiography (Huxley) **67**:11
Physiologie du mariage; ou, Méditations de philosophie éclectique sur le bonheur et le malheur conjugal (Balzac) **5**:28, 32, 42, 78, 83; **53**:22
Physiology and Calisthenics (Beecher) **30**:16
The Physiology of Common Life (Lewes) **25**:288, 296, 310-11, 317-18
The Physiology of Marriage (Balzac)
See *Physiologie du mariage; ou, Méditations de philosophie éclectique sur le bonheur et le malheur conjugal*
"The Physiology of Versification" (Holmes) **14**:111, 127
The Phytologia; or, Philosophy of Agriculture and Gardening (Darwin) **106**:183, 218, 234, 241, 245, 274
"The Piano of Chopin" (Norwid)
See "Fortepjan Szopena"
"Le piano que baise une main frê" (Verlaine) **51**:383
"The Piano-Organ" (Levy) **59**:92
Piast Dantyszek's Poem on Hell (Slowacki)
See *Poema Piasta Dantyszka o piekle*
"The Piazza" (Melville) **3**:380, 383; **49**:392
The Piazza Tales and Other Prose Pieces, 1839-1860 (Melville) **3**:331, 361, 384; **29**:315; **93**:205, 242-44, 246-49; **123**:255, 260
Piccadilly: A Fragment of Contemporary Biography (Oliphant) **47**:266, 271, 274-76, 278-79, 284-85, 296-98
Le Piccinino (Sand) **57**:316
Die Piccolomini (Schiller)
See *Wallenstein*
Pickwick Papers (Dickens)
See *The Posthumous Papers of the Pickwick Club*
"Pico della Mirandola" (Pater) **7**:313
"Pictor Ignotus" (Browning) **19**:132; **79**:94-96
The Pictorial Ukraine (Shevchenko)
See *Zivopisnaja Ukraina*
"The Picture" (Coleridge) **99**:3, 5, 81, 83-4
The Picture (Bowles) **103**:54
"A Picture at Rustrum" (Arnold) **29**:23
"The Picture Gallery" (Freneau) **111**:134
"The Picture of a Blind Man" (Wilson) **5**:545
"Picture of an Old Man" (Bowles) **103**:88-9, 91, 93, 95
"The Picture of St. John" (Taylor) **89**:311-12, 346
"A Picture of the Times" (Freneau) **111**:140-41
The Picture; or, the Lover's Resolution (Coleridge) **99**:88-93
"Picture Song" (Pinkney) **31**:268, 273-74, 276-77, 279
A Picture-Book without Pictures (Andersen) **7**:21, 27, 36
"Pictures" (Whitman) **81**:342
The Pictures (Tieck) **5**:513
"Pictures at Wilton" (Hazlitt) **29**:144
Pictures from Italy (Dickens) **3**:146; **18**:120; **113**:69
Pictures from My Life (Macha) **46**:201, 208-10, 212
"The Pictures of Columbus, the Genoese" (Freneau) **1**:319, 322; **111**:101, 119, 141
Pictures of Sweden (Andersen) **7**:17-18
Pictures of Travel (Heine)
See *Reisebilder*
"The Picturesque and the Ideal" (Hazlitt) **29**:156
"Picturesque Travel" (Gilpin) **30**:38, 43
"A Piece of String" (Maupassant)
See "La ficelle"
Pieces, in Prose and Verse (Sigourney)
See *Moral Pieces, in Prose and Verse*
"Pied Beauty" (Hopkins) **17**:208, 215-16, 238, 244, 255-56
"Le Pied de la momie" (Gautier) **1**:355; **59**:31, 35-6, 38
"The Pied Piper of Hamelin" (Browning) **19**:98
"Pielgrzym" (Mickiewicz) **3**:404
"Pielgrzym" (Norwid) **17**:367
La pierre de touche (Augier) **31**:5, 12, 14-15, 24-5, 35
"Pierre Dupont" (Baudelaire) **29**:70
Pierre et Jean (Maupassant) **1**:446-47, 450, 452, 461, 463-64, 467, 469-71; **42**:162-217; **83**:172, 181, 188
Pierre; or, The Ambiguities (Melville) **3**:330, 333, 335-38, 341, 343-44, 347-48, 351, 354, 361, 363-64, 366-70, 372, 374-75, 380, 384-85; **12**:281, 293; **29**:315-18, 323-24, 326-27, 329-32, 334-35, 338, 344, 368; **45**:195, 210, 235, 247, 251; **49**:376, 391-92, 399, 402-03, 407, 416, 420-21; **91**:1-228; **93**:240; **123**:179, 192, 194, 204, 207-8, 241, 252, 260
Pierre qui roule (Sand) **42**:311; **57**:316
"Pierrette" (Balzac) **53**:8
Pierrot fumiste (Laforgue) **5**:281-2; **53**:291
"Pierrots" (Laforgue) **53**:279, 286-8, 290-1
"Pierrots II" (Laforgue) **53**:288
"Pierrots III" (Laforgue) **53**:288
"Pierrots, I-V" (Laforgue) **5**:277; **53**:288
"Piers Plowman" (Morris) **4**:441
Pierścień wielkiej damy (Norwid) **17**:379
"Pietro of Abano" (Tieck) **5**:525
Pietro Tasca (Dumas) **71**:217, 221-22
"Pig under the Oak" (Krylov) **1**:439
"Pigen, som traadte paa Brødet" (Andersen) **79**:77
"The Pigeons at the British Museum" (Jefferies) **47**:95

"Pijaństwo" (Krasicki) **8**:403, 407
"The Pike" (Krylov) **1**:435, 439
Pikovaya dama (Pushkin) **3**:429-30, 435-37, 442, 447-48, 452, 456, 459, 464; **83**:274-77, 279, 323, 332, 350, 354-55
"Eine Pilgerfahrt zu Beethoven" (Wagner) **9**:414, 455-56, 475; **119**:190, 192
"Pilgrim" (Mickiewicz)
See "Pielgrzym"
"The Pilgrim" (Newman) **38**:344
"The Pilgrim" (Norwid)
See "Pielgrzym"
Pilgrim Fathers (Hemans) **29**:205
"The Pilgrim of Glencoe" (Campbell) **19**:179, 181, 184, 193
The Pilgrim of Glencoe, and Other Poems (Campbell) **19**:184
Pilgrimage (Boyesen)
See *A Norseman's Pilgrimage*
Pilgrimage (Southey) **97**:269
Pilgrimage to Al-Madinah and Meccah (Burton) **42**:35, 40, 42, 52-54, 57-59, 61
"A Pilgrimage to Beethoven" (Wagner)
See "Eine Pilgerfahrt zu Beethoven"
Pilgrimage to Mecca (Burton)
See *Pilgrimage to Al-Madinah and Meccah*
"A Pilgrimage to Patrick's Purgatory" (Carleton) **3**:92
The Pilgrimage to the Giants' Mountain (Macha) **46**:201, 204
A Pilgrimage to the Holy Land (Lamartine)
See *Souvenirs, impressions, pensées, et paysages pendant un voyage en Orient, 1832-1833; ou, Notes d'un voyageur*
The Pilgrims of Hope (Morris) **4**:438, 441, 443
The Pilgrims of the Sun (Hogg) **4**:275-76, 279-80, 282; **109**:200, 204, 209, 242-44, 272
"A Pillar at Sebzevar" (Browning) **79**:157
"The Pillar of the Cloud" (Newman) **38**:343, 345-46
Pillow Problems, and other Mathematical Trifles (Carroll)
See *Curiosa Mathematica. Part II: Pillow Problems Thought Out during Wakeful Hours*
"Pillows of Stone" (Crawford) **12**:174; **127**:192-93, 195-97
"El pilluelo de París" (Larra) **130**:269
The Pilot (Cooper) **1**:197, 199-202, 207-08, 221-22; **54**:252-4, 265-6, 275
"The Pilot's Daughter" (Allingham) **25**:6-7, 24
"The Pilot's Song" (Allingham) **25**:18
Pin Money (Gore) **65**:2-5, 28
Pinakidia (Poe) **94**:229, 233
The Pine Apple and the Bee (Cowper) **94**:104
"The Pine Tree" (Andersen) **79**:62-63
"The Pines and the Sea" (Cranch) **115**:18
"The Pine's Mystery" (Hayne) **94**:149
The Pink and the Green (Stendhal)
See *Le rose et le vert*
Pink and White Tyranny (Stowe) **3**:558, 562
"A Pink Villa" (Woolson) **82**:276, 290, 343, 345
Pinocchio (Collodi)
See *Le Avventure di Pinocchio*
"Pins" (Coleridge) **90**:9
"Pinty úrfi" (Petofi) **21**:283
"The Pionéer" (Lowell) **90**:215, 219
"Pioneers! O Pioneers!" (Whitman) **4**:571-72, 580; **81**:316, 319, 339
Pioneers of France in the New World (Parkman) **12**:333, 336, 339, 341, 355, 371, 374, 376
The Pioneers; or, The Sources of the Susquehanna (Cooper) **1**:197-202, 205, 207, 221, 223; **27**:123-25, 127-29, 131-37, 139-44, 146-47, 149, 151, 153, 165, 167-69, 171-72, 178, 182-85, 187; **54**:250, 252-4, 266, 277, 280, 283, 291, 297, 301
"La Pipe" (Baudelaire) **55**:3
"La pipe" (Mallarmé) **4**:371, 373, 376
"La pipe au poète" (Corbière) **43**:13, 31
"La Pipe d'opium" (Gautier) **59**:36
"The Piper" (Blake) **13**:190-91; **37**:6
"Piping Down the Valleys Wild" (Blake) **13**:180
"Pippa Passes" (Blake) **37**:5
Pippa Passes (Browning) **19**:75, 82, 96, 103, 110, 113; **79**:140, 146, 148, 156, 161, 166, 181, 190
Pique Dame (Pushkin) **27**:379
Piquillo Alliaga (Scribe) **16**:385
Pir vo vremiachumy (Pushkin) **3**:426, 433-34, 448, 450, 452; **83**:263, 265-66, 285, 338, 351
"La pirámide" (Faustino) **123**:351
"Piranése, contes psychologiques, à propos de la monomanie réflective" (Nodier) **19**:384, 400
"The Pirate" (Brontë) **109**:47
"The Pirate" (Ueda Akinari)
See "Kaizoku"
Pirate (Marryat) **3**:317, 320
"Piroskaf" (Baratynsky) **103**:17, 23-4
"Pisa's Leaning Tower" (Melville) **3**:363
"Pisemski, Turgenev and Goncharov" (Pisarev)
See "Pisemskij, Turgenev, i Goncarov"
"Pisemskij, Turgenev, i Goncarov" (Pisarev) **25**:338, 346, 352
Pis'ma (Dostoevsky) **119**:90
"Pis'ma iz Dagestana" (Bestuzhev) **131**:160
Pisma k tyotenke (Saltykov) **16**:343, 345, 358, 374
Pisma o provintsii (Saltykov) **16**:343, 374
Pisma wszystkie (Fredro) **8**:291
Pismenica serbskoga iezika (Karadzic) **115**:83, 105
"Pis'mo" (Lermontov) **126**:217
"Pis'mo k doktoru Ermanu" (Bestuzhev) **131**:161
"Pis'mo Popa k episkopu Rochester-skomu pered ego izgnaniem" (Bestuzhev) **131**:165
"Pis'mo v redakcïiu Sovremennika" (Pavlova) **138**:47, 51
"The Pit and the Pendulum" (Poe) **1**:500, 502, 530; **16**:308-10, 332-34; **55**:136; **78**:257-58, 264; **94**:225
"Le pitre châtié" (Mallarmé) **41**:250, 291
"Pitt" (Bagehot) **10**:31
"Pity for Poor Africans" (Cowper) **94**:32
"Pity's Gift" (Lamb) **10**:398
"The Pixy and the Grocer" (Andersen)
See "Nissen hos Spekhøkeren"
Pizarre; ou, La conquête de Pérou (Pixérécourt) **39**:279, 286
Pizarro (Kotzebue)
See *Die Spanier in Peru, oder Rollas Tod*
Pizarro (Sheridan) **5**:362, 369, 371; **91**:274, 279-87
Pjesme junaĉke najstarije (Karadzic) **115**:112
Pjesme junaĉke srednjijeh vrema (Karadzic) **115**:112
"Place de la Bastille" (Rossetti) **77**:297
"A Place in Thy Memory, Dearest" (Griffin) **7**:201
"The Place Where I Was Born" (Chivers) **49**:49
"Placet" (Mallarmé)
See "Placet futile"
"Placet futile" (Mallarmé) **4**:376; **41**:291
"Plagiarism" (Murray) **63**:179
"Plagiarism" (Poe) **55**:177
"The Plague" (Schiller) **39**:340
"The Plague in Bergamo" (Jacobsen) **34**:157, 168-70, 172
Plain or Ringlets? (Surtees) **14**:349, 353, 365-67, 371, 374-75, 377-80
Plain Sermons (Newman)
See *Parochial and Plain Sermons*
The Plain Speaker: Opinions on Books, Men, and Things (Hazlitt) **29**:147, 162, 175, 185
"La plaine" (Sainte-Beuve) **5**:347
"The Plainest City in Europe" (Jefferies) **47**:136
"The Plains" (Petofi)
See "Az alföld"
"Plaint of the Missouri Coon" (Field) **3**:208
"Plainte d'automne" (Mallarmé) **4**:371, 373
"Plainte de cyclope" (Leconte de Lisle) **29**:217
"Plan" (Austen)
See "Plan of a Novel"
Plan de travaux scientifiques nécessaires pour reorganiser la société (Comte) **54**:210
Plan for an Army (Cobbett) **49**:113
"A Plan for an Universal Peace" (Bentham) **38**:67
Plan for the Conduct of Female Education in Boarding Schools (Darwin) **106**:193-94, 242, 245
"Plan of a Novel" (Austen) **95**:78-8,
Plan of Theological Study (Schleiermacher) **107**:268, 279
"A plank of flesh" (Lonnrot) **53**:339
Plans of Education (Reeve) **19**:415
"La planta nueva, o el faccioso" (Larra) **130**:194, 201, 221
"The Planting of the Apple Tree" (Bryant) **6**:165, 169, 171, 182
Plastik (Herder) **8**:314
"Plato" (Emerson) **1**:294; **98**:143-44, 147
Plato (Sacher-Masoch)
See *Plato's Love*
Plato and Platonism: A Series of Lectures (Pater) **7**:301-03, 308-10, 323; **90**:243-44, 257, 261, 273, 284, 288, 295, 301, 325, 333-34
"Plato: New Readings" (Emerson) **98**:68
"Plato the Philosopher to his friend Theon" (Freneau) **111**:144-45, 154-55
"Platonic Love" (Sacher-Masoch) **31**:292, 297
"Platonisme" (Verlaine) **51**:361
"Plato's Aesthetics" (Pater) **90**:325
Plato's Love (Sacher-Masoch) **31**:287, 292, 310
Plautus im Nonnenkloster (Meyer) **81**:139
Play (Robertson) **35**:334, 336, 340, 351-52, 357, 362, 365, 369, 371
"Players" (Crabbe) **121**:83, 91
The Playfellow (Martineau) **26**:310-11, 323; **137**:255-57, 262
"Playing Old Sledge for the Presidency" (Harris) **23**:150
Plays and Poems (Boker) **125**:28, 33, 38, 58, 76, 81-82, 84, 86
The Plays of Clara Gazul (Mérimée)
See *Théâtre de Clara Gazul*
Plays on the Passions (Baillie) **71**:3-5, 8-9, 12-13
A Plea for a Miserable World . . . (Webster) **30**:413
"Plea for Beauty" (Ingelow) **39**:256
"A Plea for Captain John Brown" (Thoreau) **7**:385-6, 406; **21**:329, 331, 347, 350, 370
"A Plea for Gas Lamps" (Stevenson) **5**:388-89
"The Plea of the Midsummer Fairies" (Hood) **16**:201, 205, 208, 210, 215, 218, 221, 225-27, 229-33
The Plea of the Midsummer Fairies, Hero and Leander, Lycus the Centaur, and Other Poems (Hood) **16**:200-02, 233, 240
"Pleasant Days of My Childhood" (Traill) **31**:328
"Pleasant Memories of Pleasant Lands" (Sigourney) **87**:321
Pleasant Memories of Pleasant Lands (Sigourney) **21**:296, 299; **87**:321
"The Pleasure-Boat" (Dana) **53**:158
"The Pleasures of a College Life" (Horton) **87**:95
"The Pleasures of Hope" (Campbell) **19**:162-63, 165, 169, 171, 174-75, 178-81, 184-85, 189, 191-93, 195-99
The Pleasures of Hope, with Other Poems (Campbell) **19**:176-77
"The Pleasures of Melancholy" (Warton) **118**:351
The Pleasures of Memory (Rogers) **69**:68-9, 74-5, 77-8, 80-3, 85-92
"Pleasures of Spring" (Clare) **9**:98-99

"A Pledge to Hafiz" (Taylor) **89**:305
Les pléiades (Gobineau) **17**:65-9, 91-3, 96, 98, 100, 103-04
Les Pleurs (Desbordes-Valmore) **97**:12, 26, 29, 39
"Pleurs dans la nuit" (Hugo) **3**:263
Plighted Troth (Darley) **2**:128
"Plorata Veris Lachrymis" (Barnes) **75**:72
"Plots and Counterplots" (Alcott)
See "V.V.: or Plots and Counterplots"
Plots and Counterplots: More Unknown Thrillers of Louisa May Alcott (Alcott) **58**:3
"The Ploughboy Is Whooping Anon Anon" (Wordsworth) **12**:393
"Plovec" (Pavlova) **138**:50
"Plovets" (Pavlova) **138**:4, 16
"Le plus beau dîner du monde" (Villiers de l'Isle Adam) **3**:581
"Le plus bel amour de Don Juan" (Barbey d'Aurevilly) **1**:74-75
"Plus de chants" (Desbordes-Valmore) **97**:6, 10
"Plus de politique" (Beranger) **34**:28
"Plutarch, Charon and a Modern Bookseller" (Montagu) **117**:182
"Pluviôse irrité contre la ville entière" (Baudelaire) **55**:70
Po und Rhein (Engels) **85**:83
"The Poacher" (Hood) **16**:234
"The Pobble Who Has No Toes" (Lear) **3**:308-09
"Pocahontas" (Sigourney) **21**:298, 303; **87**:342
Pocahontas, and Other Poems (Sigourney) **87**:321, 326, 330, 332, 342
Pochi versi inediti (Manzoni) **98**:276
"Początek broszury politycznej" (Norwid) **17**:372
"Pod oknom" (Preseren) **127**:298
"Podas Okus" (Gordon) **21**:156, 160, 163, 166, 173, 181
The Podesta's Daughter (Boker) **125**:7, 21, 82
"podrazhaniye" (Bestuzhev) **131**:150
"podrazhaniye Gete" (Bestuzhev) **131**:150
"Podrazhaniye pervoy satire Bualo" (Bestuzhev) **131**:181
"Podrazhatelyam" (Baratynsky) **103**:3
"Podrobnyi otchet o lune" (Zhukovsky) **35**:406
Podrostok (Dostoevsky) **2**:167, 170, 175, 204; **7**:80, 103; **21**:101-02, 118; **33**:165, 170, 178-79, 182; **43**:92, 95
Podróż na Wschód—Podróż do Ziemi Swietej z Neopolu (Slowacki) **15**:374
"Podvig Ovechkina i Shcherbiny za Kavkazom" (Bestuzhev) **131**:182
"Poem" (Ridge) **82**:199
"A Poem for Children, with Thoughts on Death" (Hammon) **5**:262, 264-65
"Poem of Apparitions in Boston in the 73rd Year of These States" (Whitman) **31**:419, 425; **81**:329
"Poem of the Road" (Whitman) **81**:329
A Poem on the Bill Lately Passed for Regulating the Slave Trade (Williams) **135**:333
"Poem on the memorable victory obtained by the gallant capt. Paul Jones, or the Good Man Richard, over the Seraphis, etc. under the command of capt. Pearson" (Freneau) **1**:314, 317, 319; **111**:143
A Poem, on the Rising Glory of America (Freneau) **1**:314, 316, 319, 324; **111**:139, 156
"Poem Read at the Dinner Given to the Author by the Medical Profession" (Holmes) **14**:128
"Un poema" (Silva) **114**:294
Un poema (Silva) **114**:262, 270
Poema Piasta Dantyszka o piekle (Slowacki) **15**:355, 358-59
"Los poemas de la carne" (Silva) **114**:300
Los poemas de la carne (Silva) **114**:267
"Poème de la femme" (Gautier) **59**:19
Poëmes (Vigny) **7**:484
"Poëmes antiques" (Vigny) **102**:379
Poèmes antiques (Baudelaire) **6**:102
Poèmes antiques (Leconte de Lisle) **29**:212-17, 221-25, 231, 233, 235-43
Poèmes antiques et modernes (Vigny) **7**:480-81, 483-84; **102**:366, 368, 373
Poèmes barbares (Baudelaire) **6**:102
Poèmes barbares (Leconte de Lisle) **29**:212, 215-17, 221-25, 235
Poèmes d'Edgar Poe (Mallarmé) **41**:269
Poèmes en prose (Mallarmé) **4**:377
Poèmes et légendes (Nerval) **1**:484
Poèmes et poésies (Leconte de Lisle) **29**:226, 230-31, 237
"Poëmes judaïques" (Vigny) **102**:379
"Poëmes modernes" (Vigny) **102**:379
"Poèmes philosophiques" (Vigny) **102**:336
Poemes Philosophiques (Vigny) **102**:378
Les Poèmes saturniens (Verlaine) **2**:617, 619, 622-24, 628-31; **51**:352, 354-56, 359, 361-62, 365, 386-87
Poèmes tragiques (Leconte de Lisle) **29**:221-25, 235
"Poems" (Cooke) **5**:132
Poems (Allingham) **25**:24, 26
Poems (Arnold) **6**:32, 44; **29**:12, 27, 53; **89**:43, 85-6, 92; **126**:46, 111
Poems (Barbauld) **50**:9
Poems (Bécquer)
See *Rimas*
Poems (Brontë) **71**:165-66; **102**:24
Poems (Browning) **1**:112, 117, 129
Poems (Clare)
See *The Poems of John Clare*
Poems (Coleridge) **90**:7, 15, 19-21, 26, 29
Poems (Coleridge)
See *The Poems of Samuel Taylor Coleridge*
Poems (Cooke) **110**:12
Poems (Cowper) **8**:102, 113; **94**:77
Poems (Crabbe) **26**:78, 102; **121**:8-9, 11, 23, 34, 72, 83
Poems (Cranch) **115**:15, 22, 26, 28, 34, 40, 42, 55
Poems (Desbordes-Valmore)
See *Pósies*
Poems (Dyer) **129**:113, 116
Poems (Emerson) **1**:285, 295; **38**:185; **98**:177, 179-82, 184
Poems (Ferguson) **33**:279, 285, 287, 290, 299
Poems (Hayne) **94**:137, 139, 141, 148, 151, 167
Poems (Hemans) **71**:271-72
Poems (Hogg)
See *The Works of the Ettrick Shepherd*
Poems (Holmes) **14**:98, 100-01, 127
Poems (Ingelow)
See *Poems by Jean Ingelow*
Poems (Keats) **8**:321-22, 324-25, 331-32, 340; **73**:152, 182, 186, 192, 208, 290, 311-12, 314; **121**:141, 215-16
Poems (Lanier) **6**:236
Poems (Longfellow) **2**:472-73
Poems (Lowell) **2**:502-03, 511, 515; **90**:215, 220
Poems (Meyer)
See *Gedichte*
Poems (Opie) **65**:175, 182
Poems (Patmore) **9**:326-28, 336, 348
Poems (Pavlova)
See *Stikhotvoreniia*
Poems (Pinkney) **31**:267, 270, 273
Poems (Poe) **55**:162; **97**:184; **117**:195, 235, 280
Poems (Ridge) **82**:174, 185, 199, 201
Poems (Rogers) **69**:77
Poems (Rossetti) **2**:557-58
Poems (Rossetti) **4**:490, 492-93, 495, 497-98, 500, 502, 511; **77**:294, 302, 336-37, 340-41, 346
Poems (Runeberg)
See *Dikter*
Poems (Shelley) **18**:331
Poems (Sigourney) **21**:291, 308; **87**:321, 326, 331, 334, 337
Poems (Slowacki) **15**:363
Poems (Smith) **59**:259, 264, 312, 319, 326, 328-33
Poems (Southey) **8**:447; **97**:260, 314
Poems (Tennyson) **30**:211, 275-76; **115**:246
Poems (Timrod) **25**:359, 366, 382
Poems (Very) **9**:371-72, 379
Poems (Whittier) **8**:488; **59**:354
Poems (Williams) **135**:333-34
Poems (Wordsworth) **12**:393-94, 401, 416, 463, 468
Poems, 1792 (Dyer) **129**:112, 132, 140
Poems, 1800 (Dyer) **129**:95, 122-23, 146
Poems, 1801 (Dyer) **129**:93, 96, 120-21, 132, 136-37
Poems, 1802 (Dyer) **129**:99, 105, 107, 114, 121-23
Poems and Ballads of Heinrich Heine (Lazarus) **8**:418, 425
Poems and Essays (Very) **9**:370
Poems and Plays (Lamb) **113**:230
"Poems and Prose Pieces 1855-58" (Harpur) **114**:123
Poems and Prose Remains of Arthur Hugh Clough, with a Selection from His Letters, and a Memoir (Clough) **27**:60, 64, 70
Poems and Prose Writings (Dana) **53**:170
Poems and Songs (Kendall) **12**:179, 184-86, 190, 192
The Poems and Stories of Fitz-James O'Brien (O'Brien) **21**:234-35, 244
Poems and Translations, Written between the Ages of Fourteen and Sixteen (Lazarus) **109**:289, 304-05
Poems before Congress (Browning) **1**:120, 130; **61**:6, 11-2, 15, 24, 44
Poems by a Slave (Horton) **87**:86, 101
Poems by Currer, Ellis, and Acton Bell (Brontë) **3**:43, 62
Poems by Currer, Ellis, and Acton Bell (Brontë) **16**:63, 67, 87
Poems by Currer, Ellis, and Acton Bell (Brontë) **4**:38
Poems by Emily Dickinson (Dickinson) **77**:66-67, 75, 165, 169
Poems by James Clarence Mangan (Mangan) **27**:276, 301, 315, 318
Poems by Jean Ingelow (Ingelow) **39**:257, 263-64; **107**:118, 134, 146
Poems by Robert Lovell and Robert Southey (Southey) **97**:260
Poems by Robert Southey (Southey) **97**:260
Poems by the Way (Morris) **4**:421-23, 425, 443
Poems by Two Brothers (Tennyson) **30**:223
Poems by William Cowper, of the Inner Temple, Esq. (Cowper) **94**:92, 112, 117
Poems by William Cullen Bryant, an American (Bryant) **6**:157-60, 162
"Poems by William Morris" (Pater) **90**:296, 305-06, 308, 326
Poems, Chiefly Lyrical (Tennyson) **30**:203, 211, 275; **65**:280
Poems Descriptive of Rural Life and Scenery (Clare) **9**:72-73, 76, 78, 112; **86**:92, 110, 125, 128, 151, 153-55, 159-60, 173-74
Poems, Dialogues in Verse, and Epigrams (Landor) **14**:177
Poems Dramatic and Miscellaneous (Warren) **13**:411-13
Poems, Essays, and Fragments (Thomson) **18**:394
Poems for Our Children (Hale) **75**:284-86, 288-89, 341, 349
"Poems for the Sea" (Sigourney) **87**:321
Poems for the Times (Heine)
See *Zeitgedichte*
"Poems Founded on the Affections" (Wordsworth) **111**:323
Poems in Early Life (Harpur) **114**:144

Poems in Prose (Turgenev)
See *Stikhotvoreniya v proze*
Poems in Prose from Charles Baudelaire (Baudelaire)
See *Petits poèmes en prose: Le spleen de Paris*
Poems: Legendary and Historical (Milnes) **61**:137
Poems of 1820 (Keats)
See *Poems*
Poems of 1833 (Browning) **61**:48
Poems of 1844 (Browning) **61**:2, 4-5, 42-3, 61, 64-5, 71-2; **66**:88
Poems of 1850 (Browning) **61**:43, 49, 69
The Poems of Archibald Lampman (Lampman) **25**:217
The Poems of Arthur Hugh Clough (Clough) **27**:44
The Poems of Charlotte and Patrick Branwell Brontë (Brontë) **109**:26
Poems of Charlotte Smith (Smith) **115**:172, 176-78, 180, 182
The Poems of Edgar Allan Poe (Poe) **117**:231
The Poems of Emily Dickinson (Dickinson) **21**:7, 9, 11-12, 43
The Poems of Emily Dickinson. 3vols (Dickinson) **77**:48
The Poems of Emma Lazarus (Lazarus) **8**:419-20, 424
The Poems of Eugene Field (Field) **3**:209
The Poems of Francè Prešeren (Preseren)
See *Poezíje Dóktorja Francèta Presérna*
The Poems of Geoffrey Chaucer, Modernized (Horne) **127**:285
Poems of Gerard Manley Hopkins (Hopkins) **17**:196
Poems of Henry Kendall (Kendall) **12**:198
The Poems of Henry Timrod (Timrod) **25**:361, 378, 386
Poems of Home and Travel (Taylor) **89**:307, 309
The Poems of John Clare (Clare) **9**:96-97; **86**:103-04
The Poems of Joseph Sheridan Le Fanu (Le Fanu) **58**:251-2
Poems of Many Years (Milnes) **61**:137, 144-5
The Poems of Patrick Branwell Brontë (Brontë) **109**:25-6, 51
Poems of Philip Freneau (Freneau) **111**:139, 148-51, 153, 157, 159, 166
Poems of Rural Life in Common English (Barnes) **75**:18, 40, 69
Poems of Rural Life in the Dorset Dialect (Barnes) **75**:18, 40, 52-3, 67-81, 83, 85, 92
Poems of Rural Life in the Dorset Dialect; Third Collection (Barnes) **75**:18, 40, 69
The Poems of Samuel Taylor Coleridge (Coleridge) **54**:73; **99**:17, 22; **111**:233, 245
"Poems of Sentiment and Reflection" (Milnes) **61**:135
Poems of Sidney Lanier (Lanier) **6**:236
"Poems of the Imagination" (Wordsworth) **111**:323
Poems of the Lake George Darley (Darley) **2**:125
Poems of the Orient (Taylor) **89**:302, 304-07, 343, 346, 355, 357, 359
"Poems of the War" (Cranch) **115**:23
Poems of the War (Boker) **125**:25, 28, 33-34, 39, 42, 80-81
The Poems of Walter Savage Landor (Landor) **14**:157, 175
The Poems of William Allingham (Allingham) **25**:20
"The Poems of William Blake" (Thomson) **18**:404
Poems on American Affairs (Freneau) **111**:141
Poems, On American Affairs, and a Variety of Other Subjects, Chiefly Moral and Political (Freneau) **111**:183
"Poems on rural life etc." (Clare) **86**:174
Poems on Several Occasions (Lennox) **134**:219
Poems on Slavery (Longfellow) **45**:132, 140, 155; **103**:290
"Poems on the Naming of Places" (Wordsworth) **12**:452; **111**:233
Poems on Various Subjects (Lamb) **113**:186
Poems on Various Subjects (Rowson) **69**:141
Poems on Various Subjects, with Introductory Remarks on the Present State of Science and Literature in France (Williams) **135**:286, 314-15, 335-36
Poems Partly of Rural Life in National English (Barnes) **75**:15, 40, 69, 85
Poems Relating to the American Revolution by Philip Freneau (Freneau) **111**:157
Poems, second series (Arnold) **6**:32
Poems, second series (Dickinson) **21**:22-3
Poems, third series (Dickinson) **21**:15
"Poems to Caroline" (Brontë) **109**:10
Poems: Wherein It Is Attempted to Describe Certain News of Nature and of Rustic Manners (Baillie) **71**:1-2, 51-53
Poems Written between the Years 1768 and 1794 (Freneau) **111**:123, 147
Poe's Helen Remembers (Whitman) **19**:459
"Poesi och politik" (Almqvist) **42**:19
"Poesía viva" (Silva) **114**:301
Poesías (Casal) **131**:255-57
Poesías (Gómez de Avellaneda) **111**:3, 6, 9, 18, 27-8, 30, 43
Poesías (Martínez de la Rosa) **102**:238
Poesías (Silva) **114**:261, 294-98
"Poesías de don Francisco de la Rosa" (Larra) **130**:254
Poesías varias (Silva) **114**:315, 318
Poesie (Foscolo) **8**:267, 278
Poesie (Leopardi) **129**:218
Poesie der Griechen und Roemer (Schlegel) **45**:283, 320, 359
"Poésie; ou, Le paysage dans le Golfe de Glafenes" (Lamartine) **11**:270, 280
"Poésie sacrée" (Lamartine) **11**:269
Poesier (Wergeland) **5**:538
Poèsies (Gautier) **1**:350
Poésies (Laforgue) **53**:277
Poésies (Mallarmé) **41**:240-44, 249, 280
Poésies (Rimbaud) **82**:240
Poésies allemandes (Nerval) **1**:484
Poésies complètes (Gautier) **59**:18, 34-5, 72
Poèsies complètes (Rimbaud) **4**:472-74
Poésies de Choderlos de Laclos (Laclos) **4**:325
Les poésies de Joseph Delorme (Sainte-Beuve) **5**:333, 340-41
Poésies I, II (Lautréamont) **12**:210, 212, 215-16, 220-21, 237-41, 243-44
Poésies inédites (Desbordes-Valmore) **97**:13, 18, 20, 25-7, 29-30
Poésies novelles, 1836-1852 (Musset) **7**:256, 272, 279
"The Poet" (Bryant) **6**:182; **46**:6
"The Poet" (Cranch) **115**:5, 40-1
"The Poet" (Emerson) **1**:295, 307; **38**:173-74, 180-81, 184, 187, 189, 190; **98**:25-6, 47, 65, 114-16, 176, 181-82, 189
"The Poet" (Lampman) **25**:216
"The Poet" (O'Brien) **21**:249
"The Poet" (Pavlova) **138**:33
"The Poet" (Pushkin) **83**:249, 257
"The Poet" (Thoreau) **7**:396
Poet and Composer (Hoffmann)
See *Der Dichter und der Komponist*
"Poet and Crowd" (Pushkin) **83**:249, 257
"The Poet and His Muse" (Thomson) **18**:415, 419
"The Poet and His Songs" (Longfellow) **2**:491
"The Poet and the Throng" (Pushkin)
See "Poet and Crowd"
The Poet at the Breakfast-Table (Holmes) **14**:106, 110, 113-15, 124, 126, 132-33, 143-44, 146; **81**:102-04
"The Poet Boy's Love Wishes" (Harpur) **114**:107
"The Poet Heine" (Lazarus) **8**:426; **109**:326
"The Poet in the East" (Taylor) **89**:305
"The Poet of Love" (Chivers) **49**:44-6, 53, 55
"Poet of Poets" (Lanier) **118**:268
"The Poet of the Spring" (Crawford) **127**:202
"The Poet, the Oyster and Sensitive Plant" (Cowper) **94**:121
"El poeta y la sirena" (Casal) **131**:255
"Le poète contumace" (Corbière) **43**:6, 10-11, 18, 24, 27, 30, 32, 33
"Le poëte dans les révolutions" (Hugo) **21**:214
"Le poète décho" (Musset) **7**:274
"La poéte Mourant" (Lamartine) **11**:245, 248, 270, 280
Le poète sifflé (Grillparzer) **102**:104
"Les poètes de sept ans" (Rimbaud) **4**:466, 471-72, 474, 479, 486; **35**:271; **82**:226, 247
"Les poëtes du XVIe siècle" (Nerval) **67**:303
Les poètes maudites (Verlaine) **51**:354
Poetic and Religious Harmonies (Lamartine) **11**:283
Poetic Contemplations (Lamartine)
See *Les recueillements poétiques*
"Poetic Diction" (Wordsworth) **38**:416
"Poetic Discriptions of Violent Death" (Harpur) **114**:131
"Poetic Interpretation" (Lampman) **25**:203, 214-15
The Poetic Mirror; or, The Living Bards of Britain (Hogg) **4**:282, 284; **109**:192, 209, 240, 246-50, 258, 260, 262
"The Poetic Principle" (Poe) **1**:510-11, 526; **16**:307; **55**:132, 138, 159, 164, 170-1; **94**:220; **117**:194, 257, 04, 312-13, 335
"Poetic Sympathies" (Dyer) **129**:95, 118, 120
Poetic Works (Horton)
See *Poetical Works*
The Poetical Meditations of M. Alphonse de La Martine (Lamartine)
See *Méditations poétiques*
Poetical Pieces (Barnes) **75**:14, 69
"A Poetical Reverie" (Warren) **13**:412
Poetical Sketches (Blake) **13**:159, 171, 181-82, 184-85, 219, 239-40; **37**:3-4, 8-9, 13-14, 20, 35, 38, 40, 72
"Poetical Studies" (Harpur) **114**:144
"Poetical Versatility" (Hazlitt) **29**:148
Poetical Works (Adams) **33**:5, 7, 11, 16
Poetical Works (Browning) **79**:149, 152, 189-90
Poetical Works (Browning) **61**:12, 14-5, 24
Poetical Works (Crabbe) **121**:29, 78
Poetical Works (Hemans) **71**:271-72, 274-77
Poetical Works (Horton) **87**:101-102, 104
Poetical Works (Moore) **110**:177-80
Poetical Works (Rossetti) **77**:291-98, 303, 343, 349, 356-63
The Poetical Works (Taylor) **89**:325
Poetical Works (Whittier) **59**:371
The Poetical Works of Christina Georgina Rossetti (Rossetti) **2**:566, 572, 576; **50**:279; **66**:304, 310
The Poetical Works of James Thomson (B. V.) (Thomson) **18**:395
The Poetical Works of John Trumbull, LL.D. (Trumbull) **30**:346, 351, 376
The Poetical Works of Leigh Hunt (Hunt) **70**:257
The Poetical Works of Robert Southey, Collected by Himself (Southey) **97**:268-69, 277-80, 315, 317
The Poetical Works of Shelley (Shelley) **93**:343-46
The Poetical Works of Sydney Dobell (Dobell) **43**:45
The Poetical Works of the Late Thomas Little, Esq. (Moore) **6**:388; **110**:190
The Poetical Works of William Wordsworth (Wordsworth) **111**:234, 237, 239-43, 293, 301, 315, 338
Poetics, or a Series of Poems and Disquisitions on Poetry (Dyer) **129**:96-97, 132, 138

"Poetischer Realismus" (Ludwig) **4**:360
Poetry (Karamzin) **3**:284
Poetry (Mickiewicz) **101**:174-75
"Poetry: A Metrical Essay" (Holmes) **14**:98, 127
"Poetry and Imagination" (Emerson) **1**:295; **38**:175, 187-88; **98**:55, 58-60, 62
"Poetry and Politics" (Almqvist)
See "Poesi och politik"
Poetry and Prose (Shelley) **93**:294-95
Poetry and Tales of Edgar Allan Poe (Poe) **117**:321
Poetry and Truth out of My Life (Goethe)
See *Dichtung und Wahrheit*
"Poetry and Verse" (Hopkins) **17**:250
"Poetry and Verse" (Hugo) **17**:250
"Poetry for Children" (Sigourney) **87**:321
Poetry for Children (Lamb) **125**:329-30, 332-35, 345-46, 354, 360, 371, 373
Poetry for Children (Lamb) **10**:418; **113**:230, 286
Poetry for the People (Milnes) **61**:129, 137
"Poetry heals an ailing spirit" (Baratynsky)
See "Bolyashchiy dukh vrachuet pesnopenie..."
Poetry Notebooks (Emerson) **98**:177
"The Poetry of Byron" (Lampman) **25**:212
"The Poetry of Christina Rossetti" (Levy) **59**:86
The Poetry of Dorothy Wordsworth (Wordsworth) **25**:408, 420, 422
The Poetry of Julián del Casal (Casal) **131**:267-69, 271
The Poetry of Sacred and Legendary Art (Jameson) **43**:323-25, 327-28, 333-34, 337-8
"Poetry of the Celtic Races" (Renan) **26**:364
Poetry of the Pacific (Ridge) **82**:185
"Poets" (Hayne) **94**:160, 164
"The Poets" (Lampman) **25**:160, 173, 194, 209, 212
The Poets (Alfieri) **101**:36
"Poets and Poetry of America" (Poe) **55**:177
The Poets and Poetry of Munster (Mangan) **27**:280, 307-08, 314, 318
A Poet's Bazaar (Andersen) **7**:16-17; **79**:79, 81
"The Poet's Consolation" (Mangan) **27**:276
"A Poet's Daughter" (Halleck) **47**:57, 79, 81
"The Poet's Death" (Lermontov)
See "Smert' poeta"
"The Poet's Epitaph" (Wordsworth) **111**:242
The Poet's Fate. A Poetical Dialogue (Dyer) **129**:95, 104-5, 113-15, 118, 132
"The Poet's Feeble Petition" (Horton) **87**:102
"A Poet's Home" (Harpur) **114**:115
The Poet's Journal (Taylor) **89**:309, 346
Poet's Life (Tieck)
See *Des Dichters Leben*
"The Poet's Mind" (Tennyson) **65**:357-8
"The Poets of Seven Years" (Rimbaud)
See "Les poètes de sept ans"
The Poet's Pilgrimage to Waterloo (Southey) **8**:466; **97**:263, 269, 291
"The Poet's Soliloquy" (Cranch) **115**:43
"The Poet's Song" (Lampman) **25**:184, 192, 204, 216
"The Poet's Tale" (Longfellow) **45**:124
"The Poet's Vow" (Browning) **61**:53, 56, 58, 64-5, 67-70; **66**:56
"Poezdka v Poles'e" (Turgenev) **122**:264, 343-44, 348-49
Poezdka v Revel' (Bestuzhev) **131**:165-66, 183
Poezíje Dóktorja Francèta Presérna (Preseren) **127**:296, 300, 304, 323, 327, 333
Poganuc People (Stowe) **3**:562-63, 568
"Pogassee delo" (Leskov) **25**:247
The Poggenpuhl Family (Fontane)
See *Die Poggenpuhls*
Die Poggenpuhls (Fontane) **26**:236, 244, 256-57, 270-71, 278
"Pogibšie i pogibajuščie" (Pisarev) **25**:344
"Poiema lyriko eis ton thanato tou Lord Byron" (Solomos) **15**:386, 388, 390, 395, 397
"Poietes Apoietes" (Coleridge) **90**:15, 28
"point d'adieux" (Desbordes-Valmore) **97**:5
"Le point noir" (Nerval) **1**:486
The Point of View for My Work as an Author (Kierkegaard) **34**:201, 203-05, 238, 248, 250-55, 257-58; **78**:121, 181, 197, 215, 238
The Point of View for My Work as an Author: A Report to History (Kierkegaard)
See *Synspunktet for min Forfatter-Virksomhed*
"Point Rash-Judgment" (Wordsworth) **111**:367
"Le poison" (Baudelaire) **6**:80, 129; **55**:29, 61, 69
"A Poison Tree" (Blake) **13**:180; **37**:4, 44, 49, 53, 92
The Poison Tree (Chatterji)
See *Vishavriksha*
"The Poisoned Girl" (Solomos) **15**:393
"Pokal, Der" (Tieck) **46**:350
"Polden" (Tyutchev) **34**:400
Polemic with the Catholic Review regarding the Work of Aimé Martin (Faustino)
See *Polémica con la Revista Católica sobre la obra de Aimé Martin*
Polémica con la Revista Católica sobre la obra de Aimé Martin (Faustino) **123**:360
"Polemica cu România libera" (Eminescu) **131**:326
"The Polemics with the România libera" (Eminescu)
See "Polemica cu România libera"
"Der Polenflüchtling" (Lenau) **16**:264, 286
Les polichinelles (Becque) **3**:16
Polinice (Alfieri) **101**:4, 11, 42, 67, 69
Polinices and Virginia (Alfieri) **101**:32
The Polish Faust (Sacher-Masoch) **31**:295
"A Polish Insurgent" (Thomson) **18**:391
The Polish Mines (Pixérécourt)
See *Les mines de Pologne*
"Polish Pilgrims" (Mickiewicz)
See "Pielgrzym"
Politian (Poe) **1**:504, **55**:180-1, 209
The Political and Confidential Correspondence of Lewis the Sixteenth; with Observations on Each Letter (Williams) **135**:260, 307, 335
"Political Aspect of the Colored People of the United States" (Delany) **93**:166
"Political Biography, Hugh Gaine's Life" (Freneau) **111**:111
"Political Destiny" (Delany)
See "The Political Destiny of the Colored Race on the American Continent"
"The Political Destiny of the Colored Race on the American Continent" (Delany) **93**:100, 105, 129-30, 156, 169, 172
Political Essays (Hazlitt) **82**:105, 129
Political Essays (Lowell) **2**:515
Political Letters and Pamphlets (Cobbett) **49**:157
"A Political Molecule" (Eliot) **118**:38
"Political Reflections" (Madison) **126**:326
Political Register (Cobbett)
See *Cobbett's Weekly Political Register*
Political Tales (Saltykov) **16**:351
The Political Theology of Mazzini and the International (Bakunin) **25**:49
Political Work (Eminescu) **131**:289
Political Works (Cobbett) **49**:107, 112
"Politiciennes" (Maupassant) **83**:189
"Politics" (Emerson) **98**:116-17
"Politics" (Tennyson) **30**:295
"Politics" (Tonna) **135**:204, 210
"Politics as a Profession" (Bagehot) **10**:31
"Politique (1831)" (Nerval) **67**:331
Politisk camara optica (Almqvist) **42**:19
Die Polizei (Schiller) **69**:169, 250
"The Poll Cat" (Shaw) **15**:335
"Poll Jenning's Hair" (Cooke) **110**:35
"Pollice Verso" (Martí) **63**:102
"Pollion's Supper" (Pavlova)
See "Uzhin Polliona"
"Polly Be-en Upzides Wi' Tom" (Barnes) **75**:78
"Polly Mariner, Tailoress" (Cooke) **110**:20, 25, 33, 36, 44
Polnoe sobranie sochinenii (Zhukovsky) **35**:396
Polnoe sobranie stikhotvorenii (Baratynsky) **103**:47-9
Polnoe sobranie stikhotvoreniia (Pavlova) **138**:31-36
Polnoye sobraniye sochineniy (Bestuzhev) **131**:186
Poltava (Pushkin) **3**:413-14, 416, 422-23, 445, 452, 460-62; **27**:369; **83**:243, 246, 250, 257, 312-14, 335, 357
"Polunoščniki" (Leskov) **25**:234-36
"Polycrates" (Thomson) **18**:411
"Pomare" (Heine) **4**:252
Pomona für Teutschlands Töchter (La Roche) **121**:250, 263, 271, 297, 305-6, 325
Pompeii (Bulwer-Lytton)
See *The Last Days of Pompeii*
Pompeo in Egitto (Leopardi) **129**:347
"Pompey's Ghost" (Hood) **16**:234, 239
Ponce de Leon (Brentano) **1**:101-02
"The Ponds" (Thoreau) **7**:388; **138**:75
"Les ponts" (Rimbaud) **35**:323
"The Poor and Their Dwellings" (Crabbe) **121**:58, 62, 90
"The Poor Artist: or, Seven Eyesights and one Object" (Horne) **127**:269
The Poor Benefactor (Stifter)
See *Kalkstein*
"The Poor Bird" (Andersen) **7**:21
The Poor Book (Arnim)
See *Das Armenbuch*
The Poor Bride (Ostrovsky)
See *Bednaya nevesta*
"The Poor Clare" (Gaskell) **5**:202; **70**:182, 189, 191, 193, 196-98
The Poor Clare (Gaskell) **137**:99
"Poor Dionis" (Eminescu)
See "Sarmanul Dionis"
"The Poor Fiddler" (Grillparzer)
See *Der Arme Spielmann*
Poor Flowers (Desbordes-Valmore)
See *Pauvres fleurs*
Poor Folk (Dostoevsky)
See *Bednye lyudi*
The Poor Gentleman (Oliphant) **11**:446-7
A Poor Gentleman (Turgenev)
See *Nakhlebnik*
"The Poor Ghost" (Rossetti) **2**:558, 565
"The Poor in Church" (Rimbaud)
See "Les pauvres à l'église"
Poor Jack (Marryat) **3**:317-18, 320
"Poor John" (Andersen) **7**:21
Poor Laws and Paupers Illustrated (Martineau) **137**:302
"Poor Little Heart" (Dickinson) **21**:55
"Poor Liza" (Bestuzhev)
See "Bednaia Liza"
"Poor Liza" (Karamzin) **3**:280, 285-91
"Poor Lorraine" (Kingsley) **35**:212
The Poor Man's Friend (Cobbett)
See *Cobbett's Poor Man's Friend*
"Poor Mathew" (Lincoln) **18**:272-73
Poor Miss Finch (Collins) **1**:184; **18**:65
The Poor Musician (Grillparzer)
See *Der Arme Spielmann*
The Poor of New York (Boucicault) **41**:31, 34
"The Poor of the Borough" (Crabbe) **121**:62
"The Poor of the Land" (Martí) **63**:165
"Poor Relations" (Lamb) **10**:411, 436-37; **113**:210
Poor Relations (Balzac)
See *Les parents pauvres*
The Poor Rich Man, and the Rich Poor Man (Sedgwick) **19**:437-38, 440, 444
"Poor Scholar" (Carleton) **3**:83, 85, 87, 90, 92
"The Poor Scholar" (Hale) **75**:298

"Poor Susan" (Wordsworth) **111**:281
"Poor Thumbling" (Andersen) **7**:21, 24
"A Poor Young Shepherd" (Verlaine) **51**:381, 383-84
"The Poor-Rate Unfolds a Tale" (Robertson) **35**:370
Popanilla (Disraeli)
See *The Voyage of Captain Popanilla*
"The Pope" (Browning) **79**:111
"The Poplar" (Shevchenko)
See "Topolja"
"The Poplar-Field" (Cowper) **8**:139; **94**:33, 38
"Poppies" (Coleridge) **31**:71
"Popular Discontent" (Webster) **30**:424
The Popular Education of France (Arnold) **89**:101-02; **126**:3, 6, 77, 82, 112
"Popular Fallacies" (Lamb) **10**:411, 415
"Popular Fallacies—XIV" (Lamb) **113**:198
Popular Songs (Herder) **8**:305
Popular Stories (Grimm and Grimm)
See *Kinder-und Hausmärchen*
Popular Tales (Edgeworth) **1**:256, 267; **51**:81, 89, 135, 137
Popular Tales (Tieck) **5**:515
"Popularity in Authorship" (Clare) **9**:115, 121
"Por ahora" (Larra) **130**:204, 241
"Por que tan terca...?" (Castro) **78**:42
Porcupine's Gazette (Cobbett) **49**:113
Porcupine's Works (Cobbett) **49**:87, 107, 109
"Porog" (Turgenev) **21**:455; **122**:307-8
"O pórphyras" (Solomos) **15**:390, 399
"Porphyria's Lover" (Browning) **19**:131
"Porro Unum Est Necessarium" (Arnold) **89**:101, 103
"Le port" (Baudelaire) **29**:110
"Le port" (Maupassant) **1**:460
"Port Marsel'sky" (Pavlova) **138**:4, 16
Port Salvation (Daudet)
See *L'évangéliste*
"Portent" (Grillparzer)
See "Vorzeichen"
"The Portent" (Melville) **3**:378
"Portes et fenêtres" (Corbière) **43**:14, 31
"Portia" (Musset) **7**:265, 267, 278-79
"Le Portrait" (Baudelaire) **55**:10
"A Portrait" (Browning) **19**:96
"The Portrait" (Gogol)
See "Portret"
"The Portrait" (Hood) **16**:206
"Un Portrait" (Maupassant) **83**:181
"The Portrait" (Rossetti) **4**:492, 506, 508, 511, 518, 521-22; **77**:311, 314, 317, 348, 353-54, 358-59, 363
"Portrait by Vandyck" (Hazlitt) **29**:144
"A Portrait for Amoret" (Sheridan) **91**:233-34
"A Portrait in Six Sonnets" (Lampman) **25**:219
Portraits (Pater)
See *An Imaginary Portrait*
Portraits contemporains (Sainte-Beuve) **5**:346
Portraits Intimes of the Eighteenth Century (Goncourt and Goncourt) **7**:153
"Portret" (Gogol) **5**:219, 240-42, 248, 252-54, 256-58; **31**:103
"Portretnaia Gallereia" (Bestuzhev) **131**:165
Port-Royal (Sainte-Beuve) **5**:333-34, 336, 338-40, 349
Port-Tarascon (Daudet) **1**:236-37, 242
"Posąg i obuwie" (Norwid) **17**:373
Poshekhonskaya starina (Saltykov) **16**:343, 345-49, 351-52, 357, 359, 369, 373, 375
"Posielenie" (Slowacki) **15**:355
Pósies (Desbordes-Valmore) **97**:12, 26-7
"The Position of Poland with Respect to God and Man" (Krasiński)
See "O stanowisku Polski z Bożych i ludzkich wzgledów"
Positive Philosophy (Martineau) **26**:323; **137**:236
Positive Politics (Comte)
See *Système de Politique Positive ou Traité de Sociologie instituant la Religion de l'Humanité*
Positive Polity (Comte)
See *Système de Politique Positive ou Traité de Sociologie instituant la Religion de l'Humanité*
"A Positive Romance" (Bellamy) **4**:30; **86**:75
Positivist Calendar (Comte)
See *Calendrier positiviste*
Lo positivo (Tamayo y Baus) **1**:565, 569
"Poslanie k Baronu Del'vigu" (Baratynsky) **103**:28
"Poslaniie" (Shevchenko) **54**:383, 389
"Poslednì soud" (Macha) **46**:202
"Posledniaia smert" (Baratynsky)
See "Poslednyaya smert'"
"Poslednii poet" (Baratynsky)
See "Posledny poet"
"Poslednjaja smert" (Baratynsky)
See "Poslednyaya smert'"
"Posledny poet" (Baratynsky) **103**:13-20, 22, 36, 38-9, 46
"Poslednyaya smert'" (Baratynsky) **103**:3, 6-7, 9, 11, 13-20, 22-3, 25, 27, 35, 38-9, 46
"Le Possédé" (Baudelaire) **55**:66
The Possessed (Dostoevsky)
See *Besy*
"Possibilities" (Longfellow) **2**:492
"Die Post" (Muller) **73**:366, 383, 385, 393, 396-97
"The Post Office" (Sedgwick) **19**:446
Post-Bag (Moore)
See *Intercepted Letters; or, The Two penny Post-Bag*
"Das Posthorn" (Lenau) **16**:282
The Posthumous Papers of the Pickwick Club (Dickens) **3**:138-40, 144, 151-52, 154, 171, 176-77, 180-82; **8**:197; **18**:97, 113, 121, 133; **26**:156, 158, 167; **37**:142-5, 147-50, 153-54, 156, 164, 169, 177, 182, 184, 193-96, 198, 204-05, 208-09, 211; **86**:186, 255-56; **105**:227, 229-30, 249; **113**:9, 28, 81, 84, 91, 97, 103, 108, 118, 123-24, 127
Posthumous Poems of Percy Bysshe Shelley (Shelley) **18**:325
Posthumous Remains (Hazlitt) **82**:88
Posthumous Tales (Crabbe) **26**:103, 105, 110
Posthumous Works (De Quincey) **87**:36
Postille (Manzoni) **98**:214
"Der Postillion" (Lenau) **16**:266, 270, 282
"The Postmaster" (Pushkin)
See "Stantsionnyi smotritel"
"Postscript" (Pater) **7**:330-31; **90**:292, 323
"Postscript" (De Quincey) **87**:76-7, 79
Postscript (Kierkegaard) **125**:176-77, 209
"Postscript, Found in the Handwriting of Mr. Knickerbocker" (Irving) **19**:343
The Post-Script to Gebir (Landor) **14**:203
Le postscriptum (Augier) **31**:8, 16, 34
Post-Stage Master (Pushkin) **3**:447-48
"Postulates of Political Economy" (Bagehot) **10**:20, 30-31
"Pot de fleurs" (Gautier) **1**:344
"The Pot of Tulips" (O'Brien) **21**:239, 242-45, 249-50, 252
"The Potato" (Mickiewicz)
See "Kartofel"
"Potter's Clay" (Gordon) **21**:159, 166
"Pott's Painless Cure" (Bellamy) **4**:30-31
"Pounds, Shillings and Pence" (Clare) **86**:172
"Pour avoir peché" (Verlaine) **51**:361
Le Pour et le Contre (Feuillet) **45**:89-90
"Pour la Mort de la terre" (Laforgue) **53**:268, 271
"Pour le livre d'amour" (Laforgue) **53**:268
"Pour les pauvres" (Hugo) **21**:214
"Pourquoi mon âme est-elle triste?" (Lamartine) **11**:270
"Pourquoi seuls?" (Banville) **9**:29
"Poverty" (Thoreau) **7**:383
Poverty and Nobleness of Mind (Kotzebue)
See *Armuth und Edelsinn*
Poverty Is No Crime (Ostrovsky)
See *Bednost ne porok*
The Poverty of Philosophy (Marx)
See *Misère de la philosophie: Réponse à la philosophie de la misère de M. Proudhon*
Poverty, Wealth, Sin, and Penance of Countess Dolores: A True Story, Recorded for the Instruction and Amusement of Poor Young Ladies (Arnim)
See *Armuth, Reichtum, Schuld und Busse der Gräfin Dolores: Eine Wahre Geschichte zur lehrreichen Unterhaltung*
"Povest' o bogougodnom drovokole" (Leskov) **25**:245
"Povest' o tom, kak odin muzhik dvukh generalov prokormil" (Saltykov) **16**:342, 358, 373
Povesti Belkina (Pushkin) **3**:428, 435-3, 447; **83**:272-73, 275-76, 279, 308-16, 319, 323, 337-38, 354-55
Povisty o besrodnom Petrush (Shevchenko) **54**:391
"Povodni mož" (Preseren) **127**:308
"Power" (Emerson) **98**:9, 134-35, 151, 153-55, 185
"The Power of Fancy" (Freneau) **1**:316; **111**:100, 140, 151
The Power of Her Sympathy (Sedgwick) **98**:364
"The Power of Love" (Brontë) **71**:91
"The Power of Memory" (Preseren)
See "Sila spomina"
"Power of Music" (Wordsworth) **111**:235
"The Power of Novelty" (Freneau) **111**:134
"The Power of Prayer" (Lanier) **118**:227, 235
"The Power of Prayer" (Newman) **38**:345
The Power of Prayer in Relation to Outward Circumstances (Schleiermacher) **107**:362
"The Power of Russia" (Campbell) **19**:183, 194
"The Power of Words" (Poe) **1**:519-20; **117**:258, 267, 269
"Power of Youth" (Arnold) **29**:27
"The Powers of Nature" (Newman) **38**:305
"Powieść" (Norwid) **17**:374
"Powinszowania" (Krasicki) **8**:404
"The Powldoodies of Burran" (Maginn) **8**:441
"Powwaw" (Whittier) **8**:485
Poyezdka v Poles'ye (Turgenev) **37**:443
Poyezdka v Revel' (Bestuzhev) **131**:178-80
"A Practical Blue Stocking" (Parton) **86**:373
"The Practical Blue-Stocking" (Parton) **86**:348
Practical Education (Edgeworth) **1**:267; **51**:78-9, 82, 84, 86, 114, 138
Practical Piety; or, The Influence of the Religion of the Heart on the Conduct of the Life (More) **27**:334, 338
"Praeceptor Amat" (Timrod) **25**:360, 362, 375, 384
—Praelectiones (Keble)
See *Praelectiones Academicae Oxonii Habitae, Annis MDCCCXXXII...MDCCCXLI*
Praelectiones Academicae (Keble)
See *Praelectiones Academicae Oxonii Habitae, Annis MDCCCXXXII...MDCCCXLI*
Praelectiones Academicae Oxonii Habitae, Annis MDCCCXXXII...MDCCCXLI (Keble) **87**:142, 152, 156, 183
"Prahlad" (Dutt) **29**:120, 125, 128, 130
The Prairie (Cooper) **1**:199-200, 202, 205-07, 217, 221, 223, 228; **27**:125, 127, 130-36, 138-43, 148-50, 153-55, 172, 177, 179, 183-86; **54**:254, 265, 274, 277, 288, 291
"The Prairie States" (Whitman) **31**:432
"A Prairie Sunset" (Whitman) **81**:370-71
"The Prairie-Grass Dividing" (Whitman) **31**:430
"The Prairies" (Bryant) **6**:162, 168, 170, 172, 183, 185-86, 189, 191-92; **46**:3, 6, 19, 28, 34, 43, 47, 52, 55-6
"Praise and Prayer" (Lampman) **25**:183
"Praise for the fountain open'd" (Cowper) **94**:74
"Praise It—'tis Dead" (Dickinson) **21**:69
"Praise My Lady" (Morris) **4**:426, 444
"Praise o' Do'set" (Barnes) **75**:8, 101, 108

"The Praise of Chimney-Sweepers" (Lamb) **10**:398, 402-03, 407, 409-10, 415, 423, 426, 436; **113**:169, 235, 263
"Praise of Creation" (Horton) **87**:110
Die praktische Theologie (Schleiermacher)
See *Die praktische Theologie nach den Grundsätzen der evangelischen Kirche im Zusammenhang dargestellt*
Die praktische Theologie nach den Grundsätzen der evangelischen Kirche im Zusammenhang dargestellt (Schleiermacher) **107**:268, 284, 407
"Prayer" (Cooke) **110**:9
"Prayer" (Hale) **75**:284, 285
"The Prayer" (Isaacs)
See "La oración"
"A Prayer" (Lampman) **25**:201
"Prayer" (Lermontov) **5**:288
"A prayer" (Levy) **59**:107
"Prayer" (Mörike) **10**:446
"The Prayer" (Very) **9**:376, 385
"Prayer for Conformity to God's Will" (Rossetti) **50**:275
"The Prayer of a Lonely Heart" (Kemble) **18**:181
"The Prayer of Agassiz" (Whittier) **8**:524
"A Prayer of Columbus" (Whitman) **4**:582, 586; **31**:371, 435
Prayer on the Acropolis (Renan)
See *Prière sur l'acropole*
"Prayer Without Ceasing" (Cranch) **115**:50
"Praying Always" (Rossetti) **50**:316
Prazdnichny son—do obeda (Ostrovsky) **30**:104, 113
"Prazdnik Rima" (Pavlova) **138**:4, 13
"Le pré du déshonneur" (Maupassant) **83**:190
"The Preacher" (Whittier) **59**:356, 360
"Preambolo alla ristampa delle 'Annotazioni' nel 'Nuovo Ricoglitore' di Milano" (Leopardi) **129**:327-30
Precaution (Cooper) **1**:196; **27**:129, 171; **54**:251, 273
The Precipice (Goncharov)
See *Obryv*
Précis d'histoire modern (Michelet) **31**:235
"Præections on Poetry" (Keble) **87**:135
"The Precursor" (Patmore) **9**:341
"A Predicament" (Poe) **16**:322-23; **117**:231, 235
"Prediction" (Lermontov) **126**:228
Predigt eines Laienbruders zu Neujahr 1814 (Claudius) **75**:213, 215, 218
"Pre-eminence of the Man of Letters" (Boker) **125**:35
"Preface" (Crabbe) **121**:83, 85
"Preface" (Kierkegaard) **125**:204
"Preface" (Manzoni) **29**:275
"Preface" (Poe) **117**:305
Preface (Laclos)
See *Preface du Redacteur*
"La préface de Cromwell" (Hugo) **3**:268-69, 273; **21**:196, 202-03, 212, 228
Preface du Redacteur (Laclos) **87**:217, 221-22
"Préface Personnelle" (Comte) **54**:209-12, 239
"Préface pour la tradution d'un ouvrage de M. Wilberforce" (Staël-Holstein) **91**:340
"Preface to Cromwell" (Hugo)
See "La préface de Cromwell"
"Preface to Maria Magdalene" (Hebbel) **43**:239-40, 256, 267
"Preface to Poems" (Arnold) **6**:46-47, 69; **29**:5-7, 23, 25, 27, 36, 53
"Preface to 'Studies in the History of the Renaissance'" (Pater) **7**:338-39; **90**:324
"Preface to the Fables" (Krasicki)
See "Wstęp do bajek"
"Preface to the Lyrical Ballads" (Wordsworth) **38**:400, 408, 416; **111**:211, 213, 230, 232-33, 237, 239-40, 243-44, 272, 291-95, 298, 307-9, 311-14, 322-23, 331, 335-45, 357, 363-64, 367-70
"Preface to The Poetical Works of William Wordsworth" (Wordsworth) **111**:237-38
"Preface to 'The School of Giorgione'" (Pater) **7**:338
Prefaces (Kierkegaard)
See *Forord*
Prefaces (Wordsworth) **12**:436
"Prefatory Essay on Lyric Poetry" (Dyer) **129**:93
"Prefatory Letter on Irish Music" (Moore) **110**:181, 186-87
"Prefatory Note" (Pater) **7**:323
Preferment; or, My Uncle the Earl (Gore) **65**:20
"Prekop" (Preseren) **127**:297
"Prekrasnaja Aza" (Leskov) **25**:229, 239, 245
"Prekrasnaja carevna i ščastlivoj karla" (Karamzin) **3**:287
"Preliminary Confessions" (De Quincey) **4**:85
Preliminary Emancipation Proclamation (Lincoln) **18**:216-19, 268-70
"Preliminary Observations" (Bentham) **38**:90
"Preliminary Theses for the Reform of Philosophy" (Feuerbach)
See "Vorläufige Thesen zur Reform der Philosophie"
"Prelude" (Allingham) **25**:14
"Prelude" (Longfellow) **2**:492; **45**:115, 131, 183
Prelude (Crabbe) **121**:12
The Prelude (Wordsworth)
See *The Prelude; or, Growth of a Poets Mind: Autobiographical Poem*
The Prelude; or, Growth of a Poets Mind: Autobiographical Poem (Wordsworth) **12**:415, 419-20, 425, 429, 431, 433, 435-37, 442, 444-49, 453, 458-61, 465-66, 468, 471-73; **38**:355-71, 373-83, 385, 387-88, 390-96, 398-408, 411-13, 415-18, 420-24, 426; **111**:213, 233, 237, 245, 251, 254, 257-61, 263, 266, 273, 290, 314, 322, 332, 345-47, 350
"Prelude to the Voices of the Night" (Longfellow) **2**:472
Preludes (Pavlova)
See *Les préludes*
"Les préludes" (Lamartine) **11**:245, 248, 270
Les préludes (Pavlova) **138**:30
"Préludes autobiographiques" (Laforgue) **53**:289
"Preludes to a Penny Reading" (Ingelow) **39**:258, 264
"The Premature Burial" (Poe) **16**:308-09; **117**:322
"Le Premier Chagrin d'un enfant" (Desbordes-Valmore) **97**:29
"Le premier rayon de mai" (Gautier) **1**:348
"Le premier regret" (Lamartine) **11**:255, 270, 278, 280
"Première soirèe" (Rimbaud) **4**:471, 485; **35**:289
Les premières amours; ou, Les souvenirs d'enfance (Scribe) **16**:387
"Les premières communions" (Rimbaud) **4**:454-55, 474
Les Premières Communions (Laforgue) **53**:256
Premières poésies (Leconte de Lisle) **29**:234
"Premoère consultation" (Vigny) **7**:475
"Premonition" (Whitman) **4**:603
"Premudryi piskar" (Saltykov) **16**:374
Pre-Revolutionary France (Taine)
See *L'ancien régime*
"The Presence" (Very) **9**:381, 384
"The Present Age" (Emerson) **98**:65
The Present Age (Kierkegaard)
See *Two Ages: The Age of Revolution and the Present Age, a Literary Review*
"The Present Condition of Organic Nature" (Huxley) **67**:59
"The Present Crisis" (Lowell) **2**:506; **90**:215, 219, 221
"The Present Day" (Krasiński) **4**:305
A Present for Young Ladies (Rowson) **69**:115-17, 150
Present Position (Newman)
See *Lectures on the Present Position of Catholics in England: Addressed to the Brothers of the Oratory*
Present Position of Catholics (Newman)
See *Lectures on the Present Position of Catholics in England: Addressed to the Brothers of the Oratory*
Present Positions of Catholics (Newman)
See *Lectures on the Present Position of Catholics in England: Addressed to the Brothers of the Oratory*
"The present revolution in Spain" (Martínez de la Rosa)
See "La revolución actual en España"
"A Presentiment" (Bryant) **46**:47
"Presentiment—Is That Long Shadow—On the Lawn" (Dickinson) **21**:59
"Le Président mystifié" (Sade) **47**:313
Presidentens döttar (Bremer) **11**:17-18, 20, 30, 34-35
The President's Daughter: A Narrative of a Governess (Bremer)
See *Presidentens döttar*
El presidio político en Cuba (Martí) **63**:87, 102, 157-8
Le Pressoir (Sand) **42**:309
Prestuplenie i nakazanie (Dostoevsky) **2**:157, 159, 161-62, 167, 172, 175, 180-81, 184, 186, 188, 195-96, 203; **7**:69-116; **21**:90, 94, 100, 109, 113, 140, 144, 146; **33**:161, 165, 176-77, 194-94, 203, 207, 212, 227, 233; **43**:92, 122, 130, 144, 149, 162, 167; **119**:73, 76-7, 82, 85, 98, 132, 135, 147, 150, 154-55
Pretended Infidelity (Griboedov)
See *Svoia sem'ia, ili Zamuzhniaia nevesta*
The Pretender Dmitry and Vasily Shuysky (Ostrovsky)
See *Dmitry Samozvanets i Vasily Shuysky*
"Preternatural Beings" (Montagu) **7**:251
Le Prêtre de Némi (Renan) **26**:388, 408
Un prêtre marié (Barbey d'Aurevilly) **1**:70, 72, 77
"Pretty Dick" (Clarke) **19**:231, 233, 235
Pretty Green Bird (Gozzi)
See *L'augellin belverde*
Pretty Lessons in Verse for Good Children (Coleridge) **31**:61-2, 70-1
The Pretty Maid of the Mill (Muller)
See *Die schöne Müllerin*
Pretty Mrs. Gaston (Cooke) **5**:130
Preussen und die Konstitutionen (Eichendorff) **8**:220
Preussens ältere Geschichte (Kotzebue) **25**:140
Die preussische Militärfrage und die deutsche Arbeiterpartei (Engels) **85**:83
Le Prévaricateur (Sade) **47**:361-62
"Pride" (Coleridge) **90**:9
Pride and Overthrow (Smolenskin) **30**:189-90
Pride and Prejudice (Austen) **1**:30, 32-4, 36-8, 40, 44-7, 50-2, 56-61, 63-4, 66; **13**:51-112; **19**:2, 4-8, 14, 17, 32, 42, 55-6, 58, 66-7; **33**:28, 44, 58, 62, 64, 66, 69, 72, 76, 78, 86, 89-90, 92, 96; **51**:12, 15, 33, 35, 55; **81**:18, 48, 69, 77-9, 81-5; **95**:4, 9-11, 14, 16-8, 21, 25, 39, 45, 55-6, 58, 63, 73, 80, 83-4, 86; **119**:11, 14, 16-18, 21, 24-5, 27-8, 35-40
"The Pride of the Village" (Irving) **19**:327, 332, 334, 345-47
"La prière" (Lamartine) **11**:245, 269
Prière du Matin (Comte) **54**:213
Prière du Soir (Comte) **54**:213
"La Prière d'une mère" (Mallarmé) **41**:290
"La Prière pour Tous" (Bello) **131**:93
"La prière pour tous" (Hugo) **21**:224
Prière sur l'acropole (Renan) **26**:408, 414, 419
Prières (Comte) **54**:213
The Priest (Michelet) **31**:241
"Die Priesterinnen der Sonne" (Schiller) **39**:388
The Priestly Consecration (Tegner) **2**:613
"The Priest's Funeral" (Carleton) **3**:88, 92

Priests of Parnassus (Pushkin) **3**:423
"Prigover" (Dostoevsky) **33**:179-80
The Prime Minister (Trollope) **6**:461, 463, 466, 471, 473, 495, 500, 504, 507-08, 510; **33**:417, 421-22, 424; **101**:253, 268, 274, 290, 307, 310
"El primer beso" (Isaacs) **70**:305
El primer loco (Castro) **3**:107
Primer of Words (Whitman) **81**:287
"Primera representación de la comedia refundida y puesta en cuatro actos titulada Juez y reo de su causa o Don Jaime el Justiciero" (Larra) **130**:195
"Primety" (Baratynsky) **103**:13, 16-22
"The Primose" (Allingham) **25**:14
"The Primrose" (Clare) **9**:72
"Primrose Gold" (Jefferies)
See "Primrose Gold in Our Villages"
"Primrose Gold in Our Villages" (Jefferies) **47**:143
Prince (Alfieri)
See *Del principe e delle lettere*
"Prince Adeb" (Boker) **125**:34
"Prince Ahmed; or, The Pilgrim of Love" (Irving) **2**:372
"Prince Aldfrid's Itinerary through Ireland" (Mangan) **27**:283
The Prince and Letters (Alfieri)
See *Del principe e delle lettere*
"The Prince and the Peasant" (Martineau) **26**:323
"Prince Athanase" (Shelley) **18**:327, 340, 344
"Prince Charming of the Lime Tree" (Eminescu)
See "Prince Charming of the Linden Tree"
"Prince Charming of the Linden Tree" (Eminescu) **33**:249
"Prince Charming the Tear-Born" (Eminescu) **33**:247
Prince Csaba (Arany) **34**:8, 11
Une prince de la Bohème (Balzac) **5**:75
"Le prince de Sots" (Nerval) **1**:482-83; **67**:322, 324
Prince Deukalion (Taylor) **89**:320-24, 343, 349
Prince Dorus; or, Flattery Put out of Countenance (Lamb) **10**:418
"Prince Hamlet of Shehrigov Province" (Turgenev)
See "Gamlet ščigrovskogo uezda"
Prince Hohenstiel-Schwangau (Browning) **19**:136
Prince Michael Twerski (Slowacki) **15**:378
"Prince mort en soldat" (Verlaine) **2**:632
"A Prince of Court-Painters: Extracts from an Old French Journal" (Pater) **7**:298, 324; **90**:264, 288, 340-41, 344
The Prince of Darkness (Southworth) **26**:434
The Prince of Happy Land (Planché) **42**:292, 302
The Prince of Homburg (Kleist)
See *Prinz Friedrich von Homburg*
The Prince of Tunis (Mackenzie) **41**:184, 208-10, 212, 217
The Prince of Viana (Gómez de Avellaneda) **111**:12
Prince Otto (Stevenson) **5**:397-99, 402-03, 408-09, 433
"Prince Papillon" (Crawford) **127**:181-84, 186, 189
"The Prince Shalikov" (Pushkin) **83**:272
Prince Zerbino in Search of Good Taste (Tieck)
See *Prinz Zerbino; oder, Die Reise nach dem guten Geschmack*
"The Prince's Day" (Moore) **110**:184
The Prince's Justice (Eminescu) **33**:266
"The Prince's Progress" (Rossetti) **2**:558, 560, 562-3, 565-6, 568, 570-1, 573, 575; **50**:264, 266, 288, 291-3, 321, 324; **66**:304, 328, 356
The Prince's Progress, and Other Poems (Rossetti) **2**:556, 563, 574; **50**:271, 287; **66**:349
"The Princess" (Shevchenko)
See "Kniazhna"
"The Princess" (Tennyson) **115**:237, 240
The Princess (Shevchenko)
See *Kniazhna*
The Princess: A Medley (Tennyson) **30**:213, 219, 233, 237-38, 242, 268, 275-77, 279-80, 282-84; **65**:230-1, 234, 248, 263, 274, 324, 359-60, 362, 367-70, 373-5; **115**:255
"The Princess and the Pea" (Andersen) **7**:23, 28, 34; **79**:23-24, 50, 64-65, 80-81
Princess Brambilla (Hoffmann)
See *Prinzessin Brambilla: Ein Capriccio nach Jakob Callot*
Princess Ligovskaya (Lermontov) **47**:162-63, 225-26; **126**:156-57
"The Princess Marie" (Browning) **61**:75
"Princess Mary" (Lermontov) **5**:291, 293, 295, 297-98, 301-03; **126**:153-54, 174, 195-99, 202-3, 216
Princess of Bagdad (Dumas)
See *La princesse de Bagdad*
"The Princess on the Pea" (Andersen)
See "The Princess and the Pea"
The Princess; or, The Beguine (Morgan) **29**:396
"Princess Sabbath" (Heine) **4**:253
La princesse de Bagdad (Dumas) **9**:223, 230, 232, 243, 245
La princesse Georges (Dumas) **9**:225, 228, 230, 241-42, 246, 250
Principios del derecho de gentes (Bello) **131**:93-94, 96-97, 116, 124
Principle in Art (Patmore) **9**:349
Principles of Church Reform (Arnold) **18**:8, 19, 46, 51, 55
"Principles of Communism" (Engels) **85**:127-28
Principles of Communism (Engels) **85**:32-34, 157
"Principles of Criticism" (Symonds) **34**:336
Principles of International Law (Bello)
See *Principios del derecho de gentes*
Principles of International Law (Bentham) **38**:67
The Principles of Morals and Legislation (Bentham)
See *Introduction to the Principles of Morals and Legislation*
Principles of Political Economy, with Some of Their Applications to Social Philosophy (Mill) **11**:334-37, 350-51, 366, 375, 383; **58**:330, 351, 375, 378
Principles of Revolution (Bakunin) **25**:56
The Principles of Success in Literature (Lewes) **25**:289, 293, 296-97, 299-301, 304, 308, 316, 323, 325
Principles of the Philosophy of Law (Hegel) **46**:119, 124, 130, 186
Principles of the Philosophy of the Future (Feuerbach)
See *Grundsätze der Philosophie der Zukunft*
"The Pringle Family" (Galt) **110**:84
"The Printing Press" (Cranch) **115**:42
Prinz Friedrich von Homburg (Kleist) **2**:437-42, 444, 447, 450, 453-54, 458-59, 463-66; **37**:217, 220, 225, 227-28, 231-33, 237-38, 241, 243-44, 254-55, 263, 267, 272-74
"Prinz Louis Ferdinand" (Fontane) **26**:243
Prinz Zerbino; oder, Die Reise nach dem guten Geschmack (Tieck) **5**:517, 521, 524, 529-30
Prinzessin Brambilla: Ein Capriccio nach Jakob Callot (Hoffmann) **2**:357, 359, 361-62
"Prišla je jesenka noč" (Preseren) **127**:319
"The Prison" (Very) **9**:378
"La Prison" (Vigny) **102**:335, 340, 367
"Prison Amusements" (Clare) **86**:162
Prison and Exile (Herzen) **61**:88
"The Prison Door" (Hawthorne) **2**:331
"The Prisoner" (Brontë)
See "Julian M. and A. G. Rochelle"
"The Prisoner" (Browning) **1**:115; **61**:5
"The Prisoner" (Pushkin)
See "Uznik"
The Prisoner of Chillon, and Other Poems (Byron) **2**:64, 76, 99; **12**:139; **109**:69, 82
"The Prisoner of the Caucasus" (Lermontov) **126**:167
The Prisoner of the Caucasus (Pushkin)
See *Kavkazsky plennik*
"Prisoner of War" (Jerrold) **2**:395, 402-03
"Le Prisonnier de guerre" (Desbordes-Valmore) **97**:5
"La prisonnière et le chevalier" (Beranger) **34**:28
"Prisons" (Crabbe) **121**:87-8, 91
"Les Prisons et les prières" (Desbordes-Valmore) **97**:29
Private Galleries (Jameson)
See *Companion to the Most Celebrated Private Galleries of Art in London*
The Private Memoirs and Confessions of a Justified Sinner (Hogg) **4**:278, 280-81, 283-87; **109**:188-94, 197-98, 200, 204, 206, 209-10, 217-19, 221, 223, 229-34, 236-39, 242, 252, 255-56, 258-60, 262, 264, 270-72, 274-76, 278-82
Private Thoughts (Silva)
See *Intimidades*
The Privateersman (Marryat) **3**:320
Le prix Martin (Augier) **31**:8, 26
Priznaki vremeni (Saltykov) **16**:351
Prizraki (Turgenev) **37**:443
"Prizraki. Fantaziya" (Turgenev) **21**:415, 420, 431, 441, 451, 453; **122**:241, 243, 266, 364-66, 375
"Pro patria" (Isaacs) **70**:310
"The Problem" (Emerson) **1**:285, 296; **38**:187; **98**:180-82
"The Problem" (Timrod) **25**:362, 374
"The Problem" (Whittier) **59**:366
A Problem in Greek Ethics (Symonds) **34**:343, 353
A Problem in Modern Ethics (Symonds) **34**:343, 353,374
The Problems of Life and Mind (Lewes) **25**:282-83, 288-89, 293, 295-97, 304, 312-15, 318-19
"Problesk" (Tyutchev) **34**:389, 395, 398-99
"The Procession of Life" (Hawthorne) **2**:305, 309
"Processional of Creation" (Rossetti) **2**:566
"Proclamation" (Trumbull)
See "By Thomas Gage...A Proclamation"
"Procrastination" (Crabbe) **26**:93, 109, 120, 122, 131-32, 135-36, 151; **121**:43
La pródiga (Alarcon) **1**:12-13
"The Prodigal Son" (Hogg) **109**:281
The Prodigal Son (Becque)
See *L'enfant prodigue*
The Prodigious Adventures of Tartarin of Tarascon (Daudet)
See *Aventures prodigieuses de Tartarin de Tarascon*
"Proem" (Patmore) **9**:334
"Proem" (Thomson) **18**:403, 415, 417, 429
"Proem" (Whittier) **8**:515, 519-21, 525; **59**:351, 354, 364-5
"Proem Dedicatory, An Epistle from Mount Tmolus to Richard Henry Stoddard" (Taylor) **89**:305, 307, 359
Professional Education (Edgeworth) **1**:267; **51**:93
"Professions" (Thackeray) **43**:381
The Professor (Brontë) **3**:49-51, 54, 56, 60, 64, 68-72, 74-6, 78-9; **8**:54, 72, 75; **33**:117-19; **58**:187-9, 191, 194-7, 199, 208, 222, 224, 227; **105**:1-87
The Professor (Thackeray) **5**:470
"The Professor and the Flea" (Andersen) **79**:73-75

The Professor at the Breakfast-Table (Holmes) **14**:102, 105-06, 110, 113-15, 120, 123-24, 132-33, 137, 144, 146; **81**:98-104
A Profitable Position (Ostrovsky)
See *Dokhodnoye mesto*
"De profundis" (Browning) **16**:135
"De Profundis" (Tennyson) **30**:254, 270-72; **65**:235, 265, 272; **115**:341
"De Profundis clamavi" (Baudelaire) **6**:105; **55**:10
Progress (Robertson) **35**:335, 352, 362-66, 369
Progress and Prejudice (Gore) **65**:29, 32
"Progress in the World of Plants and Animals" (Pisarev) **25**:330
"The Progress of Art" (Hazlitt) **29**:162
"Progress of Culture" (Emerson) **98**:171
The Progress of Dulness (Trumbull) **30**:338, 340, 345, 347, 349-50, 352-53, 360-61, 363, 373-78, 381-82
The Progress of Dulness, Part First: or, The Rare Adventures of Tom Brainless (Trumbull) **30**:368, 370, 376
The Progress of Dulness, Part Second: or, An Essay on the Life and Character of Dick Hairbrain of Finical Memory (Trumbull) **30**:371, 373
The Progress of Dulness, Part Third, and Last: Sometimes Called The Progress of Coquetry; or The Adventures of Miss Harriet Simper (Trumbull) **30**:373
"The Progress of Error" (Cowper) **8**:110; **94**:29, 51, 110-12, 117
The Progress of Error (Cowper) **94**:9, 11-12, 14, 16
"Progress of Painting" (Hunt) **1**:406
Progress of Religious Ideas (Child) **6**:202-03; **73**:51, 56, 62, 70, 82, 87
"The Progress of Rhyme" (Clare) **9**:100; **86**:94, 112
The Progress of Romance, through Times, Countries, and Manners (Reeve) **19**:411-12, 415, 418
"The Progress of Science 1837-1887" (Huxley) **67**:64, 103, 105
"Progress of Social Reform on the Continent" (Engels) **85**:122
"Progress of Thought in Our Time" (Symonds) **34**:371
"Progress of Unbelief" (Newman) **38**:343
"The Progressive Realism of American Fiction" (Boyesen) **135**:22
"Der Prokurator" (Goethe) **4**:197
"Prolegomena" (Huxley) **67**:29, 62, 90, 92, 99, 102-03, 108, 110-11
Prolegomena (Kant) **27**:201, 225
"Prolog" (Heine) **54**:331, 336
"Prólogo" (Bécquer) **106**:85
"Prólogo al poema intitulado 'Bienaventurados los que lloran' de Rivas Frade" (Silva) **114**:317
"Prologue" (Browning) **79**:112-14
"Prologue" (Cooke) **5**:123
"Prologue" (Lamartine) **11**:287, 289
"Prologue" (Sheridan) **5**:371, 378
"Prologue" (Tennyson) **65**:368
"Prologue" (Verlaine) **2**:631
Prologue in Heaven (Goethe) **4**:186, 202, 205
"Prologue Intended for a Dramatic Piece of King Edward the Fourth" (Blake) **13**:239
"Prologue to Controverted Questions" (Huxley) **67**:62, 64, 66, 70-1, 96
"Prologue to King John" (Blake) **13**:181
"Prologue to Science and Christian Tradition" (Huxley) **67**:28
"Prologue—Delivered at a Greek Benefit, in Baltimore,—1823" (Pinkney) **31**:276
"Prologues to the Poem Entitled 'Blessed Are Those Who Cry' by Rivas Frade" (Silva)
See "Prólogo al poema intitulado 'Bienaventurados los que lloran' de Rivas Frade"
"Promenade" (Maupassant) **83**:228
Promenade autour d'un village (Sand) **42**:312
Promenades dans Rome (Stendhal) **23**:352, 410; **46**:269
"La promesa" (Bécquer) **106**:97, 99, 130, 135-36
"Les promesses d'un visage" (Baudelaire) **29**:77
I promessi sposi (Manzoni) **29**:253-54, 261, 263-70, 272, 275-87, 289-94, 296, 298-300, 302-11; **98**:197-98, 201, 204, 213, 216, 218-20, 228, 234-40, 249-51, 256, 258-59, 265, 267, 269-77, 283-87, 289-90
"Prometeo" (Casal) **131**:223, 228, 236
"Prometheus" (Goethe) **4**:163, 199; **34**:98
"Prometheus" (Lowell) **2**:503; **90**:195, 219, 221
"Prometheus" (Schlegel) **15**:223
Prometheus Bound, and Miscellaneous Poems (Browning) **66**:44, 47
Prometheus, the Fire-Bringer: A Drama in Verse (Horne) **127**:260, 268-69
Prometheus Unbound (Shelley) **18**:317, 319, 331-32, 334-38, 340, 343-45, 349, 352, 355, 361-65, 367-69, 374, 376-77, 380-83; **93**:256, 260-64, 267, 269-71, 278, 294, 305-06, 310-11, 313, 315, 327, 330, 343-44, 351-52
Promethidion (Norwid) **17**:367-69, 371-72, 375, 378, 380, 384-86
"The Promise" (Darley) **2**:133
The Promise of May (Tennyson) **30**:265-66
"The Promise of Sleep" (Levy) **59**:94
"Promontoire" (Rimbaud) **35**:269, 322
The Prompter; or, A Commentary on Common Sayings and Subjects, Which Are Full of Common Sense, the Best Sense in the World . . . (Webster) **30**:421-24
"Propagation of the Species, Christianity wants to bar the way" (Kierkegaard) **78**:225
"Propavšaja gramotax" (Gogol) **5**:224-25
"A Proper Trewe Idyll of Camelot" (Field) **3**:210-11
"Property" (Madison) **126**:311, 327-29
Property (Sacher-Masoch) **31**:287, 291, 294-95
"Properzia Rossi" (Hemans) **71**:296
"Prophecy" (Petofi)
See "Jövendöles"
The Prophecy of Capys (Macaulay) **42**:112
Prophecy of Dante (Byron) **12**:106
"The Prophecy of King Tamany" (Freneau) **111**:166
"The Prophecy of Samuel Sewall" (Whittier) **59**:375
"The Prophecy—To the Memory of the Brave Americans under Genera Greene, Who Fell in the Action of September 8, 1781" (Freneau) **1**:315, 323; **111**:140-41
"The Prophet" (Pushkin)
See "Prorok"
"The Prophet" (Shevchenko)
See "Prorok"
The Prophet (Taylor) **89**:315, 349
"The Prophet Unveiled" (Cranch) **115**:39, 41
Le prophète (Scribe) **16**:390, 401, 408
"The Prophetic Pictures" (Hawthorne) **2**:291, 305; **39**:186; **95**:105, 110
Prophetical Office (Newman)
See *Lectures on the Prophetical Office of the Church*
"The Prophet's Chamber" (Parton) **86**:347, 372
"The Prophet's Dream" (Chivers) **49**:47, 69
"Prophets Who Cannot Sing" (Patmore) **9**:360
Proposals (Cowper) **94**:80-5
"Proposals for the Speedy Extinction of Evil and Misery" (Thomson) **18**:393, 405, 425-27
Propria Quae Maribus (Reade) **74**:256
"Proprietors of the Olden Time" (Gogol)
See "Starosvetskie Pomeščiki"
"Prorok" (Pushkin) **3**:438, 442-43; **83**:255
"Prorok" (Shevchenko) **54**:389
Prosas (Casal) **131**:239-45, 247-53, 256, 258-59, 262-66
"Prosas breves" (Silva) **114**:300
"Proščaj, nemytaja Rossija" (Lermontov) **126**:190-91, 193
"Proscenia" (Shevchenko)
See "Prycynna"
The Prose of John Clare (Clare) **86**:96, 104, 129
The Prose of Philip Freneau (Freneau) **111**:160, 162
Prose Poems (Baudelaire)
See *Petits poèmes en prose: Le spleen de Paris*
Prose Poems (Turgenev)
See *Stikhotvoreniya v proze*
"Prose pour des esseintes" (Mallarmé) **4**:376-77, 389-90; **41**:259, 279, 289, 294
Prose Tales (Desbordes-Valmore)
See *Contes en prose*
The Prose Works of William Wordsworth (Wordsworth) **38**:425; **111**:311, 315, 336-42, 363-64, 366-70
The Prose Writings of James Clarence Mangan (Mangan) **27**:291-92
Prose Writings of William Cullen Bryant (Bryant) **46**:10-12, 38
"Proserpina" (Stagnelius) **61**:248
Proserpine (Pushkin) **3**:423
Proserpine (Shelley) **14**:268-69, 272
"Proshchanie s Kaspiem" (Bestuzhev) **131**:160
"Proshlo spolna . . ." (Pavlova) **138**:20
"Prošnja" (Preseren) **127**:298
"The Prospect" (Dwight) **13**:270, 272, 276, 278
"A Prospective Meeting" (Rossetti) **50**:295
Prospecto de un establecimiento de educación para señoritas (Faustino) **123**:354
"Prospects" (Thoreau) **7**:396
Prospects on the Rubicon (Paine) **62**:266, 334
Prospectus for an Educational Establishment for Young Ladies (Faustino)
See *Prospecto de un establecimiento de educación para señoritas*
"Prospectus of a History of English Philosophy" (Hazlitt) **82**:108
Prospectus to the Excursion (Wordsworth)
See *The Excursion, Being a Portion of "The Recluse"*
Prosper Mérimée's Letters to an Incognita (Mérimée)
See *Lettres à une inconnue*
Les Prosperites du vice (Sade)
See *Juliette; ou, Les prospérités du vice*
"Prospice" (Browning) **19**:89, 110
A Protégée of the Mistress (Ostrovsky)
See *Vospitannitsa*
"Protest against the Ballot" (Wordsworth) **12**:413
"The Protestant" (Tonna) **135**:204, 211
"Protestantism" (Newman) **38**:343
Protivorechiya (Saltykov) **16**:368
"Protus" (Browning) **19**:117
"Proud King" (Morris) **4**:417, 442
"Proud Maisie" (Scott) **15**:294, 318
"Proud Music of the Storm" (Whitman) **4**:579, 582
"The Proud Pedestrian" (Holmes) **14**:100
Proverb Stories (Alcott) **58**:47
Proverbes (Musset) **7**:258, 260
"Proverbs of Hell" (Blake) **37**:27, 55
"La providence à l'homme" (Lamartine) **11**:278
"Providence and the Guitar" (Stevenson) **5**:394
"Providential Design" (Harpur) **114**:148
"Provinces and Relations of the Arts" (Symonds) **34**:336
"The Provincial Governor" (Runeberg)
See "Landshövdingen"
A Provincial Lady (Turgenev) **21**:428
Provincial Memoirs (Faustino)
See *Recuerdos de provincia*
Provincial Recollections (Faustino)
See *Recuerdos de provincia*
The Provost (Galt) **1**:329, 331-35, 337; **110**:79, 81, 84-6, 93-4, 98, 101
"Prudence" (Emerson) **38**:152

"Les prunes" (Daudet) **1**:246
"Prussian Vase" (Edgeworth) **1**:255; **51**:87, 89
Prvi srpski bukvar (Karadzic) **115**:106
"Prycynna" (Shevchenko) **54**:371, 375
Przedświt (Krasiński) **4**:301-08, 310-11, 313, 318-19
"Przyjaciele" (Krasicki) **8**:403
"Psalm cxxxvii" (Halleck) **47**:57
"A Psalm for the Conventicle" (Kendall) **12**:200
"Psalm of Faith" (Krasiński) **4**:303
"Psalm of Good Will" (Krasiński) **4**:303-04, 307, 311
"Psalm of Grief" (Krasiński) **4**:307
"Psalm of Hope" (Krasiński) **4**:303
"A Psalm of Life" (Hayne) **94**:144
"A Psalm of Life" (Longfellow) **2**:471, 483, 493, 498; **45**:112, 115-16, 124-25, 127, 134, 139, 140-41, 144, 148, 152, 156-58, 164-65, 179, 184; **103**:285, 292-93, 295-96, 305-06
"The Psalm of Life" (Whittier) **8**:525
"Psalm of Love" (Krasiński) **4**:303, 307
"Psalm of the West" (Lanier) **6**:238, 248-49, 254, 256-60, 269; **118**:210-11, 215, 237-38, 275
"The Psalmist's Repenting" (Keble) **87**:177
"The Psalms of David" (Shevchenko)
See "Psalmy Davydovi"
"Psalmy Davydovi" (Shevchenko) **54**:383-4
"Psaumes de l'ame" (Lamartine) **11**:272
"Psicopatía" (Silva) **114**:300, 302-3, 316
Psicopatía (Silva) **114**:274
"Psicoterapéutica" (Silva) **114**:263
"Psovaja oxota" (Nekrasov) **11**:412
"Psyche" (Andersen) **7**:37; **79**:58, 60, 84, 89
Psyche (Storm) **1**:542
"Psyche Flagellated" (Meyer)
See "Die gegeisselte Psyche"
"Psyche Odes" (Patmore) **9**:349, 352, 357, 360, 362-66
"Psyche's Discontent" (Patmore) **9**:339, 360, 364
Psychology (Schleiermacher) **107**:285
Public Address (Blake) **57**:79
"A Public Dinner" (Hood) **16**:236
Public Galleries (Jameson)
See *A Handbook to the Public Galleries of Art in and near London*
"Public Opinion" (Madison) **126**:325
"Publication Is the Auction" (Dickinson) **21**:56; **77**:71
"Publius to Pollia" (Freneau) **111**:105
La pucelle de Belleville (Kock) **16**:251
Le puff; ou, Mensonge et vérité (Scribe) **16**:388
Puffery; or, Lie and Truth (Scribe)
See *Le puff; ou, Mensonge et vérité*
"The Pugsley Papers" (Hood) **16**:206-07
Pulcherie (Sand) **2**:589
"Pulvis et umbra" (Stevenson) **5**:410, 425
El puñal del godo (Zorrilla y Moral) **6**:523, 525
Punch's Complete Letter Writer (Jerrold) **2**:403, 408
Punch's Letters to His Son (Jerrold) **2**:395-96, 399, 402, 408
"Punctuality" (Carroll) **139**:61
"Punin and Baburin" (Turgenev)
See "Punin i Baburin"
"Punin i Baburin" (Turgenev) **21**:416, 437, 441; **122**:241, 243, 245, 264, 266, 342
The Purcell Papers (Le Fanu) **58**:251-3, 255, 302-4
"The Pure Spirit" (Vigny)
See *L'esprit pur*
"Půrglitz" (Macha)
See "Krivoklad"
Les puritaines d'Ecosse (Dumas) **71**:217
The Puritan and His Daughter (Paulding) **2**:527-30
"Puritanism and Drunkenness" (Faustino) **123**:276
Puritanism and the Church of England (Arnold) **126**:89-90
"The Puritan's Vision" (Holmes) **14**:101
"Purity and Love" (Newman) **38**:310
"The Purloined Letter" (Poe) **1**:518, 528, 530-31; **16**:293, 295-96, 298, 300-01, 303, 306, 315, 332; **55**:148, 155; **78**:281; **94**:188; **97**:208, 213, 238; **117**:235, 252, 254, 256, 290
"The Purple Flower of the Heather" (Thomson) **18**:407
"The Purple Jar" (Edgeworth) **1**:267; **51**:110-11, 116
"Purport" (Whitman) **31**:435
"The Pursuits of Happiness" (Mackenzie) **41**:184
"Pushkin and Belinsky" (Pisarev) **25**:332, 335, 348, 354
Puss in Boots (Planché) **42**:273, 279, 280, 288, 302
Puss in Boots (Tieck)
See *Der gestiefelte Kater*
"Pustka" (Shevchenko) **54**:364
"Put' do goroda Kuby" (Bestuzhev) **131**:160
Put Yourself in His Place (Reade) **2**:540, 542, 547-49; **74**:248-49, 251, 253-55, 258, 263-64, 284, 318
"PVs Correspondence" (Hawthorne) **2**:303
"Pyetushkov" (Turgenev) **21**:414
"Pygmalion" (Schlegel) **15**:223
"Pygmalion and the Image" (Morris) **4**:416, 447
Pym (Poe)
See *The Narrative of Arthur Gordon Pym, of Nantucket*
"The Pyramids of Egypt" (Freneau) **1**:314
"Die Pythagoräer" (Meyer) **81**:147-48
"Pytheas" (Kendall) **12**:199
"Pythona: or the Prophetess of En-Dor" (Freneau) **111**:110
"Pytor Petrovich Karataev" (Turgenev) **21**:377
"Qaïn" (Leconte de Lisle) **29**:215, 217, 221-24, 226, 229, 231, 234-36
"Qasida in praise of Ali" (Ghalib) **39**:147
"Qua Cursum Ventus" (Clough) **27**:44, 77, 79, 90, 108
Quadrille (Pavlova)
See *Kadril'*
"The Quadroon Girl" (Longfellow) **2**:483; **45**:123, 155; **103**:290
"Quae Nocent Docent" (Coleridge) **99**:22
"The Quail" (Turgenev) **122**:289
"The Quaker of the Olden Time" (Whittier) **8**:491
"A Quakers Meeting" (Lamb) **10**:408; **113**:250
"Quand l'ombre menaça" (Mallarmé) **4**:388; **41**:242
"The Quangle Wangle's Hat" (Lear) **3**:309
Quant au livre (Mallarmé)
See *L'Action restreinte*
Les quarante-cinq (Dumas) **11**:68, 74
"Quare Fatigasti" (Gordon) **21**:150, 154, 160, 164
"The Quarrel of Two Ivans" (Gogol)
See "The Tale of How Ivan Ivanovich Quarrelled with Ivan Nikiforovich"
"Quarterly" (Tennyson) **115**:235
"The Quartette" (Gautier) **1**:347
Quatre Chapitres sur la Russie (Maistre) **37**:288
Les quatre talismans (Nodier) **19**:384-85
Les quatre vents de l'esprit (Hugo) **3**:256, 258, 264; **21**:214
Quatre-vingt treize (Hugo) **3**:250-51, 253, 260, 267, 276; **10**:367; **21**:195
"Que diras-tu ce soir" (Baudelaire) **55**:59
"Que pasa o redor de min?" (Castro) **78**:41
"Quebec" (Moodie) **113**:344, 347
Queechy (Warner) **31**:333, 337, 341-43
"The Queen" (Hunt) **70**:258
"The Queen and the Working Classes" (Hunt) **70**:259
"Queen Eleanor and Fair Rosamond" (Oliphant) **61**:210, 241
"Queen Hynde" (Hogg) **4**:282-83
Queen Hynde (Hogg) **109**:205-08, 244-45, 250, 271
"Queen Mab" (Hood) **16**:224
Queen Mab (Shelley) **18**:330-32, 334, 336, 338, 342, 344, 346, 368, 374, 379; **93**:272, 294-95, 371-72
The Queen Mary (Tennyson) **30**:219, 262-64
"The Queen Must Dance" (Boker) **125**:81
The Queen of Hearts (Collins) **93**:46
The Queen of Spades (Pushkin)
See *Pikovaya dama*
"The Queen of the Army Camp" (Isaacs)
See "La reina del campamento"
The Queen of the Frogs (Planché) **42**:288, 293
"Queen of the Isles" (Tennyson) **30**:295
"Queen Oriana's Dream" (Lamb) **10**:418
"Queen Orraca and the Five Martyrs of Morocco" (Southey) **8**:474
"The Queen, the Opening of Parliament" (Hunt) **70**:259
"Queen Titania" (Boyesen) **135**:13
Queen Titania (Boyesen) **135**:13, 21, 28
"Queen Ysabeau" (Villiers de l'Isle Adam)
See "La reine Ysabeau"
Queeney Letters (Piozzi) **57**:245
The Queen's Jewelpiece (Almqvist)
See *Drottningens juvelsmycke*
The Queen's Necklace (Dumas)
See *Le collier de la reine*
The Queen's Wake (Hogg) **4**:274-76, 279, 284; **109**:204, 240, 246, 249, 270, 272
A Queer Book (Hogg) **109**:272
Quelques Détails sur les Mœurs des Grecs, des Arabes et des Turcs (Chateaubriand) **134**:4
Quelques médaillons et portraits en pied (Mallarmé) **41**:249, 269
"De quelques phénomènes du sommeil" (Nodier) **19**:400
"Qu'en avez-vous fait?" (Desbordes-Valmore) **97**:6
Quentin Durward (Scott) **15**:283, 308, 312-14; **69**:303-04, 308, 313, 316, 318, 328, 330, 332-34, 366
"Queries to My Seventieth Year" (Whitman) **31**:433
The Quest of the Absolute (Balzac)
See *La recherche de l'absolu*
"Qu'est-ce pour nous" (Rimbaud) **82**:232
"The Question" (Shelley) **18**:340, 345
"Question and Answer" (Browning) **16**:135
La question d'argent (Dumas) **9**:220-21, 224, 239-42, 246, 250-51
La question du divorce (Dumas) **9**:225-26, 244-45
"The Questioning Spirit" (Clough) **27**:41, 52, 80, 104
Questions contemporaines (Renan) **26**:377, 414
"Questions of Life" (Whittier) **8**:491, 510, 524; **59**:371
"Questions of Varying Import" (Almqvist) **42**:12
Questions politiques et sociales (Sand) **5**:318
"Qui Laborat, Orat" (Clough) **27**:55, 77, 89, 105
"Qui sait?" (Maupassant) **1**:457, 464, 468
"Quicksand Years" (Whitman) **31**:433; **81**:311
Quidam (Norwid) **17**:369, 378-79
"Quidquid volueris" (Flaubert) **62**:101
"The Quiet After the Storm" (Leopardi)
See "La quiete dopo la tempesta"
A Quiet Gentlewoman (Mitford) **4**:406
The Quiet Heart (Oliphant) **61**:209
"A Quiet Spot" (Turgenev) **21**:409, 418-20, 451; **122**:247, 280, 350
"Quiet Work" (Arnold) **6**:44; **29**:34
"La quiete dopo la tempesta" (Leopardi) **129**:219, 229, 338-41, 344, 348
Quitt (Fontane) **26**:234, 243-44, 260, 272
Quitte pour la peur (Vigny) **7**:473
La Quixotita y su prima (Lizardi) **30**:67-73, 78-9

"Quotation and Originality" (Emerson) **38**:203; **98**:185
"A rab gólya" (Arany) **34**:9, 16
"Rabbi Ben Ezra" (Browning) **19**:89, 103, 130, 152
"Rabbi Ishmael" (Whittier) **59**:361
"Der Rabbi von Bacherach" (Heine) **4**:268-69
"La rabouilleuse" (Balzac) **5**:32, 53, 75
"Die Rache" (Klopstock) **11**:238
Rachel Ray (Trollope) **6**:456, 470-71, 492, 499, 501, 515-16; **101**:235, 238-41, 309, 335
Rachel Wilde; or, Trifles from the Burthen of a Life (Moodie) **14**:241-44
"Rachel's Refusal" (Cooke) **110**:53, 58
Racine et Shakespeare (Stendhal) **23**:352, 391; **46**:307, 325
"Racing Ethics" (Gordon) **21**:179
Radharani (Chatterji) **19**:217-19, 221
The Radical (Galt) **110**:94
A Radical War Song (Macaulay) **42**:154
"Radlauf erzählt seine reise nach dem Starenberg" (Brentano) **1**:100, 104
"Raeburn's Portraits" (Stevenson) **5**:389
Rage et impuissance (Flaubert) **2**:256
"Rages de césars" (Rimbaud) **4**:465; **35**:271
Ragged Dick; or, Street Life in New York with the Boot-Blacks (Alger) **8**:15, 27, 30, 34, 37; **83**:95, 98, 104-6, 125, 127, 130-31, 135, 138-40, 142, 144, 146
"The Ragged Schools of London" (Browning)
See "A Song for the Ragged Schools of London"
Ragionamenti (Gozzi) **23**:110
Rahel, ein Buch des Andenkens fü4 ihre Freunde, Vol. II (Varnhagen von Ense)
See *Rahel, ein Buch des Andenkens für ihre Freunde*
Rahel, ein Buch des Andenkens für ihre Freunde (Varnhagen von Ense) **130**:292-94, 299-301, 303, 305, 310, 327, 329, 340-41, 344, 359, 367, 371
Rahel, ein Buch des Andenkens für ihre Freunde, Vol. I (Varnhagen von Ense)
See *Rahel, ein Buch des Andenkens für ihre Freunde*
Rahel, ein Buch des Andenkens für ihre Freunde, Vol. III (Varnhagen von Ense)
See *Rahel, ein Buch des Andenkens für ihre Freunde*
Rahel-Bibliothek: Gesammelte Werke (Varnhagen von Ense) **130**:367, 369
"Raids" (Bestuzhev)
See "Nayezdy"
"The Railroad" (Barnes) **75**:73
"The Railroad" (Nekrasov) **11**:416-17
"Railroad Song" (Chivers) **49**:41, 43
The Railway Man and His Children (Oliphant) **11**:449, 461; **61**:203-5, 242
"The Railway Station" (Lampman) **25**:172, 198, 204, 208-09
"A Rain Dream" (Bryant) **6**:165, 168, 175
"The Rainbow" (Sigourney) **21**:299
"A Rainy Day" (Hunt) **1**:417
"The Rainy Day" (Longfellow) **45**:147
"The Rainy Season in California" (Ridge) **82**:185
"The Rajah's Diamond" (Stevenson) **5**:393, 403
Rajani (Chatterji) **19**:210, 215, 217-19, 221-22, 224
Rajmohan's Wife (Chatterji) **19**:215
Rajsingha (Chatterji) **19**:210-13, 215, 217-21, 223-25
"Rakušanskij melamed" (Leskov) **25**:265-67
"Ralph Farnham's Romance" (Alger) **83**:98
"Ralph Raymond's Heir" (Alger) **8**:41, 43-44; **83**:96, 148
Ralph the Heir (Trollope) **101**:239, 249, 251, 272, 292, 309, 311, 320
"Ralph Waldo Emerson" (Cranch) **115**:33, 39
Ralph Waldo Emerson (Alcott) **1**:25
Ralph Waldo Emerson (Holmes) **14**:107; **81**:115, 117
Ralph Waldo Emerson: Essays and Lectures (Emerson)
See *Essays and Lectures*
Die Ramanzen vom Rosenkranz (Brentano) **1**:95, 102, 104
"Ramble" (Wordsworth)
See "A Winter's Ramble in Grasmere's Vale"
Rambles (Allingham) **25**:15
Rambles Among Words (Whitman) **81**:286-87, 291-96, 348-50
Rambles beyond Railways (Collins) **1**:184-85; **93**:46, 64
Rambles by Patricius Walker (Allingham)
See *Rambles*
Rambles in Germany and Italy (Shelley) **14**:260
Ramido Marinesco (Almqvist) **42**:4
Ramona (Jackson) **90**:125-26, 129-32, 134-42, 145-46, 150-55, 157, 159-60, 164, 166, 169, 171-78
"Randolph of Roanoke" (Whittier) **8**:501, 505, 508; **59**:353
Ranelagh House (Warton) **118**:308, 336, 350
"The Ranger" (Whittier) **8**:509, 518
"Rangstreit" (Grillparzer) **102**:174
"The Ransacked Grave" (Shevchenko)
See "Rozryta mohyla"
Ranthorpe (Lewes) **25**:273, 286, 293, 298, 307, 309
"Rape of Proserpine" (Tennyson) **115**:337
"Raphael" (Pater) **7**:308
"Raphael" (Whittier) **8**:486, 489
Raphael; or, Pages of the Book of Life at Twenty (Lamartine) **11**:257, 266, 278-79, 285-86, 288-89
"Raphael's deposition from the cross" (Fuller) **50**:249, 250
A Rapid Thaw (Robertson) **35**:333, 335-36
"Rappaccini's Daughter" (Hawthorne) **2**:294, 311, 319, 322, 331; **10**:308; **17**:137, 145; **23**:201, 218; **39**:198, 237; **79**:299; **95**:92, 109, 132, 136-37, 150
The Rapparee (Boucicault) **41**:28, 49, 51
"La rapsode foraine et le pardon de Saint-Anne" (Corbière) **43**:2-3, 7, 11, 13, 15, 18, 23-4, 28-30
"Rapsodie du sourd" (Corbière) **43**:13, 19, 21, 25, 27, 32-4
Raptularz (Slowacki) **15**:372
"Rapture—To Laura" (Schiller) **39**:339
"Rapunzel" (Morris) **4**:421, 423, 426, 431, 444
"Rare Ripe Garden-Seed" (Harris) **23**:159
"Raschi in Prague" (Lazarus) **8**:422; **109**:326, 337, 342
"Rasskaz ofitsera, byvshego v plenu u gorcev" (Bestuzhev) **131**:160-61, 187
"Rasskaz otca Alekseja" (Turgenev)
See "Rasskaz ottsa Aleksaya"
"Rasskaz ottsa Aleksaya" (Turgenev) **21**:420, 441; **122**:242, 265, 267, 348, 365, 367, 370, 376-78
"Rast" (Muller) **73**:366,391
Rastočitel (Leskov) **25**:248
"Rat Krespel" (Hoffmann) **2**:346, 356
"Le rat qui s'est retiré du monde" (Banville) **9**:32
"Ratbert" (Hugo) **3**:264
Ratcliff (Heine) **4**:253
The Rationale of Reward (Bentham) **38**:90, 92
"The Rationale of Verse" (Poe) **117**:335
"Rationale of Verse" (Timrod) **25**:373
De ratione, una, universali, infinita (Feuerbach) **139**:302-5, 308-9, 311-12
Ratos entretenidos (Lizardi) **30**:67
"Les rats" (Banville) **9**:16
"Rattle-Snake Hunter" (Whittier) **8**:484
Die Raüber (Schiller) **39**:299, 304, 306-11, 323-24, 326-27, 331, 334, 336, 338, 342-43, 348, 350, 354, 358, 365, 368-71, 375-76, 385, 390-94; **69**:169, 239, 275
"Die Räuberbraut" (Hebbel) **43**:253
"The Ravaged Villa" (Melville) **3**:363
"The Raven" (Poe) **1**:493, 496, 502, 512, 516-18, 522-25; **16**:305; **55**:132-3, 135, 138-9, 141, 147-8, 154, 176, 178, 208, 212-3; **97**:238, 240; **117**:192, 195, 197, 200, 203, 208, 215, 217, 226-27, 231, 236-37, 240-44, 252, 257, 264, 275-76, 278, 280-82, 287-90, 296-98, 301, 303, 309, 315, 327-29, 333-36
The Raven (Gozzi)
See *Il corvo*
The Raven, and Other Poems (Poe) **55**:174; **117**:333
"The Raven and the King's Daughter" (Morris) **4**:423
"The Raven Days" (Lanier) **118**:234, 240, 287
"A Raven in a White Chine" (Ingelow) **39**:264
The Ravens (Becque)
See *Les corbeaux*
"The Ravens of Odin" (Boyesen) **135**:5
Ravenshoe (Kingsley) **107**:186, 188-89, 192, 194-204, 206-11, 215-16, 219-21, 223-24, 226, 228-29
"The Ravenswing" (Thackeray) **14**:402
The Ravine (Goncharov) **63**:21-6
"La ravine Sainte-Gilles" (Leconte de Lisle) **29**:212, 216
Ravnikar (Preseren) **127**:314
The Raw Youth (Dostoevsky)
See *Podrostok*
A Raw Youth (Dostoevsky)
See *Podrostok*
"A Ray of Light in the Realm of Darkness" (Dobrolyubov) **5**:140-42, 151
Raymond and Agnes (Lewis) **11**:305
Rayner (Baillie) **2**:34-35, 39; **71**:5-6, 12-13
"Un rayo de luna" (Bécquer)
See "El rayo de luna"
"El rayo de luna" (Bécquer) **106**:92, 103, 108, 112-13, 115, 121, 130, 132-33
Les rayons et les ombres (Hugo) **3**:271, 273
"Rayons jaunes" (Sainte-Beuve) **5**:340, 342, 347
Razgovor v Kremle (Pavlova) **138**:3-4, 13, 31, 51
Razgovor v Trianone (Pavlova) **138**:3-4, 13, 52
"A Razor-Grinder in a Thunder-Storm" (Harris) **23**:159, 163
"Razrushenie estetiki" (Pisarev) **25**:334, 338, 340
"Razskaz" (Pavlova) **138**:49
"Razviazka 'Révizor'" (Gogol) **15**:85, 106, 110
RC (Parton)
See *Rose Clark*
Re Teodoro a Venezia (Da Ponte) **50**:78
"Le Rê ve intermittent d'une nuit triste" (Desbordes-Valmore) **97**:17-19, 23, 29
"Reaction in Germany" (Bakunin) **25**:40, 58, 62; **58**:105, 120, 130, 135
"Readen ov a Headstone" (Barnes) **75**:8
"Readers against the Grain" (Lamb) **10**:411; **113**:202
Readiana (Reade) **74**:281
"Reading" (Thoreau) **7**:402
"A Reading Diary" (Rossetti) **2**:572; **50**:277, 285, 290, 292, 320-21, 323
"Reading María" (Isaacs)
See "Leyendo a María"
"Real" (Dickinson)
See "I like a look of Agony"
Real Life in Verdopolis (Brontë) **109**:45, 49-50, 52
"Real Rest" (Brontë) **109**:31
"A Real Vision of Sin" (Thomson) **18**:403, 407, 414
The Realists (Pisarev)
See *Realisty*
Realisty (Pisarev) **25**:332-34, 337, 341, 344-48, 353
"Realities" (Lazarus) **8**:420
Realities (Linton) **41**:167
"Reality" (Lampman) **25**:204
"Reality" (Reade) **2**:549

"A Reaper and the Flowers" (Longfellow) **2**:473, 479; **45**:116, 121
"Rearrange a 'Wife's' Affection" (Dickinson) **21**:58
"Reason and Faith" (Mickiewicz) **3**:399-400
Reason and Heart (Eminescu) **33**:266
"Reasons Why the English Should Not Be Our Standard, Either in Language or Manners" (Webster) **30**:406
Rebecca; or, The Fille de Chambre (Rowson) **5**:310-12, 316; **69**:99, 102, 105, 113, 133-35, 141
The Rebel of the Family (Linton) **41**:164, 174
"Le rebelle" (Baudelaire) **29**:80; **55**:13
The Rebellion in Ghent under the Emperor Charles V (Sacher-Masoch) **31**:289
The Rebellion in the Cévennes (Tieck)
See *Der Aufruhr in den Cevennen*
"The Rebellion of the Waters" (Darley) **2**:131
The Rebels; or, Boston before the Revolution (Child) **6**:197-98, 200, 204, 208; **73**:39-40, 50, 58, 66, 74, 115
"Reburial" (Preseren)
See "Prekop"
"De Rebus Scenicis (Et Quibusdam Aliis)" (Lewes) **25**:291
"Recent English Poetry" (Clough) **27**:102-03
"Recent Social Theories" (Clough) **27**:82
"The Recent Telepathic Occurrence at the British Museum" (Levy) **59**:112
La recherche de l'absolu (Balzac) **5**:32-4, 36, 62, 73, 79; **53**:12
Die Rechte des Herzens (Ludwig) **4**:349, 351
Rechtslehre (Fichte)
See *Grundlage des Naturrechts nach Prinzipen der Wissenshaftslehre*
The Recluse (Stifter)
See *Der Hagestolz*
The Recluse of the Lake (Smith)
See *Ethelinde; or, The Recluse of the Lake*
The Recluse; or Views on Man, Nature, and on Human Life (Wordsworth) **12**:442, 445-46, 451, 459, 466, 468; **38**:362, 364-65, 368, 370, 373, 376-77, 380, 387, 399-400, 405, 411-12, 415; **111**:233, 243, 332, 347
"El recluta" (Silva) **114**:263, 300, 315
El recluta (Silva) **114**:270
"Recollection" (Musset) **7**:256
"The Recollection" (Shelley)
See "To Jane: The Recollection"
"Recollections" (Coleridge)
See "Recollections of Love"
"The Recollections" (Leopardi)
See "Le ricordanze"
"Recollections" (Norton) **47**:235
Recollections (Sedgwick) **19**:445
Recollections (Tonna)
See *Personal Recollections*
Recollections (Trelawny)
See *Recollections of the Last Days of Shelley and Byron*
"Recollections After a Ramble" (Clare) **9**:78, 123
"Recollections After an Evening Walk" (Clare) **9**:123
Recollections and Reflections (Planché)
See *Life and Recollections*
Recollections of a Literary Man (Daudet)
See *Souvenirs d'un homme de lettres*
Recollections of a Province (Faustino)
See *Recuerdos de provincia*
Recollections of a Tour Made in Scotland (Wordsworth) **25**:391, 393-94, 398, 407, 411-12, 415, 419, 423-24, 428
Recollections of a Tour Made in Scotland, A.D. 1803 (Wordsworth) **138**:199, 252-53, 255, 259, 263, 283, 289-91, 293, 310-11
The Recollections of Alexis de Tocqueville (Tocqueville)
See *Souvenirs de Alexis de Tocqueville*
Recollections of an Excursion to the Monasteries of Alcobaça and Batalha (Beckford) **16**:26
"Recollections of Belinsky" (Turgenev) **122**:276
"Recollections of Christ's Hospital" (Lamb) **113**:234
Recollections of Europe (Cooper)
See *Gleanings in Europe*
The Recollections of Geoffry Hamlyn (Kingsley) **107**:186, 189, 191-95, 205-21, 223, 229, 231-50
Recollections of Gógol (Aksakov)
See *Istoriya moega znakomstva s Gogolem*
Recollections of Literary Life; or, Books, Places, and People (Mitford) **4**:401-03
"Recollections of Love" (Coleridge) **99**:103-04
Recollections of My Youth (Renan)
See *Souvenirs d'enfance et de jeunesse*
"Recollections of Past Times and Events" (Freneau) **111**:138
"Recollections of Shakespeare" (Lazarus) **109**:294
"Recollections of Sully" (Cooke) **5**:132
"Recollections of the Antislavery Contest" (Douglass) **7**:126
"Recollections of the Arabian Nights" (Tennyson) **30**:204, 211, 223
"Recollections of the Lakes" (De Quincey) **4**:70-71
Recollections of the Lakes and the Lake Poets (De Quincey) **87**:60-1, 63
Recollections of the Last Days of Shelley and Byron (Trelawny) **85**:315, 317-18, 320, 322-24, 332-38
"Recollections of the West Indies" (Richardson) **55**:301
"Recollections of the Year 1848" (Grillparzer) **102**:77
Recollections of Tsarskoe-Selo (Pushkin)
See "Vospominanie v Tsarskom Sele"
"Reconciliation" (Hayne) **94**:144
Record of a Girlhood (Kemble) **18**:187-90
A Record of Courage and Cowardice (Ueda Akinari)
See *Tandai shoshin roku*
"Recorders Ages Hence" (Whitman) **81**:260
Records (Trelawny)
See *Records of Shelley, Byron and the Author*
Records of Later Life (Kemble) **18**:188-90
Records of Shelley, Byron and the Author (Trelawny) **85**:307, 309, 312, 314, 335
"The Records of Woman" (Hemans) **71**:261, 271, 274
Records of Woman, with Other Poems (Hemans) **29**:197, 202-03; **71**:274-79, 288-89, 291-94, 296-98, 302-04, 307
The Recreations of Christopher North (Wilson) **5**:551-52, 558, 560-62
"The Recruit" (Silva)
See "El recluta"
The Rector, and the Doctor's Family (Oliphant) **11**:454-5, 457, 459; **61**:174-5, 198, 226, 239
"Rectoral Address at St. Andrews" (Mill) **58**:327
The Rectory Umbrella (Carroll) **53**:51, 104
Recueil de morceaux détachés (Staël-Holstein) **91**:339, 358
"Recueillement" (Baudelaire) **6**:97-102; **29**:108; **55**:5, 26
Les recueillements poétiques (Lamartine) **11**:265, 271, 283
"Recuerdos de colegial" (Isaacs) **70**:311
Recuerdos de provincia (Faustino) **123**:273, 278, 291, 304, 308-9, 312, 318-25, 328-40, 344, 347, 352, 361
The Red and the Black (Stendhal)
See *Le rouge et le noir*
The Red Book (Kennedy) **2**:432
"The Red Cape" (Bestuzhev)
See "Krasnoe polryvalo"
Red Cotton Night-Cap Country (Browning) **19**:106, 140; **79**:153
"The Red Cross Corps" (Crawford) **127**:220
Red Deer (Jefferies) **47**:136
"The Red Fisherman" (Hood) **16**:221-22
"Red Hoss Mountain" (Field) **3**:208
"The Red Inn" (Balzac)
See *L'Auberge rouge*
"Red Jacket (from Aloft)" (Whitman) **81**:345
The Red Mask (Planché) **42**:275, 292
"Red Rébék" (Arany)
See "Vörös Rébék"
"Red River Voyager" (Whittier) **59**:356
"Red Roofs of London" (Jefferies) **47**:95, 132
The Red Rover (Cooper) **1**:199-200, 202, 207-08, 221; **54**:254, 275
"The Red Shoes" (Andersen) **7**:21, 23, 31, 34-35; **79**:23, 51, 53, 59-60, 67
"The Red Snake" (Adams) **33**:13
"The Redbreast and the Butterfly" (Wordsworth) **12**:395
Redburn: His First Voyage (Melville) **3**:328, 333, 337, 344-45, 360-61, 366-67, 381; **29**:324-25, 328, 340, 354, 358, 367; **45**:196; **49**:391; **91**:42, 45, 54-5, 218; **123**:166-265
Rede des toten Christus (Jean Paul) **7**:238, 240
"Die Rede über Mythologie und symbolische Anschaung" (Schlegel) **45**:308, 316, 333, 337, 356
Rede zum Schäkespears Tag (Goethe) **34**:121
Redémption (Feuillet) **45**:75, 77, 82, 88
Reden an die deutsche Nation (Fichte) **62**:16, 19, 35, 38
Redgauntlet (Scott) **15**:300-01, 304, 312, 315; **69**:304, 308, 318, 331; **110**:233, 305, 316
"Red-Jacket" (Halleck) **47**:57, 67, 69, 71, 73, 79
Red-Nosed Frost (Nekrasov)
See *Moroz krasni nos*
"The Redress: To a Young Poet" (Dyer) **129**:121, 149
The Redskins; or, Indian and Injin: Being the Conclusion of the Littlepage Manuscripts (Cooper) **1**:216-17, 219-20, 224, 226; **54**:258, 283
Redwood (Sedgwick) **19**:425-27, 429-30, 433, 439, 445, 447, 453; **98**:299, 301, 307, 321, 326, 334
"A Reed" (Browning) **61**:44
Refections (Paine) **62**:353-4
"The Reflection" (Grillparzer)
See "Das Spiegelbild"
"A Reflection in Autumn" (Clare) **9**:72
"Reflections and Remarks on Human Life" (Stevenson) **14**:335
"Reflections in the Pillory" (Lamb) **10**:420; **113**:285
"Reflections on Didactic Poetry" (Warton) **118**:353
"Reflections on Having Left a Place of Retirement" (Coleridge) **99**:5-6, 48
"Reflections on Marriage" (Kierkegaard) **125**:261
"Reflections on the Constitution, or Frame of Nature" (Freneau) **111**:109
"Reflections on the General Debased Condition of Mankind" (Freneau) **111**:105
"Reflections on the Novel" (Sade) **3**:468-69
Reflections on the Novel (Sade)
See *Idée sur les romans*
"Reflections on the Resurrection of Bodies" (Dobrolyubov) **5**:140
Reflections on World History (Burckhardt)
See *Weltgeschichtliche Bertrachtungen*
Reflections upon the Study of Asiatic Languages (Schlegel)
See *Réflexions sur l'étude des langues Asiatiques*
Reflector (Hunt) **70**:266
Reflexions (Maistre) **37**:314
"Réflexions sur la paix" (Staël-Holstein) **91**:340
"Réflexions sur la tragédie" (Constant) **6**:224-25

"Réflexions sur la vérité dans l'art" (Vigny) **7**:470; **102**:346-47, 378-79, 383
"Réflexions sur le procès de la reine" (Staël-Holstein) **91**:340
Réflexions sur le suicide (Staël-Holstein) **91**:360
Réflexions sur l'étude des langues Asiatiques (Schlegel) **15**:224
La réforme intellectuelle et morale (Renan) **26**:377, 414, 421
"A Reformer" (Hazlitt) **29**:152
"The Reformer" (Whittier) **8**:520, 530
"Reforms" (Emerson) **98**:81, 167
"Reforms of the Constitution" (Bello) **131**:124
Les Réfractaires (Vallès) **71**:315-16, 327-28
"Refuge" (Desbordes-Valmore) **97**:29
"Refuge" (Lampman) **25**:207
The Refuge of Monrepo (Saltykov)
See *Ubezhishche Monrepo*
The Refugee in America (Trollope) **30**:314, 319
"The Refusal of Aid between Nations" (Rossetti) **4**:499; **77**:293-94
A Refutation of Deism (Shelley) **18**:374
"Reg és Est" (Arany) **34**:19
Die Regentrude (Storm) **1**:536, 548-50
The Regent's Daughter (Dumas)
See *Une fille du régent*
"A régi jó Gvadányi" (Petofi) **21**:277
Regina (Keller) **2**:412-13
Reginald Dalton (Lockhart) **6**:288-89, 292-96, 302-03, 310-12
Reginald Glanshaw, or the Man, who Commanded Success (Crabbe) **121**:24, 33
Reginald Hetherege (Kingsley) **107**:192, 195, 210, 218
Register (Cobbett)
See *Cobbett's Weekly Political Register*
"Regret" (Lazarus) **8**:419
"Les regrets" (Sainte-Beuve) **5**:350
Das Reh (Tieck) **5**:519
Der Rehbock (Kotzebue) **25**:133, 136, 142-43
"Reife" (Meyer) **81**:146, 149-50
The Reign of Greed (Rizal)
See *El filibusterismo*
The Reign of Moderation and Order (Saltykov)
See *V srede umerennosti i akkuratnosti*
Reign of Terror (Gore) **65**:20
"La reina de la sombra" (Casal) **131**:257
"La reina del campamento" (Isaacs) **70**:306
La Reine Coax (Sand) **42**:314
"La reine des poissons" (Nerval) **1**:480
"La Reine Hortense" (Maupassant) **83**:168, 171
La reine Margot (Dumas) **11**:51-52, 68, 70; **71**:184-86, 189-90, 193
"La reine Ysabeau" (Villiers de l'Isle Adam) **3**:590
Reineke Fuchs (Goethe) **4**:163, 207
Reinhart Fuchs (Grimm and Grimm) **3**:217, 228
"Reise nach Frankreich" (Schlegel) **45**:336
"Reise um die Welt" (Chamisso) **82**:24, 28-30
Die Reise von Munchen nech Genua (Heine) **54**:336
Reisebilder (Heine) **4**:231, 233, 235-36, 239-40, 252, 259; **54**:320, 322, 330, 339
Reiseblätter (Lenau) **16**:270
"Reisekammeraten" (Andersen) **7**:33-4; **79**:23-24, 50, 76, 80, 86
Reiselieder (Muller) **73**:362, 387
"Reiselust" (Grillparzer) **102**:174
"Reisephantasie" (Meyer) **81**:142
"The Relation of the Individual to the State" (Thoreau) **138**:128
"The Relations of Poetry and Science" (Lanier) **118**:218
"Relics of General Chassé" (Trollope) **101**:234
Religio poetae (Patmore) **9**:340-42, 344, 349
"Religion" (Emerson) **38**:177; **98**:79, 160
"Religion a Weariness to the Natural Man" (Newman) **38**:302
Religion and Art (Wagner)
See *Die Religion und die Kunst*
"Religion and Philosophy in Germany" (Heine)
See "Zur Geschichte der Religion und Philosophie in Deutschland"
"The Religion of Numa" (Pater) **7**:317
"Religion of Socrates" (Martineau) **26**:309
The Religion of Solidarity (Bellamy) **4**:27-28, 30-31; **86**:4, 6, 8-9, 47, 70, 74, 78
"The Religion of the Day" (Newman) **38**:304-05
The Religion of the Heart (Hunt) **70**:287-88
Die Religion und die Kunst (Wagner) **9**:475
Religion within the Limits of Pure Reason (Kant)
See *Religion within the Limits of Reason Alone*
Religion within the Limits of Reason Alone (Kant) **27**:148, 208, 249
"Les religions de l'antiquité" (Renan) **26**:415
Religious Discourses by a Layman (Scott) **69**:365-66
"Religious Musings" (Coleridge) **9**:149; **54**:68-9, 71; **99**:58; **111**:264
"Religious Orders" (Brownson) **50**:53
Religious Songs (Fouqué) **2**:267
Religious Tracts (Cobbett)
See *Twelve Sermons*
Religious Training of Children in the School, the Family, and the Church (Beecher) **30**:9, 13
"La Relique" (Maupassant) **83**:168
"Reliques" (Percy) **95**:309, 340
Reliques (Percy)
See *Reliques of Ancient English Poetry: Consisting of Old Heroic Ballads, Songs, and Other Pieces of Our Earlier Poets, (Chiefly of the Lyric Kind.) Together with Some Few of Later Date*
Reliques of Ancient English Poetry: Consisting of Old Heroic Ballads, Songs, and Other Pieces of Our Earlier Poets, (Chiefly of the Lyric Kind.) Together with Some Few of Later Date (Percy) **95**:307-13, 316, 318-32, 334-40, 342-51, 354-58, 360-62, 364-65
Remains in Verse and Prose (Hallam) **110**:120-22, 141, 145
Remains of Henry Kirke White (Southey) **97**:268
"Remarks on Associations" (Channing) **17**:6
Remarks on Forest Scenery, and Other Woodland Views (Gilpin) **30**:36
"Remarks on National Literature" (Channing) **17**:31-2, 38, 50
"Remarks on the Character and Writings of Fenelon" (Channing) **17**:8, 31
"Remarks on the Character and Writings of John Milton" (Channing) **17**:4, 7-8, 12, 25, 31, 38, 41, 49
"Remarks on the 'Jagiellonid' by Dyzma Boncza Tomaszewski" (Mickiewicz) **101**:174
"Remarks on the Life and Character of Napoleon" (Channing) **17**:4, 6, 25, 31, 38
Remarks on the Slavery Question, in a Letter to Jonathan Phillips, Esq. (Channing) **17**:32
"Rember thee" (Moore) **110**:195
"Remember" (Lazarus) **109**:298
"Remember" (Rossetti) **2**:572, 574
"Remember the Glories of Brien the Brave" (Moore) **110**:182, 185
"Rememberance" (Hölderlin)
See "Andenken"
"Remembered Grace" (Patmore) **9**:359, 365
"Remembrance" (Brontë) **16**:70, 75, 80, 86-7, 122; **35**:111
"Remembrance" (Darwin) **106**:184
"Remembrance" (Opie) **65**:160
"Remembrance in Tsarskoe Selo" (Pushkin)
See "Vospominanie v Tsarskom Sele"
"Remembrance of a Summer's Night" (Ridge) **82**:174, 183
"Remembrance of Spain" (Martínez de la Rosa) **102**:228
"Remembrances" (Clare) **9**:97; **86**:168-69
"Remembrances" (Leopardi)
See "Le ricordanze"
"Reménvem" (Arany) **34**:18
"A Reminiscence" (Levy) **59**:119
"A Reminiscence of Federalism" (Sedgwick) **98**:315
Reminiscences (Carlyle) **70**:25, 72, 76
"Reminiscences at Tsarskoe Selo" (Pushkin)
See "Vospominanie v Tsarskom Sele"
Reminiscences of His Youth (Renan)
See *Souvenirs d'enfance et de jeunesse*
Reminiscences of My Childhood (Fontane)
See *Meine Kinderjahre*
Reminiscences of My Irish Journey (Carlyle) **70**:90-91, 93
"Reminiscences of New York" (Bryant) **6**:181
"Remonstrance" (Ingelow) **107**:159
"Remonstrance" (Lanier) **6**:246, 259; **118**:217, 273
"Remonstratory Ode from the Elephant at Exeter Change" (Hood) **16**:233
"Remords posthume" (Baudelaire) **6**:80; **55**:59
Remorse (Coleridge) **9**:138, 142-43, 146; **111**:197
"La rempailleuse" (Maupassant) **83**:157, 159, 161, 194, 229
"Le remplacant" (Maupassant) **83**:232
"The Renaissance" (Pater) **7**:310
The Renaissance (Gobineau)
See *La renaissance*
La renaissance (Gobineau) **17**:75, 79-80, 88, 96, 98
Renaissance in Italy (Symonds) **34**:316, 319, 321, 331, 334-35, 337, 340, 342, 344-51, 356-60, 362-65, 368, 374
The Renaissance: Studies in Art and Poetry (Pater) **7**:288-92, 294-99, 305, 308-10, 312-17, 323-24, 327, 332-34, 336-40, 342; **90**:239, 241-42, 244-45, 247-52, 254, 260-64, 269, 273-74, 276-80, 284, 286-91, 293, 298, 300, 304-06, 308-11, 315-17, 321-26, 328, 333-40
"Renan and the Jews" (Lazarus) **8**:423-24
Renate (Storm) **1**:540, 544, 546
"Rencontre" (Maupassant) **83**:181, 209
"The Rendezvous" (Lermontov) **5**:300
"Le Rendez-vous" (Maupassant) **83**:173
"The Rendition" (Whittier) **8**:530
René (Chateaubriand) **3**:112, 117, 121-26, 128, 130, 133-34; **134**:11-13, 16, 18, 24-30, 61, 63, 70-73, 77-83, 86-88, 90-92, 94-95, 112, 116-17, 119, 121, 130, 134, 143-44
Renée Mauperin (Goncourt and Goncourt) **7**:151, 153, 155, 157, 161, 164, 166-67, 181, 187-88
"Le reniement de Saint-Pierre" (Baudelaire) **6**:94, 121; **29**:104
"Renoncement" (Desbordes-Valmore) **97**:17
"Renouveau" (Mallarmé) **41**:277
The Rent Day (Jerrold) **2**:395, 401, 403
A Rent in a Cloud (Lever) **23**:292
"Renunciation" (Eminescu) **33**:265
"El reo de muerte" (Espronceda) **39**:100, 107
"A Reorganization of Society to Extirpate Sorrow" (Bellamy) **86**:65
"Les reparties de Nina" (Rimbaud) **4**:471; **35**:289-90; **82**:224
"The Repeal of the Differential Duties on Foreign and Colonial Wood" (Haliburton) **15**:128
"Repentance: A Pastoral Ballad" (Wordsworth) **111**:234, 236
Repertorio Americano (Bello) **131**:108-9, 112, 116, 118-19, 129-31
"Repetition" (Kierkegaard)
See "Gjentagelsen"
Repetition (Kierkegaard)
See *Gjentagelsen*
"Repining" (Rossetti) **2**:566; **50**:288, 293; **66**:386
"Reply" (Coleridge) **90**:27

Reply (Coleridge) **90**:20
A Reply to an Answer to Cursory Strictures (Godwin) **130**:88
Reply to the Charges in the Quarterly (Bowles) **103**:64
"A Reply to the Essay on Population" (Hazlitt) **82**:99
"Reply to the Spanish Regency" (Bello) **131**:97-98
"Reply to the Strictures of Three Gentlemen upon Carlyle" (Coleridge) **31**:64
"Reply to the Warsaw Critics" (Mickiewicz)
See "O Krytykach i Recenzentach"
A Reply to 'Z' (Hazlitt) **29**:169
"Réponse a un acte d'accusation" (Verlaine) **51**:352
"Report" (Jackson)
See "Report on the Conditions and Needs of the Mission Indians of California"
Report (Delany)
See *Report of the Select Committee on Emancipation and Colonization*
"Report of the Committee on the Question of Inheritance" (Bakunin) **58**:132
Report of the Conditions and Needs of the Mission Indians (Jackson) **90**:169
Report of the Select Committee on Emancipation and Colonization (Delany) **93**:97, 172
Report on Manufactures (Hamilton) **49**:298, 302, 324
Report on Public Credit (Hamilton) **49**:298
"Report on the Conditions and Needs of the Mission Indians of California" (Jackson) **90**:136-42, 150
Reporting Editing and Authorship: Practical Hints for Beginners (Jefferies) **47**:139, 141
"The Repose on the Flight" (Fouqué) **2**:266
"The Repository" (Murray) **63**:181, 209
"Representación de La mojiigata" (Larra) **130**:195
"Representación de La niña en casa y la madre en la máscara de Don Francisco Martínez de la Rosa" (Larra) **130**:201
"Representative Man" (Emerson) **98**:176
Representative Men: Seven Lectures (Emerson) **1**:281, 286, 288, 292-93, 299; **38**:172, 180, 206, 209, 211, 227; **98**:25, 65-6, 68-72, 155
"Reproach to Laura" (Schiller) **39**:358
"The Republic of the Pyrenees" (Taylor) **89**:312
"La république" (Beranger) **34**:29
"A Request" (Preseren)
See "Prošnja"
"Requiem" (Meyer) **81**:146
"Requiem" (Stevenson) **5**:427
"Requies" (Leconte de Lisle) **29**:235
"Requiescat" (Arnold) **6**:44
"Requiescat in Pace" (Ingelow) **39**:263; **107**:119
"Requiescat in Pace" (Milnes) **61**:136
"Requirement" (Whittier) **8**:509
"Le réquisitionnaire" (Balzac) **5**:78
Researches, Concerning the Institutions & Monuments of the Anc ient Inhabitants of America, with Descriptions & Views of Some of the Most Striking Scenes in the Cordilleras! (Williams) **135**:309
"Resentment" (Crabbe) **26**:93, 129-30; **121**:5, 36
Residence in Europe (Cooper) **54**:255
Resident Women-Students (Carroll) **139**:56
"Resignation" (Arnold) **6**:56, 74; **29**:29, 34-6; **89**:47, 88, 93; **126**:111
"Resignation" (Longfellow) **2**:475, 483; **45**:132, 140; **101**:92
"Resignation" (Schiller) **39**:331, 387
"Resistance to Civil Government" (Thoreau)
See "Civil Disobedience"
"Resolucións tomadas por le emigracion cubana de Tampa" (Martí) **63**:127-9, 137
"Resolution and Independence" (Wordsworth) **12**:418, 427, 435-36, 445, 447, 450, 455, 459, 470; **111**:218, 226
"Resolutions Taken by the Cuban Emigrants of Tampa" (Martí)
See "Resolucións tomadas por le emigracion cubana de Tampa"
"Respectability" (Browning) **19**:131
"The Respectable Folks" (Thoreau) **138**:67
"Respondez!" (Whitman) **81**:263-65
"The Response" (Whittier) **8**:489
"Respublica" (Petofi) **21**:286
La respuesta de la tierra (Silva) **114**:274
Les ressources de Quinola (Balzac) **5**:51
"The Rest" (Barnes) **75**:69
"Rest" (Kendall) **12**:183
"Rest" (Rossetti) **2**:563; **50**:271, 282, 289-90; **66**:301
"Rest at Last" (Lazarus) **109**:291
"Rest Only in the Grave" (Mangan) **27**:298
Restless Human Hearts (Jefferies) **47**:92-93, 116
The Restoration of the Works of Art to Italy (Hemans) **29**:192; **71**:261
"Resurrección" (Isaacs) **70**:310-11
"Resurrection" (Lanier) **6**:236, 238
"The Resurrection" (Manzoni) **29**:253
Resurrecturis (Krasiński) **4**:304, 307
"Resurrexit" (Silva) **114**:263-64
"Reszket a bokor..." (Petofi) **21**:285
"The Reticent Volcano Keeps" (Dickinson) **21**:82
"The Retired Cat" (Cowper) **8**:119
Retired from Business (Jerrold) **2**:403
"Retirement" (Beattie) **25**:106, 108, 111
"Retirement" (Cowper) **8**:113, 139-40; **94**:23, 27, 51, 115
"Retirement" (Timrod) **25**:372, 381
Retirement (Cowper) **94**:14, 59-65, 92
"Le retour" (Lamartine) **11**:289
"Retour dans une église" (Desbordes-Valmore) **97**:29
"La retraite" (Lamartine) **11**:245, 264
"El retrato de Felisa" (Isaacs) **70**:307
The Retreat (Warren) **13**:414
"Retribution" (Chamisso) **82**:6
Retribution; or, The Vale of Shadows: A Tale of Passion (Southworth) **26**:430-32, 435-37, 439, 442, 446-47
"Retro Me, Sathana!" (Rossetti) **4**:529
"The Retrospect" (Chivers) **49**:70
Retrospect of Western Travel (Martineau) **26**:311, 315, 318, 322, 334, 336; **137**:302, 316-18, 322, 328, 331-34, 336, 357-58, 360
The Retrospect; or, The American Revolution (Dunlap) **2**:218
Retrospection; or, a Review of the Most Striking and Important Events, Characters, Situations, and Their Consequences, Which the Last Eighteen Hundred Years Have Presented to the View of Mankind (Piozzi) **57**:233, 243, 252-3, 267, 271, 302
"The Retrospective Review" (Hood) **16**:201, 219, 233
"Retrospects and Prospects" (Lanier) **6**:245, 257, 277; **118**:218, 220, 260, 272-75
"The Return" (Macha) **46**:203
"Return at Evening" (Lenau) **16**:276
"The Return of Claneboy" (Ferguson) **33**:287, 299
The Return of Martin Fierro (Hernández)
See *La vuelta de Martín Fierro*
"The Return of Peace" (Hayne) **94**:145-46, 149
The Return of the Druses (Browning) **19**:102, 113
The Return of the O'Mahony (Frederic) **10**:183, 192-94
"The Return of the Recruit" (Isaacs)
See "La vuelta del recluta"
"Return to Spain" (Martínez de la Rosa) **102**:228
Reuben and Rachel; or, Tales of Old Times (Rowson) **5**:310-12, 314, 316-17, 320-21; **69**:103, 105-06, 113, 148-55
Reuben Sachs (Levy) **59**:77, 84-7, 91, 95-7, 101-5, 111-3, 115-9, 127-8, 130-5
"Reullura" (Campbell) **19**:176, 181
"Re-union" (Taylor) **89**:298
"Un rêve" (Bertrand) **31**:47, 54
"Le rêve du jaguar" (Leconte de Lisle) **29**:216, 224
"Le rêve d'un curieux" (Baudelaire) **29**:77, 105; **55**:12, 52, 66, 73
Le rêve et la vie (Nerval) **1**:476, 478; **67**:335
"Rêve familier" (Verlaine) **2**:617, 622
"Rêve parisien" (Baudelaire) **6**:84; **29**:92, 101; **55**:12, 23-4, 31
"Rêve pour l'hiver" (Rimbaud) **35**:271-72, 321
"Révélation" (Desbordes-Valmore) **97**:15
"The Revelation" (Patmore) **9**:347
"Revelation" (Rossetti) **50**:318
"The Revelation of all Posey" (Fuller) **50**:245
"The Revelation of the Spirit through the Material World" (Very) **9**:390
Revelations of London (Ainsworth) **13**:45
"Revel'skii turnir" (Bestuzhev) **131**:165, 172, 183, 185, 209-10
"Revenge" (Shelley) **18**:342
"Revenge of America" (Warton) **118**:356
The Revenge of Etruria (Alfieri)
See *L'Etruria vendicata*
"The Revenge of Hamish" (Lanier) **6**:236, 249, 254, 265, 269-70, 279-80; **118**:203, 238
"Les révérend pères" (Beranger) **34**:28
"Rêverie d'un passant" (Hugo) **21**:214
"Reversibilité" (Baudelaire) **55**:14, 45, 60
"Reversibilities" (Verlaine) **51**:368
"Revery" (Mallarmé) **41**:258
Rêves d'amour (Scribe) **16**:412
"Les rêves morts" (Leconte de Lisle) **29**:228, 235
"Review of Aenesidemus" (Fichte) **62**:8
"Review of Literature" (Brown) **74**:38
"The Review of the Army" (Mickiewicz) **3**:401
"Review of the Causes of the Late War" (Brontë) **109**:35
The Revival of Learning (Symonds) **34**:318-19, 346-48, 357, 363, 368, 370
"The Revival of Romanism" (Froude) **43**:214-15
Révizor (Gogol) **5**:210, 213-14, 216, 219-23, 213-34, 239, 250, 255, 257; **15**:78-114; **31**:82-4, 92, 94, 97, 99-100, 102, 106, 111-13, 116-19, 135, 139, 141, 144
The Revolt (Villiers de l'Isle Adam)
See *La révolte*
"The Revolt of Islam" (Lampman) **25**:211
The Revolt of Islam (Shelley)
See *Laon and Cythna, or the Revolution in the Golden City*
"The Revolt of the Tartars" (De Quincey) **87**:3
"Révolte" (Baudelaire) **6**:91, 113, 116, 122, 124; **55**:66, 73-4
La révolte (Villiers de l'Isle Adam) **3**:584-85
La revolte des Maures sous Philip II (Martínez de la Rosa) **102**:243-44
"La revolución actual en España" (Martínez de la Rosa) **102**:245, 248, 250
La revolución de Cuba vista desde Nueva York (Villaverde) **121**:335
La révolution (Taine) **15**:428-29, 433, 447-48, 455, 474-76
Revolution and Counter-Revolution (Engels)
See *Revolution and Counter-revolution in Germany*
Revolution and Counter-Revolution (Marx) **114**:8
Revolution and Counter-revolution in Germany (Engels) **85**:117, 132, 138-39, 141, 145-46, 150
"Revolution at Athens" (Landor) **14**:187
The Revolution in France, Considered in Respect to Its Progress and Effects (Webster) **30**:415
The Revolution of the World (Paine) **62**:254

"Revolutionary Catechism" (Bakunin) **58**:109, 135
Revolutionary Epic (Disraeli) **2**:148; **39**:67; **79**:215-16, 220, 233, 269, 275, 277
The Revolutionary Government (Taine)
See *La révolution*
The Revolutionary Question: Federalism, Socialism, and Anti-Theologism (Bakunin) **25**:48; **58**:110, 135, 140
"Revolutions" (Arnold) **29**:36
The Revolver (Fredro)
See *Rewolwer*
Revue du Salon (Goncourt and Goncourt) **7**:153
Reward (Bentham)
See *The Rationale of Reward*
The Reward of the Virtuous (Smolenskin)
See *ha-Gemul*
Rewolwer (Fredro) **8**:293
"El rey Ulises" (Isaacs) **70**:311
Reynard the Fox (Goethe)
See *Reineke Fuchs*
Reynard the Fox (Grimm and Grimm)
See *Reinhart Fuchs*
Rhapsodies (Borel) **41**:3, 5, 10, 19
The Rhapsodist (Brown) **74**:54, 67, 109-10, 115, 170, 172-74, 201
"A Rhapsody" (Clare) **9**:107; **86**:111
"Rhapsody of a Southern Winter Night" (Timrod) **25**:373
"The Rhapsody of Life's Progress" (Browning) **1**:115, 129
"Der Rhein" (Hölderlin) **16**:162, 175-6, 180, 192, 195-6
Das Rheingold (Wagner) **9**:408-09, 441, 445, 448, 454, 456, 459, 463, 466, 469; **119**:177, 186-87, 193, 197, 202-08, 212, 221-25, 228-32, 268, 277, 282, 318-20, 346, 350, 354
"Rheinische Thalia" (Schiller) **39**:338
"The Rhenish Apprentice" (Muller) **73**:350
"Rhetoric" (De Quincey) **4**:61, 81
Le Rhin (Hugo) **3**:276; **21**:201
"The Rhine" (Bowles) **103**:80
"The Rhodora" (Emerson) **1**:289, 296; **98**:177, 179
"Rhoecus" (Lowell) **2**:503, 522
"Rhoecus and the Dryad" (Hayne) **94**:158
"Rhyme" (Baratynsky)
See "Rifma"
Rhyme? And Reason? (Carroll) **139**:9, 124, 127, 129
The Rhyme and Reason of Country Life (Cooper) **129**:4, 9-10, 12, 46-47, 68-69
"The Rhyme of Joyous Garde" (Gordon) **21**:153-55, 157, 160, 163, 166-68, 170, 173-75, 183, 187-88
"Rhyme of Sir Christopher" (Longfellow) **45**:149
"The Rhyme of Sir Lancelot Bogle" (Browning) **1**:126
"The Rhyme of the Duchess May" (Browning) **1**:115, 117, 121-2, 124, 126; **61**:6, 43, 65, 67, 75
"Rhymed Criticims" (Harpur) **114**:97, 126
Rhymes of Travel, Ballads and Poems (Taylor) **89**:297, 299, 307
A Rhyming Chronicle of Incidents and Feelings (Ingelow) **39**:263; **107**:118
Ribbemont; or, The Feudal Baron (Dunlap) **2**:212-15
"Ribblesdale" (Hopkins) **17**:250
"Ribič" (Preseren) **127**:298
La ricahembra (Tamayo y Baus) **1**:570-71
"Ricaurte" (Isaacs) **70**:313
Ricciarda (Foscolo) **8**:262, 270
"The Rice Lake Plains" (Traill) **31**:327
"Rich and Rare" (Maginn) **8**:441
A Rich Man (Galt) **110**:78-9, 95
"Rich Man and Cobbler" (Krylov) **1**:439
Richard Darlington (Dumas) **11**:42-43, 47-48, 67, 71; **71**:184, 192-93
Richard Hurdis; or, The Avenger of Blood (Simms) **3**:507-09, 512-14
"Richard Redpath" (Moodie) **14**:237-38
Richard Wagner's Prose Works (Wagner) **119**:189
Richardson's War of 1812 (Richardson)
See *War of 1812*
"Un riche en Bretagne" (Corbière) **43**:3, 29
Richelieu; or, The Conspiracy (Bulwer-Lytton) **1**:139; **45**:62-4, 67, 69
The Richest Heiress in England (Oliphant) **11**:454
"Richmond Hill" (Arnold) **29**:27
Die Richterin (Meyer) **81**:163-65, 194, 196, 217
"Le ricordanze" (Leopardi) **129**:219, 228, 250, 339, 341, 356-57, 360
Riddertornet (Stagnelius) **61**:248
"The Riddle" (Auden) **79**:274-75
"Riddles: Anne and Joey A-Ta'ken" (Barnes) **75**:78
"A Ride across Palestine" (Trollope) **101**:233
"The Ride of Paul Revere" (Longfellow)
See "Paul Revere's Ride"
"A Ride over the Mountains" (Cranch) **115**:48
"The Ride Round the Parapet" (Mangan) **27**:296, 298
"Ride to Aix" (Browning) **79**:274-75
"Le rideau cramoisi" (Barbey d'Aurevilly) **1**:74, 78
"Ridiculous Distress of a Country Weekly News Printer" (Freneau) **111**:129
"Riding Together" (Morris) **4**:444
"The Ridotto" (Sheridan)
See "The Ridotto of Bath, a Panegyrick, Being an Epistle from Timothy Screw, Under Server to Messrs. Kuhf and Fitzwater, to his brother Heny, Waiter at Almack's"
"Ridotto of Bath" (Sheridan)
See "The Ridotto of Bath, a Panegyrick, Being an Epistle from Timothy Screw, Under Server to Messrs. Kuhf and Fitzwater, to his brother Heny, Waiter at Almack's"
"The Ridotto of Bath" (Sheridan)
See "The Ridotto of Bath, a Panegyrick, Being an Epistle from Timothy Screw, Under Server to Messrs. Kuhf and Fitzwater, to his brother Heny, Waiter at Almack's"
"The Ridotto of Bath, a Panegyrick, Being an Epistle from Timothy Screw, Under Server to Messrs. Kuhf and Fitzwater, to his brother Heny, Waiter at Almack's" (Sheridan) **91**:230-31, 239
Rienzi (Mitford) **4**:403
Rienzi (Wagner) **9**:401, 406, 414-16, 419, 433, 436-37, 444, 473, 475; **119**:189, 191-92, 241
Rienzi, the Last of the Tribunes (Bulwer-Lytton) **1**:138, 140, 150-51; **45**:13-15, 22, 27, 55, 57-8, 69
"Rienzi's Downfall" (Wagner) **9**:475
Rienzi's Fall (Wagner)
See "Rienzi's Downfall"
"Rifle Clubs!!!" (Tennyson) **30**:294
"Riflemen Form" (Tennyson) **30**:294
"Rifma" (Baratynsky) **103**:16, 22, 36
"Right at Last" (Gaskell) **5**:201; **70**:190
The Right Way the Safe Way, proved by Emancipation in the British West Indies and ELsewhere (Child) **73**:63
"The Rights and Duties of the Individual in Relation to the Government" (Thoreau)
See "Civil Disobedience"
The Rights of Man (Paine) **62**:247, 252-5, 257, 259, 261, 266, 270, 274-5, 277-9, 281, 285, 295-302, 312, 327-9, 331-2, 334-9, 341-3, 345-9, 351-5, 357, 359-63, 365, 369, 373-80, 385, 390-1, 393
"Rights of the Temporal" (Brownson) **50**:51
"The Rights of Woman" (Barbauld) **50**:14
"The Rights of Women" (Rowson) **5**:313, 322
"The Rill from the Town-Pump" (Hawthorne) **2**:291
"Rim" (Pavlova) **138**:53
"Rima 60/xv" (Bécquer) **106**:102
"Rima I" (Bécquer) **106**:148, 161
"Rima II" (Bécquer) **106**:106, 126-27
"Rima III" (Bécquer) **106**:105, 114, 116, 126-27, 160
"Rima IV" (Bécquer) **106**:101, 103, 125, 150
"Rima IX" (Bécquer) **106**:150
"Rima L" (Bécquer) **106**:161
"Rima LI" (Bécquer) **106**:170
"Rima LII" (Bécquer) **106**:127, 170
"Rima LVI" (Bécquer) **106**:126
"Rima LXII" (Bécquer) **106**:126
"Rima LXIX" (Bécquer) **106**:126
"Rima LXXI" (Bécquer) **106**:112, 124, 155-56
"Rima LXXII" (Bécquer) **106**:127, 150
"Rima LXXIII" (Bécquer) **106**:125
"Rima LXXIV" (Bécquer) **106**:103, 114, 159
"Rima LXXIX" (Bécquer) **106**:170
"Rima LXXV" (Bécquer) **106**:123-25, 129
"Rima LXXVI" (Bécquer) **106**:127
"Rima LXXXVI" (Bécquer) **106**:114, 124
"Rima V" (Bécquer) **106**:104, 124, 127
"Rima VI" (Bécquer) **106**:150
"Rima VII" (Bécquer) **106**:104, 160
"Rima VIII" (Bécquer) **106**:105, 116, 124, 126, 137
"Rima X" (Bécquer) **106**:110, 149-50
"Rima XI" (Bécquer) **106**:102, 108, 134
"Rima XII" (Bécquer) **106**:127, 169
"Rima XIV" (Bécquer) **106**:115, 124, 126
"Rima XVI" (Bécquer) **106**:124, 161
"Rima XXI" (Bécquer) **106**:102
"Rima XXIII" (Bécquer) **106**:151
"Rima XXIV" (Bécquer) **106**:127, 150
"Rima XXIX" (Bécquer) **106**:150, 169
"Rima XXVI" (Bécquer) **106**:106
"Rima XXVII" (Bécquer) **106**:128
"Rima XXX" (Bécquer) **106**:170
"Rima XXXIV" (Bécquer) **106**:150
"Rima XXXVII" (Bécquer) **106**:126-27
Rimas (Bécquer) **106**:92, 96, 99, 101, 109-10, 112, 118, 123, 125, 130, 137, 142, 167-75
Las rimas (Bécquer)
See *Rimas*
Rimas (Casal) **131**:255, 269-71
Rimas (Echeverria) **18**:147-49, 152-54
"Rimas II" (Bécquer)
See "Rima II"
"Rimas III" (Bécquer)
See "Rima III"
"The Rime" (Coleridge)
See *The Rime of the Ancient Mariner: A Poet's Reverie*
"The Rime of the Ancient Mariner" (Coleridge)
See *The Rime of the Ancient Mariner: A Poet's Reverie*
The Rime of the Ancient Mariner: A Poet's Reverie (Coleridge) **9**:130-32, 138-44, 146, 148-53, 156, 158-59, 164-67, 175-77, 179-89, 191, 194, 204, 210-12; **54**:65-132; **99**:2, 4-7, 19, 25, 41, 56, 65-6, 89, 94, 101, 104; **111**:197, 199-200, 239, 248-51, 256, 259, 289-95, 305-9, 311-16, 322, 332
"The Rime of the Ancient Waggoner" (Maginn) **8**:438
The Rime of the Ancyent Marinere (Coleridge)
See *The Rime of the Ancient Mariner: A Poet's Reverie*
Rime of the Merrie Devil of Edmonton (Horne) **127**:255
Rimes dorées (Banville) **9**:18
Rinaldo Rinaldini (Dunlap) **2**:211
"The Ring" (Baratynsky)
See "Persten'"
"The Ring" (Tennyson) **30**:226; **115**:247
"The Ring and the Book" (Tennyson) **115**:235
The Ring and the Book (Browning) **19**:80-3, 88, 90, 92, 94-6, 98, 102, 110-11, 114, 118-

19, 126-28, 133, 135, 142, 148, 152, 154-58; **79**:111, 116-21, 123, 125-27, 129-34, 149-53, 156, 161, 163-66, 180, 182, 184, 187, 189-90
The Ring and the Book (Tennyson) **115**:269
"The Ring and the Books" (Gordon) **21**:179
The Ring Cycle (Wagner)
See *Der Ring des Nibelungen*
Der Ring des Nibelungen (Wagner) **9**:409-10, 412-14, 416-17, 419, 421-22, 424-29, 433, 435, 437-38, 440-42, 444-50, 452, 458-60, 462-65, 469-71, 473-74; **119**:175, 182-83, 185-88, 190, 195-98, 203-17, 219-31, 233-38, 241-43, 248, 259, 264, 274-83, 289-93, 295, 300, 305, 308-11, 316-23, 329, 346-56
"Der Ring des Polylcrates" (Schiller) **39**:330, 337, 388
"The Ring Fetter" (Cooke) **110**:34, 41, 46, 51, 56, 58, 65
"The Ring Given to Venus" (Morris) **4**:448
Ring of Gyges (Hebbel)
See *Gyges und sein Ring: Eine Tragödie in fünf Acten*
"The Ring of Polycrates" (Schiller)
See "Der Ring des Polylcrates"
The Ring of the Nibelung (Wagner)
See *Der Ring des Nibelungen*
"Ringan and May" (Hogg) **4**:282-83
Ringan Gilhaize (Galt) **1**:333-34; **110**:107-12
"Rings" (Barnes) **75**:46
"Río Moro" (Isaacs) **70**:309
The Riot; or, Half a Loaf Is Better than No Bread (More) **27**:358-59
"Rioters" (Martineau) **26**:309
The Rioters (Martineau) **137**:264-65, 267
"Rip Van Winkle" (Irving) **2**:366-68, 376-79, 381-83, 386, 389-92; **19**:327-29, 331-39, 341, 345, 347-48, 350; **95**:227, 235-36, 240, 243, 245, 247, 249-50, 265, 283, 286, 300
Rip Van Winkle (Boucicault) **41**:31
"Rippling Water" (Gordon) **21**:160, 181
Riquet with the Tuft (Planché) **42**:278-80, 287, 298
"The Rise and Fall of the European Drama" (Lewes) **25**:302
Rise and Fall of the Free City-States of Greece (Humboldt) **134**:186
"Rise and Progress of Navigation" (Rowson) **69**:115
"Rise O Days from Your Fathomless Deeps" (Whitman) **81**:313, 330
The Rise of Iskander (Disraeli) **39**:24, 40, 46; **79**:214-14, 228, 274-75;
Risen from the Ranks; or, Harry Walton's Success (Alger) **8**:24; **83**:104, 131
"The Rising Glory of America" (Brackenridge) **7**:54, 57
"The Rising Glory of America" (Freneau) **111**:101, 113, 157-58
"The Rising of the Nations" (Chivers) **49**:75
The Rising Son; or, The Antecedents and Advancements of the Colored Race (Brown) **2**:48-51, 53; **89**:161, 163-64
"Rispah" (Bryant) **6**:162
Rite of the Graces (Foscolo) **97**:53
"Der Ritt in den Tod" (Meyer) **81**:142, 207-09
"The Ritter Bann" (Campbell) **19**:176, 190
Ritter Blaubart (Tieck) **5**:513, 515, 517, 521-23
"Ritter Glück" (Hoffmann) **2**:345, 361
"Ritter Kurts Brautfahrt" (Goethe) **4**:192
"The Rival Painters. A Tale of Rome" (Alcott) **83**:5
The Rival Races; or, The Sons of Joel (Sue)
See *Les mystères du peuple*
"The Rival Roses" (Crawford) **12**:172; **127**:182, 184
The Rivals (Griffin) **7**:195, 201, 213-14, 218
The Rivals (Sheridan) **5**:354-55, 357-63, 365, 369-73, 375-76, 378-83; **91**:236-37, 239-41, 245-48, 251-54, 256-64, 266-70
"The River" (Bryant) **6**:175
"The River" (Hayne) **94**:159, 161-62
"River" (Patmore) **9**:326-27, 348
"The River and the Hill" (Kendall) **12**:178
"The River, By Night" (Bryant) **46**:22
"The River Cherwell" (Bowles)
See "To the River Cherwell, Oxford"
"The River Gwash" (Clare) **9**:72
"The River Itchin" (Bowles)
See "To the River Itchin, Near Winton"
"River of beauty flowing through the life" (Fuller) **50**:250
"The River of Death" (Cranch) **115**:49
"The River Path" (Whittier) **8**:531
"The River Rhone" (Longfellow) **45**:121
"The River Swelleth More and More" (Thoreau) **7**:383
"Rivers Don't Gi'e Out" (Barnes) **75**:88
La rivoluzione francese del 1789 e la rivoluzione italiana del 1859: Osservazioni comparative (Manzoni) **98**:216, 276-78
"The Rivulet" (Bryant) **6**:159, 169; **46**:8, 13, 15, 39, 48
"Rivulet" (Whitman) **4**:551
"Rizpah" (Bryant) **46**:43
"Rizpah" (Kendall) **12**:192
"Rizpah" (Tennyson) **30**:245
Rjeĉnik (Karadzic) **115**:77, 104
"Road along the Precipice in Czufut-Kale" (Mickiewicz)
See "Droga nad przepascic w Czufut-Kale"
"The Road from Station almala to the Post at Mugansa" (Bestuzhev)
See "Doroga ot stantsii Almaly do posta Mugansy"
"The Road to Avernus" (Gordon) **21**:155, 160, 163, 167-68, 187-88
The Road to Ruin (Holcroft) **85**:192-93, 195, 204-07, 209, 221-23, 225, 234, 239
"The Road to Russia" (Mickiewicz) **3**:401
"A Road-side Post-office" (Cooper) **129**:71
Rob of the Bowl: A Legend of St. Inigoe's (Kennedy) **2**:429-33
Rob Roy (Scott) **15**:300, 303-04; **69**:310, 313; **110**:305
"The Robber" (Clare) **86**:103
"The Robber" (Opie) **65**:159
The Robber Brothers (Pushkin)
See *Bratya Razboiniki*
The Robbers (Schiller)
See *Die Raüber*
"The Robber's Song to His Mistress" (Ridge) **82**:180
"A Robbery" (Leskov)
See "Grabež"
The Robbery (Dunlap) **2**:214
"Robert Burns" (Halleck) **47**:56, 65, 69, 71, 78, 83
"Robert Burns" (Thomson) **18**:414
Robert der Teufel (Nestroy) **42**:225-26
Robert Guiskard, Herzog der Normänner (Kleist) **2**:437-38, 440-43, 445; **37**:217, 219, 223, 229, 255, 267, 272
Robert le Diable (Scribe) **16**:390, 408, 411
"Robert of Lincoln" (Bryant) **6**:165, 169, 182
"Robert Slender's Idea of a Visit to a Modern Great Man" (Freneau) **111**:134
"Robert Slender's Idea of the Human Soul" (Freneau) **111**:132
Robert the Devil (Scribe)
See *Robert le Diable*
"The Robin" (Very) **9**:380
"The Robin and the Violet" (Field) **3**:205
"Robin Redbreast" (Allingham) **25**:7
Robinson Crusoë (Pixérécourt) **39**:278-79, 281-82
"Los robles" (Castro) **3**:103
"La Roche" (Mackenzie)
See "The Effects of Religion on Minds of Sensibility. Story of La Roche"
"The Rock and the Sea" (Tyutchev)
See "The Sea and the Cliff"
Rock Crystal (Stifter)
See *Bergkristall*
"The Rock of Cader-Idris" (Hemans) **71**:277, 306
"Rock of the Candle" (Griffin) **7**:198
"The Rock-a-by-Lady" (Field) **3**:210
The Rockite, an Irish Story (Tonna) **135**:203
The Rocky Mountains; Or, Scenes, Incidents, and Adventures in the Far West (Irving) **95**:258
The Rod, the Root, and the Flower (Patmore) **9**:344, 354, 363-64
"De røde Sko" (Andersen) **79**:76
Roderick: The Last of the Goths (Southey) **8**:454-56, 459, 461, 469-71, 474, 476, 478-79; **97**:261-62, 268-69, 278-79, 291, 293-94, 297-300, 330-338
"Rodina" (Lermontov) **5**:295; **126**:144, 190-91, 213
"Rodina" (Nekrasov) **11**:412, 418, 420
"Rodman the Keeper" (Woolson) **82**:294-95, 297, 300-02
Rodman the Keeper: Southern Sketches (Woolson) **82**:268-69, 272-73, 283, 292-94, 299, 303-04, 306-07, 338-39
"Rodolph" (Pinkney) **31**:267, 269-70, 273, 275-77, 279, 281
"Roger Bontemps" (Beranger) **34**:34
"Roger Malvin's Burial" (Hawthorne) **2**:298; **23**:201; **39**:197, 200; **79**:311; **95**:115, 147
A Rogue's Life (Collins) **93**:38
"Le Roi candaule" (Gautier) **1**:344-45; **59**:10-11, 13-14, 31-3
"Le roi de Bicêtre" (Nerval) **1**:483, 485; **67**:335
Le roi de Ladawa (Slowacki) **15**:368
"Roi d'Yvetot" (Beranger) **34**:39
Le roi Pépin (Dumas) **71**:219
Le roi s'amuse (Hugo) **3**:236, 239, 241, 261-62, 269
Les rois en exil (Daudet) **1**:233-37, 239-41, 243-44, 247, 250-51
"Roisin Dubh" (Mangan) **27**:307, 318
Roland Cashel (Lever) **23**:292, 295, 301, 311
"The Role of the National Literature in the Public Spirit" (Eminescu) **33**:257
"The Role of the Semitic Peoples in the History of Civilization" (Renan) **26**:421
"The Role Played by Labor in the Transition from Ape to Man" (Engels) **85**:38-42, 95
"The Roll of Fame" (Chivers) **49**:51
"The Roll of the Kettledrum; or, The Lay of the Last Charger" (Gordon) **21**:154, 156, 159, 177, 181
"Rolla" (Musset) **7**:255, 258-64, 274
"Le roman" (Maupassant)
See *Etude sur le roman*
"Roman" (Rimbaud) **35**:290; **82**:224
Roman (Dobell) **43**:40, 42, 44, 49-51, 53-6, 59-60, 62, 74
"Roman and Olga" (Bestuzhev)
See "Starinnaia povest'—Roman i Ol'ga"
The Roman and the Teuton (Kingsley) **35**:246, 253
Le Roman de Charles Cecil (Charriere) **66**:126
Le Roman de la momie (Gautier) **1**:340, 342, 344-45, 347; **59**:6, 12, 56, 58-59, 61
Le Roman d'un Jeune Homme Pauvre (Feuillet) **45**:74-5, 78-9, 84-5, 87-9
Roman Elegies (Goethe)
See *Römische Elegien*
"The Roman Fountain" (Meyer)
See "Der römische Brunnen"
The Roman Matron (Tieck)
See *Vittoria Accorombona*
"Roman Rose-Seller" (Crawford) **12**:161
Roman tragique (Nerval) **1**:486; **67**:325, 328-31
Roman v pismakh (Pushkin) **3**:447; **83**:319-20, 323, 331
Roman v semi pis'makh (Bestuzhev) **131**:172, 210-11
"Romance" (Poe) **117**:195, 227, 231-32, 240, 244, 260

"Romance" (Scott) **110**:285-6
Romance and Reality (Landon) **15**:156-58, 164
"Le romance de Doña Blanca" (Leconte de Lisle) **29**:225
A Romance in Letters (Pushkin)
See *Roman v pismakh*
"The Romance in Real Life" (Sedgwick) **98**:304
The Romance of a Mummy (Gautier)
See *Le Roman de la momie*
Romance of a Poor Young Man (Feuillet)
See *Le Roman d'un Jeune Homme Pauvre*
The Romance of a Shop (Levy) **59**:76-7, 86-7, 90, 92, 95, 98, 102-5, 108, 113-5, 119
"The Romance of Britomarte" (Gordon) **21**:149, 154-56, 160, 163, 175, 183, 188
"Romance of Immortality" (Hawthorne) **2**:335
Romance of Ladybank (Oliphant) **11**:447
"A Romance of the Age" (Browning)
See "Lady Geraldine's Courtship"
The Romance of the Forest (Radcliffe) **6**:403-06, 409, 411, 413-16, 419-20, 423-27, 429-31, 435, 443-45; **55**:226, 228-35, 244-5, 250, 252-8, 261; **106**:283, 341-45, 349
"A Romance of the Ganges" (Browning) **61**:30-1, 64-5, 67,70
"Romance of the Lily" (Beddoes) **3**:34
Romance of the Republic (Child) **6**:203-05, 209; **73**:54, 63, 72, 84
"The Romance of the Swan's Nest" (Browning) **1**:113, 125; **61**:43, 65, 73; **66**:44
"The Romance of Travelling" (Hale) **75**:356, 359
A Romance of Vienna (Trollope) **30**:319
Romancero (Heine)
See *Romanzero*
Romances sans paroles (Verlaine) **2**:617, 620-21, 623, 629-32; **51**:350, 352-53, 355, 357, 359, 361-63, 365-66, 368, 370, 376-77, 379-85, 387
Romanees and Ballads (Mickiewicz)
See *Ballady i Romanse*
"Romanes Lecture" (Huxley) **67**:4
"Romania's Historical Development" (Eminescu)
See "Dezvoltarea istorica a României"
Romano Lavo-Lil: Word Book of the Romany; or, English Gypsy Language (Borrow) **9**:46-47
Romans et Contes (Gautier) **59**:36-7
Romanstudien (Ludwig) **4**:357, 359-60
Romantic Ballads (Borrow) **9**:54
A Romantic Idea (Planché) **42**:294
"The Romantic School" (Heine)
See "Die Romantische Schule"
The Romantic School (Heine)
See "Die Romantische Schule"
"Romantic Sunset" (Baudelaire)
See "Le coucher du soleil romantique"
"Romanticism" (Pater) **90**:292, 294, 322-23, 325
Romanticism (Mickiewicz)
See *Romantycznoś*
"Die Romantische Schule" (Heine) **4**:233-34, 252, 259, 264; **54**:337, 344
Romantycznoś (Mickiewicz) **3**:393, 399
"Romantyczność" (Mickiewicz) **3**:405
"The Romany Girl" (Emerson) **1**:279; **38**:193
The Romany Rye: A Sequel to "Lavengro" (Borrow) **9**:45-6, 48, 51-6, 60-3, 65, 66-9
Romanzen (Heine) **4**:248, 250
Romanzen und Bilder (Meyer) **81**:146, 152, 199, 208
Romanzero (Heine) **4**:238-39, 240-41, 247, 252-56, 268
"The Romaunt of Margret" (Browning) **61**:53, 56, 58, 64-5, 70-1, 74
"The Romaunt of the Page" (Browning) **1**:115, 117, 124; **61**:43, 64-7, 70-5; **66**:56
"Rome" (Gogol) **5**:227, 256; **31**:137
"Rome" (Pavlova)
See "Rim"
"Rome and the World" (Brownson) **50**:54
"The Rome Egg Affair" (Harris) **23**:151
Rome, Naples, et Florence (Stendhal) **23**:352, 410
Romeo et Juliette (Dumas) **71**:218
Romeo und Julia auf dem Dorfe (Keller) **2**:411-17, 424
"Rome's Holiday" (Pavlova)
See "Prazdnik Rima"
Romiero (Baillie) **2**:39-40; **71**:3
"Romilly and Wilberforce" (Landor) **14**:166
"Der römische Brunnen" (Meyer) **81**:200-01
Römische Elegien (Goethe) **4**:165, 176, 193, 207
Romola (Eliot) **118**:49, 58-60, 62, 105, 129, 136
Romulus (Dumas) **71**:210
"Ronald and Helen" (Thomson) **18**:405-06
"Roncesvalles" (Bécquer) **106**:158
"Ronda" (Silva) **114**:294
"La ronde sous la cloche" (Bertrand) **31**:49
"Rondeau" (Hunt) **1**:423; **70**:264
"Rondeau" (Musset) **7**:267
"The Rooks" (Barnes) **75**:34, 40
Rookwood (Ainsworth) **13**:15-18, 20-1, 29, 31-2, 34-7, 40
"The Room in the Dragon Volant" (Le Fanu) **9**:317; **58**:251, 264, 266, 302
"Root Bound" (Cooke) **110**:16
Rootbound (Cooke)
See *Root-Bound and Other Sketches*
Root-Bound and Other Sketches (Cooke) **110**:18, 21, 39, 43
"The Roots of the Mountains" (Morris) **4**:435, 437
"The Rope" (Baudelaire)
See "La corde"
"The Ropewalk" (Longfellow) **2**:492; **45**:162, 167, 187
"Rory and Darborgilla" (Mangan) **27**:275
"Ros Gheal Dubh" (Mangan) **27**:307-08
"Rosa" (Harpur) **114**:138
"La Rosa Blanca" (Martí) **63**:84
"La rosa de pasión" (Bécquer) **106**:90
"Rosa Mystica" (Hopkins) **17**:191
Rosa; or, The Black Tulip (Dumas)
See *La tulipe noire*
Rosa; ou, L'ermitage du torrent (Pixérécourt) **39**:291, 295
"Rosabelle" (Scott) **15**:318
"Rosalie" (Allston) **2**:21
"Rosalie Lee" (Chivers) **49**:46, 49, 52-3, 74
"Rosalie Prudent" (Maupassant) **83**:215-16
Rosaliens Briefe (La Roche) **121**:242, 250, 265-66, 269-71, 276, 279, 325-26
Rosalind and Helen (Shelley) **18**:313, 329, 336, 343-44
"Rosamund" (Ingelow) **39**:258, 264
Rosamund, A Sequel To Early Lessons (Edgeworth) **51**:78, 81, 108, 110
Rosamund Gray (Lamb) **10**:397, 400, 404-05, 409, 411; **113**:230, 281, 284
"Rosanna" (Edgeworth) **1**:265; **51**:87
"Roscoe" (Irving) **2**:392; **19**:350; **95**:265
"The Rose" (Cowper) **8**:119
"Rose" (Sainte-Beuve) **5**:333
Rose and Ninette (Daudet)
See *Rose et Ninette*
The Rose and the Key (Le Fanu) **58**:273
"The Rose and the Rainbow" (Crawford) **12**:172; **127**:182
Rose and the Ring (Thackeray) **5**:454, 469
"Rose Aylmer" (Landor) **14**:176, 183, 193, 199
Rose, Blanche, and Violet (Lewes) **25**:273-74, 286, 293, 298
Rose Clark (Parton) **86**:324, 333-35, 337, 339-44, 366-67
"La rose de l'infant" (Hugo) **3**:273
"The Rose Did Caper on Her Cheek" (Dickinson) **21**:63
"The Rose Elf" (Andersen) **7**:34
Rose et Blanche (Sand) **2**:606; **42**:316-17, 352-53, 355
Le rose et le vert (Stendhal) **23**:410, 419
Rose et Ninette (Daudet) **1**:237, 239, 244, 251
The Rose Family. A Fairy Tale (Alcott) **58**:48
Rose in Bloom (Alcott) **6**:18; **58**:4, 69; **83**:28, 47
"A Rose in His Grace" (Crawford) **127**:181, 188
A Rose in June (Oliphant) **11**:439, 447; **61**:173, 206-7
"Rose Knows Those Bows' Woes" (Hood) **16**:222
"Rose Lorraine" (Kendall) **12**:193, 201
"Rose Mary" (Rossetti) **4**:499-501, 505-07, 512-13, 518-19, 526-27, 531-32; **77**:326, 328-30
"The Rose of a Nation's Thanks" (Crawford) **127**:153, 221
"The Rose of Newport" (Meyer)
See "Die Rose von Newport"
"Rose on the Heath" (Goethe)
See "Heidenröslein"
"Die Rose von Newport" (Meyer) **81**:207, 209
"Rose Wreath" (Klopstock) **11**:230
"Les Roseaux" (Desbordes-Valmore) **97**:15
"The Rosebud" (Keble) **87**:176
"Rose-Morals" (Lanier) **118**:215
"Rosenzeit" (Mörike) **10**:451
Roses de Noël (Banville) **9**:29-30
"Les Roses de Saadi" (Desbordes-Valmore) **97**:13, 20, 27
"Les roses d'Ispahan" (Leconte de Lisle) **29**:224
Roslavlev (Pushkin) **3**:435
"Rosmowa wieczorna" (Mickiewicz) **3**:405
Rosmunda (Alfieri) **101**:8, 38
"Le rossignol" (Lamartine) **11**:255
"Le Rossignol" (Verlaine) **51**:361
"Rosy O'Ryan" (Child) **73**:132-34
"Rosz verseimröl" (Petofi) **21**:278
"Rotation Method" (Kierkegaard) **125**:178, 193, 207-8, 280
"Die Rotentaler Herren" (Gotthelf) **117**:44, 48, 58
Rothelan (Galt) **1**:334
"A Rotting Corpse" (Baudelaire)
See "Une charogne"
Les Roués innocents (Gautier) **1**:350; **59**:12
Le rouge et le noir (Stendhal) **23**:348-49, 352-54, 356-64, 369-70, 373-74, 376-77, 383-89, 392-93, 395-98, 400, 404-05, 408-09, 411-12, 415-18, 420-24, 426; **46**:251-330
Rough and Ready; or, Life among the New York Newsboys (Alger) **8**:15, 37
"A Rough Rhyme on a Rough Matter" (Kingsley) **35**:228
Roughing It in the Bush (Moodie) **113**:292-93, 295-304, 306-8, 311, 318, 323-38, 344-54, 358-49, 361, 364, 367-74
Roughing It in the Bush; or, Life in Canada (Moodie) **14**:215-41, 243-44
"La rouille" (Maupassant) **83**:231-32
Round about a Great Estate (Jefferies) **47**:103, 111-12, 133, 137, 142
"The Round Table" (Tennyson) **65**:241
Roundabout Papers (Thackeray) **5**:466, 473, 485, 490, 506-07; **43**:350
"The Rounded Catalogue Divine Complete" (Whitman) **31**:435
"Rousseau" (Hölderlin) **16**:194
"Rousseau and the Sentimentalists" (Lowell) **2**:509
La route de Thèbes (Dumas) **9**:231, 246
"A Route of Evanescence" (Dickinson) **21**:31, 49; **77**:95, 121
"The Route to the Town of Kuba" (Bestuzhev)
See "Put' do goroda Kuby"
A Rover on Life's Path (Smolenskin)
See *ha-To'eh be-darke ha-hayim*
"The Royal Ascetic and the Hind" (Dutt) **29**:123, 126, 130
"The Royal Jubilee" (Hogg) **109**:200

"A Royal Poet" (Irving)
See "The Royal Poet"
"The Royal Poet" (Irving) **19**:347, 350; **95**:266
"A Royal Princess" (Rossetti) **66**:331
The Royal Suitors (Horne) **127**:256
"Royalists of Peru" (Gore) **65**:21
"Royauté" (Rimbaud) **4**:484; **35**:322, 324-25
"Roz goniné" (Arany) **34**:24
"Rozmowa" (Mickiewicz) **101**:185
"Rozryta mohyla" (Shevchenko) **54**:378
Der Rubin: Ein Märchen-Lustspiel in drei Acten (Hebbel) **43**:258, 289
"Rückblick" (Muller) **73**:392,394
"Rückblick in die Jahre der Kindheit" (Brentano) **1**:105
Rudin (Turgenev) **21**:388, 397-98, 400, 412-13, 418-19, 426, 432, 436-38, 442, 444-46, 448, 455, 457; **37**:364, 379, 382, 402, 444; **122**:249, 251-52, 254, 256, 261, 265, 271-72, 288, 292, 298, 303, 315
"Rudokop" (Pavlova) **138**:3-4, 12, 21, 33
Rudolf von Hapsburg und Ottokar von Bohmen (Kotzebue) **25**:137
Rudolph (Beddoes) **3**:33
Rudolph Prinz von Korsika (Nestroy) **42**:224
La Rue (Vallès) **71**:377
La Rue à Londres (Vallès) **71**:372-73, 375-76, 378
"Rue de l'eperon" (Banville) **9**:32
Une rue de Paris et son habitant (Balzac) **5**:51
"Une Ruelle de Flandres" (Desbordes-Valmore) **97**:14
"The Ruffian Boy" (Opie) **65**:162, 171
Rufus and Rose; or, The Fortunes of Rough and Ready (Alger) **8**:37
Rugantino (Lewis) **11**:305
"Ruhelechzend" (Heine) **4**:256
"The Ruin of the Year" (Lampman) **25**:210
"The Ruined Chapel" (Allingham) **25**:24
"The Ruined Cottage" (Wordsworth) **12**:397; **38**:362, 364, 390; **111**:241, 260-61, 263-68, 282
"The Ruined Inn" (Petofi)
See "A csárda romjai"
Les ruines de Babylone; ou, Le massacre des barmécides (Pixérécourt) **39**:276-77, 279, 290
"The Ruins of Ithaca" (Bryant) **6**:165
"Les ruisseau" (Banville) **9**:29
Rule and Misrule of the English in America (Haliburton) **15**:122, 128
"Rules and Directions how to Avoid Creditors, Sheriffs, Constables, etc" (Freneau) **111**:132
"Rules and Regulations" (Carroll) **139**:32, 61
"Rules how to get through a crowd" (Freneau) **111**:135
"The Rumble of Wheels" (Turgenev) **122**:293
"Rumors from an Aeolian Harp" (Thoreau) **7**:382
"Run to Death" (Levy) **59**:106-7
"The Runaway Slave at Pilgrim's Point" (Browning) **1**:118; **61**:9, 33-4, 43, 66-8
"Der Runenberg" (Tieck) **5**:514, 517, 519, 524-25, 529; **46**:339-45, 347-50, 360, 363, 365, 374-75, 377, 387-88, 390-92, 414
Runic Poetry (Percy)
See *Five Pieces of Runic Poetry Translated from the Islandic Language*
Runic Poetry translated from the Islandic Language (Percy)
See *Five Pieces of Runic Poetry Translated from the Islandic Language*
"Le Runoïa" (Leconte de Lisle) **29**:223, 225-26
Rupert's Ambition (Alger) **83**:114
"Rural Architecture" (Wordsworth) **111**:234
"Rural Felicity" (Hood) **16**:235
"Rural Funerals" (Irving) **2**:381; **19**:334
Rural Hours. By a Lady (Cooper) **129**:3-6, 9-10, 12-17, 19-22, 24-26, 28, 34-35, 37-39, 41-54, 57-59, 62, 65-68, 72-75, 77-78, 82-89
"Rural Life in England" (Irving) **19**:328, 334
"Rural Morning" (Clare) **9**:113
The Rural Muse (Clare) **9**:79-80, 85; **86**:125, 160
"A Rural Picture" (Harpur) **114**:144
Rural Rambles. By a Lady (Cooper) **129**:4, 68-69
Rural Rides (Cobbett) **49**:97, 99, 101, 105-08, 110, 114, 116, 118, 120, 122, 130-34, 140, 142, 145, 147, 150, 153-55, 159-60, 163-65, 168, 171
Rural Walks (Smith) **115**:173, 210
"Rusalka" (Lermontov) **5**:287
Rusalka (Pushkin) **3**:415, 434; **83**:333, 339
Une Ruse (Maupassant) **83**:229
La Ruse de l'amour (Sade) **47**:360-61
The Rush-Light (Cobbett) **49**:109
Ruslan and Lyudmila (Pushkin)
See *Ruslan i Lyudmila*
Ruslan i Lyudmila (Pushkin) **3**:409-11, 413, 415, 417, 421, 423, 443, 445, 450; **27**:379; **83**:242-43, 245, 247, 250, 332, 349
Der Russe in Deutschland (Kotzebue) **25**:133, 138-40, 145, 147
Russia (Gautier) **59**:5
"Russia and Revolution" (Tyutchev)
See "La Russie et la Révolution"
The Russiade (Hogg) **109**:271
"The Russiade; a Fragment of an Ancient Epic Poem" (Hogg) **4**:280; **109**:250
"Russian and Germany" (Tyutchev) **34**:382
"The Russian at a Rendez-Vous" (Chernyshevsky) **1**:162
"Russian Christianity versus Modern Judaism" (Lazarus) **8**:419, 421-22, 428; **109**:303, 306, 310, 319, 329, 336, 344
"Russian Civilization As Concocted by Mr. Zherebtsov" (Dobrolyubov) **5**:140
A Russian Gentleman (Aksakov)
See *Semeinaia khronika*
"Russian Geography" (Tyutchev) **34**:381
"A Russian Hamlet" (Turgenev)
See "Gamlet ščigrovskogo uezda"
"The Russian Historical Novel" (Dobrolyubov) **5**:140
"The Russian Language" (Turgenev)
See "Russkii iazyk"
Russian Life in the Interior (Turgenev)
See *Zapiski okhotnika*
A Russian Pelham (Pushkin) **3**:435, 447; **83**:273
The Russian People and Socialism (Herzen)
See *Le peuple russe et le Socialisme*
A Russian Schoolboy (Aksakov) **2**:13-14
"The Russian Tale and the Tales of Gogol" (Belinski) **5**:97
Russian Women (Nekrasov) **11**:400, 404-05, 409, 414-18
"La Russie et la Révolution" (Tyutchev) **34**:382-83, 404
"Russkie vtorostepennye poety" (Nekrasov) **11**:422-24
"Russkii iazyk" (Turgenev) **21**:420; **122**:308, 313
"Rustem and Zorav" (Zhukovsky) **35**:378
"Rustic Childhood" (Barnes) **75**:15, 85
Rustic Songs (Muller)
See *Ländliche Lieder*
"Rustic Venus" (Maupassant)
See "La venus rustique"
"Rusticus Dolens; or, Inclosures of Common" (Barnes)
See "The Common A-Took In"
"Rusticus Emigrans or Over Sea to Settle" (Barnes) **75**:43-4, 101
"Rusticus gaudens" (Barnes)
See "The 'Lotments"
"Rusticus Res Politicas Animadvertens" (Barnes)
See "The New Poor Laws"
"Ruszaj z Bogiem" (Norwid) **17**:373
"Ruth" (Crabbe) **26**:124
"Ruth" (Hood) **16**:219, 225-27, 234
"Ruth" (Wordsworth) **12**:402; **111**:213, 245, 294
Ruth (Gaskell) **5**:180-83, 185, 187-89, 191, 196-97, 204; **70**:119, 123, 146, 149-51, 185, 188, 190, 196, 198, 200, 219; **97**:127, 134; **137**:40, 167
"Ruth, A Short Drama From the Bible" (Barnes) **75**:70, 73-4
Ruth Hall (Parton)
See *Ruth Hall and Other Writings*
Ruth Hall and Other Writings (Parton) **86**:312, 316, 318, 320, 323-26, 328-35, 337, 339, 341-44, 346-47, 352-57, 359-62, 366-69, 373-74, 376-77
"Ruth's Secret" (Alcott) **83**:5
"Ruususolmu" (Kivi) **30**:51
Ruy Blas (Hugo) **3**:254, 257, 261, 269
"Rybak" (Zhukovsky) **35**:397, 407
"Rycar' na čas" (Nekrasov) **11**:400, 416, 418-20
Rzecz o wolności słowa (Norwid) **17**:369
"s persidskogo" (Bestuzhev) **131**:150
"S polyany korshun podnyalsya" (Tyutchev) **34**:398, 400
S togo berega (Herzen)
See *Vom andern Ufer*
A Sa Majesté le tzar Nicolas (Comte) **54**:211
"Sa Majesté Très Chrétienne" (Clough) **27**:103
"Saadi" (Emerson) **1**:296; **98**:179
"Saatyr" (Bestuzhev) **131**:151
Sab (Gómez de Avellaneda) **111**:8-9, 12, 14-18, 20-2, 29, 33-6, 38-9, 42-6, 54-62, 64, 69-72, 74-5
"The Sabbath Bell" (Sigourney) **21**:310
"Sabbath Bells" (Clare) **9**:105
"Sabbath Lays" (Barnes) **75**:70, 74
"A Sabbath Scene" (Whittier) **59**:364, 366
"Sabbath Sonnet" (Hemans) **71**:270
"The Sabbath's-Day Child" (Coleridge) **90**:33
"The Sabbatia" (Very) **9**:372
"¿Sabéis por qué la amo?" (Isaacs) **70**:307
The Sack of Rome (Warren) **13**:412-14, 418-19, 424, 429-30, 436
"Sacra fames" (Leconte de Lisle) **29**:222, 230
Sacred and Legendary Art (Jameson)
See *The Poetry of Sacred and Legendary Art*
Sacred Dramas: Chiefly Intended for Young Persons, the Subjects Taken from the Bible (More) **27**:332
"The Sacred Fire" (Meyer)
See "Das heilige Feuer"
Sacred Hymns (Manzoni)
See *Inni Sacri*
"The Sacred marriage" (Fuller) **50**:249, 251
Sacred Melodies (Moore) **6**:382
"Sacred Memories" (Lanier) **118**:241
"Sacred Pleasure" (Mallarmé) **41**:254, 259
"Sacred Poetry" (Keble) **87**:153
Sacred Songs of Novalis (Novalis)
See *Geistliche Lieder*
"Sacred to the Memory of Lord Nelson" (Hemans) **71**:272
"Sacrifice" (Emerson) **1**:290
Sacrificial Death (Kotzebue)
See *Der Opfertod*
"The Sad Fortunes of the Rev. Amos Barton" (Eliot) **4**:92, 98, 117, 120, 125; **23**:57; **41**:101, 106-09; **89**:228; **118**:103
"Sadly Wails the Wind" (Pavlova)
See "Grustno veter voet"
"Sad Occurrence That Took Place in the Year 1809" (Zhukovsky) **35**:384
"The Sad Wind of Autumn Speaks to the Trees..." (Petofi)
See "Beszel a fákkal..."
"Säerspruch" (Meyer) **81**:140-41, 148-49, 155-56
"Safe in their Alabaster Chambers" (Dickinson) **77**:71
"The Saga of Ahab Doolittle" (Taylor) **89**:338
"The Saga of King Olaf" (Longfellow) **45**:115, 132, 137, 145, 148-49, 155
The Saga of Mankind (Almqvist)
See *Människosläkets saga*

"sāgare tari" (Dutt) **118**:30
Un Sage (Maupassant) **83**:831
"Sages" (Mickiewicz) **3**:399
"La sagesse" (Lamartine) **11**:254
Sagesse (Verlaine) **2**:617-21, 624-25, 627-28, 632; **51**:351-53, 355-59, 364-65, 368, 370, 372, 376, 382, 384, 388
Saggio sopra gli errori popolari degli antichi (Leopardi) **129**:230-31
Sägner (Runeberg)
See *Fänrik Ståls sägner*
"Said the Canoe" (Crawford) **12**:156, 167, 171; **127**:171-73, 179-81, 200-02
"Said the Daisy" (Crawford) **12**:156
"Said the Skylark" (Crawford) **12**:161, 171
"Said the Thistle-Down" (Crawford) **127**:170
"Said the West Wind" (Crawford) **12**:156
"Said the Wind" (Crawford) **12**:161
"The Sail" (Lermontov) **126**:129, 144, 223
"The Sailer" (Dyer) **129**:96
"Sailing Beyond Seas" (Ingelow) **39**:264; **107**:123-24
"The Sailing of the Sword" (Morris) **4**:431
"The Sailor" (Allingham) **25**:7-8
"Sailor" (Crabbe) **26**:100
"The Sailor" (Mickiewicz) **3**:392
"The Sailor" (Pavlova)
See "Plovec"
"A Sailor" (Rogers) **69**:67
The Sailor (Shevchenko)
See *Matros*
"The Sailor Boy" (Tennyson) **65**:373, 376
"The Sailor Uncle" (Lamb)
See "Elizabeth Villiers: The Sailor Uncle"
"The Sailor's Funeral" (Sigourney) **21**:304
"The Sailor's Mother" (Wordsworth) **12**:426; **111**:273-74
"The Sailor's Relief" (Freneau) **111**:134
The Saint (Meyer)
See *Der Heilige*
"Saint Agnes of Intercession" (Rossetti) **4**:504, 510; **77**:241, 331-34, 336
"Saint Benoit Joseph Labre" (Verlaine) **51**:359
"Saint Cecilia" (Kleist)
See *Die heilige Cäcilie; oder, die Gewalt der Musik*
"Saint Guido" (Jefferies) **47**:137
"St. John's Eve" (Gogol)
See "Večer nakanune Ivana Kupala"
"Saint Julien" (Flaubert)
See *La légende de Saint-Julien l'Hospitalier*
"Saint Monica" (Smith) **23**:321, 323; **115**:119, 121
"Saint Olaf's Fountain" (Boyesen) **135**:5
Saint Patrick's Eve (Lever) **23**:275-76, 307
Saint Paul (Renan) **26**:372, 402, 408, 420-21
"St. Petersburg Notes of 1836" (Gogol) **31**:137
"Saint Romualdo" (Lazarus) **109**:294
"Saint the First" (Cooke) **110**:18, 35
"Saint the Second" (Cooke) **110**:18
Saint-Anne (Charriere) **66**:125, 172, 178
"Sainte" (Mallarmé) **4**:378
"La sainte alliance des peuples" (Beranger) **34**:29
" Sainte Cécile jouant sur l'aile d'un chérubin" (Mallarmé) **41**:289-90
"A Sainte-Beuve" (Banville) **9**:26
"Sainte-Pélagie en 1832" (Nerval) **67**:332, 336
"Saintliness the Standard of Christian Principle" (Newman) **38**:305
"The Saints' Rest" (Dickinson)
See "Of Tribulation These Are They"
The Saint's Tragedy (Kingsley) **35**:204, 209, 211-13, 218-19, 222, 226, 249
"Saint-Tupetu de Tu-pe-tu" (Corbière) **43**:28
La Saisiaz (Browning) **19**:106, 110-12, 134
Une saison en enfer (Rimbaud) **4**:453-54, 456-66, 468-74, 476-83, 486; **35**:266, 270-71, 275-78, 282-83, 289,291, 294, 297-98, 302, 304-05, 307, 309-13, 314-15, 317, 320-21; **82**:218-30, 232-34, 236-38, 240-45, 247-48, 250, 252-55, 257, 259-60, 262-63
"Sakontalá" (Tyutchev) **34**:412
Die Salamandrin und die Bildsäule (Wieland) **17**:410-11
Salambo (Flaubert)
See *Salammbô*
Salammbô (Flaubert) **2**:226-8, 230-4, 236-9, 242-4, 246-7, 249, 251-2, 255-6; **10**:125, 145; **19**:268, 273, 276-8, 299-300, 302, 304, 307-8, 313, 317; **62**:80, 92, 98, 109-20, 123; **66**:293; **135**:77-86, 88-103, 109, 111-15, 117-19, 121-29, 131, 133-38, 141-43, 145-53, 155-57, 166-67, 169-78, 180-84
"Salas y Gomez" (Chamisso) **82**:6, 21, 27, 30
"A Sale" (Maupassant) **1**:457
"The Sale of the Pet Lamb" (Collins) **93**:63
Salem Chapel (Oliphant) **11**:429-31, 445, 447-9, 454-7, 459, 463; **61**:162-9, 172, 174-7, 180, 183, 197-8, 202, 216, 226-7
"Salida del señor Nicanor Puchol en Pelayo" (Larra) **130**:250
Salisbury Plain (Wordsworth) **111**:253, 261, 263-65, 267-68, 273, 311
La salle d'armes (Dumas) **11**:58
"Sally Parson's Duty" (Cooke) **110**:35
Salmagundi (Irving) **95**:219, 221-23, 225-27, 275, 291-93, 295-96
Salmagundi; or, The Whim-Whams and Opinions of Launcelot Langstaff, Esq., and Others (Irving and Paulding) **2**:525
Salmagundian Essays (Irving) **95**:219-21
"Salomé" (Casal) **131**:223, 225-26, 235, 265-66, 268
"Salomé" (Laforgue) **5**:269-71, 274, 278, 280-1; **53**:292, 293-4
"Salome" (Lamb) **125**:375-76
Der Salon (Heine) **4**:235, 262, 264, 268-69
Le salon de 1845 (Baudelaire) **29**:79-80
Le salon de 1846 (Baudelaire) **6**:81; **29**:100; **55**:8, 36
Le salon de 1859 (Baudelaire) **29**:79; **55**:43
The Salon; or, Letters on Art, Music, Popular Life, and Politics (Heine)
See *Der Salon*
"Salut" (Mallarmé) **41**:294
"Salut au Monde!" (Whitman) **4**:571, 578, 594; **31**:390, 398-99, 431; **81**:312, 319-20
"Salvator" (Dumas) **71**:185
Salvator Rosa (Hoffmann) **2**:340
Sam Slick's Wise Saws and Modern Instances; or, What He Said, Did, or Invented (Haliburton) **15**:126-27, 132, 135-36, 145
The Same Old Story (Goncharov)
See *Obyknovennaya istoriya*
Samlade skrifter (Stagnelius) **61**:248
Samlede digte (Andersen) **7**:19
Samlede Vaerker (Kierkegaard)
See *Soren Kierkegaards Samlede Vaerker*
Sämmtlich Werke (Schlegel) **45**:361
Sämmtliche Werke (Wieland) **17**:392-93
Sam's Chance; and How He Improved It (Alger) **83**:132-33, 139
"Samson" (Blake) **13**:182
Samson (Dumas) **71**:217
"Samson Agonistes" (Cooke) **110**:9
Samson's Anger (Vigny)
See "La colère de Samson"
Sämtliche Werke (Claudius) **75**:182-84, 201
Sämtliche Werke (Grillparzer) **102**:101, 106, 118, 170, 172, 187-88
Samuel Zborowski (Slowacki) **15**:360, 365, 371-72, 375-77
"San Antonio bendito" (Castro) **78**:40
"San Antonio de Bexar" (Lanier) **6**:245
San Francesco a Ripa (Stendhal) **23**:349
"San Juan de los Reyes" (Bécquer) **106**:146
Sancho García (Zorrilla y Moral) **6**:525
Sancho Saldaña (Espronceda) **39**:100, 110
"Sanct Joseph der Zweite" (Goethe) **4**:194, 197
"Sanctity the Token of the Christian Empire" (Newman) **38**:308
"Sanctuary" (Lenau) **16**:263, 277
Das Sanctus (Hoffmann) **2**:346
"Sandalphon" (Longfellow) **45**:116, 146
"Sandels" (Runeberg) **41**:314, 324-25
Sanditon—Fragments of a Novel (Austen) **1**:41-42, 46-47, 51-52, 54, 60-61; **33**:70, 72, 75, 77, 93; **95**:49; **119**:12, 18, 42-3, 46-7
"The Sandman" (Andersen)
See "Ole Lukōie"
"Sandro Botticelli" (Pater) **90**:334
"Sands at Seventy" (Whitman) **4**:563
"The Sands of Dee" (Kingsley) **35**:218-19, 226, 232
Le sang de la coupe (Banville) **9**:18-19
Le sanglot de la terre (Laforgue) **5**:275, 282-3; **53**:258-9, 269, 277, 279, 287, 289-90, 293
"Les Sanglots" (Desbordes-Valmore) **97**:8, 18, 20, 24
"Sanity of True Genius" (Lamb) **10**:432; **113**:218, 252
"Santa Cruz" (Freneau)
See "The Beauties of Santa Cruz"
"Santa Filomena" (Longfellow) **45**:116
"Santa Leocadia" (Bécquer) **106**:158
"Santo Domingo" (Douglass) **7**:126
Sapho (Daudet) **1**:237, 239, 242-44, 248-49, 251
Sapho (Staël-Holstein)
See *Sappho*
"Sapphics" (Lampman) **25**:202
Sappho (Daudet)
See *Sapho*
Sappho (Grillparzer) **1**:382-85, 387, 389, 397; **102**:81, 85, 91, 104, 108, 116-17, 147, 154-56, 180, 187
Sappho (Staël-Holstein) **91**:326, 359
Sappho's Slipper (Sacher-Masoch) **31**:298
"Sappho's Song" (Landon) **15**:165
"Sara la Baigneuse" (Hugo) **3**:261
Sara Videbeck (Almqvist)
See *Det går an*
Sarah de Berenger (Ingelow) **39**:261, 264; **107**:112-19, 124
Sarah; or, The Exemplary Wife (Rowson) **5**:311-13, 316, 319; **69**:103, 105, 113-14, 137
Sardanapale (Becque) **3**:16
Sardanapalus (Byron) **2**:66, 70, 79-81, 99; **12**:139; **109**:65, 102
Sardonic Tales (Villiers de l'Isle Adam)
See *Contes cruels*
"Sári néni" (Petofi) **21**:285
"Sarmanul Dionis" (Eminescu) **33**:245-47; **131**:315-17, 319, 334
"Sarmis" (Eminescu) **131**:290
Sarmisthā (Dutt) **118**:5, 20
Sarrasine (Balzac) **5**:46; **35**:22, 68-9-70
Sartor Resartus (Carlyle) **70**:7, 9, 22-24, 26-27, 31, 36-47, 49, 53, 56-58, 62-76, 87-88, 93, 95, 97-102, 108
"Sarum Close" (Patmore) **9**:362
"Sarum River" (Patmore) **9**:335
"Sasha" (Nekrasov) **11**:404, 407
"Sashka" (Lermontov)
See *Sashka*
Sashka (Lermontov) **126**:133-34, 138, 154
Satan: A Libretto (Cranch) **115**:17-18, 23, 26, 35-6, 55
Satanstoe; or, The Littlepage Manuscripts (Cooper) **1**:219-21; **54**:258, 279
"Satire III" (Eminescu) **131**:328-29
"A Satire on Satirists" (Horne) **127**:257
Satires (Krasicki)
See *Satyry*
Satiry v proze (Saltykov) **16**:368, 374
"The Satrap-Bear" (Saltykov) **16**:358
"Saturday in Holy Week" (Droste-Hülshoff) **3**:203
"Saturnian Poem" (Verlaine) **51**:368, 372
Saturnine Poems (Verlaine)
See *Les Poèmes saturniens*
"Le satyre" (Hugo) **3**:273; **21**:226
Satyry (Krasicki) **8**:398, 401, 403-07

"Saul" (Browning) **19**:111, 119, 129-32, 139; **79**:94, 102, 111
Saul (Alfieri) **101**:18-19, 22, 32, 41, 50, 54, 56, 79, 83, 87-8
"Le saule" (Musset) **7**:256, 273
Saulo (Isaacs) **70**:311-12
"Le Saut du berger" (Maupassant) **83**:169
"Le saut du Tremplin" (Banville) **9**:16, 25
"De Sauty" (Holmes) **14**:129
"La sauvage" (Vigny) **7**:472-73, 479-80; **102**:336
Sauvée (Maupassant) **83**:230
"Sauvegarde" (Mallarmé) **41**:294-98, 300, 304-05
"The Savage Landowner" (Saltykov) **16**:358
"Savannah Sesqui-Centennial Ode" (Hayne) **94**:145, 152
"Savitri" (Dutt) **29**:120-21, 124, 126, 128, 131
Savonarola (Lenau) **16**:263, 266, 268-70, 272-75, 279-81, 285
Savoyen, Nizza und der Rhein (Engels) **85**:83
"Say, by What Chance" (Pushkin)
See *Skazhi, Kakoi sud'boi*
"Say Not the Struggle Naught Availeth" (Clough) **27**:75, 77, 79
"Say, Tell Me . . ." (Bestuzhev)
See "Ty skazhi, govori . . ."
"The Scamper of Life" (Harpur) **114**:144
The Scandal (Alarcon)
See *El escándalo*
"The Scandinavian in the United States" (Boyesen) **135**:33
"Scar" (Woolson) **82**:273
Scarlet and Black (Stendhal)
See *Le rouge et le noir*
The Scarlet Letter (Hawthorne) **2**:295-96, 298, 305, 307, 309-12, 314-18, 320-32; **10**:269-317; **17**:110-12, 114, 116, 120, 122, 124, 128-29, 132, 146-147, 151-53, 156-57; **23**:168-69, 177-78, 183-84, 194-97, 205, 213-14, 220; **39**:167-68, 176-77, 180, 185, 187, 189-90, 195-97, 200, 220-22, 225, 227, 236-37, 239-40, 247, 249; **79**:290-92, 299, 308-11, 313, 327, 332; **95**:91, 109, 120, 123, 151, 170, 176, 178, 213
The Scarlet Shawl (Jefferies) **47**:91-92, 97, 116
Scaroni (Beddoes) **3**:38
"Sčast' e v dvux ètažax" (Leskov) **25**:258-59
Scattered Pages (Renan) **26**:422
"A Scene" (Clare) **9**:72
"A Scene" (Pavlova) **138**:35-36
"A Scene along the Rio de Las Plumas" (Ridge) **82**:184
Scene from Faust (Pushkin) **3**:446
"A Scene in a Workhouse" (Tonna) **135**:217
Scene in an Armchair (Musset)
See *Un spectacle dans un fauteuil*
"A Scene on the Banks of the Hudson" (Bryant) **46**:19-20, 38-41, 43
"Scènes" (Rimbaud) **82**:233
"Scenes and Hymns of Life" (Hemans) **71**:270
Scenes and Hymns of Life, with Other Religious Poems (Hemans) **29**:201
Scenes and Shadows of Days Departed, a Narrative (Bowles) **103**:54
"Scenes at a Target-Shooting" (Taylor) **89**:308
Scènes de la vie de province (Balzac) **5**:28-9, 31-2, 36; **53**:10, 31
Scènes de la vie militaire (Balzac) **5**:31-2
Scènes de la vie orientale (Nerval)
See *Voyage en Orient*
Scènes de la vie Parisienne (Balzac) **5**:28-29, 31, 36
Scènes de la vie politique (Balzac) **5**:31
Scènes et Comédies (Feuillet) **45**:88-9
Scènes et Proverbes (Feuillet) **45**:88
"Scenes from Life in Town" (Sedgwick) **19**:444
"Scenes from Politian" (Poe) **117**:227
Scenes from Russian Life (Turgenev)
See *Zapiski okhotnika*
"Scenes in Canada" (Moodie) **14**:243
"Scenes in My Native Land" (Sigourney) **87**:321
"Scenes in the Wood" (Lazarus) **109**:291
Scenes of Clerical Life (Eliot) **4**:92-93, 95, 97-98, 102, 109-10, 114, 116-17, 120-21, 123, 126-27, 142, 152, 154; **13**:290; **23**:80; **41**:99, 103; **49**:216, 237; **89**:228; **118**:60, 103-4
Scenes of Military Life (Balzac) **5**:31-32
Scenes of Parisian Life (Balzac)
See *Scènes de la vie Parisienne*
Scenes of Political Life (Balzac)
See *Scènes de la vie politique*
Scenes of Provincial Life (Balzac)
See *Scènes de la vie de province*
The Scented Garden (Burton) **42**:29
"Scented Herbage of My Breast" (Whitman) **4**:575; **31**:387, 402, 416
The Sceptic (Moore) **6**:395; **110**:171
The Sceptic, a Poem (Hemans) **29**:192-93, 195, 202; **71**:261
Schach von Wuthenow (Fontane) **26**:236, 240, 243, 245-46, 254, 259, 270-71
"Schastlivaiia oshibka" (Goncharov) **63**:48
Schattenreise abgeschiedener Stunden von Offenbach nach Weimar und Schönebeck im Jahre (La Roche) **121**:242
Der Schatz (Mörike) **10**:456
"Schatzgräber" (Goethe) **4**:192
Die Schauspielerin (Hebbel) **43**:230
"Schelm von Bergen" (Heine) **4**:256
"Die Schenke am See" (Droste-Hülshoff) **3**:200
Scherz, Satire, Ironie und tiefere Bedeutung (Grabbe) **2**:271-81, 283-84, 286-88
"Scherz und Satire" (Droste-Hülshoff) **3**:200
"Der Schiffsjunge" (Lenau) **16**:278
"An Schillers Nachruhm" (Raimund) **69**:16
Schillers Werke, Nationalausgabe (Schiller) **69**:225, 237-39, 257, 271-77
Der Schimmelreiter (Storm) **1**:541-42, 544, 549-51
"Schlacht" (Hölderlin) **16**:174
"Die Schlacht im Loener Bruch" (Droste-Hülshoff) **3**:195-97, 199, 201
Schleiermacher's Soliloquies (Schleiermacher)
See *Monologen: Eine Neujahrsgabe*
"Die schlimmen Monarchen" (Schiller) **39**:338, 356, 386-88
Der Schlimm-heilige Vitalis (Keller) **2**:416
"Das SchloBß Boncourt" (Chamisso) **82**:30
"Das Schloss Dürande" (Eichendorff) **8**:222
"Schlußwort" (Boyd) **102**:175
Der Schmied seines Glückes (Keller) **2**:414-15, 424
Schmucker's Psychology (Brownson) **50**:27
"The Schnellest Zug" (Field) **3**:208
"Schnitterlied" (Meyer) **81**:140, 142, 148, 152-57, 206
"Scholar and Carpenter" (Ingelow) **39**:255-56; **107**:122
"The Scholar Gypsy" (Arnold)
See "The Scholar-Gipsy"
"The Scholar-Gipsy" (Arnold) **6**:42, 44, 50-52, 65-66, 72; **29**:6-7, 32-3, 37; **89**:7, 9, 46, 49, 53, 88-99; **126**:52, 75, 83, 111
The Scholars of Arneside (Martineau) **137**:250
"The Scholasticism of the Nineteenth Century" (Pisarev)
See "Sxolastiki xix veka"
"Die Schöne Buche" (Mörike) **10**:454
Der schöne Bund (La Roche) **121**:326
Die schöne Kellnerin von Bacharach (Muller) **73**:361
Die schöne Müllerin (Muller) **73**:350, 355, 360, 363, 365-68, 373, 380, 382, 389, 396
Schönes Bild der Resignation (La Roche) **121**:249
"Schönheit" (Hölderlin) **16**:185
"Schön-Rohtraut" (Mörike) **10**:453
School (Robertson) **35**:333-34, 336, 340, 345-46, 351-52, 357, 362, 364-66, 369, 371-72
"The School Boards: What They Can Do, and What They May Do" (Huxley) **67**:92
"School Days" (Whittier) **59**:360, 371
The School for Arrogance (Holcroft) **85**:192-93, 206-07, 218-21, 225, 234
The School for Scandal (Holcroft) **85**:237
The School for Scandal (Sheridan) **5**:355-72, 374-78, 380, 382-83; **91**:233-34, 242-43, 251, 253-54, 256, 258, 260-64, 266-70, 272
The School for Widows (Reeve) **19**:412, 415
A School History of Germany (Taylor) **89**:342
"The School of Giorgione" (Pater) **90**:242, 323, 335
The School of Giorgione (Pater) **7**:326
"The School Question" (Brownson) **50**:54
School Song Book (Hale) **75**:286, 349
"The School-Boy" (Blake) **13**:182; **37**:14, 33, 45, 72
"The Schoolboy" (Nekrasov) **11**:404
The Schoolfellows (Jerrold) **2**:395, 401
The Schoolmaster (Gotthelf)
See *Leiden und Freuden eines Schulmeisters*
"The Schoolmaster's Progress" (Kirkland) **85**:265
"The Schoolmistress Abroad" (Hood) **16**:209
Schools and Universities on the Continent (Arnold) **126**:6, 115-16
The Schools: Basis for the Prosperity and for the Republic in the United States (Faustino)
See *Las escuelas, base de la prosperidad y de la república en los Estados Unidas*
"Der Schosshund" (Klopstock) **11**:238
"Der Schrecken im Bade" (Kleist) **37**:237
Das Schreibepult, oder Die Gefahren der Jugend (Kotzebue) **25**:147
Die Schreibfeder (Grillparzer) **102**:188-89
Schriften (Goethe) **34**:123
Schriften (Novalis) **13**:359-60, 362
Schriften (Tieck)
See *Ludwig Tieck's Schriften*
The Schroffenstein Family (Kleist)
See *Die Familie Schroffenstein*
"Der Schuß von der Kanzel" (Meyer) **81**:184
"Schulmeister Klopfstock und seine fünf Söhne" (Brentano) **1**:100
Der Schutzgeist (Kotzebue) **25**:134, 136
Der Schützling (Nestroy) **42**:232, 243, 254
"An Schwager Kronos" (Goethe) **4**:192
"Der Schwarze in der Zuckerplantage" (Claudius) **75**:183
"Der schwarze See" (Lenau) **16**:283
"Die Schwarze Spinne" (Gotthelf) **117**:6-11, 13, 15, 32, 36, 43-6, 48-9, 52
"Schwarzschattende Kastanie" (Meyer) **81**:209
Der Schweizerische Robinson; oder, Der schiffbrüchige Schweizerprediger und seine Familie (Wyss) **10**:466-73
"Schwüle" (Meyer) **81**:199, 201-02
"Science and Culture" (Huxley) **67**:28, 44, 61, 63-4, 69-72, 83, 87
"Science and Morals" (Huxley) **67**:60, 62, 97
Science Lectures for the People (Huxley) **67**:85
The Science of English Verse (Lanier) **6**:237, 240, 245, 247, 250, 252, 256, 263-65, 269-70, 279; **118**:200, 203, 205, 216-17, 219, 239, 263-66, 286-87, 294
The Science of Ethics as Based on the Scienc of Knowledge (Fichte)
See *Das System der Sittenlehre nach den prinzipen der Wissenschaftslehre*
"The Science of History" (Froude) **43**:184, 191
The Science of Knowledge (Wissenschaftslehre) (Fichte) **62**:40-1, 43, 52, 56
Science of Logic (Hegel) **46**:190
The Science of Rights (Fichte)
See *Grundlage des Naturrechts nach Prinzipen der Wissenshaftslehre*
"Scientific and Pseudo-Scientific Realism" (Huxley) **67**:69, 73
"Scientific Education" (Huxley) **67**:64
"Scientific Education: Notes of an After-Dinner Speech" (Huxley) **67**:85-6

Scientific Memoirs (Huxley) **67**:33
"The Scientific Poltroons" (Fourier) **51**:185
Scientific Religion (Oliphant) **47**:288-89, 291, 293-94
"A Scientific Vagabond" (Boyesen) **135**:11-12, 19
"The Scientific Ways of Treating Natural Law" (Hegel)
See "Über die wissenschaftlichen Behandlungsarten des Naturrechts"
"Scientifique" (Banville) **9**:31
Scinde; or the Unhappy Valley (Burton) **42**:37-8
The Scotch Parents (Hays) **114**:175
Scotch Recollections (Wordsworth)
See *Recollections of a Tour Made in Scotland*
"Scotch Songs" (Baillie) **2**:41
"A Scot's Mummy" (Hogg) **109**:258, 260
"Scottish Ballads" (Smith) **59**:309
Scottish Pastorals (Hogg) **109**:268
"Scottish Weaver" (Sigourney) **87**:326
The Scout (Simms) **3**:508
"A Scrap, from a Keg, of Hezekiah Salem's Sermons" (Freneau) **111**:135
Scrap-Bag (Alcott)
See *Aunt Jo's Scrap-Bag*
"Scraps" (Austen) **119**:13
"Scrap-stall of Paris" (Gore) **65**:21
"A Screw Loose" (O'Brien) **21**:236, 247
"Scrisoarea a treia" (Eminescu) **33**:248, 252, 271
"Scrisorile" (Eminescu) **33**:245, 250
"The Sculptor" (Baratynsky)
See "Skul'ptor"
"Scutari" (Milnes) **61**:138
The Scuttled Ship (Reade) **2**:544
Se Gefylsta (Barnes) **75**:40
"A se stesso" (Leopardi) **129**:219-20, 251, 308, 350, 355-56
"Sea" (Boyesen) **135**:47
"The Sea" (Bryant) **6**:175
"The Sea" (Taylor) **89**:314
The Sea (Michelet)
See *La mer*
"Sea and Sky" (Muller) **73**:352
"The Sea and the Cliff" (Tyutchev) **34**:383, 404
"The Sea and the Skylark" (Hopkins) **17**:212, 220, 225, 257
"A Sea Dialogue" (Holmes) **14**:129; **79**:23, 35, 40, 42, 51-52, 59, 62, 65, 73-74, 76
"A Sea Dream" (Darley) **2**:133
"A Sea Dream" (Whittier) **8**:513
"Sea Dreams" (Tennyson) **30**:233
The Sea Gull (Caballero)
See *La gaviota: Novela de costumbres*
"Sea Gulls in Flight" (Meyer)
See "Möwenflug"
"A Sea Has Wakened Up" (Petofi)
See "Föltámadott a tenger"
The Sea Lions; or, The Lost Sealers (Cooper) **1**:208, 221-22; **27**:142; **54**:275-7
"The Sea of Death" (Hood) **16**:208, 234
"The Sea said 'come' to the Brook" (Dickinson) **77**:93
Sea Spray and Smoke Drift (Gordon) **21**:150, 163, 170, 173, 179, 181
"The Sea View" (Smith)
See "Sonnet 83"
"The Sea-Bride" (Darley) **2**:134
"Sea-Drift" (Whitman) **4**:563, 606
"The Sea-Fairies" (Tennyson) **30**:204, 223, 241
"The Sealed Angel" (Leskov)
See "Zapečatlennyj angel"
"The Sea-Limits" (Rossetti) **4**:491-92, 512; **77**:310
"The Seamstress" (Galt) **110**:114
The Search after Happiness: A Pastoral Drama (More) **27**:332
Seashells from the island of Rugen (Muller)
See *Muscheln von der Insel Rügen*
"Sea-Shore" (Emerson) **1**:296
"A Seashore Drama" (Balzac)
See "Un drame au bord de la mer"
The Seaside and the Fireside (Longfellow) **2**:475, 492-93, 495; **45**:116, 153; **101**:92
Sea-side Studies at Ilfracombe, Tenby, the Scilly Isles, and Jersey (Lewes) **25**:280, 288, 296, 308, 310-12
A Season in Hell (Rimbaud)
See *Une saison en enfer*
"Season Tokens" (Barnes) **75**:70
The Seasons (Hogg) **109**:268
"The Seasons Moralized" (Freneau) **1**:317
The Season-Ticket (Haliburton) **15**:126, 136, 145
"The Sea-Spell" (Hood) **16**:234
"Seaweed" (Longfellow) **2**:492; **45**:116, 146, 148, 154; **103**:298
"Seaweed" (Lowell) **2**:509
Sebastian of Portugal (Hemans) **29**:201
"Sebastian van Storck" (Pater) **7**:298, 307, 312
"Sebe lyubeznogo ishchu" (Bestuzhev) **131**:148
"Seclusion" (Mörike) **10**:446
"Second" (De Quincey) **87**:77
"The Second Birth-Day" (Sigourney) **21**:310
A Second Book of Verse (Field) **3**:205-06, 208
The Second Brother (Beddoes) **3**:26, 29, 33, 35-36, 38-39
Second Brutus (Alfieri)
See *Bruto secondo*
"The Second Day" (Longfellow) **45**:138
"Second Dialogue for Three Young Ladies" (Rowson) **69**:115
"Second Epistle" (Eminescu) **131**:332
Second Inaugural Address (Lincoln) **18**:222-23, 235, 238, 246-48, 250-54, 257, 266-67
"Second Love" (Timrod) **25**:375
Second Love; or, Beauty and Intellect (Trollope) **30**:331
The Second Marriage: A Comedy on Ambition (Baillie) **2**:31, 34; **71**:64
The Second Part of Tom White the Postboy; or, The Way to Plenty (More) **27**:347
"A Second Psalm of Life" (Longfellow)
See "The Light of Stars"
"Second Sight" (Hemans) **71**:277
The Second Son (Oliphant) **61**:216-7
"The Second Spring" (Newman) **38**:310
"Second Sunday after Easter" (Keble) **87**:177
"Second Sunday after Trinity" (Keble) **87**:118, 159
"Second Sunday in Advent" (Droste-Hülshoff) **3**:202
"Second Sunday in Lent" (Keble) **87**:177
"Second Thoughts" (Pater) **7**:295, 336
Second Tour (Wordsworth)
See *Journal of My Second Tour in Scotland*
The Second Youth of Theodora Desanges (Linton) **41**:168, 175-76
seconda minutia (Manzoni) **98**:263, 267
La seconde année; ou, À qui la faute? (Scribe) **16**:394
La Seconde boussole (Fourier) **51**:171
"The Secret" (Brontë) **105**:54
"The Secret Drawer, or the Story of a Missing Will" (Alger) **83**:96
"Secret Faults" (Newman) **38**:304
"Secret Love" (Clare) **9**:89, 95
"Secret Love" (Opie) **65**:160
"The Secret of Lord Singleworth" (Norwid)
See "Tajemnica Lorda Singleworth"
The Secret of Swedenborg: Being an Elucidation of His Doctrine of the Divine Natural Humanity (James) **53**:192-3, 204-9, 214, 225, 229-30, 232, 234
"The Secret of the Sea" (Longfellow) **2**:493; **45**:116, 144, 153; **101**:92
"The Secret of the Stars" (Holmes) **14**:128
"Secret Parting" (Rossetti) **4**:498
Secret Service (Planché) **42**:292
Le secrétaire intime (Sand) **2**:599; **42**:358
"Les secrets de la Princesse de Cadignan" (Balzac) **5**:59
Secrets of the Magazine Prison-House (Poe) **55**:136
"Sed buenos!" (Isaacs) **70**:313
"Sed non satiata" (Baudelaire) **29**:99; **55**:33, 44
"The Seducer's Diary" (Kierkegaard)
See "Diary of the Seducer"
Seduction (Holcroft) **85**:205-06, 216-18, 234, 237
"Seein' Things at Night" (Field) **3**:208
"Seeing the World" (O'Brien) **21**:236, 247
"Seek and Find" (Rossetti) **2**:568, 572; **50**:271, 273-6, 289, 318, 320; **66**:331, 362
"Seeking Rest" (Rossetti) **50**:311-2
"Das Seelchen" (Meyer) **81**:201, 206
"Der Seelenkranke" (Lenau) **16**:281-82
Seelenwanderung (Kotzebue) **25**:136
"Seemorgen" (Lenau) **16**:283
"The Seer on Death" (Hayne) **94**:153
"Segen und Unsegen" (Gotthelf) **117**:43, 58
Segunda parte (Lizardi) **30**:68
The Seige of Murány (Arany)
See *Murány ostroma*
"Die Seitenwunde" (Meyer) **81**:207
Seitsemän veljestä (Kivi) **30**:46-51, 53, 55, 62-5
Seken tekake katagi (Ueda Akinari) **131**:18, 45-46, 58, 67
"Selbstbiographie" (Raimund) **69**:12
Selbstbiographie (Grillparzer) **102**:101, 103, 105, 107, 143, 148, 167, 180
Selbstbiographie (Kopitar) **117**:91, 122
"A Select Party" (Hawthorne) **2**:297-98
"Select Poems" (Sigourney) **87**:321
Select Poems (Sigourney) **87**:326, 331, 337
Select Poems of Rural Life in the Dorset Dialect (Barnes) **75**:40
Select Poems of William Barnes (Barnes) **75**:10, 23, 40, 95
Selected Correspondence (Marx) **114**:22
Selected Letters and Journals of George Crabbe (Crabbe) **121**:88
Selected Passages from Correspondence with My Friends (Gogol) **5**:212, 230, 238, 243, 257; **15**:100; **31**:111, 120, 127, 129, 133, 135-36, 139
"Selected Poems" (Browning) **79**:142, 189
Selected Poems (Emerson) **98**:177
Selected Poems of William Barnes (Barnes) **75**:40, 52, 54
Selected Satirical Writings (Saltykov) **16**:376
Selected Stories of Isabella Valancy Crawford (Crawford) **12**:170
Selection (Hemans) **71**:277
Selection from the Papers of the Devil (Jean Paul) **7**:227
A Selection from Unpublished Poems (Barnes) **75**:18, 40
The Selection of a Tutor (Fonvizin)
See *Lavengro: The Scholar—The Gypsy—The Priest*
Selections (Browning) **79**:149
Selections from Jonson (Symonds) **34**:342
"Self-Communion" (Brontë) **4**:44-45, 56; **71**:91; **102**:24
"Self-Conquest" (Parton) **86**:347
"The Self-Consumed" (Griffin) **7**:214
"Self-Culture" (Channing) **17**:21
"Self-Deception" (Arnold) **29**:34
"Self-Dependence" (Arnold) **29**:34
"Selfia" (Isaacs) **70**:304, 307
"The Selfish Crotaire" (Griffin) **7**:214
"Self-Love and Benevolence" (Hazlitt) **29**:169, 172-73
Self-Made (Southworth) **26**:436, 439-40
"Self-Made Men" (Douglass) **7**:126; **55**:108, 123
"Self-Portrait" (Foscolo) **8**:279
Self-Raised; or, From the Depths (Southworth) **26**:434, 439, 447
"Self-Reliance" (Emerson) **1**:305, 307; **38**:169, 173-75, 204-05, 208-09, 224-27; **98**:9, 18-19, 27, 31-7, 61, 65, 72, 82, 89, 93, 98, 107, 109, 111-14, 116, 136, 151, 186, 191

"Selige Sehnsucht" (Goethe) **34**:98
"Selim" (Wieland) **17**:418
"Sella" (Bryant) **6**:165, 169, 171, 187; **46**:4, 21, 47
"La semaine Sainte" (Lamartine) **11**:245, 264, 269
Semeinaia khronika (Aksakov) **2**:11-18
"Semele" (Cooke) **110**:9
Semeynaya kartina (Ostrovsky) **30**:101; **57**:195, 206-8
The Semi-Attached Couple (Eden) **10**:103-08, 110
The Semi-Detached House (Eden) **10**:103, 105-10
"Semper eadem" (Verlaine) **51**:387
"Sen" (Mickiewicz) **101**:161, 164, 185-86
"Sen Cezary" (Krasiński) **4**:306, 313
Sen srebrny Salomei (Slowacki) **15**:348, 352, 371, 378, 380
"Sending" (Arnold) **6**:67
Sendung (Goethe)
See *Theatralische Sendung*
Senilia (Turgenev)
See *Stikhotvoreniya v proze*
El señor Saco con respecto a la revolución de cuba (Villaverde) **121**:335
"Sensation" (Rimbaud) **4**:467, 478; **35**:275, 282
Sense and Sensibility (Austen) **1**:30, 32-4, 37, 39, 41, 44, 46-7, 50-1, 53-4, 59-61, 63-4, 66; **13**:67, 73, 76, 96-8, 106-07; **19**:4, 6, 32, 38, 42, 44; **33**:66, 68-9, 74, 76, 90-3, 96; **51**:12, 16, 47, 55; **81**:1-90; **95**:2-3, 11-12, 16-17, 21, 56, 74, 76, 79-80; **119**:14, 17-18, 21, 24-5, 27, 34-5, 37, 39, 42, 45, 48, 51
Sensibility (More) **27**:332, 336
"The Sensitive Man and the Cold Man" (Karamzin) **3**:281
The Sensitive Plant (Shelley) **18**:319, 330, 334, 339, 343-44, 349, 358-59, 362-63
"Sensitiveness" (Newman) **38**:343-44
"The Sensory and Motor Nerves" (Lewes) **25**:287
"The Sentences" (Patmore) **9**:330-31
"A Sentiment of Spring" (Zhukovsky) **35**:403, 407
"Sentimental Colloquy" (Verlaine)
See "Colloque sentimental"
Sentimental Education: A Young Man's History (Flaubert)
See *L'éducation sentimentale: Histoire d'un jeune homme*
"Sentimentalisme" (Villiers de l'Isle Adam) **3**:590
"Sentimentality" (Villiers de l'Isle Adam)
See "Sentimentalisme"
"El sentimiento religioso" (Martínez de la Rosa) **102**:254
The Sentry, and Other Stories (Leskov) **25**:230-31
"Separate Ways" (Ichiyō)
See "Wakare-Michi"
The Separated Wife (Sacher-Masoch) **31**:290-91, 297-98, 301
The Separation (Baillie) **2**:40-41
"Separation of Church and State" (Brownson) **50**:51
I sepolcri (Foscolo) **8**:262, 264-65, 267-70, 272; **97**:50-2, 55, 57-9, 62-4, 67-8, 78, 83-4, 86-8, 97-9
Les sept cordes de la lyre (Sand) **2**:588; **42**:314, 368-73
"Les sept vieillards" (Baudelaire) **6**:79, 116, 129-30; **29**:100, 104, 114; **55**:16, 19, 28, 35, 37-42, 67
"September" (Clare) **9**:112, 116; **86**:130
"September Gale" (Holmes) **14**:101
"September in Australia" (Kendall) **12**:183, 185-86, 191, 199-201
"September in Toronto" (Crawford) **127**:198-99
"Septembermorgen" (Mörike) **10**:448
"September's Baccalaureate" (Dickinson) **21**:67
"September's End" (Petofi)
See "Szeptember végén"
Septimius Felton, or the Elixir of Life (Hawthorne) **2**:307-08, 315, 319-21, 324, 335
"Septuagesima Sunday" (Keble) **87**:172, 202
The Sepulchres (Foscolo)
See *I sepolcri*
"Sequel" (Mallarmé) **41**:254
"A Sequel to an Evening at a Caucasian Spa in 1824" (Bestuzhev)
See "Sledstvie vechera na kavkazskikh vodakh v 1824 godu"
Sequel to Drum-Taps (Whitman) **4**:580
A Sequel to Early Lessons (Edgeworth) **51**:81
La sera del dì di festa (Leopardi) **129**:229, 232
"The Seraph and the Poet" (Browning) **61**:43
"The Seraphim" (Browning) **1**:122; **61**:4-5, 48, 52-7, 61; **66**:71
The Seraphim, and Other Poems (Browning) **1**:112, 126; **61**:4, 8, 41-2, 48, 50-3, 61; **66**:44, 83
Séraphita (Balzac) **5**:46, 49, 81; **35**:55; **53**:28, 31
A Serbian Book of Folk Songs (Karadzic)
See *Narodna srbska pjesnarica*
Serbian Dictionary (Karadzic)
See *Srpski rječnik*
Serbian Grammar (Karadzic)
See *Srpska gramatika*
"Serenada" (Pavlova) **138**:4, 50
"Serenade" (Allingham) **25**:6
"A Serenade" (Brontë) **105**:55
"La sérénade" (Nerval) **67**:306
"A Serenade" (Pavlova)
See "Serenada"
"Serenade" (Pinkney) **31**:268, 273-74, 279
"Serenade" (Timrod) **25**:366, 385
"A Serenade at the Villa" (Browning) **19**:127
Serenades in Ritor Nelles (Muller) **73**:352
Series of Lay Sermons (Hogg) **109**:231
A Series of Plays: In Which It Is Attempted to Delineate the Stronger Passions of the Mind, Each Passion Being the Subject of a Tragedy and a Comedy (Baillie) **2**:31-32, 39-43, 30-31, 38-43, 36, 39-43; **71**:1-2, 16, 19, 28, 31-32, 51-53
Sermon in a Churchyard (Macaulay) **42**:116
"The Sermon of St. Francis" (Longfellow) **45**:139
Sermons (Arnold) **18**:3, 18, 27
Sermons and Tracts (Channing) **17**:4
Sermons Bearing on Subjects of the Day (Newman) **38**:304, 306-07, 309; **99**:224
Sermons of Blair (Blair) **75**:116, 123, 129-32
Sermons Preached on Various Occasions (Newman) **38**:309-11
"Le Serpent" (Sade) **47**:313, 351
"The Serpent" (Very) **9**:387
"The Serpent Is Shut Out from Paradise" (Shelley) **93**:307-08
"Le serpent qui danse" (Baudelaire) **55**:9, 28-9
The Serpent Woman (Gozzi)
See *La donna serpente*
"La Serre" (Maupassant) **83**:229
The Servant (Shevchenko)
See *Naimychka*
The Servant Girl (Shevchenko)
See *Naimychka*
"La servante au grand coeur" (Baudelaire) **29**:80; **55**:23, 64
La servante du roi (Musset) **7**:258
"Servaz und Pankraz" (Gotthelf) **117**:44, 51, 56-8
Servian Folks' Songs (Runeberg) **41**:309
"The Service" (Thoreau) **7**:379-81; **138**:70, 117, 119, 123
Servitude et grandeur militaires (Vigny) **7**:467-68, 471-74, 476-78, 485; **102**:336-37, 353, 378
"Ses purs ongles très haut dèdiant leur onyx" (Mallarmé)
See "Sonnet en -yx"
Seth's Brother's Wife (Frederic) **10**:182-83, 187-88, 191, 193-95, 200-04, 207, 209-13, 216
"The Setting Sun" (Clare) **86**:156
"The Settle an' the Girt Wood Vire" (Barnes) **75**:70, 77, 82
"The Settlement" (Slowacki)
See "Posielenie"
"The Settler, or the Prophecy Fulfilled" (Richardson) **55**:299
"Settlers at Home" (Martineau) **26**:323
The Settlers at Home (Martineau) **137**:256, 260
"The Settlers Settled; or, Pat Connor and His Two Masters" (Traill) **31**:326
Seven Brothers (Kivi)
See *Seitsemän veljestä*
The Seven Champions of Christendom (Planché) **42**:290, 293, 301
The Seven Gables (Hawthorne)
See *The House of the Seven Gables*
The Seven Hills (De Mille) **123**:123
782 (Dickinson) **77**:151
715 (Dickinson) **77**:163
757 (Dickinson) **77**:50
745 (Dickinson) **77**:64
709 (Dickinson) **77**:71
791 (Dickinson) **77**:150
797 (Dickinson) **77**:92, 95
738 (Dickinson) **77**:63
712 (Dickinson) **77**:49, 96, 163, 173
728 (Dickinson) **77**:95
721 (Dickinson) **77**:140, 144
722 (Dickinson) **77**:84
Seven Legends (Keller)
See *Sieben Legenden*
"The Seven Old Men" (Baudelaire)
See "Les sept vieillards"
"Seven Sisters" (Wordsworth) **12**:393
The Seven Strings of the Lyre (Sand)
See *Les sept cordes de la lyre*
"The Seven Vagabonds" (Hawthorne) **2**:305
"The Seven Wonders of the World" (Cranch) **115**:42
1754 (Dickinson) **77**:132
1720 (Dickinson) **77**:119
76 (Dickinson) **77**:74
72 (Dickinson) **77**:121-22
"Severed and Gone" (Brontë) **71**:106
"Severed Selves" (Rossetti) **77**:313
"The Sewing Bird" (O'Brien) **21**:234
"The Sexton's Adventure" (Le Fanu) **9**:321
"The Sexton's Daughter" (Shevchenko)
See "Tytarivna"
"The Sexton's Hero" (Gaskell) **137**:4, 38
Sexual Inversion (Symonds) **34**:343
"Sfinks" (Pavlova) **138**:13, 33, 48
A Shabby Genteel Story (Thackeray) **5**:482, 506; **14**:402, 408; **43**:359
"The Shadow" (Andersen)
See "Skyggen"
"The Shadow" (Clough) **27**:55, 79, 87
"A Shadow" (Longfellow) **45**:121
"Shadow, a Parable" (Poe) **1**:497-98, 513; **16**:306, 331; **117**:268
"The Shadow and the Light" (Whittier) **8**:493
"Shadow of Dorothea" (Rossetti) **66**:307
Shadow Tree Shaft (Robertson) **35**:330, 333, 335-36, 356, 369
"Shadows" (Milnes) **61**:145
"Shadows All" (Hayne) **94**:166
Shadows and Sunbeams (Parton) **86**:350-52
Shadows of Society (Sacher-Masoch) **31**:294
"Shadows of Taste" (Clare) **9**:104; **86**:113, 130
Shadows of the Clouds (Froude) **43**:192-93, 209
"Shadows of the Mountain Pine" (Cooke) **5**:132
"Shadows of the Pine Forest" (Cooke) **5**:132
Shadowy images of a journey to the Harz Mountains and Saxony (Andersen) **79**:79
"Shaftesbury Feäir" (Barnes) **75**:67, 98

"The Shaker Bridal" (Hawthorne) **2**:327; **10**:316
"Shakespear" (Herder) **8**:315
Shakespear Illustrated (Lennox) **23**:228, 231, 261-65; **134**:271, 292
"Shakespeare" (Arnold) **29**:4, 35; **89**:95
"Shakespeare" (Longfellow) **45**:186
"Shakespeare" (Very) **9**:370, 379, 382
"Shakespeare, a Poet Generally" (Coleridge) **99**:87
Shakespeare and His Forerunners: Studies in Elizabethan Poetry and Its Development from Early English (Lanier) **6**:240, 245; **118**:290, 294
"Shakespeare Once More" (Lowell) **2**:509
"Shakespeare; or, The Poet" (Emerson)
See "Shakespeare, the Poet"
Shakespeare Papers (Maginn) **8**:435, 440
"Shakespeare, the Poet" (Emerson) **1**:295; **98**:70, 108, 112
Shakespearean Criticism (Coleridge) **99**:102, 105
Shakespeares Behandlung des Wunderbaren (Tieck) **5**:520, 526; **46**:332
"Shakespeare's Judgment Equal to His Genius" (Coleridge) **99**:86
Shakespeares Mädchen und Frauen (Heine) **4**:244, 246, 265
Shakespeare's Treatment of the Marvelous (Tieck)
See *Shakespeares Behandlung des Wunderbaren*
Shakespeare's Vorschule (Tieck) **5**:511, 520; **46**:359
Shakespeare-Studien (Ludwig) **4**:351-52, 358, 366, 368
"Shakespeare—the Man" (Bagehot) **10**:57
"The Shaking of the Pear Tree" (Craik) **38**:119
"Shakspeare's Critics, English and Foreign" (Lewes) **25**:285, 305
"Shameful Death" (Morris) **4**:426
"Shameless" (Thomson) **18**:411
"Shamus O'Brien" (Le Fanu) **9**:298-99
"Shane Fadh's Wedding" (Carleton) **3**:89-90, 92
"Shanid Castle" (Griffin) **7**:194, 196
Shannondale (Southworth) **26**:431
"The Shark" (Solomos)
See "O pórphyras"
"Sharp Snaffles" (Simms) **3**:508
Sharps and Flats (Field) **3**:209
The Shaughraun (Boucicault) **41**:27-30, 34, 39, 43, 49, 51, 53
Shawl Straps (Alcott) **83**:34
"Shchi" (Turgenev) **122**:308, 312
She and He (Sand)
See *Elle et lui*
"She bore it till the simple veins/Traced azure on her hand" (Dickinson) **77**:162-63
"She Came and Went" (Lowell) **90**:214
"She Died at Play" (Dickinson) **21**:55
"She dwelt among th'untrodden ways" (Wordsworth) **111**:323, 327-28
"She Is Far from the Land" (Hood) **16**:236
"She Is Far from the Land" (Moore) **6**:391
"She Lay as If at Play" (Dickinson) **21**:42-3
"She Sleeps!" (Isaacs)
See "Ella duerme!"
"She Was Good for Nothing" (Andersen)
See "Hun duede ikke"
"She Was No Good" (Andersen)
See "Hun duede ikke"
A Sheaf Gleaned in French Fields (Dutt) **29**:120, 127-28
"Shed No Tear!" (Keats) **8**:360
"The Sheep and the Dogs" (Krylov) **1**:435
"The Shekh" (Taylor) **89**:302-03
"A Shelf in my Bookcase" (Smith) **59**:307, 309-10, 315, 317, 323, 337
"The Shell" (Chivers) **49**:71
"Shelley" (Thomson) **18**:406, 414
"The Shepherd" (Blake) **37**:3, 38, 57, 65, 72, 78, 92
"The Shepherd Girl" (Kivi)
See "Paimentyttö"
"The Shepherd of King Admetus" (Lowell) **90**:194
The Shepherd of Salisbury Plain (More) **27**:333, 338, 347-49, 358
The Shepherd Prince (Mapu)
See *Ahavat Zion*
"Shepherd Sandy" (Krylov) **1**:439
"The Shepherdess and the Chimney Sweep" (Andersen) **7**:22, 34; **79**:23, 40, 42, 58, 87
"The Shepherdess and the Sheep" (Andersen)
See "Hyrdinden og Skorsteensfeieren"
"The Shepherd's Brow, Fronting Forked Lightning" (Hopkins) **17**:246, 262
The Shepherd's Calendar (Hogg) **109**:202, 256
The Shepherd's Calendar, with Village Stories, and Other Poems (Clare) **9**:78-79, 84, 96, 103-04, 106-07, 111-12, 114, 116, 123; **86**:93-105, 110, 125, 130, 154, 156, 160, 165, 168-69, 174
"The Shepherd's Hut" (Vigny) **7**:474
"Shepot grustnyj, govor tajnyj" (Pavlova) **138**:54
Sheppard Lee (Bird) **1**:84-86, 88, 91
"Sheridan" (Landor) **14**:166
The Sheriff's Ball (Barham) **77**:6
"She's All My Fancy Painted Him" (Carroll) **139**:33
"She's Up and Gone, the Graceless Girl" (Hood) **16**:219
The Shield (Cooper) **129**:67
Shifting for Himself; or, Gilbert Greyson's Fortunes (Alger) **8**:16, 43
"Shikubi no egao" (Ueda Akinari) **131**:21-22, 57-58, 88
"Shinel" (Gogol) **5**:218-20, 227, 229-30, 235-36, 238-39; **31**:88
"The Ship of Earth" (Lanier) **6**:236; **118**:217
"The Ships of San Juan" (Silva)
See "Los maderos de San Juan"
The Shipwreck (Mackenzie) **41**:184
"Shiramine" (Ueda Akinari) **131**:13, 24-25, 27, 32, 38, 40-41, 46, 48-49, 53, 87
Shiramine (Ueda Akinari) **131**:64-65, 69
Shirley (Brontë) **3**:46-9, 52, 55-7, 59-61, 64-5, 67, 69-71, 74-6; **8**:54-5; **33**:103, 117-18, 122, 129, 143; **58**:153-246; **105**:2, 6, 54-6, 73
"The Shirt Collar" (Andersen) **79**:23, 34
Shodo kikimimi sekenzaru (Ueda Akinari) **131**:18, 45, 60, 86
"The Shoes of Fortune" (Crawford) **127**:188
Shoes of Fortune (Andersen) **79**:3
"The Shoes That Were Danced to Pieces" (Grimm and Grimm) **3**:227
"Shooting Niagra: And After?" (Carlyle) **70**:93
"Shop" (Browning) **19**:87, 96
"Short Prose" (Silva)
See "Prosas breves"
Short Prose Poems (Baudelaire)
See *Petits poèmes en prose: Le spleen de Paris*
Short Stories by Alexandre Dumas (Dumas) **71**:219
Short Studies on Great Subjects (Froude) **43**:178-79, 189-90, 203-04
"The Shot" (Pushkin)
See "Vystrel"
The Shot from the Pulpit (Meyer)
See "Der Schuß von der Kanzel"
"Should We Temper Our Words" (Eminescu) **131**:326
Shou-tzu p'u (Li Ju-chen) **137**:206
"Shponka's Dream" (Gogol) **15**:89
"Shrodon Feäir" (Barnes) **75**:77
"The Shrubbery" (Cowper) **8**:138
"The Shy Man" (Barnes) **75**:8-9
"Si j'étais petit oiseau" (Beranger) **34**:44
"Si l'aurore" (Leconte de Lisle) **29**:235
"Si vienes a mi campo" (Isaacs) **70**:309
"Siberia" (Mangan) **27**:296, 298, 311-13
"Sibrandus Schafnaburgensis" (Browning) **19**:96; **79**:94, 99, 101
Sibylline Leaves (Coleridge) **9**:137, 139, 146, 159; **54**:121; **111**:292
"Sic Itur" (Clough) **27**:108
"Sic Semper Liberatoribus, March 13, 1881" (Lazarus) **109**:343
"'Sic transit gloria mundi'" (Dickinson) **21**:62
"Sic Vita" (Thoreau) **138**:75, 117
"The Siciliam Captive" (Hemans) **71**:296
A Sicilian Romance (Radcliffe) **6**:406, 409-15, 419-20, 424, 426, 444-45; **55**:225, 229-31, 242-4, 278; **106**:349
The Sicilian Vespers (Scribe)
See *Les vêpres siciliennes*
"Sicily Burns's Wedding" (Harris) **23**:155, 159, 161-62
"The Sick Author" (Freneau) **111**:134
"A Sick Bed" (Bryant) **6**:165; **46**:22
"The Sick in Heart" (Lenau) **16**:276
"The Sick King in Bokhara" (Arnold) **6**:72; **29**:26, 35
"The Sick Rose" (Blake) **37**:16, 26, 42-3, 50, 57, 82, 84-7, 92, 96-7
"The Sick Stockrider" (Gordon) **21**:149-51, 154-55, 158-59, 161, 163, 166, 170-72, 174-77, 181-83, 187
The Sickness unto Death (Kierkegaard)
See *Sygdommen til Døden*
Sidney (Symonds) **34**:342
Sie trägt die Schuld (Arnim) **123**:8
Sieben Legenden (Keller) **2**:411-12, 414, 416
Siebenundsiebzig Gedichte aus den hinterlassenen Papieren eines reisenden Waldhornisten (Muller) **73**:368
"Les siècles maudits" (Leconte de Lisle) **29**:224
The Siege (Baillie) **2**:36; **71**:5-6, 12
"The Siege of Ancona" (Landor) **14**:183
The Siege of Corinth (Byron) **2**:63, 72, 89, 95-96; **12**:139; **109**:102
The Siege of Derry; or, Sufferings of the Protestants: A Tale of the Revolution (Tonna)
See *Derry: A Tale of the Revolution in 1688*
"The Siege of Roxburgh" (Hogg) **109**:204
The Siege of Valencia (Hemans) **29**:196, 201; **71**:261, 267, 269, 275-76, 278, 291
"The Siege of Vienna" (Chivers) **49**:69
Siegfried (Wagner) **9**:417, 441, 448-49, 454-55, 459, 464, 466, 469-70; **119**:180, 186, 197, 205-10, 213, 222, 228-31, 268, 274, 278-79, 282, 289, 305-06, 321, 345
"Siegfried's Death" (Wagner)
See *Siegfrieds Tod*
Siegfrieds Tod (Hebbel) **43**:235, 238
Siegfrieds Tod (Wagner) **9**:445, 463; **119**:186, 316
"Siempre contigo" (Isaacs) **70**:308
"Sierra Morena" (Karamzin) **3**:285, 287-89
"The Siesta" (Bryant) **6**:172
"The Sifting of Peter" (Longfellow) **45**:128, 131
"Sigh" (Mallarmé)
See "Soupir"
"Sigh On, Sad Heart" (Hood) **16**:218
"Sighing for Retirement" (Clare) **9**:120
"A Sight in Camp in the Daybreak Gray and Dim" (Whitman) **31**:403, 431; **81**:323, 331
"Sight of the Hills from the Kozłowa Steppes" (Mickiewicz)
See "Widok gór ze stepów Kozłowa"
"The Sight of the Ocean" (Very) **9**:376
"Sights from a Steeple" (Hawthorne) **2**:291-92; **23**:170
"The Sightseer" (Krylov) **1**:435
"El Siglo en blanco" (Larra) **130**:196
"The Sign" (Villiers de l'Isle Adam)
See "L'intersigne"
"Sign from the West" (Cranch) **115**:51
"Signatur des Zeitalters" (Schlegel) **45**:338

"The Signet Ring" (Baratynsky) **103**:2
"The Significance of Swedish Poverty" (Almqvist)
See "Svenska fattigdomens betydelse"
La Signora Fantastici (Staël-Holstein) **91**:360
"Signs of the Times" (Carlyle) **70**:7, 39, 44, 73-74, 78, 80-82
Sigurd der Schlangentöter (Fouqué) **2**:265, 267
Sigurd Ring (Stagnelius) **61**:253, 257-8
Sigurds Rache (Fouqué) **2**:265
"Sila spomina" (Preseren) **127**:298, 323
Silas Marner, the Weaver of Raveloe (Eliot) **4**:99-100, 102-03, 106, 109-11, 114, 117, 119, 121, 123, 126-27, 131, 147-52; **13**:289, 291, 293; **23**:51, 56-7, 80; **41**:55-155; **49**:197, 213; **89**:215, 239; **118**:40, 43, 49, 59-60, 104-5, 107-8
Die silberne Hochzeit (Kotzebue) **25**:141
Silcote (Kingsley)
See *Silcote of Silcotes*
Silcote of Silcotes (Kingsley) **107**:189, 192-93, 209, 221-24, 226, 228
Silcotes (Kingsley)
See *Silcote of Silcotes*
"Silence" (Nekrasov) **11**:406
"Le silence" (Vigny) **7**:481
"Silence, a Fable" (Poe) **1**:513; **16**:306, 312, 331, 336; **94**:240; **117**:268, 281, 283, 308
"The Silence of Faith" (Harpur) **114**:144
"The Silent Melody" (Holmes) **14**:109
"Silent Noon" (Rossetti) **4**:514; **77**:312
"Silent O Moyle" (Moore) **6**:391
"Silent Sea" (Mickiewicz)
See "Cisza morska"
"Silentium" (Tyutchev) **34**:381, 386, 412
"Silford Hall; or, The Happy Day" (Crabbe) **26**:136; **121**:4
"Silhouettes" (Kierkegaard) **125**:205-9, 214, 248, 250-51
"Silly Novels by Lady Novelists" (Eliot) **23**:98; **118**:188-89
"Silly Shore" (Crabbe) **26**:102
"Silly Steve" (Petofi)
See "Bolond Istók"
"Silva a la Agricultura de la Zona Tórrida" (Bello) **131**:93-94
Silva de romances viejos (Grimm and Grimm) **3**:221
"Silva to the Agriculture of the Torrid Zone" (Bello)
See "Silva a la Agricultura de la Zona Tórrida"
Silvas Americanas (Bello) **131**:92-93, 109
The Silver Box (Dumas) **9**:234
The Silver Dream of Salomea (Slowacki)
See *Sen srebrny Salomei*
"The Silver Mine" (Hale) **75**:297, 362
"Silver Wedding" (Clough) **27**:106
"A Silvia" (Leopardi) **129**:219, 228-29, 328, 343, 350, 357-58
Simhat hanef (Smolenskin) **30**:189-90, 195-96
Simon (Sand) **2**:589, 599
"Simon Lee" (Wordsworth) **111**:198-200, 202, 211, 224, 228, 248, 251, 253, 277, 279-83, 287, 314, 323, 348-50, 359-60, 366-67, 369
"Simon Lee, the Old Huntsman" (Wordsworth) **12**:387, 428, 434, 445-46
Simon Verde (Caballero) **10**:72
"Simone" (Musset) **7**:256, 258
"Simple agonie" (Laforgue) **5**:280; **53**:289
"Simple Frescoes" (Verlaine)
See "Simples Fresques"
A Simple Heart (Flaubert)
See *Un coeur simple*
"Simple Simon" (Andersen) **7**:34; **79**:25
A Simple Story (Inchbald) **62**:131-40, 142, 149, 154-6, 158-9, 163-8, 178-81, 186, 188, 191
"Simple Susan" (Edgeworth) **1**:265; **51**:79
Simple Tales (Opie) **65**:171, 174, 179-81, 197
"Simples Fresques" (Verlaine) **51**:370, 381-82
The Simpleton (Reade) **2**:541, 545, 549; **74**:255, 257, 260, 263-65, 284
Simsone Grisaldo (Klinger) **1**:429
Sin and Sorrow Are Common to All (Ostrovsky)
See *Grekh da beda na kogo ne zhivyot*
"Sincerity and Hypocrisy" (Newman) **38**:306
"Sindhu" (Dutt) **29**:124-25, 127, 129-30
"Sinfonia Eroica" (Levy) **59**:109
"Sing On, Sad Heart" (Hood) **16**:233
"Sing, Sweet Harp" (Moore) **110**:186
"The Singer" (Zhukovsky) **35**:384-85
"The Singer in the Kremlin" (Zhukovsky) **35**:379
"The Singer in the Prison" (Whitman) **4**:561
"The Singers" (Longfellow) **2**:491-92
"The Singers" (Turgenev) **21**:413, 418, 420; **37**:379; **122**:280
"The Singing, Soaring Lark" (Grimm and Grimm) **3**:227
"The Singing Spirit" (Ridge) **82**:183-84
The Single Hound (Dickinson) **21**:22-3, 29-30, 33
Singleheart and Doubleface (Reade) **2**:547, 549; **74**:260, 263
Sing-Song: A Nursery Rhyme-Book (Rossetti) **2**:557, 565, 571; **50**:271, 288-9, 301, 304-7; **66**:330, 341
"Singular Dream from a Correspondent" (Hogg) **109**:279
"Singular Passage in the Life of the Late Dr. Harris" (Barham) **77**:36
Sink or Swim; or, Harry Raymond's Resolve (Alger) **8**:36, 42-43
"The Sinking Ship" (Rimbaud)
See "L'eclatante victoire de Saarebrück"
Das Sinngedicht (Keller) **2**:412, 414, 416, 421-23
Sins of Government, Sins of the Nation (Barbauld) **50**:4
Sintram and His Companions (Fouqué) **2**:261-63, 265, 268
"Siope" (Poe) **16**:292; **94**:240
Sir Andrew Wylie of That Ilk (Galt) **1**:329, 332-33, 335, 337; **110**:77-80, 84-6, 95-6
"Sir Brasil's Falcon" (O'Brien) **21**:234, 242
Sir Brook Fossbrooke (Lever) **23**:292, 303, 308
Sir Charles Grandison, or The Happy Man (Austen) **119**:30-1
"Sir David Graeme" (Hogg) **109**:268
Sir Eldred of the Bower (More) **27**:332, 336
"Sir Eustace Grey" (Crabbe) **26**:78-9, 81, 111, 118, 123, 126, 134; **121**:5, 9-10, 24, 26, 34
"Sir Federigo's Falcon" (Longfellow)
See "The Falcon of Ser Federigo"
"Sir Galahad" (Tennyson) **30**:223; **65**:305
"Sir Galahad: A Christmas Mystery" (Morris) **4**:426, 431, 444
"Sir Giles' War-Song" (Morris) **4**:444
Sir Harry Hotspur of Humblethwaite (Trollope) **6**:460, 470, 484; **101**:251, 309, 312-13
Sir Henry Tunstall (Brontë) **109**:29
"Sir Humphrey Gilbert" (Longfellow) **2**:493; **45**:153
Sir James Mackintosh (Macaulay) **42**:115, 122
Sir Jasper Carew (Lever) **23**:292
Sir John Chiverton (Ainsworth) **13**:15
Sir John Eliot (Forster) **11**:102, 115
"Sir Maurice" (Baillie) **2**:42
"Sir Peter Harpdon's End" (Morris) **4**:423, 425-26, 432, 441, 444
Sir Ralph Esher; or, Memoirs of a Gentleman of the Court of Charles II (Hunt) **1**:410
Sir Robert's Fortune (Oliphant) **61**:203, 210-1
"Sir Thomas Browne" (Pater) **90**:337
Sir Thomas More; or, Colloquies on the Progress and Prospects of Society (Southey) **8**:462-65, 467; **97**:266, 286
Sir Tom (Oliphant) **61**:204, 211
Sir Walter Finch et son fils William (Charriere) **66**:124-5, 137, 161, 164
"Sir Walter Raleigh" (Thoreau) **138**:120, 123
"Sir Walter Scott" (Carlyle) **70**:7
"Sir William Montague" (Austen) **119**:13
"The Sire de Malétroit's Door" (Stevenson) **5**:394, 408, 415, 431
The Siren (Sacher-Masoch) **31**:301
"Síri dal" (Madach) **19**:369
The Sister (Lennox) **23**:231
"Sister Anne" (O'Brien) **21**:236, 243-44
Sister Anne (Kock)
See *Soeur Anne*
"Sister Helen" (Browning) **1**:124
"Sister Helen" (Rossetti) **4**:491, 493, 497-99, 505-07, 512, 514, 518-19, 523, 526-27, 529-30; **77**:337, 348
"Sister Louise de la Misericorde" (Rossetti) **66**:305
"Sister Maude" (Rossetti) **2**:555, 575; **50**:270; **66**:312, 352
"The Sister of Charity" (Griffin) **7**:196, 202
Sister Philomene (Goncourt and Goncourt)
See *Soeur Philomène*
"Sister St. Luke" (Woolson) **82**:273, 302
"The Sisters" (Crabbe) **26**:118, 130
"The Sisters of Albano" (Shelley) **59**:151
Sisters of Charity Abroad and at Home (Jameson) **43**:305, 327
"The Sister's Trial" (Alcott) **83**:8
"Sistrum" (Fuller) **50**:247-8
"Sita" (Dutt) **29**:126
Sitaram (Chatterji) **19**:210-11, 213-14, 216-22, 224
"Situation of the House" (Gilpin) **30**:40
689 (Dickinson) **77**:66
640 (Dickinson) **77**:64, 67, 96
646 (Dickinson) **77**:131
690 (Dickinson) **77**:119
698 (Dickinson) **77**:89
692 (Dickinson) **77**:163-64
670 (Dickinson) **77**:97
673 (Dickinson) **77**:94
664 (Dickinson) **77**:63
613 (Dickinson) **77**:81
634 (Dickinson) **77**:101
636 (Dickinson) **77**:51
603 (Dickinson) **77**:184
612 (Dickinson) **77**:131
629 (Dickinson) **77**:121
627 (Dickinson) **77**:80
622 (Dickinson) **77**:162
Six Lectures to Working Men (Huxley) **67**:59
Six Moral Tales from Jules Laforgue (Laforgue)
See *Moralités légendaires*
Six Political Discourses Founded on the Scripture (Brackenridge) **7**:44
"The Six Servants" (Grimm and Grimm) **3**:227
Six to One: A Nantucket Idyll (Bellamy) **4**:30; **86**:9-11, 79
"Six Weeks at Heppenheim" (Gaskell) **5**:201-02; **70**:187
1651 (Dickinson) **77**:92, 95
1604 (Dickinson) **77**:93
1607 (Dickinson) **77**:149
1670 (Dickinson) **77**:148
1677 (Dickinson) **77**:92
1660 (Dickinson) **77**:140
1620 (Dickinson) **77**:119
"The Sixth Sunday after Epiphany" (Keble) **87**:203
"The Sixth Sunday after Trinity" (Keble) **87**:177, 202
67 (Dickinson) **77**:119
"A Sixty-Drop Dose of Laudanum" (Mangan) **27**:291, 303
"The Size of the World" (Schiller) **39**:336
"Sizhu zadumchiv i odin" (Tyutchev) **34**:399
Skabelsen, mennesket, og messias (Wergeland) **5**:536, 538-42
Skällnora kvarn (Almqvist) **42**:19
Skällnora Mill (Almqvist)
See *Skällnora kvarn*
"Skazanie o Fyodore—Khristianine i o druge

ego Abrame—zhidovine" (Leskov) **25**:245, 265, 267
Skazhi, Kakoi sud'boi (Pushkin) **83**:333
Skazka dlya detey (Lermontov) **126**:136, 138-39, 154
"Skazka o Mertvoy Tsarevne" (Pushkin) **3**:446; **83**:281
"Skazka o Rybake i Rybke" (Pushkin) **3**:446; **83**:284-85
"Skazka o Tsare Sultane" (Pushkin) **3**:443, 446; **83**:278-79
"Skazka o Zolotom Petushke" (Pushkin) **27**:379; **83**:277-80, 282-85
Skazki (Pushkin) **3**:446, 459
Skazki (Saltykov) **16**:346, 349, 351, 373-75
"The Skeleton in Armor" (Longfellow) **2**:472, 493; **45**:99, 103, 110, 116, 144, 153
"The Skeleton's Cave" (Bryant) **6**:180-81
"The Skeptics" (Lenau) **16**:276
"A Sketch" (Byron) **109**:82
A Sketch (Halleck) **47**:57
Sketch (Sigourney)
See *Sketch of Connecticut, Forty Years Since*
The Sketch Book (Irving)
See *The Sketch Book of Geoffrey Crayon, Gent.*
The Sketch Book of Geoffrey Crayon, Gent. (Irving) **2**:365-77, 379-84, 386-90, 392; **19**:326-51; **95**:223, 226-28, 232, 234, 236-38, 240, 243, 245, 249, 264-69, 273-80, 291, 293-94, 296-97
"A Sketch in the Manner of Hogarth" (Patmore) **9**:329
Sketch of 1842 (Darwin)
See *On the Origin of Species by Means of Natural Selection or the Preservation of Favoured Races in the Struggle for Life*
Sketch of Connecticut, Forty Years Since (Sigourney) **21**:301, 313-16; **87**:320, 338-39, 341-43
"Sketch of the Present Situation of America, 1794" (Murray) **63**:213
"Sketches" (Clare)
See "Sketches in the Life of John Clare"
"Sketches" (Sigourney) **87**:321
Sketches (Crèvecoeur)
See *Sketches of Eighteenth Century America: More "Letters from an American Farmer"*
Sketches (Newman)
See *Historical Sketches*
Sketches (Sigourney) **21**:289
Sketches Among the Poor (Carlyle) **70**:185, 193
Sketches among the Poor (Gaskell) **137**:38, 47, 54
Sketches and Essays (Hazlitt) **29**:148
Sketches and Studies in Italy (Symonds) **34**:333, 364
Sketches and Studies in Italy and Greece (Symonds) **34**:333, 337, 364
Sketches by Boz of Every-Day Life and Every-Day People (Dickens) **3**:138; **8**:200; **37**:165, 168, 176-77, 180, 183-85, 187, 195, 198-99; **105**:353; **113**:63, 91, 98, 118, 124
Sketches from a Hunter's Album (Turgenev)
See *Zapiski okhotnika*
Sketches from History (Godwin) **14**:53
"Sketches from the Country" (Moodie) **14**:231
"Sketches in the Life of John Clare" (Clare) **86**:152-53, 155, 170-75
"Sketches of a History of Carsol" (Brown) **74**:49
Sketches of American Character (Hale) **75**:296, 319, 349
"Sketches of American History" (Freneau) **111**:166
Sketches of American Policy . . . (Webster) **30**:403
Sketches of Eighteenth Century America: More "Letters from an American Farmer" (Crèvecoeur) **105**:102-06, 122, 124-25, 127, 139, 152, 157, 162-64, 182
Sketches of English Character (Gore) **65**:21
Sketches of English literature: With Considerations on the Spirit of the Times, Men, and Revolutions (Chateaubriand)
See *Essai sur la littérature Anglaise et considérations sur le génie des hommes, des temps et, des révolutions*
"Sketches of Female Biography" (Rowson) **5**:318; **69**:115-16
"Sketches of India" (Lanier) **118**:214-15
"Sketches of my Life" (Clare)
See "Sketches in the Life of John Clare"
Sketches of Provincial Life (Saltykov)
See *Gubernskie ocherki*
"Sketches of Russian Life in the Caucasus" (Lermontov)
See *Geroi nashego vremeni*
Sketches of Switzerland (Cooper) **54**:256
Sketches of the Gogol Period of Russian Literature (Chernyshevsky) **1**:160-61, 166
Sketches of the Principal Picture Galleries in England (Hazlitt) **82**:156-58, 161
Sketches of the State of Manners and Opinions in the French Republic, Towards the Close of the Eighteenth Century in a Series of Letters (Williams) **135**:260, 302, 304-6, 335
"Sketches on Different Subjects" (Freneau) **111**:129
"Skipper Ireson's Ride" (Whittier) **8**:493, 496, 506, 508-10, 513, 515-16, 519, 521-22, 526, 530; **59**:356-8, 360, 365, 371
"Skomorox Pamfalon" (Leskov) **25**:239, 245-46
"The Skull" (Baratynsky)
See "Cerep"
"Skulls" (Turgenev) **21**:452
"Skul'ptor" (Baratynsky) **103**:29
Skupoi rytsar (Pushkin) **3**:433-34, 447-48, 452, 454; **83**:263-64, 285-88, 338-39, 351, 353
"The Sky A-Clearèn" (Barnes) **75**:17
"The Sky Is Low, the Clouds Are Mean" (Dickinson) **21**:7
"Sky-Blue Flower" (Eminescu)
See "Floare albastra"
"Skyggen" (Andersen) **7**:23, 26, 37; **79**:23, 28, 40, 42, 51, 53, 63, 66, 68, 72
"The Skylark" (Hogg) **109**:200-01
"The Skylark Leaving Her Nest" (Clare) **9**:80, 94, 117
"The Skylark Sings" (Petofi)
See "Pacsirtaszót hallok megint"
"Skyrockets" (Baudelaire)
See "Fusées"
Sky-Walk, or the Man Unknown to Himself (Brown) **22**:28; **74**:15, 54, 67-8, 76, 92, 133, 155, 175; **122**:116
Slander (Scribe)
See *La calomnie*
"Slang in America" (Whitman) **4**:576; **81**:286
"The Slantèn Light o' Fall" (Barnes) **75**:7
The Slaughter House (Echeverria)
See "El matadero"
"The Slave" (Horton) **87**:102, 104
"The Slave Ships" (Whittier) **8**:489, 509-10, 515
"The Slave Singing at Midnight" (Longfellow) **103**:290
"The Slave Trade" (Williams) **135**:255, 286, 300
"The Slaveholder" (Very) **9**:383
"Slaveholder's Sermon" (Douglass) **7**:123
The Slave-King (Hugo)
See *Bug-Jargal*
"The Slaver" (Allingham) **25**:6
"Slavery" (Horton) **87**:99, 102
Slavery (Channing) **17**:24, 32, 35
"Slavery in Massachusetts" (Thoreau) **7**:386; **21**:329-31, 370
"Slavery in New England" (Sedgwick) **98**:317
The Slavery of Husbands (Ostrovsky) **30**:96
Les Slaves (Mickiewicz) **101**:166-73
"The Slave's Complaint" (Horton) **87**:94, 98, 101, 109-10
"The Slave's Dream" (Longfellow) **45**:155
Slaves in Algiers; or, A Struggle for Freedom (Rowson) **5**:309-10, 313, 318; **69**:103, 140-46, 157-63
"The Slaves of Martinique" (Whittier) **8**:510
"A Slave's Reflections the Eve Before His Sale" (Horton) **87**:102
"The Slave's Story" (Harpur) **114**:144, 148-50, 152
"Slavyanka" (Zhukovsky) **35**:403, 405-06
The Slaying of Meghanada (Dutt)
See *Meghnādbadh Kābya*
"Sledstvie vechera na kavkazskikh vodakh v 1824 godu" (Bestuzhev) **131**:156
"Sleep" (Mickiewicz)
See "Sen"
"Sleep and Poetry" (Keats) **8**:343, 345, 354-55, 364-65, 368, 391; **73**:142, 152, 157-58, 174, 181-82, 203, 206-208, 214, 216, 225-26, 254-56, 260, 311, 322, 324, 339; **121**:100-102, 105-6, 118, 122, 136-37, 141, 147-48, 215
"Sleep Did Come Wi' The Dew" (Barnes) **75**:101
"The Sleep of Sigismund" (Ingelow) **39**:258
"The Sleeper" (Poe) **1**:512; **55**:181; **117**:192, 196, 217, 221, 233, 278, 281-82, 298, 334
"The Sleeper" (Thomson) **18**:417
"The Sleepers" (Whitman) **4**:571, 579, 584, 596, 602; **31**:404-05, 412-14, 416-19, 421-25, 433; **81**:236, 258, 320, 342, 351
"Sleeping at Last" (Rossetti) **66**:343
The Sleeping Bards (Borrow) **9**:54
"The Sleeping Beauty" (Tennyson) **30**:211
Sleeping Beauty in the Wood (Feuillet)
See *Belle au Bois Dormant*
The Sleeping Beauty in the Wood (Planché) **42**:273, 277, 279, 288-89, 294, 296
The Sleepwalker (Scribe)
See *La somnambule*
"Sleepy Hollow" (Irving)
See "The Legend of Sleepy Hollow"
"The Sleigh-Bells" (Moodie) **113**:346
"Slepaya" (Shevchenko) **54**:367, 376, 386, 391
"A Slight Error" (Leskov)
See "Malen' kaja ošibka"
"A Slip of the Pen" (Levy) **59**:113
"Slipyi" (Shevchenko) **54**:388-9
"Slovo od mladosti" (Preseren) **127**:293, 297, 329-30, 332, 334
Slow and Sure; or, From the Street to the Shop (Alger) **8**:45
Śluby panieńskie; czyli, Magnetyzm serca (Fredro) **8**:285-87, 289-90, 292-93
"The Sluggish Smoke Curls Up from Some Deep Dell" (Thoreau) **7**:383
"A Slumber Did My Spirit Steal" (Wordsworth) **111**:323-24, 328
"Small Family Memories" (Cooper) **129**:4, 15, 41, 66
The Small House at Allington (Trollope) **6**:457-58, 463, 470, 486, 491, 497, 499-502, 509, 515, 517; **101**:235, 237-38, 266, 306, 308, 313, 319, 321
The Small Life of Poe (Chivers) **49**:66
Smarh (Flaubert) **2**:255; **62**:72; **135**:172
Smarra; ou, Les démons de la nuit (Nodier) **19**:377-78, 381-83, 387-89, 392, 398-401, 404
"Smert" (Baratynsky) **103**:7, 10, 16
"Smert' poeta" (Lermontov) **5**:295; **47**:158, 166; **126**:144, 218, 224
The Smiles Gone (Keller)
See *Das Verlorene Lachen*
"The Smiling Death's-Head" (Ueda Akinari)
See "Shikubi no egao"
"Smoke" (Thoreau) **7**:355, 370
Smoke (Turgenev)
See *Dym*

The Smoker Mixer (Jerrold) **2**:403
"Smotri kak na rechnom prostore" (Tyutchev) **34**:399
"Smugglers and Poachers" (Crabbe) **121**:6
"Smuggler's Leap" (Barham) **77**:36
"Snachala mysl', voploshchena" (Baratynsky) **103**:47
"The Snail and the Rosebush" (Crawford) **127**:188
"The Snake of the Cabin" (Simms) **3**:501
"The Snake-Bit Irishman" (Harris) **23**:159
The Snark (Carroll)
See *The Hunting of the Snark: An Agony in Eight Fits*
Snarleyyow; or, The Dog Fiend (Marryat) **3**:317, 319-21
"Sneedronningen" (Andersen) **7**:22-3, 28, 34; **79**:23, 26-7, 59
"Sneewittchen" (Grimm and Grimm) **3**:224-25
Snegurochka (Ostrovsky) **30**:97, 104, 111, 119; **57**:206-7, 220-3
"Snip-Snap" (Cooke) **110**:35
The Snob Papers (Thackeray) **5**:445, 463, 486
"The Snob Royal" (Thackeray) **43**:388
The Snobs of England (Thackeray)
See *The Book of Snobs*
"La snova zdes' pod sen'iu krova" (Pavlova) **138**:15
"Snow" (Lampman) **25**:204
"The Snow Image: A Childish Miracle" (Hawthorne) **2**:311, 322, 329, 332; **39**:236
The Snow Maiden (Ostrovsky)
See *Snegurochka*
"The Snow Queen" (Andersen)
See "Sneedronningen"
"The Snow Queen, a Folk Tale in Seven Parts" (Andersen)
See "Sneedronningen"
"Snow Shower" (Bryant) **6**:165, 169; **46**:4, 21
"Snow Song" (Moodie) **14**:218
"Snow Storm" (Clare) **9**:123; **86**:110, 167-69
"The Snow Storm" (Emerson) **1**:295; **98**:46, 177, 179, 181
The Snowball (Tamayo y Baus)
See *La bola de nieve*
Snow-Bound: A Winter Idyl (Whittier) **8**:496, 501-03, 508-11, 513-14, 516, 518-20, 522-24, 526, 530-32; **59**:354, 356-8, 360-1, 366, 371-2, 374-6, 378-80, 385-91
"The Snowdrop" (Allingham) **25**:14
"Snowfall" (Vigny)
See "La neige"
"Snowflakes" (Hawthorne) **2**:298, 305
"Snow-flakes" (Longfellow) **45**:130
"The Snow-Messengers" (Hayne) **94**:167-68
"The Snowstorm" (Pushkin)
See "Metel"
"Snow-White" (Grimm and Grimm)
See "Sneewittchen"
"A Snowy Day" (Ichiyō)
See "Yuki no Hi"
"Snowy Mountains" (Tyutchev) **34**:389
"Snubbing a Snob" (Haliburton) **15**:136
"So again I see you" (Tyutchev)
See "Itak, opyat uvidelsya ya s vami"
"So Fresh and Frail" (Eminescu)
See "Atît de frageda"
"So Help Me, Thou, O Lord!" (Slowacki) **15**:365
"So I Pull My Stockings Off" (Dickinson) **21**:58
"So Long!" (Whitman) **31**:433; **81**:338
"So, there are moments in life" (Tyutchev)
See "Tak, v zhizni est mgnoveniya"
"The Soaring Swan" (Chivers) **49**:48, 52
"Sobaka" (Turgenev) **21**:399, 409, 415, 420, 431, 440-41; **122**:241-42, 244, 265, 267-68, 293, 310, 337, 342, 344, 348-49, 365, 368-70, 377-78
"Soberba" (Castro) **78**:2
Soborjane (Leskov) **25**:228-29, 232, 234, 238-39, 268
Sobranie russkikh stikhotvorenii (Zhukovsky) **35**:394
Sobranie socinenij v cetyrex tomax (Lermontov) **126**:189-92
"Sobre la indolencia de los Filipinos" (Rizal) **27**:410, 419, 425, 427
De sobremesa (Silva) **114**:262-63, 267, 274, 276-77, 280, 284, 286-90, 292, 294, 296, 299-300, 303-5, 308, 315-22
Sochineniya v dvukh tomakh (Bestuzhev) **131**:178-87
Sochineniya v dvukh tomakh, Vol. 1 (Bestuzhev) **131**:209, 211-13
"Social Aspects of the German Romantic School" (Boyesen) **135**:6
The Social Cancer (Rizal)
See *Noli me tangere*
Social Strugglers: A Novel (Boyesen) **135**:14, 22-23, 31, 42-43, 62-63
"The Social War" (Mérimée) **6**:353
"Socialism: Its Growth and Outcome" (Morris) **4**:425
Socialism: Utopian and Scientific (Engels)
See *Die Entwicklung des Sozialismus von der Uopie zur Wissenschaft*
Society (Robertson) **35**:330, 333-34, 336, 338, 340-41, 345, 347, 349, 352-53, 355-57, 360, 362, 363, 365-72
"Society" (Thoreau) **138**:116
"Society and Solitude" (Emerson) **98**:68
Society and Solitude (Emerson) **1**:280; **38**:209; **98**:54
Society in America (Martineau) **26**:307, 309, 311, 314, 318, 322, 334-38, 355, 357-58; **137**:236, 281, 302, 304, 306, 309, 312, 315-24, 327-30, 332-33, 358, 360-61
"Society in the Bush" (Traill) **31**:327
Society the Redeemed Form of Man, and the Earnest of God's Omnipotence in Human Nature: Affirmed in Letters to a Friend (James) **53**:193, 204-5, 207-8, 210, 212, 228, 230, 233, 236, 240
Sočinenija (Pisarev) **25**:344
Sodome et Gomorrhe (Sade) **3**:482
Soeur Anne (Kock) **16**:245, 249, 251-53
Soeur Philomène (Goncourt and Goncourt) **7**:151-52, 161, 175-76, 181, 187, 189
"Les soeurs de charité" (Rimbaud) **4**:455; **35**:280-82, 290-91; **82**:230, 233
"Les soeurs Rondoli" (Maupassant) **83**:194-95, 201, 203
"The Sofa" (Cowper) **8**:110-11, 120, 128-29; **94**:30, 124
Sofonisba (Alfieri) **101**:13, 15, 18-19, 39
"Softer-Mother's Tale" (Wordsworth) **12**:386
"Soggarth Aroon" (Banim and Banim) **13**:128-29
"Die Söhne Haruns" (Meyer) **81**:209
"Sohrab and Rustum" (Arnold) **29**:23, 32, 37; **6**:31, 34, 42, 44, 50, 54, 66, 68, 72
Sohrab and Rustum (Arnold) **89**:14, 28
"Soia" (Castro) **78**:42
"Le soir" (Lamartine) **11**:245, 264, 269
"Le soir de la jeunesse" (Sainte-Beuve) **5**:347
"Soir historique" (Rimbaud) **35**:323; **82**:232, 248
Les Soirées de St. Petersbourg ou entretiens sur le gouvernement temporel de la Providence (Maistre) **37**:282, 284, 286, 292, 294-95, 297-98, 300, 305-08, 313-18, 322
"Sokrates und Alkibiades" (Hölderlin) **16**:162
"Sokratics in the Strand" (Levy) **59**:86, 94, 108-9, 111
"Sol natal" (Desbordes-Valmore) **97**:18-19
"Soldatgossen" (Runeberg) **41**:312, 316, 325, 328
"Solde" (Rimbaud) **35**:290, 309, 312, 322-23
"The Soldier" (Hemans) **71**:279
"The Soldier and the Pard" (Taylor) **89**:301
"The Soldier Boy" (Maginn) **8**:434
"The Soldier Boy" (Runeberg)
See "Soldatgossen"
The Soldier of Seventy-Six (Dunlap) **2**:211, 213, 218
"The Soldier's Dream" (Campbell) **19**:179, 181, 187, 193
"The Soldier's Funeral" (Southey) **97**:312, 315
"The Soldier's Grave" (Landon) **15**:161
"The Soldier's Return" (Opie) **65**:158
"Soldier's Song" (Taylor) **89**:309-10
"The Soldier's Tomb" (Isaacs)
See "La tumba del soldado"
"The Soldier's Well" (Shevchenko)
See "Moskaleva Krynycja"
"The Soldier's Wife" (Southey) **97**:312, 315
"Le soleil" (Baudelaire) **29**:100; **55**:15, 35-6, 56, 65
"Soleil couchant" (Banville) **9**:31
"Soleil et chair" (Rimbaud) **4**:455, 485; **35**:280, 282; **82**:230
"Soleils couchants" (Verlaine) **2**:631; **51**:385
"A Solemn Thing It Was I Said" (Dickinson) **21**:57; **77**:67
"Solemnity" (Mallarmé)
See "Solennité"
"Solennité" (Mallarmé) **41**:254-55, 282-83
Soliloquies (Schleiermacher)
See *Monologen: Eine Neujahrsgabe*
"Soliloquy of Mr. Broadbrim" (Parton) **86**:352
"Soliloquy of the Spanish Cloister" (Browning) **79**:163, 165, 170
"Le solitaire" (Lamartine) **11**:255
"The Solitary Reaper" (Wordsworth) **12**:431, 456, 463-66
"The Solitary Sparrow" (Leopardi)
See "Il Passero Solitario"
"Solitude" (Carroll) **139**:30
"Solitude" (Clare) **9**:77-78
"La solitude" (Lamartine) **11**:245
"Solitude" (Lampman) **25**:208-09
"Solitude" (Maupassant) **42**:202-03
"Solitude" (Sigourney) **21**:310
"Solitude" (Thoreau) **7**:352, 408
Soll und Haben (Freytag) **109**:144-45, 147-54, 157-62, 164-67, 172, 177, 180-83
Soll und Haben, der klassische Kaufmannsroman (Freytag)
See *Soll und Haben*
Le solliciteur; ou, L'art d'obtenir des places (Scribe) **16**:382
"¿Solo amistad?" (Isaacs) **70**:308
"Solo de lune" (Laforgue) **5**:277; **53**:293
"Solomon" (Woolson) **82**:286, 293, 333
Solomon (Klopstock) **11**:226
"Solovei i Kukushka" (Pushkin) **83**:304
"Solution" (Emerson) **38**:192
"Solvet seclum" (Leconte de Lisle) **29**:222
"Sombre récit, conteur plus sombre" (Villiers de l'Isle Adam) **3**:589-90
"Sombre Tale, Sombre Teller" (Villiers de l'Isle Adam)
See "Sombre récit, conteur plus sombre"
El sombrero de tres picos (Alarcon) **1**:12-13, 15-18
"Some Account of my Kin, my Tallents and Myself" (Clare) **86**:173
"Some Account of Stonehenge, the Giant's Dance" (Poe) **94**:229
Some Account of the Greek Christian Poets (Browning) **66**:44
"Some Account of the Latter Days of the Hon. Richard Marston of Dunoran" (Le Fanu) **58**:272
"Some Account of Thomas Tucker" (Cooke) **110**:20, 43, 48-9
"Some Arrows Slay but Whom They Strike" (Dickinson) **21**:56
Some Articles on the Depreciation of Silver and on Topics Connected with It (Bagehot) **10**:20
"Some Comments on Didacticism in Stories and Novels" (Dobrolyubov) **5**:140

"Some Feasts and Fasts" (Rossetti) **50**:285
"Some Observations on the Historical Development of Honour" (Herzen) **61**:101
"Some Passages in the Life of a Lion" (Poe) **16**:322
Some Passages in the Life of Mr. Adam Blair, Minister of the Gospel at Cross-Meikle (Lockhart) **5**:286, 288, 292, 294-96, 302-03, 306-07, 310-13
"Some Strange Disturbances in an Old House on Augier Street" (Le Fanu) **9**:317
"Some Thoughts on the Abodes, Life and Social Conditions of the Poor, especially in Dorsetshire" (Barnes) **75**:102
"Some War Memoranda" (Whitman) **4**:554
"Some Words with a Mummy" (Poe) **94**:240
"Some Work for Immortality" (Dickinson) **21**:38
Somebody's Neighbors (Cooke) **110**:19, 21, 26, 33-6, 39, 43-4
"Something" (Andersen)
See "Noget"
"Something Gathers Up the Fragments" (Traill) **31**:328
"Something on the Sciences, Arts, and Enlightenment" (Karamzin)
See "Nečto o naukax, iskusstvax, i proveščenii"
"Something to Write About" (Andersen) **79**:30
"Sometimes a light surprises" (Cowper) **94**:69
"Sometimes with One I Love" (Whitman) **4**:554
"Somewhere or Other" (Rossetti) **50**:295
"Sommeil" (Corbière)
See "La litanie du sommeil"
"Le sommeil du condor" (Leconte de Lisle) **29**:210, 212, 216-17, 223
"Ein Sommer tagstraum" (Droste-Hülshoff) **3**:203
"Sommerfuglen" (Andersen) **79**:69
"Die Sommernacht" (Klopstock) **11**:220, 236
"Sommernacht" (Meyer) **81**:151
"La Somnambule" (Vigny) **102**:335
La somnambule (Scribe) **16**:382, 391
"Son" (Bestuzhev) **131**:151
"Son" (Shevchenko) **54**:379-80, 382
"Son" (Turgenev) **21**:415, 435, 441, 452; **122**:243, 245-47, 266-67, 269, 364-65, 368, 371, 375-78
"The Son" (Very) **9**:378
"Le son du cor s'afflige vers les bois" (Verlaine) **51**:355
A Son Excellence Reschid-Pascha ancien grand vizir de l'Empire Ottoman (Comte) **54**:211
"Son na more" (Tyutchev) **34**:389, 404, 408-09
"The Son of Arminius: A Tale of Ancient Rome" (Moodie) **113**:310
The Son of Cromwell (Scribe)
See *Le fils de Cromwell; ou, Une Restauration*
"The Son of Darkness" (Krasiński)
See "Syn ceniów"
The Son of his Father (Oliphant) **61**:203, 205, 210
"The Son of Man" (Lazarus) **109**:337
A Son of the Forest: The Experience of William Apes, a Native of the Forest (Apess) **73**:4-5, 7-10, 14-15, 27-28, 31
The Son of the Soil (Oliphant) **11**:446, 449; **61**:203
"Sonderbarer Rechtsfall" (Kleist) **37**:237
Sonetje nesreče (Preseren) **127**:295-96, 304, 330
"Sonetni venec" (Preseren) **127**:293, 295, 298, 305, 308
"Sonetos negros" (Silva) **114**:301
Sonety Krymskie (Mickiewicz) **3**:389-90, 393-94, 399, 402-05; **101**:157, 183, 187, 190-92
"Song" (Browning) **79**:94, 101, 174
"Song" (Clare) **86**:114
"Song" (Coleridge) **90**:27
"Song" (Moore) **110**:192
"Song" (Pinkney) **31**:273-74, 277, 280
"Song" (Poe) **117**:280
"Song" (Rossetti) **2**:575; **50**:288-9
"A Song" (Shevchenko)
See "Dumka"
"Song" (Taylor) **89**:300
"Song" (Tennyson) **30**:245, 276, 279
"The Song" (Very) **9**:380
"Song and Praise" (Very) **9**:376
"Song at Sunset" (Whitman) **4**:601; **31**:391
"Song by Julius Angora" (Brontë) **16**:79, 121
"Song by Siegfried" (Beddoes) **3**:34
"Song for All Seas, All Ships" (Whitman) **31**:431
"Song for Autumn" (Lenau) **16**:276
"A Song for Occupations" (Whitman) **4**:577; **31**:419, 425, 443, 445; **81**:246, 250, 322, 342, 363
"A Song for the Future" (Harpur) **114**:166
"Song for the New Year's Eve" (Bryant) **6**:165
"Song for the Night of Christ's Resurrection" (Ingelow) **39**:266; **107**:148
"A Song for the Ragged Schools of London" (Browning) **61**:67
"Song from the Inner Life" (Chivers) **49**:72
"Song I am wearing away like the Snow in the Sun" (Opie) **65**:166
"Song III" (Barbauld) **50**:14
"Song Last Day" (Clare) **86**:114, 153
"A Song of Autumn" (Gordon) **21**:151, 155-56, 159-60, 176, 188
The Song of Bacchus (Pushkin) **83**:279
"The Song of Elaine" (Lanier) **118**:241
"A Song of Eternity in Time" (Lanier) **6**:244
"The Song of Fionnuala" (Moore) **6**:399
The Song of Hiawatha (Longfellow) **2**:477, 481, 483-84, 486-87, 494-96, 498; **45**:102-03, 106, 110-11, 114, 119-20, 128, 134, 136, 139, 144-45, 147, 149-150, 157-59, 166-69, 171-80, 187-88, 190; **101**:93-150; **103**:277, 283-84, 301, 304, 308
"Song of Isbrand" (Beddoes) **3**:34
"A Song of Joys" (Whitman) **4**:577, 601
"Song of LeVerrier on Discovering a New Planet" (Chivers) **49**:72
"A Song of Liberty" (Blake) **13**:169, 184, 214, 221; **57**:29-30, 40, 58
The Song of Los (Blake) **13**:184-85, 192-93, 221-22, 226-27; **37**:35
"Song of Love" (Lamartine)
See "Chant d'amour"
"A Song of Love" (Lanier) **118**:217
"A Song of Love Triumphant" (Turgenev)
See "Pesn' torzhestvuyushchey lyubvi"
"The Song of Marion's Men" (Bryant) **6**:165, 169, 172, 182
"The Song of Morphine" (Casal)
See "La canción de la morfina"
"Song of My Cid" (Bello) **131**:92
"The Song of My Heart" (Kivi) **30**:51
"Song of Myself" (Whitman) **31**:368-70, 375-76, 378-80, 385-87, 389-90, 392-93, 401-05, 409, 411-13, 416-21, 424-29, 435-36, 441, 443, 445; **4**:544, 562-63, 568, 571, 576, 579, 581-84, 589, 593-600, 602-04; **81**:23, 239-40, 247-8, 250, 258, 261-3, 269, 271, 276, 279-82, 299, 302-03, 307-8, 310, 312-13, 315-16, 318-20, 322, 327, 333, 340,
"The Song of Ninian Melville" (Kendall) **12**:191
"The Song of Pan" (Lampman) **25**:167
"Song of Pitcairn's Island" (Bryant) **6**:172
"Song of Praise" (Clare) **9**:76
"Song of Prudence" (Whitman) **81**:338
"The Song of Rahéro: A Legend of Tahiti" (Stevenson) **5**:410, 428
"The Song of Scandinavian Warriors" (Tyutchev)
See "Pesn skandinavskix voinov"
"Song of Slaves in the Desert" (Whittier) **59**:369, 372
The Song of Solomon, Newly Translated (Percy) **95**:313, 320, 336, 338, 360
"Song of Songs" (Barnes) **75**:99
Song of Songs (Daudet) **1**:237
"Song of Sorrow" (Keats) **73**:152
"Song of the Answerer" (Whitman) **4**:591; **31**:425, 431
"The Song of the Axe" (Crawford) **12**:158
"Song of the Banner at Daybreak" (Whitman) **4**:576; **81**:317
"The Song of the Bell" (Schiller) **38**:305, 337, 370
"The Song of the Bower" (Rossetti) **4**:491, 496-97, 510; **77**:328
"Song of the Broad-Axe" (Whitman) **4**:567, 571-72, 580; **31**:387, 392-93; **81**:322
"The Song of the Cattle Hunters" (Kendall) **12**:179, 183, 191, 195
"The Song of the Chattahoochee" (Lanier) **6**:236, 238-39, 249, 264-65, 270; **118**:203, 232, 238, 240, 265, 268, 275
"The Song of the Croaker" (Alger) **8**:16; **83**:112
"The Song of the Dogs" (Petofi)
See "A kutyák dala"
"The Song of the Earth" (Boker) **125**:7, 78
"Song of the Exposition" (Whitman) **4**:601
"A Song of the Future" (Lanier) **6**:244
"The Song of the Greek Amazon" (Bryant) **6**:172; **46**:7
"Song of the Greeks" (Campbell) **19**:179
"Song of the Lithuanian Legion" (Slowacki) **15**:349
The Song of the Merchant Kaláshnikov (Lermontov)
See *Pesnya pro tsarya Ivana Vasilievicha, molodogo oprichnika i undalogo kuptsa Kalashnikova*
"Song of the Middle Watch" (Ingelow) **107**:124
Song of the Night (Leopardi)
See "Canto notturno di un pastore errante dell'Asia"
"Song of the Open Road" (Whitman) **4**:582, 592, 596; **31**:387, 393, 431, 443; **81**:257, 278, 299, 314
"The Song of the Philaretians" (Mickiewicz) **3**:398
"The Song of the Poor Man" (Zhukovsky) **35**:402
"Song of the Redwood Tree" (Whitman) **4**:579; **31**:392
"A Song of the Rolling Earth" (Whitman) **4**:576; **31**:391; **81**:329
"Song of the sea" (Meyer)
See "Der Gesang des Meeres"
"Song of the Shingle Splitters" (Kendall) **12**:191, 195
"The Song of the Shirt" (Hood) **16**:205, 207-10, 212, 215, 220-21, 224-28, 231, 233-34, 236-38
"The Song of the Shirt" (Kingsley) **35**:227
"Song of the Sower" (Bryant) **6**:165; **46**:19
"Song of the Stars" (Bryant) **6**:161, 178, 190; **46**:6, 39
"Song of the Stream-Drops" (Lampman) **25**:200
"Song of the Stygian Naiades" (Beddoes) **3**:32, 34, 41
"The Song of the Surf" (Gordon) **21**:150, 154, 160, 164, 166, 176
"The Song of the Treadmill" (Holmes) **14**:99
"The Song of the Triumphant Love" (Turgenev)
See "Pesn' torzhestvuyushchey lyubvi"
Song of the Tsar Ivan Vasilievich, the young oprichnik and the bold Merchant Kalashnikov (Lermontov)
See *Pesnya pro tsarya Ivana Vasilievicha, molodogo oprichnika i undalogo kuptsa Kalashnikova*
"Song of the Universal" (Whitman) **31**:389-90
"The Song of the Vermonters" (Whittier) **8**:526
"Song of the Wanderer" (Nekrasov) **11**:407

"The Song of the Wolves" (Petofi)
See "A farkasok dala"
The Song of Tzar Ivan Vasiljevich, His Young Life-Guardsman, and the Valiant Merchant Kaláshnikov (Lermontov)
See *Pesnya pro tsarya Ivana Vasilievicha, molodogo oprichnika i undalogo kuptsa Kalashnikova*
"Song on Captain Barney's Victory" (Freneau) **1**:319
"Song: Rarely, Rarely, Comest Thou, Spirit of Delight" (Shelley) **18**:340, 344, 372
"Song to a City Girl" (Clare) **9**:77
Song to Joy (Schiller)
See *Lied an die Freude*
"Song, Venus" (Lazarus) **8**:426
"Song, Was it for this I dearly loved thee" (Opie) **65**:160
"Song, Yes, thou art changed" (Opie) **65**:160
"Le songe" (Sainte-Beuve) **5**:346
"Le songe de Polyphile" (Nerval) **67**:335
Songes (Almqvist) **42**:15-16, 20
"Songs" (Chivers)
See "Songs of the Heart"
"Songs" (Taylor) **89**:300
Songs, by the Ettrick Shepherd (Hogg) **109**:250
"Song's Eternity" (Clare) **9**:88, 97, 124
Songs For Children (Hale) **75**:286
"Songs for Strangers and Pilgrims" (Rossetti) **50**:286
"Songs for the Soldiers" (Crawford) **127**:153, 220-21
Songs from the Gulf of Salerno (Muller)
See *Lieder aus dem Meerbusen von Salerno*
Songs from the Mountains (Kendall) **12**:185, 187, 192, 197
"Songs in a Cornfield" (Rossetti) **50**:288
Songs of a Semite: The Dance to Death, and Other Poems (Lazarus) **8**:415, 421, 423-24; **109**:289, 304, 310, 318, 326-27, 331, 343-44
Songs of a Troubadour (Zorrilla y Moral)
See *Cantos del trovador*
"Songs of Aldhelm" (Lanier) **118**:217
Songs of Ensign Stål (Runeberg)
See *Fänrik Ståls sägner*
Songs of Experience (Blake) **13**:159, 163, 165, 172, 202, 218-22, 226, 240-43, 254; **57**:49; **127**:40, 75, 80
Songs of Innocence (Blake) **13**:159, 162, 171-72, 179-82, 191, 210-11, 218-19, 221, 239-43, 250-51; **57**:26; **127**:31, 75
Songs of Innocence and of Experience: Shewing the Two Contrary States of the Human Soul (Blake) **13**:159, 163, 184, 188-89, 218; **37**:1-99; **57**:50, 57, 93; **127**:75, 79, 82
Songs of Labor, and Other Poems (Whittier) **8**:495, 500-01, 506, 512, 517; **59**:350, 355, 357-8, 370
"The Songs of our Fathers" (Hemans) **71**:264
"Songs of Parting" (Whitman) **4**:546
"Songs of Semite" (Lazarus) **109**:341, 344
"Songs of Seven" (Ingelow) **39**:257, 264; **107**:119-20, 122, 146
"Songs of the Affections" (Hemans) **71**:261, 289
Songs of the Affections (Hemans) **71**:275, 277, 279, 293, 303-04, 307
Songs of the Army of the Night (Adams) **33**:2-8, 10-13, 15-18, 22, 24-5
Songs of the Domestic Affections (Hemans) **29**:205
"Songs of the Heart" (Chivers) **49**:48, 57
"Songs of the Ingenues" (Verlaine)
See "La chanson des ingénues"
"Songs of the Months" (Martineau) **26**:309
"Songs of the Night Watches" (Ingelow) **39**:264
"Songs of the Pixies" (Coleridge) **99**:18, 54
"Songs of the Voices of Birds" (Ingelow) **39**:264-65; **107**:122-23
Songs of the Western Slavs (Pushkin) **3**:452
Songs of Travel (Stevenson) **5**:419, 428
"Songs of Twilight" (Hugo) **3**:261
"Songs with Preludes" (Ingelow) **39**:264; **107**:119
Songs without Words (Verlaine)
See *Romances sans paroles*
"Song—Sweet Indian Maid" (Ridge) **82**:181
The Son-in-Law of M. Poirier (Augier)
See *Le gendre de Monsieur Poirier*
Sonnailles et clochettes (Banville) **9**:20, 30-31
Die Sonnenjungfrau (Kotzebue) **25**:135-37, 147
Sonnenklarer Bericht, A Report, Clear as the Sun, for the General Public on the Real Essence of the Latest Philosophy: An Attempt to compel the Reader to Understand (Fichte) **62**:4, 34
"Sonnet" (Cranch) **115**:6
"Sonnet" (Hayne) **94**:160-61
"Sonnet" (Keats) **8**:343, 349
"Sonnet" (Tennyson) **30**:205
"Sonnet 1" (Smith) **115**:152, 156
"Sonnet 2" (Smith) **115**:124, 204-5, 215
"Sonnet 3" (Smith) **115**:153
"Sonnet 4" (Smith) **115**:153, 173, 177, 180, 202-3
"Sonnet 5" (Smith) **115**:154, 177-78
"Sonnet 9" (Smith) **115**:156
"Sonnet 10" (Smith) **115**:177
"Sonnet 12" (Smith) **115**:154, 218
"Sonnet 26" (Smith) **115**:178
"Sonnet 27" (Smith) **115**:177
"Sonnet 30" (Smith) **115**:178
"Sonnet 31" (Smith) **115**:206
"Sonnet 32" (Smith) **115**:152, 178, 215
"Sonnet 33" (Smith) **115**:178
"Sonnet 34" (Smith) **115**:177
"Sonnet 36" (Smith) **115**:125, 154
"Sonnet 42" (Smith) **115**:206
"Sonnet 44" (Smith) **115**:123, 153-54, 197-99, 205
"Sonnet 45" (Smith) **115**:178
"Sonnet 47" (Smith) **115**:153, 176-77
"Sonnet 48" (Smith) **115**:154, 182
"Sonnet 55" (Smith) **115**:177
"Sonnet 57" (Smith) **115**:212, 217
"Sonnet 62" (Smith) **115**:217
"Sonnet 66" (Smith) **115**:176-77, 216
"Sonnet 67" (Smith) **115**:216
"Sonnet 68" (Smith) **115**:152
"Sonnet 70" (Smith) **115**:199
"Sonnet 77" (Smith) **115**:153
"Sonnet 79" (Smith) **115**:177, 218-19
"Sonnet 83" (Smith) **115**:210
"Sonnet 84" (Smith) **115**:177, 182
"Sonnet 89" (Smith) **115**:216
"Sonnet 90" (Smith) **115**:153, 216
"Sonnet 91" (Smith) **115**:216
"Sonnet 92" (Smith) **115**:210, 216
"Sonnet à Sir Bob" (Corbière) **43**:13
"Sonnet allégorique de lui-même" (Mallarmé) **41**:289, 291-92
"Sonnet boiteux" (Verlaine) **2**:631
"Sonnet CCLIV" (Boker) **125**:89
"Sonnet CCLXIII" (Boker) **125**:89
"Sonnet CCLXXI" (Boker) **125**:89
"Sonnet CCLXXV" (Boker) **125**:90
"Sonnet CCLXXX" (Boker) **125**:91
"Sonnet CCLXXXII" (Boker) **125**:91
"Sonnet CCXXXIX" (Boker) **125**:89
"Sonnet CCXXXVIII" (Boker) **125**:89
"Sonnet CIX" (Boker) **125**:89
"Sonnet CLXXX" (Boker) **125**:89
"Sonnet CXLVIII" (Boker) **125**:90
"Sonnet CXXIII" (Boker) **125**:84
"Sonnet CXXIV" (Boker) **125**:84
"Sonnet CXXXII" (Boker) **125**:90
"Sonnet CXXXIII" (Boker) **125**:90
"Sonnet CXXXIV" (Boker) **125**:90
"Sonnet CXXXVI" (Boker) **125**:90
"Sonnet en -yx" (Mallarmé) **4**:389; **41**:242-43, 289, 292-93
"Sonnet: England in 1819" (Shelley) **18**:375
"Sonnet II" (Boker) **125**:90
"Sonnet LIV" (Boker) **125**:89
"Sonnet LXIV" (Boker) **125**:85
"Sonnet LXX" (Boker) **125**:88
"Sonnet LXXI" (Boker) **125**:89
"Sonnet LXXII" (Boker) **125**:89
"Sonnet LXXIV" (Boker) **125**:89
"Sonnet LXXVIII" (Boker) **125**:89
"Sonnet LXXXVIII" (Boker) **125**:89
"Sonnet No. Three" (Smith) **59**:332
"Sonnet on Leaving Winchester" (Bowles) **103**:68
"Sonnet on the Approach of Autumn" (Opie) **65**:160
"Sonnet on the Fate of Poetic Genius in a Sordid Community" (Harpur) **114**:102
"Sonnet on the Mexican War" (Cranch) **115**:22
"Sonnet on the Nile" (Hunt) **70**:248
"Sonnet on the Ryne" (Bowles) **103**:85
"Sonnet to Hope" (Williams) **135**:255
"Sonnet to My Brothers" (Keats) **8**:345
"Sonnet to My Country" (Isaacs) **70**:306
"Sonnet to Solitude" (Keats) **8**:345
"Sonnet to the Moon" (Williams) **135**:255
"Sonnet to Twilight" (Williams) **135**:255, 333
"Sonnet to Zante" (Poe) **117**:217
"Sonnet Written at Tinemouth, Northumberland" (Bowles) **103**:85, 87, 90, 92-4
"Sonnet XLII" (Boker) **125**:88
"Sonnet XLV" (Boker) **125**:89
"Sonnet XXIII" (Boker) **125**:85
"Sonnet XXV" (Boker) **125**:85
"Sonnet XXVII" (Boker) **125**:84
"Sonnet XXXI" (Boker) **125**:89
Sonnets (Foscolo) **97**:62
Sonnets (Mallarmé) **4**:380
Sonnets (Mickiewicz)
See *Sonety Krymskie*
Sonnets: A Sequence on Profane Love (Boker) **125**:82-83
Sonnets and Canzonets (Alcott) **1**:22, 25
Sonnets, and Other Poems (Hayne) **94**:138-39
"'Sonnets, attempted in the Manner of 'Contemporary Writers'" (Coleridge) **111**:353
"Sonnets by Nehemiah Higginbottom" (Coleridge) **111**:353
"Sonnets for Pictures" (Rossetti) **77**:303, 344
Sonnets from the Crimea (Mickiewicz)
See *Sonety Krymskie*
Sonnets from the Portuguese (Browning) **1**:115, 122-4, 129; **16**:130-54; **61**:34, 43; **66**:44, 90-1
The Sonnets of Michelangelo and of Campanella (Symonds) **34**:334, 336
Sonnets of Unhappiness (Preseren)
See *Sonetje nesreče*
The Sonnets of William Wordsworth (Wordsworth) **12**:414
Sonnets on the War (Dobell) **43**:62
Sonnets on the War (Smith) **59**:293, 312, 319-20
Sonnets, written chiefly in Picturesque Spots (Bowles)
See *Sonnets written chiefly on Picturesque Spots during a Tour*
Sonnets written chiefly on Picturesque Spots during a Tour (Bowles) **103**:59-60, 72, 78, 85-7
"Sonnet—Silence" (Poe) **1**:528
"Sonnet—To Science" (Poe) **117**:215, 227, 231-32, 234, 242, 260, 281
"Le Sonneur" (Mallarmé) **41**:250, 281, 290
"Der Sonntag des Grossvaters" (Gotthelf) **117**:6
"Sonntags" (Meyer) **81**:205
Sons of Kings (Gobineau)
See *Les pléiades*
The Sons of Usna (Chivers) **49**:76, 78-9
"Soothsay" (Rossetti) **4**:509, 514, 518
Sophia (Lennox) **23**:228-29, 233-34; **134**:271

Sophie ou les sintiments setrcts (Staël-Holstein) **91**:326-27, 340, 358
Sophonisba (Alfieri)
See *Sofonisba*
"Sopra il monumento di Dante" (Leopardi) **129**:219, 316, 328
"Sopra il ritratto di una bella donna" (Leopardi) **129**:226, 246, 289, 291, 310
The Sorceress (Oliphant) **11**:454
La sorcière (Michelet) **31**:208, 220, 222-24, 230, 245, 258
"Sorcières espagnoles" (Mérimée) **6**:366
Sordello (Browning) **19**:75, 77-8, 102, 105, 109-10, 118, 120, 149-51; **79**:96, 132, 140, 146-47, 149, 164, 180-82, 185-86, 189-90
Søren Kierkegaard's Journals and Papers (Kierkegaard)
See *Papirer*
Soren Kierkegaards Samlede Vaerker (Kierkegaard) **78**:157-66, 168-69; **125**:260, 265
Sorgen ohne Noth und Noth ohne Sorgen (Kotzebue) **25**:145, 147
"Soročinskaja jamarka" (Gogol) **5**:218, 250, 256; **31**:110
"Sorrow" (Lampman) **25**:187
The Sorrows and Joys of a Schoolmaster (Gotthelf)
See *Leiden und Freuden eines Schulmeisters*
"Sorrows for the Death of a Favourite Tabby Cat" (Clare) **9**:77
"The Sorrows of Chatterton" (Harpur) **114**:137, 145
"The Sorrows of Rosalie" (Norton) **47**:239, 246, 248
The Sorrows of Rosalie and other Poems (Norton) **47**:251, 260
The Sorrows of Switzerland (Bowles) **103**:54, 70
The Sorrows of Young Werther (Goethe) **4**:162-63, 167, 169-71, 173, 176, 178, 188-91, 198-201
"Sortes Virgilianæ" (Timrod) **25**:361
Sortilege and Astrology (De Quincey) **4**:78
"Sotnyk" (Shevchenko) **54**:368
"Les Soucis matériels" (Baratynsky) **103**:16
"Soul and Country" (Mangan) **27**:296, 300
"The Soul Has Bandaged Moments" (Dickinson) **21**:76, 81; **77**:97
"Soul of Poets" (Keats) **8**:360
"The Soul of the Revolution" (Martí) **63**:166
"The Soul of the Rose" (Silva)
See "El alma de la rosa"
"The Soul of Wine" (Baudelaire)
See "L'ame du vin"
"The Soul Selects Her Own Society" (Dickinson) **21**:43
"The Soul should always stand ajar" (Dickinson) **77**:157
"The Soul Would Like to Be a Star" (Tyutchev) **34**:389
"Soul-Advances" (Hayne) **94**:138
"Soul's Beauty" (Rossetti) **4**:514-15; **77**:326
"The Soul's Expression" (Browning) **61**:5, 9, 43; **66**:85
"Souls of Songs" (Meyer)
See "Liederseelen"
"The Soul's Opportunities" (Very) **9**:388
"A Soul's Tragedy" (Browning) **19**:102, 113; **79**:153-54
"Soul-Sickness" (Very) **9**:397
"Sound Morality: Or, Practical Religion as distinguished from Theoretical Religion" (Hogg) **109**:231
"Sound o' Water" (Barnes) **75**:88
"The Sound of Home" (Lenau) **16**:277
"Sound Sleep" (Rossetti) **50**:267
Soundings From the Atlantic (Holmes) **81**:102, 104
"Sounds" (Thoreau) **7**:392, 402-4
"Soup from a Sausage Skewer" (Andersen)
See "How to Cook Soup upon a Sausage Pin"
"Soupir" (Mallarmé) **41**:250, 267-72, 279, 281
"La source" (Leconte de Lisle) **29**:245
"La source dans les bois" (Lamartine) **11**:279
Source of Positive Pleasure (Polidori)
See *Essay on the Source of Positive Pleasure*
"The Sources of Danger to the Republic" (Douglass) **7**:126
"Sous la table, dialogue bachique sur plusieurs questions de haute morale" (Gautier) **59**:10, 27
"Sous l'èpais Sycomore" (Leconte de Lisle) **29**:224
"Le sous préfet aux champs" (Daudet) **1**:238, 252
"Sous un portrait de Corbière" (Corbière) **43**:31, 33
"Sous-préfet in the Fields" (Daudet)
See "Le sous préfet aux champs"
"The South" (Lazarus) **8**:420
South Carolina Exposition and Protest (Calhoun) **15**:26-7, 50, 55
"South Carolina to the States of the North" (Hayne) **94**:144, 148
"The South Devil" (Woolson) **82**:272, 301
"The South Sea House" (Lamb) **10**:415, 435-36; **113**:199, 224, 235, 244, 267
"A South Sea Islander" (Adams) **33**:4
"The South Sea Sisters" (Horne) **127**:260
"The Southdown Shepherd" (Jefferies) **47**:134
"A Southern Night" (Arnold) **6**:72; **29**:26-7
"Southern Prose" (Lanier) **6**:267
"Southey and Landor" (Landor) **14**:166, 195
"Southey and Porson" (Landor) **14**:194-95
Soutien de famille (Daudet) **1**:251
"A Souvenir" (Holmes) **14**:100
"Souvenir" (Maupassant) **83**:181
"Souvenir" (Musset)
See "Le souvenir"
"Le souvenir" (Musset) **7**:258, 263, 272, 275, 280
"Souvenir de la nuit du quatre" (Hugo) **3**:262
"Le souvenir d'enfance; ou, La vie cachée" (Lamartine) **11**:255, 269-70, 278-79
Souvenir des vielles guerres (Hugo) **3**:264
Souvenirs (Goncharov) **63**:3
Souvenirs de Alexis de Tocqueville (Tocqueville) **7**:426-29, 446, 454-56; **63**:299, 304, 335, 369, 371
Souvenirs de jeunesse (Nodier) **19**:376, 384-85
Souvenirs de la révolution (Nodier) **19**:385
Souvenirs de la Révolution française (Williams) **135**:285, 289-90, 315-20, 336
Souvenirs de voyage (Gobineau) **17**:79-80, 93, 103
Souvenirs dégotisme (Stendhal) **23**:410, 411-12
Souvenirs d'enfance et de jeunesse (Renan) **26**:382, 386-87, 391-93, 398, 405-06, 408, 413, 415, 418, 421-22
Les Souvenirs d'un étudiant pauvre (Vallès) **71**:363
Souvenirs d'un homme de lettres (Daudet) **1**:241
"Souvenirs d'un vieux professeur allemand" (Renan) **26**:413
Souvenirs d'une favorite (Dumas) **71**:218
Souvenirs, impressions, pensées, et paysages pendant un voyage en Orient, 1832-1833; ou, Notes d'un voyageur (Lamartine) **11**:249, 251, 267, 289
"Souvenirs occulte" (Villiers de l'Isle Adam) **3**:589-90
"The Sovereignty of Ethics" (Emerson) **98**:66
"Sovremennoe" (Tyutchev) **34**:396
Sovremyonnaya idilliya (Saltykov) **16**:359, 361, 369, 373-74
"The Sower" (Very) **9**:384
Sowers Not Reapers (Martineau) **137**:267, 269
Sowing the Wind (Linton) **41**:157, 164-166, 170-71
The Spaewife (Galt) **1**:333-34
The Spagnoletto (Lazarus) **8**:418-19, 421, 425; **109**:289
Spain (Gautier)
See *España*
"Spain—The Confessional" (Browning) **79**:94
"The Spaniand" (Wergeland)
See "Spaniolen"
"The Spaniards in Denmark" (Mérimée)
See "Les Espagnols en Danemark"
Spaniards in Odense (Andersen) **79**:11
The Spaniards in Peru; or, The Death of Rolla (Kotzebue)
See *Die Spanier in Peru, oder Rollas Tod*
Die Spanier in Peru, oder Rollas Tod (Kotzebue) **25**:130, 141, 144-45, 148-49
"Spaniolen" (Wergeland) **5**:536, 540
Spanisches Theater (Schlegel) **15**:230
The Spanish Curate (Planché) **42**:273
"The Spanish Drama" (Lewes) **25**:285
The Spanish Drama: Lope de Vega and Calderon (Lewes) **25**:324
The Spanish Father (Mackenzie) **41**:184, 208-12
Spanish Grammar (Bello) **131**:93
The Spanish Gypsy (Eliot) **4**:102-04, 107, 109, 113-15, 140; **13**:333-34; **23**:52, 67, 88; **118**:58, 130, 166, 173
"A Spanish Love Song" (Kendall) **12**:181, 193
"The Spanish Military Nun" (De Quincey) **87**:15, 55-7
The Spanish Moors (Pixérécourt)
See *Les maures d'espagne; ou, Le pouvoir de l'enfance*
"The Spanish Nun" (De Quincey) **4**:74-75
The Spanish Story of the Armada and Other Essays (Froude) **43**:187
The Spanish Student (Longfellow) **2**:480, 482, 484, 497; **45**:113-14, 133, 135, 144, 148
"The Sparrow" (Isaacs)
See "El gorrión"
"The Sparrow" (Turgenev) **21**:452; **122**:289, 293
"The Sparrow's Nest" (Wordsworth) **12**:431
Spartacus, A Roman Story (Moodie) **113**:310, 319
"The Spartan Boy" (Lamb) **125**:348
"The Spartan Mother and Her Son" (Hemans) **71**:271
"The Spasmodic or German School" (Carroll) **139**:125
"Spätboot" (Meyer) **81**:203
"Spätjahr" (Meyer) **81**:140-41, 145-46, 148-50, 155
"Der Spaziergang" (Schiller) **39**:305, 337, 380
Speaking Likenesses (Rossetti) **50**:271, 276, 301; **66**:331
"Speak roughly to your little boy" (Carroll) **139**:29
"A Spec in China" (Horne) **127**:260
"Special Pleading" (Lanier) **6**:238, 242, 247; **118**:203, 215
"Special Report" (Arnold) **89**:110
Specimen (Cowper) **94**:82-3
Specimen Days (Whitman) **4**:577-78, 582, 588; **31**:403; **81**:275, 316-18, 338, 358, 369
"Specimen of an Induction" (Keats) **8**:345; **73**:151, 311
"Specimen of an Induction to a Poem" (Keats) **73**:158
Specimens of English Dramatic Poets Who Lived About the Time of Shakespeare (Lamb) **10**:391, 398, 405, 421-22, 427, 431-32, 434-35, 438; **113**:230, 255-59, 278
Specimens of the British Poets, with Biographical and Critical Notices, and an Essay on English Poetry (Campbell) **19**:171, 175, 200
Specimens of the Later English Poets (Southey) **97**:267
Un spectacle dans un fauteuil (Musset) **7**:260, 267

"Le spectacle interrompu" (Mallarmé) **4**:371
"Spectacle rassurant" (Hugo) **3**:273
"The Spectacles" (Poe) **55**:147; **117**:322
"The Spectre around Me" (Blake) **13**:181, 232
"The Spectre Bridegroom" (Irving) **2**:382-83; **19**:327-29, 341, 344, 348
The Spectre Lover (Southworth) **26**:434
"The Spectre of Tappington" (Barham) **77**:35, 41
The Spectre of Tappington (Barham) **77**:4, 7, 10
"The Spectre of the Cattle Flat" (Harpur) **114**:141, 148-50
"The Spectre Pig" (Holmes) **14**:101, 121, 127-28
"The Spectre Ship" (Whittier) **8**:485
"Spectre Warriors" (Whittier) **8**:485
"Spectres" (Leconte de Lisle) **29**:224
Speculations on Metaphysics (Shelley) **93**:354-55
"Speculations on Morals" (Shelley) **93**:374
"Speech Concerning Mythology" (Schlegel)
See "Die Rede über Mythologie und symbolische Anschaung"
Speech for Shakespeare's Anniversary (Goethe)
See *Rede zum Schäkespears Tag*
"Speech of a Water Nymph" (Darwin) **106**:182
Speeches (Schleiermacher)
See *Über die Religion: Reden an die Gebildeten unter ihren Verächtern*
Speeches on Religion (Schleiermacher)
See *Über die Religion: Reden an die Gebildeten unter ihren Verächtern*
Speeches on Religion to Its Cultured Despisers (Schleiermacher)
See *Über die Religion: Reden an die Gebildeten unter ihren Verächtern*
"Speeches to the Basle Congress" (Bakunin) **58**:132
The Spell (Brontë) **33**:127
"Spell-Bound" (Morris) **4**:419
A Spelling Dictionary (Rowson) **69**:115
Spelling-Book, with Appropriate Lessons in Reading and with a Stepping Stone to English Grammar (Cobbett) **49**:160
"The Spells of Home" (Hemans) **71**:264
"Spelt from Sibyl's Leaves" (Hopkins) **17**:198, 231, 238, 243, 246-48, 255-56
The Spendthrift (Ainsworth) **13**:41
The Spendthrift (Jerrold) **2**:402
The Spendthrift (Leskov)
See *Rastočitel*
The Spendthrift (Raimund)
See *Der Verschwender*
"Spenser" (Boker) **125**:35
"Speranza" (Ingelow) **39**:258
"Sperm" (Silva)
See "Zoospermos"
"The Sphinx" (Emerson) **1**:285, 289, 295-96; **38**:169, 187, 189; **98**:177-86
"The Sphinx" (Pavlova)
See "Sfinks"
"The Sphinx" (Poe) **16**:332
Le Sphinx (Feuillet) **45**:77, 79, 82, 87, 89
Le Sphinx rouge (Dumas) **71**:220
"The Sphinx's Children" (Cooke) **110**:3, 18-19
The Sphinx's Children (Cooke)
See *The Sphinx's Children and Other People's*
The Sphinx's Children and Other People's (Cooke) **110**:19, 21, 26, 33-7, 39, 43
"The Spider and the Fly" (Vigny)
See *Cinq-Mars; ou, Une conjuration sous Louis XIII*
"A Spider Sewed at Night" (Dickinson) **21**:76
"Das Spiegelbild" (Grillparzer) **102**:174
Der Spiegelritter (Kotzebue) **25**:146
"Spiel mannslied" (Keller) **2**:421
Spielmann (Grillparzer)
See *Der Arme Spielmann*
"Der Spinnerin Lied" (Brentano) **1**:96, 102, 105
Spinning-Wheel Stories (Alcott) **58**:50-1
"Spinoza and the Bible" (Arnold) **29**:55
"Spinozianism" (Schleiermacher) **107**:328
Spiridion (Sand) **2**:582, 585, 587, 598, 600; **42**:319-20, 372; **57**:315, 360, 375
"A Spirit Haunts the Year's Last Hours" (Tennyson) **30**:211
"Spirit Independent of Matter" (Murray) **63**:207
Spirit of Discovery (Bowles) **103**:54-5
The Spirit of Hebrew Poetry (Herder)
See *Vom Geist der ebräischen Poesie*
Spirit of Peers and People: A National Tragi-Comedy (Horne) **127**:252-53, 256, 263
"The Spirit of the Age" (Kennedy) **2**:432
"The Spirit of the Age" (Mill) **11**:369
The Spirit of the Age (Hazlitt) **29**:148, 152, 164, 166-67, 170, 174, 188; **82**:102-03, 106, 108-09, 112-13, 123, 125, 127
Spirit of the Age (Horne) **127**:236, 239-40, 245
Spirit of the Age (Martínez de la Rosa)
See *Espíritu del siglo*
"The Spirit of the Glen" (Hogg) **109**:203
The Spirit of the Reeds (Bird) **1**:87
"Spirit Whose Work Is Done" (Whitman) **4**:543; **81**:315
Spirite (Gautier) **1**:345, 352, 354-55; **59**:12-14, 33-6, 39, 42, 44, 71
"The Spirit's Blasted Tree" (Scott) **15**:255
"Spirits Everywhere" (Mangan) **27**:273
"Spirits of the Dead" (Poe) **117**:264, 280
"A Spirit's Return" (Hemans) **71**:303
"The Spirit's Trials" (Froude) **43**:192
Spiritual Creation (James) **53**:195, 204, 233
"Spiritual Diary" (Cowper) **94**:27, 30
"Spiritual Laws" (Emerson) **38**:149, 174, 224, 226-27; **98**:37, 107, 110-11
"Spiritualism and Materialism" (Lewes) **25**:314
Der spiritus familiaris des Rosstäuschers (Droste-Hülshoff) **3**:196, 200-01
"Der Spitzwegsche Rahmen" (Gotthelf) **117**:55
"Spleen" (Baudelaire)
See "Le spleen"
"Le spleen" (Baudelaire) **29**:83-4, 87, 103, 112; **55**:13, 49-52, 61, 65, 70
"Spleen" (Verlaine) **51**:383
Le spleen de Paris (Baudelaire)
See *Petits poèmes en prose: Le spleen de Paris*
"Spleen et Idéal" (Baudelaire) **55**:15, 51, 56-66, 73
"Spleen I" (Baudelaire) **55**:44, 64
"Spleen II" (Baudelaire) **55**:44
"Spleen IV" (Baudelaire) **55**:44-6
Splendeurs et misères des courtisanes (Balzac) **5**:63, 75-76
"Splendor of Falling Day" (Whitman) **4**:544
Splendors and Miseries of a Courtesan (Balzac)
See *Splendeurs et misères des courtisanes*
"The Splenetic Indian" (Freneau) **111**:133
"The Spoken Thought Becomes a Lie" (Tyutchev)
See "Silentium"
"Sponsa Dei" (Patmore) **9**:339, 352, 354, 359, 361-62
"Spontaneity or Instinct" (Emerson) **1**:293
"Spontaneous Me" (Whitman) **31**:372
Sporting and Social Recollections (Surtees) **14**:377
A Sportsman's Sketches (Turgenev)
See *Zapiski okhotnika*
"The Spotted Dog" (Trollope) **101**:235
"Spravedlivyj čelovek" (Leskov) **25**:228
"Sprich aus der Ferne" (Brentano) **1**:104
"Spring" (Baratynsky)
See "Vesna, vesna! kak vozdukh chist!..."
"Spring" (Barnes) **75**:34
"Spring" (Blake) **13**:182; **37**:3, 9, 13, 41, 61, 71-2, 74-6, 92
"Spring" (Hood) **16**:235
"Spring" (Hopkins) **17**:191, 220
"Spring" (Hunt) **1**:417
"Spring" (Lanier) **118**:259
"Spring" (Rossetti) **2**:575
"Spring" (Thoreau) **7**:399, 404-5; **138**:95-96, 129, 186, 192
"Spring" (Timrod) **25**:364, 372, 376, 382-83, 386, 388
"Spring" (Tyutchev)
See "Vesna"
"Spring and Boils" (Shaw) **15**:335
"Spring and Fall" (Hopkins) **17**:236, 243-44, 246, 256
"Spring and Tyranny" (Lanier) **118**:217
"Spring Calm" (Tyutchev)
See "Vesennee uspokoenie"
"A Spring Chanson" (Smith) **59**:308, 321
Spring Freshets (Turgenev)
See *Veshnie vody*
"Spring in Town" (Bryant) **6**:161
"Spring is Come" (Allingham) **25**:9
"Spring Longing" (Lazarus) **109**:292
"Spring Quiet" (Rossetti) **2**:574
"The Spring returns, the pewit screams" (Clare) **86**:90
"Spring Songs" (Clare) **9**:121
"Spring Songs" (Symonds) **34**:323
"Spring, spring! how pure the air!..." (Baratynsky)
See "Vesna, vesna! kak vozdukh chist!..."
"Spring Storm" (Tyutchev) **34**:288, 389, 401
"Spring Waters" (Tyutchev) **34**:389, 391
The Spring Wreath (Arnim)
See *Clemens Brentanos Frühlingskranz aus Jugendbriefen ihm geflochten, wie er selbst schriftlich verlangte*
"The Springs" (Hale) **75**:300
"Spring's Bedfellow" (Morris) **4**:434
"Springtime's Glances" (Lenau) **16**:276, 278
Spring-Torrents (Turgenev)
See *Veshnie vody*
"Sputnica feia" (Pavlova) **138**:16, 49
The Spy (Hogg) **109**:200, 203-04, 246, 258, 261-62
The Spy: A Tale of the Neutral Ground (Cooper) **1**:194-97, 200, 202, 207, 221-23; **27**:123-24, 137, 171; **54**:249, 251-2, 264-5, 273, 277, 280, 287, 299-300
"The Squabble of the Sea Nymphs; or, The Sacrifice of the Tuscararoes" (Warren) **13**:412, 414, 431
The Squandors of Castle Squandor (Carleton) **3**:85-86, 89-90
The Square Table (Sigourney) **87**:325
"Squaudered Lives" (Taylor) **89**:309
"Le squelette laboureur" (Baudelaire) **29**:101, 103; **55**:12, 35
The Squire (Krasicki)
See *Pan Podstoli*
Squire Arden (Oliphant) **61**:216
"The Squire in the poem" (Crabbe) **121**:65
"Squire Maurice" (Smith) **59**:321, 331, 333
"Squire Paine's Conversion" (Cooke) **110**:24, 33-4
"Squire Thomas; or, The Precipitate Choice" (Crabbe) **26**:93; **121**:40
"Squire Toby's Will" (Le Fanu) **9**:312
"The Squire's Story" (Gaskell) **70**:188
The Squire's Story (Barham) **77**:4
Srpska gramatika (Karadzic) **115**:83
Srpske narodne pjesme (Karadzic) **115**:77-80, 100, 112
Srpske narodne poslovice (Karadzic) **115**:78-9
Srpski rječnik (Karadzic) **115**:83
SS (Parton)
See *Shadows and Sunbeams*
"St. Agnes Eve" (Tennyson) **115**:235
"St. Alban's Abbey" (Radcliffe) **6**:412; **55**:224
"St. Andrew's Anniversary" (Brackenridge) **7**:56
"St. Augustine in April" (Lanier) **6**:232; **118**:212
St. Bartholomew's Eve (Newman) **99**:249
"St. Brandan" (Arnold) **6**:44, 66

St. Cecilia, or the Power of Music (Kleist)
See *Die heilige Cäcilie; oder, die Gewalt der Musik*
"St. Clair Flats" (Woolson) **82**:272, 285, 293, 333
St. Clair; or, The Heiress of Desmond (Morgan) **29**:389-90
St. Cupid (Jerrold) **2**:402-03
St. Domingo: Its Revolutions and Its Patriots (Brown) **2**:47-48, 52
"St. Edmond's Eve" (Shelley) **18**:342
"St. George's Hospital" (Landon) **15**:161
St. Giles and St. James (Jerrold) **2**:398-400, 402, 405
St. Irvyne; or, The Rosicrucian (Shelley) **18**:307, 341
St. Ives: Being the Adventures of a French Prisoner in England (Stevenson) **5**:419
"The St. James Phenomenon" (Hunt) **1**:423
St John in Patmos (Bowles) **103**:54-5, 61
St. Leon: A Tale of the Sixteenth Century (Godwin) **14**:37, 40, 42, 44-5, 47, 50, 52, 55-6, 58-60, 68-78, 80-3; **130**:29, 60, 151, 169
"St. Luke the Painter" (Rossetti) **77**:308
"St. Margaret's Eve" (Allingham) **25**:7
"St. Martin's Summer" (Browning) **19**:88
"St. Mary of the Lowes" (Hogg) **109**:202
"St. Michael's Chapel" (Lazarus) **109**:297
St. Michael's Mount (Bowles) **103**:54, 60, 70
St. Patrick's Day; or, The Scheming Lieutenant (Sheridan) **91**:240-41
"St. Paul and Protestantism" (Arnold) **126**:109
St. Paul and Protestantism; with an Introduction on Puritanism and the Church of England (Arnold) **29**:8, 15-16, 20; **126**:63-64, 89-90
"St. Paul's Characteristic Gift" (Newman) **38**:305
"St. Petersburg" (Mickiewicz) **3**:401
St. Ronan's Well (Scott) **15**:277, 289
"St. Simeon Stylites" (Tennyson) **30**:279, 281; **65**:270
"St. Valentine's Day" (Patmore) **9**:343, 349, 357
St. Valentine's Day; or, The Fair Maid of Perth (Scott) **15**:270, 283, 300, 309, 313; **69**:313, 369
"St. Winefred's Well" (Hopkins) **17**:185, 190
Stadier paa Livets Vej (Kierkegaard) **34**:200-01, 222-223, 238, 261, 263; **78**:173, 178, 181, 227, 238; **125**:184-85, 190-92, 198, 201, 209, 248, 258-68
"Die Stadt" (Storm) **1**:547
"The Staff and Scrip" (Rossetti) **4**:505, 518-19, 523, 527, 529-31; **77**:326, 328-30, 348
The Stag King (Gozzi)
See *Il re cervo*
"The Stage and the Spirit of Reverence" (Carroll) **53**:122
"The Stage Coach" (Irving) **19**:328
"Stage Illusion" (Lamb) **10**:410, 432, 434
Stages on Life's Way (Kierkegaard)
See *Stadier paa Livets Vej*
"The Stag-Eyed Lady" (Hood) **16**:234-35
"Stagnant Waters" (Pisarev) **25**:338
Les stalactites (Banville) **9**:2, 14, 18-19, 26, 28-29
"Stalwart the Bushranger" (Harpur) **114**:136
"Stances à la Malibran" (Musset) **7**:261-62, 280
"Stand by the Flag" (Foster) **26**:288
"The Standards" (Patmore) **9**:334, 339-40, 359, 362
Ständchen in Ritornellen aus Albano (Muller) **73**:362
"Den standhaftige Tinsoldat" (Andersen) **7**:23, 28-9, 34, 37, 39; **79**:21, 23, 33, 40, 51, 58, 62-4, 70-1, 76, 82
"Stangers Yet" (Milnes) **61**:136, 141-2, 152
"Stansy" (Baratynsky) **103**:8-9
"Stantsionnyi smotritel" (Pushkin) **3**:435, 464; **83**:272, 323, 327-29, 337, 354-55
"Stanza" (Clare) **9**:111
"Stanzas" (Baratynsky)
See "Stansy"
"Stanzas" (Cranch) **115**:32, 35
"Stanzas" (Moore) **110**:177
"Stanzas" (Poe) **117**:264
"Stanzas from the Grande Chartreuse" (Arnold) **29**:4, 6-7, 28, 32-3, 38; **89**:46, 51-2, 88, 96-7
"Stanzas in Memory of Edward Quillinan" (Arnold) **29**:22, 37
"Stanzas in Memory of the Author of 'Obermann'" (Arnold) **29**:4, 6-7, 22-3, 31, 36, 38
"Stanzas Meditated in the Cloisters of Christ's Hospital" (Dyer) **129**:96
"Stanzas Occasioned by certain absurd, extravagant, and even blasphemous panegyrics and encomiums on the character of the late gen. Washington" (Freneau) **111**:160
"Stanzas Occasioned by the Ruins of a Country Inn" (Freneau) **111**:145
"Stanzas on Coming of Age" (Hood) **16**:236
"Stanzas on Peele Castle" (Wordsworth) **12**:431, 436, 447, 469
"Stanzas on the Battle of Navarino" (Campbell) **19**:183
"Stanzas On the Decease of Thomas Paine" (Freneau) **111**:160
"Stanzas on the Fate of Henry Percy" (Brontë) **105**:55
"Stanzas on the Great Western Canal of the State of New York" (Freneau) **111**:102
"Stanzas on the Threatened Invasion" (Campbell) **19**:191
"Stanzas Subjoined to the Yearly Bill of Mortality of the Parish of All Saints, Northampton" (Cowper) **8**:119
"Stanzas Suggested By Matthew Arnold's 'Stanzas from the Grande Chartreuse'" (Thomson) **18**:406, 414, 424
"Stanzas to Cynthio" (Opie) **65**:160
"Stanzas To F S O" (Poe) **55**:212
"Stanzas to Malibran" (Musset)
See "Stances à la Malibran"
"Stanzas to the Memory of Gen. Washington" (Freneau) **111**:160
Stanzas to the Memory of the Late King (Hemans) **29**:192
"Stanzas to Tolstoi" (Pushkin) **83**:256
"Stanzas Written in Dejection-December 1818, Near Naples" (Shelley) **18**:344, 370-71, 373; **93**:308
"Stanzas written under Aeolus's Harp" (Opie) **65**:156
"Stanzas.—April, 1814" (Shelley) **93**:307
"Stapfen" (Meyer) **81**:199, 204-05, 209
"The Star and the Water-Lily" (Holmes) **14**:128
The Star Chamber (Ainsworth) **13**:45
"The Star Gazer" (Cranch) **115**:5, 40
"Star in the East" (Paine) **62**:325
The Star of Seville (Kemble) **18**:179-80
"Staratelno my nablyudaem svet..." (Baratynsky) **103**:9
"Starinnaia povest'—Roman i Ol'ga" (Bestuzhev) **131**:167, 175, 182-83
"The Starless King's Son" (Eminescu) **33**:264
"Starlight in the Odenwald" (Taylor) **89**:298
"The Starlight Night" (Hopkins) **17**:185, 191, 195, 216, 247
"Starosvetskie Pomeščiki" (Gogol) **5**:209, 218-19, 231, 245-47, 254-55
"The Stars Are with the Voyager" (Hood) **16**:222
"Starukha" (Pavlova) **138**:12, 54
"Starting from Paumanok" (Whitman) **4**:568-600, 603; **31**:389-90, 392-93, 398; **81**:246, 265, 319, 353
Starye gody v sele Plodomasove (Leskov) **25**:228, 232
"Starye portrety" (Turgenev) **21**:453-54; **122**:246
"State and Religion" (Wagner) **9**:414
"The State of German Literature" (Carlyle) **70**:39, 63, 94
State Papers vol.13, Children's Employment (Horne) **127**:266
State Trials (Cobbett) **49**:163
"The Stately Homes of England" (Hemans) **71**:283, 305
"Statesman and Thinker" (Krylov) **1**:439
The Statesman's Manual (Coleridge) **9**:135
"The Statesman's Secret" (Holmes) **14**:128
The Statesmen of the Commonwealth of England: With a Treatise on the Popular Progress in English History (Forster) **11**:115
"The Stationmaster" (Pushkin)
See "Stantsionnyi smotritel"
Statism and Anarchism (Bakunin) **25**:47, 49; **58**:144, 146
"La Statue amoureuse" (Gautier) **59**:35, 38-40
"The Statue and the Bust" (Browning) **19**:79, 114, 127, 129, 131
The Statue Guest (Pushkin)
See *Kamennyi gost'*
Statute Establishing Religious Freedom in Virginia (Jefferson) **103**:123, 221, 223
Statute of Virginia for Religious Freedom (Jefferson)
See *Statute Establishing Religious Freedom in Virginia*
"Stay, Summer Breath" (Foster) **26**:287
The Steadfast: Story of A Saint and A Sinner (Cooke) **110**:21, 24, 39, 50, 56, 58, 66
"The Steadfast Tin Soldier" (Andersen)
See "Den standhaftige Tinsoldat"
"The Stealing Magpie" (Herzen) **10**:334, 350; **61**:108
"The Stealthy School of Criticism" (Rossetti) **77**:341-42
The Steam boat (Galt) **1**:333, 335; **110**:84-6, 114
"The Steamboat" (Baratynsky)
See "Piroskaf"
"The Steamer" (Baratynsky)
See "Piroskaf"
"La steaua" (Eminescu) **33**:251
Der Stechlin (Fontane) **26**:234, 241, 243-45, 248, 256-57, 261, 269-71, 275, 278
"The Steed and Its Rider" (Krylov) **1**:435
"Steele and Addison" (Landor) **14**:165
Steht Homer z. Ex. unterm Spruch des Aristoteles & Compagnie? (Claudius) **75**:196
"Stella" (Mowatt) **74**:219, 234-35
"Stella" (Nin) **7**:23, 29
Stella (Goethe) **4**:164, 174, 219-20; **34**:71-2
"Stella Maris" (Symonds) **34**:323, 338-39, 350-51
Stello: A Session with Doctor Noir (Vigny)
See *Les consultations du Docteur Noir: Stello; ou, les diables bleus, première consultation*
Stello, ou les Diables bleus (Vigny)
See *Les consultations du Docteur Noir: Stello; ou, les diables bleus, première consultation*
Sténie (Balzac) **5**:88
Stenka Razine (Mérimée) **65**:85
Stephen Calvert (Brown) **122**:53
Stephen the Great (Eminescu) **131**:292
Stephen the Younger (Eminescu) **33**:264-65
"The Step-Mother" (Parton) **86**:349
"Stepnoj korol' Lir" (Turgenev)
See "Son"
"Stepnoy Korol 'Lir" (Turgenev) **21**:401, 408, 414, 416-17, 420, 422, 427, 435, 440-41; **122**:264, 266, 268
"The Steppes of Akkerman" (Mickiewicz)
See "Stepy Akermańskie"
"Stepy Akermańskie" (Mickiewicz) **3**:404

"Die sterbende Meduse" (Meyer) **81**:207
"Stern Disappointment" (Moodie) **113**:348
Sterne's Maria (Dunlap) **2**:213
"The Stethoscope Song" (Holmes) **81**:107
"The Steward" (Turgenev) **21**:377
"Steyermark" (Taylor) **89**:298
Æsthetics (Schleiermacher) **107**:285
Stick to Your Own Station (Ostrovsky)
See *Ne v svoi sani ne sadis!*
Stikhotvoreniia (Pavlova) **138**:34
Stikhotvoreniia Poèmy Proza Pis'ma (Baratynsky) **103**:47
Stikhotvoreniya v proze (Turgenev) **21**:414, 420, 431, 441, 452-55; **37**:443; **122**:243, 280, 283, 289, 293, 306-8, 312
"Still and bright, in twilight shining" (Brontë) **109**:28, 36
"The Still Small Voice" (Ridge) **82**:181
"The Still Small Voice" (Very) **9**:387
"Stillborn" (Baratynsky)
See "Nedonosok"
"The Still-Born" (Very) **9**:378
Ein Stiller Musikant (Storm) **1**:540
"A still-Volcano-Life" (Dickinson) **77**:145-46
Stilpo und seine Kinder (Klinger) **1**:429
"Stimme des Kindes" (Lenau) **16**:281
"Stimme des Volks" (Hölderlin) **16**:191
Stimmen der Völker in Liedern (Herder)
See *Volkslieder*
"Stimmung" (Meyer) **81**:152
Stine (Fontane) **26**:235-36, 240, 244, 248, 251-53, 258-59, 270-71
"The Stinger" (Leskov)
See "Jazvitel' nyj"
"The Stirrup-Cup" (Lanier) **6**:236, 249, 254; **118**:238, 273, 275
Stockholm, Fountainebleau, et Rome (Dumas)
See *Christine; ou, Stockholm, Fountainebleau, et Rome*
"Stoic and Hedonist" (Lampman) **25**:165, 190, 219
"Stojit' v seli Subotovi" (Shevchenko) **54**:382
The Stolen Child (Galt) **1**:334
"A Stolen Letter" (Collins) **1**:187
"Stolen Waters" (Carroll) **139**:30, 126-27
"The Stolen White Girl" (Ridge) **82**:175, 180
The Stone Guest (Pushkin)
See *Kamennyi gost'*
"Stone of Night" (Blake) **37**:80
"Stonehenge" (Radcliffe) **6**:412
"The Stone-Pit" (Clare) **9**:117
Stones of Many Colors (Stifter)
See *Bunte Steine*
The Store Boy (Alger) **83**:112
Storia compendiosa della vita di Lorenzo da Ponte (Da Ponte) **50**:97
"Storia del genere umano" (Leopardi) **129**:243, 265, 297
Stories (Andersen)
See *Eventyr, fortalte for børn*
Stories from Life (Craik) **38**:119
Stories from the Italian Poets, with Lives of the Writers (Hunt) **1**:413
Stories of Ensign Stål (Runeberg)
See *Fänrik Ståls sägner*
Stories of the Canadian Forest (Traill)
See *Lady Mary and Her Nurse; or, A Peep into the Canadian Forest*
Stories of the Old Dominion (Cooke) **5**:125, 127, 131
Stories of the Orphan Petrush (Shevchenko)
See *Povisty o besrodnom Petrush*
Stories of the Study (Galt) **1**:334; **110**:114
Stories to a Child (Ingelow)
See *Stories Told to a Child*
Stories Told for Children (Andersen)
See *Eventyr, fortalte for børn*
Stories Told to a Child (Ingelow) **39**:264; **107**:119, 161, 163-64
"The Storks" (Andersen) **7**:29; **79**:23
"The Storm" (Baratynsky)
See "Burya"
"Storm" (Lampman) **25**:193, 207, 220
"The Storm" (Mickiewicz)
See "Burza"
The Storm (Ostrovsky)
See *Groza*
"Storm in the Fens" (Clare) **86**:110
"A Storm in the Mountains" (Harpur) **114**:96, 98, 105, 120-21, 125, 144, 158, 161-62, 164
"Storm of Thunder among Mountains" (Hogg) **109**:202, 206
"Storm on Lake Asquam" (Whittier) **8**:520
"The Storm Rages Ever More Violently" (Tyutchev)
See "Vse bešennej burja"
"Storm Song" (Taylor) **89**:300
Storm-beat Maid (Baillie) **71**:53-4,
Storming the Bastille (Dumas)
See *Ange Pitou*
"The Stormy Morning" (Muller)
See "Der stürmische Morgen"
"A Story" (Pavlova)
See "Razskaz"
"Story for a Child" (Lermontov) **5**:288
"A Story from the Dunes" (Andersen) **7**:33; **79**:82, 88
The Story of a Famous Old Jewish Firm (Thomson) **18**:426
"Story of a Feather" (Jerrold) **2**:395-96, 399, 401-02, 404
"The Story of a Mother" (Andersen)
See "Hisbrien om en Moder"
The Story of a Puppet (Collodi)
See *Le Avventure di Pinocchio*
"The Story of a Russian Officer in Captivity among the Mountaineers" (Bestuzhev)
See "Rasskaz ofitsera, byvshego v plenu u gorcev"
"The Story of a Shipwreck" (Gordon)
See "From the Wreck"
The Story of a Town (Saltykov)
See *Istoriya odnogo goroda*
"A Story of a Wedding Tour" (Oliphant) **61**:205, 210-11
"The Story of an Affinity" (Lampman) **25**:199, 201, 219-20
"The Story of an Outcast" (Boyesen) **135**:11, 20-21, 25
Story of Belkis and Solomon (Nerval) **1**:475
"A Story of Doom" (Ingelow) **39**:256, 262, 265
A Story of Doom and Other Poems (Ingelow) **39**:257, 264, 266; **107**:118, 124, 147, 149, 155-57, 159
"The Story of Father Alexis" (Turgenev)
See "Rasskaz ottsa Aleksaya"
"The Story of Gamber-Ali" (Gobineau)
See "Histoire de Gambèr-Aly"
"The Story of Glaucus the Thessalian" (Hayne) **94**:144, 153-54, 156-59
The Story of Goethe's Life (Lewes)
See *The Life and Works of Goethe*
The Story of Juliette; or, Vice Amply Rewarded (Sade)
See *Juliette; ou, Les prospérités du vice*
"The Story of Julius" (Brown) **74**:140
The Story of Kennett (Taylor) **89**:311, 343, 346-50
"The Story of Lieutenant Ergunov" (Turgenev)
See "Istoriya leytenanta Ergunova"
Story of Margaretta (Murray) **63**:209-14
The Story of My Heart (Jefferies) **47**:94-6, 101, 105, 111, 115, 119, 121, 123-25, 129, 132-34, 136-38, 143
The Story of My Life (Andersen) **79**:4, 18, 21
The Story of My Life (Sand)
See *Histoire de ma vie*
The Story of Norway (Boyesen) **135**:8
"A Story of Pennsylvania" (Taylor) **89**:359
"A Story of Psyche" (Griffin) **7**:214
"The Story of Rhodope" (Morris) **4**:417, 447
"The Story of Rimini" (Hunt) **1**:410-12, 414, 421
The Story of Rimini (Hunt) **70**:250, 253, 263, 267, 282
The Story of Sigurd the Volsung, and the Fall of the Niblungs (Morris) **4**:417-18, 420-21, 428, 430-33, 435, 443
"The Story of the Forest" (Eminescu) **131**:296
"The Story of the Four Little Children Who Went Round the World" (Lear) **3**:297
"The Story of the Glittering Plain, Which Has Been Also Called the Land of Living Men or the Acre of the Undying" (Morris) **4**:425, 436-37, 440
"Story of the Island of Cuba" (Bryant) **6**:181
"The Story of the Just Caspar and Fair Annie" (Brentano)
See "Geschichte vom braven Kasperl und dem schönen Annerl"
"Story of the Lost Reflection" (Hoffmann) **2**:341
"Story of the Physician and the Saratoga Trunk" (Stevenson) **5**:394
"The Story of the Seven Families from the Lake Pipple-Popple" (Lear) **3**:307
"The Story of the Star-Travelling Magus" (Eminescu)
See "The Tale of the Magus Travelling in the Stars"
"The Story of the Three Bears" (Southey) **8**:470, 475; **97**:271, 289-90, 292, 323-29
"The Story of the Unknown Church" (Morris) **4**:429
"The Story of the Young Italian" (Irving) **2**:370, 382, 390; **19**:332
"Story of the Young Man with the Cream Tarts" (Stevenson) **5**:394, 413
"The Story of the Young Robber" (Irving) **2**:390; **19**:344
"The Story of Toby" (Melville) **45**:204
"Story of Two Highlanders'" (Hogg) **109**:248
The Story of Venus and Tannhäuser (Beardsley) **6**:137-38, 144-47, 149-50, 152-54
"The Story Teller" (Hawthorne) **79**:320
"The Story Teller at Fault" (Griffin) **7**:198
"A Story without a Tail" (Maginn) **8**:438-39
"The Stout Gentleman" (Irving) **2**:389; **95**:227
The Stout Gentleman (Irving) **95**:226
Strafford (Browning) **19**:75, 78, 102; **79**:146, 189
"The strains we hear in foreign lands" (Moodie) **113**:344
The Strange Case of Dr. Jekyll and Mr. Hyde (Stevenson) **5**:398, 400, 402-05, 408, 413, 415, 418, 421, 427, 429, 433-37; **14**:311-40; **63**:261, 269
"The Strange Child" (Hoffmann) **2**:351
"Strange Disturbances on Aungier Street" (Le Fanu)
See "Some Strange Disturbances in an Old House on Augier Street"
"A Strange Event in the Life of Schalken the Painter" (Le Fanu) **9**:312, 314, 318-20, 322
"Strange Fits of Passion Have I Known" (Wordsworth) **12**:445, 464; **111**:226, 323-24, 327-28
The Strange Gentleman (Dickens) **37**:153
A Strange History (Lewes) **25**:291
"The Strange Lady" (Bryant) **6**:186; **46**:4
A Strange Manuscript Found in a Copper Cylinder (De Mille) **123**:107 , 108-19, 123-24, 126, 128-34, 138-42, 144, 146-49, 151, 153, 158, 160
"A Strange Story" (Turgenev)
See "Strannaya istoriya"
A Strange Story (Bulwer-Lytton) **1**:150-51; **45**:22-3, 47
"The Strange Story of Korah, Dathan, and Abiram, Numbers, Chap. XVI, Accounted For" (Paine) **62**:325
"The Stranger" (Lewis) **11**:302
The Stranger (Bird) **1**:90

The Stranger (Kotzebue)
See *Menschenhass und Reue*
Stranger (Sheridan) **5**:362
"The Stranger: Being a Further Portion of the Recluse, A Poem" (Hogg) **4**:282; **109**:192, 247
"The Stranger in Louisiana" (Hemans) **71**:264
"The Stranger's Vision" (Brady) **41**:312-13
"Strannaya istoriya" (Turgenev) **21**:399, 408, 416, 435, 441, 453; **122**:242, 365, 369, 371, 378
"Strannik" (Pavlova) **138**:14
"Strashnoe gadanie: Rasskaz" (Bestuzhev) **131**:149, 156, 158-59, 210, 212-13
"Strašnaja mest" (Gogol) **5**:218, 223-25, 230-31, 249, 251, 256-57; **31**:76, 120
"Strast' sprosit" (Bestuzhev) **131**:165
"Stratford-on-Avon" (Irving) **2**:381; **19**:327, 347; **95**:265-67
"Stratton Water" (Rossetti) **4**:506, 518, 523; **77**:326, 337-38
"Stray Echoes from the Elder Sons of Song" (Kendall) **12**:197
"Stray Walks" (Clare) **86**:142
"The Strayed Reveller" (Arnold) **6**:44, 51, 70-71, 74; **29**:25-6, 29, 35; **89**:91; **126**:111
The Strayed Reveller, and Other Poems (Arnold) **6**:28, 30-31, 70; **29**:34; **89**:88
"The Stream of Life" (Bryant) **46**:7
"The Stream's Secret" (Rossetti) **4**:492, 495, 501, 505, 510, 513, 518, 520, 525-27; **77**:308, 338, 357-58, 361
"The Street" (Kendall) **12**:183
"The Street of the Hyacinth" (Woolson) **82**:275, 293, 296-97, 308
"Streets" (Verlaine) **51**:374
The Streets of London (Boucicault) **41**:32
Streets of the World (Sala) **46**:246
"The Street-Singer" (Allingham) **25**:6
Der Streit über das Judenthum in der Musik (Freytag) **109**:180
Stretton (Kingsley) **107**:188-89, 192-93, 197, 209, 212, 227-28
"The Stricken South to the North" (Hayne) **94**:144
"The Strictness of the Law of Christ" (Newman) **38**:305
Strictures on the Modern System of Female Education, with a View of the Principles and Conduct Prevalent among Women of Rank and Fortune (More) **27**:333, 339, 341, 350, 353, 355
"Strife and Peace" (Ingelow) **39**:263
Strife and Peace; or, Scenes in Norway (Bremer) **11**:17, 19, 22, 24
"The String Token" (Barnes) **75**:36
"The Striped Snaik" (Shaw) **15**:335
The Stripling (Baillie) **2**:40-41; **71**:7
Striving for Fortune (Alger) **8**:30
"The Stroll to Grasmere" (Wilson) **5**:561
Strong and Steady; or, Paddle Your Own Canoe (Alger) **8**:43, 46; **83**:104, 107, 145
Strong as Death (Maupassant)
See *Fort comme la mort*
"Stronger Lessons" (Whitman) **31**:434
"Struck, Was I, Nor Yet by Lightning" (Dickinson) **21**:54
"The Struggle for Existence in Human Society" (Huxley) **67**:28, 97-8, 105, 109
"Struggle for Life" (Daudet) **1**:238
"The Struggle for Life" (Pisarev)
See "Bor'ba za žizn"
"Struggle for Survival" (Pisarev)
See "Bor'ba za suščestvovanie"
"The Struggles of Conscience" (Crabbe) **26**:93; **121**:40
Struggling Upward, and Other Works (Alger) **8**:20-21, 31, 36; **83**:94
Stuart of Dunleath (Norton) **47**:247-49, 255, 257-58
"Stučit!" (Turgenev)
See "Stuk...stuk...stuk"
The Student (Freytag)
See *Die Gelehrte*
"The Student of Salamanca" (Irving) **2**:368, 387, 389-90
"The Student of the Dead Languages" (Freneau) **1**:317
"A Student's Diary" (Brown) **74**:35
Studien (Stifter) **41**:359-60, 366-69, 375-77, 384, 391
Studies (Ludwig) **4**:348-49
Studies (Stifter)
See *Studien*
"Studies by the Sea" (Smith) **115**:119
Studies for Stories (Ingelow) **39**:259, 264; **107**:119
"Studies for Two Heads" (Lowell) **2**:507; **90**:220
Studies in Animal Life (Lewes) **25**:288, 296-97, 310-11
Studies in German Literature (Taylor) **89**:340
Studies in Religious History (Renan)
See *Etudes d'histoire religieuse*
Studies in the History of the Renaissance (Pater)
See *The Renaissance: Studies in Art and Poetry*
Studies of Plant Life in Canada; or, Gleanings from Forest, Lake and Plain (Traill) **31**:316-17, 328
"Studies of Roman History" (Mérimée) **6**:352
Studies of the Greek Poets (Symonds) **34**:332-33, 337, 351, 356, 366, 371
"Studies on the Situation" (Eminescu) **33**:273; **131**:328
"Studium-Aufsatz" (Schlegel)
See "Über das Studium der griechischen Poesie"
"Study of Hands: Hands of an Empress and of an Assassin Contrasted" (Gautier) **1**:342
"The Study of Poetry" (Arnold) **6**:55, 57-58, 69, 72; **29**:42-3, 45-6, 59; **89**:32, 38, 85-6, 89, 100, 112; **126**:114-15
"A Study of Provincial Life" (Eliot)
See *Middlemarch: A Study of Provincial Life*
The Study of Psychology (Lewes)
See *The Problems of Life and Mind*
"Stuk...stuk...stuk" (Turgenev) **21**:401, 416, 420, 441; **122**:243-44, 264, 364
"Die Stunden der Weihe" (Klopstock) **11**:234
"Les stupra" (Rimbaud) **35**:291, 296
Sturm und Drang (Klinger) **1**:429-31
"Der stürmische Morgen" (Muller) **73**:384, 392
"Stutgard" (Hölderlin) **16**:161, 163
"Das Stuttgarter Hutzel männlein" (Mörike) **10**:447, 456-57
"The Stwonen Porch" (Barnes) **75**:103
"Stygmat" (Norwid) **17**:370-71, 379, 381
"Style" (Lampman) **25**:213
"Style" (Pater) **7**:299, 308, 324-25, 328, 339; **90**:241, 251, 323
"Style" (De Quincey) **4**:61
"Le Style épistolaire" (Maupassant) **83**:228
"Sub Rosa-Crux" (Fuller) **50**:245, 249
The Subjection of Women (Mill) **11**:349, 356, 360, 366, 375, 388-89, 392-93; **58**:360, 379
"Subjugation of Switzerland" (Wordsworth) **12**:431
"Sublime Was the Warning" (Moore) **110**:182
"Sublimity of Composition" (Beattie)
See *Dissertations Moral and Critical: On Memory and Imagination; On Dreaming; The Theory of Language; On Fable and Romance; On the Attachments of Kindred; Illustrations on Sublimity*
Suborneur (Sade) **47**:361
"Substance and Shadow" (Newman) **38**:344-45
Substance and Shadow; or, Morality and Religion in Their Relation to Life: An Essay upon the Physics of Creation (James) **53**:199-200, 204, 217, 228-30, 236
"The Suburbs of the Capital" (Mickiewicz) **3**:401
Success (Alcott) **58**:37
"Success in Fiction" (Oliphant) **61**:221
Success in Literature (Lewes)
See *The Principles of Success in Literature*
"Success Is Counted Sweetest" (Dickinson) **21**:73
Success, or a Hit If You Like It (Planché) **42**:290
"The Succession of Forest Trees" (Thoreau) **7**:411
"Le succube" (Balzac) **5**:78
Such Things Are (Inchbald) **62**:142-3, 145-9, 147, 149, 184-5
"Sudden Life" (Rossetti) **4**:516
"Sueño de gloria: Apoteosis de Gustavo Moreau" (Casal) **131**:219, 224, 228-29, 236, 244, 266, 268-69
"Sueta suet" (Baratynsky)
See "Vanitas Vanitatum"
The Suffering of Young Werther (Goethe)
See *Die Leiden des jungen Werthers*
"The Sugar Plum Tree" (Field) **3**:206
Suggestions for Establishing an English Art Theatre (Planché) **42**:276
"Suggestions on Arithmetic" (Parton) **86**:375
Suggestions Respecting Improvements in Education (Beecher) **30**:2, 14, 23
The Suicide Club (Stevenson) **5**:393-94, 403, 408, 417
Le suicide; ou, Le vieux sergent (Pixérécourt) **39**:287
"Suil Dhuv the Coiner" (Griffin) **7**:197, 201, 207, 212, 217
A Suitable Match (Fontane)
See *Irrungen, Wirrungen*
A Suitable Place (Ostrovsky)
See *Dokhodnoye mesto*
"The Suliote Mother" (Hemans) **71**:295
"Sullen Clouds Have Disappeared from the Fair Sky" (Mickiewicz) **3**:398
Sultan Wampum, oder Die Wünsche (Kotzebue) **25**:147
"Sultry Day" (Meyer)
See "Schwüle"
"The Sumac Gatherers" (Cooke) **5**:133
Sumerki (Baratynsky) **103**:12, 16, 26, 28, 46
A Summary View of the Rights of British America (Jefferson) **11**:166, 173, 179, 192, 199; **103**:144, 210-11
"Summer" (Bryant) **46**:9
"Summer" (Clare) **9**:119; **86**:97
"The Summer Bower" (Timrod) **25**:364, 367, 372
"Summer by the Lakeside" (Whittier) **8**:519-20
"The Summer Camp" (Taylor) **89**:300-01
"Summer Days or, the Young Wife's Affliction" (Parton) **86**:346
"Summer Evening" (Clare) **86**:131
"A Summer Evening" (Lampman) **25**:183, 211
"Summer Evening" (Tyutchev)
See "Letnij vecer"
"A Summer Evening Churchyard" (Shelley) **93**:307, 326
"A Summer Evening's Dream" (Bellamy) **4**:31; **86**:75
"A Summer Idyl" (O'Brien) **21**:246
"Summer Images" (Clare) **9**:80, 86, 96, 105, 117, 119
Summer in London (Fontane) **26**:233
A Summer in Skye (Smith) **59**:295, 299, 303, 311-2, 314, 316, 319, 321-3, 333-4, 337, 340
A Summer in the Sahara (Fromentin)
See *Un été dans le Sahara*
"Summer Longings" (Foster) **26**:289, 295
"A Summer Mood" (Hayne) **94**:144, 159, 161
"Summer Morning" (Clare) **9**:72, 74, 119; **86**:130
"A Summer Night" (Arnold) **6**:72; **29**:25-6, 31, 34, 36; **89**:98

"A Summer Night" (Kivi)
See "Kesäyö"
"Summer Night" (Klopstock)
See "Die Sommernacht"
A Summer Night (Krasiński) **4**:306
"Summer Night. Variations of Certain Melodies" (Taylor) **89**:318-19
Summer on the Lakes, in 1843 (Fuller) **5**:154-55, 157-58, 163-64, 168, 170; **50**:235-8, 241-4, 217-8
"A Summer Pilgrimage" (Whittier) **59**:366
"A Summer Ramble" (Bryant) **6**:187; **46**:2
Summer Rambles (Jameson)
See *Winter Studies and Summer Rambles in Canada*
"The Summer Sea" (Kingsley) **35**:226
"Summer Storm" (Lowell) **2**:507
"Summer Wind" (Bryant) **6**:159, 168, 176; **46**:6, 43
"Summer—We All Have Seen" (Dickinson) **21**:69
"The Sun" (Baudelaire)
See "Le soleil"
"The sun has gone down" (Clare) **86**:118
"The Sun kept setting-setting-still" (Dickinson) **77**:163-64
La Sunamite (Staël-Holstein) **91**:359-60
"The Sunbeam" (Hemans) **71**:264
"Sunbeams and Shadows" (Hugo) **3**:261
"Sunday" (Kivi)
See "Sunnuntai"
"Sunday Afternoon" (Dickinson)
See "From All the Jails the Boys and Girls"
"Sunday at Hampstead" (Thomson) **18**:391-92, 395, 397, 409, 411-12, 417
"Sunday at Home" (Hawthorne) **2**:291-92; **39**:230
"A Sun-Day Hymn" (Holmes) **81**:100, 107
The Sunday School (More) **27**:345
"Sunday up the River" (Thomson) **18**:390-92, 395-97, 404-05, 408-09, 411-12, 414, 417, 421
"Sunday Walks" (Clare) **86**:142
"A Sunday with Shepherds and Herdboys" (Clare) **9**:117
"The Sundering Flood" (Morris) **4**:424-25, 438
"Sundown" (Longfellow) **45**:130
"Sun-Down Poem" (Whitman) **4**:546
"Sunlight and Flesh" (Rimbaud)
See "Soleil et chair"
"Sunlight in a London Square" (Jefferies) **47**:95, 136
"Sunlight on the Sea" (Gordon) **21**:150, 160, 175
"Sunnuntai" (Kivi) **30**:51
Sunny Memories of Foreign Lands (Stowe) **3**:547
"Sun-Painting and Sun-Sculpture" (Holmes) **81**:102
"Sunrise" (Lanier) **6**:237-38, 240, 243, 246-47, 253-54, 256, 265, 268, 281; **118**:204, 219, 221, 223-24, 232, 239-40, 268-71, 273, 275
"Sunrise" (Lazarus) **8**:420
"Sunrise" (Tyutchev) **34**:404
A Sunrise Song" (Lanier) **118**:224
"The Sun's Shame" (Rossetti) **4**:491, 499
"A Sunset" (Clare) **9**:121
"Sunset" (Lanier) **118**:238
"Sunset and Sunrise on Lake Ontario: A Reminiscence" (Traill) **31**:328
"Sunset at les Eboulements" (Lampman) **25**:179, 185-86, 190
"Sunset in the Forest" (Meyer)
See "Abendrot im Walde"
"Sunset Visions" (Clare) **9**:121
"Sunshine and Young Mothers" (Parton) **86**:350
Sunshine through the Clouds (Lewes) **25**:291
"Sunthin' in the Pastoral Line" (Lowell) **2**:520, 522
"The Superannuated Man" (Lamb) **10**:392, 415; **113**:198-99, 248
The Supernaturalism of New-England (Whittier) **8**:487, 509
"A Superscription" (Rossetti) **4**:491; **77**:357
"Superstition" (Hogg) **109**:244
"Supper at the Mill" (Ingelow) **39**:255-56, 262-65, 268; **107**:119, 122
"Supplement to the Travelling Sketches" (Heine)
See "Nachträge Zu den Reisebildern"
"Supposed Confessions of a Second-Rate Sensitive Mind not in unity with itself" (Tennyson) **30**:252; **65**:270, 274, 368; **115**:237, 239
"The Supreme Sacrifice" (Lazarus) **109**:337
"Supreme Surrender" (Rossetti) **4**:498
"Sur la destruction des monuments en France" (Hugo) **21**:221
"Sur la femme" (Laforgue) **53**:291
Sur l'eau (Maupassant) **1**:446, 451, 453; **83**:163, 201
Sur les générations actuelles (Senancour) **16**:438, 441, 445-47
"Sur les Lettres de deux Grecs" (Chateaubriand) **134**:8
"Sur les œuvres complètes de Byron" (Vigny) **102**:379
"Sur l'herbe" (Verlaine) **2**:628-30; **51**:378, 387
"Sur l'image du Christ écrasant le mal" (Lamartine) **11**:279
"Sur un album" (Gautier) **59**:18
"Sur une défunte" (Laforgue) **5**:280; **53**:292
Sur une statue de Ganymede (Verlaine) **51**:363
Surfaceism; or, the World and its Wife (Gore) **65**:21
"The Surgeon's Daughter" (Scott) **15**:308-09
"Surgi de la croupe et du bond" (Mallarmé)
See "Une dentelle s'abolit"
"Une Surprise" (Maupassant) **83**:182
"Surprised by Joy" (Wordsworth) **12**:466
Surrey of Eagle's-Nest; or, The Memoirs of a Staff Officer Serving in Virginia (Cooke) **5**:124, 126-35
"Sursam Corda" (Rossetti) **50**:313
"Sursum Corda" (Emerson) **1**:296
"Sûryâ" (Leconte de Lisle) **29**:241
Susan (Austen) **119**:17-18, 45
"Susan Yates" (Lamb)
See "First Going to Church"
"Suspense" (Dickinson)
See "Elysium Is as Far as To"
Suspiria de profundis (De Quincey) **4**:61, 63-64, 66, 80, 83, 86-87, 89; **87**:3-16, 22, 31, 33, 36-7, 52, 75, 77
"Susquehanna" (Crèvecoeur) **105**:152-55, 157-60
Sut Lovingood (Harris)
See *Sut Lovingood: Yarns Spun by a "Nat'ral Born Durn'd Fool"*
"Sut Lovingood, A Chapter from His Autobiography" (Harris) **23**:160
"Sut Lovingood Come to Life" (Harris) **23**:151
"Sut Lovingood Lands Old Abe Safe at Last" (Harris) **23**:159
"Sut Lovingood, on the Puritan Yankee" (Harris) **23**:151, 153
Sut Lovingood: Yarns Spun by a "Nat'ral Born Durn'd Fool" (Harris) **23**:133, 135, 137-40, 142, 144-49, 156-57, 159-60, 162-64
"Sut Lovingood's Adventures in New York" (Harris) **23**:149, 160
"Sut Lovingood's Allegory" (Harris) **23**:152
"Sut Lovingood's Big Dinner Story" (Harris) **23**:160
"Sut Lovingood's Big Music Box Story" (Harris) **23**:160
"Sut Lovingood's Chest Story" (Harris) **23**:159
"Sut Lovingood's Daddy 'Acting Horse'" (Harris) **23**:139, 141, 153, 158, 161, 163-64
"Sut Lovingood's Dog" (Harris) **23**:157, 159
"Sut Lovingood's Hog Ride" (Harris) **23**:160
"Sut Lovingood's Love Feast ove Varmints" (Harris) **23**:150
"Sut Lovingood's Sermon" (Harris) **23**:159
Sut Lovingood's Travels with Old Abe Lincoln (Harris) **23**:137
"Suteishimaru" (Ueda Akinari) **131**:21-22, 58
"Sutherland's Grave" (Kendall) **12**:181, 199
"Sut's New-Fangled Shirt" (Harris) **23**:140, 158, 163
"The Suttee" (Cooke) **110**:9
"Suzon" (Musset) **7**:256, 267
"Svalen" (Wergeland) **5**:536, 541
"Svartsjukans nätter" (Runeberg) **41**:309, 317
Svea (Tegner) **2**:611-14
"Sveaborg" (Runeberg) **41**:312, 323-24
"Svedger" (Stagnelius) **61**:248
Svegder (Stagnelius) **61**:253, 258-9
"Sven Duva" (Runeberg) **41**:315, 322, 325, 328
"Svenska fattigdomens betydelse" (Almqvist) **42**:14, 18-19
"Sventura" (Foscolo) **8**:266
"Svetlana" (Zhukovsky) **35**:379, 389, 394, 398, 400-01
"Svidanie" (Turgenev) **122**:264
"Svinedrengen" (Andersen) **7**:23, 32, 34, 32, 34; **79**:23-4, 30, 40-2, 51-2, 64, 70-2
"Svoenravnoe prozvanie..." (Baratynsky) **103**:11
Svoi lyudi—sochtemsya! (Ostrovsky) **30**:97-9, 104-05, 109-13, 117; **57**:195, 197, 199, 207-8, 213-4, 218-21
Svoia sem'ia, ili Zamuzhniaia nevesta (Griboedov) **129**:172-73
"Svyataya noch na nebosklon vzoshla" (Tyutchev) **34**:393, 397, 405
"Swabian Popular Song" (Mangan) **27**:290
"The Swallow" (Smith) **115**:119
"The Swallow" (Wergeland)
See "Svalen"
Swallow Barn; or, A Sojourn in the Old Dominion (Kennedy) **2**:428-35
"The Swallow Leaves Her Nest" (Beddoes) **3**:34
"Swamp Robin" (Lanier) **118**:242
"The Swan" (Baudelaire)
See "Le cygne"
"The Swan" (Hemans) **71**:270
"The Swan" (Tyutchev)
See "Lebed"
"The Swan's Nest" (Andersen) **7**:21
"The Swans of Lir" (Griffin) **7**:198
"Swart Among the Buckeyes" (Boyesen) **135**:12, 19
"Swarthy Wastelands, Wild and Woodless" (Kendall) **12**:179
"The Swashbuckler" (Turgenev)
See "The Duelist"
"Swayne Vonved" (Borrow) **9**:54
Swear Not at All (Bentham) **38**:92, 97
"Swedenborg; or, The Mystic" (Emerson) **98**:92, 100
"Sweep Song" (Blake) **13**:161
"The Sweep's Complaint" (Hood) **16**:236, 239
"Sweet Mary Dove" (Clare) **86**:89
"Sweet Meat Has Sower Sauce or, the Slave-Trader in the Dumps" (Cowper) **94**:32
"Sweet Sunday Bells" (Allingham) **25**:24-5
"Sweet Susan" (Clare) **86**:89
"The Sweethearts" (Andersen) **79**:58, 66
"The Sweetness of Life" (Lampman) **25**:188
Swellfoot (Shelley)
See *Oedipus Tyrannus; Or Swellfoot the Tyrant*
Swellfoot the Tyrant (Shelley)
See *Oedipus Tyrannus; Or Swellfoot the Tyrant*
Świeczka zgasta (Fredro) **8**:285
"The Swift" (Very) **9**:387
"The Swiftest Runners" (Andersen) **7**:25
"Swilcar Oak" (Darwin)
See "Address to the Swilcar Oak"

"The Swimmer" (Gordon) **21**:151, 156-57, 160, 163, 167, 176, 183, 187-88
"The Swimmer" (Pavlova)
See "Plovets"
"The Swineherd" (Andersen)
See "Svinedrengen"
"Swineherd" (Crawford) **127**:188
"The Swing" (Kivi)
See "Keinu"
"The Swiss Artist" (Brontë) **109**:35
The Swiss Family Robinson (Wyss)
See *Der Schweizerische Robinson; oder, Der schiffbrüchige Schweizerprediger und seine Familie*
Switrigail oder Beiträge zu der Geschichte von Lithauen, Russland, Polen, und Preussen (Kotzebue) **25**:140
"Switzerland" (Arnold) **6**:44; **29**:34; **89**:14-20, 48
"The Switzer's Wife" (Hemans) **71**:275, 291
"The Sword" (Crawford) **127**:171
The Sword and the Distaff; or, "Fair, Fat, and Forty" (Simms)
See *Woodcraft; or, Hawks about the Dovecote*
"Sxolastiki xix veka" (Pisarev) **25**:337, 345
"A s'y méprendre" (Villiers de l'Isle Adam) **3**:590
"Syberie" (Norwid) **17**:373
Sybil; or, The Two Nations (Disraeli) **2**:144-45, 147-54; **39**:4, 6, 9-12, 15-17, 19-20, 22-7, 30-31, 33-5, 38, 41, 44-51, 56-59, 61-4, 69, 73, 75-6, 78, 80; **79**:195-97, 199, 212-13, 222, 234-36, 238-39, 244-45, 247-50, 252-55, 257-59, 261-64, 269, 271, 279, 281-82
"Sybille" (Mitford) **4**:400
Sybille (Feuillet)
See *Histoire de Sybille*
"The Sycamores" (Whittier) **8**:516
"The Sydney International Exhibition" (Kendall) **12**:187, 191, 200, 202-03
Sygdommen til Døden (Kierkegaard) **34**:178, 192, 200, 224, 226-29, 231-32, 238, 264; **78**:124-27, 140-43, 152, 175, 182-83, 185-86, 188-90, 193, 195, 238, 242; **125**:206, 241, 244, 253, 256, 284
"The Sylphs of the Seasons" (Allston) **2**:19, 21-22, 24, 26
The Sylphs of the Seasons, with Other Poems (Allston) **2**:19-21, 24
"Sylvan Musings. In May" (Hayne) **94**:160
Sylvandire (Dumas) **71**:203
"Sylvia" (Musset) **7**:258
Sylvia; or, The May Queen (Darley) **2**:125-27, 129-30, 133
Sylvia's Lovers (Gaskell) **5**:185, 188, 190, 192, 196-98, 201, 204-06; **70**:120, 123-24; 129, 132-33, 185, 187, 189, 196, 198, 200-02, 205-06, 209, 212-13; **137**:3-4, 40
Sylvie and Bruno (Carroll) **2**:106-8, 111, 115, 117, 121-2; **53**:40, 56-7, 84, 86, 89-90, 104-9, 113, 115; **139**:4-5, 21-27, 45, 52-53, 89, 120, 126, 136-37, 139, 147
Sylvie and Bruno Concluded (Carroll) **2**:107, 111, 115, 121-2; **53**:105; **139**:4-5, 14, 21-22, 45, 53, 89, 139
Sylvie: Recollections of Valois (Nerval) **1**:475-80, 482, 485, 487, 489; **67**:303-04, 311, 315, 318, 320, 323-25, 333-35, 348, 351, 354, 356-57, 360, 363
Sylvoe (Herder) **8**:299
"The Symbol and the Saint" (Field) **3**:205
Symbolic Logic (Carroll) **53**:110, 122
Symbolic Logic, Part I: Elementary (Carroll) **139**:8-9, 80, 84, 145
"Symbolism and Language" (Cranch) **115**:9
"Sympathy" (Lazarus) **109**:295
"Sympathy" (Thomson) **18**:400-01
"Sympathy" (Thoreau) **7**:355; **138**:116
"Symphonic Studies" (Lazarus) **109**:291-92
"Symphonie en blanc majeur" (Gautier) **59**:19
Symphonie littéraire (Mallarmé) **4**:396; **41**:269, 278
"The Symphony" (Lanier) **6**:232, 235, 237-38, 243-44, 248-49, 251, 253-54, 257-59, 263, 265, 269, 274, 277, 279; **118**:203, 206-7, 213, 218, 223-24, 229, 236-38, 240, 259-62, 265, 267-68, 270, 279
Symphony in C Major (Wagner) **119**:189
Sympneumata (Oliphant) **47**:289-93, 295
"Symptoms of Love" (Opie) **65**:156
"Syn cieniów" (Krasiński) **4**:306, 313
Synspunktet for min Forfatter-Virksomhed (Kierkegaard) **125**:176, 209, 229, 234
Synthèse Subjective ou Système universel des conceptions propres a l'état normal de l'Humanité (Comte) **54**:211, 214
Synthetic Philosophy (Brownson) **50**:27
Synthetic Psychology (Brownson) **50**:27
"The Syrens" (Lowell) **2**:502, 507
"Syrinx" (Kendall) **12**:192
Syskonlif (Bremer) **11**:23-24, 34-35
System der gesammten Philosophie und der Naturphilosophie insbesondere (Schelling) **30**:175-77
Das System der Sittenlehre nach den prinzipen der Wissenschaftslehre (Fichte) **62**:30, 34, 47, 58
System der Wissenschaft: 1. Theil. Der Phänomenologies des Geistes (Hegel) **46**:60-1, 70, 73-4, 86, 89-90, 102, 104-06, 108, 112, 140, 147, 150, 162, 164-73, 175-78, 187, 189
System des transcendentalen Idealismus (Schelling) **30**:122-24, 126-28, 146, 155, 166, 176-81
A System of Christians Ethics on the Principles of the Evangelical Church (Schleiermacher) **107**:267
"The System of Doctor Tarr and Professor Fether" (Poe) **16**:312; **55**:147
The System of Ethical Theory according to the Principles of Wissenschaftslehre (Fichte)
See *Das System der Sittenlehre nach den prinzipen der Wissenschaftslehre*
A System of Logic, Ratiocinative and Inductive: Being a Connected View of the Principles of Evidence and the Methods of Scientific Investigation (Mill) **11**:329-30, 332, 337, 339, 341, 349-51, 358, 365, 375-76, 380, 383; **58**:319, 321-4, 327, 337, 341, 375
System of Positive Philosophy (Comte)
See *Système de Politique Positive ou Traité de Sociologie instituant la Religion de l'Humanité*
"System of the Heavens" (De Quincey) **87**:7
System of Transcendental Idealism (Schelling)
See *System des transcendentalen Idealismus*
A System of Vegetables (Darwin) **106**:232, 274
Système de Logique Positive ou Traité de philosophie mathématique (Comte) **54**:211
Système de Politique Positive ou Traité de Sociologie instituant la Religion de l'Humanité (Comte) **54**:199, 203, 205, 210, 212, 235-8, 241-2, 244
Syzygies (Carroll) **139**:57
"Szabadság, szerelem" (Petofi) **21**:279
"A szájhösök" (Petofi) **21**:280
"Szczęsacliwość filutów" (Krasicki) **8**:407
"Széchenyi emlékezete" (Arany) **34**:16
"Szécsi Mária" (Petofi) **21**:264, 267
"Szeptember végén" (Petofi) **21**:260, 285
"A szerelem, a szerelem" (Petofi) **21**:283
"Szerelem átka" (Petofi) **21**:264
Szerelem Gyöngyei (Petofi) **21**:285
"Szeretlek, kedvesem" (Petofi) **21**:285
"Szomjas ember tünödése" (Petofi) **21**:283
"Szondi két apródja" (Arany) **34**:15, 20
"Szüleim halálára" (Petofi) **21**:286
"Ta voix" (Banville) **9**:29
"Taarnvægteren" (Andersen) **79**:77
"A táblabíro" (Petofi) **21**:277
A Table of the Springs of Action (Bentham) **38**:55-7, 84, 90
Table Talk (Cowper) **94**:19, 51-3, 58-9
Table Talk (Pushkin) **3**:436; **83**:270, 274
Le Tableau de Paris (Vallès) **71**:342-43, 373
Tableau historique et critique de la poésie Française et du théâtre Français au seizième siècle (Sainte-Beuve) **5**:338, 349
Tableaux de siège (Gautier) **1**:344
"Tableaux parisiens" (Baudelaire) **6**:113, 115, 122-24; **55**:15-16, 35, 37-42, 65-6, 73
"the Tables Turned" (Wordsworth) **111**:202, 209, 225, 255, 281, 283, 285, 314
"Table-Talk" (Cowper) **8**:110, 120; **94**:25-8, 112, 129
Table-Talk (Alcott) **1**:21, 23-26
Table-Talk (Coleridge) **9**:157, 159
Table-Talk (Hazlitt) **29**:141, 147, 167, 169, 171, 187; **82**:88, 90, 115, 142, 144, 146
Tablets (Alcott) **1**:23-26
Tablettes romantiques (Nodier) **19**:378
"Tábori képek" (Madach) **19**:369
"Tact" (Emerson) **1**:285
Tafellieder (Muller) **73**:353, 387
"Ein Tag aus Noltens Jugendleben" (Mörike) **10**:451-52
"Tag, schein' herein" (Meyer) **81**:143
Tagalog Nobility (Rizal) **27**:420
Tagebuch einer Reise durch die Schweitz (La Roche) **121**:242, 299, 301
Tagebuch einer Reise durch Holland und England (La Roche) **121**:242, 299, 302-6
Tagebücher (Grillparzer) **102**:101-02, 105-07, 111, 168-72
Tagebücher (Hebbel) **43**:252-53, 255, 261, 263
"Einem Tagelohner" (Meyer) **81**:155
"Täglich zu singen" (Claudius) **75**:190
"Ta-Hsüeh" (Clague)
See "The Latest Decalogue"
Le tailleur de pierres de Saint-Point (Lamartine) **11**:286
"The Tain Quest" (Ferguson) **33**:278-79, 283, 289, 293
Taine's On Intelligence (Taine)
See *De l'intelligence*
"Tajemnica Lorda Singleworth" (Norwid) **17**:369, 379, 382
"Tak, v zhizni est mgnoveniya" (Tyutchev) **34**:399
"Take delight: all passes by!" (Baratynsky)
See "Naslazhdaytes: vsyo pokhodit!..."
"Take Your Heaven Further On" (Dickinson) **21**:54, 57
Takekurabe (Ichiyō) **49**:331, 336-37, 341, 344-47, 350, 353
"Taken from my Mothers singing" (Clare) **86**:108
Taking by Storm (Lewes) **25**:291
"The Taking of the Redoubt" (Mérimée)
See "L'enlèvement de la rédoute"
"Taking up the Fair Ideal" (Dickinson) **21**:56
Talanty i poklonniki (Ostrovsky) **30**:103, 111, 115, 117; **57**:212-4, 216-7, 220
Talbot Harland (Ainsworth) **13**:36
"A Tale" (Verlaine) **51**:368
The Tale (Eminescu) **33**:266
"A Tale about Myself" (Herzen) **61**:108
"Tale for Girls" (Rossetti) **50**:289
A Tale of a Man of Valour (Ueda Akinari)
See *Masurao monogatari*
"The Tale of a Trumpet" (Hood) **16**:218-19, 235
"The Tale of Good Queen Bess" (Hogg) **4**:283
"The Tale of How Ivan Ivanovich Quarrelled with Ivan Nikiforovich" (Gogol) **2**:228, 234, 250; **31**:110-11, 114, 117, 119; **5**:219, 227, 231, 242, 249-51
"A Tale of Jerusalem" (Poe) **55**:185
A Tale of Mystery (Holcroft) **85**:199, 212, 224-25, 235, 237

A Tale of Paraguay (Southey) **8**:460; **97**:264, 273, 276
"A Tale of Passions; or, The Death of Despina" (Shelley) **14**:267
"Tale of Romance" (Keats) **8**:322
"A Tale of Terror" (Hood) **16**:221
"The Tale of the Dead Princess and the Seven Heroes" (Pushkin)
See "Skazka o Mertvoy Tsarevne"
"The Tale of the Female Vagrant" (Wordsworth) **12**:386-87
"The Tale of the Fisherman and the Fish" (Pushkin)
See "Skazka o Rybake i Rybke"
The Tale of the Golden Cockerel (Pushkin)
See "Skazka o Zolotom Petushke"
A Tale of the House of the Wolfings and All the Kindreds of Mark (Morris) **4**:425
"Tale of the Indians" (Maturin) **6**:325, 334
"The Tale of the Lime Tree" (Eminescu) **33**:247
"The Tale of the Magus Travelling in the Stars" (Eminescu) **33**:246, 264; **131**:287
"The Tale of the Monk and the Jew Versified" (Paine) **62**:321
"Tale of the Monk Felix" (Longfellow) **45**:113
"A Tale of the Ragged Mountains" (Poe) **55**:201; **94**:240
"Tale of the Spaniard" (Maturin) **6**:334
"The Tale of the Squint-Eyed Left-Handed Smith from Tula and the Steel Flea" (Leskov)
See "Levša"
"The Tale of the Three Pictures" (Fouqué) **2**:266
"Tale of the Tsar Berendeia" (Zhukovsky) **35**:390
"The Tale of the Tsar Sultan" (Pushkin)
See "Skazka o Tsare Sultane"
A Tale of the Tyne (Martineau) **137**:264, 267
"The Tale of Theodore the Christian and His Friend Abraham the Jew" (Leskov)
See "Skazanie o Fyodore—Khristianine i o druge ego Abrame—zhidovine"
"A Tale of Trials" (Opie) **65**:171
A Tale of Two Cities (Dickens) **3**:154-55; **8**:168; **18**:114, 120, 131; **26**:168, 171, 178, 228; **86**:186-267; **105**:254; **113**:20, 53-4, 103, 118
"The Tale of Two Ivans" (Gogol)
See "The Tale of How Ivan Ivanovich Quarrelled with Ivan Nikiforovich"
"The Talent for Silence" (Lewes) **25**:290
Talents and Admirers (Ostrovsky)
See *Talanty i poklonniki*
Tales (Cowper) **8**:103
Tales (Crabbe) **26**:93, 102, 111, 114, 119, 128, 130-31, 134-35, 138, 148, 150-51; **121**:4-6, 10-11, 25, 43, 61, 73-4, 78, 83-4
Tales (Hogg)
See *The Works of the Ettrick Shepherd*
Tales (Runeberg)
See *Fänrik Ståls sägner*
Tales (Wilson) **5**:564, 567
"Tales and Essays for Children" (Sigourney) **87**:321
"Tales and Historic Scenes" (Hemans) **71**:261
Tales and Historic Scenes in Verse (Hemans) **29**:192, 202; **71**:274-76, 289, 291, 293-95
Tales and Sketches (Norton) **47**:246, 248
Tales and Sketches (Sedgwick) **19**:440
Tales and Stories by Mary Wollstonecraft Shelley (Shelley) **14**:264; **59**:155
Tales by Belkin (Pushkin)
See *Povesti Belkina*
Tales by Edgar A. Poe (Poe) **1**:495; **16**:293-94, 296
Tales by the O'Hara Family (Banim and Banim) **13**:116-32, 141
Tales for the Pemberton Children (Opie) **65**:173
Tales from Shakespear (Lamb) **125**:301-7, 320, 352, 354, 358
Tales from Shakespeare, Designed for the Use of Young Persons (Lamb) **10**:386, 402, 406, 417, 420, 422, 439; **113**:159, 199, 278, 286
Tales from Two Hemispheres (Boyesen) **135**:8, 12, 24-26, 30
Tales in Verse (Crabbe) **121**:34, 36, 39-40, 65
Tales in Verse (Holcroft) **85**:199-200, 212-13
Tales of a Grandfather (Scott)
See *The History of Scotland*
Tales of a Traveller (Irving) **2**:369-71, 374, 379, 381-82, 384, 387, 389-90; **19**:331-33, 341, 344; **95**:280
Tales of a Wayside Inn (Longfellow) **2**:481, 484, 487-88, 492, 495-96; **45**:113-14, 119, 124, 128, 132, 137-38, 140, 144-45, 147, 149, 160, 162, 185, 187-88
"Tales of an Englishman" (Brontë) **109**:47
Tales of Ensign Stål (Runeberg)
See *Fänrik Ståls sägner*
Tales of Fashionable Life (Edgeworth) **1**:257, 261, 267-68; **51**:75, 89, 93, 130, 137, 140
Tales of Ireland (Carleton) **3**:83, 88, 91
The Tales of Ivan Belkin (Pushkin)
See *Povesti Belkina*
Tales of My Landlord (Scott) **15**:259, 304, 309-10, 321-22; **69**:299
Tales of My Neighborhood (Griffin) **7**:215, 218
Tales of Mystery and Imagination (Poe) **16**:309, 311
Tales of Old Travel Re-Narrated (Kingsley) **107**:209
Tales of Orris (Ingelow) **39**:263
Tales of Real Life (Opie) **65**:171
Tales of Spain and Italy (Musset)
See *Contes d'Espagne et d'Italie*
Tales of the Court of Vienna (Sacher-Masoch) **31**:294
Tales of the Folio Club (Poe) **55**:185
Tales of the Grotesque and Arabesque (Poe) **1**:492-93, 520-21; **16**:291-92, 296; **55**:132; **94**:239
Tales of the Hall (Crabbe) **26**:100, 103, 108, 115-16, 128-31, 134, 136, 142, 149; **121**:6, 12, 14, 34, 84
Tales of the Heart (Opie) **65**:164, 171, 174, 179, 197-8
"Tales of the Inn Kitchen" (Irving) **19**:328
Tales of the Juryroom (Griffin) **7**:204
Tales of the Munster Festivals (Griffin) **7**:193, 197, 204, 207, 210-12, 216-17
"Tales of the Province House" (Hawthorne) **2**:303
Tales of the Queen of Navarre (Scribe)
See *Les contes de la reine de Navarre*
Tales of the Russian Court (Sacher-Masoch) **31**:294
Tales of the Spring Rain (Ueda Akinari)
See *Harusame Monogatari*
Tales of the Wars of Montrose (Hogg) **4**:279
Tales of Wonder (Lewis) **11**:296-97, 302
Tales Told for Children (Andersen)
See *Eventyr, fortalte for bøorn*
"Taliessin" (Tennyson) **30**:294
"Le talion" (Leconte de Lisle) **29**:225-26
"Le Talion" (Sade) **47**:313
Der Talisman (Nestroy) **42**:220-21, 223, 232, 239, 242, 245-47, 249, 251-53, 264
The Talisman (Scott) **15**:312; **69**:303-04, 313-14, 316, 319, 328, 332-34
"The Talking Lady" (Mitford) **4**:401, 408
"The Talking Oak" (Holmes) **14**:109
"Talking Oak" (Tennyson) **30**:215
"Tall Ambrosia" (Thoreau) **7**:384
"The Tall Woman" (Alarcon)
See "La mujer alta"
"Taller moderno" (Silva) **114**:299, 301
"Talleyrand" (Landor) **14**:166
Tamakatsuma (Motoori) **45**:277
Tamakushige (Motoori) **45**:276-79
"Taman" (Lermontov) **5**:290-91, 295, 297, 300-02, 305-06; **126**:145, 150-51, 153-54, 157, 195-96, 199
"Tamango" (Mérimée) **6**:354, 360, 365-6, 369; **65**:56, 60, 66, 113
Tamaris (Sand) **57**:316
"Tamarlane" (Poe) **1**:492, 527; **117**:195, 224-25, 227, 244, 260, 264, 266, 269, 280
Tamarlane, and Other Poems, By a Bostonian (Poe) **1**:514; **55**:207; **117**:224
The Tambov Treasurer's Wife (Lermontov)
See *Tambovskaya kaznacheysha*
Tambovskaya kaznacheysha (Lermontov) **126**:134, 136
"Tamerton Church-Tower" (Patmore) **9**:328-29
Tamerton Church-Tower, and Other Poems (Patmore) **9**:328, 348
"The Taming of the Shrew" (Lamb) **125**:305
"The Tampa Resolution" (Martí)
See "Resoluciónes tomadas por le emigracion cubana de Tampa"
"Tampa Robins" (Lanier) **6**:236, 238-39, 243, 255; **118**:273, 275
The Tamworth Reading Room (Newman) **38**:324; **99**:261, 273, 278-79, 301
"Tan solo dudas y terrores sieto" (Castro) **78**:41
Tancred; or, The New Crusade (Disraeli) **2**:140-41, 144-45, 147-48, 150-54; **39**:3-4, 6, 16-17, 20, 23-4, 26-7, 29-31, 34-5, 39-42, 44-5, 47, 50-1, 56, 64, 69, 75-7, 80; **79**:195, 212-15, 222, 232-33, 235, 239, 257-60, 263-64, 266-67, 269, 276
Tandai shoshin roku (Ueda Akinari) **131**:20, 51, 60, 81-83
Tändeleien und Erzählungen (Claudius) **75**:191-92
The Tangled Skein (Carroll) **2**:107
A Tangled Tale (Carroll) **139**:57
Tanglewood Tales for Girls and Boys: Being a Second Wonder-Book (Hawthorne) **2**:302, 306, 313; **17**:149-50; **23**:214;
Tanhauser (Wagner)
See *Tannhäuser*
"Tannhaüser" (Lazarus) **8**:412-14, 420, 425-26; **109**:289-90, 294, 319, 321
Tannhäuser (Nestroy) **42**:225
Tannhäuser (Wagner) **9**:401, 403, 406, 414-16, 418-19, 421, 434, 437, 450, 452, 454-55, 462-63, 469, 473-74; **119**:172, 176, 178, 181, 185, 192, 195, 198, 240, 244, 267-68, 274, 302, 328
"Tante Tandpine" (Andersen)
See "Auntie Toothache"
"Tanto e tanto nos odiamos" (Castro) **78**:2
Das Tanzlegendchen (Keller) **2**:416
Tarare (Da Ponte) **50**:83-4
"Taras Bulba" (Gogol) **5**:209, 218-20, 227, 230, 240, 242, 248-49, 251, 256; **31**:122
"Tarasova nic" (Shevchenko) **54**:360, 371-4
"La tarde azul" (Isaacs) **70**:304
"Tardy George" (Boker) **125**:33, 39, 81
"Tarr and Fether" (Poe)
See "The System of Doctor Tarr and Professor Fether"
"The Tartars" (De Quincey) **4**:75
"The Tartarus of Maids" (Melville) **3**:354
"Tartuffe's Punishment" (Rimbaud)
See "Le châtiment de Tartuff"
The Tashkentsians (Saltykov)
See *Gospoda Tashkentsy*
The Task (Cowper) **8**:96-97, 99, 102-06, 109-20, 122-23, 125, 127-29, 132-33, 138; **94**:46-51, 65, 76-7, 79, 84, 92-6, 98, 100-01, 119-120, 124, 126-30
Task of the Historian (Humboldt)
See *Über die Aufgabe des Geschichtschreibers*
"Tasso and His Sister" (Hemans) **71**:306-07
"Tasso to Leonora" (Thomson) **18**:396
"'Tas-tis, tas-tis' na silenciosa noite" (Castro) **78**:41
"Tat'jana Borisovna i ee plemjannik" (Turgenev) **122**:264
The Tatler (Hunt) **70**:288
Tatsachen des Bewusstseins (Fichte) **62**:34

Tattered Tom; or, The Story of a Street Arab (Alger) **8**:42, 45; **83**:129, 140, 145
"Der Taucher" (Schiller) **39**:388
"Taurus in Lynchburg Market" (Harris) **23**:159, 163
"Taüschung" (Muller) **73**:366, 383, 390, 392-93, 396-97
"Távolból" (Petofi) **21**:276
Tchitchikoff's Journey; or Dead Souls (Gogol) **5**:210-11, 213-14, 218-20, 222-24, 226-27, 229-31, 234, 239-40, 243-44, 247-48, 250, 253-57; **15**:80, 88-9, 98-100, 105; **31**:72-148,
"De Te" (Gordon) **21**:155, 159-60, 164, 176, 183
"Le Te Deum du Ier Janvier" (Hugo) **3**:276
Tea Table (Coleridge) **90**:20
"Tea-Ballad" (Warren) **13**:414
"Teachers' Migration" (Faustino) **123**:274
"The Teaching and Sayings of Bacon" (Bestuzhev)
See "Uchenie—aforizmy iz Bekona"
"Teapots and Quails" (Lear) **3**:306
"The Tear of a Wife" (Parton) **86**:350
"Tears" (Tyutchev) **34**:387-88
"Tears" (Whitman) **4**:567, 571, 580; **31**:431
Tears (Desbordes-Valmore)
See *Les Pleurs*
"Tears and Roses" (Muller) **73**:352
"Tears, Idle Tears" (Tennyson) **30**:246, 248, 279, 283; **115**:364, 366
Teatral'nyi raz'ezd posle predstavleniia novoi komedii (Gogol) **15**:83-4, 98, 106, 108, 110
"Teatros" (Larra) **130**:228, 247-48, 273
"Tece voda v synje more" (Shevchenko) **54**:372
"Technical Education" (Huxley) **67**:55-6
Die Technik des Dramas (Freytag) **109**:137, 140-43
Technik des Dramas (Freytag)
See *Die Technik des Dramas*
Technique of the Drama (Freytag)
See *Die Technik des Dramas*
Teckningar utur hvardagslifvet (Bremer) **11**:33, 35
Tecumseh; or, The Warrior of the West: A Poem of Four Cantos with Notes (Richardson) **55**:293, 302, 311-3, 317, 329-32, 335, 343
"Tegnér's Drapa" (Longfellow) **45**:132, 155, 190
Tékéli; ou, Le siège de Montgatz (Pixérécourt) **39**:274, 277, 279, 283-84, 287
"The Telegraph and Telephone" (Cranch) **115**:42
Telemachus (Planché) **42**:273, 278, 286, 298-99
"Telka" (Field) **3**:210
"Tell All the Truth but Tell It Slant" (Dickinson) **21**:75; **77**:160
Tell Truth and Shame the Devil (Dunlap) **2**:214, 217
"Telling the Bees" (Whittier) **8**:493, 506, 509-10, 513, 517, 519-21, 531; **59**:356, 358, 360, 369, 371, 373-4
"The Tell-Tale Heart" (Poe) **1**:500; **16**:295, 301, 303, 309-10, 315-16, 319, 328-29, 331-32, 336; **55**:172, 202; **78**:256-63, 265-70, 272-75, 277-86, 289-90, 294, 296-300; **97**:180; **117**:320, 322-23
"The Temeraire" (Melville) **123**:258
Temper (Morgan) **29**:390
Temper, or, Domestic Scenes (Opie) **65**:169, 173-4, 179
"Temperance Address Delivered before the Springfield Washington Temperance Society" (Lincoln) **18**:278
"Temperance Movement" (De Quincey) **4**:61
"The Tempest" (Browning) **61**:35-7
"The Tempest" (Lamb) **125**:303
"Un tempête sous un crâne" (Hugo) **10**:354, 357, 366, 378
"Le temple" (Lamartine) **11**:269
The Temple (Darwin)
See *The Temple of Nature; or Origin of Society*
The Temple of Independence (Dunlap) **2**:213
"The Temple of Infamy" (Harpur) **114**:144
The Temple of Nature; or Origin of Society (Darwin) **106**:185-86, 190-92, 195-97, 199-200, 203, 207, 209-10, 212, 214, 216, 218, 221, 228-29, 232-34, 237, 239-40, 242, 244-45, 247-52, 254-56, 259-60, 262-66, 269, 274, 277-78
"The temple soared" (Fuller) **50**:246
Templos de España (Bécquer)
See *Historia de los Templos de España*
The Temptation (Krasiński) **4**:306
Temptation and Atonement (Gore) **65**:21
The Temptation of Pescara (Meyer)
See *Die Versuchung des Pescara*
The Temptation of St. Anthony (Flaubert)
See *La tentation de Saint Antoine*
"10 de octubre!" (Martí)
See "October 10!"
Ten Letters to Dr. Joseph Priestly, in Answer to His Letters to the Inhabitants of Northumberland (Webster) **30**:405
"Ten piedad de mi" (Isaacs) **70**:310-11
Ten Tales (Maginn) **8**:440, 442-43
"Ten Years Ago" (Clarke) **19**:233
Ten Years' Exile (Staël-Holstein)
See *Dix années d'exil*
Ten Years from the Life of a Woman; or, Bad Advice (Scribe)
See *Dix ans de la vie d'une femme; ou, Les Mauvais Conseils*
"The Tenant" (Very) **9**:376
The Tenant of Wildfell Hall (Brontë) **4**:38-43, 47-54, 56; **71**:73-4, 90, 104-05, 109-10, 112, 126, 134, 137, 141, 143-45, 147, 154-55, 157, 159, 164, 167, 169, 174, 179; **102**:1-73
Tenants of Malory (Le Fanu) **9**:301, 302, 304, 311; **58**:271, 295, 303
The Tender Recollections of Irene McGillicuddy (Oliphant) **47**:288
"Les Ténèbres" (Baudelaire) **55**:10
"Tènébres" (Gautier) **1**:340, 350
Une ténébreuse affaire (Balzac) **5**:74
"Tengerihántás" (Arany) **34**:21
"Tennyson's Poems" (Mill) **58**:368
"The Tent on the Beach" (Whittier) **8**:509, 520; **59**:350
The Tent on the Beach, and Other Poems (Whittier) **8**:501
Tentation (Feuillet) **45**:87-90
La tentation de Saint Antoine (Flaubert) **2**:220, 227, 229-31, 233-4, 236-9, 243-6, 255-6; **10**:125, 132, 155-6; **19**:278; **62**:69, 76, 79, 82, 90-2, 96, 98-9, 111; **66**:262, 269-72; **135**:77, 84, 126, 172
The Tenth Haycock (Martineau) **137**:250
"Teon i Eskhin" (Zhukovsky) **35**:379, 398
"The Terek's Gifts" (Lermontov) **126**:142
"Teresa" (Isaacs) **70**:306
Térésa (Dumas) **11**:42-43, 47, 67
"Teresa di Faenza" (Lazarus) **109**:292
"A természet vadvirága" (Petofi) **21**:278
"Terminus" (Emerson) **1**:279, 289, 296; **98**:177, 184
Ternove (Gobineau) **17**:79
"Terpsichore" (Holmes) **14**:101
Terpsichore (Herder) **8**:313
"The Terrace at Berne" (Arnold) **6**:44; **29**:34; **89**:4, 7
La terreur prussienne (Dumas) **71**:210
"A Terrible Disappointment" (Petofi)
See "Irtóztató csalódás"
"The Terrible Divination: A Story" (Bestuzhev)
See "Strashnoe gadanie: Rasskaz"
"The Terrible Doubt of Appearances" (Whitman) **4**:562
"A Terrible Night" (O'Brien) **21**:236, 245-46, 252
The Terrible Temptation (Reade) **2**:541, 546, 549; **74**:243, 248-49, 255, 263-64, 284
"A Terrible Vengeance" (Gogol)
See "Strašnaja mest"
"A Terribly Strange Bed" (Collins) **93**:64
"Tessa's Surprise" (Alcott) **6**:16
"The Test" (Bestuzhev)
See "Ispytaniye"
"Le testament" (Maupassant) **1**:458
"Testament" (Shevchenko)
See "Zapovit"
Testament (Comte) **54**:213
A Testament (Sacher-Masoch) **31**:295
"Testament de Champavert" (Borel) **41**:5-7
Le Testament d'un blagueur (Vallès) **71**:357
"The Testament of Cathaeir Mor" (Mangan) **27**:297-98
"El testamento" (Larra) **130**:249
Testigo de bronce (Zorrilla y Moral) **6**:523
"Tête de faune" (Rimbaud) **4**:458
"La tête de Kenwarc'h" (Leconte de Lisle) **29**:225
La tête de mort; ou, Les ruines de Pompeïa (Pixérécourt) **39**:272, 278-79, 283, 289-90
"Tetemrehívás" (Arany) **34**:21
Les têtes du serail (Hugo) **3**:234
Tetralogy (Wagner) **9**:437
Teutonic Mythology (Grimm and Grimm)
See *Deutsche Mythologie*
Teverino (Sand) **2**:589, 599; **42**:310, 320; **57**:315-6
Textbook of Literature for Russian Youth (Gogol) **31**:95, 106, 125, 136
"Tezkomyslnot" (Macha) **46**:202
Thackeray (Trollope) **101**:345
Thalaba the Destroyer (Southey) **8**:447-49, 451, 453, 456, 461, 474, 476-77; **97**:260-61, 268, 275, 278-79, 281, 293-97, 307, 322, 332, 336
"Thamurīos Marching" (Browning) **79**:106, 113, 115-16, 174
"Thanatopsis" (Bryant) **6**:158-60, 163-65, 168-74, 176-79, 182-83, 187-90, 192; **46**:2-4, 8-9, 17, 19-23, 29, 34, 37, 41, 44, 49-51, 53
"Thanks in Old Age" (Whitman) **31**:434
"Thanks to meddling malice" (Baratynsky) **103**:47-9
"Thar's More in the Man Than Thar Is in the Land" (Lanier) **6**:264; **118**:227-28, 230, 235
That Boy of Norcott's (Lever) **23**:292
"That Enough Is as Good as a Feast" (Lamb) **10**:428
"That Letter" (Bellamy) **4**:30-31
"That Nature Is a Heraclitean Fire and of the Comfort of the Resurrection" (Hopkins) **17**:190, 214, 244, 246, 250, 253, 256
"That Pig Morin" (Maupassant) **1**:460
"Thatchen O' the Rick" (Barnes) **75**:77
Theages oder Unterredungen von Schönheit und Liebe (Wieland) **17**:401, 419
Theaterg'schichten (Nestroy) **42**:243
Theatralische Sendung (Goethe) **90**:102-04
Théâtre choisi (Pixérécourt) **39**:278, 280-83, 288
Théâtre de Clara Gazul (Mérimée) **6**:350, 353-4, 356, 362; **65**:44, 49, 54-6, 63, 79-82, 85, 87, 90, 95
Théâtre d'Eugène Scribe, dediéà ses collaborateurs (Scribe) **16**:381
Théâtre mystère comédies et ballets (Gautier) **59**:35
The Theatrical Recorder (Holcroft) **85**:235
"Thébaide" (Gautier) **1**:350
"The Theban Sphinx" (De Quincey) **87**:53, 57
"Their Height in Heaven Comforts Not" (Dickinson) **21**:38
"Theism" (Mill) **11**:358, 378-79
"Thekla at her Lover's Grave" (Hemans) **71**:303
"Thekla's Answer" (Arnold) **29**:35
"Thekla's Song" (Harpur) **114**:144
"Them Ku Klux" (Lanier) **118**:227, 231
"Themself Are All I Have" (Dickinson) **21**:58

"Then She Bore Pale Desire" (Blake) **13**:240
"Les thénardiers" (Hugo) **10**:375
"Theodicaea Novissima" (Hallam) **110**:120, 141-46
Theodora Desanges (Linton)
See *The Second Youth of Theodora Desanges*
"Théodore de Banville" (Mallarmé) **41**:281
"Theodric: A Domestic Tale" (Campbell) **19**:175, 179, 181, 184, 190, 193, 197
Theodric: A Domestic Tale, and Other Poems (Campbell) **19**:175
Theogonie nach den Quellen des classischen, hebräischen und christlichen Alterthums (Feuerbach) **139**:242
Theogony (Feuerbach)
See *Theogonie nach den Quellen des classischen, hebräischen und christlichen Alterthums Feuerbach*
Theokritos, Bion, und Moschos (Mörike) **10**:449
The Theological Works of Thomas Paine (Paine) **62**:325
Theology Explained and Defended in a Series of Sermons (Dwight) **13**:265, 269, 272
"The Theology of the Seven Epistles of St. Ignatius" (Newman) **38**:311
"Theon and Aeschines" (Zhukovsky)
See "Teon i Eskhin"
"A Théophie Gautier" (Banville) **9**:26, 28
"Théophile Gautier" (Baudelaire) **29**:70
Theophrastus Such (Eliot) **118**:118
Théorie de l'unité universelle (Fourier) **51**:161
Théorie des quatre mouvements (Fourier) **51**:156, 161, 163, 171, 174
Theorie und Geschichte der Red-Kunst und Dicht-Kunst (Wieland) **17**:417, 419
"Theories of Food" (Lewes) **25**:287
Theories of Surplus Value (Marx) **114**:8, 70
Theory of a True Poetical Language (Chivers) **49**:54
"Theory of Colours" (Goethe) **4**:209-10
"Theory of Greek Tragedy" (De Quincey) **87**:74-5, 78
Theory of Legislation (Bentham) **38**:66, 68, 70
Theory of Life (Coleridge) **9**:197
"A Theory of Poetry" (Timrod) **25**:365, 373, 378, 380
The Theory of Science in its General Lines (Fichte)
See *Die Wissenschaftslehre in ihrem allgemeinen Umrisse*
"Theory of the Vertebrate Skull" (Huxley) **67**:4
"Theosophy" (Novalis) **13**:404
"Therania" (Allingham) **25**:9, 18
"There" (Herzen)
See "Elena"
"There" (Verlaine) **51**:371-72
"There Are Thousands" (Petofi)
See "Ezrivel terem"
"There Are Those Favorites of Inspiration" (Pavlova)
See "Est' liubimtsy vdokhnovenii"
"There came a day at summer's full" (Dickinson) **77**:58, 156
"There Came a Wind Like a Bugle" (Dickinson) **21**:81; **77**:97
"There Goes, There Drones the Green Noise, the Noise of Spring" (Nekrasov) **11**:411
"There Had Been Wars" (Shevchenko)
See "Buvaly voiny"
"There Is a Fountain" (Cowper) **8**:127
There is a Time to Plant (Smolenskin)
See *Et la-ta'at*
"There Is Another Loneliness" (Dickinson) **21**:69
"There Is in the Light of Autumn Evenings" (Tyutchev) **34**:393
"There is melody in the sea waves" (Tyutchev)
See "Pevuchest est v morskikh volnakh"
"There Is Mist on the Mountain" (Scott) **15**:318
There Is No Natural Religion (Blake) **37**:55; **57**:53, 91; **127**:5, 31, 123
"There Is Not a Spot in this Wide Peopled Earth" (Moodie) **113**:308
"There Should Have Been Roses" (Jacobsen) **34**:170-72
"There Stands in the Village of Subotiv" (Shevchenko)
See "Stojit' v seli Subotovi"
"There Was a Boy" (Wordsworth) **38**:405, 408
"There Was a Child Went Forth" (Whitman) **4**:584, 602; **31**:403-04, 425, 445; **81**:314, 358-59, 364, 368
Therefore (Mallarmé)
See *Igitur*
"There's a Certain Slant of Light" (Dickinson) **21**:42, 75
"There's a Good Time Coming" (Foster) **26**:295
"There's a rare Soul of Poetry which may be" (Harpur) **114**:115
"There's Been a Death in the Opposite House" (Dickinson) **21**:43
"There's Dr. Clash" (Blake) **37**:29
"There's Rest" (Moodie) **113**:345
"Theresa" (Keller) **2**:412
Thérèse Aubert (Nodier) **19**:376, 381, 384-85
"Thermopylae" (Brontë) **109**:28
"These Are the Nights that Beetles Love" (Dickinson) **21**:82
"These Carols" (Whitman) **4**:602
"These I Singing in Spring" (Whitman) **31**:387
"These Prairies Glow with Flowers" (Bryant) **6**:165
Theses on Feuerbach (Marx) **114**:36, 69
Theseus and Ariadne (Planché) **42**:287
Thessalonica (Brown) **74**:15, 49, 82-3; **122**:119
"Thestylis" (Leconte de Lisle) **29**:219
"They Put Us Far Apart" (Dickinson) **21**:38
"They Taught Me, and It Was a Fearful Creed" (Bryant) **46**:21
"Thick-Headed Thoughts" (Gordon) **21**:168
"Thick-Sprinkled Bunting" (Whitman) **81**:318
"The Thief" (Nekrasov) **11**:407
Things As They Are; or, The Adventures of Caleb Williams (Godwin) **14**:36, 40-5, 47-53, 55-9, 61-2, 68-85, 87, 92-3; **130**:1-190
"Things Necessary to the Life of a Woman" (Warren) **13**:412, 415
Things Seen (Hugo)
See *Choses vues*
"Thinking Proletariat" (Pisarev) **25**:339
Thiodolf, the Islander (Fouqué) **2**:266, 268
"The Third Day" (Longfellow) **45**:138
"The Third Epistle" (Eminescu)
See "Scrisoarea a treia"
"Third Letter to Marcie" (Sand) **42**:358
"The Third of February, 1852" (Tennyson) **30**:294
"The Third Part of Christabel" (Maginn) **8**:438
"Third Sunday in Advent" (Keble) **87**:177
"Third Sunday in Lent" (Keble) **87**:157
"The Third Voice" (Carroll) **139**:128
The Thirteen (Balzac)
See *Histoire des treize*
1356 (Dickinson) **77**:89
1347 (Dickinson) **77**:94
1377 (Dickinson) **77**:153
1364 (Dickinson) **77**:123
1339 (Dickinson) **77**:96
1331 (Dickinson) **77**:77
"The Thirty Flasks" (Mangan) **27**:291, 302
Thirty Poems (Bryant) **6**:165
Thirty Years Later, the War, or Insurrection of El Chacho (Faustino) **123**:274
Thirty Years of Paris and of My Literary Life (Daudet)
See *Trente ans de Paris*
This Book Belongs to the King (Arnim)
See *Dies Buch Gehört dem König*
"This City and This Country" (Blake) **37**:29
"This Compost" (Whitman) **31**:368, 370, 402, 404, 408; **81**:258
"This Frog He Would Awooing Ride" (Blake) **37**:29
"This Life" (Arany)
See "Ez az élet"
"This Lime-Tree Bower My Prison" (Coleridge) **54**:71; **99**:2, 28, 37, 101, 104
This Must Be Said, So Let It Be Said (Kierkegaard) **34**:238
"This twilight seems a veil of gause and mist" (Clare) **86**:120, 129
"Tho' the Last Glimpse of Erin" (Moore) **110**:186, 194, 198
Thomas à Becket (Darley) **2**:128, 130
Thomas Carlyle (Froude) **43**:181, 189, 197-98, 215-221
"Thomas Carlyle and His Works" (Thoreau) **138**:124, 127
"Thomas Davis: An Elegy" (Ferguson) **33**:288
"Thomson and Cowper" (Hazlitt) **29**:166
"Thoralf and Synnöv" (Boyesen) **135**:10, 18
"Thora's Song" (Gordon) **21**:173
"Thoreau" (Emerson) **98**:73
"Thoreau" (Lowell) **90**:202, 206, 220-21
"The Thorn" (Wordsworth) **12**:386-87, 403, 430, 445; **111**:200-3, 207-8, 210-12, 223, 244, 263, 283, 291-92, 294, 312-13, 315-16, 338, 356, 367-69
"Thorns for the Rose" (Parton) **86**:347
"The Thorns in the Geate" (Barnes) **75**:73
"The Thorny Path of Honor" (Andersen) **7**:21; **79**:84, 89
"Thorp Green" (Brontë) **109**:38
"Those Evening Bells" (Moore) **110**:197
"Those Who Have Perished and Those Who Are Perishing" (Pisarev)
See "Pogibšie i pogibajuščie"
"Thou Art Indeed Just, Lord" (Hopkins) **17**:225
"Thou Art the Eyes by Which I See" (Very) **9**:384
"Thou Mother with Thy Equal Brood" (Whitman) **4**:586; **31**:390
"Thou Orb Aloft Full-Dazzling" (Whitman) **31**:391
"Thou Shalt Hear the Judgement of the Fool" (Turgenev) **37**:385
Thou Shalt Not Lie (Grillparzer)
See *Weh dem, der lügt!*
"Thou who dost smile" (Boker) **125**:82
"Thought" (Allston) **2**:26
"Thought" (Lermontov) **47**:166
"Thought for Michael Angelo" (Horne) **127**:255, 271
"Thought May Well Be Ever Ranging" (Clough) **27**:105
"A Thought of Columbus" (Whitman)
See "A Prayer of Columbus"
"The Thought of Death" (Symonds) **34**:323
"A Thought on Book-Binding" (Melville) **123**:255
"A Thought on Thoughts" (Browning) **61**:22
"The thoughtful dragon" (Lonnrot) **53**:339
"The Thoughtful Ones" (Almqvist)
See "De fundersamme"
"Thoughts" (Amiel)
See "Pensées"
"Thoughts" (Arany)
See "Gondolatok"
"Thoughts" (Whitman) **31**:433
Thoughts (Joubert)
See *Pensées, essais, maxmimes, et correspondance de Joseph Joubert*
Thoughts, A Series of Sonnets (Harpur) **114**:95, 105, 107-8, 120, 138
"Thoughts and Doings" (Huxley) **67**:49
"Thoughts and Fancies" (Coleridge) **90**:26-7
"Thoughts at the Funeral of a Respected Friend" (Sigourney) **21**:309
"Thoughts at the Grave of Sir Walter Scott" (Sigourney) **21**:301
"Thoughts for Mourners" (Sigourney) **87**:337
"Thoughts from Various Authors" (Bestuzhev)
See "Mysli iz raznykh avtorov"

Thoughts in verse on Christian children; their ways and their privileges (Keble)
See *Lyra Innocentium: Thoughts in Verse on Christian Children, Their Ways, and Their Privileges*
Thoughts of a Recluse (Wright) **74**:362
"Thoughts on a Tomb" (Zhukovsky) **35**:377, 402-03, 405
Thoughts on Art, Philosophy, and Religion (Dobell) **43**:60
"Thoughts on Beauty and Art" (Barnes) **75**:28, 55, 65-6
Thoughts on Death and Immortality. From the Papers of a Thinker, along with an Appendix of Theological-Satirical Epigrams (Feuerbach)
See *Gedanken über Tod und Unsterblichkeit, aus den Papieren eines Denkers, nebst einem Anhang theologischsatyrischer Xenien, herausgegeben von einem seiner Freunde*
Thoughts on English Prosody (Jefferson) **11**:190; **103**:105
Thoughts on Government (Adams) **106**:11, 13
Thoughts on Man: His Nature, Productions, and Discoveries (Godwin) **14**:50, 62, 66; **130**:26-27, 36-37, 40
"Thoughts on My Sick-Bed" (Wordsworth) **138**:284-85, 313
"Thoughts on Myth, Epic, and History" (Grimm and Grimm) **3**:219
Thoughts on Purity of Election (Milnes) **61**:138
"Thoughts on Reading" (Whitman) **81**:239
"Thoughts on Sunday Morning" (Fuller) **5**:170
Thoughts on the Importance of the Manners of the Great to General Society (More) **27**:332-33, 337
"Thoughts on the Soul" (Dana) **53**:158, 175
"Thoughts Suggested at the Bazaar at Kingston House" (Barnes) **75**:42
"Thousand-and-Second Tale of Scheherazade" (Poe) **94**:240
Thraliana: The Diary of Mrs. Hester Lynch Thrale (Later Mrs. Piozzi), 1776-1809 (Piozzi) **57**:236, 240, 251-3, 257-9, 261, 263, 265-70, 284, 287-91, 293, 297, 299, 304
"Thränenregen" (Muller) **73**:364, 370-72, 375
"Thrawn Janet" (Stevenson) **5**:403, 431, 434; **63**:228, 274
3 (Dickinson) **77**:120
"The Three" (Wergeland) **5**:537
Three Ages (Martineau) **137**:269
"The Three Bears" (Southey)
See "The Story of the Three Bears"
The Three Clerks (Trollope) **6**:453, 463, 465, 470-71, 492, 499-500, 511-12, 514; **101**:235, 253, 266, 275, 329, 333
The Three Cousins (Trollope) **30**:330
Three Cutters (Marryat) **3**:317, 320
"Three Encounters" (Turgenev)
See "Three Meetings"
"The Three Enemies" (Rossetti) **2**:562-3, 576; **50**:272; **66**:305
"The Three Eras of Libbie Marsh" (Gaskell)
See "Libbie Marsh's Three Eras"
Three Essays on Picturesque Beauty (Gilpin) **30**:41-3
Three Essays on Religion (Mill)
See *Nature, the Utility of Religion, and Theism*
"The Three Fishers" (Kingsley) **35**:218, 226, 232
"The Three Flowers" (Allingham) **25**:8
"The Three Friends" (Gordon) **21**:149, 151, 155, 161, 163
"The Three Friends" (Lamb) **10**:389
"Three Friends of Mine" (Longfellow) **2**:492; **45**:132
The Three Friends—A Socialist Tragedy (Horne) **127**:255
"Three Gipsies" (Lenau) **16**:264
"Three Graces of Christian Science" (Martineau) **26**:349
"The Three Graves" (Coleridge) **9**:148; **111**:291-92
"The Three Graves" (Wordsworth) **111**:291-92
"The Three Guides" (Brontë) **4**:45
"The Three Half Crowns" (Mangan) **27**:303
311 (Dickinson) **77**:93
315 (Dickinson) **77**:76, 114, 180, 184
352 (Dickinson) **77**:119
349 (Dickinson) **77**:64
391 (Dickinson) **77**:173, 184
392 (Dickinson) **77**:84
374 (Dickinson) **77**:66
376 (Dickinson) **77**:80
306 (Dickinson) **77**:51
365 (Dickinson) **77**:67
366 (Dickinson) **77**:65
313 (Dickinson) **77**:84
338 (Dickinson) **77**:77
334 (Dickinson) **77**:108, 146
339 (Dickinson) **77**:148, 173
336 (Dickinson) **77**:64, 147
303 (Dickinson) **77**:51, 66
326 (Dickinson) **77**:130
322 (Dickinson) **77**:63
302 (Dickinson) **77**:84
"The Three Hundredth Anniversary of the University of Jena" (Taylor) **89**:308
"The Three Hypotheses Respecting the History of Nature" (Huxley) **67**:27
"The Three Kings" (Longfellow) **45**:128, 139
"The Three Ladies of Sorrow" (De Quincey) **4**:77-78
"Three Lectures to Swiss Members of the International" (Bakunin) **58**:132
Three Märchen of E. T. A. Hoffman (Hoffmann) **2**:345
The Three Maupins; or, The Eve of the Regency (Scribe)
See *Les Trois Maupin; ou, La Veille de la Régence*
"Three Meetings" (Turgenev) **21**:388, 399, 407, 418, 431, 451; **122**:242, 244, 247
Three Mile Cross (Mitford) **4**:404
"The Three Mountains" (Cranch) **115**:49
"The Three Musicians" (Beardsley) **6**:145-46
Three Musketeers (Dumas)
See *Les trois mousquetaires*
The Three Musketeers; or, The Feats and Fortunes of a Gascon Adventurer (Dumas)
See *Les trois mousquetaires*
"Three Nuns" (Rossetti) **2**:566; **50**:284, 322
"The Three Offices of Christ" (Newman) **38**:305
Three Oranges (Gozzi)
See *L'amore delle tre melarance*
"Three Palms" (Lermontov)
See "Tri palmy"
"Three Palm-Trees" (Lermontov)
See "Tri palmy"
"The Three Peasants" (Krylov) **1**:435
The Three Perils of Man; or, War, Women, and Witchcraft (Hogg) **4**:285-86; **109**:200, 204, 206-09, 269, 271
The Three Perils of Woman; or, Love, Learning, and Jealousy (Hogg) **4**:277; **109**:200, 204-06, 208-17, 234
Three Plays (Barlach) **84**:105
Three Poems (Slowacki)
See *Trzy poemata*
"Three Portraits" (Turgenev)
See "Tri portreta"
"Three Raps" (Turgenev)
See "Stuk...stuk...stuk"
The Three Righteous Combmakers (Keller)
See *Die drei gerechten Kammacher*
"The Three Sisters" (Austen) **11**:72; **119**:13
"The Three Sisters" (Hogg) **109**:200
"Three Souls" (Pavlova)
See "Tri dushi"
"Three Stages" (Rossetti) **2**:572; **50**:284, 291; **66**:307, 311
"Three Sundays in a Week" (Poe) **16**:323, 325
"Three Sunsets" (Carroll) **139**:29-30
The Three Sunsets, and Other Poems (Carroll) **139**:29, 31, 127
"The Three Suns of Budrys" (Mickiewicz) **3**:398
Three Tales (Flaubert)
See *Trois contes: Un coeur simple; La légende de Saint-Julien l'hospitalier; Hérodias*
"The Three Tasks" (Carleton) **3**:89, 92
"Three Thoughts" (Ferguson) **33**:290
Three Thoughts of Henryk Ligenza (Krasiński)
See *Trzy myśli pozostale po ś.p. Henryku Ligenzie*
"Three Visions Occasioned by the Birth and Christening of His Royal Highness" (Hunt) **70**:260
"3 Voices" (Carroll)
See "The Three Voices"
"The Three Voices" (Carroll) **2**:111; **139**:34, 124-30
"Three Warnings to John Bull before He Dies. By an Old Acquaintance of the Public" (Piozzi) **57**:240, 298, 304
"The Three Waterfalls" (Lanier) **118**:286
"The Three Witnesses" (Patmore) **9**:335
Three Years in Europe; or, Places I Have Seen and People I Have Met (Brown) **2**:46-50, 52-3, 55; **89**:143, 163-64, 166-68, 181
"Three years she grew in sun and shower" (Wordsworth) **111**:227, 323-24, 328
The Three-Cornered Hat (Alarcon)
See *El sombrero de tres picos*
"Three-Fingered Jack, l'Obi" (Borel) **41**:4, 6, 13
"The Threefold Destiny" (Hawthorne) **2**:303
"Threnody" (Chivers) **49**:50
"Threnody" (Emerson) **1**:285, 296; **38**:150; **98**:177, 179, 181-82
"The Threshold" (Turgenev)
See "Porog"
"The Thrill Came Slowly Like a Boon For" (Dickinson) **21**:58
"Through a Glass Darkly" (Clough) **27**:63
"Through Baltimore" (Taylor) **89**:311
"Through Death to Love" (Rossetti) **4**:517
Through the Looking-Glass and What Alice Found There (Carroll) **2**:107-8, 111-5, 117-20; **53**:37-115; **139**:5, 7, 22-26, 35, 37, 39, 44-45, 51-53, 57, 59, 80-81, 83-89, 92-96, 98, 107-21, 124-26, 131, 133-41, 143, 148, 150-58
"Through Those Old Grounds of Memory" (Dickinson) **21**:77
"Throughout the City. The Center for Store Clerks" (Casal)
See "A través de la ciudad. El centro de dependientes"
A Throw of the Dice Never Will Abolish Chance (Mallarmé)
See *Un coup de dés jamais n'abolira le hasard*
A Throw of the Dice Will Never Abolish Chance (Mallarmé)
See *Un coup de dés jamais n'abolira le hasard*
"The Thrush in a Gilded Cage" (Cranch) **115**:41
"Thumbelina" (Andersen)
See "Tommelise"
"Thumbling" (Andersen)
See "Poor Thumbling"
"Thunder Storm" (Clare) **86**:112, 120-21
"The Thunder Storm" (Hale) **75**:286
"Thunder-gust" (Cranch) **115**:5
"A Thunderstorm" (Lampman) **25**:210
The Thunderstorm (Ostrovsky)
See *Groza*
"Thursday" (Thoreau) **7**:400
"Thursday Before Easter" (Keble) **87**:201

"Thus for Entire Days" (Foscolo)
See "Cosi gl'interi giorni"
"Thy Beauty Fades" (Very) **9**:381
"Thy Brother's Blood" (Very) **9**:377, 387
Thyestes (Foscolo) **97**:73
"Thyoné" (Leconte de Lisle) **29**:239, 245
"Thyrsis" (Arnold) **6**:37, 42, 50-51, 72; **29**:38; **89**:21, 49
"A tf" (Silva) **114**:301
"Tibby Hyslop's Dream" (Hogg) **4**:283
"Tibby Johnson's Wraith" (Hogg) **109**:280
"Tiber, Nile, and Thames" (Rossetti) **77**:296
Tiberius (Adams) **33**:5-8
"Tiberius and Vipsania" (Landor) **14**:176
"The Tide Rises, The Tide Falls" (Longfellow) **2**:492; **45**:186-87
"The Tide River" (Kingsley) **35**:226
"La tierra de Córdoba" (Isaacs) **70**:312-13
"La tierra madre" (Isaacs) **70**:313
Tieste (Foscolo) **8**:262; **97**:48
"The Tiger" (Blake)
See "The Tyger"
Tiger and Hyena (Petofi)
See *Tigris és hiéna*
"Tiger-Lilies" (Lanier) **118**:252, 254
Tiger-Lilies (Lanier) **6**:231, 232, 245, 248, 251, 264, 266-67, 273, 277; **118**:200-201, 217, 219, 227-28, 237, 250-55, 257-59, 261-62, 265, 267, 269, 282, 284-86
"Tight Boots" (Shaw) **15**:335
Tigris és hiéna (Petofi) **21**:284
"Til en gran" (Wergeland) **5**:540
"The Tillers" (Lamartine)
See "Les laboureurs"
Tilottama Sambhav Kāvya (Dutt) **118**:5
"Timbuctoo" (Tennyson) **30**:283; **65**:258-9, 271, 274
Timbuctoo (Hallam) **110**:148-50, 152
Time (Engels) **85**:6
Time Flies (Rossetti) **66**:305-6, 331, 341-2
"The Time of the Barmecides" (Mangan) **27**:278, 285-86, 292, 296, 298
"A Time of Unexampled Prosperity" (Irving) **95**:256
"Time, Real and Imaginary" (Coleridge) **9**:149
A Time to Plant, and a Time to Pluck up That Which is Planted (Smolenskin)
See *Et la-ta'at*
Time Works Wonders (Jerrold) **2**:395, 397, 401-06
"The Time-Piece" (Cowper) **8**:110-11, 115, 128-29; **94**:27, 30, 120
"The Times" (Barnes) **75**:23, 43-4, 96, 101, 105, 108-09
"Times o' Year" (Barnes) **75**:20, 26, 68
"Time's Revenges" (Browning) **79**:94, 102
Timoleon (Melville) **3**:351, 363, 379; **91**:184
Timoleone (Alfieri) **101**:8, 32, 38, 42
"Timon of Athens" (Lamb) **125**:304
Timothy Crump's Ward (Alger) **8**:41; **83**:96, 142, 146
Timour the Tartar (Lewis) **11**:306
The Tin Box (Alger) **8**:43-44; **83**:92
"The Tin Soldier" (Andersen)
See "Den standhaftige Tinsoldat"
"The Tinder-Box" (Andersen)
See "Fyrtøjet"
"The Tinker" (Wordsworth) **111**:203-4
"The Tint I Cannot Take—Is Best" (Dickinson) **21**:83
"A tintásüveg" (Petofi) **21**:283
"Tintern Abbey" (Wordsworth)
See "Lines Composed a Few Miles Above Tintern Abbey"
"The Tippler and His Horse" (Muller) **73**:353
"The Tippler to His Bottle" (Horton) **87**:89
"Tired Memory" (Patmore) **9**:349, 358
"Tiresias" (Tennyson) **30**:235, 280, 293
Tiriel (Blake) **13**:183, 218-21; **37**:14, 20, 22
Tirocinium; or, Review of Schools (Cowper) **8**:98; **94**:8-9, 14-16, 19-21
"'Tis April and the morning, love" (Clare) **86**:87
"'Tis Finished" (Very) **9**:387
"'Tis Opposites Entice" (Dickinson) **21**:69
'Tis Sixty Years Since (Scott)
See *Waverley; or, 'Tis Sixty Years Since*
"'Tis so appalling-it exhilirates sic" (Dickinson) **77**:75-76
"'Tis the Last Glass of Claret" (Maginn) **8**:441
"'Tis the Last Rose of Summer" (Moore) **6**:397; **110**:196
"The Tisza" (Petofi) **21**:285
Titan (Jean Paul) **7**:226, 232-33, 236, 238-40
The Tithe Proctor: Being a Tale of the Tithe Rebellion in Ireland (Carleton) **3**:85-86, 90
"Tithonus" (Tennyson) **30**:220, 239, 279-80, 283; **65**:358-9; **115**:237, 240
"Titmouse" (Emerson) **1**:284, 296; **38**:186; **98**:184
Tiw: or, a View on the Roots and Stems of the English as a Teutonic Tongue (Barnes) **75**:26-7, 40, 65
"Ætna" (Cowper) **94**:117
"To" (Halleck) **47**:57
"To—" (Keats) **73**:154
"To—" (Lanier) **6**:237
"To—" (Moore) **110**:177
"To ——" (Pinkney) **31**:276
"To—" (Poe) **55**:214; **117**:242, 280
"To—" (Smith) **59**:320
"To a Bavarian Girl" (Taylor) **89**:298
"To a Caty-Did" (Freneau) **1**:317, 322; **111**:141
"To a Certain Civilian" (Whitman) **31**:360; **81**:314
"To a Child" (Longfellow) **2**:493; **45**:155
"To a China Tree" (Chivers) **49**:48
"To a Cloud" (Bryant) **6**:161
"To a Comet" (Harpur) **114**:144
"To a Common Prostitute" (Whitman) **31**:403, 428, 432
"To a Comrade" (Corbière) **43**:14
"To a Dead Woman" (Meyer)
See "Einer Toten"
"To a False Friend" (Hood) **16**:216
To a Former Goethe Disciple (Heine)
See *An einen ehemaligen Goetheaner*
"To a Fragment of Cotton" (Sigourney) **87**:346-48
"To a Friend" (Arnold) **6**:44; **29**:35
"To a Friend" (Keats) **73**:147, 231-32
"To a Friend" (Novalis) **13**:364
"To a Friend Who Asked How I Felt When the Nurse First Presented My Infant to Me" (Coleridge) **99**:37
"To a Fringed Gentian" (Bryant) **6**:169, 172, 193; **46**:7-9
"To A. G. A." (Brontë) **16**:122
"To a Gipsy Child by the Sea-shore" (Arnold) **29**:4, 35; **89**:95
"To a Highland Girl" (Wordsworth) **12**:434
"To a Honey Bee" (Freneau) **1**:315
"To a Katydid" (Holmes) **14**:100
"To a Lofty Beauty Edith Southey, from her Poor Kinsman" (Coleridge) **90**:6, 26
"To a Magnate" (Pushkin) **3**:443
"To a Maniac" (Opie) **65**:160
"To a Millionaire" (Lampman) **25**:194
"To a Mocking Bird Singing in a Tree" (Ridge) **82**:184
"To a Moralist" (Schiller) **39**:339
"To a Mosquito" (Bryant) **6**:161, 167; **46**:7
"To a Mountain" (Kendall) **12**:185, 187, 189-90, 198, 200
"To a Nightingale" (Smith)
See "Sonnet 3"
"To a Nun" (Solomos) **15**:393
"To a Passing Woman" (Baudelaire)
See "A une passante"
"To a Persian Boy" (Taylor) **89**:357
"To a Polish Mother" (Mickiewicz) **3**:398
"To a Republican Friend" (Arnold) **29**:34
"To a Rosebud in Humble Life" (Clare) **9**:74
"To a Russian Landowner" (Gogol) **31**:138
"To a Shred of Linen" (Sigourney) **21**:299, 301, 310; **87**:346-48
"To a Skylark" (Shelley) **18**:319, 329, 336, 355, 361-62
"To a Southern Statesman" (Whittier) **8**:519
"To a Star Seen at Twilight" (Ridge) **82**:184
"To a Stream" (Darley) **2**:133
"To a Waterfowl" (Bryant) **6**:158, 162-63, 168-70, 172-74, 177, 183-84, 190, 192; **46**:3, 6, 23, 32, 41, 43-4, 47, 53-4
"To a Western Boy" (Whitman) **4**:575
"To a Winter Scene" (Clare) **86**:110
"To a Young Ass" (Coleridge) **54**:71
"To a Young Gentleman Residing in France" (Warren) **13**:413
"To a Young Lady on Showing an Excellent Piece of Painting, Much Faded" (Warren) **13**:413
"To a Young Lady Who Requested the Author to Draw Her Character" (Trumbull) **30**:345, 349
"To —, After Reading a Life and Letters" (Tennyson) **65**:381
"To All" (Very) **9**:383
"To Allegra Florence in Heaven" (Chivers) **49**:38, 40, 51, 56
"To Allegra in Heaven" (Chivers)
See "To Allegra Florence in Heaven"
"To Amine" (Mangan) **27**:278
"To an Aeolian Harp" (Mörike) **10**:446
"To an Angry Zealot" (Freneau) **111**:113
"To an April Daisy" (Clare) **9**:74
"To an Author" (Freneau) **111**:142, 181
"To an Echo on the Banks of the Hunter" (Harpur) **114**:107-8, 115, 117, 144
"To an Enthusiast" (Dyer) **129**:107
"To an Insect" (Holmes) **14**:128
"To an Insignificant Flower" (Clare) **9**:123
"To an Old Man" (Freneau) **111**:144
"To an Ultra-Protestant" (Lampman) **25**:194
"To an Unknown Friend" (Nekrasov) **11**:418
"To Anna" (Opie) **65**:160
"To Anna" (Rowson) **69**:128
"To Anne" (Rowson) **69**:120
"To Autumn" (Keats)
See "Ode to Autumn"
"To Autumn Robin" (Clare) **9**:80
"To Baratynsky" (Pavlova)
See *A. D. Baratynskoy*
"To Bayard Taylor" (Lanier) **6**:248
"To Be or Not to Be" (Blake) **37**:29
"To Beethoven" (Lanier) **118**:286
"To Blazes!" (Petofi)
See "Lánggal égo"
"To Bogdanovic" (Baratynsky)
See "Bogdanovicu"
"To Brighton" (Jefferies) **47**:134-35
"To Brown Dwarf of Rügen" (Whittier) **8**:529
To Buonaparte, the Liberator (Foscolo) **97**:49
"To Byron" (Keats) **73**:145, 148
"To Carmen Sylva" (Lazarus) **109**:339
"To Cecilia" (Chivers) **49**:71
"To Charles Cowden Clarke" (Keats) **73**:318, 331
"To Charlotte Cushman" (Lanier) **118**:215
"To Chaucer" (Lampman) **25**:172, 184, 193, 217
"To Cole, the Painter, Departing For Europe" (Bryant) **46**:55
"To Constantia Singing" (Shelley) **18**:344, 370
"To Count Razumsky" (Pushkin) **83**:272
"To Cuban Women" (Gómez de Avellaneda)
See "A las cubanas"
"To Damascus" (Kendall) **12**:181, 192
"To Death" (Shelley) **18**:342
"To Delvig" (Baratynsky) **103**:10
"To Dependence" (Smith)
See "Sonnet 57"
"To Die Takes Just a Little While" (Dickinson) **21**:42; **77**:163
"To Dr. Moore" (Williams)
See "An Epistle to Dr. Moore"

"To Dr. Thomas Shearer" (Lanier) **118**:219
"To E" (Levy) **59**:94, 102, 120
"To E. FitzGerald" (Tennyson) **30**:280
"To E. Milkeev" (Pavlova) **138**:14
"To Ebert" (Klopstock)
See "An Ebert"
"To Edward Williams" (Shelley) **18**:369
"To Eliza" (Horton) **87**:110
"To Elizabeth Linley" (Sheridan) **91**:232
"To Ellen" (Emerson) **38**:189
"To Emir Abdel-Kader" (Norwid) **17**:368
"To England" (Adams) **33**:4
"To England" (Boker) **125**:31, 33
"To Ennui" (Halleck) **47**:76
"To Eva" (Emerson) **98**:92, 96
"To Evening" (Foscolo)
See "Alla sera"
To Every Sage His Share of Folly (Ostrovsky)
See *Na vsyakogo mudretsa dovolno prostoty*
"To F. W. N." (Newman) **38**:343
"To Fancy" (Keats) **8**:355
"To Fancy" (Smith)
See "Sonnet 47"
"To Fanny" (Keats) **8**:362; **73**:154
"To Fausta" (Arnold) **29**:35
"To Fidelio, Long Absent on the Great Public Cause, Which Agitated All America in 1776" (Warren) **13**:413
"To Fight Aloud Is Very Brave" (Dickinson) **21**:37, 56
"To Florence" (Foscolo) **8**:278
"To Foreign Lands" (Whitman) **31**:426
"To Gentlemen: A Call to Be a Husband" (Parton) **86**:362
"To George Cruikshank..." (Arnold) **29**:4
"To George Eliot" (Woolson) **82**:311
"To George Sand: A Recognition" (Browning) **61**:5
"To (Georgiana)" (Pinkney) **31**:280
"To Get the Final Lilt of Songs" (Whitman) **31**:434
"To Gladstone" (Crawford) **127**:223
"To Gogol" (Shevchenko)
See "To Hohol"
"To Governor Johnstone, one of the British Commissioners, on his late letters and offers to bribe certain eminent characters in America, and threatening afterwards to appeal to the public" (Paine) **62**:321
"To Hampstead" (Hunt) **70**:291, 293-94, 297
"To Harriet" (Shelley) **18**:358
"To hear an Oriole sing" (Dickinson) **77**:110
"To Helen" (Poe) **1**:492, 528; **16**:330; **117**:196, 207-10, 212, 227, 231, 235-37, 242-44, 280-82, 287, 309, 332
"To Henrique. Pray and Hope!" (Isaacs)
See "A Henrique. Ora y espera!"
"To Henry" (Opie) **65**:160
"To Henry George in America" (Adams) **33**:25
"To Him that Was Crucified" (Whitman) **31**:372
"To His Distant Lady" (Foscolo)
See "Alla sua donna lontana"
"To His Friend on Her Recovery" (Foscolo)
See "All' amica risanata"
To his lady (Leopardi)
See "Alla sua donna"
"To His Watch" (Hopkins) **17**:235
"To Hohol" (Shevchenko) **54**:380
"To Homer" (Keats) **73**:194; **121**:129, 141
"To Honoria, on Her Journey to Dover" (Warren) **13**:413
"To Hope" (Hood) **16**:234
"To Hope" (Keats) **73**:311, 334
"To Hope" (Smith) **115**:156
"To Hope" (Williams) **135**:336
"To Ianthe: With Petrarca's Sonnets" (Landor) **14**:199
"To Imitators" (Baratynsky)
See "Podrazhatelyam"
"To Iurev" (Pushkin) **83**:308
"To J. W." (Emerson) **1**:296; **98**:179
To James Russell Lowell on his Fiftieth Birthday (Cranch) **115**:35
"To Jane: The Invitation" (Shelley) **18**:357-58, 362, 369, 371-73; **93**:309
"To Jane: The Keen Stars Were Twinkling" (Shelley) **18**:369-70; **93**:309
"To Jane: The Recollection" (Shelley) **18**:357-58, 362, 369, 371-73; **93**:309
"To Jarifa in an Orgy" (Espronceda)
See "A Jarifa en una orgía"
"To Joachim Lelewel" (Mickiewicz) **3**:398
"To Joanna" (Wordsworth) **111**:219
"To John Ruskin" (Adams) **33**:25
"To Joseph Brenan" (Mangan) **27**:301
To Joy (Schiller)
See *Lied an die Freude*
"To Julia" (Barnes) **75**:70
"To Julia" (Boker) **125**:82
"To K.A. Sverbeevaya" (Baratynsky) **103**:10
"To know just how He suffered-would be dear" (Dickinson) **77**:162
"To Konsin" (Baratynsky)
See "K Konsinu"
"To Ladies' Eyes" (Moore) **110**:185
"To Lady H—, On an Old Ring Found at Tunbridge-Wells" (Moore) **110**:177
"To Lallie" (Levy) **59**:110
"To Laura" (Kendall) **12**:183
"To Laura" (Sheridan) **91**:232
To Laura (Foscolo) **97**:48-9
"To Laura, and a Love Elegy to Laura" (Opie) **65**:160
"To Laura, Melancholy" (Schiller) **39**:339
"To Leigh Hunt" (Keats) **73**:312
"To Literary Aspirants" (Parton) **86**:374
"To Lizzie" (Ridge) **82**:180
"To Lorenzo" (Opie) **65**:160
"To Lothario" (Opie) **65**:160
"To Louis Napoleon" (Boker) **125**:25
"To Luigia Pallavicini, Thrown from Her Horse" (Foscolo)
See "A Luigia Pallavicini caduto da cavello"
"To M. ł. on the Day of Taking Her Holy Communion" (Mickiewicz) **3**:399-400
"To M. L. S." (Poe) **117**:242, 280
"To Marcia" (Freneau) **111**:133
"To Marguerite" (Arnold) **89**:19
"To Marguerite—Continued" (Arnold) **29**:34-5; **89**:16, 18-19, 48, 88, 95, 119
"To Marie with a Copy of the Translation of Faust" (Taylor) **89**:326
To Marry or Not to Marry (Inchbald) **62**:144-6, 185
"To Mary" (Cowper) **8**:116, 123; **94**:34
To Matija Čop (Preseren)
See *Matiju Čopu*
"To Meet So Enabled a Man" (Dickinson) **21**:50
"To Melancholy" (Smith)
See "Sonnet 32"
"To M.H." (Wordsworth) **111**:219
"To Mie Tirante" (Darley) **2**:133
"To Mihril" (Mangan) **27**:290
"To Miss Macartney" (Cowper) **94**:23, 26
"To Miss R. B." (Fuller) **5**:169
"To Mr. —" (Warren) **13**:431
"To Mr. Arthur Aikin" (Dyer) **129**:136, 138-40, 143-44
"To Mr. West on his Translation of Pindar" (Warton) **118**:356
"To Mrs Henry T—ghe, On Reading Her 'Psyche'. 1802" (Moore) **110**:178
"To Mrs. King" (Cowper) **94**:27
"To Muscovite Friends" (Mickiewicz)
See "Do przyjaciól Moskali"
"To My Brother George" (Keats) **73**:331
"To My Class, On Certain Fruits and Flowers Sent Me in Sickness" (Lanier) **118**:218-19
To My Convalescent Friend (Foscolo)
See *Ode all'amica risanata*
"To My Daughter C." (Isaacs)
See "A mi hija Clementina"
"To My Father" (Stevenson) **5**:401
"To My Father on His Birthday" (Browning) **61**:27, 30, 34
"To My Fellow Countrymen" (Shevchenko)
See "Poslaniie"
"To My Friend, the Poet" (Pushkin) **83**:271
"To My Friends" (Arnold) **89**:20
"To My Friends" (Pushkin) **83**:256
"To My Friends, on Sending Schiller's 'Ode to Joy'" (Tyutchev) **34**:392, 395
"To my Friends, who ridiculed a tender Leave-taking" (Arnold) **89**:20
"To My Lyre" (Smith) **115**:155-56
"To My Mother" (Chivers)
See "To My Mother in Heaven"
"To My Mother" (Hayne) **94**:160
"To My Mother" (Poe) **117**:227, 242
To My Mother (Castro)
See *A mi madre*
To My Mother (Hayne) **94**:134
"To My Mother in Heaven" (Chivers) **49**:50, 70
"To My Muscovite Friends" (Mickiewicz)
See "Do przyjaciól Moskali"
"To My Native Land" (Mangan) **27**:296, 299
"To My Niece" (Wordsworth) **138**:310
"To My Old Friend Peter Schlemihl" (Chamisso) **82**:9
"To My Old Readers" (Holmes) **14**:128
"To My Old Schoolmaster" (Whittier) **59**:360, 371-3
"To My Sister" (Gordon) **21**:154, 160-61, 173
"To My Sister" (Whittier) **59**:371, 387
"To My Sister" (Wordsworth) **12**:445
"To My Son" (Arany)
See "Fiamnak"
"To N." (Tyutchev) **34**:389
"To N. M. Yazykov" (Baratynsky) **103**:4
"To N. V. Gogol, 3 July 1847" (Belinski) **5**:101, 110-11
"To Night" (Shelley) **18**:362
"To N.N." (Tyutchev) **34**:394
"To Oblivion" (Smith)
See "Sonnet 90"
"To Old Roscoff" (Corbière)
See "Au vieux Roscoff"
"To One Afar" (Taylor) **89**:298
"To One in Paradise" (Poe) **117**:217, 227, 233, 237, 243, 280-81, 299, 308
"To Osnovjanenko" (Shevchenko)
See "Do Osnovjanenka"
"To Our Ladies of Death" (Thomson) **18**:392, 397-98, 403, 409, 412-13, 418, 421, 424
"To Peter Porcupine" (Freneau) **111**:129
"To Princess Z.A. Volkonskaya" (Baratynsky)
See "Knyagine Z.A. Volkonskoy"
"To R. B." (Hopkins) **17**:225, 260, 262
"To Rhea" (Emerson) **38**:169, 191
"To Richard Wagner" (Lanier) **118**:217, 286
To Russian, Polish and All Slav Friends (Bakunin)
See *To the Russian, Polish, and All the Slav Countries*
"To Sarah" (Fuller) **50**:247
"To Science" (Poe) **55**:151; **78**:282
"To Seem the Stranger Lies My Lot" (Hopkins) **17**:192, 261-62
"To Sensibility" (Williams) **135**:255
"To Silvia" (Leopardi)
See "A Silvia"
"To Sir Robert Smyth: What is Love" (Paine) **62**:324
"To Sleep" (Keats) **73**:196-97
"To Some Ladies" (Keats) **73**:311
"To Spring or Concerning the Antique Fables" (Leopardi)
See "Alla primavera o delle favole antiche"
"To Superstition" (Warton) **118**:356
"To Sylvia" (Levy) **59**:95
"To the Apennines" (Bryant) **6**:164; **46**:47
"To the Apollo on my pin" (Fuller) **50**:246
"To the Aurora Borealis" (Cranch) **115**:8, 32, 54

"To the Body" (Patmore) **9**:339, 354, 359, 363
"To the Cam" (Dyer) **129**:93
"To the Canary Bird" (Very) **9**:380, 390-91
To the Citizens of the United States (Paine) **62**:271
"To the Coat of Arms of New Granada" (Isaacs)
See "Al escudo de armas de Nueva Granada"
"To the Coterie" (Baratynsky)
See "Kotterii"
"To the Cricket" (Lampman) **25**:208
"To the crowd life's daily cares are sweet" (Baratynsky)
See "Tolpe trevozhny den' priveten"
"To the Daisy" (Wordsworth) **12**:395
"To the Dandelion" (Lowell) **90**:190, 215
"To the Dead and the Living" (Shevchenko)
See "Poslaniie"
"To the Driving Cloud" (Longfellow) **45**:168; **101**:122; **103**:282
"To the Duke of Wellington" (Arnold) **29**:35
"To The Dying Clad" (Longfellow) **101**:122
"To the Eternal Memory of Kotljarevs'kyj" (Shevchenko)
See "Na vicnu pamjat' Kotljarevs' komu"
"To the Evening Star" (Blake) **37**:40
"To the Evening Star" (Campbell) **19**:188
"To the Evening Wind" (Bryant) **6**:159, 169, 176, 183
"To the Face seen in the Moon" (Fuller) **50**:249-50
"To the Flowers of Heidelberg" (Rizal)
See "A las flores de Heidelberg"
"To the Fossil Flower" (Very) **9**:376, 380
"To the Friend F. I." (Eminescu) **131**:294, 297
"To The Fringed Gentian" (Bryant) **46**:3
"To the Girls" (Preseren)
See "Dekletam"
To the Goddess Misfortune (Foscolo) **97**:52
"To the Goddess of Botany" (Smith)
See "Sonnet 79"
"To the Grasshopper and the Cricket" (Hunt) **70**:263
"To the Great Metropolis" (Clough) **27**:103, 114
"To the Hesitating Purchaser" (Stevenson) **63**:229
"To the Hon. J. Winthrop, Esq." (Warren) **13**:413, 431
"To the Hon Mrs Norton, the Poetess, on Meeting Her at Frampton House" (Barnes) **75**:85
"To the Humming Bird" (Very) **9**:379
"To the Hungarian Youth" (Petofi)
See "A magyar ifjakhoz"
"To the Immortal Memory of the Halibut on which I dined This Day" (Cowper) **94**:122
"To the Infant Princess" (Hunt) **70**:259
"To the Ingleeze Khafir Calling Himself Djaun Bool Djenkinzun" (Mangan) **27**:284, 311-13
"To the King" (Krasicki)
See "Do króla"
"To the King of England" (Paine) **62**:322, 324
"To the Ladies: A Call to Be a Wife" (Parton) **86**:363
"To the Leaven's Soil They Trod" (Whitman) **81**:313
"To the Lord Viscount Forbes" (Moore) **110**:171
"To the Magnolia Grandiflora" (Cranch) **115**:46
"To the Memory of Bem, a Funeral Rhapsody" (Norwid)
See "Bema pamięci żałobny rapsod"
To the Memory of Canning (Coleridge) **90**:16
"To the Memory of Iu. P. Vrevskaia" (Turgenev)
See "Pamiati Iu. P. Vrevskoi"
"To the Memory of the Brave Americans" (Freneau)
See "The Prophecy—To the Memory of the Brave Americans under Genera Greene, Who Fell in the Action of September 8, 1781"
"To the Moon" (Leopardi)
See "Alla Luna"
"To the Moon" (Smith)
See "Sonnet 4"
"To the Moon" (Zhukovsky)
See "K mesyatsu"
"To the Muse" (Foscolo)
See "Alla musa"
"To the Nation" (Petofi)
See "A nemzethez"
"To the National Assembly" (Petofi)
See "A nemzetgyüléshez"
"To the Nightingale" (Clare) **9**:123
"To the Nightingale" (Cowper) **8**:120
"To the Ottawa River" (Lampman) **25**:184, 210
"To the Past" (Bryant) **6**:162
"To the People" (Hugo) **3**:262
"To the Philosopher" (Baratynsky)
See "Mudrecu"
"To the Poet" (Preseren)
See "Pevcu"
"To the Poet" (Pushkin) **83**:249, 257
To the Poet in Whittier (Hayne) **94**:144
"To the Poets Who Only Read and Listen" (Holmes) **14**:132
"To the Portrait of 'A Lady'" (Holmes) **14**:99
"To the Prophetic Soul" (Lampman) **25**:216
To the Public (Villaverde) **121**:335
"To the Pure All Things Are Pure" (Very) **9**:385
"To the Queen" (Blake) **16**:182
"To the Queen" (Hunt) **70**:259
"To the Queen" (Tennyson) **30**:295; **65**:258, 265, 271, 350, 353, 373
"To the Rainbow" (Campbell) **19**:181-82, 192, 198
"To the Reader" (Baudelaire)
See "Au lecteur"
"To the Recording Angel" (Sheridan) **91**:232
"To the Rescue" (Carroll) **2**:107
"To the River Cherwell, Oxford" (Bowles) **103**:79-80, 82, 88-9, 92, 94
"To the River Itchin, Near Winton" (Bowles) **103**:72, 76, 80, 83-4, 86
"To the River Otter" (Coleridge) **99**:17
"To the River Wainsbeck" (Bowles)
See "To the River Wensbeck"
"To the River Wensbeck" (Bowles) **103**:72, 80
To the Russian, Polish, and All the Slav Countries (Bakunin) **25**:64; **58**:135
"To the Sayers of Words" (Whitman) **81**:329
"To the Sea!" (Isaacs)
See "Al mar!"
"To the Sea" (Pushkin)
See "K moriu"
"To the Small Celandine" (Wordsworth) **12**:395
"To the Snipe" (Clare) **86**:144
"To the Sons of Labor" (Adams) **33**:25
"To the South Downs" (Smith)
See "Sonnet 5"
"To the Spirit of Keats" (Lowell) **2**:522
"To the Spirit of Poesy" (Harpur) **114**:94, 144
"To the Star" (Eminescu) **33**:246
"To the States" (Whitman) **31**:426
"To the Sultan's Accession" (Pushkin) **83**:272
"To the Sun" (Smith)
See "Sonnet 89"
"To the Tsar once was it said" (Pushkin) **83**:272
"To the Unknown Eros" (Patmore) **9**:339, 359, 364
"To the Utilitarians" (Wordsworth) **12**:446
"To the Warbling Vireo" (Lampman) **25**:207
"To the Warsaw Critics" (Mickiewicz)
See "O Krytykach i Recenzentach"
"To the Working-Classes of Great-Britain" (Engels) **85**:184
"To the Young Poets" (Hölderlin)
See "An die jungen Dichter"
"To Think of Time" (Whitman) **4**:600; **31**:419, 421, 424-25, 443; **81**:342, 361-62
"To Time" (Clare) **86**:160
"To Tirzah" (Blake) **13**:202, 221, 243; **37**:44, 47, 49, 53, 57, 90-1
"To Torrismond" (Warren) **13**:430
"To Turgenev, in Answer to His Letter" (Zhukovsky) **35**:402
"To Two Friends" (Tyutchev) **34**:388, 395
"To Two Sisters" (Tyutchev) **34**:394
"To V. and R." (Isaacs)
See "A Virginia y Rufino"
To Verdener (Jacobsen) **34**:158, 168, 172
"To Vernon Lee" (Levy) **59**:120
"To Virgil" (Tennyson) **30**:286
"To What Serves Mortal Beauty" (Hopkins) **17**:197, 243
"To Whom This May Come" (Bellamy) **4**:30; **86**:70, 75
"To Wilhelmina" (Lanier) **6**:237
"To William Wordsworth Composed on the Night after His Recitation of a Poem on the Growth of the Individual Mind" (Coleridge) **54**:127; **99**:104
"To Winter" (Blake) **13**:219
"To Wordsworth" (Hemans) **71**:288
"To Wordsworth" (Landor) **14**:198
"To Yazykov" (Baratynsky)
See "To N. M. Yazykov"
"To You" (Silva)
See "A tí"
"To You" (Whitman) **31**:426
"To Zante" (Foscolo)
See "A Zacinto"
"To Zante" (Poe) **117**:308
"A Toast" (Preseren)
See "Zdravljica"
"Le toast des gallois et des bretons" (Lamartine) **11**:271
"Toast funèbre" (Mallarmé) **4**:387-89, 396; **41**:272
"Tobias Correspondence" (Maginn) **8**:439
"Tobler's Ode to Nature" (Goethe)
See "Goethe's Botany: The Metamorphosis of Plants"
"A Toccata of Galuppi's" (Browning) **19**:117, 153; **79**:106, 108-09, 164
"Toc...toc...toc" (Turgenev)
See "Stuk...stuk...stuk"
Der Tod am Hochzeitstage (Nestroy) **42**:224, 229
"Der Tod, das ist die kühle Nacht" (Heine) **4**:256
Der Tod des Dichters (Tieck) **46**:397
Der Tod des Empedokles (Hölderlin) **16**:162
"Der Tod des Erzbischofs Engelbert von Köln" (Droste-Hülshoff) **3**:197, 202
Todesgedanken (Feuerbach)
See *Gedanken über Tod und Unsterblichkeit, aus den Papieren eines Denkers, nebst einem Anhang theologischsatyrischer Xenien, herausgegeben von einem seiner Freunde*
"Der Tod fürs Vaterland" (Hölderlin) **16**:174
"To-Day" (Hugo) **3**:253
"To-Day" (Krasiński) **4**:307
"Today" (Very) **9**:378
"Tofenfeier" (Schiller) **39**:386
The Toilers of the Field (Jefferies) **47**:112, 119, 137
The Toilers of the Sea (Hugo)
See *Les travailleurs de la mer*
"Toilette of a Hebrew Lady" (De Quincey) **4**:69
"La toison d'or" (Gautier) **1**:345, 350; **59**:13, 31-2
Toldi (Arany) **34**:4-6, 10-11, 14, 16, 18, 20, 23
Toldi estéje (Arany) **34**:4, 6, 8, 10, 14, 16, 18
Toldi szerelme (Arany) **34**:4, 10, 14, 18
"A tölgyek alatt" (Arany) **34**:21
"Der Tolle Invalide auf dem Fort Ratonneau" (Arnim) **5**:13, 15-16, 18, 21-24
"Tolpe trevozhny den' priveten" (Baratynsky) **103**:16-17
Tom Brace (Alger) **8**:43

Tom Burke of "Ours" (Lever) **23**:285, 292, 299-301, 303, 305-07, 309
Tom Temple's Career (Alger) **8**:34
Tom the Bootblack; or, The Road to Success (Alger) **8**:20, 33, 45; **83**:142, 148
Tom Tracy (Alger) **83**:113
"The Tomb at San Praxed's" (Browning)
See "The Bishop Orders His Tomb at San Praxed's"
"The Tomb of B." (Isaacs)
See "La tumba de Belisario"
"The Tomb of Charlemagne" (Taylor) **89**:298
"The Tomb of Edgar Poe" (Mallarmé)
See "Le tombeau d'Edgar Poe"
"The Tomb of Madame Langhans" (Hemans) **71**:304
"Les tombales" (Maupassant) **83**:171-72, 194, 197
"La Tombe lointaine" (Desbordes-Valmore) **97**:7
"Le tombeau d'Edgar Poe" (Mallarmé) **4**:376; **41**:280, 289, 291
"Le tombeau d'Edgard Poe" (Mallarmé)
See "Le tombeau d'Edgar Poe"
"Le tombeau d'une mère" (Lamartine) **11**:270
Un tombeau pour Anatole (Mallarmé) **41**:248, 251, 275, 289
"The Tombs in the Abbey" (Lamb) **10**:408; **113**:173, 177, 179
"Tommatoo" (O'Brien) **21**:234, 239, 242-43
"Tommelise" (Andersen) **7**:28-9; **79**:23, 31, 50, 58, 70-1, 76, 81
"Tommy's Dead" (Dobell) **43**:48
"Tomorrow" (Edgeworth) **51**:88-9
"To-morrow" (Longfellow) **45**:121
"To-morrow" (Sigourney) **21**:298
"Tom's Garland" (Hopkins) **17**:189, 225
"The Tone of a Koto" (Ichiyō)
See "Koto no Ne"
Tony Butler (Lever) **23**:292, 303
"Too Late" (Arnold) **89**:49
"Too Late" (Browning) **19**:131
"Too Late" (Cooke) **110**:20, 30, 34, 37, 43-4, 47, 49
"Too Late" (Lenau) **16**:276
"Too Long, O Spirit of Storm" (Timrod) **25**:362, 373
The Too Many (Alfieri)
See *I troppi*
"Too Much" (Mörike) **10**:446
"The Top and the Ball" (Andersen) **79**:23, 34, 69
"Topografía de la Provincia de Cumaná" (Bello) **131**:129
"Topography of the Province of Cumaná, Venezuela" (Bello)
See "Topografía de la Provincia de Cumaná"
"Topolja" (Shevchenko) **54**:373, 389
Topsy Turvy Talk (Fredro)
See *Trzy po trzy*
"The Torch" (Whitman) **4**:592
Torlogh O'Brien (Le Fanu) **58**:275
Törnrosens bok (Almqvist) **42**:4, 9-10, 15
"The Torpedoes of Progress" (Fourier) **51**:180
Torquato Tasso (Goethe) **4**:162-63, 166-67, 169, 172, 190, 192, 211, 218-21; **34**:75, 90
"Torquemada" (Longfellow) **2**:481; **45**:137, 145, 161
Torquemada (Hugo) **3**:261, 264, 269-70
"Torquil and Oona" (Smith) **59**:333
The Torrents of Spring (Turgenev)
See *Veshnie vody*
Torrismond (Beddoes) **3**:29, 32, 34, 36, 38-39
Torso (Herder) **8**:313
"La tortuga y la hormiga" (Lizardi) **30**:68
"La torture par l'espérance" (Villiers de l'Isle Adam) **3**:587
"The Tortured Heart" (Rimbaud)
See "La coeur volé"
"Tory Pledges" (Moore) **110**:172
"To—'s Picture" (Moore) **110**:177
"Der tote Achill" (Meyer) **81**:199, 206, 209
"Die Tote Clarissa" (Klopstock) **11**:240
"Das tote Kind" (Meyer) **81**:143
"Die toten Freunde" (Meyer) **81**:199, 203
"Touch My Honour, Touch My Life" (Griffin) **7**:215
"Touching 'Never'" (Rossetti) **50**:298
"The Touchstone" (Allingham) **25**:6
La tour de Nesle (Dumas) **11**:42-43, 47, 57, 63, 75, 79, 89-90; **71**:184, 186, 190, 193, 209, 232, 249
La tour de Percemont (Sand) **2**:596
"Tour en Belgique" (Gautier) **1**:352
A Tour of Switzerland, or a View of the present State of the Governments and Manners of those Contons, with comparative Sketches of the present State of Paris (Williams) **135**:260, 302, 306, 334-35, 342
"A Tour of the Forest" (Turgenev) **21**:415, 420, 441
A Tour on the Prairies (Irving) **2**:372, 376-77, 380, 382; **95**:253, 280
Tour to the Lakes (Gilpin) **30**:28, 43
Tourmaline (Stifter) **41**:357, 360-62, 364
"Tournament at Reval" (Bestuzhev)
See "Revel'skii turnir"
"The Tournament: Joust First Being the Right Pleasant Joust betwixt Heart and Brain" (Lanier) **6**:254; **118**:238, 259-60
"Toussaint l'ouverture" (Whittier) **8**:515; **59**:364
Toussaint l'ouverture (Lamartine) **11**:258
"Tout entière" (Baudelaire) **55**:29
"Toute mon âme" (Banville) **9**:29
La Tovr Saint-Jacques (Dumas) **71**:193
"Towards a History of Religion and Philosophy in Germany" (Heine)
See "Zur Geschichte der Religion und Philosophie in Deutschland"
"Towards Democracy" (Whitman) **31**:371
Tower Hill (Ainsworth) **13**:36, 40
The Tower of London (Ainsworth) **13**:26, 28, 31-6, 39-40, 43-44, 48-49
The Tower of Nesle (Dumas)
See *La tour de Nesle*
"The Tower of the Dream" (Harpur) **114**:99-100, 105, 144
"The Town" (Martineau) **26**:353
"The Town" (Pushkin)
See "Gorodok"
Town and Country (Trollope) **30**:330-31
"A Town and Country Mouse" (Cooke)
See "A Town Mouse and a Country Mouse"
Town Geology (Kingsley) **35**:232
"A Town Mouse and a Country Mouse" (Cooke) **110**:34, 42, 44
The Town of Lucca (Heine) **54**:319
The Town of the Cascades (Banim) **13**:130
"The Toys" (Patmore) **9**:343, 349, 358
"Tract" (Newman)
See *Tracts for the Times*
"Tract 73" (Newman) **99**:220-22
"Tract 83" (Newman) **99**:220, 222
"Tract 85" (Newman) **99**:221, 225
Tract 90 (Newman) **38**:291, 294, 299-300, 315, 318, 320-21
"Tract One" (Newman)
See *Tracts for the Times*
"Tract XC" (Newman)
See *Tracts for the Times*
Tracts (Keble)
See *Tracts for the Times*
Tracts (Newman)
See *Tracts for the Times*
The Tracts (Newman)
See *Tracts for the Times*
"Tracts and Essays on Several Subjects" (Freneau) **111**:132
"Tracts for the Times" (Keble) **87**:132
Tracts for the Times (Keble) **87**:192-93, 199
Tracts for the Times (Newman) **99**:220, 264
Tracts of the Times (Newman)
See *Tracts for the Times*
Tracy's Ambition (Griffin) **7**:197-98, 201, 209, 213-14, 216, 218
"Trades" (Crabbe) **26**:140
Traditions of Palestine (Martineau) **26**:309-10, 326; **137**:336
"Traduzione de'due primi canti dell'Odissea di Ippolito Pindemonte" (Foscolo) **97**:89
"Una tragedia y un ángel" (Bécquer) **106**:144
The Tragedies of Maddelen, Agamemnon, Lady Macbeth, Antonia, and Clytemnestra (Galt) **1**:327
The Tragedy of Count Alarcos (Disraeli) **39**:67; **79**:269, 277-78;
"The Tragedy of Donohoe" (Harpur) **114**:94, 114, 138
The Tragedy of Man (Madach)
See *Az ember tragédiája*
Tragedy of the Conspiracy of Venice (Martínez de la Rosa)
See *La conjuración de Venecia*
"The Tragic" (Emerson) **38**:193-94
"The Tragic in Ancient Drama Reflected in the Tragic in Modern Drama" (Kierkegaard) **125**:198, 203, 205-6, 208, 212-14, 248, 280
Der Tragödie erster Teil (Goethe)
See *Faust. Die Erster Teil*
Traidor, inconfeso, y mártir (Zorrilla y Moral) **6**:523
"Trailing Arbutus" (Cooke) **110**:9, 15
Train Boy (Alger) **83**:142
"The Training" (Whittier) **59**:364, 373
Training in Christianity (Kierkegaard) **78**:124-25, 154-55, 229, 238
"Training in Relation to Health" (Lewes) **25**:310
Traité de l'association domestique-agricole (Fourier) **51**:156, 161, 172
Traité des écritures cunéiformes (Gobineau) **17**:65
Traité sur les Sacrifices (Maistre) **37**:308
"Le traitement du docteur Tristan" (Villiers de l'Isle Adam) **3**:590
Traités de Législation civile et pénale (Bentham) **38**:24-5, 66
"The Traitor" (Bestuzhev)
See "Izmennik"
"Traits" (Sigourney)
See *Traits of the Aborigines of America*
Traits and Stories of the Irish Peasantry (Carleton) **3**:85, 83-86, 88-94
Traits of American Life (Hale) **75**:296, 319, 349, 356-62
"Traits of Indian Character" (Irving) **95**:265-66, 269
Traits of the Aborigines of America (Sigourney) **21**:304; **87**:340-42
"Tramps of the Night" (Bertrand) **31**:54
"Tranquilization" (Tyutchev) **34**:389
"Transcendency" (Emerson) **1**:282
Transcendental Philosophy (Schelling)
See *System des transcendentalen Idealismus*
"Transcendental Wild Oats" (Alcott) **58**:12, 69; **83**:35
"'Transcendentalism'" (Browning) **19**:131; **79**:141-42
"Transcendentalism" (Cranch) **115**:32, 64
"The Transcendentalist" (Emerson) **38**:209, 227-30; **98**:114
"Transformation" (Shelley) **14**:264, 267; **59**:154-5; **103**:344
The Transformation (Brown)
See *Wieland; or, The Transformation*
Transformation; or, The Romance of Monte Beni (Hawthorne)
See *The Marble Faun; or, The Romance of Monte Beni*
"The Transient and the Permanent in the Sick-Room" (Martineau) **137**:283
"Transition" (Emerson) **38**:190

Translations from Alexander Petőfi, the Magyar Poet (Petofi) **21**:259
Translations from Camoens and Other Poets, with Original Poems (Hemans) **29**:192
Translations from Horace (Brontë) **109**:26
"The Transmigration of Souls" (Baratynsky) **103**:3
"Transplanted" (Dickinson)
See "As If Some Little Arctic Flower"
"A Transplanted Boy" (Woolson) **82**:276, 297, 344-45
"A Transport One Cannot Contain" (Dickinson) **21**:79
"Transpositions d'art" (Gautier) **59**:19
Tran-Tran (Tamayo y Baus) **1**:571
"Trapping a Sheriff" (Harris) **23**:159, 161, 163
"Le Trappiste" (Vigny) **102**:335, 367
"Tras una enfermedad" (Casal) **131**:239
"Die Traube" (Meyer) **81**:146, 149-50
"Trauerode" (Schiller) **39**:386
Trauerspiel in Sizilien (Hebbel)
See *Ein Trauerspiel in Sizilien: Tragicomödie in einem Act, nebst einem Sendschreiben an H. T. Rötscher*
Ein Trauerspiel in Sizilien: Tragicomödie in einem Act, nebst einem Sendschreiben an H. T. Rötscher (Hebbel) **43**:237, 257, 275
Der Traum ein Leben (Grillparzer) **1**:384-85, 390, 398; **102**:93, 105, 107, 110-12, 115-17, 172, 185, 187
"Traum und Erwachen" (Chamisso) **82**:27
"Traumbilder" (Heine) **4**:248-49, 257, 259
Les travailleurs de la mer (Hugo) **3**:248-50, 252-53, 255, 258-59, 264, 267, 270-71; **10**:367; **21**:195, 199, 213
Travel Letters (Petofi)
See *Úti levelek*
The Traveller Returned (Murray) **63**:184-5, 193, 195, 199, 201, 214
The Travellers (Sedgwick) **19**:447
"The Travelling Companion" (Andersen)
See "Reisekammeraten"
"Travelling in Victoria" (Kingsley) **107**:232, 240
Travels (Burton) **42**:36
Travels (Faustino) **123**:273-74
Travels from Hamburgh, through Westphalia, Holland, and the Netherlands, to Paris (Holcroft) **85**:198-99, 207, 212, 215, 235
Travels from Moscow through Prussia, Germany, Switzerland, France, and England (Karamzin) **3**:279
Travels in America (Chateaubriand)
See *Voyage en Amérique*
Travels in Greece, Palestine, Egypt, and Barbary, during the Years 1806 and 1807 (Chateaubriand)
See *Itinéraire de Paris à Jérusalem et de Jérusalem à Paris, en allant par la Grèce, et revenant par l'Egypte, a Barbarie, et l'Espagne*
Travels in New-England and New-York (Dwight) **13**:267-69, 271-73, 276-77
"Travels in the Land of Not" (Emerson) **1**:308
Travels of an Irish Gentleman in Search of a Religion (Moore) **6**:396
"The Travels of the Four Children" (Lear) **3**:297
Travels round the World (Chamisso) **82**:5
Travels with a Donkey in the Cévennes (Stevenson) **5**:387-88, 397, 410
"A través de la ciudad. El centro de dependientes" (Casal) **131**:274, 280
The Treasure (Mörike)
See *Der Schatz*
Treasure Island (Stevenson) **5**:394, 397, 399-400, 402-05, 407, 409, 415, 417, 422, 425, 429-39; **14**:318; **63**:220-76
"The Treasures of the Deep" (Hemans) **71**:264
"Treatise on a Pair of Tongs" (Mangan) **27**:291
A Treatise on Ancient and Modern Literature (Staël-Holstein)
See *De la littérature considérée dans ses rapports avec les institutions sociales*
A Treatise on Cobbett's Corn (Cobbett) **49**:110, 114, 151-52
The Treatise on Despair (Kierkegaard)
See *Sygdommen til Døden*
Treatise on Domestic and Agricultural Association (Fourier)
See *Traité de l'association domestique-agricole*
A Treatise on Domestic Economy for the Use of Young Ladies at Home and at School (Beecher) **30**:14-15, 17-24
"Treatise on Morals" (Shelley) **18**:376; **93**:340
A Treatise on the Influence of the Passions upon the Happiness of Individuals and Nations (Staël-Holstein)
See *De l'influence des passions sur le bonheur des individus et des nations*
"Treatise upon the Origin of Language" (Herder) **8**:305
"The Treaty of Friendship" (Andersen) **79**:89
"The Tree" (Very) **9**:380, 387, 391
"Tree Burial" (Bryant) **46**:4, 19, 22
"The Tree of Liberty" (Harpur) **114**:166
"The Tree of Life" (Dutt) **29**:122
"Trees Be Company" (Barnes) **75**:36
"Treize ans" (Barbey d'Aurevilly) **1**:76
Tremordyn Cliff (Trollope) **30**:319
Trente ans de Paris (Daudet) **1**:236
Trente-six ballades joyeuses (Banville) **9**:18, 25
Tres amores (Gómez de Avellaneda) **111**:28, 53
"Tres Fechas" (Bécquer) **106**:97, 99, 103, 106, 115, 120, 130-32, 149, 156, 159
"Los tres no son más que dos y el que no es nada vale por tres—mascarada política" (Larra) **130**:195-96, 223, 254
Le trésor d'Arlatan (Daudet) **1**:251-52
"Le trésor de al caverne d'Arcueil" (Borel) **41**:13
Trésor des fèves et fleur des pois (Nodier) **19**:385
"Treu Kätchen" (Ludwig) **4**:353
Ein Treuer Diener Seines Herrn (Grillparzer) **1**:384, 387; **102**:90, 111, 168, 172, 180, 184
Der Treulose (Nestroy) **42**:257
"Tri dushi" (Pavlova) **138**:32-34, 50
"Tri palmy" (Lermontov) **5**:287, 295; **126**:142
"Tri portreta" (Turgenev) **21**:377, 414, 417-18; **122**:241, 266, 350
"Tri putnika" (Zhukovsky) **35**:398
"Tri vstreči" (Turgenev) **122**:268
"A Triad" (Rossetti) **2**:561; **50**:298, 321-2; **66**:330
The Trial of Abraham (Wieland) **17**:390
"The Trial of Mamachtaga" (Brackenridge) **7**:55
"The Trial of the Dead" (Sigourney) **21**:299
"Trials of a Travelling Musician" (Moodie) **14**:235
"The Trials of Arden" (Brown) **74**:186
The Trials of Margaret Lyndsay (Wilson) **5**:547-49, 554, 558, 561, 564, 567, 569
"Trials of Temper" (Hogg) **4**:283
Trials of the Human Heart (Rowson) **5**:311-12, 314, 316, 319; **69**:103-05, 113, 136-39
The Tribes of Ireland (Mangan) **27**:314-15
Tribulat Bonhomet (Villiers de l'Isle Adam) **3**:583, 586, 588
"Tribuneaux rustiques" (Maupassant) **1**:448; **83**:174
"Tribute to the Memory of a Dog" (Wordsworth) **12**:430
"La tricoteuse" (Crawford) **12**:169-70
"Trifles" (Emerson) **38**:145
Trilby (Du Maurier) **86**:278-81, 285-88, 292, 294, 296-307
Trilby; ou, Le lutin d'Argail (Nodier) **19**:377, 381, 384-86, 388, 392-93, 395, 400-01
Trilogie der Leidenschaft (Goethe) **4**:201
The Trimph of Infidelity (Dwight) **13**:263, 269-70, 272-73, 278-79
"Trinitas" (Whittier) **59**:356
"Triomphe" (Banville) **9**:31
"A Trip from Åbo" (Runeberg) **41**:313
"A Trip to Ischia" (Taylor) **89**:313
A Trip to Niagara; or, Travellers in America (Dunlap) **2**:212-13
A Trip to Parnassus; or the Judgement of Apollo (Rowson) **69**:109-11, 117, 141
A Trip to Scarborough (Sheridan) **5**:359, 382; **91**:242
"A Trip to Stony Lake" (Moodie) **113**:348
Trip to the Orient (Nerval)
See *Voyage en Orient*
"A Trip to Walpole Island and Port Sarnia" (Richardson) **55**:314, 317
"Tripetown: Twenty Minutes for Breakfast" (Harris) **23**:159
Tristan and Isolde (Wagner)
See *Tristan und Isolde*
Tristan de Roux (Dumas) **9**:234
Tristan und Isolde (Wagner) **9**:404, 406, 408, 412-13, 416, 419, 421, 439-40, 442-43, 446, 450, 452-58, 460, 464-65, 467, 470; **119**:172, 182, 185, 198, 210, 228, 240, 244-46, 268-69, 293, 295-96, 303, 312-15, 349
"Triste" (Silva) **114**:294
"Los tristes" (Castro) **78**:21
"Tristesse" (Desbordes-Valmore) **97**:6, 29
"Tristesse" (Gautier) **1**:350
"Tristesse" (Lamartine) **11**:254
"Tristesse" (Musset) **7**:275
"Les tristesses de la lune" (Baudelaire) **6**:80
Tristia ex Ponto (Grillparzer) **102**:174
"Tristissima nox" (Casal) **131**:267
"Tristitia" (Patmore) **9**:349, 358
Tristram (Arnold)
See *Tristram and Iseult*
"Tristram and Iseult" (Arnold) **6**:32, 34, 42, 44, 54, 66-68, 72-75; **29**:6-7, 23, 31, 33, 35
Tristram and Iseult (Arnold) **89**:3-12
"Trisyllabic Feet" (Bryant) **6**:178
"Der Triumf der Liebe" (Schiller) **39**:386
"Triumph Der Empfindsamkeit" (Goethe) **4**:200
The Triumph of Life (Shelley) **18**:326, 329, 336, 339, 346, 349-53, 355, 360-65, 373, 379, 382-83; **93**:322, 333, 341, 344, 354
"The Triumph of Mind Over Body" (Brontë) **109**:30
"The Triumph of Poetry" (Dyer) **129**:97
"The Triumph of Woman" (Southey) **8**:447
"Triumphal Arch" (Meyer)
See "Der Triumphbogen"
"A Triumphal Arch, Erected in Honor of Kotzebue" (Schlegel) **15**:223
"The Triumphal Banquet" (Schiller) **39**:305
"Der Triumphbogen" (Meyer) **81**:140, 153-54, 156, 199
"The Triumphs of Bacchus" (Pushkin) **3**:415
"Trockne Blumen" (Muller) **73**:363, 365, 373
Trois ans en Asie (Gobineau) **17**:71
Trois contes: Un coeur simple; La légende de Saint-Julien l'hospitalier; Hérodias (Flaubert) **2**:227, 233, 257-9; **62**:108; **135**:93, 109, 145
Les Trois Femmes (Charriere) **66**:124-6, 134, 136-7
"Les trois filles de Milton" (Villiers de l'Isle Adam)
See "Les filles de Milton"
Les Trois Maupin; ou, La Veille de la Régence (Scribe) **16**:412-13
Les trois mousquetaires (Dumas) **11**:50, 52, 58, 63-65, 68, 70, 72-73, 75-76, 80, 86-90; **71**:184, 186, 188-89, 198, 201, 209-10, 228, 232
"Trojka" (Nekrasov) **11**:412
"The Troll Garden" (Kingsley) **35**:240
"Tropical Landscape" (Silva)
See "Paisaje tropical"
"The Trosachs" (Wordsworth) **12**:417

"Le trou du serpent" (Gautier) **1**:350
The Troubadour, Catalogue of Pictures, and Historical Sketches (Landon) **15**:161, 166, 168
"Troubadour Song" (Hemans) **71**:275
La troublante (Dumas) **9**:246
"Troubled about Many Things" (Dickinson)
See "How Many Times These Low Feet Staggered"
"Troubles of the Day" (Barnes) **75**:20
A Troublesome Lodger (Mayhew) **31**:158
Trouled Waters (Ichiyō)
See *Nigorie*
"Troy Town" (Rossetti) **66**:305
"Troy Town" (Rossetti) **4**:492, 498, 505, 511, 518, 526-27, 530; **77**:326-28, 330, 337, 340
Les Troyens (Scribe) **16**:407
"The Truce of Piscataqua" (Whittier) **59**:371
"True" (Cooke) **110**:57
"True and False Comforts" (Cowper) **94**:72
"The True and Froggy Art of Swimming" (Horne) **127**:262
The True and the False (Tennyson) **65**:379
The True and the False Waldemar (Arnim)
See *Der Echte und der falsche Waldemar*
The True History of Joshua Davidson, Christian and Communist (Linton) **41**:167, 169-70
"The True in Dreams" (Cranch) **115**:22
"The True Life" (Lampman) **25**:219
"The True Light" (Very) **9**:372, 385, 390
The True Remedy for the Wrongs of Woman (Beecher) **30**:16, 24-5
The True Story of My Life (Andersen) **7**:15, 23
"A True Tale of the Wiltshire Labourer" (Jefferies) **47**:116, 119
"True Woman" (Rossetti) **77**:312
"True Worshippers" (Martineau) **26**:309
"Truls, the Nameless" (Boyesen) **135**:11, 19
"A Trumpet of Our Own" (Ridge) **82**:195
"Der trunkene Gott" (Meyer) **81**:207
"Truth" (Baratynsky)
See "Istina"
"The Truth" (Blake) **13**:165
"The Truth" (Cowper) **8**:110, 120; **94**:26, 28-9, 111-12, 114
"The Truth" (Lampman) **25**:160-61, 194, 199, 212, 218
"Truth" (Lampman) **25**:163
Truth (Cowper) **94**:10, 14, 16, 51, 53-5, 58-9
"The Truth About the United States" (Martí) **63**:167
"Truth as the Fountain of Beauty in Dramatic Literature" (Tamayo y Baus) **1**:565
"Truth Crushed to Earth" (Bryant) **6**:165
"Truth of Intercourse" (Stevenson) **5**:389; **63**:271, 275
"Truxton's Victory" (Rowson) **5**:322
Try and Trust (Alger) **83**:92
The Tryal (Baillie) **2**:31, 43; **71**:1, 6, 51, 56, 59-67
"Tryzna" (Shevchenko) **54**:379, 386, 390-2, 395
Trzy myśli pozostale po ś.p. Henryku Ligenzie (Krasiński) **4**:306, 313
Trzy po trzy (Fredro) **8**:287-90, 293
Trzy poemata (Slowacki) **15**:358
"The Tsar, Knitting his brows" (Pushkin) **83**:272
"Tsar, nash, nemets russkiy . . ." (Bestuzhev) **131**:181
"Tsar Nikita" (Pushkin) **3**:443, 451
"Tsar Sultan" (Pushkin)
See "Skazka o Tsare Sultane"
"Tschia" (Lamartine) **11**:245, 270, 283
Tsuzurabumi (Ueda Akinari) **131**:20
Tsyganka (Baratynsky)
See *Nalozhnitsa*
Tsygany (Pushkin) **3**:409-12, 416, 421, 424, 433, 444-45, 447-48, 451, 453, 458-59, 462; **27**:386, 392; **83**:243, 245, 250, 334, 357
"Tu imagen de María" (Isaacs) **70**:309
"Tu mettrais l'univers entier dans tu ruelle" (Baudelaire) **29**:103; **55**:56
"Tubber Derg; or, The Red Well" (Carleton) **3**:85, 89, 92, 96
"Tuci" (Lermontov) **126**:190-91
"Tudor Tramp" (Crawford) **12**:169-70
"Tuesday before Easter" (Keble) **87**:177
La tulipe noire (Dumas) **11**:60, 68, 74, 77
"La tumba de Belisario" (Isaacs) **70**:312
"La tumba del soldado" (Isaacs) **70**:311
"Tündérálom" (Petofi) **21**:264, 279
Tündérálom (Madach) **19**:371
"The Tune of Seven Towers" (Morris) **4**:419, 426, 431-32
"Tupejnyi xudožnik" (Leskov) **25**:239
Turandot (Gozzi) **23**:107, 112-14, 119-23, 125-29
"Le turco" (Banville) **9**:16
"Turgenev, Pisemsky, and Goncharov" (Pisarev)
See "Pisemskij, Turgenev, i Goncarov"
"The Turkish Lady" (Campbell) **19**:179, 181
The Turkish Wonder (Gozzi)
See *Il mostro turchino*
"The Turn of the Day" (Barnes) **75**:33
"Turner's Old Téméraire, under a Figure Symbolizing the Church" (Lowell) **2**:512
"The Turn-Out" (Martineau) **26**:309
The Turn-out (Martineau) **137**:251, 264-65
"The Turnstile" (Barnes) **75**:8
"El turpial" (Isaacs) **70**:303
"Turtle Soup" (Carroll) **139**:37
"The Tuscan Maid" (Allston) **2**:21, 26
Tutte le opere (Leopardi) **129**:313, 315-16
Tutte le opere (Manzoni) **29**:306; **98**:214
"Twaddle on Tweedside" (Wilson) **5**:550
"Twas a Long Parting—But the Time" (Dickinson) **21**:56, 79
Twas All for the Best (Bird) **1**:87, 89, 93
"Twas but a Babe" (Sigourney) **21**:309
"Twas like a Maelstrom" (Dickinson) **77**:114-15
"twas warm-at first-like Us" (Dickinson) **77**:162-64
"The Tweed Visited" (Bowles) **103**:80
"Tweil" (Barnes) **75**:7, 79
1258 (Dickinson) **77**:81
1254 (Dickinson) **77**:68
1247 (Dickinson) **77**:109
1209 (Dickinson) **77**:89
1210 (Cantor) **77**:93
1225 (Dickinson) **77**:75
Twelve Original Hibernian Melodies (Morgan) **29**:390
Twelve Sermons (Cobbett) **49**:110, 114, 123, 152, 156, 160
"The Twelve Sleeping Maidens" (Zhukovsky) **35**:379, 389, 391, 398
Twelve Years (Northup)
See *Twelve Years a Slave, Narrative of Solomon Northup, a Citizen of New York, Kidnapped in Washington City in 1841, and Rescued in 1853, from a Cotton Plantation Near the Red River in Louisiana*
Twelve Years a Slave, Narrative of Solomon Northup, a Citizen of New York, Kidnapped in Washington City in 1841, and Rescued in 1853, from a Cotton Plantation Near the Red River in Louisiana (Northup) **105**:358-94
"Twenty Ballads by a Swiss" (Meyer)
See "Zwanzig Balladen von einem Schweizer"
25 Years After (Andersen) **79**:11
24 (Dickinson) **77**:84
Le 24 février (Dumas) **71**:192
"Twenty Golden Years Ago" (Mangan) **27**:281, 292, 296, 298
Twenty Poems in Common English (Barnes) **75**:40
Twenty Years After; or, The Further Feats and Fortunes of a Gascon Adventurer (Dumas)
See *Vingt ans après*
Twenty-Five Village Sermons (Kingsley) **35**:205
"The Twenty-Second of December" (Bryant) **46**:47
"Twenty-third Sunday after Trinity" (Keble) **87**:177
"Twice" (Rossetti) **2**:565, 570; **50**:267, 287, 313, 318; **66**:342
Twice Round the Clock, or the Hours of the Day and Night in London (Sala) **46**:232-33, 237, 244-50
Twice-Told Tales (Hawthorne) **2**:291-94, 299, 303, 305, 319, 321-22; **10**:272, 274; **39**:235-36; **79**:295-96, 307-09; **95**:106, 111
"Twilight" (Halleck) **47**:57, 61
"Twilight" (Levy) **59**:94
"Twilight" (Norton) **47**:238, 240
"Twilight" (Silva)
See "Crepúsculo"
"Twilight" (Tyutchev) **34**:402
"Twilight" (Whitman) **31**:434; **81**:370
Twilight (Baratynsky)
See *Sumerki*
"Twilight Calm" (Rossetti) **2**:576
"Twilight Night" (Rossetti) **50**:288
The Twilight of the Gods (Wagner)
See *Die Götterdämmerung*
"The Twin Brothers" (Eminescu) **33**:265
"Twinkle, twinkle little Bat" (Carroll) **139**:29
Twin Roses (Mowatt) **74**:221
"The Twins" (Eminescu) **131**:286-87, 290-91, 296, 346
The Twins (Shevchenko)
See *Blyzniata*
"Twins of Macha" (Ferguson) **33**:279, 285
"A Twist-Imony in Favour of Gin-Twist" (Maginn) **8**:441
2 (Dickinson) **77**:120
The Two Admirals (Cooper) **1**:208, 221; **54**:258, 263
Two Ages (Kierkegaard)
See *En literair Anmeldelse. To Tidsaldre*
Two Ages: The Age of Revolution and the Present Age, a Literary Review (Kierkegaard) **34**:200, 239, 269; **78**:176, 238
"The Two April Mornings" (Wordsworth) **12**:420; **111**:325, 349-50
"The Two Armies" (Timrod) **25**:361, 388
"Two Augurs" (Villiers de l'Isle Adam)
See "Deux augures"
"Two Brothers" (Baillie) **2**:42
"The Two Brothers" (Carroll) **139**:33-34
"The Two Butlers of Kilkenny" (Maginn) **8**:440
"Two Canadian Poets" (Lampman) **25**:213-14, 216
"Two Charades" (Rossetti) **66**:341
The Two Chiefs of Dunboy (Froude) **43**:192-96
"The Two Children" (Brontë) **16**:93
"Two Choices" (Rossetti) **50**:310
"Two Countrymen" (Krylov) **1**:439
"Two Days' Solitary Imprisonment" (Bellamy) **4**:30
"The Two Deserts" (Patmore) **9**:358
Two Discourses at the Communion on Fridays (Kierkegaard) **34**:205, 239
"The Two Dogs" (Grillparzer)
See "Die beiden Hunde"
"The Two Dragoons" (Runeberg) **41**:314
Two Dramas from Calderón (FitzGerald) **9**:276
"The Two Drovers" (Scott) **110**:232
"Two Early French Stories" (Pater) **7**:338
Two Edifying Discourses (Kierkegaard) **34**:224, 258; **125**:210
"Two Enigmas" (Rossetti) **66**:341
"Two Farms in Woone" (Barnes) **75**:43-4, 93, 101
"Two Fates" (Baratynsky)
See "Dve doli"
"The Two Fishermen" (Moodie) **14**:231
The Two Foscari (Byron) **2**:66, 79-80, 92; **109**:99, 102
Two Foscari (Mitford) **4**:403

Two Friends (Turgenev) **21**:418; **37**:435; **122**:246, 350
"The Two Generals" (Trollope) **101**:264
"The Two Gentlemen of Verona" (Lamb) **125**:304-5
"The Two Graves" (Bryant) **46**:3
"The Two Grenadiers" (Heine) **4**:242-43
"2 Harps" (Allingham) **25**:7
"The Two Heirs" (Mérimée) **6**:354
"The Two Herd-Boys" (Taylor) **89**:342
280 (Dickinson) **77**:76
288 (Dickinson) **77**:112
281 (Dickinson) **77**:75
286 (Dickinson) **77**:91
283 (Dickinson) **77**:66
211 (Dickinson) **77**:149
258 (Dickinson) **77**:84
255 (Dickinson) **77**:163
251 (Dickinson) **77**:152
253 (Dickinson) **77**:119
252 (Dickinson) **77**:119
A Twofold Life (Pavlova)
See *Dvoinaia zhizn'*
249 (Dickinson) **77**:149
241 (Dickinson) **77**:162
246 (Dickinson) **77**:65
214 (Dickinson) **77**:93, 119
296 (Dickinson) **77**:63, 147
293 (Dickinson) **77**:50, 64
271 (Dickinson) **77**:67
273 (Dickinson) **77**:184
272 (Dickinson) **77**:68
216 (Dickinson) **77**:71
239 (Dickinson) **77**:96
232 (Dickinson) **77**:173
"Two in the Campagna" (Browning) **19**:112; **79**:162
"The Two Ivans" (Gogol)
See "The Tale of How Ivan Ivanovich Quarrelled with Ivan Nikiforovich"
"The Two Kinds of Poetry" (Mill) **58**:321-2, 324, 329, 363
"Two Landowners" (Turgenev) **122**:293, 350
"Two Lengths Has Every Day" (Dickinson) **21**:77
"Two Letters to Lord Byron" (Bowles) **103**:54
"The Two Little Skeezucks" (Field) **3**:208
The Two Martyrs (Chateaubriand)
See *Les martyrs; ou, Le triomphe de la religion Chrétienne*
The Two Mentors (Reeve) **19**:408, 412, 415
Two Minor Ethico-Religious Treatises (Kierkegaard) **78**:238
"Two Mollies: A City Sketch" (Boyesen) **135**:13
"Two Muses" (Klopstock) **11**:231
"Two National Songs to the Same Measure" (Harpur) **114**:144
Two Nights Before the Full Moon (Ichiyō)
See *Jusan'ya*
"The Two Pages of Szondi" (Arany)
See "Szondi két apródja"
"The Two Painters" (Allston) **2**:20-21
"The Two Peacocks of Bedfont" (Hood) **16**:218
The Two Piccolomini (Schiller)
See *Wallenstein*
"The Two Poplar Trees" (Desbordes-Valmore)
See "Les Deux peupliers"
"The Two Portraits" (Timrod) **25**:361
"Two Pursuits" (Rossetti) **66**:305
"Two Quatrains" (Turgenev)
See "Dva chetverostishiia"
"The Two Races of Men" (Lamb) **10**:392, 409-11, 428, 436; **113**:173-75, 199
"Two Red Roses across the Moon" (Morris) **4**:426, 431, 444
"The Two Rivers" (Longfellow) **45**:130
"Two Roses and a Ring" (Crawford) **127**:189
"Two Sails" (Meyer)
See "Zwei Segel"
"Two Saints" (Cooke) **110**:16, 55, 57-8
The Two Scars (Fredro)
See *Dwie blizny*
"Two Scenes from the Life of Blondel" (Lowell) **2**:511
Two Sermons on the Interpretation of Prophecy (Arnold) **18**:18
The Two Shoemakers (More) **27**:345, 358
"The Two Sides of the River" (Morris) **4**:421
"Two Sides to a Tortoise" (Melville) **3**:383
Two Sisters (Stifter)
See *Zwei Schwestern*
"Two Sisters of Mercy" (Baudelaire)
See "Les Deux Bonnes Soeurs"
"The Two Skulls" (O'Brien) **21**:242
"Two Sonnets" (Thomson) **18**:392
"Two Sonnets: Harvard" (Holmes) **14**:129
"The Two Sons" (Opie) **65**:173
"The Two Spirits: An Allegory" (Shelley) **18**:362; **93**:304
Two Stories of the Seen and Unseen (Oliphant) **61**:174
"The Two Swans" (Hood) **16**:218, 227, 231
"Two Swimmers Wrestled on the Spar" (Dickinson) **21**:63
"The Two Terrors" (Levy) **59**:94
"The Two Thieves" (Wordsworth) **111**:235
Two Thoughts of Death (Rossetti) **50**:287
"The Two Travellers" (Bryant) **46**:42
"Two Trees Were We" (Barnes) **75**:70
"The Two Villages" (Cooke) **110**:3, 9, 41
"Two Voices" (Ferguson) **33**:290
"The Two Voices" (Ingelow) **39**:256
"The Two Voices" (Tennyson) **30**:226-28, 233, 253, 276-77, 281; **65**:241, 243, 249, 267, 270-1; **115**:236-37, 252, 256-57, 261
"The Two Watchers" (Whittier) **8**:493
"Two Ways of Telling A Story" (Ingelow) **107**:150
The Two Wealthy Farmers (More) **27**:345
"The Two Widows of Hunter's Creek" (Traill) **31**:324
Two Women (Gómez de Avellaneda)
See *Dos mujeres*
"The Two Worlds" (Newman) **38**:345
Two Worlds (Jacobsen)
See *To Verdener*
Two Years Ago (Kingsley) **35**:208, 211, 215, 220, 230-32, 235, 241-42, 244, 246-49, 251, 253-57
"The Two-Days-Old Baby" (Blake)
See "Infant Joy"
Twopenny Trash (Cobbett)
See *Cobbett's Twopenny Trash*
"Ty skazhi, govori . . ." (Bestuzhev) **131**:181
"Ty, utselevshii v serdtse nishchem" (Pavlova) **138**:21, 55
"Ty vse, chto serdtsu milo" (Pavlova) **138**:11
"Ty zrel ego v krugo bol shogo sveta" (Tyutchev) **34**:389, 404
"The Tyger" (Blake) **13**:180-81, 222, 227-29, 231-33, 243, 247; **37**:3-4, 7, 10, 13, 18, 27, 33, 43, 49, 51, 54-7, 62, 69, 77-8, 82, 84-5, 93
Tylney Hall (Hood) **16**:201, 205
"Typee" (Melville) **49**:391
Typee: A Peep at Polynesian Life (Melville) **3**:325-30, 332-34, 337-42, 344, 347, 349, 355-56, 359-60, 363-65, 370-71, 384; **12**:255, 257, 259; **29**:323-24, 331, 335, 338, 354, 367-68; **45**:193-257; **91**:9, 33, 42, 44-5, 55, 63, 122, 212; **123**:187, 192-93, 211, 232, 238-39, 251-52
Les Types de Paris (Mallarmé) **41**:249
"Tyranny" (Lanier)
See "Spring and Tyranny"
Tyrocinium (Cowper)
See *Tirocinium; or, Review of Schools*
"Tytarivna" (Shevchenko) **54**:389
"U Boha za dvermy lezhala sokyra" (Shevchenko) **54**:390
Über Anmut und Würde (Schiller) **69**:206
"Über das Dirigiren" (Wagner) **9**:475
"Über das Erhabene" (Schiller) **39**:363, 367, 380-81, 386-86; **69**:209-10, 266
Über das Genie (Claudius) **75**:195-96, 205, 209-10, 212-14, 219
"Über das Marionettentheater" (Kleist) **2**:446-47, 451, 454-55, 458, 461-62; **37**:226-27, 233, 246, 249-50, 264-65, 267
"Über das Pathetische" (Schiller) **39**:377
"Über das Studium der griechischen Poesie" (Schlegel) **45**:310-12, 319-20, 326-27, 331, 342, 357-60, 366
Über das Wesen der menschlichen Freiheit (Schelling)
See *Philosophische Untersuchungen über das Wesen der menschlichen Freiheit und die damit zusammenhängende Gegenstände*
"Über das Wesen des Drama" (Grillparzer) **102**:104
"Über den Ausbruck: 'Stilles Verdienst'" (Claudius) **75**:211
Über den Begriff der Wissenschaftslehre (Fichte) **62**:29
"Über den Dualis" (Humboldt) **134**:199
"Über den Entwurf zu einer neuen Konstitution für die Juden" (Humboldt) **134**:208, 210
"Über den Gebrauch des Chors in der Tragödie" (Schiller) **69**:181
"Über den Geist der Menschheit" (Humboldt) **134**:194
Über den Geschlechtsunterschied und dessen Einfluss auf die organische Natur (Humboldt) **134**:171
Über den Nationalcharakter der Sprachen (Humboldt) **134**:206
"Über den Unterschied der Dichtungsarten" (Hölderlin) **16**:177
Über den Ursprung der Sprache (Herder) **8**:314
Über den Zusammenhang der tierischen Natur des Menschen mit seiner geistigen (Schiller) **39**:394
"Über die allmähliche Verfertigung der Gedanken beim Reden" (Kleist) **2**:458; **37**:225, 250-2
Über die Aufgabe des Geschichtschreibers (Humboldt) **134**:157
"Über die Diotima" (Schlegel) **45**:358, 373
"Über die Grenzen des Schönen" (Schlegel) **45**:357
"Über die Heide" (Storm) **1**:548
"Über die Kupferstiche" (Tieck) **5**:520
Über die männliche und weibliche Form (Humboldt) **134**:171
Über die nothwendigen Grenzen beim Gebrauch schöner Formen (Schiller) **69**:250
Über die Philosophie der Sprache, und des Worts (Schlegel) **45**:301
Über die Religion: Reden an die Gebildeten unter ihren Verächtern (Schleiermacher) **107**:262, 265-66, 274, 318-19, 331-32, 334-36, 339, 343, 345, 347-51, 353, 355-56, 358, 361, 376, 382-83, 396-98, 401, 405, 408-09
Über die Schriften des Lukas: Ein kritischer Versuch (Schleiermacher) **107**:268, 369
Über die Sprache und Weisheit der Indier (Schlegel) **45**:288, 300, 316
"Über die Unsterblichkeit der Seele" (Claudius) **75**:210, 216
"Über die Unverständlichkeit" (Schlegel) **45**:335, 343, 375-76, 379, 381-82
"Über die Verfahrungsweise des poetischen Geistes" (Hölderlin) **16**:177
"Über die verschiedenen Arten zu dichten" (Hölderlin) **16**:177
Über die Verschiedenheiten des menschlichen Sprachbaues (Humboldt) **134**:206
Über die vierfache Wurzel des Satzes vom zureichenden Grunde (Schopenhauer) **51**:278, 328
"Über die weiblichen Charaktere in den griechischen Dichtern" (Schlegel) **45**:358

Über die Wirkung der Dichtkunst auf die Sitten der Völker in alten und neven Zeiten (Herder) **8**:316
"Über die wissenschaftlichen Behandlungsarten des Naturrechts" (Hegel) **46**:110
"Über ein Sprichwort" (Claudius) **75**:213
Über Garantien (Eichendorff) **8**:220
"Über Lessing" (Schlegel) **45**:359
"Über naïve und sentimtalische Dichtung" (Schiller) **39**:337, 347, 366, 370, 381, 391; **69**:187, 208, 257
Über Polen (Heine) **54**:336
Über Recensenten Unfug (Kotzebue) **25**:135
Über Religion (Humboldt) **134**:192
Über Sprach und Dichtkunst (Klopstock) **11**:228, 233-34
Ubezhishche Monrepo (Saltykov) **16**:345, 358, 373-75
"Übungen im Stil" (Claudius) **75**:210, 218
"Uchenie—aforizmy iz Bekona" (Bestuzhev) **131**:165, 168
Udolpho (Radcliffe)
See *The Mysteries of Udolpho*
Ueber das Wesen des Gelehrten (Fichte) **62**:35
Ueber den Grund unseres Glaubens an eine göttliche Weltregierung (Fichte) **62**:34
Ueber dramatische Kunst und Litteratur (Schlegel) **15**:205, 209, 212, 218, 223, 228, 230-35, 241
Ueda Akinari zenshu (Ueda Akinari) **131**:21
"Uezdnyj lekar" (Turgenev) **122**:264-65
Ugetsu Monogatari (Ueda Akinari) **131**:2-6, 9, 12-17, 19, 21-23, 30-31, 35-39, 41, 45-53, 57, 60-64, 67-70, 72-74, 76-77, 85-88
"The Ugly Duckling" (Andersen)
See "Den grimme Ælling"
"Ugly Princess" (Kingsley) **35**:206
"Ugolino" (Mickiewicz) **101**:162-64
Uiyamabumi (Motoori) **45**:277
"Ukazi" (Preseren) **127**:298
"Ukrainian Duma" (Slowacki) **15**:368
"Ulalume" (Poe) **1**:503, 509, 512, 519; **16**:305; **55**:141, 160; **94**:233; 192, 195-96, 207, 211, 217, 221, 226-27, 236-40, 242-43, 246-47, 264, 277-78, 280-81, 288, 297-98, 309-11, 316, 334
"Der Uli" (Meyer) **81**:140, 146, 148
Uli der Knecht: Elin Volksbuch (Gotthelf)
See *Wie Uli der Knecht glücklich wird*
Uli der Pächter (Gotthelf) **117**:4, 6-8, 17-18, 24, 27, 32-3, 35, 39
"Ulmarra" (Kendall) **12**:192
"Uloola" (Kendall) **12**:192, 201
Ulric the Farm Servant: A Story of the Bernese Lowlands (Gotthelf)
See *Wie Uli der Knecht glücklich wird*
Ulrich der Empfindsame (Tieck) **5**:519
"Ultima canto di Saffo" (Leopardi) **129**:340
"La última ilusión" (Casal) **131**:242
"Ultimatum" (Kierkegaard) **125**:202, 210, 213, 234, 254
Ultime lettere di Jacopo Ortis (Foscolo) **8**:260-65, 267, 269, 273, 275, 277-78; **97**:49-50, 53, 62, 70-80, 82-4, 88, 97
"El último adiós y nosotros, inos morimos o qué hacemos?" (Larra) **130**:205, 231, 241, 243
"El último arrebol" (Isaacs) **70**:308
"Ultra cœlos" (Leconte de Lisle) **29**:226, 228, 235
"Ulysses" (Tennyson) **30**:213, 223, 239, 242, 257, 276, 279-80, 283; **65**:376; **115**:235, 240, 275
Ulysses (Lamb) **113**:278
"Umeršee soslovie" (Leskov) **25**:258
"Umoregi" (Ichiyō) **49**:334, 342
Umsonst (Nestroy) **42**:242, 245, 250
"A un vincitore nel pallone" (Leopardi) **129**:328
"A una dama burlada" (Espronceda) **39**:116
"A una estrella" (Espronceda) **39**:86, 100, 102-04, 108-11, 113, 116, 118-19
Der Unbedeutende (Nestroy) **42**:220, 244, 246-47, 263
Das Unbehagen (Grillparzer) **102**:216
"The Uncanny Guest" (Hoffmann) **2**:342
"Uncle and Aunt" (Barnes) **75**:13, 48
"Uncle and Nephew" (O'Brien) **21**:236, 247
"The Uncle and Nephew" (Opie) **65**:159
"Uncle Ben's Attack of Spring Fever, and How He Got Cured" (Parton) **86**:351
"Uncle Jack" (Nekrasov) **11**:421
"Uncle Jim's Baptist Revival Hymn" (Lanier) **118**:227, 235
"Uncle Joe and His Family" (Moodie) **14**:231
"Uncle Josh" (Cooke) **110**:43
"Uncle Out O' Debt and' Out O' Danger" (Barnes) **75**:70
Uncle Silas: A Tale of Bartram-Haugh (Le Fanu) **9**:299-314, 316-17; **58**:251, 254, 256, 266, 269-71, 274-5, 286-9, 291-303, 306-13
Uncle Tom's Cabin; or, Life among the Lowly (Stowe) **3**:537-53, 555-61, 563; **50**:328-407
"Uncle's Dream" (Dostoevsky) **2**:168, 203
The Uncommercial Traveller (Dickens) **18**:111; **113**:68
"The Unconscious Life" (Cranch) **115**:68
Under a Mask (Boker)
See *The World a Mask*
Under Ground (Carroll)
See *Alice's Adventures Under Ground*
"Under the Cloudy Sky" (Eminescu) **33**:265
"Under the Glacier" (Boyesen) **135**:13, 19, 27
Under the Hill (Beardsley)
See *The Story of Venus and Tannhäuser*
Under the Hill, and Other Essays in Prose and Verse (Beardsley) **6**:147
Under the Lilacs (Alcott) **6**:18, 20; **58**:41, 49-50
"Under the Oaks" (Arany)
See "A tölgyek alatt"
Under the Pine (Hayne) **94**:136
"Under the Pine. To the Memory of Henry Timrod" (Hayne) **94**:159, 165
"Under the Rose" (Rossetti) **2**:558
"Under the Violets" (Holmes) **14**:109, 128, 132
"Under the Willow" (Andersen) **7**:21, 29, 32
"Under the Willow She's Sleeping" (Foster) **26**:295
Under the Willows, and Other Poems (Lowell) **2**:509; **90**:198
"Under the Willow-Tree" (Andersen) **79**:82
"Under the Window" (Preseren)
See "Pod oknom"
Under Which Lord? (Linton) **41**:167
"An Undertaker" (Hood) **16**:206
"The Undertaker" (Pushkin)
See "Grobovshchik"
Underwoods (Stevenson) **5**:400-01, 428; **63**:239-40
"Undine" (Eminescu) **131**:286-87
Undine (Fouqué) **2**:262-63, 265-69
Undine (Hoffmann) **2**:345
The Undivine Comedy (Krasiński) **4**:300, 302-09, 311-22
"The Undying One" (Norton) **47**:233, 239, 251
The Undying One and Other Poems (Norton) **47**:235, 246, 252, 260
"A une jeune tribun" (Gautier) **59**:18
Unexplored Syria (Burton) **42**:37
"The Unexpress'd" (Whitman) **31**:435
"The Unfaithful Servants" (Very) **9**:383
"The Unfaithful Village Girl" (Isaacs)
See "La aldeana infiel"
"The Unfinished Poem" (Krasiński) **4**:304, 307
"The Unforeseen" (Baudelaire)
See "L'imprévu"
"The Unfortunate" (Shevchenko)
See "Tryzna"
"The Unfortunate" (Turgenev)
See "Neschastnaya"
"The Unfortunates" (Nekrasov)
See "Nesžastnye"
"Ungeduld" (Muller) **73**:364, 370-71
Die Unglücklichen (Kotzebue) **25**:146-47
"Unha vez tiren un cravo" (Castro) **78**:41
"The Unhappiest Man" (Kierkegaard) **125**:207-9
"The Unhappy" (Nekrasov) **11**:404-05
"An Unhappy Girl" (Turgenev)
See "Neschastnaya"
Unhappy Valley (Burton)
See *Scinde; or the Unhappy Valley*
Die unheilbringende Zauberkrone (Raimund) **69**:8, 12, 16, 22, 24, 27, 36-38, 44-6, 48-9, 52
"Der Unheimliche Gast" (Hoffmann) **2**:353
Die Uniform des Feldmarschalls Wellington (Kotzebue) **25**:136
"Union Means Power" (Eminescu) **33**:272
"Union of Church and State" (Brownson) **50**:54
"The Unioners" (Barnes)
See "The Times"
"Unitarian Christianity: Discourse at the Ordination of the Rev. Jared Sparks" (Channing) **17**:34
"Unitarian Christianity Most Favorable to Piety: Discourse at the Dedication of the Second Congregational Unitarian Church in New York" (Channing) **17**:35, 39
"Universal Goodness" (Clare) **9**:120
"Universal Money" (Bagehot) **10**:31
"The Universe" (Poe) **117**:304, 309, 320
"Universities: Actual and Ideal" (Huxley) **67**:92
"University Preaching" (Newman) **38**:302, 304
"University Sermon" (Newman) **99**:298
"University Sermon X" (Newman) **99**:298
"University Sermon XI" (Newman) **99**:298
"University Sermon XII" (Newman) **99**:298
"University Sermons" (Newman)
See *Fifteen Sermons Preached before the University of Oxford*
"University Subjects" (Newman)
See *The Idea of a University, Defined and Illustrated*
"The Unknown" (Hale) **75**:358, 361-2
"The Unknown Dead" (Timrod) **25**:360, 388
The Unknown Eros, and Other Odes I-XXXI (Patmore) **9**:333, 336-39, 342-43, 346-47, 352, 354-55, 357-59, 361-62, 364
"The Unknown Masterpiece" (Balzac)
See "Le Chef d'oeuvre inconnu"
"The Unknown Way" (Bryant) **6**:175; **46**:38, 42, 48
"The Unknown Woman" (Villiers de l'Isle Adam)
See "L'inconnue"
"Unmaßgebliche Betrachtung" (Kleist) **37**:274
"The Unmarried Mother" (Preseren)
See "Nezakonska mati"
"Ünneprontók" (Arany) **34**:5
L'uno (Alfieri) **101**:45, 73
"The Unparalleled Adventure of One Hans Pfaall" (Poe) **1**:500; **16**:292, 300, 303, 313, 321, 335
"An Unprotected Female at the Pyramids" (Trollope) **101**:233, 235
Unpublished Poems (Desbordes-Valmore)
See *Poésies inédites*
"Unquiet Sleeper" (Whittier) **8**:845
"Unreal Words" (Newman) **38**:304
"The Unreaped Row" (Nekrasov) **11**:409
"Unrest" (Lampman) **25**:187
"Unseen Buds" (Whitman) **31**:435
"Unshriven" (Gordon) **21**:160
Die Unsichtbare Loge (Jean Paul) **7**:232, 238, 240
"Unspoken Language" (Sigourney) **21**:298
"The Unstamped Press in London" (Horne) **127**:253
"The Untainted Heart" (Preseren)
See "Neiztrohnjeno srce"
"Unter den Sternen" (Meyer) **81**:147
"Unter Sternen" (Keller) **2**:421

Unterhaltungen deutscher Ausgewanderten (Goethe) **4**:196
Unterm Birnbaum (Fontane) **26**:236, 243, 272
"Unterricht" (Klopstock) **11**:238
"Until the Very End" (Arany)
See "Mindvégig"
"Unto Like Story—Trouble Has Enticed Me" (Dickinson) **21**:64
"'Unto Me?' I Do Not Know You" (Dickinson) **21**:58; **77**:160
"Unto Myself I Reared a Monument" (Pushkin) **83**:249
"Die unüberwindliche Flotte" (Schiller) **39**:388
"An Unusual Story" (Goncharov)
See "Neobyknovennaya istoriya"
"Unveiled" (Hayne) **94**:148-49, 166
Unverhofft (Nestroy) **42**:220
Die Unvermählte (Kotzebue) **25**:145
"Unwahrscheinliche Wahrhaftigkeiten" (Kleist) **37**:237
Unwiederbringlich (Fontane) **26**:234, 236-37, 239-40, 244, 251-53, 259-60
"Der Unzufriedene" (Grillparzer) **102**:192
"Up at a Villa-Down in the City, as Distinguished by an Italian Person of Quality" (Browning) **79**:170
"Up Hill" (Rossetti) **2**:555, 562, 572, 575; **50**:272, 283, 317; **66**:301
"Up in the Blue Ridge" (Woolson) **82**:273, 299, 302
"Up the Airy Mountain" (Allingham)
See "The Fairies"
"Up the Country": Letters Written to Her Sister from the Upper Provinces of India (Eden) **10**:103-04
Up the Rhine (Hood) **16**:229
"Up to the Star" (Eminescu)
See "La steaua"
"The Upas Tree" (Pushkin)
See "Anchar"
Upbuilding Discourses (Kierkegaard) **125**:233
"An Up-Country Township" (Clarke) **19**:250
"Upon a fitful dream of passion" (Taylor) **89**:300
"Upon a Very Ancient Dutch House on Long Island" (Freneau) **111**:148, 151
"Upon parting" (Preseren)
See "K slovesu"
"Upon the Anatomy and Affinities of the Medusae" (Huxley) **67**:4
"Upon the Bank at Early Dawn" (Thoreau) **7**:383
"Upon the Lonely Moor" (Carroll) **139**:34
"Upon the Strange Attempt Made on the Lives of Her Majesty" (Hunt) **70**:259
"Upon This Bank at Early Dawn" (Thoreau)
See "Upon the Bank at Early Dawn"
The Upper Rhine: The Scenery of Its Banks and the Manners of Its People (Mayhew) **31**:192
The Upright Men (Tamayo y Baus)
See *Los hombres de bien*
The Uprising in the Cévennes (Tieck)
See *Der Aufruhr in den Cevennen*
Uramurasaki (Ichiyō) **49**:349
Urania: A Rhymed Lesson (Holmes) **14**:100
"Uranii" (Tyutchev) **34**:387-88
"Uranothen" (Chivers) **49**:50
"Urara" (Kendall) **12**:192
Urdu-i-M'ualla (Ghalib) **39**:161
Urfaust (Goethe) **4**:204; **34**:68, 73, 85-6, 94-5, 121-24, 127
"Uriel" (Emerson) **98**:177, 179-81
Urizen (Blake)
See *The Book of Urizen*
"La urna" (Casal) **131**:255
Urne (Feuillet) **45**:88
Der Ursprung der Familie, des Privateigenthums und des Staats (Engels) **85**:6, 9, 12-13, 15, 19, 31, 94-97, 118; **114**:83
Ursula (Keller) **2**:412
Ursule Mirouët (Balzac) **53**:8
"Das Urteil des Paris" (Wieland) **17**:427, 429
"Der Urwald" (Lenau) **16**:269, 278, 283
"The Use and Abuse of Political Terms" (Mill) **58**:320
"The Use of Conflict" (Bagehot) **10**:45
Used Up (Boucicault) **41**:30
Useful and Instructive Poetry (Carroll) **139**:32, 61
Useless Memoirs of the Life of Carlo Gozzi (Gozzi)
See *Memorie inutili della vita di Carlo Gozzi*
"Uses of Great Men" (Emerson) **98**:68, 70, 72
Ustep (Mickiewicz)
See *The Digression*
"The Usurpations of Reason" (Newman) **38**:304, 307
"Uta no homare" (Ueda Akinari) **131**:21-22, 59
Úti jegyzetek (Petofi) **21**:277-78, 280
Úti levelek (Petofi) **21**:277-78, 280
Utilitarianism (Mill) **11**:372, 378, 380, 385; **58**:319, 333-4, 342, 350, 379
"Utility of Religion" (Mill) **11**:358, 378; **58**:327
"Utopie" (Lamartine) **11**:271
"Utoplena" (Shevchenko) **54**:360, 389-90
"Utrumque Paratus" (Arnold) **29**:35
"Utsusemi" (Ichiyō) **49**:354
Œuvres complètes de Jules Laforgue (Laforgue) **53**:277
"Uxa bez ryby" (Leskov) **25**:265, 267
"Uzhin Polliona" (Pavlova) **138**:13, 50
"Uznik" (Pushkin) **83**:351
"Uznik" (Zhukovsky) **35**:398
V chuzhom piru pokhmelye (Ostrovsky) **30**:100, 102-03, 110, 113, 115
"V den' imenin" (Bestuzhev) **131**:150
"V derevne" (Tyutchev) **34**:414
"V dni bezgranichnykh uvlecheniy..." (Baratynsky) **103**:4, 21
"V doroge" (Nekrasov) **11**:412, 420
V srede umerennosti i akkuratnosti (Saltykov) **16**:345, 358, 374
"V tolpe. . ." (Pavlova) **138**:20
Les vacances de Pandolphe (Sand) **42**:346-47, 349
Väd är kärlek? (Almqvist) **42**:17
Vade-Mecum (Norwid) **17**:365, 371-74, 377, 379, 386
Vadim (Lermontov) **5**:294, 296; **47**:162-63, 191-92, 224; **126**:156, 214
"Vadimov" (Bestuzhev) **131**:161
"Vadrózsák" (Madach) **19**:368
"Vae Victis" (Gordon) **21**:164
Vagabond Tales (Boyesen) **135**:13, 29-30
"Vagabonds" (Rimbaud) **4**:477, 482; **35**:293-94, 322; **82**:226
Vagabunduli Libellus (Symonds) **34**:337, 365
"The Vain Owl and the Elf" (Crawford) **12**:172; **127**:181-82, 184, 189
"Vain Virtues" (Rossetti) **4**:491, 499
Vala (Blake)
See *The Four Zoas: The Torments of Love and Jealousy in the Death and Judgement of Albion the Ancient Man*
"Válasz kedvesem levelére" (Petofi) **21**:285
"Valdek" (Macha) **46**:201
"Valdice" (Macha) **46**:201
"The Vale of Esthwaite" (Wordsworth) **111**:293
"The Vale of Tears" (Leskov)
See "Judol'"
"The Valediction" (Cowper) **94**:25
"Valedictory Stanzas to Kemble" (Campbell) **19**:179, 191
Valentin: A French Boy's Story of Sedan (Kingsley) **107**:192-93, 209
"A Valentine" (Poe) **117**:242
Valentine (Sand) **2**:581, 585-86, 588-89, 596-98, 604-07; **42**:314-15, 317, 335, 339-40, 349, 354, 356, 357, 386; **57**:311-3, 316-20, 327-8, 333, 335-7, 339, 347-8, 350, 355, 368, 371
Valentine M'Clutchy, the Irish Agent; or, Chronicles of the Castle Cumber Property (Carleton) **3**:83, 85-87, 89-90, 94-96
Valentine; ou, Le séduction (Pixérécourt) **39**:272, 277, 279, 284
Die Valentine: Schauspiel in fünf Aufzügen (Freytag) **109**:138
"Valentines" (Allingham) **25**:24
"Valentine's Day" (Lamb) **10**:436; **113**:245
Valentine's Eve (Opie) **65**:162, 173-4, 179, 197
Valérie (Scribe) **16**:386-88
"Valerik" (Lermontov) **5**:295; **126**:189
Valerius: A Roman Story (Lockhart) **6**:287, 292-96, 302, 310-12
Valet an meine Leser (Claudius) **75**:198, 214-16
"Valete Omnia" (Chivers) **49**:74
"The Valiant Soldiers" (Truth) **94**:338
Valkyrie (Wagner)
See *Die Walküre*
Vallé2s (JUles)-Séverine: Correspondance (Vallès) **5**:374, 376
"La Vallée de la Scarpe" (Desbordes-Valmore) **97**:6
"The Valley of Baca" (Lazarus) **109**:337
"The Valley of the Shadow of Death" (Carroll) **139**:29-30, 126
"The Valley of Unrest" (Poe) **117**:264, 272-75, 281-82, 306-8
"Le vallon" (Lamartine) **11**:269, 282
Valperga; or, The Life and Adventures of Castruccio, Prince of Lucca (Shelley) **14**:252-53, 261, 265, 267, 270-71, 274-75, 289-90, 292-93; **59**:144, 154, 192-3; **103**:331-32, 335, 338-40, 342, 346
Value of Criticism (Sacher-Masoch) **31**:286
Value, Price, and Profit (Marx) **114**:10
Valvèdre (Sand) **42**:312, 335, 340; **57**:311
"Vamos bebendo" (Castro) **78**:2
"The Vampire" (Baudelaire)
See "Les métamorphoses du vampire"
"Le Vampire" (Baudelaire)
See "Les métamorphoses du vampire"
The Vampire (Boucicault) **41**:32
Le Vampire (Dumas) **71**:210-11, 213-15
Le vampire (Nodier) **19**:378, 383
Le Vampire nouvelle traduite de l'anglais de Lord Byron (Polidori)
See *The Vampyre: A Tale*
Der Vampyr Eine Erzahlung aus dem Englischen des Lord Byron Nebst einer Schilderung seines Aufenthaltes in Mytilene (Polidori)
See *The Vampyre: A Tale*
The Vampyre (Byron) **109**:121
The Vampyre: A Tale (Polidori) **51**:193-96, 199, 201-05, 207-09, 211-29, 231-32, 234, 237-41
Vanda (Norwid) **17**:366-67, 369, 379
"Vanddraaben" (Andersen) **79**:68, 74, 89
"Vande Mataram" (Chatterji) **19**:216, 220, 222, 227
"Vane's Story" (Thomson) **18**:396-97, 400-01, 403, 405-06, 408, 411-13, 420, 424
Vane's Story, Weddah and Om-el-Bonain, and Other Poems (Thomson) **18**:392
Vanina Vanini (Stendhal) **23**:408; **46**:294, 307
"The Vanishers" (Whittier) **59**:375-7
"Vanitas Vanitatum" (Baratynsky) **103**:29
Vanitas Vanitatum (Brontë) **71**:91
Vanity Fair: A Novel without a Hero (Thackeray) **5**:444-50, 452-54, 457-61, 464, 466-69, 471-78, 480, 482-84, 486-90, 492-95, 497-501, 503-04, 506; **14**:387-439; **43**:349-50, 356-57, 361-62, 368, 372, 374, 376-77, 379, 389, 393
"The Vanity of Existence" (Freneau) **1**:317; **111**:141, 144
"Vanna's Twins" (Rossetti) **66**:330
The Variation of Animals and Plants under Domestication (Darwin) **57**:147, 168, 170
"Variations lyriques" (Banville) **9**:16

Variations sur un sujet (Mallarmé) **41**:249
Varieties in Prose (Allingham) **25**:15
"Varios caracteres" (Larra) **130**:193
"Various Verses" (Silva)
See "Versos varios"
Varnak (Shevchenko) **54**:392-3
"Den vartige Dreng" (Andersen) **79**:76
"Vásárban" (Arany) **34**:21
Vasconselos (Simms) **3**:507-08
"Le vase" (Leconte de Lisle) **29**:239
"Le vase étrusque" (Mérimée) **6**:352-4, 360, 367, 369-70; **65**:55, 57-8, 62-3, 100, 102, 104, 113, 128
"The Vase of Ibu Mokil" (Lampman) **25**:167
"Vashti the Queen" (Crawford) **12**:155
Vasilisa Melentyevna (Ostrovsky) **30**:101; **57**:206-7
Vassall Morton (Parkman) **12**:346, 349
"Vastness" (Tennyson) **30**:228, 280; **115**:341-42
"Vaterländische Gesänge" (Hölderlin) **16**:180
Vathek (Beckford) **16**:15-25, 27-39, 41-7, 49-57, 59
"The Vaudois' Wife" (Hemans) **71**:303
Vautrin (Balzac) **5**:75
"Vdol' Fontanki-reki" (Bestuzhev) **131**:181
"Ve, pensamiento!" (Isaacs) **70**:305
"The Veairies" (Barnes) **75**:75
"Večer nakanune Ivana Kupala" (Gogol) **5**:231, 236, 251
"Vecher na bivuake" (Bestuzhev) **131**:175, 185, 210
"Vecher na kavkazskikh vodakh v 1824 godu" (Bestuzhev) **131**:156, 158
Vechera ná khutore bliz Dikanki (Gogol) **5**:209, 218-19, 227, 231, 235, 242, 248-49; **15**:95, 98
Vechny muzh (Dostoevsky) **2**:168, 175, 188, 203; **33**:178; **119**:156
"Veder Napoli poi Mori" (Corbière) **43**:33
"The Veiled Hippolytus" (Pater) **7**:303
"The Veiled Prophet of Khorassan" (Moore) **6**:379, 381, 393; **110**:203-4, 210, 212, 214, 216-17, 221, 224-25
"Veiled Prophet of Korassan" (Moore)
See "The Veiled Prophet of Khorassan"
"La Veillée" (Maupassant) **83**:172, 228
"La veillée" (Sainte-Beuve) **5**:347
"La veillée de Vincennes" (Vigny) **7**:478
"Veillées" (Rimbaud) **35**:311; **82**:230, 232
Veillées des Antilles (Desbordes-Valmore) **97**:12
"Veils" (Cranch) **115**:26-9, 35
Veinte años despues (Dumas)
See *Vingt ans après*
"Vejeces" (Silva) **114**:299, 301-3
"Vellen O' the Tree" (Barnes) **75**:76, 95
"Die Veltlinertraube" (Meyer) **81**:141-42, 150, 155
"Velykyj l'ox" (Shevchenko) **54**:368, 381, 388
"The Venale Muse" (Baudelaire)
See "La Muse vénale"
La vendée (Trollope) **6**:514; **33**:417; **101**:264
"Une vendetta" (Maupassant) **1**:469; **83**:208, 210-12, 222
"A vendre" (Maupassant) **83**:181
"Venecïia" (Pavlova) **138**:16, 49
"Venedigs erster Tag" (Meyer) **81**:209
"Venere" (Eminescu) **33**:265
"Veneris pueri" (Landor) **14**:181
Venetia (Disraeli) **2**:138-39, 143, 149; **39**:22, 24-5, 29, 40, 46, 52, 65-8, 75; **79**:223-28, 230, 233, 269, 272-73, 276-77
The Venetian Bracelet, The Lost Pleiad, A History of the Lyre, and Other Poems (Landon) **15**:158, 161, 166
Venetian Epigrams (Goethe) **4**:173
A Venetian Night (Musset)
See *La nuit Vénitienne; ou, Les noces de laurette*
Vengeance (Fredro)
See *Zemsta*
"La vengeance d'une femme" (Barbey d'Aurevilly) **1**:75, 77-78
Vengeance d'une Italienne (Scribe) **16**:381
The Vengeance of the Covenant (Smolenskin)
See *Nekam berit*
The Vengeance of the Goddess Diana (Hayne) **94**:144
"Vengeance of the Welshmen of Tirawley" (Allingham) **25**:13
"The Vengeance of the Welshmen of Tirawley" (Ferguson) **33**:278, 289, 294, 301, 305
"Venice" (Longfellow) **45**:121
"Venice" (Pavlova)
See "Venecïia"
"Venice" (Rogers) **69**:71
"Venice, an Italian Song" (Longfellow)
See "Venice"
"Venice in the East End" (Jefferies) **47**:95, 136
"Venice's First Day" (Meyer)
See "Venedigs erster Tag"
Venoni; or, The Novice of St. Mark's (Lewis) **11**:305
"Le vent froid de la nuit" (Leconte de Lisle) **29**:222, 228, 235-36
"La venta de los gatos" (Bécquer) **106**:97, 99
"Ventajas de las cosas a medio hacer" (Larra) **17**:275; **130**:197, 223
"La ventana" (Silva) **114**:301, 303
La ventana (Silva) **114**:271
"Une vente" (Maupassant) **1**:448
La Vénus à la fourrure (Sacher-Masoch)
See *Venus im Pelz*
"Venus Anadeomena" (Casal) **131**:236, 267
"Vénus anadyomène" (Rimbaud) **4**:471
"Venus and Madonna" (Eminescu) **131**:287, 330-31
"La Vénus de Milo" (Leconte de Lisle) **29**:222, 224, 238-39
"La Vénus d'Ille" (Mérimée) **6**:353-5, 357, 359, 361, 363, 366, 368-71; **65**:50, 52-4, 56-61, 87, 96, 98, 100-01, 103, 114-15, 118, 123, 129-32, 140
Venus im Pelz (Sacher-Masoch) **31**:285, 287-88, 291-94, 296-98, 300-03, 305, 307, 309-12
Venus in Furs (Sacher-Masoch)
See *Venus im Pelz*
"The Venus of Ille" (Mérimée)
See "La Vénus d'Ille"
"La venus rustique" (Maupassant) **1**:455
"Venus's Looking-Glass" (Rossetti) **2**:561, 576
"Der Venuswagen" (Schiller) **39**:339
Les vêpres siciliennes (Scribe) **16**:408
"Véra" (Villiers de l'Isle Adam) **3**:581, 590
"Vera i neverie. Stsena iz poemy" (Baratynsky) **103**:8
"Vérandah" (Leconte de Lisle) **29**:215
"Die Verbannten" (Droste-Hülshoff) **3**:193
Die Verbannung aus dem Sauberreiche (Nestroy) **42**:224
"Verborgenheit" (Mörike) **10**:458
"Verdad y poesía" (Casal) **131**:259
"The Verdict" (Dostoevsky)
See "Prigover"
"El verdugo" (Espronceda) **39**:85, 100, 107-09, 113-14, 118
El verdugo (Balzac) **5**:78; **53**:25
"Véres napokról álmodom" (Petofi) **21**:286
Verflucht sei der Acker um deinetwellen (Claudius) **75**:191
Der Verfolgte (Fouqué) **2**:266
"Vergänglichkeit" (Lenau) **16**:282
"Die Vergeltung" (Klopstock) **11**:238
Der verhängnisvolle Faschingsnacht (Nestroy) **42**:225-26, 228-29, 240
Die Verkehrte Welt (Tieck) **5**:517, 522-24, 529-30, 532
"Der Verlassene Mägdlein" (Mörike) **10**:453
Die Verlobung (Tieck) **5**:514
Die Verlobung in St. Domingo (Kleist) **2**:456, 462; **37**:245, 247-49, 253-55
Die verlorene Handschrift (Freytag) **109**:153, 158, 175, 177-78
Das Verlorene Lachen (Keller) **2**:415, 421, 423
"Das verlorene Schwert" (Meyer) **81**:209
"Vermächtnis" (Goethe) **4**:172
Vermischte Schriften (Heine) **4**:235, 240, 256, 265
"The Vernal Ague" (Freneau) **111**:153-54
Veronika (Storm) **1**:539-40
Le Verre d'eau; ou, Les Effets et les causes (Scribe) **16**:388-89, 395-96, 401-03, 405-07, 413-14
"Le Verrou" (Maupassant) **83**:176
Vers de circonstance (Mallarmé) **41**:247-50
"Vers dorés" (Nerval) **1**:476, 478, 486; **67**:307
"Vers nouveaux et chansons" (Rimbaud) **82**:240
Vers pour être calomnié (Verlaine) **51**:362
Verschiedene (Heine) **4**:249-50
"Verschiedene Deutung" (Lenau) **16**:269, 283
Der Verschwender (Raimund) **69**:5-6, 8-10, 13, 15, 18, 26, 38, 43-6, 48, 50-3
Der Verschwiegene wider Willen (Kotzebue) **25**:136
Die Verschwörung des Fiesco zu Genua (Schiller) **39**:309-12, 323, 327, 334, 361, 368, 375, 392-94; **69**:169, 239, 263
Verse Tales (Desbordes-Valmore)
See *Contes en vers*
Verses (Rossetti) **2**:559, 561, 576; **50**:271, 284-6
"Verses Addressed to Laura" (Sheridan) **91**:233
"Verses by Lady Geralda" (Brontë) **71**:165
"Verses for Being Vilified" (Verlaine) **51**:372
"Verses, Made at Sea, in a Heavy Gale" (Freneau) **111**:147, 178-81
The Verses of Frederick the Great (Sacher-Masoch) **31**:291
Verses on the Death of the Revd Mr Charles Churchill (Beattie) **25**:122, 124
"Verses on the Exile of the Prince Imperial" (Jefferies) **47**:121
"Verses on the New Year" (Webster) **30**:421
Verses on Various Occasions (Newman) **38**:314; **99**:256
"Verses on War" (Paine)
See "Verses to a Friend After a Long Conversation on War"
Verses Supposed to be Written by Alexander Selkirk (Cowper) **94**:32-38
"Verses to a Friend After a Long Conversation on War" (Paine) **62**:322
Verses to John Howard (Bowles) **103**:54, 70
"The Verses to Memory of a Young Friend" (Lamb) **113**:193
"Verses to the Memory of Garrick" (Sheridan) **91**:234
"Verses written at Bath on Finding the Heel of a Shoe" (Cowper) **94**:119
Versi inediti (Manzoni) **98**:276
"Versions from the Irish" (Ferguson) **33**:287
"Versöhnender, der du nimmer geglaubt ..." (Hölderlin) **16**:162, 166, 168-69, 171, 176
Die Versöhnung, oder Bruderzwist (Kotzebue) **25**:147, 155
Versos Libres (Martí) **63**:105-6
Versos sencillos (Martí) **63**:63, 105, 107-10, 167
"Versos varios" (Silva) **114**:300
Versuch einer Kritik aller Offenbarung (Fichte) **62**:8, 33, 40
"Ein Versuch in Versen" (Claudius) **75**:193
"Versuch über den verschiedenen Styl in Goethe's früheren und späteren Werken" (Schlegel) **45**:309, 327
Versuche des Ignaz Mácha, Die (Macha) **46**:200
Die Versuchung des Pescara (Meyer) **81**:135-37, 153, 164, 166-67, 181, 194
"Vertige" (Rimbaud) **4**:462
Vertraute Briefe über Friedrich Schlegels Lucinde (Schleiermacher) **107**:268, 325, 376, 379, 382
Die Verwandtschaften (Kotzebue) **25**:145
Verwickeltegeschicht (Nestroy) **42**:234-35
"Der verwundete Baum" (Meyer) **81**:200
"Verwünschung" (Grillparzer) **102**:174

Very Hard Cash (Reade)
See *Hard Cash: A Matter-of-Fact Romance*
"The Very Image" (Villiers de l'Isle Adam)
See "A s'y méprendre"
Very Young and Quite Another Story (Ingelow) **39**:264
"Veselie i gore" (Baratynsky) **103**:11
"Vesennee uspokoenie" (Tyutchev) **34**:411
Veshnie vody (Turgenev) **21**:399-401, 411, 413-14, 416, 419, 431, 435, 437-41; **37**:424; **122**:242, 245, 247, 249, 265-67, 326-31, 338, 348, 362, 364
"Vesica piscis" (Patmore) **9**:359
"Vesna" (Baratynsky)
See "Vesna, vesna! kak vozdukh chist!..."
"Vesna" (Tyutchev) **34**:388, 398, 400, 405
"Vesna, vesna! kak vozdukh chist!..." (Baratynsky) **103**:11, 13
Vešnie vody (Turgenev)
See *Veshnie vody*
The Vespers of Palermo (Hemans) **29**:196, 201, 206; **71**:261, 267
"Vestíbulo: Retrato de Gustavo Moreau" (Casal) **131**:219, 223, 227-29, 236, 266, 268-70
"The Veteran" (Runeberg)
See "Veteranen"
"Veteranen" (Runeberg) **41**:321
The Veto on Love (Wagner) **9**:414
"Vezde i vsegda" (Pavlova) **138**:4, 17, 52
Viaggo sentimentale di yorick lungo la Francia e l'Italia (Foscolo) **8**:263-64
Viajes por España (Alarcon) **1**:12
Viajes por Europa, África i América, 1845-1847 (Faustino) **123**:282, 322, 330, 347, 378
Vicaire des Ardennes (Balzac) **5**:58
The Vicar of Bullhampton (Trollope) **6**:465; **101**:235, 312, 319, 342
The Vicar of Wrexhill (Trollope) **30**:308, 319
"The Vices of the Constitution" (Madison) **126**:296
"Vices of the Political System of the United States" (Madison) **126**:297
"Vicksburg" (Hayne) **94**:149
Le Vicomte de Bragelonne (Dumas) **71**:184, 189, 222, 242
The Victim of Prejudice (Hays) **114**:174-75, 182, 189, 191, 197, 200, 206-8, 210, 215-16, 218-20, 222-23, 226-30, 233-34, 251-57
"Victims of Progress" (Boyesen) **135**:49
"Victor and Vanquished" (Longfellow) **45**:139
"Victor Hugo's Romances" (Stevenson) **5**:415; **63**:239-40
Victor; ou, L'enfant de la forêt (Pixérécourt) **39**:273, 276
Victor Vane, the Young Secretary (Alger) **8**:17, 46
Victoria (Rowson) **5**:309, 315, 321; **69**:99, 102-03, 105, 111, 119-22, 125, 127, 135, 141
"A Victorian Rebel" (Morris) **4**:436
"Victoria's Tears" (Browning) **61**:8, 61
The Victories of Love (Patmore) **9**:349, 352
"Victorieusement fui" (Mallarmé) **41**:291
"Victory" (Lazarus) **8**:419
"Victory Comes Late" (Dickinson) **21**:39
"Victory in Defeat" (Patmore) **9**:358, 365
Vida de Abrán Lincoln (Faustino) **123**:274-75
Vida de Dominguito (Faustino) **123**:319, 338
"Vida de Quiroga" (Faustino) **123**:378
Vida y hechos del famoso caballero Don Catrín de la fachenda (Lizardi) **30**:69-73, 78-9
"Videnie" (Tyutchev) **34**:389, 404-05, 407-09
"Vid'ma" (Shevchenko) **54**:368, 389
Une vie (Maupassant) **1**:442, 445-46, 452-54, 456, 463, 465-69; **42**:167-69, 174, 189; **83**:169, 172, 182, 227, 230
"La Vie antérieure" (Baudelaire) **6**:83; **55**:5
"Vie de Byron" (Lamartine) **11**:270
Vie de Henri Brulard (Stendhal) **23**:352, 368, 376, 378-79, 410-12, 416, 422; **46**:261, 270, 277, 281, 320, 325
La vie de Jésus (Renan) **26**:365, 367-72, 377, 401-05, 407-11, 414, 418, 420
"Vie de Joseph Delorme" (Sainte-Beuve) **5**:346
La Vie de Polinchinelle et ses Nombreuses Aventures (Feuillet) **45**:93
Vie de Rancé (Chateaubriand) **134**:15, 18, 99
Vie de Rossini (Stendhal) **23**:352
"La vie de voyage" (Gobineau) **17**:69-70, 104
La vie d'une comédienne (Banville) **9**:19
"La vie et la mort du Capitaine Renaud; ou, La canne du jour" (Vigny) **7**:473, 478
Vie, poésies, et pensées de Joseph Delorme (Sainte-Beuve) **5**:335, 346
"Vieille chanson du jeune temps" (Hugo) **3**:263
Une vieille maîtresse (Barbey d'Aurevilly) **1**:70
"Viel kraftzfüsselnder Bücklinge" (Preseren) **127**:315
"Vields By Watervalls" (Barnes) **75**:31
La vielle fille (Balzac) **5**:33-4, 46, 65, 71; **53**:29
"Viendome perseguide por la alondra" (Castro) **78**:40
Vienna and the Austrians (Trollope) **30**:310
"Vier Jahreszeiten" (Goethe) **4**:193
Vier Schauspiele von Shakespeare (Tieck) **5**:520
"Vierge folle" (Rimbaud) **35**:317-318; **82**:230, 241-42, 245
"Vies" (Rimbaud) **82**:242
"Vies I" (Rimbaud) **35**:322
"Vies II" (Rimbaud) **35**:297, 322
"Le vieux drapeau" (Beranger) **34**:28, 38, 44
"Le vieux vagabond" (Beranger) **34**:38
A View of the English Stage (Hazlitt) **29**:174, 188; **82**:125
"View of the Mountains from the Kozlov Steppes" (Mickiewicz)
See "Widok gór ze stepów Kozłlowa"
"A View on Russian Literature in 1847" (Belinski) **5**:99, 109, 105, 108-09, 116
Views Afoot: or Europe seen with Knapsuck and Staff (Taylor) **89**:297, 363
The Views and Reviews in American History, Literature, and Fiction (Simms) **3**:501
Views of Labour and Gold (Barnes) **75**:23, 40, 51-2, 60, 66, 102, 107
"Views of Life" (Brontë) **4**:45
Views of Society and Manners in America (Wright) **74**:373, 377-78
"The Vigil in Aiden" (Chivers) **49**:71, 73
"Vigil of the Annunciation" (Rossetti) **50**:291
"Vigil Strange I Kept on the Field One Night" (Whitman) **81**:301, 321-22, 330
"La vigne de Naboth" (Leconte de Lisle) **29**:215, 226-28
"La vigne et la maison" (Lamartine) **11**:272, 284-85, 289
"Vigny" (Mill) **58**:333
Vijnan rahasya (Chatterji) **19**:225
"Világosságot!" (Petofi) **21**:285
"Le vilain" (Beranger) **34**:28
"De vilde Svaner" (Andersen) **7**:26, 29, 32-3; **79**:23-4, 63, 76, 88
"The Village" (Crabbe) **121**:52, 83
"The Village" (Pushkin) **83**:333
"The Village" (Turgenev)
See "Derevnia"
The Village (Crabbe) **26**:77-81, 83, 86, 101-02, 106, 110-11, 116-18, 120, 122, 124, 127, 131-34, 137, 140-41, 143, 145-48, 151; **121**:8-10, 16, 18, 26, 28-30, 59, 63-6, 72-3, 75, 83-4, 88
Le Village (Feuillet) **45**:75, 88-9
"The Village Band" (Krylov) **1**:439
"The Village Beau" (Mitford) **4**:401
"The Village Blacksmith" (Hayne) **94**:144
"The Village Blacksmith" (Longfellow) **2**:472-73, 493; **45**:99, 116, 135, 148, 152, 179; **103**:285, 293, 295
"The Village Churchyard" (Zhukovsky)
See "Thoughts on a Tomb"
The Village Coquette (Dickens) **37**:153
Village Disputants (More) **27**:359
"Village Doctor" (Turgenev) **21**:378
The Village Fool (Arany)
See *A falu bolondja*
"The Village Garden" (Levy) **59**:89, 102
"A Village Lear" (Turgenev)
See "Stepnoy Korol 'Lir"
"Village Lovers" (Turgenev) **21**:378
"The Village Merchant" (Freneau) **1**:314
"Village Minstrel" (Clare) **9**:76-77, 97, 102, 113; **86**:129, 157
The Village Minstrel, and Other Poems (Clare) **9**:76-78, 84, 97, 112, 115; **86**:89-90, 103, 108, 110, 113, 125, 154, 159-60, 173-74
"The Village of Balmaquhappel" (Hogg) **4**:284
"Village of Goryukhino" (Pushkin)
See *Istoriia sela Goriukhino*
The Village of Stepanchikovo (Dostoevsky)
See *The Friend of the Family*
The Village on the Heath (Stifter)
See *Das Haidedorf*
Village Politics, by Will Chip (More) **27**:333, 342-45, 349, 359
"The Village Register" (Crabbe)
See "The Parish Register"
A Village Romeo and Juliet (Keller)
See *Romeo und Julia auf dem Dorfe*
The Village Verse-book (Bowles) **103**:54
"La ville enchantée" (Banville) **9**:16
La Ville Noire (Sand) **42**:312-13
"Villes" (Rimbaud) **4**:473; **35**:269, 290, 322; **82**:238
"Villes I" (Rimbaud) **35**:309, 313; **82**:232
Villette (Brontë) **3**:49-61, 63-4, 67-74, 76, 80; **8**:54-5, 72, 75; **33**:102-57; **58**:171, 179, 187, 194-96, 199, 205; **105**:4, 6-7, 45-6, 64, 66, 71, 73, 75
Villette (Eliot) **118**:132
Le vin (Baudelaire) **6**:116, 122, 124; **55**:62, 66
"Le vin de l'assassin" (Baudelaire) **29**:104; **55**:62
"Le vin des amants" (Baudelaire) **29**:104-05; **55**:43-4
"Le vin des chiffoniers" (Baudelaire) **6**:96; **29**:112
"Vinden fortæller om Valdemar Daae og hans Døttre" (Andersen) **79**:77
"Vindicación" (Larra) **17**:273
Vindication (Hays) **114**:231
A Vindication of Catholic Morality (Manzoni)
See *Osservazioni sulla morale cattolica*
Vindication of Congress (Hamilton)
See *A Full Vindication of the Measures of Congress*
Vindication of the English Constitution (Disraeli) **39**:6, 25-6; **79**:211, 215, 269-70, 275;
Vindiciae Ecclesiae Anglicanae (Southey) **97**:265-66
The Vindictive Man (Holcroft) **85**:199, 212-13, 237
"Vineta" (Muller) **73**:352, 359
Vingt ans après (Dumas) **11**:58, 63, 65, 68, 73-74, 76; **71**:203
Vingt jours en Sicile (Renan) **26**:417
"Vino" (Nekrasov) **11**:412, 414
The Vintage of Burgundy (Rogers) **69**:66-7, 73
Viola tricolor (Storm) **1**:540
"La viole de gamba" (Bertrand) **31**:47, 49
"The Violet" (Very) **9**:376, 380
"The Violin" (Cranch) **115**:6
"Violina" (O'Brien) **21**:249-50
"The Violinist" (Lampman) **25**:167, 204
Virgil (Warton) **118**:337
"The Virgin" (Meyer)
See "Die Jungfrau"
"The Virgin" (Thoreau) **7**:383
The Virgin and the Nun (Keller)
See *Die Jungfrau und die Nonne*
The Virgin as Knight (Keller)
See *Die Jungfrau als Ritter*

"The Virgin Mary to the Child Jesus" (Browning) **61**:8, 10, 61
"Virgin Mother Mary mild" (Fuller) **50**:245, 247
Virgin Soil (Turgenev)
See *Nov'*
Virginalia (Chivers)
See *Virginalia or Songs of My Summer Nights*
Virginalia or Songs of My Summer Nights (Chivers) **49**:43, 47-9, 52, 73-6
Virginia (Alfieri) **101**:8, 38, 42-3
Virginia (Macaulay) **42**:111
Virginia (Tamayo y Baus) **1**:570-71
Virginia: A History of the People (Cooke) **5**:127, 131, 135
Virginia and Magdalene (Southworth) **26**:432
"Virginia and Paul" (Villiers de l'Isle Adam)
See "Virginie et Paul"
The Virginia Bohemians (Cooke) **5**:125, 127, 131-32, 135
"La 'Virginia' del Páez" (Isaacs) **70**:308
"The 'Virginia' of the Páez River" (Isaacs)
See "La 'Virginia' del Páez"
Virginia; or, The Roman Father (Mackenzie) **41**:207-09
"A Virginia Romana" (Leopardi) **129**:329, 332
"A Virginia y Rufino" (Isaacs) **70**:311
The Virginian Comedians; or, Old Days in the Old Dominion (Cooke) **5**:121, 123, 126-35
The Virginians: A Tale of the Last Century (Thackeray) **5**:460-61, 481, 485, 488, 500; **14**:452; **43**:363, 388
Virginibus Puerisque, and Other Papers (Stevenson) **5**:388-90, 395, 397, 402-05, 410, 413-14, 425
"Virginie et Paul" (Villiers de l'Isle Adam) **3**:590
La Virtu indiana (Leopardi) **129**:347
"Virtue and Vice" (Thomson) **18**:392
Vishavriksha (Chatterji) **19**:204-06, 209, 212-15, 217-21
"The Visible Church for the Sake of the Elect" (Newman) **38**:305
"A Vision" (Clare) **9**:100, 102-03; **86**:87, 90, 114
"The Vision" (Southey) **97**:281
Vision (Tyutchev)
See "Videnie"
The Vision (Beckford) **16**:37, 47-50
"The Vision Beautiful" (Longfellow) **45**:128
"La vision de Brahma" (Leconte de Lisle) **29**:222-23, 241-42
"La vision de Charles XI" (Mérimée) **65**:48, 53-4, 57-8, 87, 99, 115
La vision de Dante (Hugo) **3**:270
"La vision de Snorr" (Leconte de Lisle) **29**:225, 227
"La visión del Castillo" (Isaacs) **70**:308-09
The Vision of Columbus (Barlow) **23**:3, 12, 14-16, 18-20, 22, 26, 29, 32, 37, 40, 42
"A Vision of Connaught in the Thirteenth Century" (Mangan) **27**:296, 298, 301, 311-13
"A Vision of Conor O'Sullivan" (Mangan) **27**:308
"The Vision of Don Quixote" (Eminescu)
See "Viziunea lui don Quijote"
"The Vision of Dry Bones" (Moodie) **113**:316-17
"Vision of Hell" (Borrow) **9**:54
"A Vision of Horns" (Lamb) **10**:411
The Vision of Judgment (Byron) **2**:67, 72, 75, 78, 81, 91-94; **12**:102, 138; **109**:105
A Vision of Judgment (Southey) **8**:458, 461, 463-64; **97**:259, 264, 273, 277
"A Vision of Poesy" (Timrod) **25**:361, 364-66, 369, 372-74, 378, 383-84
"A Vision of Poets" (Browning) **1**:113, 115, 117, 127; **61**:4
"A Vision of Purgatory" (Maginn) **8**:440
"The Vision of Sin" (Tennyson) **30**:223, 233, 249-50, 254; **115**:236
"The Vision of Sir Launfal" (Lowell) **2**:507, 515, 516, 522
The Vision of Sir Launfal (Lowell) **90**:193, 209-10, 215-17
"The Vision of Sudden Death" (De Quincey) **4**:82-83
"The Vision of the Castle Ranch" (Isaacs)
See "La visión del Castillo"
"The Vision of the Fountain" (Hawthorne) **2**:298
"The Vision of the Goblet" (Boker) **125**:78
A Vision of the Last Judgment (Blake) **13**:219, 246; **37**:4, 28; **57**:24, 67, 74, 79; **127**:7, 16, 71, 125, 127, 131, 137
"A Vision of the Mermaids" (Hopkins) **17**:190-91, 195, 215, 222
"The Vision of the Night, A Fragment" (Freneau) **111**:152
"A Vision of Twilight" (Lampman) **25**:204
"The Vision of Vanity" (Mackenzie) **41**:184
"The Vision; or, Prospect of the Future Happiness of America" (Dwight) **13**:270, 272, 276, 278-79
"The Visionary" (Brontë) **16**:74-5, 86
"Visions" (Turgenev) **21**:399
Visions (Borrow) **9**:54
"Visions: A Fantasy" (Turgenev)
See "Prizraki. Fantaziya"
"Visions in the Smoke" (Gordon) **21**:160-61, 165, 180
Visions of the Daughters of Albion: The Eye Sees More Than the Heart Knows (Blake) **13**:163, 183, 218, 220-21, 223, 232-33, 251-52; **37**:22; **127**:11, 60, 82
Visions of the Past (Dutt) **118**:31
"The Visit" (Austen) **119**:13
"The Visit" (Very) **9**:378
"A Visit to Grosse Isle" (Moodie) **14**:243
A Visit to India, China and Japan in the year 1853 (Taylor) **89**:346
"A Visit to Portugal" (Andersen) **79**:79
"A Visit to the Autocrat's Landlady" (Holmes) **81**:98
Une visite à Bedlam (Scribe) **16**:391
"La Visite au hameau" (Desbordes-Valmore) **97**:8
Une visite de Noces (Dumas) **9**:223, 225-26, 230, 232-33, 242
"Visitors" (Irving) **2**:372
Visits and Sketches at Home and Abroad (Jameson) **43**:304, 317, 320, 323, 337
"Visits to St. Giles" (Tonna) **135**:204
"Visszatekintés" (Arany) **34**:16, 19
Vita (Alfieri) **101**:14, 25, 41, 52, 56-7, 59, 64-5, 67-70, 73, 75, 78-80, 83
La vita solitaria (Leopardi) **129**:229-33
"Vitre bujnyj" (Shevchenko) **54**:375
"Vittoria Accoramboni" (Symonds) **34**:348
Vittoria Accorombona (Tieck) **5**:517, 532; **46**:365, 374-76, 381, 397
La viuda de Padilla (Martínez de la Rosa) **102**:226, 230, 245, 252
"La vivandière" (Beranger) **34**:29
Vivia; or, The Secret of Power (Southworth) **26**:438
"Vivia Perpetua" (Lampman) **25**:169, 220
Vivian (Edgeworth) **1**:267-68; **51**:88-90
Vivian Grey (Disraeli) **2**:136-39, 142-43, 145-46, 148-50; **39**:3, 20-2, 24-5, 30-3, 39-40, 42, 44-6, 50-2, 65-6, 74-5, 78; **79**:199-202, 214, 218, 226-27, 232, 257, 270-72, 274, 276, 279
"Vivian to His Correspondents" (Lewes) **25**:290
"Vivien" (Tennyson) **65**:226, 315-6, 359
Viviparous Quadrupeds of North America, The (Audubon) **47**:13, 33-8, 45-6, 51-2
"The Vixen" (Clare) **9**:117; **86**:131
"Vixerunt" (Herzen) **10**:338
"Viy" (Gogol) **5**:224, 226-27, 242, 248-49, 251, 256-58; **31**:120, 122
"Viziunea lui don Quijote" (Eminescu) **131**:348
"Vladimir Beltov" (Herzen) **61**:109
Vladimir den Store (Stagnelius) **61**:248, 251, 261, 263
Vladimir the Great (Stagnelius)
See *Vladimir den Store*
"Vladyčnyj sud" (Leskov) **25**:258-59, 265-67
"Vlas" (Nekrasov) **11**:400, 407, 412-13, 421
Vließ (Grillparzer)
See *Das goldene Vließ*
The Vocation of Man (Fichte)
See *Die Bestimmung des Menschen*
"La voeux stériles" (Musset) **7**:256
Voevoda: Son na Volge (Ostrovsky) **57**:206-7
"Die Vogelhütte" (Droste-Hülshoff) **3**:197
Die Vogelscheuche (Tieck) **5**:519
"The Voice" (Arnold) **29**:35
"The Voice and the Peak" (Tennyson) **30**:271-72
"A Voice from the Dungeon" (Brontë) **4**:44
A Voice from the Factories (Norton) **47**:260
"A Voice from the Nile" (Thomson) **18**:421
"The Voice in the Pines" (Hayne) **94**:144, 149
"The Voice in the Wild Oak" (Kendall) **12**:189
"The Voice of a Spirit" (Schiller) **39**:306
"The Voice of Autumn" (Bryant) **6**:176
"Voice of By-Gone Days" (Foster) **26**:287
"A Voice of Encouragement—A New Year's Lay" (Mangan) **27**:300, 317
"Voice of Flowers" (Sigourney) **87**:321
"A Voice of Nature" (Clare) **9**:110
The Voice of Nature (Dunlap) **2**:211
"Voice of Spring" (Hemans) **29**:200
"The Voice of the Ancient Bard" (Blake) **13**:181; **37**:19, 45, 72
"The Voice of the Native Oak" (Harpur) **114**:116
"Voice of the People" (Hölderlin)
See "Stimme des Volks"
"The Voice of Things" (Silva)
See "La voz de las cosas"
"The Voice of Thought" (Chivers) **49**:58, 72
"Voice out of the Sea" (Whitman) **4**:546
"The Voice that Stands for Floods to Me" (Dickinson) **21**:77
"The Voiceless" (Holmes) **14**:109, 132; **81**:97
"Voices from the Canadian Woods: The White Cedar" (Traill) **31**:327
"Voices of Earth" (Lampman) **25**:194, 204
Voices of Freedom (Whittier) **8**:489, 495, 504-05, 509-16; **59**:353, 357-8
"Voices of the Night" (Longfellow) **2**:471; **45**:112, 115, 127, 131, 133-34, 151-52, 154, 183-84; **103**:293, 295
"Voices of the Pines" (Hayne)
See "The Voice in the Pines"
"The Voices that Be Gone" (Barnes) **75**:59
"Void in Law" (Browning) **61**:7, 45, 66
Les voiles nors (Gobineau) **17**:104
"Voitel' nica" (Leskov) **25**:228, 235, 238-39, 246, 260, 263-65
La voiture de masques (Goncourt and Goncourt) **7**:153
"La Voix d'un ami" (Desbordes-Valmore) **97**:28
"La Voix perdue" (Desbordes-Valmore) **97**:6-7
"Vojtina ars poetikájából" (Arany) **34**:16
Vol. 1 (Sochineniya v dvukh tomakh) (Bestuzhev)
See *Sochineniya v dvukh tomakh, Vol. 1*
Vol. I (Prosas) (Casal)
See *Prosas*
Vol. II (Prosas) (Casal)
See *Prosas*
Vol. III (Prosas) (Casal)
See *Prosas*
"Les Voleurs" (Mérimée) **65**:121-2
Volki i ovtsy (Ostrovsky) **30**:100, 103, 113, 115; **57**:213-4, 220
"Volksglauben in den Pyrenäen" (Droste-Hülshoff) **3**:203
Volkslieder (Herder) **8**:299, 310, 315
Volksmärchen (Tieck) **46**:334
Vollständige Ausgabe durch einem Verein von Freunden des Verewigten (Hegel) **46**:139

Vollständige ausgabe letzter Hand (Goethe) **34**:125
"Vol'nost': Oda" (Pushkin) **3**:455; **83**:253, 305
"Voltaire" (Carlyle) **70**:61
Volume the First (Austen) **1**:46; **119**:13
Volume the Second (Austen) **119**:13
Volume the Third (Austen) **119**:13
"Voluntaries" (Emerson) **1**:279, 285, 290, 296; **98**:39, 177, 182-83
"The Volunteer" (Hood) **16**:237
The Volunteers (Rowson) **69**:140-41
"La volupté" (Baudelaire) **55**:74
Volupté (Sainte-Beuve) **5**:328, 333, 335, 337, 348, 351
"The Voluptuary Cured" (Griffin) **7**:214
Voluptuousness (Sainte-Beuve)
See *Volupté*
Vom andern Ufer (Herzen) **10**:326-7, 332, 334-7, 339-40, 344, 346
"Vom ästhetischen Werte der griechischen Komödie" (Schlegel) **45**:312, 324, 334, 358
Vom Geist der ebräischen Poesie (Herder) **8**:297, 300, 303, 305-06, 316
"Vom Gewissen: In Briefen an Andres" (Claudius) **75**:218
Vom Ich als Princip der Philosophie (Schelling) **30**:128, 164
"Vom Vaterunser" (Claudius) **75**:217
"Vom Wert des Studiums der Griechen und Römer" (Schlegel) **45**:310, 357
Von den Lebensaltern einer Sprache (Herder) **8**:317
"Von der Seele" (Schlegel) **45**:338
"Von der Überlegung: Eine Paradoxe" (Kleist) **37**:249, 266
Von deutscher Art und Kunst (Herder) **8**:309-10
"Von Essen" (Runeberg) **41**:314
Von heut und ehedem (Storm) **1**:544
"Von hohen Menschen" (Jean Paul) **7**:240
"Von Jung" (Poe) **16**:322
"Von Kempelen and His Discovery" (Poe) **16**:313
"Von Konow" (Runeberg) **41**:314
"Von Projekten und Projektmachern" (Claudius) **75**:203
Von Ranke (Macaulay)
See *Essay on Ranke*
"Von Törne" (Runeberg) **41**:314
Von Zwanzig bis Dreissig (Fontane) **26**:235, 247-49
Vor dem Sturm: Roman aus dem Winter 1812 auf 13 (Fontane) **26**:236-37, 243, 250-52, 261, 267, 270-71, 274-75, 278
"Vor dem Tor" (Goethe) **4**:215, 221
"Vor der Ernte" (Meyer) **81**:146, 152-53, 157, 206
"Vor einer Büste" (Meyer) **81**:207
"Vor Gericht" (Goethe) **34**:71
"Vord lys!" (Wergeland) **5**:539
"Vorläufige Thesen zur Reform der Philosophie" (Feuerbach) **139**:293, 331
Vorlesungen über die Aesthetik (Hegel) **46**:181-82, 186-87
Vorlesungen über die Geschichte der Philosophie (Hegel) **46**:166, 192
Vorlesungen über die Methode des academischen Studium (Schelling) **30**:167
Vorlesungen über die Philosophie der Geschichte (Hegel) **46**:110
Vorlesungen über die Philosophie der Religion, nebst iener Schrift über die Beweise vom Dasein Gottes (Hegel) **46**:162, 186
Vorlesung über das Wesen der Religion: Nebst Zusätzen und Anmerkungen (Feuerbach) **139**:289, 293
"Vörös Rébék" (Arany) **34**:21
Vorschule der Aesthetik: Nebst einigen Vorlesungen in Leipzig über die Parte ien der Zeit (Jean Paul) **7**:223, 225-26, 234, 237-38, 242
"Vorwurf an Laura" (Schiller) **39**:357
"Vorzeichen" (Grillparzer) **102**:175
Vospitannitsa (Ostrovsky) **30**:98-9, 102, 104, 111, 115; **57**:198, 209-10, 218-20
"Vospominanie v Tsarskom Sele" (Pushkin) **3**:423; **83**:258
"Vostochnaia Legenda" (Turgenev) **122**:312
"Vot vernyi spisok vpechatlenii" (Baratynsky) **103**:47
"Votive Offering" (Meyer)
See "Weihgeschenck"
"The Vow" (Fouqué) **2**:266
"The Vow of the Chrysanthemum" (Ueda Akinari)
See "Kikuka no chigiri"
"Vox Ecclesiae, Vox Christi" (Rossetti) **77**:292-93, 295, 297
"Vox Populi" (Longfellow) **45**:134
"Vox populi" (Villiers de l'Isle Adam) **3**:590
"Le voyage" (Baudelaire) **6**:90, 93, 101, 109, 116-17, 123-24; **29**:78, 90, 105, 107; **55**:3-4, 6, 12, 26, 29, 43, 49-50, 52-53, 65-8, 73, 78
"The Voyage" (Irving) **95**:265
Voyage (Crèvecoeur)
See *Voyage dans la Haute Pennsylvanie et dans l'Etat de New-York not generally known; and conveying some idea of the late and present interior circumsances of the British Colonies in North America.*
"Le voyage à Cythère" (Baudelaire) **6**:91, 109, 116-17; **29**:74, 84, 104; **55**:4, 29, 31, 33, 73-6, 78-80
Voyage aux eaux des Pyrénées (Taine) **15**:411, 431, 450, 452
Voyage dans la Haute Pennsylvanie et dans l'Etat de New-York not generally known; and conveying some idea of the late and present interior circumsances of the British Colonies in North America. (Crèvecoeur) **105**:94-5, 104
"Voyage de Noce" (Maupassant) **83**:173
"Voyage du jeune anacharsis" (Nerval) **67**:320
Voyage en Amérique (Chateaubriand) **3**:134; **134**:41-45, 47, 80, 95, 127
Voyage en Egypte (Fromentin) **10**:229; **125**:106-7, 109-11, 139-40
Voyage en Espagne (Gautier) **1**:339, 341, 344
Voyage en Italie (Chateaubriand) **134**:18, 20, 92
Voyage en Italie (Gautier) **59**:47-55
Voyage en Italie (Taine) **15**:417, 452
Voyage en Orient (Flaubert) **62**:113-5, 117, 123
Voyage en Orient (Nerval) **1**:475-76, 479-80, 483, 485; **67**:302-03, 312, 323, 333-34, 336, 357, 363-64, 366-72, 375
Voyage en Russie (Gautier) **1**:344
The Voyage of Captain Popanilla (Disraeli) **2**:149, 153; **39**:3, 33, 39, 46, 48-9, 52-5, 72-3, 75; **79**:269-71
The Voyage of Columbus (Rogers) **69**:68, 70-1, 74, 83
"The Voyage of Maeldune" (Tennyson) **30**:223
"The Voyage of Telegonus" (Kendall) **12**:181, 190, 192, 201-02
The Voyage of the Beagle (Darwin)
See *The Zoology of the Voyage of the Beagle*
The Voyage of the Fregate Pallada (Goncharov) **1**:366, 370, 373; **63**:3-4, 27
"The Voyage of Timberoo-Tabo-Eede, an Otaheite Indian" (Freneau) **111**:133
A Voyage to Arzrum (Pushkin) **3**:436
A Voyage to Boston (Freneau) **111**:139
"Voyage to Cythera" (Baudelaire)
See "Le voyage à Cythère"
"Voyage to England" (Irving) **19**:328, 350-51
A Voyage to the Holy Land (Slowacki)
See *Podróż na Wschód—Podróż do Ziemi Swietej z Neopolu*
"The Voyager's Song" (Pinkney) **31**:273, 279
Voyages (Flaubert) **135**:84
Voyages (Gautier) **59**:51
Voyages and Travels . . . (Galt) **1**:327; **110**:76, 94
"Voyance" (Verlaine) **51**:382
"Les Voyelles" (Rimbaud) **4**:452-53, 469, 472, 475, 482; **35**:323; **82**:227, 248, 256, 258
Voyevoda (Ostrovsky)
See *Voevoda: Son na Volge*
"La voz de las cosas" (Silva) **114**:299, 301
"La voz del silencio" (Bécquer) **106**:112, 114
Vrajānganān Kāvya (Dutt) **118**:5
"Vse bešennej burja" (Tyutchev) **34**:415
"Vse mysl' da mysl'!..." (Baratynsky) **103**:25-9
"Vsegda i vezde" (Bestuzhev) **131**:150
"La vœu suprême" (Leconte de Lisle) **29**:228, 235
La vuelta de Martín Fierro (Hernández) **17**:162-69, 171-72, 176-79
"La vuelta del combate" (Bécquer) **106**:110
"La vuelta del recluta" (Isaacs) **70**:305
"Vuelva ud. mañana" (Larra) **130**:230
The Vultures (Becque)
See *Les corbeaux*
"V.V.: or Plots and Counterplots" (Alcott) **58**:39; **83**:6
"Vystrel" (Pushkin) **3**:435, 452; **83**:272, 323-27, 337, 354
"Vzoshla zaria..." (Zhukovsky) **35**:406
"Wachusett" (Thoreau)
See "A Walk to Wachusett"
Waclaw (Slowacki) **15**:348, 358
Wacousta; or, The Prophecy: A Tale of the Canadas (Richardson) **55**:288, 290, 292, 294, 299-300, 303-5, 312-27, 329, 332-40, 342-4, 346-65, 369-76
Wage-Labor and Capital (Marx) **114**:10
"The Wager" (Crabbe) **26**:93; **121**:4-5
A Wager (Tamayo y Baus) **1**:571
"The Waggon A-Stooded" (Barnes) **75**:78
The Waggoner (Wordsworth) **12**:409, 422, 451
Die Wahlverwandtschaften (Goethe) **4**:168, 172-73, 176, 178, 188, 193, 201, 223; **34**:98
Die Wahlverwandtschaften (Grillparzer) **102**:172
Wahrheit aus Jean Paul's Leben (Jean Paul) **7**:229-30
"The Waif" (Longfellow) **2**:474
"The Wail and Warning of the Three Khalandeers" (Mangan) **27**:278, 284-85
Wait and Hope (Alger) **8**:44
"Waiting by the Gate" (Bryant) **6**:193
"Waiting for Dead Men's Shoes" (Moodie) **14**:236
"A Waitress" (Woolson) **82**:290
"Wakacje" (Norwid) **17**:373
"Wakaremichi" (Ichiyō)
See "Wakare-Michi"
"Wakare-Michi" (Ichiyō) **49**:336-37, 347-48, 350-51, 353-54
"The Wake" (Shevchenko)
See "Tryzna"
The Wake (Hogg)
See *The Queen's Wake*
"Wakefield" (Hawthorne) **2**:292
"Wakerejimo" (Ichiyō) **49**:341
"Walcourt" (Verlaine) **51**:370, 382, 384
"Wald und Höhle" (Goethe) **4**:214
Der Waldbrunnen (Stifter) **41**:375, 379
Waldeinsamkeit (Tieck) **5**:519
"Waldemar Daa and His Daughters" (Andersen)
See "The Wind Tells of Valdemar Daae and His Daughters"
Walden; or, Life in the Woods (Thoreau) **7**:349-53, 357, 361, 363, 369-70, 373-7, 379-82, 385-411; **21**:319-20, 322, 328-30, 340, 343-5, 350-3, 358, 360-1, 369-70, 372; **61**:278-390; **138**:66-68, 74-75, 78, 80, 82-85, 87-89, 95-97, 99, 102-3, 115, 119, 123-26, 128-31, 134, 137, 140-41, 144, 146-50, 155-58, 162, 164, 166-67, 170, 177, 182-83, 186, 188-89, 191-93
Der Waldgänger (Stifter) **41**:343, 353

"Wald-Idylle" (Mörike) **10**:449
"Die Waldkapelle" (Lenau) **16**:278
Der Waldsteig (Stifter) **41**:361, 366, 377
Waldwinkel (Storm) **1**:540
"A walesi bárdok" (Arany) **34**:8, 10, 15, 21
"The Walk" (Schiller)
See "Der Spaziergang"
"A Walk at Sunset" (Bryant) **46**:3, 13
"Walk in the Woods" (Clare) **9**:123
"A Walk Through the Franconian Switzerland" (Taylor) **89**:308
"The Walk to Dummer" (Moodie) **14**:231, 239
"A Walk to Railway Point" (Traill) **31**:327
"A Walk to Wachusett" (Thoreau) **21**:372; **138**:106, 118, 120, 124, 159-63, 165-67
"Walking" (Thoreau) **7**:394; **21**:372; **138**:71, 135, 162, 167
"Walking in Scotland" (Keats) **8**:360
"Walking to the Mail" (Tennyson) **115**:240
A Walking Tour (Andersen) **79**:86
"Walking Tours" (Stevenson) **5**:413
"Walking with God" (Cowper) **94**:73
"Walks in the Wheat-fields" (Jefferies) **47**:140, 143
Die Walküre (Wagner) **9**:409, 414, 416-17, 419, 448, 454, 456, 459, 466, 469-70, 473; **119**:186-87, 201-07, 222, 228-31, 277, 282, 309, 320, 347, 349-51, 354-55
"A Wall Flower" (Levy) **59**:92
"Wallace" (Hemans) **71**:261
"Wallace" (Hogg) **109**:200
Wallenrod (Mickiewicz)
See *Konrad Wallenrod*
Wallenstein (Coleridge) **111**:232
Wallenstein (Schiller) **39**:314, 316, 318-20, 322, 324, 326, 328, 337, 341-46, 348, 352, 361, 364, 367-69, 372-73, 375-78, 380, 385; **69**:169, 189, 194, 243-44, 272, 275
Wallenstein's Camp (Schiller)
See *Wallenstein*
Wallenstein's Death (Schiller)
See *Wallenstein*
Wallenstein's Lager (Schiller)
See *Wallenstein*
Wallenstein's Tod (Schiller)
See *Wallenstein*
"The Wallflower" (Wergeland) **5**:538
Wallstein (Constant) **6**:213, 224
"Walpurgisnacht" (Goethe) **4**:214-15
"The Walrus and the Carpenter" (Carroll) **2**:112; **53**:40, 43, 54, 73, 93, 96, 113; **139**:29, 38, 137
"The Walse" (Sheridan) **91**:233
"Walstein's School of History" (Brown) **74**:170, 172, 175-76
Walt and Vult; or, The Twins (Jean Paul)
See *Flegeljahre: Eine Biographie*
Walt Whitman: A Study (Symonds) **34**:365
"Walt Whitman, an American" (Whitman) **4**:540, 545-46, 548, 556
"Walter" (Droste-Hülshoff) **3**:195-96
Walter Savage Landor (Forster) **11**:102-03, 120, 125-27, 129-31
Walter Scott et La Princesse Clèves (Stendhal) **23**:392
Walter Sherwood's Probation; or, Cool Head and Warm Heart (Alger) **8**:24, 43
"Walter Wilson" (Hale) **75**:298
"Wanda" (Vigny) **7**:473, 478, 484; **102**:380
"Wandelnde Glocke" (Goethe) **4**:192
"Der Wanderer" (Hölderlin)
See "Versöhnender, der du nimmer geglaubt ..."
"Wanderer" (Pavlova)
See "Strannik"
"The Wanderer" (Pushkin) **83**:279
The Wanderer (Brontë) **109**:29
The Wanderer (Sacher-Masoch) **31**:291-92
A Wanderer Astray on the Path of Life (Smolenskin)
See *ha-To'eh be-darke ha-hayim*
"The Wanderer from the Fold" (Brontë) **16**:86
"The Wanderer of the Wold" (Lewis) **11**:302-03
The Wanderer; or, Female Difficulties (Burney) **12**:19, 21-2, 28, 30, 32-4, 46-7, 51-4, 56-9, 62-4; **54**:18-19, 21, 25-7, 29-31, 36-9, 50-2; **107**:10, 13, 16
"The Wanderers" (Morris) **4**:427
"Wander-füße" (Meyer) **81**:155
The Wandering Boys (Pixérécourt)
See *Le pèlerin blanc; ou, Les orphelins du hameau*
The Wandering Heir (Reade) **2**:541-42, 547, 549; **74**:256, 263-65
"The Wandering Jew" (Muller) **73**:351
The Wandering Jew (Sue) **1**:555-60
"Wandering Knight's Song" (Lockhart) **6**:297
The Wandering Minstrel (Mayhew) **31**:156, 158-59
"Wandering Willie" (Stevenson) **5**:428
Wanderings in Spain (Gautier)
See *Voyage en Espagne*
Wanderings in Three Continents (Burton) **42**:35
"The Wanderings of Cain" (Coleridge) **54**:79; **111**:240, 291
The Wanderings of Ulysses (Lamb) **10**:406
The Wanderings of Warwick (Smith) **23**:323; **115**:166
Wandering—with Pleasure but not without Morals (Shevchenko)
See *Matros*
Wanderjahre (Goethe)
See *Wilhelm Meisters Wanderjahre; oder, Die Entsagenden*
Wanderlieder (Muller) **73**:365-67, 387
Wanderlieder eines rheinischen Handwerksburschen (Muller) **73**:362, 380
"Das Wandern ist des Müllers Lust" (Muller) **73**:350, 379, 381, 383
"Wanderschaft" (Muller) **73**:364, 368
"Wanderschaft, Wandernder Dichter" (Eichendorff) **8**:213
"Die Wanderung" (Hölderlin) **16**:174-76
Wanderungen durch die Mark Brandenburg (Fontane) **26**:234, 261, 263, 270
"Der Wandrer" (Goethe) **4**:211, 214
"Wandrers Sturmlied" (Goethe) **4**:212
Wandsbeck, eine Art von Romanze (Claudius) **75**:196
Der Wandsbecker Bote (Claudius) **75**:192, 195, 201
"The Waning Moon" (Bryant) **46**:4
Wann-Chlore (Balzac)
See *Jane la pâle*
"The Wants of the Times" (Brownson) **50**:47
"War" (Channing) **17**:33
"War" (Crawford) **12**:174; **127**:215, 218-19, 221, 227
"War" (Lampman) **25**:167, 203
War (Robertson) **35**:335, 354, 361, 364-65
"War and Peace: A Poem" (Hemans) **71**:272-73
"The War and the Commune" (Mazzini) **34**:281
War Memoranda (Whitman) **81**:317
War of 1812 (Richardson) **55**:301-2, 311-2, 317, 330, 347
The War of Chocim (Krasicki)
See *Wojna Chocimska*
War of the Norns and the Asas (Grundtvig) **1**:401
"The War of the Turcomans" (Gobineau)
See "La guerre des Turcomans"
"War Song" (Moore) **6**:398
War Sonnets (Smith)
See *Sonnets on the War*
The War Widow (Frederic) **10**:188
War with the Saints (Tonna) **135**:207
Warbeck (Schiller) **69**:169
The Ward (Ostrovsky)
See *Vospitannitsa*
The Warden (Trollope) **6**:452-53, 464-66, 470-71, 476, 494, 497, 499, 510, 512, 514, 517; **33**:362, 365, 374-75, 382, 387-88, 395-96, 416, 418-20, 424; **101**:232, 235, 243, 253, 263, 266, 275, 280, 287, 307, 318, 329, 30
"Wardour Street" (Morris) **4**:434
"Ware kara" (Ichiyō) **49**:336-37
"Waring" (Browning) **79**:100
The Warlord: Dream on the Volga (Ostrovsky)
See *Voevoda: Son na Volge*
"Warning" (Grillparzer)
See "Warnung"
"The Warning" (Longfellow) **45**:147, 155
"The Warning Voice" (Mangan) **27**:296, 299-300, 316
"Warnung" (Grillparzer) **102**:175
"The Warrigal—Wild Dog" (Kendall) **12**:183
"The Warrior's Return" (Opie) **65**:160-1, 175
"Warsaw" (Grillparzer)
See "Warschau"
"Warschau" (Grillparzer) **102**:175
War-Song for the Scanian Reserves (Tegner) **2**:613
"Warum gabst du uns" (Goethe) **4**:193
"Was ist deutsch?" (Wagner) **119**:291
"Was My Brother in the Battle" (Foster) **26**:288
"Was the Earl of Beaconsfield a Representative Jew?" (Lazarus) **8**:419, 424; **109**:297, 302-03, 306, 319, 327
"Was wär' ich ohne dich gewesen?" (Novalis) **13**:362
"The Washers of the Shroud" (Lowell) **2**:514; **90**:193, 198
"Washing-Day" (Barbauld) **50**:14-16
"A Washington" (Gómez de Avellaneda) **111**:4
"Washington" (Landor) **14**:166
Washington Irving Journals and Notebooks, Vol. II (Irving) **95**:276, 278-79
Washington Irving Letters Volume I 1802-23 (Irving) **95**:273-79
"Wasps in a Garden" (Lamb) **125**:346, 360
"Wasserflut" (Muller) **73**:384, 396
Der Wassermensch (Tieck) **5**:519
"Die Wassernot im Emmental" (Gotthelf) **117**:4
"Waste Not, Want Not" (Edgeworth) **1**:265; **51**:87
"Wat o' the Cleuch" (Hogg) **109**:246, 249
Wat Tyler (Southey) **8**:455, 458, 467; **97**:250, 259, 263-64, 267, 293, 312-17
"The Watch" (Mickiewicz) **3**:398
"The Watch" (Turgenev)
See "Časy"
The Watch Dog (Fredro)
See *Brytan bryś*
"The Watcher" (Le Fanu)
See "The Familiar"
"The Watching of the Falcon" (Morris) **4**:416, 447-48
The Watchman (Coleridge) **111**:253
"The Water Colley" (Jefferies) **47**:136
"Water Color" (Verlaine)
See "Aquarelles"
"The Water Crowfoot" (Barnes) **75**:22, 28, 37
"The Water Crowvoot" (Barnes)
See "The Water Crowfoot"
"Water Drops" (Sigourney) **87**:321
"Water Flows into the Blue Sea" (Shevchenko)
See "Tece voda v synje more"
"The Water Lady" (Hood) **16**:225
"The Water Lillies" (Moodie) **113**:316
"The Water Nymph" (Lermontov)
See "Rusalka"
The Water Nymph (Pushkin)
See *Rusalka*
"The Water of Life" (Grimm and Grimm) **3**:222
"The Water of the Wondrous Isles" (Morris) **4**:425, 436, 438
The Water-Babies: A Fairy-Tale for a Land-Baby (Kingsley) **35**:220, 227, 232, 235, 246, 249, 251, 254-55, 258-60
"The Waterfall" (Baratynsky) **103**:6, 10
"The Waterfall and the Eglantine" (Wordsworth) **111**:323
"Water-Lilies" (Clare) **9**:117
"The Waterlily" (Crawford) **12**:172; **127**:181-86, 189, 193-94

"The Water's Flow" (Muller)
See "Wasserflut"
The Water-Witch; or, The Skimmer of the Seas (Cooper) **1**:200, 207-08, 221-22; **54**:255
The Watsons (Austen) **1**:36, 42, 46, 50-52, 54, 60; **13**:99; **119**:18, 26, 30, 45-6
Wau-Nan-Gee; or, The Massacre at Chicago (Richardson) **55**:304, 313, 321
"Wava, The Fairy of the Shell" (Crawford) **127**:181-84, 189, 193
Waverley Novels (Scott) **15**:275-76, 278-79, 284, 289, 292, 294-95, 300, 306-07, 309-10, 318, 320-22, 325
Waverley; or, 'Tis Sixty Years Since (Scott) **15**:257-59, 263, 266-67, 269-70, 274-75, 285-87, 289, 300-03, 307, 310, 313, 315-16, 318, 321, 323; **69**:296-97, 299-300, 303-04, 308, 318-20, 378, 391; **110**:230-345
"The Waves" (Taylor) **89**:300
The Waves (Grillparzer) **1**:385
"The Waving of the Corn" (Lanier) **6**:238; **118**:203
"Way Down upon the Swanee River" (Foster)
See "Old Folks at Home"
"Way of the Soul" (Tennyson) **115**:313
"The Way of the World" (Rossetti) **66**:342
The Way towards the Blessed Life; or, The Doctrine of Religion (Fichte)
See *Die Anweisung zum seligen Leben, oder auch die Religionslehre*
The Way We Live Now (Trollope) **6**:460-61, 464, 471, 477, 480, 482, 487, 489, 497, 500, 507, 511-13; **33**:417, 424; **101**:216, 221, 251, 253, 256, 266, 273, 275, 279-81, 283, 286-88, 290, 292, 308, 311-12, 319, 326-28
"Wayconnell Tower" (Allingham) **25**:8
The Ways of the Hour (Cooper) **1**:220; **54**:259, 262-3, 300
"The Wayside Dream" (Taylor) **89**:298-99
"Wayside Flowers" (Allingham) **25**:14
"The Wayside Inn" (Turgenev)
See "The Inn"
Wayside Inn (Longfellow)
See *Tales of a Wayside Inn*
"The Wayside Well" (Allingham) **25**:6, 8, 24
We and Our Neighbors; or, The Records of an Unfashionable Street: A Sequel to "My Wife and I" (Stowe) **3**:554, 562
"We Are Coming Father Abraham, 300,000 More" (Foster) **26**:298
"We Are Seven" (Wordsworth) **12**:387, 414, 430; **111**:202, 209, 223, 228, 252, 314, 316, 348, 358
"We Break the Glass" (Pinkney) **31**:279-80
"We May Roam Through the World" (Moore) **110**:185
"We Parted" (Lermontov) **5**:299
"We Play at Paste" (Dickinson) **21**:43
"We studiously observe the world..." (Baratynsky)
See "Staratelno my nablyudaem svet..."
"We Two, Each Other's Only Pride" (Sheridan) **91**:232
"We Two, How Long We Were Fool'd" (Whitman) **4**:601; **31**:389
"We Watched Her Breathing" (Hood) **16**:233
"The Weaker Vessel" (Parton) **86**:350
"The Weaker Vessel" (Patmore) **9**:340, 344
"Weal and Woe in Garveloch" (Martineau) **26**:336
Weal and Woe in Garveloch (Martineau) **137**:240, 250
"Wealth" (Crawford) **127**:215-16, 218-19
"Wealth" (Emerson) **98**:8-9, 113, 135
"Wealth and Poverty" (Ueda Akinari)
See "Himpukuron"
"Weariness" (Longfellow) **45**:116-17, 131
Wearing of the Gray (Cooke) **5**:130, 135
"Weary in Well-Doing" (Rossetti) **50**:268, 316
"Weary of the Bitter Ease" (Mallarmé)
See "Las de l'amer repos"
"The Weary Soul" (Milnes) **61**:136
"The Weathercock" (Muller) **73**:385
"The Weaver" (Lampman) **25**:206, 216
"Wechsel" (Hölderlin) **16**:185
"Weddah and Om-el-Bonain" (Thomson) **18**:392, 397, 401, 403, 405, 408
"The Wedding" (Lamb) **10**:410
"Wedding and Funeral" (Hale) **75**:296
The Wedding Day (Inchbald) **62**:144, 150
"Wedding Hymn" (Lanier) **6**:237; **118**:242
"The Wedding Knell" (Hawthorne) **2**:291; **10**:316; **79**:296; **95**:105
"The Wedding of Maksim Crnojević" (Chappel) **115**:92
"The Wedding of Marko Kraljeviĉ" (Karadzic) **115**:91
Weder Lorbeerbaum noch Bettlestab (Nestroy) **42**:239-40
"Wednesday" (Thoreau) **7**:352
"Wednesday Before Easter" (Keble) **87**:201
Weeds and Wildings, with a Rose or Two (Melville) **3**:379-80
"A Week in a Village" (Clare) **86**:92
"A Week on Capri" (Taylor) **89**:313
A Week on the Concord and Merrimack Rivers (Thoreau) **7**:348, 352, 361, 369-70, 375, 377-8, 381, 388-90, 400, 405, 410-1; **21**:322, 344-6, 369-70, 372; **61**:283, 288, 296-7, 302, 306, 309, 315, 326, 335, 339, 342-3, 348, 352, 375; **138**:66-67, 71-72, 74-81, 83-92, 94-109, 111-12, 114-31, 133-42, 144-45, 148-53, 155-63, 165-67, 169-71, 174-78, 182-86, 188-92
"Weep On, Weep On" (Moore) **110**:187
"The Weepen Leady" (Barnes) **75**:76
"Weeping Willow" (Sigourney) **87**:321
"Der Wegweiser" (Muller) **73**:391, 393, 396-97
Weh dem, der lügt! (Grillparzer) **1**:384; **102**:106, 131, 139, 168, 172, 184, 186, 188, 190, 192
"Das Weib des Admirals" (Meyer) **81**:142
"Das weiBe Spitzchen" (Meyer) **81**:144
Der weibliche Jakobiner-Klubb (Kotzebue) **25**:143, 147
"Weighed in the Balance" (Woolson) **82**:322
"A Weight with Needles on the Pounds" (Dickinson) **21**:64
"Der Weiher" (Droste-Hülshoff) **3**:203
"Weihgeschenck" (Meyer) **81**:199, 205, 209
Die Weihnachtsfeier: Ein Gespräch (Schleiermacher) **107**:268, 350, 363, 376, 398, 400
"Weimar and its Dead" (Taylor) **89**:308
"Weimar in June" (Taylor) **89**:325
"Der Weingott" (Hölderlin) **16**:176
"Weinhtrunk an die toten Freunde" (Klopstock) **11**:236-37
"Weinsegen" (Meyer) **81**:146
Weir of Hermiston (Stevenson) **5**:416-19, 427, 429-34
"Weird Gathering" (Whittier) **8**:485
"The Weird Lady" (Kingsley) **35**:218
Weird Women (Barbey d'Aurevilly)
See *Les diaboliques*
Weisthümer (Grimm and Grimm) **3**:216
"Welcome" (Very) **9**:388
"Welcome and Parting" (Goethe)
See "Willkommen und Abschied"
"The Welcome Home" (Opie) **65**:172
"Welcome, Wild North-Easter!" (Kingsley) **35**:212, 219
"The Well at the World's End" (Morris) **4**:424-36, 438
"Well! Dad's Dead" (Harris) **23**:142, 146, 160
"The Well of Pen-Morfa" (Gaskell) **5**:205; **70**:185, 190
We'll Settle It Among Ourselves (Ostrovsky)
See *Svoi lyudi—sochtemsya!*
"Well! Thou Art Happy" (Byron) **2**:77
"Welland River" (Morris) **4**:431, 444
"Welldean Hall" (Hogg) **4**:283; **109**:203, 279
"Wellington's Funeral" (Rossetti) **4**:518; **77**:296-7
Welsh Melodies (Hemans) **29**:205; **71**:261
"The Welshmen of Tirawley" (Ferguson)
See "The Vengeance of the Welshmen of Tirawley"
Die Welt als Wille und Vorstellung (Schopenhauer) **51**:245, 249, 270-71, 287, 292, 294, 302, 311-12, 315-16, 318, 321, 324, 344-46
Die Weltalter (Schelling) **30**:141, 170
Weltgeschichtliche Bertrachtungen (Burckhardt) **49**:5, 7-9, 16, 19, 22
"Wen Gott betrügt, ist wohl betrogen" (Clough) **27**:103, 107
"Wenden Castle" (Bestuzhev)
See "Zamok Venden"
"Wenn der lahme Weber träumt, er webe" (Brentano) **1**:105
"Wenn der Sturm das Meer umschlinget" (Brentano) **1**:104
"Went Hwome" (Barnes) **75**:53
The Wept of Wish-ton-Wish (Cooper) **1**:199, 221-22; **54**:255, 262
"Wer ist der Verräter?" (Goethe) **4**:194
Wer ist schuldig? (Grillparzer) **102**:78
"Die Werbung" (Lenau) **16**:264, 285
"Das Werden im Vergehen" (Hölderlin) **16**:178
"We're a Million in the Field" (Foster) **26**:288
"Werke: Hamburger Ausgabe" (Goethe) **90**:42-4, 103, 106-07
Werke und Briefe (Arnim) **38**:12
Werner (Byron) **2**:67, 79-80, 90
Werther (Hays) **114**:177
Das Wesen der Religion (Feuerbach) **139**:241-42, 289, 293
Das Wesen des Christentums (Feuerbach) **139**:236, 242, 246, 251-53, 260, 266, 271, 274-81, 283, 286-87, 289-90, 293-94, 297-98, 309, 313, 316-25, 329, 334, 337, 339, 343
"The West Shetucket Railroad" (Cooke)
See "The West Shetucket Railway"
"The West Shetucket Railway" (Cooke) **110**:18, 32, 44
"The West Wind" (Bryant) **6**:176; **46**:45
Westbrook, The Outlaw; or, The Avenging Wolf. An American Border Tale (Richardson) **55**:304, 364-6
West-Eastern Divan (Goethe)
See *West—östlicher Divan*
The Western Boy (Alger) **83**:148
Western Clearings (Kirkland) **85**:260, 263, 265, 270, 284, 301
Western Home, and Other Poems (Sigourney) **87**:326
The Western Journals of Washington Irving (Irving) **2**:382
"Westminster Abbey" (Irving) **2**:381; **19**:347
"Westminster Bridge" (Wordsworth) **12**:431
West—östlicher Divan (Goethe) **4**:173, 193
Westward Ho! (Kingsley) **35**:209, 211, 215-18, 220, 222, 228-31, 233, 235, 241, 243-44, 249, 252, 255-57
Westward Ho! (Paulding) **2**:527-30
"Wetterleuchten" (Meyer) **81**:153, 199, 204, 209
"Wettgesang" (Schlegel) **15**:229
"Weyla's Song" (Mörike)
See "Gesang Weylas"
The Whale (Melville)
See *Moby-Dick; or, The Whale*
"The Wharf Rat" (O'Brien) **21**:234
"What Am I without Thee?" (Lanier) **118**:231
"What Befell" (O'Brien) **21**:245
"What Can an Old Man Do But Die?" (Hood) **16**:219
"What Can It Mean?" (Delany) **93**:157
"What Daddy Does Is Always Right" (Andersen)
See "What Father Does is Always Right"
"What Dick and I Did" (Barnes) **75**:78
"What Do Poets Want with Gold?" (Lampman) **25**:160, 188, 200, 216

"What Does an Author Need?" (Karamzin) **3**:289
"What Does It Mean?" (Delany) **93**:157
"What Father Does" (Andersen)
See "What Father Does is Always Right"
"What Father Does is Always Right" (Andersen) **7**:34; **79**:88
"What for Us, My Heart, Are Pools of Blood" (Rimbaud) **4**:486
"What Had I Been If Thou Were Not?" (Novalis)
See "Was wär' ich ohne dich gewesen?"
"What I Lived For" (Thoreau) **7**:352, 381
"What Is a Classic" (Sainte-Beuve) **5**:350
"What is Beauty?" (Child) **73**:77
What Is Enlightenment? (Kant) **27**:219, 231, 237
"What Is Fancy?" (Lamb) **125**:354
"What Is He?" (Disraeli) **79**:215
"What Is Heaven" (Dickinson)
See "What Is 'Paradise'"
"What is Life?" (Chivers) **49**:69
"What is Life?" (Clare) **86**:156
What is Love? (Almqvist)
See *Väd är kärlek?*
"What Is Oblomovism?" (Dobrolyubov) **5**:140-41, 145, 147, 149, 151
What Is Orientation in Thinking? (Kant) **27**:220
"What Is 'Paradise'" (Dickinson) **21**:41
"What Is Past, What Is Lost, What Is Gone" (Pavlova) **138**:34
"What Is Poetry" (Mill) **11**:384; **58**:319, 323-5, 329, 332, 363, 366, 368
"What is Poetry?" (Timrod) **25**:380
"What Is Really My Belief?" (Landor) **14**:201
"What is the People?" (Hazlitt) **29**:184
"What is the preferable method or system for writing history?" (Martínez de la Rosa)
See "¿Cuál es el método o sistema preferible para escribir la historia?"
"What Is There in the Distant Hills" (Clare) **9**:124
What Is to Be Done? Tales about New People (Chernyshevsky)
See *Chto delat'?*
"What Mr. Robinson Thinks" (Lowell) **90**:218
"What Must a Fairy's Dream Be" (Foster) **26**:287
"What old Johanne told" (Andersen)
See "Hvad gamle Johanne fotalte"
"What One Says to the Poet on the Subject of Flowers" (Rimbaud)
See "Ce qu'on dit au poète à propos de fleurs"
"What Santa Claus Brought Me" (O'Brien) **21**:246
"What Shall I Call You" (Petofi)
See "Minek nevezzelek"
"What Ship Puzzled at Sea" (Whitman) **31**:388
"What strains are these?" (Baratynsky)
See "Chto za zvuki?"
"What the Birds Said" (Whittier) **8**:517; **59**:358
"What the Black Man Wants" (Douglass) **7**:130
"What the Lord Lyndhurst Really Was" (Bagehot) **10**:58
"What the Moon Saw" (Andersen) **7**:29
"What the Old Man Does is Always Right" (Andersen)
See "What Father Does is Always Right"
"What the Tortoise said to Achilles" (Carroll) **139**:80, 83
"What the Voice Said" (Whittier) **8**:530
"What, Then, Does Dr. Newman Mean?" (Kingsley) **35**:229
"What Things Exist?" (Bentham) **38**:93
"What Use Are Black Brows to Me?" (Shevchenko) **54**:374
"What Use are you, Days" (Baratynsky)
See "Na chto vy, dni"
"What Was It? A Mystery" (O'Brien) **21**:235-36, 238, 240, 242, 245-46, 248-51, 253
What Will He Do with It? (Bulwer-Lytton) **1**:151; **45**:22, 69
"What Would I Give?" (Rossetti) **2**:575
"What's This?" (Corbière)
See "Ça?"
"What's This Uproar Again?" (Petofi)
See "Mi lárma ez megént?"
"When All the World is Young, Lad" (Kingsley) **35**:227
"When Even the Voice of Thoughts Is Silent" (Eminescu) **33**:247
"When He Who Adores Thee" (Moore) **6**:391
"When I Am Dead, My Dearest, Sing No Sad Songs for Me" (Rossetti) **2**:563
"When I Have Fears That I May Cease to Be" (Keats) **73**:161, 193-94, 256
"When I Heard at the Close of Day" (Whitman) **81**:330
"When I Saw You" (Eminescu) **33**:265
"When I was a youth my shouts..." (Baratynsky)
See "Byvalo, otrok, zvonkim klikom..."
"When I Was Young" (Parton) **86**:373
"When I was young, with ringing call..." (Baratynsky)
See "Byvalo, otrok, zvonkim klikom..."
"When in Death I Shall Calm Recline" (Moore) **6**:389
"When Israel Came Out of Egypt" (Clough) **27**:41, 106
"When Lilacs Last in the Dooryard Bloom'd" (Whitman) **4**:544, 559, 561, 569, 571, 579-80, 582, 592, 595, 602; **31**:368, 370, 385, 388-91, 404-05, 408, 432; **81**:255, 257-58, 268, 271, 331, 366-70
"When Old Corruption First Begun" (Blake) **13**:182; **37**:29
"When Our Deteriorating Strength" (Tyutchev)
See "Kogda drjaxlejušcie sily"
"When Panting Sighs the Bosom Fill" (Clough) **27**:52, 106
"When Soft September" (Clough) **27**:104
"When Sparrows build" (Ingelow) **107**:122
"When the Blacksmith Leaves his Forge..." (Bestuzhev)
See "Kak idyot kuznets da iz kuznitsy . . ."
"When the Kye Comes Hame" (Hogg) **4**:286; **109**:269
"When the Sea Gives Up Its Dead" (Ingelow) **39**:268
When the Spaniards Were Here (Andersen) **79**:16
"When the Yellowing Fields Billow" (Lermontov) **5**:295
"When to Great Chastisers" (Pavlova)
See "Kogda karateliam velikim"
"When We Husked the Corn" (O'Brien) **21**:245
"When will the darkness disappear..." (Baratynsky)
See "Kogda ischeznet omrachenie"
"When Will the Day Come?" (Dobrolyubov) **5**:140, 149
"When Youthful Hope Is Fled" (Lockhart) **6**:296
"Whenever I Remember" (Eminescu) **131**:296
"Where am I now?" (Crabbe) **121**:82
"Where Be You Going, You Devon Maid?" (Keats) **8**:360
"Where Does the Day Begin?" (Carroll) **53**:51
"Where Gleaming Fields of Haze" (Thoreau) **7**:384
"Where I Have Lost, I Softer Tread" (Dickinson) **21**:55
"Where is the sweet whisper..." (Baratynsky)
See "Gde sladkiy shyopot..."
Where It Is Thin, There It Breaks (Turgenev) **21**:428, 432
"Where Liberty Was Born" (Chivers) **49**:51
"Where Shall We Bury Our Shame?" (Moore) **110**:186
"Wherefore" (Lazarus) **8**:418
"Wherefore" (Lermontov) **5**:299
"Where's Agnes?" (Browning) **61**:45
"Whereto?" (Preseren)
See "Kám?"
"Wherever I Go and Look" (Eichendorff) **8**:210
"Which Is the True One?" (Baudelaire)
See "Laquelle est la vraie?"
Whigs and Whiggism: Political Writings by Benjamin Disraeli (Disraeli) **39**:69; **79**:269;
Whims and Oddities (Hood) **16**:202, 205, 208, 213, 219
Whimsicalities (Hood) **16**:217, 238
"A Whirl-Blast from behind the Hill" (Wordsworth) **12**:446
"A Whisper in the Dark" (Alcott) **58**:75
"Whisperings in the Wattle-Boughs" (Gordon) **21**:154, 160-61, 173, 181
"Whispers of Heavenly Death" (Whitman) **81**:309
Whispers to a Bride (Sigourney) **87**:321-22, 338
"White an' Blue" (Barnes) **75**:17, 22, 46
The White Cat (Planché) **42**:273, 288-89
The White Doe of Rylstone; or, The Fate of the Nortons (Wordsworth) **12**:400, 407-08, 422, 460, 466
"The White Eagle" (Leskov)
See "Belyj orel"
"White Exploit" (Dickinson) **77**:68
"White Lies" (Opie) **65**:162, 171, 179
White Lies (Reade) **2**:534, 536, 549; **74**:245, 258, 264-64, 312
"White Margaret" (Lampman) **25**:183, 220
"White Mountains" (Whittier) **8**:485
"White Nights" (Dostoevsky) **33**:201
"The White Old Maid" (Hawthorne) **2**:292, 322
"White Peak" (Ueda Akinari)
See "Shiramine"
"The White Road up Athirt the Hill" (Barnes) **75**:87
"The White Rose" (Martí)
See "La Rosa Blanca"
"The White Ship" (Rossetti) **4**:499-500, 506-08, 518, 525-26, 532
The White Woman (Scribe)
See *La dame blanche*
Whitehall; or, The Days of George IV (Maginn) **8**:432, 436, 441
White-Jacket; or, The World in a Man-of-War (Melville) **3**:328, 332-34, 337, 339, 342, 345, 347-49, 359-61, 363, 365, 371, 373; **12**:281; **29**:318, 322, 325, 327-28, 331-34, 340-41, 345, 348, 350, 354, 358, 360-64, 367-69, 372, 374, 378; **45**:243, 254; **49**:391-92; **91**:42-3, 45, 55, 186; **123**:177, 184, 204, 211, 232, 235, 239
Whiteladies (Oliphant) **11**:441, 446; **61**:212
"Whiteness" (Isaacs)
See "Albor"
"Whither?" (Muller)
See "Wohin?"
"Whitman" (Thomson) **18**:407
"Whitsuntide an' Club Walken" (Barnes) **75**:95
"The Whitsuntide Fire" (Kivi)
See "Helavalkea"
Whittier on Writers and Writings (Whittier) **59**:364
"Who Can Be Happy and Free in Russia?" (Nekrasov)
See "Komu na Rusi zhit khorosho"
"Who curseth Sorrow knows her not at all" (Crawford) **127**:151-52
Who Has Seen the Wind (Rossetti) **50**:306
"Who Hath Ears to Hear Let Him Hear" (Very) **9**:381
Who Is Guilty? (Grillparzer)
See *Wer ist schuldig?*
"Who is Now Reading This?" (Whitman) **81**:332
"Who Is the People?" (Hazlitt) **82**:129
"Who Is This Woman...?" (De Quincey) **4**:88
Who Is to Blame? (Herzen)
See *Kto vinovat?*

"Who Killed Zebedee?" (Collins) **1**:188
"Who Learns My Lesson Complete" (Whitman) **31**:419, 425
"Who Shall Deliver Me?" (Rossetti) **2**:572
"Who Was Lost and Is Found" (Oliphant) **61**:202, 222
"Who was She?" (Taylor) **89**:325
"Who Will Say the World is Dying?" (Kingsley) **35**:219
"Who Would be the Last Man" (Parton) **86**:351
"Whoever Wants to Wander to Foreign Lands" (Eichendorff) **8**:210
Whom to Marry and How to Get Married! or, The Adventures of a Lady in Search of a Good Husband (Mayhew) **31**:160-61, 178, 191
Who's to Blame? (Newman) **38**:324
Who's Your Friend (Planché) **42**:278
"Why Did I Laugh Tonight" (Keats) **73**:173, 194, 202, 217
"Why Distant Objects Please" (Hazlitt) **82**:158
"Why Do Ye Call the Poet Lonely?" (Lampman) **25**:216
"Why I Am a Liberal" (Browning) **19**:110
"Why Lombard Street Is Sometimes Highly Excited and Sometimes Very Dull" (Bagehot) **10**:22
"Why Mr. Disraeli Has Succeeded" (Bagehot) **10**:31, 58
"Why Should We Hurry—Why Indeed?" (Dickinson) **21**:66
"Why the Heroes of Romances Are Insipid" (Hazlitt) **29**:148
"Why the Little Frenchman Wears His Arm in a Sling" (Poe) **16**:292, 323-24
"Why—Do They Shut Me Out of Heaven" (Dickinson) **21**:53, 56
The Wide, Wide World (Warner) **31**:332-33, 337-41, 343-49, 352-55
"Widok gór ze stepów Kozłlowa" (Mickiewicz) 3:404; **101**:188-89
"The Widow" (Southey) **97**:315
"The Widow and Her Son" (Irving) **19**:327, 348; **95**:232, 237
The Widow Barnaby (Trollope) **30**:314, 319-20
"The Widow Goe" (Crabbe) **26**:132
The Widow Grey (Crabbe) **121**:33
The Widow Lerouge (Gaboriau)
See *L'affaire Lerouge*
The Widow Married: A Sequel to the Widow Barnaby (Trollope) **30**:314, 320, 322
"The Widow McCloud's Mare" (Harris) **23**:159
"The Widow of Crescentius" (Hemans) **71**:293
Widow of Padilla (Martínez de la Rosa)
See *La viuda de Padilla*
"The Widow of Zarephath" (Sigourney) **21**:309
The Widow's Marriage (Boker) **125**:21, 36, 58
"The Widow's Son" (Irving)
See "The Widow and Her Son"
The Widow's Son (Southworth) **26**:433
"Widow's Song" (Pinkney) **31**:270
"The Widow's Tale" (Crabbe) **26**:93, 129-30, 135
"A Widow's Tale" (Oliphant) **61**:205, 209, 211-2
"The Widow's Trials" (Parton) **86**:347
The Widow's Vow (Inchbald) **62**:143, 145-6, 148
Wie Anne Bäbi Jowäger haushaltet und wie es ihm mit dem Dokterngeht (Gotthelf) **117**:5, 7-8, 15, 17, 19, 23, 32, 35, 38-9, 52
"Wie Christen eine Frau gewinnt" (Gotthelf) **117**:6, 25
"Wie fünf Mädchen im branntwein jämmerlich umkommen" (Gotthelf) **117**:44, 51, 58
"Wie Joggeli eine Frau sucht" (Gotthelf) **117**:6, 35
Wie Uli der Knecht glücklich wird (Gotthelf) **117**:4, 7-8, 18, 24, 32, 35-6, 38, 40, 43
"Wie wenn am Feiertage ..." (Hölderlin) **16**:161, 173, 175, 190-91, 195
"Wiederkehr" (Hölderlin) **16**:185
Wieland; or The Transformation (Brown) **22**:4-8, 11-14, 16-17, 19-20, 22-31, 33-40, 48-52, 54-5; **74**:4-7, 9-10, 13, 15-18, 21, 36-7, 41, 46-7, 49-51, 53-6, 60-1, 64, 68-70, 75-7, 80, 82-3, 92-5, 98, 103-05, 107-08, 110-12, 117, 120, 122-26, 129-30, 133-34, 137, 141-47, 149-50, 155-56, 159, 161, 163-64, 196-203; **122**:1-168
Wielki cztowiek do matych interesbw (Fredro) **8**:285
"Wielkie-słowa" (Norwid) **17**:374
"The Wife" (Irving) **2**:376-77, 392; **19**:327-28, 331, 334, 348, 350; **95**:232, 237, 249, 265, 277
The Wife (Norton) **47**:248, 255
"The Wife A-Lost" (Barnes) **75**:7, 73
"Wife and Two Children, Sleeping in the Same Chamber" (Hood) **16**:216
"The Wife A-Prais'd" (Barnes) **75**:73
"A Wife at Daybreak I Shall Be" (Dickinson) **77**:143
Wife Murderer; or, The Clemenceau Tragedy (Dumas)
See *L'affaire Clémenceau: Mémoire de l'accusé*
"The Wife of Asdrubal" (Hemans) **71**:294
"The Wife of Brittany" (Hayne) **94**:148-149, 153-58
The Wife of Claude (Dumas)
See *La femme de Claude*
"Wife to Husband" (Rossetti) **50**:267
"A Wife's Duty" (Opie) **65**:171-3, 179, 182
The Wife's Trial (Lamb) **10**:404
The Wigwam and the Cabin (Simms) **3**:501-02, 505-06, 508, 510
"Wild Apples" (Thoreau) **7**:378
The Wild Ass' Skin (Balzac)
See *La peau de chagrin*
Wild Bee of Australia: A Series of Poems with Prose Notes (Harpur) **114**:120, 122
"Wild Flower of Nature" (Petofi)
See "A természet vadvirága"
"Wild Flowers" (Campbell) **19**:181
"Wild Flowers" (Jefferies) **47**:102, 137
The Wild Goose Chace (Dunlap) **2**:213-14
"The Wild Honey Suckle" (Freneau) **1**:314-17, 322-23; **111**:133, 141, 159
The Wild Irish Boy (Maturin) **6**:317, 322, 328, 331, 336, 341-42, 346
The Wild Irish Girl (Morgan) **29**:386, 388-91
"Wild Kangaroo" (Kendall) **12**:191
Wild Life in a Southern County (Jefferies) **47**:88, 96-97, 103, 105, 108, 111-12, 121, 133, 136-37, 142
Wild Money (Ostrovsky)
See *Beshenye dengi*
"Wild Nights—Wild Nights" (Dickinson) **21**:43, 49, 58, 77; **77**:149
"The Wild Swans" (Andersen)
See "De vilde Svaner"
Wild Wales: Its People, Language, and Scenery (Borrow) **9**:45-49, 51, 54-56, 66
"Wild Wind" (Shevchenko)
See "Vitre bujnyj"
"The Wilderness and Our Indian Friends" (Moodie) **14**:231
Der Wildfang (Kotzebue) **25**:133, 145, 155
Wildfell Hall (Brontë)
See *The Tenant of Wildfell Hall*
"The Wild-Flower Nosegay" (Clare) **9**:84
"Wildflower Song" (Blake) **13**:173
"Wildgoose Lodge" (Carleton) **3**:85, 91, 96
"Die Wildschützen" (Ludwig) **4**:365
Wilhelm Meister (Goethe) **90**:47-52, 57-64, 79-82, 85-6, 88, 102, 105
Wilhelm Meister (Gotthelf) **117**:22
Wilhelm Meister's Apprenticeship (Goethe)
See *Wilhelm Meisters Lehrjahre*
Wilhelm Meisters Lehrjahre (Goethe) **34**:59, 74-5, 88-9, 133; **90**:38-122
Wilhelm Meister's Travels (Goethe)
See *Wilhelm Meisters Wanderjahre; oder, Die Entsagenden*
Wilhelm Meisters Wanderjahre (Goethe)
See *Wilhelm Meisters Wanderjahre; oder, Die Entsagenden*
Wilhelm Meisters Wanderjahre; oder, Die Entsagenden (Goethe) **34**:73-4, 88-9, 94; **90**:43, 105
Wilhelm Tell (Schiller) **39**:306, 321-22, 325, 330, 337, 346-47, 361, 368, 372, 377, 380, 385; **69**:168-283
"Wilhelm von Schwerin" (Runeberg) **41**:312, 325-26
"Wilhemina" (Woolson) **82**:272, 286, 305, 307, 333
"The Will" (Edgeworth) **51**:89-90
"Will" (Hayne)
See "The Will and the Wing"
"Will" (Tennyson) **65**:250
"The Will" (Very) **9**:387
A Will (Sacher-Masoch) **31**:287
"The Will and the Wing" (Hayne) **94**:145
The Will and the Wing (Hayne) **94**:134, 160
"The Will as Vision" (Pater) **7**:336
The Will in Nature (Schopenhauer)
See *Der Wille in der Natur*
"Will o' the Mill" (Stevenson) **5**:415, 418, 424, 431
"The Will of the People" (Boker) **125**:39
"Will Waterproof's Lyrical Monologue" (Tennyson) **30**:234
Der Wille in der Natur (Schopenhauer) **51**:294, 296-97
"William Bailey" (Crabbe) **26**:109
"William Bond" (Blake) **13**:172; **37**:22
"William Cowper" (Bagehot) **10**:40
William Lovell (Tieck) **5**:513, 515, 517-18, 522-23, 525, 527-28; **46**:375, 382, 384, 397-401, 409-11
"William Penn" (Herzen) **10**:348
William Shakespeare (Hugo) **3**:258, 273-74
"William Tell" (Bryant) **46**:47
William Tell (Schiller)
See *Wilhelm Tell*
"William the Silent" (Douglass) **7**:126
"William Wilson" (Poe) **1**:492, 506; **16**:303, 314-16, 319, 329, 331, 336; **55**:194-5; **78**:260; **97**:180; **117**:213
"William's Views" (Hazlitt) **29**:144
"Willie and Katie, A pastoral" (Hogg) **109**:268
"Willie Has Gone to the War" (Foster) **26**:285
"Willie We Have Missed You" (Foster) **26**:298
"Willie Winkie" (Andersen) **79**:23, 28, 34
Willing to Die (Le Fanu) **9**:299; **58**:273-5, 295, 301, 303
"Willkommen und Abschied" (Goethe) **4**:195
"The Willow and the Red Cliff" (Morris) **4**:429
"Willowwood" (Rossetti) **4**:496, 500-01, 512; 77;313, 339, 358
"Will's Will and His Two Thanksgivings" (Cooke) **110**:35
"Willst du, ich soll Hütten bauen?" (Grillparzer) **102**:174
"Willy Gilliland" (Ferguson) **33**:299
Willy Reilly and His Dear Coleen Bawn (Carleton) **3**:85, 87, 90
"Wilt Thou Be Gone, Love?" (Foster) **26**:298
"Wilton Harvey" (Sedgwick) **19**:445
"Winckelmann" (Pater) **7**:305, 312, 339; **90**:273, 296, 298, 300-01, 303, 305-06
"Wind" (Dobell) **43**:46
"The Wind" (Morris) **4**:419, 423, 431-32, 444
"The Wind and Stream" (Bryant) **6**:165, 176; **46**:20
"Wind and Wave" (Patmore) **9**:349, 357
"The Wind Flower" (Very) **9**:372, 380
"The Wind Has Such a Rainy Sound" (Rossetti) **50**:306
"Wind of the West Arise" (Darley) **2**:128
"The Wind Tells of Valdemar Daae and His Daughters" (Andersen) **7**:33, 35

"The Wind Tells the Story of Valdemar Daa and his Daughters" (Andersen)
See "The Wind Tells of Valdemar Daae and His Daughters"
"The Wind Waves o'er the Meadows Green" (Clare) **9**:111
Wind, Where Have You Been (Rossetti) **50**:306
"Wind-Clouds and Star-Drifts" (Holmes) **14**:125, 129; **81**:103, 105
"The Windhover" (Hopkins) **17**:185, 198, 206, 211, 216, 221, 225, 232, 236-39, 246, 254-55, 257-60
"The Winding Banks of Erne" (Allingham) **25**:20-1
"Windlass Song" (Allingham) **25**:8
"The Window" (Silva)
See "La ventana"
"Window Wat's Courtship" (Hogg) **4**:283
"Windows" (Hunt) **1**:417
"The Windows" (Mallarmé)
See "Les fenêtres"
"The Winds" (Bryant) **6**:175-76; **46**:7, 47
"Winds of Heaven" (Jefferies) **47**:101
"The Wind's Story" (Andersen) **7**:29
"The Wind's Tale" (Andersen)
See "The Wind Tells of Valdemar Daae and His Daughters"
Windsor Castle (Ainsworth) **13**:28, 31-2, 34, 36, 40, 43, 47-48
"The Wine Bibber's Glory" (Maginn) **8**:441
"Wine of Cyprus" (Browning) **61**:43
"The Wine of the Assassin" (Baudelaire)
See "Le vin de l'assassin"
Wine, Women, and Song (Symonds) **34**:323, 337
The Wing-and-Wing; or, Le Feu-Follet (Cooper) **1**:221-22; **54**:258
"Winged Hours" (Rossetti) **4**:498
"Winged Sphynx" (Fuller) **50**:247-8
Wingolf (Klopstock) **11**:235, 237
"Wings" (Lazarus) **8**:420
"Winter" (Clare) **9**:106; **86**:98, 110, 160-61
"Winter" (Lampman) **25**:189, 204
"Winter" (Patmore) **9**:349, 357
"Winter" (Smith) **59**:315-6, 322
Winter Day (Baillie) **71**:52
"The Winter Evening" (Cowper) **8**:120, 128; **94**:23, 26, 28, 30, 44, 127, 129-30
"Winter Evening" (Lampman) **25**:180, 197, 204, 211
"Winter Evening" (Pushkin)
See "Zimniy Vecher"
Winter Evening Tales: Collected among the Cottagers in the South of Scotland (Hogg) **4**:276
"Winter Fields" (Clare) **86**:160
"Winter Hues Recalled" (Lampman) **25**:160, 164, 181, 192, 194, 200
"Winter Hunt" (Grillparzer)
See "Jagd im Winter"
A Winter in Russia (Gautier)
See *Voyage en Russie*
"A Winter in the Country" (Hale) **75**:298
The Winter Journey (Muller)
See *Die Winterreise*
"Winter Joys" (Hale) **75**:294
"The Winter Landscape" (Mitford) **4**:401
"Winter Morning's Walk" (Cowper) **8**:119, 129; **94**:24, 27
"Winter: My Secret" (Rossetti) **50**:299, 312
"A Winter Night" (Barnes) **75**:15, 97
"Winter Night" (Lenau) **16**:276
"The Winter Night" (Very) **9**:387
Winter Notes on Summer Impressions (Dostoevsky) **2**:195; **33**:234; **119**:73, 132
"A Winter Piece" (Bryant) **6**:168-69; **46**:43, 45, 47
A Winter Piece: Being a Serious Exhortation, with a Call to the Unconverted, and a Short Contemplation on the Death of Jesus Christ (Hammon) **5**:262-63, 265
"Winter Rain" (Rossetti) **2**:575
"A Winter Scene" (Bryant) **46**:21
Winter Studies and Summer Rambles in Canada (Jameson) **43**:304, 312, 321, 323, 328-45
"The Winter Theatres" (Lewes) **25**:291
"Winter Thought" (Lampman) **25**:166
"Winter Uplands" (Lampman) **25**:172, 185, 200, 210
"Winter Visitors" (Thoreau) **7**:378, 408
"A Winter Walk" (Thoreau) **138**:121
"The Winter Walk at Noon" (Cowper) **94**:27, 29-30
"Winter Winds Cold and Blea" (Clare) **9**:111
Wintermarchen (Heine)
See *Deutschland: Ein Wintermärchen*
"Winternacht" (Keller) **2**:421
Die Winterreise (Muller) **73**:350-52, 360, 365-66, 373, 375, 380, 382-84, 387-96
"A Winter's Day" (Leskov)
See "Zimnij den'"
"Winter's gone the summer breezes" (Clare) **86**:87
"A Winter's Ramble in Grasmere Vale" (Wordsworth) **25**:421; **138**:229-32
Winter's Tale (Heine)
See *Deutschland: Ein Wintermärchen*
"The Winter's Walk" (Norton) **47**:238, 241, 245
Winterslow: Essays and Characters Written There (Hazlitt) **29**:148
"Winter-Store" (Lampman) **25**:183, 187, 204
"Wintertag" (Meyer) **81**:147
"Wirkung in die Ferne" (Goethe) **4**:192
Der Wirrwarr (Kotzebue) **25**:142
"Das Wirtshaus" (Muller) **73**:394, 396
Wisbur (Stagnelius) **61**:253, 256-7
"Wisdom" (Cowper) **94**:75
Wisdom (Verlaine)
See *Sagesse*
"Wisdom and Innocence" (Newman) **38**:308
Wisdom and Language of India (Schlegel)
See *Über die Sprache und Weisheit der Indier*
"Wisdom as Contrasted with Faith and with Bigotry" (Newman) **38**:307
"The Wisdom of Ali" (Taylor) **89**:302, 304
"Wise in her Generation" (Levy) **59**:92, 95, 112
The Wise Man of the East (Inchbald) **62**:144, 146-8
"A Wish" (Arnold) **29**:34
"The Wish" (Eminescu) **131**:287
"The Wish" (Lermontov) **126**:142
"A Wish" (Rogers) **69**:67, 79
Wishing-Cap Papers (Hunt) **1**:417; **70**:279, 282
Die Wissenschaftslehre in ihrem allgemeinen Umrisse (Fichte) **62**:34
Wit and Wisdom from West Africa: A Collection of 2,859 Proverbs, Being an Attempt to Make Africans Delineate Themselves (Burton) **42**:35
"A Witch" (Barnes) **75**:75
"The Witch" (Shevchenko)
See "Vid'ma"
The Witch (Lamb) **10**:401
The Witch (Michelet)
See *La sorcière*
"Witch Aunt" (Lamb) **10**:402
"A Witch in the Nursery" (Horne) **127**:268
"The Witch of Atlas" (Shelley) **18**:326-27, 329, 345, 357-58, 362-63
"The Witch of East Cliff" (Moodie) **14**:231
"Witch of Fife" (Hogg) **4**:275, 280, 282-83, 285; **109**:240, 243, 248, 270, 279
"The Witch of Fyfe" (Southey) **8**:472
"The Witch of Hebron" (Harpur) **114**:99, 105, 144-46
"The Witch of Wenham" (Whittier) **8**:509, 529
"The Witch-Bride" (Allingham) **25**:18
Witchcraft (Baillie) **2**:40-41
"Witches, and Other Night Fears" (Lamb) **10**:410, 429, 437; **113**:173, 177-78, 200, 219, 250-51
The Witches' Frolic (Barham) **77**:7, 9, 41
"The Witches of Traquir" (Hogg) **109**:279
"A Witch's Chant" (Hogg) **4**:282; **109**:201
"The Witch's Daughter" (Whittier) **8**:515; **59**:351, 356, 371
"With a Flower" (Dickinson)
See "I Hide Myself within My Flower"
"With a Guitar, to Jane" (Shelley) **18**:362, 369-70
"With a lively sense of greeting" (Tyutchev)
See "Zhivym sochuvstviem priveta"
"With a Rose That Bloomed on the Day of John Brown's Martyrdom" (Alcott) **58**:48
"With Antecedents" (Whitman) **81**:335
"With Garments Flowing" (Clare) **86**:87
"With Graceful Seat and Skilful Hand" (Clough) **27**:106
"With Muted Strings" (Verlaine) **51**:374
With Trumpet and Drum (Field) **3**:205-06
"With Two Words" (Meyer)
See " Mit zwei Worten"
"With Whom Is No Variableness, Neither Shadow of Turning" (Clough) **27**:84, 100
"Withdrawal" (Mörike)
See "Verborgenheit"
"Within a Budding Grove" (Browning) **79**:167
"Within my Garden, rides a Bird" (Dickinson) **77**:121
Within the Precincts (Oliphant) **61**:204, 209, 240, 243
Without a Dowry (Ostrovsky)
See *Bespridannitsa*
"Without Her" (Rossetti) **4**:514
"Withstanders" (Barnes) **75**:9
Witiko (Stifter) **41**:337, 339, 344, 346, 356, 358-60, 364, 369-75, 391
The Witlings (Burney) **54**:35
"The Witnesses" (Longfellow) **2**:483; **45**:123, 155; **103**:290
"Wives" (Irving) **95**:235, 237
Wives and Daughters (Gaskell) **5**:185-86, 188, 190, 192-93, 197-98, 201, 203-06; **70**:120, 123, 129, 132, 182, 185, 187, 193, 197, 199-200, 214; **97**:110, 113, 124; **137**:54, 167
Wives as They Were and Maids as They Are (Inchbald) **62**:144-9, 185
"The Wives of the Dead" (Hawthorne) **2**:322
The Wizard's Son (Oliphant) **11**:442-3, 446-9, 454; **61**:216
"Woak Hill" (Barnes) **75**:8, 13, 46, 48
"Woak Wer Good Enough Woonce" (Barnes) **75**:69, 82
Woe from Wit (Griboedov)
See *Gore ot Uma*
"Woe to the Double-Tongued" (Tennyson) **30**:293
"Wohin?" (Muller) **73**:350, 363-64, 369, 374
Wojna Chocimska (Krasicki) **8**:398
"A Wold Friend" (Barnes) **75**:9
"The Wold Waggon" (Barnes) **75**:82-3
"The Wold Wall" (Barnes) **75**:20, 26, 67-8
"Wolf and Hound" (Gordon) **21**:155, 158-59, 164-65, 176, 183, 188
"The Wolf and the Cat" (Krylov) **1**:435
"Wolfert Webber" (Irving) **2**:390; **19**:337
"Wolfert's Roost" (Irving) **2**:384; **19**:331
Wolves and Sheep (Ostrovsky)
See *Volki i ovtsy*
"Woman" (Crabbe) **26**:78
"Woman" (Emerson) **98**:166-69, 171-72
"Woman" (Gogol) **5**:258; **31**:137
"Woman" (Halleck) **47**:57, 78, 81
Woman (Michelet)
See *La femme, la famille, et le prêtre*
"Woman and Fame" (Hemans) **71**:296-97
Woman and Her Master (Morgan) **29**:396-97
"Woman . . . Apple of Discord" (Eminescu) **131**:288
A Woman Hater (Reade) **2**:547, 549; **74**:254-57, 264-65, 284, 289
Woman in the Nineteenth Century (Fuller) **5**:156-57, 163-65, 168, 171-73; **50**:217, 228-235, 243, 245-51, 253-60
"The Woman in White" (Dumas) **71**:185

The Woman in White (Collins) **1**:173-75, 178-83, 187-88, 191; **18**:61, 63-5, 67, 69, 72, 78-9; **93**:2-3, 7-12, 14, 19-20, 24-7, 30, 33-4, 46-7, 50, 52-6, 58-9, 61-3, 65-6, 86-91
The Woman Never Vexed (Planché) **42**:273
"Woman of Arles" (Daudet) **1**:238
The Woman of Paris (Becque)
See *La Parisienne*
The Woman of the Pharisees (Caballero)
See *La Farisea*
A Woman of Thirty (Balzac)
See *La femme de trente ans*
"The Woman of Three Cows" (Mangan) **27**:283, 310-11
"The Woman of Zakynthos" (Solomos)
See "I gynaika tis Zakynthos"
"Woman on the Field of Battle" (Hemans) **71**:275, 293
Woman; or, Ida of Athens (Morgan) **29**:386, 396
"Woman Question" (Brownson) **50**:56
Woman Snake (Gozzi)
See *La donna serpente*
"Woman the Poet of Nature" (Hale) **75**:324-25
"A Woman Waits for Me" (Whitman) **31**:402; **81**:329
"Woman! when I behold thee" (Keats) **73**:147
The Woman's Kingdom (Craik) **38**:122, 132
"A Woman's Last Word" (Browning) **19**:127, 131, 155, 158; **79**:163
A Woman's Life (Maupassant)
See *Une vie*
Woman's Record; or, Sketches of All Distinguished Women, from "The Beginning" Till A.D. 1850. (Hale) **75**:280, 283, 303-05, 307-09, 317, 335-42, 349, 353, 355, 360-61
"A Woman's Revenge" (Barbey d'Aurevilly)
See "La vengeance d'une femme"
The Woman's Reward (Norton) **47**:248, 255
"A Woman's Shortcomings" (Browning) **61**:43
A Woman's Thoughts about Women (Craik) **38**:126-27, 129, 130
"Women" (King)
See "La mujer"
"Women and Club Life" (Levy) **59**:92
"Women and Money" (Parton) **86**:351
"Women and Roses" (Browning) **19**:127
"Women as They Are" (Rowson) **69**:129
Women as They Are; or, The Manners of the Day (Gore) **65**:20, 22
"Women of Cairo" (Nerval) **1**:475
The Women of the North (Stagnelius) **61**:248, 253
Women; or, Pour et contre (Maturin) **6**:320-23, 328, 332-33, 335, 340-43, 347
"Women Politicians" (Maupassant)
See "Politiciennes"
"A Women's Love and a Wife's Duty" (Opie) **65**:172
Women's Songs (Karadzic)
See *Ženske pjesme*
"Wonder is not precisely Knowing" (Dickinson) **77**:77
Wonderland (Carroll)
See *Alice's Adventures in Wonderland*
Wonder Stories Told for Children (Andersen)
See *Eventyr, fortalte for bøorn*
A Wonder-Book for Girls and Boys (Hawthorne) **2**:299, 301, 306, 313; **17**:149-50; **23**:214
The Wonderful History of Peter Schlemihl (Chamisso)
See *Peter Schlemihls Wundersame Geschichte*
Wonderful Tales (Andersen)
See *Eventyr, fortalte for bøorn*
Wonderful Tales for Children (Andersen)
See *Eventyr, fortalte for bøorn*
The Wonderous Tale of Cocky, Clucky, and Cackle (Brentano)
See *Gockel, Hinkel, und Gackeleia*
"The Wondersmith" (O'Brien) **21**:234-39, 242, 249-51, 253
"A Wondrous City" (Baratynsky)
See "Chudnyy grad poroy solyotsya..."
"A wondrous city at times emerges..." (Baratynsky)
See "Chudnyy grad poroy solyotsya..."
The Wondrous Tale of Alroy (Disraeli) **2**:138; **39**:3, 22, 24, 39-40, 42, 46, 66; **79**:202-07, 211, 214-18, 227-28, 233, 269, 273-74, 282
The Wondrous Tale of Ikey Solomons (Barham) **77**:6
"The Wood beyond the World" (Morris) **4**:425, 437
The Wood Daemon (Lewis) **11**:305
Wood Magic (Jefferies) **47**:93-94, 101, 112, 124-27, 129-31, 137
"The Wood Nymph" (Andersen) **79**:82, 84
"The Wood of Saint John" (Silva)
See "Los maderos de San Juan"
Woodcraft; or, Hawks about the Dovecote (Simms) **3**:507-09, 513-14
"The Woodcutter" (Leskov)
See "Povest' o bogougodnom drovokole"
"The Woodcutter's Hut" (Lampman) **25**:186, 188, 202, 218
"Wooden Steeds" (Verlaine)
See "Chevaux de bois"
The Woodlands; or, A Treatise on the Preparation of the Ground for Planting (Cobbett) **49**:110, 114, 132, 151
"The Woodlark" (Lanier) **118**:241
"The Woodman and the Nightingale" (Shelley) **18**:373
"The Woodman's Daughter" (Patmore) **9**:327, 348
"Woodnotes" (Emerson) **1**:296-99; **38**:169, 178
"Woodnotes II" (Emerson) **38**:184, 186-87; **98**:179
"The Woods" (Ridge) **82**:185
"The Woodspurge" (Rossetti) **4**:491, 512, 516, 526; **77**:308
Woodstock (Scott) **15**:309, 316; **69**:304
"The Woody Hollow" (Barnes) **75**:95
"The Wooing of Gheezis" (Crawford) **127**:214
"The Wooing of Hallbiorn" (Morris) **4**:421, 434
The Woolgatherer (Hogg) **4**:285
"Woone smile mwore" (Barnes) **75**:7
"A Word about America" (Arnold) **126**:95
"A Word about Tom Jones" (Lewes) **25**:306
"A Word dropped careless on a Page" (Dickinson) **77**:107
"A Word for the Novel Writers" (Moodie) **113**:296
"A Word on Fools" (Bestuzhev)
See "Nechto o gluptsakh"
"A Word on the Drama" (Hebbel)
See "Mein Wort über das Drama"
"A Word to the Elect" (Brontë) **4**:51
"A Word to the Public" (Bulwer-Lytton) **1**:155
Words (Whitman) **81**:286-87
"The Words of Rosalind's Scroll" (Browning) **61**:69
"Wordsworth" (Arnold) **89**:86
"Wordsworth" (Pater) **7**:306, 338; **90**:296, 298, 305
"Wordsworth" (Whittier) **59**:364
"Wordsworth, Tennyson, and Browning; or, Pure, Ornate, and Grotesque Art in Poetry" (Bagehot) **10**:30, 57, 62
"Wordsworth's Poetry" (De Quincey) **4**:61
"Work" (Lamb) **10**:405
Work (Browning) **66**:44
Work: A Story of Experience (Alcott) **6**:16; **58**:10-5, 17-9, 21-3, 28, 37, 49, 69, 81-5, 87-8; **83**:6, 9, 30, 33, 57
"Work and Contemplation" (Browning) **61**:43
"The Work and Mission of My Life" (Wagner) **119**:189
"Work without Hope" (Coleridge) **9**:159
"The Workhouse Clock" (Hood) **16**:209, 228, 235, 239
Working Notes (Dickens) **113**:130, 133, 137
"The Workingman's Drink" (Baudelaire) **6**:83
Works (Baillie) **71**:16-17
Works (Byron) **109**:123, 126
Works (Eminescu) **131**:295, 297, 319
Works (Hazlitt) **82**:97-101
Works (Lanier) **118**:248
Works (Mackenzie) **41**:184, 213
Works (Moore) **110**:181
Works (Pisarev)
See *Sočinenija*
Works (Tonna)
See *The Works of Charlotte Elizabeth*
Works IV, Posthumous Poems (Eminescu) **33**:266
Works V (Eminescu) **33**:266
"Works and Days" (Emerson) **1**:280, 290; **38**:150
The Works and Life of Walter Bagehot (Bagehot) **10**:31
The Works of Alexander Hamilton (Hamilton) **49**:308
The Works of Charles and Mary Lamb (Lamb) **125**:345-50, 375
The Works of Charles and Mary Lamb (Lamb) **10**:389
The Works of Charles Lamb (Lamb) **113**:180-81, 184, 186, 202-05, 279-81
The Works of Charlotte Elizabeth (Tonna) **135**:193, 195
The Works of Francis Parkman (Parkman)
See *France and England in North America*
The Works of Gerald Griffin (Griffin) **7**:196
Works of Jeremy Bentham (Bentham) **38**:53-4, 80, 90, 92
The Works of John C. Calhoun (Calhoun) **15**:25
Works of Love (Kierkegaard)
See *Kjerlighedens Gjerninger*
Works of Love: Some Christian Reflections in the Form of Discourses (Kierkegaard) **34**:178, 192, 197, 202, 211, 224; **78**:142, 185, 215, 239
The Works of Maria Edgeworth (Edgeworth) **1**:258
Works of Peter Porcupine (Cobbett)
See *Porcupine's Works*
Works of Shakespeare (Blair) **75**:129-30, 132
The Works of the Ettrick Shepherd (Hogg) **4**:279; **109**:192, 200-01, 203-05, 207, 274
The Works of Thomas Carlyle (Carlyle) **70**:64
Works of Virgil (Warton) **118**:353
The Works of William Blake, Poetic, Symbolic, and Critical (Blake) **127**:3
"The World" (Rossetti) **2**:561; **66**:305
"The World" (Very) **9**:387
The World a Mask (Boker) **125**:20-21, 28, 36, 58, 82
"The World and the Quietist" (Arnold) **29**:34-5
"The World and the Soul" (Harpur) **114**:100, 126, 166
The World as Will and Idea (Schopenhauer)
See *Die Welt als Wille und Vorstellung*
The World as Will and Representation (Schopenhauer)
See *Die Welt als Wille und Vorstellung*
The World before Them (Moodie) **14**:226
"The World Below the Brine" (Whitman) **31**:431
"A World for a Sonnet" (Isaacs)
See "Un mundo por un soneto"
The World in a Man-of-War (Melville)
See *White-Jacket; or, The World in a Man-of-War*
"The World of Dreams" (Crabbe) **26**:118, 126, 139; **121**:81-2
"The World. Self-Destruction" (Rossetti) **50**:285
The World Well Lost (Linton) **41**:166
"The World-feels Dusty/When We stop to Die" (Dickinson) **77**:163
Worldly Apes with a Smattering of Various Arts (Ueda Akinari)
See *Shodo kikimimi sekenzaru*

Worldly Monkeys with Ears for the Arts (Ueda Akinari)
See *Shodo kikimimi sekenzaru*
"The World's Convention" (Whittier) **8**:491
World's End (Jefferies) **47**:93
"The World's Epigram" (Allingham) **25**:6
"The World's Justice" (Lazarus) **109**:311, 336-37
"The World-Soul" (Emerson) **1**:296
"Wormwood and Night-Shade" (Gordon) **21**:150, 154, 160, 167, 181
"Worship" (Emerson) **38**:149
"Die Worte des Glaubens" (Schiller) **39**:388
"The Worth of Hours" (Milnes) **61**:136
The Worthies of Yorkshire and Lancashire (Coleridge) **90**:15
Worthy of Pity (Fredro)
See *Godzien litości*
Wotton Reinfred (Carlyle) **70**:44
"Would I Die or Should You Die" (Eminescu) **131**:294
"Would I Knew" (Allingham) **25**:7, 18
"Wound in the Side" (Meyer)
See "Die Seitenwunde"
"The Wound-Dresser" (Whitman) **4**:558, 582; **81**:313, 320-22
"The Wounded Hussar" (Campbell) **19**:190, 193
Woyzeck (Büchner) **26**:4, 7, 9-11, 14, 16-22, 25-7, 35-9, 41-2, 45-7, 49, 55-7, 62, 65, 67, 69
"The Wrath of Samson" (Vigny)
See "La colère de Samson"
"The Wreath and the Chain" (Moore) **110**:177, 180
"Wreath of Sonnets" (Preseren)
See "Sonetni venec"
"Wreath the Bowl" (Moore) **110**:190
"The Wreck" (Wergeland) **5**:537
"The Wreck of Rivermouth" (Whittier) **8**:506, 509, 513, 529
"The Wreck of the Deutschland" (Hopkins) **17**:183-84, 186, 188, 194-95, 202, 207-09, 215, 217, 220, 222, 224-25, 229-32, 238-39, 242-43, 245-46, 250-58, 260
"Wreck of the Emelie" (Clare) **9**:125
"The Wreck of the Hesperus" (Longfellow) **2**:472, 493; **45**:99, 116, 135, 140, 144, 153, 155, 158, 179-80; **103**:298
The Wrecker (Stevenson) **5**:411, 415, 522
The Wretched (Hugo)
See *Les misérables*
"The Wretched Dionysos" (Eminescu)
See "Sarmanul Dionis"
Writer's Diary (Dostoevsky)
See *Dnevnik pisatelya*
"Writing Under Difficulties" (Parton) **86**:373
Writings (Hallam) **110**:120
Writings (Jefferson) **103**:195, 198
Writings (Lowell) **90**:220
Writings (Novalis)
See *Schriften*
The Writings of James Madison (Madison) **126**:278
The Writings of John Greenleaf Whittier (Whittier) **8**:506
The Writings of Henry David Thoreau (Thoreau) **138**:67
"Written at Bamborough Castle" (Bowles) **103**:67
"Written at Bignor Park in Sussex, in August, 1799" (Smith)
See "Sonnet 92"
"Written at Exmouth, midsummer 1795" (Smith)
See "Sonnet 68"
"Written at Midnight" (Rogers) **69**:68
written at midnight on the River St. Lawrence (Moodie) **113**:345
"Written at Ostend. July 22, 1787" (Bowles) **103**:68, 72
"Written at Rome, 1833" (Emerson) **38**:190
"Written at the Close of Spring" (Smith)
See "Sonnet 2"
"Written at Tinemouth" (Bowles)
See "Sonnet Written at Tinemouth, Northumberland"
"Written at Tinemouth, Northumberland, After a Tempestuous Voyage" (Bowles)
See "Sonnet Written at Tinemouth, Northumberland"
"Written in a Bible" (Coleridge) **90**:32
"Written in a tempestuous night, on the coast of Sussex" (Smith)
See "Sonnet 66"
"Written in a Thunderstorm" (Clare) **9**:102
"Written in Autumn" (Clare) **9**:121
"Written in Emerson's Essays" (Arnold) **29**:34
"Written in Germany, On one of the coldest days of the Century" (Wordsworth) **111**:235
"Written in Spring" (Allston) **2**:26
"Written in the Church-Yard at Middleton in Sussex" (Smith)
See "Sonnet 44"
"Written in the Cloisters of Christ's Hospital" (Dyer) **129**:148
"Written in the First Leaf of a Child's Memorandum-Book" (Lamb) **125**:347, 361
"Written on a Marble" (Barbauld) **50**:16
"Written on the Day" (Keats) **73**:147, 253, 332
"Written on the sea shore.—October, 1784" (Smith)
See "Sonnet 12"
The Wrong Box (Stevenson) **5**:409
The Wrongs of Woman (Tonna) **135**:195-96, 199-200, 207-17, 220-21, 223-25
The Wrongs of Woman, Part I (Tonna)
See "Milliners and Dressmakers"
The Wrongs of Woman, Part II (Tonna)
See "The Forsaken Home"
The Wrongs of Woman, Part III (Tonna)
See "The Little Pin Headers"
The Wrongs of Woman, Part IV (Tonna)
See "The Lace Runners"
The Wrongs of Women (Tonna)
See *The Wrongs of Woman*
"The Wryneck's Nest" (Clare) **86**:133
"Wstęp do bajek" (Krasicki) **8**:402
"Die wunderbare Rede" (Meyer) **81**:154
"Die Wunderlichen Nachbarskinder" (Goethe) **4**:196
"Wunsch" (Meyer) **81**:150
"Die Wurmlinger Kapelle" (Lenau) **16**:275, 282
Wuthering Heights (Brontë) **16**:63-9, 71-5, 77-8, 80, 82-3, 85-6, 88-90, 92-7, 100-01, 103, 105-17, 122-26; **35**:107-97
Wyandotté; or, The Hutted Knoll (Cooper) **1**:204-05, 217; **54**:258, 277, 280
Wychowanka (Fredro) **8**:293
Wylder's Hand (Le Fanu) **9**:299, 301-03, 309, 311-12, 316-18; **58**:251, 266, 268-9, 271-4, 288-9, 301
"Wynken, Blynken, and Nod" (Field) **3**:205-06, 209-10, 212
"Wyoming" (Halleck) **47**:65, 71
The Wyvern Mystery (Le Fanu) **58**:273-4
"Xan" (Castro) **78**:2
"Xantippe" (Levy) **59**:92, 102, 104, 106-7
Xantippe and Other Verse (Levy) **59**:86, 92, 106-7
Xenien (Goethe) **4**:193
Xenien (Schiller) **39**:362
"Xenophanes" (Emerson) **1**:297; **98**:179
"Xenophanes" (Lampman) **25**:184
"Xigante scos olmos" (Castro) **78**:3
"Ximenes" (Polidori) **51**:233
Ximenes, The Wreath, and Other Poems (Polidori) **51**:201
Xudoznik (Shevchenko) **54**:362, 365, 371, 381, 387, 390, 392, 396-8
"A xusticia pola man" (Castro) **78**:42
"A XXX dedicándole estas poesías" (Espronceda) **39**:108-09
Yager's Songs and Poems of the War of 1813 (Fouqué) **2**:267
"Yak by vy znaly panychi" (Shevchenko) **54**:394
Yakov Pasynkov (Turgenev) **21**:414, 418; **122**:242, 245, 268
"Yamiyo" (Ichiyō) **49**:353
"Yamizakura" (Ichiyō) **49**:334, 341
Yankee Chronology (Dunlap) **2**:211, 213, 218
A Yankee in Canada, with Anti-Slavery and Reform Papers (Thoreau) **7**:361; **21**:347, 353; **61**:339
The Yankey in London (Tyler) **3**:571-72, 574
"Yardley Oak" (Cowper) **8**:102, 116, 118-23, 139-40; **94**:39, 119
Yarns (Harris)
See *Sut Lovingood: Yarns Spun by a "Nat'ral Born Durn'd Fool"*
"Yarrows" (Wordsworth) **12**:431
Yasaisho (Ueda Akinari) **131**:19, 45
Yasumikoto (Ueda Akinari) **131**:20, 51
"Yazykovu" (Baratynsky)
See "To N. M. Yazykov"
"Ye Mariners of England" (Campbell) **19**:165, 168, 179, 181-82, 185, 190-93, 195-96
"Ye Wearie Wayfarer" (Gordon) **21**:159-61, 173, 177, 179-80
A Year at Hartlebury; or, The Election (Disraeli) **39**:74
"The Year Clock" (Barnes) **75**:32
A Year in the Sahel (Fromentin)
See *Un année dans le sahel*
"The Year LVII of the Republic, One and Indivisible" (Herzen) **10**:338
A Year of Consolation (Kemble) **18**:182-83
The Year of Our Lord (Droste-Hülshoff) **3**:194
"A Year's Courtship" (Timrod) **25**:361-62
A Year's Life (Lowell) **2**:502, 515; **90**:221
Years of Childhood (Aksakov) **2**:12-16
The Years of Childhood of Bagrov, the Grandson (Aksakov)
See *Years of Childhood*
A Year's Residence in America (Cobbett) **49**:110, 113, 120, 153
A Year's Residence in the United States (Cobbett)
See *A Year's Residence in America*
"A Year's Spinning" (Browning) **66**:60
"Years, You Years to Come" (Arany)
See "Evek, ti még jövendőévek"
"Yeast" (Huxley) **67**:83
Yeast (Kingsley) **35**:202-04, 209, 211-15, 219-22, 226-28, 230-31, 233-36, 241-42, 244, 246-53, 255
The Yellow Dwarf (Planché) **42**:273, 278-79, 288-89, 292, 294, 296
The Yellow Mask (Collins) **1**:180
"The Yellow Violet" (Bryant) **6**:158, 169, 193; **46**:3, 6, 25, 40-1
"The Yellow Violet" (Very) **9**:372
"Yellow Wagtail's Nest" (Clare) **9**:85
"Yellowhammer's Nest" (Clare) **9**:85
The Yellowplush Correspondence (Thackeray) **5**:444, 447, 450, 465, 469, 481, 506
The Yellowplush Papers (Thackeray) **5**:481; **14**:420; **43**:381
The Yemassee (Simms) **3**:499-500, 502, 506-08, 511-12, 514
"Yermolai and the Miller's Wife" (Turgenev) **122**:293-94
"Yermolay and the Miller's Wife" (Turgenev)
See "Yermolai and the Miller's Wife"
"Yeshcho listok iz dnevnika gvardeyskogo ofitsera" (Bestuzhev) **131**:186
Yevgeny Onegin (Pushkin) **3**:409-15, 417-18, 421-25, 431-34, 436-48, 451, 455, 459, 461-62, 464; **27**:361-405; **83**:243, 245-47, 249-51, 269-70, 304-05, 308, 318-19, 323, 33, 334-38, 350, 353-54, 357, 361, 372-73
"The Yew Trees" (Wordsworth) **12**:452

"Yey" (Bestuzhev) **131**:150
"Yid Somersault" (Leskov)
See "Židovskaja kuvyrkalegija"
Yin-chien (Li Ju-chen) **137**:206
"Yo cantar, cantar, canté" (Castro) **78**:55, 59
Yö ja päivä (Kivi) **30**:53
"Yo quiero ser cómico" (Larra) **130**:248-49
"Yoke and Star" (Martí)
See "Yugo y Estrella"
"Yonnondio" (Whitman) **31**:434; **81**:345, 347
"Yorktown Centennial Lyric" (Hayne) **94**:145
"You Add Tomorrow to Your Days" (Eminescu) **33**:246
"You Are All That Is Dear To My Heart" (Pavlova)
See "Ty vse, chto serdtsu milo"
"You are old, Father William" (Carroll) **139**:29
"You Ask Me, Why, Though Ill at Ease" (Tennyson) **30**:293
You Can't Live As You Want To (Ostrovsky)
See *Ne tak zhiví kak khóchetsya*
"You, dead, dead, dead" (Verlaine) **51**:372
"You Felons on Trial in Courts" (Whitman) **31**:372
"You Lingering Sparse Leaves of Me" (Whitman) **31**:434
"You saw him in society circles" (Tyutchev)
See "Ty zrel ego v krugo bol shogo sveta"
"You saw him in the mundane spheres" (Tyutchev)
See "Ty zrel ego v krugo bol shogo sveta"
"You So Much Tortured Me with Words of Love" (Eminescu) **131**:287
You Suffer Through No Fault of Your Own (Ostrovsky) **57**:209-10
"You Who Have Lived on in My Beggarly Heart" (Pavlova) **138**:34
"You Will Hear the Judgment of a Fool" (Turgenev) **122**:283
"You Would Place the Whole Universe in Your Alley" (Baudelaire)
See "Tu mettrais l'univers entier dans tu ruelle"
"Yound Death" (Rossetti) **50**:292
"Young Achilles" (Symonds) **34**:356
The Young Acrobat (Alger) **83**:118
The Young Adventurer; or, Tom's Trip across the Plains (Alger) **8**:25
"Young America" (Halleck) **47**:71
Young America (Halleck) **47**:80
Young and Handsome (Planché) **42**:275, 288
The Young Bank Messenger (Alger)
See *A Cousin's Conspiracy*
"The Young Bear Hunter" (Kivi)
See "Nuori Karhunampuja"
Young Benjamin Franklin (Mayhew) **31**:193
The Young Countess; or, Love and Jealousy (Trollope) **30**:330
The Young Duke (Disraeli) **2**:137, 144, 146, 147; **39**:3, 22, 24-6, 28, 30-1, 33, 39-40, 45-6, 51-2, 65-8, 75-6; **79**:200-202, 214-15, 227, 239, 270-71
The Young Emigrants; or, Pictures of Canada, Calculated to Amuse and Instruct the Minds of Youth (Traill) **31**:320-21
The Young Explorer (Alger) **8**:43
"A Young Fir-Wood" (Rossetti) **4**:491
"The Young Giant" (Grimm and Grimm) **3**:227
"Young Goodman Brown" (Hawthorne) **2**:293, 297-98, 310, 317, 324, 327, 329, 331, 333; **10**:300; **17**:137; **23**:202; **39**:180; **79**:311, 317-18; **95**:91, 93-8, 100, 105, 107-10, 112, 114-16, 118-20, 123-29, 132-34, 137-40, 146-48, 150-51, 155-60, 162-63, 167-70, 176-80, 184, 186, 188, 190, 192-93, 195-96, 198, 204, 210, 213
Young Heads and Young Hearts (Desbordes-Valmore)
See *Jeunes Têtes et jeunes coeurs*
"The Young Italian" (Irving)
See "The Story of the Young Italian"
"Young Kennedy" (Hogg) **109**:280
"The Young Lady-Peasant Girl" (Pushkin)
See "Baryshnia-krest'ianka"
Young Love (Trollope) **30**:329
"The Young Mahometan" (Lamb)
See "Margaret Green: The Young Mahometan"
The Young Married Couple (Griboedov)
See *Molodye suprugi*
The Young Master Carpenter (Tieck)
See *Der junge Tischlermeister*
Young Men and Old Women (Inchbald) **62**:144-5
The Young Miner (Alger) **8**:40
Young Mrs. Jardine (Craik) **38**:122
Young Musgrave (Oliphant) **11**:446
The Young Musician (Alger) **8**:43
The Young Outlaw (Alger) **8**:42
The Young Philosopher (Smith) **23**:326, 330, 333; **115**:136, 144, 147-48
"Young Poet" (Crabbe) **26**:102
"The Young Queen" (Browning) **61**:61
"The Young Robber" (Irving)
See "The Story of the Young Robber"
The Young Salesman (Alger) **8**:46; **83**:114
The Young Sculptor (Mayhew) **31**:159
"The Young Serf" (Taylor) **89**:342
"Young Soult" (Brontë)
See "Young Soult's Poem"
"Young Soult's Poem" (Brontë) **109**:35
"Young Tirel" (Meyer)
See "Jung Tirel"
Young Tom Hall (Surtees) **14**:351, 378-80
Young Wives (Griboedov)
See *Molodye suprugi*
The Younger Son (Trelawny)
See *Adventures of a Younger Son*
"Your Image of Mary" (Isaacs)
See "Tu imagen de María"
"Your love to me appears in doubtful signs" (Boker) **125**:82
"Youth and Age" (Coleridge) **9**:159
"Youth and Art" (Browning) **19**:131
"Youth and Calm" (Arnold) **6**:75; **29**:31, 37; **89**:25
"Youth and Love" (Stevenson) **5**:428
"Youth and Manhood" (Timrod) **25**:381
Youth of Jefferson (Cooke) **5**:121, 124, 128-29
"The Youth of Man" (Arnold) **6**:51; **29**:27, 34
"The Youth of Nature" (Arnold) **6**:51, 56; **29**:34, 36; **89**:99
"The youth once gaily cried" (Baratynsky)
See "Byvalo, otrok, zvonkim klikom..."
"Youth, thou art fled" (Coleridge) **90**:27
"Youthful Dreams" (Lenau) **16**:277
"Youth's Agitations" (Arnold) **29**:27
Youth's First Step in Geography (Rowson) **69**:116
Yugalanguriya (Chatterji) **19**:217-19
"Yugo y Estrella" (Martí) **63**:87
"Yuki no Hi" (Ichiyō) **49**:335, 342, 353
"Yuku Kumo" (Ichiyō) **49**:344, 353
"Yunost" (Bestuzhev) **131**:150
"Yveline Samoris" (Maupassant) **83**:194-96, 220-21
"Yvette" (Maupassant) **1**:443, 457, 463-64; **83**:194-96, 220
"Z. Marcas" (Balzac) **5**:51
"Z pamiętnika" (Norwid) **17**:375
"Za bairakom bairak" (Shevchenko) **54**:389
"Za chainym stolom" (Pavlova) **138**:22-27, 35-36, 47
Za kulisami: Tyrtej (Norwid) **17**:379
"Zabytaja derevnja" (Nekrasov) **11**:412-13
"Zagadka" (Norwid) **17**:373
"Zagon" (Leskov) **25**:258
Zahme Xenien (Goethe) **4**:173, 193
"Zajačij remiz" (Leskov) **25**:229, 231-32, 234, 238-39
"Zakoldovannoe mesto" (Gogol) **5**:231; **31**:120
"Zamok Eyzen" (Bestuzhev) **131**:175, 184, 187, 208-10, 213
"Zamok Neigauzen" (Bestuzhev) **131**:171, 183, 185, 209
"Zamok Venden" (Bestuzhev) **131**:169, 175, 183-84, 208-10
Zampa der Tagdieb (Nestroy) **42**:225
Zanoni (Bulwer-Lytton) **1**:140-41, 147, 150, 153; **45**:3, 5-7, 19, 23, 47-54, 69-70
Zanzibar (Burton) **42**:40-1
El zapatero y el rey (Zorrilla y Moral) **6**:523, 525-26
"Zapečatlennyj angel" (Leskov) **25**:228, 233, 238
Zapiski iz mertvogo doma (Dostoevsky) **2**:160-63, 168, 203; **7**:73, 80, 90, 106; **21**:107; **33**:161; **43**:164; **119**:90
Zapiski iz podpol'ya (Dostoevsky) **2**:161, 172, 184, 189, 195, 201-02; **7**:80, 90, 107, 116; **21**:116, 129-30, 145-46; **33**:158-243; **43**:92, 122; **119**:147, 156
Zapiski ob uzhenyi ryby (Aksakov) **2**:16
Zapiski okhotnika (Turgenev) **21**:378, 388, 399-400, 406, 409, 413, 416-18, 420-21, 432, 435, 437, 441, 446-48, 451, 454; **37**:364, 379, 393, 401-02, 430, 438; **122**:241, 247, 256, 260, 263-66, 275-76, 279, 293-94, 306, 348, 350
Zapiski ruzheynago okhotnika (Aksakov) **2**:16
Zapiski starucha (Fredro) **8**:293
Zapolya: A Christmas Tale (Coleridge) **9**:143, 159
"Zapovit" (Shevchenko) **54**:384, 390
"Zapustenie" (Baratynsky) **103**:11-12
Zaputannoye delo (Saltykov) **16**:368
Zaragoza (Martínez de la Rosa) **102**:225
Zastrozzi (Shelley) **18**:306, 341-42; **93**:272
"Zatiš'e" (Turgenev) **122**:268
"Die Zauberei im Herbste" (Eichendorff) **8**:226
"Zauberlehrling" (Goethe) **4**:192
"Der Zauberleuchtturm" (Mörike) **10**:455
Der Zauberring (Fouqué) **2**:265-68
"Zaunno" (Bestuzhev) **131**:172
Zawisza czarny (Slowacki) **15**:371-72, 380
Zawisza the Black (Slowacki)
See *Zawisza czarny*
Zaxudalyj rod (Leskov) **25**:228, 232, 238, 245
"Zdes, gde tak vyalo svod nebesnyy" (Tyutchev) **34**:400
"Zdravljica" (Preseren) **127**:299, 329, 332, 334
"Zeal and Love" (Newman) **38**:343
"Żegluga" (Mickiewicz) **3**:403
"Die Zeichen" (Meyer) **81**:155
Zeim, re dei genii (Gozzi) **23**:119
"Zeinab and Kathema" (Shelley) **93**:336
Die Zeit Constantins des Grossen (Burckhardt) **49**:10, 15-6, 23, 32-4
"Zeitbilder" (Droste-Hülshoff) **3**:193, 200
Zeitgedichte (Heine) **54**:345, 348
"Der Zeitgeist" (Hölderlin) **16**:191
Zeitgeist und Bernergeist (Gotthelf) **117**:4, 6-7, 14-15, 17-18, 22, 32, 34
"Železnaja volja" (Leskov) **25**:239
"Zelyóny shum" (Nekrasov) **11**:413, 417, 420-21
The Zemganno Brothers (Goncourt)
See *Les frères Zemganno*
Zemsta (Fredro) **8**:285-87, 289-90, 292-93
The Zenana, and Minor Poems of L. E. L. (Landon) **15**:161
Ženske pjesme (Karadzic) **115**:112
"Zephyrus and Flora" (Barbauld) **50**:13
Der Zerbrochene Krug (Kleist) **2**:439-41, 443-45, 454, 457, 461, 463; **37**:226, 229, 233, 237, 239, 241, 243-44, 253-55, 267, 270-73
Der Zerrissene (Nestroy) **42**:220, 223, 251, 257
Zerstreute Blätter (Herder) **8**:313
Die Zerstreuten (Kotzebue) **25**:136
"Zgubljena vera" (Preseren) **127**:298, 323
"Zhelanie" (Zhukovsky) **35**:403, 407
Zhenit'ba; Sovershenno neveroyatnoye sobitye (Gogol) **5**:218, 224, 231, 251; **15**:84-5, 98
"Zhivym sochuvstviem priveta" (Tyutchev) **34**:404
Zibaldone (Leopardi) **129**:222-23, 225-26, 228, 230, 234-39, 241-43, 248, 255-60, 264-68,

272, 276-77, 279-82, 291, 295-96, 298, 302-6, 314, 316-19, 322-26, 330-32, 339-41, 343, 346-48
"Zid" (Turgenev) **122**:267
"Židovskaja kuvyrkalegija" (Leskov) **25**:265-67
"Die Zigeunerin" (Ludwig) **4**:353
Zigzags (Gautier)
See *Caprices et zigzags*
"The Zilver-Weed" (Barnes) **75**:38
"Zimnij den'" (Leskov) **25**:232
"Zimniy Vecher" (Pushkin) **3**:443
The Zincali; or, An Account of the Gypsies of Spain (Borrow) **9**:36-40, 42, 66
Zinzendorff, and Other Poems (Sigourney) **21**:292, 307; **87**:321, 326, 337, 340, 342
"Zitten Out the Wold Year" (Barnes) **75**:77
"Ziua de mâine" (Eminescu) **131**:361
Zivopisnaja Ukraina (Shevchenko) **54**:379
Zivot i obicaji naroda srpska (Karadzic) **115**:79
Zizine (Kock) **16**:248
Złota czaszka (Slowacki) **15**:352, 354, 371
La Zobeide (Gozzi) **23**:108, 119, 123, 126
"Żona modna" (Krasicki) **8**:403, 407
"A Zong" (Barnes) **75**:71
The Zoology of the Voyage of the Beagle (Darwin) **57**:113, 116
The zoonomia; or, Laws fo Organic Life (Darwin) **106**:185-86, 191-92, 203, 205, 208-11, 216-21, 228, 233-34, 236, 240, 242, 245, 247, 252, 260, 269, 274-78
"Zoospermos" (Silva) **114**:263, 319
Zoospermos (Silva) **114**:273
"Zoraida" (Isaacs) **70**:310
Zrzędnosc i przecora (Fredro) **8**:284-85
"Zu der Edlen Jagd" (Gordon) **21**:159
Zu ebener Erde und erster Stock (Nestroy) **42**:231-32, 236, 238-41, 257
"The Zucca" (Shelley) **18**:370
"Zukunftsmusik" (Wagner) **119**:198
Zulma (Staël-Holstein) **91**:340, 358
Zum ewigen Frieden: Ein philosophischer Entwurf (Kant) **27**:228-29, 236, 238
"Zum neven Jahr" (Mörike) **10**:455
"Zummer" (Barnes) **75**:6
"Zummer an'Winter" (Barnes) **75**:9 32
"Zummer Stream" (Barnes) **75**:22, 59
"Zummer Thoughts in Winter Time" (Barnes) **75**:22, 32
"Zunsheen in the Winter" (Barnes) **75**:32
Zur Chronik von Grieshuus (Storm) **1**:540-41, 546
"Zur Geschichte der Religion und Philosophie in Deutschland" (Heine) **4**:255, 263, 264, 266; **54**:321, 336-7, 340
Zur kritik der politischen Ökonomie (Marx) **17**:289, 302, 304, 318, 321-22, 335; **114**:8, 10, 37, 70, 78, 80, 82, 84-5
"Zur Literargeschichte" (Grillparzer) **102**:118
Zur Literargeschichte (Grillparzer) **102**:142
Zur Philosophie und Wissenschaft der Nature (1) (Schopenhauer) **51**:297
Die Zürcher Novellen (Keller) **2**:412, 414, 416, 422
"Zürchersee" (Klopstock) **11**:234, 237-38
Die Zurückkunft des Vaters (Kotzebue) **25**:140
"Zver'" (Leskov) **25**:239
"Zvezdocka" (Baratynsky) **103**:28
"Zwanzig Balladen von einem Schweizer" (Meyer) **81**:199, 209
"Zweckprosa" (Gotthelf) **117**:92
"Zwei Johannes würmchen" (Klopstock) **11**:238
"Zwei Polen" (Lenau) **16**:286
Zwei Schwestern (Stifter) **41**:334, 343, 366
"Zwei Segel" (Spencer) **81**:201
"Die Zweifler" (Lenau) **16**:272, 275, 287
Der Zweikampf (Kleist) **2**:456, 458, 461; **37**:237-38, 246, 249, 253-55
"Zwiegesprach" (Meyer) **81**:147
Die Zwillinge (Klinger) **1**:429
Zwischen Himmel und Erde (Ludwig) **4**:346-50, 354-55, 357-58, 360-61, 363-64, 367-68
Zwölf Mädchen in Uniform (Nestroy) **42**:236
Zwölf moralische Briefe (Wieland) **17**:417-18
Zwolon (Norwid) **17**:367, 371, 379
"Zyuleyka, S persidskogo" (Bestuzhev) **131**:150